THE SIXTIES

THE SIXTIES

AS REPORTED BY The New York Times

Edited by
Arleen Keylin
and
Laurie Barnett

Introduction by
TOM WICKER

Arno Press
New York 1980

A Note to the Reader
Original copies of *The New York Times* were not available to the publisher. This volume, therefore, was created from 35mm microfilm.

Library of Congress Cataloging in Publication Data
Main entry under title:

The Sixties.

"As reported by the New York Times."
1. History, Modern—1945- —Sources
I. Keylin, Arleen. II. Barnett, Laurie. III. New York Times.
D1050.S59 909.82 80-84
ISBN 0-405-13085-6

Book design by Stephanie Rhodes

Editorial Assistant: Jonathan Cohen

Manufactured in the United States of America

CONTENTS

INTRODUCTION

Ordinarily, people and nations more nearly disguise—in humbug or in myth, in pretensions or in illusions—than reveal themselves. But in the 1960s, the United States of America began to disclose something of a more essential self, enough so that the old false face probably will never quite fit again.

"Will the real Mr. X please stand up?" a quiz show host of the time used to demand, but the unmasking of a nation was not quite like that. It was more as if a wrecking ball were swinging relentlessly against a false front. Before they could recover from or even grasp the effect of one blow, it seemed to many Americans in the Sixties, they were hit with another, harder than before. The old facade had been in place a long time, though loosened somewhat by the Depression and by World War II; it was not to be shaken easily. Mom, apple pie, baseball, the flag, Sunday school—these were hailed as the verities of a nation that saw itself regularly portrayed in benign Norman Rockwell cover illustrations for the old *Saturday Evening Post* (which, rather symbolically, went out of business in the Sixties). Happy families, so the faith decreed, lived in a sort of perpetual Thanksgiving Day atmosphere, the older generations beaming generously upon the young; "togetherness," beginning as an advertising slogan, had been a sort of national theme in the Fifties. Eager bread-winners, through hard work and faith in the system, would always get ahead. Citizen soldiers would spring to arms when needed, but only in a righteous cause. Boys and girls might pitch a little woo, but only in the front porch swing.

Everybody found spiritual peace in church, so they said, and believed that the poor ought to be too proud to take charity. Justice would be done, eventually if not now; J. Edgar Hoover and the cops protected the rich and the poor alike, from communism as well as crime. Riots were unthinkable. The President was revered. America, the land of the free and the home of the brave, was also the leader of the Free World. And Americans were proud of that role and sure they could handle it, the way they had handled the Indians and the Nazis. Sometimes, some of that was true. But it was essentially a false identity, and the events of the Sixties blew it away. Perhaps the first blow was the revelation in 1960 that President Eisenhower, the national father figure, had lied publicly and officially when he insisted that the U-2, shot down over the Soviet Union, had been on a weather mission.

After that, the wrecking ball never seemed to stop. John Kennedy, who had seemed to reenforce so many stereotypes—the tough idealist, the son of the melting pot who made it to the top, the man who proved the nation was unbigoted enough to elect a Roman Catholic President—could promise in his inaugural that "We shall pay any price, bear any burden, meet any hardship, support any friend, oppose any foe to assure the survival and the success of liberty." But the first fruit of that was the Bay of Pigs fiasco; then the Cuban missile crisis gave those who had thrilled to his words a sense of their ultimate terrifying meaning; and the war in Vietnam became their most corrosive legacy.

Meanwhile, the civil rights movement, culminating in the great March on Washington and Martin Luther King's memorable speech from the steps of the Lincoln Memorial, also seemed to confirm the nation's picture of itself—even though in raising the hopes of some it raised the hackles of others. Wrong was being righted, if somewhat slowly; and Bull Connor's Birmingham police dogs were only the expected Southern exception that proved the rule. Then Watts, Hough, Newark, Detroit and dozens of other American cities exploded in flame and hatred as the last half of the Sixties turned into "the long hot summer;" and the National Commission on Civil Disorders painted the new picture that few could deny any longer. "Our nation," the commission concluded, "is moving toward two societies, one black, one white—separate and unequal." Nor was it only the burning of the cities that laid bare the hot streak of violence so near the core of American experience. "Violence," H. Rap Brown had said amid the flames, "is as American as cherry pie." And so it suddenly seemed, with John Kennedy's brain shattered by gunfire on a sunlit day in Dallas, and Robert Kennedy blown down in a moment of triumph by a strange, uprooted boy—while, one by one, gunmen and the furies destroyed Malcolm X, Medgar Evers, Martin King, each in his differing way embodying the hopes and capacities of American blacks.

It was in the Sixties, too, that Harold Teen, Andy Hardy and Miss Teenage America variously sat in at the dean's office, took to the streets in protest of war and anonymity, told Mom and Pop to shove it, took of for Haight-Ashbury and turned on to drugs. In the process, said Senator Eugene McCarthy—who almost became President as one result—"the spirit of America, largely through its young people, was renewed and revitalized." Not everyone agreed, by a long shot. Quite a few of its elders and some of its won generation thought the youth movement of the Sixties was rude, self-centured, naive, more destructive of old values than revolutionary, and counter-productive to liberal reform. It is still disputed whether the greater patriotism was shown by those who went unquestioningly to war in Vietnam or by those who questioned that war enough to go to Canada instead. However they were regarded, the young activists of the Sixties undeniably had their effect—notably in making the war eventually impossible to continue (at least American troops' participation in it), and in forcing older generations into reluctant recognition that, in a theme song of the era, "The Times, They Are a-Changin'," and the change could no more be stopped or ignored than King Canute could halt the waves.

In 1962, for example, a woman named Rachel Carson published a book called "The Silent Spring," arguing that a combination of unthinking technical "progress" and uncaring citizens was resulting in the destruction of nature's order and making the world more and more unliveable. That was the seminal event of an environmental revolution that reshaped the nation's consciousness of the world it had to live in. In 1963, another woman, Betty Friedan, published "The Feminine Mystique," and her book, too, helped set off a revolution—the strongest and most successful feminist movement in American history. Beginning in the Sixties, thousands of women were out of the kitchen and into virtually every aspect of American business and social life. It would not be long before they were a part of the ultimate male sanctum—the locker rooms of sports teams. Freed by The Pill from the ancient discipline of fear, women, too, were participating in still another revolution of changing generations and mores—a sexual revolution that made pre-marital sex, "living together" without marriage, "open marriage," avowed homosexual relationships and easy divorce more nearly the norm than the old iron expectations of courtship, marriage and living "happily ever after."

Everywhere one looked there was change. The Beatles brought a new music to a generation hungry for it; professional football, swift and violent as the times, became a new Sunday religion; and the television that brought it into the living room evolved into a sort of national nervous system. Even the once invincible New York Yankees, rather like the nation's old image of itself, sagged into disarray. That most revered of American symbols, the Presidency, came in the Sixties to seem remote, unrestrained, untouchable; and Presidents Johnson and Nixon became the first to have to wonder whether they could safely visit certain places. But in no dimension of their self-image were Americans forced to a more radically different view than in their conception of their country's power and place in the world.

Vietnam did that. Americans had believed that they could go anywhere and do anything, given their technological "knowhow," military might and righteous purposes. But when the impulse to bring sewage systems and the ballot box to the villages of Vietnam was frustrated, it turned swiftly into the savage reaction of free-fire zones. Failure begat My Lai; the body count proved no substitute for the accustomed American victory. Americans had to face what no President would admit—that they had lost a war. And in wondering why, at least some came to the conclusion that they should never have fought it, and had done so more from arrogance and ignorance than the righteousness their leaders had claimed. Others concluded that, for dark and unclear reasons, American power had not been unleashed. Neither view was fit for a Rockwell illustration. This disillusionment was accompanied at home by numerous indications that the sainted Hoover and the cop on the corner had feet of clay and fists of iron. Blacks, political dissidents, the peace movement, marchers and demonstrators—all had reason to claim that their rights were being violated, their privacy invaded, their heads cracked, their Constitution ignored.

Even the one true faith of pre-Sixties Americans—in technology—turned out to have a dark side. If they led the world in color television, as Nixon had boasted to Khrushchev, and could hitch the computer and the rocket in tandem to put a man on the moon within a decade after John Kennedy had announced the goal, still with all their electronics and all their gadgets they could not subdue a few tough little men in black pajamas in Vietnam. Many brooded over a paradox: the talents and skill that could produce jet aircraft and Telstar seemed inevitably to bring napalm and nuclear waste as well. Technological progress, moreover, was not least at fault in the environmental battles that erupted in the Sixties. Many came to believe that it was also at the root of a sort of dehumanized new urban life that placed superhighways, refrigerated air and frozen food too high in man's scale of values.

Change in the Sixties, as at any other time in man's history, was not universally accepted, or widely approved; and even for those who did approve, change was not always an unmixed blessing. Sexual revolution, for an ironic example, was accompanied by an explosion of pornography and a revival of street prostitution. Environmental gains could mean loss of jobs and higher prices. Movements spawned counter-movements. Black gains, followed by the "long hot summer," gave birth to Richard Nixon's Southern Strategy and to George Wallace's spectacular forays into the national consciousness. The drug culture evoked harsh police action and prison sentences. The Okie from Muskogee was as much a part of the youth scene as the Flower Child—the one immortalized in country music, the other in "Hair," the Tribal Love-Rock Musical. Hawks and doves became accepted terms for opposed views, not just on Vietnam but on the nation's role in the world. Feminism met its predictable response from male chauvinist pigs—and from women who preferred a more traditional role as well as from men who resented being as stereotyped as women had been. "Hardhats" beat up peace marchers; priests broke the law to protest the war.

So, one by one, stereotypes were broken in the Sixties, illusions were shattered, pretensions fell away. But what identity was it that came out of the closet of the past? Even now, in the perspective of a far different decade, it is difficult to say. Certainly the extremes of the Sixties have long faded—the younger siblings of the Flower Children are quietly at work in the classroom, the black movement is quiescent, President Carter's White House is not surrounded by demonstrators. Some major changes of the Sixties now seem endangered—affirmative action has become "reverse discrimination," many environmental gains are being rolled back, the feminist movement has not been able to win ratification of the Equal Rights Amendment.

But defeat in war, the murder of heroes, the collapse of institutions and attitudes, the rebellion of a generation and the revolt of a race—the essential stuff of the Sixties and of this evocative book—are bound to leave their scars and corrosions. They seem to me to have left a nation less sure of itself, less careless of power, more concerned with values (if not confident of value), somewhat more sensitive to history and mortality, but rather resentful of these intrusions on former comforts and certainties. Such a nation would certainly be flawed by comparison to the old Norman Rockwell vision; hence it would be more human, in a real sense more likeable. Being no longer sure of what to do and what to think it might also be less able to act—or perhaps less willing. Put another way, with some hesitation, maybe the nation has grown up a little, even if it still pines for its romantic youth.

Now, readers of this book can relive the Sixties through its headlines. No doubt some will take a different view than mine. Most probably won't find it necessary to judge the times or the nation. But I'd be willing to bet that most who lived through those events, the sad and the stirring alike, will feel in retrospect—as I do—that they wouldn't have missed a day of it.

Tom Wicker

1960

"All the News That's Fit to Print"

The New York Times.

LATE CITY EDITION

U. S. Weather Bureau Report (Page 91) forecasts: Occasional rain today; rain ending tonight. Partly cloudy tomorrow. Temp. range: 47—40; yesterday: 45—29.9.

NEWS SUMMARY AND INDEX, PAGE 91

SECTION ONE

VOL. CIX....No. 37,234. NEW YORK, SUNDAY, JANUARY 3, 1960. TWENTY-FIVE CENTS

25c outside New York City, its suburban area and Long Island. Higher in air delivery cities.

MAYOR PLEDGES FULL-SCALE STUDY OF TRANSIT CRISES

One Aim Is to Eliminate Strike Threats—Public Is 'Sick of Them,' He Says

15-CENT FARE PROMISED

Wagner Points to Burden on Budget—Notes Authority Is Creature of the State

Text of Wagner's statement is printed on Page 63.

By STANLEY LEVEY

Mayor Wagner announced yesterday that he had ordered the City Administrator's office to prepare "a comprehensive plan for dealing with the city's transportation problem."

The Mayor said the plan, designed to eliminate New York's biennial transit labor crises, would be "the most thorough-going study yet made of transportation" here.

To begin with, Mr. Wagner said, there will be a report on what the study should cover and what is needed to do the job.

Then, he declared, "I will set in motion the necessary machinery for working out our solutions, utilizing in this effort the best thinking in the community, state, region and nation."

Atmosphere of Crisis

The Mayor acted just two days after settlement of labor disputes between the Transport Workers Union and the Transit Authority and seven private bus companies.

The agreements were reached at City Hall as a 5 A. M. New Year's Day strike deadline approached, and with the usual atmosphere of crisis and pressure.

Both settlements were possible only as a result of financial assistance from the city. Mayor Wagner made $6,500,000 a year available to the authority to pay for the cost of its police force for two years. And he has promised to compensate the private lines for transporting school children at cut-rate fares.

'Terrible Ordeal' Cited

The authority-union contract calls for wage increases of 18 to 25 cents over two years plus welfare benefits that bring the total hourly cost to about 40 cents, or $35,000,000. The private lines package grants total benefits worth nearly 36 cents an hour, for a total cost of about $4,000,000.

In announcing his plan for a transportation study, the Mayor said he and the people of the city were "sick and tired of this periodic anxiety, uncertainty, pressure and near-panic."

"It simply doesn't make sense," he declared, "for the people of the city to go through this terrible ordeal every year or every second year.

"It prevents orderly development of a good transportation

Continued on Page 63, Column 5

President and Aides Work on Messages to Congress

The President with Maurice H. Stans, director of Bureau of the Budget, at Augusta. Associated

By FELIX BELAIR Jr.

Special to The New York Times.

AUGUSTA, Ga., Jan. 2—A blanket of fog over the Augusta National Golf Club kept President Eisenhower indoors again today for a busy round of official duties. Just after 8 A. M., the President conferred with White House aides from Washington on his State of the Union Message and his annual Budget Message. He will deliver the first message to Congress in person next Thursday. The budget document will be ... Jan. 18. Before these major ... President worke... hour on routine official corresp...ence, ac-

Continued on Page 40, Column 1

BORDER BUILD-UP RUSHED IN INDIA

Army Reinforced and Roads Built Near Tibet—Peiping Stand Is Unchanged

By PAUL GRIMES

Special to The New York Times.

NEW DELHI, India, Jan. 2—A massive campaign is under way to strengthen northeastern India against any further Chinese Communist aggression.

Army troops and paramilitary police units are being reinforced. Supply lines are being strengthened and are handling as much modern arms and equipment as India's limited resources will allow.

Top priority has been given to the construction and improvement of roads and communications. New roads are pushing into mountainous jungles that until last summer were considered nearly impenetrable.

Meanwhile, Communist China's latest note on its border claims against India has emphasized how far apart the two countries are in the dispute.

Note Termed Friendly

Indian sources here conceded privately that the Chinese Foreign Ministry's note of Dec. 26 appeared friendlier than early Peiping messages. Yet they noted that Peiping's claims to more than 40,000 square miles of Indian territory appeared as firm as ever.

India's defensive determination was strikingly evident to this reporter in a two-week tour of the Northeast. The tour included Himalayan highlands less than thirty-five miles from the Tibetan frontier. It included the Indian protectorate of Sikkim, sandwiched between Tibet and Nepal, and the hill city of Shillong, the command post and brain center for the remote North East Frontier Agency.

Prime Minister Jawaharlal Nehru has warned that any aggression against Sikkim would be considered an attack on India. He has rejected Peiping's claims to more than 32,000

Continued on Page 2, Column 3

Bonn Charges Plot To Smear Republic With Anti-Semitism

By ARTHUR J. OLSEN

Special to The New York Times.

BONN, Germany, Jan. 2—The West German Government charged tonight that a wave of anti-Semitic incidents during the holiday season was a result of a deliberate effort to defame the republic.

A written statement made no attempt to identify the source of the alleged anti-German campaign.

It said that the police authorities were making every effort to track down the "wire-pullers" responsible for more than a dozen incidents of swastika painting and other acts of hooliganism with anti-Semitic or neo-Nazi overtones.

Several more incidents were reported today in widely separated parts of the country.

Statement by Government

The Government statement said:

"The Federal Government and the whole German people have followed with greatest indignation reports about the desecration of Jewish places of worship and the smearing of public and private buildings with emblems and slogans of National Socialism.

"There are signs that these actions in various parts of the country are part of a concerted plan to defame the Federal Republic in the eyes of the world public. The German police authorities are conducting extensive inquiries to identify the wire-pullers behind the acts.

"The police authorities will do everything they can to bring the guilty people to justice and prevent the repetition of incidents of this kind."

Government officials believe that some of the incidents, unheard of since the end of World War II in Germany, may be examples of "juvenile stupidities," presumably inspired by the wide publicity given to the desecration of a Cologne synagogue on Christmas Day.

Three members of the Rightist radical German Reichs party have been charged in connection with the Cologne incident.

Continued on Page 4, Column 4

BENSON DRAFTING 40C CUT IN WHEAT

Price Supports Geared to Open Market Planned to Reduce Surplus

By WILLIAM M. BLAIR

Special to The New York Times.

WASHINGTON, Jan. 2—The Administration is planning to ask for sharply lower price supports on wheat and an expansion of aid to low-income farmers.

Secretary of Agriculture Ezra Taft Benson has tentatively decided to seek a drop in price supports on wheat to about $1.37 a bushel under a new formula geared to open market prices. This would be 40 cents below the $1.77-a-bushel support announced for the 1960 wheat crop under the parity formula in effect for two decades.

President Eisenhower and Mr. Benson have asked Congress to abandon the parity concept as the basis for price supports. But they have not yet outlined proposals for a support level on wheat. They also want all acreage and marketing controls removed from wheat.

However, it is understood that Mr. Benson has in mind a level of 75 per cent of the average market price of the three years immediately preceding a crop year. This plan would become effective with the 1961 crop if approved by Congress.

Based on the average of the last three years of about $1.85 a bushel, this level would be about $1.37 a bushel.

If Mr. Benson compromised at

Continued on Page 58, Column 4

EISENHOWER WARY ON PLAN TO WIDEN CIVIL RIGHTS LAW

Unlikely to Press Congress for U. S. Vote Registrars to Protect Negroes

By ANTHONY LEWIS

Special to The New York Times.

WASHINGTON, Jan. 2—The Administration will not press for early Congressional action on a proposal to appoint Federal registrars in Southern areas where Negroes are denied the right to vote.

That was the key recommendation in the Civil Rights Commission report last Sept. 8. It has been made a rallying cry by civil rights organizations, and it is already looming as a major political issue in the new session of Congress.

Congress reconvenes next Wednesday. The President will deliver his State of the Union Message Thursday and submit his budget Jan. 18.

Early Action Seen

No program has been fixed for either house, but the Senate is expected to hold an early debate on Federal aid for school construction. Other big issues of the session are likely to include farm policy, Government bond interest rates and improved Social Security benefits.

The civil rights issue will be waiting in the wings. By all indications it will not wait long.

The Senate majority leader, Lyndon B. Johnson of Texas, has promised to call civil rights legislation up for debate in mid-February. In the House, backers are working, with good hopes of success, to dislodge a bill from the Rules Committee.

The Administration has not fixed its position on civil rights. But official thinking indicates strongly that it will stand pretty much on the relatively modest proposals made by President Eisenhower last year.

Bill Whittled Down

A truncated version of the 1959 package was approved by the House Judiciary Committee last summer and is now in the Rules Committee. The House bill would:

¶Permit inspection of state voting records by the Justice Department and require preservation of the records for two years.

¶Make it a Federal crime to interfere with court school desegregation orders by violence or threats.

¶Make it a Federal crime to cross state lines in flight from prosecution for bombing or burning any building.

¶Authorize Federal schooling for children or military personnel in communities where schools have been closed to avoid integration.

In addition to these provisions, President Eisenhower had called for technical assistance to communities ending school segregation and for creation of a permanent commission against job discrimination by Government contractors. The Judiciary

Continued on Page 54, Column 1

Another Democrat Enters Contest

Associated Press Wirephoto

Senator John F. Kennedy at his news conference yesterday

KENNEDY IN RACE; BARS SECOND SPOT IN ANY SITUATION

Formal Announcement Cites Confidence He Will Win Election as President

CHALLENGES SYMINGTON

Insists All Aspirants Should Be Willing to Test Their Strength in Primaries

Text of Kennedy statement will be found on Page 44.

By RUSSELL BAKER

Special to The New York Times.

WASHINGTON, Jan. 2—Senator John F. Kennedy made it official today.

He told a news conference that he was a candidate for the Democratic Presidential nomination and was convinced that he could win both the nomination and the election.

At the same time Democratic leaders who believe that his following can be consolidated behind the Democratic ticket if Mr. Kennedy is given the Vice-Presidential nomination were given a sober warning.

If he is rejected for top place on the ticket, the Senator said, he will refuse to accept the Vice-Presidential nomination "under any condition."

'Not Subject to Change'

This decision, he added, "will not be subject to change under any condition."

The 42-year-old Massachusetts Democrat, first serious Roman Catholic contender for the Presidency since Alfred E. Smith ran in 1928, delivered his long-expected announcement to a crowded news conference in the Senate Caucus Room.

Of the many Democratic contenders, Senator Hubert H. Humphrey of Minnesota is the only other who has announced his candidacy for the Presidential nomination.

Regarding religion, Mr. Kennedy said:

"I would think that there is really only one issue involved in the whole question of a candidate's religion—that is, does a candidate believe in the Constitution, does he believe in the First Amendment, does he believe in the separation of church and state. When the candidate gives his views on that question, and I think I have given my views fully, I think the subject is exhausted."

Audience Applauds

An audience of about 300 supporters and friends applauded various answers to the reporters, giving the session the flavor of a political rally. Mrs. Kennedy also attended the conference.

Mr. Kennedy has been openly campaigning for the Democratic nomination for months. Thus today's ceremonial announcement came as no surprise.

At present the Senator is the acknowledged front-runner in

Continued on Page 44, Column 1

Party's Debate on Kennedy Takes Note of Catholic Vote

By JAMES RESTON

Special to The New York Times.

WASHINGTON, Jan. 2—Senator John F. Kennedy was in the center of a controversy within the Democratic party tonight as a result of his flat and "final" statement that he would not accept the Vice-Presidential nomination "under any condition."

This was interpreted by leaders of his party as both a temporary tactical move, and as a threat, and it raised once more the question of his powerful political support among Roman Catholics.

Those who saw the Senator's public rejection of the Vice-Presidential nomination today as merely a tactic regarded it as a perfectly justifiable move to protect his campaign for the Presidential nomination.

Those, however, who really did take his statement as a "final" rejection of the Vice-Presidential nomination regarded it as something far more ominous: as a warning to the Democratic leaders not to think they can reject his bid for the Presidency on religious grounds and still retain the backing of his supporters by giving him the Vice-Presidential nomination.

Facts Widely Known

The facts of this controversy among Democratic leaders are widely known. Though they are seldom discussed in public they are as follows:

In the Democratic Presidential race of 1956, when Senator Kennedy sought and almost got the Vice-Presidential nomination, Theodore Sorensen, who was and still is the Senator's assistant, made a detailed study of voting records to demonstrate that a Catholic Vice-Presidential candidate would be an advantage to the Democratic ticket.

Early in that 1956 race, the Senator's father, former Ambassador Joseph P. Kennedy, opposed his son's campaign for the Vice-Presidency on the ground that President Eisenhower was probably going to win and that, if Senator Ken-

Continued on Page 44, Column 2

DEMOCRATS PRESS CUT IN STATE TAX

Little Chance Seen for Plan, but It Is Expected to Give Party Campaign Issue

By DOUGLAS DALES

The Democratic minority in the Legislature will make a reduction in the state income tax a main goal in its 1960 legislative program.

Tax relief will be sought chiefly through a restoration of exemptions that existed prior to changes enacted last year. The Legislature will convene Wednesday.

Little chance is seen that the Democratic proposals will succeed, but they will provide campaign ammunition next November, when a new Legislature will be elected.

The principal obstacles to an increase in the allowances for personal exemptions are the loss of revenue that would result and the efforts of the Rockefeller administration to achieve conformity between state and Federal tax practices.

The Democratic drive for a tax cut was announced in a statement yesterday by Michael H. Prendergast, state chairman, and Senator Joseph Zaretzki and Assemblyman Anthony J. Travia, the minority leaders.

They proposed that the personal exemption allowance be restored to $2,500 for a married couple and $1,000 for a single person. They also urged that the "head of family" category, with a $2,500 exemption, be restored.

With the establishment of the

Continued on Page 64, Column 4

MAN FOUND SLAIN, SECOND WOUNDED

Police Hunt 3 in Shootings at 13th St. and Ave. A

One man was killed and another wounded in a fusillade of bullets fired early today on the lower East Side.

The police believe they were shot by three men, who fled.

The dead man was found lying on the curb at the northeast corner of Thirteenth Street and Avenue A. He had three bullet wounds in the back of the head and another in his chest.

The dead man's last name was tentatively listed by the police as Parisi. A car registered in the name of Mario Parisi of 1651 East Seventh Street, Brooklyn, was found near the scene.

The second man staggered eight blocks to the Fifth Street police station to report the shooting. He had two bullet wounds, one in the left arm and the other in the left hand.

The wounded man was Carl Radosti, 35, of 170 Fenimore Street, Brooklyn.

Authorities began investigating a report that three young men were seen hurrying into the hallway of 211 Avenue A.

Continued on Page 51, Column 1

Soviet Is Believed Ahead of U. S. In Explosions for Peaceful Use

By GLADWIN HILL

Special to The New York Times.

LOS ANGELES, Jan. 2—Some of the nation's foremost atomic researchers are ruefully convinced that the Russians have quietly forged far into the lead in another important field of science.

This is the application of tremendous explosions to peaceful engineering purposes, such as mining and the development of waterways.

In this field, over the last four years, the Russians apparently have accomplished some things the United States is still talking about doing.

The advance is not just technical. In some spectacular experiments, the Russians evidently have added greatly to the scanty amount of scientific knowledge about specialized explosive phenomena.

Intelligence reports and sketchy Soviet publications about this work, for instance, have become of prime interest and concern among scientists working for the Atomic Energy Commission at the University of California Radiation Laboratory at Livermore.

This laboratory, where the hydrogen bomb development was centered, is the headquarters of the A. E. C.'s Plowshare Project for peaceful applications of nuclear explosions.

A recent and hitherto undisclosed laboratory assessment of the Soviet work concludes that

Continued on Page 28, Column 4

School Integration Has Passed Its Crisis, Negro Leader Says

All-Out Resistance Yielding to Legal Skirmishing, Marshall Declares

By WAYNE PHILLIPS

The period of crisis and massive resistance to school integration has passed, according to the Negro attorney who won the Supreme Court decision outlawing racial segregation in public schools.

In its place, says Thurgood Marshall, has come a period of token integration, legal maneuver and what he calls "a lot of fast play around second base."

The 51-year-old attorney gave his view of what lies ahead in the school-integration controversy on the eve of his departure for his first trip to Africa.

He flew to Liberia last Friday to attend the inauguration of President William V. S. Tubman of Liberia. He will travel for two months before returning to the seventeenth-floor office in the Coliseum Tower from which he supervises the nationwide legal struggle of the Negro for equality.

Mr. Marshall, a graduate of the Howard University Law School, has been an attorney for the National Association for the Advancement of Colored People since 1934. Since 1950 he has been director-counsel of that organization's legal defense and educational fund.

The fund provides legal assistance to Negroes who are

The New York Times

Thurgood Marshall

Contnued on Page 52, Column 1

Doctors Find Christmas Strains Make Season Unhappy for Many

By JOHN A. OSMUNDSEN

Relief from the pressure of having to be happy during the holidays is beginning to brighten the lives of many persons who react violently against Christmas, according to a current medical journal.

Hives, overeating, crying jags, dishonesty, sexual deviation and just plain orneriness are said to be some of the "Christmas reactions" that those people develop around Thanksgiving and carry on until after the first of the year.

Underlying those difficulties are the rituals or "rules" of Christmas, four Utah physicians and psychiatric social workers wrote in the December issue of American Practitioner and Digest of Treatment.

Those rules, they said, require that everyone celebrate, renew family ties, exchange gifts, put up holiday decorations, have a special Christmas dinner, and—above all be happy.

The trouble is, the physicians observed, that all those rules cannot be observed by everyone, often compounding existing psychological difficulties.

In another way, such seasonal symptoms stem from the dual nature of Christmastime, according to the report.

To some, they wrote, Christmas is a time to relax and indulge oneself, to become a child again for a while.

To others, the holiday is only a reminder that life is tough enough the rest of the year.

Either way, the season is

Continued on Page 35, Column 1

Today's Sections

*Included in all copies in the New York metropolitan area and adjacent territory.

Index to Subjects

Anthony Perkins and Janet Leigh starred in Alfred Hitchcock's *Psycho.*

Jack Lemmon starred in Billy Wilder's comedy, *The Apartment.*

Paul Newman masqueraded as an Arab in a scene from *Exodus.*

1960

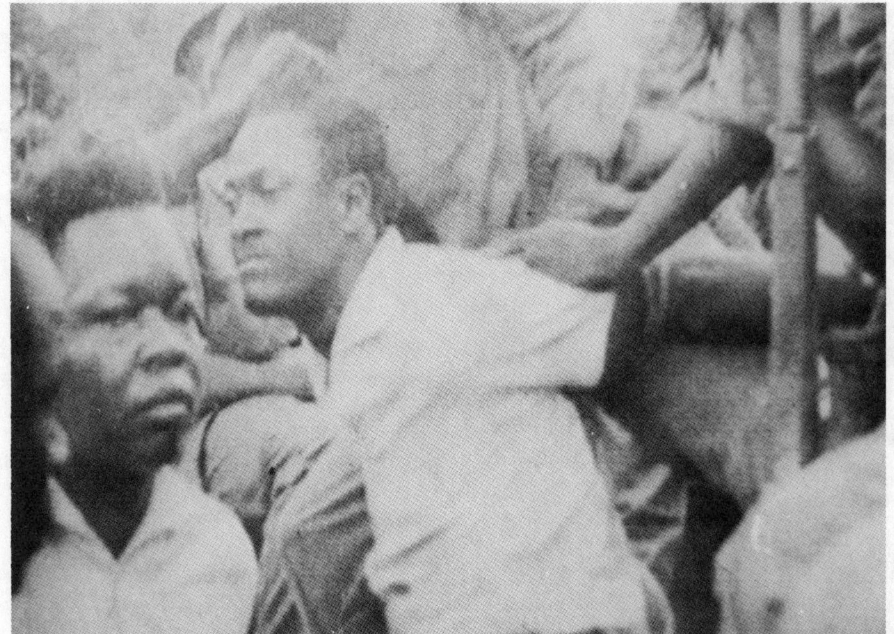

Premier Lumumba was captured by troops of Col. Mobutu and taken to jail as a traitor.

On Dec. 16, the nation was shocked by the death of 133 persons when a United Airlines DC-8 collided with a TWA Super Constellation over New York harbor and plowed into a Brooklyn street.

Discontent in Algiers led to a revolt against France in 1960.

"All the News That's Fit to Print"

The New York Times.

LATE CITY EDITION
U. S. Weather Bureau Report (Page 69) forecast: Partly cloudy early today, fair this afternoon, tonight and tomorrow.
Temp. range: 38—27; yesterday: 35.7—29.9.

VOL. CIX..No. 37,264. | NEW YORK, TUESDAY, FEBRUARY 2, 1960. | FIVE CENTS

10 cents beyond 50-mile zone from New York City except on Long Island. Higher in air delivery cities.

STATE'S BUDGET 2 BILLION, WITH 32 MILLION SURPLUS; TAX CUT DEMANDS LIKELY

REVENUE RISE DUE

Pay-as-You-Go Fiscal Policy Is Outlined by Rockefeller

Excerpts from budget message are on Pages 26 and 27.

By LEO EGAN
Special to The New York Times.

ALBANY, Feb. 1—Governor Rockefeller submitted to the Legislature today a pay-as-you-go budget that contemplates record state expenditures and tax collections.

For the new fiscal year starting April 1 the Governor estimated general fund expenditures at $2,035,000,000. This is $32,000,000 more than the state is spending in the current fiscal year. And the over-all surplus also was put at $32,000,000.

Other expenditures to be met out of tax collections were estimated by the Governor at $22,000,000. This is $8,000,000 more than is being spent for such purposes this year.

The $40,000,000 total rise in state spending contemplated is the smallest increase that has occurred from one year to another since 1953.

Mr. Rockefeller's budget recommendations were contained in a fifty-three-page special message read by a relay of clerks to a specially convened joint session of the Senate and Assembly. Since most members had printed copies, few of the elected members of the two chambers listened to the formal reading.

2 Other Funds Supported

Besides the general fund, two other state funds are supported by tax revenues. They are the war bonus and mental hygiene fund, established to pay off the state bonus to World War II veterans and to finance a state hospital construction program, and the highway account, established to pay off bonds issued for highway, parkway and grade-crossing construction.

The highway bond account is financed by the gasoline and Diesel fuel tax increases that the Legislature voted last year. The war bonus and mental hygiene fund is financed by one-tenth of income tax collections and one-fifth of cigarette tax collections.

Combined tax collections for

Continued on Page 27, Column 2

Pressure to Spend More Expected by Both Parties

Message Received With Little Comment—Only Morhouse Lauds It—Levitt Urges Added Aid for Schools

By DOUGLAS DALES
Special to The New York Times.

ALBANY, Feb. 1—Governor Rockefeller's expectation that revenues will exceed expenditures in the fiscal year starting April 1 is almost certain to bring new demands for tax relief and for spending beyond the level he proposed.

Pressure is anticipated from both Republicans and Democrats.

The budget was received today with portentous silence by the legislative leaders of both parties. The absence of the normal praise from Republican leaders was viewed as particularly significant.

The only unstinted praise for the budget came from L. Judson Morhouse, the Republican State Chairman. He called it "an unparalleled achievement in courageous, competent executive leadership" and suggested that "it should cause the rest of the nation to take careful notice."

The principal Democratic comment came from State Controller Arthur Levitt, who declared that the budget bore out his prediction that Governor Rockefeller had underestimated revenues in the year now ending by $80,000,000.

Mr. Levitt, the only elected Democrat in the state administration, referred to the document as "an austere budget that does not respond to the needs of the people, particularly in education." He said also that the budget included a "'delay of essential capital construction."

Asked whether he thought that a tax cut should be granted, the Controller said that he would favor such relief when "it was practical and feasible" but

Continued on Page 27, Column 1

MEYNER SUBMITS RECORD BUDGET

No New Taxes for Running Expenses Foreseen—Aid to Rails Not Included

By GEORGE CABLE WRIGHT
Special to The New York Times.

TRENTON, Feb. 1—Gov. Robert B. Meyner presented a record budget to the Legislature today.

It called for expenditures of $431,365,104 in the fiscal year beginning July 1. This is $24,212,000 more than in the current year.

Mr. Meyner stressed in his accompanying message that the budget would require no new taxes "for our operations."

He conceded, however, that there were multimillion-dollar capital improvements for which the state could not wait longer. He left to the Legislature the problem of how these should be financed. Thus, he did not rule out tax increases in the new year.

The Governor read his message this afternoon at a joint session of the Senate and Assembly.

He noted that the record spending would be met by anticipated total resources of $432,475,057. He proposed that a supplemental appropriation of $3,893,000 be drawn from existing state treasury balances.

New Jersey will end the current fiscal year with a treasury reserve of only $3,989,409, the smallest in more than two decades, and possibly close the new fiscal year with but $1,109,953.

Continued on Page 28, Column 2

Prosecutor Seeking Grand Jury Inquiry In Maniscalco Case

Matters brought out by a state inquiry's hearings on Borough President Albert V. Maniscalco and other Staten Islanders "must be presented to a grand jury," District Attorney John M. Braisted Jr. of Richmond said yesterday.

He declined to indicate what he thought the grand jury ought to do about any phase of the testimony taken last week by the State Commission on Governmental Operations of the City of New York, headed by Otto L. Nelson Jr.

At the sessions, Whitney North Seymour Jr., chief commission counsel, had charged that the Borough President had given and received favors in relations with builders. Mr. Maniscalco denied any wrongdoing and maintained that he had been serving his borough.

'Further Inquiry' Cited

Mr. Braisted said arrangements had been made with Mr. Seymour to turn over to his office all exhibits "together with any other pertinent additional information wh'ch may be forthcoming."

"The hearings indicated," he said, "that a further investigation will have to be made by this office into certain of the matters included in the hearings."

Both Borough President Maniscalco and District Attorney Braisted are Democrats, elected with Liberal party endorsement.

The District Attorney said his present staff—which includes four assistant district attorneys—"lacks the necessary manpower to conduct the

Continued on Page 31, Column 2

PENNSY GRANTED JERSEY FARE RISE

10,000 Commuters Affected —New Haven Plea Gains

The Interstate Commerce Commission in Washington granted commuter fare increases averaging 28 per cent yesterday to the Pennsylvania Railroad. The new rates are effective today.

The railroad, which made its request for more money on Dec. 30, reported that about 10,000 riders using the main line to Trenton and the Rahway-South Amboy line would be affected.

Commuters between Philadelphia and New York, however, will face increases of only 16 per cent.

In another action yesterday, a preliminary I. C. C. decision supported an application by the New York, New Haven and Hartford Railroad for a 10 per cent interstate commutation fare increase.

The commission voted, however, to study whether the new rate "should remain indefinitely."

A request for a 10 per cent intrastate fare rise by the New Haven is now before the New York Public Service Commission.

The I. C. C.'s action indicated that the New Haven would be allowed to put the increases in effect at midnight tomorrow.

It had been argued by the Pennsylvania Railroad that higher fares were justified to bring them into line with those

Continued on Page 24, Column 6

Civil Right Hearings Scheduled This Week by House Rules Unit

By RUSSELL BAKER
Special to The New York Times.

WASHINGTON, Feb. 1—The House Rules Committee agreed today to take up a civil rights bill this week and act on it without "dilly," "delay" or "dally."

With this concession to rising political pressure, the main barrier to the passage of a rights bill by the House appeared to be overcome.

It remained doubtful, however, whether the House could act in time to put a bill before the Senate by Feb. 15, the date on which the Senate leadership is committed to start action on civil rights legislation.

Today's action followed weeks of political maneuver by non-Southern Democrats to force the bill out of the rules committee, where it had been gathering dust.

Debate within the committee reflected some of the political pressure generated by the contest as Republicans and Southern Democrats hotly denied Northern charges that they had conspired to keep the bill "bottled up."

Representative Clarence J. Brown of Ohio, speaking for the Republicans, complained that they had been "blatherskittered all over the land" as oppressors of minorities when, in fact, their House membership had voted 164—19 for the Civil Rights Act of 1957.

The committee chairman, Representative Howard W. Smith of Virginia, charged that the real villains of the piece were the Northerners, and par-

Continued on Page 20, Column 2

WAGNER CHARGES NELSON'S REPORT PLAYED POLITICS

Assails Timing in City Study —Gerosa Calls Fiscal Section Unrealistic

Text of Mayor's statement will be found on Page 31.

By PETER KIHSS

Mayor Wagner denounced the Nelson Commission's report on the city's affairs yesterday as "a partisan political document paid for out of the taxpayers' money."

City Controller Lawrence E. Gerosa assailed the state investigating group's proposals for fiscal changes as an impractical application of hindsight.

The inquiry—formally called the State Commission on Government Operations of the City of New York and informally labeled "the Little Hoover Commission"—made public its first report to the Governor and Legislature on Sunday. Otto L. Nelson Jr. is its chairman.

The report charged that the city government, "taken as a whole, does not manifest the appetite, willingness or capacity" to reform fundamental weaknesses.

Fiscal Plan Given

It proposed revisions in cash flow, investment and debt programs by which it said the city could save $8,000,000 the first year, and at least $88,000,000 cumulatively in five years.

Replying to the Mayor and Controller, Chairman Nelson said he for one had been animated by "a very genuine desire for improvement in New York City government."

Mr. Nelson, a vice president for housing for the New York Life Insurance Company, said experts had drawn up the fiscal plan.

Noting that he was a resident of Princeton, N. J., Mr. Nelson observed, "I couldn't run for office if I wanted to." He added: "Of all the elected officials of the City of New York that appeared at our conferences, the Mayor was the only one who indicated there was any need for some improvement."

Wagner Is Bitter

Mayor Wagner, in a bitter statement issued at City Hall, complained that he had received the 143-page report only yesterday morning.

He said he would have it studied, and "if there is anything worth while in it, we will ignore the lack of amenities and will adopt the recommendations anyhow."

In a news conference later at his company office, 51 Madison Avenue, Mr. Nelson noted that in a letter sending the report to the Mayor and Controller, he had offered the services of his commission and staff to aid city studies.

The Mayor charged the report had been "timed to justify the commission's own continued

Continued on Page 31, Column 4

A Moskvich in Your Future? Soviet and U.S. Dealer Hope So

Associated Press
The four-cylinder Moskvich will carry four passengers

Special to The New York Times.

MOSCOW, Feb. 1—The Soviet Government announced this evening that it had given a United States automobile dealer an exclusive franchise for the distribution of 10,000 Moskvich cars in the United States in the next two years.

The dealer was identified as Robert Castle, chairman of Andrea Motors, Inc. No addresses were given. [Efforts to determine Mr. Castle's home city or the location of the Andrea Motors concern were unsuccessful.]

The Moskvich is the smallest of four passenger cars in production here. It is a four-cylinder, four-passenger car, somewhat like the West German Opel of several years ago.

The car's name, Moskvich, translates as Muscovite, a resident of Moscow. The car has been sold in countries of the Soviet bloc, Austria and Scandinavia.

The Moskvich factory here turned out about 70,000 cars last year, more than half of the total number of passenger cars produced in the Soviet Union.

The Government press agency Tass said Mr. Castle had signed a contract with Avtoeksport, a Soviet foreign trade corporation. It provides for the delivery of 5,000 cars this year beginning in early summer and 5,000 next year, with spare parts.

In the past exports of Soviet automobiles have been hampered by shortages of spare

Continued on Page 12, Column 4

ALGERIAN INSURGENTS SURRENDER; LEADER IS FLOWN TO JAIL IN PARIS; DE GAULLE SEEKS DECREE POWERS

DEPUTIES CALLED

Session Today to Act on Request—Basic Problems Remain

By HENRY GINIGER
Special to The New York Times.

PARIS, Feb. 1—President de Gaulle prepared, in effect, today to assume special powers to consolidate his victory over the European insurrection in Algeria.

The Cabinet called Parliament into session at 5 P. M. tomorrow, when it will be asked to give the Government power to legislate by decree.

The action was taken by the Cabinet, meeting under General de Gaulle, shortly after the European insurgents had ended eight days of open defiance of authority and surrendered to the French Army.

Tonight one of their leaders, Pierre Lagaillarde, a fiery 28-year-old Deputy, was flown to Paris to face justice. His principal associate, Joseph Ortiz, was reported to be in flight. A third, Robert Martel, also was missing.

Many Feeling Relief

Most Frenchmen tended to settle back with the relieving thought that President de Gaulle and their nation had weathered a grave crisis. But there was hardly a political observer or politician in Paris who did not think that the basic problems—the cohesion of the Government, the obedience of the army, the struggle over Algerian policy and, finally, the Algerian war, the great breeding ground of the trouble—remained.

The Cabinet decision was a clear indication that political leaders considered that much remained to be done to take in hand all the elements of dissidence and subversion that had threatened France's democracy and civil peace.

Assembly to Hear Debré

It will be Premier Michel Debré who will go before the National Assembly tomorrow, but it will be General de Gaulle who will effectively rule. More than ever before, he stands alone as the country's only effective political power and its only bulwark against chaos.

Hesitant, fumbling, divided, many of its members in sympathy with Algiers' political goals, the Government was kept in line last week only by the President's strength of character. A Cabinet shake-up is in prospect, although it is not expected to take place until he

Continued on Page 2, Column 3

Associated Press Radiophoto
INSURRECTION ENDS: Pierre Lagaillarde (arrow), insurgent leader, walking at the head of his forces yesterday as they came out from behind barricades in Algiers.

TWO ARE IN HIDING

Army Permits Most of the Dissidents to Save Face

Text of Algiers commander's communiqué on Page 3.

By THOMAS F. BRADY
Special to The New York Times.

ALGIERS, Feb. 1—The European uprising collapsed here today and its principal leader was flown to prison in Paris. Another leader was in flight and a third was mysteriously out of sight.

A face-saving formula was provided by the French Army command, which agreed to let the insurgent rank and file keep their arms by remaining "at the disposition of the army in operational units to be attached for the time being to the First Paratroop regiment of the Foreign Legion."

Those who wanted simply to go home were permitted to lay down their arms and walk away.

Home guardsmen, who had been an important element in the week-long hold-out in the middle of Algiers, were ordered to report to their battalion headquarters.

Prosecution Foreseen

The collapse came fifteen hours after insurgent loudspeakers closed down last night, proclaiming that the defenders of the barricades would die rather than surrender.

Pierre Lagaillarde, bearded 28-year-old extremist Deputy of the French National Assembly and an insurgent leader, was taken into army custody. He was not permitted to choose a face-saving course of action because it is expected he will be prosecuted.

He was sent to Paris by plane tonight to be held in Santé Prison, where the French Government first incarcerated Mohammed Ben Bella, Algerian nationalist leader. Mr. Ben Bella's organization, the National Liberation Front, advocates Algerian independence.

The uprising by the Europeans was an attack on President de Gaulle's policy of self-determination for Algeria.

A warrant has been issued for the arrest of Joseph Ortiz, a tavernkeeper and chief of a lo-

Continued on Page 3, Column 1

U. S. Expects Soviet To Have 150 ICBM's In '61 for 3-1 Lead

By JOHN W. FINNEY
Special to The New York Times.

WASHINGTON, Feb. 1—The Soviet Union will have at least 150 intercontinental ballistic missiles in operational readiness in 1961, according to the latest intelligence estimates of the United States.

If the estimates are correct, the Soviet Union will have at least a three-to-one superiority over the United States in intercontinental missiles. In the coming year, the United States will have fewer than fifty ICBM's ready to fire.

This predicted superiority in Soviet missile strength became known today as Secretary of Defense Thomas S. Gates Jr. once again went before Congress to defend the adequacy of the Administration's defense budget, particularly for the production of intercontinental missiles. He testified before the Senate Appropriations Committee.

Mr. Gates conceded that the Soviet Union "may enjoy, at times, a moderate numerical superiority" in ballistic missiles during the next three years.

Mr. Gates insisted, however, that the Soviet numerical advantage in long-range missiles "will not produce a gap in our deterrent power" because of "the versatility and strength of

Continued on Page 16, Column 3

ISRAELI JETS FIGHT MIG'S FROM SYRIA

Cairo Reports Troops Are Set to March—Ben-Gurion Threatens New Attack

Special to The New York Times.

TEL AVIV, Israel, Feb. 1—Israeli and Syrian jets clashed today as week-long border fighting continued.

Armed Syrians were reported to be refortifying positions that Israelis had smashed earlier today in a disputed demilitarized border zone.

Premier David Ben-Gurion told the Knesset (Parliament) in Jerusalem that the Israelis might be compelled to use force again to evict the Syrians from the area.

[Armed forces of the United Arab Republic were reported Monday by the Middle East News Agency, semi-official Arab press service, to be ready to move soon toward the Egyptian-Israeli border in the Sinai Desert, according to an Associated Press dispatch from Cairo.]

Meanwhile, Israeli forces were on the alert against a possible Syrian reprisal for the attack, during which the Arab village of Tawafik was said to have been destroyed by Israeli raiders.

The Israelis counted three

Continued on Page 8, Column 3

British Defense Outlay to Soar To a Record $4,536,000,000

By DREW MIDDLETON
Special to The New York Times.

LONDON, Feb. 1—Britain will increase defense expenditures this year by more than a third of a billion dollars to the highest peacetime level in her history, authoritative sources said tonight.

The Government's Defense White Paper, to be presented to the House of Commons later this month, will call for increases of between £120,000,000 ($336,000,000) and £150,000,000 ($420,000,000), officials said.

Defense Minister Harold Watkinson's estimates thus will break away from the figure of £1,500,000,000 ($4,200,000,000) that has been the average since the fiscal year 1957-58. The estimates presented last year totaled £1,514,000,000.

The explanation for the rise in fiscal 1960-61 may be found in the theme sounded in most of Prime Minister Macmillan's speeches in the last twelve months. Britain is trying to achieve a relaxation of tensions, Mr. Macmillan has said, and will continue working to that end with the Soviet Union. But he invariably has warned that Britain must keep her guard up in the meantime.

There are three principal reasons why keeping a guard up will be more expensive this year than last: the cost of the nuclear deterrent is increasing, great emphasis is being placed on the re-equipment of conventional forces and there has been a general increase in costs, especially labor costs.

Britain, a Defense Ministry

Continued on Page 17, Column 6

AFRICAN CONTROL OF KENYA IS SEEN

Long-Range British Plans Worry Whites at Talk

By WALTER H. WAGGONER
Special to The New York Times.

LONDON, Feb. 1—Iain Macleod, Secretary of State for the Colonies, proposed today that Kenya be brought to independence under a parliamentary system that, "as time goes on," would guarantee the majority Africans the predominant voice.

The Colonial Secretary outlined his views as the Kenya constitutional reform conference entered its third week, and after a week in which forty-six delegates had spoken at length on or around the issue of the East African colony's future.

The exact nature of Mr. Macleod's proposals was not made known. He asked that they be regarded as confidential and delegation leaders in the main tried to respect his request.

But from their reactions, it was apparent that the Colonial Secretary went further in his recommendations for Kenya's ultimate self-government and independence than either of the

Continued on Page 6, Column 3

NEWS INDEX

"All the News That's Fit to Print"

The New York Times.

LATE CITY EDITION

U. S. Weather Bureau Report (Page 42) forecasts: Mostly fair and continued cold today, tonight and tomorrow. Temp. range: 34—17; yesterday: 33—14.8.

VOL. CIX..No. 37,303. NEW YORK, SATURDAY, MARCH 12, 1960. 10 cents beyond 50-mile zone from New York City except on Long Island. Higher in air delivery cities. FIVE CENTS

U.S. ROCKET PUT INTO SUN ORBIT WILL BE FIRST TO GATHER DATA DEEP IN INTERPLANETARY SPACE

SENATE DELETES SCHOOL PROVISION FROM RIGHTS BILL

Liberals Join Southerners to Kill, 49-35, Plan to Curb Integration Violence

LABOR MEN INTERVENE

Act After Lausche Succeeds in Broadening Section So That Unions Are Covered

By JOHN D. MORRIS
Special to The New York Times.

WASHINGTON, March 11—The Senate killed a major section of the Administration's civil rights bill today as organized labor intervened against new provisions.

An unusual coalition of liberal and Southern Democrats struck out the section by a vote of 49 to 35. The section would have made it a Federal crime to use violence or threats to obstruct school desegregation orders of Federal courts.

The liberals turned against it when Senator Frank J. Lausche, Democrat of Ohio, won Senate approval of an amendment broadening it to cover obstruction of all Federal court orders, including those against labor unions.

The Lausche amendment was adopted on a ballot of 65 to 19. The Senate then killed the entire section by approving a motion to table it by Senator Wayne Morse, Democrat of Oregon.

'Hole' in Bill Seen

The effect, according to Senator Everett McKinley Dirksen of Illinois, the Republican leader and sponsor of the Administration bill, was to plow "a good big nuclear hole" in the measure.

The proposal, as originally drafted, was designed to deal with mob action against school desegregation such as occurred at Little Rock, Ark., and Clinton, Tenn., in 1956.

Senator Lausche sought to broaden it on the ground that the principle of equal application of the law would be violated by singling out a particular type of court order for application of the proposed anti-obstruction penalties.

Some of the most avid proponents of stiff civil rights legislation, their legal backgrounds rising to the fore, agreed with him.

When it became evident that a majority of the Senate felt the same way, word circulated in the lobbies that leaders of the American Federation of Labor and Congress of Indus-

Continued on Page 10, Column 4

Goldfine Indicted By U. S. as Evader Of $790,000 Taxes

Associated Press
Bernard Goldfine

By The Associated Press.

BOSTON, March 11—Federal indictments charging tax evasions aggregating more than $790,000 were returned here today against Bernard Goldfine, whose gift-giving forced the resignation in 1958 of Sherman Adams as the Assistant to President Eisenhower.

Mr. Adams, a former New Hampshire Governor, resigned after a Congressional investigation had disclosed he had been lavishly entertained at

Continued on Page 44, Column 3

EX-FARM OFFICIAL ADMITS PROFITING

Portland, Ore., Supervisor Was a Silent Partner in Grain Storage Concern

By WILLIAM M. BLAIR
Special to The New York Times.

WASHINGTON, March 11—A former supervisor of Government-owned surplus farm stocks acknowledged today that he had made a profit of $83,250 from a silent partnership in a company that stored Federal grain without investing any of his own money.

Earl C. Corey, who resigned under pressure from the Department of Agriculture Jan. 22, also told Senate investigators he owned stock in one of the country's largest grain companies.

The profit from the storage concern in the Pacific Northwest came in a three-year period, 1956-59, while he was director of the Agriculture Department's commodity office in Portland, Ore. The Portland office is a major office in the storage of the Government's multi-billion-dollar stocks of wheat and other grains. It handles price support and storage operations in seven Western states.

Net Gain Is Listed

The subcommittee estimated that Mr. Corey had made a net gain of $113,853 since 1955. Of this amount, it listed $83,250 from the storage company and the remainder on stock in a California grain company that he purchased for $3,020 in 1955.

Confronted with Federal regulations on conflict of interest, Mr. Corey swore under oath he was unaware of them until mid-1959 although he had held jobs under three Secretaries of Agriculture. Asked whether any Agriculture Department official had ever inquired about his out-

Continued on Page 44, Column 4

EISENHOWER ASKS POSTAL RATE RISE

Urges 5 Cents on First Class —Bill's Passage Doubted

Summary of suggested rises is printed on Page 9.

By FELIX BELAIR Jr.
Special to The New York Times.

WASHINGTON, March 11—Postal rate increases intended to yield about $550,000,000 a year in added revenues were urged by President Eisenhower today.

In a special message to Congress he said it was "imperative" to enact the higher rates and put an end to Post Office losses of $2,000,000 every working day and a resulting $600,000,000 Federal subsidy to mail users annually.

"Responsibility in the handling of our public affairs demands prompt action, in this session, to restore the Post Office Department to its traditional posture of budgetary good sense," the President said.

Summerfield in Appeal

His urgent message was followed promptly by another from Postmaster General Arthur E. Summerfield recommending specific rate increases including most of those rejected by Congress last year. Legislative leaders indicated the proposal had even less chance of passage in this election year despite a move in the House to link it to the pending bill increasing pay of postal workers.

Under the President's package plan, first-class letter rates

Continued on Page 9, Column 1

94 Million in Roads Speeded to Aid Fair

By BERNARD STENGREN

The full cooperation of Federal and state officials with the city was pledged yesterday to speed the construction of $94,000,000 in arterial highways to the site of the 1964 New York World's Fair.

Among the other developments affecting the fair, to be held in Flushing Meadow Park, Queens, were these:

¶Efforts were pressed to clear the "conflict of interest" problem for city employes who may work for the fair corporation.

¶The fair corporation obtained, rent-free for a year, the seventy-sixth floor of the Empire State Building for use as executive offices.

Those matters and others concerning the fair were discussed by officials yesterday at

Continued on Page 11, Column 2

WEST RESTRICTS SOVIET MISSIONS IN GERMAN AREAS

Travel Curbs Set by U.S. and Britain in Reprisal for Move on Passes

By SYDNEY GRUSON
Special to The New York Times.

BONN, Germany, March 11—The United States and British Army commanders in West Germany ordered sharp travel restrictions today against the Soviet military missions attached to their forces.

The Soviet mission with the French forces has been confined to Baden-Baden since early February, when the Russians paralyzed the work of the Allied missions attached to the Soviet forces in East Germany.

They did this by demanding that the Allied missions accept new documents for travel in the "German Democratic Republic" rather than in the "Soviet Zone of Occupation," as specified in the old passes.

Gen. Clyde D. Eddleman, the American commander, restricted the Soviet group to the vicinity of Frankfurt, where the mission has its headquarters.

Restriction by British

Gen. Sir James Cassel restricted the mission with the British forces to the vicinity of Buende a small town that is the mission headquarters, and Herford, a larger town, seven miles away.

The United States and British actions finally aligned the three Western Allies in the same position, though for a time during the day it appeared that the Russians were deliberately trying to divide the Americans and the British.

Joint action had been decided upon by Washington and London. General Eddleman proceeded as planned early in the morning. But the British received word through a liaison officer in East Berlin that they would be given a reply today to their protest of Feb. 19 rejecting the new passes.

The British held off. Later today a Soviet officer delivered an oral message to General Cassell. Without disclosing the contents, the British Embassy here said that it did not constitute a reply and that General Cassell had given orders to restrict the Soviet mission.

Others Await Reply

The United States and France had protested at the same time as the British. So far as was known tonight, neither the American nor the French commander in Germany had received any communication from the Soviet commander.

Ostensibly the work of the missions has been to maintain liaison between the various commands concerned. In effect the missions are engaged in overt military intelligence and there is more or less a gentleman's agreement whereby each side works the other's territory without too much interference.

Washington is known to be considering withdrawing the

Continued on Page 4, Column 2

UNKNOWN PROBED

Pioneer V Expected to Refine Maps of Solar Regions

By WALTER SULLIVAN

For the first time, man sent a "live" messenger on its way deep into the solar system yesterday.

It should help answer many of the fundamental questions regarding the role that the sun plays in our lives. It might even provide a more accurate yardstick for measuring distances within the solar system.

Not only is Pioneer V one of the most elaborately equipped scientific laboratories hurled into space, but it also should be able to report on what is going on far beyond the earth-moon system.

Starting Point Uncertain

Some believe, for instance, that the earth-moon system extends its influence a considerable distance into space. No one knows, as yet, where true interplanetary space begins.

Two vehicles, the Soviet's first cosmic rocket (Mechta) and Pioneer IV, have already become artificial planets. In effect, however, they "fell" into orbit around the sun after their radios had gone dead. At that time they were not far beyond the moon, and from then on they were no longer of value to science.

In any case, Pioneer V is headed far beyond the region where the earth's gravity, magnetism and reflected radiation have any appreciable influence.

From time to time, and with great frequency at the climax of the sunspot cycle, the sun erupts, sending clouds of gas into space. A day or two later violent magnetic storms may break out on earth.

Still Many Mysteries

Electric currents, sufficient to fuse telegraph instruments, flow between the continents and auroral displays flicker in the heavens. Furthermore, the great outer radiation belt around the earth seems to collapse, then suddenly expands to huge dimensions.

Much has been learned with earth satellites and ground observations. But the shape, composition and magnetic characteristics of the clouds from the sun are a mystery.

The nature of interplanetary space is unknown, although it has recently been proposed that the corona, or solar atmosphere, extends out as far as the earth's own orbit.

Some believe that gigantic nuclear accelerators exist in space between the earth and

Continued on Page 2, Column 6

Associated Press Wirephoto

TELL OF SATELLITE: National Aeronautics and Space Administration scientists, at left, at Washington news conference. From the front are Dr. William Duke, Maj. John Richards, Dr. Abe Silverstein and Dr. Homer E. Newell Jr. In foreground is duplicate of Pioneer V satellite, which was sent into orbit. Flat extensions contain solar cells.

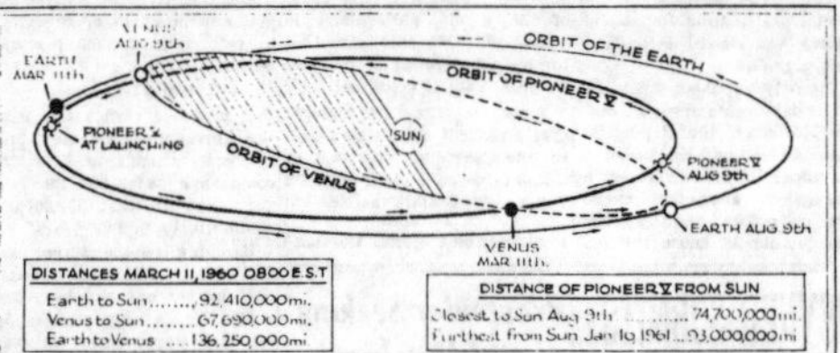

The New York Times. Adapted from Scientific American, with data from Hayden Planetarium and Space Technology Laboratories.

SKY PATHS: Orbits of the earth, Venus and Pioneer V are shown. Satellite will be closest to orbit of Venus about Aug. 9. However, the exaggerated tilt of the orbital planes of the earth and Venus, in drawing, makes the distance on that date seem larger. The actual tilt is about 3.4 degrees. Satellite's path is near plane of earth's orbit.

TAKES A NEW PATH

Course of the Vehicle Is Between Orbits of Earth and Venus

By JOHN W. FINNEY
Special to The New York Times.

WASHINGTON, March 11—The United States today shot a 94.8-pound sphere, packed with scientific instruments, into an unending orbit around the sun between the planetary paths of Earth and Venus.

The artificial planetoid, named Pioneer V, will explore realms of interplanetary space not yet traversed by space vehicles. It will also demonstrate the feasibility of communicating with the earth over interplanetary distances of 50,000,000 miles and more.

The sphere is twenty-six inches in diameter. It carries five principal scientific experiments. It was successfuly launched by a Thor-Able rocket fired from Cape Canaveral, Fla., at 8 A. M.

Built Around Thor

The launching rocket was built around the Air Force's Thor intermediate-range ballistic missile, which produces 165,000 pounds of thrust at take-off. All three stages of the rocket burned to within one second of their scheduled time.

By the time the final stage stopped burning, at an altitude of about 300 miles, the payload had been accelerated to a velocity of 24,869 miles an hour. This was 150 miles an hour below the planned velocity, but it was still enough for the sphere to escape the earth's gravitational hold and to go into an elliptical orbit around the sun.

By 8:05 A. M. tomorrow, officials estimated, Pioneer V will be 187,150 miles from the earth. It is on the first leg of a 527,000,000-mile, 311-day trip around the sun. Its instruments and radio equipment were reported to be functioning perfectly.

Velocity Reduced

As the sphere soared upward in a dog-legged path away from the earth, its velocity was quickly reduced by the gravitational pull of the earth.

By midafternoon its speed was less than 8,000 miles an hour. It will pick up speed again, however, as it is caught, like a weight on the end of a string, in the sun's much more powerful gravitational field.

In its orbit around the sun, the sphere will be traveling at an average speed of about 70,000 miles an hour, in comparison with 66,500 miles an hour for Earth and 78,000 miles an hour for Venus.

On the basis of preliminary tracking information, the Na-

Continued on Page 2, Column 1

NINE NATIONS SEE NEED TO LIFT AID

Japan Joins Western Lands in Agreement—Bold Plan for Africa Sought

By PAUL HOFMANN
Special to The New York Times.

WASHINGTON, March 11—Seven Western nations and Japan agreed today with the United States on the necessity of stepping up aid to underdeveloped countries.

Delegates from the nine countries decided at their first meeting, which ended tonight after three days, to harmonize their assistance projects and to make them more efficient. A bold approach to Africa's economic needs was agreed to be in the common interest.

The nine capital-exporting countries that make up the new Development Assistance Group decided to keep in touch in Washington on foreign aid questions. The group will meet again in Bonn, Germany, in about three months.

Members of the group are Belgium, Britain, Canada, France, Italy, Japan, Portugal, West Germany and the United States.

Egidio Ortona, chief Italian delegate to the United Nations

Continued on Page 6, Column 2

Ben-Gurion Asserts West Could Assist A Peaceable Egypt

Special to The New York Times.

WASHINGTON, March 11—David Ben-Gurion, Premier of Israel, said today that the West could contribute to the development of the United Arab Republic if Cairo would resolve to live in peace with its neighbors.

The Israeli leader met with members of the Senate Foreign Relations Committee and several other invited Senators for an hour and forty-five minutes this morning.

Afterward, at a news conference, he summarized the substance of his informal discussion with the Senators.

Calls Peace Key to Future

"If Egypt will be satisfied to live in peace with its neighbors—not only its Jewish neighbors, but its Arab neighbors as well—it may do a great deal to persuade the West to help their country, to change their country to a healthy, educated country," Mr. Ben-Gurion said.

This objective could be achieved, he added, if only the Egyptian leaders "would apply their energies to that and not to negative objectives, such as making war and dominating other peoples."

Mr. Ben-Gurion recalled that the Middle East was "the cradle of civilization" and ex-

Continued on Page 5, Column 5

WEST TO PROPOSE LIMIT ON FORCES

To Ask Ceiling of 2,100,000 Men for Soviet and U. S. at Geneva Parley

By A. M. ROSENTHAL
Special to The New York Times.

PARIS, March 11—The West plans to propose at the disarmament conference opening in Geneva Tuesday that the Soviet Union and the United States limit their military manpower to 2,100,000 men each.

This ceiling would go into effect in the second of the three phases of the Western plan and would be followed by more manpower cuts in the third stage. The 2,100,000 figure is 400,000 less than proposed by the West in 1957 as the preliminary manpower ceiling.

Under the five-power Western plan, the Soviet Union and the United States would eventually cut their armed forces to the level required for the maintenance of internal security.

U. N. Provisions Invoked

But until an international police force was set up the powers would be allowed to keep enough troops to live up to the obligations undertaken under the United Nations Charter, according to unofficial reports here. The Western powers regard the North Atlantic Treaty Organization as within the self-defense provisions of the Charter, and this part of the plan apparently was written with NATO defenses in mind.

The Western disarmament plan, agreed to in a revised version yesterday, does not state specific manpower ceilings for Britain and France.

The plan would require those two countries to reduce their forces' strength. But France, heavily engaged in Algeria, is not ready at the moment to commit herself in advance to specific figures. The importance

Continued on Page 4, Column 6

Dr. Roy Chapman Andrews Dies; Explorer and Naturalist Was 76

He Discovered Dinosaur Eggs in Asia in 1920's—Headed Natural History Museum

By The Associated Press.

CARMEL, Calif., March 11—Dr. Roy Chapman Andrews, explorer and naturalist, died here tonight of a heart attack at Peninsula Community Hospital. He was 76 years old.

Dr. Andrews, who had been living in retirement for several years in near-by Carmel Valley, gained world fame in the Nineteen Twenties through a series of expeditions to Central Asia. He was former director of the American Museum of Natural History in New York.

Ability Plus Showmanship

Dr. Andrews combined scientific ability with the showmanship necessary to obtain public financial support for exploration ventures of true scientific importance.

For three decades he was a lecturer and author, and the popular ideal of a romantic explorer; it was he who found the first 10,000,000-year-old dinosaur eggs in the Gobi Desert and exhibited to an awed public great leg bones of the biggest

Associated Press
Dr. Roy Chapman Andrews

ancient monsters known to have walked the earth.

The acclaim that came to Dr. Andrews was sometimes criticized by more stolid scientific workers, but he turned it to the advantage of man's understanding of his earth. He raised funds for and led a great many large-scale expeditions to little-known corners of the world.

His integrity as a scientist was proved by his colleagues, who through the years elected

Continued on Page 21, Column 2

Suit Says Powell Bars Whites From Selling Liquor in Harlem

By RALPH KATZ

The Liquor Salesmen's Union charged in Supreme Court yesterday that Representative Adam Clayton Powell Jr. had "advised" Harlem retail store owners that they would be picketed unless they bought from Negro salesmen.

The charge was made in a motion by the union for a temporary injunction to restrain the Metropolitan Package Store Association, Inc., and its executive director, Gerald F. Dunne, "from instructing any of the members of the association to cease purchasing from white salesmen."

In support of the motion, Local 2 of the union submitted affidavits from white liquor salesmen alleging that store owners had told them they could no longer buy from them. The affidavits asserted that a list of approved salesmen had been sent out by the National Association for the Advancement of Colored People.

One salesman, Sidney R. Barrett, with ten years of service in Harlem, said that store owners had told him they were acting "pursuant to directives of the Metropolitan Package Store Association."

Another salesman, Sol Berkoff, said in his affidavit:

"They [the store owners] were also told by Congressman Powell that after the Harlem pressure groups take care of the liquor industry, they will take care of the 'milk and bread' business."

Max Drexel, executive secretary of the union, asserted in his affidavit that the union admitted to membership all qualified persons without regard to race, creed or color. "This applica-

Continued on Page 10, Column 8

NEWS INDEX

GEROSA ACCUSED OF 'ABOUT-FACE'

Beame Charges Controller Gave Facts He Disowns

By PAUL CROWELL

Controller Lawrence E. Gerosa was accused yesterday of seeking to disown by "an amazing about-face from the facts" an attack on a state commission's proposals to improve the city's fiscal procedures.

The charge was made by Budget Director Abraham D. Beame, who had been named by Mr. Gerosa Thursday as the author of a statement issued in the name of Mr. Gerosa and Mayor Wagner.

This statement attacked the report by the State Commission on Governmental Operations of the City of New York, calling its proposals "pie in the sky." The statement was published in newspapers of Feb. 13 and 14.

In his statement Thursday Mr. Gerosa said that he had agreed to have his staff work with Mr. Beame in preparing an answer to the proposals but that he had been "under the impression" that the material was for use at a legislative hearing.

He also said that Mr. Beame had told him, when questioned

Continued on Page 12, Column 5

"All the News That's Fit to Print"

The New York Times.

LATE CITY EDITION

U. S. Weather Bureau Report (Page 46) forecasts: Chance of rain today and tonight. Windy, chance of rain tomorrow. Temp. range: 56—45; yesterday: 63.6—45.5.

VOL. CIX....No. 37,324. NEW YORK, SATURDAY, APRIL 2, 1960. 10 cents beyond 50-mile zone from New York City except on Long Island. Higher in air delivery cities. FIVE CENTS

U.S. ORBITS WEATHER SATELLITE; IT TELEVISES EARTH AND STORMS; NEW ERA IN METEOROLOGY SEEN

U. N. COUNCIL BIDS HAMMARSKJOLD ACT ON SOUTH AFRICA

France and Britain Abstain —Ecuador's Plan to Halt Race Violence Wins, 9-0

OUTBREAKS DEPLORED

Lodge Praises Program— Secretary General May Meet Fourie Today

Excerpts from U. N. Council debate are on Page 2.

By LINDESAY PARROTT
Special to The New York Times.

UNITED NATIONS, N. Y., April 1—The Security Council asked Secretary General Dag Hammarskjold today to consult with the Government of South Africa with a view to curbing racial violence there.

The council adopted a moderate draft resolution, introduced by Ecuador, "deploring" recent outbreaks near Capetown and Johannesburg and requesting the Secretary General to "make arrangements" to provide that the United Nations Charter be upheld.

The vote was 9 to 0 with two abstentions—Britain and France. The French representative, Armand Bérard, told the council that although his nation disapproved of racial segregation under South Africa's apartheid policy, he had "serious misgivings" that the council had gone beyond the functions assigned it by the Charter.

Abstentions Not a Veto

Sir Pierson Dixon of Britain raised the same objection. The abstentions of the two nations did not constitute a veto. Under Security Council practice, it takes an adverse vote by one of the five permanent members to block the adoption of a resolution.

A spokesman for the United Nations said this evening that Mr. Hammarskjold would undertake "urgent consideration" of the responsibilities assigned to him by the Council's action.

It was understood that he might talk first with Bernardus G. Fourie, head of the South African delegation here, and later communicate, through him or directly, with the Union Government.

A member of the South African delegation said that instructions regarding the next step had been sought from his Government. South African representatives, however, let it be understood that the initiative rested with Mr. Hammarskjold.

'No Plans' for Talks

Mr. Fourie, as he left United Nations headquarters tonight, said that he had "no plans" to talk with Mr. Hammarskjold. The Secretary General, he said, would be welcome in South Africa if he chose to go there. But Mr. Fourie was not sure that his Government would be willing to discuss its policy of apartheid, the main target in the Security Council debate.

Some sources, however, said that a meeting between the South African representative and Mr. Hammarskjold had been tentatively set for 11:30 A. M. tomorrow, pending instructions from Pretoria.

Ecuador's delegate, Dr. José A. Correa, made plain during today's discussion that one purpose of his resolution was to give the Secretary General the freest possible hand in talks

Continued on Page 3, Column 1

U. S. and Soviet Set For Air Route Talks

By WILLIAM J. JORDEN
Special to The New York Times.

WASHINGTON, April 1—The Soviet Government has informed Washington that it is ready to negotiate for regular airline traffic between the United States and the Soviet Union.

A note received from Moscow today was in answer to a suggestion made by the United States Government in October, 1958. The Soviet message said Soviet representatives would be prepared to enter into talks at a time and place convenient to both Governments.

Officials here welcomed this indication that the Soviet Union was now willing to have the United States join the list of

Continued on Page 46, Column 6

3 Africans Killed As Mob Marches On Jail in Durban

By LEONARD INGALLS
Special to The New York Times.

JOHANNESBURG, South Africa, April 1—Three persons were killed and five wounded today when the police fired on African rioters who surged to the center of Durban, South Africa's major Indian Ocean port.

Today's loss of life in Durban came after a night of disturbances in several parts of South Africa. At least two Africans were shot dead last night by the police in outbreaks of violence in Johannesburg. An African policeman died today from stab wounds he received last night, during disturbances at Natal Spruit, about twelve miles east of Johannesburg.

Several thousand Africans from Cato Manor, the African slum about two miles outside Durban, began a march on the city just after noon today. A similar attempt had been turned back yesterday. They were met by the

Continued on Page 3, Column 2

U.S. WARNS SOVIET ON SPACE DANGER

Charges 'Propaganda' Bars Steps at Geneva to Avert Orbiting of A-Bombs

By A. M. ROSENTHAL
Special to The New York Times.

GENEVA, April 1—The United States, charging that Soviet "propaganda" was blocking the disarmament conference, appealed to Moscow today to negotiate immediately on space-age dangers before the world reached the "point of no return."

Inside and outside the conference room the United States delegation pushed aside three weeks of diplomatic gentility and got tough—sharply and deliberately tough. It said the Soviet plan for disarmament would not meet United Nations goals. Although the United States avoided the word "rejection," the meaning was plain.

But blended with this planned sharpening of position was the appeal to Moscow to work for an agreement to prevent the launching of nuclear bombs into space before it was too late.

Just thirty inspectors, said the United States, are all that are needed to keep watch on launching sites in the United States and the Soviet Union. Delay much longer, the United States warned, and the danger of bombs in orbit around the earth might become a reality beyond control.

An answer came from the Soviet Union in a matter of minutes. It was this: The United States concentrates on controlling space dangers be-

Continued on Page 4, Column 4

MAYOR'S BUDGET UP 160 MILLIONS; TAX CUT POSSIBLE

2.3 Billion Total May Bring a Lower Rate on Realty— Hearings Open Friday

Excerpts from Mayor's budget message, Page 12.

By PAUL CROWELL

Mayor Wagner submitted to the Board of Estimate yesterday a record executive expense budget of $2,338,857,547 for the fiscal year starting July 1.

Despite the new high in spending, there may be a reduction in the real estate tax rate because of increases in property assessments.

The proposed budget is the second to pass the $2,000,000,000 mark and the fourteenth in succession to rise above the $1,000,000,000 level. It is $160,266,357 larger than the current expense budget of $2,178,591,190.

Realty Pays Half

Under the budget real estate taxpayers would be required to contribute $1,026,860,822, the first time this figure has gone above $1,000,000,000 in a single year.

This is $48,394,385 more than real estate is currently paying. But, according to the Mayor, this is only 43.9 per cent of the entire budget expense, compared with 44.91 per cent in the current budget.

Although no responsible city official would say so "for the record," it was strongly hinted that the current basic real estate tax of $4.16 on each $100 of assessed valuation would be reduced at $4.15 for 1960-61. It was said that the reduction would be possible because of the substantial increase in assessed valuations over the city.

General Fund Crucial

A few optimists expressed the opinion that the rate might even drop to $4.14 if the city's general fund revenues exceed the $795,668,000 estimated in the Mayor's budget calculations.

Such an increase would reduce by an equivalent amount the contribution required of real estate taxpayers as a whole. The ultimate bill for individual property owners will vary according to individual assessments despite any decrease in tax rates.

The proposed budget produced yet another "first." For the first time in the city's history its annual bill for interest and principal payments on its debt is more than $400,000,000—a $25,080,731 rise over the 1959-60 bill bringing it to $401,652,504.

In general this debt is incurred in financing projects under the city's other budget—the capital budget, which operates on a calendar-year basis and provides for public improvements of a permanent nature.

The Mayor's proposed expense budget, which covers day-

Continued on Page 13, Column 1

Continued on Page 13, Column 1

SENT BY SATELLITE: One of TV pictures from Tiros I. Dark area, lower right, is St. Lawrence River and Gulf.

Associated Press Wirephotos

CLOUDS: White mass is cloud cover on U. S. and Canada. Pictures were made by a camera with a wide-angle lens.

2 CAMERAS IN USE

270-Pound Vehicle to Transmit Pictures for 3 Months

By RICHARD WITKIN
Special to The New York Times.

CAPE CANAVERAL, Fla., April 1—The first artificial satellite able to provide detailed photographs of the earth's weather was fired into orbit here today by the United States.

Two television cameras looking down from an altitude of about 450 miles made initial pictures of the earth's cloud patterns during the satellite's second orbital trip.

Four pictures, taken by the wider-viewing and therefore less-precise camera of the two, were proudly distributed this evening by the National Aeronautics and Space Administration. The space agency has over-all responsibility for the project.

The pictures showed the cloud cover that lay over the Northeast United States and the adjacent area of Canada this morning. They also showed an identifiable outline of the gulf of the St. Lawrence River. The curvature of the earth was clearly recognizable.

2 Storms Photographed

In Washington Dr. Harry Wexler, director of research of the Weather Bureau, said officials at Fort Monmouth, N. J., had reported that the satellite had taken photographs of a storm moving into the Middle West, a New England storm and the "cloud bridge" connecting the two.

Before being made public, the pictures had been taken to the White House by Dr. T. Keith Glennan, the head of the space agency.

The President told him:

"The earth doesn't look so big when you see that curvature."

He said also:

"I think it's a marvelous development."

Vast Gains Envisioned

It was understood that the second camera, with a narrow-angle lens for taking pictures with finer detail, was also working successfully. It may be that, for reasons of security, such pictures will not be released immediately.

For weather experts, today's successful launching held some of the promise that the discovery of the telescope must have held for astronomers in the seventeenth century.

The 270-pound satellite, named Tiros I, offered a means

Continued on Page 2, Column 1

1,014 BILLS LEFT FOR ROCKEFELLER

Gains and Losses Seen for Governor—Session May Have Hurt Mahoney

Summary of the 1960 session is printed on Page 10.

By WARREN WEAVER Jr.
Special to The New York Times.

ALBANY, April 1—The adjournment of the Legislature early today left conflicting and confused opinions as to who had won and who had lost politically in the 1960 session.

When the lawmakers filed wearily out of the Capitol this morning, they also left behind a legacy of 1,014 bills on Governor Rockefeller's desk.

The Governor did not wait to find out what problems the legislators had passed on to him. He left for New York City, a few hours after the session adjourned at 1:36 A. M. to fly to Venezuela tonight.

[The Governor left Idlewild Airport for Caracas at 10:24 P. M. He was to join his family on his Venezuelan ranch.]

Mr. Rockefeller's post-session vacation will be a short one this year. He is due back in the state next Thursday for a visit to the Jamestown Community College and a Republican dinner in that city.

Actually, the 1960 Legislature approved 1,389 bills between the time it convened on Jan. 6 and adjournment this morning. Of these, however, the Governor had already signed 346 into law and vetoed twenty-nine others.

The number of bills approved this year set a record, just edging out the previous high of

Continued on Page 11, Column 1

APPROXIMATE AREA in TV photos, shown on a globe

NIXON WEIGHS BID TO ROCKEFELLER

Keeps Door Open for Later Appeal That the Governor Be His Running Mate

By W. H. LAWRENCE
Special to The New York Times.

WASHINGTON, April 1—Vice President Nixon has indicated that he has an open mind on a possible approach to Governor Rockefeller as a prospective Vice-Presidential running mate.

Mr. Nixon let it be known, however, that he had made no overtures to the New York Governor and that he planned none in the immediate future.

Mr. Rockefeller has declared in the strongest terms that under no circumstances would he run for Vice President now that he has bowed out of the active race for the Presidency.

But many Republicans, including former Gov. Thomas E. Dewey of New York, feel that a Nixon-Rockefeller ticket would be "ideal" for the G. O. P. in 1960. They have expressed the hope that Mr. Rockefeller can be persuaded to reconsider.

Mr. Nixon, it was said, feels that Governor Rockefeller's initial decision not to accept second place on the ticket was quite sincere.

But Mr. Nixon recalled that a similar stand was taken by Earl Warren, then Governor of California and now Chief Justice of the United States, before

Continued on Page 24, Column 2

Trujillo Quits Party To Spur Opposition

By United Press International.

CIUDAD TRUJILLO, Dominican Republic, April 1—Generalissimo Rafael Leonidas Trujillo Molina resigned today as leader and member of the Dominican party, the political coalition that helped keep him in power here for more than thirty years.

The Dominican strong man said at a meeting of the party's executive board that his decision stemmed from a desire to see more political parties established in the Dominican Republic.

"No one wants to form new parties while I remain in the Dominican party," General Trujillo told the board members, who asked him to withdraw his

Continued on Page 9, Column 4

FAIR HOUSING ACT UPHELD BY COURT

Justice Steuer Rejects Suit Claiming the 'Right' to Discriminate in City

The constitutionality of the city's Fair Housing Practices Law was upheld yesterday by State Supreme Court Justice Aron Steuer.

The court rejected a suit by Edmond Martin, a real estate man of 16 Christopher Street, who had contended that the 1958 statute, commonly known as the Sharkey-Brown-Isaacs law, was an unjustified interference with his right to conduct business.

"The individual must yield to what legislative authority deems is for the common good," Justice Steuer ruled.

The action was the first legal test of the measure, which became effective on April 1, 1958. The law was the first of its kind in the country to prohibit discrimination because of race, religion or national origin in the rental or sale of private housing not receiving Government aid.

Sign Caused Dispute

Mr. Martin became involved in litigation after he displayed a sign in his Greenwich Village office that said he would refuse to show apartments to Negroes, on constitutional grounds. He was summoned to appear before the city's Commission on Intergroup Relations to answer a complaint that he had violated the Fair Housing Practices Law.

Referring to the statute, which is listed in city regulations as "Local Law 80," Justice Steuer said:

"Just because a man is a Negro he is not, ipso facto, a desirable tenant. But the statute does not say that. It says the converse—because a man is a Negro he is not, ipso facto, an undesirable tenant."

The justice said it had long been recognized that the state had the power to make regulations on rental housing. He pointed out that statutes now

Continued on Page 11, Column 2

NEWS INDEX

News Summary and Index, Page 25

SENATE REJECTS A REFEREE CURB

Anger Marks Rights Debate as Kefauver Plan Fails— Courts to Set Hearings

By RUSSELL BAKER
Special to The New York Times.

WASHINGTON, April 1—In an afternoon of angry personal quarreling, the Senate killed the Kefauver amendment to the civil-rights bill today. The vote was 69 to 22.

The amendment, sponsored by Senator Estes Kefauver, Democrat of Tennessee, would have weakened the bill's voting-referee provision by permitting local authorities to participate in procedures for registering Negro voters.

Its opponents charged that it would have made it possible for hostile local authorities to intimidate Negro applicants.

Instead of killing it outright, the Senate voted to substitute a single sentence sponsored by Senator John A. Carroll, Democrat of Colorado. This says only that the courts shall set the time and place for the referees to hear applicants.

'Neither Adds Nor Subtracts'

Senator Kenneth B. Keating, Republican of New York, observed that this was "meaningless" since the courts would normally have such power anyhow. The Justice Department, Mr. Keating said, believed that the Carroll amendment "neither adds to nor subtracts from" the bill.

After disposing of the Kefauver amendment the Senate leadership immediately opened a holding operation calculated to prevent more changes in the bill and force matters to an early end.

This set off a series of bitter personal disputes, the first in seven weeks of strong but bloodless oratory on the Senate floor.

After the vote Senator Lyndon B. Johnson of Texas, the Democratic leader, announced that he hoped to dispose of more amendments today and suggested that Senator Jacob K. Javits, Republican of New York, get things rolling by offering one of his.

Mr. Javits had prepared an amendment giving statutory authority to the President's Commission Against Discrimi-

Continued on Page 21, Column 4

Cubans and Poles Sign Trade Treaty

By TAD SZULC
Special to The New York Times.

HAVANA, April 1—Cuba announced last night a far-reaching trade pact with Poland. Cuba will receive industrial plants and equipment, ships, planes and helicopters on credit and in exchange for goods.

The United States has refused to sell Cuba any helicopters, contending that they might be used for military purposes. This led Premier Fidel Castro to denounce Washington's position and to send a formal protest. Cuba said she needed the helicopters for agriculture.

The Cuban-Polish agreement, signed by Foreign Minister Raul Roa and Poland's Deputy Minister of Foreign Trade, Francis-

Continued on Page 8, Column 3

F.B.I. AGENT NAMED A HOFFA MONITOR

Judge Refuses to Approve Resignation of Maher

By JOSEPH A. LOFTUS
Special to The New York Times.

WASHINGTON, April 1—Terence F. McShane, a special agent of the Federal Bureau of Investigation for nine years, was named today as a monitor of the International Brotherhood of Teamsters.

Mr. McShane resigned from the F. B. I. yesterday to accept appointment by Judge F. Dickinson Letts of United States District Court. He was sworn in today by Judge Letts.

He succeeds Lawrence T. Smith, who was discharged by Judge Letts.

Judge Letts also notified James R. Hoffa, president of the Teamsters, that he was refusing to accept the resignation of Daniel B. Maher as a monitor and therefore he could not consider Mr. Hoffa's nomination of William E. Bufalino, Detroit teamster leader, to succeed Mr. Maher.

The third member of the board of monitors is Martin F. O'Donoghue, the chairman.

Mr. McShane said that as an F. B. I. agent he had worked on cases involving the Teamsters, Mr. Hoffa and his associates. He emphasized, however,

Continued on Page 48, Column 7

Head of Nation's Household Answers Census Man

Associated Press Wirephoto

President Eisenhower replies to questions of Louis J. Alexis, census director of the District of Columbia, at the White House. The eighteenth ten-year census began yesterday.

By RICHARD E. MOONEY
Special to The New York Times.

WASHINGTON, April 1—Eisenhower, Dwight D., reported to two high-ranking census takers today that he was the head of his household, male, white, married, and born in October, 1890.

Thus began the eighteenth ten-year census of the population of the United States. It will provide the record on which the next decade's representation in Congress will rest, and the basis for countless plans, theories and decisions that will be developed at varied levels of Government, business and the academic world. The President gave the facts of his life, his

Continued on Page 15, Column 1

"All the News That's Fit to Print"

The New York Times.

LATE CITY EDITION

U. S. Weather Bureau Report (Page 95) forecasts: Cloudy, rain today, tonight. Clearing gradually tomorrow. Temp. range: 64-54; yesterday: 66-6-54.8.

NEWS SUMMARY AND INDEX, PAGE 95

SECTION ONE

VOL. CIX—No. 37,360. NEW YORK, SUNDAY, MAY 8, 1960. 35c outside New York City, its suburban area and Long Island. 50c in 17 Western states, Canada; higher in air delivery cities. TWENTY-FIVE CENTS

U. S. CONCEDES FLIGHT OVER SOVIET, DEFENDS SEARCH FOR INTELLIGENCE; RUSSIANS HOLD DOWNED PILOT AS SPY

JOHNSON ARRIVES IN WEST VIRGINIA AS CLIMAX NEARS

Texan Declines to Choose Between Humphrey and Kennedy in Primary

VOTE DRIVES WINDING UP

City of Clarksburg Invaded by Politicians, High School Bands and Rotarians

By WAYNE PHILLIPS

Special to The New York Times.

CLARKSBURG, W. Va., May 7—Senator Lyndon B. Johnson, an undeclared candidate for President, flew into West Virginia today as the climax approached in the state's Presidential preference primary.

He announced that he would not state a preference between the two Democratic candidates in the primary, Senator Hubert H. Humphrey of Minnesota and Senator John F. Kennedy of Massachusetts.

He described the candidates as "colleagues of mine, both of whom I have the greatest respect and affection for." And he added, "Either one of them would be far superior to anything that the Republican party can possibly offer."

Candidates Everywhere

"I didn't come down here to tell you how to make your decision," he said. "I look forward with confidence to your decision, whatever it may be."

The city of Clarksburg that welcomed him appeared like a rather soggy finale to "The Music Man." For it was also playing host to thirty-three high school bands, a Rotary convention, and an army of hopeful candidates for almost every public office from constable to President of the United States.

No one counted the number of trombones in the bands to see if there were seventy-six. But Clarksburg is about the same size as Mason City, Iowa, which inspired the Broadway musical. And the light rain that fell discouraged none of those who had traveled from miles around to see what was going on.

Humphrey's Sister Stumps

While the crowd was waiting for the bands to parade down Main Street, Mrs. Frances Humphrey Howard, a sister of Senator Humphrey, was passing out coffee and doughnuts on the steps of the County Courthouse.

Near by, one of the many local candidates who was moving through the crowd greeting old friends and trying to make new ones, was Ralph J. Keister, who is running for the state's House of Delegates.

There are more than 200 candidates on the Democratic ballot in this county alone, and nearly that many on the Republican ballot. Together with family and friends, that made a sizable number of people here

Continued on Page 47, Column 2

Nixon Shifts Tactics To Combat Kennedy

By The Associated Press.

WASHINGTON, May 7—Vice President Nixon reshaped his campaign plans today on the theory that Senator John F. Kennedy would win the West Virginia primary Tuesday and go on to win the Democratic Presidential nomination.

Herbert G. Klein, Mr. Nixon's press secretary, told the newsmen that if the belief was accurate, Mr. Nixon, as the expected Republican nominee, would be competing against a single opponent instead of half a dozen Democratic Presidential possibilities.

Mr. Klein indicated that if this turned out to be the case, Mr. Nixon, in drafting his speeches during the coming weeks, would concentrate more on Senator Kennedy. Even if Senator Hubert H. Hum-

Continued on Page 46, Column 3

N.A.A.C.P. TO FIGHT CURBS AT BEACHES

Plans 'Wade-In' Campaign at Tax-Maintained Resorts From Jersey to Texas

Special to The New York Times.

ATLANTA, May 7—The National Association for the Advancement of Colored People announced today a "wade-in" campaign against segregation on Southern beaches.

The association's executive secretary, Roy Wilkins, said "hundreds and thousands of miles" of beaches and public parks were maintained with tax funds.

Negroes, he said, pay taxes and "they get hot just like white people do." They like to swim to cool off and with the prospect of warm weather ahead "they intend to do it this summer" from Cape May, N. J., to Brownsville, Tex., he said.

Between Cape May, on the Atlantic, and Brownsville, on the Gulf of Mexico, is a coastline that touches eleven states that practice segregation. North of Cape May, public facilities are generally integrated.

Cites Biloxi Incident

The wade-in drive, Mr. Wilkins told a news conference, was spurred by the recent attempt of Negroes to use a public beach at Biloxi, Miss. They were attacked by whites and for a time authorities feared serious rioting.

Mr. Wilkins met here at the Waluhaje Apartments with state presidents and secretaries of the association from Arkansas, Florida, Georgia, Louisiana, Mississippi, North Carolina, South Carolina, Oklahoma, Tennessee and Virginia.

Besides the beach demonstrations and a continuation of the group's efforts to break down lunch-counter segregation, Mr. Wilkins said the conference had reviewed plans to increase voter registration and N. A. A. C. P. membership and to speed the process of school desegregation.

He pointed out that the civil rights law signed by President Eisenhower this week required establishment of a pattern of discrimination before Federal referees could step in to guarantee Negro voting rights.

Many to Seek Vote

As a result, he said, local N. A. A. C. P. officials will urge Negroes to "apply in numbers."

He also cited recent gains in registration, which he attributed to a strong campaign by the organization and particularly its youth chapters.

A Florida representative reported that 4,000 Negroes had been added to the registration rolls at Tampa since Feb. 1. They are now registered in the only South Carolina county—McCormick—that had no Negro registrants, according to Mr. Wilkins.

He said the N. A. A. C. P. would continue to provide guidance, counseling and financial and legal support for the student sit-in demonstrations against lunch-counter segregation.

Mr. Wilkins also said the association "will not indulge in criticism of other groups or individuals" involved in the movement but would concentrate on increasing its own activities.

This apparently was a reference to attacks on the N. A. A. C. P. by some elements in the Southern Christian Leadership Conference, a Negro ministers' organization headed by the Rev. Dr. Martin Luther King Jr. of Atlanta. Dr. King attended today's session but left early for another meeting.

On school desegregation, Mr.

Continued on Page 67, Column 6

DERBY CAPTURED BY VENETIAN WAY

Bally Ache Defeated by 3½ Lengths at Louisville

Venetian Way, owned by Isaac Blumberg, won the $158,950 Kentucky Derby yesterday at Churchill Downs in Louisville by three and a half lengths. Bally Ache ran second and Victoria Park third. Tompion, the 11-to-10 favorite, finished fourth in the field of thirteen 3-year-old colts. Bill Hartack rode the winner a mile and a quarter in 2 minutes 2 2/5 seconds. Venetian Way paid $14.60 for $2.

In other sports:

BASEBALL

The New York Yankees beat the Kansas City Athletics, 4 to 1, on the five-hit pitching of Ralph Terry. The Boston Red Sox defeated the Detroit Tigers, 5 to 0, as Bill Monbouquette pitched a one-hitter. The San Francisco Giants downed the Pittsburgh Pirates, 6 to 5, and tied them for first place in the National League.

CHESS

Mikhail Tal, a 23-year-old Latvian, won the world championship from Mikhail Botvinnik of Leningrad.

Details In Section 5.

LONDON TROUBLED

Fears That U.S. Stance for Summit Parley Will Be Injured

By DREW MIDDLETON

Special to The New York Times.

LONDON, May 7—The United States position at the summit conference and in the global contest with the Soviet Union may be seriously weakened by the plane incident in Russia, diplomats said today.

The damage to the United States abroad has been heightened by the first hasty denial of spying on the Soviet Union and the subsequent admission forced from the Eisenhower Administration. At first, Allied diplomats thought the Soviet version would be accepted only by the Left-Wing circles, neutralists and pacifists of Europe, Asia and Africa.

The State Department's later acknowledgment of the nature of the plane's mission, even though it was unauthorized by the authorities in Washington, means that distrust of the United States will spread beyond those circles.

'Bad Luck' Evident

The Foreign Office had no official comment on Mr. Khrushchev's charges. This Government has not been informed by the Administration about the incident.

Beneath the diplomatic explanation that it was a United States affair there clearly was concern over what was considered to be rather offhand treatment of a stanch supporter of the Administration at a critical moment.

The British are clearly worried about what professionals call "bad luck" and by the effect of the incident on the diplomatic position of the United States, Britain and France at the summit meeting. The immediate effect in this field, it was said, is that Mr. Khrushchev's report will raise doubts all over the world about the true willingness of the United States to work for a reduction of tensions.

The Image of Eisenhower

The British and their European allies seldom read the fine print in Presidential and Senatorial speeches. Consequently, they have perhaps been too impressed by what they considered American readiness to work for such a relaxation.

The European image of General Eisenhower, supported by his speeches abroad last September and December, is that of a man of peace and goodwill. The latest incident is said to

Continued on Page 24, Column 5

'CONFESSION' CITED

Khrushchev Charges Jet Was 1,200 Miles From the Border

Excerpts from the Khrushchev speech are on Page 24.

By OSGOOD CARUTHERS

Special to The New York Times.

MOSCOW, May 7—Premier Khrushchev jubilantly reported today the capture of the pilot of a United States plane that he said had been shot down on May Day. He said the Americans had admitted attempting to carry out a photo-reconnaissance mission all the way across the Soviet Union from Pakistan to Norway.

Mr. Khrushchev said the American was being held and probably would be tried, presumably for espionage, in Moscow.

The Premier said the plane had been shot down by a Soviet rocket near Sverdlovsk, 1,200 miles from the Afghan-Soviet border.

To wildly cheering Deputies of the Supreme Soviet, who had been called into a three-day session to pass on internal legislation, Mr. Khrushchev cried: "We have parts of the plane and we also have the pilot, who is quite alive and kicking. The pilot is in Moscow and so are the parts of the plane."

Provocation Implied

He implied once again that he felt that the United States military had sent the plane across the Soviet Union as a provocation aimed at sabotaging the summit conference, which is scheduled to open a week from Monday in Paris. But he indicated that he still intended to meet with the Western leaders and play host to President Eisenhower. Mr. Khrushchev said, however, that the incident was "bad preparation" for the East-West talks.

He displayed a handful of large photographs of what he said was part of the "espionage equipment" taken from the plane's wreckage and from the pilot.

This was Mr. Khrushchev's reply to the State Department's contention that the plane may have been a weather reconnaissance aircraft that has been missing on a high-altitude flight over northeastern Turkey after the pilot, Francis Gary Powers of Jenkins, Ky., had reported trouble with his oxygen equipment.

The Soviet leader said the plane had taken a cluster of photographs of industrial cen-

Continued on Page 25, Column 1

Associated Press Radiophoto

ACCUSES PILOT: Premier Khrushchev displaying before the Supreme Soviet in Moscow one of the views of Soviet territory he said had been obtained by United States flier.

ACTION EXPLAINED

Officials Say Danger of Surprise Attack Forces Watch

Text of the State Department statement is on Page 29.

By JAMES RESTON

Special to The New York Times.

WASHINGTON, May 7—The United States admitted tonight that one of this country's planes equipped for intelligence purposes had "probably" flown over Soviet territory.

An official statement stressed, however, that "there was no authorization for any such flight" from authorities in Washington.

As to who might have authorized the flight, officials refused to comment. If this particular flight of the U-2 was not authorized here, it could only be assumed that someone in the chain of command in the Middle East or Europe had given the order.

President Clears Statement

"It appears," said the statement, "that in endeavoring to obtain information now concealed behind the Iron Curtain, a flight over Soviet territory was probably undertaken by an unarmed civilian U-2 plane."

The statement was issued by the State Department after clearance by President Eisenhower. It came at the end of a day of uneasy silence. All through the day the highest officials of the Government had worked on an answer to Premier Khrushchev's charges that the United States had been caught red-handed in an aerial-intelligence operation behind the Soviet borders.

The statement contained what was probably the first official admission that extensive intelligence activities were being conducted along the Soviet frontiers. It gave no assurance that these activities would be curbed in the future.

Soviet Activity Cited

But it justified this intelligence work on several grounds. "The Soviet Union," it pointed out, "has not been lagging behind in this field." Furthermore, it said, the excessive secrecy practiced by the Russians and their refusal to accept a United States plan for mutual protection against surprise attack obliged the free world to take every precaution.

"It is in relation to the danger of surprise attack that planes of the type of the unarmed civilian U-2 aircraft have made flights along the frontiers of the

Continued on Page 28, Column 4

VOROSHILOV QUITS AS CHIEF OF STATE

Brezhnev, Khrushchev Aide, Rising in Party Councils, Succeeds Marshal, 79

By MAX FRANKEL

Special to The New York Times.

MOSCOW, May 7—Leonid I. Brezhnev, a 54-year-old Communist party functionary, was chosen today to succeed 79-year-old Marshal Kliment Y. Voroshilov as titular chief of state of the Soviet Union.

Marshal Voroshilov, a slight and wizened figure in the otherwise robust ranks of the Soviet hierarchy, resigned because of health in an emotional scene at the close of today's session of the Supreme Soviet, this country's version of a parliament. The move was not unexpected.

The retiring chief of state was praised, decorated and finally kissed on both cheeks by Premier Khrushchev and by his successor. Minutes later the Premier, who remains undisputed leader of the Soviet Government and the Communist party, nominated Mr. Brezhnev.

The nature of Marshal Voroshilov's illness is not known.

Long a Revolutionary Symbol

Marshal Voroshilov was a Bolshevik revolutionary for a decade before his faction seized power in 1917. To nearly all Russians he has been a popular symbol of stability and national dignity. He was associated with Lenin and the revolution, with the growth of the Red Army and the civil war, with Stalin, the defense of Leningrad and the defeat of Germany in World War II.

Mr. Brezhnev, on the other hand, represents a new generation of Soviet figures, men who were born in this century and are now coming into their own. They were weaned on the machines, in industry, agriculture and politics.

A personable and respected figure in party circles and a particularly steadfast ally of Mr. Khrushchev in recent years, Mr. Brezhnev will continue to serve also as one of the six important secretaries of the Communist party.

Heads Executive Group

Mr. Brezhnev's new post carries the formal title of Chairman of the Presidium of the Supreme Soviet of the Soviet Union. This Presidium, distinct from the ruling Presidium of the Communist party, to which Marshal Voroshilov also belongs, is a committee of thirty-two men who are collectively the Soviet Executive.

Hitherto the office of chairman of this group has been one of little formal power. But because its occupant proclaims all laws and decrees, receives foreign envoys and in ceremony and fact represents the entire nation he has come to be known abroad as the "Soviet President."

Russians place his portrait on

Continued on Page 30, Column 4

Underground Atom Blasts Set by U.S. to Aid Detection

By E. W. KENWORTHY

Special to The New York Times.

WASHINGTON, May 7—President Eisenhower announced today a six-fold expansion of the United States program to improve the detection of underground nuclear explosions. The President said that the expanded program, known as Project Vela, would involve a series of underground nuclear explosions of various sizes in different kinds of geological formations.

The announcement was made this morning at Gettysburg, Pa., by James C. Hagerty, the President's press secretary.

The President explained that the explosions would be limited

Text of White House statement is printed on Page 34.

to those "essential to a full understanding of both the capabilities of the presently proposed detection system and the potential for improvements in this system."

All Underground Blasts

He emphasized that all the explosions would be conducted underground "under fully contained conditions and would produce no radioactive fall-out."

Officials here also stressed that the planned explosions would not be used in any way for the development of nuclear weapons. There was no intention, they insisted, to end the present moratorium on weapons testing, which is now being renewed on a month-to-month basis.

The officials emphasized also that the decision to conduct such tests was not a pre-summit maneuver and that the timing of the announcement had not been determined by the disclosure of Premier Khrushchev

Continued on Page 35, Column 1

INTELLIGENCE ACTS ADMITTED BY U.S.

Both Soviet and American Efforts in Field Cited in Statement on Plane

By JACK RAYMOND

Special to The New York Times.

WASHINGTON, May 7—The United States statement today on the plane downed in the Soviet Union contained the first official Government disclosure that this country was engaged in aerial intelligence efforts.

Heretofore such activities have been only hinted at through announcements of Soviet activities and military strength.

For example, it was the United States that first announced Soviet atomic and hydrogen bomb explosions. The United States has consistently made public, officially or indirectly, statistical estimates of Soviet military strength, including missiles.

The State Department's announcement called attention to both the United States' own intelligence-gathering efforts and those of the Soviet Union, saying that these are "certainly no secret."

Planes Active in Turkey

It has been known for many years that in Turkey the United States has sent aircraft high into the skies, equipped with radar and various electronic instruments, to seek to learn secrets of the Soviet nuclear explosions, missile-launching bases and other military materials.

The United States has constructed giant radar antennas in Turkey, which it has used to study Soviet missile launchings with considerable accuracy. So acute have the United States "ears" become that the State Department was able in 1958 to release a tape recording of Soviet pilots talking to each other over their intercommunication systems as they prepared for an attack on a United States Air Force transport plane.

Officials today would not amend the story they issued at that time that the Air Force C-130, which was downed by the Russians, had accidentally flown over the Soviet border. President Eisenhower hinted then that the Soviet Union might have lured the Air Force craft over Soviet territory with a false radio signal.

Similar efforts by airborne reconnaissance efforts off the

Continued on Page 26, Column 1

John Reed Kilpatrick, 70, Dies; Headed Madison Square Garden

Arena President From 1933 to 1955—Was Soldier, Builder and Athlete

John Reed Kilpatrick, honorary chairman of Madison Square Garden and its president from 1933 to 1955, died yesterday of cancer in Roosevelt Hospital. He was 70 years old.

His most recent political activity had been as national chairman of the Citizens for Eisenhower and Nixon organization in the 1956 campaign.

At his death he was chairman of the New York City Committee of the American Cancer Society. He had been active in the group for fourteen years and had served as its president for nine.

Mr. Kilpatrick, who had been an outstanding athlete at Yale, served with distinction in both World Wars and was a retired brigadier general of the Army Reserve. He also had been a construction executive and had been active in politics and public service.

Mr. Kilpatrick was the man who bailed the Garden out of red ink during the depression and kept it profitable thereafter.

He was extraordinarily equipped for the job of president, and later chairman, of the corporation that ran the largest indoor sports arena in New York. He had been a great athlete in his youth and a sports fan all his life. He was a big, bulky, exuberant, extroverted, democratic man; a wealthy, successful, friendly man; a very intelligent, well educated man; a New York Athletic Club-type of man; in short, the best Madison Square Garden-type of man.

John Reed Kilpatrick was

John Reed Kilpatrick

Continued on Page 86, Column 3

Cuba Is Exchanging Envoys With Soviet

By TAD SZULC

Special to The New York Times.

HAVANA, May 7—Cuba and the Soviet Union formally resumed diplomatic relations tonight.

A communiqué issued by Foreign Minister Raul Roa said these relations had in fact been "tacitly" re-established through Moscow's recognition of Fidel Castro's revolutionary Government on Jan. 1, 1959, and through the trade pact signed here last Feb. 13 by Anastas I. Mikoyan, a Soviet First Deputy Premier, and the Castro Government.

By the new agreement, Cuba and the Soviet Union are exchanging ambassadors in completion of the diplomatic formality.

A few hours before the announcement, Vladimir Bazikin, the Soviet Ambassador to

Continued on Page 19, Column 4

Today's Sections

Index to Subjects

Nikita Khrushchev and Andrei Gromyko at the UN General Assembly session.

Khrushchev insisted that this exhibited equipment came from our U-2 spy plane.

Fidel Castro gave Khrushchev a warm greeting when they both visited the United Nations.

Francis Gary Powers, U-2 pilot, was sentenced to 10 years at his Moscow spy trial.

"All the News That's Fit to Print"

The New York Times.

LATE CITY EDITION

U. S. Weather Bureau Report (Page 78) forecasts: Cloudy, cool, some rain today and tonight. Cloudy and mild tomorrow. Temp. range: 55—48; yesterday: 60.1—45.9.

VOL. CIX....No. 37,363. © 1960, by The New York Times Company. Times Square, New York 36, N. Y. NEW YORK, WEDNESDAY, MAY 11, 1960. 10 cents beyond 50-mile zone from New York City except on Long Island. Higher in air delivery cities. FIVE CENTS

KENNEDY WINNER OVER HUMPHREY IN WEST VIRGINIA

RIVAL QUITS RACE

Minnesotan to Seek Re-election to Senate —He Lauds Victor

By W. H. LAWRENCE
Special to The New York Times.

CHARLESTON, W. Va., Wednesday, May 11—Senator John F. Kennedy of Massachusetts won a smashing upset victory in yesterday's West Virginia's Presidential preferential primary.

The Senator promptly forecast that he would be nominated at the Democratic National Convention, which starts July 11.

His "significant and clear-cut" victory was conceded at 1 A.M. Eastern standard time (2 A.M. New York time) by Senator Hubert H. Humphrey of Minnesota.

Senator Humphrey also announced that he would withdraw from the race for the Democratic Presidential nomination. For Senator Kennedy, a Roman Catholic it was a surprising victory in a state where it had appeared that anti-Catholic sentiment had made Senator Humphrey the pre-primary favorite.

Turnout Is Heavy

The Associated Press, reporting on returns from 1,168 of 2,750 precincts, gave:

Kennedy 93,341
Humphrey 60,889

Observers estimated that 400,000 of the 670,000 registered Democrats had turned out to vote on a raw, chilly day.

[In the Nebraska primary, Mr. Kennedy and Vice President Nixon received impressive popular support. Mr. Kennedy was the only Presidential candidate entered. Mr. Nixon was backed by write-in votes.]

Senator Kennedy flew here from Washington after the vote trend had established him as the probable winner. He told a television audience that the West Virginia vote had demonstrated that his religion was not a major issue with the nation's voters.

He said the results here should go far toward "quieting" the concern he said some Democratic leaders had felt about nominating a Catholic for the Presidency. The vote here, Senator Kennedy said, demonstrated that religion would not be a dominant issue if he were picked by the Democrats to run against Vice President Nixon, the expected Republican Presidential nominee.

Senator Kennedy said the West Virginia primary was "the

Continued on Page 31, Column 1

Mayor Asks Speed On Rezoning Plan

By CHARLES G. BENNETT

Mayor Wagner served notice yesterday on opponents of the proposed new zoning law that the statute was long overdue and should be enacted.

The Mayor's declaration was the most unequivocal one favoring rezoning that he has made since the City Planning Commission undertook its zoning study more than three years ago.

His statement, however, came in the face of mounting criticism of some of the zoning proposals, some of it from members of the Board of Estimate.

Mr. Wagner emphasized his endorsement of rezoning in a 3,000-word policy speech delivered yesterday at a luncheon of the Committee for Modern Zoning, a pri-

Continued on Page 42, Column 3

F.P.C. HEAD DENIES INFLUENCE CHARGE

Kuykendall Heard at House Inquiry—Defends Actions on Gas Rate Increases

By ANTHONY LEWIS
Special to The New York Times.

WASHINGTON, May 10—The chairman of the Federal Power Commission defended himself today against charges of having been swayed by influence-peddlers and of having neglected consumer interests in favor of natural gas companies.

Jerome K. Kuykendall spent a long day before the House Special Subcommittee on Legislative Oversight. The group opened an inquiry into the power commission.

The subcommittee counsel, Robert W. Lishman, brought out that $506,000,000 in supposedly "temporary" gas rate increases were still in effect because the F. P. C. had never got around to reviewing them.

Provisions for Refunds

The companies are allowed to collect the increases pending commission review, but they must refund any part of the rise later found improper. Some of the cases listed by Mr. Lishman had been before the commission since 1954.

"Isn't it a fact," Mr. Lishman asked, "that these companies can come in and get temporary increase on top of temporary increase—five or six at a time?"

Mr. Kuykendall agreed that that was so, adding that it was "a deplorable situation." The reason, he explained, is simply the enormous backlog of work facing the power commission—the biggest workload of any regulatory agency, he said.

The hearing focused on one case in which an F. P. C. examiner had found that the Colorado Interstate Gas Company owed its customers a refund of $50,000,000 but the customers

Continued on Page 14, Column 4

DONEGAN ASSAILS POLITICAL BIGOTRY

Bishop Asks Ban on Religion in Presidential Campaign

By GEORGE DUGAN

The Right Rev. Horace W. B. Donegan, Bishop of the Protestant Episcopal Diocese of New York, told churchgoers yesterday that religion had no part in the Presidential election of 1960.

"We are not electing a Protestant, a Roman Catholic or a Jew—we are electing a President of these United States," he said.

His words bore special significance as voters went to the polls in the West Virginia primary yesterday to choose between Senator John F. Kennedy of Massachusetts, a Roman Catholic, and Senator Hubert H. Humphrey of Minnesota, a Protestant.

The Bishop's address before the annual convention of the diocese on the grounds of the Cathedral Church of St. John the Divine was regarded by observers as one of the most forthright of his career.

In addition to his plea to keep religion out of the Presidential campaign he scored the South African policy of apartheid as "morally unsupportable, spiritually unpardonable and shamefully tragic in its consequences."

Bishop Donegan's comments

Continued on Page 32, Column 5

Nashville Integrates Six Lunch Counters

Special to The New York Times.

NASHVILLE, Tenn., May 10—Lunch counters were desegregated today in six department and variety stores in downtown Nashville.

It was believed to be the first such general action in the South outside of a few cities in Texas.

The move followed a carefully prepared agreement that was reached by merchant and Negro leaders last Friday after four weeks of negotiation. Efforts to achieve an understanding had been under way since the last Negro sit-in demonstrations April 12, when a near-riot resulted.

The decision was a well-guarded secret. No announcement was made and Nashville newspapers and radio and television stations had agreed not to publicize the transition.

In accordance with the agree-

Continued on Page 15, Column 1

Atom-Powered Submarine Circles Earth in 84 Days

Associated Press Wirephoto (U. S. Navy)

Capt. Edward L. Beach as he first told crew on Feb. 17 of plans for underwater voyage

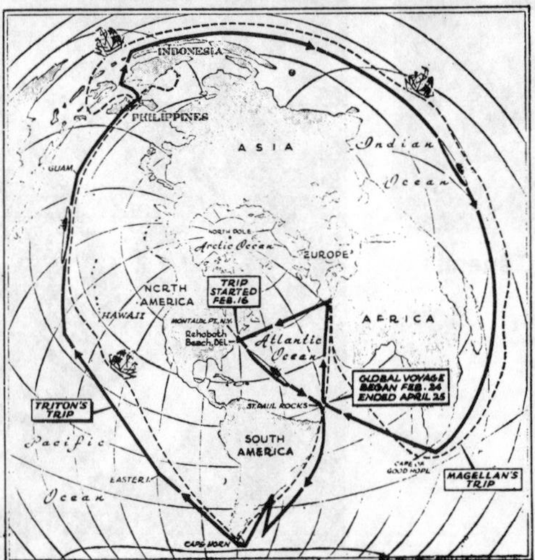

The New York Times — May 11, 1960

Triton's 41,500-mile voyage included 30,708 miles on circumnavigation route, much the same course as the one sailed by Magellan in a three-year cruise more than 420 years ago.

Triton Goes Around Globe Submerged, Retracing the Route Sailed by Magellan

$16,300,000 SLATED FOR SCHOOL RISES

Theobald Gives Salary Plan, but Teachers Ask More—Board Re-elects Silver

By LEONARD BUDER

A new salary schedule for teachers was proposed yesterday by Dr. John J. Theobald, the Superintendent of Schools. It is intended to put the city school system in a better position to attract and retain staff members.

Dr. Theobald presented the details of the $16,300,000 proposal to the Board of Education at its annual meeting. The plan, which would grant annual increases of $200 to $400 to the city's teachers and various amounts to other employes, follows the lines indicated last week by the Superintendent when he met with teacher leaders.

Pension Aid Adds to Rise

Because of the city's recent decision to pay part of the pension contributions of city employes, the school staff will receive a further increase in take-home pay. For teachers, this will mean $120 to $207, after tax deductions. The total increases for teachers, starting July 1, thus will range from $323 to $607, according to the system's estimates.

However, the United Federation of Teachers, which has threatened a work stoppage starting next Tuesday, and the Teachers Union said yesterday that they were not satisfied with the proposed increases.

The federation called for a $400 increase in the basic starting salary and $600 in top salaries. The union also asked for other salary adjustments that would raise the maximum paid to teachers with extra preparation to $10,000, or $900 above the proposed amount.

Charles H. Silver was elected to another term as president of the board. He is a retired textile executive and has been a

Continued on Page 25, Column 3

Skipper Is Decorated—Log Tells Drama of Global Journey

Excerpts from the Triton's log appear on Page 26.

By FELIX BELAIR Jr.
Special to The New York Times.

WASHINGTON, May 10 — The world's largest submarine, the nuclear-powered U. S. S. Triton, surfaced off the Delaware coast just before dawn today after a submerged voyage around the world.

The distance covered under water was 41,500 miles, a great deal more than the distance around the globe. The voyage lasted eighty-four days.

Behind the 7,750-ton twin-engined submersible as she eased her rust-streaked and slimy hull above the Atlantic surf was a record of circumnavigating the globe over much the same route taken by Ferdinand Magellan, sixteenth century explorer—but in a fraction of the time taken by Magellan.

In sixty-one days, the most powerful submarine ever built cruised 30,708 miles over Magellan's route, from St. Paul Rocks off the northeast coast of Brazil.

She was submerged all the time except for two brief periods when she "broached" the surface, showing about five feet of her superstructure above the ocean.

With her 183 officers and men, including half a dozen scientists and technicians, the Triton left her base at New London, Conn., on Feb. 16. She reached St. Paul Rocks on Feb. 24.

Then she rounded Cape Horn and cruised deep and fast across

Continued on Page 27, Column 1

NEWS INDEX

LINCOLN CENTER FINDS COSTS SOAR

Estimate for Arts Project Up From 75 Million to 100 —More Aid Sought

By PETER KIHSS

The estimated cost of the Lincoln Center for the Performing Arts has climbed well above $100,000,000. However, only $59,177,219 has been pledged so far toward a $75,000,000 fund-raising goal, which was initially expected to cover virtually all costs.

Appeals for further aid from the city government are among proposals now being considered. The center's board of directors has had a committee studying the financing problem for several months, but as yet it has not come up with a solution.

One proposal being considered is for the city to assume some of the cost of $12,000,000 to $14,000,000 for the projected home for the City Center of Music and Drama and the $7,000,000 Library-Museum of the Performing Arts. However, neither the City Center nor the New York Public Library has formally joined Lincoln Center.

Many Changes in Plans

The plans and financing arrangements have undergone many revisions over the years. Some changes have been made because of increases in construction costs since the general estimates were made in 1957. Even now detailed plans have yet to be drawn for several units. Other increases have resulted from changes in concepts.

Construction costs throughout the city have increased 9.2 per cent since September, 1957—when the Lincoln Center fund-raising campaign began—to March, 1960, according to the F. W. Dodge Corporation's Dow Building Cost Calculator.

Lincoln Center's cost increases have become known piecemeal. Asked for comment, John W. McNulty, director of public relations, would say only that "financial problems are now

Continued on Page 25, Column 1

U.S. VOWS TO DEFEND ALLIES IF RUSSIANS ATTACK BASES; SOVIET TO TRY PILOT AS SPY

MOSCOW PROTESTS

Will Exhibit Plane—U. S. Asks Interview With Jailed Flier

Texts of the Soviet and U. S. notes are on Page 4.

By OSGOOD CARUTHERS
Special to The New York Times.

MOSCOW, May 10 — The Kremlin told the United States today that it would bring to trial an American pilot shot down over the Soviet Union on May 1 while on a reconnaissance mission.

In an official note of "emphatic protest" the Soviet Union threatened that it would take "retaliatory measures" against any repetition of American intelligence flights over its territory.

At the same time the United States Embassy in Moscow delivered a brief note to Foreign Minister Andrei A. Gromyko requesting an interview with the pilot, Francis Gary Powers.

Premier Khrushchev has declared that Mr. Powers was captured after his single-engine U-2 plane was shot down by a rocket near the Urals industrial center of Sverdlovsk.

Plane Exhibit Prepared

Meanwhile, the Soviet Union was setting the stage for a public display of some of the wreckage of the plane it described as the downed American aircraft. It was expected that the exhibition would be preceded by a news conference.

Pieces of a plane, including part of an unmarked wing and other pieces of twisted metal, were set up in the building of the chess club in Gorky Park. Other objects purported to be equipment from the wreckage were set on pedestals.

Today's Soviet protest note did not give any more detail about the incident than had been disclosed by Mr. Khrushchev. It said an investigation by Soviet experts of available data had "incontrovertibly established" that Mr. Powers, a civilian pilot from Pound, Va., was flying a plane based in Turkey and sent through Pakistan into the Soviet Union "with hostile purposes."

No Trial Date Given

"Pilot Powers, about whose fate the Embassy of the United States of America inquired in its note of May 6, is alive and, as indicated in the aforementioned speech of Chairman of the U. S. S. R. Council of Ministers, N. S. Khrushchev, will be brought to account under the laws of the Soviet state," the note asserted.

It did not indicate when the trial would take place or on what precise charges Mr. Powers would be tried.

The Soviet note said that in light of the plane incident United States authorities "apparently seek to return the state of American-Soviet relations to the worst times of cold war and to poison the international situation before the summit

Continued on Page 4, Column 2

U. S. Photographed Soviet Spy Planes

By JACK RAYMOND
Special to The New York Times.

WASHINGTON, May 10—The United States has photographed Soviet jet planes on aerial reconnaissance over Western military bases all over the world, Pentagon authorities said today.

However, the highest available sources said they were unaware of any Soviet efforts to fly such missions over the continental United States.

The United States has never downed a Soviet reconnaissance plane, a high military official said. He explained that United States interceptor planes were operating under strict orders not to fire on Soviet reconnaissance aircraft unless they are fired on.

Most of the Soviet efforts at surveillance from the air have occurred in the Pacific, according to Defense Depart-

Continued on Page 4, Column 5

CONGRESS UNITED ON SOVIET CHARGE

Hails Speeches by Johnson and Cannon, Democratic Chiefs, on Need to Spy

Text of Senator Johnson's talk will be found on Page 3.

By JOHN D. MORRIS
Special to The New York Times.

WASHINGTON, May 10—Congress engaged in a pre-summit display of unity today in response to the Soviet Union's protests against aerial espionage by the United States.

The demonstration took the form of bipartisan applause and praise of speeches in the Senate and House by Lyndon B. Johnson of Texas, the Senate Democratic leader, and Representative Clarence Cannon, Democrat of Missouri.

Both speakers made the point that espionage was a "cold war" necessity. Both assailed Premier Khrushchev for his belligerent reaction to the May 1 flight over the Soviet Union of a United States U-2 photo-reconnaissance plane.

Shooting Down Denied

Representative Cannon, in addition, declared that the plane had not been shot down, as Premier Khrushchev contended. Mr. Cannon said its capture had resulted either from a mechanical defect or some "physiological defect" of the pilot.

Mr. Cannon, as chairman of the House Appropriations Committee, was among the representatives who received a secret briefing on the plane incident yesterday from Secretary of State Christian A. Herter and Allen W. Dulles, director of the Central Intelligence Agency.

Senator Johnson's statement as well as Mr. Cannon's showed a closing of Congressional ranks in support of the Administra-

Continued on Page 3, Column 1

WASHINGTON FIRM

Clears Other Nations of All Responsibility in Plane Incident

By WILLIAM J. JORDEN
Special to The New York Times.

WASHINGTON, May 10—The United States pledged today to help defend its allies if they were attacked by Soviet missiles.

This was Washington's answer to Premier Khrushchev's threat yesterday to strike at bases used by the United States for aerial surveys of Soviet territory.

The United States Government also said that other countries had no responsibility for the recent flight of a U-2 jet reconnaissance plane that went down in the vicinity of Sverdlovsk nine days ago. Mr. Khrushchev said the flight began in Pakistan and was to have ended in Norway.

The statement of United States policy was made by Lincoln White, State Department spokesman. Like previous pronouncements on the U-2 incident, today's statement was approved by Secretary of State Christian A. Herter.

President to See Press

President Eisenhower will have a news conference tomorrow morning. The U-2 incident will undoubtedly be its center of interest. Meanwhile, it was understood that there was no intention at the Central Intelligence Agency to look for scapegoats in the affair. Premier Khrushchev had identified Francis Gary Powers, the U-2 pilot, as a C. I. A. agent.

Asked about Mr. Khrushchev's warning to other countries that permitted the United States to use their facilities, Mr. White replied:

"It is typical that the Soviet Government singles out as the objective of its threats those smaller countries of the free world who bear no responsibility for the recent incident."

When asked what the United States would do if Mr. Khrushchev carried out his threat, Mr. White replied:

"The United States has undertaken certain commitments in the multilateral and bilateral arrangements for the common defense existing between this Government and those which once again appear to be subjected to a policy of intimidation by the Soviet Government."

"There should be no doubt that the United States will

Continued on Page 3, Column 1

SOUTH AFRICA TIE TO BRITISH SHAKEN

Poll on Republic Could Peril Commonwealth Status

By THOMAS P. RONAN
Special to The New York Times.

LONDON, May 10—South Africa's continued membership in the Commonwealth was put in doubt today.

This became apparent during a discussion at the Commonwealth Prime Ministers' conference of South Africa's status if it becomes a republic. Its Government is planning a referendum to determine whether this step should be taken but it has not yet named a date.

Upon becoming a republic, South Africa, like India and Pakistan, would no longer owe allegiance to Queen Elizabeth II but would simply recognize her as head of the Commonwealth.

This would apply unless South Africa decided to drop out of the Commonwealth or the other countries barred it.

At today's session Ghana notified the conference that in conformity with her recent plebiscite she planned to become a republic on July 1 but wished to remain in the Commonwealth. The representatives

Continued on Page 9, Column 1

Turkey Acts to Cut Off Funds Of Menderes' Student Foes Here

The foreign exchange privileges of eight Turkish students here have been rescinded by the Turkish educational attaché, it was disclosed yesterday.

The attaché's office offered no explanation of the action. However, a spokesman for the students said the order, sent in letter form to each of the group, grew out of the participation of the students in a demonstration outside the United Nations in connection with the recent student uprising in Turkey.

"The letters were sent—the reason is a secret," a spokesman for the educational attaché said last night.

The students' spokesman said that the order would not work a hardship on those with private sources of income here, but that students depending on official sources would be hard put to remain in New York.

There are approximately 100 Turkish students enrolled in New York educational institutions. Not all the eight who received the notifications are dependent upon Turkish Government sponsorship, it was said.

The eight students were in a group that picketed the United Nations headquarters May 2 in support of the demonstrations by students in Turkey against the Government of Premier Adnan Menderes. The Turkish outbreaks followed close after the student demonstrations in South Korea that led to the resignation of President Syngman Rhee.

A Turkish student, discussing the effects of the educational attaché's action, said that some of the eight students received tuition and living expenses under Turkish Government scholarships. Others get the money from their parents, he said, but

Continued on Page 17, Column 3

"All the News That's Fit to Print"

The New York Times.

LATE CITY EDITION

U. S. Weather Bureau Report (Page 82) forecasts: Early showers, clearing later today; mostly fair tonight and tomorrow. Temp. range: 78—62; yesterday: 77.0—61.5.

VOL. CIX..No. 37,370. | © 1960, by The New York Times Company. Times Square, New York 36, N. Y. | NEW YORK, WEDNESDAY, MAY 18, 1960. | 10 cents beyond 50-mile zone from New York City except on Long Island. Higher in air delivery cities. | FIVE CENTS

SUMMIT CONFERENCE BREAKS UP IN DISPUTE; WEST BLAMES KHRUSHCHEV'S RIGID STAND; HE INSISTS ON EISENHOWER SPYING APOLOGY

PASSENGER GAINS AND CITY SUBSIDY END TRANSIT LOSS

Board Expects $4,000,000 Surplus June 30 Instead of Deficit of $116,000

By STANLEY LEVEY

Thanks to more riders and city subsidies, the Transit Authority expects to end the present fiscal year on June 30 with a surplus of $4,000,000, instead of a deficit of $116,000.

Most of the help from the city had been anticipated in planning for 1959-60. But the sharp upturn in passenger revenues had not.

While the agency was pleased with the development, it had no explanation for it yesterday beyond the suggestion that new buses and subway cars were responsible.

"We just have more riders," Charles L. Patterson, chairman of the authority, said happily.

The prospect of a big surplus apparently made firm a previous pledge by the authority that the present 15-cent bus and subway fare would be held at least until Jan. 1, 1962. On that date contracts between the agency and the Transport Workers Union expire.

City Subsidies Counted On

The projected $4,000,000 surplus was based on the records for the first nine months of the fiscal year. From last July 1 to March 31 the authority's revenues exceeded its expenses by $2,865,021. In the same period of the preceding year the agency had a $7,822,603 deficit and it finished that fiscal year with a total deficit of $10,200,000.

Last spring, when the authority drew up its 1959-60 operating budget, it expected to end the year with a deficit of $116,000. The officials knew then that they could count on the

Continued on Page 21, Column 3

U. S. Sues to Open Biloxi Beach to All

Special to The New York Times.

WASHINGTON, May 17—The Justice Department sued Biloxi, Miss., today in a move to open the Gulf coast beach there to Negroes.

Three weeks ago, on the week-end of April 23, a group of about forty Negroes tried to swim at the beach. They were chased by white men with clubs. It has been reported that Negroes are not permitted to swim anywhere on the twenty-six-mile beach.

Gunfire and street fights in Biloxi followed the episode. Two white men and eight Negroes were wounded by bullets. Several Negroes who had tried to use the beach were arrested and fined $25 each for "disturbing the peace."

The Justice Department suit was based on the fact that

Continued on Page 22, Column 1

SOVIET SHIFT SEEN

'Warmed-Up Cold War' Awaited—Khrushchev Will Stop in Berlin

By SYDNEY GRUSON

Special to The New York Times.

PARIS, May 17 — Western diplomats here expressed the belief today that Premier Khrushchev's break with President Eisenhower signaled a major change in Soviet policy. One Frenchman suggested that this tended toward a "warmed-up cold war."

The change will become apparent quickly, these diplomats believe, perhaps even in a session of the Supreme Soviet, the parliament in Moscow, that Mr. Khrushchev is expected to summon on his return home.

Meanwhile, the Soviet Premier plans to stop in Berlin on his way back to Moscow. His meetings in Berlin with East Germany's Communist leaders are expected by Western diplomats to open some new phase in the Soviet campaign to resolve the Berlin issue.

Soviet-Bloc Parley Predicted

Soviet sources here said Mr. Khrushchev would also call together the Soviet Union's Eastern European allies to consider the consequences of the rupture with President Eisenhower and the failure of the Paris summit conference.

The Russians have been threatening to sign a separate peace treaty with East Germany and place access to West Berlin in East German hands unless the West negotiates a Berlin settlement.

Bits and pieces purporting to show the Soviet leader's plans and intentions were being dropped here all day by Communist sources. But nothing was forthcoming to answer clearly the major question bedeviling Allied diplomats:

What led the Soviet Premier to torpedo the summit conference before it ever got going?

Internal Pressures Seen

Two theses are being exchanged among the diplomats. They are essentially contradictory, but a common thread runs through them. It is that Mr. Khrushchev is under stronger pressure from his political opponents throughout the Communist bloc and not only in the Soviet Union than at any time since he won power.

The favored thesis was that Premier Khrushchev arrived here Saturday with his position frozen, that a decision had been taken in Moscow beforehand to break up the conference by posing what were patently inacceptable conditions to the President of the United States.

The minority view was that something happened to force a policy switch on Mr. Khrushchev during the week-end.

Mr. Khrushchev made what was generally regarded as a conciliatory statement on arriving here Saturday but utterly abandoned that attitude the next day.

In that connection some

Continued on Page 15, Column 5

United Press International Radiophoto

TRANQUIL INTERLUDE: President Eisenhower and Prime Minister Macmillan stroll about the grounds of the villa in Marnes-la-Coquette, where the President lived in 1951 and 1952 as the commander of the North Atlantic Treaty Organization forces in Europe.

Radiophoto of The New York Times (by Erich Lessing—Magnum)

WIELDING THE AXE: Premier Khrushchev chops wood near Sézanne, France.

KENNEDY SWEEPS MARYLAND'S VOTE

Gets 70% of Total in Routing Morse for Sixth Straight Primary Triumph

By W. H. LAWRENCE

Special to The New York Times.

BALTIMORE, May 17—Senator John F. Kennedy won a landslide victory in Maryland's Democratic primary today to enlarge his claim to the Presidential nomination.

The young Massachusetts contender polled about 70 per cent of the vote and picked up twenty-four first-ballot delegate votes at the national convention opening in Los Angeles July 11.

There was no contest in the Republican preferential primary.

Senator Kennedy overwhelmed Senator Wayne Morse of Oregon and Maryland politicians who had urged a vote for an uninstructed delegation to demonstrate support for the Presidential aspirations of Senator Stuart Symington of Missouri, Senator Lyndon B. Johnson of Texas and Adlai E. Stevenson of Illinois

Returns from 1,354 of 1,356 precincts gave:

Kennedy 199,362
Morse 49,323

Mr. Kennedy jumped far ahead in the first precinct to report, and built his lead steadily in every section.

Mr. Morse took his worst beating in Baltimore, which casts about half the Democratic vote, trailing his rival by a plurality in excess of 73,000.

The Oregonian received about 17 per cent of the vote, or 50 per cent less than the expectation he voiced Sunday, when he conceded defeat in advance.

For Senator Kennedy this was his sixth straight primary victory and an impressive show of strength before his final

Continued on Page 30, Column 4

2 NETWORKS FIGHT FREE TV DEBATES

But Would Give Candidates Time Under Own Plans

By TOM WICKER

Special to The New York Times.

WASHINGTON, May 17—Adlai E. Stevenson's idea for a series of television debates between the major Presidential candidates encountered stiff opposition today from the TV industry and the opposition party.

Dr. Frank Stanton, president of the Columbia Broadcasting System, and David C. Adams, senior vice president of the National Broadcasting Company, resisted Mr. Stevenson's proposal that the networks be required by law to grant free time to the candidates.

However, both said that their networks would make free time available voluntarily, under certain circumstances.

Bill Before Senate Unit

Mr. Stevenson's "great debate" plan is embodied in S. 3171, a bill pending before the Communications Subcommittee of the Senate Interstate and Foreign Commerce Committee. The group heard and questioned the former Governor of Illinois yesterday and Dr. Stanton today.

It also received today a written statement from Mr. Adams and took written testimony against the bill from Vice President Nixon, former President Herbert Hoover and Thomas E. Dewey, twice a Republican Presidential candidate.

Mr. Adams will be questioned at an afternoon session tomorrow. His statement today described S. 3171 as "the wrong way to go about doing the right thing." The bill, he said, is "discriminatory" and "confiscatory." It is not needed, he went on, because N. B. C. already proposes to "invite the major Pres-

Continued on Page 29, Column 3

DEMOCRATS HINT 'BLUNDERS' PROBE

But Mansfield and Johnson Emphasize United Front During Crisis in Paris

By RUSSELL BAKER

Special to The New York Times.

WASHINGTON, May 17—Democratic Congressional leaders created a temporary united front behind President Eisenhower today for the duration of the summit crisis but hinted at possible investigations to come.

Senator Mike Mansfield of Montana, the Senate's deputy Democratic leader, said that questions about Administration "blunders" preceding the Paris conference "must be asked," but only "at the proper time."

While the President is still in Paris and the Soviet Union is threatening to create a fresh German crisis that could bring "all peoples to the edge of catastrophe" is not the right time, he told the Senate.

Lyndon B. Johnson of Texas, the Democratic Senate leader, agreed that first priority should be given to maintaining a united national front behind the President in the present period of uncertainty.

Johnson Bars Division

"If there have been mistakes, responsibility will be assessed coolly and objectively," he said. "But one mistake that we cannot afford to make right now is to weaken the free world by division within our own ranks."

Behind these speeches by the Senate's two Democratic leaders was the conviction that to permit a great national debate at this point might strengthen Premier Khrushchev's indictment of the United States Government and further embarrass President Eisenhower.

By tacit agreement with the leadership, most Congressional Democrats suspended criticism of the Administration and waited nervously for further developments in Paris.

Many Republicans were conceding today that even if the Administration got out of Paris without additional trouble, the party had been politically hurt for the election campaign ahead.

Moreover, the calm that Senators Johnson and Mansfield and Speaker Sam Rayburn have

Continued on Page 14, Column 5

The Western Communique

By The Associated Press.

PARIS, May 17—Following is a joint communiqué issued tonight by Britain, France and the United States:

The President of the United States, the President of the French Republic and the Prime Minister of the United Kingdom take note of the fact that because of the attitude adopted by the Chairman of the Council of Ministers of the Soviet Union it has not been possible to begin, at the summit conference, the examination of the problems which it had been agreed would be discussed between the four chiefs of state or government.

They regret that these discussions, so important for world peace, could not take place. For their part, they remain unshaken in their conviction that all outstanding international questions should be settled not by the use or threat of force but by peaceful means through negotiation. They themselves remain ready to take part in such negotiations at any suitable time in the future.

PRELATE IN CUBA DENOUNCES REDS

Archbishop Urges Fight—Stand Could Bring Death

By R. HART PHILLIPS

Special to The New York Times.

HAVANA, May 17—A pastoral letter attacking communism and urging Cuban Roman Catholics to combat this "enemy within our gates" has been issued by the Archbishop of Santiago de Cuba, Msgr. Enrique Pérez Serantes.

The letter, which the Archbishop ordered read in churches of his archdiocese of Oriente Province, was published in Havana today by Información and El Crisol, Cuba's only independent newspapers. The Government press and radio ignored the pastoral.

This letter has special significance since anti-communism has been declared by the Government of Premier Fidel Castro to be synonymous with "counter-revolutionary activities," punishable by death before a firing squad or long imprisonment.

Castro's Ranks Split

The letter caused a sensation in the island, particularly since Archbishop Pérez Serantes has long been a close friend of Premier Castro and is credited with having saved the life of the revolutionary leader in 1953.

At that time, following an unsuccessful attack by Dr. Castro and a group of young revolutionaries on the Moncava army post of Santiago de Cuba, the Archbishop protected Dr. Castro and obtained assurances for his life from the authorities while others of the group were being hunted down and killed on sight.

Communism is a major issue in Cuba and has split the ranks of Premier Castro's own revolutionary followers. The issue has

Continued on Page 6, Column 3

LUMUMBA RISING AS A CONGO RULER

Defies Belgians as He Builds Power in Interior Region

By HOMER BIGART

Special to The New York Times.

STANLEYVILLE, Belgian Congo, May 17—Belgian authority is collapsing in part of the Congo.

Patrice Emergy Lumumba, Congolese nationalist leader, is taking over as virtual dictator of this city and much of the Stanleyville and Eastern Provinces.

Not even the arrival of Belgian troop reinforcements is likely to halt the rapid erosion of the colonial administration's authority. Forty-five days before Congolese independence the Belgian administration already seems subservient to the nationalists.

Ban on Meetings Defied

M. Lumumba saw reports of troops arrivals at the Kamina military base in Katanga Province as an "attempt to intimidate the voters and influence the election in favor of Belgian selected candidates." He said he had sent a telegram to King Baudouin of the Belgians demanding the recall of the troops. He did not seem unduly worried, however.

Yesterday, in a moment of painful humiliation for the Belgian settlers, M. Lumumba defied a ban on public meetings. He did it in the heart of the city that jailed him last October for inciting riots.

The incident marked the beginning of a triumphal tour by M. Lumumba of the region north of Stanleyville. There, in villages deep in the equatorial forest, he demanded and received assurances from Belgian officials that watchers from his party, the National Congolese Movement, would be allowed at

Continued on Page 5, Column 3

COLLAPSE FEARED FOR GENEVA TALK

Summit Breakdown Likely to Affect Nuclear-Test and Arms Discussion

By A. M. ROSENTHAL

Special to The New York Times.

PARIS, May 17—The East-West negotiations in Geneva on disarmament and on a nuclear test ban were collapsing today.

Premier Khrushchev's decision to boycott the summit meeting convinced Western diplomats that the chances for agreement on disarmament or the ending of nuclear tests had been blown to bits and would take considerable time to paste together again.

The West was going on the assumption that the Soviet Union would not immediately call off the two sets of negotiations.

Russians were saying that the Khrushchev tactics at the summit did not mean that the Geneva talks would be called off. But the opinion of diplomats here was that the political foundation for agreement had been smashed.

American sources said tonight that the prospects for both conferences had been pushed back, if not destroyed. Foreign Secretary Selwyn Lloyd of Britain said the breakdown at the summit need not wreck the two Geneva meetings.

The Western delegations were expecting the Soviet Union to take the issue of the U-2 reconnaissance plane to Geneva and make it their political centerpiece at the disarmament negotiations. Moscow has repeatedly said that the West is more interested in espionage than dis-

Continued on Page 15, Column 7

CHARGES TRADED

Allies Leave the Door Open to New Talk—Soviet Scores U.S.

By DREW MIDDLETON

Special to The New York Times.

PARIS, May 17—The summit conference died tonight. The leaders of the West said Premier Khrushchev had killed it. The Russians blamed the United States.

President Eisenhower, Prime Minister Macmillan and President de Gaulle feel "complete disgust" at the attitude the Soviet delegation has taken here in the last two days, James C. Hagerty, White House press secretary, reported.

In a communiqué issued this evening, the three Western chiefs declared that the Soviet leader's attitude had made it impossible to begin examination of the problems that it had been agreed should be discussed.

Apology Was Demanded

Premier Khrushchev had refused to meet with the Western leaders, on the invitation of President de Gaulle, unless Presdnt Eisenhower apologized for United States espionage flights over the Soviet Union. This the President was not prepared to do.

The meeting, so long prepared and so anxiously awaited, expired in an atmosphere of gloomy foreboding. Diplomats of the three Western powers feared the world situation would deteriorate.

The Western leaders pledged their support to a settlement of all outstanding international issues by negotiation rather than by the use or threat of force. The United States, Britain and France remain ready for such negotiations "at any suitable time in the future," a communiqué said.

Soviet in Sharp Attack

A few minutes after the communiqué had been made public, a group of leading Soviet editors answered it with a sharp denunciation of the United States. The conference foundered, a Soviet statement said, because "aggressive actions" of the United States Government and the Administration's failure to accept responsibility had "torpedoed the conference which the peoples of the whole world were awaiting with such hopes."

The Western leaders will meet again tomorrow afternoon after a preliminary conference between their foreign ministers, Christian A. Herter, Selwyn Lloyd and Maurice Couve de Murville. These meetings, Western diplomats said, will review

Continued on Page 14, Column 1

Jovial Khrushchev Has Rural Holiday

By OSGOOD CARUTHERS

Special to The New York Times.

PARIS, May 17 — Premier Khrushchev spent a happy day outdoors in France today despite all the efforts of the Western leaders to get him indoors for a session of the summit conference.

With seeming abandon, the leader of the Soviet Union spent the day doing the things he wanted to do when he came to France on a state visit two months ago. Meanwhile, the tense and anxious leaders of the West waited for him to save the summit from catastrophe.

Mr. Khrushchev held sidewalk and barnyard news conferences. He dashed up to startled Frenchmen and shook their

Continued on Page 15, Column 3

KHRUSHCHEV STEP REKNITS NATO TIE

Allies Feel Premier Carried U-2 Exploitation Too Far

By ROBERT C. DOTY

Special to The New York Times.

PARIS, May 17—Soviet intransigence, applied this time to bringing the summit conference to a halt, has again served to restore the cohesion of the North Atlantic Treaty Organization.

The conclusion of NATO secretariat officials of the United States and of smaller powers today was that Premier Khrushchev had again badly overplayed his hand in exploitation of Soviet grievances arising from the downing of the United States U-2 reconnaissance plane over the Soviet Union May 1.

The same officials were unwilling to predict the long-term effects on the Atlantic alliance of the events since Sunday. New, heavy Soviet pressure on Berlin—one of the possibilities—would reimpose severe strains on the military and political resources of NATO.

But for the present at least, resentment of Soviet tactics here has largely overshadowed Allied impatience with the

Continued on Page 14, Column 7

Vatican Paper Proclaims Right Of Church to Role in Politics

Special to The New York Times.

ROME, May 17—L'Osservatore Romano, the Vatican newspaper, declared today that the Roman Catholic hierarchy had "the right and the duty to intervene" in the political field to guide its flock. It rejected what it termed "the absurd split of conscience between the believer and the citizen."

The pronouncement was in a front-page editorial described by the Vatican Press Service as "authoritative." It was presented in a special make-up that L'Osservatore Romano usually reserves for semi-official statements emanating from its Vatican superiors, as distinct from its own editorial opinion.

The article clearly referred to the political situation in Italy, where some left-of-center elements in the dominant Christian Democratic party, which enjoys Vatican backing, have recently advocated collaboration with Left-Wing Socialists, against the advice of the Roman Catholic Episcopacy.

However, L'Osservatore Romano made it plain that the pronouncement was valid for Roman Catholic laymen everywhere. It deplored "the great confusion of ideas that is spreading, especialy in some nations, among Catholics with regard to the relations between Catholic doctrine and social and political activities, and between the ecclesiastical hierarchy and

Continued on Page 31, Column 1

NEWS INDEX

1960

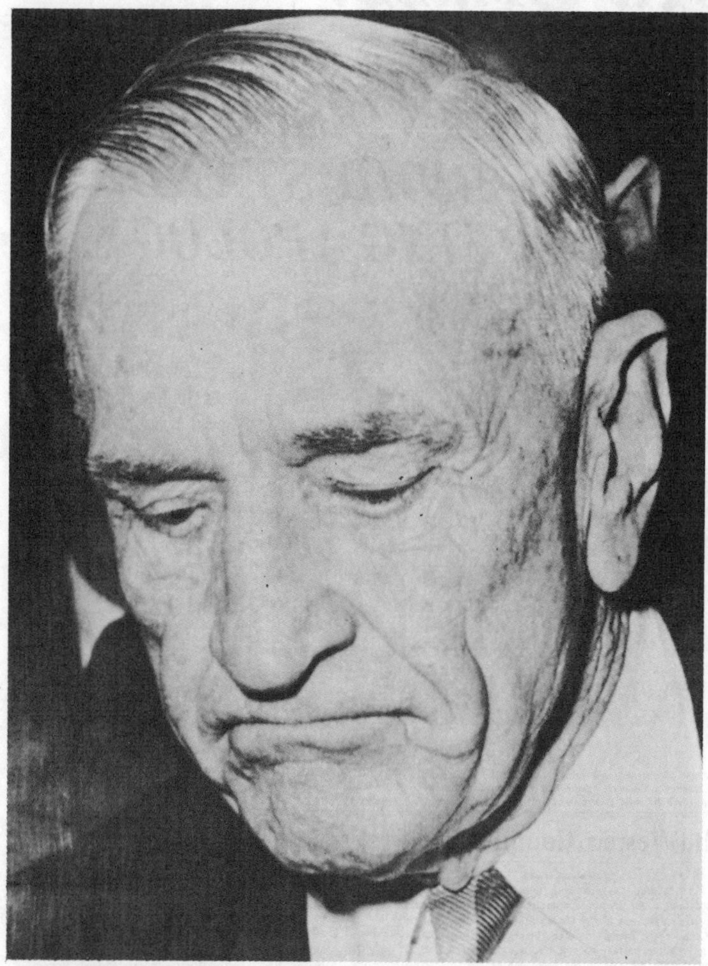

Casey Stengel retired at 70, after a Yankee shakeup.

Bill Russell made a substantial contribution to the defeat of the St. Louis Hawks when the Boston Celtics won their fourth championship in five years.

Ted Williams hit his 521st homer for the Boston Red Sox and announced his retirement after nineteen years with the team.

Cheers exploded on the field when Bill Mazeroski hit a ninth-inning homerun, earning the Pittsburgh Pirates their first World Series' title since 1925.

"All the News That's Fit to Print"

The New York Times.

LATE CITY EDITION
U. S. Weather Bureau Report (Page 54) forecasts: Cloudy, chance of showers today. Fair, cooler, less humid tomorrow.
Temp. range: 84—72; yesterday: 83.2—70. Temp.-Hum. Index: high 70's; yesterday: 78.

VOL. CIX—No. 37,427. NEW YORK, THURSDAY, JULY 14, 1960. FIVE CENTS

10 cents beyond 50-mile zone from New York City except on Long Island. Higher in air delivery cities.

KENNEDY NOMINATED ON THE FIRST BALLOT; OVERWHELMS JOHNSON BY 806 VOTES TO 409

Security Council Authorizes U. N. Force to Aid Congo

PEACE UNIT VOTED

U. S. and Soviet Clash in Debate—Belgians Asked to Pull Out

Congolese texts, resolution, debate excerpts, Page 4.

By THOMAS J. HAMILTON
Special to The New York Times.

UNITED NATIONS, N. Y., Thursday, July 14 — The Security Council authorized Secretary General Dag Hammarskjold today to organize and send a United Nations force to the Congo.

The vote was eight in favor and none against, with Britain, France and Nationalist China abstaining.

The vote was taken at 3:03 A. M., nearly six and a half hours after the Security Council, at the request of Mr. Hammarskjold, began its urgent night session. The decision was delayed by bitter exchanges between the United States and Soviet representatives, Henry Cabot Lodge and Arkady A. Sobolev. The Council adjourned at 3:24 A. M.

Outcome Was Uncertain

The outcome remained uncertain until the last. It was known that Britain, France and Nationalist China would abstain. They objected to a provision in the resolution, which was introduced by Tunisia, calling for the withdrawal of Belgian troops from the Congo.

The withdrawal recommendation was included on the demand of the Soviet Union and the African states. However, word was passed during the long meeting that the Soviet Union and Poland had not received instructions on the Tunisian proposal, and would therefore abstain if the United States insisted upon a vote at this meeting.

This belief was strengthened after Walter Loridan, the Belgian representative, announced that Belgian troops would be withdrawn from the Congo when the United Nations force is able to provide "effective" maintenance of order.

Mr. Sobolev termed this statement unsatisfactory. He introduced amendments condemning Belgian "armed aggression" in the Congo, stating that the Belgian forces must be withdrawn "immediately," and limiting participation in the United Nations force to the other African states.

The first two amendments were rejected 7 to 2, with only the Soviet Union and Poland

Continued on Page 4, Column 3

Belgian Commandos Rout Congo Troops at Airport

Bunche Meets With Both Sides to Try to Halt Clashes—Congolese Open Fire on Convoy of Refugees

By HENRY TANNER
Special to The New York Times.

LEOPOLDVILLE, the Congo, July 13—Belgian commandos occupied Leopoldville's airport today and then clashed with Congolese troops. At least six Congolese and two Belgians were killed.

Belgian forces occupied the airport at midmorning. They went into action after Congolese soldiers had moved into the airport and had threatened to interfere with the evacuation of Belgian civilians by Sabena, the Belgian airline.

[Leopoldville was reported by press associations to be under the control of Belgian troops, but there was uncertainty over the extent of control. Congolese troops opened fire Wednesday night on a convoy of 300 Belgians heading for the airport, Reuters said the Congo Government had declared that a "state of war" existed with Belgium. The Congo has asked Ghana to send troops.

[In Brussels, the Belgian Government said it would keep troops at key points in the Congo.]

Dr. Ralph J. Bunche, United Nations Under Secretary, met with Congolese authorities and Ambassador Jean van den Bosch of Belgium this afternoon in an effort to halt the clashes.

Dr. Bunche was reported to have been called in by the Congolese to mediate a cease-fire between them and the Belgians. He left the United States Embassy, where he has an office, in the early afternoon with the blue United Nations flag flying

Continued on Page 3, Column 2

MOSCOW BIDS U. N. CONVENE AT ONCE ON RB-47 INCIDENT

Says Flights by U. S. Planes With Reconnaissance Aim Are Threat to Peace

By OSGOOD CARUTHERS
Special to The New York Times.

MOSCOW, July 13—The Soviet Union called today for an urgent meeting of the United Nations Security Council to discuss its charges of United States "aggressive actions."

The Soviet complaint derived from the shooting down of a United States RB-47 reconnaissance plane off the Soviet coast in the Barents Sea on July 1.

[In a statement from the summer White House at Newport, R. I., the United States backed a full investigation by the United Nations of the "wanton shooting down" of the plane.]

Moscow called for the United Nations meeting in a cablegram sent by Foreign Minister Andrei A. Gromyko today to the president of the Security Council, José A. Correa of Ecuador.

Hammarskjold Gets Copy

The message, a copy of which was sent to Secretary General Dag Hammarskjold, charged that the United States flights constituted "a serious threat to the preservation of peace."

The United States has denied that the RB-47 plane had violated Soviet territorial waters as alleged by the Kremlin.

The Soviet request came on the heels of a statement yesterday by Premier Khrushchev that his Government might take the matter of the plane before the Security Council.

He said he did not expect that the Security Council, which he described as an "instrument" of the United States, would take any action satisfactory to the Soviet Union. However, he said he thought it was necessary to raise the question there anyway if only to "discredit the dishonest judges once more."

Mr. Gromyko's cablegram, which he said would be followed by an explanatory letter, noted that the Security Council had discussed the previous plane incident, in which a U-2 reconnaissance jet was shot down deep inside Soviet territory on May 1.

The message asked the Security Council to "take such measures as appear necessary to put an end to these dangers

Continued on Page 6, Column 5

AFTER THE VICTORY: Senator John F. Kennedy of Massachusetts heads for rostrum at Los Angeles Memorial Sports Arena to address the Democratic National Convention.

Associated Press Wirephoto

LONG DRIVE WINS

Wyoming's Vote Puts Bostonian Over Top Before Acclamation

Kennedy's talk on Page 14; nominating speeches, 16.

By W. H. LAWRENCE
Special to The New York Times.

LOS ANGELES, Thursday, July 14—Senator John F. Kennedy smashed his way to a first-ballot Presidential nomination at the Democratic National Convention last night and won the right to oppose Vice President Nixon in November.

The 43-year-old Massachusetts Senator overwhelmed his opposition, piling up 806 votes to 409 ballots for his nearest rival, Senator Lyndon B. Johnson of Texas, the Senate majority leader. Senator Kennedy's victory came just before 11 o'clock last night [2 A. M. Thursday, New York time].

Then the convention made it unanimous on motion of Gov. James T. Blair Jr. of Missouri, who had placed Senator Stuart Symington of Missouri in nomination.

'We Shall Win'

Senator Kennedy, appearing before the shouting convention early today, pledged he would carry the fight to the country in the fall "and we shall win."

He thanked his defeated rivals for their generosity and appealed to all of their backers to keep the party strong and united in a tremendously important election. He spoke directly of Senators Johnson and Symington and the favorite sons, but made no reference to Adlai E. Stevenson.

The third session of the national convention adjourned after his speech. The next session will convene at 5 P. M. today.

Little Wyoming, well down the roll-call, provided the decisive fifteen votes that gave victory to Senator Kennedy. Two favorite-son states, Minnesota and New Jersey, waited in vain to give the on-rushing Kennedy bandwagon the final shove.

When Wyoming came in with its vote, the Kennedy total had mounted to 765 votes, or four more than the 761 votes required for nomination.

It was a tremendous victory for Senator Kennedy. Mr. Johnson, the Senate majority leader, had fought desperately to reverse a Kennedy tide that had been running for months. But Senator Johnson quickly telephoned his congratulations to

Continued on Page 14, Column 1

KISHI IS STABBED AT HOME IN TOKYO

Japan's Premier Is Reported Not Badly Hurt—Ikeda Chosen His Successor

By RICHARD J. H. JOHNSTON
Special to The New York Times.

TOKYO, Thursday, July 14—Premier Nobusuke Kishi was attacked by an assassin and stabbed in the thigh within an hour after his apparent successor had been elected by his party.

The Premier was attacked at a reception in his official residence. The attacker was identified by the authorities as Taizo Aramaki, a Rightist, about 45 years old.

Mr. Kishi was removed to a nearby hospital, where it was announced that his condition was not serious.

His assailant was arrested.

The police established the time of the attack as 2:30 P. M. This would be within forty minutes of Mr. Kishi's departure from Hibiya Hall in Downtown Tokyo, where the Liberal-Democratic party convention had been held.

The reception at the Premier's home was arranged to honor Hayato Ikeda, who, less than an hour before had been elected in the convention of the governing party as its new president, replacing Mr. Kishi who had resigned in the convention a short time before.

Mr. Ikeda, now Trade Minister, backs the Kishi policies.

The attack on the 63-year-old Premier was an ironic twist in the turbulent politics of recent months in Japan.

On June 23 he had announced

Continued on Page 11, Column 2

Peru Urges O.A.S. Debate Red Threat; U.S. Favors Parley

Special to The New York Times.

WASHINGTON, July 13 — Peru has suggested that the foreign ministers of the American nations meet soon to consider the Soviet threat to inter-American unity and democracy in the Western Hemisphere.

Informed sources said the Peruvian initiative was welcomed by the United States and that Washington would support the proposal. It is believed that the Peruvian suggestion will be considered at a meeting this week of the Council of the Organization of American States.

The Peruvian suggestion was circulated today among representatives of the twenty-one members of the O.A.S. It was also the subject of urgent consultation at embassies and in the State Department.

Peru's proposal was couched in careful diplomatic language, but its meaning was clear. The message stressed the necessity for the continued solidarity of the countries of this hemisphere. It called for the defense of the regional system in inter-American affairs and of democratic principles.

There was no specific refer-

Continued on Page 12, Column 5

JOHNSON PLEDGES HELP TO KENNEDY

He Assures Candidate of His Full Support and Issues a Call for Party Unity

By JOHN D. MORRIS
Special to The New York Times.

LOS ANGELES, July 13—Senator Lyndon B. Johnson accepted tonight "with all my heart" Senator John F. Kennedy's nomination for President.

The Texan, who had watched the convention proceedings by television in his suite at the Biltmore Hotel, issued a four-paragraph statement just as the first ballot ended. It had been prepared as Montana and some other Mountain States failed to provide expected shifts to the Johnson banner.

The statement follows:

"The delegates have made their decision and I accept it with all my heart.

"Senator Kennedy has my sincere congratulations, and my solemn assurance that in the coming months of this campaign, no one will be more dedicated than I—no one will work harder than I to make doubly sure of what all Democrats here and throughout the country know must come about for the good of the nation and the free world—that John F. Kennedy will be elected the next President of the United States.

"We have a winner—he has proved it here.

"Now, let our party unite behind our candidate—let us sweep the country this November, so that in January Demo-

Continued on Page 15, Column 6

Symington Heavy Favorite For Second Place on Ticket

By LEO EGAN
Special to The New York Times.

LOS ANGELES, July 13—Senator Stuart Symington became a heavy favorite for the Vice-Presidential nomination tonight following Senator John F. Kennedy's first-ballot nomination for President. The Missouri delegation was the first to swing into line behind Senator Kennedy after the New Englander had clinched the nomination for first place.

At the Kennedy headquarters in the Biltmore Hotel it was announced that the Presidential nominee would meet with those under consideration for Vice President and with party leaders from all sections of the country before going to bed.

Before the convention opened, he had promised the New York delegation, which was an important factor in his victory, that he would consult with its leaders before making a choice on second place.

Senator Symington parried questions about the Vice-Presidential nomination with the comment that the matter was entirely up to Senator Kennedy.

Good Word for Jackson

Although the Missouri Senator was regarded as the front runner for the Vice-Presidential nomination, two others were receiving serious consideration.

They were Gov. Orville L. Freeman of Minnesota, who had placed the New Englander in nomination, and Senator Henry M. Jackson of Washington State.

At a meeting of the Washington delegation today, Robert F. Kennedy, the Senator's brother and floor manager, said that Senator Jackson was his (Robert's) personal choice for the place but that political considerations might force his brother to turn elsewhere.

Governor Freeman had also been informed that those around Senator Kennedy had a high regard for him and that he would be acceptable as a Vice-Presidential candidate.

Up to the hour of Senator Kennedy's nomination, Senator Symington and Representative Charles A. Brown of Missouri, his campaign manager, were declaring that Senator Symington was not a candidate. But few delegates expected him to

Continued on Page 15, Column 6

STEVENSON GIVEN A WILD RECEPTION

His Nomination Touches Off Roaring Demonstration—It Lasts 25 Mintues

By WILLIAM M. BLAIR
Special to The New York Times.

LOS ANGELES, July 13—A wild, emotional demonstration for Adlai E. Stevenson shook the Democratic National Convention tonight.

As the name of the man who led the Democrats in 1952 and 1956 was placed before the convention, the galleries erupted in a screaming roar that dwarfed all that went before.

A rip-roaring nominating speech by Senator Eugene J. McCarthy, an "egghead" from Minnesota, set off the nearest thing to hysteria that this convention has seen.

Although the demonstrators obviously were full of enthusiasm, it was also obvious that the demonstration was at least partly contrived.

It took the convention chairman, Gov. LeRoy Collins of Florida, twenty-five minutes to slow down the stamping, shouting show to get seconding speeches.

Supporters Storm Floor

Stevenson supporters from outside the convention stormed the floor, some apparently gaining entrance by ruses, to call for the man who said he did not come West to seek the nomination.

Chanting, placard-waving demonstrators jammed the aisles while the galleries suddenly came alive with thousands of placards and hundreds of demonstrators going round and round in a deafening din.

The bobbing, weaving demonstrators on the floor, many of them young persons, caused many delegates to cover their ears. And many covered their heads with their hands as the Stevenson rooters bounced a giant, white papier-mâché ball through the air. The ball represented a snowball intended to dramatize the "Draft Stevenson" effort.

For the most part, the delegates appeared unmoved by the

Continued on Page 15, Column 2

HOGAN WILL PRESS A NEW JACK TRIAL

Fall Date to Be Asked Today in Borough Chief's Case

By PETER FLINT

A date for a new trial for Borough President Hulan E. Jack of Manhattan on charges of conflict of interest and conspiracy will be requested by District Attorney Frank S. Hogan today in the Court of General Sessions.

Since the court is now in summer recess, with only three of the nine judges sitting, the prosecutor is expected to ask for a date in the fall.

Mr. Jack's first trial ended last Thursday night when the jury failed to agree on a verdict after two days of deliberation and was discharged.

Mr. Jack's lawyer, Carson DeWitt Baker, said he would request an immediate trial. But he expressed the view that Mr. Hogan would "have his way as usual," and that the new trial probably would begin in October.

Mr. Baker also expressed "firm conviction" that the Borough President would continue his self-suspension from office until the case was resolved. Mr.

Continued on Page 25, Column 5

Union Forcing Plant To Return to City

By A. H. RASKIN

An arbitrator has ordered a New York clothing manufacturer to reopen his closed factory here and to pay the Amalgamated Clothing Workers union more than $200,000 in damages for having moved his work to Mississippi.

The employer, who lost a court fight to block arbitration, made it clear yesterday that he would resist the unusual award through new litigation.

The union is confident that recent decisions of the United States Supreme Court strengthening the power of arbitrators and limiting the right of judges to upset their awards will bar a successful challenge.

Jacob S. Potofsky, president of the Amalgamated, hailed the award as proof that "runaway

Continued on Page 55, Column 4

2 Planes Down Off Philippines; 86 of 88 Aboard Saved From Sea

Two Lost as U. S. Airliner Ditches—Island DC-3 Also Crashes, 30 on It Safe

The New York Times July 14, 1960
Sites of crash of U. S. plane (1) and Philippines plane (2)

By United Press International.

MANILA, Thursday, July 14 —An American airplane and a Philippine passenger plane went down at sea in separate accidents today with a total of eighty-eight persons aboard. But eighty-six were reported safe after swift, dramatic rescue from shark-dangerous waters.

At least thirty-four Americans were aboard one of the planes, a Northwest Orient Airlines DC7-C on the last leg of a New York-to-Manila flight with fifty-one passengers and a crew of seven.

United States air force amphibious planes from Clark Field reported the rescue of fifty-six persons from the Northwest plane. One person was reported killed and one missing.

In the southern Philippines, 500 miles from Manila between the islands of Negros and Mindanao, a Philippines Airlines plane on an inter-island flight ditched in shallow water near land and all thirty passengers and crew members were picked up.

Passengers on the Northwest airliner included Dr. Rodrigo L. Sarmiento, Filipino surgeon banished from the United States for the confessed killing of a Brooklyn nurse, Margaret Kabal. Dr. Sarmiento was among the survivors.

The Northwest plane, which had come from New York via Seattle, Anchorage, Tokyo and Okinawa, crash-landed near the little island of Jimalog, of the Potillo group about 150 miles northeast of Manila, after a propeller "ran away" and fell off and a wing caught fire.

Capt. David Rall, 53 years old of Seattle, deliberately put the plane down at sea after radioing at 4:20 A. M. [4:20 P. M.

Continued on Page 12, Column 4

Plan to End Strike On L.I.R.R. Offered

Governor Rockefeller's fact-finding board proposed an arbitration plan last night to bring an immediate end to the Long Island Rail Road strike.

The plan was rejected almost at once by the union's negotiating committee. It charged that most arbitrators had been "so brainwashed by the propaganda of the Association of American Railroads and the National Association of Manufacturers" that labor could not trust them.

The rejection will be reviewed by the 1,350 strikers at a meeting this morning, but union leaders said they would "bet a million dollars that the men will turn the idea down unanimously."

The company said the union's reaction made further study of the plan seem academic. It

Continued on Page 20, Column 2

F.H.A. INVESTMENT OPENED TO PUBLIC

Individuals Invited to Deal in U. S.-Insured Mortgages

By RICHARD E. MOONEY
Special to The New York Times.

WASHINGTON, July 13—The Government invited individuals today to invest in mortgages insured against loss by the Federal Housing Administration.

It was, in effect, an offer of a long-term investment that could earn the investor more than 5 per cent and would be paid off by the Government if the mortgage went into default. The yields of representative stocks and bonds currently are lower than 5 per cent.

Investment in an F. H. A.-insured mortgage would not be riskless. The investor would have to hold his investment until the mortgage was paid off, by the homebuyer or F. H. A., if he were to realize the full return. If he sold out before that, he might sell at a loss.

Besides being an attractive offer, and a break with policy of twenty-five years' standing, today's action was the Government's third stimulant to sagging activity in home building in as many months.

In April, the F. H. A. reduced

Continued on Page 55, Column 4

NEWS INDEX

"All the News That's Fit to Print"

The New York Times.

LATE CITY EDITION

U. S. Weather Bureau Report (Page 50) forecast: Sunny and pleasant today; cool tonight. Mostly fair tomorrow. Temp. range: 78—64; yesterday: 80.5—69. Temp.-Hum. Index: 72; yesterday: 74.

VOL. CIX..No. 37,434. NEW YORK, THURSDAY, JULY 21, 1960. FIVE CENTS

10 cents beyond 50-mile zone from New York City except on Long Island. Higher in air delivery cities.

2 POLARIS MISSILES FIRED BY SUBMERGED SUBMARINE; HIT MARK 1,150 MILES OFF

ACCURACY HAILED

Tests Are First Held Underseas—Message Sent to President

By HANSON W. BALDWIN

Special to The New York Times.

ABOARD U. S. S. OBSERVATION ISLAND, off Cape Canaveral, Fla., July 20—The Navy opened a new chapter in warfare today as a submarine—for the first time—successfully fired a ballistic missile from under water.

About three hours later the nuclear submarine successfully launched another Polaris to the same target area.

The first twenty-eight foot, two-stage Polaris rocket was launched from the U. S. S. George Washington at 1:39 P. M. It flew eastward more than 1,000 nautical miles, or 1,150 statute miles, in less than fourteen minutes to its impact area half way between Bermuda and Puerto Rico.

The Navy described the flight, which has major strategic implications, as highly successful. Unofficial sources said the accuracy of the Polaris was "remarkable."

Message Is Sent

A message from Comdr. James B. Osborn, who commanded the George Washington, to the President, the Chief of Naval Operations and others jubilantly summarized today's test. The message read:

"Polaris—from out of the deep to target. Perfect."

A Polaris missile was also successfully launched yesterday from a pad ashore at Cape Canaveral.

Jubilant naval officers from Admiral Arleigh A. Burke, Chief of Naval Operations, down to ensigns concluded that the Polaris "had it made"; that the nation's newest weapons system, a nuclear tipped missile, would be ready for actual tactical use on schedule late this fall.

Rear Admiral William F. Raborn Jr., director of the Navy's Special Projects Office, which developed the Polaris missile, said he considered the mating of the missile and the nuclear submarine the "most significant happening in weaponry since the day when the airplane first flew."

"I believe," he said, "that it will be just as important as the airplane was to the defense of our country."

Admiral Raborn said that the two successful tests today

Continued on Page 3, Column 5

Associated Press Wirephoto

ON ATLANTIC MISSILE RANGE: The second of two rockets fired from a submarine rises near Cape Canaveral.

'60 Federal Budget Shows $1,068,101,353 Surplus

By RICHARD E. MOONEY

Special to The New York Times.

WASHINGTON, July 20—The Federal budget showed a surplus of $1,068,101,353 in the fiscal year 1960, which ended last June 30. It was a spectacular improvement over the $12,400,000,000 deficit of the previous year. The surplus resulted largely from a sharp post-recession rebound in tax revenues and a string of unforeseen events that reduced expenditures.

The surplus was also better than had been expected, because of chance circumstances and a broad array of small, purposeful savings.

The first word on the surplus came this morning from President Eisenhower's vacation quarters at Newport, R. I. The President called it "a very encouraging turnaround" from the previous year and a "demonstration of fiscal responsibility."

He said it "reinforces economic strength here at home and reaffirms to the world that the United States intends to run its financial affairs on a sound basis."

3d Surplus in 7 Years

The surplus was the third, and smallest, in the seven years of the Eisenhower Administration. However, the fact that it was a surplus, in the wake of the nation's largest peacetime deficit, is something to which Republican campaign orators will point with pride.

Except in the years at the end of the two World Wars, there has never been a sharper one-year improvement in the budget picture in dollar terms. It was a substantial, if not a record, improvement in terms of percentage, relative to the over-all size of the budget. It came about principally because of developments over which the Government's control was indirect at best.

The detailed results, announced here by the Treasury and the Budget Bureau, were

Continued on Page 12, Column 4

KENNEDY NAMES 3 CAMPAIGN AIDES

White, Bailey and Reinsch Get Key Posts—Visit by Stevenson Is Slated

By JOSEPH A. LOFTUS

Special to The New York Times.

HYANNIS PORT, Mass., July 20—Three top slots in the Kennedy-Johnson campaign organization were filled today.

The appointments were:

Byron R. White of Denver, national chairman of Citizens for Kennedy.

John M. Bailey of Hartford, personal liaison between Senator John F. Kennedy, the Presidential nominee, and state and county political leaders.

J. Leonard Reinsch of Atlanta, director of radio and television.

With his vacation already on a part-time basis, Mr. Kennedy devoted several hours to talks with advisers on campaign schedules. Whether he will open his campaign with a Labor Day speech in Cadillac Square, Detroit, as some other Democratic Presidential nominees have done, will probably be announced tomorrow.

The Senator put in a call from his Hyannis Port summer home for his ticket partner, Senator Lyndon B. Johnson, at Johnson City, Tex., but missed him. Mr. Johnson had left for a rest in Mexico.

Johnson Side Attends

Apparently the two have not talked directly since both left Los Angeles last week-end. James H. Rowe, a Washington lawyer who was an adviser to Mr. Johnson in the nomination race, came today for the conference on campaign schedules and remained over night.

The three Kennedy homes on the shores of Nantucket Sound will be a political headquarters for the next few weeks, possibly until the road campaign actually gets under way. Telephone employes were installing a switchboard today and the list of visitors for the next ten days grew longer.

Friday's visitors will include former Gov. W. Averell Harriman of New York, to talk about foreign policy particularly and state politics, and Representative Frank Thompson Jr. of New Jersey, who will direct a national registration campaign.

Next week's visitors will include Senator Henry M. Jackson of Washington, the new Democratic National Chairman, and Adlai E. Stevenson.

The development of a Citizens-

Continued on Page 12, Column 2

L.I.R.R. PEACE PLAN REJECTED BY LINE

Company Fears Fare Rise —Trainmen Would Accept

By EMANUEL PERLMUTTER

Long Island Rail Road workers accepted a Federal mediation proposal to end their eleven-day-old strike yesterday, but the company rejected it.

The railroad turned down a clause in the eight-point mediation package whereby the Brotherhood of Railroad Trainmen would agree to a 2½-cent-an-hour wage cut to help pay for the five-day week it is seeking.

Thomas M. Goodfellow, president of the road, said the wage cut would reduce the $350,000 annual cost of the shorter week by only one-third. He said the company would have to pass $208,000 on to the public in increased fares, a course it refused to follow.

Mr. Goodfellow said the method of financing the shorter week should be submitted to arbitration, a solution he has urged before and since the strike.

However, the 1,350 striking trainmen have refused to arbitrate this issue. They refused again yesterday at a meeting in the Knights of Columbus Hall at Lynbrook, L. I.

Francis A. O'Neill Jr., Chair-

Continued on Page 28, Column 1

Zeckendorf Drops 52d St. Hotel Site

By GLENN FOWLER

William Zeckendorf yesterday gave up his plan to build a 2,000-room hotel bearing his name on the Avenue of the Americas just north of Rockefeller Center.

He turned over his lease on the east blockfront between Fifty-first and Fifty-second Streets to the Uris Buildings Corporation, New York's largest builder of office space. Uris will erect a forty-two-story skyscraper on the site, which is in one of the most active building areas in the city.

Webb & Knapp, Inc., of which Mr. Zeckendorf is president, will realize $8,500,000 by disposing of the hotel site. But expenses incurred in the year and a half since the inception

Continued on Page 10, Column 4

NIXON REPORTED TO FAVOR THREE FOR SECOND SPOT

Would Take Lodge, Morton or Seaton—Gov. Hatfield to Get a Major Role

By LEO EGAN

Special to The New York Times.

CHICAGO, July 20 — Vice President Nixon, serenely confident of his own nomination for President, was reported on good authority today to have limited the field of possible running mates to three.

They are Henry Cabot Lodge, 58 years old, the United States Ambassador to the United Nations; Thruston B. Morton, 52, Republican National Chairman and a Senator from Kentucky, and Fred A. Seaton, 48, Secretary of the Interior.

At least a half-dozen others, including Governor Rockefeller, are figuring in pre-convention speculation here as possibilities. But none is given more than an outside chance.

Gov. Mark O. Hatfield of Oregon was reported today as Mr. Nixon's choice to put his name in nomination. Governor Hatfield, like Governor Rockefeller, scored an upset victory in 1958. A year ago he had been mentioned as a likely Vice-Presidential possibility if Governor Rockefeller won the Presidential nomination.

A Change of Mind

Leonard W. Hall of Oyster Bay, L. I., Mr. Nixon's campaign manager, said at a news conference today that Mr. Rockefeller would have to indicate a change of mind before he could be considered for the Vice-Presidential nomination. The New York Governor has insisted he would not accept such a designation.

Mr. Hall, a former Republican National Chairman, ridiculed a contention being made in behalf of a "Draft Rockefeller" group that Mr. Nixon cannot win.

It is not going to be a romp, he said, but the Vice President will come through because voters resent the "cynicism" shown by Democrats. Every one of the fifty states will be debatable territory in the campaign, he added.

Two Directions Cited

Senators John F. Kennedy and Lyndon B. Johnson, the Democratic nominees for President and Vice President, have voting records that run in one direction and a platform that runs in another, he said.

Mr. Hall predicted that Vice President Nixon would receive a minimum of 1,000 first-ballot votes out of the 1,331 represented in the convention. He would need 666 for nomination.

Mr. Rockefeller's position at the convention is scheduled for clarification Sunday night, when New York's ninety-six delegates hold their first meeting here.

Senator Jacob K. Javits of New York said today he was

Continued on Page 13, Column 2

U. S. WARNS SOVIET IN U.N. ON CONGO, PLEDGES ACTION TO BAR INTRUSION; CONGOLESE BIDS BELGIANS GET OUT

LUMUMBA BACKED

Cabinet Votes Appeal for Forces to End 'All Aggression'

By HENRY TANNER

Special to The New York Times.

LEOPOLDVILLE, the Congo, July 20—The Congo Cabinet decided today "to appeal immediately to the Soviet Union or any other country of the African-Asian bloc to send troops to the Congo" unless the United Nations Security Council took effective action tonight to expel the Belgian troops.

A communique from Premier Patrice Lumumba's office reported the decision. [There was no word of Congolese action after the indecisive night session of the Security Council.]

It was not immediately known whether the mention of "African-Asian bloc" was intended to include Communist China.

The communiqué said the first mission of troops from the Soviet Union or the Asian-African bloc would be to "peacefully bring about the evacuation of Belgian forces."

Such troops would also be used to contribute to the maintenance of order in the Congo in accordance with the wishes of the Congo Government, and to "prevent all aggression from outside," the communiqué said.

Senate Against Soviet Bid

On Monday the Congolese Senate voted unanimously to reject Soviet military intervention. This followed an announcement by the Chief of State and the Premier that they had given the Belgians an ultimatum to leave, failing which Moscow would be asked to send troops.

[Meanwhile, the crash of a Belgian plane in the Congo, in which thirty-four soldiers were killed, resulted in the disclosure that Belgian troops were still being sent to the area, according to an Associated Press report from Brussels.]

Premier Lumumba commented on today's Cabinet decision in a dramatic news conference in the presence of Dr. Ralph J. Bunche, Under Secretary of the United Nations.

Premier Lumumba accused the United Nations of dragging its feet and deferring to the Belgians. "We want to expose the hypocrisy of certain powers," he said.

He declared he had received assurances from Premier Khrushchev that Soviet intervention would get the Belgians out of

Continued on Page 5, Column 1

The New York Times

CONGO DELEGATE: André Mandi, a foreign officer, is greeted by Secretary General Dag Hammarskjold at U. N.

RUSSIAN IS FIRM

Insists Brussels Pull Men Out in 3 Days —Vote Deferred

Excerpts from Hammarskjold report and debate, Page 4.

By THOMAS J. HAMILTON

Special to The New York Times.

UNITED NATIONS, N. Y., Thursday, July 21—The United States served notice this morning that "we will do whatever may be necessary" in association with other United Nations members, to keep Soviet troops out of the Congo.

Henry Cabot Lodge issued this warning in the Security Council after Vasily V. Kuznetsov, a Soviet First Deputy Foreign Minister, had introduced a resolution calling for the immediate cessation of Belgium's "armed intervention" and the withdrawal of Belgian forces from the Congo within three days.

Thomas Kanza, the Congolese representative, called on the council to recommend the withdrawal of Belgian forces "as rapidly as possible."

[In Brussels, Premier Gaston Eyskens warned that Belgium might have to review her relations with the United Nations if she was accused of aggression in the Congo by the world organization, according to United Press International.]

Soviet Warning Noted

Mr. Lodge did not say specifically that the United States was determined to exclude Soviet troops. However, he prefaced his statement with the remark that there had been reports that the Soviet Union might "intervene in the Congo directly with troops," and that the position of the United States on this point was "unequivocably clear."

"With other United Nations members we will do whatever may be necessary to prevent the intrusion of military forces not requested by the United Nations," Mr. Lodge emphasized.

Mr. Lodge's statement was prompted by the decision of the Congolese Government yesterday to issue an immediate appeal for help to the Soviet Union "or any other country of the African-Asian bloc" unless the Security Council took prompt effective action. The session began at 9:15 P. M. and continued until 1:05 A. M. without a vote.

The Council will resume de-

Continued on Page 5, Column 4

Paris and NATO Rule Out Soviet Move Into the Congo

By ROBERT C. DOTY

Special to The New York Times.

PARIS, July 20 — The French Government and the North Atlantic alliance both indicated today that they would oppose interference from any source with the United Nations mission to re-establish order in the Congo.

A communiqué of the French Cabinet made clear its opposition "to any unilateral intervention whatever, as well as to the competition of influences that might occur as a result of these [Congo] events."

The Permanent Council of the North Atlantic Treaty Organization refrained from any public comment on a meeting almost exclusively devoted to a study of the Congo situation.

But it was clear that the first sign of Soviet intention to give the Congo military aid would produce North Atlantic support for a warning to the Kremlin. Premier Patrice Lumumba of the Congo said in Leopoldville that he would appeal for Soviet aid unless the United Nations Security Council took really effective action.

Step May Be Embarrassing

Some Western officials doubted that the Soviet Union would heed such an appeal. Instead, they saw the possibility that a formal Congo request might prove to be a political and strategic embarrassment for Premier Khrushchev.

This reasoning runs along these lines:

To intervene, the Russians would have to repudiate an engagement taken when they voted for the Security Council resolution setting up a United Nations force to restore order in the Congo. Secretary General Dag Hammarskjold clearly stated before the vote that forces of non-African states that are members of the Security Council would not participate. It was in this context that the Soviet representative voted for the resolution.

Assuming that the Soviet leaders decided to brush aside these juridical obstacles to So-

Continued on Page 9, Column 1

U. S. STUDIES ROLE OF REDS IN AFRICA

Experts Find Soviet Bloc's Economic Aid to Guinea Is Pattern for Congo

By DANA ADAMS SCHMIDT

Special to The New York Times.

WASHINGTON, July 20—In the light of the Congo crisis, State Department officials are anxiously studying the problem of Soviet penetration of the African continent.

The officials called Ambassador Clare H. Timberlake by telephone to check reports that the Congolese Cabinet had decided to invite Soviet or other troops to help oust the Belgians unless the United Nations acted promptly to get Belgian forces out of the Congo.

Mr. Timberlake asserted that, according to his information, the Cabinet had as yet made no final decision to call in Soviet troops.

Lincoln White, State Department press officer, made public this conversation with the evident intention of counteracting alarmist reports. Other officials indicated that they thought Premier Patrice Lumumba of the Congo was using the Belgian troop issue and the threat of Soviet intervention to unite his supporters and hasten United Nations action.

Troop Shipment Doubted

The officials said they thought the Soviet Union was more likely to provide the Congolese with advisers, technicians and credits than to send them troops.

This is the pattern the Soviet bloc has used in Guinea. American experts expect the pattern to be repeated wherever Africans reject Western assistance or the West is unable to keep up with African development aspirations.

Many African leaders who have visited the United States in recent months have shown that they were impressed by the economic help the Soviet bloc has given Guinea.

While the United States has for one year been negotiating with Guinea for agreements on

Continued on Page 7, Column 1

Guggenheim Museum Director Resigns in Difference of 'Ideals'

Sweeney Revised Wright's Design for Building Before Opening Last October

By SANKA KNOX

A conflict that has been simmering for some time between James Johnson Sweeney, director of the Solomon R. Guggenheim Museum, and the foundation that runs the museum has boiled over. Mr. Sweeney has resigned.

The newest shift at the museum, now housed in Frank Lloyd Wright's controversial building, brought an acknowledgment from both sides yesterday that they were motivated by differing "ideals."

Neither side offered any explanation of what the differing ideals were and neither Mr. Sweeney nor Harry F. Guggenheim, the president of the foundation, could be reached after a formal statement had been sent out.

Mr. Sweeney's short letter of resignation, dated June 24, said merely that he was resigning because of the difference between ideals held by the museum "and my own ideals, which I feel I have a responsibility to follow."

The resignation will be effective on Aug. 15.

Mr. Guggenheim's statement, while expressing gratitude for Mr. Sweeney's services, implied that such services were no longer needed in view of the foundation's plan to broaden "the scope of its activities" and said that the foundation would "require new approaches to the objectives sought by the founder."

"Mr. Wright's creation, an architectural achievement of great moment, has proved to be not only unusually well

Continued on Page 18, Column 7

The New York Times

James Johnson Sweeney

CASE ON TRUJILLO IMPRESSES PANEL

O. A. S. Unit Hears Charges of Plot in Caracas

By JUAN de ONIS

Special to The New York Times.

CARACAS, Venezuela, July 20—The Organization of American States fact-finding mission completed today its investigation of Venezuela's charges that the Dominican Republic organized the attempted assassination of President Romulo Betancourt here June 24.

The members of the mission were clearly impressed by testimony given to them privately by prisoners here that Generalissimo Rafael Leonidas Trujillo Molina, Dominican dictator, had personally provided arms and instructions for the bombing, in which the President was seriously burned and two persons were killed. The mission will submit a report, probably within a week, to the council of the O. A. S. A meeting of American foreign ministers has been called to consider Venezuela's charges that the Dominican dictatorship is a threat to the peace of the hemisphere.

The chairman of the mission, Vicente Sanchez Gabito of Mexico, remained here today while the other members, representing Argentina, Panama and

Continued on Page 2, Column 7

4 Guilty of Slaying Boys in Playground

Four teen-aged youths have been found guilty of the slaying of two 16-year-old boys in a West Forty-sixth Street playground last August.

An all-male jury in the Court of General Sessions last night brought out verdicts of first-degree murder on two counts and attempted first-degree murder on a third count against two youths, Salvador Agron, 16 years old, of 75 Hudson Street, Brooklyn, and Luis Antonio Hernandez, 17, of 524 West 134th Street. Both face mandatory death sentences.

At 2:50 o'clock this morning the jury returned separate decisions against the two other defendants, Francisco Cruz, 18,

Continued on Page 14, Column 1

NEWS INDEX

Martin Milner and George Maharis were the adventurers in *Route 66.*

Mitch Miller drew huge audiences for NBC with his famous *Sing Along* shows and kept the public enchanted until 1964 when the novelty finally wore off.

David Brinkley and Chet Huntley sparked the public with the *Huntley-Brinkley Report* and top-rated coverage of the 1960 conventions, bringing NBC's news rating to its height.

"All the News That's Fit to Print"

The New York Times.

LATE CITY EDITION
U. S. Weather Bureau Report (Page 54) forecasts Mostly fair and warm today, tonight and tomorrow.
Temp. range: 84—65; yesterday: 72.9—68.9
Temp.-Hum. Index: 76; yesterday: 71.

VOL. CIX..No. 37,441. NEW YORK, THURSDAY, JULY 28, 1960. FIVE CENTS
10 cents beyond 50-mile zone from New York City except on Long Island. Higher in air delivery cities.

NIXON IS GIVEN NOMINATION BY ACCLAMATION AFTER GOLDWATER GETS 10 LOUISIANA VOTES; CANDIDATE PICKS LODGE FOR SECOND PLACE

SANITATION UNION QUITS IN PROTEST; GARBAGE PILES UP

5,000 March on City Hall as Wage Talks Break Off —Walkout May Go On

By LAYHMOND ROBINSON

Thousands of tons of refuse were left lying on city streets yesterday when angry sanitation workers suddenly stopped work to protest a breakdown in wage negotiations with the city.

The Sanitation Department reported that at least 4,000 of the 5,000 garbage collectors, street cleaners and incinerator employes on the day shift had failed to report for duty at 7 A. M. They may not report today, either.

Instead, the shouting, chanting city employes, augmented by 1,000 fellow workers who were on vacation or had days off, marched to City Hall.

They besieged the building for several hours, created a traffic jam and gave a 100-man police detail some anxious moments in holding the surging crowd behind barricades. However, there was no violence, though the police took the precaution of locking the doors of City Hall.

Meeting Collapses

Later in the day, a collapse of a hastily arranged meeting between union and city negotiators brought predictions that the walkout, which the union has denied is a strike, might last for some time.

Last night, as a result of the walkout, Traffic Commissioner T. T. Wiley announced that alternate-side parking rules would be lifted here today. Motorists may ignore signs that normally prohibit parking on Thursdays between 8 A. M. and 11 A. M. and 11 A. M. and 2 P. M. The department has not decided yet what it will do about parking regulations tomorrow.

City Demands Return

At the meeting between union and city negotiators, the spokesmen for the city, acting under instruction from the Board of Estimate, demanded that the men return to work before negotiations were resumed. Union negotiators rejected the demand and vowed to stay out until the city came up with a better offer on wages and fringe benefits.

The state's Condon-Wadlin Law prohibits strikes by Civil Service employes but Mayor Wagner would not say yesterday whether he viewed the stoppage as a strike, nor would he say whether the law would be invoked for the first time here.

Union members did not report for the night shift. The Sanitation Department said only a handful had showed up for night duty, which begins at 4 P. M. Usually about 700 men work the night shift in the summer.

The Sanitation Commissioner warned the men involved that they would be docked a day's pay for each day they refused

Continued on Page 11, Column 4

Stock Margin Rate Is Cut To 70% by Reserve Board

Officials Deny Reduction From 90% Is Aimed at Shoring Up the Market—Economic Significance Minimized

By TOM WICKER
Special to The New York Times.

WASHINGTON, July 27—The margin requirement for purchases of stocks was reduced from 90 to 70 per cent today by the Federal Reserve Board.

The reduction is effective tomorrow. It reflects the belief of the board of governors of the Federal Reserve that stock market credit is relatively stable at this time.

The margin requirement governs the minimum cash payment a stock buyer must make. As an example, today's action will reduce from $900 to $700 the amount of cash that must be put up for each $1,000 of stock.

The reduction also applies to short sales, in which a trader borrows stock and sells it in the hope of buying it back later at a lower price and thus making a profit.

The margin requirement is a device by which the Federal Reserve attempts to prevent excessive use of credit in the stock market. A spokesman said today the board of governors "just thinks 70 per cent will do it" under today's conditions.

The price of common stocks has declined recently. But the spokesman denied that today's action was an attempt to shore up prices or to stimulate credit and speculative activity.

He conceded, however, that since a trader could pick up more stock with the same amount of money, beginning tomorrow, the reduction might have an initial effect on the volume of transactions.

Despite the fact that the latest change before today's in margin requirements—an advance from 70 to 90 per cent on Oct. 16, 1958—came when the

Continued on Page 37, Column 1

CHIEFS CONSULTED

Bricker Is Expected to Place U.N. Aide in Nomination

By LEO EGAN
Special to The New York Times.

CHICAGO, Thursday, July 28—Henry Cabot Lodge, delegate to the United Nations, was picked today by Vice President Richard M. Nixon to be his running mate.

Mr. Nixon revealed his preference a few hours after he himself had been nominated for President by the Republican convention.

Mr. Nixon came out of his room and made this announcement:

"I have reached a decision that I shall recommend to the convention Henry Cabot Lodge."

He said he would call Mr. Lodge at his New York home and ask if he would accept. He said he expected the decision to be affirmative.

Mr. Nixon made the announcement at 2:20 A. M. Central daylight time (3:20 A. M. New York time).

His decision all but assured Mr. Lodge's nomination for Vice President when the convention votes tonight on that post.

Mr. Nixon made the selection in consultation with leading Republicans in a meeting that began at his hotel about a half hour after the adjournment of last night's session of the convention.

Choice Not Unanimous

New York was represented at the meeting by L. Judson Morhouse, its Republican State Chairman.

The choice of Mr. Lodge was far from unanimous. However, Mr. Nixon insisted upon the Presidential nominee's right to choose his running mate.

Earlier yesterday, Mr. Nixon had listed the 58-year old former Massachusetts Senator as one of the four front runners for the vice-presidential nomination.

The three others were:

Senator Thruston B. Morton of Kentucky, the 52-year-old Republican National Chairman.

Representative Walter H. Judd of Minnesota, now 61 years old, who delivered the keynote address to the convention on Monday.

Robert B. Anderson, the 50-year-old Secretary of the Treasury, a former Texas Democrat who became an Eisenhower Republican in 1952.

To offset Midwest opposition to Mr. Lodge, an arrangement was reported to have been made to have former Senator John W. Bricker of Ohio place his name in nomination. And Representative Gerald Ford of Michigan, a

Continued on Page 12, Column 5

Associated Press Wirephoto

AFTER THE DELEGATES VOTED: Vice President and Mrs. Nixon at their hotel in Chicago last night with their daughters, Patricia, left, 14 years old, and Julie, 12.

UNITY IS STRESSED

Goldwater Withdraws and Asks Backing for the Nominee

Hatfield's speech, Page 12; Goldwater text, Page 14.

By W. H. LAWRENCE
Special to The New York Times.

CHICAGO, Thursday, July 28—Vice President Richard M. Nixon swept to a first-ballot Republican Presidential nomination last night and the right to face Democratic Senator John F. Kennedy in the November election.

Early today, Mr. Nixon chose Henry Cabot Lodge, chief United States delegate to the United Nations, as his Vice-Presidential running mate.

Mr. Nixon received 1,321 votes on the polling of state delegations. Senator Barry Goldwater of Arizona received ten votes, cast by members of the twenty-six-vote Louisiana delegation even after the Arizonan had asked withdrawal of his name from consideration.

At the end of the roll-call, Louisiana moved to make Mr. Nixon's choice unanimous, but balked at changing its ten votes from the Goldwater to the Nixon column without a poll. When the roll-call vote was announced as 1,321 to 10, the Arizona delegation then moved to make the nomination unanimous, and this was done by acclamation.

Goldwater Asks Unity

The convention decision pits the 47-year-old Vice President against the 43-year-old Senator from Massachusetts. Mr. Nixon is the first Vice President in the history of the modern two-party system to win a Presidential nomination in his own right.

Senator Goldwater made the dramatic appearance of the night, calling upon all conservatives to back Mr. Nixon in November and avoid any party split or stay-at-home nonvoting attitude that would help Democrats "dedicated to the destruction of this country."

Withdrawing his own name from consideration for the Presidency, the Arizona Senator, an avowed conservative, said he had been campaigning for Mr. Nixon's nomination for the last six years and would fight for his election in November.

Lecture to Conservatives

"Let us put our shoulders to the wheel of Dick Nixon and push him over across the line," Senator Goldwater said.

He lectured conservatives sternly, telling them they must "grow up" and get to work "if we want to take this party back some day—and I think we can."

He said the Democratic party no longer was the party of Jefferson, Jackson and Wilson but now was ruled by "Bowles, Galbraith and Reuther." His references were to Representative Chester Bowles of Connecticut; Kenneth Galbraith, Harvard economist, and Walter P. Reu-

Continued on Page 12, Column 1

FRENCH 'SLIGHTS' ANGER ADENAUER

He Will Leave for Week-End Paris Talks Only Because His Hand Was Forced

By SYDNEY GRUSON
Special to The New York Times.

BONN, Germany, July 27—Chancellor Adenauer will fly to Paris for talks with President de Gaulle Friday, but in a furious mood and only because the French forced his hand.

Both Paris and Bonn announced the meeting this afternoon and said the main subject of the talks would be the political integration of Western Europe.

But the background to this laconic announcement was far more dramatic. The Chancellor had been infuriated by a number of what he considers slights to West Germany by France and had determined not to go through with the meeting this week-end.

The French, aware of his mood, let it be known last night to West German reporters in Paris and to some French newspapers that the meeting was on.

Apparently rather than permit a crack for all the world to see in the painfully restored French-German friendship, the keystone of his European policy,

Continued on Page 2, Column 5

British Earl Named Foreign Secretary In Cabinet Shuffle

By DREW MIDDLETON
Special to The New York Times.

LONDON, July 27 — Prime Minister Macmillan chose the Earl of Home as Britain's new Foreign Secretary today in a major reconstruction of the Conservative Government.

Selwyn Lloyd leaves the Foreign Office to become Chancellor of the Exchequer. A successful tenure there would improve Mr. Lloyd's prospects as the future Prime Minister.

Lord Home (whose name is pronounced Hume) is the first peer to be Foreign Secretary since Lord Halifax held the office twenty years ago. The official announcement of his appointment this evening brought to a climax the mounting criticism of the last five days.

Mr. Macmillan will be forced to defend his choice against the Labor party's censure in a House of Commons debate tomorrow night.

The objections to the appointment of Lord Home were based on two points. First, the critics said, the Foreign Secretary should be a member of the House of Commons and answerable in the House to any questions on foreign policy. Second, the objectors maintained, there was nothing in Lord Home's career to justify the appointment.

The first newspaper comment

Continued on Page 2, Column 2

NIXON BOLSTERS ROCKEFELLER TIE

New York Delegation Greets Him Warmly — Governor to Campaign Anywhere

By WARREN WEAVER Jr.
Special to The New York Times.

CHICAGO, July 27—At political sword points only a week ago, Governor Rockefeller and Vice President Nixon joined today in a powerful demonstration of concord.

Mr. Nixon made a special morning trip two miles up Michigan Avenue to visit his new-found supporters in the New York delegation. The delegation endorsed him unanimously, if belatedly, yesterday.

The Governor went to the Sheraton Towers lobby to greet Mr. Nixon, like classmates at a reunion. Beaming, he escorted him to the closed caucus. They posed for pictures with arms around each other.

Mr. Rockefeller said the Vice President's visit had given the New Yorkers "a final inspiration and emotional lift."

"We're with you all the way," he promised.

Mr. Nixon was hardly less enthusiastic about the Governor. He pleaded with the New York

Continued on Page 14, Column 5

13 Dead in Chicago Crash Of 'Copter on Airport Run

By The Associated Press.

CHICAGO, July 27—A helicopter carrying passengers between airports suddenly lost power and plunged in a mass of flames into a suburban cemetery tonight. All thirteen persons aboard were killed. Wreckage was scattered over a wide area.

A swath of clipped tree tops almost 600 feet long indicated that the pilot had tried to gain altitude.

Witnesses said the craft, an S-58, carrying eleven passengers and a crew of two, stopped in air, zigzagged a moment and then plummeted, shooting flames.

The helicopter, owned by Chicago Helicopter Airways, Inc., was on an eleven-minute trip from Midway Airport on the Southwest side to O'Hare International Airport on the Northwest side.

Falls Near River

It plunged into the Forest Home Cemetery north of Roosevelt Road near the Des Plaines River. The crash site is between suburban Maywood and Forest Park.

An officer of the helicopter company landed near the crash scene and said that the pilot of the downed craft was Capt. Robert Meyer, 37 years old. The names of the other victims were not immediately available.

However, a company spokesman said "no one of national importance was known to be aboard." He apparently referred to the fact the Republican National Convention is meeting in Chicago.

The helicopter, which has a capacity of fourteen, including

Continued on Page 55, Column 2

ROBERT KENNEDY EASES SPLIT HERE

Candidate's Brother Wins Prendergast's Approval of Independent Group

By CLAYTON KNOWLES

Robert F. Kennedy came to New York yesterday and brought Michael H. Prendergast around to an agreement that an independent citizens' committee could work effectively in the state for the election of Senator John F. Kennedy as President.

Mr. Prendergast, the Democratic state chairman, reversed his earlier opposition to such an auxiliary campaign unit during a two-and-a-half hour luncheon meeting with Mr. Kennedy, who is the manager of his brother's campaign for the Presidency.

Carmine G. De Sapio, Democratic national committeeman, who sat in on the session at the Hampshire House, was asked if he, too, was satisfied.

"One hundred per cent!" he said with emphasis.

The conference was one of five important meetings that Mr. Kennedy held during a busy day with representatives of virtually every shade of thinking within the Democratic party.

The session with Mr. Prendergast was of particular importance because Mr. Prendergast had understood originally in talks with Senator Kennedy that the campaign would be run strictly through the Democratic state organization.

Later, when the Senator agreed to establishing a Citizens for Kennedy committee here, Mr. Prendergast viewed the enterprise as competitive with the regular organization's work. He also viewed the individuals

Continued on Page 16, Column 1

Iran Cuts Cairo Tie In Dispute on Israel

By Reuters.

TEHERAN, Iran, July 27—Iran severed diplomatic relations with the United Arab Republic today and gave Cairo's Ambassador here twenty-four hours to get out of the country.

The severance was announced by Foreign Minister Abbas Aram after he had served the expulsion order on the Ambassador, Mahmoud Hammad.

Mr. Aram said the decision to oust Mr. Hammad was made after President Gamal Abdel Nasser attacked Shah Mohammed Riza Pahlevi of Iran yesterday in a speech at Alexandria. President Nasser assailed the Shah for his statement Saturday that Iran had recognized Israel.

The Iranian Foreign Minister described President Nasser as

Continued on Page 5, Column 1

The New York Times

PROTEST AT CITY HALL: Employes of the Department of Sanitation rally against the breakdown of wage talks

Key Issues in Congo Awaiting U.N. Chief

By HENRY TANNER
Special to The New York Times.

LEOPOLDVILLE, the Congo, July 27 — Secretary General Dag Hammarskjold is likely to be successful in paving the way for the peaceful entry of United Nations forces into Katanga Province, diplomatic observers here predict.

Mr. Hammarskjold is scheduled to arrive here tomorrow from Brussels. Katanga, which has declared its independence of the Congo, is expected to be the dominant issue in his consultations here. He will spend four or five days talking with Congolese, Belgian and United Nations officials.

Katanga is now controlled by Belgian forces that went there at the request of the provincial Premier, Moise Tshombe. Mr.

Continued on Page 3, Column 3

NEWS INDEX

Eisenhower Is Firm For Middle of Road

By DONALD JANSON
Special to The New York Times.

CHICAGO, July 27 — President Eisenhower emphasized today the superiority of a middle political course over right or left extremes.

He denounced the Socialist philosophy of a "fairly friendly European country" he said he had been reading about in the last few weeks.

"The experiment of almost complete paternalism" there, he said, has resulted in a sharp rise in the suicide rate, "more than twice our drunkenness," and a "lack of moderation discernible on all sides."

It was believed that he had alluded to Sweden. Her suicide rate is 19.9 for every 100,000 persons, compared with ten in

Continued on Page 14, Column 4

1960

Nixon faced Kennedy in one of their televised debates. It is believed that Nixon's poor showing contributed to his defeat.

Richard M. Nixon conceded the presidential election to John F. Kennedy as a very sad Pat Nixon looks on.

The Kennedy campaign gave Americans the chance to greet the most charismatic leader in modern times.

Burt Lancaster won an Oscar for his dramatic role in *Elmer Gantry.*

Marilyn Monroe and Clark Gable in *The Misfits*, which was released after Gable's death in 1960.

"All the News That's Fit to Print"

The New York Times.

LATE CITY EDITION

U. S. Weather Bureau Report (Page 36) forecasts: Chance of rain today and tonight. Warmer, possible showers tomorrow.

Temp. range: 76—67; yesterday: 75.5—65.8. Temp.-Hum. Index: low 70's; yesterday: 71.

VOL. CIX...No. 37,457. © 1960, by The New York Times Company. Times Square, New York 36, N. Y. NEW YORK, SATURDAY, AUGUST 13, 1960. 10 cents beyond 50-mile zone from New York City except on Long Island. Higher in air delivery cities. FIVE CENTS

BALLOON SATELLITE ORBITS; RELAYED MESSAGE HERALDS NEW COMMUNICATIONS ERA

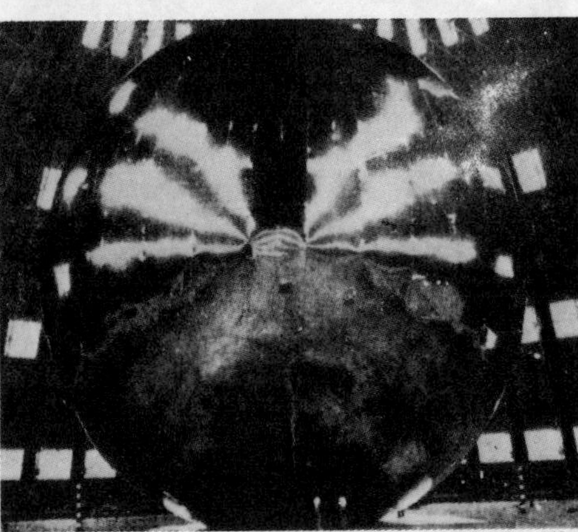

National Aeronautics and Space Administration, via Associated Press

SPACE VEHICLE: A balloon of the type sent into orbit dwarfs technicians, center

U.N. TROOPS ENTER KATANGA IN FACE OF NEW DEFIANCE

Hammarskjold Averts Move to Block the Landing of 7 Planes With Him

CROWD JEERS SWEDES

Tshombe Greets Secretary Warmly—Two Men Hold Preliminary Discussion

By HENRY TANNER

Special to The New York Times.

ELISABETHVILLE, the Congo, Aug. 12—Katanga Province accepted United Nations troops today with a last gesture of defiance. Secretary General Dag Hammarskjold refused to change his plans, however.

On instructions from the Katanga Government the airport control tower told the pilot of Mr. Hammarskjold's plane to land but withheld clearance for seven troop-carrying planes that followed.

Five trucks, a bus, a fire engine and a big excavator had been posted along the runway at the last moment. Their operators were to have been ordered to move into the path of the troop carriers once the lead plane had landed. About 200 Katanga troops also were on hand.

Airport officials said Mr. Hammarskjold's pilot had radioed back that unless all eight planes were permitted to land the Secretary General would fly back to Leopoldville.

Tshombe Clears Way

Katanga's President, Moise Tshombe, who was waiting on the landing field apron with his ministers and two Belgian diplomats, then instructed the control tower to give clearance to all the planes.

Mr. Tshombe said that there had been a misunderstanding and that the control tower had been acting on instructions given several days ago.

The acceptance of United Nations troops was a reversal of the stand Katanga had taken earlier. The province, which has declared its independence from the Congo, has insisted that United Nations forces were not needed because its own forces, assisted by Belgian troops, were able to keep order.

Katanga authorities refused to let United Nations civilian specialists leave a plane that landed at Elisabethville last Saturday. This led to an urgent session of the Security Council, which adopted a resolution call-

Continued on Page 2, Column 1

U.N. CHIEF OFFERS WIDE AID TO CONGO

Would Lend Experts in Many Fields—Vows Neutrality

Additions to Hammarskjold's report on Congo, Page 2.

By LINDESAY PARROTT

Special to The New York Times.

UNITED NATIONS, N. Y., Aug. 12 — Secretary General Dag Hammarskjold assured the Security Council and the leaders of the Congo today that the United Nations force there would maintain a completely neutral role in the new republic's internal quarrels.

At the same time, he announced a wide program for assistance to the Congo Government, going considerably beyond the technical aid the international organization has offered thus far to under-developed nations.

He said the United Nations, if requested, would furnish an adviser to each Cabinet Minister in the Congo to provide expert guidance on such subjects as agriculture, communications, public health, foreign trade, labor and public administration.

The Secretary General, in an addition to his second report to the Security Council on the Congo crisis, conceded that his plan for assistance would "go further" than the traditional method of technical assistance. It would also be more sweeping, he said, than the Operational and Executive Personnel program that he has pushed for several years.

This program, known as

Continued on Page 2, Column 4

Associated Press Radiophoto

U. N. CONFERENCE IN THE CONGO: Dag Hammarskjold, center, Secretary General, with Dr. Ralph J. Bunche, Under Secretary, and Maj. Gen. Carl Carlsson von Horn, head of U. N. force. Mr. Hammarskjold left later for Elisabethville, in Katanga.

U. S. Decides to Maintain Its Role in Test-Ban Talks

Special to The New York Times.

WASHINGTON, Aug. 12—The Administration, despite increasing impatience over the lack of progress toward a prohibition of tests of nuclear weapons, decided today against making any precipitate move that might break up the negotiations in Geneva.

The issue was considered by President Eisenhower at a National Security Council meeting this morning at the White House.

According to State Department sources, the President received varying counsel from his principal advisers on the course the United States should follow in the negotiations and whether the Administration should proceed with a planned series of underground nuclear explosions to improve detection.

Thomas S. Gates Jr., Secretary of Defense, and John A. McCone, Atomic Energy Commission chairman, were reported to have urged that the United States conduct the explosions, even without Soviet concurrence.

Herter Opposed Move

Secretary of State Christian A. Herter was said to have argued against any precipitate move to proceed with the tests on the ground that the United States would risk censure in the United Nations and possibly alienate the African-Asian bloc.

These two views, according to State Department sources, were discussed without decision at a meeting late yesterday of the Committee of Principals, the policy-making body on a test ban.

The principals are the Secretaries of Defense and State, the A. E. C. chairman, the director of the Central Intelligence Agency and the President's scientific adviser.

The President and the Security Council, it was reported, reached no clear decision on whether to conduct the tests

Continued on Page 3, Column 5

MOSCOW STEPS UP ANTI-SPY ACTIONS

Tells Another U. S. Student to Leave After Accusing Him of Provocations

By OSGOOD CARUTHERS

Special to The New York Times.

MOSCOW, Aug. 12—Another American student on tour in the Soviet Union has been accused of hostile and provocative activities and has been ordered to leave the country, the Moscow press reported today.

The tourist is James Shultz, a 21-year-old university student from Otis, Kan.

The report was seen as part of the Kremlin's mounting propaganda campaign to drive home its accusations that the United States is using tourism and every other means to carry out a national policy of espionage and provocation against the Soviet Union.

Reports Come Almost Daily

The report was buried in an article in the Communist youth newspaper Komsomolskaya Pravda about the American student who was expelled from the country yesterday on espionage charges.

The Soviet press has been bringing out such cases almost daily as the time approaches for the espionage trial Wednesday of Francis Gary Powers, pilot of the United States U-2 jet that was downed May 1 in the Soviet Union.

[Mr. and Mrs. Oliver W. Powers, the pilot's parents, arrived in Moscow early Saturday, hoping to see their son, The Associated Press said.]

Mr. Shultz, touring the Soviet Union with twelve other persons under the sponsorship of the Bureau of International Youth Travel of the Young Men's and Women's Christian Associations, "conducted anti-

Continued on Page 4, Column 3

Cuba Clamps Down On Travel Abroad

By R. HART PHILLIPS

Special to The New York Times.

HAVANA, Aug. 12—Cuba acted today to tighten exit regulations for residents who seek to leave the island.

Military exit permits now held by residents were canceled. The permits are needed to leave the island.

Foreign tourists are not affected, since they are not required to have the permits.

No official reason was announced for the cancellation. It was reported that the move would give the Cuban police a better means for checking on American residents of Cuba as well as Cubans.

Revolución, a semi-official newspaper, said the exit permits had been canceled to "put an end to counter-revolutionary propaganda and to prevent con-

Continued on Page 13, Column 5

JERSEY APPROVES UTILITY RATE RISE

$10,163,000 Gas, Electric Increase Will Affect 80% of State's Population

Special to The New York Times.

NEWARK, Aug. 12—The Public Service Electric and Gas Company, which serves four-fifths of the population of New Jersey, was granted a $10,163,000-a-year rate increase today.

The increase, approved by the Board of Public Utility Commissioners, amounted to about a 7 per cent rise in the company's revenue. It was only a little more than one-quarter of the amount the company had sought, however.

The increase will not become effective until after a hearing on Sept. 19 on a new tariff schedule the company was told to submit by Sept. 2. Until then it will not be possible to say how the increase will affect home owners and industries.

The board based its action on the premise that the company was entitled to a 6.25 per cent rate of return.

Hearings Began in '58

In rejecting the request for the larger increase, amounting to $37,498,709, the board said the rates as proposed were "unjust and unreasonable in that they yield an excessive return."

Public hearings on the rate increase were held on ninety-six days between the first hearing on July 2, 1958, and the final session last March 30. The record contains 7,664 pages of transcript, in addition to prepared text submitted by the company and those who opposed the increase.

The case, according to Ralph L. Fusco, president of the board, has been the longest in the agency's fifty-year history.

The proposed increase was opposed by the Federal General

Continued on Page 12, Column 3

X-15 Climbs to 131,000 Feet; 'Fantastic Up Here,' Pilot Says

Rocket-Ship Flier Weightless Almost a Minute as He Sets Altitude Record

By The Associated Press.

EDWARDS AIR FORCE BASE, Calif., Aug. 12—A test pilot rode the rocket ship X-15 today to a record height of 131,000 feet—nearly twenty-five miles—then radioed back from the fringe of space:

"This is really fantastic up here."

Maj. Robert M. White of the Air Force raced weightless for nearly a minute as the dartlike research plane, out of sight from observers at this desert test center, carried man higher than he had ventured before.

Back on the ground the 36-year-old pilot, with nearly 5,000 hours in the air, spoke feelingly of his experience:

"It was a very deep blue, but not exactly like night. There was distinct contrast. Your view encompasses three distinct bands — the earth, the light blue of the sky and then the very deep blue of extreme altitude. It was very impressive.

"I was impressed by the feeling of altitude—the height above ground. At the altitude I nor-

Associated Press

Maj. Robert M. White

mally fly, 40,000 to 50,000 feet, I can see, oh, maybe, hundreds of square miles. This time I took in ten times that much. I couldn't see any definite curvature of the earth, but I expect photographs would show it.

"I would have no qualms about going higher."

Higher, perhaps to 100 miles, is where he is expected to go when the X-15 is equipped with

Continued on Page 7, Column 1

REPUBLICANS SEE SENATE BEING RUN TO HELP KENNEDY

Nixon Joins in the Attack—Johnson Denies Charge—Javits Maps Rights Bid

By TOM WICKER

Special to The New York Times.

WASHINGTON, Aug. 12—Republicans carried the attack to the Democrats in the Senate today, as mounting political pressures began to irritate members on both sides of the aisle.

Senator Jacob K. Javits pledged unremitting efforts to pass civil rights legislation during the remainder of the session. The New York Republican told Democrats it was "clear to the country" that they were opposed to action in that field.

Two other Republican Senators, Kenneth B. Keating, also of New York, and Hugh Scott of Pennsylvania, berated the Democratic Presidential nominee, Senator John F. Kennedy of Massachusetts, for flying to New York late yesterday. They said the Senate was being run for his political benefit.

Vice President Nixon joined the attack late in the day. He said Senator Kennedy was "directing the Senate for his own purposes."

Wage Bill Debated

The statement was issued by Herbert G. Klein, the Vice President's press secretary. Mr. Nixon, the Republican Presidential nominee, did not appear on the Senate floor during any of the day's political flurries or during the desultory debate on the Kennedy bill to raise the minimum wage from $1 to $1.25 an hour and broaden coverage. Debate on the bill took up most of the Senate's day.

Senator Kennedy, who was on the floor during the Keating-Scott attack, appeared unperturbed. He smiled, lounged in his seat and let his colleagues respond to the Republican taunt.

Other Senators were not so relaxed. Edgy tempers, whetted by the tense political situation in the chamber, showed particularly in an unimportant but acrimonious debate over what hour the Senate would set for adjournment Saturday night.

In the course of that exchange, the majority leader, Lyndon B. Johnson, the Democratic Vice-Presidential nominee, struck back at Vice President Nixon for the Scott-Keating attack on Senator Kennedy.

Javits Against Russell

Senator Johnson noted that Mr. Nixon would make a flying trip to Maine tomorrow and observed—with his tongue ill-concealed in his cheek—that he hoped no one on his side of the aisle would "denounce" the Vice President for that.

Civil rights—the Senate's traditional sore spot—set off the hottest round of the day. It pitted Senator Javits against Senator Richard B. Russell, Democrat of Georgia.

Senator Russell opened hostilities by blocking the Senate's usual "morning hour"—a period for brief statements, tributes and similar matters, usually limited to three minutes each. He said he had been informed that Senator Javits would seek action on a civil rights bill during the morning hour and "I do not propose to be caught here with a three-minute limitation of debate."

He said Senator Javits's effort was political and called it a

Continued on Page 8, Column 7

Fire and Blast Kill Five on Navy Ship

Special to The New York Times.

CHARLESTON, S. C., Saturday, Aug. 13—An explosion and fire killed five men aboard a Navy minesweeper off Savannah, Ga., last night.

A spokesman at the naval base here confirmed that the blast had occurred about 6 P.M. aboard the Exultant. He said that other ships had rushed to the scene, and that the fire had been brought under control. But he would give no further details.

The Coast Guard at Savannah located the vessel as seventy miles southeast of there.

The Exultant is a wooden-hulled minesweeper of the Agile class, bearing a normal complement of seventy-two to seventy-four men. She is 171 feet long and weighs 750 tons. She was launched in 1953. She had left

Continued on Page 8, Column 4

FARM BILL FADES FOR THIS SESSION

House Leaders Act to Drop Price-Support Measure —Passage Unlikely

Special to The New York Times.

WASHINGTON, Aug. 12. — The prospect of major farm legislation at this Congressional session virtually disappeared today.

An informal meeting of leaders of the House Agriculture Committee decided against price-support legislation that would affect 1960 crops. They said it would be impractical to act now on a Senate-passed wheat bill.

Harold D. Cooley, the North Carolina Democrat who is the committee chairman, said there was "still some hope" that a voluntary land reserve plan might be pushed through the House.

This measure would permit farmers to withdraw land from production voluntarily and receive payment in kind. That is, they would be given 55 or perhaps 60 per cent of the commodity they might have harvested, supplied from existing Government-held surpluses.

Sources in the Senate indicated that this plan would not be received favorably there. The Senate leadership in both parties has made it clear that the House must take the initiative on major farm legislation if there is to be any.

Mr. Cooley said the informal

Continued on Page 15, Column 2

Washington to Hail Retrieved Capsule In Ceremony Today

By RICHARD WITKIN

The Air Force capsule retrieved from orbit on Thursday was scheduled to be flown to Washington on Saturday for a round of ceremonies that probably will end at the White House on Monday.

Gen. Thomas D. White and Lieut. Gen. Bernard A. Schriever, Air Force Chief of Staff and head of research respectively, will head the committee when the prize arrives at Andrews Air Force Base, Md., aboard a C-130 cargo plane.

Officials are reported to be discussing arrangements whereby the capsule, first man-made object known to have been recovered from orbital flight, probably will be shown to President Eisenhower on Monday.

Will Preserve Secrecy

News photographers will be allowed their first close-up pictures at a news conference at Andrews Base scheduled for Saturday. Classified equipment carried by the capsule was to have been removed at Moffett Naval Air Station, Calif., on the homecoming trip from Hawaii.

Escorting the package with the tenderest of loving care was a six-foot, 200-pound colonel for whom the successful recovery ended sixteen months of the greatest frustration.

The colonel, Charles G. ("Moose") Mathison, had been directing "the great capsule chase" since the first Discoverer launchings.

He had coordinated launch-

Continued on Page 7, Column 1

PRESIDENT HEARD

His Talk Spans U. S. —Object Glitters in Sky Like a Star

By JOHN W. FINNEY

Special to The New York Times.

WASHINGTON, Aug. 12—The United States, in a triumphant day in the exploration of space, introduced a new era in world communications today by placing in orbit a balloon satellite 100 feet in diameter.

The inflatable satellite is the largest man-made object yet placed in orbit. It was launched from Cape Canaveral, Fla., in the early morning hours as the forerunner of a new mode of communications by which messages and eventually television broadcasts will be relayed across oceans by way of satellites.

Called Echo I, the satellite immediately proved its worth by bouncing a recorded message by President Eisenhower, in crystal-clear fashion, between stations in Goldstone, Calif., and Holmdel, N. J., a distance by land of 2,400 miles.

Two Other Milestones

The 136-pound satellite, glittering in the night skies with the brilliance of a bright star, started its journey 1,000 miles above the earth as the United States passed two other important milestones in the exploration of space:

¶The X-15 airplane, an experimental forerunner for space ships, was piloted by Air Force Maj. Robert M. White to an altitude of 131,000 feet over Edwards Air Force Base in California. It is the highest altitude yet achieved by man.

¶The Air Force returned and recovered the first payload from an orbiting satellite. The Discoverer capsule, recovered yesterday from the Pacific Ocean 330 miles northwest of Hawaii, was scheduled to arrive here tomorrow.

'Significant Step'

In his recorded message relayed by Echo I, President Eisenhower described the satellite's launching as "one more significant step in the United States program of space research and exploration."

As the satellite, launched at 5:39 A. M. Eastern Daylight Time, was completing its first orbit and was passing over the central United States, the Jet Propulsion Laboratory's station at Goldstone, Calif., started transmitting the President's 127-word message. The radio signals bounced off the satel-

Continued on Page 6, Column 1

2,000 Americans Are Stranded In Europe by Strike of Seamen

By The Associated Press.

LONDON, Aug. 12—An emergency airlift started tonight to fly home more than 2,000 American tourists stranded by a growing strike of British seamen.

Thousands of British and French tourists were also without transportation. The strike caused chaos in more than a score of usually busy ports.

The strikers, defying their union leaders, scored two major victories.

They forced the Cunard Company to abandon all hope of getting the Queen Mary out of Southampton. She carried 1,020 New York-bound passengers. In France, 815 more were waiting to join her.

Then they kept the 25,000-ton Canadian Pacific liner Empress of Britain tied up in Liverpool. She had been due to sail for Montreal this evening with 1,000 passengers, most of them Americans.

The strike is led by a union splinter group, the National Seamen's Reform Movement. The strikers want an increase of 4 pounds ($11.20) on the basic monthly wage of £33 5s ($93) instead of the increase of 50 shillings ($7) that union leaders had accepted.

Thirty-nine ships due to sail from British ports today were held up while 123 left on schedule. The crew of the Cunarder Carinthia has voted to strike when she reaches Liverpool tomorrow. The next big test will occur when the Queen Elizabeth docks at Southampton from New York next week.

A hunt started for passenger space on transatlantic airliners, already packed at the height of the tourist season. Cunard took three planes under charter from Pan American and British Overseas Airways. Canadian Pacific started a ferry service with its own aircraft.

Stranded passengers stayed in the liners, maintained by skeleton staffs.

Strikers and owners saw the Queen Mary's fate as crucial to the future of the strike. A strike leader said: "If we can hold the Mary more men will want to support us all over the country."

A Cunard official said: "If the Mary gets away the strike bubble will be burst."

Cunard accused the strikers of "crude and completely unjustified disregard of the wel-

Continued on Page 38, Column 5

NEWS INDEX

Rafer Johnson won the decathlon at the Olympics in Rome.

Wilma Rudolph wore a brace on her leg at eight. At twenty, she brought home 3 gold medals from Rome and was the fastest woman ever. She won the 100 meters in 11 flat, the 200 meters in 22.9 and anchored the 400-yard relay.

Floyd Patterson made a comeback and defeated Ingemar Johansson to regain his heavyweight title.

"All the News That's Fit to Print"

The New York Times.

LATE CITY EDITION
U. S. Weather Bureau Report (Page 46) forecasts: Mostly fair today and tonight. Variable cloudiness tomorrow.
Temp. range: 74—59; yesterday: 69.7—57.7.

VOL. CX. No. 37,499. | NEW YORK, SATURDAY, SEPTEMBER 24, 1960. | 10 cents beyond 50-mile zone from New York City except on Long Island. Higher in air delivery cities. | FIVE CENTS

KHRUSHCHEV ASKS HAMMARSKJOLD OUSTER; WOULD SUBSTITUTE A 3-BLOC DIRECTORATE; HERTER SEES 'DECLARATION OF WAR' ON U. N.

MAYOR DECLARES POLICE HEAD FREE OF RELIGIOUS BIAS

Yields on Call for Apology in Holy Days Case—Lehman Defends Commissioner

By WAYNE PHILLIPS

Mayor Wagner last night backed down on his demand that Police Commissioner Stephen P. Kennedy apologize for questioning the religious sincerity of Jewish policemen who wanted time off for Rosh ha-Shanah.

The two officials had an hour-and-a-half conference at Gracie Mansion, the Mayor's residence, after which aides took six hours to draft a four-paragraph statement spelling out their agreement.

The Commissioner, the statement said, "reiterated his statement that there was no intention to insult the Jewish community or any part of it or any faith."

The Mayor, it continued, has "full confidence" in Mr. Kennedy's administration of the department, and "can affirm that he is without any trace of bigotry or prejudice."

It also said that Stanley Lowell, chairman of the Commission on Intergroup Relations, had discussed the matter with representatives of the New York Board of Rabbis.

Statement Is Amended

The first version of the Mayor's statement, issued at City Hall shortly before 11 P. M., said:

"Mr. Lowell told me that knowing their attitude he is convinced they will accept this statement and consider the matter closed."

A few minutes later, after a call from Mr. Lowell, this was amended to read that he "anticipates" such an acceptance.

Officials of the New York Board of Rabbis, who would be authorized to comment, were unable to do so last night because of their observance of the Sabbath.

Rosh ha-Shanah began at sundown Wednesday and ended at sundown last night, when the Sabbath began.

It was learned that the board would have a statement after sundown today, when the Sabbath ends.

Earlier in the day, former Gov. Herbert H. Lehman came to the Commissioner's defense.

"I have never seen any indication whatsoever that he is anti-Semitic or a bigot of any

Continued on Page 12, Column 6

NIXON IS ACCUSED OVER 'LAND GRAB'

Senator Says He Backs Plan to Give States U. S. Tracts

By PETER BRAESTRUP
Special to The New York Times.

WASHINGTON, Sept. 23—Senator James E. Murray, Montana Democrat, accused Vice President Nixon tonight of agreeing to back "give-away" legislation to transfer Federal public lands to the states.

The Senator, chairman of the Senate Interior and Insular Affairs Committee, cited a report by an Arizona newspaper carrying an announcement by Gov. Paul Fannin that the Vice President had agreed to back a "notorious land grab bill if he [Mr. Nixon] is elected President."

Democrats were prepared to use the issue during the campaign. Senator Barry Goldwater, Republican of Arizona, was reported to have "sounded out" Mr. Nixon on the proposal.

In a statement, Senator Murray said:

"This outrageous proposal was buried so deep by Congress a decade ago, it seemed unthinkable that it would ever come up again. But apparently

Continued on Page 15, Column 1

The New York Times

BLAMES BELGIUM: President Kwame Nkrumah of Ghana demands an all-African U. N. force in the Congo with orders to support Patrice Lumumba as Premier.

Kennedy Charges Nixon Is Selling America Short

By RUSSELL BAKER
Special to The New York Times.

SALT LAKE CITY, Sept. 23—Senator John F. Kennedy struck back hard today against Vice President Nixon's assertion that he was debasing the prestige of the United States. Mr. Nixon, the Senator declared before a crowd of thousands in downtown Denver, is "selling America short" and "peddling complacency" across the country by arguing that the country could not improve on its performance of the last seven years.

Tonight, ending a day of campaigning in Wyoming, Colorado and Utah, Mr. Kennedy spoke in the Mormon Tabernacle. He praised the Mormons for their contributions to the American culture.

Cites Debt to Mormons

"I am particularly in their debt tonight for their successful battle to make religious liberty a living reality," he said, "for having proven to the world that different faiths of different views could flourish harmoniously in our midst, and for having proven to the nation in this century that a public servant devout in his chosen faith was still capable of undiminished allegiance to our Constitution and national interest."

This was a reference to Utah's late Republican Senator, Reed Smoot, a Mormon. Mr. Smoot, Mr. Kennedy said, was challenged in his right to a

Continued on Page 16, Column 2

G. O. P. FARM PLAN ALTERED BY NIXON

Program Built on Benson's Calls for Strong Controls and Support Revision

Excerpts from Nixon speech appear on Page 14.

By WILLIAM M. BLAIR
Special to The New York Times.

SIOUX FALLS, S. D., Sept. 23—Vice President Nixon held out to farmers today the Administration's basic farm policy, with some modifications, as his method of putting the farm economy on an even keel.

However, Mr. Nixon did not mention Secretary of Agriculture Ezra Taft Benson, designer of the Administration's policy. The Vice President has broken with the Secretary, but mainly on political grounds rather than on basic farm policy, as was evident in his speech today.

Mr. Benson is unpopular in the Midwest and Mr. Nixon's careful exposition of his views obviously was aimed at creating for himself a friendlier and warmer climate with his farm audience.

[On Friday the White House announced that Secretary Benson would leave Oct. 20 to tour South America. The trip, to be made at President Eisenhower's request, will take him out of the country during the climactic days of the election campaign.]

Although Mr. Nixon foresaw a stiff control program for surplus crops in the immediate future, he deemed such action a necessary first step toward freeing the farmer from Government controls and eliminating the high cost of current farm programs.

During the "transition" period toward a freedom for farmers to grow what they wish for market, his plan provides for consumption-promoting devices to reduce price-depressing surpluses.

For the first time in the campaign, voters have perhaps more of a clear-cut choice in farm

Continued on Page 14, Column 3

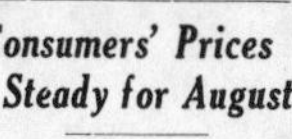

Consumers' Prices Steady for August

By RICHARD E. MOONEY
Special to The New York Times.

WASHINGTON, Sept. 23—The United States Consumer Price Index held steady in August.

It was the first month since January in which the index did not rise. Most of the monthly increases this year have been so small that they could be described as "virtually no change." But by the same token, a single month of absolutely no change did not mean that the slight upward trend had come to an end.

Ewan Clague, Commissioner of Labor Statistics, indicated today that he saw more of the past in the future. That is, he saw no forces that would bring prices down substantially in the next few years, but rather a mixture of forces that might

Continued on Page 36, Column 2

NKRUMAH SPEAKS

Proposes All-African Force in Congo—Backs Lumumba

Excerpts from Nkrumah talk and Belgian reply, Page 2.

By DANA ADAMS SCHMIDT
Special to The New York Times.

UNITED NATIONS, N. Y., Sept. 23—President Kwame Nkrumah of Ghana urged the United Nations today to delegate its functions in the Congo to the independent African states.

He proposed that the United Nations command and troops in the Congo be restricted to Africans and that Patrice Lumumba be supported as the head of the Congo's only legitimate Government.

In the first major speech by an African leader before the fifteenth General Assembly of the United Nations, the Ghanaian President proposed that the Security Council name a committee of independent African states to administer future financial and technical aid to the Congo.

A Problem for Africans

"The Congo," he declared, "is an acute African problem which can be solved by Africans only."

Mr. Nkrumah denounced Col. Joseph D. Mobutu, as a "fake." And he blamed "colonialist intrigue" for the fact that a document of reconciliation **"drafted in the presence of my Ambassador in Leopoldville"** had not been signed by Mr. Lumumba and President Joseph Kasavubu.

Mr. Nkrumah's hour-long speech drew enthusiastic applause especially from the Soviet bloc. Premier Khrushchev, who was the next speaker, caught Mr. Nkrumah's hand and shook it as the African President returned to his seat.

Mr. Nkrumah wore African dress. An orange, gold, green and brown cloth was slung over his left shoulder, somewhat in the manner of a Roman toga. His colleagues wore European clothes.

In great detail the President of Ghana reviewed the origins of the Congo's disorders. He criticized Belgium at every step.

"What has happened in the Congo," he said, "has more than

Continued on Page 2, Column 4

AMERICAN ANGRY

Eisenhower Supports Aide in Defense of U. N. Secretary

Text of the Herter statement is printed on Page 10.

By DAVID ANDERSON

Secretary of State Christian A. Herter described Premier Khrushchev's speech before the General Assembly yesterday as "an all-out attack, a real declaration of war against the structure, the personnel and the location of the United Nations."

President Eisenhower indicated in Washington that he was in full agreement with this opinion.

James C. Hagerty, the White House press secretary, announced that while the President would make no formal statement on the speech, he was fully aware of what Mr. Herter and James J. Wadsworth, United States' delegate, had to say about it.

Crisis Seen for U. N.

Mr. Wadsworth declared on the Assembly floor that the Soviet Union was attempting "to destroy the office and the very structure of the Secretary General and the Secretariat and through it to destroy the United Nations."

"It must face this crisis head on," he said. "If it does not, it will fail."

Mr. Herter was so irritated by the Soviet leader that he reacted at once by word and deed. What he said and did at that time was recalled by him less than an hour later when he spoke before the Foreign Press Association at a luncheon in the Waldorf-Astoria Hotel. He said:

"Immediately after the speech concluded I went behind the rostrum to Secretary General Hammarskjold's office. He and the President of the General Assembly, Mr. [Frederick H.] Boland, were there. The first question that I asked him was whether or not under the procedural rules of the United Nations it was possible to call for an immediate vote of confidence in the Secretary General.

"That is what I would like to have seen done, if it had been

Continued on Page 10, Column 3

Nasser Arrives to Attend U. N.; Will Meet Eisenhower Monday

Associated Press

President Gamal Abdel Nasser, left, at Idlewild airport, where he was met by Foreign Minister Mahmoud Fawzi.

By FOSTER HAILEY

President Gamal Abdel Nasser of the United Arab Republic arrived in New York yesterday to attend the United Nations General Assembly.

He expressed hopes that the Assembly sessions would create a favorable climate to establish peace on a sound basis and said he brought warm greetings to the United States from the people of his country.

In Washington, the White House announced that President Eisenhower would meet President Nasser as well as Prime Minister Jawaharlal Nehru of India Monday afternoon in New York. President Eisenhower will return here that day to address a dinner meeting for Roman Catholic charities. It will be the first meeting of Presidents Eisenhower and Nasser.

President Nasser's four engined Comet jet, chartered from the Government-owned United Arab Airlines, arrived at New

Continued on Page 12, Column 1

The New York Times

BLAMES THE U. N.: Premier Khrushchev demands the United Nations be taken out of the United States and Secretary General Hammarskjold be taken out of U. N.

Delegates Expect No Vote On Proposals by Premier

By LINDESAY PARROTT
Special to The New York Times.

UNITED NATIONS, N. Y., Sept. 23—Western and "uncommitted" nations said today that they doubted that Premier Khrushchev's proposals to change the United Nations would get to a vote in the General Assembly.

Spokesmen were reserved on the Premier's suggestions that the post of Secretary General be replaced by a committee and that the headquarters be moved to Geneva, Vienna or Moscow.

Western states, as was expected, condemned Mr. Khrushchev's statement as a declaration of "war to the death" against the United Nations as it is presently constituted.

Calls It a Blunder

Some Asian and African nations, in assessing the Soviet approach this afternoon, seemed to back off from the suggestions made by Mr. Khrushchev. Representatives of Ceylon, Tunisia and others felt that the attack on the Secretary General would not be supported by most Asian and African nations.

One African spokesman called Mr. Khrushchev's approach a "Soviet blunder." An Asian spokesman said that he and his associates were "stunned" by the bitterness of the Soviet leader's attack and thought that the Russian Premier had "over played his hand."

Mr. Khrushchev, when he ended his address this afternoon, got more than one minute's applause, both from the Assembly floor and from the

Continued on Page 11, Column 5

NEUTRALIST BLOC FORMING AT U. N.

Tito Meets Nkrumah and Indian in Buffer Moves—Wants Nehru to Lead

By JACK RAYMOND
Special to The New York Times.

UNITED NATIONS, N. Y., Sept. 23—A neutralist grouping among the delegates to the United Nations General Assembly began taking shape today.

President Kwame Nkrumah of Ghana met President Tito at the Yugoslav leader's residence. V. K. Krishna Menon, Defense Minister of India, conferred with Koca Popovic, the Yugoslav Foreign Minister, and also saw Marshal Tito.

The Yugoslav Communist leader has appealed for a buffer of uncommitted nations, including especially the new African nations, between the "extremes" of the United States and the Soviet Union.

Tito to Visit Ghana

The first results of the moves came tonight after the Tito-Nkrumah meeting. Marshal Tito accepted an invitation from Mr. Nkrumah to visit Ghana. The date is expected to be worked out later.

Mr. Nkrumah also gave his support to Marshal Tito's efforts to form the neutralist grouping with an emphatic "Yes" as they emerged from the talks at the headquarters of the Yugoslav delegation to the United Nations at 854 Fifth Avenue.

Ako Adjei, the Ghanaian Foreign Minister, described the goal of the efforts as "positive neutrality"—a term made popular by Marshal Tito after his 1948

Continued on Page 11, Column 4

Trujillo Rules Out Visit to U. N. Now

Generalissimo Rafael Leonidas Trujillo Molina of the Dominican Republic "will probably not" attend the United Nations General Assembly, an aide said yesterday.

The aide, Otto Vega, made the comment in a cablegram from Ciudad Trujillo to The New York Times. The Times had sent a cablegram to General Trujillo asking whether he still planned to attend the session.

On Aug. 4, the General's name was submitted to the United Nations as Permanent Representative for the Dominican delegation. This was some time before Premier Khrushchev and other heads of government decided to attend.

Señor Vega said that the most pressing reason for General Trujillo's change of mind

Continued on Page 11, Column 2

PREMIER IS HARSH

Suggests U. N. Leave City and Urges All Colonies Be Freed

Text of Khrushchev's address is on Pages 6, 7, 8 and 9.

By THOMAS J. HAMILTON
Special to The New York Times.

UNITED NATIONS, N. Y., Sept. 23—Premier Khrushchev, in a fighting speech, demanded today that Secretary General Dag Hammarskjold get out of the United Nations and suggested that it might be a good idea for the United Nations to get out of the United States.

His call for Mr. Hammarskjold's ouster was linked to a plan for reorganizing the Secretary General's office by replacing it with a three-man body representing the West, the Communist bloc and the neutral nations.

Mr. Khrushchev's speech in the General Assembly's opening debate ranged over a wide area of problems.

The Soviet Premier upbraided the Western powers for refusing to accept his disarmament proposals, and he submitted a draft treaty under which the General Assembly would put them into effect in three stages over a period of at least four years. In general, his disarmament proposals offered nothing substantially new.

Speaks for 2 Hours

Mr. Khrushchev was on the rostrum for two hours and twenty minutes, and his speech totaled about 19,000 words. In addition, he submitted to the General Assembly, but did not read, two documents on disarmament and a longer "Declaration of Granting Independence to Colonial Countries and Peoples."

Mr. Khrushchev's speech retained none of the friendly tone he had displayed toward President Eisenhower and the United States when he submitted his proposal for global disarmament here a year ago. He remarked, sarcastically, that the President, who did not refer to the U-2 plane in his conciliatory address here yesterday, had, perhaps, "forgotten" about it.

Other points made by Mr. Khrushchev were these:

¶He declared that continuation of flights of United States planes over Soviet territory "can at any moment plunge mankind into a third World War."

¶He repeated his suggestion that another Big Four summit conference be held "within a

Continued on Page 9, Column 1

AIR DEFENSE UNITY ACHIEVED BY NATO

Allies Agree on Set-Up for West European Command

By WILLIAM J. JORDEN
Special to The New York Times.

WASHINGTON, Sept. 23—The North Atlantic allies have quietly taken three important steps to strengthen the command structure and military effectiveness of the North Atlantic Treaty Organization.

Diplomatic sources here disclosed the following today:

¶Members of the Western alliance have agreed to establish a unified air defense command for Western Europe.

¶The Central Army Group in West Germany, composed of United States, German and French troops, has been transferred to the alliance's command and henceforth will be at the disposal of NATO Land Forces, Europe.

¶Arrangements have been completed under which French forces in West Germany will be able to participate in the alliance's system of nuclear weapons on the same basis as other forces in it.

The latter development will permit assignment of weapons

Continued on Page 13, Column 3

NEWS INDEX

News Summary and Index, Page 25

In 1960, ***The Flintstones*** made their debut in the first prime-time cartoon series. This Hanna-Barbara production launched the trend for "adult" cartoon programming.

Andy Griffith played the sheriff on the *Andy Griffith Show*, which also paved the way for the young Ron Howard (his son, Opie), who emerged later as a popular teen-aged star.

"All the News That's Fit to Print"

The New York Times.

LATE CITY EDITION
U. S. Weather Bureau Report (Page 45) forecasts: Mostly fair today and tonight. Partly cloudy and milder tomorrow. Temp. range: 66—50; yesterday: 65—49.4.

VOL. CX..No. 37,513. NEW YORK, SATURDAY, OCTOBER 8, 1960. 10 cents beyond 50-mile zone from New York City except on Long Island. Higher in air delivery cities. FIVE CENTS

KHRUSHCHEV SAYS SUMMIT AFTER U. S. VOTE IS PRICE FOR STATUS QUO IN BERLIN

PREMIER DISPUTED

An Aide of Macmillan Denies Assurance of Big 4 Talk

Excerpts from Khrushchev's speech are on Page 2.

By THOMAS J. HAMILTON
Special to The New York Times.

UNITED NATIONS, N. Y., Oct. 7—Premier Khrushchev threatened today to sign a peace treaty with East Germany unless he was assured that the Western Big Three agreed to meet with him shortly after the United States Presidential election or voiced wish to do so.

Assurance that such a meeting would be arranged was given to him by Prime Minister Macmillan of Britain, the Soviet Premier said. This was interpreted as meaning a Big Four summit meeting would be held soon after the election. A British spokesman denied this.

Mr. Khrushchev emphasized that if arrangements for a summit meeting held good he would keep his promise not to take unilateral action regarding Germany or West Berlin. He added, however, that if there was no agreement on the date and no desire for one, the Soviet Union and other countries would sign a separate treaty with East Germany.

Berlin's Status Threatened

"That will mean the end of the occupation regime in West Berlin also," he declared.

However, this renewal of Soviet threats regarding West Berlin was overshadowed by the question whether Mr. Khrushchev was correct in his statement that Mr. Macmillan had "assured" him that a summit meeting would be held.

John Russell, a spokesman for Mr. Macmillan, said tonight that "no such positive assurance" had been given to Mr. Khrushchev by Mr. Macmillan. Mr. Russell conceded, however, that, as he had previously stated, "the possibility of another summit conference some time in 1961 was indeed implicit" in the talks between Mr. Macmillan and Mr. Khrushchev.

There was no word on whether the British Government had asked President de Gaulle whether he would agree to a summit meeting early next year. It was assumed that Mr. Macmillan, in view of protocol requirements, would not have asked the opinions of the two major candidates for the Presidency, Vice President Nixon and Senator John F. Kennedy.

Messrs. Nixon and Kennedy, in their television debate this evening both said they would not participate in a summit meeting unless the Soviet Union met prior conditions.

Mr. Khrushchev made his statement at a luncheon given for him by the United Nations Correspondents Association.

Mr. Macmillan, who returned to London early this week, told Mr. Khrushchev during their talks here that he hoped a sum-

Continued on Page 2, Column 4

French Ask A-Bomb Veto On Use by West Anywhere

De Gaulle Details His Views on Defense —Again Insists on 'National' Force in Contrast to NATO Integration

By ROBERT C. DOTY
Special to The New York Times.

PARIS, Oct. 7—President de Gaulle stated publicly today for the first time that France intended to seek veto rights over the use anywhere of nuclear weapons by the West.

This position, which has long been the subject of semi-secret and inconclusive exchanges by Paris, Washington and London, was detailed by the French President in a speech at Grenoble.

"So far as her defense is concerned, France believes that defense has a national character," he said. "With respect to nuclear armament, she intends to have her own instrument."

"France intends that if, by misfortune, atomic bombs were to be dropped in the world," he went on, "none should be dropped by the free world's side unless she should have accepted it, and that, from her soil, no atomic bomb should be launched unless she herself should have decided it."

In these few remarks President de Gaulle stated the core of his position on the North Atlantic Treaty Organization that has embroiled him with West Germany, his principal Continental ally, with the United States and Britain, and with a considerable part of French political opinion.

In the pursuit of his goal of a "national" defense, President

Continued on Page 3, Column 7

TV JURY CHARGES 20 WITH PERJURY IN QUIZ INQUIRY

Group Questioned Included Van Doren, Mrs. Nearing and Bloomgarden

By JACK ROTH

A New York County grand jury has returned second-degree perjury charges against twenty to twenty-five contestants on two television quiz shows.

The District Attorney's office said yesterday that since none of the accused had been arrested yet, it would be illegal to make their names public.

Among those who are known to have been questioned by the special television grand jury that returned the charges were Charles Van Doren, the former Columbia University instructor; Vivienne Nearing, who defeated Mr. Van Doren on the show "Twenty-one," Hank Bloomgarden and Elfrida Von Nardroff.

All those against whom the grand jury acted, it was learned yesterday, had appeared on either "Twenty-One" or "Tic Tac Dough" and all were money winners.

Questioned on Coaching

It was reported that the defendants were accused of lying before a grand jury when they testified under oath that they had never received assistance from anyone connected with the programs prior to their appearances.

The special panel that has been hearing evidence, the fourth July, 1960 hold-over grand jury, handed up a number of documents to General Sessions Judge Charles Marks, who had empaneled the jurors.

He directed the panel to continue its deliberations into other television matters and subsequently, it was learned, he signed an order directing that the District Attorney's office follow the mandate of the grand jury and file informations against the defendants.

All were accused, in one-count informations, of perjury in the second degree. This is a misdemeanor, punishable on conviction by a year in jail and a $500 fine.

Jury 'Sanctity' at Stake

First-degree perjury is defined as perjury committed in connection with a material fact and is punishable by five years in prison. Second-degree perjury is described as perjury that does not fall into the category of first-degree perjury.

A number of judges expressed the belief that one "strong reason" the grand jury had acted in the matter was because "it was felt that the sanctity of the grand jury system must be upheld."

The life of the television panel is supposed to expire on Oct. 28, but one report said that the life of the panel would be extended.

Assistant District Attorney Joseph Stone has been conduct-

Continued on Page 46, Column 3

HERTER CONSULTS WARSAW LEADER

Secretary and Gomulka Are Said to Have Discussed Possible U.S. Aid Rise

By JACK RAYMOND
Special to The New York Times.

UNITED NATIONS, Oct. 7—Secretary of State Christian A. Herter and Wladyslaw Gomulka, the First Secretary of the Communist party of Poland, conferred for half an hour today.

It was understood that they had discussed possible increases in United States economic aid to Poland. The United States has provided $650,000,000 in economic assistance to Poland in the last four years, including $426,300,000 worth of surplus agricultural products for which payment was accepted in Polish currency.

Last year, almost directly as a consequence of United States dissatisfaction with Polish support of Soviet policies, the United States agreed to provide only half of a $100,000,000 request for non-agricultural economic assistance.

M. Gomulka is the only Communist chief of the Soviet bloc with whom the United States has had a high-level contact since the United Nations General

Continued on Page 2, Column 8

2 IN CREW VANISH AFTER RAIL CRASH

Wreck of Central Freights Delays Thousands Here —Conductor Killed

By IRA HENRY FREEMAN

The Hudson Division of the New York Central was blocked for nine hours yesterday after a moving freight train rammed a halted one in the Bronx.

Immediately after the crash, the engineer and fireman of the oncoming train disappeared, and the railroad was still trying to locate them last night with the aid of the police. A railroad official said the engineer had run through a stop signal.

The wreck occurred about an hour on the bank of the Harlem River, a quarter of a mile below the Marble Hill Station.

The moving freight, an outbound one, plowed into the rear of the one stopped on the tracks. The conductor of the stalled train was killed and a brakeman was injured.

Cars blocking the tracks forced inbound trains on the division to stop at Marble Hill, and more than 11,000 commuters from the lower Hudson River valley were delayed in reaching the city during the morning rush hours.

The stalled commuters had to

Continued on Page 48, Column 3

Bronx Wreck Blocks Central, Delays Commuters

Freight cars criss-cross tracks below Marble Hill Station (at right of bridge in rear)

The New York Times (by Arthur Brower)

At the station, service is terminated and commuters are transferred to the IRT subway

Adenauer Clashing With Erhard Again

By SYDNEY GRUSON
Special to The New York Times.

BONN, Germany, Oct. 7—Chancellor Adenauer and Dr. Ludwig Erhard, the Vice Chancellor and Minister of the Economy, are engaged in another blazing political dispute.

It is a many-sided clash involving specific economic issues and also the Chancellor's well-known antipathy to the Minister as his successor.

The specific issues are the trade sanctions against Communist East Germany ordered by Dr. Adenauer last week and the effort by the Chancellor and representatives of big industry to bypass Dr. Erhard in deciding upon measures to meet the dangers of inflation here.

When the latest Communist squeeze on Berlin began, Dr. Adenauer was on holiday and Dr. Erhard headed the Govern-

Continued on Page 8, Column 2

NIXON AND KENNEDY CLASH ON TV OVER ISSUE OF QUEMOY'S DEFENSE; U-2 'REGRETS' AND RIGHTS ARGUED

The New York Times (by John Orris)

REPUBLICAN: Vice President Nixon as he appeared last night on TV screen.

DEMOCRAT: Senator John F. Kennedy taking part in telecast from Washington.

EXCHANGES SHARP

Senator Is Accused of 'Woolly Thinking'— He, Too, Is Tough

Nixon-Kennedy transcript is on Pages 10 and 11

By RUSSELL BAKER
Special to The New York Times.

WASHINGTON, Oct. 7—Vice President Nixon and Senator John F. Kennedy raised the campaign temperature tonight, clashing sharply on foreign policy and civil rights in the second of their nation-wide television debates.

The question of who won will have to await the surveys of voters, but the equally nagging question for Republicans—of how Mr. Nixon would "project" after his unhappy appearance in the first debate—was answered immediately. The Vice President did not have the thin, emaciated appearance that worried Republicans across the nation during the first debate.

One of the high points of tonight's debate was a direct conflict between the Presidential candidates over policy for dealing with the islands of Quemoy and Matsu off the Chinese mainland.

Criticizes Vagueness

Mr. Kennedy took the position that the islands were militarily worthless and, lying virtually in a harbor on the Communist mainland, were indefensible.

Moreover, he said, Administration vagueness about whether the islands would be defended in case of Communist attack created a dangerous uncertainty for the Chinese about this country's intentions. While Taiwan (Formosa) should certainly be defended, he indicated, he favored a pull-back from Quemoy and Matsu by the Chinese Nationalists.

Mr. Nixon denounced this as "the same kind of woolly thinking that led to disaster in Korea." He insisted that the islands should be held. "These two islands are in the area of freedom," he said. To give them up, he argued, would only encourage the Communists to press their drive on Taiwan.

The question was not of "two tiny pieces of real estate," he said, but a matter of principle.

Johnson Is Nixon Target

In a long running exchange over civil rights, Mr. Nixon denounced the Democratic Vice-Presidential candidate, Senator Lyndon B. Johnson of Texas, as a man who had voted against most of the civil rights proposals in the Democratic platform and "who opposes them at the present time."

Although Mr. Johnson contends that, as Democratic Senate leader, he is responsible for the only two civil rights bills to be enacted since the Reconstruction period after the Civil War, Mr. Kennedy did not expand on this issue.

Instead, Mr. Kennedy charged

Continued on Page 12, Column 1

SCHENECTADY ASKS AID IN G. E. STRIKE

Emergency Is Proclaimed —Company Calls on Court to Bar Mass Picketing

Special to The New York Times.

SCHENECTADY, N. Y., Oct. 7—City officials here declared a state of emergency today after thousands of striking workers sealed off the General Electric Company main plant.

Mayor Malcolm Ellis and City Manager Arthur Blessing said the 152-man police force could not deal with a situation where "serious violence might occur at any time." Eleven persons were arrested, but no one was injured, in picket-line rushes.

Late this afternoon General Electric moved for a court order prohibiting mass picketing. The union will be required on Monday to show cause why such an injunction, limiting picketing, should not be issued.

Production Halted

The company also filed with the National Labor Relations Board a complaint charging that the union had engaged in unfair labor practices. A similar charge was filed today in connection with picket-line outbreaks at a G. E. plant in Syracuse.

For the second day plant production was at a standstill. Only a dozen persons were able to smash their way through dense picket lines manned by members of Local 301 of the International Union of Electrical Workers.

The emergency declaration came on the sixth day of the union's nation-wide strike against fifty-five General Electric plants. The company is attempting to keep its installations open despite the walkout, but union pickets have pre-

Continued on Page 13, Column 4

Kennedy Protests Lighting And Cold and Wins on Both

By W. H. LAWRENCE
Special to The New York Times.

WASHINGTON, Oct. 7—Short-lived disagreements over blinding lights and a frigid studio developed tonight just before Vice President Nixon and Senator John F. Kennedy made their second joint nation-wide television appearance.

Democrats were the complainants in both instances, contending that steps taken to improve Mr. Nixon's television appearance were unfair to Senator Kennedy.

The studio had been chilled to 64 degrees to relieve Mr. Nixon's heavy perspiration problem that contributed to his generally unsatisfactory physical appearance on television last week.

Senator Kennedy tested the flood lighting from both his own lectern and Mr. Nixon's before the show began. He complained that four bright lights shone directly into his eyes from his own position but only one bright light hit him directly when he stood in Mr. Nixon's spot.

Adjustments Made

After the complaints, network officials adjusted the lighting to Senator Kennedy's satisfaction, and an engineer turned up the thermostat to a 70-degree temperature in the studio.

At the end of an hour-long show, the consensus among studio observers was that Mr. Nixon's make-up artist and lighting experts had done a better job for him than last time and that the physical image projected by the cameras was a vast improvement over the debate from Chicago on Sept. 26

The Vice President wore what was described as "a mild amount of make-up."

Senator Kennedy, as before, declined all make-up assistance and appeared before the nation without applying powder.

While partisans for both sides

Continued on Page 12, Column 3

JOBLESS LIKELY TO SHOW DECLINE

September Figure Expected to Disclose Drop Was Greater Than Usual

By RICHARD E. MOONEY
Special to The New York Times.

WASHINGTON, Oct. 7—The official monthly estimate of unemployment is expected to show that the number of jobless declined more than usual in September.

The Labor Department will not release the estimates until Monday morning. But a source who has been right before suggested that Monday's report would show 3,400,000 unemployed in September, against 3,800,000 in August.

There is a political facet to the report on unemployment, of course, in the election campaign and the effect, real or imagined, that a good or bad report might have.

The political factor crops up every second year, as the general elections approach. Neither Vice President Nixon nor Senator John F. Kennedy mentioned the report due Monday in their television debate tonight.

Pre-vote Report Due

If past form is followed, there will be one more report on the job situation before the vote. The report is regularly issued on about the tenth day of each month, except in election years, when Democratic and Republican Administrations alike have found that they were able to complete the statistical work a little earlier in November.

Unemployment almost always declines in July, August, September and October, even in recession years. It has dropped in eleven of the thirteen post-war Septembers, mostly by 150,000 to 250,000. If the drop this time were greater than this, the seasonally adjusted percentage rate of unemployment would also be reduced. Assuming a 400,000 drop in unemployment this time, it is estimated that the rate would drop to 5.4 per cent, from 5.9 per cent in August. There

Continued on Page 13, Column 7

British Believe Ghana Intends To Nationalize Foreign Assets

Special to The New York Times.

LONDON, Oct. 7—A report that the Government of Ghana planned to nationalize all foreign business enterprises caused considerable anxiety here today.

A dispatch from The News Chronicle's correspondent in Accra said that the nationalization would begin May 1 and be completed in three years. It said that representatives of the concerns, including seventy owned by British interests, had been told this by a Ghana official at a private meeting.

The Commonwealth Relations Office said it had received no communication from the Ghana Government, but was asking Sir Arthur Snelling, the British High Commissioner in Accra, about it.

A spokesman for the United Africa Company said, after the regular weekly meeting of the concern's board of directors, that the company was aware that proposals were being discussed in Ghana for the establishment of a national cooperative organization that would take over all imports and distributive trades.

"According to the company's information, these proposals have been drawn up in certain Government circles, but have not yet been before the Cabinet," the spokesman said.

"It appears that the proposals affect equally all private enterprise, Ghanaian and expatriate, large and small."

The United Africa Company, a subsidiary of Unilever, is an importing business that deals in a wide range of goods. Until last year, it purchased about 16 per cent of Ghana's total annual cocoa crop. Cadbury's,

Continued on Page 4, Column 5

NEWS INDEX

Labor Sues to Halt Erie Line's Merger

By The Associated Press.

WASHINGTON, Oct. 7—Railway labor sought today to block the merger of the Erie and Lackawanna Railroads until the Interstate Commerce Commission guaranteed the jobs of union members.

A petition filed in the United States District Court in Detroit contended that the I. C. C. violated the Interstate Commerce Act when it approved on Sept. 13 the merger of the lines into the nation's twelfth largest railroad.

The unions asked the court to issue an order preventing the merger from going into effect as scheduled Oct. 17 until the question of labor protective conditions could be worked out.

Judge Thomas P. Thornton set a hearing on the request for next Wednesday and asked that

Continued on Page 23, Column 2

"All the News That's Fit to Print"

The New York Times.

LATE CITY EDITION
U. S. Weather Bureau Report (Page 93) forecasts: Cloudy, periods of rain today. Partly cloudy, colder tomorrow.
Temp. range: 55—41; yesterday: 53.8—40.4.

VOL. CX..No. 37,546. NEW YORK, THURSDAY, NOVEMBER 10, 1960. 10 cents beyond 50-mile zone from New York City except on Long Island. Higher in air delivery cities. FIVE CENTS

KENNEDY'S VICTORY WON BY CLOSE MARGIN; HE PROMISES FIGHT FOR WORLD FREEDOM; EISENHOWER OFFERS 'ORDERLY TRANSITION'

DEMOCRATS HERE SPLIT IN VICTORY; LEHMAN ASSAILED

De Sapio Accepts Challenge for Party Control—Mayor Claims Leadership

Text of De Sapio statement appears on Page 43.

By LEO EGAN

Less than twenty-four hours after the polls closed, the political coalition that gave Senator John F. Kennedy New York's forty-five electoral votes began coming apart at the seams.

Its disintegration was signaled by Carmine G. De Sapio in a statement assailing former Gov. Herbert H. Lehman, key figure in the Democratic reform group, and Alex Rose, Liberal party master of strategy.

The statement accepted Mr. Lehman's election night challenge to a finish fight for control of the party organization in the city and state.

At the same time it appeared to rule out any chance of a Democratic-Liberal party coalition for next year's Mayoral election in New York City and for the Governorship election in the state in 1962 if Mr. De Sapio remains in control of the party machinery.

Kennedy's Delicate Problem

Mr. De Sapio, leader of Tammany and Democratic National Committeeman for New York, consulted Michael H. Prendergast, the Democratic State Chairman, and a number of party leaders in the city and upstate before issuing his statement.

The collapse of the coalition so soon after it achieved its goal gave President-elect Kennedy a delicate political problem before he takes office. At some stage soon he will have to decide whom in New York to consult about appointments for the new Administration.

Thus, in so far as New York is concerned, the election appeared to raise as many questions as it settled. Control of the Democratic party machinery is one of them. Among the others are: What is Mayor Wagner's political future? And what is Governor Rockefeller's?

When told of Mr. De Sapio's statement last night, Mayor Wagner commented that he in-

Continued on Page 43, Column 1

Registration Set-Up Called Faulty Here

By DOUGLAS DALES

Political leaders voiced dissatisfaction yesterday over the way permanent personal registration functioned here Tuesday in its first test in a Presidential election.

Charges were made that thousands of persons had been disfranchised because they were unable to convince election inspectors that they had registered and were eligible to vote.

How many voters may have been so affected was concededly a guess. But a check of the Supreme Courts in the five boroughs indicated that more than 1,300 persons had gone before the justices for orders directing the inspectors to permit them to vote.

"There was a minimum of 10,000 denied the right to vote," Abraham Gellinoff,

Continued on Page 43, Column 5

ASSEMBLY DELAYS U.N. CONGO DEBATE

Postpones It Indefinitely, 48-30, as Soviet Backs Step—U. S. Move Fails

By KATHLEEN TELTSCH
Special to The New York Times.

UNITED NATIONS, N. Y., Nov. 9—The General Assembly voted tonight to postpone the debate on the Congo indefinitely.

The 48-to-30 vote, with eighteen abstentions, was on a surprise move made by Ghana with the help of Guinea and Nigeria and the enthusiastic support of the Soviet bloc.

The United States tried to avoid the adjournment vote by asking for a suspension of the session until delegates could ponder the unexpected request.

Western sources said privately that Ghana's initiative appeared to have been prompted in part by the presence here of President Joseph Kasavubu of the Congo and the likelihood that the Assembly's Credentials Committee would agree to his request for the seating of a Congolese delegation of his supporters.

A Two-Hour Wrangle

Ghana, Guinea, India and five other states have joined in sponsoring a resolution that aims instead at having the Assembly seat a delegation designated by the deposed Congolese Premier, Patrice Lumumba.

The Assembly acted after a two-hour wrangle marked by two table-thumping demonstrations by the Soviet bloc and also by Ghana, both in protest against the efforts of Foreign Minister Pierre Wigny of Belgium to defend his country's position on the Congo issue.

The adjournment request was made by Alex Quaison-Sackey, Ghana's chief delegate. He appealed to the Assembly to hold off any further debate pending the efforts of a fifteen-member Asian-African commission to reconcile the clashing political factions in the Congo and restore some governmental stability.

He said that the commission probably would leave for the Congo in a week and that further acrimonious debate in the Assembly would only hamper the conciliation effort.

However, the adjournment as voted did not stipulate how long the debate should be suspended. United States sources said tonight that they understood this to mean that discussion could

Continued on Page 3, Column 1

ATOM BILL BEATEN IN FRENCH SENATE

Debre to Push Compromise on Nuclear Force Plan

By W. GRANGER BLAIR
Special to The New York Times.

PARIS, Thursday, Nov. 10—The Senate early today rejected President de Gaulle's project for an independent French nuclear striking force.

By a vote of 186 to 83, with seventeen abstentions, this conservative Upper House approved a procedural motion to table the national nuclear deterrent bill that had been passed to it by the National Assembly Oct. 27.

Although the Senate's action was a stinging blow to President de Gaulle and a sharp indication of mounting parliamentary opposition, it did not mean that the Government's measure would not eventually become law.

It was announced after the vote that Premier Michel Debré would call for the creation of a mixed committee of Senators and Deputies to work out a compromise measure. Should this conference committee fail to find a compromise, the Government would resubmit its measure to the Assembly for a second reading, and virtually certain approval. The measure would then become law with or without Senate's approval.

The Senate motion to table

Continued on Page 8, Column 1

NEWS INDEX

WINNER'S PLEDGE

Family Is With Him as He Vows to Press Nation's Cause

Text of Kennedy's statement is printed on Page 36.

By HOMER BIGART
Special to The New York Times.

HYANNIS, Mass., Nov. 9—Senator John F. Kennedy accepted in solemn mood today his election as President.

He pledged all his energy to advancing "the long-range interests of the United States and the cause of freedom around the world."

He made this pledge inside the flag-decked Hyannis Armory at 1:45 P. M., an hour after Vice President Nixon, his Republican opponent, had conceded defeat.

His wife, Jacqueline, stood at his side as the 43-year-old President-elect faced 300 newsmen and massed batteries of TV cameras and gave his victory statement to the nation.

Behind him were arrayed the Kennedy family: his father, former Ambassador Joseph P. Kennedy; his mother, three sisters and three brothers.

No Sign of Jubilation

The Kennedys showed no evidence of jubilation. All wore expressions of solemnity. Mr. Kennedy's margin of victory was too slender to stir much elation. Some of his aides acknowledged disappointment over the startlingly narrow gap in the popular vote.

Mr. Kennedy, after responding to applause with a diffident bow and a smile, first read the telegram from Mr. Nixon conceding defeat and extending congratulations. The Senator had stayed up until 3:50 A. M. awaiting this concession and had gone to bed disappointed when the Vice President withheld it.

Replies to Nixon

Mr. Nixon wired the President-elect that all the nation would give him "united support" in the next four years.

Mr. Kennedy replied to Mr. Nixon:

"I know that the nation can continue to count on your unswerving loyalty in whatever effort you undertake, and that you and I can maintain our long-standing cordial relations in the years ahead."

Mr. Kennedy then read a congratulatory message from President Eisenhower.

In his message the President informed Mr. Kennedy that he would shortly receive suggestions from the President as to the change-over of responsibilities for national leadership.

To this Senator Kennedy had replied:

"I am grateful for your wire and good wishes. I look forward to working with you in the near future. The whole country is hopeful that your long ex-

Continued on Page 36, Column 7

United Press International Telephoto

THE MESSAGES WERE CONGRATULATORY: Senator John F. Kennedy displaying telegrams at Hyannis, Mass. With him are Mrs. Kennedy, his parents and Robert F. Kennedy, left, and R. Sargent Shriver, a brother-in-law.

KHRUSHCHEV NOTE SALUTES KENNEDY

Message of Congratulations Asks for Negotiations on Tensions in World

Text of Khrushchev message will be found on Page 42.

By The Associated Press.

MOSCOW, Nov. 9—Soviet Premier Khrushchev congratulated Senator John F. Kennedy today for his Presidential victory.

He expressed hope that Soviet-United States relations would "again follow the line along which they were developing in Franklin Roosevelt's time."

He urged negotiations aimed at easing the international situation.

[In Bonn, Chancellor Konrad Adenauer said he planned to go to Washington early next year for conferences with Mr. Kennedy.]

Mr. Khrushchev's statements in a congratulatory message to Mr. Kennedy coincided with Moscow's insistence that the policies of President Eisenhower had suffered a rebuff in the election.

The Soviet press contended that the election proved "the American people have blackballed the policy of the 'cold war' and the arms race, that they want changes and expect Washington to pursue a reasonable course in international affairs, a course dictated by life and the balance of forces now prevailing in the world." Mr.

Continued on Page 42, Column 4

Electoral Vote by States

	Rep.	Dem.		Rep.	Dem.		Rep.	Dem.
Alabama	..	5*	Louisiana	..	10	Ohio	25	..
Alaska	..	..	Maine	5	..	Oklahoma	8	..
Arizona	4	..	Maryland	..	9	Oregon	6	..
Arkansas	..	8	Mass.	..	16	Penna.	..	32
California	..	..	Michigan	..	20	Rhode Island	..	4
Colorado	6	..	Minnesota	..	11	So. Carolina	..	8
Conn.	..	8	Mississippi	**	**	So. Dakota	4	..
Delaware	..	3	Missouri	..	13	Tennessee	11	..
Florida	10	..	Montana	4	..	Texas	..	24
Georgia	..	12	Nebraska	6	..	Utah	4	..
Hawaii	..	..	Nevada	..	3	Vermont	3	..
Idaho	4	..	New Hamp.	4	..	Virginia	12	..
Illinois	..	27	New Jersey	..	16	Washington	9	..
Indiana	13	..	New Mexico	..	4	W. Virginia	..	8
Iowa	10	..	New York	..	45	Wisconsin	12	..
Kansas	8	..	No. Carolina	..	14	Wyoming	3	..
Kentucky	10	..	North Dakota	4	..	Total	185	300

*Five electors are pledged to Kennedy and six unpledged.
**Eight electors not pledged to vote for party candidates.

LIBERALS SUFFER SETBACK IN HOUSE

G. O. P. Picks Up 22 Seats to Aid Conservative Bloc

By JOHN D. MORRIS

The House of Representatives will have a more conservative tinge in the Eighty-seventh Congress.

Inroads into the present House Democratic majority of 283 to 154 scored by the Republicans in Tuesday's elections promised to strengthen their conservative coalition with Southern Democrats.

The liberal legislative program to be submitted early next year by the new Democratic President, John F. Kennedy, may consequently face handicaps in the new Congress, which convenes Jan. 3.

In the Senate, Republicans cut the Democratic margin by two seats, to 64 to 36. That chamber remains predominantly liberal in membership, although conservatives dominate key committee posts.

Gubernatorial Shifts

The Democrats achieved a net gain of one governorship and now control thirty-four of the fifty state houses. In twenty-seven gubernatorial contests the Democrats won fifteen and the Republicans twelve, with an exchange of party control in thirteen.

In the House races, nearly complete unofficial returns showed that the Democrats had elected 257 House candidates and the Republicans 175, with five contests still in doubt.

The Republicans captured twenty-nine seats held by Democrats and lost seven of their own, for a net gain of at least twenty-two. For a bare numerical majority of 219 they would have had to achieve a net gain of sixty-five.

Among the eleven states of the Old Confederacy the Republicans maintained their hold on seven seats of the Eighty-

Continued on Page 38, Column 4

NIXON WIRE GIVES HIS 'BEST WISHES'

Sends Kennedy a Message —500 in Capital Hail Him

By BILL BECKER
Special to The New York Times.

LOS ANGELES, Nov. 9—Vice President Nixon conceded today the Presidential election of his Democratic opponent, Senator John F. Kennedy.

About twelve hours after the polls had closed, the Vice President sent the following telegram to Senator Kennedy at Hyannis Port, Mass.:

"I want to repeat through this wire the congratulations and best wishes I extended to you on television last night. I know that you will have the united support of all Americans as you lead the nation in the cause of peace and freedom in the next four years."

Read by Aide

The telegram was read to newsmen by Mr. Nixon's press secretary, Herbert G. Klein, at 9:45 A. M., Pacific standard time (12:45 P. M., Eastern standard time).

The Vice President did not make a personal appearance. Mr. Klein said Mr. Nixon was resting with Mrs. Nixon and their two daughters in their suite at the Ambassador Hotel.

It was obvious that the Vice President had considered his remarks late on election night a virtual concession.

[A crowd of several hundred greeted Mr. Nixon as he arrived Wednesday night at Andrews Air Base, near Washington, after a flight of four and a half hours from Los Angeles.]

Mr. Nixon remained in seclusion most of the morning although Mr. Klein said he was up about 6 A. M. after little more than three hours of sleep. The secretary said Mr. Nixon

Continued on Page 42, Column 5

PRESIDENT SENDS WIRE TO KENNEDY

He Felicitates Senator and Orders Agency Chiefs to Cooperate With Him

By FELIX BELAIR Jr.
Special to The New York Times.

AUGUSTA, Ga., Nov. 9—President Eisenhower congratulated President-elect John F. Kennedy today on his election and then invited him to designate representatives to participate in all Federal policy discussions to assure an "orderly transition" to the new Administration.

The text of the President's telegram was withheld here at the request of Mr. Kennedy. But President Eisenhower is understood to have told the President-elect that he had instructed all heads of Federal departments and agencies to "cooperate fully" with Mr. Kennedy's representatives.

President Eisenhower arrived here for his customary fall holiday in midafternoon after a two-hour flight from Washington.

The President's message of congratulation to Mr. Kennedy was sent from the White House just before he took off for his favorite vacation retreat here at Augusta National Golf Club.

He also sent messages to the defeated Republican candidate, Vice President Nixon, and his running mate, Henry Cabot Lodge, as well as Vice President-elect Lyndon B. Johnson.

In his telegram to Mr. Nixon

Continued on Page 42, Column 7

RESULTS DELAYED

Popular Vote Almost Even—300-185 Is Electoral Tally

By JAMES RESTON

Senator John F. Kennedy of Massachusetts finally won the 1960 Presidential election from Vice President Nixon by the astonishing margin of less than two votes per voting precinct.

Senator Kennedy's electoral vote total stood yesterday at 300, just thirty-one more than the 269 needed for election. The Vice President's total was 185. Fifty-two additional electoral votes, including California's thirty-two, were still in doubt last night.

But the popular vote was a different story. The two candidates ran virtually even. Senator Kennedy's lead last night was little more than 300,000 in a total tabulated vote of about 66,000,000 cast in 165,826 precincts.

That was a plurality for the Senator of less than one-half of 1 per cent of the total vote—the smallest percentage difference between the popular vote of two Presidential candidates since 1880, when James A. Garfield outran Gen. Winfield Scott Hancock by 7,000 votes in a total of almost 9,000,000.

End Divided Government

Nevertheless, yesterday's voting radically altered the political balance of power in America in favor of the Democrats and put them in a commanding position in the Federal and state capitals unknown since the heyday of Franklin D. Roosevelt.

They regained control of the White House for the first time since 1952 and thus ended divided government in Washington. They retained control of the Senate and the House of Representatives, although with slightly reduced margins. And they increased their hold on the state governorships by one, bringing the Democratic margin to 34—16.

The President-elect is the first Roman Catholic ever to win the nation's highest office. The only other member of his church nominated for President was Alfred E. Smith, who was defeated by Herbert Hoover in 1928.

Faces Difficult Questions

Despite his personal triumph, President-elect Kennedy is confronted by a number of hard questions:

¶In the face of such a narrow victory how can he get through the Congress the liberal program he proposed during the campaign?

¶Can so close an election produce any impetus for loosening the conservative coalition of Republicans and Southern Democrats which has blocked most liberal legislation in the House?

¶Will the new President be able successfully to claim a mandate for legislation such as the $1.25 minimum wage, Fed-

Continued on Page 35, Column 1

10 Irish Soldiers Slain in Congo When U.N. Patrol Is Ambushed

By PAUL HOFMANN
Special to The New York Times.

LEOPOLDVILLE, the Congo, Nov. 9 — A patrol of eleven Irish soldiers of the United Nations force in the Congo was ambushed in the northern part of Katanga Province yesterday. The bodies of four men were sighted.

[The United Nations Command said that ten soldiers had been slain in the ambush, Reuters reported. The Irish Army announced in Dublin that one private had survived the attack. Reports received by the United Nations in New York said the surviving soldier was "badly wounded," according to United Press International.]

The patrol belonged to the Irish Thirty-third Battalion, which has headquarters in the industrial city of Albertville. The battalion, with a strength of about 550 men, is responsible for maintaining order in a vast area of North Katanga. The region has been the scene of intertribal warfare and clashes between Baluba tribesmen and the gendarmerie controlled by Moise Tshombe, President of Katanga.

United Nations officials here were unable to say who had attacked the Irish patrol. The ambush occurred south of Niemba, a village between Albertville and Kabalo. The zone is described as "Baluba country," but it is not known whether Baluba tribesmen were responsible for the assault.

Announcing the loss, a United Nations spokesman said it brought the toll of dead in the international force in the Congo to about thirty since the world organization's troops arrived

Continued on Page 2, Column 3

Vatican Calls Kennedy Election Proof of American Democracy

By ARNALDO CORTESI
Special to The New York Times.

ROME, Nov. 9—The election of Senator John F. Kennedy, a Roman Catholic, to the Presidency was received with keen satisfaction in the Vatican today.

During the campaign the Vatican remained neutral. Its newspaper, L'Osservatore Romano, abstained from all comment lest it be accused of siding with one candidate against the other.

Today the editor of the newspaper, former Italian Deputy Raimondo Manzini, said:

"Kennedy's victory strengthens the appreciation for the high democratic principles of freedom that guide American public life and assure access to the highest office to every citizen regardless of social class, race, or religion.

"The effective support given by large numbers of Protestant citizens to a Catholic considered suitable for the Presidency has been significant in this respect. Catholics are, of course, satisfied at the solemn confirmation of the principle that the office of President is open to a son of the Catholic Church, which enjoys such large prestige in the United States. Catholics have, however, always admired Nixon's irreproachable attitude of deferential respect for the Catholic hierarchy."

Senator Kennedy's victory was announced under large headlines by the whole morning press in Italy today. In most newspapers it took precedence over the results of the provincial and municipal elections that were held in Italy over the week-end.

Government circles received the news without astonishment

Continued on Page 38, Column 7

1961

Jackie Kennedy set the style for the American woman of the sixties.

"All the News That's Fit to Print"

The New York Times.

LATE CITY EDITION
U. S. Weather Bureau Report (Page 66) forecasts: Mostly fair, seasonably cold today and tonight. Fair, warmer tomorrow.
Temp. range 38—25; yesterday: 35—31.

VOL. CX..No. 37,601. | © 1961 by The New York Times Company. Times Square, New York 36, N. Y. | NEW YORK, WEDNESDAY, JANUARY 4, 1961. | 10 cents beyond 50-mile zone from New York City except on Long Island. Higher in air delivery cities. | FIVE CENTS

U.S. BREAKS ITS DIPLOMATIC TIES WITH CUBA AND ADVISES AMERICANS TO LEAVE ISLAND; EISENHOWER CITES 'VILIFICATION' BY CASTRO

REGIME IS SCORED

People Suffer Under 'Yoke of Dictator,' President Says

Texts of President's statement and notes are on Page 3.

By E. W. KENWORTHY
Special to The New York Times.

WASHINGTON, Jan. 3—The United States formally terminated diplomatic and consular relations with Cuba tonight.

President Eisenhower announced the break with the Government of Premier Fidel Castro in a statement issued at the White House at 8:30 o'clock.

The break came a day and a half after the Cuban Government had delivered a note to the United States Embassy in Havana demanding that the staff of the embassy and the consulate there be reduced to eleven persons within forty-eight hours.

The President said in his statement:

"There is a limit to what the United States in self-respect can endure. That limit has now been reached."

Normal Situation 'Impossible'

The action of the Castro Government, the President said, "can have no other purpose than to render impossible the conduct of normal diplomatic relations with that Government."

Therefore, the President said, he had instructed the Secretary of State to deliver a note to the Cuban Embassy here announcing the formal ending of relations.

The President added that "this calculated action on the part of the Castro Government is only the latest of a long series of harassments, baseless accusations and vilification."

President Eisenhower said in his statement that the friendship of the United States for the Cuban people "is not affected" by the breaking of diplomatic relations with the Castro regime.

Sympathy Expressed

"It is my hope and my conviction," the President said, "that in the not too distant future it will be possible for the historic friendship between us once again to find its reflection in normal relations of every sort."

"Meanwhile," the President said, "our sympathy goes out to the people of Cuba now suffering under the yoke of a dictator."

The United States requested the Government of Cuba, in turn, to withdraw "as soon as possible" the entire Cuban personnel in the Cuban Embassy in Washington and in all Cuban consular offices in the United States.

In a note to the Cuban Government, Secretary of State Christian A. Herter stated that it was requesting the Government of Switzerland to assume

Continued on Page 3, Column 1

Associated Press Radiophoto

NO ENTRY: Portion of the crowd in front of the U. S. Embassy in Havana as Cubans sought visas yesterday. When they discovered that the visa section of the embassy had been closed, there were cries of protest and dismay.

U. S. Will Help Evacuate Its Citizens Living in Cuba

Special to The New York Times.

HAVANA, Wednesday, Jan. 4—The United States Embassy last night urged all Americans in Cuba to leave the island. A statement issued by the press attaché said that "all American citizens are urged to depart from Cuba immediately unless compelling reasons oblige them to remain."

The embassy has arranged for a ferry of the West Indies Fruit and Steamship Company to sail from Havana to West Palm Beach today and Friday to evacuate the Americans.

Additional extra flights to Miami from the José Marti International Airport will augment the facilities for departure today and tomorrow.

Cuba Guarantees Safety

The Castro regime, in a note delivered this morning to the United States Chargé d' Affaires, Daniel M. Braddock, pledged the "most absolute guarantees" for the safety of all American citizens in Cuba, including diplomatic or consular officials "as well as residents or tourists."

Meanwhile, thousands of Cubans who for months have been seeking visas to the United States were dismayed yesterday by the Cuban-United States crisis.

A long line of Cubans appeared as usual at the United States Embassy early in the morning after Premier Fidel Castro had ordered a cut in the embassy staff. They found the

Continued on Page 3, Column 6

CASTRO'S CABINET DRAFTING A REPLY

Emergency Session Called After U. S. Acts—Premier Says 'Cuba Is Alert'

By R. HART PHILLIPS
Special to The New York Times.

HAVANA, Jan. 3—Premier Fidel Castro, President Osvaldo Dorticós Torrado and members of the Cuban Cabinet met in the Presidential Palace tonight at 10:30 to draft a reply to the United States' break in diplomatic relations with Cuba.

The reply will be delivered to the United States Embassy here soon, according to a statement by Dr. Carlos Olivares, Cuba's Foreign Under Secretary.

The Cabinet meeting ended without any announcement.

The Cuban people learned of the United States move tonight when the announcement was made over all radio stations.

The announcer said that "according to cables received President Eisenhower had broken off diplomatic relations with Cuba on the pretext of the order of the Revolutionary Government that he withdraw his 300 spies in the embassy from Cuba."

"Being discovered in his criminal plans of terrorism Eisenhower has responded with the habitual shamelessness of imperialism," the announcer declared.

The announcer said the radio would keep the people informed

Continued on Page 3, Column 5

KENNEDY AVOIDS ROLE IN DECISION

Rusk Turns Down Herter Move to Link Democrats to Break With Cuba

By JAMES RESTON
Special to The New York Times.

WASHINGTON, Jan. 3—The Eisenhower Administration took full responsibility tonight for the diplomatic break with Cuba.

Secretary of State Christian A. Herter yesterday informed Dean Rusk, who will succeed him in less than three weeks, of the President's decision, but he did not seek the advice of the leaders of the incoming Administration on what should be done.

Mr. Herter asked Mr. Rusk whether the incoming Democratic Administration wished to associate itself with the break. Mr. Rusk replied after consultations with President-elect John F. Kennedy that in the absence of complete information on all the relevant factors the new Administration did not feel that it could participate in the decision.

Both parties thus found themselves in an extremely delicate position. The Republicans were well aware of the fact that they were taking a decision that would greatly complicate the problems of the Kennedy Administration in the early days of its responsibility after the inauguration Jan. 20.

At the same time, they did not feel that they could avoid responsibility for reacting quickly to Premier Fidel Castro's demand that the United States diplomatic mission in Cuba should be reduced to eleven persons.

The Democrats were equally

Continued on Page 4, Column 3

CONGRESS OPENS WITH CONFLICTS ON PROCEDURES

Filibuster Curbs Sought in Senate—Colmer's Purge Is Believed Certain

By RUSSELL BAKER
Special to The New York Times.

WASHINGTON, Jan. 3—The Eighty-seventh Congress convened today amid clashes in both houses over rules of procedure.

In the Senate, proponents of tighter curbs on the rules of debate opened a battle to make it easier to cut off filibusters. The skirmishes ended inconclusively with a decision to postpone further action until tomorrow.

In the House of Representatives, Speaker Sam Rayburn was reported to have completed arrangements for removing Representative William M. Colmer, Democrat of Mississippi, from the Rules Committee and replacing him with a member who would reinforce the Texas Democrat's leadership.

Pledges by Leaders

The Senate session was marked by a clash between Vice President Nixon and Richard B. Russell. The Georgia Democrat, leader of the Southern bloc, normally gets deference from the chair. Twice, however, Mr. Nixon used his gavel against him with authority.

In the House's traditional opening procedures, Mr. Rayburn and Charles A. Halleck of Indiana, the Republican minority leader, made pledges to work for responsible government.

Behind the scenes, however, a liberal-conservative fight for control of the Rules Committee continued unabated. Mr. Rayburn was assured of the necessary votes in the Democratic Committee on Committees to help purge Mr. Colmer.

This presumably would create a Rules Committee majority favoring critical parts of President-elect John F. Kennedy's program, Capitol observers described the Rayburn plan as "replacing a 'no' man with a 'yes' man."

Friction in Caucus

Meanwhile, Senate Republicans joined Democrats in a standing ovation for the new and only woman member on the Democratic side, Mrs. Maurine Neuberger of Oregon.

Mr. Nixon's duty on the rostrum was to administer the oath to each Senator elected in November.

A Senate Democratic caucus this morning brought more friction. As expected, Mike Mansfield of Montana was elected to succeed Vice President-elect Lyndon B. Johnson as majority leader, and Hubert H. Humphrey of Minnesota was named assistant leader.

Mr. Mansfield, however, created a surprise when he announced that he wanted the

Continued on Page 24, Column 3

Legislators Choose Mahoney, Carlino

By WARREN WEAVER Jr.
Special to The New York Times.

ALBANY, Jan. 3—Senators and Assemblymen descended on the capital tonight to prepare for the opening of the 1961 legislative session here tomorrow.

The Republican majorities in the Senate and Assembly held separate caucuses to choose their leaders and housekeeping officers for the next two years.

The Democrats chose their own nominees at separate sessions, but since the Republicans control both houses their nominations were equivalent to election.

There were no surprises. Senator Walter J. Mahoney of Buffalo was chosen temporary President of the Senate, the official title of the majority leader, a post he has held for the last seven years. In the Assembly, Joseph F.

Continued on Page 14, Column 1

L.I.R.R. SEEKS AID TO AVERT 'CRISIS'

Says It Will Be Unable to Meet April Payroll—Two Rail Walkouts Cited

By CLARENCE DEAN

The Long Island Rail Road appealed yesterday for financial help to avert what it said was an impending crisis.

A statement by Thomas M. Goodfellow, president of the line, declared that unless the help was forthcoming the railroad would be unable to meet its payroll by the last week in April.

The present indications, Mr. Goodfellow said, are that the carrier's deficit by the end of this year will exceed $4,000,000.

If there is no financial help, Mr. Goodfellow said, three alternatives will arise: "a whopping fare increase," a cut in maintenance "to rock bottom" or "an arbitrary 12 per cent slash in the number of commuter trains." He declined to suggest specifically what kind of financial help the road wanted.

He attributed the railroad's predicament to unforeseen emergencies, chiefly a twenty-six-day strike on the Long Island last summer and a subsequent twelve-day shutdown of Pennsylvania Station as a result of a strike against the Pennsylvania Railroad.

For last October and Novem-

Continued on Page 67, Column 2

U. S. SAYS SOVIET AND RED VIETNAM AID LAOS REBELS

Asserts 180 Air Drops Were Made in Nineteen Days—President Sees Advisers

Text of the State Department statement is on Page 8.

By WILLIAM J. JORDEN
Special to The New York Times.

WASHINGTON, Jan. 3—The United States Government charged today that the Soviet Union and North Vietnam were guilty of "extensive participation" in military operations against the Government of Laos.

To bolster its charge, the State Department released a listing of Communist supply flights over Laos, serial numbers of Soviet planes engaged in the airlift, dates and places of air drops to the anti-Government rebels and other details.

The department said the two Communist powers had carried out more than 180 air sorties into Laos in the nineteen days from Dec. 15 through Jan. 2 to drop supplies and personnel to pro-Communist forces. It said that "substantial numbers" of North Vietnamese had been parachuted into Laos to help the rebels.

Elaboration Is Declined

A department spokesman would not elaborate on the numbers. Nor would he use the term "aggression" to describe the Communists' activities.

The charges against the Communist states were attributed to "hard evidence," however. Today's bill of particulars detailed earlier general charges of Communist intervention in Laos.

The catalogue of Communist involvement should be read, officials said, with the strong statement issued by the United States Government three days ago in mind. On Saturday the State Department warned that the Government would take "the most serious view" of intervention in Laos by the Chinese Communists, North Vietnamese "or others" in support of the anti-Government rebels.

Today's Government statement on Laos was issued soon after a special briefing on the Laos situation for President Eisenhower by his top diplomatic, military and intelligence advisers. It was the third White House conference on Laos in four days.

On Capitol Hill a group of House members also received an up-to-date report on developments in Laos. John M.

Continued on Page 8, Column 5

Belgian Assembly Defeats Socalists; Violence Continues

By HARRY GILROY
Special to The New York Times.

BRUSSELS, Belgium, Jan. 3—The Belgian House of Representatives rejected today a motion to withdraw the proposed new law to raise taxes and tighten up the social security administration, against which 500,000 Socialist workers are striking.

Leo Collard, president of the Socialist party, and Achille van Acker, a former Premier, presented the motion. It was defeated by a vote of 121 to 83 with 1 abstention.

The House gave the Government three votes of confidence before adjourning at 8 P. M. until 2 P. M. tomorrow. The votes followed three critical speeches by Socialists and one by a Communist member on the conduct of public affairs and on the treatment of strikers.

The votes were taken in a calm parliamentary atmosphere that contrasted with an unruly session in which the measure was last discussed Dec. 23, and even more with the street demonstrations that turned up new

Continued on Page 12, Column 3

Associated Press Wirephoto

WELCOME TO WASHINGTON: Lyndon B. Johnson, right, Vice President-elect, receives William A. Blakley, successor as Democratic Senator from Texas. With them at Capitol is Benjamin A. Smith 2d of Massachusetts, President-elect Kennedy's successor.

I.T.T. Voices Hopes On H-Bomb Power

By GENE SMITH

Experiments that might lead to a "low-cost nuclear fusion process" were announced here yesterday by the International Telephone and Telegraph Corporation.

No details were given, but the experiments apparently deal with a concept that many nuclear experts have not considered promising. The company said the experiments had been conducted "for a number of years" but made no claim of success.

The problem of producing a controlled and sustained nuclear fusion, and thus harnessing the reaction of the hydrogen bomb, is the goal of many experiments being conducted both here and abroad.

Temperatures of millions of degrees Centigrade are neces-

Continued on Page 10, Column 6

Hammarskjold Flying to Congo To Try to End Factional Strife

By JAMES FERON
Special to The New York Times.

UNITED NATIONS, N. Y., Jan. 3—Secretary General Dag Hammarskjold left for the Congo today in an attempt to end the civil disorders threatening the work of the United Nations force there.

His departure, which had been delayed a day to study disorders in Kivu Province, remained uncertain until two hours before he left because of the changing situation in Laos.

At New York International Airport, Mr. Hammarskjold said he did not intend to visit Laos on this trip but that he might return to the United Nations earlier than he had planned if the Laotian situation required his presence here.

The Secretary General was warmly applauded by a large crowd in the main lobby of the airline terminal. His plane left for Leopoldville at 5:55 P. M.

He will spend two days in the Congo and will talk with members of the eleven-nation United Nations Conciliation Commission, the Congo Government and United Nations force leaders. Technically, the visit is only a side trip on the way to South Africa, where the Secretary General will spend eight days studying racial segregation.

However, United Nations sources suggested that Mr. Hammarskjold's principal concern now was the "developing civil war" in the Congo. They felt that continuing strife between opposing Congolese factions could put the United Nations force in an untenable

Continued on Page 12, Column 5

Cuban U.N. Charge To Get Stern Reply

By LINDESAY PARROTT
Special to The New York Times.

UNITED NATIONS, N. Y., Jan. 3—The United States will follow up its break in relations with Cuba by sharply rejecting in the Security Council tomorrow Cuban charges of American "aggressive intentions."

Representatives of Western delegations here tonight expressed some surprise at the United States severance of relations. The American delegation, during the day, had been in contact with allied nations over the Cuban charges. It was understood, however, that the question discussed was largely whether opposition should be offered to Cuba's request to put the issue on the agenda.

The Council is to meet at 10:30 A. M. at the request of Foreign Minister Raul Roa of

Continued on Page 4, Column 4

NEWS INDEX

"All the News That's Fit to Print"

The New York Times.

LATE CITY EDITION
U. S. Weather Bureau Report (Page 58) forecasts: Some cloudiness today, tonight and tomorrow. Temp. range: 45—32; yesterday: 44—29.

VOL. CX..No. 37,609. NEW YORK, THURSDAY, JANUARY 12, 1961. 10 cents beyond 50-mile zone from New York City except on Long Island. Higher in air delivery cities. FIVE CENTS

PORT WALKOUTS TO CUT SHIPMENT OF FOOD BY HALF

Ferry Tie-Up and Boycott Slow Produce and Meat Movement to Trickle

STOCK STILL PLENTIFUL

Leaders of the Strike Weigh Spread of Picketing as Peace Talks Bog Down

By A. H. RASKIN

The harbor strike tightened its grip on the city's distribution lifeline yesterday as new peace efforts failed.

Market Commissioner Anthony Masciarelli warned that the refusal of other unions to cross picket lines set up by the 660 strikers on railroad ferryboats and tugboats would cut off half of the city's normal deliveries of fresh fruit, vegetables and meat today.

However, he assured housewives that the food supply remained plentiful, and he expressed confidence that alternate delivery routes would be developed before there was any emergency. Milk, staples and fuel oil were relatively unaffected.

Leaders of the two-day-old walkout considered a spread of their picketing to other East Coast ports to block diversion of export-import cargo tied up by the New York stoppage. Their study of the legality of such a move came as an embargo on the rail movement of foreign trade through this city was made virtually complete. Other rail freight movements were reduced to a trickle.

Injunction Weighed

The eleven railroads affected by the shutdown of their marine operations explored the possibility of obtaining injunctions to break the boycott of rail freight by sympathetic truck drivers, railroad freight handlers, longshoremen and other workers.

Lawyers for the carriers were asked to determine whether the honoring of picket lines at freight yards, where none of the striking harbor employes normally worked, constituted an illegal secondary boycott under the Taft-Hartley and Landrum-Griffin Acts. Union officials defended the picketing as legal.

The 30,000 New Jersey commuters who usually use the nine strikebound ferryboats to get to their jobs in Manhattan again managed to find substitute transportation, but not without

Continued on Page 16, Column 4

PORT UNIT'S TOLLS CRITICIZED BY U.S.

Charges and Officials' Pay Linked at Tobin Trial

By JOSEPH C. INGRAHAM
Special to The New York Times.

WASHINGTON, Jan. 11—The high salaries of top officials of the Port of New York Authority and continuation of tolls on bridges long after they had been paid for were linked by the Government today as an unfair burden on interstate travelers.

The assertion was made at the trial of Austin J. Tobin, executive director of the authority, on a charge of criminal contempt of Congress. Mr. Tobin defied a subpoena of the House Judiciary subcommittee calling for some of the agency's confidential records.

The case is being heard without a jury by Judge Luther W. Youngdahl in Federal court here.

Judge Seeks Clarification

The judge constantly broke into the argument advanced by Assistant United States Attorney William Hitz to seek enlightenment on what he called two crucial questions.

Why, Judge Youngdahl asked, did it take Congress so long to decide to investigate the agency's practice of using surplus bridge tolls to aid less profitable projects?

Mr. Hitz acknowledged that the practice was thirty years old and agreed with the judge's statement that "if it was basically, philosophically and economically wrong in 1931, it was wrong today."

Mr. Hitz stressed that it had taken a long time for the "mingling" of funds to reach sizable

Continued on Page 16, Column 5

Mayor Moves to Revamp Medical Services of City

Heyman Heads 17-Man Group to Study Health and Hospital Set-Up

By MORRIS KAPLAN

Mayor Wagner moved yesterday to reorganize the city's health and hospital services.

He announced the formation of a group to overhaul the administration of medical services. David M. Heyman, philanthropist and retired banker, was named chairman and sixteen other members were selected.

The group was directed to present detailed measures to reorganize the city's medical services, taking future needs into account, and to develop plans to integrate municipal services with those provided by voluntary and private institutions.

"The city now spends some $275,000,000 a year to protect and improve the health of its citizens," the Mayor said. "We employ over 40,000 people in this work and operate many institutions, including twenty-seven health centers and twenty-eight hospitals with a total of 19,024 beds.

"This is a big enterprise and I intend to make sure we are running it as efficiently as possible, while maintaining highest levels of medical care."

The group, the Task Force on Organization of Medical Services, will study previous proposals to eliminate waste and duplication and will suggest changes.

Medical management experts, for instance, have recently dis-

Continued on Page 26, Column 6

Fabian Bachrach

David M. Heyman

Soviet Indicates a Desire To Avoid War Over Laos

By WILLIAM J. JORDEN
Special to The New York Times.

WASHINGTON, Jan. 11—Western diplomats here reported today that the Soviet Union had indicated in discussions with the United States that it did not wish to push the critical situation in Laos to the brink of war.

This interpretation is being placed on remarks made yesterday by the Soviet Ambassador, Mikhail A. Menshikov, in a talk with Secretary of State Christian A. Herter.

As reports of the conversation circulated in the diplomatic community, guarded and carefully qualified relief was noticeable.

[Another move to solve the Laotian crisis was reported in London, where Britain has received a proposal that a new control commission be sent to Laos. The new group would consist of representatives of India, Indonesia and Burma.]

Danger Appears Lessened

Diplomats in Washington believed the danger of a serious flare-up in Laos was less now than it had been a few days earlier. They noted, however, that Moscow apparently had not departed from any of its basic positions on Laos.

To deal with the dangerous situation, the Soviet envoy repeated yesterday Moscow's suggestion that a conference of interested parties be held immediately to settle the Laotian crisis. This would revive the 1954 Geneva meeting that ended the Indochina war. Another

Continued on Page 3, Column 2

WAGNER PRAISES RECORD IN OFFICE

Calls It 'Possibly the Most Outstanding' for City—Bid for 3d Term Seen

By CHARLES G. BENNETT

Mayor Wagner last night described the record of his seven years in office as "possibly the most outstanding one in the history of the city."

His assertion, coupled with a long list of accomplishments in office, was seen as laying the foundation for a race for reelection this year.

The Mayor enumerated his achievements in a 2,000-word address to the Citizens Budget Commission, a civic group. The occasion was the commission's annual dinner at the Waldorf-Astoria Hotel. The tone and style of the Mayor's talk reminded many of those present of a political platform.

The forum the Mayor selected for emphasizing his accomplishments was considered significant. The Citizens Budget Commission is a frequent sharp critic of the city administration's fiscal policies.

Mr. Wagner called his audience "men and women who make a vocation, or an avocation, out of viewing government—sometimes helping government, sometimes passing judgment on government." He said he valued their opinions highly.

"I know this is a political year ahead," the Mayor said.

Continued on Page 27, Column 2

Cuba's Mobilization Limits Cane Harvest

By R. HART PHILLIPS
Special to The New York Times.

HAVANA, Jan. 11—Cuba's sugar harvest is off to a slow start because thousands of workers in the civilian militia have been mobilized to repel a "Yankee invasion."

Grinding has started at only thirty of the 161 mills on the island, according to the National Agrarian Reform Institute.

The shortage of cane cutters is so acute that the Federation of Sugar Workers asked today for "volunteers" to perform a "patriotic duty." The federation opened an office at the Palace of Workers for the registration of the "volunteers."

At some places on the island women were said to have been attempting to cut cane without great success.

For many years the harvest of Cuba's sugar crop, her prin-

Continued on Page 8, Column 3

Navy Plans Underwater Range For Missile Tests Off Bahamas

Project Will Include a Base on Island Britain Leased in Destroyer Exchange

By JACK RAYMOND
Special to The New York Times.

WASHINGTON, Jan. 11—The United States is preparing to build an underwater missile range off the Bahamas as part of an effort to counter the growing Soviet submarine threat.

The new range will include a small land base on Great Exuma, site of one of the bases leased from Britain for ninety-nine years during World War II in exchange for American destroyers.

It will provide testing facilities for various torpedoes, new types of underwater missiles, sonar tracking and communications that can be used against submarines.

The anti-submarine warfare test range, dubbed AUTEC for Atlantic Underwater Test and Evaluation Center, will cost about $100,000,000. A related program of oceanographic surveys is also planned.

The anti-submarine warfare research and development efforts hold high Pentagon priorities, Navy sources said.

The Navy now has officially confirmed its belief that the Soviet Union has some submarines, "which include a growing

The New York Times Jan. 12, 1961

Navy testing area (cross)

number probably capable of launching ballistic missiles."

There have been unofficial published reports of Soviet missile-carrying submarines. Premier Khrushchev said last October that the Soviet Union had "atomic-powered submarines armed with rockets" similar to the United States' Polaris submarines.

At that time, the Navy Department would not comment, although unofficially it indicated its willingness to accept Premier Khrushchev's statement at face value.

Now an official information circular, prepared last month,

Continued on Page 12, Column 8

GEORGIA STUDENTS RIOT ON CAMPUS; TWO NEGROES OUT

University Suspends Them 'for Their Safety'—Police Tear Gas Quells Mob

By CLAUDE SITTON
Special to The New York Times.

ATHENS, Ga., Thursday, Jan. 12 — About 600 students and a few outsiders rioted last night at the University of Georgia. Early today university officials announced that two Negro students, targets of the demonstration, had been suspended.

A university official said the action was taken for their safety and that of the student body until "it is safe and practical for them to return."

The affected students are Charlayne Alberta Hunter, 18 years old, and Hamilton E. Holmes, 19, both of Atlanta. They began classes only yesterday under a Federal court order that brought the first desegregation in the state's public education system.

Riot Rages for an Hour

A howling, cursing mob laid siege late last night to the dormitory in which Miss Hunter was living. The riot raged out of control for nearly an hour before the police broke it up with tear gas and fire hoses.

A number of students were arrested. Other students and a few patrolmen were injured. One of these was a girl in Miss Hunter's dormitory.

The city police declined to say how many students had been jailed.

For some time after the rioters had been driven from the dormitory—Myers Hall—U. S. Highway 441 was a no man's land half a block below the building. Youths hurled bricks at passing cars and rolled logs into the road.

At the height of the rioting members of the Ku Klux Klan appeared on the scene in mufti to distribute copies of their racist publication, The Rebel. They were led by Calvin F. Craig, Grand Dragon of the Georgia Klan.

Troopers Not at Scene

University officials and a city police force of forty men found themselves almost powerless to stem the disorder and numerous calls were placed to the Georgia highway patrol barracks here for help.

The answer to one caller's plea was a polite "Thank you," but no troopers were dispatched to the scene.

Following the university's decision to suspend the two students, Miss Hunter was led from the dormitory in tears at 12:20 A. M. by Dean of Men William Tate and highway patrolmen. She and her luggage were placed in a patrol car and driven away.

Dean of Students Joseph A. Williams said that both Miss Hunter and Mr. Holmes, who was living off the campus, would

Continued on Page 20, Column 1

DILLON FORESEES A BUDGET DEFICIT

Notes 'Possibility' in 1962 During Senate Hearing—Expects No Tax Cut

By RICHARD E. MOONEY
Special to The New York Times.

WASHINGTON, Jan. 11—C. Douglas Dillon, who will be Secretary of the Treasury in the Kennedy Administration, said today that there might be a deficit in the Federal budget next year.

His statement to the Senate Finance Committee came as the White House was announcing that President Eisenhower would propose that next year's budget be balanced.

Mr. Dillon said that balancing the budget was "highly important." In boom times, he said, there should be budget surpluses "higher than in the immediate past" and big enough to offset recession deficits.

Tax Revenues Declining

"Every thing we do depends on having a sound economy, which in turn means a sound fiscal system," he said. But he noted the "possibility" of a deficit in the fiscal year 1962—beginning next July 1—because tax revenues were declining, particularly those on corporate profits.

Asked whether he would recommend a tax cut if that would create a budget deficit, Mr. Dillon noted that there were schools of thought for and against such action. He said he had "no present intention" to recommend it.

He also said he had no intention to recommend that Congress give the President power to adjust tax rates temporarily to combat recession, as was suggested to President-elect John F. Kennedy last week by his anti-recession task force.

Mr. Dillon, aware of Con-

Continued on Page 18, Column 4

U. N. Sends Troops To Bar Katanga War

By PAUL HOFMANN
Special to The New York Times.

LEOPOLDVILLE, the Congo, Jan. 11—The United Nations command moved reinforcements into northern Katanga today to prevent what it termed an acute danger of civil war.

About 600 Moroccan and other troops of the world organization's Congo force (battalion strength) were reported on the march to the area of Manono, which was invaded this week by Congolese National Army detachments supporting Patrice Lumumba, the imprisoned former Premier.

A spokesman for the United Nations declared here that it was "attempting to contain the situation" by preventing clashes between the pro-Lumumba troops and the gendarmerie of Moise Tshombe, President of separatist Katanga Province.

The United Nations headquar-

Continued on Page 4, Column 5

Associated Press Wirephoto

SUSPENDED: Charlayne Alberta Hunter is led from the University of Georgia campus

Rayburn Abandons Purge, Seeks Bigger Rules Panel

By JOHN D. MORRIS
Special to The New York Times.

WASHINGTON, Jan. 11—Speaker Sam Rayburn announced plans today to enlarge the House Rules Committee, instead of purging a Southern Democratic member, to prevent the obstruction of President-elect John F. Kennedy's legislative program.

The Texas Democrat disclosed the change in tactics at a news conference, and predicted that the House would accept his proposal. It calls for the addition of three members—two Democrats and a Republican—to the twelve-man committee. The division under present rules is eight Democrats and four Republicans.

Mr. Rayburn, as chief Democratic leader of the House, said he had decided on an enlargement of the committee as "the painless way" of solving the problem and "the way to embarrass nobody if they didn't want to be embarrassed."

Has Blocked Bills

The committee, which screens major bills before they reach the floor, has been dominated in recent sessions by a coalition of two Southern Democrats and the four Republican members.

The coalition, by bringing about tie votes of 6 to 6, has been able to block, delay or force modification of much legislation favored by liberals.

The Rayburn enlargement plan is designed to give the Democratic leadership control of the vital panel by the addition of two party regulars. This

Continued on Page 18, Column 6

KENNEDY WARNED OF SPACE SETBACK

Task Force Says Soviet Will Probably Orbit Man First—Asks Reorganization

Excerpts from space report to Kennedy are on Page 14.

By W. H. LAWRENCE
Special to The New York Times.

PALM BEACH, Fla., Jan. 11—A task force on space programs warned President-elect John F. Kennedy today that the United States was lagging behind the Soviet Union in ballistic missiles and outer-space exploration.

The group said that the lag in developing powerful booster rockets made it "very unlikely that we shall be first in placing a man into orbit around the earth."

The nine-member group, headed by Dr. Jerome B. Wiesner of the Massachusetts Institute of Technology, said that more money would not suffice to catch up with the Soviet. It called for reorganization of the missile and space programs.

[At the civilian space agency's Langley Research Center near Hampton, Va., officials defended Project Mercury, the United States' effort to place a man in orbit. They conceded, however, that the program would cost more than $400,000,000, or about twice the original estimate.]

Named Aide to Kennedy

Dr. Wiesner, an early expert in radar and the development of weapons systems, was selected by Mr. Kennedy today to be Special Assistant to the President for Science and Technology. He will succeed Dr. George B. Kistiakowsky, also of M. I. T., who has held the post under President Eisenhower.

The President-elect, at the same time, asked other members of the President's Science Advisory Committee to continue to serve in the new Administration.

The task force was critical of the Eisenhower Administration's performance in developing missiles and planning outer-space exploration.

"The nation's ballistic missile program is lagging," the report

Continued on Page 14, Column 1

DE GAULLE SPURS ALGERIA REFORMS

Says Vote Shows Plan Must Be Applied Unreservedly

By W. GRANGER BLAIR
Special to The New York Times.

PARIS, Jan. 11—President de Gaulle declared today that the national referendum favoring provisional autonomy for Algeria had shown that his liberal policy "must be applied without reserve in its spirit as in its letter."

This was General de Gaulle's first public reaction to the referendum since the balloting ended Sunday.

The President's plans for Algeria were endorsed by 72 per cent of those who voted on both sides of the Mediterranean and were rejected by 25 per cent. Spoiled ballots accounted for 3 per cent. The combined abstentions amounted to 25.8 per cent of those eligible to vote.

General de Gaulle's views on the referendum were announced to the press by Louis Terrenoire, the Minister of Information, after a Cabinet meeting devoted mainly to analyzing the vote and approving the initial steps to be taken to give Algeria provisional autonomy in advance of ultimate political self-determination.

The initial steps did not include the establishment of an

Continued on Page 3, Column 5

NEWS INDEX

SENATE SHELVES FILIBUSTER CURB; VOTE IS 50 TO 46

2 Proposals to Limit Debate Are Sent to Committee—Liberals Doubt Change

MANSFIELD WINS IN TEST

Two-Thirds Rule to Govern on Any Bill That Panel Sends Back to Floor

By TOM WICKER
Special to The New York Times.

WASHINGTON, Jan. 11—By only four votes, the Senate decided today to delay a showdown on ending the filibuster, the principal weapon of Southerners against civil rights legislation.

Liberal Senators freely predicted that there would be no further chance in this Congress or the next to eliminate it.

The vote was 50 to 46 in favor of a motion to send to the Rules Committee two proposals that would have made it easier for debate to be ended on civil rights and other controversial legislation.

Parties Closely Divided

The narrow majority was made up of thirty-two Democrats and eighteen Republicans. Voting to keep the matter on the floor for an early showdown on one or both of the two proposals were thirty-one Democrats and fifteen Republicans.

Senator Mike Mansfield of Montana, the Democratic floor leader and a co-sponsor of the motion passed today, gave the Senate a pledge that the Rules Committee would send back to the floor one of the proposals to limit debate during the 1961 session.

Mr. Mansfield is the committee chairman. His group is considered likely to approve a plan put forth by Senator Clinton P. Anderson of New Mexico that would shut off debate upon the affirmative vote of three-fifths of those present and voting.

Liberals Note Rule

Liberal Senators — among them Mr. Mansfield's assistant leader, Senator Hubert H. Humphrey of Minnesota—pointed out that whatever plan the Rules Committee approved would have to be debated under the rule now in force. It provides that debate may be ended only by two-thirds of those present and voting.

That was the factor that made today's vote crucial. The liberals were armed with an advisory opinion by Vice President Nixon, the Senate's presiding officer, that led them to believe they could end debate at the opening of a new Congress by a majority of all Senators.

By the time a rules change proposal comes back from the

Continued on Page 19, Column 4

U. S. URGED TO ACT TO RAISE PRESTIGE

Report to President Calls for Bigger Effort Overseas

By FELIX BELAIR Jr.
Special to The New York Times.

WASHINGTON, Jan. 11—Substantial and progressive expansion of United States information activities abroad to bolster the nation's prestige was urged in a report by a Presidential study group made public today.

A heavily abridged version of the full report to President Eisenhower found that present programs and expenditures were inadequate for coping with the world-wide Communist propaganda apparatus. It avoided any estimate of the cost of the expanded effort, but said:

"The scale of the total United States information effort will have to be progressively expanded for some time to come. There is urgent need for substantial increases in the critical areas of Africa and Latin America."

The report as released made no direct evaluation of the level of American prestige abroad although even the abridged version embracing only 40 per cent of the full document offered considerable evidence that it had slipped significantly in recent years.

At one point the report ob-

Continued on Page 11, Column 5

"All the News That's Fit to Print."

The New York Times.

LATE CITY EDITION
U. S. Weather Bureau Report (Page 44) forecasts: Chance of snow flurries, cold today and tonight. Fair and cold tomorrow.
Temp. range: 21—6; yesterday: 19—10.

VOL. CX..No. 37,618. | NEW YORK, SATURDAY, JANUARY 21, 1961. | FIVE CENTS

10 cents beyond 50-mile zone from New York City except on Long Island. Higher in air delivery cities.

KENNEDY SWORN IN, ASKS 'GLOBAL ALLIANCE' AGAINST TYRANNY, WANT, DISEASE AND WAR; REPUBLICANS AND DIPLOMATS HAIL ADDRESS

24-Hour Snowstorm Ties Up City Area; Schools Closed

COLD TO CONTINUE

Northeast Is Crippled by Heavy Drifts—Deaths Total 47

By RUSSELL PORTER

Cold and windy weather plagued the city yesterday in the wake of a twenty-four-hour snowstorm that almost paralyzed the East.

The bitter wind here hampered the removal of the ten-inch snow, intensified suffering and delayed the restoration of normal travel.

Continued cold was predicted for the week-end, with the possibility of snow flurries today. Clear skies were expected tomorrow.

The temperature dropped to 9 degrees here at 2 A. M. today and went lower in the suburbs. A high in the twenties was expected this afternoon. The wind, which was twenty miles an hour yesterday afternoon was expected to drop to ten to fifteen miles an hour today.

Schools and colleges were closed in the city and other parts of the stormbound East. Many factories and business offices were shut down or forced to work with short staffs.

Travel Disrupted

Highways were blocked, auto traffic was slowed, cars were marooned in snow banks, rail and bus traffic was suspended or slowed, air travel was all but halted, mail service was interrupted and funerals were canceled.

The Associated Press counted at least forty-seven deaths attributed to the storm, including twenty in Pennsylvania, six in New York, two in New Jersey and five in Connecticut. Most of the deaths were caused by storm-induced traffic accidents and overexertion from shoveling snow.

Two Navy men and a civilian were in a truck that went off a pier into Jamaica Bay at Floyd Bennett Field in Brooklyn early yesterday. One body was found last night.

Drifts Up to 10 Feet

Although the Weather Bureau measured ten inches of snow near its Rockefeller Center office, it said the fall varied from six to twelve inches throughout the city. Wind-blown drifts were as high as ten feet in the city and suburbs.

The Weather Bureau labeled the storm a near blizzard here because the wind did not maintain the steady thirty-to-forty-mile-an-hour velocity of a blizzard. Some gusts reached fifty miles an hour, however, and the temperature dropped as low as 12 degrees early yesterday.

The storm was the city's second major one of the winter. In the first, on Dec. 11 and 12, a total of seventeen inches fell.

The new snowfall, although lighter, was considered worse in places because of the heavy drifting.

The new snowstorm began

Continued on Page 14, Column 1

Associated Press Wirephoto

NEW PRESIDENT TAKES THE OATH: John Fitzgerald Kennedy taking the oath of office yesterday. Administering it is Chief Justice Earl Warren, and holding the Bible is James R. Browning, Clerk of the Supreme Court. In the foreground, from the left, are Mrs. Kennedy; Mrs. Warren; outgoing President Eisenhower; Mrs. R. Sargent Shriver, a sister of President Kennedy; Dean Rusk and, at right, Lyndon Baines Johnson, who was sworn in as Vice President. Partly hidden behind Mrs. Shriver is Adlai E. Stevenson.

SNOW KEEPS MANY FROM JOBS IN CITY

Airport Drifts Stop Flights—Highway Traffic Light, With Some Roads Shut

By McCANDLISH PHILLIPS

Tens of thousands of people in the metropolitan area solved their transportation problems yesterday by evading them. They stayed at home.

For the most part, the brave, the bold and the resourceful were able to get to work. But they were often delayed and in many cases had to use alternate routes.

Others, who had stayed at hotels in the city overnight, had little trouble reaching their offices.

Long-distance travelers faced greater difficulties.

Snow clogged runways at the three major airports, bringing air traffic almost to a halt. Instead of the normal 1,600 arriving and departing flights there were twelve—six at New York International Airport and six at Newark.

This situation began to be reversed by late afternoon, and La Guardia and the two other airports reported virtually normal operations. Some flights were being canceled, however,

Continued on Page 15, Column 1

Unions Reject Plea to Halt Rail Ficketing for 10 Days

By A. H. RASKIN

Leaders of the crippling harbor strike rejected early today a plea by Governor Rockefeller for a ten-day halt in their picket blockade of railroad terminals and freight yards.

The Governor had made his appeal on the basis that snow-clogged highways had aggravated the peril to the city's lifeline created by the pickets' cut-off of rail commutation and food and freight movements.

The three striking unions asserted that compliance with the Governor's request would strip them of their only effective weapon without requiring any "comparable sacrifice" by the railroads.

They said the withdrawal of pickets by the 664 ferry and tug crewmen would "completely tip the scale in favor of the employers and obviously encourage an even more unyielding position on their part."

The marine strikers were so irked by the Governor's move that they urged the New York City Central Labor Council to call a meeting of all unions here to censure him. The rail tug unions asserted that he had intervened on the side of management in a manner that endangered the security and the bargaining status of all labor.

The rejection of the armistice plan came a few minutes after new settlement negotiations sponsored by the Governor had ended in failure. The peace talks will be resumed at 10:15 A. M. today, but there was no indication last night that they were making any progress.

The outlook was for a rapid intensification of the strikers'

Continued on Page 15, Column 5

CASTRO SUGGESTS AMITY WITH U. S.

Premier, in Citing Kennedy's Inaugural, Says Cuba Is Ready to 'Begin Anew'

By R. HART PHILLIPS

Special to The New York Times.

HAVANA, Jan. 20 — Premier Fidel Castro said tonight that the Cuban Government would "begin anew" in its relations with the United States.

The Premier stressed, however, that Cuba would hold the United States responsible for improving relations between the countries.

The Castro Government began here a demobilizing of the militia forces called up against an alleged threat of a United States "invasion."

Dr. Castro noted that President Kennedy had urged in his Inaugural Address that the United States' adversaries "begin anew the quest for peace."

"For our part," Premier Castro declared, "we are going to begin anew."

"However, we will ask nothing from Washington, nor did we expect any favors or economic assistance from Washington," he asserted. "We have no resentment of the past, but we will wait for the action of the Kennedy Administration. We

Continued on Page 4, Column 4

Inaugural Widely Praised By Both Sides of Congress

By JOHN D. MORRIS

Special to The New York Times.

WASHINGTON, Jan. 20—President Kennedy was widely acclaimed in Congress today for an Inaugural that stirred Republicans as well as Democrats. Diplomats and other public figures also joined in the praise.

The outgoing President, Dwight D. Eisenhower, said his successor's address was "fine, very fine."

Among the other Republican comment was that of Everett McKinley Dirksen, the Senate minority leader, who described the speech as "inspiring" and "a very compact message of hope."

Charles A. Halleck, the House Republican leader, said:

"I was much impressed."

Monroney Calls It Best

Any prize for the most glowing reaction would probably have gone to Senator A. S. Mike Monroney of Oklahoma, who led forces seeking the nomination of Adlai E. Stevenson, one of the country's most eloquent orators, at the Democratic National Convention last July.

Senator Monroney called the speech "the best Inaugural Address I have heard in my lifetime." He said he had heard twelve in all, starting with Woodrow Wilson's second in 1917.

He and a number of others,

Continued on Page 8, Column 6

EISENHOWER FINDS NEW LIFE 'GREAT'

Drives to Gettysburg Farm as Private Citizen After a Luncheon in His Honor

By FELIX BELAIR Jr.

Special to The New York Times.

GETTYSBURG, Pa., Jan. 20—Dwight D. Eisenhower left the official Washington scene today and became an elder statesman.

At the same time the curtain fell on his fifty years of public service as soldier and President and a new life as a private citizen began.

Mr. Eisenhower appeared lighthearted and no little relieved to be rid of the burdens of office, and he expressed his mood several times during the afternoon.

"Great, fine," he said when asked how he liked the idea of retiring from public life.

After President Kennedy's Inaugural, Mr. Eisenhower went to the 1925 F Street Club in Washington for a farewell luncheon given in his honor by Lewis L. Strauss, former chairman of the Atomic Energy Commission.

It had been a bitterly cold morning for everybody and the cocktails and champagne flowed freely inside. The host was having trouble getting his guests away from the bar until Mr. Eisenhower put down his glass

Continued on Page 12, Column 1

SOVIET SHAKE-UP SEEKS FOOD RISE

Khrushchev Orders Changes in Supply and Distribution

By OSGOOD CARUTHERS

Special to The New York Times.

MOSCOW, Jan. 20—Premier Khrushchev has ordered a sweeping reorganization of supply and distribution in Soviet agriculture.

He has ordered the setting up of new agencies as middlemen between industry and the farms to insure a better supply of equipment to agriculture and a better return distribution of food to the people.

The Premier's proposals were adopted two days ago by the ruling Central Committee of the Communist party after having been outlined in a lengthy speech three days ago in the Kremlin at a plenary session of the committee.

The proposals were aimed at ending the lag in the growth of agriculture and at working out ways of better satisfying the demands of the populace for meat, milk, butter and eggs as well as the usual fare of bread and potatoes.

The most drastic divergence from the traditional Soviet sys-

Continued on Page 3, Column 2

KHRUSHCHEV SEES HOPE FOR ACCORD

Message to Kennedy Urges Drive to Ease Tensions

By Reuters.

LONDON, Jan. 20—Premier Khrushchev and President Leonid Brezhnev of the Soviet Union cabled President Kennedy an Inauguration Day message today extending the hope for a "radical improvement" in Soviet-American relations.

They hoped, the Soviet news agency Tass reported, that joint efforts of the United States and the Soviet Union would improve relations and therefore "make healthier the entire international climate."

[British Government officials, politicians and the press joined Friday in hailing President Kennedy's Inaugural Address. They admired its content and acclaimed its "style and flair" as symbolizing a new, dashing and dynamic approach to the world's problems.]

The cable from the Russian leaders said:

"Dear Mr. President, we congratulate you upon your inauguration. We avail ourselves of the opportunity to express the

Continued on Page 10, Column 8

Inquiry Mystified by Jet Wreck That Killed 4 on Take-Off Here

By RICHARD WITKIN

Investigators failed yesterday to turn up any solid clue as to why an Aeronaves de Mexico jet airliner crashed on take-off from a snow-whipped runway here Thursday evening.

They found only that the DC-8 had not been overloaded, that the snowstorm had not dropped the ceiling or visibility below the legal minimum for take-offs, and that the pilot evidently had tried to stop the plane by reversing thrust on all four engines.

Most observers thought it amazing that 102 of the 106 persons on board managed to escape before the plane went up in flames. The four who died were all members of the Mexican crew: two pilots, an engineer and a woman purser.

The jet, taking off to the northeast on the 10,000-foot Runway 7 at International Airport, ripped out a 100-foot-wide section of a steel fence at the end of the strip. It then tore through a wire mesh cyclone fence in the field beyond, struck a car as it crossed Rockaway Boulevard, and came to rest in a marshy area about 900 feet from the runway.

Many of the 102 survivors were interviewed by Civil Aeronautics Board officials during the day.

George Van Epps, C. A. B. chief in the Northeast region,

Continued on Page 16, Column 5

Capital Paraders Don Overcoats To Pass in White House Review

By RUSSELL BAKER

Special to The New York Times.

WASHINGTON, Jan. 20—President Kennedy had warned that it wouldn't be easy on "the New Frontier" and, for 32,000 marchers in today's inauguration parade, it wasn't.

A Siberian wind knifing down Pennsylvania Avenue in the wake of last night's snowfall turned majorettes' legs blue, froze baton twirlers' fingers and drove beauty queens to flannels and overcoats.

"This," said Cathy Magda, Miss Florida from Fort Lauderdale, "is the coldest parade I can ever remember."

Under her gown, she confided, she was wearing flannel pajamas.

Fear of chilblains visibly reduced attendance along the mile-and-a-half route from the Capitol to the White House but the big and ebullient Clan Kennedy obviously had the time of its life.

The President's younger brother Robert, the new Attorney General, rode down the avenue seated high on the back of his open car, hair tossing in the wind, waving and laughing in exuberant spirits.

The President's sister Eunice brought her movie camera to the reviewing stand in front of the White House and had her brother pose in the foreground as she panned across the

Continued on Page 9, Column 4

NATION EXHORTED

Inaugural Says U. S. Will 'Pay Any Price' to Keep Freedom

Text of Inaugural Address will be found on Page 8.

By W. H. LAWRENCE

Special to The New York Times

WASHINGTON, Jan. 20—John Fitzgerald Kennedy assumed the Presidency today with a call for "a grand and global alliance" to combat tyranny, poverty, disease and war.

In his Inaugural Address, he served notice on the world that the United States was ready to "pay any price, bear any burden, meet any hardship, support any friend, oppose any foe to assure the survival and the success of liberty."

But the nation is also ready, he said, to resume negotiations with the Soviet Union to ease and, if possible, remove world tensions.

"Let us begin anew," Mr. Kennedy declared. "Let us never negotiate out of fear. But let us never fear to negotiate."

Asks Aid of Countrymen

He called on his fellow-citizens to join his Administration's endeavor:

"Ask not what your country can do for you—ask what you can do for your country."

At 12:51 P. M., he was sworn by Chief Justice Earl Warren as the nation's thirty-fifth President, the first Roman Catholic to hold the office.

Ten minutes earlier, Lyndon Baines Johnson of Texas took the oath as Vice President. It was administered by Sam Rayburn, Speaker of the House of Representatives.

At 43 years of age, the youngest man ever elected to the Presidency, Mr. Kennedy took over the power vested for eight years in Dwight D. Eisenhower, who, at 70, was the oldest White House occupant.

President Kennedy alluded to this change of generation in his Inaugural.

'Torch Has Passed'

He said:

"Let the word go forth from this time and place, to friend and foe alike, that the torch has been passed to a new generation of Americans—born in this century, tempered by war, disciplined by a hard and bitter peace, proud of our ancient heritage—and unwilling to witness or permit the slow undoing of those human rights to which this nation has always been committed, and to which we are committed today at home and around the world."

A blanket of 7.7 inches of newly fallen snow, bitter winds and a sub-freezing temperature of 22 degrees held down the crowds that watched the ceremonies in front of the newly

Continued on Page 8, Column 1

5 Dances Conclude Capital Festivities

By DAVID HALBERSTAM

Special to The New York Times

WASHINGTON, Jan. 20—Some of them brought formals and tuxedos thousands of miles, then stayed in their hotels. Some of the women shivered in their fashionable and frail gowns while some of their men wore long johns under their white-tie formals at the Inaugural Ball here tonight.

The ball was the last official event of a crowded two-and-a-half-day schedule of social politicking, or political-socializing, and the exhausting pace began to show tonight.

It was cold again, and windy, and there were traffic problems. If there was any redeeming part about tonight's weather as far

Continued on Page 11, Column 8

NEWS INDEX

"All the News That's Fit to Print"

The New York Times.

LATE CITY EDITION

U. S. Weather Bureau Report (Page 74) forecasts: Rain and fog early today; fair, mild this afternoon, tonight, tomorrow. Temp. range: 50—32; yesterday: 36—27.

VOL. CX...No. 37,642. | NEW YORK, TUESDAY, FEBRUARY 14, 1961. | FIVE CENTS

10 cents beyond 50-mile zone from New York City except on Long Island. Higher in air delivery cities.

LUMUMBA MURDERED IN KATANGA; HIS BACKERS PREDICT A CIVIL WAR; U. N. CHIEF CALLS FOR FULL INQUIRY

KENNEDY INVITES BUSINESS TO JOIN IN 'FULL ALLIANCE'

Advises Industrialists Their Success Is 'Intertwined' With Administration's

STRESSES 3 PROBLEMS

Asks Plant Modernization, More Economic Growth and Price Stability

Excerpts from Kennedy talk appear on Page 22.

By RICHARD E. MOONEY
Special to The New York Times.

WASHINGTON, Feb. 13—President Kennedy appealed to business today for "a full-fledged alliance" with his Administration.

"Your success and ours are intertwined," he said.

Mr. Kennedy, four Cabinet officers and Vice President Johnson presented their case to a special one-day session of the National Industrial Conference Board, an organization of business and industry devoted to economic research.

Secretary of State Dean Rusk took note of a campaign to scuttle United States membership in the twenty-nation Organization for Economic Co-operation and Development. Senate hearings on the organization start tomorrow. He gave assurances that the organization "will have nothing to do with tariff-making."

Goldberg Offers Assurance

Secretary of Labor Arthur J. Goldberg gave assurances that the Administration would not try to force predetermined wage settlements on labor and industry and that anti-recession programs would be "sound" in their size and "responsible" in their financing.

In short, the President and his principal officers addressed themselves to a number of objections that they felt business men held against the Administration.

Indeed, Mr. Kennedy prefaced his prepared speech with a light-hearted reference to the assumed political leanings of his audience.

"It would be premature to ask your support in the next election," he said, "and it would be inaccurate to thank you for it in the past."

Areas of Concern Listed

The speech was devoted primarily to "three areas of common concern" that the President said must receive the full attention of a business-Government alliance—economic growth, plant modernization and price stability.

By implication the President also gave an estimate that his proposals would add about $3,000,000,000 to the Federal Budget next year, without counting programs financed outside the Budget, such as Social Security.

In this matter, too, he injected a jest. He said that $3,000,000,000 would pay for all his anti-recession, health and education proposals next year, with enough left over "to start closing what the Democrats and this Administration used to call the missile gap." He was referring to the controversy over whether there is a gap between

Continued on Page 22, Column 7

Price Supports for Cotton Expected to Be Increased

Freeman Is Likely to Act This Week—Domestic Rise Viewed as Leading to Call for Higher Textile Tariffs

By TOM WICKER
Special to The New York Times.

WASHINGTON, Feb. 13—Secretary of Agriculture Orville L. Freeman is expected to announce this week an increase in the cotton support price. It could have broad economic implications.

Congressional sources expect a support level of about 81 per cent of parity, which is the standard set by law to give farmers a fair return for their costs. Such a support level would represent an increase of about 2 cents a pound above last year's average market price of 30 cents a pound and would portend an increase of slightly more than 2 cents on this year's market.

The expected support price would increase the cost of domestic cotton to the United States textile industry, which already pays 6 cents a pound more than foreign manufacturers.

Such an effect could lead, in turn, to an increased flow of low-cost textile imports into the United States. And that development would probably cause domestic textile men to bring more pressure in Congress for tariff or quota protection from foreign competition.

Additionally, a cotton support price increase might signal Administration efforts to raise support prices on other farm commodities.

Already, a program has been proposed that would add about 24 cents to the corn support level. "All these other folks are expecting increases too," a Congressional source reported. "After all, this Administration promised a better farm income."

In another development Secretary Freeman announced another injection of funds into the farm economy. He said $35,000,-

Continued on Page 26, Column 3

Udall Asks 'Vigorous' Plan To Increase Public Power

By DAVID HALBERSTAM
Special to The New York Times.

WASHINGTON, Feb. 13—The Secretary of the Interior indicated today a policy of increased public power under the Kennedy Administration. Secretary Stewart L. Udall issued a memorandum on public power calling for "a vigorous program of full development and maximum utilization of our total energy to meet the nation's growing demands."

He favored a return to the five-point development program first announced by the Truman Administration in 1946.

The memorandum called for "expanding the planned activities of the department to make possible the timely construction of new projects and facilities." However, it outlined no specific projects.

The major significance of the statement was said to be in its stand for public power, as contrasted with the attitude of the previous Administration.

A Campaign Issue

The Eisenhower Administration was regarded as suspicious of public power. It advocated a "partnership" between the Government and private enterprise on power projects. Rural cooperatives, however, felt that the partnership was weighted in favor of private business.

Thus, during his campaign, President Kennedy attacked the Eisenhower Administration on public power-conscious areas as having a record of "no new starts."

Mr. Udall's statement was regarded by some officials in his department as a start toward fulfilling Mr. Kennedy's campaign pledges on new power starts.

It was also regarded as part of the Kennedy economic pro-

Continued on Page 62, Column 1

DEMOCRATS NAME HUGHES IN JERSEY

Nomination for Governor Is Virtually Assured by Vote of 20 County Leaders

By GEORGE CABLE WRIGHT
Special to The New York Times.

TRENTON, Feb. 13—Former Superior Court Judge Richard J. Hughes was named the Democratic organization's candidate for Governor today.

The designation, tantamount to nomination, was made by the unanimous vote of party leaders from twenty of the twenty-one counties at a conference with Gov. Robert B. Meyner.

Mayor John J. Grogan of Hoboken, the only other aspirant with any party support, withdrew from the race a few hours before the selection of Mr. Hughes. Thus Mr. Hughes is not expected to have any major opposition for the nomination in the April 18 primary election.

Commenting on his candidacy tonight, Mr. Hughes said:

"I am very happy. It is with a deep sense of humility that I accept this honor. I promise the Democratic party and all of its voters that I will do my best to deserve it."

Mr. Hughes said he would hold a press conference in about ten days.

Dennis F. Carey, party leader in Essex, the state's most populous county, was in Florida and did not send a representative to the conference with the Governor, which was held at the Executive Mansion in Princeton this morning. He has been at

Continued on Page 29, Column 4

HOGAN SUPPORTS DE SAPIO'S STORY OF '58 CONVENTION

Prosecutor Affirms Charge That Mayor and Harriman Behaved Like 'Bosses'

By CLAYTON KNOWLES

District Attorney Frank S. Hogan said yesterday that "the two persons who tried to be bosses and acted like bosses at the Democratic state convention at Buffalo in 1958 were Mayor Wagner and Governor Harriman."

In a battle at the convention, Mr. Hogan won the nomination for United States Senator with the support of Carmine G. De Sapio. In an interview, the District Attorney supported the account of behind-the-scenes maneuvering there that was given by Mr. De Sapio in his television-radio defense Sunday.

Mr. Hogan even elaborated on the story. He said that W. Averell Harriman, now a roving United States Ambassador, "shook his fist at me at the demanded that I withdraw."

"He told me that if I did not withdraw," Mr. Hogan recalled, "the Mayor would place Thomas Murray's name in nomination and that he, the Governor, would take the floor to support Mr. Murray."

Harriman Has No Comment

Reached by telephone in Washington, Ambassador Harriman said he had no comment.

Mr. Hogan was emphatic, however, in declaring that Mr. De Sapio had been accurate in saying that he, the prospective nominee, had been "threatened and bullyragged."

"These are the only words that could truthfully describe what the Mayor and Governor tried to do to me," he declared. "I was not privy to everything that happened there, but I was an interested party. And to my personal knowledge, the two persons who tried to be bosses and acted like bosses at the Democratic state convention at Buffalo in 1958 were Mayor Wagner and Governor Harriman."

The prosecutor gave these views when asked whether there was anything in the charges and suggestions made by Mr. De Sapio in his broadcast that merited investigation by the District Attorney's office.

Mr. Hogan said he did not think there was anything to investigate at this point.

Asked About Council Vote

The District Attorney then was asked whether he saw any reason to investigate the suggestion by Mr. De Sapio that City Investigation Commissioner Louis I. Kaplan had brought pressure on Councilmen Earl Brown and Daniel S. Weiss to get their votes for Edward R. Dudley, the Mayor's candidate for Borough President.

"If specifics were given, there conceivably might be," Mr. Hogan replied, "but on the basis of what we have now, such action would be far-fetched and might involve our office in a charge that we were getting involved in a partisan political squabble."

The Hogan statement added

Continued on Page 28, Column 3

URGES U. N. INQUIRY: Dag Hammarskjold, Secretary General, before Security Council yesterday.

CALLS FOR CAUTION: Adlai E. Stevenson, chief U. S. delegate, calls for conciliation, not revenge.

The New York Times (by Patrick A. Burns)

ASSAILS U. N. STAFF: Valerian A. Zorin of the Soviet Union says bid for inquiry seems hypocritical.

SITE KEPT SECRET

Province Says Tribal Foes Killed 2 Aides With Ex-Premier

Text of Katanga communiqué is printed on Page 16.

By PAUL HOFMANN
Special to The New York Times.

LEOPOLDVILLE, the Congo, Feb. 13—Patrice Lumumba, deposed Premier of the Congo, was killed yesterday by tribesmen, the Katanga radio announced today.

The broadcast said Mr. Lumumba, who was 35 years old, and two associates were murdered by inhabitants of a village they had passed while in flight. The three men had been in the custody of Katanga authorities acting on behalf of the Leopoldville Government, which Mr. Lumumba opposed, until they escaped Thursday night.

[A spokesman for the Katanga Provincial Government refused to identify the village where Mr. Lumumba was killed and where he was buried. He said that vengeance might be taken against the tribal inhabitants.]

The village where the three men were killed was said to be in the area of Katanga known to be violently opposed to the policies of the late Premier.

Slain Associates Identified

The two other victims with Mr. Lumumba were identified as Maurice Mpolo, Minister of Youth in the Lumumba Government, and Joseph Okito, vice president of the suspended Congolese Senate.

Congolese followers and foreign supporters of Mr. Lumumba's policies predicted that civil war would result from his death. Fears arose that new anti-white violence might break out in Eastern Province and other areas dominated by pro-Lumumba forces.

The United Nations disclosed today it had warned President Moise Tshombe of Katanga that the responsibility would rest with him if United Nations troops clashed with his forces, which are fighting rebels in Katanga.

Force by U. N. Hinted

The warning was interpreted as reflecting new orders to United Nations detachments in Katanga to use force if necessary to stop the operations of Mr. Tshombe's troops.

A United Nations note to Mr. Tshombe was said to have requested that he halt his offensive against Baluba tribesmen in the northern part of his province who oppose his regime.

The announcement that Mr. Lumumba was dead was received with outward calm in Leopoldville, the capital of the Congo.

The news was first broadcast by the radio station in Brazzaville, in the former French Congo across the Congo River.

A United Nations spokesman voiced "shock and horror" over the news. He said, "The slay-

Continued on Page 15, Column 1

MOSCOW REPORTS PROBE ON COURSE

Vehicle Radios Back Data on Ground Command as It Speeds Toward Venus

By SEYMOUR TOPPING
Special to The New York Times.

MOSCOW, Feb. 13—A Soviet space rocket streaked along on its course toward Venus today.

When the instrument-loaded vehicle reaches the vicinity of Venus in May, Soviet scientists said, it should radio back a wealth of data on the mysterious, cloud-shrouded planet.

[On both sides of the Iron Curtain, European scientists and newspapers hailed the Soviet rocket shot. Some termed it the greatest space achievement since the first sputnik was launched.]

Prof. Viktor Bazykin, director of the Moscow Planetarium, estimated that the station would pass near Venus at a point about 62,000,000 miles from the earth and then go into orbit around the sun.

Prof. Bazykin said in an interview that the task of sending an interplanetary station to the area of Mars would be of the same "order of difficulty" as the Venus probe.

The Moscow Radio announced tonight that the interplanetary station at noon Moscow time (4 A. M. Eastern Standard time) was 488,900 kilometers (about 300,000 miles) from the earth.

Twenty-four hours earlier, at noon the day of its launching from an earth satellite, the station was 126,300 kilometers (78,300 miles) in space.

The announcement said the earth satellite had been orbited yesterday with precision and that the rocket launched from it also had put the "automatic interplanetary station" into a precise trajectory.

The wording of the announce-

Continued on Page 8, Column 3

Hammarskjold Statement Is Denounced by Russian

By LINDESAY PARROTT
Special to The New York Times.

UNITED NATIONS, N. Y., Feb. 13—Secretary General Dag Hammarskjold called today for a full investigation of the death of Patrice Lumumba, deposed Premier of the Congo, and two of his aides.

The Secretary General, speaking before the Security Council as it resumed hearings on the Congo situation, asserted that

Statements at U. N. on death, of Lumumba, Page 17.

the case "is of such a character and significance as to render necessary a full and impartial investigation."

Mr. Hammarskjold announced that he would speak to the eleven-nation body later regarding possible further action by the United Nations in view of the new crisis.

The declaration by Mr. Hammarskjold was strongly criticized by Valerian A. Zorin, the Soviet delegate. The Soviet Union has "not the slightest confidence in the Secretary General or in his staff," Mr. Zorin said.

Proposal Held 'Hypocritical'

The proposal for an investigation appears "hypocritical," the Russian asserted, in so far as the inquiry would be made by Mr. Hammarskjold, the United Nations Secretariat and the United Nations command in the Congo. He implied that these agencies were equally responsible with the "colonists" for the death of Mr. Lumumba and his two ministers, Maurice Mpolo and Joseph Okito.

Adlai E. Stevenson, new chief of the United States' delegation, expressed regret over the slayings and called for attempts at reconciliation in the Congo rather than revenge.

Word of former Premier Lumumba's death was received here just before the Council con-

Continued on Page 17, Column 1

KENNEDY SHOCKED BY CONGO SLAYING

Capital Distressed by Report—Fears Setback to Effort to Map New Approach

By DANA ADAMS SCHMIDT
Special to The New York Times.

WASHINGTON, Feb. 13—President Kennedy expressed "great shock" today when news of the death of Patrice Lumumba was telephoned to him.

This comment, reported by Pierre Salinger, Presidential press secretary, epitomized official Washington's reaction to the announcement at Elisabethville, capital of Katanga, that the former Congo Premier and two associates had been "massacred."

The Administration's African specialists were distressed at the prospect that their efforts to promote a new constructive approach to the Congo problem out of confusion at the United Nations and in Africa would be swept away in a new wave of violence and passion.

But another school of thought contended that, grim as was Mr. Lumumba's end, the Congo would be better off without him.

New Soviet Gains Feared

The prevailing view, however, was that the West would be blamed by many Congolese for the killing and that the Soviet Union would make new gains at the United Nations and in Africa. Among the consequences feared were the following:

¶That the Soviet Union would launch a new drive to discredit the United Nations operation in the Congo and to oust Secretary General Dag Hammarskjold.

¶That a massacre of about 3,000 whites, most of them Belgians, would break out in Eastern and Kivu Provinces, which are controlled by Mr. Lumumba's lieutenants, Antoine Gizenga and Anicet Kashamura.

¶That such violence would provoke renewed Belgian intervention and in its turn a demand for further United Nations intervention, thus bringing the

Continued on Page 16, Column 8

Residents of Westchester Battle For Right to Leave Boots in Hall

Special to The New York Times.

WHITE PLAINS, Feb. 13—It is courtesy to leave footgear at the door in Japan; it is cleanliness to park the brogans on Dutch doorsteps; it is an invitation to shine the leather when shoes are left in places like the corridors of French hotels; it is a mark of reverence to leave foot coverings outside the Pakistani masjid.

But some residents discovered with dismay today that footgear left in hallways was considered sloppiness in North White Plains.

Occupants of the 160 dwelling units in Edgebrook Garden Apartments, a $2,000,000 co-operative near the Bronx River Parkway, have been leaving their soggy boots and overshoes in the hallways in an attempt to keep the heavy recent snows outside the home.

But the nine-member board of directors decided that the overshoe collections meant cluttered corridors.

Today the residents had to go down to the cellar and untangle a huge heap of footgear to get back their boots and rubbers.

Footgear flew in many directions. Words also flew.

Mrs. Irving Monk, the wife of a sales executive, mimeographed a protest and distributed it to every apartment.

"The confiscation of boots is a grotesque distortion of the power to legislate," Mrs. Monk said. "The very idea of having one's wearing apparel snatched from one's door is appalling. The sight of men gathering boots by the cartons and trans-

Continued on Page 32, Column 3

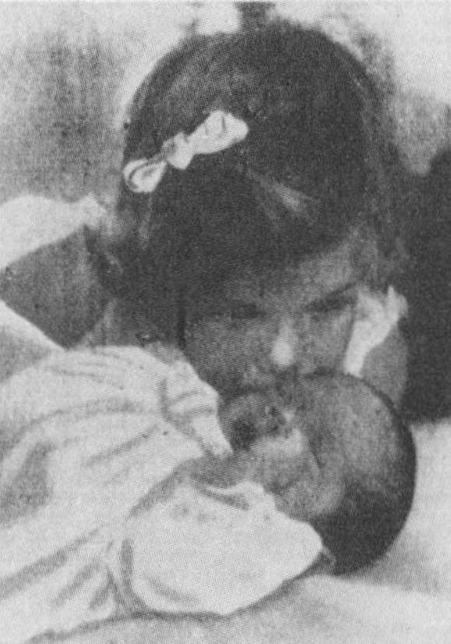

Associated Press Wirephoto

KISSING KIN: Caroline Kennedy, 3-year-old daughter of President and Mrs. Kennedy, with her brother, John F. Kennedy Jr. The photograph, made some weeks ago when the Kennedys were at Palm Beach, was released yesterday at the White House. Picture was made by Richard Avedon.

Beer Union Agrees to Lay-Offs To Help Put Ruppert's in Black

By RALPH KATZ

An agreement has been reached between management and a union to help pull the Jacob Ruppert Brewery out of the red by cutting labor costs $1,000,000 a year.

The plan, a union counter-proposal, was made public yesterday by I. Philip Sipser, counsel for the Brewery Workers Joint Board, and officials of three teamster locals, which represent 800 production and distribution employes.

It calls for workers to take five-week lay-offs during the year on a rotating basis, reducing the labor bill by about 10 per cent. The locals have said the remaining force would continue to produce the brewery's normal annual output of 1,200,000 barrels of beer.

Management personnel would take a salary cut of at least 10 per cent under the plan. Murray Vernon, chairman of the board, has agreed to reduce his $50,000-a-year salary to $25,000, a management spokesman said.

The plan also calls for an inducement to the fifty-five to sixty men 65 years old or older to accept retirement. Such workers who retire by April 1 would receive $20 a week for a year from the company in addition to regular retirement benefits.

Workers eligible for retirement after April 1 would also get the bonus.

The union plan was devised after management had proposed the elimination of forty-eight

Continued on Page 31, Column 2

NEWS INDEX

News Summary and Index, Page 39

Albania Red Leader Says U.S. Plots War

By Reuters.

BELGRADE, Yugoslavia, Feb. 13—Gen. Enver Hoxha, Communist party leader in Albania, accused the United States today of complicity in a recent plot to overthrow the Albanian regime.

General Hoxha said the plot also involved Yugoslavia and Greece "working together with the United States Sixth Fleet and a group of Albanian traitors."

The Communist leader's charges were made in a speech to the fourth congress of the Albanian Communist party at Tirana. The general warned that the West, under the leadership of President Kennedy, was "preparing for the third World War."

The belligerent speech placed the small Balkan nation firmly behind Communist China and

Continued on Page 6, Column 8

"All the News That's Fit to Print"

The New York Times.

LATE CITY EDITION

U. S. Weather Bureau Report (Page 61) forecasts: Mostly fair today and tonight. Chance of rain tomorrow. Temp. range: 43—30; yesterday: 44—36.

VOL. CX....No. 37,644. NEW YORK, THURSDAY, FEBRUARY 16, 1961. 10 cents beyond 50-mile zone from New York City except on Long Island. Higher in air delivery cities. FIVE CENTS

KENNEDY WARNS OF RISKS OF WAR IN A UNILATERAL ACTION IN CONGO; HAMMARSKJOLD FIRM; RIOT IN U.N.

18 U.S. SKATERS AMONG 73 DEAD IN A JET CRASH

BELGIAN DISASTER

All Lost When Plane Falls at Brussels—49 Americans

By HARRY GILROY

Special to The New York Times.

BRUSSELS, Belgium, Feb. 15—A Sabena Airlines Boeing 707 jet crashed near the Brussels Airport early today, killing seventy-three persons, including the eighteen members of the United States figure-skating team.

The plane, en route from New York, plunged to earth after it had twice circled the airport. The dead included the sixty-one passengers, the crew of eleven, and a farmer in the field where the plane fell.

The passengers included forty-nine Americans, a Swiss, a Frenchman, a German, a Canadian, a Nicaraguan and seven Belgians.

The American figure-skating team was on its way to a world championship meet in Prague. Its members included Mrs. Maribel Vinson Owen, 49 years old, of Winchester, Mass., and her two daughters, both of them champions. Mrs. Owen was the United States figure-skating champion nine times. On the current trip she was the coach for her daughters.

Worst Sabena Crash

The crash was the worst ever suffered by Sabena. It also marked the first time any passengers had been killed in a Boeing 707 accident. The last serious Sabena crash occurred May 18, 1958, when a DC-7C crashed at Casablanca, killing fifty-six passengers and nine crew members.

The four-engine jet came in sight of the control tower shortly before 10 A. M. in a cloudless sky. The plane, which had left New York at 7:30 P. M. yesterday, would have landed at once except that another plane was moving along the runway to take off, an airport official said.

Persons in the little farming hamlet of Berg, northeast of Brussels, saw the airliner circling overhead at an altitude of about 600 feet. Officials at the control tower were also watching the plane with field glasses.

Suddenly the plane fell. An airport official placed the time at 10:05 A. M.

Plane Strikes Farmer

The plane came down at a 70 degree angle onto a small farm field. It plunged into a grove of trees, narrowly missing three houses. It struck Theo de Laet, a young farmer noted as an amateur cyclist, killing him. A piece of debris tore a leg off another farmer, Marcel Lauwers.

Parts of the plane were thrown 200 yards but the bulk of the airliner burst into flames, preventing anyone from approaching until firemen arrived from the airport.

William de Swarte, director general of Sabena, said tonight that "something must have gone wrong with the controls of the plane." He said the plane

Continued on Page 18, Column 1

Meany Denounces Foes of Wage Rise

By A. H. RASKIN

Special to The New York Times.

BAL HARBOUR, Fla., Feb. 15—George Meany called today for higher wages as the key to national prosperity and economic growth.

The president of the American Federation of Labor and Congress of Industrial Organizations derided arguments that wage increases had been responsible for pricing United States goods out of world markets.

His talk at a luncheon of the federation's Maritime Trades Department in the Americana Hotel was an indirect reply to moves by some White House advisers to put the brakes on wage increases as a means of spurring recovery and combating competition.

Mr. Meany took specific exception to a suggestion by Sen-

Continued on Page 21, Column 2

GEROSA PREDICTS NO NEW TAXATION

Says General Fund Will Be 872 Million—Criticizes Mayor on Estimating

By CHARLES G. BENNETT

Controller Lawrence E. Gerosa estimated yesterday that the city's general fund would reach a record total of $872,636,000 for the fiscal year beginning next July 1. This, he said, "indicates there will be no need for new taxes of any kind."

At the same time, Mr. Gerosa criticized a proposal by Mayor Wagner that the Mayor's office take over the estimation of general fund receipts. A "spending Mayor," the Controller said, "could have one of his subordinates tailor-make the estimate to fit his spending needs."

The general fund consists of miscellaneous revenues—largely the proceeds from licenses, permits, water charges and excise taxes—including the 3 per cent retail sales tax. Other sources of revenue are the real estate tax and money received from the state and Federal Governments.

Mr. Gerosa also reported that business in New York City in 1960 "appeared to run against the nation-wide tide of economic contraction." He made a guarded prediction that the city's prosperity would continue.

The Controller's prediction on the general fund forecast a cash carry-over of $67,560,000 from 1960-61, plus funds withdrawn from the stabilization reserve. Mr. Gerosa forecast that

Continued on Page 25, Column 1

PRESIDENT CALLS SPEED ESSENTIAL TO COMBAT SLUMP

Renews Plea to Congress—Says 'Recession' Is Right Word for Business Lag

By RICHARD E. MOONEY

Special to The New York Times.

WASHINGTON, Feb. 15—President Kennedy said tonight that anyone who considered all the available evidence would agree that "it is necessary to take action" to combat the recession.

He spoke, at his news conference, in reply to a Republican charge that he had overstated the nation's economic problems for political reasons. [Question 12, Page 16.]

He defended the use of the word "recession" to describe the present situation, and called once again for quick Congressional action on his economic proposals—unemployment compensation, aid to depressed areas and other measures.

He also announced two lesser stimulating actions that will be taken under existing authority—a speed-up in post office construction and a liberalization of the criteria for awarding defense contracts to small businesses.

Cites '58 Recession

The President said he saw "no necessity or desirability of minimizing our problems." There has been a recession for "some months," and the difficulty is compounded by the fact that the country never fully recovered from the 1958 recession, he said.

He called for the cooperation of the leaders of both parties in Congress. And he took exception to the view of the Senate Republican leader, Everett McKinley Dirksen of Illinois, that the State of the Union message had had no more impact than "a snowflake falling on the bosom of the Potomac."

In his opening statement at the news conference, Mr. Kennedy reviewed all the economic actions taken by his Administration, and all the proposals it had made.

Wants Action 'This Winter'

"This country is most concerned about the very serious problem of unemployment which we have faced this winter," he stated. He said he was hopeful "that we can move forward this winter so that some relief can be given to our fellow Americans."

Mr. Kennedy cited five statistics to underscore his belief that "it is necessary to take action"—inventories of 1,000,000 unsold new automobiles, more than 5,500,000 unemployed workers, 600,000 of this jobless group who have exhausted their unemployment-benefit rights, slack operations in the steel industry and a decline in over-all business activity since the middle of last year.

"I hope we can get action as soon as possible," he said. "We want to see the American economy get back on its feet."

The President also said tonight that his Administration

Continued on Page 17, Column 2

VIOLENCE AT U. N.: United Nations guards battle with demonstrators in gallery of Security Council chamber

Associated Press

Khrushchev Urges 'Strict' Arms Curbs In Wire to Kennedy

By SEYMOUR TOPPING

Special to The New York Times.

MOSCOW, Feb. 15—Premier Khrushchev told President Kennedy today that any disarmament agreement should include "strict international control."

The Soviet leader urged a speedy solution of the disarmament problem in a telegram acknowledging the congratulations extended by the President on the launching of the Soviet Venus rocket.

Noting that Mr. Kennedy, in his inaugural address, had proposed a pooling of efforts in the struggle against disease, the conquest of space and the development of culture and trade, Mr. Khrushchev said:

"We consider that the solution of the disarmament problem would provide conditions favoring the earliest realization of these noble tasks before mankind. And we would like every country to exert every effort for the solution of this problem with the establishment of such strict international controls that no one could arm in secret and commit aggression."

Mr. Khrushchev also said:

"All are in agreement that the solution of the disarmament problem depends to a great extent on the agreement

Continued on Page 6, Column 1

RIOT IN GALLERY HALTS U.N. DEBATE

American Negroes Ejected After Invading Session—Midtown March Balked

More than two dozen persons were injured yesterday when a group made up mostly of American Negroes set off the most violent demonstration inside United Nations headquarters in the world organization's history.

About sixty men and women burst into the Security Council chamber, interrupting the session, and fought with guards in a protest against United Nations policies in the Congo and the slaying of Patrice Lumumba, former Congo Premier.

Last night, 200 demonstrators virtually took over the north side of Forty-second Street in a march from First Avenue westward across Manhattan, chanting "Congo, yes! Yankee, no!"

When they refused to abandon an advance toward Times Square, mounted policemen charged the demonstrators at Sixth Avenue and Forty-third Street and dispersed them.

Groups Anti-Colonialist

The demonstrators inside the Security Council chamber included members of the United African Nationalist Movement, the Liberation Committee for Africa and On Guard, groups apparently of nationalist and anti-colonialist hue.

The public was excluded for the rest of the day and will be barred again today.

Later, picketing outside the United Nations on First Avenue at Forty-third Street appeared

Continued on Page 10, Column 2

U. N. Chief Tells Russians He Won't Be Forced Out

By LINDESAY PARROTT

Special to The New York Times.

UNITED NATIONS, N. Y., Feb. 15—Secretary General Dag Hammarskjold told the Soviet Union today that he would not be driven out of his post. His resignation and the substitution of a three-man committee for the office of Secretary General, which have been demanded by the

Statements at U. N. on Congo are on Pages 12 and 13.

Russians, would destroy the world organization at its most critical moment, he said.

The Swedish diplomat told the Security Council that he meant to stay on as long as the organization needed him.

The Council's debate on the Congo crisis was interrupted by what officials here called the worst outbreak it ever has witnessed. Shortly before noon, as the new United States representative, Adlai E. Stevenson, was making his first major address to a United Nations body, thirty or more demonstrators started a minor riot in the spectators' gallery.

Lumumba Death Protested

The demonstrators, many of them Negroes, were protesting the murder of Patrice Lumumba, the deposed Congolese Premier.

The day's debate in the Council seemed to indicate that, despite friendly gestures by the new United States Administration and by the Kremlin, the American and Soviet delegations were as far apart as ever on the crucial questions of the Congo and of the "cold war."

The discussion of the Congo situation was adjourned just before 7 tonight and will be resumed at 11 A. M. tomorrow.

Mr. Stevenson said that a statement issued last night in Moscow and a draft resolution laid before the Council today by Valerian A. Zorin, the chief Soviet delegate, constituted a "declaration of war" on the United Nations. The resolution would call for an end of United Nations operations in the Congo within a month. The Soviet Union, in its Moscow statement, also declared its non-recognition of Mr. Hammarskjold as Secretary General.

Mr. Hammarskjold, defending his record in carrying on United Nations operations in the Congo, said he had done his

Continued on Page 10, Column 1

POLISH MOB SACKS BELGIAN EMBASSY

Rioters Assault Diplomats in Protest on Lumumba—Files Are Burned

By ARTHUR J. OLSEN

Special to The New York Times.

WARSAW, Feb. 15—A mob of young Poles, protesting the death of Patrice Lumumba, sacked the Belgian Embassy today and assaulted diplomats who tried to defend it.

The demonstrators fed a bonfire on the street outside the four-story building with papers and files thrown from the embassy windows.

Bricks and cobblestones shattered virtually every window in the building, which also houses the Netherlands Embassy. Furniture was broken and marred with crimson dye.

At the end of the twenty-minute foray, the four Belgian diplomats and local employes of the embassy were crimson stained with dye and shaken but uninjured.

Second Attack on Building

The mid-afternoon assault was the second "spontaneous" demonstration against Belgium in eighteen hours. Last night a mob of nearly 1,000, mostly youngsters from Warsaw Polytechnic Institute, hurled stones at the embassy building and shouted and orated against the "murderers" of Mr. Lumumba.

The Polish Government was actively encouraging today the spirit of indignation over the death of the Congolese politician. Premier Jozef Cyrankiewicz sent a telegram of condolence to Antoine Gizenga, whom he addressed as Vice Premier of the Congolese Government.

The President of the Sejm (Parliament) denounced the slaying. Polish members of the Interparliamentary Union issued a statement of protest. The official press excoriated "colonialists" and "imperialists" in vengeful terms.

About fifty riot policemen were on duty at the Belgian Embassy in a residential section of Warsaw when the crowd began forming at 1:30 P. M. Witnesses said that most of the protestors arrived in buses. A

Continued on Page 11, Column 3

ALLIES IN ACCORD

Strong Stand Backed as West Appraises Soviet Position

Transcript of news conference and summary, Page 16.

By W. H. LAWRENCE

Special to The New York Times.

WASHINGTON, Feb. 15—President Kennedy pledged tonight that the United States would defend the Charter of the United Nations by opposing any attempt by any Government to intervene unilaterally in the Congo.

The President declared at a nationally televised news conference that massive, unilateral intervention by any country would bring with it "risks of war."

He did not mention the Soviet Union, but it was obvious his statement was directed to the Soviet leadership in the light of its newest attack on the United Nations operation in the Congo and on Secretary General Dag Hammarskjold.

President Kennedy spoke in cautious diplomatic language, but a solemn and careful appraisal of the situation was made here with the principal Western allies before he spoke.

Decision Is Reached

This produced agreement that a strong position was necessary and strategically possible since the Western allies are closer to the Congo than the Soviet Union. Accordingly a decision was reached to speak out at once in the hope of deterring the Soviet Union from intervening unilaterally.

The President declared he was "seriously concerned at what appears to be a threat of unilateral intervention in the internal affairs of the Republic of the Congo."

"I find it difficult to believe," he added, "that any Government is really planning to take so dangerous and irresponsible a step."

Then he made clear his intention to defend the United Nations authority in the Congo and his belief that the only legitimate government for that country was that of President Joseph Kasavubu.

Nehru's Stand Endorsed

President Kennedy endorsed his strong agreement with India's Prime Minister Jawaharlal Nehru, that it would be "a disaster" if the United Nations left the Congo.

The overriding concern of the half-hour news conference, held in the auditorium of the new State Department building, was the deepening crisis in the Congo and the threat posed to the United Nations by yesterday's declaration by the Soviet Union that it no longer would recognize Mr. Hammarskjold or the Kasavubu Government with which the United Nations has been dealing.

President Kennedy discussed the Congo with a carefully drafted statement he read be-

Continued on Page 10, Column 8

Nehru Offering U.N. Congo Combat Force

Special to The New York Times.

NEW DELHI, India, Feb. 15—India has offered to send "combat" troops to assist the United Nations command in the Congo.

Prime Minister Jawaharlal Nehru told Parliament today that the offer had been made in response to a request from the world body some weeks ago. He said a reply had been sent saying that India believed the United Nations should continue to function in the Congo, but that it should be made more effective.

If that could be done, Mr. Nehru said, "we would get over our reluctance and help the United Nations even by sending some combat troops." India now has some troops in the Congo. She has described these as noncombatant personnel.

Mr. Nehru said the reply had

Continued on Page 11, Column 6

Reds Virtually Lift Berlin Entry Curbs

Special to The New York Times.

BERLIN, Feb. 15—East Germany announced today a virtual lifting of restrictions on the entry of West Germans into East Berlin.

The announcement, from Communist police headquarters, said that effective at midnight tonight it would "simplify and ease" the regulations under which West Germans have been required since last fall to obtain special permits to enter East Berlin.

High-ranking sources in West Berlin said the Communists in effect had agreed to lift their ban under the impact of West German threats to take sharp measures of reprisal. These sources said the East German announcement was phrased so as to allow the Communists to "save face."

Dr. Kurt Leopold, West Ger-

Continued on Page 2, Column 7

ON FATAL FLIGHT: Members of U. S. figure-skating team at Idlewild Tuesday before departure for Brussels. Front row, from left: Deane McMinn, coach; Laurence Owen, Stephanie Westerfield and Rhode Michelson. Others, bottom to top, from left: Douglas Ramsey, Gregory Kelley, Bradley Lord, Maribel Owen, Dudley S. Richards, William H. Hickox, Ray Hadley, Laurice Hickox, Dallas Pierce, Ila Hadley, Roger Campbell, Diane Sherbloom, Donna Lee Carrier, Robert Dineen and Patricia Dineen. Plane was Sabena jet.

Associated Press

U. S. Backs 3d Loan For New Haven Line

By ROBERT E. BEDINGFIELD

The New York, New Haven and Hartford Railroad will be able to meet its $1,500,000 payroll tomorrow, thanks to another lifeline tossed to it by the Federal Government.

The Interstate Commerce Commission agreed yesterday to guarantee a $3,500,000 unsecured bank loan that the carrier said it needed to meet immediate obligations and avert bankruptcy. The railroad had asked for a guarantee of a $5,000,000 loan, but the commission scaled down the amount.

The New Haven is obtaining the loan from a group of banks headed by the Chase Manhattan. The loan carries a 5 per cent interest rate and matures Nov. 3. The Interstate Commerce Commission has guaranteed payment of both interest and principal to the lenders under the

Continued on Page 34, Column 2

"All the News That's Fit to Print."

The New York Times.

LATE CITY EDITION

U. S. Weather Bureau Report (Page 84) forecasts: Mostly fair, mild today and tonight. Some cloudiness, mild tomorrow. Temp. range: 55—35; yesterday: 40—33.

VOL. CX..No. 37,658. © 1961 by The New York Times Company. Times Square, New York 36, N. Y. NEW YORK, THURSDAY, MARCH 2, 1961. 10 cents beyond 50-mile zone from New York City except on Long Island. Higher in air delivery cities. FIVE CENTS

EXTENSION OF AID TO JOBLESS VOTED BY HOUSE, 392-30

Parties Join on Payroll-Tax Plan That Will Provide 13 Additional Weeks

SENATE IS READY TO ACT

Hearings on Minimum Wage Continue—G.O.P. Critical of Proposal's Scope

By TOM WICKER

Special to The New York Times.

WASHINGTON, March 1 — Both parties joined today in the House of Representatives to give quick passage to President Kennedy's plan to extend unemployment compensation.

It was the first major bill to be passed by either house in the Eighty-seventh Congress.

The vote was 392 to 30, with twenty-eight Republicans and two Democrats in opposition. Voting for it were 248 Democrats and 144 Republicans.

The measure would provide up to thirteen weeks of extra unemployment benefits for workers who have used up their regular payments from state plans. For that purpose it provides that $927,000,000 be raised by a two-year increase of four-tenths of 1 per cent in the Federal unemployment tax on employers.

Added Sum Provided

An additional sum of $63,000,000 would be provided from Federal revenues for out-of-work former Federal employes and former service men.

Debate was desultory and required only two hours and sixteen minutes. A half-hour of that time was devoted to discussing the rule against amendments under which the bill was being considered.

Representative Wilbur D. Mills of Arkansas, the Democratic chairman of the Ways and Means Committee, said he understood the Senate Finance Committee would open hearings on the bill Monday.

However, Senator Harry F. Byrd, Democrat of Virginia and chairman of the Senate committee, said he expected to start hearings the middle of next week, although the committee might take up the measure as early as Tuesday.

Mr. Mills told the House he hoped it could be on the President's desk, ready for signature, by March 15. In that event, he said, payments can begin in many cases on April 1.

Meanwhile, hearings on the

Continued on Page 13, Column 1

Federal Order to Tighten Ban on Job Discrimination

Kennedy Says He Will Act in a 'Few' Days—Reorganization Is Expected for 2 Government Committees

By ANTHONY LEWIS

Special to The New York Times.

WASHINGTON, March 1—The Administration will move soon to stiffen enforcement of the policy against racial discrimination in hiring by the Government or its contractors.

President Kennedy told his news conference today that he hoped to issue an executive order "in the next few days." He said the order would "strengthen the employment opportunities, both in and out of the Government, for all Americans." [Question 5, Page 12.]

The executive order, it was learned, will reorganize two committees set up by President Eisenhower to deal with job discrimination.

One of these, the Committee on Government Contracts, has worked for the hiring of Negroes by companies doing business with the Government. The other, working inside the Government itself, is the Committee on Government Employment Policy.

If present Administration plans prevail, the Kennedy order will combine the two committees. The feeling is that putting authority in one place will be more effective.

The language of the Eisenhower executive orders setting up the programs against discrimination in hiring will also be clarified and strengthened.

The Committee on Government Contracts has no enforcement powers itself. If a contractor violates his pledge not to discriminate in hiring, the committee can do nothing.

The committee can ask the contracting agency of the Government—for example the Defense Department—to cancel the contract. But no contract ever has been canceled. Or the committee could ask the Justice

Continued on Page 14, Column 7

PENTAGON STUDY ASKS A BUILD-UP OF ALL DEFENSES

President Says It Proposes More Conventional Arms—He Denies Policy Shift

By JACK RAYMOND

Special to The New York Times.

WASHINGTON, March 1 — The Pentagon has completed a reappraisal of defense strategy and has recommended a "general strengthening of our armed forces," President Kennedy said at his news conference today.

The President said the recommendations prepared for him by Secretary of Defense Robert S. McNamara included proposals to augment conventional military forces. [Question 1, Page 12.]

However, no decision has been reached that would indicate a shift in the United States policy of reliance on nuclear weapons, Mr. Kennedy declared. [Question 25.]

At the same time, he expressed hope for an agreement with the Soviet Union on a ban on nuclear-weapons testing when talks are resumed in Geneva March 21. [Question 14.]

Over-All Problem Knottier

Over-all disarmament, he said, is a knottier problem that requires preparations at least until this summer before the Administration's policy position is developed.

Meanwhile, John J. McCloy, his disarmament adviser, is working on a proposal to establish a permanent, well-staffed disarmament agency under the direction of the White House or the State Department, the President disclosed. [Question 16.]

The questioning of President Kennedy on defense policies was prompted by an article in The Washington Star, which was officially characterized as "inaccurate." The article purported to reveal the contents of a memorandum prepared for Secretary McNamara by Secretary of State Dean Rusk.

Would Alter NATO Stand

According to the report in The Star, Secretary Rusk proposed abandoning nuclear retaliation as a means of coping with various forms of hostilities, including a "massive attack" on Europe.

Such a policy, if adopted, would alter the standing policy of the North Atlantic Treaty Organization, which authorizes the use of nuclear weapons, if necessary, to meet any form of Soviet military aggression in Europe.

The President said the "gist" of the Secretary's memorandum was a desire to "see conventional forces strengthened, not only in Western Europe, but throughout the world."

Secretary Rusk testified on the subject at a closed meeting of the Senate Foreign Relations Committee yesterday, but he made it clear that he did not

Continued on Page 12, Column 2

Recruits Flocking to Join Corps

Rafer Johnson Asks to Serve—Work by Staff Is Heavy

By DAVID HALBERSTAM

Special to The New York Times.

WASHINGTON, March 1 — Rafer Johnson, the Olympic decathlon champion, has volunteered to join the Peace Corps announced today by President Kennedy.

Forrest Evashevski, former football coach at the University of Iowa and once a noted blocking back at the University of Michigan, will soon take a job at the headquarters of the corps in Washington.

Sally Bowles, daughter of Under Secretary of State Chester Bowles, and Nancy Gore, daughter of Senator Albert Gore of Tennessee, are already at work at corps headquarters.

Today, within an hour or two after President Kennedy had announced the establishment of the Peace Corps on a pilot basis, the switchboard at headquarters could not handle the calls from volunteers and inquirers.

The response to the idea of a voluntary organization in which American men and women could help the developing countries of the world has exceeded all expectations.

President Kennedy is reported to have received more letters about the peace corps than about any other issue — some 6,000 letters of suggestion, inquiry and open application. None mentions salary.

Ed Bayley, who is serving temporarily as public relations director for the corps, said that "not only do we get letters from young people who want to

Continued on Page 13, Column 1

Forrest Evashevski

Associated Press

Rafer Johnson

Sally Bowles

Associated Press

Nancy Gore

KENNEDY SETS UP U. S. PEACE CORPS TO WORK ABROAD

Creates Pilot Plan and Asks Congress to Establish a Permanent Operation

RECRUITS TO GET NO PAY

President Aims to Have 500 on Job by the End of '61—Training Will Be Pushed

Transcript of news conference, Page 12; message, 13.

By PETER BRAESTRUP

Special to The New York Times.

WASHINGTON, March 1 — President Kennedy issued an executive order today creating a Peace Corps. It will enlist American men and women for voluntary, unpaid service in the developing countries of the world.

The order set up the Peace Corps on a "temporary pilot basis." President Kennedy also sent Congress a message requesting legislation to make the corps permanent.

Announcing the move at his news conference, the President described the Peace Corps as a "pool of trained American men and women sent overseas by the United States Government or through private organizations and institutions to help foreign governments meet their urgent needs for skilled manpower."

The President's expressed hope was to have 500 to 1,000 Peace Corps workers "in the field by the end of this year."

Shriver Heads Planners

The Administration's planning effort on the Peace Corps has been headed since late January by R. Sargent Shriver, a Chicago business man and civic leader who is the President's brother-in-law. The President said today that a decision on who would head the agency would be made "in several days." [Question 4, Page 12.]

Life in the Peace Corps, the President stressed, "will not be easy." Members will work without pay but they will be given living allowances. They will live at the same level as the inhabitants of the countries to which they are sent.

The President emphasized that "we will send Americans abroad who are qualified to do a job," particularly those with technical skills in teaching, agriculture and health.

"There is little doubt," the President said in his subsequent message to Congress, "that the number of those who wish to serve will be far greater than our capacity to absorb them."

President Kennedy first broached his version of the Peace Corps idea in a campaign speech at San Francisco last Nov. 2. Previously, Senator Hubert H. Humphrey, Democrat of

Continued on Page 13, Column 7

KENNEDY INSISTS ON ECONOMIC AIDS

Finds No Upward Move Now —Says All Measures in Program Are Needed

By RICHARD E. MOONEY

Special to The New York Times.

WASHINGTON, March 1—President Kennedy said today it would be "premature to make a judgment that our economy is on the rise."

Citing reports of continued heavy unemployment and "most serious" situations in various sections, he emphasized at his news conference that all the economic programs he had submitted to Congress were needed.

He expressed hope that "we will see the economy move up in the spring and summer," but said that predictions could not be made now. [Question 2, Page 12.]

Leading Government economists have refrained from making predictions, but have noted trends that may be signals of better times. These are the stock-market boom, rising prices for industrial materials and a diminished rate of inventory reduction by manufacturers.

Higher Peaks Sought

The Administration is not just directing its efforts at turning the economy upward, however. It believes that activity was not high enough even when it was highest last spring. Its programs, therefore, are aimed at recovery and then higher peaks of business activity.

Mr. Kennedy touched on two other economic matters:

¶He revealed "with some satisfaction" that the gold supply held steady the last week for the first time since last July. It is $17,372,500,000, compared with $19,200,000,000 then. Some experts believe there has even been an inflow lately.

¶He said he would send his Budget Message to Congress March 23. It will include proposals for matching his spending requests with revenues to pay for them.

The President opened his con-

Continued on Page 12, Column 5

SCREVANE NAMED AS DEPUTY MAYOR

Sanitation Chief Succeeding O'Keefe, Who Resigns to Return to Business

By CHARLES G. BENNETT

Sanitation Commissioner Paul R. Screvane was named Deputy Mayor by Mayor Wagner yesterday.

He will succeed Paul T. O'Keefe, who resigned yesterday after more than two years in the office. Mr. O'Keefe will resume his former association with the real estate concern of James Felt & Co.

The post of Deputy Mayor pays the same as that of Sanitation Commissioner, $25,000 a year.

Mr. Screvane, who is 46 years old and a career man in city government, will take over as Deputy Mayor tomorrow after being sworn in by Mayor Wagner at City Hall at 10:30 A. M. His headquarters, now 125 Worth Street, will be in City Hall's west wing, next to Mayor Wagner's office.

Mayor Wagner said he would announce a new Sanitation Commissioner tomorrow morning before he swore in Mr. Screvane as Deputy Mayor.

The Sanitation Commissionership is expected to go to 49-year-old Frank J. Lucia, Chief of Staff of the operations division of the Sanitation Department, who, like his chief, is a career man in city service.

Mayor Wagner announced also that he had "worked out

Continued on Page 31, Column 2

FRANCE RESTRICTS ARMY IN ALGERIA

Political and Police Powers Cut—Leaders at Rabat Urge Peace Efforts

By ROBERT C. DOTY

Special to The New York Times.

PARIS, March 1—The French Government took steps today to reduce the political and police power of the French Army in Algeria as a new effort began to end the rebellion there by negotiation.

Limitation of the role of the French Army has been a principal demand of the rebel Provisional Government. The Cabinet action was interpreted as a conciliatory gesture to encourage the rebels to negotiate an end to the rebellion, now in its seventh year.

[King Hassan II of Morocco, President Habib Bourguiba of Tunisia and leaders of the Algerian nationalist rebel regime, conferring in Rabat, issued a statement early Thursday calling for "direct negotiation between the French Government and the Algerian Provisional Government in the framework of total decolonization."]

The French Cabinet approved a series of decrees proposed by Louis Joxe, Minister for Algeria.

One ended the arbitrary power of the military to order administrative detention of suspected Moslem nationalists without formal charges. Henceforth detention orders must be approved by civil authorities.

Continued on Page 6, Column 2

President Backs Williams On 'Africa for Africans'

By W. H. LAWRENCE

Special to The New York Times.

WASHINGTON, March 1—President Kennedy said today that Africa should belong to the people who feel they are Africans. Backing up the controversial "Africa for the Africans" statement of G. Mennen Williams, Assistant Secretary of State for African Affairs, the President said with emphasis at his news conference: "I do not know who else Africa should be for." [Question 12, Page 12.]

Like Mr. Williams, a former Governor of Michigan who is on his first diplomatic assignment abroad, the President recognized as Africans "all those who felt that they were Africans, whatever their color might be, whatever their race might be."

By this definition, he appeared to exclude those African residents who still felt they were more British, French, Belgian or Portuguese than they were African.

Anti-Colonial Tone Noted

The President's statement thus seemed to have a more clearly anti-colonial ring than most United States Government statements of the past.

Mr. Williams' remark was made Feb. 20 when he arrived in Nairobi, Kenya, on his tour of African nations. He said the United States backed the theory of "Africa for the Africans."

He said later that by "Africans" he meant all who have made their homes in Africa, including Europeans and Asians.

President Kennedy expressed his support of Mr. Williams at a crowded news conference of 358 reporters, broadcast later

Continued on Page 4, Column 5

ADENAUER TO SEE KENNEDY IN APRIL

Accepts His Invitation for 12th and 13th—President Firm on Bonn Aid Pledge

By E. W. KENWORTHY

Special to The New York Times.

WASHINGTON, March 1 — President Kennedy announced at his news conference today that Chancellor Adenauer had accepted his invitation to visit Washington April 12 and 13.

The West German leader's visit will come just a week after that of Prime Minister Macmillan. The State Department said that it had no information yet on what officials would accompany the 85-year-old Chancellor.

Mr. Kennedy's talks with Dr. Adenauer will cover the whole range of problems facing the North Atlantic alliance, including the question of "equitable shares" in the common defense burden and aid to less-developed nations.

Clear Acceptance Seen

Officials here indicated that the President would certainly raise again the principle of "systematic budgetary contributions" for foreign aid by West Germany—a principle that the Administration assumed the Bonn Government had accepted as a result of the talks here two weeks ago with Dr. Heinrich von Brentano, the West German Foreign Minister.

At his news conference today President Kennedy said that the West German Government then "clearly accepted" the responsibility of making aid to under-developed nations available "on a continuing basis."

The question of how much West Germany would do, the President said, is a matter for the Bonn Government to determine and a subject for discussion.

Continued on Page 2, Column 6

CATHOLIC BISHOPS MAP SCHOOL FIGHT

Prelates Confer on How to Resist Kennedy Aid Plan

By JOHN D. MORRIS

Special to The New York Times.

WASHINGTON, March 1 — The highest United States prelates of the Roman Catholic Church met here today to plan what is expected to be a vigorous fight against President Kennedy's school-aid program.

The churchmen sat as the administrative board of the National Catholic Welfare Conference. The board consists of the five United States Cardinals and ten Bishops and Archbishops who head departments of the conference.

The unpublicized one-day session coincided with a new statement by President Kennedy opposing Federal aid to parochial or other sectarian schools at the elementary and secondary level.

"There isn't any room for debate on that subject," the President said at his news conference. "It is prohibited by the Constitution, and the Supreme Court has made that very clear. Therefore there would be no possibility of our recommending it." [Question 23 Page 12.]

Officials of the Catholic conference declined to discuss any aspect of the board's meeting. A spokesman would not even confirm reports that the prelates had convened.

From other sources, it was learned that the regular annual session, usually held at Easter, had been moved ahead a month because of the pressing nature of the school-aid question.

Indications were that the prelates had drafted a "Catholic position" on the issue, which

Continued on Page 14, Column 2

Building of Schools Under Inquiry Here

By LEONARD BUDER

Investigations by the state and the city are being made into the operations of the Board of Education's multi-million-dollar school construction program.

The separate inquiries are being conducted by the State Investigation Commission and the City Department of Investigation. They are reported to be centering on possible irregularities in the award of school-building contracts and in the inspection of work performed by private concerns for the school board.

Among the matters known to be under investigation, it was learned yesterday, are these:

¶Whether political considerations and possible kickbacks and pay-offs have resulted in preferential treatment for certain con-

Continued on Page 18, Column 4

Return of Eisenhower's 5 Stars Given Support by the President

Krpm Taronis from Magnum

Former President Eisenhower in 1951 during his final military assignment as Supreme Commander of military forces of North Atlantic Treaty Organization. Inset shows how he preferred to wear stars of General of the Army.

Special to The New York Times.

WASHINGTON, March 1—President Kennedy gave his official backing today to legislation to restore the lifetime rank of General of the Army to former President Dwight D. Eisenhower.

He told his news conference that he had conveyed his backing for the five-star rank in letters to the chairmen of the Senate and House Armed Services Committees. They are Senator Richard B. Russell and Representative Carl M. Vinson, both Georgia Democrats.

Mr. Kennedy said that the former President's "outstanding military record and his long public service to our country in war and peace" made it appropriate that Congress restore the rank to him. [Opening statement, Page 12.]

Mr. Eisenhower resigned his rank in 1952 when he was nomi-

Continued on Page 14, Column 3

Negroes Say Conditions in U. S. Explain Nationalists' Militancy

Following is the second of two articles on extremist groups seeking to rouse American Negroes to a more militant attitude in their efforts to obtain equality.

By ROBERT L. TEAGUE

"Mere crumbs from the tables of an abundant society have made millions of black men angry. That's why there was a riot at the U. N. the other day, and why the black nationalist movement is growing and becoming more militant in New York and everywhere else."

These are the words of James Lawson, president of the United African Nationalist Movement, who was one of forty-three persons interviewed last week on black nationalism.

The forty-three, nearly all Harlem Negroes, echoed Mr. Lawson's analysis again and again. But as to specific goals and the way to seek them, there is a diversity of opinion. However, none advocated violence, "except in self-defense."

As an example of how far the opinions range, the Black Muslims are opposed to integration. They say they will settle for nothing less than a separate sovereign state.

The Muslim aims were described by the leader of Temple of Islam No. 7 on 116th Street. He is called Minister Malcolm X.

At a Lenox Avenue restaurant, one of several businesses owned and operated by Muslims, Minister Malcolm explained the "X." He said: "All who follow Mr. [Elijah] Mu-

Continued on Page 17, Column 1

HOUSE VOTES FUND FOR RED INQUIRIES

Backs Unit on Un-American Activities by 412 to 6

By United Press International.

WASHINGTON, March 1 —The House of Representatives, in an endorsement of its Committee on Un-American Activities, gave the investigating group $331,000 today to carry on its work in the current year. The vote was 412 to 6 for the appropriation.

The action followed an exchange in which the committee chairman, Francis E. Walter, charged that Representative James Roosevelt apparently did not share the view that communism was evil and un-American.

Mr. Roosevelt, Democrat of California, had charged in the Congressional Record that the committee was "a bad institution, which has tended to grow worse in its depredations on our liberties as well as on our democratic reputation in the world."

Mr. Walter, Democrat of Pennsylvania, discussing Mr. Roosevelt's statement, told the House:

"I was staggered at the extent to which it was based on faulty reasoning, distortion, falsehood and total failure to comprehend even remotely the nature of communism.

"The only way I can interpret

Continued on Page 8, Column 3

NEWS INDEX

Sophia Loren and Eleanora Brown starred in Vittorio DeSica's *Two Women.* Loren won an Oscar for her performance.

James Darren, Stanley Baker, David Niven, Gregory Peck, Anthony Quinn, and Anthony Quail in *Guns of Navarone.*

George Chakiris was the leader of "The Sharks" in *West Side Story*, a modern version of Shakespeare's love-story, *Romeo and Juliet.*

"All the News That's Fit to Print"

The New York Times.

LATE CITY EDITION
U. S. Weather Bureau Report (Page 74) forecasts:
Mostly fair today.
Fair tonight and tomorrow.
Temp. range: 56—42; yesterday: 55—42.

VOL. CX..No. 37,705. NEW YORK, TUESDAY, APRIL 18, 1961. 10 cents beyond 50-mile zone from New York City except on Long Island. Higher in air delivery cities. FIVE CENTS

ANTI-CASTRO UNITS LAND IN CUBA; REPORT FIGHTING AT BEACHHEAD; RUSK SAYS U. S. WON'T INTERVENE

CARIBBEAN STRIFE: Rebel forces attacking Cuba landed in Las Villas Province in the area of Bahia de Cochinos (1, and A on the inset map). Other anti-Castro landings were said to have taken place in area of Santiago de Cuba (2) and in Pinar del Rio (3).

The New York Times April 18, 1961

PREMIER DEFIANT

Says His Troops Battle Heroically to Repel Attacking Force

The texts of Castro appeals are printed on Page 14.

By TAD SZULC
Special to The New York Times.

MIAMI, Tuesday, April 18—Rebel troops opposed to Premier Fidel Castro landed before dawn yesterday on the swampy southern coast of Cuba in Las Villas Province.

The attack, which was supported from the air, was announced by the rebels and confirmed by the Cuban Government.

After fourteen hours of silence on the progress of the assault, the Government radio in Havana broadcast early today a terse communiqué signed by Premier Castro announcing only that "our armed forces are continuing to fight the enemy heroically."

The announcement, made shortly before 1 A. M., said that within the next few hours details of "our successes" would be given.

The communiqué came amid a wave of rebel assertions of victories, new landings and internal uprisings. The rebel spokesmen were acclaiming important progress in new landings in Oriente and Pinar del Rio Provinces, but none of these reports could be confirmed.

Government Reports Battle

The Government communiqué said a battle had been fought in the southeastern part of Las Villas Province, where yesterday morning's landings occurred.

Although the communiqué was signed by Premier Castro, the Cuban leader has not spoken to his nation since the attack began. An earlier communiqué, issued yesterday, reported the rebel landings.

In a communiqué issued last night, the Revolutionary Council, the top command of the rebel forces, said merely that military supplies and equipment were landed successfully on the marshy beachhead. The communiqué added that "some armed resistance" by supporters of Premier Castro had been overcome.

Premier Castro was reported to have escaped injury in an early-morning air raid yesterday near the beachhead.

The Revolutionary Council's announcement spoke of action in Matanzas Province, indicating that the rebels might have

Continued on Page 14, Column 1

Rusk Declares Sympathy Of Nation for Castro Foes

By JAMES RESTON
Special to The New York Times.

WASHINGTON, April 17—Secretary of State Dean Rusk expressed today the sympathy of the American people for those who struck against Castroism in Cuba, but emphasized "there is not and will not be any intervention there by United States forces."

The Administration did not deny that it was giving material support to the raiding parties, but this aid was undoubtedly on a much smaller

Transcript of Rusk's news conference is on Page 18.

scale than originally planned here and the landings in Cuba were much smaller than excited reports of "invasion" suggested.

No more than 200 to 300 men were involved in the week-end landings on the vast coastline of Cuba, according to reliable information reaching here.

In fact, the landings of the last forty-eight hours were not designed to get a lot of fighting men on the ground, but to provide supplies for the anti-Castro underground already operating there as a result of at least six other landings that have taken place over the last few months.

Refugees Assume Control

In the last ten days, the Cuban refugees have assumed control of the operations against Premier Fidel Castro. Accordingly, official Washington could not be sure of the fate of all the small parties that went ashore.

Secretary Rusk was extremely cautious in his remarks on the situation at his news conference this morning. What happens in Cuba, he said, is for the Cuban people to decide. He added, however, that the Administration was "not indifferent" to the intrusion of the "Communist conspiracy" into this hemisphere and promised to "work together with other governments of this hemisphere to meet efforts by this conspiracy to extend its penetration." [Opening statement, Page 18.]

On this point, considerable attention was being paid here

Continued on Page 18, Column 1

MOSCOW BLAMES U. S. FOR ATTACK

Izvestia Asserts 'American Hirelings' Invade Cuba—Khrushchev Confers

By SEYMOUR TOPPING
Special to The New York Times.

MOSCOW, April 17—The Soviet Union charged tonight that the United States was responsible for the landing in Cuba by what it described as "American hirelings."

Izvestia, the Soviet Government newspaper, contended that plans for landing anti-Castro forces in Cuba had been worked out and inspired by "American imperialists."

"On all continents voices now are crying out determinedly for an end to the armed aggression against Cuba and for the defense of the freedom and independence of the Cuban people," Izvestia said.

At his vacation retreat in Sochi on the Black Sea, Premier Khrushchev conferred on the Cuban crisis with Foreign Minister Andrei A. Gromyko. A formal Government statement is expected tomorrow.

Atmosphere Is Tense

An atmosphere of tension gripped the Soviet capital after the announcement at 4 P. M. by the Moscow radio that "an armed intervention against Cuba had begun."

It was felt by most Western experts that the Soviet reaction would be confined to strong diplomatic representations, complaints in the United Nations and a propaganda onslaught against the United States.

Some observers recalled that in a speech here July 10, Mr. Khrushchev had declared: "Figuratively speaking, if need be, Soviet artillerymen can support the Cuban people with their rocket fire, should the aggressive forces in the Pentagon dare to start intervention against Cuba."

The Soviet leader also had noted that the United States was no longer out of range of Soviet missiles.

Western experts said that Mr. Khrushchev's statement seemed to have more applicability to an invasion of Cuba by United States forces than to an attack of the type being under-

Continued on Page 17, Column 2

ROA CHARGES U.S. ARMED INVADERS

Tells U.N. That C.I.A. Aided Attacks—'Aggression' Is Denied by Stevenson

Excerpts from Stevenson and Roa statements, Page 16.

By THOMAS J. HAMILTON
Special to The New York Times.

UNITED NATIONS, N. Y., April 17—Dr. Raul Roa, Foreign Minister of Cuba, charged today that his country had been invaded this morning "by a force of mercenaries, organized, financed and armed by the Government of the United States."

Dr. Roa told the General Assembly's Political Committee that the attack had been launched from points in Florida and Guatemala under the direction of the Central Intelligence Agency, which he called the "Gestapo." The Gestapo was the Nazi security police force.

He continued to use terms made familiar to nazism by calling Dr. José Miró Cardona, head of the anti-Castro Cuban Revolutionary Council, the "gauleiter." Gauleiters were regional party leaders under the Nazis.

Florida Launching Denied

Adlai E. Stevenson, chief United States delegate, said in reply that "the United States has committed no aggression against Cuba and no offensive has been launched from Florida or from any other part of the United States."

[In Guatemala, the Government denied that it had participated in any attack on Cuba.]

Just before the debate ended late this evening Dr. Roa charged that two jet planes from a United States carrier had escorted a Cuban rebel plane to safety this afternoon. He also alleged that forces from the United States Naval Base at Guantanamo had entered Oriente Province, where

Continued on Page 17, Column 1

Walker Is Relieved of Command While Army Checks Birch Ties

Special to The New York Times.

WASHINGTON, April 17—The Army said today that Maj. Gen. Edwin A. Walker had been relieved of his command in Germany while an investigation was made into reports that he had been indoctrinating his troops with the views of the John Birch Society.

The announcement said that Secretary of the Army Elvis J. Stahr Jr. had ordered General Walker transferred immediately from command of the front-line Twenty-fourth Division "pending the outcome of an official investigation."

The investigation will involve "certain published statements and actions of General Walker," the Army said.

General Walker was ordered transferred to the headquarters of the United States Army in Europe at Heidelberg, Germany, the Army said.

The announcement did not mention the Birch Society. However, officials acknowledged that the transfer and investigation had been prompted by allegations that the 51-year-old general had been urging the views of the Right-Wing group upon his troops for the last six months.

The Overseas Weekly, a privately owned newspaper distributed among American troops in Europe, reported last week that General Walker had instituted a special troop-indoctrination program using materials and publications of the society.

General Walker accused the newspaper yesterday of being "immoral, unscrupulous, corrupt and destructive." The newspaper stood by its original report and said that its charges

Continued on Page 24, Column 6

CHANTING CUBANS BACK CASTRO HERE

1,000 in Midtown March Dispersed by Police

Nearly 1,000 chanting, sign-bearing pro-Castro Cubans demonstrated last night outside the United Nations and the United States Mission to the United Nations and in the Times Square area.

Heavy police details had kept the crowds behind barriers most of the day and no violence erupted until a smaller group of pro-Castro Cubans blocked pedestrian traffic in Times Square. The police made two arrests and two policemen were injured during a brief scuffle with the demonstrators.

Many of the demonstrators carried Cuban flags and pictures of Dr. Castro as they marched from the United Nations Plaza along Forty-second Street to the corner of Eighth Avenue and Forty-third Street.

An emergency police signal brought ten radio cars and ten mounted policemen to that area. The crowd then broke up into four factions and departed in different directions.

A few minutes later, at 8 P. M., a smaller group of demonstrators formed on the sidewalk on Broadway between

Continued on Page 14, Column 5

NEWS INDEX

SUPREME COURT UPHOLDS UNIONS AGAINST N. L. R. B.

It Upsets Board's Ruling That Contracts Illegally Force Membership

MAILERS' PACTS BACKED

New York Printers' Local and California Teamsters Win on Agreements

By ANTHONY LEWIS
Special to The New York Times.

WASHINGTON, April 17—A series of decisions by the National Labor Relations Board designed to prevent the compelling of union membership was struck down today by the Supreme Court.

The court disposed of a group of major labor cases that will affect dozens of others pending in the lower courts and before the labor relations board. The court did the following things in its principal rulings:

¶It upheld, 6 to 2, contracts of the International Typographical Union with newspapers that provided that the foreman of the composing room or mail room must be an I. T. U. member and must handle all hiring in his operation.

¶By the same vote, it upheld a provision in I. T. U. contracts that made the I. T. U. "general laws" applicable unless in conflict with Federal or state laws.

¶By the same vote, it held there was nothing illegal in bargaining agreements that provided that casual workers, both union and nonunion, be hired through a union-operated hiring hall.

¶It killed, 7 to 1, an N. L. R. B. ruling making labor and management refund to employes all union dues collected under an agreement found to constitute an illegal closed shop.

Douglas Writes Opinion

Justice William O. Douglas wrote the opinion of the court in all the cases. There was an eight-man court because Justice Felix Frankfurter took no part in the decisions.

Two cases settled long disputes over standard contracts sought by the typographical union. The first of these involved the New York Mailers' Union 6, which is affiliated with the I. T. U., and The New York Daily News and The Wall Street Journal.

The contract specified that mail room foremen must be members of the I. T. U. and must do the hiring. The N. L. R. B. had ruled that the foremen clause was a coercive device to make sure that only union members were hired and that it was thus a violation of the Taft-Hartley Law.

Justice Douglas wrote today that first, the contract said no foreman should be disciplined by the union for carrying out the publisher's instructions, and he concluded that the foreman remained the employer's agent despite his union membership.

Second, Justice Douglas said, the court would "not assume" that the foremen clause would produce discrimination in favor of union members in the absence of actual proof of discrimination.

The N. L. R. B. was thus left free to bring a case to show that

Continued on Page 27, Column 3

Jersey Votes Today In Primary Election

By GEORGE CABLE WRIGHT
Special to The New York Times.

TRENTON, April 17 — New Jersey residents will nominate major party candidates for Governor tomorrow, along with candidates for ten of twenty-one State Senate seats and for all sixty seats in the Assembly.

Also at stake will be the nominations for a number of county and local posts.

The polls will open at 7 A. M. and close at 8 P. M.

Interest will center on the balloting for the Republican nomination for Governor. A bitter three-way contest for the nomination came to a close tonight with television and radio appeals by the participants.

They are James P. Mitchell, the former Secretary of Labor, and State Senators Walter H. Jones of Bergen County and

Continued on Page 38, Column 1

U. S. Finds Soviet's Reply On Laos Is Unsatisfactory

Rusk Says Note Is Unclear on Timing and Verification of Cease-Fire—Calls Issue 'Very Critical'

By E. W. KENWORTHY
Special to The New York Times.

WASHINGTON, April 17—Secretary of State Dean Rusk said today that the new Soviet note on Laos did not satisfy the United States on the timing and verification of a cease-fire.

This, Mr. Rusk said at his news conference, is a "very critical matter" in any attempt to bring "the situation to a peaceful and satisfactory conclusion." [Introductory statement, Page 18.]

The Soviet note "clarifying" Moscow's first reply to the British proposals of March 23 was delivered to Sir Frank Roberts, the British Ambassador, yesterday. The British Embassy informed Mr. Rusk of the contents of the reply last night.

The British had proposed a three-step procedure—a call for a cease-fire by Britain and the Soviet Union, the co-chairmen of the 1954 Geneva Conference that brought the Indochinese war to an end; verification of the cease-fire by the three-nation International Control Commission, which observed the carrying out of the Geneva accord in Laos, and a fourteen-nation conference to set up a neutral, independent Laotian Government.

It was the British intention that these steps should take place in quick order. But Britain and the United States had made clear that there could be no conference until a cease-fire was in effect.

In one respect the Soviet note represented an advance over the earlier response, according to informed sources here. Previously Moscow had indicated that the cease-fire and the conference must take place simultaneously—or very nearly so.

In yesterday's note, these

Continued on Page 2, Column 3

HIGH COURT VOIDS CAFE'S NEGRO BAN

Holds Private Restaurant on State Land in Delaware Cannot Refuse Service

Special to The New York Times.

WASHINGTON, April 17—The Supreme Court held today that a privately operated restaurant situated in a publicly owned parking garage in Wilmington, Del., could not refuse to serve Negroes.

Six justices agreed on that result. The three others thought the case should have been sent back to the Delaware Supreme Court for clarification of its views on state law.

The decision is a significant one because of the light it throws on the established doctrine that only "official action" is covered by the Fourteenth Amendment. The Constitution does not prohibit racial discrimination by private persons or enterprises.

The court concluded that the Government of Delaware was sufficiently involved in this private enterprise, the restaurant, to bring it under the Constitution. In the view of observers here, the court broke at least some new ground in reaching that conclusion.

Justice Tom C. Clark wrote the opinion of the court. He was joined by Chief Justice Earl Warren and Justices Hugo L. Black, William O. Douglas and William J. Brennan Jr.

A separate concurring opinion, resting on quite different grounds, was filed by Justice Potter Stewart. Dissents suggesting that the court should

Continued on Page 26, Column 1

HAUSNER ATTACKS EICHMANN'S PLEA

Israeli Prosecutor Details His Charges After Ex-Nazi Says He Is Not Guilty

Text of decision and Hausner excerpts are on Page 23.

By HOMER BIGART
Special to The New York Times.

JERUSALEM (Israeli Sector), April 17—Attorney General Gideon Hausner began an attack today on Adolf Eichmann's plea of innocence at his trial for responsibility in the killing of millions of Jews.

Earlier in the day Eichmann lost a challenge to the court's jurisdiction and entered his not-guilty plea when the trial was resumed after the week-end recess. Eichmann's plea for a hearing on his kidnapping from Argentina was rejected by the court.

"In the sense of the indictment I am not guilty," Eichmann had told the three Israeli judges.

He made his statement of innocence in a precise but toneless voice in reply to charges that he had planned the annihilation of 6,000,000 European Jews for the Nazis during World War II.

From the qualified nature of his plea, it was clear that Eichmann's defense would be based on the contention that he was a mere cog in the machinery of genocide and that he was bound by higher orders when he delivered the Jews to death camps.

Standing rigidly erect and

Continued on Page 23, Column 7

GIZENGA OFFICERS ACCEPT MOBUTU AS ARMY'S CHIEF

Kasavubu Agrees to Reform Troops—Signs Accord on Congo-U.N. Cooperation

By HENRY TANNER
Special to The New York Times.

LEOPOLDVILLE, the Congo, April 17—Congolese Army headquarters announced tonight that field commanders operating under the control of the Leftist regime of Antoine Gizenga had recognized the authority of Maj. Gen. Joseph D. Mobutu as military commander in chief.

General Mobutu is the commander of the Central Government's forces.

The announcement said officers of the Gizenga regime had recognized General Mobutu during a conference at Bundoki, on the border of Eastern Province. The province is controlled by Mr. Gizenga.

The announcement also said a cease-fire had been ordered all along the border of Eastern and Equator Provinces.

Here in Leopoldville President Joseph Kasavubu and representatives of Secretary General Dag Hammarskjold signed an agreement on reorganization of the Congolese Army and the withdrawal of some foreign advisers.

Resolution 'Accepted'

The Congolese President and his Government "accepted" the Security Council resolution of Feb. 21 with the "understanding" that the United Nations, in implementing the resolution, respected the sovereignty of the Congo Republic.

The announcement on the military agreement did not say whether Gen. Victor Lundula, who has been commanding Mr. Gizenga's forces, took part in the conference.

Despite rumors of rivalry between him and Mr. Gizenga, General Lundula has consistently stressed his loyalty to his civilian superiors in Stanleyville, capital of Eastern Province.

General Mobutu left Leopoldville a week ago for the border area where the military conference took place. Talks between the two sides had continued intermittently for several weeks with and without his participation.

Kasavubu Plan Backed

In accepting the Security Council resolution the Leopoldville Government "recognized" the necessity for reorganizing the Congolese National Army. It reaffirmed President Kasavubu's earlier proposal that the reorganization take place with United Nations assistance, but under his personal authority as chief of state.

The agreement called for the United Nations to give assistance to the President so that "all foreign civil officials, military and paramilitary mercenaries and political advisers who have not been engaged under his authority" will be

Continued on Page 4, Column 3

Eisenhowers Are Welcomed Home to Pennsylvania

United Press International Telephoto

General and Mrs. Eisenhower in Harrisburg with Gov. David L. Lawrence of Pennsylvania

By The Associated Press.

HARRISBURG, Pa., April 17—Thousands of persons welcomed former President Dwight D. Eisenhower and Mrs. Eisenhower home to Pennsylvania today. The gathering was the state's official welcome for General Eisenhower, who left the White House Jan. 20. The former President, looking tanned and rested after a six-week vacation in California, was obviously touched. Gov. David L. Lawrence, a Democrat, headed the state and city officials on the platform. The Eisenhowers have a farm home in Gettysburg, thirty-five miles southwest of this capital city. It is the only home they have ever owned. They left for home by car after the ceremonies.

"All the News That's Fit to Print"

The New York Times.

LATE CITY EDITION
U. S. Weather Bureau Report (Page 77) forecasts: Variable cloudiness today and tonight. Mostly fair tomorrow.
Temp. range: 56—38; yesterday: 44—38.

VOL. CX..No. 37,706.

NEW YORK, WEDNESDAY, APRIL 19, 1961.

10 cents beyond 50-mile zone from New York City except on Long Island. Higher in air delivery cities.

FIVE CENTS

KENNEDY WARNS KHRUSHCHEV ON CUBA AFTER RUSSIAN VOWS HELP TO CASTRO; MIGS AND TANKS ATTACK BEACHHEAD

MITCHELL DEFEATS JONES IN JERSEY IN G.O.P. PRIMARY

Former Secretary of Labor Nominated for Governor After Running Behind

DEMOCRATS FOR HUGHES

He Beats Token Opposition —Nixon and Rockefeller to Join Campaign

By LEO EGAN

James P. Mitchell, Secretary of Labor in the Eisenhower Administration, came from behind last night to capture the Republican nomination for Governor in New Jersey.

He had trailed State Senator Walter H. Jones of Bergen County, his principal rival, until the half-way mark in the tabulation of the results in the spirited primary. Thereafter he steadily increased his lead.

With returns tabulated from 4,173 of the state's 4,396 election districts, Mr. Mitchell had 190,883 votes to 151,509 for Senator Jones.

Former Vice President Richard M. Nixon telephoned his congratulations to Mr. Mitchell at 11:30 P. M., when the victory, which had seemed wobbly earlier, was assured.

Meyner Backed Hughes

Mr. Mitchell will face former Superior Court Judge Richard J. Hughes of Trenton in the November election. Judge Hughes had only token opposition from two little-known rivals in the Democratic primary. He had the backing of Gov. Robert B. Meyner and all twenty-one of the Democratic county organizations.

Both Mr. Mitchell and Judge Hughes are Roman Catholics. This means that New Jersey, which has never had a Catholic Governor, will choose one in November.

Mr. Mitchell's primary victory was a major gain for Senator Clifford P. Case and former Senator H. Alexander Smith, who had persuaded him to enter the race.

Twelve of the twenty-one Republican county organizations in the state had backed Senator Jones, three had backed Mr. Mitchell and three, Senator Wayne Dumont Jr. of Warren County, the third major entry. The three remaining were neutral.

Although all but lost sight of in the campaign, Mr. Mitchell had a third rival. He was Louis Berns of Oradel, who is almost

Continued on Page 42, Column 2

EXTENSION SLATED FOR RIGHTS GROUP

Kennedy Will Ask Congress to Keep Commission

By ANTHONY LEWIS
Special to The New York Times.

WASHINGTON, April 18—The Administration will ask Congress to extend the life of the Civil Rights Commission, which is now scheduled to go out of business next November.

The approach of the date set by statute for the end of the operation has already led the commission to begin winding up its work. It was disclosed today that the commission planned to let its seven investigators go on May 1.

Dr. John M. Hannah, chairman of the group, explained to a House Appropriations subcommittee that the dismissal of the investigators was only "realistic." He said there would be no time to act before next November on anything the investigators turned up now.

The Civil Rights Commission was created by the Civil Rights Act of 1957, with a two-year term of life. In 1959 it was extended by Congress for two years.

A request for a further ex-

Continued on Page 27, Column 5

NEWS INDEX

Union Is Canceling Its Plan to Boycott Japanese Textiles

Special to The New York Times.

WASHINGTON, April 18—The Amalgamated Clothing Workers notified the White House today that it was calling off its boycott of Japanese textiles used in the manufacture of men's clothing. The boycott had been scheduled to start May 1.

Jacob S. Potofsky, union president, said he had acted at the request of President Kennedy and "in the national interest."

Mr. Kennedy, at a recent news conference, said the Government was studying textile problems, including imports, and would regret unilateral action by any group to impose boycotts while the study was in progress.

Arthur J. Goldberg, Secretary of Labor, relayed the President's request to Mr. Potofsky, who discussed it with the union board.

Mr. Kennedy said today he was gratified by the union's action. The union, with 385,-

Continued on Page 22, Column 4

SENATE REJECTS WAGE BILL CUTS

Defeats 4 Moves to Limit Scope—Kennedy Forces Expect Passage Today

By TOM WICKER
Special to The New York Times.

WASHINGTON, April 18—Senate Democrats and liberal Republicans easily defeated today four proposals that would have limited the Administration's bill to increase the minimum wage and extend its coverage.

The first item on tomorrow's agenda will be an hour's debate on the bill, followed by a vote on the chief threat to it. This is an amendment by Senator A. S. Mike Monroney, Democrat of Oklahoma, that would limit the bill's coverage to retail and service enterprises operating in two or more states.

The Administration forces, strengthened by their coalition with the liberal Republicans, were confident they could defeat the Monroney proposal, though not so easily as they won today's battles. They expected final passage tomorrow.

College Aid Backed

Meanwhile, the Administration's education program made its first progress in Congress when a House subcommittee approved a $2,400,000,000 college aid bill.

The Kennedy wage bill is almost intact after three days of debate and voting. Only minor amendments have been accepted.

It would increase the minimum wage from $1 an hour to $1.15 in four months, and to $1.25 two years after that, for about 24,000,000 workers already covered, mostly in manufacturing.

It would provide a minimum of $1 an hour, with increases to $1.25 in four years, for about 4,063,000 retail, service and construction workers not now covered.

Its key provision is a requirement that the minimum wage be paid by retail and service enterprises doing a $1,000,000 annual business and importing more than $250,000

Continued on Page 23, Column 3

Congress Gets Kennedy's Plan For Urban Post in the Cabinet

By PETER BRAESTRUP
Special to The New York Times.

WASHINGTON, April 18—President Kennedy asked Congress today to create a Cabinet-level Department of Urban Affairs and Housing.

He expressed hope for "prompt action," but both Administration officials and Capitol Hill sources indicated a cautious approach.

The new Secretary of Urban Affairs and Housing, President Kennedy said, would be able to "present the nation's housing and metropolitan development needs to the Cabinet and will, by virtue of his position, provide the necessary leadership in coordinating the many Federal programs in these fields."

If Congress creates the department, it is understood President Kennedy plans to nominate Dr. Robert C. Weaver to head it. Dr. Weaver, head of the Housing Home Finance Agency, would be the first Negro to hold Cabinet rank.

The President made his request in letters to Vice President Johnson, the Senate's presiding officer, and Sam Rayburn, Speaker of the House of Representatives.

In his letters, President Kennedy said that two of the nation's high-priority problems were "preventing the appalling deterioration of many of our urban areas" and "insuring the availability of adequate housing for all segments of our population."

In an accompanying memorandum, Budget Director David E. Bell noted that the bill set forth a proposed declaration of "national urban affairs and

Continued on Page 29, Column 1

REBELS HARASSED

Havana Reports Raid by B-26 but Asserts It Was Driven Off

By TAD SZULC
Special to The New York Times.

MIAMI, April 18—The forces of Premier Fidel Castro appeared tonight to have mounted a major, tank-led offensive designed to dislodge rebel fighters from their narrow beachhead on the marshy southern coast of Cuba.

An announcement over Cuban television said that "news of victory" would be broadcast within a few hours.

The Havana radio reported late tonight that a B-26 bomber had attacked the city earlier in the evening.

According to the radio, the bomber appeared over the city at 8:20 and dropped a bomb on the military base of San Antonio de los Banos. The plane was then reported to have made several strafing passes over the city.

Plane Strafes City

The Cuban radio said that the bomb had missed its mark and that the strafing passes had done no serious damage. It said that anti-aircraft batteries had opened fire on the plane and that the plane had then flown off to the north.

The plane might have taken off from Guatemala or other airfields in the Caribbean.

[The apparent arrest of several Americans in Havana was reported from the United States Naval Base at Guantanamo Bay.]

Although the Havana regime maintained official silence about the operations in Las Villas Province, where anti-Castro troops landed before dawn yesterday, a communiqué from the rebels' Revolutionary Council said that Soviet-built tanks and Mig jet fighters were attacking its units.

The communiqué spoke of a "rapidly expanding area already being liberated by the revolutionary command," but there were no indications that the invaders had succeeded in capturing the town of Jaguey Grande, across the provincial line in Matanzas Province, which seemed to be their immediate target.

Revolt's Extent Unclear

Deep concern was developing here over the immediate and long-range political repercussions of a possible failure of the rebel landing operation in southern Cuba.

If the rebel attempt to establish a foothold on Cuban territory is defeated—and this was a possibility that was begrudgingly being accepted in some anti-Castro quarters here—it could deal a demolishing blow to the entire exile movement and help to consolidate Dr. Castro's position.

There were no indications whether masses of Cubans had rebelled against Premier Castro at the news of the first landing,

Continued on Page 15, Column 1

PREMIER IS GRIM

Bids U. S. Halt Attack —Thousands Storm Moscow Embassy

By SEYMOUR TOPPING
Special to The New York Times.

MOSCOW, April 18—Premier Khrushchev told President Kennedy today that the Soviet Union would render the Castro regime "all necessary assistance" to beat back the rebel attacks on Cuba.

In an urgent message to Mr. Kennedy the Russian leader called upon the United States to halt the attacks so as to avert the danger of "a conflagration which it will be impossible to cope with."

He placed responsibility for the air bombings of Cuban bases Saturday and the landings in Cuba on the United States.

[Premier Chou En-lai of Communist China, in a cablegram to Premier Castro, pledged Peiping's support to "the Cuban people" in resisting the attacks, The Associated Press reported.]

Embassy Is Attacked

Two and one-half hours after Mr. Krushchev's message was handed to the United States chargé d'affaires, thousands of organized students and workers carrying anti-American banners and hurling stones and ink bottles converged on the United States Embassy in a protest demonstration that continued until late tonight.

Hundreds of Soviet militiamen backed by mounted police and unarmed soldiers fought off repeated assaults on the embassy that were led at times by African, Asian and Latin-American students of the Friendship University.

The demonstrators were allowed, however, to drape a Cuban flag and pro-Castro banners on the front of the defaced building.

Will Aid Fight on Rebels

Without making clear in his message to President Kennedy what form Soviet aid to the Castro forces might take, Mr. Khrushchev stated:

"As to the Soviet Union, there should be no misunderstanding of our position: We shall render the Cuban people and their Government all necessary assistance in beating back the armed attack on Cuba.

"We are sincerely interested in a relaxation of international tension, but if others aggravate it, we shall reply in full measure."

Premier Khrushchev's message contained no reference to what he has described as his

Continued on Page 14, Column 1

SOVIET URGES U. N. TO ASSIST CASTRO

Calls for Action to Disarm Cuban Rebels in U. S.

By THOMAS J. HAMILTON
Special to The New York Times.

UNITED NATIONS, N. Y., Wednesday, April 19—The Soviet Union proposed last night that the General Assembly request all members of the United Nations to provide the "necessary assistance," if requested by Cuba, to repulse the "aggression" there.

Under a resolution introduced by Valerian A. Zorin, the Soviet representative, the Assembly would also request the "immediate disarming" of all "counter-revolutionary bands" stationed on the territory of the United States and other countries.

The Soviet draft resolution would condemn the "aggressive actions" of the United States and other countries "from whose territory the invasion is being carried out" and request all members of the United Nations to stop assistance to such groups.

Mr. Zorin introduced the Soviet proposal after Adlai E. Stevenson, the United States representative, had struck back angrily against the "innuendos,

Continued on Page 16, Column 5

Associated Press Radiophoto
PROTEST IN MOSCOW: Police push back crowd in front of the United States Embassy

The Exchange of Messages

Statement by Premier Khrushchev

By The Associated Press.

MOSCOW, April 18—Premier Khrushchev's message today to President Kennedy:

Mr. President, I address this message to you at an hour of anxiety fraught with danger to world peace. An armed aggression has begun against Cuba.

It is not a secret to anyone that the armed bands which invaded that country had been trained, equipped and armed in the United States of America. The planes which bomb Cuban cities belong to the United States of America, the bombs they drop have been made available by the American Government.

Here in the Soviet Union all this arouses a natural feeling of indignation on the part of the Soviet Government and Soviet people.

Once recently we exchanged views through our representatives. We spoke about the common desire of both sides to make joint efforts to improve the relations between our countries and avert the danger of war.

Your statement of a few days ago to the effect that the United States would not take part in military operations against Cuba produced the impression that the top echelons of the United States are aware of the consequences of aggression against Cuba to world peace and to the United States itself.

How are we to understand what is really being done by the United States now that the attack on Cuba has become a fact?

Action Still Possible

It is yet not too late to prevent the irreparable. The Government of the United States still can prevent the flames of war kindled by the interventionists on Cuba from spreading into a conflagration which it will be impossible to cope with.

I earnestly appeal to you, Mr. President, to call a halt to the aggression against the Republic of Cuba. The military techniques and the world political situation now are such that any so-called "small-war" can produce a chain reaction in all parts of the world.

As to the Soviet Union, there should be no misunderstanding of our position: we shall render the Cuban people and their Government all necessary assistance in beating back the armed attack on Cuba.

We are sincerely interested in a relaxation of international tension, but if others aggravate it, we shall reply in full measure. And, in general, it is hardly possible to handle matters in such a way as to settle the situation and extinguish the conflagration in one area and kindle a new conflagration in another.

I hope that the United States Government will take into account these considerations of ours, prompted as they are by the sole concern for not allowing steps which could lead the world to a military catastrophe.

The Answer by President Kennedy

Special to The New York Times.

WASHINGTON, April 18—President Kennedy's answer to Premier Khrushchev:

Mr. Chairman:

You are under a serious misapprehension in regard to events in Cuba. For months there has been evident and growing resistance to the Castro dictatorship.

More than 100,000 refugees have recently fled from Cuba into neighboring countries. Their urgent hope is naturally to assist their fellow Cubans in their struggle for freedom. Many of these refugees fought alongside Dr. Castro against the Batista dictatorship; among them are prominent leaders of his own original movement and government.

These are unmistakable signs that Cubans found intolerable the denial of democratic liberties and the subversion of the 26 of July Movement by an alien-dominated regime. It cannot be surprising that, as resistance within Cuba grows, refugees have been using whatever means are available to return and support their countrymen in the continuing struggle for freedom. Where people are denied the right of choice, recourse to such struggle is the only means of achieving their liberties.

I have previously stated and I repeat now that the United States intends no military intervention in Cuba. In the event of any military intervention by outside force we will immediately honor our obligations under the inter-American system to protect this hemisphere against external aggression.

The Spirit of Liberty

While refraining from military intervention in Cuba, the people of the United States do not conceal their admiration for Cuban patriots who wish to see a democratic system in an independent Cuba. The United States Government can take no action to stifle the spirit of liberty.

I have taken careful note of your statement that the events in Cuba might affect peace in all parts of the world. I trust that this does not mean that the Soviet Government, using the situation in Cuba as a pretext, is planning to inflame other areas of the world. I would like to think that your Government has too great a sense of responsibility to embark upon any enterprise so dangerous to general peace.

I agree with you as to the desirability of steps to improve the international atmosphere. I continue to hope that you will cooperate in opportunities now available to this end.

A prompt cease-fire and peaceful settlement of the dangerous situation in Laos, cooperation with the United Nations in the Congo and a speedy conclusion of an acceptable treaty for the banning of nuclear tests would be constructive steps in this direction.

The regime in Cuba could make a similar contribution by permitting the Cuban people freely to determine their own future by democratic processes and freely to cooperate with their Latin-American neighbors.

I believe, Mr. Chairman, that you should recognize that free peoples in all parts of the world do not accept the claim of historical inevitability for Communist revolution. What your Government believes is its own business; what it does in the world is the world's business. The great revolution in the history of man, past, present and future, is the revolution of those determined to be free.

PRESIDENT IS FIRM

Tells Soviet U. S. Will Not Permit Meddling —Asks Laos Truce

By WALLACE CARROLL
Special to The New York Times.

WASHINGTON, April 18—President Kennedy warned the Soviet Union tonight that the United States would tolerate no outside military intervention in Cuba.

The President reacted in less than ten hours to a threat by Premier Khrushchev to give the Castro regime "all necessary assistance" in repelling attacks by anti-Castro forces.

In an icily worded message, the President rebuffed Mr. Khrushchev's request that the United States suppress the efforts of the anti-Castro exiles who are trying to maintain a beachhead in Cuba.

The President also took up the Soviet Premier's implied threat to stir up trouble in other parts of the world. If the Soviet Union sincerely wants to improve the international atmosphere, Mr. Kennedy said, it should accept a cease-fire in Laos, cooperate with the United Nations in the Congo and agree to reasonable proposals for a ban on tests of nuclear weapons.

Communism Rejected

The President went beyond immediate issues to reject Soviet claims to the inevitable triumph of communism.

"The great revolution in the history of man, past, present and future, is the revolution of those determined to be free," Mr. Kennedy declared.

Secretary of State Dean Rusk handed the President's message to the Soviet Ambassador, Mikhail A. Menshikov, at 7 P. M. The message answered a communication from Premier Khrushchev that was given to the United States Embassy in Moscow this morning.

"You are under a serious misapprehension in regard to events in Cuba," Mr. Kennedy told the Premier.

The Castro dictatorship, he said, is "an alien-dominated regime." This was a restrained reiteration of the American contention that Dr. Castro's Government is under Soviet domination. Many Cubans, the President said, have found the denial of liberties intolerable and have turned to resistance against Dr. Castro.

"Where the people are denied the right of choice," the President said, "recourse to such struggle is the only means of achieving their liberties."

The President then replied to

Continued on Page 12, Column 1

LAOTIAN CANCELS WASHINGTON TRIP

Souvanna Phouma Declines to Defer Rusk Talks

By W. H. LAWRENCE
Special to The New York Times.

WASHINGTON, April 18—Prince Souvanna Phouma of Laos abruptly canceled today his trip to Washington to discuss with officials an easing of the Laotian crisis.

The cancellation arose out of a conflict of schedules. Originally expected in Washington tonight, the Prince postponed his arrival by one day, and this meant he would be here for consultations only on Thursday. Secretary of State Dean Rusk already had agreed to speaking appearances then in Atlanta and Weleska, Ga.

The Prince was to interrupt his visit in the Soviet Union to visit Washington. He planned to return to Moscow after the conferences here.

State Department officials said that when the Thursday conflict developed "discreet" suggestions were made to the Prince that he finish his talks in Moscow and come here from there.

While it had been expected that President Kennedy also would receive Prince Souvanna

Continued on Page 8, Column 1

Eichmann Is Portrayed as Crueler Than Himmler

By HOMER BIGART
Special to The New York Times.

JERUSALEM (Israeli Sector), April 18—Adolf Eichmann was portrayed today as crueler and more relentless than his

Excerpts from the Hausner charges are on Page 20.

Gestapo chief, Heinrich Himmler, in pressing for the annihilation of European Jews.

In a hushed courtroom, Attorney General Gideon Hausner, the chief prosecutor, wound up his opening statement with words that rang like an Old Testament phrase:

"And the judges of Israel will

Prosecutor Says Gestapo Chief Criticized Death March

pronounce true and righteous judgment. Mr. Hausner said he would prove "an astonishing thing"—that Himmler himself had reprimanded Eichmann for organizing a death march of Jews from Budapest in late 1944.

Hundreds committed suicide or died of typhus during the forced march toward the Austrian frontier, the prosecutor said, and it took an order from Himmler to make Eichmann call a halt to the brutal operation.

Israel called her first witnesses at the afternoon session. An Israeli police captain, Avner Less, testified that he had taken a tape-recorded declaration from Eichmann, made willingly by the prisoner after he was brought to Israel last May.

This recording, part of the police interrogation of Eichmann, which runs close to 1,000,000 words, will be played at tomorrow's court session. The prosecution asserts that the recording is highly incriminating, proving that Eichmann, by his own admissions, played a key role in the annihilation of Jews.

Members of the prosecution said the deposition would also

Continued on Page 20, Column 1

1961

Floyd Patterson was declared the winner over Ingmar Johansson in a hotly contested match.

Roger Maris surpassed Babe Ruth's home-run record of 60 by one home-run.

"All the News That's Fit to Print"

The New York Times.

LATE CITY EDITION

U. S. Weather Bureau Report (Page 62) forecast: Cloudy, warm, chance of rain late today or tonight and tomorrow. Temp. range: 61—48; yesterday: 70—47.

VOL. CX..No. 37,723. NEW YORK, SATURDAY, MAY 6, 1961. 10 cents beyond 50-mile zone from New York City except on Long Island. Higher in air delivery cities. FIVE CENTS

U. S. HURLS MAN 115 MILES INTO SPACE; SHEPARD WORKS CONTROLS IN CAPSULE, REPORTS BY RADIO IN 15-MINUTE FLIGHT

LAUNCHING: Rocket lifts the capsule

RETURN: Astronaut rides in one of helicopters carrying his Mercury capsule to the Lake Champlain

Associated Press Wirephotos

SAFE ABOARD: On the Lake Champlain's deck, Comdr. Alan B. Shepard Jr. views capsule he occupied

ASTRONAUT: Commander Shepard removes space suit.

IN FINE CONDITION

Astronaut Drops Into the Sea Four Miles From Carrier

Excerpts from radioed reports by Shepard, Page 8

By RICHARD WITKIN

Special to The New York Times.

CAPE CANAVERAL, Fla., May 5—A slim, cool Navy test pilot was rocketed 115 miles into space today.

Thirty-seven-year-old Comdr. Alan B. Shepard Jr. thus became the first American space explorer.

Commander Shepard landed safely 302 miles out at sea fifteen minutes after the launching. He was quickly lifted aboard a Marine Corps helicopter.

"Boy, what a ride!" he said, as he was flown to the aircraft carrier Lake Champlain four miles away.

Extensive physical examinations were begun immediately.

Tonight doctors reported Commander Shepard in "excellent" condition, suffering no ill effects.

Major U. S. Step

The near-perfect flight represented the United States' first major step in the race to explore space with manned space craft.

True, it was only a modest leap compared with the once-around-the-earth orbital flight of Maj. Yuri A. Gagarin of the Soviet Union.

The Russian's speed of more than 17,000 miles an hour was almost four times Commander Shepard's 4,500. The distance the Russian traveled was almost 100 times as great.

But Commander Shepard maneuvered his craft in space—something the Russians have not claimed for Major Gagarin.

All in all, the Shepard flight was welcomed almost rapturous-

Continued on Page 8, Column 1

JOHNSON TO MEET LEADERS IN ASIA ON U. S. TROOP USE

President Says Decision on South Vietnam Action Will Await Report

TALKS SET IN CAPITALS

Ngo Dinh Diem Is Expected to Seek American Units to Deter Red Attack

Transcript of news conference and summary, Page 14.

By WILLIAM J. JORDEN

Special to The New York Times.

WASHINGTON, May 5—President Kennedy said today that the assignment of United States armed forces to South Vietnam would be one of several important matters Vice President Lyndon B. Johnson would discuss on his coming trip to Asia [Opening statement and Question 1, Page 14.]

The President confirmed that the possibility of sending United States troops to Southeast Asia was under study. He indicated that the final decision would depend on the results of Mr. Johnson's talks in Saigon with President Ngo Dinh Diem and others.

Mr. Kennedy said at a news conference that a special task force in the Government was working on problems related to helping South Vietnam maintain its independence. The question has been considered by the National Security Council as well, he said.

Vital Assignment

Mr. Johnson is expected to leave next Tuesday for the Far East. He also will meet with top Government officials in Bangkok, Thailand; Manila, and other capitals.

The President today described the Johnson mission as "an extremely important assignment."

It is widely assumed here that President Ngo will ask for the assignment of at least a token force of United States troops and regard it as a guarantee of United States' involvement should his country be attacked in force by the Communist North.

Mr. Kennedy did not touch on the matter today, but it is known that the Government is also considering the possibility of sending a similar token force to Thailand. The latter is allied to the United States in the

Continued on Page 3, Column 4

Talks Open in Laos On Truce Details; Meeting 'Friendly'

By JACQUES NEVARD

Special to The New York Times.

HIN HEUP, Laos, May 5—Military representatives of the pro-Western Laotian Government and the pro-Communist Pathet Lao rebels held a preliminary conference here today on machinery for continuing the cease-fire that became effective Wednesday.

The conference lasted one hour and five minutes and was described as "friendly."

According to a Laotian Army spokesman, Col. Oudom Sananikone, the meeting did not take up any political questions.

There appeared to be few tangible results of the talks, but Colonel Oudom Sananikone stressed that the meeting was a preliminary one.

He said that the first Pathet Lao request was that the next meeting take place at Namone, thirty-five miles north of here

Continued on Page 3, Column 2

2 BILLION AID PLAN FOR BRAZIL IS NEAR

U. S. Presses World-Wide Program of New Loans and Debt Deferments

By TAD SZULC

Special to The New York Times.

WASHINGTON, May 5—An international financial rescue package worth more than $2,000,000,000 is being prepared for Brazil. Negotiations, already well advanced, involve the United States, six Western European countries, Japan and the International Monetary Fund.

The agreements, which may be announced late next week, call for new loans totaling nearly $630,000,000. About $340,000,000 of this is to be provided by the United States. The remainder will take the form of a postponement in the repayment of much of Brazil's huge foreign debt.

This international financial operation, the largest ever involving a Latin-American country and one of the largest anywhere in postwar years, is designed to provide President Janio Quadros with extra time and resources to reorganize his economy.

Broad Effort in View

The United States is playing a key role in putting together the Brazilian package. It will also supply separate smaller loans to bolster the economies of Venezuela and Bolivia. Venezuela, which is facing serious budget difficulties, expects to receive soon an initial loan of $50,000,000.

Besides these emergency measures to assist the economies of individual Latin-American republics, the United States moved today to call a special inter-American conference to blueprint long-range economic and social development programs.

President Kennedy announced at his news conference that the United States' delegation to the Council of the Organization of American States had been in-

Continued on Page 17, Column 1

NIXON ASKS DRIVE TO OFFSET SOVIET

Bids Kennedy Rally America to a Fresh Foreign Policy

Excerpts from Nixon speech are printed on Page 2.

By AUSTIN C. WEHRWEIN

Special to The New York Times.

CHICAGO, May 5—Former Vice President Richard M. Nixon urged President Kennedy today to rally the American people for a new start in American foreign policy.

Mr. Nixon called for a "searching reappraisal of the free world's ability, particularly America's ability, to deal with the kind of aggression in which Communists are now engaging."

He further revealed that he had given President Kennedy the "assurance that I will support him to the hilt in backing positive action he may decide is necessary to resist Communist aggression."

[President Kennedy, meanwhile, sent his nuclear test-ban negotiator back to Geneva with an implied warning that the United States might not continue the talks much longer without some prospect of a safeguarded treaty.]

To meet such threats, the former Vice President said that the United States should be prepared to act alone if swift action were needed while machinery for collective action was being set up.

The lesson of Cuba and Laos, he said, is this:

"We must never talk bigger than we are prepared to act.

"When our words are strong and our actions are timid, we

Continued on Page 2, Column 3

Kennedy Plans Aid To Retrain Jobless And Spur Recovery

By PETER BRAESTRUP

Special to The New York Times.

WASHINGTON, May 5—The Kennedy Administration expects to ask Congress for at least $75,000,000 to provide retraining for the long-term unemployed. Other new anti-recession measures also are being considered.

The key question that President Kennedy has yet to decide is whether to break the Administration's self-imposed limit on Federal spending in an effort to stimulate the economy and spur employment.

The $75,000,000 program for retraining workers who have been laid off by technological change and by the decay of their own industries will not materially affect the budget. Nor will the President's orders to the Pentagon to channel more defense contracts to small

Continued on Page 19, Column 2

MAYOR IS UPHELD ON CHARTER LAW

But Court Reverses Ban on Action by Council, Opening Way to Rival Proposals

By RONALD MAIORANA

Mayor Wagner's right to appoint a Charter Revision Commission was upheld by Justice Irving Saypol yesterday in State Supreme Court.

However, Justice Saypol ruled invalid part of the law under which the Mayor had acted. This part excluded the City Council from Charter-revision activity.

Lawyers said the ruling appeared to make possible the enactment of the City Council's own plan for a Charter Revision Commission. Thus, it is conceivable, they said, that two competing Charters—one drawn by the Mayor's commission and the other by a commission created by the Council—could be submitted to the voters Nov. 7.

In a twenty-two-page decision that caused confusion at City Hall Justice Saypol ruled that the section of the state law that had the effect of bypassing the City Council was invalid because it was an improper delegation of legislative power. He said: "The newly enacted au-

Continued on Page 32, Column 1

Shepard Had Periscope: 'What a Beautiful View'

By JOHN W. FINNEY

CAPE CANAVERAL, Fla., May 5—"All systems go * * * Everything A-O.K. * * * Mission very smooth * * * What a beautiful view! * * * Coming in for a landing."

These were the reports of Comdr. Alan B. Shepard Jr. as he rode the capsule Freedom 7 115 miles up into space today in the United States' first step toward manned exploration of space. His "A-O.K." is a rocket engineer term meaning double O.K. or perfect.

In a calm, methodical way he reported back by radio on every detail of his fifteen-minute flight, even during the moments of greatest stress as his capsule accelerated from the launching pad and then quickly decelerated upon re-entering the earth's atmosphere.

And there were moments of excitement in his voice, such as when he viewed much of the Eastern Coast of the United States through a periscope from 115 miles up in space.

"What a beautiful view!" he exclaimed into a microphone inside his visored space helmet and then, according to instructions, he returned to scientific observations to report that the cloud cover was three- to four-tenths and was obscuring much of the coast up through Cape Hatteras.

Three-to-four-teenths cloud cover is a description used by

Continued on Page 10, Column 1

NATION TO WIDEN ITS SPACE EFFORTS

Kennedy Wants More Funds —He Telephones Shepard to Offer Congratulations

Texts of Kennedy statement and call to Shepard, Page 11

By DAVID HALBERSTAM

Special to The New York Times.

WASHINGTON, May 5—An even greater effort in the exploration of space was promised today by President Kennedy.

On the day of this country's first manned space flight, he told a news conference he would make an additional request for appropriations for its space program this year.

"We are going to make a substantially larger effort in space," he declared. [Question 1, Page 14.]

Earlier in the day the President telephoned his personal congratulations to Comdr. Alan B. Shepard Jr., the nation's first space traveler, in a call from the White House to the aircraft carrier Lake Champlain.

The President also congratulated the commander's wife and his six fellow-astronauts.

Commander Shepard will visit Washington Monday. There will be a ceremony at noon on

Continued on Page 11, Column 7

PRESIDENT TO ASK INCOME TAX CUTS

Drop Next Year Is Planned, Dillon Tells House Unit

By JOHN D. MORRIS

Special to The New York Times.

WASHINGTON, May 5—The Kennedy Administration plans to lay before Congress next year a tax reform program that will include reduction of individual income taxes.

Secretary of the Treasury Douglas Dillon told the House Ways and Means Committee of the plan today but gave no details. He made it clear, however, that taxpayers with high incomes would probably be among the chief beneficiaries of a proposed reduction in rates.

"I think those in high brackets deserve relief," he said.

Mr. Dillon was questioned for nearly three hours, mainly by Republican committee members, as he completed three days of testimony on tax-revision legislation being sought now by the Administration.

The pending proposals include $1,700,000,000 a year in special tax credits for business enterprises to encourage modernization and expansion of plant and equipment. Tax laws on foreign income, business expense accounts and stock dividends

Continued on Page 22, Column 3

Elizabeth Visits Pope in Vatican

Associated Press Wirephoto

Pope John XXIII in private audience with Queen Elizabeth

By ARNALDO CORTESI

Special to The New York Times.

ROME, May 5—Pope John XXIII received Queen Elizabeth II and Prince Philip in a private audience today with traditional pomp and ceremony. The meeting was marked by extreme cordiality. Addressing the Queen in French, the Pope said that relations between Britain and

Continued on Page 19, Column 6

14 Dead, 57 Hurt by Tornado; 2 Towns in Oklahoma Hard Hit

By The Associated Press.

POTEAU, Okla., May 5—A vicious tornado tore through two tiny eastern Oklahoma communities near here tonight, killing at least fourteen persons and injuring fifty-seven.

Ten were reported dead at Howe and four at Reichert. The death toll could go higher as rescue workers dug into the debris.

There was a report that a light plane—trying to avoid the massive storm cloud—crashed after a wing tore off. The highway patrol said that a woman who lived in the area reported she saw the plane go down west of Heavener near Summerfield

It was a grim anniversary for this rolling, wooded area some 200 miles southeast of Oklahoma City. Just one year ago twelve were killed when a twister destroyed most of the downtown area of Wilburton.

Tornadoes had plagued Oklahoma for two days, but until tonight there had been only one fatality from the scores of funnels sighted.

Two of the dead were babies. One father died with his 3-month-old son and a mother with her 14-month-old boy.

Tiny farms are scattered throughout the twister-pounded

Continued on Page 62, Column 6

NEWS INDEX

Nation Exults Over Space Feat; City Plans to Honor Astronaut

By ROBERT CONLEY

The successful flight of America's first astronaut, Comdr. Alan B. Shepard Jr., roused the country yesterday to one of its highest peaks of exultation since the end of World War II.

The achievement brought relief from the strain of hearing about the Soviet Union's success in orbiting a man, feelings of new hope for the future from Maine to Hawaii and dancing in the streets at New York's Columbus Circle.

"Wonderful," "Tremendous," "The greatest thing that ever happened," thousands of persons said as the reaction took hold across the country.

Knots of people crowded sidewalks to watch television screens in store windows. Others jumped up to cheer, pounded friends on the back, ran into neighbors' houses or fell silent.

"He made it," a woman gasped in Chicago, then broke into tears. "He made it."

New York City laid plans for the "most fabulous" ticker tape welcome ever given—one that a city official said would be "even bigger than the one for Charles Lindbergh."

In Washington, Congressmen moved to bestow the nation's

Continued on Page 11, Column 5

Adolf Eichmann listened to his witnesses' testimony behind the protection of the glass-enclosed booth, but no expression of remorse or fear was ever displayed, even at the end.

Pablo Picasso celebrated his 80th birthday on the French Riviera where an exhibition of his works and a bullfight were staged in his honor.

A *Freedom Rider* bus was fire-bombed by white crowds in Atlanta.

"All the News That's Fit to Print"

The New York Times.

LATE CITY EDITION

U. S. Weather Bureau Report (Page 95) Forecasts: Variable cloudiness today and tonight. Rather cloudy tomorrow. Temp. range: 66—80; yesterday: 70—80.

NEWS SUMMARY AND INDEX, PAGE 95

SECTION ONE

VOL. CX....No. 37,738. NEW YORK, SUNDAY, MAY 21, 1961. THIRTY CENTS

400 U.S. MARSHALS SENT TO ALABAMA AS MONTGOMERY BUS RIOTS HURT 20; PRESIDENT BIDS STATE KEEP ORDER

FORCE DUE TODAY

Agents to Bear Arms —Injunction Sought Against the Klan

Texts of U. S. and Alabama statements on Page 78.

By ANTHONY LEWIS

Special to The New York Times.

WASHINGTON, May 20—The Federal Government dispatched 400 marshals and other armed officers to Alabama tonight to restore order in areas that were torn by racial violence.

The Government acted after a mob of white persons attacked a racially mixed group of bus riders in Montgomery, Ala. The disorders lasted two hours. At least twenty of the riders were beaten.

Attorney General Robert F. Kennedy announced the Federal action in a telegram to Alabama officials. He said it was necessary to "guarantee safe passage in interstate commerce."

Marshals Due by Noon

The 400 Federal marshals will be in Montgomery by noon tomorrow, a Justice Department spokesman said. He said they would have arm bands for identification and would carry sidearms as well as tear-gas bombs and riot clubs or night sticks.

Mr. Kennedy disclosed also that he would ask the Federal Court in Montgomery "to enjoin the Ku Klux Klan, the National States Rights Party, certain individuals and all persons acting in concert with them from interfering with peaceful interstate travel by buses."

A Justice Department spokesman said that there were reports of Ku Klux Klan and Negro groups converging on Montgomery County and that he was afraid of larger scale problems than had already developed.

Attacks Deplored

The Attorney General acted immediately after President Kennedy issued a statement deploring the mob attacks.

The President said the situation in Alabama was "a source of the deepest concern to me as it must be to the vast majority of the citizens of Alabama and all Americans."

"I have instructed the Justice Department to take all necessary steps," the President added.

He called on Gov. John Patterson of Alabama and other state and local officials "to exercise their lawful authority to prevent any further outbreaks of violence."

"I hope that state and local officials in Alabama will meet their responsibilities," the President said. "The United States

Continued on Page 78, Column 8

Associated Press Wirephoto

ALABAMA STREET SCENE: A Negro student, who arrived in Montgomery aboard bus carrying anti-segregation riders from Birmingham, being beaten yesterday by white men.

Freedom Riders Attacked By Whites in Montgomery

By The Associated Press.

MONTGOMERY, Ala, May 20—Street fighting that left at least twenty persons beaten with clubs and fists raged for two hours here today after a white mob had attacked a busload of Freedom Riders.

The fighting broke out and subsided three times before the police, unable to restore order by other methods, tossed tear gas bombs into the crowds.

The mob, which at times numbered about 1,000, attacked the white and Negro bus riders within an instant after the Greyhound bus pulled into the downtown station from Birmingham at 10:15 A. M.

The violence engulfed some bystanders, too. These included a representative of the United States Justice Department and of President Kennedy who had tried to rescue a white girl from the mob.

Slugged From Behind

John Seigenthaler, 32 years old, also a representative of Attorney General Robert F. Kennedy, was taken to a hospital with a cut behind his ear. He was slugged from behind as he struggled to help the besieged girl, one of the Freedom Riders.

At least four out-of-town reporters and photographers were beaten as they attempted to film the rioting. Others had their cameras smashed.

Four white persons were arrested after the police arrived.

Tonight, Attorney General MacDonald Gallion said that a state court judge had ordered the arrest of twenty-one Freedom Riders for contempt of an injunction he issued yesterday.

Mr. Gallion said that at his request Circuit Court Judge Walter B. Jones had "issued an order to show cause why twenty-one Freedom Riders should not be jailed for con-

Continued on Page 78, Column 4

ALGERIA TALKS ON; FRANCE DECLARES 30-DAY CEASE-FIRE

REBELS CRITICAL

Call Step 'Blackmail'— 6,000 Will Be Freed From Internment

By ROBERT C. DOTY

Special to The New York Times.

EVIAN-LES-BAINS, France, May 20—France opened peace negotiations with the Algerian Moslem rebels here today with the announcement of a thirty-day cease-fire.

France also announced other measures designed to demonstrate her will for a settlement of the Algerian war.

The rebel Provisional Government, branding the French action as "pure propaganda," "blackmail" and "a movement of diversion," said its fight would continue. It called the cease-fire order a unilateral action.

Transfer of Ben Bella

The other French measures included transfer of Ahmed Ben Bella, Deputy Premier of the Provisional Government, and four associates from a fortress off the Breton coast to more liberal "controlled residence" in the Château de Turquant, in the Maine et Loire Department, near Saumur.

The Government liberated a sixth Algerian, Mohammed Lacheraf, captured with Mr. Ben Bella and the others in October, 1956, when a French ruse took their airplane into Algiers instead of their destination, Tunis.

The French also promised the liberation in the next four weeks of 6,000 Algerians detained for nationalist activity, acceleration of financial and technical aid under President de Gaulle's development plan and the return to their homes of some of the hundreds of thousands of Algerians "regrouped" to remove them from rebel influence in the hills.

Conference Is Guarded

All of this was communicated to Belkacem Krim, Foreign Minister of the rebel Government and leader of the Algerian delegation, in the first meeting of the long-sought conference. It was held in the closely guarded Hôtel du Parc facing on the neatly landscaped shore of Lake Geneva in this summer resort and spa.

France's moves were conveyed by Louis Joxe, Minister for Algerian Affairs and leader of the French delegation.

The order to the French Army in Algeria ends offensive operations against the rebels at 6 o'clock tonight and directs it, for the period of a month, to engage only in operations of legitimate self-defense or pursuit of the perpetrators of acts of terrorism.

The order, the announcement

Continued on Page 4, Column 3

United Press International Radiophoto

ALGERIAN ARRIVES: Belkacem Krim, the head of the nationalist delegation, just before meeting French.

ADENAUER PRODS DE GAULLE ON TIES

But Is Said to Fail in Plea for Use of Forces in NATO —Berlin Is Discussed

By SYDNEY GRUSON

Special to The New York Times.

BONN, Germany, May 20—Chancellor Adenauer sought today to persuade President de Gaulle to adopt a more cooperative attitude toward the North Atlantic Treaty Organization. Reliable sources said the Chancellor had failed.

Drawing on the experiences of his recent meetings in Washington with President Kennedy, the Chancellor was said to have told General de Gaulle, who arrived today by air, that fears about American intentions toward the defense of Europe were unjustified.

The two government chiefs "agreed on the need to strengthen the alliance and on the necessity of the alliance for the defense" of both their countries, Dr. Karl Carstens, Secretary of State in the West German Foreign Office, said at a news conference after the day-long talks ended.

No Accord on Details

But, according to reliable sources, this agreement in principle was not accompanied by agreement on the all-important details. President de Gaulle has "not changed his mind" about refusing to intergrate French forces, a French source said.

In addition to NATO, the two government leaders discussed the stalled negotiations among the six Common Market countries on the next steps for European unity and the likelihood that President Kennedy and Premier Khrushchev will discuss the German and Berlin problems when they meet in Vienna next month.

On the European question, Dr. Carstens said, General de Gaulle and Dr. Adenauer agreed that the ties among France, West Germany, Italy, the Netherlands, Belgium and Lux-

Continued on Page 34, Column 1

KHRUSHCHEV GIVES CONSUMER GOODS EQUAL ROLE NOW

Premier Indicates Soviet Will Shift Emphasis in Industrial Production

By OSGOOD CARUTHERS

Special to The New York Times.

MOSCOW, May 20—Premier Khrushchev said today his Government was beginning to turn greater attention to consumer goods and would no longer give priority to the production of heavy industry.

"Now we consider our heavy industry as built," Mr. Khrushchev declared at a reception in honor of officials and exhibitors of the large British Trade Fair that opened in Moscow yesterday.

"So we are not going to give it priority," Premier Khrushchev continued. "Light industry and heavy industry will develop at the same pace."

The Soviet leader's impromptu remarks indicated that a decision to level off the development of heavy and light industry had already been made. This would mean a considerable alteration in the original project figures of the seven-year plan that is to end in 1965.

Wide Changes Predicted

The indications were that the question of a shifted emphasis in production was being thoroughly studied by Mr. Khrushchev and his aides in preparation for the twenty-second Congress of the Soviet Communist party at which sweeping and dramatic changes are predicted.

The mass of Soviet consumers has noted a steady but gradual increase in the last few years in the availability of clothing and necessary household goods. However, the distribution system still makes ordinary necessities and the few available luxuries hard to get and prices are high.

Premier Khrushchev had been asked by some of the British business men at the party given by the Soviet Ministry of Foreign Trade in the House of Receptions what he was doing about supplying his people with more consumer goods.

Heavy Work Came First

"I can declare that we understand perfectly well the good things about light industry," he replied. He added, however, that the Communist rulers of the country had determined that the Soviet Union must develop heavy industry first.

"This was not, he said, because the Soviet people did not appreciate quality clothing and other things, but because they had to produce the proper basis for developing industry first.

"Now we consider that we have created that base," Mr. Khrushchev declared.

This remark indicated a significant change in the thinking among the Soviet leadership and its top planners.

Even in these last days the Soviet press and other propaganda outlets have continued to emphasize to the public the

Continued on Page 25, Column 1

KOREA PRESIDENT RETURNS TO POST; CABINET SWORN IN

Coup Leader Now Premier —Action by Yun Eases Seoul Legal Situation

By BERNARD KALB

Special to The New York Times.

SEOUL, Korea, Sunday, May 21—Military rule was formally introduced in South Korea today with the swearing in of a Cabinet of fourteen men, all from the armed forces.

The legal path for the new Government was cleared when President Posun Yun resumed late yesterday the post as head of state that he had resigned Friday.

The Cabinet pledged firmness in meeting the national crisis and vowed to strengthen the republic's ties with the United Nations.

Chang in Defense Post

The Cabinet, hand-picked by the military junta that rose to power in a coup here early Tuesday, replaces the Cabinet of Premier John M. Chang. Dr. Chang, elected to office last August, resigned under pressure Thursday.

Heading the new Government is Lieut. Gen. Chang Do Young, the 38-year-old Army Chief of Staff. General Chang, who led the coup, also becomes Minister of Defense.

General Chang in a speech to the ministers told them to direct all their energies and efforts toward the earliest realization of the goals of the revolution—the nation's economic and political reform, a stepped-up fight on communism and the eventual unification of Korea.

New Government's Pledge

As the new Cabinet under General Chang was installed, each Minister took an oath as follows:

"I do solemnly pledge to the people that I will concentrate my efforts upon strengthening national power for the unification of the nation, developing the national economy, preserving national independence and freedom, strengthening the ties with the United Nations and friendly countries and overcoming the national crisis through the strengthening of power and effectiveness to combat communism and complete the elimination of corruption and social evils, acting in the basis of the patriotic spirit of the glorious armed forces."

It was apparent that the 63-year-old President Yun had been pressured by the military leaders into resuming his office. His continuance in the Presidency preserves South Korea's diplomatic relations with the United States and other countries.

A spokesman at the Presidential Palace said the military junta argued that acceptance of the President's resignation would have created embarassing international complications.

Had the President stuck by his resignation, the junta, whose take-over was opposed by the United States Embassy

Continued on Page 3, Column 5

THREAT SILENCES MIGRANT WITNESS

U. S. Hearings on Farming Workers End Here With Testimony on Abuses

By MURRAY ILLSON

A woman who was scheduled to testify about conditions among migrant farm workers on eastern Long Island refused to do so yesterday because, she said, she had been threatened.

Representative Herbert Zelenko, Manhattan Democrat, made the announcement as he ended two days of hearings by a House Labor subcommittee into conditions among the migrant workers. He declined to identify the woman other than to say that she was a "crew leader" among the workers in the area of Riverhead, L. I.

He said that staff members of the subcommittee, of which he is chairman, were investigating the source of the asserted threat.

17-Hour Day Reported

Earlier two women migratory workers from the South had told the subcommittee they had been severely exploited by potato growers and male crew leaders. One of the women testified her crew leader slapped his workers and kept them drunk and in debt by selling them cheap wine at exorbitant prices.

In sworn affidavits, the women said they had worked as potato graders seventeen hours a day, six days a week, and that after various deductions—for rent, food, "union dues" and other items— they never had netted more than $18 a week. Usually, they said, they got no more than $3 to $8 in cash.

Mr. Zelenko said a report of the two days' testimony would

Continued on Page 36, Column 1

NEGROES FACING TEST IN SUBURBS

Major Shift From the City Poses Housing Question —Progress Is Noted

By CLARENCE DEAN

One of the major, although quieter, phases in the battle for racial equality in housing appears to be shaping up in the New York suburbs.

There are indications the contest will grow in intensity and, possibly, bitterness for many years. However, there are many hopeful signs.

On Sept. 1, New York state's new law against discrimination in housing goes into effect. A similar measure is pending before the New Jersey Legislature. Connecticut adopted such legislation in 1959, and has been implementing it.

All of this has, or will have, the effect of extending to much private housing the legal bars against discrimination that have existed in publicly financed housing. It will mean a Negro cannot be rejected in a privately financed apartment house or housing development solely because of his color.

This legislative activity coincides with a substantial increase in the suburban Negro population.

A Rise in Suburbs

In 1950, the nonwhite population of the New York suburban area was 5.3 per cent of the total; in 1960, it was 6.8 per cent. There were nearly 250,000 more Negroes in the suburban area in 1960 than in 1950. The total now is approximately 550,000. With favorable economic conditions, the increase may be expected to continue.

Already portents have begun to appear.

There has been some panic selling by white property owners in at least two communities, Freeport, L. I., and Teaneck, N. J.

In Stamford, Conn., two Negroes have been accepted as tenants in upper-grade apartment houses, and in Greenwich, a Negro has bought a house in a white neighborhood but in each instance only after intervention by the Connecticut Commission on Civil Rights.

But the panic selling in Freeport and Teaneck was arrested, if not halted, by citizen groups. And, in the Stamford-Green-

Continued on Page 79, Column 4

Sports News

HORSE RACING

Carry Back rallied from far back yesterday and won the $178,700 Preakness at Pimlico by three-quarters of a length. Globemaster ran second and Crozier third in the field of nine 3-year-olds. Carry Back, who won the Kentucky Derby two weeks ago, again was ridden by Johnny Sellers. The time for the mile and three-sixteenths was 1 minute 57 3/5 seconds. Carry Back was the even-money favorite. The colt is owned by Mrs. Jack Price and trained by her husband. He earned $126,200.

BASEBALL

The Indians beat the Yankees again, 4—3, at Cleveland and dropped the New Yorkers to fourth place in the American League. Boston defeated Detroit, 4—3, in ten innings; Baltimore topped Washington, 4—3, and Minnesota shut out Kansas City, 2—0. In the National League, Los Angeles subdued San Francisco, 4—3; Milwaukee whipped Cincinnati, 9—5; Chicago blanked St. Louis, 1—0, and Pittsburgh downed Philadelphia, 4—3.

ROWING

The Navy heavyweights and the Harvard lightweights took the Eastern varsity sprint titles at Worcester, Mass.

Details in Section 5.

10,000 Here Parade The Nation's Might

By RICHARD J. H. JOHNSTON

The military establishment paraded its strength here yesterday before admiring civilians in celebration of Armed Forces Day.

The sun shone brightly and flags and standards fluttered in an eight-mile-an-hour wind as units of soldiers, airmen, marines and sailors swung down Fifth Avenue from Ninety-third Street to Sixty-second, beginning at 2 P. M.

The last element passed the reviewing stand at Sixty-ninth Street at 3:30 P. M. The march was led by a detail of six mounted New York City policemen, led by a mounted sergeant.

Behind the prancing horses

Continued on Page 38, Column 1

M'CLOY INDICATES A-TALKS MAY FAIL

He Expresses Pessimism in Report to Senate Unit

By JACK RAYMOND

Special to The New York Times.

WASHINGTON, May 20—President Kennedy's disarmament adviser has indicated to the Senate Foreign Relations Committee that the nuclear weapons test ban negotiations with the Russians in Geneva may fail.

John J. McCloy, the President's adviser, expressed his pessimism in a letter accompanying a lengthy review of the United States' negotiating positions for a test ban treaty. The details may be "academic," he observed.

It was also learned today that a Congressional delegation, including leaders of the Joint Atomic Energy Committee, had been urged by the White House to go to Geneva next week.

The group will leave Wednesday for what may be the critical negotiating effort in the test ban talks before President Kennedy's scheduled meeting with Premier Khrushchev in Vienna June 3 and 4.

The President, it is known,

Continued on Page 24, Column 1

PLAN TO RELOCATE JOBLESS CHARTED

President Will Ask Program in an Economic Message

By JOSEPH A. LOFTUS

Special to The New York Times.

WASHINGTON, May 20—For the first time, the Federal Government will propose an attack on the problem of chronic unemployment areas by relocating workers and their families.

A message on the state of the economy, now in the drafting stage, will propose additionally a training and retraining program for the unemployed and for youths who have not charted a vocation or career.

Policy advisers had hoped that the program might help 100,000 workers in all the new categories of assistance, but this total may be scaled down. The message is expected to go to Congress in a week or ten days.

President Kennedy is also said to believe that in view of current and prospective economic circumstances, there is no need to use extraordinary

Continued on Page 47, Column 4

Ransom to Free Cuba's Captives Pushed by Miro and 3 Americans

Exile Leader Hopeful

By SAM POPE BREWER

Special to The New York Times.

MIAMI, May 20—Dr. José Miró Cardona told Cuban negotiators today that he hoped to see enough money raised in the next seventy-two hours to ransom about 1,000 prisoners now held by Cuba.

The exile leader, confined to his bed with a lung affliction, received ten young Cuban prisoners captured by Premier Fidel Castro's forces during the abortive rebel landing in Cuba April 17.

He promised the support of the Cuban Revolutionary Council, which he heads, for the fund-raising effort.

The prisoners, who were said

Continued on Page 16, Column 5

Tractor Fund Sought

By DAMON STETSON

Special to The New York Times.

DETROIT, May 20—Walter P. Reuther, Mrs. Franklin D. Roosevelt and Dr. Milton S. Eisenhower offered today to assume the responsibility for raising funds to provide 500 tractors for Cuba if Premier Fidel Castro would free 1,000 imprisoned Cuban rebels.

In an address at a rally of students and farmers in Havana on Wednesday, Premier Castro said he was willing to trade the captured members of the invasion force of April 17 for 500 bulldozers and tractors with caterpillar treads.

Mr. Reuther, Mrs. Roosevelt and Dr. Eisenhower made their

Continued on Page 19, Column 1

Today's Sections

Index to Subjects

"All the News That's Fit to Print"

The New York Times.

LATE CITY EDITION

U. S. Weather Bureau Report (Page 70) forecasts: Partly cloudy, showers today, tonight and tomorrow. Temp. range: 79—56; yesterday: 79—67.

VOL. CX...No. 37,749. | © 1961 by The New York Times Company. Times Square, New York 36, N. Y. | NEW YORK, THURSDAY, JUNE 1, 1961. | 10 cents beyond 50-mile zone from New York City except on Long Island. Higher in air delivery cities. | FIVE CENTS

KENNEDY AND DE GAULLE AGREE TO DEFEND BERLIN; DISCUSS ASIA AND AFRICA

Associated Press Radiophoto

GUARD OF HONOR: President Kennedy and President de Gaulle are accompanied by Republican Guard as they ride from Orly Airport to the Quai d'Orsay in French capital.

PRESIDENTS MEET

Stand Firm on Soviet Threat—Parisians Hail Kennedys

Statements by de Gaulle and Kennedy are on Page 11.

By ROBERT C. DOTY
Special to The New York Times.

PARIS, May 31 — President Kennedy and President de Gaulle proclaimed today their "complete identity of view" on Western action to counter any threat to Berlin by the Soviet Union.

In view of the position on Berlin authoritatively attributed to General de Gaulle on the question, this meant that the two leaders apparently had reached agreement to go to war if necessary to maintain Western rights in the divided city.

Pierre Salinger, White House press secretary, and Pierre Baraduc, spokesman for the French Foreign Ministry, reported agreement on Berlin as a result of the thirty-seven-minute conversation between the two leaders just before they lunched together today.

In an hour-and-fifty-minute conversation after lunch, Mr. Kennedy and General de Gaulle began discussions of problems in Southeast Asia, notably Laos, and in Africa.

Welcome Is Colorful

The state visit by President and Mrs. Kennedy got off to a colorful start.

After their arrival at Orly Airport at 10:20 A. M. (5:20 A. M. Eastern Daylight Time), they rode in a motorcade through flag-decked streets.

The morning was bright and sunny and 500,000 or 1,500,000 cheering Parisians—depending on whether skeptical professional estimates or enthusiastic official figures were followed—lined the streets.

The two Presidents had three occasions to exchange complimentary words in public—at the airport, in luncheon toasts, and in a final exchange at a formal state dinner at the Elysée palace tonight.

At the dinner, Mr. Kennedy made a strong statement on the interdependence of France and the United States and pledged that "American forces will remain in Europe as long as they are required, ready to meet any threat with whatever response is needed."

Taken in the context of the earlier talks on Berlin, this seemed to be a commitment to go all the way—including, ap-

Continued on Page 10, Column 1

Western Big Three Confer On Tough U.S. Berlin Plan

By SYDNEY GRUSON
Special to The New York Times.

BONN, Germany, May 31—The United States, Britain and France have begun consultations in Washington on American proposals to strengthen plans to meet a new Berlin crisis. A White House group headed by Dean Acheson, former Secretary of State, worked out the proposals on President Kennedy's orders, reliable sources here said.

The President was reported to have been dissatisfied with the need, under the current plans, for the Western Big Three to consult at almost every step of their reaction to Soviet or East German moves against West Berlin.

The sources said the United States now was seeking agreement for a whole series of measures that the Allies might have to take. Britain has always resisted this kind of advance commitment, it was said.

The French Attitude

Diplomats here believe that France is unlikely to oppose the new American proposals. President de Gaulle is known to advocate the most uncompromising front to the Russians on the Berlin question. When he was here ten days ago, he assured Chancellor Adenauer he would urge this view on President Kennedy.

As they have been from the start of the Berlin crisis in 1958, when Premier Khrushchev first proposed the transformation of West Berlin into a demilitarized

Continued on Page 10, Column 2

BEN-GURION FIRM ON IMMIGRATION

Reiterates View on Zionism in Cordial Meeting Here With U. S. Leaders

By IRVING SPIEGEL

Premier David Ben-Gurion spoke to American Zionist leaders here yesterday in a congenial atmosphere and held fast to his view that Zionism means nothing less than "aliyah"—immigration to Israel.

The Zionist leaders included Dr. Nahum Goldmann, president of the World Zionist Organization, and Rabbi Irving Miller, chairman of the American Zionist Council, the representative body of all Zionist groups in the country.

The setting was 515 Park Avenue, site of the offices of the Zionist Council and the Jewish Agency for Israel and various other groups. Before delivering two talks in the building, Mr. Ben-Gurion exchanged warm greetings with Dr. Goldmann and other Zionist leaders.

Free Exchange Stressed

Speaking first at a joint session of leaders of the Council and the executives of the agency, the Israeli leader said that the Zionist movement could not be the only link between Jews in America and Israel. He added that Israel welcomed close relationships between the Jewish people and other groups.

Mr. Ben-Gurion stressed the right of a free exchange of opinions between himself and Zionist leaders. He said this could only be accomplished in such nations as the United States and Israel with strong adherence to democratic ideals and principles.

"Such differences can be conducted in a friendly spirit," he asserted.

On frequent occasions Mr. Ben-Gurion has said that a good Zionist is one who goes to Israel. Zionist leaders in the United States have replied that the role of the world Zionist movement was not only to aid

Continued on Page 3, Column 5

Jobless Total Falls But Rate Hits 6.9%

Special to The New York Times.

WASHINGTON, May 31—A high unemployment rate of nearly 7 per cent continued in May for the sixth straight month despite seasonal rises in jobs, the Labor Department reported today.

Between mid-April and mid-May employment rose seasonally by 1,044,000 to 66,778,000. This total was 400,000 below that for May, 1960.

The number of unemployed Americans declined, also seasonally, by 194,000 to 4,768,000, as farm and construction work picked up last month.

But the seasonally adjusted unemployment rate increased from 6.8 to 6.9 per cent.

Asked if these May statistics

Continued on Page 19, Column 1

FRENCH GENERALS GET 15-YEAR TERM IN ALGERIA MUTINY

Challe and Zeller Sentenced for Leadership of Rising—Stripped of Decorations

By HENRY GINIGER
Special to The New York Times.

PARIS, May 31 — Former Gens. Maurice Challe and André Zeller were sentenced today to fifteen years in prison for their leadership of the military mutiny in Algeria last month.

A high military tribunal of nine distinguished jurists, generals and admirals thus ended a three-day trial. The relative leniency of their decision contrasted with the furor and anger that the generals had provoked when they seized power in Algiers early in the morning of April 22. Four days later their mutiny collapsed.

Both men had been liable to the death sentence, but the state prosecutor, Antonin Besson, said he could not see his way clear to demand it. Instead he asked for twenty years for each on the ground that there were extenuating circumstances.

Indulgence for the Army

To a large extent the indulgence shown was for the French Army itself, personified by the two generals on trial.

The three days of hearings gave the impression of a conscience-stricken military arm now living in despair because it had promised the Algerian people that it would keep Algeria French. Now it is the instrument of a policy that seeks a settlement with the Moslem rebels on the basis of Algeria's independence.

Challe and Zeller listened to their sentences without expression and their partisans in the courtroom remained silent.

The prison terms were accompanied by a court decision stripping the two men of all their decorations, including that of the Legion of Honor. They had already been deprived of their rank of full general by President de Gaulle during the mutiny.

Appeals Not Possible

The sentences cannot be appealed, but they can be commuted by the President. Challe, who is 55 years old, and Zeller, who is 63, will live their years of disgrace probably in a fort or fortress where they will be able to receive visits, newspapers and mail.

Tonight they were taken in a pouring rain back to their cells in Santé prison in Paris. Challe smoked a pipe on the way out of the Palace of Justice and appeared relaxed, as did Zeller.

Before M. Besson began his summation, the court clerk read a letter from Paul Delouvrier, who was Delegate General in Algeria during 1959 and 1960 when Challe was supreme commander.

M. Delouvrier said he still had esteem for Challe because of his high motives in acting

Continued on Page 4, Column 3

New Submarine-Finder Project Could Blunt the Role of Polaris

Mid-Atlantic Laboratory Acts to Trace Undersea Craft Through Their Sounds

By WALTER SULLIVAN

A program to develop what may become the underwater equivalent of the North American radar-warning system was announced today.

The effort, under way in secret for a considerable time, is known as Project Artemis. Its success would be a mixed blessing.

If, as now seems possible, the United States can develop equipment to locate a submarine under the pack ice of the Arctic Ocean, so, eventually, can the Soviet Union. The deterrent effect of nuclear-powered submarines carrying Polaris missiles would be considerably reduced if they could no longer move in secret.

At present, however, it is thought that the Soviet Union lags far behind the United States in this field of research.

The prime contractor for the study is the Hudson Laboratories, operated by Columbia University at Yonkers in behalf of the Office of Naval

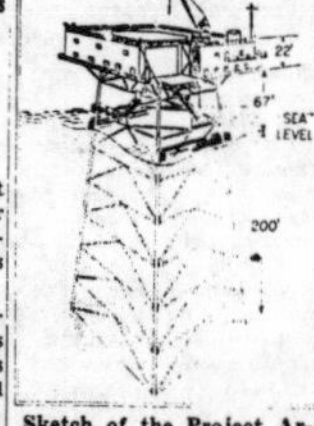

Sketch of the Project Artemis tower near Bermuda.

Research. Thirty university, industrial and government scientific groups are taking part.

Columbia and other participants in the project were permitted by the Navy to announce the program.

Among the project's chief tools are a midocean laboratory on a tower thirty miles from Bermuda and a 17,000-ton tanker modified so that she can raise and lower an immense sound generator into the sea.

This "sound transducer" is five stories high and weighs

Continued on Page 16, Column 4

TRUJILLO SHOT DEAD BY ASSASSINS; HIS REGIME REPORTS ARMY RULES; DOMINICAN CRISIS STUDIED BY U.S.

RUSK DELAYS TRIP

He Stays in Capital to Follow Events—Coup Is Doubted

By WILLIAM J. JORDEN
Special to The New York Times.

WASHINGTON, May 31—Secretary of State Dean Rusk delayed his departure for Europe today at President Kennedy's request. The President asked Mr. Rusk to follow developments in the wake of the assassination of the Dominican dictator, Generalissimo Rafael Leonidas Trujillo Molina.

The President talked by telephone from Paris with Secretary Rusk.

Officials here said they presumed the Secretary of State would be able to leave Washington in time to participate in the Vienna conference between President Kennedy and Premier Khrushchev. Those talks open Saturday.

Mr. Rusk and his top aides were studying reports from every available source on General Trujillo's death. The more important questions being asked here were:

Who planned and carried out the Trujillo assassination? What group or individual now holds political power? Does the death of General Trujillo mean a shift in the Dominican Republic's political orientation? If so, in which direction, Left or Right?

Balaguer Reports Death

There were reports that the assassination was carried out by military elements as part of an attempted coup d'état. But the glowing tribute to the dead ruler broadcast by Caribe radio in Ciudad Trujillo indicated that anti-Trujillo forces were not in control in the Dominican capital.

The decree reporting General Trujillo's death was issued in the name of President Joaquin Balaguer. Officials took this as a further indication that there had been no overthrow of the Government.

President Balaguer's statement that "the Dominican Army is in control of the situation" was open to a variety of interpretations. It could mean that the army has seized power. Or it could indicate that there had been an unsuccessful armed effort by Dominican or foreign elements to capture the capital.

Officials here said it was not yet clear what the situation was in the Dominican capital, although available evidence indicated there had been no important changes in the Government.

The first report that Trujillo had been murdered reached Washington early this morning.

Continued on Page 14, Column 5

Associated Press

ASSASSINATED: Generalissimo Rafael Leonidas Trujillo Molina, the dictator of the Dominican Republic.

NEWS HELD A DAY

Murder of Dictator Laid to a General Seeking Revenge

Texts of the proclamation and decree are on Page 14.

By PETER KIHSS

Generalissimo Rafael Leonidas Trujillo Molina, dictator of the Dominican Republic since 1930, was assassinated Tuesday night.

The death of the 69-year-old Caribbean strongman was announced over the signature of Dr. Joaquin Balaguer, who became President last August. The announcement of the assassination by the Dominican Caribe radio at 5:45 P. M. yesterday, New York time, gave no details.

Dr. Balaguer also is reported to have said the army was in control.

From San Juan, P. R., The Associated Press said information reaching there from responsible sources was that the generalissimo had been shot.

Seven persons in an automobile were said to have attacked him at 10 P. M. Tuesday as he was driving to Ciudad Trujillo from his home in San Cristobal.

Killing Laid to Revenge

The National Broadcasting Company reported last night that a disgruntled army general seeking revenge had carried out the assassination.

In a telephone call from Ciudad Trujillo, NBC's John Hlavacek said General Trujillo had been shot from ambush by a band of seven men headed by Gen. Juan Tomas Diaz.

One of the assassins was killed and several others captured, Mr. Hlavacek reported. The general and several survivors escaped to the mountains, where 1,000 troops were reported waiting.

The general was believed to have acted to avenge some wrong done to his family.

The Associated Press reported that the police went at 4:30 A. M. to the home of Roman Catholic Bishop Thomas F. Reilly, a United States citizen who has been under house arrest in the capital as a result of his quarrels with the regime. Bishop Reilly was reported to have been taken away but later

Continued on Page 14, Column 1

Foes of Trujillo Riot Here, Wrecking Consulate Room

By EMANUEL PERLMUTTER

Enemies of the Trujillo regime rioted yesterday at the Dominican Consulate offices in Rockefeller Center. As a result of the disorders, thirty-one men were taken to the West Forty-seventh Street police station and charged with disorderly conduct.

Despite the violence that took place in the consulate and in the street, no one was injured.

Most of the men arrested were part of a group that had forced its way into the third floor reception room seeking confirmation of General Trujillo's death from Consul General Luis R. Mercado. The men announced their intention to take possession of the offices at 1270 Avenue of the Americas.

When Dr. Mercado said he had no information for them and returned to the consulate's inner offices, the Trujillo foes began their disturbances.

Outer Room Wrecked

They tore pictures from the wall, broke a water cooler, overturned a small telephone switchboard and threw books around the room. They were prevented from entering the inner suite by Detective Walter Maidhof and Patrolman Joseph De Rosa, who had been assigned to guard the consulate.

The approximately twenty-five men who entered the consulate reception room were part of a crowd of about 200 enemies of the Trujillo regime who had gathered outside the building at 5 P. M.

The disorders inside brought more than fifty policemen to the scene. More than 2,000 pedestrians, homeward bound at rush hour, stopped to watch. The police kept the Trujillo foes in the street until two patrol wagons arrived.

The police reinforcements also prevented thirty Trujillo foes who had made their way to the third floor from entering the reception room to aid their associates.

Dr. Mercado said after the disturbance that he would cooperate with the police in any action they took against the rioters. He said he had no comment to make about General Trujillo's death or his own plans.

Police Commissioner Michael Murphy went to the consulate and conferred with Dr. Mercado for twenty minutes. The Consul General left his office at 7:40 P. M. with a police bodyguard.

The men who took part in

Continued on Page 15, Column 2

MAYOR DEMANDS SCHOOL REPAIRS

Tells Board to Act 'or Else' as He Institutes Drive on Red-Tape Procedures

By LEONARD BUDER

An angry Mayor Wagner told the Board of Education yesterday to speed school repairs—"or else."

After a ninety-minute meeting at City Hall with top school and other city officials, the Mayor declared:

"I do not intend to let bureaucratic red tape make our school problem look bad. I do not intend to let this kind of red tape make our schools actually bad."

Mr. Wagner announced he had ordered school officials to embark on an emergency program to expedite necessary repairs, and he promised that the funds would be found to finance such a program.

"There will be no red tape, we'll get action or else," the Mayor said in issuing his order. He indicated that disciplinary action would be taken against anyone found derelict in duty.

He also indicated that he did not consider the nine-member school board responsible for the situation, but rather administrative red tape and a "slowness" in procedure. The Mayor has the power to remove board members, after bringing charges and holding a

Continued on Page 27, Column 1

U.S. Fails to Enjoin Birmingham Police

By The Associated Press.

MONTGOMERY, Ala., May 31—A Federal judge rejected today a request by the Justice Department for a no-violence injunction against the Birmingham, Ala., police, but warned sternly against further violence toward Freedom Riders.

In its action the Government sought to prohibit the police from allowing mobs to interfere with Freedom Riders and other interstate passengers.

The court also refused to keep in force a temporary restraining order against one of three Ku Klux Klan factions.

Still pending before United States District Judge Frank M. Johnson Jr. in Montgomery is a Government request for a con-

Continued on Page 23, Column 3

PUPIL PLAN GIVEN TO NEW ROCHELLE

Integration Method Set—Town Official Sees Chaos

Text of Kaufman decree is printed on Page 24.

By EDWARD RANZAL

Federal Judge Irving R. Kaufman ordered New Rochelle yesterday to let any child transfer out of the predominantly Negro Lincoln Elementary School.

He had previously ruled that the school had been deliberately created and maintained as a segregated institution.

His order yesterday, outlining principles to be followed in desegregation, rejected a plan submitted under protest by a majority group of the New Rochelle Board of Education. This plan would have offered temporary transfers to selected pupils.

Judge Kaufman said no administrative measures could be allowed to preserve segregation. "There is no room in the Constitution for any concept of inferior citizenship," he said.

In New Rochelle, Merryle Stanley Rukeyser, president of the Board of Education, said compliance would cause "chaos" in the school system. He said the board would appeal to the United States Court of Appeals.

The judge refused to stay his order pending an appeal. Un-

Continued on Page 24, Column 1

NEWS INDEX

1961

President Kennedy held the first televised press conference on a nationwide basis.

John F. Kennedy sat for the first time in the seat of presidency.

U.S. Attorney General, Bobby Kennedy said his biggest job was to fight against organized crime.

Shirley Booth starred as *Hazel*, the Baxter family maid. The supporting cast included Whitney Blake, Don DeFore, and Bobby Buntrock.

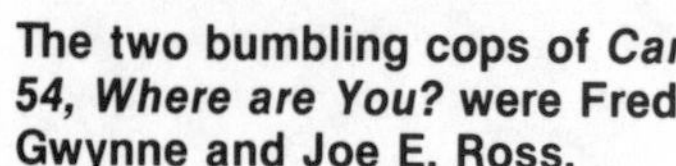

The two bumbling cops of *Car 54, Where are You?* were Fred Gwynne and Joe E. Ross.

E. G. Marshall and Robert Reed with one of their clients, (Sam Jaffe) in one of the most popular courtroom series to hit the small screen, *The Defenders.*

"All the News That's Fit to Print"

The New York Times.

LATE CITY EDITION

U. S. Weather Bureau Report (Page 95) forecasts: Mostly fair, less humid today; fair and cool tonight and tomorrow.
Temp. range: 76—60; yesterday: 79—64. Temp.-Hum. Index: near 70; yesterday: 74.

SECTION ONE

NEWS SUMMARY AND INDEX, PAGE 95

VOL. CX..No. 37,752.

NEW YORK, SUNDAY, JUNE 4, 1961.

35c outside New York City, its suburban area and Long Island. 50c in 17 Western states, Canada; higher in air delivery cities. THIRTY CENTS

KENNEDY AND KHRUSHCHEV STRESS PROBLEM OF LAOS IN 4-HOUR TALK; DISCUSSION 'FRANK AND COURTEOUS'

Associated Press Wirephoto

MEETING IN VIENNA: President Kennedy talking with Premier Khrushchev yesterday at residence of United States Ambassador. Meeting continued after lunch at residence.

PARLEY IS LIVELY

Soviet Veto Proposal a Topic in Vienna—More Talks Today

President Schaerf's welcome and Kennedy reply, Page 26.

By JAMES RESTON

Special to The New York Times.

VIENNA, June 3—President Kennedy and Premier Khrushchev held today what was described as a "frank and courteous" four-hour discussion of the troubled world relationships between the United States and the Soviet Union.

A statement issued by the official spokesmen of the two countries at a joint news conference said special attention had been paid to the Southeast Asian country of Laos, whose Government is facing a Communist-backed rebellion.

It is understood that this produced some lively discussion of the recent Soviet insistence on a veto over the control of the present "cease-fire" in that country, but no agreement.

In fact, while the atmosphere of the conversations was apparently more cordial than had been expected after the rising controversies of the last few months, no agreements were expected or reached on any of the topics discussed.

Randolph Churchill 'Bored'

The leaders' discussions will be continued tomorrow.

At the end of the mammoth news conference this evening—broken up by Randolph Churchill, son of the former British Prime Minister, who forced his way out of the closed conference room because he was "bored"—it was not possible for the official spokesmen to agree on how to characterize the results of the day's talks.

Mikhail A. Kharlamov, chief of the press department of the Soviet Foreign Office, described the conversations as "fruitful." Pierre Salinger, White House press secretary, said he preferred to stand on his previous description of the meeting as "frank and courteous."

Fruitful or not, the meetings at least avoided both the false optimism of the first summit meeting of 1955 and the angry Soviet denunciations of the ill-fated U-2 summit meeting in Paris last year.

The unexpectedly small Soviet delegation arrived here by slow train yesterday complaining that the United States seemed determined to turn the Vienna meeting into a propaganda circus, but the President insisted personally today on precisely the opposite approach.

He greeted Mr. Khrushchev

Continued on Page 26, Column 1

TRUJILLO ASSERTS 60 ARE NOW HELD IN FATHER'S DEATH

New Military Chief Asserts No Disorders Exist—He Pledges 1962 Elections

DENIES ANTI-U. S. VIEW

Dominican Exiles Charge Regime Is Carrying Out a 'Wave of Terror'

By SAM POPE BREWER

Special to The New York Times.

CIUDAD TRUJILLO, Dominican Republic, June 3—Lieut. Gen. Rafael Trujillo Jr. declared today that the Dominican authorities were holding fewer than sixty suspects in connection with the assassination of his father, Generalissimo Rafael Leonidas Trujillo Molina.

General Trujillo, who now holds the key position in the country as commander of the armed forces, said that the whole country was calm and there was no disorder anywhere.

[However, in San Juan, P. R., anti-Trujillo exiles reported that a "wave of terror" was continuing in the Dominican Republic and that strong guerrilla activities were under way.]

General Trujillo pledged the full support of all armed services to the Government of President Joaquín Balaguer and its pro-Western policies. He promised to keep the military services out of politics. He and the President pledge that next year's scheduled elections would be held.

He Backs Amnesty Plan

General Trujillo said he supported a decree published earlier this week offering amnesty to all Dominican citizens living abroad who had political charges against them. The Government said this move was designed to let all Dominicans vote in elections here next year.

He repudiated the suggestion that he might personally be hostile to the United States. General Trujillo said, "I would like to assure you that this is a lie spread by reactionary persons."

In a news conference later, President Balaguer said that lifting the present diplomatic and economic sanctions by the Organization of American States against the Dominican Republic would be the best way to further a liberal policy here.

Señor Balaguer said he had already invited American nations to "witness" Presidential

Continued on Page 3, Column 5

School Aide Is Suspended; City Bars 24 Contractors

Inspector Accused of Taking $3,000—Payola Laid to 30 Others—Queens Jury Sifts Building Practices

By LEONARD BUDER

A supervisory inspector in the city school system's Bureau of Construction was suspended last night for allegedly accepting about $3,000 in cash from twenty-four mechanical contractors. He was said to have admitted taking the money.

Mayor Wagner immediately barred the twenty-four concerns from doing business with the city pending further investigation.

The inspector's suspension came shortly after it was learned that thirty Board of Education inspectors were under investigation for allegedly accepting gifts from construction concerns.

The announcement of the suspension was made by Mayor Wagner at Gracie Mansion.

The Mayor also disclosed that a Queens County Grand Jury had been conducting an investigation of various aspects of the school construction and maintenance program of the Board of Education.

The suspended employe is Francis X. Ficarra of 348 Hutchinson Avenue, Mount Vernon, N. Y., an $8,500-a-year supervisor of mechanical installations. He has been employed by the board since 1948.

Mr. Ficarra, the Mayor said, allegedly accepted money over a four-year period.

Mr. Ficarra, reached at his home by telephone, said he was stunned by news of his suspension. He said he had heard nothing about it until told by his wife a few minutes earlier and could not comment because he did not know the details.

The Mayor, in a written statement, said that earlier in the day he had received a report from Commissioner of Investi-

Continued on Page 62, Column 4

WAGNER OUTLINES 6-POINT PROGRAM TO AID HOSPITALS

First Steps in Trussell Plan Designed to Cut Shortage in Personnel and Service

By PAUL CROWELL

Mayor Wagner yesterday announced six steps that had been taken or were about to be taken to hire more physicians and technicians and to extend municipal hospital services.

The Mayor said the steps were to implement some of the recommendations that Dr. Ray E. Trussell, Commissioner of Hospitals, had made for solving the most pressing of the hospital service problems.

Remedial action on other problems will be taken soon, the Mayor said.

Dr. Trussell's over-all program, which has the Mayor's approval, is aimed at raising medical-care standards, overcoming critical shortages of medical personnel, coping with the problems of plant obsolescence and maintenance and strengthening various auxiliary services in the system.

Concern Over Reports

Mr. Wagner said he was concerned over recent reports by both public and private agencies calling attention to the decline in the quality of service given in some city hospitals.

He said he was determined to take all steps necessary to assure modern medical care for persons "who must turn to municipal hospitals for treatment."

During the day the Mayor and Dr. Trussell spent an hour inspecting Bellevue Hospital's facilities for psychopathic patients.

The Mayor said overcrowding was the most serious problem there. He said the first step toward a solution would be taken Tuesday when twenty-six female patients would be transferred to the city hospital in Elmhurst, Queens.

Details of Program

Mr. Wagner also announced these actions for the over-all municipal hospital program:

¶The five county medical societies have been enlisted to expedite the recruiting of paid part-time physicians to meet staff shortages.

The coordinating council of the societies is sending letters to about 17,000 physicians urging their cooperation. The city has already appropriated $200,000 for staffing costs, and $1,000,000 more will be available, starting July 1, for part-time physicians.

¶A special committee has been named to handle the problem of supplying technical and scientific personnel, now in short supply. The committee consists of City Administrator Charles H. Tenney, chairman; Budget Director Abraham D. Beame and City Personnel Director Theodore H. Lang.

¶A start has been made on the hiring of full-time directors and assistants at Harlem Hospital in Manhattan and Morrisania Hospital in the Bronx. The $25,000-a-year directors and their assistants will be chosen

Continued on Page 43, Column 1

Con Ed and Union Accused Of Bias Against Negroes

By STANLEY LEVEY

The Consolidated Edison Company and the union representing its 20,000 employes were accused yesterday of discrimination against Negroes. The charges were made by three Negro witnesses during a hearing of the House Committee on Education and Labor, headed by Representative Adam Clayton Powell Jr., Democrat of Manhattan, at the Federal Building in Foley Square.

The three witnesses listed one company division after another in which they said no Negro was employed or where Negro representation was nominal. They said 3,400 Negroes were employed by the company. All are members of the union, an affiliate of the American Federation of Labor and Congress of Industrial Organizations.

Charges Are Denied

While neither the company nor the union was given an opportunity to reply at the hearing, company and union spokesmen later denied the charges.

The hearing was told by Harrison W. Smith, an assistant foreman in the plant construction department of the utility, that "Negroes are restricted to the most menial jobs at Con Edison—mops, brooms, picks, shovels and jackhammers." Mr. Smith has been a Con Ed employe for twelve years.

Griffin Simmons, who has been with the company for nine years, testified that Local 1-2 of the Utility Workers Union, representing Consolidated Edison workers, was "Jim Crow and lily white from top to bottom." This was in reply to a question from Mr. Powell regarding the union's policy.

Representative Powell called the answer "the best I have ever received to a question."

Mr. Simmons said "not a

Continued on Page 79, Column 1

U. S. SHIPS PATROL DOMINICAN AREA

Marines on Stand-by Alert —O. A. S. Acts Tomorrow on Mission to Island

By JACK RAYMOND

Special to The New York Times.

WASHINGTON, June 3—United States naval units patrolled the Caribbean waters off the Dominican Republic today as diplomats prepared for a vote here Monday in the Organization of American States.

The move in the O. A. S. consists of an attempt, backed by the United States, to send a committee to the Dominican Republic to determine whether the regime "still" constitutes a threat to the peace and security of the Western Hemisphere.

Government sources said the naval patrols, including aircraft carriers and a sizable marine force, had been ordered on a "stand-by" basis. The order was attributed to possible tension arising out of the assassination of Generalissimo Rafael Leonidas Trujillo Molina Tuesday night.

A high Government official stressed that there was no present intention of landing marines or making any effort to evacuate the 5,200 American citizens in the Dominican Republic.

The official said that al-

Continued on Page 3, Column 1

FRANCO CONDEMNS WESTERN POLICIES

Delivers Attack in Address to Cortes—Terms Spain's System 'Wave of Future'

By BENJAMIN WELLES

Special to The New York Times.

MADRID, June 3—Generalísimo Francisco Franco launched a scathing attack here today on Western policy, on capitalism, on liberalism and on democracy in general.

He declared that Spain's own brand of "organic" democracy represented the wave of the future, whereas the Western world, hamstrung by "party politics," was heading for disaster.

The 68-year-old dictator expressed his views in an hour-long speech at the formal opening of the new three-year term of the Spanish Cortes, or Parliament. He read his speech while seated, in uniform, on a red-cushioned chair.

Denounces Democracy

Every sally by General Franco against the West, against democracy, liberalism and capitalism was greeted with roars of approval by the mass of black-shirted Falangist Deputies who dominate the 588-member chamber.

General Franco informed the hand-picked "Procuradores," or Deputies, that in the new Cortes session his regime would present for their "approval" a new Law of Information. Since 1937 the Spanish press and all public expression have been controlled by one of the most

Continued on Page 35, Column 3

Kennedy Faces Problem In Britain on Berlin Issue

By DREW MIDDLETON

Special to The New York Times.

LONDON, June 3—A problem in persuasion faces President Kennedy when he arrives here tomorrow. The British Government remains to be persuaded that the West should draw a line in West Berlin over which the Soviet Union cannot step without provoking Allied military action.

The United States Administration, qualified sources said, believes this line must be drawn if an early Soviet attempt to pluck West Berlin out of the Allied sphere of influence is to be averted.

The British object that no one can foretell the nature and scope of the pressures the Soviet Union is expected to exert upon Berlin this year and that political and military tactics must be shaped to meet circumstances as they arise.

At the moment, the British Government is disinclined to agree to determining the size or direction of an Allied military effort on behalf of Berlin. Nor will it be so inclined until the scope of Soviet and East German efforts to oust the West from Berlin is clear.

U. S. Held Not Satisfied

But Britain, it can be said on high authority, is prepared to agree on a point of principle beyond which the West cannot be pushed on Berlin. This has failed to satisfy the United States, the sources acknowledged.

Foreign Office sources directed attention to a note delivered by the British Ambassador to the Soviet Foreign Ministry in Moscow today that was termed an example of Allied solidarity on Berlin.

The note rejected a Soviet complaint over the establishment by the West German Government of an agency in Berlin supervising the banking system there.

The note also emphasized the

Continued on Page 24, Column 4

FIRST LADY WINS KHRUSHCHEV, TOO

Premier, at Dinner, Says He'd Like to Shake Her Hand Before Kennedy's

By The Associated Press.

VIENNA, June 3—Premier Khrushchev met Mrs. John F. Kennedy in the splendor of Schoenbrunn Palace tonight and a twinkle lit up his eyes.

"Mr. Khrushchev," a photographer asked, "won't you shake hands with Mr. Kennedy for us?"

With a grin, Premier Khrushchev nodded toward the President's wife, Jacqueline, stately and beautiful in a long white gown, and replied:

"I'd like to shake her hand first."

The occasion was the state dinner given by Austria in the country residence of the former Habsburg emperors.

6,000 at Palace Gates

More than 6,000 Viennese crowded around the floodlit gates of the 267-year-old palace to watch the leaders of East and West enter.

Premier Khrushchev, dressed in a plain dark suit and a checked gray tie, arrived first. He was accompanied by his wife, Mme. Nina Petrovna Khrushchev, who wore a dark silk dress laced with a faint golden thread.

President and Mrs. Kennedy arrived ten minutes later—and five minutes late.

"The American princess," exclaimed a woman in the crowd, referring to Mrs. Kennedy.

President Kennedy went to Premier Khrushchev as soon as he saw him and apologized for having been late. The Soviet leader graciously accepted.

Leaders Appear Fresh

Despite six hours together earlier in the day, Mr. Khrushchev, who is 67 years old, and President Kennedy, 44, looked remarkably fresh.

Waiters in knee breeches and gold braid moved through the corridors and across the spacious rooms bearing silver trays laden with drinks.

The heavy scent of spring flowers, lavishly banked through the old palace, floated into every room.

President Adolf Schaerf of Austria welcomed the Khrushchevs and the Kennedys and members of their delegations.

President Kennedy made a striking figure beside his blue-eyed wife and the shorter Khrushchevs. The President found

Continued on Page 26, Column 4

Anti-Violence Law Is Passed in Tokyo

Special to The New York Times.

TOKYO, June 3—The ruling Liberal Democrats and the moderate Social Democrats defied strong Socialist party opposition today and passed their anti-violence bill in a stormy session of the lower house.

The bill is aimed at controlling all acts of political violence, including demonstrations near the Diet (Parliament) building and courts.

In an attempt to obstruct the opening of the session, the Socialists blocked Speaker Ichiro Kiyose from reaching the dais and calling for a vote. However, he exercised his duties from a seat on the chamber's floor.

Immediately after the lower house's approval by a majority standing vote, the bill was for-

Continued on Page 9, Column 1

SHERLUCK, 65 TO 1, FIRST IN BELMONT

Carry Back Is 7th in Upset Watched by Eisenhowers

Sherluck, paying $132.10 for $2, won the $148,650 Belmont Stakes yesterday. Owned by Jacob Sher and ridden by Braulio Baeza, the longest-priced 3-year-old in the field of nine beat Globemaster, the runner-up, by two lengths and a quarter in the ninety-third running of the mile-and-a-half race timed in 2 minutes 29 1/5 seconds. Guadalcanal was third and Carry Back, the Kentucky Derby and Preakness winner who was the 9-20 favorite to take racing's triple crown, finished seventh. General and Mrs. Eisenhower were among the 51,586 racegoers at Belmont Park. Mrs. Eisenhower presented the Belmont Stakes trophy.

BASEBALL

The White Sox beat the Yankees, 6—5, in the thirteenth inning at Chicago on Roy Sievers' home run. Third-place New York lost ground as the American League's leading Tigers beat the Minnesota Twins, 3—1, at Detroit, and the second-place Indians routed the Los Angeles Angels, 9—4, at Cleveland. In the National League, the Chicago Cubs upset Cincinnati, 10—7; Milwaukee trounced St. Louis, 9—3, and Pittsburgh trimmed Philadelphia, 5—1.

BOXING

Emile Griffith of New York retained the world welterweight championship. Griffith stopped Gaspar Ortega of Mexico in the twelfth round of a scheduled fifteen-round bout at Los Angeles in his first title defense.

Details in Section 5.

Associated Press Wirephoto

PREPARING FOR ACTION: Combat-ready marines load equipment aboard carrier Boxer in Norfolk, Va. Carrier, normally used as an attack transport, is being readied for possible action in the Caribbean near Dominican Republic.

Today's Sections

Index to Subjects

"All the News That's Fit to Print"

The New York Times.

LATE CITY EDITION

U. S. Weather Bureau Report (Page 44) forecasts: Mostly fair, hot, humid, chance of showers late today, part of tomorrow. Temp. range: 94—75; yesterday: 93—72. Temp.-Hum. Index: low 80's; yesterday: 82.

VOL. CX. No. 37,800. | NEW YORK, SATURDAY, JULY 22, 1961. | 10 cents beyond 50-mile zone from New York City except on Long Island. Higher in air delivery cities. | FIVE CENTS

FRENCH OCCUPY BIZERTE; TUNIS ASKS FOREIGN HELP; CEASE-FIRE URGED IN U. N.

FIGHTING IS HEAVY

Casualty Toll High—Tunisians Seize Oil Pipeline Terminal

By Reuters

BIZERTE, Tunisia, Saturday, July 22—The commander of the French naval base here declared last night that French forces had captured the city of Bizerte.

The announcement, by Admiral Maurice Amman, came after French troops had battered their way into the heart of the city, three miles northeast of the naval base. The Tunisians suffered heavy casualties.

Although the French claimed victory, a Tunisian Government spokesman said early today the fighting was continuing. He said the Tunisian garrison in Bizerte "holds a great part of the town."

As the French forces moved to occupy Bizerte, President Habib Bourguiba said in Tunis he had instructed all Tunisian Embassies to accept foreign volunteers to fight against the French in Tunisia.

[Mr. Bourguiba appealed to "all brother nations to come take part in the battle of Bizerte," it was reported.]

The Tunisian President also said the Government had seized the French coastal oil installation at La Skhira in eastern Tunisia. La Skhira is the terminal port for the oil pipeline from the Edjele wells in the Sahara.

150 Reported Dead

By THOMAS F. BRADY

Special to The New York Times.

BIZERTE, July 21—The French attacked this city today with troops, tanks and planes.

But after day-long fighting, the Governor's residence was still holding out against the French assault. Heavy firing and explosions could be heard from the central sector and the Arab quarter of Bizerte.

Tunisian sources said military and civilian Tunisian casualties totaled at least 150 today.

About 110 Tunisians were reported killed in the fighting in

Continued on Page 5, Column 3

The New York Times July 22, 1961

THE TUNISIAN BATTLE: The French claimed Bizerte (1). Tunisians seized La Skhira oil works (2). There was fighting near Saharan Edjele field (3).

U.S. WILL SPONSOR AIRLIFT OF CUBANS

Will Pay Havana-to-Miami Passage for 20,000 if Castro Allows Exit

By The Associated Press.

WASHINGTON, July 21—The United States Government announced tonight that it would sponsor a free airlift for more than 20,000 Cubans seeking to come to the United States.

The State Department said that, starting tomorrow, Pan American World Airways would sharply increase its flights to Havana to bring in the waiting Cubans at the rate of 1,000 a day.

The United States Government expects to pay about $350,000 out of its emergency foreign aid fund to finance the mass airlift. The White House has approved the action.

The State Department said the step was being taken because the Cubans had been unable to pay American dollars for the flight to Miami. Instead, they have had only Cuban pesos—unusable to pay their fares on such flights.

Obstacles Possible

Lincoln White, the State Department's press officer, who made the announcement, said no assurance had been received from Premier Fidel Castro as to whether he would let the Cubans out. The United States has not told Dr. Castro about the plan, Mr. White added.

This raised questions about obstacles the airlift might encounter.

The approximately 20,000 Cubans eligible for the flights are those who have visas or waivers issued by the United States Government. Most are relatives

Continued on Page 7, Column 2

U. S. DRAFTS PLEA

Resolution Will Seek Troop Withdrawal on Both Sides

Excerpts from U. N. debate appear on Page 2.

By SAM POPE BREWER

Special to The New York Times.

UNITED NATIONS, N. Y., July 21—Tunisia and France put their conflicting accounts of the Bizerte crisis before the Security Council today.

Armand Bérard of France renewed a French offer to accept an immediate cease-fire, to be followed by negotiations when conditions had returned to normal. This was made at the close of the session as he spoke in rebuttal of some of the charges made.

Mongi Slim of Tunisia said a cease-fire would be possible only on the basis of a French agreement to leave Tunisia. All the day's speakers agreed on the need for a cease-fire, though they differed in their views on responsibility for the situation.

Seven Nations Speak

Seven nations spoke in today's session, which was summoned hastily in response to a cablegram yesterday from the Tunisian Government charging French aggression. In order, they were Tunisia, France, the United States, the United Arab Republic, Turkey, the Soviet Union and Liberia.

All speakers urged a cease-fire in the growing conflict, but Mr. Slim said it was unacceptable without the withdrawal of French troops.

The United States called for an immediate cease-fire and for the return of all troops to their previous positions as a prelude to negotiations for a permanent settlement. Charles W. Yost, Deputy United States representative, presented this as an appeal to France and Tunisia.

U. S. Works on Accord

The United States delegation was working on a draft resolution incorporating those steps.

Dr. Leopoldo Benites, of Ecuador, this month's President of the Security Council, adjourned the meeting at 8:08 P. M. It will resume at 10 A. M. tomorrow.

During the meeting a message from the Tunisian Government was circulated to the eleven members of the Council. It reported a "very dangerous worsening of the situation." The message, addressed to Secretary General Dag Hammarskjold, was signed by Dr. Sadok Mokkadem, Tunisian Secretary for Foreign Affairs.

The message referring to conditions as of last night, said

Continued on Page 2, Column 3

RUSK TELLS ALLIES OF U.S. PLANNING FOR BERLIN CRISIS

Confers With Three Powers' Diplomats on Measures to Increase Readiness

By E. W. KENWORTHY

Special to The New York Times.

WASHINGTON, July 21—Secretary of State Dean Rusk conferred today with British, French and West German diplomats on measures to increase the West's readiness to meet a Berlin crisis.

Attending the late afternoon meeting were Viscount Hood, British Minister; Claude Lebel, French Minister Counselor, and Dr. Wilhelm Grewe, West German Ambassador. The British Ambassador, Sir Harold Caccia, and the French Ambassador, Hervé Alphand, were out of town.

At his news conference Wednesday President Kennedy said the National Security Council would conclude on Wednesday afternoon its review of actions to be taken to strengthen the military position of the United States and these decisions would be communicated to its allies this week.

Coordination Is Outlined

Officials said that in addition to disclosing the projected United States moves, Secretary Rusk had suggested in general terms the coordinated actions that the Administration hoped its principal allies would take.

The meeting lasted forty-five minutes. Afterward Dr. Grewe said Mr. Rusk had presented "the Administration's ideas." There was not much discussion, Dr. Grewe said, because "it was the type of meeting where you don't have a great exchange."

He said he was certain West Germany would "step up its defense efforts" if the Council of the North Atlantic Treaty Organization decided this should be done.

West Germany's assigned goal in the alliance is twelve divisions. It now has seven divisions, six of them at full strength. The United States would like West Germany to speed the completion of the seventh and form three more as quickly as possible.

Kennedy Stressed Tension

At his news conference President Kennedy had stressed that the Western alliance was probably facing a period of mounting tensions in relations with the Soviet Union extending beyond the Berlin question, and that it was therefore necessary to consider "what we can in common do."

Tomorrow Secretary of Defense Robert S. McNamara and Gen. Lyman L. Lemnitzer, Chairman of the Joint Chiefs of Staff, will fly to Paris to brief representatives of the Atlantic alliance on United States plans.

They will be accompanied by Paul H. Nitze, Assistant Secretary of Defense for International Security Affairs, and Thomas K. Finletter, United States delegate to NATO headquarters.

Tuesday evening President Kennedy will address the nation

Continued on Page 6, Column 4

U.S. AGAIN FIRES MAN INTO SPACE; CAPSULE LOST AFTER SEA LANDING, BUT ASTRONAUT SWIMS TO SAFETY

Associated Press Wirephoto

Helicopter at right tries vainly to lift space capsule, Liberty Bell 7, from the Atlantic after space flight

Associated Press Wirephoto From N. A. S. A.

Capt. Virgil I. Grissom, behind capsule, waves after trip

United Press International Telephoto From N. A. S. A.

Captain Grissom, aboard carrier, talks with the President

Unplanned Swim Leaves Grissom a 'Little Uneasy'

By JOHN W. FINNEY

Special to The New York Times.

CAPE CANAVERAL, Fla., July 21—Within a half-hour, Capt. Virgil I. Grissom, the second United States astronaut, floated in two elements. For five minutes of his sixteen-minute ride into space he was in the weightless condition of space flight. Then for two to four minutes he floated in his silvery space suit in the Atlantic Ocean.

The first experience, he said, was thrilling. The unexpected dunking left him "a little uneasy," he reported after having been landed by helicopter on the aircraft carrier Randolph. His first words after landing were:

"Give me something to blow my nose. My head is full of sea water."

Why Captain Grissom was forced to end his 118-mile-high trip into space with a swim for his life was a critical question being asked by space agency officials. And for the moment there was no certain answer.

One moment the astronaut was waving to the rescue helicopter overhead through the "picture window" of his capsule, bobbing upright in gentle seas. The next moment the escape hatch had blown from the side of the Liberty Bell 7 capsule, letting water pour into it and forcing the astronaut to swim away from his craft, which was sinking rapidly in 2,800 fathoms—more than three miles—of water.

For more than two minutes, the astronaut, who was described by Comdr. Alan. B. Shepard Jr. as more of a "floater" than a swimmer, was forced to tread water. Around him spread the

Continued on Page 8, Column 3

HATCH BLOWN OFF

Mishap Not Explained—Grissom Reported in Good Condition

Text of Grissom conversation with base, Page 9.

By RICHARD WITKIN

Special to The New York Times.

CAPE CANAVERAL, Fla., July 21—Virgil I. Grissom became the nation's second space explorer today.

The Air Force captain rocketed aboard a Mercury capsule on an arching flight that took him 118 miles into the sky and 303 miles out into the Atlantic.

But the flight was denied complete success. A mishap forced the 35-year-old astronaut to take an unplanned swim and resulted in the sinking of the $2,000,000 capsule with precious films aboard.

From the take-off at 8:20 A. M., Eastern daylight time, until the capsule landed in the ocean sixteen minutes later, the mission appeared as successful as the nearly perfect journey of the nation's first space traveler, Navy Comdr. Alan B. Shepard Jr., on May 5.

Capsule Ships Water

Minutes later, for reasons unknown, explosive bolts blew out the side hatch of the bobbing capsule before a Marine helicopter overhead could hook on and lift the capsule upright.

This hooking-on procedure was provided so that water would not pour into the open hatch when the seventy explosive bolts blew off the cover.

Captain Grissom said he had not pulled the plunger that controls the bolts. The cover blew off before the helicopter had had a chance to lift the capsule to its upright position.

Water rolled into the capsule immediately, and the captain floated out. Two to four minutes later he was hauled to safety by a second helicopter. He had swallowed more sea water than he would have liked. He was somewhat shaky. But he was essentially in excellent condition.

Some observers interpreted the following radio exchange between the capsule and the helicopter as indicating that Captain Grissom had, in fact,

Continued on Page 8, Column 1

SOVIET SAYS NAVY HAS ATOMIC EDGE

Warns U.S. It Has More and Faster Submarines of Missile-Firing Type

By SEYMOUR TOPPING

Special to The New York Times.

MOSCOW, July 21—The Soviet Government newspaper Izvestia declared today that the Soviet Union had a larger and faster fleet of rocket-launching nuclear submarines than the United States.

In the midst of the growing controversy over Berlin, Izvestia asserted that the Soviet Navy boasted "atomic submarines armed with the mightiest rockets of various types."

It was not said, however, whether the Soviet submarines were capable—like the United States Polaris submarines—of launching missiles under water.

The references to nuclear submarines were made in a political commentary written by Observer, a signature reserved for authoritative pronouncements.

Robert Kennedy Scored

It attacked Robert F. Kennedy, the United States Attorney General, for a speech made July 15 at the launching of the Polaris submarine John Marshall at Newport News.

In that speech, the Attorney General, President Kennedy's brother, warned Mr. Khrushchev that the United States could "be pushed too far." He cautioned against "underestimating the American people."

Izvestia denounced the Attorney General as one of a group of United States leaders who had created "military hysteria" over Berlin and had threatened the Soviet Union.

Izvestia contended that Soviet nuclear submarines operated "not at a lesser but at a greater speed than United States submarines and were not fewer in

Continued on Page 7, Column 2

BROOKLYN YOUTH SLAIN OVER DIME

Congresswoman Tours Area After Stomp Killing

An 18-year-old Brooklyn youth was stomped to death in an argument over a dime last night.

Less than three hours after the slaying, Representative Edith Green, Democrat of Oregon, began a scheduled tour of Brooklyn, including the neighborhood where the murder occurred, to study juvenile delinquency conditions.

The victim, Judge Sanders of 939 Lafayette Avenue, was playing handball with his brother Matthew, 17, in a playground at Greene and Stuyvesant Avenues in the Bedford-Stuyvesant section.

According to the police, the brothers heard a cousin involved in a noisy dispute with three other youths at the far end of the playground. The argument was over borrowing 10 cents, the police said.

When the Sanders brothers went to investigate, the older one was attacked by the trio. He was punched and kicked,

Continued on Page 12, Column 2

6,406 APARTMENTS SLATED FOR CITY

Estimate Board to Weigh 9 Middle-Income Projects

By PAUL CROWELL

Proposals for the construction $115,100,000 worth of middle-income housing will go before the Board of Estimate next Thursday.

J. Clarence Davies Jr., chairman of the New York City Housing and Redevelopment Board, said yesterday that the proposals, for 6,406 residential apartments in nine projects, constituted the "biggest single program of middle-income housing ever advanced at once in the city, the state or the nation."

Mr. Davies said the nine projects, all by private builders, would be completed within the next five years. He said 2,043 of the apartments would be available within the year, and the rest would be completed in two to five years.

The Board of Estimate has been asked to review the projects and give them final approval. The plans provide for tax abatement and mortgage loans by the city for the benefit of the builders. The state's

Continued on Page 22, Column 4

ARGENTINA TO GET $204,500,000 AID

U. S. and World Bank Will Grant Development Loans

By TAD SZULC

Special to The New York Times.

WASHINGTON, July 21—Argentina will be granted $204,500,000 in loans for industrial development by the United States and the International Bank for Reconstruction and Development.

It was authoritatively stated today that agreements in principle on the loans had been negotiated here by United States and World Bank officials and an Argentine mission headed by Ambassador Adalbert Krieger Vasena.

Washington also agreed to send a trade mission to Argentina to help her expand her exports to the United States. In addition, Washington will send specialists to Argentina to determine whether the United States ban on the entry of Argentine meat because of foot-and-mouth disease can be lifted for cooked meats.

Surplus Issue Solved

Argentina believes the resumption of substantial exports to the United States can go far to help with her balance-of-payments problems and her financial requirements for imports of industrial equipment.

The negotiators also worked out a solution of the long-standing problem of Argentina's concern that United States loans and donations of surplus commodities, particularly wheat, were threatening her sales abroad.

They agreed to arrange for consultations every six months to determine whether the dis-

Continued on Page 3, Column 1

Strikers Stone Vans at Aqueduct, but Races Go On

Associated Press

Strikers attempt to prevent a horse van from entering the Aqueduct race track in Queens

By STANLEY LEVEY

More than 1,200 stablehands went on strike yesterday at the Aqueduct race track for union recognition and economic gains. Vans carrying horses to the track were stoned and six pickets were arrested on charges of disorderly conduct. However, the violence failed to halt the day's nine-race program. The walkout involved grooms, exercise boys and hot walkers—men who walk horses to cool them off after races and workouts. The New York Racing Association said that today's nine-race card would be held. Taking no chances, however, the association set up an emergency program of

Continued on Page 16, Column 2

NEWS INDEX

1961

Major Yuri Gagarin helped the Russians beat the U.S. in the space-race when he made the first single-orbit flight on April 12, beating the U.S. by a month.

Shepard's flight on TV at the White House

1961

Chrysler introduced Valiant, one of the first compact cars.

The Chevrolet Corvair, along with Ford's popular Falcon were the Valiant's competition.

Dress buyers swarmed over to Oleg Cassini's spring showing to inspect a line of dresses from one of the First Lady's designers.

"All the News That's Fit to Print"

The New York Times.

LATE CITY EDITION
U. S. Weather Bureau Report (Page 44) forecasts:
Fair and cool today and tonight.
Fair and milder tomorrow.
Temp. range: 78—60; yesterday: 79—64.
Temp.-Hum. Index: low 70's; yesterday: 75.

VOL. CX—No. 37,823. NEW YORK, MONDAY, AUGUST 14, 1961. FIVE CENTS

SOVIET TROOPS ENCIRCLE BERLIN TO BACK UP SEALING OF BORDER; U.S. DRAFTING VIGOROUS PROTEST

Associated Press Wirephoto

NO EXIT: An East German couple walks away from barbed-wire barrier on border between East and West Berlin. East German troops blocked their entry to West Berlin.

SPECIAL SESSION SET FOR AUG. 21 ON SCHOOL ISSUE

Governor Expected to Seek to Limit Mayor's Power in Appointing Board

FISCAL CHANGES LIKELY

System May Get Right to Raise Funds—Residence Rules in Question

By WARREN WEAVER Jr.
Special to The New York Times.

ALBANY, Aug. 13—Governor Rockefeller today called a special session of the Legislature for Monday, Aug. 21, to provide fresh leadership and guidance for the New York City school system.

The Governor issued a one-sentence call for the Senate and Assembly to meet in the Capitol at noon a week from tomorrow to deal with "legislation pertaining to the structure, management, supervision and control" of the city's schools.

He provided no further information on the action he would urge upon the lawmakers. It was learned, however, that the administration proposals would include bills to do the following:

¶Strip the Mayor's office of its unrestricted power to appoint members of the Board of Education.

¶Abolish the requirement that members of the board live in certain boroughs and the practice of their having to get "clearance" from their county political leaders as a condition of eligibility.

¶Provide a reconstituted Board of Education with power to raise and spend funds without political interference.

¶Authorize the Board of Regents to supersede the present Board of Education with an interim board. The interim board would set education policy until a permanent unit, selected under a new system, could take office.

The Governor's chief adviser in his effort to reorganize the Board of Education is the state Education Commissioner, Dr. James E. Allen Jr. Their plan calls for legislation to set up an advisory committee or council of a dozen or more outstanding New York City educators, lawyers and laymen.

Membership on this council

Continued on Page 16, Column 1

8 CEZANNE WORKS STOLEN IN FRANCE

Art Valued at $2,000,000 Taken From Exhibition

By W. GRANGER BLAIR
Special to The New York Times.

PARIS, Aug. 13—Eight paintings by Paul Cézanne were stolen early today. The theft occurred at an exhibition of the postimpressionist's works at Aix-en-Provence, in southern France.

The value of the stolen canvases was unofficially estimated to be about $2,000,000.

The burglary thus equaled in value, if not in size, the theft twenty-eight days ago of fifty-seven modern art works from the Annonciade Museum in Saint-Tropez, on the French Riviera.

All the Cézannes taken had been lent to the Aix-en-Provence exposition by European and United States museums and private collectors.

'Card Players' Taken

The stolen works were: "The Card Players," a version showing two figures, from the Louvre in Paris; a portrait of Marie Cézanne, sister of the painter, from the St. Louis Municipal Museum; a still life of a leg of mutton, from the Zurich, Switzerland, Museum, and a still life of a teapot, from the Cardiff Museum in Britain.

Also, a landscape near Aix, showing Caesar's tower, from a private collection; "Water Reflections," from a collector in Milan, Italy; "Seated Peasant," from Sidney Simon of New York, and "The Skulls [Les Crânes]," from Mme. Marianne Feilchenfeldt of Zurich.

The paintings were stolen, probably around 4 A. M., from the Vendôme Pavilion, a 287-year-old mansion built for the Duc de Mercoeur, who was Car-

Continued on Page 2, Column 3

Mayor Still Weighs Dismissal of Board

By GENE CURRIVAN

Deputy Mayor Paul R. Screvane said yesterday Mayor Wagner was committed to remove the members of the Board of Education if this was recommended by his newly appointed board of inquiry.

Mr. Screvane, who appeared on the "Searchlight" program on WNBC-TV, was asked if he thought the public had lost so much confidence in the board that it should either resign or be removed by the Mayor.

"If this is the decision of the three-man group we now have, and this decision can be made very quickly, the Mayor is already committed to do precisely that," he said.

Concerning a report that the

Continued on Page 16, Column 4

2 MAYORAL RIVALS ASK MORE JUDGES

Lefkowitz and Levitt Tell a Bar Group Congestion in Courts Must Be Eased

By LAYHMOND ROBINSON

Two aspirants for Mayor joined yesterday in calling for an increase in the number of judges in the city and state to ease court congestion.

In letters to a bar group that had solicited their views, State Controller Arthur Levitt, a Democratic contender, and Attorney General Louis J. Lefkowitz, Republican candidate, both urged more judgeships.

Neither, however, estimated how many more judgeships there should be. Their letters went to the New York State Association of Plaintiffs' Trial Lawyers.

Two Albany Attempts Fail

Bills to set up new judgeships in New York City were scuttled in the last two sessions of the Legislature when Republicans and Democrats could not agree on the number of posts or the persons who would fill them.

In his letter to Joseph Kelner, president of the 2,100-member bar association, Mr. Levitt called the court congestion problem a "serious menace" to justice.

Mr. Lefkowitz said the city and state deserved "a judicial system which provides an expeditious, economical and efficient administration of justice," and that "an increase in the number of judges is an important facet of this over-all program."

In releasing the Levitt and Lefkowitz statements, Mr. Kelner did not make clear whether he had also asked for Mayor Wagner's views on the subject.

A spokesman for the Mayor, who is running as an independ-

Continued on Page 17, Column 4

AID DEBATE DUE IN HOUSE TODAY; STIFF FIGHT SEEN

Mansfield Expects Senate to Approve Measure by Middle of the Week

By LLOYD GARRISON
Special to The New York Times.

WASHINGTON, Aug. 13—Senator Mike Mansfield, the majority leader, predicted today that the foreign-aid bill would pass the Senate by mid-week without any major changes.

But the bill, with its controversial request for $8,800,000,000 in long-term borrowing authority, is likely to meet much stiffer resistance in the House. The House is scheduled to take up the measure tomorrow and to continue debate on it for the rest of the week.

Senator Mansfield predicted that "the usual amendments" aimed at cutting the bill would be offered this week. But he contended that "we'll just about hold the amount of the bill as it now stands."

The Senate Foreign Relations Committee has cut $436,000,000 from the President's request for $4,762,500,000, leaving a total of $4,326,500,000.

Further Cut Doubted

It was this figure that Senator Mansfield predicted would pass without any significant change.

The heart of the bill is an Administration request for authority to borrow $8,800,000,000 from the Treasury over the next five years to finance long-term overseas loans.

Last Friday, by a seventeen-vote margin, the Senate defeated an amendment offered by Senator Harry F. Byrd, Democrat of Virginia. The amendment would have required the President to go to the House and Senate appropriations committees each year for the money.

The measure is likely to contain an amendment representing a compromise proposal made last week by Senator J. W. Fulbright in an effort to win liberal Republican votes against the Byrd amendment.

Review Plan Expected

The compromise by the chairman of the Senate Foreign Relations Committee would give Congress the right to review for a thirty-day period all loans over $10,000,000. But it would not give Congress the right to veto such loans.

The Administration wants the reviewing period shortened to fifteen days. It would also like to limit the review to loans above $15,000,000, to lessen the paper work.

However, the Arkansas Democrat's compromise is expected to go through unaltered.

Over the week-end the Administration sought to counter

Continued on Page 5, Column 1

ALLIES IN ACCORD

Britain and France Due to Join in Challenge on German Action

Text of Rusk's statement on Berlin appears on Page 7.

By TAD SZULC
Special to The New York Times.

WASHINGTON, Aug. 13—Secretary of State Dean Rusk charged today that the East German closing of the West Berlin border was a double violation of agreements between the Soviet Union and the Western powers.

In a statement issued with President Kennedy's approval, Mr. Rusk declared "these violations of existing agreements will be the subject of vigorous protest through appropriate channels."

Mr. Rusk said that the travel ban was in contravention of accords on free circulation within the city and of a decision by a four-power meeting of foreign ministers in 1949 assuring access to Berlin from what are now the former occupation zones.

Allied Access Unaffected

He noted, however, that the Communist measures did not "thus far" interfere with the access by the Western Allies to Berlin.

The threat that this may occur later has been raised by the Soviet Union's announcement that it will sign a peace treaty with East Germany and turn over to East Germany the control of routes to the disputed city.

[In London and Paris officials viewed the East German action with extreme concern. Britain denounced the new restrictions as a violation of Berlin's four-power status.]

According to a State Department spokesman, a protest is expected to be made tomorrow in similar notes to be handed by the United States, British and French military commanders in Berlin to their Soviet counterpart.

There was also the possibility, diplomatic sources indicated, that the protest delivered by the military commanders might promptly be followed with a direct protest to the Soviet Union by the Western Allies.

With the closing of the bor-

Continued on Page 7, Column 1

TEAR GAS IS USED

Reds' Police Disperse Crowds—Workers Kept From Jobs

Soviet bloc communiqué, East German decree, Page 6.

By SYDNEY GRUSON
Special to The New York Times.

BERLIN, Monday, Aug. 14—Two battle-ready Soviet Army divisions were reported to have ringed Berlin yesterday in support of East Germany's sudden and dramatic closing of the border between East and West Berlin.

The Soviet divisions were said to have armor and artillery with them. Other Soviet Army divisions among the estimated total of twenty in East Germany were reported on the move throughout the restive country.

The new Communist measures shut off West Berlin to East Berliners and East Germans. They did not affect the movement from West Berlin into the Communist-controlled Eastern sector of the city or the vital communications linking West Berlin to West Germany.

Barrier Effective

According to preliminary reports to West Berlin authorities, none of the 53,000 East Berliners with jobs in West Berlin had crossed the border by 9 A. M. today. Also, it was reported, no refugees had reached West Berlin under the cover of darkness.

The East German action brought angry exchanges yesterday between East Berliners and the Communist People's Police near some of the thirteen border crossing points left open.

Smoke and tear-gas bombs and water hoses were used to disperse one crowd of several hundred youths who had taunted the police and armed Communist factory brigades trying to explain the necessity for the new measures.

Rope Barrier at Gate

At one border point, the East German police also hurled tear gas to break up a crowd of West Berliners facing them across the road. The crowd melted into side streets until the gas had cleared, but then most of them came back. The police then left them alone.

As the night wore on, the Berliners drifted to their homes. Along toward dawn, fewer than 100 young people stood behind the rope barricade put up about fifty yards from the Brandenburg Gate. Approximately 200 West Berlin riot policemen were on guard in parked trucks.

Today, there were no reports of early morning incidents from either side of the border, the West Berlin police reported, and both halves of the divided city began to come to life under a gray cloud-filled sky with no indication that trouble was in the offing.

Under an order of the East

Continued on Page 6, Column 1

ADENAUER IS SURE ALLIES WILL REACT

Tells Germans Reds' Berlin Decree Will Be Countered —Economic Step Hinted

By GERD WILCKE
Special to The New York Times.

BONN, Germany, Aug. 13—Chancellor Adenauer assured Germans on both sides of the Iron Curtain tonight that Bonn "with its Allies will take the necessary measures" to counter the Communists' closing of the border between East and West Berlin.

In a statement issued after consultation with some of his top advisers, Dr. Adenauer said:

"It is the law of the hour to meet the challenge from the East firmly but calmly and to do nothing that can worsen the situation."

Although Dr Adenauer did not say what counter-measures the West was contemplating, it was generally felt here that economic sanctions might be high on the list.

Dr. Adenauer suggested at election rallies last week that the Communist bloc could be hurt economically if Western trade was cut off. Premier Khrushchev, he said, would use different language if the partners of the North Atlantic

Continued on Page 6, Column 3

Closing of Border Is Seen As First of Soviet Moves

By SEYMOUR TOPPING
Special to The New York Times.

MOSCOW, Aug. 13—The closing of the border between East and West Berlin was regarded by informed Western observers here today as the first in a series of acts the Soviet Union will take in respect to Berlin.

These observers also viewed the Berlin action as signifying that Premier Khrushchev had decided irrevocably to conclude a separate peace treaty with East Germany.

Mr. Khrushchev has been under pressure from East Germany for years to curb the westward flow of refugees by sealing the Berlin border. For reasons of broader policy, the Soviet Premier withheld his consent.

Mr. Khrushchev apparently felt that any one-sided abrogation of the four-power accord on free movement within Berlin would prejudice the chances of the West's joining in a peace treaty that would recognize the status quo in Eastern Europe.

Action Was Expected

It has been regarded as inevitable, however, that the border would be closed if a heavy flow of refugees continued from East to West Germany through Berlin.

The draining away of East German manpower through the West Berlin refugee centers was dislocating the economy of the Communist state.

According to well-informed sources, three factors counted in Mr. Khrushchev's decision to restrict the transit of Germans across the border at this time:

¶Mr. Khrushchev came to the conclusion that the West would not join in any peace treaty that would recognize the division of Germany and that he must sign a separate treaty with the East Germans.

¶There was concern that the flight of the refugees would reach dangerous and unmanageable proportions before the

Continued on Page 7, Column 4

MOOD OF BERLIN: CONTROLLED FURY

Sunday Motorists Flocking to Checkpoints Jarred by Sight of Guns

By HARRY GILROY
Special to The New York Times.

BERLIN, Aug. 13—At times today East Berlin looked like a new tourist attraction. Then it was a war camp. Next it was the picture of an ominous mob with a flicker of revolt in the air.

West Berlin was alternately a family strolling in its Sunday best, a woman crying.

It depended on where you moved and what you stumbled upon. The 3,300,000 people of this metropolis were put under sudden violent strain when the East German regime sealed the East-West Berlin border.

Churchgoers answered the call of church bells in the morning in what was described as the usual Sunday attendance. Some references were made from the pulpits to the "serious events." There was a large attendance at vesper services.

Communist Units Eyed

In the cool dawn only a dozen Berliners gathered on each side of the Brandenburg Gate and at other crossing points between East and West Berlin to look at the spectacle of Communist policemen, soldiers and "factory fighting groups" deploying as if to stand off an approaching army.

By noon, thousands of West Berlin motorists were jamming the approaches to the gateways with their cars and everyone seemed to be out for a look.

Hundreds of these cars drove through the East Berlin checkpoints, with the occupants receiving snappy salutes from the East German guards, and went on to make the main streets of East Berlin more crowded and lively than they are on ordinary days.

These motorists were in for a shock. In the Marx-Engels Platz stood twenty-seven big military trucks, most of them filled with troops holding submachine guns.

Continued on Page 7, Column 5

U. S. Is Preparing Disarmament Plan

John J. McCloy, President Kennedy's chief adviser on disarmament, disclosed yesterday that the United States was working on a "far-reaching" disarmament plan.

Mr. McCloy said the plan would be ready for presentation some time this fall and was being discussed with this country's allies. He asserted that it would be premature to reveal any of its details now.

Mr. McCloy was interviewed on the National Broadcasting Company's television program "Meet the Press."

Mr. McCloy, who recently talked privately with Premier Khrushchev at the Soviet leader's villa near Sochi on the Black Sea, also made the following observations:

¶His impression was that Mr. Khrushchev knew very well

Continued on Page 7, Column 7

Emergency Aid Plan Given Latin Parley

By EDWARD C. BURKS
Special to The New York Times.

PUNTA DEL ESTE, Uruguay, Aug. 13 — The United States today pledged prompt emergency aid to Latin-American nations and then reported that all significant issues of the Inter-American Economic and Social Conference had been settled.

Preliminary calculations showed that about $150,000,000 could be quickly available in existing foreign-aid funds for projects described as of an emergency nature.

But United States officials here said that considerably more could be earmarked for emergency projects out of the more than $1,000,000,000 that President Kennedy has promised in Latin-American aid under his Alliance for Progress programs

Continued on Page 5, Column 3

'61 Ball May (or May Not) Account for Homers

Conclusion Reached Through Analysis Is Inconclusive

Engineers' report on baseballs used in majors, Page 19.

By HOWARD M. TUCKNER

Baseball fans, who are swiveling their heads like spectators at a tennis match as home-run balls fly by, are asking:

"Is the 1961 ball the same ball that Babe Ruth hit?"

Scientific tests show that maybe it is, and maybe it isn't.

With both Mickey Mantle and Roger Maris threatening Ruth's 1927 record of sixty home runs—and even 150-pound weaklings casually smashing the ball into the bleachers—the players, the fans and particularly the loyalists who do not want to see the Sultan of Swat dethroned are looking suspiciously at that little ball.

And after what Maris and Mantle did yesterday—Mantle hit his forty-fifth homer, Maris his forty-fourth and forty-fifth—these suspicions are bound to intensify. Both New York Yankee sluggers are comfortably ahead of Ruth's record pace.

By common consent of the romanticists of the "Golden Era" of baseball, the 1961 ball is "livelier" than the ones Ruth belted thirty-four years ago. But for the realists, those fans waiting eagerly for the Mantles and the Marises to get past

The New York Times

Stephen E. Taub, an engineer, uses an explosive-driven ram in making baseball comparison tests in Central Park.

the magic mark of sixty and who insist, like broken records, that "records are made to be broken," the ball is really no better; the players are better.

The New York Times decided to subject some baseballs—a total of seven, including a vintage ball of 1927, a 1936 ball and one from the current batch at Yankee Stadium—to scientific analysis.

The tests, made by technicians who had no rooting inter-

Baseball Hit by Ruth Not Unlike Those of '36 or Today

est in the outcome, were undertaken by Foster D. Snell, Inc., consulting chemists and engineers, at 29 West Fifteenth Street.

After subjecting two of the balls to surgical dissection, and all of them to battering by an explosive-driven Remington Arms Ram, to deformation measurements with a vernier caliper, to study by a rubber technologist and to similar probings, the technologists do not find anything in any of the balls to show clearly that a home run has been easier to hit in any one period of baseball than in any other period.

The two technicians who conducted the experiments, Robert W. Batey, the company's director of special evaluations, and Stephen E. Taub, the firm's acting director of engineering, reached this conclusion:

"The 1961 ball is slightly larger, slightly lighter and slightly livelier than one 1927 ball."

(The 1961 ball studied by the experts was donated by the New York Yankees and the 1927 ball was a treasure piece that Babe Ruth smacked for a homer at the Stadium.)

The technicians, adding a quick postscript to their "conclusion," went on to say that

Continued on Page 19, Column 1

NEWS INDEX

"All the News That's Fit to Print"

The New York Times.

LATE CITY EDITION
U. S. Weather Bureau Report (Page 54) forecasts: Mostly fair and warm today; clear tonight. Warm tomorrow.
Temp. range: 90—66; yesterday: 85—64.
Temp.-Hum. Index: near 80; yesterday: 77.

VOL. CX..No. 37,840. NEW YORK, THURSDAY, AUGUST 31, 1961. 10 cents beyond 50-mile zone from New York City, except on Long Island. Higher in air delivery cities. FIVE CENTS

SOVIET RESUMING ATOMIC TESTS; KENNEDY SEES PERIL TO WORLD; SAYS U.S. HANDS ARE NOW FREED

DEAN IS RECALLED

Washington May Act in U. N. to Condemn Move by Moscow

The White House statement is printed on Page 5.

By MAX FRANKEL
Special to The New York Times.

WASHINGTON, Aug. 30—The United States declared itself freed tonight from its promise not to conduct nuclear tests, but it withheld any definite decision on the resumption of testing.

President Kennedy responded to the announcement of Soviet intentions to resume testing by immediately recalling Arthur H. Dean, the chief United States negotiator at the Geneva test ban talks.

The Soviet action, the White House said, "leaves the United States under the necessity of deciding what its own national interests require."

The White House said the Soviet decision would be met with "deepest concern and resentment" throughout the world.

It accused Moscow of creating a hazard to every human being by increasing the dangers of nuclear fall-out, of disregarding mankind's desire for a halt in the arms race and of threatening the entire world by increasing the dangers of "a thermonuclear holocaust."

'Hypocrisy' Condemned

"The Soviet Government's decision to resume nuclear weapons testing indicates the complete hypocrisy of its professions about general and complete disarmament," the White House declared.

President Kennedy and his aides reacted within three hours after they had confirmation of the Soviet decision. They had been prepared for the news by the interception of a Soviet radio transmission to Central Asia, betraying the Soviet move.

Even before final confirmation was received, the President met at 5:25 P. M. at the White House with Secretary of State Dean Rusk, Allen W. Dulles, director of the Central Intelligence Agency, and McGeorge Bundy, his special assistant for security affairs. They conferred for twenty minutes and later kept in touch by telephone.

The apparent purpose of their cautious, noncommittal statement was to let the Soviet Union dominate the unfavorable

Continued on Page 5, Column 1

WEST IS BLAMED

Moscow Cites Berlin Tensions—Boasts of Superbomb Project

Soviet statement on nuclear tests appears on Page 4.

By SEYMOUR TOPPING
Special to The New York Times.

MOSCOW, Thursday, Aug. 31 — The Soviet Union announced early today it would resume testing of nuclear weapons.

The Government statement said also that Soviet scientists had worked out projects for creating a series of superpowerful nuclear bombs with an explosive force equivalent to 20,000,000 to 100,000,000 tons of TNT.

Moscow asserted it had been compelled to undertake these testing plans because of what it described as the threatening attitude of the United States and its allies in the Berlin dispute.

It warned that the Soviet Union possessed rockets capable of delivering a superbomb "to any point on the globe from which an attack on the Soviet Union or other Socialist [Communist] countries can be launched."

Faster Arms Race Expected

The rockets were described as "similar to those which Maj. Yuri Gagarin and Maj. Gherman Titov used for their unrivaled cosmic flights around the earth."

The Soviet decision to break the moratorium on nuclear testing, which started in 1958, was expected here to accelerate the East-West nuclear weapons race.

The United States warned the Soviet Union in a note June 17 that its national security would not allow for the indefinite suspension of testing in the absence of a treaty to bar the testing of nuclear weapons.

The moratorium had been subject to a year-to-year renewal pending the outcome of negotiations in Geneva by the United States, Britain and the Soviet Union on a test ban treaty.

Geneva Talks Stalled

The Soviet delegate at the Geneva talks, Semyon K. Tsarapkin, has brushed aside new Western proposals aimed at breaking the deadlock in negotiations for a system of controlling and supervising any test ban treaty. Mr. Tsarapkin insisted that any such ban must be made part of an agreement on general and complete disarmament.

It has been the feeling of Western experts here for some time that Soviet intransigence at the Geneva negotiating table had been due to a desire to resume testing.

These Western sources reasoned that the Soviet Union wanted to undertake testing again because the United States, prior to the moratorium, had developed a more sophisticated arsenal of nuclear

Continued on Page 4, Column 2

Berlin Reds Hold Four in U. S. Army Car 75 Minutes

Associated Press Radiophoto

United States tanks and armored personnel carriers lined up yesterday on Friedrichstrasse at the dividing line between the Soviet and United States sectors of Berlin.

By SYDNEY GRUSON
Special to The New York Times.

BERLIN, Aug. 30—A United States Army car with a captain and three sergeants was held in East Berlin for seventy-five minutes today. The incident brought American tanks rumbling to the border line, their guns pointing down the street from West Berlin into Communist territory. The right front window of the car was smashed. The United States Army's Berlin command said that an East Berlin motorcycle policeman had used a truncheon to break it. The policeman was overheard telling one of his officers that he had broken the window with his fist after his

Continued on Page 3, Column 5

I.C.C. PROPOSES SUBSIDY BY U.S. FOR RAILROADS

NEW HAVEN CITED

Agency Asserts Every Passenger Line Is in Same Plight

Excerpts from I. C. C. report will be found on Page 18.

Special to The New York Times.

WASHINGTON, Aug. 30—The Interstate Commerce Commission today advocated direct Federal subsidies to sustain essential railroad passenger services.

The plan would provide Federal funds to railroads to offset losses in carrying passengers, plus further support equal to any tax relief the railroads receive locally. The plan would cost $52,000,000 at the start.

Everett Hutchinson, chairman of the I. C. C., made the proposal in testimony before the Senate surface transportation subcommittee.

Senator Warren G. Magnuson, Democrat of Washington, chairman of the Senate Interstate Commerce Committee, said: "I would think the proposal would not meet with too much approval because that would lead to nationalization in time, and that's what we would like to avoid."

Report Is Released

Mr. Hutchinson's recommendation reflected a conclusion reached by the I. C. C. in investigating the New York, New Haven and Hartford Railroad. A report on the study was issued at the time of the Senate hearing.

After reviewing the "decline and fall" of the New Haven, the report by the commission said the outlook was bleak for the nation's railroads, especially those in the East. It then outlined a program to aid railroad passenger service generally. Legislation would be sought from Congress to carry out the program, the commission said.

If prompt and vigorous action is not taken, the commission said, a number of other railroads may be forced to go into reorganization, as the New Haven has.

"We believe that the time has come for the formulation of a

Continued on Page 18, Column 4

Three States Set Up Transportation Unit

By CHARLES GRUTZNER

A Tri-State Transportation Committee was appointed yesterday by Governor Rockefeller of New York, Gov. Robert B. Meyner of New Jersey and Gov. John Dempsey of Connecticut.

While the major problem is how to save and improve commuter railroad service, the new committee has been directed also to come up with solutions to problems of motor traffic, air travel and freight transportation.

The committee is to make its first report, covering matters that require early action, by Nov. 1. It will make periodic reports and recommendations to the three Governors on a variety of problems, with a first over-all interim report on long-range solutions due by Sept. 1, 1963.

The Governors made a joint

Continued on Page 17, Column 1

MILITARY LEADERS DECLARE GOULART MUST NOT RETURN

Rule Uut Compromise Plan to Allow Him to Assume Brazilian Presidency

By EDWARD C. BURKS
Special to The New York Times.

RIO DE JANEIRO, Thursday, Aug. 31—Brazil's top military leaders declared flatly last night that they would not allow Vice President João Goulart to return to the country "in the present situation."

Their decision was announced in a manifesto as Brazil appeared to stand at the brink of violence or even civil war over the question of a successor to Dr. Janio Quadros, who resigned the Presidency Friday.

[Vice President Goulart flew to New York from Paris Wednesday and left six hours later by air for Panama. He said he expected to receive in Panama last-minute information to determine his course from there.]

In their declaration, Brazil's War, Navy and Air Force ministers seemed to rule out a compromise plan proposed by a Congressional committee that would allow Senhor Goulart to return as a figurehead President under a changed style of government. The change would set up a parliamentary regime with a Premier as head of government.

Ideology Is Cited

The three ministers said Senhor Goulart had demonstrated clearly his leftist ideological tendencies and his admiration for Communist China and the Soviet Union.

The ministers reiterated their contention that it would be "absolutely inconvenient in the present situation" for Senhor Goulart to return.

In Senhor Goulart's home state of Rio Grande do Sul, Gov. Leonel Brizola, who is Senhor Goulart's brother-in-law, ordered three small ships sunk in the narrow entrance to Porto Alegre harbor to keep the navy from sending in warships.

Commander Rebels

The top military leader there, Gen. José Machado Lopes, Third Army commander was refusing to take orders from the military ministers and was supporting Senhor Goulart's cause.

The manifesto issued by the military ministers said that Senhor Goulart's accession to power would unleash agitation, tumult and even bloody clashes.

The ministers added that the armed forces were deeply convinced that during such a period democratic institutions would fall "and with them justice, liberty, social peace and all the highest standards of our Christian culture."

The statement said further:

"In the Presidency of a regime which gives ample authority to the chief of government,

Continued on Page 10, Column 2

HOUSE VOTE KILLS SCHOOL AID PLAN

Coalition Bars Compromise Bill on Construction With a Margin of 242-169

By JOHN D. MORRIS
Special to The New York Times.

WASHINGTON, Aug. 30—The House of Representatives killed the Administration's compromise school construction bill today, 242 to 169.

The unexpectedly one-sided vote was a stunning defeat for President Kennedy and a major victory for the House coalition of Republicans and conservative Democrats.

It came on a motion by Representative Adam Clayton Powell Jr., Democrat of Manhattan, for consideration of the bill. Without debate, the House defeated the motion and thus wiped out any hope for passage of new school-aid legislation this session.

President Kennedy accepted the action as final for this session. He told his news conference, however, that "we will be back again next year" with further recommendations. [Question 2, Page 10.]

He conceded that even then it would be difficult to get a bill through Congress and would "require a good deal of goodwill on all sides."

"The only one who loses today," he said, "is not the Administration but the school children who need assistance."

The central provision of the three-part compromise bill, sponsored by Representative

Continued on Page 17, Column 5

Clay Will Return to Berlin To Represent President

Special to The New York Times.

WASHINGTON, Aug. 30—President Kennedy announced today that Gen. Lucius D. Clay would return to West Berlin next month as his personal representative to enhance the nation's "resources of judgment and action" in that city.

The President also disclosed that the foreign ministers of the United States, Britain, France and West Germany would resume their planning for the Berlin crisis in Washington Sept. 14.

Transcript of news conference and summary, Page 10.

Mr. Kennedy made his announcements at the start of his news conference, which was dominated by the subject of Berlin.

The President described the situation there as "fraught with danger," promised to use all means to find a peaceful settlement but said he had no indication from Moscow so far that made him optimistic about the prospects. [Questions 1 and 22, Page 10.]

General Clay, retired, who was military governor of Germany when an Allied airlift broke the Communist blockade of Berlin in 1948-49, will go to Berlin with the rank of ambassador Sept. 15. This will be two days before the West German elections, in which Berlin has become an issue.

The President said he and Secretary of State Dean Rusk had "unusual confidence" in General Clay. That confidence appears to have been magnified by the tumultuous reception given by West Berliners to Vice

Continued on Page 2, Column 3

PRESIDENT SENDS NOTE TO NEUTRALS

Message to Belgrade Talks Cites Common Interest in Peace and Freedom

By TOM WICKER
Special to The New York Times.

WASHINGTON, Aug. 30 — President Kennedy said today that the nonaligned nations that will open a conference at Belgrade Friday shared with the United States a commitment to "a world at peace in which nations have the freedom to choose their own political and economic systems."

Mr. Kennedy's remarks at his news conference appeared to be an effort to identify the United States with the basic interest of the nonaligned nations.

He carefully avoided, however, any effort to influence them on specific issues such as Berlin.

Instead, Mr. Kennedy said he was sending a message to the conference that included the following passage:

"We believe that the peoples represented at this conference are committed to a world society in which men have the right and freedom to determine their own destiny, a world in which one people is not enslaved by the other and in which the powerful do not devour the weak.

"The American people share that commitment. We have pledged the influence of this nation to the abolition of exploitation in all its forms."

This was viewed here as a tacit appeal for the conference to take a strong stand on national self-determination and an effort to associate the United States with that position in advance.

The President opened his message to the meeting by declaring that "it is always encouraging when responsible world

Continued on Page 3, Column 2

GOVERNOR ORDERS WELFARE INQUIRY

State Study Is to Bolster 'Public Confidence'—Panel Headed by Gillespie

Special to The New York Times.

ALBANY, Aug. 30—Governor Rockefeller appointed a special investigating commission today to make a broad study of public welfare in the state.

The eleven-member commission is headed by S. Hazard Gillespie of New York, a former president of the state Bar Association. Mr. Rockefeller directed all state and local agencies, local welfare commissioners and law enforcement officers to cooperate.

The Governor, in a television interview in New York on WNBC-TV, denied that his decision had been prompted by the national attention given to the city of Newburgh as a result of its stringent new welfare code.

Views on Newburgh Plan

The Newburgh program, of which the Governor has expressed disapproval, has won the support of many conservative Republicans in New York State and elsewhere.

[The Newburgh City Council voted Wednesday to protest a Federal order delaying temporarily a $3,000,000 urban-renewal project.]

The Governor said it was time for a "fresh perspective" on the entire welfare issue.

He emphasized the need to maintain "public confidence" in the welfare program, saying:

"In such public confidence lies the hope of the unfortunates, and this confidence depends upon the conviction of the people of the state that their dollars are expended in a manner best calculated to further the social and humanitar-

Continued on Page 25, Column 4

MAYOR PROMISES FIGHT ON SHARKEY

Says He Would Oust Him as Council Majority Leader

By LEO EGAN

Mayor Wagner declared yesterday that if he was re-elected he would take action to remove Joseph T. Sharkey as the majority leader of the City Council. Mr. Sharkey is the Democratic leader of Brooklyn.

Mr. Wagner's pledge was made in a statement issued from City Hall. The statement described Mr. Sharkey as the "Brooklyn puppet" of Carmine G. De Sapio, the Manhattan (Tammany) leader.

The strong language used by the Mayor in his attack on Mr. Sharkey took many Democrats by surprise. Mr. Wagner had remained on good terms with the Brooklyn leader long after he broke with Mr. De Sapio earlier this year.

In May the Mayor broke an out-of-state speaking engagement to attend the annual Brooklyn Democratic fund-raising dinner at the St. George Hotel in Brooklyn. On that occasion he described Mr. Sharkey as "one of the most enlightened and responsible political leaders our state and city have ever known."

Mr. Sharkey, who is now backing state Controller Arthur Levitt against Mr. Wagner for the Democratic nomination for Mayor, responded in kind on that occasion. He told the 2,100 Democrats who had paid $100 a plate to attend the dinner "We can take pride in the record of a city administration that has made tremendous strides in housing, schools and hospitals."

Mr. Wagner, in now declaring

Continued on Page 34, Column 2

Met May Request Government Funds

By RALPH KATZ

The Metropolitan Opera Association may seek government subsidies to save it from "the threat of eventual bankruptcy," Anthony A. Bliss, president of the association, said yesterday.

Mr. Bliss touched briefly on this possibility in testimony at the opening of arbitration proceedings involving the opera association and the American Federation of Musicians on contract renewal terms.

Secretary of Labor Arthur J. Goldberg conducted the two-hour session at the Federal Courthouse in Foley Square. He gave the parties until Sept. 15 to submit to him written opinions of the issues and supporting material for their respective positions. He told the union and the association to send copies of their submissions to each

Continued on Page 24, Column 4

Atlanta Integration Is Peaceful; Louisiana School Law Is Upset

Racists' Moves Fail

By CLAUDE SITTON
Special to The New York Times.

ATLANTA, Aug. 30—Public school desegregation came peacefully today to Atlanta and Georgia despite efforts by a handful of racists to disrupt the changeover.

The violence and the jeering mobs that marked compliance with the Supreme Court's 1954 decision in other Southern cities were notably absent in Atlanta as nine Negroes entered four white high schools.

[At his news conference, President Kennedy congratulated Atlanta and Georgia for the "responsible, law-abiding manner" in which the change had taken place. "I strongly urge the officials and citizens of all communities which face this difficult transition in the coming weeks and months to look closely at what Atlanta has done," he said.]

Four suburban youths and an avowed member of the American Nazi party were arrested when they appeared at two of the schools. The police said they had failed to leave areas that had been ruled off limits under six security measures ordered by Chief Herbert T. Jenkins.

They were taken before Judge Luke Arnold of the Municipal Court three hours later. He found them guilty of disturb-

Continued on Page 15, Column 3

Federal Court Acts

Excerpts from court decision are printed on Page 14.

By The Associated Press.

NEW ORLEANS, Aug. 30—A three-judge Federal court struck down Louisiana's school-closing law today. The law had permitted citizens of school districts to vote to abandon public schools that were faced with desegregation orders.

[In Washington, the Senate voted a two-year extension of the Civil Rights Commission.]

The Federal court said that the Louisiana school-closing law was part of a "single, carefully constructed design" that included a grant-in-aid program to assist private segregated schools. But it did not rule the grants illegal.

The opinion was handed down by Judge John Minor Wisdom of the Court of Appeals for the Fifth Circuit and District Judges J. Skelly Wright and Herbert W. Christenberry.

All three of the judges, who sat as a special court, are from New Orleans.

"This is not the moment in history for a state to experiment with ignorance," the opinion said. "When it does, it must

Continued on Page 14, Column 5

Survey of 500,000 Will Study Role of Diet in Heart Disease

By WALTER SULLIVAN
Special to The New York Times.

HONOLULU, Aug. 30—A project involving 500,000 Americans is being planned to determine the role of diet in producing heart disease.

The survey, sponsored by the National Heart Institute, is to be preceded by five years of pilot studies.

As now envisaged, it may require the Government to provide a large portion of the weekly food requirements of tens of thousands of families.

Only in this way, it is suspected, can adequate control be kept over the participants' food intake.

The reduction in the food bills of those taking part would help compensate them for faithful adherence to the rules of the survey.

Plans for the project have been disclosed here by Dr. Frederick J. Stare, Professor of Nutrition at Harvard University and deputy chairman of the committee organizing the project. He believes it will be one of the costliest surveys ever carried out.

The organizing committee is headed by Dr. Irvine H. Page, director of research at the Cleveland Clinic in Ohio. According to Dr. Stare, the project has strong backing in Congress, where large appropriations will have to be passed, and is supported by the food industry as well.

At a meeting some months ago, attended by the presidents of many of the nation's food companies, leading heart and nutrition specialists presented their problem. The goal is to

Continued on Page 28, Column 1

Kennedy Asks Steel Not to Raise Prices

By RICHARD E. MOONEY
Special to The New York Times.

WASHINGTON, Aug. 30 — The Administration made its first public effort today to head off the possibility of a steel price increase this fall.

President Kennedy voiced concern at his news conference that an increase would set off an inflationary spiral, impair business recovery and affect the balance of international payments.

He expressed hope that the industry's leaders would recognize their "public responsibilities" and hold the line. (Questions 10 and 16, Page 10.)

Talk of a price increase centers on the automatic raise due to steel workers Oct. 1. It is the second of two automatic increases awarded by the one contract that settled the long 1959

Continued on Page 11, Column 2

NEWS INDEX

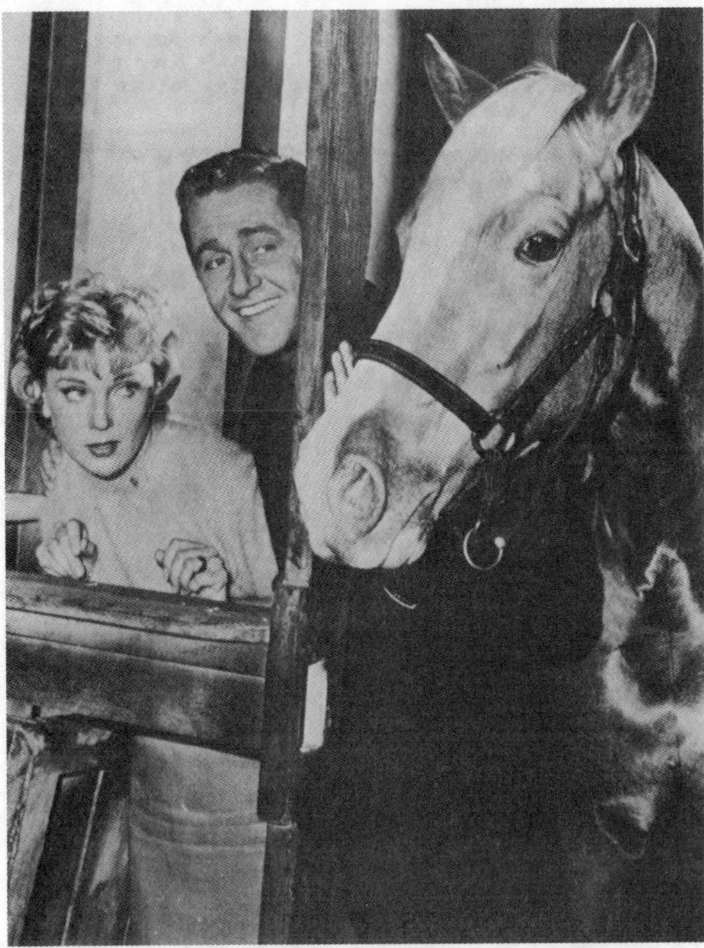

Mister Ed was the horse that talked in the zany comedy that starred Alan Young and Connie Hines.

Ben Casey, starring Vincent Edwards in the title role, was another popular series among the epidemic of medical shows.

Mary Tyler Moore (bottom left) became everybody's sweetheart in the *Dick Van Dyke Show.* The rest of the lovable cast included (top, left to right) Richard Deacon, Rose Marie, and Morey Amsterdam.

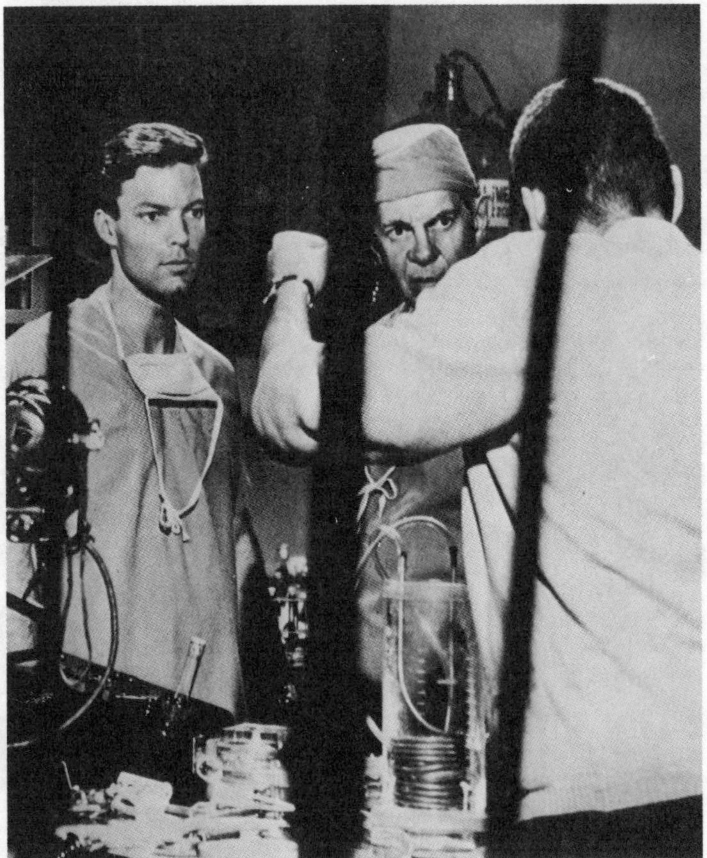

Richard Chamberlain played the handsome *Dr. Kildare* to Raymond Massey's Dr. Gillespie on the program which emerged as one of the most successful medical shows.

The Berlin Wall, a 25-mile sector of barbed wire and concrete, was one more communist-devised flash point in the cold war.

Refugees from East Germany arrived in the West just before the border was closing.

The U.S. sent GIs down Berlin's East-West checkpoints as a sign of commitment to West Berlin.

"All the News That's Fit to Print"

The New York Times.

LATE CITY EDITION

U. S. Weather Bureau Report (Page 69) forecasts: Considerable cloudiness today; occasional rain tonight, tomorrow. Temp. range: 72—59; yesterday: 71—49. Temp.-Hum. Index: middle 60's; yesterday: 66.

VOL. CXI..No. 37,859. NEW YORK, TUESDAY, SEPTEMBER 19, 1961. 10 cents beyond 50-mile zone from New York City except on Long Island. Higher in air delivery cities. FIVE CENTS

HAMMARSKJOLD DIES IN AFRICAN AIR CRASH; KENNEDY GOING TO U.N. IN SUCCESSION CRISIS

Associated Press Radiophoto

Rescue workers study wreckage of the Secretary General's plane in Northern Rhodesia

The New York Times

Secretary General Dag Hammarskjold

12 OTHERS KILLED

Lone Survivor Reports Explosions on Flight to Tshombe Talks

By DAVID HALBERSTAM

Special to The New York Times.

NDOLA, Northern Rhodesia, Sept. 18—Secretary General Dag Hammarskjold of the United Nations was killed today with twelve other persons in the crash of a plane carrying him to a meeting with President Moise Tshombe of Katanga Province. The meeting had been called in an effort to end the fighting in Katanga.

The bodies of the Secretary General and his staff were found about four miles from the Ndola airport in Northern Rhodesia. The plane had been scheduled to land at the airport last night.

[The Associated Press said that mistaken identity and tight security led it to report erroneously Sunday night that Mr. Hammarskjold's plane had reached Ndola.]

The site of the crash is close to the border of the Congolese province of Katanga. The Congo is an area that has demanded much of Mr. Hammarskjold's time and patience in the last fifteen months.

Crash Stuns U. N. Aides

The news of the crash stunned this area. Earlier today United Nations officials at Elisabethville seemed dazed as they kept hearing reports that Mr. Hammarskjold had not arrived in Ndola.

[The Associated Press reported that the lone survivor, Harold M. Julian, a United Nations security guard, said that a series of explosions had preceded the crash. He also said that the plane had turned away from a landing, apparently on Mr. Hammarskjold's orders.]

At near-by Kitwe, in Northern Rhodesia, President Tshombe was holding a news conference and was saying that he hoped to meet in a few minutes with the Secretary General and end the war when a newsman said:

"President Tshombe, Mr. Hammarskjold is dead. His body lies not far away in the wreckage of his airplane."

Mr. Tshombe's face reflected shock and horror seemed to show in his eyes.

Tshombe Expresses Regret

"I regret it very much if what you say is true," he said. "He was a man who enjoyed the respect of many African nations and I had hoped to reach a settlement with him that would leave Katanga free."

Earlier in his news conference Mr. Tshombe had attacked United Nations policy in the Congo.

Mr. Hammarskjold's plane was a United Nations DC-6B. It left Leopoldville yesterday. Much concerning the crash remains inexplicable.

The Secretary General's plane apparently crashed after it had circled the Ndola airport twice and had been waved in. No one here could offer any explanation for the crash.

It was believed that the plane might have taken a circuitous route to avoid the Katanga area, which is patrolled by one Katanga jet fighter. This might account for the plane's late arrival here and it might account for some fatigue on the part of the pilot.

There apparently was only one survivor, a man who was found severely burned and in a delirious state near the plane. He was taken to a hospital.

Those who have been trying to end the Katanga fighting believe that Mr. Hammarskjold's death was a terrible blow to hopes for a truce.

Mr. Tshombe has refused to meet with United Nations officials in Elisabethville, the Ka-

Continued on Page 14, Column 1

MAYOR APPOINTS 9 CIVIC LEADERS AS SCHOOL BOARD

Group Is Due to Be Sworn Today but Injunction Is Sought to Bar Change

By PAUL CROWELL

Mayor Wagner named a new nine-member Board of Education yesterday to replace the present board, which goes out of existence tomorrow.

The new board, which like the old one is unsalaried, is scheduled to be sworn in at City Hall today at 3:30 P. M., but there may be a last-minute hitch.

Two members of the outgoing board moved in Supreme Court late yesterday to have the Legislature's recent action dismissing the old board declared illegal and to prevent Mayor Wagner, in the meantime, from swearing in the members of the new board this afternoon.

A legal representative of the city will appear at the Brooklyn court at 10 o'clock this morning to contest both the complaint and the appeal for an injunction against the Mayor.

'Red Letter Day'

For his own part, before the legal action was instituted, Mayor Wagner expressed the hope that the swearing-in ceremony scheduled for the new board members this afternoon would mark "a red letter day for the City of New York for all the days to come."

He expressed the belief that "this can be the best board our city has ever had, possibly the best board any city ever had."

The board has seven members from Manhattan, and one each from Brooklyn and Queens.

The board was chosen from a list of twenty-six recommended by an eleven-man panel set up by the state on Aug. 21. A special session of the Legislature had passed a law to dissolve the present board and pave the way for a new one.

Appointees Listed

The Mayor's appointees are:

Brendan Byrne, public relations man, 85-19 118th Street, Kew Gardens, Queens.

James B. Donovan, lawyer, 35 Prospect Park West, Brooklyn.

Lloyd K. Garrison, lawyer, 133 East Sixty-fourth Street.

John F. Hennessy, engineer, 144 East Thirty-ninth Street.

Morris Iushewitz, labor leader, 386 Park Avenue South.

Samuel R. Pierce, lawyer, 2225 Fifth Avenue.

Anna M. Rosenberg, public relations consultant, 1136 Fifth Avenue.

Max J. Rubin, lawyer, 101 West Fifty-fifth Street.

Clarence O. Senior, economist and sociologist, 15 Claremont Avenue.

In announcing the appointments, the Mayor said that he had chosen the board "without regard to politics."

"I do not even know the political affiliations of those I have selected," he said, "except in the cases where I have had previous personal knowledge." It was

Continued on Page 30, Column 5

Militia Seizes 176 In Cuban Outbreak

Special to The New York Times.

HAVANA, Sept. 18—Militiamen in plainclothes who had mingled with the crowd arrested 176 persons last night after a demonstration had broken out during a religious procession near here.

Eighteen demonstrators were injured, three seriously, when the militiamen swung clubs they had hidden in their clothing.

The outburst occurred one week after a larger anti-Government demonstration before a Havana church. Seven were injured, one fatally, by the militia and many were arrested in that demonstration.

The new incident took place a few hours after 136 priests had been deported from Cuba

Continued on Page 13, Column 1

New Group Seeks Funds to Purchase And Repair Slums

By MARTIN ARNOLD

A nonprofit organization has been set up here to offer inducements to private investors to buy and improve slum tenements.

The organization, headed by former Deputy Mayor Paul T. O'Keefe, would select the buildings, find buyers and repair, operate and maintain the tenements.

Private investors would own the buildings and would collect profits agreed upon between them and the organization.

8 to 10 Per Cent Profit

The profits usually would be 8 to 10 per cent. Many unimproved slum tenements now bring profits up to 25 per cent.

Laurance S. Rockefeller, son of the late John D. Rockefeller Jr., has agreed to invest up to $250,000 in tenements to get the program started.

Mr. Rockefeller will not be part of the organization. A spokesman said last night that Mr. Rockefeller had agreed to help the program because he felt it was "a way to get responsible private money that will be reasonably rewarded into such housing."

The Rockefeller spokesman and other supporters of the program emphasized that the project would not be charitable or philanthropic. Rather,

Continued on Page 25, Column 1

3 STATES TO GET U. S. TRANSIT AID

New Committee Wins Pledge of Support From 2 Bodies at Orientation Meeting

By LLOYD GARRISON

Special to The New York Times.

WASHINGTON, Sept. 18—The newly created Tri-State Transportation Committee won Government support today for its plans to improve transport and commuter service in the New York metropolitan area.

Committee members from New York, New Jersey and Connecticut met for more than three hours with representatives of the Housing and Home Finance Agency and the Bureau of Public Roads.

Dr. William J. Ronan, secretary to Governor Rockefeller, said the meeting had been called to explain the aims of the group and to seek Federal cooperation. He described the session as "very heartening." The committee did not ask for specific amounts of money, he added, but would undoubtedly seek financial support "sometime soon."

Government participants in the meeting indicated funds would be made available if requested.

Anxious to Aid

"This is the kind of program we would like to assist," said Morton J. Schussheim, assistant administrator for program policy at the Housing and Home Finance Agency. The agency is involved in transportation problems through its urban renewal program.

His enthusiasm was echoed by another Federal representative, Edward H. Holmes, assistant commissioner of the Bureau of Public Roads.

Dr. Ronan acted as regional spokesman at the meeting. The New Jersey delegation was led by Highway Commissioner Dwight R. G. Palmer and the Connecticut by Carl LaLumia, executive aide to Gov. John Dempsey.

Roger H. Gilman, on leave from the Port of New York Authority to serve as executive director of the committee, attended the meeting but departed immediately after it had ended.

The tri-state committee was established three weeks ago to study and make recommendations on improving commuter service and to attack also problems of motor traffic, air travel and freight transportation. Its

Continued on Page 18, Column 3

Adenauer Begins Efforts To Form Coalition in Bonn

By SYDNEY GRUSON

Special to The New York Times.

BONN, Germany, Sept. 18—Chancellor Adenauer began fighting for his political life today as a result of his party's heavy losses in the West German elections.

With the Christian Democratic Union's parliamentary majority wiped out yesterday, the 85-year-old Chancellor lost no time in seeking a coalition with the Free Democratic party led by Dr. Erich Mende. The Free Democrats made the biggest gain in the election.

Dr. Adenauer rejected the bid of Willy Brandt, West Berlin's Mayor, for a national coalition embracing the Social Democrats as well as the two other parties.

A coalition with the Socialists, the Chancellor said at a news conference, "would not correspond with our democratic feeling."

The big question was not whether Dr. Adenauer could set the terms for a coalition but whether he could survive the demands for his retirement and his replacement as Chancellor by Dr. Ludwig Erhard, the 64-year-old Minister of Economics.

There was considerable speculation that the Free Democrats would agree to Dr. Adenauer's continuing as Chancellor for a limited period—just long enough to carry the onus for accepting the hard decisions facing West Germany.

With the long, bitter campaign and the vote at last out of the way, a beginning was in sight for the long-awaited public discussion of these decisions.

The Free Democrats' news service, commenting on the election results, which left the party holding the balance of power, said:

"An epoch of German postwar history has ended. The coming months and years will destroy many illusions and place extraordinary demands on our people."

The statement reflected a continuing but decreasing reluctance to specify the demands. Two are accepted by almost all West German officials as inevitable: the acceptance of the Oder-Neisse border as Germany's frontier with Poland and some form of de facto recognition for Communist East Germany, with all that means to the loss of hope for the reunification of Germany.

No one here is yet sure whether the West Germans are

Continued on Page 3, Column 5

2D SOVIET ROCKET FIRED 7,500 MILES

Lands in Same Pacific Area as Shot Last Wednesday

By THEODORE SHABAD

Special to The New York Times.

MOSCOW, Sept. 18 — The Soviet Union fired a second rocket 7,500 miles into the central Pacific yesterday.

An announcement today by Tass, Soviet press agency, said that the dummy of the rocket's last stage had landed "in the immediate proximity" of the spot where the first rocket of the current series hit the water last Wednesday.

Today's brief Tass statement emphasized the accuracy of the Soviet shots. It referred to the "high-precision control system" of the rocket and called it "another big achievement of Soviet rocketry."

[In Washington, the Atomic Energy Commission announced that the Soviet Union on Monday exploded its thirteenth nuclear device since it resumed testing Sept. 1. The yield of the atmospheric explosion was "on the order of a megaton" and the site was "in the vicinity of Novaya Zemlya," the commission said.]

The present series of test shots was announced on Sept. 10. Ships and planes were advised to keep away from the target area, 1,000 miles southwest of Hawaii, during the

Continued on Page 8, Column 1

VIETNAM REBELS BURN CITY IN RAID

Regime Says 1,000 Reds Took Part in Attack

By The Associated Press.

SAIGON, Vietnam, Tuesday, Sept. 19—More than 1,000 Communist rebels attacked and burned the capital of Phuoc Vinh Province, sixty miles north of Saigon early yesterday, the Government said today.

It was believed to be the largest rebel assault so far in South Vietnam's civil war.

The province chief, an army major, and his deputy and a large number of Government civil guardsmen were killed.

About fifty wounded were rushed to Saigon hospitals after the rebels withdrew under attack.

The Government announcement said the Viet Cong guerrillas stormed the capital at 1 A. M. yesterday in a move to liberate rebels taken prisoner.

The Viet Cong held the town for several hours in pre-dawn darkness, burning and ransacking several provincial buildings.

One source estimated 1,500 Viet Cong took part in the attack, the first on a provincial capital.

It also marked a new height in violence in the areas north of Saigon where the rebels were said to be building strength.

Phuoc Thanh is a newly created province in a largely upland forest and rubber-growing

Continued on Page 3, Column 7

ACTING SECRETARY IS SOUGHT AT U. N.

Delegates Favoring Proposal to Appoint Mongi Slim—Assembly Meets Today

By THOMAS J. HAMILTON

Special to The New York Times.

UNITED NATIONS, N. Y., Sept. 18—On the eve of the opening of the United Nations General Assembly session, a move was developing to have Mongi Slim of Tunisia take over the coordination of the Secretariat until the election of a successor to Dag Hammarskjold.

The death of Mr. Hammarskjold saddened delegates to the General Assembly, which will open its sixteenth session tomorrow afternoon.

Delegates and members of the Secretariat mourned the death of an able diplomat who had helped bring about compromise solutions of dangerous issues in an age of nuclear stalemates.

Long Struggle Feared

There were grave forebodings of a long struggle over the choice of a Secretary General who would be acceptable to both the Soviet Union and the Western powers.

The interim plan gained momentum after Dr. Ali Sastroamidjojo of Indonesia, Mr. Slim's only competitor for President of the sixteenth session of the Assembly withdrew this afternoon on the understanding that the African-Asian group would support him for President next year.

Frederick H. Boland of Ireland, who was President of the fifteenth session, and a number of Asian, African and European delegates are understood to favor the plan, under which Mr. Slim would, in effect, become Acting Secretary General.

Mr. Boland will call the sixteenth session to order at 3 P. M. tomorrow. Its formal business will be limited to the election of Mr. Slim and the vice presidents and committee chairmen, who will serve under Mr. Slim as the Assembly's Steering Committee.

Soviet May Force Demand

The United States and some Western delegations declined to comment on the plan, which so far is still in the informal stage. However, other delegates expressed the belief that it would be accepted without opposition unless the Soviet Union decided to force an immediate showdown on its demand for the liquidation of the office of Secretary General and the substitution of a three-man directorate.

A Soviet spokesman said today that his delegation would press this demand, which was submitted to the General Assembly by Premier Khrushchev a year ago, at the impending session.

Although the Soviet delegate, Valerian A. Zorin, refused to join other members of the Security Council in praising Mr.

Continued on Page 16, Column 2

President to Assure U. N. U. S. Backs a Single Chief

By JAMES RESTON

Special to The New York Times.

WASHINGTON, Sept. 18—President Kennedy decided tonight to intervene personally in the constitutional crisis created at the United Nations by the death of Secretary General Dag Hammarskjold.

The White House announced that the President would address the General Assembly in New York, probably Friday. His purpose in doing so is to reassure the delegates and Secretariat that the United States supports the United Nations and is determined to do everything possible to maintain the executive authority of the office of the Secretary General.

The President's plan to address the United Nations was made known after he had paid a tribute to Mr. Hammarskjold, in which he said:

"I am hopeful that the members of the United Nations, recognizing his untiring labors, will attempt in the coming sessions and in the years to come to try to build the United Nations into the effective instrument for peace which was Dag Hammarskjold's great ambition."

Interim Plan Sought

As for the crisis at the United Nations, the United States believes that an interim arrangement must be made quickly, with the concurrence of the Soviet Union if possible, to enable the office of the Secretary General to carry out the past instructions of the world organization.

This is an urgent matter in the Congo, where United Nations troops in secessionist Katanga Province have been under fire and must be reinforced quickly.

Officials here and in New York were in constant consultation today about how this could be done in the face of the Soviet Union's opposition to the

Continued on Page 16, Column 1

KATANGA IMPERILS MAIN U. N. AIR BASE

Loss Would Be Second Big Defeat—Tshombe Units Claim Capture of 500

Special to The New York Times.

ELISABETHVILLE, the Congo, Sept. 18—United Nations troops guarding the big air base at Kamina, in Katanga Province, were reported under heavy fire today and in danger of being overwhelmed by their Katangan attackers.

[According to The Associated Press, Katangan military radio messages reported the capture of the Kamina base and the surrender of its 500 Irish and Swedish defenders.]

The loss of the air base would be the second major defeat for the United Nations in the six days of fighting here. This morning, the surrender of a garrison of 158 Irish troops was completed at Jadotville, sixty-five miles north of Elisabethville.

With the military situation deteriorating, United Nations forces here spent an anxious morning waiting for news of Secretary General Dag Hammarskjold. Word of his death brought sorrow to the already grim band of United Nations soldiers and officials.

Outside this capital of Katanga, the secessionist forces are more numerous than those

Continued on Page 14, Column 6

French to End the Occupation Of Bizerte City, Starting Today

By THOMAS F. BRADY

Special to The New York Times.

TUNIS, Sept. 18—French and Tunisian representatives agreed today on a plan for the withdrawal of French troops from the city of Bizerte and its environs.

The withdrawal will start tomorrow morning and continue through Saturday.

Negotiations leading to the troop pullback began after a proposal by President Habib Bourguiba of Tunisia Sept. 7 to permit the French to maintain their naval-air base near Bizerte for the duration of the Berlin crisis if they would agree to a timetable for the eventual evacuation of the base.

The occupation of Bizerte and the surrounding area began July 20 when French forces moved against Tunisian troops and civilians who were barricading roads leading to the base entrance. Fighting had broken out July 19 after France defied a Tunisian demand for a promise to evacuate the base.

In return for ending of the city's occupation, the Tunisians have guaranteed to the French the right of circulation among the scattered military installations in the Bizerte region and freedom of movement through the entrance channel from the Mediterranean Sea to the Lake of Bizerte, on which the installations are situated.

The first concrete step toward a solution of the Bizerte dispute was an exchange of prisoners Sept. 10.

The second step was the agreement just achieved on a military withdrawal to the positions held before the July

Continued on Page 2, Column 3

NEWS INDEX

"All the News That's Fit to Print"

The New York Times.

LATE CITY EDITION
U. S. Weather Bureau Report (Page 50) forecasts: Fair and warmer today and tonight. Partly cloudy and warmer tomorrow. Temp. range: 73—50; yesterday: 69—50.

VOL. CXI... No. 37,870. NEW YORK, SATURDAY, SEPTEMBER 30, 1961. FIVE CENTS

SYRIA QUITS UNITED ARAB REPUBLIC AND SETS UP INDEPENDENT REGIME; NASSER ABANDONS MILITARY ACTION

CABINET IS NAMED

Conservative Premier Heads Civilian Rule —Vote Promised

By The Associated Press.

BEIRUT, Lebanon, Saturday, Sept. 30—Syria won independence by force of arms from the United Arab Republic yesterday and a new conservative regime promised today that there would be elections and constitutional rule.

President Gamal Abdel Nasser, in Cairo, decided not to oppose the revolt with force. The uprising was a tremendous blow to his dreams of an "Arab nation" that would encompass the Arab world.

The foundation from which Mr. Nasser had launched his program of Arab unity—the merger of Syria and Egypt in the United Arab Republic—fell apart in less than four years.

The new Premier, Dr. Mahmoun al-Kuzbari, a 48-year-old conservative lawyer and law professor, proclaimed Syria independent and declared that the Government emerging from a two-day officers' revolt had the people's full support.

Pledges for the Future

In a fifteen-minute broadcast over the Damascus radio, Dr. Kuzbari said the revolutionary command in Damascus had "finished its mission at this point" and had returned "to the normal functions of defending the country."

He promised that his all-civilian Government would "prove itself true to the aims and support of the people"—apparently meaning elections. He also pledged "a true and democratic life" for Syria and promised to "lead the country within four months to a constitutional stage."

"Syria again affirms to the Arabs that she is the bastion of Arabism," the Premier said.

He charged that Egypt had dominated the United Arab Republic and had "liquidated loyal [Syrian] nationalist elements, especially in the army."

Friendly Relations Sought

Before making his speech, Dr. Kuzbari received members of the foreign consular corps and told them Syria wanted to establish diplomatic relations with all friendly countries.

The Syrians' victory came yesterday after Mr. Nasser had called off Egyptian army, air and naval forces sent to crush the revolt and, in a speech, had bitterly admitted the temporary defeat of his principles of Arab unity.

In a broadcast yesterday, the Damascus radio declared that "the regime of tyranny has gone forever."

It accused President Nasser of having turned Syria into a prison in nearly four years of union in the United Arab Republic and it disputed his claim to Arab nationalism.

Syria, which is separated from Egypt by 150 miles of Jordanian and Israeli territory, was given a subordinate role as a result of the union with Egypt. Mr. Nasser's socialization program conflicted with the interests of the Syrian business community, which had flourished under a system of free enterprise.

Before President Nasser's speech, a Damascus broadcast announced that 200 Egyptian paratroopers attempting an airborne invasion had been wiped out at Latakia, Syria's chief port. Another broadcast said 120 commando invaders had been captured. Both broadcasts apparently described the same action.

Aleppo, a major city in the north, was reported in rebel hands. On Thursday Mr. Nasser

Continued on Page 2, Column 1

U. A. R. PRESIDENT AT CAIRO RALLY. Gamal Abdel Nasser, center, with Field Marshal Abdel Hakim Amer, at left, and Vice President Kamal Eddine Hussein. Marshal Amer had returned earlier from Syria, after having been trapped by the rebels. (Associated Press Radiophoto)

WAGNER ACCEPTS INQUIRY ON ETHICS OF HIS FUND RALLY

Directs Lindenbaum to Give a Full Report on Details of Realty Luncheon

PANEL MEETS THURSDAY

Will Take Up Charges Then—Lefkowitz and Gerosa Renew Their Attacks

Mayor Wagner agreed yesterday to a Board of Ethics inquiry into the way that gifts to his political campaign had been solicited from persons who have business with city agencies.

At a news conference in City Hall, the Mayor said:

"This matter ought to go to the Board of Ethics. I am cooperating fully with the board."

Mr. Wagner said he had directed Abraham M. Lindenbaum, a member of the City Planning Commission who presided at the controversial fund-raising luncheon Wednesday, to make a full report to the Board of Ethics.

Mr. Wagner's announcement came after his two principal opponents in the mayoral race had demanded that he disclose the facts in the case, and two civic organizations had demanded that Mr. Lindenbaum resign from the Planning Commission.

Pledges Asked

At the luncheon, Mr. Lindenbaum had called upon forty-three builders and real estate men, some of whom do business with the city, to rise in turn and say how much each would pledge to the Wagner campaign fund.

As the Mayor looked on, campaign pledges of $500 to $5,000 were made. The total was about $25,000.

Yesterday the Mayor declined, when asked, to say whether he thought the city's Code of Ethics had been violated.

"That is up to the Board of Ethics to decide," he said. "It would be improper for me to comment on it now before the board takes up the matter."

Cloyd Laporte, the chairman of the five-member board, said the case would be considered at the next regular meeting, on Thursday. But he said the board had power only to advise, not to punish.

Mayor Wagner denied that the contributors could expect favors from the city government.

"That has never happened

Continued on Page 29, Column 2

NEW CHIEFS MOVE TAMMANY'S HOME

Cavanagh Says Fresh Start in Smaller Office Is Aim

By DOUGLAS DALES

Moving men put dollies under the desk of Carmine G. De Sapio at 331 Madison Avenue yesterday as the new leaders of the New York County Democratic Committee began to take over Tammany Hall.

In a sudden move, quickly executed, party records and usable furniture were moved last night to new party headquarters in the Chatham Hotel, 33 East Forty-eighth Street.

The shift in Democratic headquarters—the third in this century—was inspired by Mayor Wagner, who officially took command of the party on Wednesday when he brought about the election of Edward F. Cavanagh Jr. as chairman of the New York County Committee.

"We don't need that big shop over there and we wanted to get off to a new, efficient, fresh start," said Mr. Cavanagh, who is on leave as Fire Commissioner to manage the Mayor's campaign for re-election.

As to the suddenness of the move to close the doors of Tammany Hall, he said:

"It was fast. But that's the way I am. I wanted the place cleared by 6 o'clock."

The time schedule was not met, however. At that hour, the movers were still crating records and getting furniture into moving vans. But they were under orders to stay on the job all night if necessary to clear the eight-room suite.

At the Chatham, which is in

Continued on Page 13, Column 2

N. L. R. B. Backs a Device To Skirt Union-Shop Ban

Reverses Previous Stand—Rules That Indiana 'Right-to-Work' Law Does Not Forbid Payments in Lieu of Dues

By JOHN D. MORRIS
Special to The New York Times.

WASHINGTON, Sept. 29—The National Labor Relations Board, in a reversal of policy, ruled today that the agency shop is legal in Indiana, a "right-to-work" state.

By a 4-to-1 vote, the board reconsidered and reversed a 3-to-2 decision of last Feb. 20 in a case involving the General Motors Corporation and the United Automobile Workers.

Under agency-shop agreements, nonunion employes must pay the union sums equal to union fees and dues to keep their jobs.

The agency shop is designed to ease the impact on labor unions of so-called "right-to-work" state laws, which bar union-shop agreements. Under the union shop, employes are required to join the union within a specified time to hold their jobs.

The new ruling had no direct effect on agency-shop agreements in eighteen other states with right-to-work laws. But it established the principle that such state laws, in the board's opinion, do not necessarily bar agency-shop agreements.

The decision left unanswered the question whether the agency shop would be legal in a state with a right-to-work law that specifically prohibits it. Nothing in the Indiana statute specifically deals with the agency-shop device.

The majority opinion was signed by two new board members appointed by President Kennedy and two holdover appointees from the Eisenhower

Continued on Page 13, Column 4

Lefkowitz Assails Kaplan After Questioning on Bids

By LEONARD BUDER

City Investigation Commissioner Louis I. Kaplan was questioned for ninety minutes yesterday by two assistants of the State Attorney General about an alleged conspiracy by school contractors to rig bids.

Mr. Kaplan appeared under subpoena and was given another to return next Friday.

Louis J. Lefkowitz, the Attorney General, who was not present during the interrogation, said that in the opinion of members of his staff, "the testimony given by Commissioner Kaplan raises serious doubts as to the course of conduct followed by him in this matter."

Asked to elaborate, Mr. Lefkowitz would say only: "Some answers were not always the same. There was some variance."

Meeting 'Friendly' to Kaplan

On the other hand, Mr. Kaplan told newsmen that he had had a "very friendly meeting" with Mr. Lefkowitz' two assistants and that he had answered every question.

The State Investigation Commission has scheduled a meeting Wednesday at which Mr. Kaplan's role in the investigation of Joseph R. Weiss, the suspended Deputy Superintendent of Schools, will be discussed. The commission indicated it had no plans to subpoena either man, but might invite them to appear.

The Attorney General issued the first subpoena to Mr. Kaplan two weeks ago. Mr. Lefkowitz asserted that this was necessary because the Commissioner had failed to give him information about an alleged scheme by eleven plumbing con-

Continued on Page 29, Column 2

KENNEDY WEIGHS AGED-CARE DRIVE

Aides Would Carry Fight to Key Cities by Holding Seminars on Issues

By RUSSELL PORTER
Special to The New York Times.

NEWPORT, R. I., Sept. 29—President Kennedy is considering a plan to sponsor seminars in key cities to build public support for medical care for the aged and other Administration proposals.

Another objective would be to learn what domestic legislation the public thinks should be asked of Congress next year. A third goal would be to explain what was accom[illegible]shed in this field at the last [illegible]ession of Congress.

Reports that such a program is under study were confirmed today by members of the White House staff who are with the President on his working vacation here. The plans are being made by Lawrence F. O'Brien, President Kennedy's chief liaison with Congress, and reports are being forwarded to the President.

It is expected that the time and place of the first seminar will be announced in a week or so. Cooperation from Democratic Governors and party chairmen in various states is being arranged.

The plan is that Cabinet members and other high officials from Washington will be included on Federal teams to appear at the seminars. These will be one-day meetings in major cities, with the public invited to join in the discussions. The subjects will include housing, urban affairs, aid for

Continued on Page 13, Column 7

Mets Name Stengel As Manager for '62

Casey Stengel is returning to town.

The colorful, 71-year-old Stengel, baseball's most successful manager, agreed yesterday to a one-year contract as manager of the New York Mets. The Mets will begin play next year in the expanded National League.

In the twelve years from 1949 through 1960, Stengel managed the Yankees to ten American League pennants and seven world championships. The Yankees did not renew his contract for 1961, and he spent the year out of baseball.

Stengel will be reunited with George M. Weiss, the Mets' president. Weiss was the Yankee general manager during Stengel's tenure.

Weiss said Stengel insisted on a contract of only one year.

Details on Page 18.

U. S. SAID TO PLAN NEW NOTE ASKING KHRUSHCHEV VIEW

Kennedy Wants More Details on Soviet's Berlin Stand Than Given by Gromyko

By MAX FRANKEL
Special to The New York Times.

WASHINGTON, Sept. 29—President Kennedy will probably send a personal message to Premier Khrushchev next week to obtain a more precise indication of Moscow's approach to formal East-West negotiations on Berlin and Germany.

A possible White House visit has been suggested to Andrei A. Gromyko, the Soviet Foreign Minister, although no final arrangements have been made. The usefulness of Presidential intervention in the "exploratory talks" with Mr. Gromyko will be reviewed tomorrow following his third meeting with Secretary of State Dean Rusk in New York.

It is expected here that the Rusk-Gromyko talks will move to Washington next week and that at their conclusion Mr. Gromyko will call on the President before returning to Moscow.

Gromyko Going Home

The Soviet diplomat now plans to leave the United States early in the week of Oct. 8, one week before the start of the twenty-second Soviet Communist party Congress in Moscow. He will not play a major role at the Congress but his report may influence the tone of Mr. Khrushchev's discussion of the Berlin crisis with Communist leaders from all parts of the world.

President Kennedy is expected to return to Washington Monday from a week's vacation.

Some sign from Moscow that the Russians intend to discuss more than their own formula for peace in Germany in a meeting with Western representatives later this fall is one of the basic conditions established by the Western powers for the negotiations.

Bonn and Paris Suspicious

Washington believes it will need more of an indication than Mr. Gromyko has given so far if France and West Germany are to be persuaded of the wisdom of direct bargaining with the Soviet Union.

The rising suspicion in Paris and Bonn that the United States may be promoting undisclosed deals behind the allies' backs disturbs the Administration greatly. The Allied Ambassadors still meet almost daily at the State Department with high United States officials and, it is said, are briefed on all developments.

But the continuing talk here of a compromise German settlement, when none is yet clearly in sight, has encouraged the

Continued on Page 8, Column 6

SOVIET PROTESTS AUTOBAHN PATROL

Berlin Commandant Assails U. S. Increase in Police Forces on the Highway

By DAVID BINDER
Special to The New York Times.

BERLIN, Sept. 29—The Soviet Union has protested increased patrolling of the Autobahn between Berlin and West Germany by the United States military police.

The protest was made last Sunday by Col. Andrei I. Solovyev, the Soviet commandant in East Berlin, to Maj. Gen. Albert E. Watson, the United States commandant, two days after the patrols had been increased.

An official United States spokesman explained today that the military police patrols had been increased following an incident in which the East German Communist police detained two American soldiers who were on their way from West Berlin to West Germany Sept. 21.

The soldiers were taken off the Autobahn about twenty-three miles inside East Ger-

Continued on Page 8, Column 4

Jordan and Turkey Swiftly Recognize New Syrian Regime

By Reuters.

AMMAN, Jordan, Sept. 29—Jordan promptly recognized the Syrian rebels today in the latest move in this country's quarrel with President Gamal Abdel Nasser of the United Arab Republic.

The action came after an emergency Cabinet meeting in the morning, presided over by King Hussein and attended by leading officials outside the Cabinet.

After the meeting, Premier Bahjat Abdul Kadhr Talhouni sent a telegram to Damascus, reading: "I congratulate and support you and express Jordan's pride in your blessed revolution."

[Turkey also recognized the new Syrian regime, The Associated Press said from Ankara.]

The Jordanian Government also placed its broadcasting facilities at the service of the Syrian rebels.

"Jordan's King, Government and people are very pleased to see Syria regain her real place in the Arab heart and as a base for true Arab nationalism," Mr. Talhouni, who is Foreign Min-

Continued on Page 2, Column 4

NASSER DIRECTS PLEA TO SYRIANS

Urges People to Preserve 'Rights' and Denounces 'Capitalists' on Coup

By JAY WALZ
Special to The New York Times.

CAIRO, Sept. 29—President Gamal Abdel Nasser told Egyptians tonight that he had called off armed resistance to the Syrian coup against the United Arab Republic. He appealed to the Syrian people to preserve "the rights they have earned" through union with Egypt.

Addressing a cheering throng in Republic Square, President Nasser termed the new insurgent regime in Damascus a "reactionary element" seeking once more to hang a yoke of "capitalist exploitation" around the necks of 5,000,000 Syrians.

"I am sure the people will not give up the rights they have earned in the last four years," he said.

"I am sure the Syrian army will not be an agent of capitalist exploiters," the President said.

Mr. Nasser spoke a few hours after the dissenting officers who led yesterday's coup in Damascus had announced the formation of an all-civilian Cabinet headed by Dr. Mahmoun al-Kuzbari.

Mr. Nasser said scornfully that the Kuzbari Cabinet had been set up to give the capitalists "what they want." Sarcastically, he noted that King Hussein of Jordan had been the "first to congratulate and recognize the new Damascus Government."

"This proves the intention of

Continued on Page 2, Column 5

Signs of Ghana Drift To Left Worry U. S.

By LLOYD GARRISON
Special to The New York Times.

WASHINGTON, Sept. 29—United States Administration sources expressed concern today over indications that Ghana was inching more and more toward a pro-Soviet position in foreign affairs and a Marxist dictatorship at home.

The latest cause for concern was the Ghanaian move yesterday for a major shake-up in the Government. The call for the resignation of K. A. Gbedemah, Minister of Health, and Kojo Botsio, Agricultural Minister, was seen as eliminating almost all remaining moderate influence on President Kwame Nkrumah. Mr. Gbedemah complied with the call and resigned today.

The shake-up indicated a victory for a rising group of young

Continued on Page 3, Column 4

Nations Join in Tribute to Hammarskjold at State Funeral in Sweden

Pallbearers carry coffin of Dag Hammarskjold to family grave site at Uppsala after the service at the cathedral (Associated Press Radiophoto)

By WERNER WISKARI
Special to The New York Times.

UPPSALA, Sweden, Sept. 29—Dag Hammarskjold, acclaimed as "the devoted servant of all mankind," was buried here today in the presence of representatives of those he had served. The state funeral accorded the United Nations Secretary General by the Swedish Government, with King Gustaf VI Adolf and Queen Louise in attendance, became almost a world funeral. For among the 2,000 mourners in the flower-banked Uppsala Cathedral were United Nations leaders, members of foreign governments and diplomats. There were Mongi Slim of Tunisia, President of the United Nations General Assembly, and Nathan Barnes of Liberia, President of the Security Council. There were Dr. Sture C. Linner of Sweden, head of the United Nations operations in the Congo, and

Continued on Page 25, Column 2

NEWS INDEX

Ernest Hemingway was with his wife Mary at Sun Valley, shortly before he died.

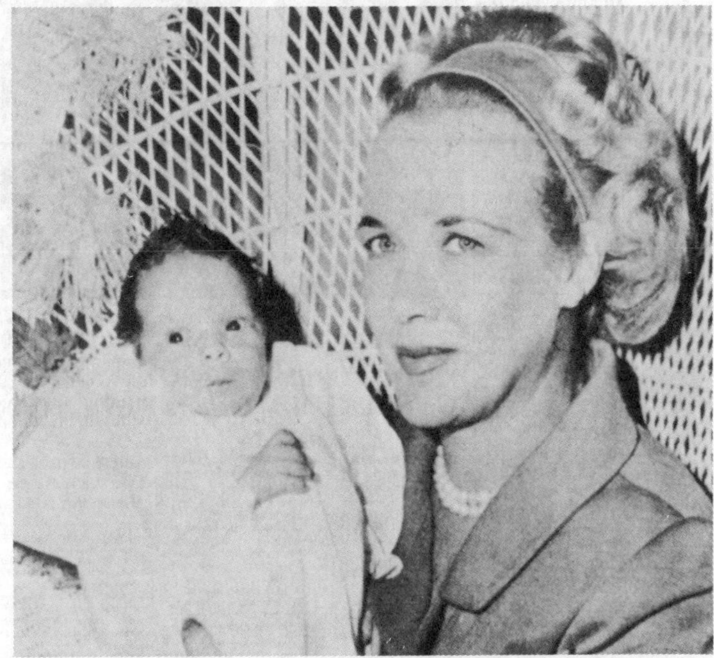

John Clark Gable, son of the late actor Clark Gable, posed with his mother, Mrs. Kay Gable, for his first picture.

Sammy Davis, Jr. and his Swedish wife May Britt carried their new-born baby home on July 5.

Rudolf Nureyev, who defected from the Soviet Union in 1961, appeared at a London charity ballet with Dame Margot Fonteyn and ballerina, Rosella Hightower.

"All the News That's Fit to Print"

The New York Times.

LATE CITY EDITION
U. S. Weather Bureau Report (Page 96) forecasts: Snow mixed with rain, then rain today, tonight, tomorrow. Milder tomorrow. Temp range: 39—30; yesterday: 32—14.

NEWS SUMMARY AND INDEX, PAGE 95

SECTION ONE

VOL. CXI..No. 37,948.
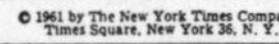
NEW YORK, SUNDAY, DECEMBER 17, 1961. 35c beyond 50-mile zone from New York City, except on Long Island. 50c beyond 200-mile zone from New York City; higher in air delivery cities. THIRTY CENTS

U.N. TAKES KATANGA CAMP, ADVANCES IN HEAVY FIGHT; TSHOMBE FLEES CAPITAL

BATTLE NEAR END

President of Province Is Offered Asylum in Rhodesia

By HENRY TANNER
Special to The New York Times.

LEOPOLDVILLE, the Congo, Dec. 16—United Nations troops made a systematic advance in all parts of Elisabethville today against Katangese forces.

Military observers here predicted the early end of the fighting and said the United Nations force appeared to be within reach of complete control of the capital of Katanga.

Today Swedish United Nations troops captured Camp Massart, the principal Katangese military post in Elisabethville, in bitter fighting, United Nations headquarters here announced.

Haven Offered Tshombe

President Moise Tshombe of Katanga was reliably reported to have fled from Elisabethville to Kipushi, a Katangese town on the border of Northern Rhodesia. He has been offered political asylum by Prime Minister Sir Roy Welensky of the Federation of Rhodesia and Nyasaland.

United Nations troops were advancing on Mr. Tshombe's residence, on the central post office and on Hotel Leopold II in the downtown area, according to reliable unofficial reports reaching Leopoldville this afternoon.

An official report by a United Nations spokesman made no reference to fighting in the downtown area, but said that United Nations troops had captured the Lido Hotel, a wooded park area on the outskirts of the city, in addition to Camp Massart.

Ethiopian Troops Gain

The Lido area had been an important Katangese stronghold.

The Ethiopian troops who captured the area shortly before dawn were said to have come under heavy fire from near-by private houses and buildings belonging to the Union Minière du Haut-Katanga, the large Belgian mining concern.

Four Ethiopians were killed and four were wounded by fire from the Union Minière Institute, a spokesman added. The United Nations issued five warnings during the day, telling the snipers to cease fire or face retaliation. The spokesman said the sniping continued.

The spokesman also announced that Irish troops had begun a direct assault on a strategic underpass in the city but desisted

Continued on Page 2, Column 3

DESTRUCTION IN KATANGA: Flames rising from railroad cars set afire by U. N. troops in Elisabethville silhouette two Katangese soldiers in province's capital. Associated Press Radiophoto

Thant Says a Truce Now Would Be Major Setback

BY RICHARD EDER
Special to The New York Times.

UNITED NATIONS, N. Y., Dec. 16—U Thant, Acting Secretary General, said today that a cease-fire in Katanga at the present time between United Nations and Katangese forces "would be a serious setback for the United Nations."

Mr. Thant gave this opinion to the Advisory Committee on the Congo, a group made up of the nineteen countries that have contributed contingents to the United Nations' Congo operation.

It was the first time he had met formally with the group since fighting began Dec. 5 in Elisabethville, the capital of the Congo's secessionist Katanga Province.

The committee, which met for four hours, was reported to have given enthusiastic support to the Acting Secretary General.

[Pope John XXIII appealed Saturday to "all those who can and must intervene" to work together to re-establish peace in the Congo. The Vatican said the appeal was addressed to the leaders of the nations in the United Nations and particularly to President Kennedy.]

Mr. Thant's Advisory Committee expressed publicly its appreciation for United States cooperation with the United Nations.

In addressing the committee, Mr. Thant noted the appeal for a cease-fire that was made earlier this week by Britain. He disclosed that similar appeals had been made by Belgium,

Continued on Page 3, Column 1

8 COUNTRIES ASK A U.N. BOND ISSUE

200 Million Would Be Sought to Avert Financial Collapse —Red Bloc Fights Plan

By ROBERT CONLEY
Special to The New York Times

UNITED NATIONS, N. Y., Dec. 16 — A $200,000,000 bond issue was proposed today by eight small nations in a dramatic move to head off the United Nations' impending financial collapse.

Their efforts were attacked immediately by the Soviet bloc as an attempt to put a "mortgage" on the United Nations.

The eight sponsors would have the General Assembly authorize Acting Secretary General Thant to sell the bonds to governments, national banks and approved nonprofit institutions or associations.

None of the bonds would be sold to the public, in the belief that it would be beneath the dignity of the world organization to base its financial stability on the generosity of a few individuals.

The bond action would mark the first time that the United Nations would go outside the organization for money to assure its continued effectiveness.

The bonds would be issued for a twenty-five-year period at an annual interest of 2 per cent.

Such a radical step was

Continued on Page 4, Column 2

KENNEDY, ON VISIT, HAILS VENEZUELA AS AIDING LIBERTY

Urges End of 'All Tyranny' Within South America—Betancourt Is Praised

FARM PROJECT OPENED

President Cheered on Route in Caracas Where Nixon Was Attacked in '59

Texts of speeches by Kennedy and Betancourt, Page 37.

By JUAN de ONIS
Special to The New York Times.

CARACAS, Venezuela, Dec. 16—President Kennedy arrived in Caracas today and received a cheering welcome. He issued a call for the "elimination of all tyranny" from South America.

Mr. Kennedy drove into Caracas from Maiquetía Airport after his arrival from San Juan, Puerto Rico, along roads lined with steel-helmeted soldiers whose bayoneted rifles were pointed at the welcoming crowd.

The strict security measures were taken by the Venezuelan Government to avoid the possibility of a repetition of the incident in 1959, when Vice President Richard M. Nixon was attacked by a mob here.

Mrs. Kennedy Acclaimed

President Kennedy was not the only one to be acclaimed by the Venezuelans as he in turn hailed Venezuela. In an appearance at an agrarian reform project at La Morita, on the outskirts of Caracas, Mrs. Kennedy received an ovation when she spoke to the crowd in nearly perfect Spanish.

Tomorrow, the Kennedy party goes to Bogota, Colombia.

It was at the La Morita project that President Kennedy issued his call for an end to tyranny. He said that the "new spirit of this hemisphere requires the elimination of all tyranny until this is a continent from north to south of free men living under a system of liberty."

Scores Dictatorships

In that connection, Mr. Kennedy went out of his way to praise the regime of President Romulo Betancourt of Venezuela, which overthrew dictatorial rule three years ago.

The President said in his speech, broadcast and televised nationally: "I do not share the belief of some that dictatorship is necessary for economic progress."

The crowd of thousands of farmers cheered.

There was no sign of hostility at any point on President Kennedy's route through Caracas, the same as that used by Mr. Nixon. The throngs that turned out had been largely organized

Continued on Page 36, Column 1

AMONG FRIENDS IN VENEZUELA: President Kennedy with some of the crowd yesterday at La Morita, on the edge of Caracas, where he spoke at an agrarian reform rally. Associated Press Radiophoto

RUSK SEES FRANCO AND PRAISES SPAIN AS ANTI-RED ALLY

Also Acclaims Ties Linking Washington and Madrid With Latin America

By BENJAMIN WELLES
Special to The New York Times.

MADRID, Dec. 16—Secretary of State Dean Rusk praised Spain warmly here today as an ally of the United States in the world's defense against Communist aggression.

He also cited the continuing importance of what he termed the "triangle" relationship between the United States, Spain and the eighteen Spanish-speaking nations of Latin America whose culture, religion and language are of Spanish origin.

The Secretary's friendly references to Spain were highly gratifying to officials here. The regime of Generalissimo Francisco Franco, with whom Mr. Rusk conferred today, is far more responsive to such personal gestures by high United States officials than to the "nuts and bolts" question of continuing American military and economic aid.

Gesture Was Awaited

Spain has been awaiting a public gesture by the Kennedy Administration and her gratification over Mr. Rusk's visit and over his expressions of association was quickly reflected in a speech by Foreign Minister Fernando Maria Castiella.

The Foreign Minister forecast at a luncheon for Mr. Rusk and the American party in his official residence here that there would be no major problems when talks begin next year on continued use by the United States of the four large United States-built air bases constructed in Spain at a cost exceeding $400,000,000.

Secretary Rusk arrived this morning in a special jet aircraft from the recent United States-British-French-West German and North Atlantic Treaty Organization meetings in Paris.

Dulles Visit Recalled

During his six-hour visit he held a private ninety-minute talk with General Franco, attended the official luncheon in his honor and managed to tour the Prado Museum before taking off shortly after 5 P. M. direct for Washington.

[Secretary Rusk returned to Washington by air Saturday evening.]

Mr. Rusk's visit to Madrid continued the precedent of the late Secretary of State John Foster Dulles, who flew here first in 1958 to inform General Franco similarly of the results of the Paris NATO Council meeting that year.

Spain is not a member of the Atlantic alliance but is already indirectly linked to it through her defense ties with two members — the United States and Portugal.

Sources close to the talks reported later that Mr. Rusk had won General Franco's full ap-

Continued on Page 42, Column 3

Wagner Warns Governor On Rent-Control 'Jokers'

By CHARLES G. BENNETT

Mayor Wagner told Governor Rockefeller yesterday in a letter that the city would be "proud and happy" to take over rent control from the state next May 1 provided "there are no jokers in the cards being dealt."

In a letter, the Mayor ridiculed many of the Governor's housing policies and proposals. At one point he called on the Governor to "stop playing politics with human misery."

The Mayor also declared that if the city took over rent control it would "keep it clean,

Wagner letter to Rockefeller will be found on Page 62.

which is more than the state has done."

Mayor Wagner's letter was in reply to one the Governor sent Thursday in which Mr. Rockefeller said the state would transfer rent control to the city on May 1. The Governor said the state would pay "the reasonable cost" of administering control, based on the state's own cost experience.

The present state outlay is just under $4,000,000 a year.

Morhouse Critical

L. Judson Morhouse, the Republican state chairman, said the Mayor's letter indicated he had not read Mr. Rockefeller's proposal, "or at least did not read it carefully."

The proposal, he said, would transfer to the city "full authority to set the amount of rents and to draft all rent-control regulations, with the state paying for the administrative costs."

In writing that the city would take over only without "jokers" the rent control function the state is "abdicating," Mayor Wagner asserted that "one such joker is already apparent in your offer pegging the state's share of rent control administrative expenses at the old level."

The correct procedure, accord-

Continued on Page 62, Column 3

KHRUSHCHEV GIVES WARNING ON CROPS

Asserts Farm Officials Face Ouster From Party Unless Production Is Raised

By THEODORE SHABAD
Special to The New York Times.

MOSCOW, Dec. 16 — Premier Khrushchev was reported today to have threatened farm officials with dismissal from the Communist party if they refused to follow his proposals for raising Soviet agricultural output.

Mr. Khrushchev has been engaged in a campaign to improve the livestock feed base by replacing hay and oats with higher yielding fodder crops such as corn, sugar beets and beans.

Press accounts published today said the Premier also had told an agriculture conference here Thursday that Soviet cities were suffering a meat shortage because of the failure of the farms to increase livestock output.

Shift to Hogs Urged

Production should be increased swiftly in the next few years, Mr. Khrushchev said, by shifting from beef cattle to more prolific hogs and by using sugar beets as hog feed.

Since Moscow has begun to import large amounts of cane sugar from Cuba there appears to have developed a sugar glut in what was previously an important beet sugar producing nation. The Government has therefore found it possible to divert some of its sugar beet planting to strengthen its deficient feed supply.

The Premier lashed out especially at farm officials of the Leningrad area, which together with other parts of central and northern European Russia had sent 11,000 delegates to the farm conference.

Premier Khrushchev asserted that a state farm director named

Continued on Page 20, Column 4

FEDERATION WINS IN TEACHER VOTE

Gets Two-Thirds of Ballots in 3-Way Election to Pick Bargaining Agent Here

By RALPH KATZ

The United Federation of Teachers last night won the right to represent the city's 43,500 public school teachers in collective bargaining.

The results of the three-day election gave the union 20,045 of a total of 33,119 votes.

The Teachers Bargaining Organization was second with 9,770 votes, and the Teachers Union was third with 2,575 votes.

There were 662 votes for no union. Sixty-seven ballots were voided.

The United Federation of Teachers, an affiliate of the American Federation of Labor and Congress of Industrial Organizations, struck the city's elementary and secondary schools for one day—on Nov. 7, 1960—in a demand for a collective bargaining election.

Demands Listed

The strike was called off when Mayor Wagner appointed a three-member board of mediation. Since then, the union has achieved its major goal—the election of a bargaining agent. It has now drawn up a list of bargaining demands on wages, pension improvements and working conditions.

Charles Cogen, president of the union, said last night that he would press for an early start on bargaining talks with the Board of Education. He said he expected to set a pattern for "the teaching profession in schools throughout the nation.

The vote was conducted by the Honest Ballot Association for the city's elementary and

Continued on Page 67, Column 1

Sports News

FOOTBALL

Syracuse did all its scoring in the second half yesterday and beat Miami of Florida, 15—14, in the Liberty Bowl before 15,712 spectators at Philadelphia. The running of Ernie Davis, the all-America halfback, paced the rally.

Kansas trounced Rice, 33—7, before 52,000 fans in the Bluebonnet Bowl at Houston. Ken Coleman and Roger McFarland led the running attack for the winners.

Two Southwest Conference teams chose new head coaches. Texas A. and M. signed Hank Foldberg and Southern Methodist appointed Hayden Fry.

The Baltimore Colts upset the San Francisco Forty-Niners, 27—24, on the passing of Johnny Unitas. The Forty-Niner loss allowed the Detroit Lions to clinch second place in the Western Conference of the National Football League.

HORSE RACING

Gyro won the $11,900 City of Coral Gables Handicap by two and a quarter lengths at Tropical Park. Gyro ran six furlongs in 1 minute 9 seconds and paid $3.40 for $2 to win.

HOCKEY

George Armstrong scored three goals as the Toronto Maple Leafs turned back the New York Rangers, 4 to 2.

Details in Section 5.

Ban on Reds Ended By City University

By MILTON BRACKER

The ban on speeches by known Communists on city college campuses was reversed yesterday.

The Administrative Council of the City University ruled that each college could approve or disapprove invitations to members of the Communist party. This is the same rule that had been in effect before the ban was imposed on Oct. 26.

In reversing itself, the five-man council cited a report on the issue by the Committee on the Bill of Rights of the Association of the Bar of the City of New York. The report concluded:

"Accordingly, it is our considered opinion that a faculty or administration of the City University is legally entitled to permit known United States Communist party members

Continued on Page 59, Column 3

Dr. King Among 265 Negroes Seized in March on Albany, Ga., City Hall

Demonstrators, under arrest after a rally in behalf of jailed Negroes, move through business area in Albany, Ga. Associated Press Wirephoto

By CLAUDE SITTON
Special to The New York Times.

ALBANY, Ga., Dec. 16—The Rev. Dr. Martin Luther King Jr., 264 other Negroes and one white youth were arrested today as they marched on City Hall for a prayer demonstration. All were jailed.

There was no violence, despite the tension aroused by week-long racial controversy and the breakdown of negotiations between white and Negro leaders aimed at restoring this city of 56,000 persons to normal. Today's demonstration was mainly in protest against the city's refusal to release hundreds of other Negroes held in earlier arrests.

The city police and state highway patrolmen herded the demonstrators through the heart of the business district and into an alley beside the City Hall. Thousands of whites and Negroes in the Saturday afternoon shopping crowds watched in relative

Continued on Page 46, Column 3

Diem to Cooperate With U.S. on Reform

By JACK RAYMOND
Special to The New York Times.

WASHINGTON, Dec. 16 — The United States and South Vietnam will set up joint operations in intelligence, military strategy and the surveying of social and economic conditions in the Southeast Asian country, it was reported today.

These moves were part of a program of administrative changes that the South Vietnamese government is understood to have accepted in return for President Kennedy's assurance of increased United States assistance in the fight against communism and flood disaster.

President Kennedy and President Ngo Dinh Diem of South Vietnam discussed the aid problem in letters that were released early yesterday. In his letter the South Vietnamese President

Continued on Page 27, Column 1

Today's Sections

Index to Subjects

1962

"All the News That's Fit to Print"

The New York Times.

LATE CITY EDITION

U. S. Weather Bureau Report (Page 46) forecasts: Cloudy, windy and cold today; fair and colder tonight. Fair tomorrow. Temp. range: 30—18; yesterday: 43—33.

VOL. CXI..No. 38,003. © 1962 by The New York Times Company. Times Square, New York 36, N. Y. NEW YORK, SATURDAY, FEBRUARY 10, 1962. 10 cents beyond 50-mile zone from New York City except on Long Island. Higher in air delivery cities. FIVE CENTS

POWERS IS FREED BY SOVIET IN AN EXCHANGE FOR ABEL; U-2 PILOT ON WAY TO U. S.

Associated Press

Francis G. Powers

The New York Times

Col. Rudolf Abel

TRANSFER IS MADE

American Student Is Also Released in East Germany

By TOM WICKER

Special to The New York Times.

WASHINGTON, Saturday, Feb. 10 — Francis Gary Powers has been released by the Soviet Union in exchange for the release of Col. Rudolf Abel, the convicted Soviet spy, the White House announced at 3:20 A. M.

Frederic L. Pryor, an American student held by East German authorities since August, 1961, also has been released. He was turned over to the American authorities in Berlin.

Mr. Powers, the White House said, is in Berlin en route to the United States.

Colonel Abel was deported and has been released in Berlin.

Result of Long Effort

The White House announcement said that efforts to obtain Mr. Powers' release had been under way for some time. It added that the United States, in its recent efforts, had had the "cooperation and assistance" of James B. Donovan, a New York lawyer.

The announcement of the releases and the exchange with the Soviet Union was made by Pierre Salinger, the President's press secretary, at a White House news conference just after 3 A. M.

Mr. Powers was downed in a U-2 plane while making a high-altitude reconnaissance flight over the Soviet Union in May, 1960. At a Moscow trial later he pleaded guilty to espionage charges and was sentenced to ten years—three in prison and seven in a prison colony.

The U-2 incident occurred just before a Big Four summit meeting was to have taken place in Paris. After reaching Paris, Premier Khrushchev unloosed a barrage of diatribe against the United States and used the incident to disrupt the planned meeting.

Colonel Abel was convicted in the United States of espionage charges in 1957 and given

Continued on Page 2, Column 2

SHELTER PROGRAM FOR COMMUNITIES SENT TO CONGRESS

U. S. Would Pay All or Part of Cost of Structures for 20,000,000 People

$450,000,000 IS SOUGHT

Schools, Hospitals or Other Nonprofit Groups Would Be Eligible for Funds

By PETER BRAESTRUP

Special to The New York Times.

WASHINGTON, Feb. 9—The Kennedy Administration asked Congress today for authority to pay all or part of the costs of neighborhood fall-out shelters for 20,000,000 people over the next few years.

The proposed legislation would clear the way for the Office of Civil Defense to help authorities and schools, hospitals and other nonprofit institutions finance public shelters holding fifty or more persons.

Pentagon spokesmen released the text of the bill and an accompanying letter by Defense Secretary Robert S. McNamara. Both documents were sent to Capitol Hill late yesterday.

"This bill," Mr. McNamara wrote, "will help coordinate [state and local] programs into an efficient and effective defense against enemy attack."

Concedes Many Would Die

Originally, the President was to have sent the explanatory letter to Congress. However, White House spokesmen indicated that Mr. Kennedy would discuss the civil defense program at a later date.

Although many people would die in a nuclear attack, regardless of defense measures, Mr. McNamara said, "we can develop our program of civil defense to increase the number of people who can create the base for recovery after an attack."

Details of any program, Mr. McNamara continued, "must change as the forces and technology of weapons change, but the essential elements [remain] the same." These elements, he said, are a warning system, fall-out shelters, and advance preparations for post-attack recovery.

Essentially, the Administration has geared its civil defense effort for the fiscal year 1963 to its belief that the Soviet Union has only a limited ability to deliver large thermonuclear weapons on target in the United

Continued on Page 10, Column 2

BUCKLEY TO RUN FOR HOUSE AGAIN

'Not Worried' Over Possible Primary Election Contest

Representative Charles A. Buckley of the Bronx said yesterday he would run for re-election this year despite Mayor Wagner's opposition.

The Mayor has called Mr. Buckley a "political boss" and has undertaken to force him out of his post as the Democratic leader of Bronx County, following Mr. Buckley's endorsement of the Mayor's opponent in the primary election last year.

President Kennedy, however, has been overtly friendly to Mr. Buckley. The Representative is chairman of the important Public Works Committee of the House of Representatives and was one of the first leading New York Democrats to support Mr. Kennedy for the Presidential nomination in 1960.

Sat With President

Despite the political feud between the Mayor and Mr. Buckley, the President invited the Representative to sit beside him during one half of the Army-Navy football game in Philadelphia last fall. Mr. Wagner was the President's companion during the other half.

There had been speculation that Mr. Buckley, a 71-year-old former Alderman who has served in the House since 1935, would step aside this year rather than face a primary election fight for the Democratic nomination.

Leaders of the reform faction in the Democratic party in the Bronx are planning to nominate a candidate to oppose Mr. Buckley at a convention tentatively

Continued on Page 19, Column 7

United Press International Telephoto

DISCUSSES INQUIRY: Senator Strom Thurmond, right, South Carolina Democrat, at news conference yesterday. At the left is J. Fred Buzhardt Jr., his legislative aide.

City Bids States and U. S. Join on New Haven Aid

By CHARLES G. BENNETT

Mayor Wagner proposed last night that Federal, state and city representatives meet to decide what could be done to save the New York, New Haven and Hartford Railroad.

He said he agreed with President Kennedy that state and local governments must share the responsibility for keeping the New Haven running.

"We in New York City have accepted our share of this responsibility and will continue to share the burden," Mr. Wagner said.

The Mayor issued his call for the meeting after a telephone conversation with Gov. John A. Notte Jr. of Rhode Island. Earlier in the day, he said, Governor Notte had discussed the railroad situation with Governors Rockefeller of New York, John N. Dempsey of Connecticut and John A. Volpe of Massachusetts.

Early Meeting Expected

At City Hall it was expected that the proposal for a meeting would be accepted and that the conference would be held soon.

Last night a spokesman for the New Haven said the railroad had been notified by Governor Notte in a letter that a meeting of the four Governors and Mayor Wagner could be expected in March to look into the railroad's plight.

The officials, Governor Notte wrote, are concerned over "apparent inconsistencies" in recent statements by the three court-appointed trustees of the carrier.

In an interview published Wednesday, Richard Joyce Smith, one of the trustees, was quoted as saying that the New Haven had enough cash to continue operating its passenger service indefinitely. The assertion was quickly questioned by

Continued on Page 19, Column 7

MAYOR QUITS CLUB OVER BIAS CHARGE

He Notes Allegations That the New York A. C. Bars Negroes and Jews

By RICHARD P. HUNT

Mayor Wagner resigned from the New York Athletic Club yesterday amid a dispute over whether the club discriminates against Negroes and Jews in admitting new members.

The Mayor's one-sentence letter of resignation gave no reason for his quitting the club, where his late father had been a member and where his late mother once worked.

But Mr. Wagner said at a news conference in City Hall that he had heard "allegations" about the club's policy.

"I thought the best move would be not to be in a position where, if the allegations were true, I would be a member," he said.

John F. X. Condon, public relations director of the club, denied that there was any discrimination in its membership policy. He said that some Jews were among the approximately 9,500 members, but that he knew of no Negro members.

Accused by 2 Groups

About a month ago the Anti-Defamation League listed the club as "discriminating" in membership policy. And a spokesman for the National Association for the Advancement of Colored People said yesterday it had "protested" the club's policy.

Although the Mayor did not say where he had heard the "allegations" about the New York Athletic Club, it was learned that his resignation stemmed indirectly from an effort to boycott the club's annual indoor track meet next Friday.

Jackie Robinson, the first Negro to play in the major leagues, and James L. Hicks, executive editor of the Amsterdam News, a weekly newspaper serving the Negro community, are urging the boycott.

They have sent letters to sixty-five Negro and Jewish athletes urging them to withdraw from this year's New York Athletic Club Games at Madison Square Garden because of what they call the club's "unfair policy towards Negroes and Jews."

Mr. Condon said there had been no indications so far that any athletes were withdrawing from the meet. "We will run the games, boycott or no boycott," he declared.

The meet, which has been held regularly since 1868, is one of the big indoor track

Continued on Page 48, Column 5

Morristown Finds Quiet Way to Spur School Integration

By JOSEPH O. HAFF

Special to The New York Times.

MORRISTOWN, N. J., Feb. 9—This city of 17,000 has quietly tackled the problem of school segregation with a plan to distribute its Negro pupils more widely.

The plan has been marked, residents say, by a policy of complete frankness by the Board of Education and a spirit of cooperation and understanding throughout the city.

Under the plan, a predominantly Negro grade school will house only the school system's seventh and eighth grades. The children in that school from kindergarten through the sixth grade will be distributed among the three other grade schools.

Morristown's grade school enrollment of 1,810 includes 547 Negroes, of whom 341 attend the Lafayette School in a section known as The Hollow. Forty-two white children are attending the Lafayette School, making the ratio about eight Negro pupils to each white pupil.

In two of the three other grade schools, the ratio is reversed, while in the third, there are about five white pupils to each Negro.

Alerted to the dangers of the "neighborhood" school by the difficulties that New Rochelle, N. Y., had been facing, the local Board of Education last June

Continued on Page 24, Column 5

NEWS INDEX

THURMOND SAYS LETTER VANISHED AT MARINE OFFICE

It Showed Up Later on Desk of Shoup, Senator Reports —General Is Silent

By JACK RAYMOND

Special to The New York Times.

WASHINGTON, Feb. 9—A "purloined letter" case developed today in the Senate's investigation of Pentagon speech censorship and troop indoctrination.

The mystery centered on Senator Strom Thurmond's charge that when one of his aides visited Marine Corps headquarters last November, a letter disappeared from his briefcase "while his head was turned."

The letter, according to the South Carolina Democrat, showed up afterward on the desk of Gen. David M. Shoup, commandant of the Marine Corps. But when the Senator asked the general how it had happened, Senator Thurmond said, the officer replied:

"I cannot reveal that information. The Secretary of the Navy has directed me not to furnish that information."

Shoup Is Silent

Senator Thurmond, in a speech on the Senate floor late yesterday, said he still did not know the answer. At marine headquarters today, a spokesman said that General Shoup would not comment.

The Senator did not say flatly that anyone had stolen the letter. He merely underscored the mystery surrounding its travels from his aide's briefcase to the marine commandant's desk.

The letter contained reports, addressed to the Senator's office, of alleged prohibitions against anti-Communist programs at West Coast military installations. It also contained the names of officers who might testify on the subject.

Thus a new controversy developed in the efforts of the Special Senate Preparedness Subcommittee to investigate charges that military leaders have been restricted in their attempts to speak out against communism. The Senate panel is also studying charges that troop indoctrination against communism has been inadequate.

Senator Thurmond, a member of the subcommittee, which is headed by Senator John Stennis, Democrat of Mississippi, pressed the original charges.

Censors' Names a Problem

In the course of the hearings, however, a dispute arose over whether Pentagon officials should disclose the names of censors responsible for specific speech alterations. The dispute was resolved when President Kennedy invoked the doctrine of Executive privilege to withhold the information.

A second controversy arose when General Shoup complained over the quizzing of a group of marines on "cold war" subjects by investigators associated with the subcommittee. The marines filled in a questionnaire that asked identification of such individuals as Frol R. Kozlov and the meaning of dialectical materialism.

Mr. Kozlov is a secretary of the Communist party of the Soviet Union. Dialectical materialism is the official Soviet theory that the course of history is dominated by class

Continued on Page 9, Column 1

ARMS AIDE WARNS ON LETTING SOVIET BEAT U.S. TO TESTS

Key Kennedy Adviser Says Last Soviet Blasts in Air Made Substantial Gain

By MAX FRANKEL

Special to The New York Times.

WASHINGTON, Feb. 9—President Kennedy's chief disarmament adviser said today the United States could not afford to let the Soviet Union stage another series of nuclear tests before the United States itself resumes testing in the atmosphere.

William C. Foster, director of the United States Arms Control and Disarmament Agency, said the latest analyses of last fall's Soviet test series showed "that the Soviets achieved some substantial gains."

Unless there is an effective treaty banning all tests and offering safeguards against secret preparations for tests, Mr. Foster declared, the Russians could again surprise the West with a program of experiments that might well tip the balance of nuclear power in their favor.

Since no one here any longer expects the Russians to agree to a well-inspected ban on tests, Mr. Foster's statement had the effect of confirming reports that the Administration had decided to proceed with its tests.

Loss of Superiority Feared

Another Soviet series before the United States tests again, he said, "might actually give them a superiority in the anti-missile and other strategic areas."

At his news conference Wednesday President Kennedy hinted that he had decided to resume testing in the atmosphere, but he did not state the military imperatives so clearly.

The President also appeared to have raised his terms for a treaty to ban tests by demanding guarantees against secret Soviet preparations for future major test series. It was an attempt to explain the President's comments and to justify them with the United States' diplomatic posture that prompted Mr. Foster's statement, in the form of a letter to the editor of The Washington Post and Times-Herald.

Most observers here believe that the United States will soon announce plans to resume atmospheric testing. The President said his studies — presumably on what kind of a program to conduct—should be completed by the end of the month.

Last Chance Offered

Partly in response to British pressure and partly out of concern for public opinion here and abroad, Washington agreed to join London in giving the Russians a final chance to sign a treaty banning tests and providing for controls and inspection.

The general expectation is that Moscow will refuse to sign now, though it may agree to continue negotiations as part of the general disarmament discussions due to start in Geneva March 14.

What the Administration feared most was a last-minute "acceptance" by the Soviet Union of last September's offer by the West to prohibit tests in the atmosphere even without inspection.

That offer no longer stands.

Continued on Page 8, Column 4

Soviet Rebuffed on Berlin In Effort to Curb Flights

Special to The New York Times.

BERLIN, Feb. 9—The Russians have tried and failed over the last forty-eight hours to restrict the Western Allied air traffic in the three twenty-mile wide flight corridors to Berlin.

The West also rebuffed Col. Andrei I. Solovyev, the Soviet commandant, today when he tried to enter the United States sector at the Friedrichstrasse crossing en route to a meeting at British headquarters.

The United States has barred Colonel Solovyev from its sector in retaliation for East German restrictions against American officials' entry into East Berlin.

An Allied statement said the Soviet Union had demanded temporary exclusive use of one of the air corridors for yesterday and of the two others this morning.

The Allies rebuffed the Soviet demand and flew both military and civilian craft without incident.

Major Probing Is Seen

The Soviet move was considered by Allied officials as a major probing of their determination on the sensitive air-access issue in the Berlin crisis.

Gen. Lucius D. Clay, President Kennedy's personal representative in Berlin, defied the Russians this morning and flew to Bremen, West Germany, along the northern air corridor during the period that the Soviet had demanded its exclusive use for military maneuvers.

The general had been in consultation with the President and with Secretary of State Dean Rusk ever since the Soviet controller at the Berlin air safety center first raised the demand last Wednesday.

On his return to Berlin tonight, General Clay said the Soviet move might have been the "first attempt to get the Allies out of the air corridors." He added: "We shall keep the planes flying."

His plane had flown to Bremen at an altitude of 6,000 feet. No Soviet activity in the air was seen.

"They wanted to harass us, but we did not let ourselves be harassed," General Clay added.

The Allies flew all the scheduled commercial flights in and

Continued on Page 6, Column 5

ROBERT KENNEDY DEBATES LEFTIST

Invites Tokyo Unionist to Visit 'Imperialist' U. S.—Reaches Taipei on Tour

By A. M. ROSENTHAL

Special to The New York Times.

TOKYO, Saturday, Feb. 10—Attorney General Robert F. Kennedy faced the startled chief of Japan's massive Left-wing labor union yesterday and challenged him to visit the United States and find out for himself whether it was really an "imperialist" land of "monopoly capital."

"Come and see," urged Mr. Kennedy, waving a finger at the labor leader and bouncing up and down in his chair with eagerness. "Give us a fair shake!"

Across the table, begging off from the trip, sat Akira Iwai, 39-year-old secretary general of Sohyo, a national union of 4,000,000 members.

Sohyo, affiliated with the strongly Marxist Socialist party of Japan, is one of the nation's most powerful political forces.

[Mr. and Mrs. Kennedy reached Taipei, Taiwan, Saturday morning on a flight that was to take them later in the day to Hong Kong, The Associated Press said.]

Mr. Kennedy had awakened just after dawn yesterday, the last full day of his Japanese visit. After bouncing from a judo school to an ice rink to factories to a news conference, he was looking a little weary by the time he walked into the hotel to meet with the Sohyo delegation. The meeting with organized Japanese labor was

Continued on Page 2, Column 2

ISRAEL DEVALUES POUND TO 3 TO $1

Subsidies Ended Also in Act to Strengthen Exports

By LAWRENCE FELLOWS

Special to The New York Times.

JERUSALEM (Israeli Sector), Feb. 9—Israel devalued her currency today as part of a broad program aimed at increasing exports.

Finance Minister Levi Eshkol announced the devaluation in a broadcast on the state radio at 4 P. M., an hour after the last business concerns in Israel had closed for the beginning of the Sabbath at sundown.

The new rate of exchange, which Mr. Eshkol said would take effect at midnight, is three Israeli pounds to the dollar. The old official rate was 1.8 Israeli pounds to the dollar.

Subsidies Drew Criticism

The new rate, the Finance Minister announced, will be uniform and applies to exports of goods and services, imports and capital transfers.

The old rate was supported with premiums and subsidies that aided Israel's young industries but drew criticism from international banking organizations and foreign producers, who complained that Israel was competing unfairly with them for world markets.

The cold reception Israel has got from the European Common Market countries helped bring on the decision to cast off these main supports of Israeli industry. Israel will now be in a better position to seek an accommodation with the market and continue to sell her goods in its member-states, which are France, West Germany, Italy, Belgium, the

Continued on Page 9, Column 3

Associated Press Radiophoto

TOUCH FOOTBALL is the game taught by Attorney General Robert F. Kennedy to a group of Japanese youngsters in compound of U. S. Embassy in Tokyo. Mr. Kennedy and his wife are on first leg of international goodwill tour.

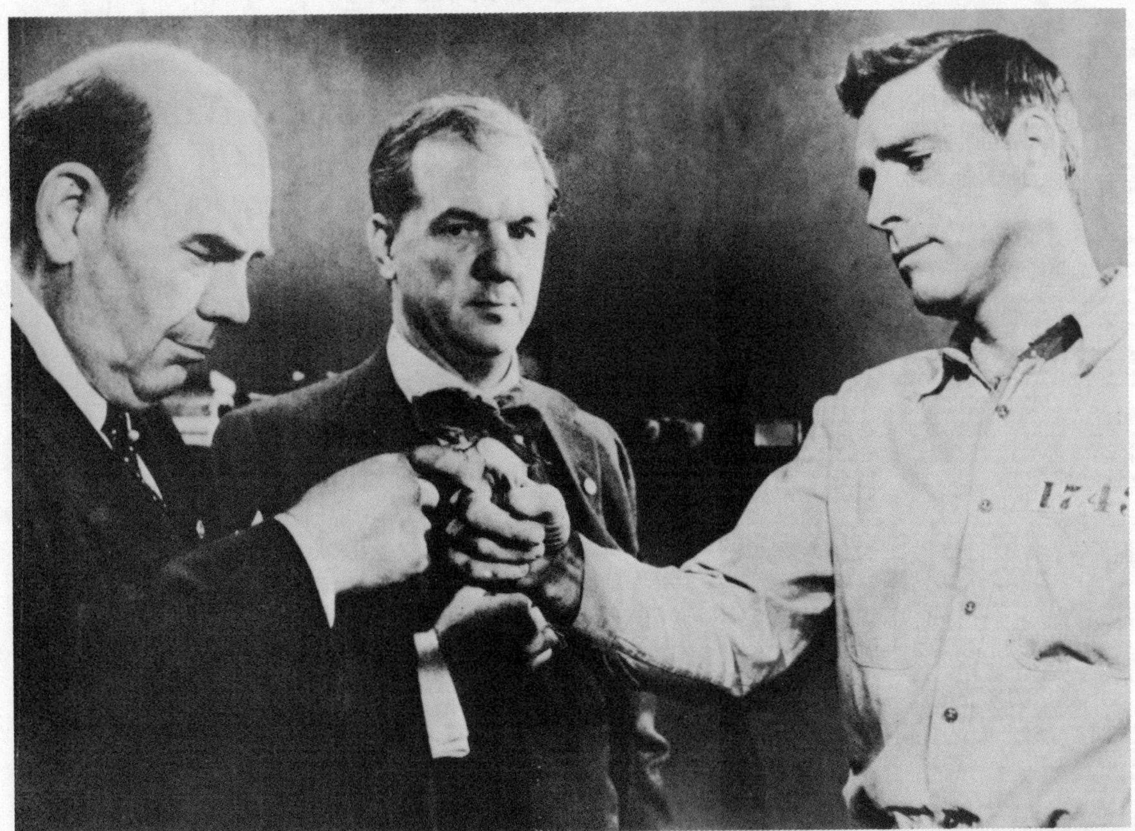

Burt Lancaster starred as the unusual convict who became a noted ornithologist in prison. James Westerfield and Karl Maiden are also seen in this scene from *Birdman of Alcatraz.*

Peter O'Toole in *Lawrence of Arabia.*

"All the News That's Fit to Print"

The New York Times.

LATE CITY EDITION
U. S. Weather Bureau Report (Page 57) forecasts: Fair today and tonight. Fair and warmer tomorrow. Temp. range: 51—31; yesterday: 49—35.

VOL. CXI..No. 38,040. NEW YORK, MONDAY, MARCH 19, 1962. FIVE CENTS
10 cents beyond 50-mile zone from New York City except on Long Island. Higher in air delivery cities.

ALGERIAN CEASE-FIRE IS SIGNED; DE GAULLE BIDS FRANCE BACK IT; SALAN APPEALS FOR RESISTANCE

CABINET TO MEET

French Leader Says He Will Ask People to Ratify Accord

Text of de Gaulle's address is printed on Page 11.

By HENRY GINIGER
Special to The New York Times.

PARIS, March 18—President de Gaulle appealed to the French people tonight to support the peace accords reached today between French and Algerian negotiators. They will be presented to the Cabinet at a meeting tomorrow.

The French leader hailed the accords on radio and television. He announced that he would soon ask the people to ratify the accords. This is expected to take place in a referendum in France, probably April 8.

France was reported extremely calm tonight as the country received the momentous news of the end of its last colonial war.

Paris Under Guard

Paris was heavily guarded against the possibility of trouble. This was particularly true of the Elysée Palace, from which General de Gaulle spoke. His message was recorded this afternoon, although it is believed to have been ready for days.

The President directly and by implication made clear that he saw the accords as the start of a new and difficult phase of the Algerian problem. What is on everyone's mind here, including the President's, is the violent opposition, expressed through terroristic and subversive means, of most of the European population of Algeria to the application of the agreements.

But the mechanism to apply the accords, which had waited so long to be put into action, began functioning despite the obstacles.

Cabinet Will Meet

Tomorrow afternoon the French Cabinet will meet under General de Gaulle to draw up decrees and instructions to put the agreements into effect in Algeria. These include the naming of a French High Commissioner, the appointment of an executive body, formation of an

Continued on Page 11, Column 1

ANNOUNCES THE CEASE-FIRE: President de Gaulle appearing on French television
Associated Press Radiophoto

ACCORD AT EVIAN

Truce in 7-Year War Is in Effect Today—Future Tie Defined

Summary of truce agreement will be found on Page 10.

By ROBERT C. DOTY
Special to The New York Times.

EVIAN-LES-BAINS, France, March 18 — A cease-fire ending the Algerian war was signed here today by French and Algerian rebel delegations.

The document terminating the rebellion after seven years, four months and eighteen days will go into effect throughout Algeria at noon tomorrow (6 A. M. Eastern standard time). The signing took place at 5:30 P. M.

The accord ended the long fight between the French Republic and the Algerian rebels' National Liberation Front for control of the vast North African territory.

It opened a new phase in the resistance of the Secret Army Organization, made up of extremist Europeans, to a policy certain to lead to an independent, predominantly Moslem Algeria.

Referendum Provided

Only after France and the nationalists have mastered the bloody terror unleashed by the Secret Army will the settlement become really operative.

The accord covers the process by which Algerians will vote on their own political future in four to six months and the cooperation between France and the independent Algeria that will result from a self-determination referendum.

Included also are guarantees for the rights of the 1,000,000 Europeans living among 9,000,000 Moslems; an interim political regime; provisions for a continued French military presence in Algeria; joint exploitation of oil and other minerals in the Sahara, and a broad amnesty for military and political prisoners on both sides.

Joxe Announces Accord

The accord was announced here shortly after 6:30 P. M. by Louis Joxe, French Minister for Algerian Affairs. M. Joxe has shepherded it through four open conferences and one secret meeting since June, 1960.

The settlement came at the end of twelve days of hard bargaining here with a rebel delegation headed by Belkacem Krim, Deputy Premier and Interior Minister of the rebels' Provisional Government.

An hour and a half after the announcement here, President de Gaulle went on the state radio and television networks in France and Algeria to proclaim the settlement and to call for massive backing of the Government's Algerian policy in a referendum to be held, probably early next month, in France.

At Aubonne, in Switzerland, the rebel delegation held a news conference to present its version of the accord. It coincided in all essentials with the French announcement.

M. Joxe's statement gave no

Continued on Page 10, Column 3

Challenge in Algeria: The Secret Army

This is the first of four articles on the Secret Army Organization by a correspondent recently returned from a six-week inquiry in Algeria.

By BENJAMIN WELLES
Special to The New York Times.

MADRID, March 18—Settlement of the long Algerian rebellion leaves France with the problem of reconciling the Europeans in Algeria to the cease-fire — particularly the Secret Army Organization, whose avowed purpose is to wreck the agreement and keep the country French.

Even before the cease-fire agreement, the Secret Army, known by its initials in French as the O. A. S., seized virtual control of the major cities of Algeria in open defiance of President de Gaulle.

With the creation of a National Committee of French Resistance in Algeria and a secret National Council of Resistance in France, announced today, the O. A. S. is in full rebellion against the de Gaulle Government.

Both the National Committee and National Council presumably are led by the same clandestine group of extremist army officers and civilians who form the O. A. S. Supreme Council, or Conseil Supérieure de l'O.A.S.

Except for former Generals Raoul Salan and Edmond Jouhaud, no members of the Supreme Council have been publicly identified.

Within Algeria the new National Committee appears to be preparing a Provisional Central Power to exercise French sovereignty over "liberated areas."

These areas presumably will include Algiers, Oran and other cities where the O. A. S. is supreme.

These cities in time may become linked strong points or even a military redoubt along the Algerian coast in which the Secret Army Organization will wage guerrilla warfare against both the de Gaulle regime and

Continued on Page 12, Column 1

TRUCE NO PEACE, BEN KHEDDA SAYS

Premier of Algerians Cites Threat From Rightists in Period of Cease-Fire

By United Press International.

TUNIS, March 18—Benyoussef Ben Khedda, Premier of the Algerian Provisional Government, said tonight that the French-Algerian cease-fire did not mean peace in Algeria, because of danger from the Secret Army Organization.

Mr. Ben Khedda, in a radio address in French and Arabic, ordered his forces to stop fighting at noon tomorrow. He also paid tribute to the Moslem nationalists who died in the seven-year war.

He spoke about fifteen minutes, coming on the air half an hour after President de Gaulle's broadcast of news of the cease-fire from Paris.

Mr. Ben Khedda described the cease-fire as a "great victory for the Algerian people." But he continued:

"The period of the cease-fire is not the peace because there is the danger the Fascist hordes of the Secret Army Organization will increase the bloodshed in their fight for a French Algeria."

He accused the French civil and military authorities "to this day" of being "more or

Continued on Page 10, Column 8

Strikes Sweeping Algeria As Rightists Protest Pact

By PAUL HOFMANN
Special to The New York Times.

ALGIERS, Monday, March 19—Algeria's big cities were almost paralyzed this morning by a general strike ordered by European extremists as a protest against the cease-fire in the Algerian war.

Electric current was cut in Algiers before dawn, plunging the city into darkness. The only lights were those of ships in the harbor.

The strike was heralded by explosions in various parts of the city.

In Oran, former Gen. Raoul Salan, leader of the Secret Army Organization of European extremists was heard on a television wavelength yesterday ordering "French forces" to harass "the enemy" in cities and in the countryside. He urged Europeans to join his underground forces in the interior.

French Troops Alerted

The French Army threw huge forces into the streets of Algiers and the other large cities. The troops were under orders to return massive fire at every shot fired against them.

The extremists' strike order appeared to have been obeyed by virtually all European settlers, and by many Moslems who live or work in predominantly European neighborhoods.

The French Army moved fresh reinforcements into the streets and into positions at key installations this morning.

At 8 A. M. (2 A. M., Eastern

Continued on Page 12, Column 5

KENNEDY PRAISES 'HISTORIC' ACCORD

Statement by White House Sees a 'Sound Basis' for Progress in Algeria

By JACK RAYMOND
Special to The New York Times.

WASHINGTON, March 18—The White House hailed the French - Algerian cease - fire agreement today as a "historic accomplishment."

In a statement approved by President Kennedy, hope was expressed that the opportunity "will be quickly seized" to carry out the settlement of the Algerian nationalist rebellion.

Pierre Salinger, White House press secretary, issued the statement, which said:

"The United States supports these efforts toward a mutually beneficial solution and welcomes the agreement. It provides a sound basis for a friendly and fruitful relationship between Algeria and France and it presents an opportunity for all residents of Algeria to contribute constructively toward the future.

"The conclusion of the cease-fire agreement between French authorities and representatives of the F. L. N. is an historic accomplishment made possible by the vision, statesmanship and moderation demonstrated by all concerned.

"It is to be hoped that the opportunity will be quickly seized and that the wisdom in which the agreement was

Continued on Page 11, Column 7

MAHONEY CLEARS CITY'S 3 BUS BILLS; PASSAGE TONIGHT

He Will Seek Action Later to Keep Franchises and Fares Out of Politics

CONSPIRACY IS CHARGED

G.O.P. Leader Calls Mayor, Quill and Weinberg 'Unholy Triangle' in Tie-Up Here

By DOUGLAS DALES
Special to The New York Times.

ALBANY, March 18—Senator Walter J. Mahoney said today that the three bills to permit New York City to take over the strikebound Fifth Avenue Coach Lines would receive final passage tomorrow night.

The Republican majority leader added, however, that other bills to provide safeguards on fares and franchises would be introduced some time this week.

He said the additional bills were needed "to prevent trafficking in franchises and fare increases which promote the political aspirations of any individual, faction or party."

Separating the issues will prevent the three-day delay that would ensue if the three basic bills, already approved by the Assembly, were amended.

Reply to Wagner

In a statement replying to charges yesterday by Mayor Wagner that he was stalling on the bus legislation, Senator Mahoney said the present bus crisis "stems from the prolonged political conspiracy between the Mayor and Michael J. Quill [international president of the Transport Workers Union]."

"They have now been joined into an unholy triangle by Harry Weinberg," he added.

Mr. Weinberg is president of the Fifth Avenue company.

All three men, Senator Mahoney said, stand to benefit from the strike.

The Republican leader, who held up final action on the bus legislation last Thursday, said the bills had never been a prerequisite for settling the strike, which, he added, was clearly illegal.

6,500 Employes Idle

Nor, he said, has the legislation been a requirement for the exploration of legal means to settle the strike.

The strike, which has idled 6,500 employes since March 1 and forced 1,500,000 daily riders to seek other means of transportation, came after twenty-nine senior employes were laid off. The company said the layoffs were the first move toward reducing the work force by 1,500.

Senate approval of the bus bills tomorrow is expected to enable the New York City Transit Authority to resume service on the bus routes by Thursday. The authority has

Continued on Page 23, Column 3

Kheel Asked to End Surface Line Strike

By STANLEY LEVEY

The Fifth Avenue Coach Lines demanded yesterday that Theodore W. Kheel, impartial chairman of the transit industry, immediately order employes of its subsidiary, Surface Transit, Inc., back to work.

The demand was made in a letter to Mr. Kheel from Lawrence I. Weisman, executive vice president of the line.

Mr. Weisman made no mention of the parent company, which operates most of the north-south and crosstown routes in Manhattan. Surface Transit runs all routes in the Bronx and ten in Manhattan.

Mr. Kheel said he had requested an answer from John F. O'Donnell, counsel for the Transport Workers Union. The union went on strike

Continued on Page 22, Column 3

WEST WILL OFFER NEW ATOMIC PLAN

U.S. and Britain to Suggest at Geneva a Pact With Control Aspects Eased

By MAX FRANKEL
Special to The New York Times.

GENEVA, March 18 — The United States and Britain plan to offer this week another refinement of their conditions for a treaty to ban nuclear testing.

Experts in Washington and London are said to be revising the Western plan again to minimize, as much as President Kennedy will allow, the international controls to which the Soviet Union has objected so vehemently.

There is not much hope in Western circles here that Moscow will accept any form of outside inspection to police a test ban. The new offer is being prepared primarily to satisfy world opinion that there is no room for bargaining in the month that remains before the start of United States nuclear tests in the atmosphere.

The scaled-down Western proposals will be presented to the Soviet Foreign Minister, Andrei A. Gromyko, by Secretary of State Dean Rusk and the British Foreign Secretary, the Earl of Home.

Talks Scheduled on Berlin

The three foreign ministers, who arrived a week ago to open a seventeen-nation disarmament conference, have given themselves another week to set in motion a useful East-West dialogue looking toward a reduction of tension.

Before he returns to Washington next week, Mr. Rusk is expected to confer at least twice more in private with Mr. Gromyko. Mr. Rusk will continue the search for a solution of the Berlin problem.

United States officials believe the Russians share their desire to continue a discussion of Berlin. The United States officials expect Mr. Gromyko to be under new instructions for the next round of talks when they dine at the Soviet villa here Tuesday evening.

Much of Mr. Rusk's remaining time here will be taken up in informal conferences with the Russians and representatives of eight nonaligned nations. The neutrals want to isolate the main differences in rival Communist and Western plans for general and complete disarmament.

The neutral nations also ap-

Continued on Page 8, Column 3

PERON'S BACKERS SCORE WIDE GAINS IN ARGENTINE VOTE

Win Buenos Aires Province From Frondizi Men—Move Weighed by Military

By EDWARD C. BURKS
Special to The New York Times.

BUENOS AIRES, Monday, March 19—Peronist parties were well on the way early today to sweeping victories in yesterday's congressional and provincial elections.

Substantial returns soon after midnight gave the Peronists the prospect of winning at least thirty-two and perhaps forty of the eighty-six seats at stake in the balloting for the Chamber of Deputies.

Peronists apparently had swept to victory in Buenos Aires Province, where a third of the Argentina population lives. They had elected a Peronist labor leader, Andres Framini, 47 years old, as Governor of the province.

Intervention Possible

The parties supporting the exiled former dictator, Juan D. Peron, who was ousted by a military coup in 1955, were running up victories at the expense of President Arturo Frondizi's Intransigent Radical party and the Popular Radicals.

Argentina's Army, Navy and Air Secretaries—all emphatically anti-Peron—were in an emergency meeting during the night.

There have been repeated reports that the Federal Government, at the military's insistence, would intervene to forestall any outright attempts to restore Peronism even on a provincial basis.

The military leaders, a month ago, put pressure on the Frondizi Government to take a stand against Fidel Castro's Cuban regime after Argentina had abstained in a key vote at the Americas' foreign ministers conference in Punta del Este, Uruguay.

Link With Communists

Peronist factions have been linked with the Communists here in recent years; and the service chiefs are alert to prevent General Peron's followers from regaining control in the country.

Dr. Frondizi had Peronist support when he was first elected President in 1958. He has acted against Peronism in labor and political affairs since then; and the Peronists have fought the President in return.

The Peronist gain in the count of votes was conceded for the Government by Interior Minister Alfredo Vitolo.

Senor Framini, claiming a decisive success in Buenos Aires Province, declared:

"The people have won. General Peron (who is now in Spain) will return."

Senor Framini added that his plans for running the province of Buenos Aires were "the

Continued on Page 17, Column 1

CITY TO GET RIGHT OF SLUM SEIZURE

Albany Bill Will Allow It to Take Rent for Repairs

By LAYHMOND ROBINSON
Special to The New York Times.

ALBANY, March 18 — The Legislature is ready to approve this week a bill giving New York City the power to seize and repair slum properties.

This anti-slum measure, known as the receivership bill, has been sought by the Wagner administration for five years. In that time it had been the focal point of political battles in city elections as well as in the Republican-controlled Legislature.

The measure before the Legislature is a Republican-sponsored compromise version of the city's bill. It was worked out in consultation with city housing officials by Senator MacNeil Mitchell, Republican of Manhattan, its sponsor in the upper house.

Mayor Wagner described the compromise version last night as "not wholly satisfactory, but one that we can live with." He said it would give the city a sorely needed weapon for clearing up serious violations in slum buildings when the owner refuses to do so.

Mr. Mitchell said the Repub-

Continued on Page 25, Column 1

Track Study Assails 7-Day Work Week

By EMANUEL PERLMUTTER

Extensive improvements in the working and living conditions of grooms, exercise boys and "hot walkers" at the state's thoroughbred race tracks were recommended yesterday by an official commission of inquiry.

The commission was appointed by Governor Rockefeller last Aug. 25 as part of the settlement of a five-week strike of backstretch workers at Aqueduct, Belmont and Saratoga.

Major recommendations called for elimination of the seven-day work-week, abolition of dormitory overcrowding, better welfare coverage, improvement in the keeping of work schedule records by employers and the

Continued on Page 42, Column 1

Premier Votes in Soviet Election

Premier Khrushchev voting at a polling station in Moscow
Associated Press Radiophoto

By THEODORE SHABAD
Special to The New York Times.

MOSCOW, March 18—Today was Election Day in the Soviet Union, with a single slate of Communist-approved candidates placed before the voters. Election Day, which began at 6 A. M., was snowy and overcast in Moscow. But the gloom caused by the weather was partly dispelled by red flags and bunting and music blaring from loudspeakers. Premier Khrushchev cast his ballot in midmorning in Precinct 52 of the Frunze Election District, a block from the Kremlin wall. A correspondent for Reuters

Continued on Page 6, Column 3

Integration Forces in Suburbs Mount Drive on a Broad Front

By MILTON BRACKER

Racial segregation is under attack in the New York suburbs. The campaign involves pressures that are new to the North, and their impact is being felt by whites and Negroes in scores of communities.

Racial attitudes are being reexamined. Some harden. Some adjust as patterns of daily life change.

The problem affects every suburban area — New Jersey, Westchester County, Long Island and Connecticut. And it is growing, as an attorney for the National Association for the Advancement of Colored People indicated a few weeks ago. Asked if there was "something in the works" for a Long Island village, he said with a smile:

"I would say that something is in the works for the entire North."

The lawyer, Wilfred V. Reape Jr. of Westbury, L. I. put into one sentence a development already expressed in law suits, hearings, conferences, boycotts, sit-ins and a program to train more lawyers in the specialized requirements of fighting segregation in Northern communities.

Last month, for example, there were pickets, a boycott

Continued on Page 42, Column 3

Tshombe's Meeting With Adoula Opens

By HENRY TANNER
Special to The New York Times.

LEOPOLDVILLE, the Congo, March 18—The Premier of the Congo, Cyrille Adoula, and Moise Tshombe, President of Katanga Province, opened long-delayed talks today on ways to end Katanga's secession.

The meeting, which had been preceded by two days of wrangling over security measures and questions of protocol, began in a suprisingly relaxed atmosphere.

Mr. Tshombe traveled without escort from United Nations headquarters, where he is staying, to the Premier's residence on the bank of the Congo River. He was driven by United Na-

Continued on Page 2, Column 3

NEWS INDEX

"All the News That's Fit to Print"

The New York Times.

LATE CITY EDITION
U. S. Weather Bureau Report (Page 65) forecasts: Fair and warm today, tonight and tomorrow.
Temp. range: 83—65; yesterday: 84—48.

VOL. CXI..No. 38,078. | NEW YORK, THURSDAY, APRIL 26, 1962. | 10 cents beyond 50-mile zone from New York City except on Long Island. Higher in air delivery cities. | FIVE CENTS

U.S. OPENS A-TESTS IN AIR WITH BLAST OF MEDIUM YIELD

DAWN SHOT FIRED

Device Is Dropped From a Plane Near Christmas Island

By JOHN W. FINNEY
Special to The New York Times.

WASHINGTON, April 25—The United States resumed nuclear testing in the atmosphere today by setting off an intermediate-size explosion near Christmas Island in the Pacific.

The explosion took place at about 10:45 A. M. (Eastern Standard Time), just as dawn was beginning to light the overcast skies above the equatorial atoll in the Central Pacific.

Rising through the overcast, the mushroom-shape cloud symbolized a new competitive phase in the atomic arms race and the frustration of more than three years of effort to reach an international agreement to prohibit atomic testing.

It was the first atmospheric explosion by the United States since Oct. 30, 1958, just before a voluntary moratorium went into effect. The moratorium came to an abrupt end last Sept. 1, when the Soviet Union resumed atmospheric testing, a step that led to today's long-debated action by the United States.

25 to 30 Tests Expected

The explosion today was the first in a series called Operation Dominic. The series is expected to consist of twenty-five to thirty explosions over the Pacific in the next two to three months.

In the first test, the nuclear device was dropped from a plane and detonated high over one of the coral atolls of the British-controlled island.

The explosion was described by the Atomic Energy Commission as in "the intermediate-yield range." This meant that its explosive force was more than twenty kilotons — the equivalent of the force of 20,000 tons of TNT—and less than one megaton, or 1,000,000 tons of TNT.

Christmas Island is just north of the Equator and 1,200 miles south of Hawaii.

Statement Is Terse

The test was announced in this terse, one-paragraph statement issued by the Atomic Energy Commission about three hours after the explosion:

"A nuclear test detonation took place at 10:45 A. M. E. S. T. today in the vicinity of Christmas Island. The detonation was in the intermediate-yield range. The device was dropped from an airplane. The test was the first detonation in Operation Dominic, now under way in the Pacific."

In line with its desire to hold to a minimum publicity about the experiments, the Administration supplied no statement explaining why the United States had resumed atmospheric testing. Rather, it rested its case on President Kennedy's speech March 2. In that speech, Mr. Kennedy declared that it would be militarily necessary to

Continued on Page 12, Column 1

Neutrals at Geneva Are Warned by U.S. Against a Walkout

Special to The New York Times.

GENEVA, April 25 — The United States has warned the neutralist delegations at the disarmament conference here against walking out of the talks because of its resumption of nuclear tests in the atmosphere.

The United States, it was learned, said such an action would be considered unfriendly because the United States negotiators continued talks with the Soviet spokesmen about a treaty to ban tests and also went ahead with the disarmament parley despite the Soviet tests in September.

Valerian A. Zorin, the leader of the Soviet delegation, was not immediately available for comment on the United States test today in the Pacific. However, when

Continued on Page 12, Column 5

EXPLOSION STIRS WORLD REACTION

West Europe Supports Tests as Soviet Assails Them—Tokyo Students March

The resumption of nuclear tests in the atmosphere yesterday touched off world-wide cries of denunciation and disapproval, regret and moral support.

Communists bitterly assailed the move. Pacifists protested. But those who backed Washington's decision said the Soviet Union, by its testing late last year, had left the United States no choice.

In Tokyo, students marched on the United States Embassy to protest. The police threw a cordon around the embassy after Left-wing organizations had called for a daily series of demonstrations against the United States.

In Western Europe, according to The Associated Press, many newspapers expressed regret that the United States had resumed testing. But they blamed the Soviet Union for not having agreed to a system of international inspection and control.

"President Kennedy's decision to resume tests in the atmosphere is a tragedy," said Britain's Daily Mirror. "It means the nuclear arms race is again in full spate. But the world must realize the responsibility for this tragedy is not Kennedy's. It is Khrushchev's."

In Austria, the mass-circula-

Continued on Page 14, Column 1

PROTEST IN TOKYO: Police disperse demonstration against U. S. nuclear testing by the Leftist Zengakuren student association outside the grounds of the U. S. Embassy. *Associated Press Radiophoto*

Nation's Monitors Watch for Fall-Out

By MARJORIE HUNTER
Special to The New York Times.

WASHINGTON, April 25 — A network of sampling and testing stations throughout the country will keep Americans posted on whether they are in danger from nuclear fall-out.

Government officials, from President Kennedy on down, have said repeatedly they do not expect fall-out from the current tests to reach dangerous levels.

The Public Health Service has had its sampling program functioning since the Russians renewed their tests last fall.

The Government maintains about sixty air monitoring stations. There is at least one in every state and Puerto Rico. They operate around the clock.

In addition, sixty milk-collecting stations are at work. Milk samples are tested at regional laboratories in Las Vegas, Nev.;

Continued on Page 13, Column 2

REFORM OF COURTS SIGNED INTO LAW BY ROCKEFELLER

22 Bills Implement First Big Reorganization in State in More Than a Century

MAIN CHANGES IN CITY

3 New Tribunals Established Here and 5 Abolished—Judges to Get $25,000

By DOUGLAS DALES
Special to The New York Times.

ALBANY, April 25—Twenty-two bills providing for the first major reorganization of the court structure of the state in more than a century were signed by Governor Rockefeller today. The reorganization will become effective Sept. 1.

The legislation, probably the most significant achievement of the 1962 session, is the culmination of studies that began nine years ago with the creation of a Commission on the Courts, headed by Harrison Tweed of New York City.

The product of this commission was a new judiciary article in the State Constitution that was approved by the voters last November. The package of bills signed today implements this article.

While the court reorganization plan has been referred to as providing a "unified statewide court system," the principal changes will take place in New York City, where only the county Surrogate Courts will remain unchanged.

New Administrative Board

Outside the city, the principal change is the establishment of county Family Courts, which will be part of a state-wide Family Court system.

Among the outstanding features of the reorganization is a provision for placing the administration of the principal courts in the state under a new administrative board composed of the Chief Judge of the Court of Appeals and the Presiding Justices of the four Appellate Divisions of the Supreme Court.

The Presiding Justices of the Appellate Division will have direct supervision over the courts within their districts. To assist in carrying out their functions, they will appoint one or more administrators from among the judges in their districts.

Other principal changes effected by the new laws are these:

¶In New York City, there will be three new courts—the Family, city-wide Civil and city-wide

Continued on Page 21, Column 1

The New York Times (by Larry Morris)

DISTINGUISHED VISITOR: Prime Minister Macmillan of Britain is welcomed at Idlewild by Adlai E. Stevenson, delegate to the United Nations. Mr. Macmillan will address American Newspaper Publishers Association today.

MACMILLAN HERE ON WAY TO TALKS WITH PRESIDENT

Says They Will Have 'Plenty' to Discuss — Will Press European Unity Concept

Prime Minister Macmillan arrived in New York last night on his way to Washington for week-end talks on world problems with President Kennedy.

"We have plenty to talk about," he said, smiling, as he alighted from a British Overseas Airways plane at New York International Airport at 5:50 P. M.

"We are always in touch all the time, but there is nothing like a personal discussion," he added, in reference to the Saturday and Sunday meetings in Washington. "I am looking forward to them."

One topic undoubtedly will be the nuclear test series that the United States began yesterday in cooperation with the British in the Pacific. The first test preceded Mr. Macmillan's arrival by a few hours.

Other Items on Agenda

Other topics that undoubtedly will be on the agenda will be Britain's proposed membership in the European Common Market and her concept of political confederation with Europe.

Mr. Macmillan was in good humor as he alighted with his party of twelve, and other passengers, from the scheduled jet flight. He was dressed in a light gray business suit and was hatless.

"I am very glad to be back in New York," he said. "The last time I was here was at the end of 1960 for the General Assembly meeting of the United Nations. At that time I had some agreeable discussion with [Premier] Khrushchev."

The Prime Minister said he was here primarily to address the American Newspaper Publishers Association tonight.

"It's a great occasion," he added. "Since I will be speaking then, the less I say now the better."

Mr. Macmillan then went on to comment about his forthcoming consultations with the President.

Fortunate Ties Cited

"I was fortunate to have an intimate relationship with President Eisenhower and equally as fortunate to have a close friendship with President Kennedy," he said. "We made a start early last year when we discussed world affairs in London and later in Bermuda. Now I'm here today for the same purpose."

After his Washington talks, Mr. Macmillan will fly to Toronto and Ottawa for discussions with the Canadian Prime Minister, John Diefenbaker.

Mr. Macmillan was met at the airport by the British Ambassadors to Washington and to the United Nations, Sir David Ormsby Gore and Sir Patrick Dean, respectively; A. M. Williams, the British Consul General in New York, and Adlai E. Stevenson, the United States permanent delegate to the United Nations. Mr. Macmillan and Mr. Stevenson are old friends.

After the brief greetings at the airport, Mr. Macmillan and his entourage left in a fleet of six cars for the Hotel Carlyle, Madison Avenue and Seventy-sixth Street, where he will stay while in New York. A fairly

Continued on Page 10, Column 1

Khrushchev Forms New Agency on Aid

By THEODORE SHABAD
Special to The New York Times.

MOSCOW, April 25—Premier Khrushchev disclosed today that he had established a high Government agency to coordinate the Soviet Union's expanding program of foreign trade and economic aid.

He has placed at its head a relative newcomer to the upper echelon of the Soviet hierarchy, Mikhail A. Lesechko, a planning official.

The importance of the new foreign trade and aid commission was made clear by the fact that it was established at the highest level of the Soviet Government. Its formal name is the Commission of the Presidium of the Council of Ministers for Foreign Economic Matters.

The agency, which has apparently been operating quietly for some time, was the

Continued on Page 11, Column 1

TRAVEL BAN ENDS FOR G.I. FAMILIES

Pentagon to Resume Paying Dependents' Way Abroad —6,000 to Go Monthly

By FELIX BELAIR Jr.
Special to The New York Times.

WASHINGTON, April 25 — The Defense Department lifted its ban on Government-paid travel by military dependents today. The action will permit families to join thousands of service men in Europe.

In announcing the resumption of dependents' travel allowances, Defense Secretary Robert S. McNamara said about 6,000 wives and children would be going abroad monthly by the end of May.

They will replace about the same number of dependents returning to this country with service men whose involuntary extensions of duty during last summer's Berlin crisis have been terminated.

Reasons for the Ban

Government travel authorizations for dependents of service men were cut off on Oct. 9. The Pentagon said at the time that the action was required to make available space on planes and ships for the movement of 40,000 troop reinforcements and supplies made necessary by the Russian threat to the Western position in Berlin.

When that movement was completed, the ban was retained to ease the outflow of gold and dollars adding to the deficit in this country's balance of payments. That calculation reflects the difference between United States receipts and expenditures on foreign transactions.

In his formal announcement of the department's action, Mr. McNamara said:

"It is the general policy of the Department of Defense that service personnel serving overseas should not be separated from their families except during emergencies or for short

Continued on Page 8, Column 3

ALGIERS MOSLEMS, GOADED BY BLAST, BEAT EUROPEANS

Act After Trap Kills Two—Own Leaders and French Troops Join to Calm Them

By HENRY TANNER
Special to The New York Times.

ALGIERS, April 25—Secret Army Organization terrorists were able to provoke Moslem crowds into retaliatory attacks on Europeans for the first time here today.

French soldiers and Moslem members of "vigilante committees," taking their orders from the Algerian Provisional Government in Tunis, intervened immediately and succeeded in calming the crowds before much harm could be done.

Nevertheless, a European woman was severely beaten and a number of other persons were manhandled. But these were the only victims of crowd action.

Observers agreed that the effective intervention of soldiers and Moslem vigilantes, in a joint effort, appeared to have prevented a major disaster in the form of a massive movement of angry Moslem masses from the Casbah, the old Moslem quarter, into the neighboring European quarter. However, tension remained high all day on the borders of the Casbah.

Stepped-Up Attack Feared

Some observers expressed fear that the terrorists of the Secret Army Organization, having come so close to their goal of provoking mass unrest in the Casbah, would step up their attack against the Moslems.

It is generally felt here that the Secret Army has suffered serious setbacks, especially in the arrest of former Gen. Raoul Salan, its leader, and that, being unable to conduct major operations, its terrorists will strike even more cruelly and at random in the coming days.

Today terrorists in Algiers killed at least fourteen persons and wounded thirty-four.

The incident that provoked the Moslem attacks started when a booby-trapped car exploded at a bus stop on the Place du Gouvernement, one of the principal points of entry into the Casbah. The heavy explosion killed two Moslems and wounded twenty-two, including a policeman.

Three Parked the Car

The car had been parked moments earlier by three persons presumed to be members of the Secret Army Organization, which is seeking to block Algerian independence.

One of the main goals of the insurgents' terror campaign is to provoke the Moslem masses into descending on the European sections of Algiers to seek vengeance. The insurgents' hope is that the French Army would then be forced to open fire on Moslems and would thus become committed to the side of the European extremists.

Until now the Moslems have shown remarkable discipline. Almost without exception they

Continued on Page 3, Column 2

Wagner Says New Taxes Will Be Needed Next Year

By PAUL CROWELL

Mayor Wagner declared yesterday that the city must be prepared to impose new special taxes next year to help meet the cost of services that were needed and desired by the public. The Mayor made it clear, however, that he did not intend to advocate the levying of any of the spe-

Text of Wagner's statement is printed on Page 36.

cial taxes the city was not now using, but has the power to levy.

He made his remarks in a statement summarizing the problems involved in his proposed 1962-63 budget of $2,771,-202,764.

Because this is a gubernatorial election year, he declared, "the most expedient tactic" might be to ignore the problem of new taxation. But, he said, he will not follow that course.

He contended that the time had come to shift the focus of public attention from the spending of money to the raising of money. There is no other answer to the city's present needs, he declared.

Taxation One Answer

"In that direction," he said, "lies one of the answers to the most pressing dilemma of the city—not only of our city but of all cities—how to raise the money to pay for the improved services and schools that we must have."

The Mayor's reference to the Governorship election, coupled with charges in his statement accusing Governor Rockefeller and the Republican-controlled Legislature of not treating the city fairly, was interpreted in some quarters as an indication that the Mayor would accept a Democratic nomination for Governor this year.

The Mayor has repeatedly said he is not a candidate.

Continued on Page 36, Column 4

MAYOR OPPOSING BUCKLEY IN HOUSE

He Is Against Any Aid to Bronx Chief—Says He Got No Truce Bid

By LEO EGAN

Mayor Wagner said yesterday that he was opposed not only to Representative Charles A. Buckley's retention as Bronx Democratic leader, but also to Mr. Buckley's renomination for Congress.

The Mayor's statement, which thus carried his feud against Mr. Buckley one step further, was made during a City Hall news conference devoted primarily to political subjects.

It was prompted by published reports that the Kennedy Administration was seeking to bring about a truce under which Mr. Wagner would give Mr. Buckley clear sailing for renomination in return for Mr. Buckley's retirement as leader.

The Mayor said he had not been approached by the Kennedy Administration on such a proposal. He declared that he did not favor Mr. Buckley's renomination. Heretofore Mr. Wagner had avoided taking any position on Mr. Buckley as a Representative.

Mayor's Plan Uncertain

Mayor Wagner was uncertain as to what role, if any, he might play in a primary fight to deny Mr. Buckley the renomination and to oust him as leader. As yet, Mr. Wagner's friends in the Bronx have not agreed among themselves on a candidate for Mr. Buckley's Congressional seat or his leadership.

"There is a great difficulty in bringing about a change in the Bronx leadership, but they certainly need new leadership," Mr. Wagner remarked.

A convention of clubs of the reform faction in Mr. Buckley's district has been called for tomorrow night to agree on a candidate to oppose Mr. Buckley for the Congressional nomination in the Sept. 7 primary.

There are three active candidates for the designation. They are Edward Gitkind, a 31-year-old industrial engineer

Continued on Page 20, Column 5

CIVIL RIGHTS FIGHT OPENED BY SENATE

Debate on Literacy Test Bill Threatens a Major Tie-Up

By ANTHONY LEWIS
Special to The New York Times.

WASHINGTON, April 25—The Senate began a major civil rights debate today that could tie it up for weeks or even months.

The majority leader, Mike Mansfield of Montana, opened up that prospect as he presented the Administration's bill to curb discriminatory literacy tests for voters. The bill would declare anyone with a sixth-grade education literate for voting purposes.

Southerners immediately began the extended talk that they had promised. They hope and expect to kill the bill by keeping it from reaching a vote. The only way to stop their talking is by a closure motion, which requires a two-thirds majority.

Senator Mansfield indicated that he would let the Senate talk on for some time. He said he would file a closure motion when he decided "that all the wisdom of which the Senate is reasonably capable has been exhausted with respect to the merits of this issue." The expectation is that he will move in about two weeks.

But Senator Mansfield went on to disclose a surprise in his strategy—the possibility of a second closure motion later.

If his first motion fails by a "substantial margin," he said, he will conclude that the Senate "prefers to avoid a confronta-

Continued on Page 24, Column 1

Vatican Set to Aid Church Unity With Non-Doctrinal Concessions

By ARNALDO CORTESI
Special to The New York Times

ROME, April 25 — The Roman Catholic Church is willing to make considerable concessions on practical grounds to meet the "separated brethren" half way in achieving Christian unity, Augustin Cardinal Bea said today.

The Cardinal, president of the Vatican's Secretariat for the Union of Christians, said, however, that the Church could not make any concessions in doctrine.

Roman Catholics believe that what the Church teaches is doctrine received from Jesus Christ, he said, and, therefore, there is no room for doctrinal concessions.

As an example of a practical matter on which the Roman Catholic Church might make concessions, he cited differences that exist between the liturgical rites of the Eastern and West-ern Roman Catholic Churches. The Eastern rite uses languages other than Latin in the mass and does not impose celibacy upon the clergy.

The Cardinal said a code of canon law for various Oriental rites was being compiled alongside the code for the Latin rite.

Addressing a foreign press luncheon, Cardinal Bea also disclosed that theological discussions between Roman Catholic specialists and specialists of other faiths had been going on for some time in Belgium, Germany, Switzerland and elsewhere.

The discussions have dealt largely with Biblical studies and have borne "truly beautiful fruits," he said.

Such theological discussions were scheduled to take place in

Continued on Page 2, Column 4

NEWS INDEX

"All the News That's Fit to Print"

The New York Times.

LATE CITY EDITION

U. S. Weather Bureau Report (Page 86) forecasts: Cloudy, cool, occasional light rain today, tonight and tomorrow.

Temp. range: 55—47; yesterday: 73—49.

NEWS SUMMARY AND INDEX, PAGE 95

SECTION ONE

VOL. CXI. No. 38,095.

NEW YORK, SUNDAY, MAY 13, 1962.

25c beyond 50-mile zone from New York City, except on Long Island. 35c beyond 200-mile zone from New York City; higher in air delivery cities.

THIRTY CENTS

U.S. SHIPS AND 1,800 MARINES ON WAY TO INDOCHINA AREA; LAOS DECREES EMERGENCY

United Press International Telephoto

ON WAY TO CONFERENCE ON CRISIS: Secretary of State Rusk, left, Under Secretary of State George W. Ball, center, and Assistant Secretary of State W. Averell Harriman arrive at White House to meet with President Kennedy on Southeast Asia crisis.

ESTES WILL MEET M'CLELLAN AIDES TO DISCUSS DEALS

Investigators Fly to Texas—Senator Hopes for Details on Links With Officials

HOLLEMAN QUESTIONED

Inquiry Turns to Goldberg Aide Who Resigned Over Gift From Financier

By PETER BRAESTRUP
Special to The New York Times.

WASHINGTON, May 12 — Two Senate investigators flew to Texas today to question Billie Sol Estes about his complex cotton and grain dealings and his relations with Federal officials.

Senator John L. McClellan, chairman of the Permanent Investigations Subcommittee, said that Mr. Estes, who has been indicted on fraud charges, might be willing to talk with the investigators.

"I don't know that he will answer all of our questions," the Arkansas Democrat said, "but we have to find out all we can from him."

[In Dallas, the two investigators said Saturday that a meeting with Mr. Estes had been scheduled, The Associated Press reported. No details of time or place were disclosed.]

In any event, the subcommittee plans to summon Mr. Estes next month for public hearings on his affairs. Mr. Estes' business records have already been subpoenaed. The 37-year-old West Texas millionaire's land, grain, cotton, and fertilizer empire collapsed after a Federal investigation.

Holleman Questioned

Other staff members of the McClellan subcommittee this morning questioned Jerry R. Holleman, who resigned late last night as Assistant Secretary of Labor. In resigning, Mr. Holleman said he had accepted a "personal gift" of $1,000 from Mr. Estes to help meet his living expenses in Washington.

Mr. Holleman's Government salary was $20,000 a year. He was responsible, primarily, for the Labor Department's programs dealing with manpower, apprenticeship training and importation of Mexican farm labor. He also served as executive vice chairman of the President's Committee on Equal Employment Opportunity.

Senator Karl E. Mundt, South Dakota Republican, a member of the McClellan panel, predicted that Mr. Holleman's resignation would not be "the last resignation, dismissal, or conviction occurring in the fast-spreading investigation." He said Mr. Holleman would be called to testify by the panel.

Mr. Holleman, former president of the Texas labor federation, said he had done Mr. Estes

Continued on Page 65, Column 1

President Puts Progress Of U. S. Up to the People

Tells Milwaukee Dinner 'We Have Many Tasks Still Undone'—Asks Support on His Social and Economic Goals

By E. W. KENWORTHY
Special to The New York Times.

MILWAUKEE, May 12—President Kennedy told a Democratic Jefferson-Jackson Day dinner tonight that the people of the United States had to decide whether their country was to stand still or move ahead.

"I think we should make up our minds," he said, "that we have many tasks still undone."

The President in particular cited medical care for the aged financed through Social Security, aid to education and steady economic growth to reduce the level of unemployment.

In his speech of nineteen minutes, the President also bore down heavily on the need to expand educational opportunities for the nation's youth. The theme brought an enthusiastic response in a state that has long boasted one of the great state universities in the nation.

"All the way in from the airport, all I saw was your children who need to be educated, who want some day to go to the university, who want some day to find a job."

He recalled that Wisconsin had originated the idea of Social Security.

These are the things "a country must do," the President said. He declared that the argument "Why doesn't the Government leave us alone?" was heard in the days of Woodrow Wilson's "New Freedom" and Franklin D. Roosevelt's "New Deal."

Mr. Kennedy made a direct appeal for the support of his programs and for the election of Congressmen who back them. "There is nothing that can be done in Washington without your support," he said.

He asserted that the election of members of Congress was

Continued on Page 47, Column 1

CHURCH IN SPAIN BACKS WORKERS ON STRIKE RIGHTS

Hierarchy Implies Franco Regime Is Lax in Handling 3-Week-Old Disputes

By BENJAMIN WELLES
Special to The New York Times.

MADRID, May 12—The powerful Spanish Roman Catholic hierarchy accused the regime of Generalissimo Francisco Franco by implication today of laxity and inefficiency in handling the three-week-old strikes of coal miners and industrial workers that have disrupted industry in the north and other regions of Spain.

The hierarchy also openly proclaimed that a strike is a "licit weapon" when negotiations by direct or syndical channels fail.

In championing the Spanish workers' right to strike, the church appeared to be opening a gulf between itself and General Franco, who has made strikes illegal and punishable by jail sentences for the last twenty-five years.

70,000 Are Still Out

At least 70,000 miners and workers are still refusing to return to work throughout the nation until the Government agrees to minimum wage demands amounting in the miners' case to 160 pesetas ($2.33) for an eight-hour working day.

The miners, who began the walkouts and whose example sparked the strikes elsewhere, are now receiving between $1.40 and $1.60 a day, which they contend is insufficient in view of rising living costs.

For weeks the regime has been torn between either conceding wage demands widely believed to be justified or appearing to lose prestige by giving way under pressure.

The church's implied rebuke was expressed editorially in today's issue of Ecclesia, the weekly publication of Catholic action and the only publication in Spain not subject to state censorship.

Primate Checks Policy

Ecclesia's editorial policy is closely supervised by the Primate of Spain, Enrique Cardinal Pla y Deniel, Archbishop of Toledo.

He has clashed publicly before with José Solís Ruiz, head of the Falange party and of the Syndical movement. The appearance of the editorial at this time was widely considered to have been carefully calculated.

The Catholic Church enjoys wide privileges in Spain and has been closely identified with the Franco regime.

In recent years, however, it has begun cautiously to dissociate itself from certain more repressive aspects of the dictatorship, such as police brutality and General Franco's continuing refusal to permit Spain's 10,000,000 workers to elect their own officials in the compulsory state-run Syndical organization.

Noting that the regime had at last lifted its own censorship

Continued on Page 30, Column 1

MOSLEM FORCES SET UP TO FIGHT ALGERIAN TERROR

30,000 Soldiers to Be Used in Algiers and Oran—Referendum July 1

By HENRY TANNER
Special to The New York Times.

ALGIERS, May 12 — The transitional executive announced tonight that 30,000 Moslem soldiers would join the fight against the terrorists of the Secret Army Organization in Algiers and Oran in the near future.

Fifteen thousand men of the newly created Local Force will go into action here in Algiers. The Local Force consists of Moslem soldiers who served in the French Army. The force's officers are French.

Fifteen battalions of tirailleurs or infantry skirmishers of the French Army will be sent to Oran. The tirailleur units consist almost exclusively of Algerians. Many of their officers and noncommissioned officers also are Algerian Moslems. A battalion is about 1,000 men strong.

Popular Vote Advanced

Sources close to the transitional executive said that the date of the popular referendum in Algeria, which is expected to approve independence, had been set for July 1. It had previously been reported for July 8.

Three weeks later, elections for a Constituent Assembly are expected to be held. A draft constitution is said to be already under preparation for submission to this Assembly. The Assembly will also name a new Government, it is believed.

The transitional executive, the predominantly Moslem body that has taken over most of the functions of local government in Algeria for the duration of the period of transition leading to independence, also decided to dissolve the Municipal Council of Oran and to replace it by a single official. In Algiers this reorganization of the city administration was made some time ago.

Statement at Rocher-Noir

The announcement of the transitional executive's decisions was made at Rocher-Noir, the administrative city thirty miles east of Algiers that is the seat both of the executive and the French High Commission.

Announcement of the large-scale anti-Secret Army measures was the first really important action by the executive since it came into being following the cease-fire between the French and the Algerian nationalists that took effect last March 19.

The executive met today and yesterday under the chairmanship of Abderrahmane Fares, its president, and in the presence of Christian Fouchet, the French High Commissioner in Algeria.

The presence of M. Fouchet was taken as an indication that

Continued on Page 12, Column 1

2,000 Boun Oum Troops Are Interned in Thailand

Special to The New York Times.

VIENTIANE, Laos, May 12—The commander of the Royal Laotian forces in the northwest and 2,000 troops—the remnants of Gen. Phoumi Nosavan's 5,000-man army in the area—crossed the Mekong River into Thailand today. They had abandoned the riverside town of Houei Sai yesterday without fighting.

A top-ranking United States military adviser here said the seven American advisers with the Laotian troops were also in Thailand.

The Laotians now interned in Thailand are commanded by Gen. Bounleut Sanichan. Interned with him and his men was Gen. La Pathammavong, commander of the garrison at Nam Tha, north of Houei Sai, which fell previously to the rebels.

Crossing in Small Boats

The action seemed to complete the pro-Communist rebels' conquest of northwestern Laos. Prince Boun Oum's Government here declared a state of emergency.

Early this morning, the royal troops were still crowding the eastern bank of the 300-yard-wide river waiting for Thai river craft and canoes to pick them up.

They apparently completed the crossing by noon. No troops were left in Houei Sai, the American officer here said. He could not tell whether the rebels had actually entered the town or not.

General Phoumi Nosavan, who is Deputy Premier and Defense Minister, flew to Rangoon, Burma, during the day for conferences with the Burmese military ruler, Gen. Ne Win. It was understood General Phoumi Nosavan was to return here at once.

Wide Communist Threat

The threat of the Communist forces in Laos closely affects Burma. Muong Sing, the royal Laotian stronghold to the north that fell the first of this week to the rebels, is in the area where the border of Burma meets Communist China.

The decision to evacuate Houei Sai was taken after some mortar bombs fell in the town Thursday night. The United States advisers here said there was no indication that there had been any fighting.

The men of the American military advisory team left Houei Sai by helicopter Friday afternoon when they found there was no longer any headquarters or any responsible Laotian officers there to work with. The whole team then moved across the river into Thailand, the American here said.

Summing up the situation, he described it as a "major blow, it can't be painted in any other colors, and it means the loss of a good sized force" of Laotian soldiers.

Neutralist leaders in Khang Khay, Prince Souvanna Phouma's administrative capital, said recently that General Phoumi

Continued on Page 3, Column 5

KENNEDY REACTS

Seeks to Counter Red Gain in Laos—Still Hopes for Coalition

By MAX FRANKEL
Special to The New York Times.

WASHINGTON, May 12—President Kennedy ordered today that United States naval, air and land forces, including a battle group of 1,800 marines, move toward the Indochinese peninsula.

The President's reaction to a major military victory by pro-Communist forces in Laos promises to be a major new phase in the attempt to save the country from Communist control.

The President was described by associates as taking an extremely serious view of the situation in Laos. They said the military movements were not just a traditional "show of force" but an effort to get into position for more direct action should it be required.

Some of the United States Marine forces are believed to be headed for Thailand, whose border has been reached by pro-Communist forces in Laos. The Pathet Lao movement broke an uneasy cease-fire this week and seized control of most of northern Laos.

Administration leaders, after two emergency meetings today, were described as still reluctant to send United States troops into Laos. At the same time, no one is yet willing to rule out

Continued on Page 3, Column 1

Bunche Bars Senate Race; Calls Stand 'Irreversible'

By RICHARD P. HUNT

Dr. Ralph J. Bunche announced yesterday that he would not consent to become a candidate for the Democratic nomination for Senator. "This position is firm and irreversible," Dr. Bunche said in a note to correspondents issued at the United Nations, where he is Under Secretary for Special Political Affairs.

Later, he added that a few minutes after the statement had been issued, Mayor Wagner had telephoned from Miami to ask that the statement be withheld until the two could talk face-to-face about Dr. Bunche's position.

"I informed the Mayor that it was too late for this," Dr. Bunche said.

He gave no reason for refusing to run. But he recalled in an interview that he recently had said of his present post: "I very much doubt if there is any better way to serve humanity, to serve one's country and the community."

O'Connor Hints at Running

Meanwhile, District Attorney Frank D. O'Connor of Queens came within a personal pronoun of saying he would seek the Democratic nomination for Governor, and Mayor Wagner said former Representative Franklin D. Roosevelt Jr. should "get out and campaign" if he wanted it.

Mr. O'Connor, in a speech at a Rensselaer County Democratic dinner in Troy, began by referring to himself as "we" eight times as a substitute for "I."

Then he went on to outline how he thought a Democrat should run against Governor Rockefeller next fall, and ended by promising: "That's the kind

Continued on Page 70, Column 3

140 AT COLUMBIA DEFY A.M.A. STAND

Physicians Among 500 on Faculty to Back Kennedy on Care for Elderly

By ALFRED E. CLARK

One hundred and forty physicians associated with the Faculty of Medicine at Columbia University have split with the American Medical Association's stand on providing health care for the aged through Social Security.

The physicians, who are on the staffs of medical schools affiliated with the Columbia-Presbyterian Medical Center, were among 500 Columbia faculty members who joined in forming a committee to support the controversial King-Anderson bill.

They signed a resolution that had been circulated since early this month by Dr. Frank Van Dyke, an Associate Professor of Administrative Medicine and secretary of the College of Physicians and Surgeons.

'Urgent Need' Cited

Dr. Van Dyke issued a statement yesterday, under the name of the Committee for Health Care of the Aged, saying:

"There is urgent need to insure that the world's wealthiest society does not neglect the medical care needs of the people who built it."

The A. M. A. has thrown its support behind the Kerr-Mills Law, now in effect, in its campaign to block adoption of the King-Anderson bill, which has the backing of President Kennedy and his Administration.

Dr. Van Dyke said he was

Continued on Page 68, Column 3

VIETNAMESE SLAY 300 REDS IN CLASH

U. S. Forces Fly Troops to Attack South of Saigon —Two Copters Downed

By United Press International.

SAIGON, Vietnam, Sunday, May 13—Waves of South Vietnamese troops flown into battle by United States helicopters killed 300 Communist guerrillas yesterday in a major attack, it was reported today. The Vietnamese troops suffered few casualities.

Two United States Army helicopters were shot down but were recovered. No Americans were injured. The downed craft were from the Fifty-seventh Helicopter Company.

Marine helicopters also participated in the action, which took place in Kien Phong Province about seventy-five miles southwest of Saigon.

Planes Find Guerrillas

Informed sources said Government Rangers, regular Army troops and Civil Guardsmen attached to the Vietnamese Seventh Infantry Division killed the 300 guerrillas in five separate clashes.

The fighting raged through areas covered by high reeds and flooded rice paddies in an operation designed to disorganize and wipe out guerrilla units.

Some of the guerrilla units were found by Vietnamese observation planes, the sources said. Attack units were dropped on the targets in waves of five to six helicopters each. The

Continued on Page 2, Column 3

Sports News

BASEBALL

The New York Mets won both games of a double-header for the first time by defeating the Milwaukee Braves at the Polo Grounds yesterday. A homer in the ninth decided each game. Hobie Landrith's wallop off Warren Spahn with a runner on base took the opener, 3-2. Spahn, who went all the way, allowed ten hits. Gil Hodges connected to break a tie and produce an 8-7 victory in the second game. With Tom Tresh and Mickey Mantle clouting home runs, the New York Yankees beat the Indians at Cleveland, 9-6.

HORSE RACING

Jaipur, the 3-4 favorite owned by George D. Widener, took the $58,600 Withers Stakes before 50,105 racegoers at Aqueduct. Green Ticket ran second and Cyrano third. Ridden by Willie Shoemaker, Jaipur ran the mile in 1 minute 35 3/5 second.

TRACK AND FIELD

The University of Oregon lowered the world four-mile relay record to 16 minutes 8.9 seconds in the West Coast Relays at Fresno, Calif. Dyrol Burleson anchored the Oregon quartet with a 3:57.9 leg. Frank Budd of Villanova University equaled the world 220-yard record of 20 seconds in a dual meet against the Quantico Marines on the Villanova (Pa.) track.

Details in Section 5.

Revised Trade Bill Asks for Negotiator

By JOHN D. MORRIS
Special to The New York Times.

WASHINGTON, May 12—The Administration's trade expansion bill has been revised to create the office of "special representative" for trade negotiations with other countries.

The House Ways and Means Committee inserted the provision yesterday in an unannounced decision. The committee is putting the final touches to the bill in closed session. It hopes to finish the job next week.

The amendment is designed to meet complaints of some members of Congress and representatives of business and agriculture over the lack of any fixed authority or responsibility, other than the President himself, in the tariff-bargaining process.

Under the expiring Recipro-

Continued on Page 53, Column 1

Thomas Hart Benton Welcomed at Ozark Birthplace

Associated Press Wirephoto

Thomas Hart Benton, center, is just a spectator as former President Harry S. Truman congratulates Charles Banks Wilson on his portrait of Mr. Benton, background, which Mr. Truman unveiled during the homecoming activities for Mr. Benton in Neosho, Mo.

By AUSTIN C. WEHRWEIN
Special to The New York Times.

NEOSHO, Mo., May 12—In a setting that could have been taken from one of his murals, Thomas Hart Benton came home today to this town in the Ozarks. At the age of 73, his return was the symbolic end of a long, often turbulent, journey to find the place of the artist in America. He received a homecoming tribute of the kind usually reserved for national heroes—like that given former President Dwight D. Eisenhower in Abilene, Kan., last week. It was tendered to him by, among others, his friend, former President Harry S. Truman, also born in a small town in

Continued on Page 87, Column 1

Doctors Transplant Human Heart Valve

By The Canadian Press.

TORONTO, May 12 — Two medical journals say Toronto surgeons have successfully transplanted parts of dead men's hearts in critically ill heart-disease victims.

The New England Journal of Medicine, one of the oldest of North America's medical publications, says in its latest edition that six persons are alive and well as a result of replacement of aortic valves at Toronto Western Hospital. This valve controls blood flow from the heart to the body.

The Journal of the Canadian Medical Association reports that one man has had his mitral heart valve replaced by the cardiac team at Toronto General Hospital. The mitral valve controls the flow between the blood chambers in the heart.

The operations, reported

Continued on Page 79, Column 4

Today's Sections

Index to Subjects

Mrs. Kennedy invited a large television audience on all three networks to a tour of the White House.

The Beverly Hillbillies was an overnight sensation even though critics labeled it the most flagrant example of TV decadence. The innocent bumpkins included Irene Ryan, Buddy Ebsen and Donna Douglas (left to right).

Ernie Kovaks appeared as a comedy guest on many shows and starred in his own show for a short time, but his brilliant career was brought to a halt in an automobile accident in 1962.

America's favorite anchorman, Walter Cronkite covered the Project Mercury space shot for CBS.

"All the News That's Fit to Print"

The New York Times.

LATE CITY EDITION
U. S. Weather Bureau Report (Page 66) forecasts: Partly cloudy today. Fair tonight. Sunny and warm tomorrow.
Temp. range: 80—61; yesterday: 85—61.

VOL. CXI . No. 38,107. | © 1962 by The New York Times Company. Times Square, New York 36, N. Y. | NEW YORK, FRIDAY, MAY 25, 1962. | 10 cents beyond 50-mile zone from New York City except on Long Island. Higher in air delivery cities. | FIVE CENTS

CARPENTER ORBITS EARTH 3 TIMES SAFELY, BUT OVERSHOOTS LANDING AREA 250 MILES; FATE IN DOUBT AN HOUR, HE IS FOUND IN RAFT

STIFF GRAIN CURB VOTED AS SENATE UPHOLDS KENNEDY

Tightest Controls in History Are Added to Farm Bill—Committee Reversed

By RUSSELL BAKER
Special to The New York Times.

WASHINGTON, May 24 — The Senate gave President Kennedy a victory on the farm bill today by voting the strictest controls in history on the production of wheat and feed grains.

Voting largely along party lines, the Senate reversed its Agriculture Committee and put the Administration's production curbs on wheat and livestock feed grains back into the farm bill.

Final Senate action on the measure is expected tomorrow after work is completed on its less controversial sections. The action will then shift to the House, where the Kennedy control program has been approved by the Agriculture Committee. The House has delayed action to see what the Senate would do.

Democrats See Victory

House Democrats predict another victory there for the President. Republican leaders contend that the production curbs will be rejected. The outlook is for a bitter, closely fought floor battle.

The President's fight in the Senate was led by Allen J. Ellender of Louisiana, Democratic chairman of the Agriculture Committee. He received important help from Senator Richard B. Russell, Democrat of Georgia, leader of the Southern bloc.

The two important votes came on Mr. Ellender's moves to write into the bill the Administration plans on wheat and feed grains.

The vote for adopting the wheat program was 53 to 36. The majority consisted of fifty-one Democrats and two Republicans—Senators John Sherman Cooper and Thruston B. Morton, both of Kentucky. Opposing it were thirty Republicans and six Democrats.

Cooper Cites Failure

Mr. Cooper said he had supported the program because "no new principle is involved." He said that wheat had been under control since 1938 and was in the heaviest surplus of all crops under Government price supports. "The present wheat program is a failure," he declared.

The vote for adopting the feed-grain program was 46 to 37. Again, it was cast largely along party lines after the Senate had beaten attempts to weaken the program. The feed-grain program applies to corn, barley, grain sorghums, rye and oats.

Broadly, the two provisions would give the farmer a choice of limiting production and receiving high Federal price supports, or of rejecting the curbs and having price-support levels

Continued on Page 20, Column 3

4.6 Billion Aid Bill Voted by House Unit

By FELIX BELAIR Jr.
Special to The New York Times.

WASHINGTON, May 24—A foreign aid authorization of $4,668,500,000 was approved today by the House Foreign Affairs Committee for the year beginning July 1.

The authorization was $210,000,000 less than President Kennedy had requested.

It included $600,000,000 for the Alliance for Progress, the program of aid to Latin-American republics other than Cuba. The legislation provided $1,800,000,000 more for economic development loans under the alliance at the rate of $600,000,000 in each of the three fiscal years beginning July 1, 1963.

The committee's action on the bill confirmed its $600,000,000 cutback in long-term authorization of funds for the alliance. President Kennedy's

Continued on Page 5, Column 3

TORNADO INJURES 25 IN WATERBURY

One Man Killed, 45 Homes Destroyed — Jersey and L. I. Lashed by Storms

A tornado swept through Waterbury, Conn., yesterday, killing one man and injuring at least twenty-five other persons. Forty-five houses were destroyed and 150 others damaged.

The tornado was one of a series of storms that battered the East with lightning, hail, high winds and heavy rain.

Falling trees toppled power lines in many parts of Brooklyn, Queens and Long Island. Eleven thousand homes were without electricity for varying periods.

A tornado also struck in central New Jersey, north of Trenton, flipping a truck on its side and uprooting trees. Other parts of the state were hit by hail, heavy rains and winds.

Commuters Drenched

In New York City, commuters on the way home from work were drenched by a sudden rainstorm. The skies quickly cleared, but at about 9 P. M. a new thunderstorm struck, accompanied by a downpour that lasted about an hour. The Weather Bureau forecast partly cloudy and mild weather for today.

A Weather Bureau spokesman said the thunderstorms were the result of an encounter between relatively cool and dry air moving in from the West and warm, moist air in the East. The effects were felt as far north as Montreal, where a tornado tore off most of the roof of the Seminary College of Holy Apostles. Nearly 200 persons were in the building, but the only casualties were three students who suffered slight cuts and bruises.

Similar storms, not directly related to those in the East, struck scattered sections of the Middle West. Hutchinson, Kan.,

Continued on Page 42, Column 6

DE GAULLE ANGRY OVER SALAN CASE; COURT IS REBUKED

Joxe Says Tribunal's Ruling Could Hurt French Forces Fighting Algeria Terror

Special to The New York Times.

PARIS, May 24 — An angry Government expressed concern today over the effect that the sentence of life imprisonment for former General Raoul Salan would have on the morale of the Government forces fighting the Secret Army Organization.

Louis Joxe, Minister for Algerian Affairs, told the Cabinet that the judgment, which has stunned the nation, could constitute a "blow to the morale" of the security forces.

President de Gaulle was understood to have expressed his anger at the judgment in the strongest terms during the Cabinet session. At the meeting, the Government took a first step to restore public liberties in Algeria after more than seven years of war restrictions.

In preparaton for the self-determination vote scheduled in Algeria for July 1, the Ministers approved an ordinance allowing free formation of parties and other political groups. Some restrictive police measures also will be abrogated.

Rightist Defeat Sighted

At the same time, the Government expressed its belief that the Secret Army Organization, which is still attempting to distrupt the Algerian cease-fire accords and prevent independence, was on its way to defeat.

Confidence was expressed that voting would be possible everywhere in Algeria on the scheduled date. The vote is expected to approve independence for Algeria in association with France.

The heaviest casualties inflicted by the Secret Army Organization have been among the gendarmerie, the republican security companies and the special undercover police units.

Salan, former chief of the terrorist underground, escaped the death penalty last night when a high military tribunal, after finding him guilty on all five counts involving his activities in Algeria, ruled that there were extenuating circumstances in his case. The judgment was expected to encourage the Secret Army organization to continue its terrorism.

Strongest Action Possible

The statement by M. Joxe at the Cabinet meeting at which General de Gaulle presided was reported by Alain Peyrefitte, Secretary of State for Information.

It clearly represented the strongest rebuke that the Government felt it could publicly deliver against the judgment, in view of the independence of judicial institutions in France.

Other elements of public life were unrestrained in their reactions to the Salan ruling. In general, the political Left was outraged and the Right was delighted.

But virtually everyone was amazed, since it had not appeared possible that the chief of the terrorist movement would get a lesser sentence than his second in command, Edmond Jouhaud, who was condemned to death by the same high tribunal slightly more than a month ago.

M. Peyrefitte disclosed after the Cabinet meeting that the Government had "envisaged the consequences that the verdict

Continued on Page 6, Column 2

N. A. S. A. via Associated Press Wirephotos

RECOVERY AND CONGRATULATIONS: Lieut. Comdr. M. Scott Carpenter is hoisted aboard a Navy helicopter from beside floating capsule after his orbital trip. Later, on the carrier Intrepid, he talks with President Kennedy.

Dean to Join Zorin In Plan to Condemn War Propaganda

By Reuters.

GENEVA, May 24—Arthur H. Dean, chief United States delegate at the seventeen-nation disarmament conference, said today that the United States and the Soviet Union planned to present a joint declaration condemning war propaganda.

Mr. Dean said that the two countries, as co-chairmen of the conference, had been working on the text of the declaration in private and, barring unforeseen problems, they would submit it to the full conference tomorrow.

He stressed that the declaration was not a ban on war propaganda, but simply a statement against it.

During earlier discussion of the question by the full conference, the West objected to the Soviet Union's proposal for a ban on war propaganda, calling it undesirable and unenforceable under American constitutional guarantees of freedom of speech and of the press.

As a counter-proposal, the United States suggested that East and West open avenues of communication and encourage the exchange of information to counter propaganda.

Mr. Dean said today that the chief Soviet delegate, Valerian A. Zorin, had submitted the

Continued on Page 4, Column 4

U.S. OFFERS PLAN FOR NEW GUINEA

Suggests Gradual Transfer From Dutch to Jakarta, Then a Plebiscite

By MAX FRANKEL
Special to The New York Times.

WASHINGTON, May 24—The United States' proposals to settle the Dutch-Indonesian dispute over Netherlands New Guinea call for a rigidly supervised plebiscite in the indefinite future, but only after Indonesians have taken over administration of the area.

This feature of the plan and the fact that Washington has taken more than an intermediary's interest in the problem seem to be resented by the Dutch and appear to account for their refusal to reopen negotiations with the Indonesians.

[In The Hague, the lower House of the Netherlands Parliament rejected Thursday night a resolution calling on the Government to accept the United States plan as the basis for a New Guinea settlement.]

Both U Thant, Acting Secretary General of the United Nations, and President Kennedy appealed yesterday for new talks to settle the issue before the current fighting in New Guinea

Continued on Page 2, Column 2

Entire Nation Gives Thanks When Astronaut Is Sighted

A sigh of relief went up across the nation yesterday following the news that Lieut. Comdr. M. Scott Carpenter had been found in a life raft in the Atlantic after his triple orbit of the earth. Until it became known that radio contact with Commander Carpenter's space capsule had been lost, the flight had aroused less interest than that of Lieut. Col. John H. Glenn Jr. last February.

The general assumption seemed to be that Commander Carpenter would safely follow Colonel Glenn's path.

In Congress and state legislative bodies, procedure was interrupted to announce the news of the astronaut's rescue. The Massachusetts House of Representatives halted for a moment of prayerful thanks.

Cheers Greet News

"Have they found him yet?" was the question asked across the country. In a restaurant in Toledo, Ohio, two dozen patrons cheered at Commander Carpenter's rescue.

"Thank God," one said.

Here, about 7,000 persons stood silently in Grand Central Terminal in front of a huge television screen when it was announced that radio contact had been lost.

They broke into cheers when word came that the 37-year-old astronaut had been sighted in the Atlantic.

Subway riders received the word over loudspeakers in stations. A storm of ticker-tape descended from buildings in Rockefeller Center. An anonymous person gave expression to his feelings by writing "Bravo Carpenter" on the typewriter in front of the Longine-Wittnauer Building on Fifth Avenue.

Mayor Sends Wire

In the ballroom of the Biltmore Hotel, Francis Cardinal Spellman opened a reception in honor of his seventy-third birthday by asking 800 women present to give thanks in prayer for the successful flight.

At City Hall, Mayor Wagner invited Commander Carpenter to a parade up Broadway, the city's traditional welcome to heroes.

"All New York City joins in paying you deserved tribute," he said in a telegram. "Your dramatic flight and rescue have thrilled all of us."

In Washington, the Senate interrupted debate on a farm bill to applaud the news that Commander Carpenter had been found. Senator Hubert H. Humphrey of Minnesota, assistant Democratic leader, paid tribute to the astronaut and those who had participated in the launching.

Senator Everett McKinley Dirksen of Illinois, the Repub-

Continued on Page 17, Column 4

RESCUE TECHNIQUE PLANNED 3 YEARS

Project Mercury Provided for Emergency Pick-Ups Outside Target Area

By JOHN W. FINNEY
Special to The New York Times

CAPE CANAVERAL, May 24—Three years of "contingency planning" by Project Mercury paid off today by assuring the safe rescue of Lieut. Comdr. M. Scott Carpenter after he had overshot his landing area by 250 miles.

In drafting plans for sending men into space, project officials attempted to develop a course of action to meet any emergency.

One of these, which became a momentarily frightening reality today, was that the astronaut and his capsule would return outside of the selected landing areas and beyond the immediate reach of the Navy recovery task force.

To meet this contingency, plans were developed for emergency rescue by airborne teams of Air Force men who would parachute to the aid of the astronaut.

This plan was put into effect today when the Aurora VII capsule landed beyond the Navy task force stationed in the prime

Continued on Page 15, Column 8

ON OCEAN 3 HOURS

Capsule Picked Up—Nose of Craft Too High on Re-entry

Excerpts from Project Mercury record are on Page 16.

By RICHARD WITKIN
Special to The New York Times.

CAPE CANAVERAL, Fla., May 24—M. Scott Carpenter became today the second American astronaut to orbit the earth.

His three-orbit trip ended, however, with a global audience suffering almost an hour's anxiety about his safe return.

It was three hours from the time his space capsule landed until he was plucked from a life raft by a rescue helicopter. And it was hours later before the capsule was picked up by the destroyer Pierce.

Tonight, on Grand Turk Island in the British West Indies, Commander Carpenter had an emotional reunion with two fellow-astronauts, John H. Glenn, who made the first orbital flight, and Walter M. Schirra.

Carried Beyond Goal

Coming down from orbit, the 37-year-old Navy test pilot was carried 250 miles beyond the intended Caribbean landing point and the recovery ships waiting to pick him up.

[In Washington, President Kennedy termed Commander Carpenter's courage and the skill of his rescuers "heart-warming to all of us." The President authorized the National Aeronautics and Space Administration to award its Distinguished Service Medal to Commander Carpenter.]

The overshoot was said to have been caused by the fact that the nose of the Aurora VII capsule was pointed too high at the time the retro or braking rockets fired to slow its speed and bring it out of orbit.

Radio communication blacked out, as it was expected to, part way in the descent. But because the capsule was beyond its target point, voice communication did not resume, as it normally would, after a gap of four or five minutes.

Millions Await Word

Project Mercury officials had immediate indications from two seconds of radar reception as the capsule disappeared over the horizon, that it had survived the searing re-entry into the atmosphere, though the astronaut's fate was unknown.

The millions following the flight by television and radio did not even have this reed to lean on, since word of the radar reception was not relayed to them by Mercury officials.

It was only after thirty-five minutes of bleak silence following the initial blackout that the public had a reassuring word.

It was announced that an automatically transmitted signal had been picked up by a Navy search plane. But even this carried no clue, for the public or officials, as to whether the capsule's parachute had popped

Continued on Page 14, Column 1

Maryland Calls Special Session As Court Orders Redistricting

By The Associated Press.

ANNAPOLIS, Md., May 24—Gov. J. Millard Tawes called a special session of the Maryland Legislature today after a court order had invalidated the distribution of seats in the House of Delegates.

Judge O. Bowie Duckett ruled in Anne Arundel County Circuit Court that the present distribution of House seats, weighed in favor of small counties, was "invidious discrimination" against the voting rights of residents of three metropolitan counties.

Governor Tawes summoned the Legislature to meet in special session at 10 A. M. tomorrow to fill "an acute constitutional void" resulting from the court order.

In anticipation of the court ruling, legislation already has been prepared by the administration to give nineteen more seats to metropolitan areas in the November election and take nineteen away from less populated areas in 1966. The present membership of the House is 123.

The Governor also had alerted legislators earlier in the week to be ready for the special session, which is expected to enact stop-gap legislation before the June 1 deadline for passage of simple bills. New jobs cannot be created in an emergency act in Maryland.

Judge Duckett did not disturb the make-up of the twen-

Continued on Page 23, Column 2

NEWS INDEX

Model Penal Code Is Approved By the American Law Institute

By ANTHONY LEWIS
Special to The New York Times.

WASHINGTON, May 24 — The American Law Institute gave final approval today to a model penal code that has been under preparation for ten years.

The code is regarded by many authorities as one of the most important recent projects in legal scholarship. Even before its completion it had begun to influence the criminal law of the states and the Federal Government.

The code is intended to take a fresh look at all of criminal law—its philosophical underpinnings, its definitions of crimes, its provisions for sentencing and correction of offenders.

The principal work on the code was done by two law professors—Herbert Wechsler of Columbia University and Louis B. Schwartz of the University of Pennsylvania. They received a standing ovation from institute members after the final vote on the code.

The Law Institute is an association of the country's most distinguished judges, law professors and practitioners. It works to codify and modernize the law. It has completed such other projects as a uniform commercial code that has been adopted by many states, including New York.

Under the institute's procedure, sections of a work such as the model penal code are prepared by the principal draftsmen, then debated in various committees and before the full membership at the annual meeting here in Washington. Then further drafts are written and rewritten until the language is finally approved.

The late Judge Learned Hand was one of the many eminent figures who took part, under this procedure, in the shaping of the penal code.

One of his arguments was that the criminal law should not punish any kind of sexual relations, normal or abnormal, between consenting adults in private. The institute adopted

Continued on Page 30, Column 1

Attempt to Fly Balloon in Space To Test Vision Is Part Success

By HAROLD M. SCHMECK Jr.
Special to The New York Times.

CAPE CANAVERAL, Fla., May 24—Lieut. Comdr. M. Scott Carpenter's attempt to fly a balloon in space today was only partly successful.

The experiment was one of the most important conducted during the three-orbit flight. It was intended to show how well a person can perceive various colors in space and also was a test of ability to judge distances and sizes against the unfamiliar black sky of the space environment.

These are points of considerable importance to the nation's moon exploration program because they could offer hints concerning the difficulties to be expected in rendezvous of a space vehicle with another object in space.

The balloon, thirty inches in diameter totally inflated, had panels of different hues—yellow, orange, flat white and phosphorescent, so that a comparison of visibility of different colors could be made. It was expected to produce a drag of only one one-hundredth or one one-thousandth of a pound on the space craft. Commander Carpenter found that an orange color called "Day Glow" showed up the best when sunlight was on it.

Rendezvous in space is expected to be important in Proj-

Continued on Page 15, Column 2

"All the News That's Fit to Print"

The New York Times.

LATE CITY EDITION
U. S. Weather Bureau Report (Page 70) forecasts: Sunny, then cloudy late today and tonight. Sunny, pleasant tomorrow. Temp. range: 90—62; yesterday: 90—65. Temp.-Hum. Index: 76—70; yesterday: 75.

VOL. CXI..No. 38,154. NEW YORK, WEDNESDAY, JULY 11, 1962. 10 cents beyond 50-mile zone from New York City except on Long Island. Higher in air delivery cities. FIVE CENTS

SATELLITE IN ORBIT BEAMS TV FROM U. S. TO EUROPE; PICTURES CLEAR IN FRANCE

The New York Times

TELECAST FROM SPACE: This picture on television screen here was produced by signals sent to Telstar satellite and then relayed back to earth. Dome in background contains tracking antenna at American Telephone and Telegraph center near Andover, Me.

Live Images Transmitted Across Ocean First Time

By RICHARD WITKIN
Special to The New York Times.

ANDOVER, Me., July 10 — Live television pictures leaped the ocean for the first time tonight when broadcasts beamed from here were relayed to France and England by way of the Telstar satellite.

The pictures were also seen on television screens in the United States.

The three major TV networks in this country broke into their evening programs to carry major portions of the initial satellite telecast.

The pictures were sent on the Telstar's sixth and seventh orbits. They were bounced back from the satellite to the originating point here, and then to a smaller horn-shaped antenna at Holmdel, N. J.

They then went out over conventional TV across the nation.

Officials Are Jubilant

Top officials of the Bell System, which built the satellite and the installation here, were jubilant over the success of their Telstar satellite.

Until the sixth orbit, Telstar's weaving paths back and forth across the Equator, to 45 degrees north and south latitude, had not brought it within line-of-sight range at Andover.

The first pictures to cross the ocean were of Vice President Johnson and other officials gathered in the Carnegie Institute auditorium in Washington.

Earlier the antenna here had beamed to the Telstar a picture of a waving American flag against a background of the domed antenna.

But the satellite, racing high above the Atlantic on a line from Haiti to Spain, was not within line-of-sight of Europe. Also, the British station was having trouble receiving signals on this sixth pass.

Music From Sound Track

On the seventh, two and a half hours later, the Europeans were too late for the flag sequence.

Accompanying the flag sequence, a sound tract played, first, "America the Beautiful," and then, "The Star Spangled Banner."

Also on the seventh orbit, the Bell System transmitted its first two-way phone conversation via the satellite.

Phone experiments on the sixth orbit had been one way because the satellite equipment had to be switched for most of the time to a television system.

On the seventh orbit, six two-way conversations were carried out simultaneously.

The satellite was in sight of here on the sixth orbit from 7:17 P. M. to 8:13 P. M., East-

Continued on Page 16, Column 5

NATION SEES TESTS

Experimental Device Launched by Space Agency for A. T. & T.

By JOHN W. FINNEY
Special to The New York Times.

WASHINGTON, July 10 — An experimental communications satellite was rocketed into orbit today in a joint Government-industry venture into space. It marked a historic, highly successful first step toward achieving a revolutionary new global communications system in space.

In a communications feat regarded as rivaling in significance the first telegraphed transmission by Samuel F. B. Morse more than a century ago, the satellite relayed the first trans-Atlantic television broadcast.

With the satellite serving as a relay station some 3,000 miles above the North Atlantic, clear television pictures were transmitted this evening from a station in Andover, Me., to stations in France and Britain.

Good Reception on Continent

The pictures were so clear that the French station said they appeared as if they had been sent from about twenty-five miles away. Reception in Britain was reported not to be as good.

On its first experimental transmission, the satellite also relayed a fifteen-minute television program that was broadcast by the three television networks into millions of American homes.

The 170-pound Telstar satellite, developed by American Telephone and Telegraph Company, pointed the way toward a day in the not too distant future when television programs, telephone calls, telegraph messages and data for electronic computers will be transmitted between

Continued on Page 16, Column 1

KHRUSHCHEV URGES SMALLER NATIONS GARRISON BERLIN

Calls on Western Big Three to Turn Over Their Part of City to New Force

SUGGESTS U.N. CONTROL

Premier Tells Peace Meeting NATO Members and Red States Could Send Units

Excerpts from Khrushchev's address are on Page 4.

By THEODORE SHABAD
Special to The New York Times.

MOSCOW, July 10—Premier Khrushchev proposed today that the United States, British and French forces in West Berlin be replaced by troops from the small nations in the North Atlantic and Warsaw alliances.

In making the proposal concerning Western occupation rights in Berlin, a principal stumbling block in United States-Soviet efforts to find a solution to the Berlin problem, Mr. Khrushchev suggested that the new occupation be under control of the United Nations.

The Premier said Norway and Denmark or the Netherlands and Belgium, all members of NATO, together with Poland and Czechoslovakia, of the Warsaw Pact group, might supply contingents for Berlin.

Addresses Peace Meeting

The proposal came in a two-and-a-half-hour speech by Mr. Khrushchev to the Communist-sponsored World Congress for General Disarmament and Peace, meeting in the Kremlin. The meeting has attracted 2,000 delegates from 100 countries.

Mr. Khrushchev repeated the Soviet demand for general and complete disarmament, but he defended Soviet nuclear testing.

He said the Soviet Union had been forced to resume tests last autumn to "cool some hotheads who proposed to finish off Russia with one blow" at a time when "the aggressive North Atlantic bloc openly threatened war over the German peace treaty."

He said "the new major series of nuclear tests that the United States Government is carrying out jointly with the British Government is a challenge to mankind."

"The matter has gone so far," he added, "that the United States is carrying out nuclear weapon tests in outer space, disregarding the fact that these experiments may have very dangerous conse-

Continued on Page 4, Column 1

Associated Press Radiophoto

ADDRESSES PEACE CONGRESS: Premier Khrushchev speaking yesterday at an international gathering in Moscow. Mr. Khrushchev stressed Soviet military resources.

U. S. Rebuffs Khrushchev On Berlin Bid and Testing

By MAX FRANKEL
Special to The New York Times.

WASHINGTON, July 10—The State Department issued two statements today dismissing Premier Khrushchev's proposals to replace Western troops in Berlin as unacceptable and describing his complaints against United States high-altitude nuclear explosions as "hypocrisy."

Defense Department sources also expressed doubt again about Mr. Khrushchev's assertion that the Soviet Union had an effective anti-missile defense.

The reactions were based on news accounts of Mr. Khrushchev's address to a world peace congress in Moscow.

The suggestion that Danish and Norwegian or Dutch and Belgian troops together with Polish and Czechoslovak forces replace United States, British and French garrisons in West Berlin was rejected by the State Department even as a basis for negotiation.

Plan Not New

The proposal was merely one of several offered previously by Moscow to reduce, eliminate or supplement with Communist troops the garrisons of the Western powers in Berlin, the department said. It added that today's specific suggestions by Premier Khrushchev had previously been turned down in private conversations.

It was not made clear here whether the proposal had come up in talks between Secretary of State Dean Rusk and Andrei A. Gromyko, the Soviet Foreign Minister, or between Mr. Rusk

Continued on Page 5, Column 1

INDIA SAYS CHINA MENACES OUTPOST

Charges Communist Soldiers Surround Base in Disputed Section of Kashmir

Special to The New York Times.

NEW DELHI, India, July 10 — An Indian note charged today that Chinese Communist troops had encircled an Indian checkpost in the Galwan Valley in the disputed Ladakh area of eastern Kashmir.

The note, a reply to a Peiping memorandum of two days ago that protested against an alleged Indian intrusion into the area, said that about 400 Chinese soldiers had encircled the base.

"They moved up threateningly quite within fifty to seventy yards of the post" the Indian message said.

Precise Position Given

The site of the Indian post, according to the note, is approximately Long. 78 degrees 38 minutes E. Lat. 34 degrees 39.45 minutes N.

The position is ten and a half miles from the boundary of the 12,000 square miles that the Chinese claimed in their map of 1956, but it is within the 2,000 additional square miles they claimed in 1960.

The Indian note warned that "if any untoward incident should now occur, the responsibility for it will entirely rest on the Government of China."

New Delhi said that the lower reaches of the Galwan Valley were not only well inside Indian territory, but also twenty-eight miles from the boundary shown in Peiping's 1956 map. Premier Chou En-lai himself acknowledged it in a letter to Prime Minister Jawaharlal Nehru as

Continued on Page 6, Column 4

ALGERIANS' TALKS FAIL TO END RIFT; BEN BELLA FIRM

Rabat Parleys Broken Off—More Due After Military Zones Clarify Views

Special to The New York Times.

RABAT, Morocco, July 10—Negotiations here to restore Algerian unity have failed and were broken off tonight.

Algerian Provisional Government sources said that talks between the rival factions would be resumed elsewhere after officials in all the willayas (military zones) had made clear their views.

The rupture in the reconciliation talks was first announced tonight by sources close to the dissident Vice Premier, Mohammed Ben Bella. These sources said that "no compromise was possible" under the present circumstances.

[In Algeria, the commander of the Liberation Army for the Oran region announced that the army would try several hundred Moslems and publicly execute those convicted of looting and kidnapping.]

Ben Bella Angered

Mr. Ben Bella was said to be angered by the announcement today from Algiers that the Transitional Executive council, which is administering Algeria on a temporary basis, had set Aug. 12 as the date for Algerian elections for a national assembly and announced an amnesty without waiting for the outcome of the negotiations here.

M'Hammed Yazid, the Provisional Government's Minister of Information and a member of the conciliation mission, announced that the meeting at Rabat had "advanced" the cause of national unity.

"We believe that all Algerian leaders will abstain in the next few days from making declarations that could be a blow to national unity, which is essential and demanded by our people," he said at the end of the talks.

Rivals in Final Meeting

The minister spoke after the final meeting of the rival factions, which came to an end at 10 P. M. He said that Mr. Ben Bella had informed Provisional Government "colleagues" of his plan to leave late tonight for western Algeria.

Members of the Vice Premier's entourage said that he would preside over a Liberation Army rally in Marnia in western Algeria tomorrow. Mr. Ben Bella is also expected to visit his mother, who lives in Marnia.

Sources close to the Provisional Government said that they considered Mr. Ben Bella's trip to Marnia as "a move toward the next meeting" with

Continued on Page 2, Column 5

FRANCO REPLACES SEVEN IN CABINET; NAMES SUCCESSOR

2d-Ranking Soldier Will Be Vice President of Council and Generalissimo's Heir

By BENJAMIN WELLES
Special to The New York Times.

MADRID, July 10—Generalissimo Francisco Franco will carry out a major Cabinet overhaul tomorrow and create the post of Vice President of the Cabinet.

The new post is to go to Capt. Gen. Agustin Muñoz Grandes, the highest ranking soldier in Spain after General Franco. The Cabinet shuffle will involve the replacement of seven of the eighteen ministers.

General Muñoz Grandes, who is 65 years old, will be designated General Franco's automatic successor as chief of the Spanish Government in the event of a "vacancy" through death or any other reason. At present General Franco, who is 69, will remain Chief of State and head of the Government.

Major Shift Noted

Political observers here agree that the Cabinet shuffle, which will be announced tomorrow in the official journal, the State Bulletin, signifies a major shift toward political and economic liberalism at a time when Spain has an application pending for eventual association with the European Economic Community.

The nomination of General Muñoz Grandes is a gesture recognizing the importance of the Spanish Army, whose key leaders favor restoration of the monarchy after General Franco relinquishes power.

General Muñoz Grandes is loyal to General Franco, but it is reliably understood that he would not oppose a monarchy under Don Juan, Count of Barcelona and pretender to the throne, after General Franco's death.

New U. S. Arms Sought

General Muñoz Grandes will continue as chief of the Central General Staff and will coordinate the equipment requirements of the three Spanish armed services. Spain's armed forces are asking for more modern United States arms in connection with the planned renegotiation of United States military base rights in Spain, which are due for renewal this September.

The following aspects of the Cabinet shuffle drew special attention from political observers:

¶The influence in the new Cabinet of the Falange, the only legal political movement in Spain, will drop sharply. Three of the four retiring civilian ministers are Falangists. The new Labor Minister, Jesus

Continued on Page 12, Column 3

PRESIDENT UPHELD ON INTERIM POSTS

U. S. Appeals Court Backs Executive Right to Name Temporary Judges

By EDWARD RANZAL

The right of the President to make interim judicial appointments when the Senate is in recess was upheld unanimously yesterday by the United States Court of Appeals.

The same constitutional power, the court held, extends to vacancies that arise while the Senate is in session.

The decision was the first by a Federal appeals court in a matter that rested squarely on the issue of Presidential interim appointments.

Because of the lack of legal precedence the court resorted to the wording of the Constitution and excerpts from the writings of Alexander Hamilton.

The question arose when a defendant convicted in a narcotics case challenged the conviction on the ground that he had been deprived of a constitutional trial. He said this was so because the trial judge had received an interim appointment from former President Dwight D. Eisenhower on Aug. 17, 1955, fifteen days after the Senate had adjourned.

The defendant, Dominic Allocco, contended that the commission of the judge, John M.

Continued on Page 20, Column 7

ADENAUER HAILS BONN-PARIS TIES

Says de Gaulle Agrees Amity Will Prevent Soviet Gains

By SYDNEY GRUSON
Special to The New York Times.

BONN, Germany, July 10—Chancellor Adenauer said today that he and President de Gaulle had agreed on the necessity of French-German relations so close that neither country could ever again make a pact with the Soviet Union against the other.

The German leader said that one of the most important results of the French-German reconciliation after World War II had been the building of a political dam "against the spread of communism in Europe."

"De Gaulle and I were clear on this point, that the future relationship should not be confined to governments but should be backed by the feelings and the will and conviction of both peoples," the Chancellor went on.

"We agreed," he said, "to lay firm foundations for this relationship so that it would become a matter of course for both peoples and so that no one later could entertain the thought of establishing relations with Russia that might in any way be directed against one of the two countries."

Dr. Adenauer took an unusual way to report on his week-long state visit to France that ended Sunday. He delivered a statement at a news conference but

Continued on Page 6, Column 3

Turin Police Check Rioting on 4th Day

By PAUL HOFMANN
Special to The New York Times.

TURIN, Italy, July 10—The police tore down barricades here today and later broke up renewed rioting to quell what they called an attempted revolt.

On the fourth day of disorders in this usually staid center of Italy's automobile industry, the violence was plainly aimed at the Government forces, but it seemed to be lessening. The disorders resulted from a labor conflict.

Officials accused Communists of what they termed an attempted "revolt against the state."

A Government spokesman said tonight the situation was under control. Disturbances were continuing on a small scale compared with the last three days.

About 2,000 people have been detained since Saturday, when

Continued on Page 3, Column 2

Moses Quits Fire Island Hearing

Charles Collingwood, opponent of road at Fire Island, speaks at hearing at Jones Beach

Walks Out as Letter Comparing Him to Hitler Is Read

By BYRON PORTERFIELD
Special to The New York Times.

JONES BEACH, L. I., July 10—Robert Moses walked out of a public hearing today when a speaker quoted a twenty-four-year-old letter comparing him to Adolf Hitler.

The comparison had been made in a satirical letter written to The New York Times by the late Elmer Davis on Oct. 3, 1938. In the excerpt read today Mr. Davis asserted that Mr. Moses "would save Fire Island the way Hitler is saving the Sudetenland."

Charles Collingwood, a Columbia Broadcasting System correspondent and chairman of the Fire Island Voters Association's committee on legislation, quoted the Davis letter. Mr.

The New York Times

Robert Moses reading Fire Island News at hearing. Later, when Mr. Collingwood quoted an old attack on him, he left.

Collingwood is a summer resident of Saltaire, on the barrier beach.

The incident occurred at a hearing on a proposed $106,400,000 program for rebuilding and stabilizing the storm-torn Atlantic shoreline from Staten Island to Montauk Point, a distance of 135 miles. Fire Island

Continued on Page 25, Column 2

Dr. King Is Jailed For Georgia Protest

By The Associated Press

ALBANY, Ga., July 10—The Rev. Dr. Martin Luther King Jr., Negro integration leader, and a fellow minister went to jail today to emphasize their nonviolent defiance of racial barriers.

Dr. King and the Rev. Ralph Abernathy, both of Atlanta, were convicted in Recorder's Court of having violated a street and sidewalk assembly ordinance by leading a street demonstration without a permit last Dec. 16.

Recorder A. N. Durden sentenced them to pay $178 fines or spend forty-five days in jail. They spurned both the fines and freedom on bond through appeals and went to jail to await assignment to prisoner street gangs.

The integrationist leader assailed both the Albany law and the court that had con-

Continued on Page 26, Column 4

C.B.S. Omits Speech By Head of A.T.&T.

The Columbia Broadcasting System omitted most of the remarks of Frederick R. Kappel, chairman of the board of the American Telephone and Telegraph Company, from its coverage last night of the satellite telecast.

Richard S. Salant, president of C. B. S. News, acknowledged that the omission was a sequel to protests by the network against A. T. & T.'s serving as producer of the historic program.

As a matter of principle, he said, C. B. S. News did not believe that the principal party in a major news story should determine how it was presented to the public.

Mr. Salant said that, under its policy, C. B. S. had turned down a bid by A. T. & T. to present a special half-hour program immediately after the for-

Continued on Page 17, Column 4

NEWS INDEX

"All the News That's Fit to Print"

The New York Times.

LATE CITY EDITION

U. S. Weather Bureau Report (Page 43) forecasts: Mostly fair, warm and humid today, tonight and tomorrow.

Temp. range: 86—69; yesterday: 85—65. Temp.-Hum. Index: 78; yesterday: 78.

VOL. CXI..No. 38,180. © 1962 by The New York Times Company. Times Square, New York 36, N. Y. NEW YORK, MONDAY, AUGUST 6, 1962. 10 cents beyond 50-mile zone from New York City except on Long Island. Higher in air delivery cities. FIVE CENTS

Marilyn Monroe Dead, Pills Near

Star's Body Is Found in Bedroom of Her Home on Coast

Police Say She Left No Notes—Official Verdict Delayed

Special to The New York Times.

HOLLYWOOD, Calif., Aug. 5—Marilyn Monroe, one of the most famous stars in Hollywood's history, was found dead early today in the bedroom of her home in the Brentwood section of Los Angeles. She was 36 years old.

Beside the bed was an empty bottle that had contained sleeping pills. Fourteen other bottles of medicines and tablets were on the night stand.

The impact of Miss Monroe's death was international. Her fame was greater than her contributions as an actress.

As a woman she was considered a sex symbol. Her marriages to and divorces from Joe DiMaggio, the former Yankee baseball star, and Arthur Miller, the Pulitzer Prize playwright, were accepted by millions as the prerogatives of this contemporary Venus.

The events leading to her death were in tragic contrast to the comic talent and zest for life that had helped to make "Seven Year Itch" and "Some Like It Hot" smash hits all over the world.

Miss Monroe's physician had prescribed sleeping pills for her for three days. Ordinarily the bottle would have contained forty to fifty pills.

The actress had also been under the care of a psychoanalyst for a year, and had called him to her home last night. He had suggested she take a drive and relax. She remained home, however.

After an autopsy the Los Angeles coroner reported that Miss Monroe's "was not a natural death." He attributed it to a drug. He added that a toxicological study, to be completed within forty-eight hours, should yield more detailed information. He refused, until then, to list the death as a suicide.

Pending a more positive verdict by Dr. Theodore J. Curphey, the coroner, the Los Angeles police refused to call the death a suicide. They said they had no idea how many pills the actress might have taken, or whether any overdose might have been accidental. Miss Monroe left no notes, according to the police.

In addition to a physical autopsy, Los Angeles had a "psychological" autopsy. Two experts will look into the psychological history of Miss Monroe.

However, the non-physical

Continued on Page 13, Column 6

Marilyn Monroe

Associated Press

COMMON MARKET AND BRITISH VOICE HOPES IN IMPASSE

Both Sides Say Gains Were Made on Role for London Before Session Ended

OCTOBER MEETING SET

Failure to Settle Question of Commonwealth Exports Is Blow to Macmillan

By EDWIN L. DALE Jr.

Special to The New York Times.

BRUSSELS, Belgium, Aug. 5—Representatives of Britain and the European Economic Community expressed disappointment and some bitterness but no discouragement today over their failure to reach full agreement on the basis for British membership in the Community.

They stressed that substantial progress had been made on major issues.

The protracted negotiations, the present session of which lasted four days, will resume early in October.

After nearly twenty-two hours of continuous effort, the negotiators gave up this morning on the key matter still impeding agreement: Britain's effort to assure markets for the agricultural imports she receives from Canada, Australia and New Zealand.

New Tariff to Be Imposed

At the end, only a few points were still unsettled in a Common Market plan designed to give some assurance to the three Commonwealth countries. Their exports, now in large part duty-free in the British market, will be subject to a new common tariff and a variable levy system for farm products if Britain joins the six-nation Community.

The plan includes world commodity agreements, a pledge of a "reasonable" farm price policy aimed at preventing overproduction and a detailed arrangement to maintain preferential treatment for all British Commonwealth countries during a transition period up to 1970.

[The inconclusiveness of the negotiations was viewed in Britain as a setback for Prime Minister Macmillan. It is believed he will now find it more difficult to hold doubtful Conservatives in line and to get an unqualified reaction from the Commonwealth Prime Ministers when they meet next month.]

Key to the Failure

The key to the failure to conclude the matter appears to have been the last-minute introduction by France of a highly complex financial issue. While hundreds of millions of dollars are potentially involved, the issue has no connection with the Commonwealth. The French made agreement on the point a condition for an over-all settlement.

The result of the work of the last four days is that the British will have the "major part" of the terms of their entry to present to the Commonwealth Prime Ministers when they meet in London Sept. 10, but not a full outline, as had been wished.

The British Government must deal with the political as well as the economic consequences

Continued on Page 4, Column 5

N.A.A.C.P. to Ask Courts To End Union Racial Bars

By JOHN D. POMFRET

Special to The New York Times.

WASHINGTON, Aug. 5—The National Association for the Advancement of Colored People is planning a major legal assault on discrimination against Negroes by labor unions. The new effort is to begin in early fall. The aim will be to create a body of judge-made law equal to that now found in the field of public education.

The N. A. A. C. P. was instrumental in creating these laws following the 1954 Supreme Court decision outlawing segregation in public schools.

Much as the association attacked the doctrine of "separate but equal" in the school segregation case, its lawyers are preparing to make the doctrine of "voluntary association" a main target in the union field.

This doctrine holds that private voluntary groups have the right to decide whom they will admit. It has been advanced by some unions as a defense against legal efforts to compel them to take in Negroes.

Role of Unions Cited

The association will argue that the doctrine does not apply to unions because they are not voluntary associations. Their certification by the National Labor Relations Board as exclusive bargaining agents, their role in collective bargaining and their control in some situations of access to jobs distinguish them from social or fraternal groups, the association will contend.

Herbert Hill, the association's labor secretary, said that the N. A. A. C. P. was going into court as a "last resort." In the seven years since it was established, he declared, the merged labor federation has been "either unwilling or unable to eliminate discrimination" by its affiliated unions.

Mr. Hill asserted that the American Federation of Labor and Congress of Industrial Organizations had given the elimination of racial discrimination by affiliated unions "a low level of priority."

"They have no understanding of the problem," Mr. Hill said. "What is progress for them is not progress for us."

A federation spokesman said that the federation "has made progress in the fight against discrimination."

"We will not be satisfied until discrimination is completely eliminated and we will continue to make progress in a trade union way undeterred by outsiders," he asserted.

Animosity between the association and the federation dates from early 1959 when the association concluded that the federation was not going to move vigorously enough to end discrimination against Negroes.

Since then, the association has assisted in building Negro caucuses inside unions to exert internal pressure and has filed complaints with Federal and state anti-discrimination agencies against unions. The legal effort now in preparation is an extension of these efforts into a new field.

The first case, according to Mr. Hill, will begin as a petition to the National Labor Relations Board to decertify a union on

Continued on Page 22, Column 8

CITY ACTS TO PAY ITS BILLS FASTER

Economies Are Expected—Tenney Says Poor Liaison Is a Cause of Delays

By PAUL CROWELL

Steps are being taken to have the city pay its bills more quickly, City Administrator Charles H. Tenney reported yesterday.

Mr. Tenney said that delays were a result, in part, of inadequate liaison between the office of the Controller and the management offices of other city agencies.

His report was based on a study requested in January by Controller Abraham D. Beame. Mr. Beame said at the time that he was convinced many individuals and companies were reluctant to bid for city business only because there were long delays in the payment of bills.

Changes Already Made

More bidders, Mr. Beame said, would mean more competition and, probably, lower prices and savings for the city.

The Tenney study, in which Mr. Beame's office took part, found that the procedures of the Controller's office in processing venders', suppliers' and contractors' bills were "basically sound."

Mr. Tenney reported that bookkeeping and record-keeping changes had already been made to shorten and simplify the handling of bills in the office of the Controller.

Mr. Tenney, who sent copies of his report to Mayor Wagner and Mr. Beame, said he would

Continued on Page 10, Column 3

PRESIDENT NAMES DEAN AT COLUMBIA TO POST ON A. E. C.

John G. Palfrey Is Second Lawyer Picked for Agency in Resolution of Dispute

Special to The New York Times.

HYANNIS PORT, Mass., Aug. 5—President Kennedy announced today his intention to appoint John G. Palfrey, dean of Columbia College, New York, as a member of the Atomic Energy Commission.

He also announced his selection, reported yesterday, of James T. Ramey, executive director of the Congressional Joint Committee on Atomic Energy, to fill another vacancy on the A. E. C. Mr. Palfrey will succeed Loren K. Olson. Mr. Ramey will succeed John S. Graham.

Mr. Palfrey and Mr. Ramey are lawyers.

Mr. Palfrey, who has done research work on the political and legal aspects of atomic energy, served three years on the staff of the office of the general counsel of the A. E. C.

Dispute Over Posts

Since the resignations of Mr. Olson and Mr. Graham July 1, the Administration and some influential members of the Joint Committee on Atomic Energy have been arguing behind the scenes over candidates for the two $22,000-a-year posts.

Some Executive Branch officials, particularly in the Atomic Energy Commission itself, had rejected candidates, including Mr. Ramey, who had been put forward by the Democrats on the Congressional committee. The Democrats then refused to accept Administration candidates.

The resolution of the dispute was regarded as a compromise. The committee Democrats got Mr. Ramey, one of "their boys." The A. E. C. got Mr. Palfrey, who had been in the office of the general counsel of the commission from 1947 to 1950.

May Serve Short Terms

Besides settling the differences between the two parties, the Administration also had to find two men who would be willing to serve as short a term as one year.

Mr. Palfrey's term officially runs to July 30, 1967, and Mr. Ramey's to June 30, 1964. But it is understood that the Administration is planning to ask Congress next year to replace the five-man commission with a single administrator.

The selection of Mr. Palfrey and Mr. Ramey presumably will satisfy fears expressed by some members of the Joint Committee that the commission was falling into the hands of scientists.

The present three members of

Continued on Page 2, Column 4

KENNEDY PRESSES FOR SAFER DRUGS

Asks Senate to Stiffen Bill to Improve Quality and Combat Health Hazard

By ALVIN SHUSTER

Special to The New York Times.

HYANNIS PORT, Mass., Aug. 5—President Kennedy asked the Senate today to strengthen its pending new drug law to insure "safer and better" drugs for the American consumer.

The President proposed a series of "essential" amendments to the Senate bill. One would enable the Government to move faster to remove from the prescription market any new drug suspected of being a hazard to public health.

Safety Goal Stressed

The proposals were substantially the same as those requested in a special message the President sent to Congress earlier this year. They were renewed today in a letter to Senator James O. Eastland, Democrat of Mississippi, who is chairman of the Senate Judiciary Committee.

Last month the committee approved a bill embodying many of the earlier proposals. But, as the President told his news conference last week, it did "not go far enough."

Accordingly, he asked Senator Eastland to amend the bill to make sure the American people were protected "against

Continued on Page 28, Column 1

BLAST IN THE ARCTIC: The Soviet Union resumed tests of nuclear weapons in the air over Novaya Zemlya (cross).

The New York Times Aug. 6, 1962

Ben Bella Ally Is Named Chief of Political Bureau

By HENRY TANNER

Special to The New York Times.

ALGIERS, Aug. 5—Mohammed Khider, Mohammed Ben Bella's closest ally, was named today as Secretary General of the powerful Political Bureau. The position is the key post on the seven-man organ of the Algerian National Liberation Front.

Mr. Khider, envoy of Mr. Ben Bella in the negotiations last week that ended a month-long crisis in the nationalist leadership, was also given charge of financial affairs and information.

Hadj Ben Alla, another close collaborator of Mr. Ben Bella, was given control of military affairs.

Mr. Ben Bella himself was put in charge of "coordination of interior affairs" with the Transitional Executive. This, too, is regarded as a key position.

Executive Has Little Power

The Transitional Executive theoretically has responsibility for the country's administration under the cease-fire agreement signed in March with France. But it has no real power of its own and is taking instructions from nationalist leaders.

Mr. Ben Bella apparently will be the man through whom the Transitional Executive will have to work in the future. Some observers said he would act as Algeria's Interior Minister until the Constituent Assembly election set for Sept. 2.

Mohammed Boudiaf, one of Mr. Ben Bella's most determined opponents, was given charge of "guidance and external affairs." He is one of the principal ideologists of the nationalist movement.

The Political Bureau is the policy-making body of the National Liberation Front, the

Continued on Page 8, Column 6

SOVIET TEST STIRS REGRET AT GENEVA

Negotiators for Ban Hope New Series Will be Last —Dean and Zorin Meet

Special to The New York Times.

GENEVA, Aug. 5—Western and neutralist delegates at the seventeen-nation disarmament conference here expressed regrets today that the Soviet Union had renewed nuclear tests. The test renewal had long been accepted here as inevitable.

Arthur H. Dean of the United States commented that the new round of testing begun by the Soviet Union was "particularly regrettable when we are trying our best to work out a test ban treaty."

"It makes our work all the more complicated," the United States negotiator said.

Arthur S. Lall of India said India was "against tests by anyone, anywhere, any time."

Renewed Effort Urged

"Although both sides are now testing," the Indian delegate said, "this should not be allowed to interfere with the efforts to get a test ban treaty. On the contrary, efforts must be redoubled because of the greater urgency of the problem."

Mr. Dean held an "inconclusive" discussion today on the test ban issue with Valerian A. Zorin, a Deputy Foreign Minister, who is Moscow's delegate at the talks.

Mr. Dean was understood to have emphasized that Moscow must agree to on-site inspections if Washington makes concessions on the controls to guarantee the observance of the projected treaty to end testing.

No arrangements were made during their ninety-minute private talk for a formal discussion of the test ban problem in full conference here.

Meeting Inconclusive

Mr. Dean and Mr. Zorin, who are co-chairmen of the conference, also failed to set a meeting of the three-power subcommittee in which the United States, Britain and the Soviet Union conduct negotiations for a treaty to outlaw atomic tests.

They met at the Soviet delegation's headquarters. No Soviet comment was immediately available. United States sources described the session as "inconclusive."

The hope among the neutralists in particular is that once the United States and the Soviet Union have completed their current tests they will consider their defense requirements satisfied and will be better prepared to compromise on a test

Continued on Page 3, Column 2

RUSSIANS RESUME A-TESTING IN AIR; BLAST 2D BIGGEST

Explosion at High Altitude Over Arctic Island Is Put in 40-Megaton Range

U. S. DEPLORES ACTION

But Voices Hope Soviet Will Still Work for a Treaty—Stresses Pending Offer

By TAD SZULC

Special to The New York Times.

WASHINGTON, Aug. 5—The Soviet Union resumed its nuclear tests in the atmosphere early today with a powerful high-altitude blast believed to have been in the forty-megaton range.

The blast, over Novaya Zemlya, in the Arctic, appeared to have been the second most potent nuclear explosion ever achieved. The record is held by the Soviet Union, which detonated last Oct. 30 a nuclear device with an explosive force estimated at the equivalent of fifty-eight megatons of TNT. A megaton is 1,000,000 tons.

The United States Government called the resumption a "somber episode," but expressed the hope that Moscow would nonetheless cooperate in working for an effective treaty prohibiting all tests of nuclear weapons.

This morning's test, at 5:08 A. M., Eastern daylight time, was first reported by Swedish and Japanese scientists. It was later confirmed, without details, by the Atomic Energy Commission here. News of the test was withheld from the Soviet people.

Issue Before Geneva Parley

The start of the Soviet test series, forecast by Moscow two weeks ago, came on the eve of the expected presentation before the seventeen-nation disarmament conference in Geneva of new and simplified United States proposals for a test ban treaty.

Moscow broke a three-year-old moratorium on nuclear testing last fall. The United States followed with an extensive series of tests underground and in the atmosphere.

In a statement made public this morning, the State Department commented that, "despite its resumption of atmospheric nuclear testing, we hope the Soviet Union will match our efforts to negotiate an effective nuclear test ban treaty."

It said that "the Soviet Union's initiation of yet another series of atmospheric tests — the second such series in less than a year—can only be regarded as a somber episode."

The statement stressed that "the series was started even as

Continued on Page 3, Column 5

TRIBES REASSERT POWER IN CONGO

Aim Is to Revise Provinces to Follow Ethnic Lines

By DAVID HALBERSTAM

Special to The New York Times.

LEOPOLDVILLE, the Congo, Aug. 5—Tribal political power is reasserting itself strongly in the Congo. It is manifest in the powerful desire of the Congolese to form new provinces along basically tribal lines.

When the Congo won independence from Belgium on June 30, 1960, there were only six major provinces in this huge country. With the sanction of Parliament, seven new provinces have been approved. A total of nineteen provinces is foreseen shortly.

Observers view the trend as essentially federalist and traditionalist and thus anti-nationalist and against the mainstream of pan-African political development. It marks, in effect, these observers believe, the failure of the late Patrice Lumumba and his nationalist movement to make any deep inroads into the traditional tribal allegiance in the Congo.

There are, the observers note, about forty ethnic groups in the Congo, of which about twenty are major groups. The new provinces are generally being developed along major ethnic lines.

The new province of South Kasai, for example, is essentially a Baluba tribal area,

Continued on Page 8, Column 4

Jamaica Now Independent After Long British Rule

Associated Press Radiophoto

Prime Minister Sir Alexander Bustamante with Princess Margaret at National Stadium

By R. HART PHILLIPS

Special to The New York Times.

KINGSTON, Jamaica, Monday, Aug. 6—Jamaica became an independent nation with dominion status within the British Commonwealth today. Princess Margaret as representative of her sister, Queen Elizabeth II, witnessed the end of the 307 years of British colonial status. About 30,000 Jamaicans jammed the big new National Stadium and cheered the raising of the new flag. On the stroke of midnight, the huge spotlights were turned off and in silence and darkness, the British flag that had flown over the island was hauled down and the green, gold and black

Continued on Page 6, Column 2

Charter Change Urged to Keep Fiscal Power of Estimate Board

The Citizens Budget Commission urged yesterday an early revision of the new City Charter to preserve the Board of Estimate's authority to control capital projects from the time a site is chosen through the appropriation of funds.

The present Charter gives the board this authority. In exercising it the board has followed a time-consuming procedure of holding public hearings on each aspect of a given capital project, from the planning stage on.

The Citizens Budget Commission recommended a single public hearing on each project, covering all its phases. It proposed that the Mayor should not initiate any project unless the Board of Estimate then approved it.

The civic organization pointed out that the new Charter, which becomes effective Jan. 1, provides for a public hearing by the Board of Estimate on all capital projects before the Mayor initiates them, but gives the board no power to disapprove them since the hearing would be held after the budget was approved.

The public hearing, the civic group contended, would therefore be "farcical and deceptive."

It proposed that the Charter be revised through a local law giving the Board of Estimate authority to approve "the site, final plans, cost estimates, major construction contracts, proposed bond issues and necessary appropriations."

As it now stands, the new Charter provides for appropriation of funds for all projects in the city's capital budget when the budget is adopted by the Board of Estimate and the City Council. The Citizens Budget Commission contended this would leave actual initiation of any project listed in

Continued on Page 10, Column 6

NEWS INDEX

The Boston Celtics picked up John Havlicek from Ohio State; he later became one of the all-time greats.

Sonny Liston became world heavyweight champion by knocking down Floyd Patterson in the first round.

The fight between Benny Paret and Emile Griffith was stopped too late by Ruby Goldstein. Paret left Madison Square Garden that night losing his title and his life.

Wilt Chamberlain helped beat the New York Knicks with an incredible score of 36 baskets and 28 free throws for an even 100 points.

"All the News That's Fit to Print"

The New York Times.

LATE CITY EDITION
U. S. Weather Bureau Report (Page 96) forecasts: Sunny and warm today and tomorrow. Clear and mild tonight.
Temp. range: 89—65; yesterday: 83—64.
Temp.-Hum. Index: 78; yesterday: 74.

VOL. CXI..No. 38,204. © 1962 by The New York Times Company. Times Square, New York 36, N. Y. NEW YORK, THURSDAY, AUGUST 30, 1962. 10 cents beyond 50-mile zone from New York City except on Long Island. Higher in air delivery cities. FIVE CENTS

JUSTICE FRANKFURTER RETIRES; KENNEDY HAILS 23-YEAR SERVICE, NAMES GOLDBERG AS SUCCESSOR

Associate Justice Felix Frankfurter

The New York Times

Secretary of Labor Arthur J. Goldberg

ILL HEALTH CITED

Justice Absent From Bench Since April Because of Stroke

Texts of Frankfurter and Kennedy letters, Page 14.

By ANTHONY LEWIS
Special to The New York Times.

WASHINGTON, Aug. 29 — Felix Frankfurter has retired from active service on the Supreme Court after twenty-three years as an associate justice.

President Kennedy made the announcement at his news conference this afternoon and said he would appoint Arthur J. Goldberg, Secretary of Labor, to the vacancy. [Opening statement, Page 10.]

Justice Frankfurter, who is 79 years old, has been away from the court since he suffered a mild stroke last April 5. He had hoped to return when the new term opens on Oct. 1, but concluded that this would be medically unwise.

Mr. Goldberg, 54, will bring to the bench a long background as a leading labor lawyer.

Confirmation Expected

He will be the fourth Jew to sit on the Supreme Court. The others have been Justice Frankfurter and Justices Louis D. Brandeis and Benjamin N. Cardozo.

The President praised Justice Frankfurter for his impact on the court and termed Mr. Goldberg "superbly qualified" as a successor.

Reaction on Capitol Hill indicated that confirmation of Mr. Goldberg would be forthcoming. Leaders of both parties expressed satisfaction with Mr. Kennedy's choice.

Speculation on a successor to Mr. Goldberg centered on W. Willard Wirtz, Under Secretary of Labor. George Meany, president of the merged labor movement, was reported to have a "very high opinion" of Mr. Wirtz' abilities.

There was the sense of history in the State Department Auditorium as the President made the announcement today, and his words reflected that feeling.

Comment by President

"Few judges have made as significant and lasting an impression upon the law," Mr. Kennedy said of Justice Frankfurter. "Few persons have made so important a contribution to our legal traditions and literature."

For many years Justice Frankfurter has been the most important spokesman on the Supreme Court for a philosophy of caution on the part of judges, of deference to the views of legislators, however unwise the judge may personally consider them.

His last major opinion was a final, great expression of this position. It was his dissent from the 6-2 decision of last March 26 holding that the apportionment of seats in state legislatures was subject to the scrutiny of Federal judges.

"There is not under our Con-

Continued on Page 14, Column 3

FEUDING TROOPS CLASH IN ALGIERS; SIX DIE IN CASBAH

Soldiers Around Capital Lay Attack on Their Patrols to Guerrilla Leader

CURFEW INVOKED IN CITY

Officer Charges Leader of Political Bureau Backed Raid in Moslem Area

By HENRY TANNER
Special to The New York Times.

ALGIERS, Aug. 29—Fighting between rival Algerian military factions broke out today in the Casbah, the city's historic Moslem section.

Troops of Willaya (military region) IV clashed with men led by Col. Yacef Saadi, a former guerrilla commander in the Casbah who is now a prominent follower of Vice Premier Ahmed Ben Bella.

Willaya IV controls Algiers and central Algeria.

The shooting started early in the afternoon when troops of Willaya IV searched houses for arms held by Colonel Saadi's men.

Five Willaya IV soldiers were killed, according to a spokesman, Lieut. Ali Alouache. Casualties among Colonel Saadi's men and among civilians were not announced. Witnesses in the Rue Rovigo, where the heaviest shooting took place, said they had seen one dead civilian.

Bureau Aide Accused

Lieutenant Alouache said Colonel Saadi's men had fired on Willaya IV patrols on orders from Mohammed Khider, Secretary General of the Political Bureau, which is now, in effect, governing the country. Mr. Ben Bella is the best known of the bureau's members, but Mr. Khider is regarded as its driving spirit.

Lieutenant Alouache called Mr. Khider an "assassin" and some of his remarks appeared to threaten armed action against the Political Bureau.

The bureau was set up after Algeria's seven-year war with France ended last March. Its establishment followed a political feud between Premier Benyoussef Ben Khedda and Vice Premier Ben Bella.

Mr. Ben Bella became a dominant figure in the bureau and a proponent of civilian rather than military control.

Willaya IV soldiers sealed off the Casbah after the shooting.

Continued on Page 4, Column 3

DE GAULLE AGREES TO A HEAVY GUARD

Also Pledges to Take Step to Insure His Succession

By ROBERT C. DOTY
Special to The New York Times.

PARIS, Aug. 29—President de Gaulle authorized today increased measures to protect his life. He also promised action to insure his succession.

The President, the target of assassination attempts last week and last year, confirmed to the Cabinet his intention to "take initiatives necessary to insure the continuity of the state, of the Republic and republican institutions." This was interpreted as a decision to seek constitutional amendments, almost certainly in the direction of a popular election of his eventual successor.

This selection by the whole nation, General de Gaulle believes, would supply the next President with the authority he has exercised by personal prestige.

Security Shift Planned

The present system provides for the naming of the President by "grand electors." They are members of Parliament, the general councils and the assemblies of overseas territories, elected representatives of municipal councils and the delegates of the member states in the French community.

General de Gaulle yielded to the pressing demands of Roger Frey, Interior Minister, that the President's safety be taken out of the hands of a small special unit under Presidential direction and turned over to the main security forces.

In the past, the President has dismissed attempts on his life with such phrases as "a joke in

Continued on Page 5, Column 1

United Press International Telephoto

DEFENDS DECISIONS IN ESTES CASE: Charles S. Murphy, Under Secretary of Agriculture, tells Senators he showed no favoritism in the treatment of Billie Sol Estes.

Cuba Puts Tight Controls On Labor to Raise Output

By United Press International.

HAVANA, Aug. 29—The regime of Premier Fidel Castro put tight controls today on the wages of Cuban workers, invoked stiff penalties for absenteeism and authorized the sharp curtailment of vacation time in an effort to increase production.

A decree signed by Maj. Augusto Martinez, the Labor Minister, emphasized that "all pay raises or any variation in the wage scale without the knowledge and approval of the Labor Ministry will be null and void."

[President Kennedy, at his news conference in Washington, rejected Congressional suggestions that the United States invade Cuba because of the reported presence there of Soviet troops.]

Transfers Authorized

The Cuban decree also authorized the transfers of workers from one establishment to another without their consent. Such transfers can be ordered as a penalty for absenteeism or because of production needs, according to the decree.

In a move that tightened control over education, the Cuban Government announced the establishment of a Committee on Extracurricular Activities to orient the thinking of children outside the classroom.

Among those on the committee are Vilma Espin, wife of Maj. Raul Castro, Armed Forces Minister; Lazaro Peña, Secretary General of the Cuban Workers Confederation and a top Communist leader, and Cesar Gomez, a leader of the Union of Young Communists.

The Government said the com-

Continued on Page 8, Column 3

SOVIET AGAIN ASKS UNCHECKED A-BAN

Plan to Stop All Tests Was Refused by West Earlier—Kennedy Does So Anew

By SYDNEY GRUSON
Special to The New York Times.

GENEVA, Aug. 29—The Soviet Union submitted to the disarmament conference today a formula for halting nuclear weapons tests that the United States and Britain have repeatedly termed unacceptable.

The formula calls for an unpoliced moratorium on underground tests and a ban on testing in the atmosphere, space and under water, all to take effect Jan. 1, 1963.

[In Washington President Kennedy rejected the Soviet proposal for a moratorium.]

The moratorium would last until a "permanent solution" was found for the problem of detecting and verifying underground tests, Vasily V. Kuznetsov, a Soviet First Deputy Foreign Minister, told the seventeen-nation conference.

Nigerian Backs Soviet Plan

To the disappointment of the United States and Britain, the Soviet call for a moratorium was supported by M. T. Mbu of Nigeria, the only delegate of the eight unaligned countries to speak at today's seventy-sixth disarmament session.

Mr. Mbu said he believed India shared Nigeria's views on the need for a moratorium if that was the way all testing could be halted.

The Soviet move was the answer to a British-American offer on Monday. That offer was a choice between a treaty banning all tests but including ob-

Continued on Page 2, Column 2

Arabia and Jordan Map Broad Merger

By The Associated Press.

AMMAN, Jordan, Aug. 29—The Kings of Saudi Arabia and Jordan, friends amid the hostilities of the Arab world, said tonight that they would merge their military forces and coordinate economic policies.

The unity moves of Kings Saud and Hussein were announced in a communiqué published here and in Saudi Arabia on a three-day meeting the monarchs held at Taif, Saudi Arabia.

Their joint statement and comments on it reflected continuing bitterness toward President Gamal Abdel Nasser of the United Arab Republic and affirmed one of the few issues on which they and other Arab leaders agree: continued enmity toward Israel.

They announced full adherence to "sacred Arab rights in

Continued on Page 6, Column 3

MURPHY DEFENDS ACTIONS ON ESTES AS FAIR AND JUST

Agriculture Aide, in Senate Hearing, Denies Showing Favoritism to the Texan

By J. ANTHONY LUKAS
Special to The New York Times.

WASHINGTON, Aug. 29—Under Secretary of Agriculture Charles S. Murphy spoke up in his own defense today in the Billie Sol Estes case.

He said that in his decisions in the case he had been guided by a desire to protect Mr. Estes' rights as well as the Government's interests.

Mr. Murphy told the Senate Permanent Subcommittee on Investigations that he had showed no favoritism toward Mr. Estes —"only the fairness and justice that every American has a right to expect from his Government."

"I think it was right to give anyone—including Billie Sol Estes—a fair chance to prove his case," he said.

Replies to Allegations

Mr. Murphy, the second-ranking official in the department, has been repeatedly named before the subcommittee as the key figure in the department's handling of the Estes case. Today was his first opportunity to state his position before the committee and to reply to allegations that he tried to help the Texas financier.

In the soft accents of his native North Carolina, Mr. Murphy read a twenty-nine-page statement and then answered questions from Senator John L. McClellan, Democrat of Arkansas, who heads the subcommittee.

Mr. McClellan's questioning was respectful but pointed. From time to time he emphasized his questions by pointing a finger directly at Mr. Murphy's face. Several times he pounded the table for further emphasis.

Testimony Will Continue

These gestures were the only open signs of tension between the two men. But few persons in the crowded Senate Caucus Room needed anything to underline the significance of the confrontation.

Senator McClellan said last week that either Mr. Murphy or Secretary of Agriculture Orville L. Freeman must have been trying to help Mr. Estes. Since the Senator had earlier praised Mr. Freeman for acting promptly when he knew all the facts, his statement was widely interpreted as an accusation against Mr. Murphy.

Mr. Murphy's testimony, which is expected to continue most of the week, is therefore widely regarded as the climax to the hearings, which the subcommittee has been holding since June 27.

Though the hearings are scheduled to continue two weeks more, the allegations that there was favoritism for

Continued on Page 16, Column 5

PRESIDENT WARNS AGAINST AID SLASH

Brands as 'Height of Folly' House Foes' Proposals to Cut Bill 1.5 Billion

Text of news conference and summary, Page 10.

By FELIX BELAIR Jr.
Special to The New York Times.

WASHINGTON, Aug. 29 — President Kennedy took issue sharply today with Congressional advocates of heavy cuts in his $4,674,000,000 foreign aid program.

The President told his news conference that "I can imagine nothing more short-sighted than to cut the heart out of this program." [Question 8, Page 10.]

House appropriations managers are demanding cuts of at least $1,500,000,000 below provisions of the authorization legislation.

The President said it struck him as "the height of folly" to appropriate $50,000,000,000 for the military establishment and additional amounts for the Atomic Energy Commission and then to cut the foreign aid program in a way that would force into the Communist bloc a number of countries whose independence was vital to the security of the United States.

"I find it very ironical," said Mr. Kennedy, "that those who make the strongest speeches

Continued on Page 10, Column 3

House Passes Works Bill To Assist Jobless Areas

By C. P. TRUSSELL
Special to The New York Times.

WASHINGTON, Aug. 29—The House passed today a $900,000,000 public works bill designed to relieve unemployment in economically depressed areas. It gave its approval by voice vote after rejecting, 221 to 192, a Republican attempt to kill the measure by sending it back to the Public Works Committee.

The bill now goes to the Senate, which passed a similar $1,500,000,000 measure last May. It is expected that the differences will be ironed out by Senate and House conferees and that President Kennedy will sign the resulting bill promptly after its ratification by both houses.

Neither the Senate nor the House bill would give the President all he asked for—$600,000,000 for immediate use on a matching basis plus $2,000,000,000 in stand-by funds for use in case of a recession.

The House measure would make the full $900,000,000 available immediately. The Senate had approved $750,000,000 in immediate appropriations and another $750,000,000 for use, if necessary, after June 30, 1963.

Matching Eased

The regular matching requirement was set in both the House and Senate bills at 50 per cent of project costs. It was argued in debate, however, that many of the more than a thousand communities declared eligible for aid would be unable, because of their depressed economies, to meet this share.

The House, by a voice vote, provided that communities unable to meet the 50 per cent requirement could get their projects by putting up 25 per cent. In some regions, it was said, the state governments could contribute this much on behalf of the communities benefited.

Although the Republicans had denounced the program as "a phony" based on "pork

Continued on Page 16, Column 1

PLAN ON DIVIDENDS BARRED IN SENATE

66-20 Poll Rejects Kennedy Proposal on Withholding —Stiff Curbs Also Fail

By JOHN D. MORRIS
Special to The New York Times.

WASHINGTON, Aug. 29 — The Senate rejected tonight President Kennedy's proposal for withholding personal income taxes on dividends and interest at the source. The vote was 66 to 20.

The action confirmed a Finance Committee recommendation to delete a House-approved withholding provision from the pending Administration tax revision bill.

Voting against the withholding plan were thirty-two Republicans and thirty-four Democrats. For it there were one Republican and nineteen Democrats.

Whether the final version of the bill will contain the disputed feature depends on compromise negotiations that will take place in a Senate-House conference committee after Senate passage of the measure. The outlook tonight was uncertain.

20% Withholding Sought

Under the House version, corporations, banks and other such institutions would be required to hold back 20 per cent of their payments of dividends and interest to stockholders and depositors. The amounts withheld would be turned over to the Treasury periodically.

Taxpayers could obtain refunds for overpayments after making final returns for the year. Those who did not expect to pay any taxes could obtain exemptions in advance of withholding.

The plan is designed to assure the collection of about $780,000,000 a year in taxes on income that is not now being reported to the Government. This would offset in part the revenue loss of $1,000,000,000 a year that the bill's other main feature would entail.

This other feature is known as the "investment incentive" plan, whereby businesses would be permitted to deduct from taxes up to $7 of every $100

Continued on Page 36, Column 5

State Bars Anthem As a School Prayer

By DOUGLAS DALES
Special to The New York Times.

ALBANY, Aug. 29 — Dr. James E. Allen, Commissioner of Education, ruled today that Hicksville, L. I., could not designate a portion of the National Anthem as an official school prayer. But he added that there was nothing to prevent reading, reciting or singing it in the schools.

In a five-page decision, the Commissioner said that a resolution adopted by the school board on June 29 clearly violated the decision by the United States Supreme Court that the use of the Board of Regents' nondenominational prayer was unconstitutional.

The crux of Dr. Allen's opinion was that the lines of "The Star-Spangled Banner" had been adopted as an "official prayer."

Dr. Allen also ruled today that

Continued on Page 18, Column 2

Lehman Endorses Regular Democrat

By LEONARD INGALLS

Former Senator Herbert H. Lehman, long identified with the reform movement in the Democratic party, endorsed a regular Democrat for re-election yesterday.

Mr. Lehman said he favored Assemblyman William F. Passannante, an ally of Carmine G. De Sapio, former leader of Tammany Hall. Mr. Passannante is opposing a reform candidate in the Democratic primary in Manhattan's First Assembly District.

Leaders in the party said Mr. Lehman's move was significant for several reasons. It was his first break with the reformers. He was said to have acted because he had been concerned about the activities of extreme elements in the reform group.

What disturbed Mr. Lehman particularly was the refusal of

Continued on Page 30, Column 2

Lower Deck of George Washington Bridge Is Opened

The New York Times

Acknowledging cheers of the crowd on the new deck are, from left: Governor Rockefeller, S. Sloan Colt, chairman of Port of New York Authority; Gov. Richard J. Hughes of New Jersey, and Linda Feria of Ridgefield, N. J., who attended as guest of Governor Hughes.

By JOSEPH C. INGRAHAM

A new era in the life of the George Washington Bridge started at 3:17 P. M. yesterday when the six-lane lower deck went into service. The opening of the second deck makes the bridge across the Hudson the only fourteen-lane vehicular crossing in the world.

At the dedication ceremony, Governor Rockefeller hailed the majestic span as a bridge of unity between New York and New Jersey. He said the second deck and the intricate network of new approach roads were symbolic of the spirit of cooperation between all levels of government and civic groups. Gov. Richard J. Hughes of New Jersey as-

Continued on Page 59, Column 2

NEWS INDEX

Johnny Carson replaced Jack Paar on *The Tonight Show* and gave NBC its most popular late-night talk-show yet. He is seen here with Ed McMahon (left).

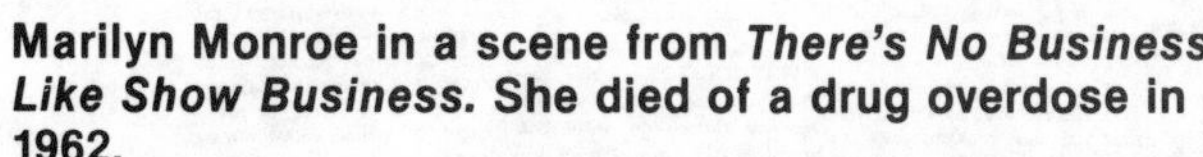

Marilyn Monroe in a scene from ***There's No Business Like Show Business.*** She died of a drug overdose in 1962.

Eleanor Roosevelt is seen talking to Adlai Stevenson, Chief U.S. Delegate to the U.N., shortly before her death. He was the only visitor outside of her family permitted to see her at the end.

"All the News That's Fit to Print"

The New York Times.

LATE CITY EDITION
Sunny today; fair and cool tonight. Mostly fair and pleasant tomorrow.
Temp. range: 70–50; yesterday: 68—54. Temp.-Hum. Index: 64; yesterday: 65.

NEWS SUMMARY AND INDEX, PAGE 95

SECTION ONE

VOL. CXII. No. 38,235. NEW YORK, SUNDAY, SEPTEMBER 30, 1962. 35¢ beyond 50-mile zone from New York City, except on Long Island. 50¢ beyond 200-mile zone from New York City, higher in air delivery cities. THIRTY CENTS

KENNEDY FEDERALIZES MISSISSIPPI'S GUARD; MOBILIZES TROOPS, ORDERS STATE TO YIELD; ADDRESSES NATION TODAY ON RACIAL CRISIS

PRESIDENT CALLS RUSK AND BRITON TO DISCUSS BERLIN

Lord Home and Envoys Will Fly to Capital Today as German Crisis Grows

By E. W. KENWORTHY
Special to The New York Times

WASHINGTON, Sept. 29—President Kennedy will meet here tomorrow with high United States and British officials to discuss the Berlin situation and other foreign policy questions.

The luncheon at the White House will be attended by Secretary of State Dean Rusk; the Earl of Home, the British Foreign Secretary; David K. E. Bruce, the United States Ambassador in London, and Sir David Ormsby Gore, the British Ambassador in Washington.

[Mr. Rusk said in New York that assertions by the Communists that they had no troops in Laos were "nonsense and the world knows it."]

Newport Trip Called Off

President Kennedy had planned to fly to Newport this afternoon and have luncheon there with the British and American officials. However, at 3 P.M. the White House said he had called off the trip.

Andrew T. Hatcher, associate press secretary, was reticent at the time about saying that the trip cancellation was related to the integration crisis in Mississippi.

The ministers and ambassadors will fly here tomorrow from New York, where they are attending sessions of the United Nations General Assembly.

The White House did not say what would be discussed. But officials here said it was obvious that Berlin and increasing tensions there would demand much of the meeting's attention.

High Administration officials have not disguised their deep concern over the lack of interest on the part of the Soviet Union in various proposals by the United States and Britain to reduce tension over Berlin. For example, Soviet officials

Continued on Page 26, Column 1

Brandt, Rockefeller and Wagner Lead Steuben March

The New York Times

Mayor Willy Brandt of West Berlin joins Mayor Wagner and Governor Rockefeller at the head of about 25,000 marchers during annual Steuben Day parade up Fifth Avenue.

By DAVID BINDER

The Bavarians yodeled, the Cologners danced a two-step, the Rhinelanders sang, the Hamburgers cried "Hummel Hummel" and the bands played Berliner melodies as 25,000 German-Americans marched up Fifth Avenue yesterday.

The occasion was the fifth annual Steuben Parade, honoring Baron Friedrich Wilhelm von Steuben, the general from Magdeburg who helped George Washington drill the Continental Army during the American Revolution. Mayor Willy Brandt of West Berlin was the honored guest. German touches were everywhere—in black corduroy carpenter costumes, gymnastic stunts

Continued on Page 52, Column 3

JOHNSON IS FINED

Barnett's Lieutenant Is Liable to a Penalty of $5,000 a Day

Text of court order finding Johnson guilty, Page 66.

By HEDRICK SMITH
Special to The New York Times

NEW ORLEANS, Sept. 29—Lieut. Gov. Paul B. Johnson Jr. of Mississippi was held in civil contempt of Federal court orders today in his state's integration crisis.

A three-judge panel of the United States Court of Appeals for the Fifth Circuit tried Mr. Johnson in absentia. He was found guilty of defying court orders forbidding any official interference with the desegregation of the University of Mississippi.

The court gave Mr. Johnson until 11 A.M. Tuesday to purge himself of contempt or face a fine of $5,000 a day. The fine is to start building up immediately, but no money is to be collected until Tuesday.

The opinion closely followed the language used in a contempt ruling yesterday against Gov. Ross R. Barnett except that Mr. Johnson is not initially subject to arrest.

Fine Might Increase

However, the court ruled that if Mr. Johnson became Acting Governor and refused to comply with its orders, he would face the same penalties as Mr. Barnett.

This means that, in such a situation, Mr. Johnson could face arrest and a fine of $10,000 a day unless he retreated and ordered Mississippi officials to comply with the court's desegregation orders.

Like Governor Barnett, Mr. Johnson did not appear at the court hearing.

There were no attorneys in court to represent him. However, the two attorneys for the state of Mississippi were in the courtroom—Charles Clarke of Jackson and John C. Satterfield of Yazoo City.

They entered no pleadings or arguments in Mr. Johnson's behalf. However, they submitted

Continued on Page 66, Column 1

Federal Troops Massing At a Base Near Memphis

Soldiers Landed by Army Helicopters for Possible Duty in Mississippi Crisis —Engineers Ordered Into State

Special to The New York Times.

MEMPHIS, Tenn., Sept. 29—Hundreds of Army troops and about 500 United States marshals were in the huge Memphis Naval Air Station near here tonight.

The Government kept flying men in during the day for a showdown next week with Gov. Ross R. Barnett of Mississippi over the court-ordered desegregation of the University of Mississippi.

[President Kennedy ordered an Army Engineer battalion to move into Mississippi to set up a tent city for 700 United States marshals, according to United Press International.]

Large Army helicopters landed 200 to 250 soldiers during the day. Newsmen were barred from the air station, 18 miles north of Memphis, but they counted 16 helicopters as they landed and discharged troops.

The Pentagon in Washington admitted that the helicopters were here.

Earlier, about 400 men had been flown in by Navy transport planes. The armed soldiers were confined to the base.

Sailors leaving the base on weekend liberty told newsmen about the soldiers' being here.

The Department of Defense denied that any paratroop units had been sent to Memphis. So did Gen. C. W. G. Rich, commander of Fort Campbell, Army base in Kentucky. It was from here that 110 men of the 70th Battalion of Engineers were sent to the air station yesterday.

Gen. H. H. Howze, commander of Fort Bragg, Army base in North Carolina, would not confirm that paratroopers had been

Continued on Page 68, Column 5

ACTS AT MIDNIGHT

President Holds Talks With Gov. Barnett but to No Avail

Text of Kennedy proclamation is printed on Page 68.

By ANTHONY LEWIS
Special to The New York Times

WASHINGTON, Sunday, Sept. 30.—President Kennedy committed the full weight of the Federal Government at midnight last night to end Mississippi's defiance of the Union.

He called the state's National Guard into Federal service.

He sent troops of the United States Army to Memphis, Tenn., to stand in reserve if more force were needed.

And he issued a proclamation calling on the Government and people of Mississippi to abandon what had become the most serious challenge to Federal authority since the Civil War.

Addresses Nation Tonight

Tonight, the President goes on the air to explain the situation to the American people. He will speak over all national television and radio networks at 7:30 New York time.

The President took what one official called his "irrevocable steps" after three telephone conversations yesterday with Governor Ross R. Barnett of Mississippi.

In a statement issued at five minutes before midnight, the acting White House press secretary, Andrew T. Hatcher, said that in the conversations "the President was unable to receive from Governor Barnett satisfactory assurances that law and order could, or would, be maintained in Oxford, Miss., during the coming week."

Crisis Over Negro Student

Oxford is the seat of the University of Mississippi. Mississippi's defiance of Federal court orders to admit a Negro, James H. Meredith, to the university, has provoked the Federal-state crisis.

Mr. Hatcher said the action was being taken at that late hour—and telegrams dispatched to the guard commanders—so that the units "will be available for service Monday." Most Guardsmen are one-day-a-week soldiers, and it will take time to mobilize them.

The regular Army troops sent to Memphis comprised 900 military policemen, especially

Continued on Page 68, Column 1

KENNEDY WISHES BEN BELLA WELL

'Warmest Congratulations' Sent as U. S. Recognizes New Algerian Regime

By PETER BRAESTRUP
Special to The New York Times

WASHINGTON, Sept. 29—President Kennedy today sent "warmest congratulations" to Ahmed Ben Bella, Premier of independent Algeria's newly formed Government.

Mr. Kennedy, who as a Senator endorsed Algerian self-rule in 1957, wished Mr. Ben Bella "every success" and said that "my Government and my people share my earnest desire to foster and extend the cordial relations that exist between our two countries."

The President's message coincided with the State Department's announcement of formal diplomatic recognition of the newly established Government of Algeria.

New Premier to Visit Here

Yesterday Mr. Ben Bella announced his Cabinet and pledged a "neutralist and nonengaged" foreign policy in a speech before the week-old National Assembly. The Assembly subsequently approved the Cabinet list, 159 to 1 with 19 abstentions.

Secretary of State Dean Rusk sent congratulations to the Algerian Foreign Minister, Mohammed Khemisti, saying that he looked forward to a meeting "in the near future."

Informed sources said today that President Kennedy and Secretary Rusk would meet with Mr. Ben Bella sometime after the Algerian Premier's arrival in the United States, possibly late next week, to head

Continued on Page 4, Column 1

Norway Criticizes Paris Plan to Build National A-Forces

By HENRY GINIGER
Special to The New York Times

PARIS, Sept. 29—The four-day state visit by King Olav V of Norway ended today with a strong attack by the Norwegian Foreign Minister, Dr. Halvard M. Lange, on national atomic striking forces in Europe such as that planned by France.

King Olav took leave of President de Gaulle this morning before flying to Oslo. He had been warmly received and responded with the same warmth in a recorded message of thanks that was broadcast over the French radio and television.

It was left to Dr. Lange, who had accompanied the King, to underline the serious divergences between the Norwegian and French Governments on Western defense. He did so in a statement to the French News Agency.

Reliance Placed on the U. S.

Dr. Lange said the Western alliance must rest on confidence among its members, for "otherwise it has no sense." He said that Norway, placing her confidence in the United States' assumption of the burden and responsibility for the West's nuclear armament, was hostile to national atomic forces in Europe.

President de Gaulle has often said that France must assume responsibility for her defense, and he and his aides have left the widespread impression that they are not wholly confident of the United States' ability or willingness to defend Western Europe.

Dr. Lange said Western Europe should assume greater shares of the burden of conventional armaments and of "help to underdeveloped nations, a

Continued on Page 23, Column 2

U.S. TELLS SOVIET TO OUST 2 AS SPIES

Says Aides at U. N. Bought Secrets From Sailor, Held Here in $100,000 Bail

By EMANUEL PERLMUTTER

The United States yesterday demanded the expulsion of two members of the Soviet delegation to the United Nations who were involved with an American sailor in an espionage plot.

In a sharply worded note to the Soviet mission, the United States said: "As host to the United Nations, the Government of the United States strongly protests the espionage activities directed against the internal security of the United States."

The Russians countered a few hours later with a note charging that Federal agents had illegally arrested, manhandled and questioned the two

Continued on Page 29, Column 1

Principals in Naval Secrets Case

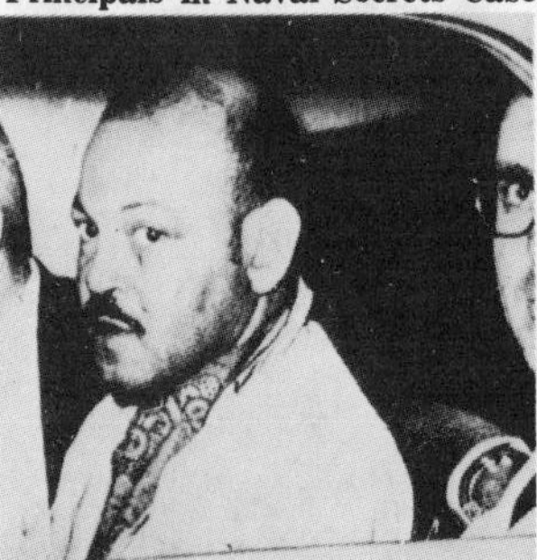

Nelson Cornelious Drummond, a Navy petty officer, sitting between Federal officers after his arrest early yesterday.

Ivan Y. Vyrodov, member of Soviet mission to the U. N.

Associated Press

Yevgeny M. Prokhorov, second secretary of mission.

Longshore Walkout Scheduled Tonight; Ships Rush to Sea

By EDWARD A. MORROW

A steady stream of ships sailed out of New York and other Atlantic and Gulf ports yesterday to avoid being caught in a longshoremen's strike that appeared certain to begin at 12:01 A.M. tomorrow.

Work on the piers continued at a record level as shipowners filed unusual weekend calls for labor with the Waterfront Commission.

The bistate agency said that 17,459 men had been hired to work 101 ships at 80 piers at time-and-a-half pay. On a normal Saturday the waterfront force is 2,000 to 3,000 men.

Sixty-two ships passed the quarantine station outbound yesterday. This number would have been even higher had not some operators decided to postpone the sailing of 12 ships until today to accept all the tonnage that could be moved off the piers before the deadline.

Cruise Liner Held Up

The 591 passengers aboard the Queen of Bermuda, which was scheduled to sail at 3 P.M. for Hamilton, Bermuda, found their cruise departure delayed until 8 A.M. this morning so the vessel could load cargo.

While the peak of the effort to get ships out has passed, a Sunday hiring record is expected to be broken today, a Waterfront Commission spokesman said.

The agency has received calls for 8,500 men to work 35 piers at double their regular pay of $3.02 an hour. The normal Sunday work force averages 1,000.

Federal mediators failed yes-

Continued on Page 44, Column 5

SUPREME COURT OPENS TOMORROW

Legislative Districting Still Among Major Problems—Goldberg to Be Sworn

Special to The New York Times

WASHINGTON, Sept. 29—The Supreme Court convenes Monday for a new term that promises to be one of high drama and significance.

Two issues that dominated the last term—legislative districting and prayers in the schools—will be back in new and difficult guises.

The court will consider such other controversial problems as restaurant segregation, contempt of Congress and censorship of books and movies.

Goldberg to Take Oath

The presence of two new justices on the bench will heighten interest. In a court that has so frequently been divided 5-to-4 in recent years, two changes in membership could shift the balance of judicial philosophies.

Arthur J. Goldberg, appointed to replace Felix Frankfurter on his retirement, is scheduled to take the oath of office Monday. Byron R. White succeeded Charles E. Whittaker last April, too late to permit any real appraisal of his views last term.

Seldom, if ever, have new members of the Supreme Court faced questions so intellectually challenging or with so great a potential impact on

Continued on Page 74 Column 3

GIANTS AND COLTS SPLIT TWO GAMES

Dodgers Clinch at Least a Tie for First Place

The league-leading Los Angeles Dodgers lost to the St. Louis Cardinals yesterday but remained a game ahead of the San Francisco Giants who split a double-header with the Houston Colts. The results assured the Dodgers of at least a tie for first place.

FOOTBALL

Army and Columbia won major college football contests in New York. Scores of leading games:

Army	9	Syracuse	2
Auburn	22	Tennessee	21
Boston Coll.	28	Villanova	13
California	22	San Jose St.	8
Colgate	23	Cornell	12
Columbia	22	Brown	20
Dartmouth	27	Mass.	3
Duke	21	S. Carolina	8
Ga. Tech	17	Florida	0
Harvard	27	Lehigh	6
Holy Cross	16	Buffalo	6
Iowa	28	Oregon St.	8
Minnesota	0	Missouri	0
Mississippi	14	Kentucky	0
Navy	20	W. & M.	16
Nebraska	25	Michigan	13
Notre Dame	13	Oklahoma	7
Ohio State	41	N. Carolina	7
Oregon	35	Utah	8
Penn	13	Lafayette	11
Penn State	20	Air Force	6
Princeton	15	Rutgers	7
Stanford	16	Mich. St.	13
Washington	28	Illinois	7
Yale	18	Conn.	14

HORSE RACING

Kelso won the $115,200 Woodward Stakes as the Aqueduct meeting ended. Jaipur was a distant second to the favorite.

Details in Section 5

U.N. Says Katanga Still Recruits Troops in Violation of Promise

BY SAM POPE BREWER
Special to The New York Times.

UNITED NATIONS, N. Y., Sept. 29—The United Nations has accused the Government of Katanga of continuing to recruit mercenaries in spite of repeated promises not to do so.

The charges were made in a letter from the chief United Nations officer in the Congo, Robert K. A. Gardiner, to President Moise Tshombe of Katanga Province dated last Tuesday and made public here last night.

[In Elisabethville President Tshombe likened the United Nations charges to "the stories of sea serpents or the abominable snowman." He said such charges always precede an attack on Katanga.]

Mr. Gardiner said the Katangese gendarmerie "has been receiving reinforcements for some time both in the form of troops and material."

He said: "I am worried to see that in spite of your affirmations that there would be no more mercenaries serving the Katangese Gendarmerie, bodies of Europeans killed in combat between the National Congolese Army and the Gendarmerie have been found."

In further support of the charges, Mr. Gardiner said that the United Nations organization in the Congo had a complete file of the names, addresses and photographs of mercenaries who had arrived in Katanga in recent months. It also has copies of payrolls signed by the men, he said.

Mr. Gardiner charged that recruiting was still being carried on through newspaper advertisements, especially in

Continued on Page 8, Column 1

Traffic Overhaul at Lincoln Sq. Called Basic to Orderly Growth

By JOSEPH C. INGRAHAM

The city was urged yesterday to overhaul traffic patterns around Lincoln Center before approving any future construction.

The proposal for traffic relief was submitted in a report by Day & Zimmerman, Philadelphia consulting engineers.

The firm was hired by the city on April 23 to conduct a $30,000 study of the effects of future developments on traffic and mass transit, with "particular emphasis on the impact that the proposed Litho City housing development would impose."

Among the principal recommendations were the following:

¶Widening and rebuilding parts of the West Side Highway.

¶Changing the traffic pattern in local streets.

¶Adding crosstown express streets and rebuilding existing ones.

¶Changing the traffic pattern within the Lincoln Center for the Performing Arts.

The Litho City project, sponsored by Local 1, Amalgamated Lithographers of America, is planned along the Hudson River between 60th and 70th Streets.

Consisting of 17 buildings of 23 and 33 stories over the New York Central's freight yards, the project would tower above the western side of Lincoln Center.

The consultants stressed that their broad traffic study had been predicated largely on the Litho City project. They noted that the original plans had called for 6,000 apartments for 15,000 to 20,000 persons, but said

Continued on Page 85, Column 3

Today's Sections

*Included in all copies in the New York metropolitan area and adjacent territory.

Index to Subjects

Joan Baez drew large audiences both as a folksinger and an activist.

Folksingers Peter, Paul and Mary hit the top of the charts in 1962.

"All the News That's Fit to Print"

The New York Times.

LATE CITY EDITION
U. S. Weather Bureau Report (Page 61) forecasts: Sunny and mild today and tonight. Increasing cloudiness tomorrow. Temp. range: 73—52; yesterday: 72—50.

VOL. CXII. No. 38,236. © 1962 by The New York Times Company. Times Square, New York 36, N. Y. NEW YORK, MONDAY, OCTOBER 1, 1962. 10 cents beyond 50-mile zone from New York City except on Long Island. Higher in air delivery cities. FIVE CENTS

NEGRO AT MISSISSIPPI U. AS BARNETT YIELDS; 3 DEAD IN CAMPUS RIOT, 6 MARSHALS SHOT; GUARDSMEN MOVE IN; KENNEDY MAKES PLEA

Khrushchev Invites Kennedy to Moscow; White House Studies Bid for Berlin Talk

Mrs. Kennedy Is Urged to Make Trip—Udall Carried Message

By JAMES RESTON
Special to The New York Times

WASHINGTON, Sept. 30—Premier Khrushchev has sent a private invitation to President Kennedy to visit the Soviet Union.

It is understood that the message was delivered to the President by Secretary of the Interior Stewart L. Udall, who recently visited the Soviet Union.

The Soviet leader first made the suggestion in a five-hour talk with Mr. Udall, after he had stressed the need for another major effort to reach an accommodation on the Berlin problem.

Later, just as Mr. Udall was leaving, Mr. Khrushchev again said that he hoped it would be possible for the President to go to Moscow and take Mrs. Kennedy along. No date was mentioned, but the invitation was passed on to the President and is now the subject of discussion within the State Department and the White House.

The New York Times
Stewart L. Udall

No decision has been reached. The project is being studied in the light of increased tension over Berlin and the growing conviction here that the Soviet Union will sign a peace treaty with the Communist East German regime, probably in mid-November.

Recent conversations between Secretary of State Dean Rusk and the Soviet Foreign Minister, Andrei A. Gromyko, about Berlin have been courteous and correct. However, they have failed to indicate any new basis for a Berlin accommodation.

The President discussed the Berlin question at luncheon today with the Earl of Home, the British Foreign Secretary. Mr. Rusk, Under Secretary of State George W. Ball, David Bruce, the Ambassador to Britain, and the British Ambassador in Washington, Sir David Ormsby Gore.

It is not known whether the Khrushchev invitation was considered. A communiqué issued from the White House later

Continued on Page 2, Column 4

U.S. and British Officials Review Parleys With Gromyko on Crisis

PRESIDENT MEETS WITH LORD HOME ON CURBING CUBA

They Agree on Peril in Rise of Communism—British Policy Shift Hinted

By TAD SZULC
Special to The New York Times

WASHINGTON, Sept. 30—President Kennedy and the Earl of Home, the British Foreign Secretary, discussed at the White House today ways of "containing further Communist expansion and subversion in the Caribbean."

The announcement in a joint statement that "they agreed on the serious nature of developments in Cuba" suggested that Britain may have altered her policy of regarding the Cuban affair as a matter of concern to the United States alone.

But it was understood that Mr. Kennedy and Lord Home were not able to work out a solution to the problem of the chartering of British and other Western Allied ships to the Soviet Union to carry petroleum and other strategic cargoes to Cuba.

Lord Home was reported to have repeated for Mr. Kennedy the standing British view that the Government had no control over privately owned shipping and that no official restrictions were possible while Britain maintained diplomatic relations with Cuba.

Role in Patrols Possible

However, diplomats indicated that Britain's possible cooperation with the United States could extend to her participation in the patrolling of the Caribbean against the movement of arms or agents from Cuba, particularly in the direction of British Guiana.

British Guiana's Prime Minister, Dr. Cheddi B. Jagan, is a Marxist and in recent months his Government has sought to increase economic and political ties with Cuba. The British Government is concerned by the situation.

President Kennedy and Lord Home also reviewed the questions of Berlin, the Congo, Laos and hopes of achieving a nuclear test ban. They were together for two hours and twenty minutes at luncheon and in an additional talk.

Lord Home and Secretary of State Dean Rusk flew here for the meeting from New York, where they were attending the sessions of the United Nations General Assembly. From the White House, British and Amer-

Continued on Page 3, Column 1

U. S. MARSHALS USE TEAR GAS IN MISSISSIPPI: Two of the marshals, armed with riot clubs and wearing gas masks and helmets, move in on the rioters on University of Mississippi campus after Federal officers hurled tear gas at the demonstrators.

United Press International Telephoto

TEAR GAS IS USED

Mob Attacks Officers —2,500 Troops Are Sent to Oxford

By CLAUDE SITTON
Special to The New York Times

OXFORD, Miss., Monday, Oct. 1—James H. Meredith, a 29-year-old Negro, was admitted last night to the University of Mississippi campus and was scheduled to enroll today in the all-white institution.

A riot broke out shortly after his arrival, and marauding bands of students and adults, many of whom were from other states, were still ranging through the campus and the town early today.

At least three men were killed, one of them unidentified. Fifty persons were being treated for various injuries in the university infirmary. Six United States marshals were shot, one was critically wounded.

Although the riot started at about 7:30 P. M., Central standard time, Army troops did not arrive until five and a half hours later. About 200 military policemen arrived from Memphis shortly after 1 A. M. (3 A. M., E. D. T.)

[Army headquarters received word early today that about 200 more persons had joined the rioting mob and that the situation on the campus was "very bad," The Associated Press reported. About 2,500 regular Army military policemen and infantrymen were converging on Oxford. Army observers in Mississippi reported to headquarters that automatic weapons fire was being aimed at the registration building.]

Marshals Besieged

A small detachment of Mississippi National Guardsmen went to the aid of a besieged force of 300 deputy marshals in the university administration building. The marshals were under the command of top Justice Department officials, including Nicholas de B. Katzenbach, deputy attorney general.

For a time, it appeared that the marshals would not be able to hold the building, which is called the Lyceum. But barrage after barrage of tear gas discouraged the rioters, and they began to break up.

A number of other Mississippi National Guardsmen had arrived early today at the armory on the eastern outskirts of town. But there was considerable delay before they began a drive to the campus.

Automobiles loaded with roughly dressed whites, some of whom were from Alabama, began pulling into the campus shortly after the state highway patrol withdrew from the campus entrances early last night.

Clouds of tear gas billowed around the Administration building.

The tree-dotted mall in front

Continued on Page 23, Column 6

SHIPPING TIED UP IN PIER WALKOUT

Longshoremen Go on Strike From Maine to Texas—U. S. Action Expected

By EDWARD A. MORROW

Longshoremen struck in all ports from Maine to Texas at 12:01 this morning as their three-year contract expired.

Leaders of the International Longshoremen's Association, representing 75,000 members, said their action was the result of a lockout. Spokesmen for the New York Shipping Association, which sets the industry pattern for the Atlantic and Gulf Coasts, called it a strike.

A Sunday work record was set in the Port of New York yesterday, with 10 times the normal number of longshoremen employed. Fifty-four ships sailed before the midnight deadline.

The strike was not expected to cause any immediate hardship on the consumer public here, but thousands of trans-Atlantic passengers arriving here this week may be inconvenienced.

No strike negotiations were set, and it was apparent that both sides expected the problem to be put on President Kennedy's desk. His probable action will be to invoke the Taft-Hartley Act to bring the longshoremen back to work during an 80-day cooling-off period.

The President can request an injunction after a finding is made that a strike endangers

Continued on Page 14, Column 4

Giants and Dodgers End Season in a Tie

The Los Angeles Dodgers and the San Francisco Giants ended the National League season in a tie for first place yesterday and will play a two-of-three game series to determine the champion. The playoff will start today in San Francisco and move tomorrow to Los Angeles.

Two eighth-inning home runs set up the pennant tie. Willie Mays walloped one that lifted the Giants to a 2-1 victory over the Houston Colts. Gene Oliver of the St. Louis Cardinals belted the homer that defeated the Dodgers, 1—0.

The winner of the playoff will meet the New York Yankees in the World Series starting in the West Coast city on Thursday. The series games in New York will be played next Sunday and Monday and, if necessary, Tuesday.

Details on Page 48.

Dutch Control Ends In West New Guinea As U.N. Takes Over

By A. M. ROSENTHAL
Special to The New York Times

HOLLANDIA, New Guinea, Monday, Oct. 1—A brief and delicate United Nations experiment in a transfer of power began here today in a public square.

More than 350 years of rule in the East by the Netherlands had turned a small European country into a great colonial power. That rule ended without pomp, and quietly passed into history today, totally defeated by Asian nationalism.

Once the Dutch ruled over all the islands and riches of the East Indies. Thirteen years ago they gave up control to the new republic of Indonesia, keeping one territory, West New Guinea, which was known as Netherlands New Guinea.

About twenty Indonesians in civilian tunics watched today as a Guatemalan official of the United Nations read the proclamation ending Dutch rule in New Guinea, and began seven months of United Nations jurisdiction that will end in the transfer of authority to Indonesia on May 1.

500 Netherlanders Remain

Also in the square were representatives of Australia, which rules the eastern half of New Guinea and is watching with some nervousness the arrival of an Asian power on her frontiers.

No flags were raised at the public ceremony. The United Nation had planned to raise its banner and the Dutch flag. But Papuans demanded the raising also of a banner symbolizing the New Guinea independence movement.

To avoid antagonizing them or the Indonesians, the United Nations dispensed with the public flag ceremony and instead merely hoisted the Dutch and United Nations banner over United Nations headquarters.

There were a few score Netherlanders in the crowd. Only about 500 of the original 2,700 Dutch officials remain in New Guinea. Most Dutch women and children have left, and a Greek ship will carry others home next week.

From today until May 1 the United Nations will be in formal control of a territory three

Continued on Page 8, Column 3

NEWS INDEX

CHOU IS ADAMANT IN SOVIET DISPUTE

Upholds Aid for 'Liberation' Wars—Speech Is Viewed as Rebuke to Moscow

Special to The New York Times

HONG KONG, Sept. 30—Premier Chou En-lai declared in Peking tonight that no one could force Communist China to change the "just stand it takes in international affairs."

His statement was interpreted here as a reply to a recent Soviet assertion that economic tasks must take precedence over political tasks in the Communist bloc. The Chinese Communists hold that the bloc should give priority to political tasks by actively aiding "liberation struggles" in various countries.

Premier Chou asserted that "imperialist reactionaries of various countries and modern revisionists" had, in collaboration with one another, "continually launched anti-Chinese campaigns in an attempt to isolate China and compel China to change the just" stand.

"But their attempt is completely futile," he said. "It is they themselves, not China, who

Continued on Page 4, Column 4

New York Times Begins Printing Western Edition in Los Angeles

Special to The New York Times.

LOS ANGELES, Sept. 30—The New York Times began printing here today a Western edition for readers in thirteen Western states, including Alaska and Hawaii.

The innovation marks the first time in the United States that a daily newspaper of general readership has been printed in two cities simultaneously. The first issue was that of Monday, Oct. 1.

The operation is being accomplished by means of a speedy method of long-distance typesetting. Text coded onto punched paper tape in New York is transmitted over telephone lines across the continent at 1,000 words a minute. The electric impulses produce a duplicate tape here, which is fed into typesetting machines.

Perforating a single tape in New York simultaneously produces tape for use in Los Angeles, and in Paris for The New York Times's two-year-old International Edition.

The Western Edition will be essentially a duplicate of The New York Times, now 111 years old. The main differences will be the exclusion of news of purely local New York interest and the additional Western advertising.

The new edition will be printed six days a week, Monday through Saturday. A morning newspaper, it will be distributed primarily by mail, arriving in cities of distribution throughout the area on the day of publication. It will also be sold on newsstands at 10 cents a copy.

Special dispatches and features from The New York Times's Sunday Edition will appear in the Western Edition. A four-page Review of the Week section will appear regularly on Mondays. The Western Edition will regularly include The New York Times's full business and financial report and market tables.

The New York Times's president and publisher, Orvil E. Dryfoos, explained that the new edition was being inaugurated "in direct response to readers' demand," as reflected in the suggestions of thousands of Western residents after the establishment of the simultaneous International Edition in Paris.

The Western Edition, Mr. Dryfoos added, "will seek to

Continued on Page 27, Column 1

BARNETT GIVES IN; PLEADS FOR CALM

Declares Mississippi Was 'Overpowered' by U. S. —Vows a Court Fight

Text of Barnett's statement will be found on Page 23.

By PETER KIHSS
Special to The New York Times

JACKSON, Miss., Sept. 30—Gov. Ross R. Barnett, declaring that his state had been "physically overpowered" by the Federal Government, gave up his fight tonight to keep a Negro out of the University of Mississippi.

In a statement issued here, the Governor announced that Mississippi would keep up a struggle in the courts against the admission of James H. Meredith, who was placed in residence at the university tonight under escort of Federal marshals.

But with the Mississippi National Guard mobilized and Federal troops entering the state to enforce the Federal court's order for Mr. Meredith's admission, Governor Barnett declared that Mississippians "must at all odds preserve the peace and avoid bloodshed."

Crowds that had been rallied earlier by the White Citizens Council here to support the Governor in his fight against racial desegregation heard broadcasts of the Governor's statement on portable transistor radios.

Crowd Is Silent

They were silent. The state's position had been crumbling for an hour or more, since Mr. Meredith had been escorted on to the university campus at Oxford.

Just before midnight Governor Barnett issued a statement that he would continue his crusade. This apparently was to counter interpretation that he had backed down. However, it did not indicate any change in his projected legal tactics.

The statement said: "I will never yield a single inch in my determination to win the fight we are all engaged in. I call on all Mississippians to keep the faith and courage. We will never surrender."

Earlier, thousands of segregationists ringed the block on which the Governor's mansion stands. They had been called there by the Citizens Council to protect the Governor against a possible Federal effort to arrest him.

But inside the mansion, Gov-

Continued on Page 23, Column 1

TONIGHT at 8:30 P.M.: "Fiorello," Complete Score. Radio Station WQXR, 1560 AM—96.3 FM.

President Asks Mississippi To Comply With U.S. Laws

By ANTHONY LEWIS
Special to The New York Times.

WASHINGTON, Sept. 30—President Kennedy appealed to the students and the people of Mississippi tonight to comply peacefully with Federal law and bring the desegregation crisis to an end. "The eyes of the nation and all the world are upon you and upon all of us," he said, "and the honor of your university and state are in the balance."

The President spoke to the nation on television less than an hour after Gov. Ross R. Barnett of Mississippi pulled back from his all-out defiance of Federal authority. The Governor indicated he would no longer attempt to block the enrollment of James H. Meredith, a Negro, at the University of Mississippi.

Kennedy's speech, proclamation, Executive order and wire to Barnett are on Page 22.

Mr. Kennedy expressed cautious hope that the great Federal-state conflict, the gravest since the Civil War, was coming to a peaceful end. He said Federal Court orders "are beginning to be carried out."

But he qualified his optimism most carefully, and indeed made clear that the Government was waiting anxiously to see how Mississippi officials and citizens behaved. There was still much concern here tonight about violence at the university in Oxford.

There were no recriminations in the President's talk, nor even a reference to Governor Barnett. It was addressed pri-

Continued on Page 22, Column 1

Morgenthau Urges Off-Track Bet Vote

By CLAYTON KNOWLES

Robert M. Morgenthau, Democratic candidate for Governor, put himself on record twice yesterday in favor of a statewide referendum on off-track betting.

He acknowledged his misgivings about the proposal, originally advanced by Mayor Wagner as a solution for city fiscal difficulties. But the candidate said his personal views would "have to be weighed against the need for additional revenues."

It has been widely estimated that legalized off-track betting would produce $100,000,000 a year in new revenue for the city and state.

In a second new stand, Mr. Morgenthau said it was his feeling that the proposal for a bonus for veterans of the Korean War was another "one of the things that should be put to the voters."

The Democratic platform

Continued on Page 34, Column 2

A.E.C. MAY CREATE ATOM-ROCKET CITY

Nevada Desert Site Studied as Nuclear Missile Work Encounters Setbacks

By GLADWIN HILL
Special to The New York Times

LOS ANGELES, Sept. 30—Unpublicized accidents, delays and disappointments in the development of a nuclear-propelled rocket are forcing the Atomic Energy Commission to consider, reluctantly, the creation of a new Oak Ridge in the Nevada Desert.

The objective of the new atomic company town would be to make the hazardous experimental work more palatable to personnel urgently needed to push along the lagging $4,000,000-a-week Rover project.

Most of the 700 persons now involved in the work have to spend four hours a day commuting between the desert test site and Las Vegas, 100 miles to the south. Living in the gambling center is expensive and it has other adverse features that commission officials acknowledge have posed morale problems and have hampered the recruiting of scientific talent.

The talent is needed to overcome a succession of problems that have afflicted what a number of leading scientists assess as one of the most important programs in the international space race.

Project Begun in 1955

Just as atomic bombs are so much more powerful than conventional explosives, so nuclear propulsion could yield two to three times the payload lift physically possible with the biggest chemical-fuel rockets. This advantage is judged indispensable by many scientific observers to getting useful payloads — such as persons — anywhere beyond the close range of the moon.

At its inception in 1955 the Rover project was envisioned as the possible answer to the projected moon landing. But slippages in the project's schedule have put this out of consideration in favor of relatively small-lift chemical-fuel rockets.

Although $257,000,000 has

Continued on Page 13, Column 1

Congress Is Driving To Quit This Week

By JOHN D. MORRIS
Special to The New York Times

WASHINGTON, Sept. 30 — Congress moves into one of the busiest weeks of its session tomorrow, with leaders pressing for adjournment by Saturday night.

The size of the foreign aid program is the main issue still to be decided. Action on tax and trade bills, among other major elements of President Kennedy's legislative program, is expected to be completed with out further time-consuming controversy.

A new fight over Federal aid to higher education is developing, however, as a result of an Administration decision to press for passage of a $972,000,000 program of aid for medical and dental schools.

A $4,422,800,000 foreign aid money bill, approved Friday b

Continued on Page 35, Column 3

"All the News That's Fit to Print"

The New York Times.

LATE CITY EDITION

U. S. Weather Bureau Report (Page 77) forecasts: Mostly sunny today. Fair tonight and tomorrow.

Temp. range: 75—54; yesterday: 74—52.

VOL. CXII..No. 38,237. © 1962 by The New York Times Company. Times Square, New York 36, N. Y. NEW YORK, TUESDAY, OCTOBER 2, 1962. 10 cents beyond 50-mile zone from New York City except on Long Island. Higher in air delivery cities. FIVE CENTS

3,000 TROOPS PUT DOWN MISSISSIPPI RIOTING AND SEIZE 200 AS NEGRO ATTENDS CLASSES; EX-GEN. WALKER IS HELD FOR INSURRECTION

Associated Press Wirephoto

PRISONERS ARE MARCHED TO ARMORY IN OXFORD: Army men escort a group of prisoners to National Guard Armory. The group had participated in a disturbance and was apprehended after the soldiers were ordered to fire at the feet of the rioters.

United Press International Telephoto

WALKER IS STOPPED BY TROOPS: Former Maj. Gen. Edwin A. Walker is detained by soldiers near the courthouse in Oxford. He was turned over to U.S. marshals and is being held in $100,000 bail on charges stemming from his role in Sunday's campus riots.

SENATE REJECTS AID CUTS AND BAN ON HELP FOR REDS

Upholds Kennedy's Authority to Assist Nations That Do Business With Cuba

By FELIX BELAIR Jr.
Special to The New York Times.

WASHINGTON, Oct. 1—The Senate decided for the Administration today in preliminary votes on the foreign aid appropriation bill, due for passage tomorrow.

It voted, 47 to 28, against cutting $785,000,000 from the $792,400,000 of military and economic aid funds that its Appropriations Committee restored to the bill the House had cut heavily.

The effect of the vote was to hold the appropriation at $4,422,800,000, as recommended by its Appropriations Committee. The Administration had requested the full amount of the authorized ceiling of $4,734,800,000 but the House cut this back to $3,630,400,000.

On a later vote, the Senate confirmed this action by rejecting a proposal by Senator Allen J. Ellender, Democrat of Louisiana, to adopt the House cut of $150,000,000 for military aid.

Votes Become Narrow

By increasingly narrow margins, however, it supported other Administration goals. For instance, it voted, 39-36 to continue the President's discretion to aid countries doing business with Cuba. Then it decided, 39-37, to give the President similar discretion to waive the ban on aiding Communist nations such as Yugoslavia and Poland.

All three proposals were sponsored by Senator William Proxmire, Democrat of Wisconsin.

They were intended, first, to cut back the separate money items in the bill to the low levels voted by the House. Second, they would have approved the House's ban on aiding any Communist countries or free nations that help the Castro regime or allow their ships to deliver cargo to Cuba.

Only with the help of Republican members was the Democratic leadership able to turn back the Proxmire attack on the President's discretionary powers. On the proposal to ban aid to nations shipping to Cuba, 12 Republicans voted with 27 Democrats to defeat the move, while 22 Democrats and 14 Re-

Continued on Page 16, Column 4

MOSCOW FOCUSING ON BLOC IN EUROPE

Rift With Chinese Believed Behind New Emphasis

By SEYMOUR TOPPING
Special to The New York Times

MOSCOW, Oct. 1—The Soviet Union has decided to pursue its program of rapprochement with Yugoslavia even at the risk of a further deterioration in relations with Communist China.

Diplomatic officials here have found evidence of this development in a comparative study of Soviet and Chinese Communist documents.

These officials believe that the ideological quarrel with Peking has caused Moscow to resolve to concentrate its resources on the consolidation of the European Communist economic bloc.

Pravda, the Communist party newspaper, published today an edited version of the communiqué issued by the Central Committee of the Chinese Communist party at the conclusion of its plenary session Friday.

The Soviet summary, which covered half a page in Pravda, omitted the strong attacks on President Tito of Yugoslavia for his so-called "modern revision-

Continued on Page 3, Column 1

Home Urges West to Help East's Coexistence Moves

By ARNOLD H. LUBASCH

The Earl of Home, Britain's Foreign Secretary, urged last night that the West pursue policies designed to help the Soviet bloc move toward genuine coexistence. He suggested that nuclear war was no longer a useful instrument of policy, that Communist doctrine was changing because of this and that Soviet society was changing even faster.

The West should recognize these facts, he said, and adapt its policies to them.

Lord Home's remarks were made at a dinner in the Waldorf - Astoria Hotel. The dinner was given by the Pilgrims of the United States, a friendship society devoted to cultivating understanding between this country and the nations of the British Commonwealth.

The organization, composed of 1,000 prominent persons, was founded in 1903. A sister organization across the Atlantic is known as the Pilgrims of Great Britain. The groups give dinners in honor of leading statesmen to promote understanding and brotherhood among nations.

Cites Soviet Ingenuity

Lord Home observed that the Russians exercise great ingenuity to reconcile their propaganda about peaceful coexistence with a program that permits limited force in certain regions to further the cause of Communist domination.

The West must be on guard against this technique, he said, and against the force that backs it up. He mentioned Berlin and South Vietnam as two areas of particular concern.

"I pray," he added, "that Cuba may never become a third."

Communist doctrine has begun to change, Lord Home

Continued on Page 2, Column 3

SPAAK REASSURES AFRICA ON TRADE

Tells Newer U.N. Members That Common Market Will Aid Their Development

By THOMAS J. HAMILTON
Special to The New York Times

UNITED NATIONS, N. Y., Oct. 1—Paul-Henri Spaak, the Foreign Minister of Belgium, assured underdeveloped countries today that they could count on the cooperation of the members of the European Economic Community in the fight for economic advancement.

In addition, Mr. Spaak appealed to the entire world to understand the "new Europe" and its goal of "world cooperation."

Mr. Spaak's policy statement in the General Assembly was addressed in the first instance to 18 newly independent African states, all former possessions of France, Belgium or Italy.

Some of the states have asked the European Economic Community, or Common Market, for status as associates.

The six members of the market — Belgium, France, West Germany, Italy, the Netherlands and Luxembourg—are negotiating with the African states in Brussels.

Success Is Predicted

Mr. Spaak predicted that these talks would be concluded successfully by the end of 1962.

He also predicted that the negotiations with Britain for her admission to the market would be successful. He said the market would then have about the same productive capacity as the United States, and more than the Soviet Union.

The Belgian Foreign Minister, who was one of the leaders in the formation of the Common Market, defended it against two charges: that it is a manifestation of "neo-colonialism," and that it is merely intended to provide economic support for the North Atlantic Treaty Organization.

Mr. Spaak devoted almost his entire speech to his explanation of the market's program. He received an ovation at the end, with African and Asian members joining.

The Belgian Foreign Minister emphasized that the exports of African associate members would be admitted duty-free to the Common Market countries, while the Africans would retain

Continued on Page 5, Column 2

KENNEDY MOVING TO END PIER TIE-UP

He Names Board of Inquiry as First Step in Obtaining Taft-Hartley Injunction

By JOHN D. POMFRET
Special to The New York Times

WASHINGTON, Oct. 1—President Kennedy took the first step today toward getting an injunction to end the Atlantic and Gulf Coast longshoremen's strike for 80 days.

Declaring that continuation of the strike would imperil the national health and safety, the President issued an Executive order naming a three-man board of inquiry to investigate the dispute and to report to him by Thursday.

[Meanwhile in New York, leaders of the nation's seven major maritime unions abandoned inter-union battling to plan support for the striking longshoremen. American seamen and officers started leaving their ships, while other unions made plans to avoid servicing foreign-flag ships entering Atlantic and Gulf ports.]

The strike, which began at 12:01 A.M. today, has tied up all ports from Searsport, Me., to Brownsville, Tex. About 75,000 members of the Internation-

Continued on Page 78, Column 5

WALKER IS FACING 4 FEDERAL COUNTS

Flown to Medical Center in Missouri to Await Trial—Bail Put at $100,000

Special to The New York Times

OXFORD, Miss., Oct. 1 — Former Maj. Gen. Edwin A. Walker was arrested today on four charges, including insurrection, for his role in last night's rioting at the University of Mississippi.

The man who commanded Federal forces during the school integration crisis at Little Rock in 1957 was held in $100,000 bail.

Unable to put up the bail, he was flown to the United States Medical Center for Federal Prisoners in Springfield, Mo., to await his trial.

[Mr. Walker, accompanied by marshals, arrived at the medical center Monday night, The Associated Press said.]

"They don't have a thing on me," Mr. Walker said after his arrest. He dictated a message to Gov. Ross R. Barnett, which said:

"Mr. Walker hopes his efforts were in your behalf and in behalf of the stand for freedom everywhere. Do nothing based on my status that is not in support of your own objectives.

Continued on Page 27, Column 3

Mississippi Aides Blamed By U.S. Officials for Riot

By ANTHONY LEWIS
Special to The New York Times.

WASHINGTON, Oct. 1 — The Federal Government asserted today that the failure of Mississippi officials to keep their word led to the bloody rioting in Oxford, Miss., last night. Attorney General Robert F. Kennedy and other spokesmen said that Gov. Ross R. Barnett and his aides had repeatedly given as-

Statements by Robert Kennedy and Eastland, Page 25.

surances that they could and would maintain order when James H. Meredith, a Negro, entered the University of Mississippi last night.

Instead, the Federal spokesmen said, the state police were withdrawn at the crucial moment of the developing mob scene. Federal troops were then called in, but two men were dead and many were injured by the time they arrived.

Senator James O. Eastland, Democrat of Mississippi, read on the Senate floor this morning a report on the rioting. He said the report had been prepared by officials of the University of Mississippi.

Eastland Orders Inquiry

Tonight, Senator Eastland directed the Senate Judiciary Committee, which he heads, to make an investigation "of all events at the University of Mississippi since U.S. marshals and Army troops moved in."

The report read by Mr. Eastland this morning sought to put the blame for the rioting on "amateurism by untrained marshals." It said that the 300 marshals at the university last night had "provoked" the crowd of 2,500 persons gathered on the campus.

The university officials also

Continued on Page 25, Column 1

BARNETT CHARGES MARSHALS ERRED

Says 'Trigger-Happy' U. S. Officers Are Responsible for Campus Bloodshed

Text of Barnett statement appears on Page 25.

By HEDRICK SMITH
Special to The New York Times

JACKSON, Miss., Oct. 1—Gov. Ross R. Barnett tonight attributed the fatal rioting at the University of Mississippi last night to "inexperienced, nervous and trigger-happy Federal marshals."

The Governor made the statement in a recorded broadcast carried by the National Broadcasting Company. In a later recorded broadcast, carried by the Columbia Broadcasting System, Mr. Barnett directly assailed President Kennedy.

"The responsibility for this unwarranted breach of the peace and violence in Mississippi rests directly with the President of the United States," he said. "He ordered armed forces to invade Mississippi and their actions were directly responsible for violence, bloodshed and death."

People Are "Enraged"

In his earlier statement, the Governor said that the people of Mississippi "are enraged, incensed—and rightly so."

"Free men do not submit meekly to the kind of treatment Mississippians received," he said.

The Governor also said that the only solution to the Mississippi integration crisis was for the Federal Government to remove James H. Meredith, a 29-year-old Negro student, from the university.

"The Federal authorities alone have the power to stop bloodshed in Mississippi," he said.

Continued on Page 25, Column 5

SHOTS QUELL MOB

Enrolling of Meredith Ends Segregation in State Schools

By CLAUDE SITTON
Special to The New York Times

OXFORD, Miss., Oct. 1—James H. Meredith, a Negro, enrolled in the University of Mississippi today and began classes as Federal troops and federalized units of the Mississippi National Guard quelled a 15-hour riot.

A force of more than 3,000 soldiers and guardsmen and 400 deputy United States marshals fired rifles and hurled tear-gas grenades to stop the violent demonstrations.

Throughout the day more troops streamed into Oxford. Tonight a force approaching 5,000 soldiers and guardsmen, along with the Federal marshals, maintained an uneasy peace in this town of 6,500 in the northern Mississippi hills.

[There were two flareups tonight in which tear gas had to be used, United Press International reported. A small crowd of students began throwing bottles at marshals outside Baxter Hall where Mr. Meredith was housed. They were quickly dispersed by tear gas. Soldiers also broke up a minor demonstration at a downtown intersection.]

200 Are Seized

The troops seized approximately 200 persons.

They were seized in the mobs of students and adults that besieged the university administration building last night and attacked troops on the town square this morning.

Among those arrested was former Maj. Gen. Edwin A. Walker, who resigned his commission after having been reprimanded for his ultra-right-wing political activity. He was charged with insurrection.

The university's acceptance of Mr. Meredith, a 29-year-old Air Force veteran, followed Gov. Ross R. Barnett's retreat from his defiance of Federal court orders that the Negro be enrolled.

The 64-year-old official, a member of the militantly segregationist Citizens Councils, had vowed he would go to jail if necessary to prevent university desegregation.

Mr. Meredith's admission marked the first desegregation of a public educational institution in Mississippi. It reduced the Deep South bloc of massive-resistance states to two —

Continued on Page 24, Column 6

Congo Flies Troops To End Kasai Revolt

By Reuters

LEOPOLDVILLE, the Congo, Oct. 1—Reliable sources said today that the central Congolese Government was flying troops to Luluabourg to put down a new revolt by supporters of Albert Kalonji in South Kasai. Luluabourg is the Government army base nearest to the diamond-rich province.

The troop movement followed the declaration by the Government of a state of emergency in South Kasai. No immediate action was planned by the United Nations.

Mr. Kalonji, self-styled "king," virtually seceded from the central Government shortly after the Congo became independent two years ago. He escaped recently from a prison near Leopoldville and returned to his capital of Bakwanga.

A United Nations spokesman,

Continued on Page 9, Column 3

Columbia Study Scores Doctors; Says Quality of Care Lags Here

Financial Sanctions Under Blue Shield Suggested in Trussell Report

By FARNSWORTH FOWLE

The medical profession is "doing little" about the quality of medical care in the metropolitan area, the state was told yesterday in an experts' report.

The report warned that the first reaction of many laymen to poor medical care "is to demand firm and drastic government action—and indeed this may occur." It said that "strong medical, hospital, community and government leadership must be asserted in the public interest."

The conclusions were contained in the final volume of the Trussell-van Dyke Report, an independent study for the state by the Columbia University School of Public Health and Administrative Medicine. It was directed by Dr. Ray E. Trussell, chairman of the school, now on leave from the school while serving as New York City's Commissioner of Hospitals, and Frank van Dyke, an associate professor at the school.

The report called on the medical profession to welcome cur-

The New York Times

Dr. Ray E. Trussell

rent efforts of management and labor toward improving medical care.

"The organized purchasers of medical and hospital care can be the strongest arm of the community in upgrading standards, and it is to the best interest of organized medicine and hospitals to work with them,"

Continued on Page 42, Column 1

Bidwell's Tax Trial Ends in Hung Jury

By DAVID ANDERSON

The tax-evasion trial of J. Truman Bidwell, former chairman of the New York Stock Exchange, ended early today with a hung jury.

The jury, which had been deliberating since 1 P.M., filed into the courtroom shortly after midnight and told Federal Judge Thomas F. Murphy that it was "hopelessly deadlocked."

Judge Murphy, who two hours earlier had rejected a similar report and had instructed the jurors to try once more, now said:

"I declare a mistrial. Unhappy as I am. I guess there is nothing else we can do."

The prosecutor, Assistant United States Attorney Stephen E. Kaufman, said the Government would now consider

Continued on Page 18, Column 3

CAMPUS A BIVOUAC AS NEGRO ENTERS

2,000 Troops Stand Guard —Meredith Eats Alone

By McCANDLISH PHILLIPS
Special to The New York Times

OXFORD, Miss., Oct. 1—The University of Mississippi campus was under military occupation today as James H. Meredith, its first Negro student, registered and attended two classes.

Two thousand of the more than 3,000 Army and National Guard troops here made the tree-studded, rolling campus look like a cross between a bivouac and a prisoner-of-war camp. More olive drab uniforms were evident on campus than student casual dress.

Mr. Meredith, who did not get his first meal on campus until supper was served to him privately tonight, was housed in an end room in Baxter Hall, a male residence dormitory. The room next door was occupied by Federal marshals.

The 29-year-old Negro was taken from his dormitory under guard at 7:45 A. M. and marched to the Lyceum, the administration building. There he was registered in 45 minutes—

Continued on Page 26, Column 1

NEWS INDEX

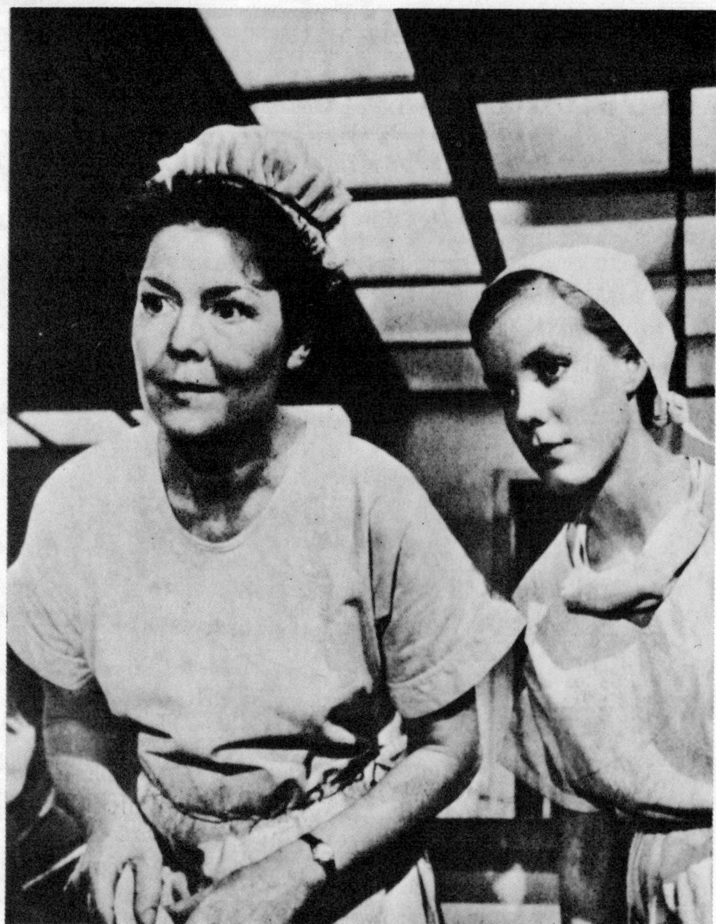

Shirl Conway and Zina Bethune starred in *The Nurses.*

Carol Burnett and Julie Andrews had occassional assistance from 20 chorus boys at Carnegie Hall, but it was the combination of this effervescent duo alone which produced one of television's fastest-flying hours.

James Drury was a cowboy known only as *The Virginian.*

"All the News That's Fit to Print"

The New York Times.

LATE CITY EDITION
U. S. Weather Bureau Report (Page 62) forecasts Mostly fair today, tomorrow. Chance of showers this morning and tonight. Temp. range: 82—65; yesterday: 78—58.

VOL. CXII..No. 38,247. NEW YORK, FRIDAY, OCTOBER 12, 1962. 10 cents beyond 50-mile zone from New York City except on Long Island. Higher in air delivery cities. FIVE CENTS

DEADLOCK ENDED, CONGRESS STRIVES TO ADJOURN TODAY

Conferees Reach Agreement on Funds for Research by Agriculture Department

RIVERS BILL IN DISPUTE

Chiefs Are Planning to Hold Both Houses in Session Tonight if Necessary

By JOHN D. MORRIS
Special to The New York Times

WASHINGTON, Oct. 11—The main obstacle to Congressional adjournment was removed today when Senate-House conferees broke a deadlock over Agriculture Department research funds.

Hopes for ending the session tonight were abandoned, however, when another conference committee failed to agree on terms of an omnibus bill on rivers, harbors and flood control.

Democratic leaders decided to give the rivers and harbors conferees a final chance to reach a compromise tomorrow. Regardless of whether an agreement resulted, they planned to hold the House and Senate all night tomorrow, if necessary, to bring the session to a close.

Delaying Tactics Expected

But strong resistance and possibly delaying tactics faced any attempt to adjourn without completing action on the bill. The measure is commonly referred to as the "pork barrel." It authorizes more than 160 projects of great political concern, particularly in an election year, to the Senators and Representatives whose states and districts stand to benefit from them.

The controversy over farm funds came to an end in midafternoon after two days of mediation by House and Senate leaders. The chief adversaries in the dispute had been Senator Richard B. Russell of Georgia and Representative Jamie L. Whitten of Mississippi, both Democrats, who headed the long-deadlocked Senate and House conferees.

At issue had been $28,653,500 in research funds that the Senate had added to the House-approved annual appropriation bill for the Agriculture Department.

A 'Debate' Is Averted

Senator Russell had threatened a prolonged adjournment-delaying "constitutional debate" on the Senate floor to strengthen his hand for a satisfactory compromise. He was especially interested in retaining five construction projects, including two in Georgia, for which the Senate had voted $1,170,000.

Representative Whitten and his colleagues gave in on that point today. But the Senators yielded and permitted the deletion of $17,500,000 of research funds that, under the Senate version, the Agriculture Department would have been authorized to distribute among various projects at its own discretion. The Senators also gave up an appropriation of $1,600,000 for a peanut marketing research facility at Dawson, Ga.

Within hours after the conference agreement, the compromise $5,487,029,500 farm appropriation bill was approved by the House and Senate and was sent to the White House.

Continued on Page 14, Column 2

President Flies Into City To Support Morgenthau

The New York Times

President Kennedy leaving the airport yesterday with Robert M. Morgenthau, Democratic nominee for Governor.

By LEO EGAN

Robert M. Morgenthau attempted yesterday to link his fortunes as Democratic-Liberal candidate for Governor to President Kennedy. He met the President at La Guardia Airport when Mr. Kennedy arrived at 2 P.M. to start a five-state tour this weekend on behalf of Democratic candidates.

With two of his running mates on this year's state ticket, Mr. Morgenthau rode to the Carlyle Hotel at 76th Street and Park Avenue with the President.

Later Mr. Morgenthau conferred privately with the President, who, he reported, gave him his "unequivocal endorsement."

They also made a series of 20-second television commercials together. The first of these will be shown here Tuesday.

Dudley With Morgenthau

With Mr. Morgenthau at the airport's Marine Terminal were Borough President Edward R. Dudley of Manhattan and Mayor John J. Burns of Binghamton. Mr. Dudley is the Democratic-Liberal candidate for Attorney General, the first Negro to be nominated for a statewide office in New York by a major party. Mr. Burns is a candidate for Lieutenant Governor.

James B. Donovan, the Democratic-Liberal candidate for the Senate against Senator Jacob K. Javits, was unable to greet the President. He returned to Miami yesterday afternoon from Cuba, where he has been negotiating for the release of prisoners captured in the ill-fated Cuban invasion last year.

Pierre Salinger, the President's press secretary, made a point of telling reporters that the President was also endorsing Mr. Donovan.

Mr. Kennedy is scheduled to visit Newark this morning to

Continued on Page 22, Column 2

PAY OFFER FINAL, FIREMEN ARE TOLD

Mayor Also Tells Police He Will Not Bow to Pressure to Raise $650 Package

Mayor Wagner told the heads of police and fire organizations yesterday that the city's offer of improvements in wages and other benefits made on Wednesday was a "final" one.

The offer had been rejected almost unanimously that night at a membership meeting of the Uniformed Firemen's Association. There seemed little doubt yesterday that the Patrolmen's Benevolent Association, which meets next Tuesday, would take the same action.

Meanwhile, 2,000 off-duty policemen and firemen picketed City Hall yesterday in a continuation of the demonstration that was begun last Tuesday. The pickets shouted, blew a loud horn and booed whenever the Mayor's name was mentioned.

In City Hall, Mayor Wagner met a half-hour with John J. Cassese, president of the Patrolmen's Benevolent Association, and Gerald J. Ryan, president of the Uniformed Firemen's Association, whom he had summoned to a conference.

"I told these two gentlemen in no uncertain terms that the city's offer was final," he said later. "I told them they had a

Continued on Page 23, Column 7

KENNEDY WARNING NATION AND ALLIES ON BERLIN CRISIS

Making Determined Effort to Convince Them of Risk of Trouble This Year

By MAX FRANKEL
Special to The New York Times

WASHINGTON, Oct. 11 — President Kennedy and his closest advisers are making a determined effort to persuade the country, the Western allies and the Russians that there is a danger of a serious diplomatic crisis over Berlin this fall and winter.

Secretary of State Dean Rusk, Secretary of Defense Robert S. McNamara and Attorney General Robert F. Kennedy are among the high officials spreading the carefully thought out forecasts of trouble.

In so doing they are acting on the most disturbing analyses of Soviet intentions here and playing down the view of some of their associates that the evidence of an impending "crunch" in Berlin is still circumstantial and far from conclusive.

Allies' Opinions Vary

The Administration is expressing its worst fears — and its determination to hold fast in Berlin — even though other allied capitals, too, are still speculating widely about Soviet intentions.

The British, generally, deny any anxiety. The French have been as unwilling to sound the alarm as they have been in other days to find hope in negotiations. The West Germans, at best, are divided.

But Washington is undeterred by these conflicting analyses. Indeed, the allies, as well as the Russians, appear to be the target of some of the crisis talk here.

Secretary Rusk related his concern over Berlin to nearly all of the 64 foreign ministers with whom he met in New York in the last two weeks. Both American and foreign reporters have been told of the Administration's worries by the White House and the State Department.

Reasons for U. S. Concern

Mr. McNamara has publicly conveyed military warnings to Moscow, including a determination to use nuclear weapons, if necessary, in any battle for Berlin. Attorney General Kennedy predicted a "great crisis" in a Las Vegas speech on Tuesday.

Authoritative United States sources, though they concede the possibility of error here, give the following reasons for their deliberate and repeated predictions of a Berlin showdown:

¶The crisis talk represents the best available estimate, in view of Premier Khrushchev's expressions of impatience to a number of foreign visitors, the build-up of Soviet insistence for an early settlement on Moscow's terms and the indicated Soviet timetable to return to the Berlin issue after the United States

Continued on Page 8, Column 4

POPE OPENS ECUMENICAL COUNCIL WITH A CALL FOR CHRISTIAN UNITY; 2,700 OF HIERARCHY IN ST. PETER'S

Associated Press Radiophoto

ECUMENICAL COUNCIL IS CONVENED: The scene in the nave of the St. Peter's Basilica yesterday as the 21st Ecumenical Council of the Roman Catholic Church was opened. Pope John XXIII is in center before the altar.

U.S. RACIAL ACTION PRAISED IN AFRICA

Firm Handling of Mississippi Crisis Said to Have Made a Favorable Impression

By DAVID BINDER
Special to The New York Times

WASHINGTON, Oct. 11—The Federal Government's firm handling of the Mississippi crisis has made a favorable impression in Africa, according to information available here.

At the height of the crisis, when United States troops and Federal marshals were dispatched to the University of Mississippi to back the registration of a Negro student, James H. Meredith, the President of Mali, Modibo Keita, cabled President Kennedy his congratulations for acting decisively.

Mr. Keita's government has developed strong ties to the Soviet bloc in recent months, so the cable, dated Oct. 1, was viewed here with surprise and pleasure.

Guinea Leaders Approve

Mr. Kennedy wired his thanks to the Mali leader last Oct. 3.

At the same time, it was reported that Guinean political leaders reacted with similar approval of the Federal actions in Mississippi.

Rather than deploring the segregationist attitudes of some Southerners, which the Guineans knew existed, they are quoted as saying, in effect: "What country in the world would mobilize a whole army to get a Negro student into college?"

These impressions contrast with the expectations of some observers here, who thought that the Mississippi crisis would

Continued on Page 20, Column 8

Pomp and Prayer Reign On Sunny Day at Vatican

By ARNALDO CORTESI
Special to The New York Times

ROME, Oct. 11—The sun burst through the rain, the greatest gathering of bishops in the history of the Roman Catholic Church filed into St. Peter's Basilica and the Ecumenical Council opened today amid the splendor of the centuries.

The ceremonies in the basilica started with the singing of the hymn "Veni Creator Spiritus" ("Come Creating Spirit"), an invocation to the Holy Ghost.

After a high mass had been celebrated by Eugene Cardinal Tisserant, dean of the Sacred College of Cardinals, and Pope John XXIII had read his address, the session closed with an apostolic blessing.

Before entering St. Peter's, the greatest church of Christendom, the Pontiff was carried on his portable throne from the bronze doors of the Vatican through St. Peter's Square. In front and behind him walked his glittering lay and ecclesiastical courts and the 2,700 "fathers of the Council."

White Robes and Miters

The Council fathers, including 81 cardinals and other prelates from 55 countries, wore white robes and had white miters on their heads. Archbishops and bishops of the Eastern Rite were distinguished by their beards and by headgear resembling crowns.

The Pope was carried in a throne of gilded wood with red upholstery. It rested on the shoulders of eight bearers in uniforms of crimson damask. Overhead floated a cream-colored canopy.

At the Pope's sides walked members of the Swiss Guards in picturesque uniforms said to have been designed by Michelangelo; noble guards in white breeches and black jackboots.

Continued on Page 19, Column 3

CHINA-INDIA CLASH WORST IN 3 YEARS

Both Sides Rushing Troops to Tibet Border Area—50 Casualties Reported

By The Associated Press.

NEW DELHI, Oct. 11—Indian and Chinese Communist troops have suffered 50 casualties in their most serious battle in three years along the disputed Tibetan border, it was reported today.

Both sides claimed a victory in the fighting, which broke out yesterday and appeared to be continuing in the high Himalayas. Communiqués in New Delhi and Peking said reinforcements were being rushed to the front.

A spokesman for the Indian Government said the Indians suffered 17 casualties and that the Communist losses were heavier.

Peking said 33 Communist soldiers were killed or wounded as the Indians "continued their reckless attacks."

Move by India Forecast

It said Chinese border guards stood firm and "aggressive Indian troops fled in confusion, leaving six bodies and arms and ammunition behind."

The Indians and Chinese both insisted that they were shooting only in self-defense.

The firing broke out even as authoritative sources in New Delhi predicted that Indian forces were about to move in an effort to oust the Chinese from Himalayan territory.

The latest fighting centered north of the Kechilang river near Chihtung, along the north-eastern frontier between India's Assam state and Chinese-occupied Tibet.

An Indian Government spokesman charged a Communist grenade hurled at an Indian outpost set the stage for a Chinese

Continued on Page 3, Column 5

PONTIFF HOPEFUL

Goal of One Church Is Distant but Urgent, He Says in Address

Text of the Pope's address is printed on Page 18.

Special to The New York Times

ROME, Oct. 11—Pope John XXIII opened the 21st Ecumenical Council today with a call for the "visible unity in truth" of all the followers of Christ.

The greatest gathering of the Roman Catholic hierarchy the world had ever seen heard the Pope's opening address in the vast splendor of St. Peter's Basilica. A great throng in St. Peter's Square witnessed the procession into the basilica.

Pope John made it clear that the goal of union of all Christians was still distant and could be attained only by degrees.

But, speaking with great confidence in the future of mankind, he expressed the goodwill of the church toward all believers in Christ and proclaimed it a duty of the church to work actively for their unity.

Pope Retains Primacy

An Ecumenical Council is the supreme deliberative body of the church, though subject to the primacy of the Pope. The gathering that opened today, known officially as Ecumenical Council Vatican II, is expected to introduce reforms in institutions, structure and procedures that may influence the worship and the lives of the more than 500,000,000 Catholics.

About 2,700 high prelates were in St. Peter's as participants and spectators. They included 81 cardinals, nine patriarchs, and almost all the archbishops, bishops, abbots and heads of religious orders in the hierarchy.

With them were 200 or so theological and other experts, who will participate in the Council meetings without voting rights.

Protestants Represented

Also present were 85 special envoys of foreign governments, including the United States Ambassador to Italy, G. Frederick Reinhardt; the entire diplomatic corps accredited to the Holy See, several hundred newspaper correspondents and a small group of especially invited observers.

In special seats were 28 delegate observers, representing the World Council of Churches, a Protestant body, and 14 non-Catholic Christian churches. They treated the Pontiff with marked deference, crowding around him to present their respects when he entered the basilica. Some participated in the religious ceremonies.

The Council was opened with

Continued on Page 19, Column 1

$1.25 Wage Voted By Estimate Board

By PAUL CROWELL

The Board of Estimate unanimously approved yesterday Mayor Wagner's bill to establish minimum wages here for employes in private business and industry.

The measure calls for the early establishment of a minimum wage of $1.25 an hour. This would be increased a year later to $1.50.

The $1.25 minimum will become effective 30 days after the Mayor signs the bill into law. He is scheduled to do so in 10 days, after a public hearing.

The bill calls for the creation of a minimum wage bureau in the city's Labor Department.

The Mayor disclosed before the Board of Estimate acted, that he had "borrowed" four minimum wage experts from the United States Department

Continued on Page 23, Column 3

A New Translation Alters Bible

Scholars Find Moses Crossed a Marsh, Not Red Sea

By LEWIS FUNKE
Special to The New York Times

PHILADELPHIA, Oct. 11 —A series of changes has been incorporated into a new translation of the five books of Moses, known as the Torah, or Pentatuch, to be issued next Jan. 28 by the Jewish Publication Society of America with headquarters in this city.

The changes will incorporate scholars' views that the commandment against taking the "name of the Lord thy God in vain" is not an injunction against profanity and that the Israelites fleeing from bondage in Egypt did not cross the Red Sea.

The translation, made by a committee of leading Jewish Bible scholars in the English-speaking world, was put directly into English from the traditional text preserved through the centuries by the Masoretic scribes.

In discussing the alteration of what is generally accepted as the Third Commandment, Dr. Harry M. Orlinsky, professor of Bible at Hebrew Union College-Jewish Institute of Religion in New York and editor-in-chief of

United Press International Telephoto

Dr. Harry M. Orlinsky holds page proofs of the new Torah

the new translation, said that the original Hebrew text was open to two interpretations.

The commandment in the King James version reads: "Thou shalt not take the name of the Lord thy God in vain; for the Lord will not hold him guiltless that taketh his name in vain."

In the new translation it has been rendered as: "You shall not swear falsely by the name of the Lord your God; for the Lord will not clear one who swears falsely by His name."

In making the change, Dr. Orlinsky said, the committee was convinced that the commandment could not be interpreted as an injunction against profanity because in that sense, it lacked both sufficient impor-

Continued on Page 20, Column 1

Watchman Service Blacklisted by State

By CHARLES GRUTZNER

A private detective service that had a virtual monopoly on supplying guards for state construction work in this city has been barred from all state jobs.

The State Department of Public Works removed the concern, Sentinel Investigation Service, Inc., from its list of approved subcontractors and is also holding up payments totaling more than $200,000 for work the company says it has performed.

This development came to light yesterday in Albany, where the company has filed liens against the department and contractors on road building and other public construction. The company, with offices at 29-46 Northern Boulevard, Long Island City, Queens, had

Continued on Page 22, Column 1

NEWS INDEX

Antifat 'Food Fad' Assailed by A.M.A.

By AUSTIN C. WEHRWEIN
Special to The New York Times

CHICAGO, Oct. 11 — The anticholesterol "food fad" is a wasted, dangerous effort, the American Medical Association said today.

The association had in mind widespread fears linking animal fats to heart attacks.

"The antifat, anticholesterol fad is not just foolish and futile; it also carries some risk," the group said.

Its five-page statement was designed as a warning both to what it called "do-it-yourself Americans" and to food processors who have built advertising campaigns on cooking oils, margarine and other foods derived from vegetable oils.

Few medical subjects have aroused more interest among

Continued on Page 34, Column 4

1962

This U-2 photo disclosed the Soviet-built missile base in Cuba's Sagua La Grande.

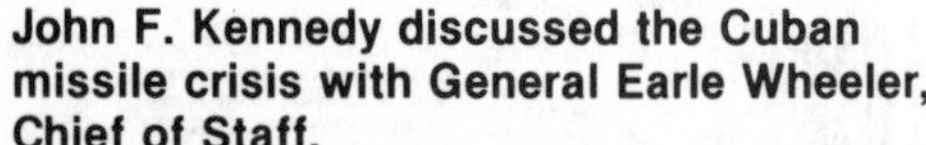

John F. Kennedy discussed the Cuban missile crisis with General Earle Wheeler, Chief of Staff.

Although he was embroiled in many crises, the President still found time for his children, Caroline and John-John.

"All the News That's Fit to Print"

The New York Times.

LATE CITY EDITION

U. S. Weather Bureau Report (Page 74) forecasts: Partly cloudy, breezy, cool today. Fair and cool tonight and tomorrow. Temp. range: 54—45; yesterday: 66—44.

VOL. CXII..No. 38,258. © 1962 by The New York Times Company. Times Square, New York 36, N. Y. NEW YORK, TUESDAY, OCTOBER 23, 1962. 10 cents beyond 50-mile zone from New York City except on Long Island. Higher in air delivery cities. FIVE CENTS

U.S. IMPOSES ARMS BLOCKADE ON CUBA ON FINDING OFFENSIVE-MISSILE SITES; KENNEDY READY FOR SOVIET SHOWDOWN

U. S. JUDGES GIVEN POWER TO REQUIRE VOTE FOR NEGROES

High Court Upholds Order Forcing the Registration of 54 in Alabama County

Special to The New York Times

WASHINGTON, Oct. 22 — The Supreme Court held today that Federal judges have the power to make state registrars put specific Negroes on the voting rolls.

Alabama had challenged an order by Federal District Judge Frank M. Johnson Jr. requiring the registration of 54 specific Negroes in Macon County, Ala. The order was upheld by the United States Court of Appeals for the Fifth Circuit.

Today the Supreme Court unanimously affirmed the disputed order. And it did so in a way that indicated once again its mood of impatience with Southern efforts to maintain denials of Negro rights.

One-Sentence Ruling

All that was before the court was an application for review of the Fifth Circuit decision. The usual alternatives would have been to deny the petition or to grant it and hear oral argument later.

Instead, the court granted review and then, summarily, affirmed the lower courts. It did so in a single sentence, with just one citation in the way of explanation.

The citation was to a decision in 1960 upholding a Federal Court order in a Louisiana voting case. There, a district judge had told Louisiana registrars to put back on their books 1,377 Negroes whose names had been removed in a purge by the segregationist Citizens Council.

Action by Congress

The Macon County case was one of the first brought by the Department of Justice under the Civil Rights Act of 1957. It is especially significant because the county is in the so-called Black Belt, with a predominantly Negro population.

In 1958, when the suit was started, virtually all of the 3,000 white persons of voting age in the county were registered. But only about 1,000 of the 12,000 potential Negro voters were actually eligible.

In a further move, the registrars resigned, and this was held to leave no defendants to be sued. Congress in 1960 handled this problem by providing

Continued on Page 24, Column 4

102 SAVED AT SEA AS PLANE DITCHES

Rescue Is Made off Alaska Minutes After Accident

By The Associated Press

SITKA, Alaska, Oct. 22—A military-charter airliner ditched in the ocean near here today, but all 102 persons aboard were saved in a quick rescue operation.

The plane, a DC-7C of Northwest Airlines, was going from McChord Air Force Base in Washington to Anchorage, Alaska. It carried 95 passengers and a crew of seven.

The rescue was reported by Northwest and the Alaska Coastal-Ellis Airline at Sitka, which also reported that there apparently were no serious injuries.

The plane went down shortly after the Federal Aviation Agency at Anchorage got word that it was being ditched because of propeller trouble.

A Coast Guard plane alighted on the water nearby; the Air Force sent two rescue planes, and small boats from Sitka, about seven miles north of the

Continued on Page 8, Column 3

Chinese Open New Front; Use Tanks Against Indians

Nehru Warns of Peril to Independence—Reds Attack Near Burmese Border and Press Two Other Drives

Special to The New York Times

NEW DELHI, Oct. 22—Prime Minister Jawaharlal Nehru told the people of India tonight that the Chinese Communist attack was a threat to their liberty.

His grave warning followed word that the advancing Chinese had opened a third front in the Himalayas, near the Burmese border, and had used tanks for the first time. Five more Indian posts fell to the Chinese on the third day of savage fighting.

Excerpts from Nehru's speech will be found on Page 2.

[A bid for negotiations for a peace accord was broadcast by the Chinese Communist radio early Tuesday, The Associated Press reported from Tokyo.]

In a broadcast, Mr. Nehru denounced the Peking regime as "a powerful and unscrupulous opponent, not caring for peace or peaceful methods."

"The time has come," he said, "for us to realize fully this menace that threatens the freedom of our people and the independence of our country."

Prime Minister Nehru said India would not abandon her economic development program and policy of nonalignment with international blocs, but called on the nation to switch "from the slow-moving methods of peacetime to those which produce results quickly."

"We must build up our military strength by all means at our disposal," he said.

The third front in the Himalayan fighting was opened early today when the Chinese attacked an Indian post at Kibitoo, on the border between

Continued on Page 3, Column 1

U.S. Bids U.N. Bar China; Denounces Attack on India

By SAM POPE BREWER

Special to The New York Times

UNITED NATIONS, N.Y., Oct. 22—Adlai E. Stevenson told the General Assembly today that Communist China's "naked aggression" against India was new proof that it was unfit for membership in the United Nations.

The chief United States representative at the United Nations spoke as the Assembly took up the perennial question of admitting Peking.

Mr. Stevenson told the members that by their actions on the Indian frontier the Chinese Communists "again show their scorn for the Charter of this organization."

The Vice President of the Philippines, Emmanuel Pelaez, told the Assembly that there were more than 40,000,000 Chinese living outside China who would become "a Trojan horse" if the United Nations accepted the Communist Government.

Mr. Pelaez said that the Chinese abroad, 1,000,000 of them in the Philippines, would be used for subversion by the Peking Government. He said they could now be controlled because the Communist Government did not have the means to get at them.

On the fighting in India, Mr. Stevenson declared: "Should there be some among us who think that perhaps the whole thing is a mistake that will right itself before long, let me point out that when a nation moves its troops with tanks and armor, it is no mistake. It is a premeditated act. It is naked aggression. And it has been going on with gathering momentum for some three years."

He quoted Prime Minister

Continued on Page 5, Column 3

U.S. SAID TO EASE KATANGA POLICY

Reported Willing to Put Off Any Economic Sanctions—Congolese Disturbed

By LLOYD GARRISON

Special to The New York Times

LEOPOLDVILLE, the Congo, Oct. 22 — Authoritative sources said today that the United States was no longer insisting that Katanga Province strictly meet the deadlines of the United Nations plan to end its secession from the Congo.

This has alarmed Congolese officials. They say that the United States shift is reflected in United Nations policy.

The United Nations plan, introduced Aug. 2 by U Thant, Acting Secretary General, was said to have been conceived largely by the United States.

As outlined by Mr. Thant, the plan's first stage called for the following timetable:

Within thirty days a program was to be decided on for the reintegration of Katanga's army into the Congolese National Army. Sixty days were to be allowed for the program to be carried out.

Recall of Missions

All Katangese foreign missions were to be recalled immediately, and all Katanga's foreign currency reserves were to be put under the control of the central Government, with 50 per cent of these reserves rebated to Katanga.

Unification of the Congo's currency was to have begun within 10 days.

Katanga was to have started immediately to share 50 per cent of her tax revenues with the central Government.

Not one of these conditions has been met.

Last week Cyrille Adoula, Premier of the central Government, declared that "the deadline for the first stage has passed." He said that it was now time for the United Nations to consider the second stage — economic sanctions.

A shift in United States policy became apparent over the weekend after the departure of George C. McGhee, Under Secretary of State for Political Af-

Continued on Page 3, Column 6

Stocks Plunge Early On Crisis, but Rally

By RICHARD RUTTER

An already badly battered stock market was hit by massive selling yesterday as talk of a new international crisis spread in Wall Street.

The selling was of dimensions reminiscent of late May when the market experienced its worst break in a generation. Yesterday, the tape ran as much as 19 minutes late before a half-hearted recovery set in that cut losses by about one-third.

Both tape lateness and volume were the greatest since July 10. Two million shares were traded in the first two hours.

Stock markets in London, Frankfurt and Brussels, following Wall Street's lead, also took large losses.

The selling was directly ascribed to news in the morning about an air of crisis in Wash-

Continued on Page 49, Column 6

SHIPS MUST STOP

Other Action Planned If Big Rockets Are Not Dismantled

By JAMES RESTON

Special to The New York Times

WASHINGTON, Oct. 22 — President Kennedy drew the line tonight, not with Cuba, but with the Soviet Union. After almost a generation of trying to keep the "cold war" from reaching a direct confrontation between United States and Soviet power, a decision has been made to force Soviet missile bases from this hemisphere at the risk of war.

This is the official interpretation of President Kennedy's speech tonight, and the orders to American forces bear it out. On the highest authority, it can be said that these orders include the following:

¶Ships carrying to Cuba weapons capable of striking the continental United States must either turn back or submit to search and seizure, or fight. If they try to run the blockade, a warning shot will be fired across their bows; if they still do not submit, they will be attacked.

¶This applies not only to ships but to any planes suspected of carrying additional offensive weapons to Cuba. There is no evidence that there are nuclear warheads in Cuba, but long-range aircraft suspected of carrying these or any other offensive weapons, will be intercepted, and instructions have been issued to do everything possible to check all Communist-bloc planes en route to Cuba via Newfoundland or Africa.

Prepared to Risk War

Even this will not satisfy the new policy announced by President Kennedy. Not only must new offensive weapons be stopped, under the President's orders, but those already in Cuba must be dismantled, or the United States will take whatever additional action is necessary, beginning with a much more rigorous blockade of such things as Cuba's essential oil supplies, to force compliance.

If this leads to Soviet retaliation, such as a counter-blockade of Berlin, the United States is prepared to risk a major war to defend its present position in the former German capital. Accordingly, American forces, not only in Berlin and West Germany but all over the world, have been placed on emergency alert. The new policy has been defined in a private communi-

Continued on Page 19, Column 1

Associated Press Wirephoto

ANNOUNCES HIS ACTION: President Kennedy speaking to the nation last night on radio and television. He told of moves to keep offensive equipment away from Cuba.

Canada Asks Inspection of Cuba; Britain Supporting Quarantine

Diefenbaker Comments

By RAYMOND DANIELL

Special to The New York Times

OTTAWA, Oct. 22 — Prime Minister John Diefenbaker of Canada declared tonight the time had come for an impartial inspection of what is happening in Cuba by eight of the "nonaligned nations."

Interrupting debate of the Canadian economic crisis in the House of Commons, Mr. Diefenbaker described President Kennedy's speech on Cuba as "somber and challenging."

"Naturally," he said, "there has been little time to give consideration to positive action that might be taken. But I suggest that if there is a desire—and I am sure there is on the part of the U.S.S.R.—to have the facts, if a group of nations, perhaps the eight comprising the unaligned members of the 18-nation disarmament committee, were given the opportunity of making an on-site inspection of Cuba to ascertain what the facts are, a major step forward would be taken."

Meanwhile it was disclosed that Canada has barred the use of her airfields, including that

Continued on Page 21, Column 2

British Note Peril

By DREW MIDDLETON

Special to The New York Times

LONDON, Oct. 22—Qualified sources said today that approval for President Kennedy's military quarantine of Cuba could be expected from the British government.

A Foreign Office spokesman declared, "Revelation of the Soviet build-up in Cuba will come as a shock to the whole civilized world."

Official comment cannot be given until after Prime Minister Macmillan and his Cabinet have discussed the President's statement.

Initial reaction among diplomats was that the President had taken the most reasonable course to frustrate what military circles regard as evident danger to the United States: a buildup of Soviet nuclear capacity in Cuba.

The danger that war might result from a Soviet attempt to break what amounts to a military blockade of Cuba is accepted. But one experienced airman expressed the general feeling this way: "War can come from any one of a number of causes,

Continued on Page 21, Column 1

TRAFFIC DELAYED AT BERLIN BORDER

Reds Start Intensive Check of Civilian Trucks an Hour Before Kennedy Speech

By SYDNEY GRUSON

Special to The New York Times

BONN, Oct. 22—The East German police began to slow down civilian traffic between West Berlin and West Germany late tonight.

About an hour before President Kennedy announced the United States countermeasures against the Soviet build-up in Cuba, the police started intensive examination of the papers of trucks moving into East German territory.

The connection, if any, between the two actions was not immediately clear. Similar harassment of civilian traffic has occurred periodically over the years. The immediate reaction in West Berlin was to consider tonight's harassment as part of the regular order of things, rather than as an advance countermeasure to the American moves against Cuba.

Nevertheless, there was deep anxiety that the Soviet Union would retaliate by causing trouble on the West's access lines to the city.

The outcome of tomorrow's meetings between Andrei A. Gromyko, the Soviet Foreign Minister, and East German Communist leaders was awaited with concern. Mr. Gromyko

Continued on Page 17, Column 3

Moscow Says U.S. Holds 'Armed Fist' Over Cuba

By SEYMOUR TOPPING

Special to The New York Times

MOSCOW, Tuesday, Oct. 23—In a broadcast before President Kennedy's speech on the missile build-up in Cuba, the Moscow radio said that the unusual activity in Washington indicated that the United States "once again was raising its armed fist over Cuba." The broadcast said there was "real hysteria" in Washington.

A Soviet reply to the United States note on Cuba that was given last night to Anatoly F. Dobrynin, the Soviet Ambassador to Washington, was expected to be delivered in 24 hours. It was expected that the reply would take the form either of a diplomatic communication or a message to President Kennedy from Premier Khrushchev.

Western observers said it appeared inevitable in view of recent Soviet statements that the reply would be a denial of any offensive Soviet intent and a charge of United States aggression against Cuba.

Veracity Questioned

The veracity of the Soviet Government was directly questioned in President Kennedy's speech, which was given after delivery of the note. The President said evidence had been obtained that Moscow was constructing offensive missile bases on Cuban territory.

The Soviet Government statement of Sept. 11, which warned the United States that an attack on Cuba would mean war, contended that the Soviet weapons supplied to Cuba were of a defensive nature.

Western observers said the crisis over Cuba would enter a critical phase when and if United States war vessels sought to halt and search a Soviet ship bound for Cuba.

A number of Soviet vessels carrying civilian goods and pos-

Continued on Page 18, Column 3

All Military Forces Mobilized by Castro

By The Associated Press

KEY WEST, Tuesday, Oct. 23—All of Cuba's military forces have been mobilized as a result "of the news from the United States," the Havana radio said today.

The broadcast said the order was issued by Premier Fidel Castro, who will address the nation later today.

"Our combat units rapidly placed themselves on a fighting basis," said the Havana broadcast.

"Hundreds of thousands of men were mobilized in the course of a few hours," added the broadcast, which followed by some hours President Kennedy's announcement of a naval blockade against Cuba.

During the evening, Havana appeared slow to react to President Kennedy's broadcast and

Continued on Page 20 Column 5

BIG FORCE MASSES TO BLOCKADE CUBA

Armada Is Under Orders to Open Fire if Necessary—All Troops Are Alerted

By JACK RAYMOND

Special to The New York Times

WASHINGTON, Oct. 22—American ships and planes began preparing tonight to impose a blockade of Cuba. United States forces are under orders to thwart any attempt to deliver offensive weapons to Havana.

A Defense Department spokesman said that a large force of ships and planes concentrating in the Caribbean area had instructions to use force if necessary, including sinking of ships, to carry out President Kennedy's orders for a "quarantine" of Cuba.

The Pentagon said also that United States military units throughout the world, including the garrison in Berlin and the nuclear-armed Strategic Air Command, had been placed "on alert."

Dependents of servicemen at the Guantanamo Bay Naval Base in Cuba have been evacuated, the department said.

Forces at Base Doubled

It added that the military forces there, which were previously put at 3,300 naval officers and men and several hundred Marines, have been doubled.

Air defense units in the United States, particularly radar warning stations, interceptor aircraft and ground-to-air missiles, "have been redeployed," the department spokesman said.

The orders for additional defense precautions were taken the spokesman continued, on the basis of aerial photographic evidence of long-range ballistic missile bases and the arrival of Soviet Ilyushin-28 bombers in Cuba.

The spokesman displayed some of the aerial photographs and pointed to some missiles sites that, he said, had been established only in the last 10 or 15 days.

He said some of the missile

Continued on Page 20 Column 1

NEWS INDEX

News Summary and Index, Page 39

PRESIDENT GRAVE

Asserts Russians Lied and Put Hemisphere in Great Danger

Text of the President's address is printed on Page 18.

By ANTHONY LEWIS

Special to The New York Times

WASHINGTON, Oct. 22 — President Kennedy imposed a naval and air "quarantine" tonight on the shipment of offensive military equipment to Cuba.

In a speech of extraordinary gravity, he told the American people that the Soviet Union, contrary to promises, was building offensive missile and bomber bases in Cuba. He said the bases could handle missiles carrying nuclear warheads up to 2,000 miles.

Thus a critical moment in the cold war was at hand tonight. The President had decided on a direct confrontation with — and challenge to — the power of the Soviet Union.

Direct Thrust at Soviet

Two aspects of the speech were notable. One was its direct thrust at the Soviet Union as the party responsible for the crisis. Mr. Kennedy treated Cuba and the Government of Premier Fidel Castro as a mere pawn in Moscow's hands and drew the issue as one with the Soviet Government.

The President, in language of unusual bluntness, accused the Soviet leaders of deliberately "false statements about their intentions in Cuba."

The other aspect of the speech particularly noted by observers here was its flat commitment by the United States to act alone against the missile threat in Cuba.

Nation Ready to Act

The President made it clear that this country would not stop short of military action to end what he called a "clandestine, reckless and provocative threat to world peace."

Mr. Kennedy said the United States was asking for an emergency meeting of the United Nations Security Council to consider a resolution for "dismantling and withdrawal of all offensive weapons in Cuba."

He said the launching of a nuclear missile from Cuba against any nation in the Western Hemisphere would be regarded as an attack by the Soviet Union against the United States. It would be met, he said, by retaliation against the Soviet Union.

He called on Premier Khrushchev to withdraw the missiles from Cuba and so "move the

Continued on Page 18, Column 1

KENNEDY CANCELS CAMPAIGN TALKS

He and Johnson Take Step to Concentrate on Crisis

By CABELL PHILLIPS

Special to The New York Times

WASHINGTON, Oct. 22—The White House announced tonight that President Kennedy and Vice President Johnson would make no further political appearances in the Congressional campaign because of the Cuban crisis.

The move by the Administration was considered evidence not only of the seriousness of the situation but also of the desire of the President to unify the country behind his blockade order and keep the issue out of partisan politics.

In this connection, the White House said the President personally informed former Republican Presidents Dwight D. Eisenhower and Herbert Hoover, as well as former Democratic President Harry S. Truman, of his decision.

And the White House announced that John J. McCloy, former disarmament adviser to the Kennedy Administration and a Republican, had been as-

Continued on Page 18, Column 7

"All the News That's Fit to Print"

The New York Times.

LATE CITY EDITION

U. S. Weather Bureau Report (Page 47) forecasts: Chance of rain, then cloudy today, tonight. Chance of rain tomorrow. Temp. range: 58—46; yesterday: 67—41.

VOL. CXII..No. 38,264. © 1962 by The New York Times Company. Times Square, New York 36, N. Y. NEW YORK, MONDAY, OCTOBER 29, 1962. 10 cents beyond 50-mile zone from New York City except on Long Island. Higher in air delivery cities. FIVE CENTS

U.S. AND SOVIET REACH ACCORD ON CUBA; KENNEDY ACCEPTS KHRUSHCHEV PLEDGE TO REMOVE MISSILES UNDER U.N. WATCH

DE GAULLE WINS 61% OF BALLOTS; ABSTENTIONS HIGH

46% of the Eligible Voters Support President's Plan on Choosing Successor

By ROBERT C. DOTY
Special to The New York Times

PARIS, Monday, Oct. 29—President de Gaulle won his referendum battle in nationwide balloting yesterday, but he suffered substantial losses of support in comparison with previous tests.

On the basis of complete unofficial returns early this morning, 61.76 per cent of the valid ballots cast were in favor of the President's proposal to elect his eventual successor by popular vote instead of by the limited college of 80,000 "notables" specified in the present Constitution.

But, with abstentions running at about 24 per cent of the electorate, General de Gaulle had only a minority—about 46 per cent — of the registered voters backing him.

Tally of Voting

Of 27,579,424 registered voters, 21,306,123 went to the polls and 20,740,649 cast valid ballots. Of these, 12,808,196 were "yes" votes and 7,932,453 were "no" votes. A total of 565,474 voters invalidated their ballots.

Most political observers, including those of the traditional French parties united against the President, indicated the belief that this was just sufficient backing to dissuade the President from carrying out his threat to resign if the voters expressed only "vague and doubtful" confidence in him.

The result, on which General de Gaulle must ponder, was that of every 100 potential voters, 46 said "yes" to the President and his proposal, 29 said "no" and 25 either did not care enough to vote or spoiled their ballots.

Gaullist and Opposition interpretations of the results varied widely, however. Premier Georges Pompidou called the "yes" majority a "massive" one.

Ballots Subtracted

By subtracting the Communist and extreme Right-Wing votes, he reached the conclusion that the traditional parties aligned against the President had been able to swing only 10 to 12 per cent of the voters into the "no" column.

Bertrand Motte, president of the Independent (Conservative) group in the dissolved National Assembly and one of the leaders of the Opposition coalition, found, however, that "the regime has been hurt." The "no" vote, he said, represented "a very important percentage of Frenchmen."

One section of the country—the southwest—deserted General deGaulle and voted "no" by varying margins. His backing

Continued on Page 3, Column 1

Associated Press Radiophoto

DE GAULLE VOTES IN REFERENDUM: President de Gaulle casting ballot in Colombey-les-deux-Eglises..

Castro Asks Guantanamo; Strives to Repair Prestige

By TAD SZULC
Special to The New York Times

WASHINGTON, Oct. 28 — Premier Fidel Castro demanded today that the United States evacuate its naval base at Guantanamo Bay. This was taken here tonight as a major point in evidence that Cuba's revolutionary leader was struggling to salvage his prestige at home and in the rest of Latin America.

United States officials and Latin-American diplomats believed the provisional accord between Washington and Moscow on the withdrawal of nuclear missiles from Cuba left the Castro regime a substantial loser in the crisis.

Therefore, it was believed here that Premier Castro would try his best to inject such sensitive issues as the fate of the Guantanamo base into the negotiations at the United Nations.

Text of the Castro statement appears on Page 19.

The United States is not prepared to discuss the status of Guantanamo with Cuba, officials said.

Officials considered the possibility that, in the light of his reactions last night and today to the United States-Soviet settlement over the bases in Cuba, he might seek to block a final agreement unless his conditions were met.

There was agreement here tonight that the realities of East-West relationships and the close danger of war in recent days had forced a solution of the bases dispute over Dr. Castro's head.

Whether or not he was fully consulted by Moscow on the

Continued on Page 19, Column 1

WARFARE ALTERS INDIA PROFOUNDLY

Nonalignment Views Are Re-examined—Many Call Menon Career Ruined

By A. M. ROSENTHAL
Special to The New York Times

NEW DELHI, Oct. 28 — The Chinese Communist invasion of India's northern frontiers has brought about profound changes in this country — in politics, in thought, in international attitudes and in the lives of the men in power.

It has, in the opinion of New Delhi's tightly knit political community, wrecked the political future of Defense Minister V. K. Krishna Menon.

At a rally today Mr. Menon said India had been forced to yield territory and that the people had to be prepared for more sacrifices and losses. The Indian Government said Chinese forces had opened an attack in a new section in the frontier region of Ladakh and had forced Indian troops out of one post by overwhelming numbers.

Chinese Drive into Ladakh

The attack today and those of the last week are apparently designed to plant the Chinese flag all across Ladakh. In the North East Frontier Agency, 800 miles to the east, there was a lull in the fighting.

Before the Chinese attacks, Mr. Menon was at the peak of his career. He had won a smashing victory at the polls in Bombay and had created a well-financed political foundation that he and his followers hoped would one day help make him Prime Minister.

Now Mr. Menon is being blamed bitterly and widely for two things—for failing to foresee the invasion and for failing to prepare Indian armed forces to meet it.

Heavy pressure is being put on Prime Minister Jawaharlal Nehru to remove Mr. Menon from the Defense Ministry. Some politicians here believe his resignation is a matter of time. Others say that his power is already being whittled away gradually by Mr. Nehru, but that the Prime Minister will

Continued on Page 13, Column 1

MCA Will Finance Shows on Broadway

By MURRAY SCHUMACH
Special to The New York Times

HOLLYWOOD, Oct. 28 — MCA, Inc., already a major power in movies, television and records, will become one of the nation's most important financiers of Broadway shows.

The aim of MCA is to finance entire shows. It will back musicals as well as dramas.

The plan to expand into Broadway became known this weekend after conferences between the president of the corporation, Lew R. Wasserman, and Milton R. Rackmil, who is president of Universal Pictures and vice chairman of MCA.

In disclosing the plan to finance shows, Mr. Wasserman explained that MCA did not intend to produce them. This approach to Broadway is novel, for MCA is not interested pri-

Continued on Page 37, Column 5

Caracas Guards Oil After 4 Red Blasts

Special to The New York Times

CARACAS, Venezuela, Oct. 28—The Government declared the rich oil-producing region around Lake Maracaibo a zone of military operations tonight and sent marines to protect oil installations. The action was taken after dynamite attacks last night by Communist terrorists.

A Government spokesman said, however, that the attacks against four electric power stations of the United States-controlled Creole Petroleum Corporation were not so serious as first feared. Creole is an affiliate of the Standard Oil Company of New Jersey.

Venezuelan authorities said earlier that the blasts, part of the Communist war of nerves and destruction against the Government of President Rom-

Continued on Page 19, Column 6

THANT SETS VISIT

He Will Go to Havana Tomorrow to Seek Castro Consent

Text of Thant note to Castro is printed on Page 18.

By THOMAS J. HAMILTON
Special to The New York Times

UNITED NATIONS, N.Y., Oct. 28—U Thant, the Acting Secretary General, will fly to Cuba Tuesday with his top assistants to discuss arrangements for a United Nations check on the dismantling of Soviet missiles and the halting of the building of bases.

Mr. Thant plans to stay in Cuba only long enough to obtain Premier Fidel Castro's acceptance of the Thant plan to send observer teams to inspect and be sure Premier Khrushchev's agreement to dismantle the missiles is complied with.

According to reliable sources, once the Acting Secretary General makes these arrangements, he will return to obtain authorization from the Security Council for the inspection program.

Mahmoud Riad of the United Arab Republic, who on Thursday will take over the monthly presidency of the Security Council from the Soviet delegate, had a talk with Mr. Thant today. Mr. Riad said he saw no need for a Council meeting until Mr. Thant returned—perhaps Thursday or Friday.

Outcome Awaited

The Council suspended its debate Thursday night to await the outcome of messages exchanged by President Kennedy and Premier Khrushchev.

Premier Castro's consent will be necessary under the precedent set in the Suez crisis of 1956.

At that time the late Secretary General, Dag Hammarskjold, ruled that President Gamal Abdel Nasser would have to agree to all arrangements for stationing United Nations forces in the United Arab Republic, including which countries might supply the troops.

Premier Castro offered to provide a Cuban plane to transport the Acting Secretary General and his aides, who are expected to include Brig. Indar Jit Rikhye of the Indian Army, a military adviser.

Mr. Thant told Premier Castro, however, that he preferred to charter his own plane. An

Continued on Page 18, Column 1

RUSSIAN ACCEDES

Tells President Work on Bases Is Halted —Invites Talks

Texts of Khrushchev notes to Kennedy and Thant, Page 16.

By SEYMOUR TOPPING
Special to The New York Times

MOSCOW, Oct. 28—Premier Khrushchev agreed today to end the construction of Soviet bases in Cuba and to dismantle Soviet rockets there, both under United Nations supervision.

In a message to President Kennedy, the Soviet leader said that he already had issued instructions for this and for crating and returning the rockets to the Soviet Union.

This was said to have been done in return for the commitments offered in a letter sent to Mr. Khrushchev yesterday by President Kennedy. The letter expressed the United States' readiness to lift the naval quarantine of Cuba and join with other nations of the Western Hemisphere in providing assurances against an invasion of the island.

Offer of Talks Welcomed

Mr. Khrushchev's message, which was broadcast at 5 P.M. Moscow time, indicated unconditional acceptance of the measures stipulated by the President to bar offensive Soviet weapons from Cuba.

The Premier also welcomed the readiness of President Kennedy to discuss a detente, or relaxation of tension, between the nations of the North Atlantic Treaty Organization and its East European Communist counterpart, the Warsaw Pact organization.

The Russian leader insisted that Soviet weapons had been introduced in Cuba solely for the defense of the island. He added that, in view of the assurances of the President, "the motives which induced us to render assistance of such a kind to Cuba would disappear."

There was no mention in the Khrushchev message of the proposal made in the Premier's communication of yesterday to the President. Mr. Khrushchev then offered to withdraw Soviet weapons from Cuba, but in exchange for similar action by the United States in respect to Turkey, where a missile base of the North Atlantic Treaty Organization is maintained.

Western observers here be-

Continued on Page 16, Column 5

The President's View

Kennedy Rejects Thesis That Outcome On Cuba Shows 'Tough Line' Is Best

By JAMES RESTON
Special to The New York Times

News Analysis

WASHINGTON, Oct. 28 — President Kennedy is looking at the Cuban crisis not as a great victory but merely as an honorable accommodation in a single isolated area of the "cold war."

War has been avoided, but the Communists retain a sanctuary in the Western Hemisphere. The Russians have withdrawn rather than fight, but this was done in an area strategically disadvantageous to them and does not mean that they would do the same in many other areas where the battlefield is disadvantageous to the West. This, at least, is the official view here.

The President is not even drawing general conclusions from this special case about the tactics of dealing with the Soviet Union in the future. To be specific, while he may be equally bold again in risking conflict in support of vital national interests, he is rejecting the conclusion of the traditional "hard-liners" that the way to deal with Moscow everywhere in the world is to be "tough," as in Cuba.

In other circles there seems to be general agreement about these rather more optimistic conclusions:

¶In modern weaponry, the Soviet Union does not feel itself ahead of the United States. If Moscow did, it would not have insisted on ending the ban on nuclear testing and it would not have taken the long gamble to establish medium and intermediate missiles in Cuba where they would be effective against the United States.

¶In the Western alliance, President Kennedy has enhanced his leadership by defying the Soviet challenge and achieving at least part of his main objectives without war.

¶In his dealings with the Russians, he has probably removed the Soviet illusion that America would not fight and thus reduced the chances of miscalculation in Moscow.

¶In the perpetual propaganda dialogue of the "cold war," it has been demonstrated that the United States did not make a deal with the Soviet Union at the expense of Turkey, while the same thing can scarcely be said about the

Continued on Page 17, Column 7

United Press International Telephoto

PRESIDENT ATTENDS MASS: Mr. Kennedy at St. Stephen's Roman Catholic Church in Washington yesterday before receiving Premier Khrushchev's message.

Plane Veers Over Soviet, Kennedy Voices Regrets

By ANTHONY LEWIS
Special to The New York Times

WASHINGTON, Oct. 28—A United States plane flew over Soviet Far Eastern territory today, but both President Kennedy and Premier Khrushchev sought to avoid tension over the incident. The President told Mr. Khrushchev that the incursion resulted from a navigational error.

"I regret this incident and will see to it that every precaution is taken to prevent recurrence," Mr. Kennedy declared.

Premier Khrushchev disclosed the incident in his letter to President Kennedy on the Cuban crisis. He recalled previous flights by U-2 reconnaissance planes over Soviet territory but used language much less bristling than the Russians had employed in earlier protests.

Plane Said to Be Unarmed

The President, for his part, went into much greater detail than usual on the reasons for the flight and adopted a reassuring tone. He gave the explanation in his response to Mr. Khrushchev's letter on the Cuban crisis.

Mr. Kennedy said the plane, "without arms or photographic equipment," was on a mission to sample the atmosphere in connection with Soviet nuclear tests. Its course was from Eielson Air Force Base in Alaska to the North Pole and back.

In turning at the pole, the President said, "the pilot made a serious navigational error that carried him over Soviet territory."

He immediately made an emergency call on open radio for navigational assistance and

Continued on Page 17, Column 8

PATROLS MAINTAIN BLOCKADE OF CUBA

Pentagon Says Its Military Precautions Continue—Air Reconnaissance Goes On

By JACK RAYMOND
Special to The New York Times

WASHINGTON, Oct. 28—The Defense Department said today that the United States was continuing its military precautions in the crisis over Cuba.

A department spokesman said that reconnaissance flights were still being carried out, presumably to verify Premier Khrushschev's announcement that he had ordered the dismantling of ballistic missiles in Cuba and a cessation of work on bases on the island.

The spokesman said also that air and sea patrols in the blockade of Cuba were being maintained. For the first time in a week of crisis, the Pentagon official referred to the military build-up carried out to meet the emergency, describing it as "quite a development of power."

Reserve Units Called Up

The Pentagon, which announced last night that 24 Air Force Reserve troop carrier squadrons were being ordered to active duty, issued implementing instructions that went into effect at 9 A.M.

The mobilization of the reserve units, which operate C-119 and C-23 troop and cargo aircraft, will affect 14,214 reservists, the Pentagon estimated.

Under special legislation that Congress passed in its last session at President Kennedy's request, the reservists may be held on active duty for a period up to one year.

The Pentagon refused to comment on a statement by Senator Kenneth Keating that he had unconfirmed reports that submarine bases were being built

Continued on Page 17, Column 1

U.S. Looks for Hint Of Shift at Kremlin

By MAX FRANKEL
Special to The New York Times

WASHINGTON, Oct. 28 — President Kennedy and his advisers weighed every word and step in the climactic moments of the Cuban blockade crisis today for possible signs of confusion and division in the Kremlin.

There was satisfaction here about the promise of an early settlement. But there was no celebration, no talk yet of an American victory or of a Russian capitulation after the announcement by Premier Khrushchev that the Soviet Union would dismantle its missile bases in Cuba.

Two considerations dictated the Administration's caution tonight.

On the one hand, the Presi-

Continued on Page 18, Column 7

CAPITAL HOPEFUL

Plans to End Blockade as Soon as Moscow Lives Up to Vow

Texts of the Kennedy statement and message are on Page 16.

By E. W. KENWORTHY
Special to The New York Times

WASHINGTON, Oct. 28—President Kennedy and Premier Khrushchev reached apparent agreement today on a formula to end the crisis over Cuba and to begin talks on easing tensions in other areas.

Premier Khrushchev pledged the Soviet Union to stop work on its missile sites in Cuba, to dismantle the weapons and to crate them and take them home. All this would be done under verification of United Nations representatives.

President Kennedy, for his part, pledged the lifting of the Cuban arms blockade when the United Nations has taken the "necessary measures," and that the United States would not invade Cuba.

U. S. Conditions Met

Essentially this formula meets the conditions that President Kennedy set for the beginning of talks. If it is carried out, it would achieve the objective of the President in establishing the blockade last week: the removal of the Soviet missile bases in Cuba.

While officials were gratified at the agreement reached on United States terms, there was no sense either of triumph or jubilation. The agreement, they realized, was only the beginning. The terms of it were not nailed down and Soviet negotiators were expected to arrive at the United Nations with a "bag full of fine print."

Although Mr. Khrushchev mentioned verification of the dismantling by United Nations observers in today's note, sources here do not consider it unlikely that the Russians may suggest that the observers be under the procedures of the Security Council.

This would make their findings subject to a veto by the Soviet Union as one of the 11 members of the Council.

No Big Gains Envisioned

United States officials did not expect a Cuban settlement, if it materialized, to lead to any great breakthroughs on such problems as inspection for a nuclear test ban and disarmament.

On the other hand, it was thought possible that a Cuban settlement might set a precedent for limited reciprocal concessions in some areas.

The break in the crisis came dramatically early this morning after a night of steadily mounting fears that events were running ahead of diplomatic efforts to control them.

The break came with the arrival of a letter from Premier Khrushchev in which the Soviet

Continued on Page 16, Column 1

Relief Felt in NATO At Cuba Relaxation

Special to The New York Times

PARIS, Oct. 28—There was great relief today within the North Atlantic Treaty Organization at Premier Khrushchev's pledge to remove Soviet missiles from Cuba. Some Governments, however, notably that of France, tended to take a cautious attitude toward the Soviet move.

The relief followed reports that concern was expressed this morning at a secret meeting of the North Atlantic Council that NATO might be drawn into the conflict if the United States moved against Cuba either through invasion or bombardment.

The concern had been caused by a message from Premier Khrushchev to President Kennedy that seemed to NATO delegates to imply the threat of

Continued on Page 16, Column 4

NEWS INDEX

"All the News That's Fit to Print"

The New York Times.

LATE CITY EDITION

U. S. Weather Bureau Report (Page 66) forecasts: Windy with chance of late showers today. Cloudy through tomorrow. Temp. range: 50–37; yesterday: 38–33.

VOL. CXII..No. 38,287. NEW YORK, WEDNESDAY, NOVEMBER 21, 1962. 10 cents beyond 50-mile zone from New York City except on Long Island. Higher in air delivery cities. FIVE CENTS

KENNEDY LIFTS BLOCKADE OF CUBA AFTER KHRUSHCHEV GIVES PLEDGE TO TAKE OUT BOMBERS IN 30 DAYS

The New York Times

AT U.N. LUNCHEON: U Thant, center, Acting Secretary General, is host at luncheon. From the left in first row are: John J. McCloy and Adlai E. Stevenson of U.S., Mr. Thant, Vasily V. Kuznetsov and Valerian A. Zorin of the Soviet Union. In the back row are, from left: Omar Loutfi, Brig. Indar Jit Rikhye, Dr. Ralph J. Bunche and Yevgeny D. Kiselev, members of the U.N. staff. They discussed the removal of Soviet planes from Cuba.

NAVY GETS ORDER

President Says Soviet Move Has Helped to Reduce Dangers

Transcript of news conference and summary, Page 10.

By TAD SZULC
Special to The New York Times

WASHINGTON, Nov. 20—President Kennedy announced tonight that he had ordered the lifting of the naval blockade of Cuba.

He did this, he explained, because he had been informed during the day by Premier Khrushchev that all the Soviet jet bombers in Cuba would be withdrawn within 30 days.

The Soviet move went "a long way toward reducing the dangers which faced this hemisphere four weeks ago," the President said at a news conference. [Opening statement, Page 10.]

Within minutes of the conference, the Pentagon said that Secretary of Defense Robert S. McNamara had ordered the Navy to end the quarantine "forthwith." The quarantine, which began Oct. 24, was designed to cut off a further Soviet build-up in what the United States had termed the offensive military potential of Premier Fidel Castro's regime.

Message From Khrushchev

The Soviet promise to withdraw 30 or so obsolescent IL-28 jet bombers from Cuba came to President Kennedy in the form of a message from Premier Khrushchev this afternoon. The message ended ten days of negotiations on their removal.

It followed by 15 hours the receipt by U Thant, Acting Secretary General of the United Nations, of a letter from Premier Castro saying that if the Soviet Union wished to remove the bombers, he would not object.

The Administration was convinced that Dr. Castro had reversed his opposition to removal of the aircraft under powerful pressure from the Soviet Union.

Earlier, he had insisted they were Cuban property and not in the same category as the Soviet missiles that have been dismantled and shipped from the island.

Meeting in Havana

United States officials noted that the letter to Mr. Thant was dispatched within hours of a suddenly convoked conference in Havana between Premier Castro and Anastas I. Mikoyan, a Soviet First Deputy Premier.

While reporting progress in the fulfillment of his agreement with Mr. Khrushchev on the withdrawal of the Soviet missiles and other offensive weapons from Cuba, Mr. Kennedy emphasized that "important parts" of his understanding with the Soviet leader on Oct. 27 and 28 "remain to be carried out."

These, he said, are inspection in Cuba of the weapons' removal and the fact that "no lasting safeguards have yet been es-

Continued on Page 10, Column 3

CHINA ORDERS CEASE-FIRE ON INDIAN BORDER TODAY; OFFERS A PULLBACK PLAN

MEETING IS URGED

Peking Says Troops Will Move 12½ Miles Behind '59 Line

Text of Red China's statement is printed on Page 2.

By Reuters.

PEKING, Wednesday, Nov. 21—Communist China announced today that it was ordering a cease-fire along the entire Indian border at midnight tonight.

A Government statement also said that, starting Dec. 1, "Chinese frontier guards will withdraw to positions 20 kilometers (12.43 miles) behind the lines of actual control which existed between China and India" on Nov. 7, 1959.

The statement said China was making the move in an effort to end hostilities, to correct the border situation and to put into effect proposals it made Oct. 24.

The Oct. 24 proposals called for 12-mile withdrawals by both sides and "peaceful negotiation" of a boundary line. India rejected them.

Warning Given to Indians

Peking warned today that it "reserved the right to fight back in self-defense" if Indian troops "continued their attacks" after the Chinese cease-fire or withdrawal. [The cease-fire will take effect at 11 A.M. Wednesday Eastern standard time.]

The withdrawal would move Chinese forces north of the McMahon line on the eastern sector of the border and from their present positions in the other sectors of the 2,000-mile Himalayan frontier, the statement said.

Hsinhua, the official Chinese Communist press agency, reported shortly after issuance of the cease-fire announcement that Premier Chou En-lai and the Chinese Foreign Minister, Marshal Chen Yi, received the Indian chargé d'affaires, P. K. Banerjee, last night.

Border Talks Proposed

The 2,000-word Government statement said that "provided that the Indian Government agreed to take corresponding measures," Indian and Chinese officials could "immediately" appoint officials to meet and discuss the troop withdrawal.

It said the two sides could also discuss the establishment of checkpoints by each side and the return of personnel captured since major fighting broke out last month.

The statement said that after the results of such talks had been implemented, Prime Minister Jawaharlal Nehru and Premier Chou En-lai could meet either in Peking or New Delhi to discuss an over-all border settlement.

Aggression Charged

The "Chinese Government sincerely hopes that the Indian Government will make a positive response," the statement said. But it added that even if India "fails to make such a response," China would take the initiative.

The statement said that, to insure normal movements for border-area inhabitants and to "forestall the activities of saboteurs and maintain order here, China will set up checkposts." The posts will be at a number of points on the Chinese side of the line of actual control and will be manned by civil policemen, the statement said.

The statement said that in the last two years Indian troops crossed the "line of actual control between China and India and nibbled Chinese territory, set up strongpoints for aggression and provoked a number of border clashes."

It said that while rejecting

Continued on Page 3, Column 1

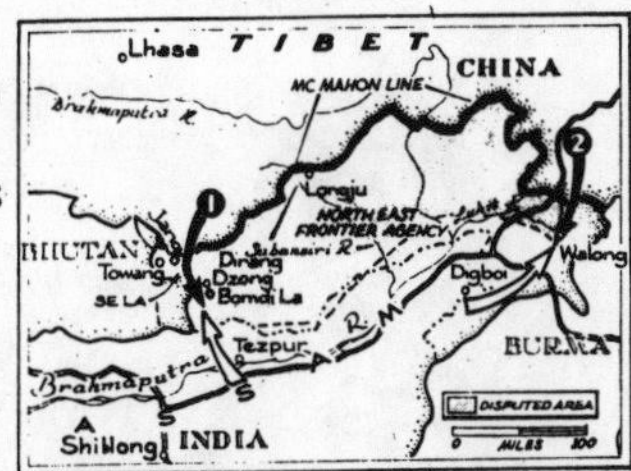

The New York Times Nov. 21, 1962

OFFER FROM PEKING: Communist China suggested a withdrawal from positions in disputed Indian border areas, where its forces were south of Bomdi La (1) and Walong (2) and were attacking near Chushul airport (3).

NEW DELHI WEIGHS A 'POSITIVE' REPLY

But India Asserts Demands Must Be Met—'Diabolical Maneuver' Is Feared

By THOMAS F. BRADY
Special to The New York Times

NEW DELHI, Wednesday, Nov. 21—The Indian Government said early today that it would "respond positively" to the Chinese Communist offer of a cease-fire and troop withdrawal if the offer met India's conditions for ending hostilities.

A Government spokesman said:

"We have received no such proposal and would like to see it in Delhi before making any comment.

"If in detail the Chinese proposal is the same as the Government of India's—namely, the restoration of the status quo as it existed before Sept. 8, 1962, when the Chinese launched their massive attacks in the North East Frontier Agency and in Ladakh—then we will respond positively."

[Prime Minister Jawaharlal Nehru told Parliament that India would continue to obtain aid from friendly countries to strengthen her defenses and economic potential, according to Reuters.]

In effect, the spokesman's statement was aimed at underling the reason why the Chinese proposal, as reported by news agencies here, was unacceptable to India.

Unofficially, some Government quarters described the

Continued on Page 3, Column 5

HARRIMAN HEADS MISSION TO INDIA

Team of High Aides Leaving Today Will Assess Arms Needs in Chinese War

By DAVID BINDER
Special to The New York Times

WASHINGTON, Nov. 20—A team of high officials headed by W. Averell Harriman, Assistant Secretary of State for Far Eastern Affairs, will fly to India tomorrow to assess her needs in her struggle against Communist China.

President Kennedy announced the mission at his news conference this evening. He also said the White House was in touch with the Indian Government on its appraisal of the Chinese cease-fire declaration and proposal to pull back troops. [Opening statement, Page 10.]

The United States team will include Paul H. Nitze, Assistant Secretary of Defense, and other officials from the Defense Department and the State Department. Mr. Kennedy said a similar mission might be sent from Britain.

Mr. Kennedy indicated that the Administration viewed the Chinese offer with extreme caution and that it was not changing its present arms aid plans for the time being.

He called the border fighting "a very serious struggle which may lead to a full-scale war if it hasn't already."

Indian sources here said that the Chinese offer was unacceptable and would be rejected in New Delhi as it was when voiced in essentially the same

Continued on Page 4, Column 3

PRESIDENT BARS BIAS IN HOUSING ASSISTED BY U.S.

Order Forbids Any Racial or Religious Discrimination —Pledge Is Fulfilled

Text of the Executive order on housing is on Page 19.

By JOHN D. MORRIS
Special to The New York Times

WASHINGTON, Nov. 20—By a long-promised "stroke of the pen," President Kennedy prohibited today racial and religious discrimination in housing built or purchased with Federal aid.

In an Executive order, he directed Federal agencies to take "all necessary and appropriate action" to that end.

Administration officials said that the order would apply principally to housing projects and apartments. When the regulations are drawn, they said, sales of private homes by individual owners will probably be exempt.

Thus, the order is unlikely to affect houses that are not in commercially developed neighborhoods. Officials indicated that F. H. A.-insured loans for home improvements will be excluded, too. And the order itself does not cover "conventional"—that is, purely private—financing at all.

Sanctions Are Provided

The order authorizes various sanctions to enforce its provisions with respect to all future construction. Enforcement with respect to existing housing will depend on persuasion and possible court action.

The President announced his action in an opening statement at his news conference tonight, a few minutes after signing the order. His action carried out a pledge he repeatedly made in his campaign for President in 1960.

Mr. Kennedy said in several campaign speeches that President Dwight D. Eisenhower could and should, "by one stroke of the pen," have prohibited discrimination in Federally aided housing.

Extent Is Uncertain

The order today covers housing financed by direct Federal loans or grants, and by private mortgages guaranteed or insured by the Federal Housing Administration, the Veterans Administration and the Farmers Home Administration, as well as property owned by the Federal Government.

This includes low-rent public housing projects, housing constructed under the urban renewal program, college housing, farm housing, the Federal community facilities program, and housing administered by the Defense Department.

There is no way of measuring how much housing will be affected. Administration officials noted that one-fourth of the new housing being constructed

Continued on Page 19, Column 3

COMMON MARKET REJECTS U.S. PLEA

Rebuffs Freeman's Request It Make Concessions on Agricultural Products

By ROBERT ALDEN
Special to The New York Times

PARIS, Nov. 22—The United States was rebuffed today in efforts to win concessions from the Common Market on American agricultural exports.

The French Minister of Agriculture, Edgard Pisani, told Orville L. Freeman, the United States Secretary of Agriculture, and other ministers gathered here at a special meeting of the Organization for Economic Cooperation and Development that the Common Market countries had no intention of retreating from agreed-upon agricultural policies.

Secretary Freeman protested in Brussels Sunday and here yesterday against what he called "unreasonable and arbitrary protectionist action" by the Common Market countries on several important American agricultural exports.

Mr. Pisani said that the Common Market countries were willing to discuss with third parties any difficulties in the agricultural domain. But he did not appear to hold out much hope of adjustment in the position adopted by the European Economic Community, as the Common Market is formally known.

The French Minister said that the problems in agricultural

Continued on Page 15, Column 3

Soviet Says Test Ban Pact Needs Only a 'Small Push'

By SEYMOUR TOPPING
Special to The New York Times

MOSCOW, Nov. 20—Izvestia declared tonight that only a "relatively small push" was needed to obtain a treaty prohibiting the testing of nuclear weapons.

The article in the Soviet Government newspaper, written by a political commentator, Vikenty A. Matveyev, indicated that Moscow still was not ready to agree to international inspection of seismic disturbances, as demanded by the United States and Britain.

Nevertheless, Western observers attached significance to the commentary because of two related developments.

It was published on the presumed terminal date of the current series of Soviet nuclear tests in the atmosphere, which began last August. Premier Khrushchev said Nov. 7 that the series would end today.

The other development was an improvement in the prospects for obtaining a Cuban settlement. United States diplomats made it clear to Moscow earlier that such a settlement was regarded by Washington as the prerequisite to substantive negotiations on other East-West issues.

Accord With Mikoyan Seen

The Moscow radio and Tass, the Soviet press agency, published tonight details of the new message from Premier Fidel Castro to U Thant, Acting Secretary General of the United Nations, in which the Cuban leader said he was agreeable to having Soviet bombers withdrawn from his country.

Dr. Castro's remark that the recently delivered IL-28 bombers should be classified as obsolete also was published by Soviet news media.

The Soviet radio's news bulletins emphasized Premier Castro's letter as an indication that he had arrived at some agreement with Anastas I. Mikoyan, a Soviet First Deputy Premier, who has been negotiating with him in Havana. It was regarded as likely that Dr. Castro had received a pledge

Continued on Page 12, Column 3

RUSK HOPES CRISIS WILL LEAD TO GAIN

Says U.S.-Soviet Exchange Opens Way to Revisions of World 'Patterns'

By ALEXANDER BURNHAM

Secretary of State Dean Rusk indicated yesterday that as a result of exchanges between the Soviet Union and the United States in the Cuban crisis a way might be open for progress on other world problems.

In a speech at a luncheon held by the Foreign Policy Association at the Waldorf-Astoria, he said:

"I suspect that we are on the front edge of significant and perhaps unpredictable events, a period in which some of the customary patterns of thought will have to be reviewed and perhaps revised—a process that will affect governments in all parts of the world."

However, he warned that the leaders of the Communist world were faced with what he called a fateful decision. That decision, he said, is whether to "pick up the great revolutionary responsibility that is waiting for them—the revolution of peace."

He also cautioned that much remained to be done before the Cuban situation was resolved. But he added, "We believe that in this period there are those on the other side who have had

Continued on Page 11, Column 2

Liquor Board Removes an Aide For Balking at Inquiry by Jury

By EMANUEL PERLMUTTER

A senior investigator for the State Liquor Authority was relieved of his duties yesterday after he had refused to waive immunity before a New York County grand jury that is investigating the agency.

The investigator, Ernest Moss, faces the loss of his job. The State Constitution specifies that a state employe who refuses to waive immunity and answer questions in a legal inquiry automatically forfeits his position.

William Phillips, assistant administrative director of the authority, said he had been informed by telephone yesterday by Assistant District Attorney Alfred J. Scotti that Mr. Moss had refused to sign a waiver.

Mr. Phillips said that as soon as the authority had been notified officially in writing of Mr. Moss's action, departmental charges would be filed against him and he would be suspended.

Mr. Moss had been requested to appear before the grand jury on Monday, but he failed to show up. He went yesterday in response to a subpoena, but when he was informed that he would be questioned about his official duties and conduct in office he refused to waive immunity. He was not interrogated.

A lawyer who joined the liquor authority on May 16, 1951, Mr. Moss was appointed to the post of senior investigator on Feb. 1, 1956. His annual salary was $8,435. He is 39 years old, married and lives at 723 East 27th Street, Brooklyn.

Another official of the Liquor Authority who is scheduled to appear before the grand jury is Martin C. Epstein, the agency's chairman. Mr. Epstein, whose left leg was amputated recently, refused to answer a subpoena in view of his health.

However, after he had been examined by a court-appointed physician, Supreme Court Justice Saul S. Streit ruled on Monday that the chairman was physically able to appear before the jurors under conditions that made allowances for his disabilities. Justice Streit directed that Mr. Epstein go before the jurors next Monday afternoon.

District Attorney Frank S. Hogan has subpoenaed records of the authority dating from Jan. 1, 1959, when Governor Rockefeller took office. Mr. Epstein was appointed by Mr. Rockefeller.

Mr. Phillips disclosed yesterday that Mr. Hogan had asked for the minutes of all meetings

Continued on Page 22, Column 3

Joint Action on Traffic Speed-up Planned by 2 Agencies in City

By RALPH KATZ

The Traffic Department and the Transit Authority are going to explore how they may ease the movement of buses and private and commercial vehicles through the city's streets.

The joint studies were announced separately yesterday by the two agencies after their top officials had met and agreed that it was too early to decide on letting buses use the major expressways.

"Transit and traffic are inseparable," Traffic Commissioner Henry A. Barnes said. "What we do to speed up traffic will help transit, and vice versa."

John J. Gilhooley and Daniel T. Scannell, members of the Transit Authority, said: "The Transit Authority and Traffic Department will cooperate fully to alleviate the traffic congestion in the city, and we are impressed with Mr. Barnes's willingness to cooperate with us."

Mr. Barnes said it was the first time the two agencies had come together to study the daily competition between 3,700 buses, 200,000 trucks and untold numbers of passenger cars for space on the city's streets.

The decision to undertake the joint studies was reached at a meeting of the heads of the authority and the Traffic Department last Friday, when the subject of discussion was the possibility of using city expressways for express bus service.

The officials agreed then that discussion of such use of the expressways was "premature," because the present speed of traffic on these roadways "was not inducive to bus service." The subject was tabled for later dis-

Continued on Page 22, Column 8

President Ending News Curbs; Defends Secrecy During Crisis

By E. W. KENWORTHY
Special to The New York Times

WASHINGTON, Nov. 20—President Kennedy assured the people and the press tonight that his Administration would not restrict information except where publication would endanger the national security.

In his first news conference since Sept. 13, Mr. Kennedy was asked three questions on the handling of information on the Cuban crisis by the Defense and State Departments. There have been widespread charges in the last week that the Administration is restricting, managing and even suppressing news.

The President referred to directives by the State and Defense Departments requiring officials to report back on any conversations with reporters.

He said there would be "a change" in the State Department directive, "because the need there is somewhat different from what it is in the Defense Department."

As for the Defense directive, he said that it had not yet been demonstrated "that this has restricted the flow of essential news of the Pentagon." [Question 14, Page 10.]

"If it does," he added, "we will change it."

He announced that the Defense Department would withdraw tonight a memorandum issued Oct. 24 to editors and radio and television directors.

The memorandum listed 12 categories of information, from troop movements to estimates of United States nuclear capabilities, that the Government considered "vital to the national security." The department had asked editors who obtained such

Continued on Page 11, Column 2

NEWS INDEX

Ray Charles won a Grammy for *I Can't Stop Loving You.*

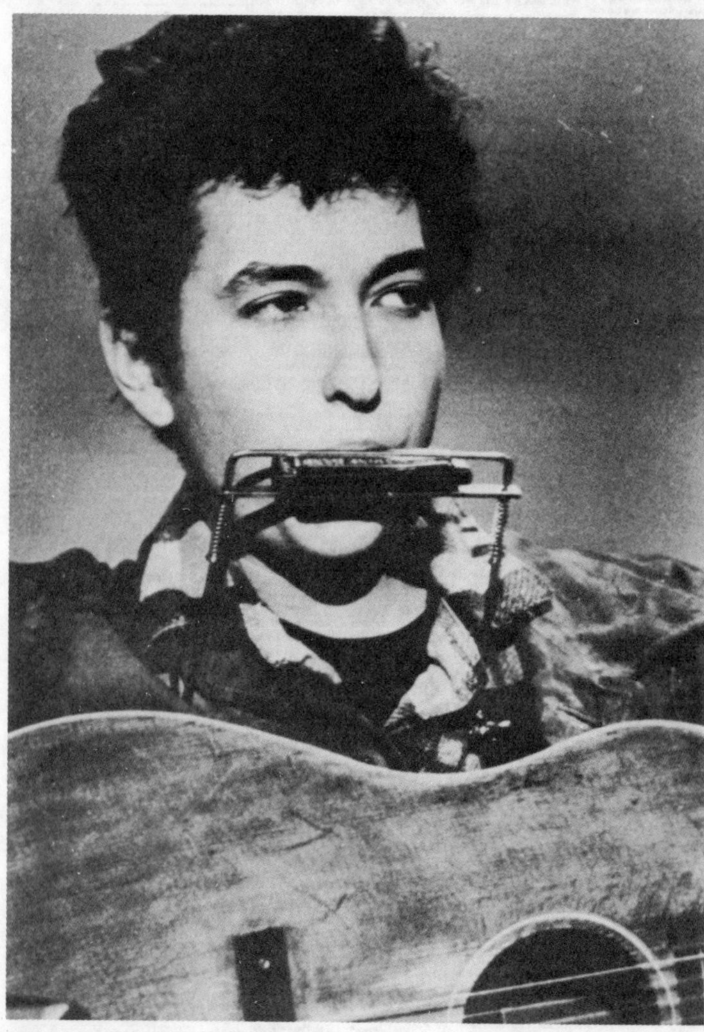

Bob Dylan began his career at a Greenwich Village coffeehouse with angry songs of social protest. Within a few months, his lyrics were becoming political slogans and he was on his way to becoming *poet laureate* of the decade.

Chubby Checker started the newest dance craze, the Twist.

1963

"All the News That's Fit to Print"

The New York Times.

VOL. CXII....No. 38,357. © 1963 by The New York Times Company. NEW YORK, WEDNESDAY, JANUARY 30, 1963. Air delivery in Alaska & Hawaii [illegible] cents; Air delivery in Canada & Mexico [illegible] cents P TEN CENTS

THE WEATHER

U.S. Weather Bureau Reports (Page 17) forecast:
Los Angeles: Cloudy with occasional rain.
San Francisco: Intermittent rain.
Seattle: Partly cloudy becoming mostly cloudy at night.

COMMON MARKET TALKS WRECKED AS FRANCE VETOES BRITISH ENTRY; BLOW TO EUROPEAN UNITY IS SEEN

PRESIDENT ASKS BROAD PROGRAM TO AID EDUCATION

Message to Congress Calls for Package Bill Costing 1.2 Billion First Year

TOTAL PUT AT 6 BILLION

Funds Would Help States in Building Schools and Raising Teachers' Pay

Excerpts from Kennedy message on education, Page 4.

By MARJORIE HUNTER
Special to The New York Times.

WASHINGTON, Jan. 29 — President Kennedy asked Congress today for a new education program that he promised would have something in it for potentially every American.

In a special message to Congress, the President called for passage of a single bill that would put $1,215,000,000 of Federal money into the nation's schools and colleges in the fiscal year beginning July 1.

Some of the programs would extend for four years. According to one estimate the total cost would be up to $6,000,000,000.

"Instead of a general aid approach that could at best create a small wave in a huge ocean," the President said, "our efforts should be selective and stimulative, encouraging the states to redouble their efforts under a plan that would phase out Federal aid over a four-year period."

Single-Package Plan

The single package represented a departure from earlier Administration efforts to aid various levels of education. During the last two years, numerous bills dealing with separate educational programs were defeated.

Administration leaders said the new bill attempted to head off the church-state fight that defeated earlier general aid measures.

However, the President did not retreat from his position that general aid on the elementary and secondary levels should be limited to public schools.

The new proposals call for funds to aid states in constructing public school buildings or improving salaries of public school teachers.

Aid to private institutions is limited to the college and university levels through student loans and matching funds for construction of academic buildings.

Items in Proposal

The bill also provides construction grants for public junior colleges; seeks to improve teacher quality through institutes and other programs; provides aid to libraries and expands vocational education and special education programs.

However, provisions for improving the quality of education, through institutes and teacher preparation programs, would be available to teachers of both public and private schools.

The President explained he was seeking a single educational package "because education cannot easily or wisely be divided into separate parts. Each part is linked to the other."

An educational official put it

Continued on Page 4, Column 7

Robert Frost Dies at 88; Kennedy Leads in Tribute

Poet Won Four Pulitzer Prizes—Took Part in 1961 Inauguration

By The Associated Press.

BOSTON, Jan. 29 — Robert Frost, dean of American poets, died today at the age of 88.

He was pronounced dead at Peter Bent Brigham hospital at 1:50 A.M.

The poet's general condition began deteriorating two days ago.

His attending physician, Dr. Roger B. Hickler, said Mr. Frost died shortly after complaining of severe chest pains and a shortness of breath. The cause of death was listed as "probably a pulmonary embolism," or blood clot in the lungs.

Dr. Hickler said that a few hours before the fatal attack Mr. Frost was "talkative and comfortable."

Not long before his death, Mr. Frost had been dictating an article on Ezra Pound from his hospital bed when he fell asleep, according to his daughter, Lesley Frost.

President Kennedy was among Government and literary figures who paid tribute to Mr. Frost.

The poet entered the hospital Dec. 3 and underwent an operation on Dec. 10 for removal of a urinary obstruction.

Subsequently he had a heart

Continued on Page 5, Column 1

Associated Press
Robert Frost

Long-Distance Rate in U.S. Cut to $1 Top After 9 P.M.

By ANTHONY LEWIS
Special to The New York Times.

WASHINGTON, Jan. 29—The Bell Telephone System agreed today to cut rates sharply on long distance calls made between 9 P.M. and 4:30 A.M. Starting about April 1, it will cost a maximum of $1 to telephone anywhere in the United States for three minutes during those hours. That will be the rate for a station-to-station call—one to a telephone number rather than a particular party.

The $1 ceiling will mean cuts up to 43 per cent below the minimum present rates, those for after 6 P.M. and on Sundays. In addition, there will be proportionate reductions below the $1 level.

The rate between New York and Los Angeles is now $1.75—nights and Sundays. It will be $1 after 9 P.M.

The New York—Chicago rate will drop from $1.15 to 70 cents after 9 P.M. and the San Francisco-Portland, Ore., rate from $1 to 65 cents.

The lower rates will begin at 9 P.M. local time in the city where the call originates.

Offsetting Reduction

Under the lower rate schedules, the charges for overtime will also be less, since they are based on a percentage of the initial three-minute charge. For example, at present a caller pays 45 cents for each extra minute on a $1.75 call between New York and Los Angeles. The new rate will be 25 cents for each extra minute on the $1.00 call.

The Federal Communications Commission announced the new rates today. It has been pressing the American Telephone and Telegraph Company and its Bell operating subsidiaries for some time to reduce the cost of long-distance tolls.

Under an agreement between the commission and the companies, they will file tariffs, effective "about April 1," incorporating what the F. C. C. called "after 9 reduced rates."

Positions Set Forth

The new tariffs will also include some small compensating increases in person-to-person rates, raising them 5 or 10 cents on calls up to 800 miles. The F. C. C. said these relatively short calls had not borne their share of costs.

Based on 1962 traffic volumes, the lower nighttime rates are expected to cost A. T. & T. $55,000,000 in revenue. The company will get $25,000,000 of that back in the person-to-person increases, for a net reduction of $30,000,000.

The commission said A.T.&T. would be able "to maintain a level of earnings on investments within the range realized by it since the last rate reduction [on interstate calls] in 1959."

In a statement issued here, A. T. & T. said: "The Bell companies are disappointed that the commission failed to recognize

Continued on Page 18, Column 3

U.S. TO INCREASE FEES FOR GRAZING

Will Use Money to Restore Lands in West—Strong Protest Expected

By WILLIAM M. BLAIR
Special to The New York Times.

WASHINGTON, Jan. 29 — The Interior Department will increase soon the fees it charges livestock producers for cattle and sheep grazing on the public domain in 10 Western states. The increase has a twofold purpose.

First, it would yield more money to help rehabilitate millions of acres of public range, which a recent study found in a "shocking condition." Range fees produced only $3,000,000 last year while the Federal Government spent nearly $12,000,000 for maintenance and management.

Second, it would establish the principle that people who use the public domain should help pay the costs whether for grazing or for recreation. The Administration will soon ask Congress to authorize new user fees to create a land conservation fund to be used to acquire and develop outdoor recreational facilities.

Cattle and sheep producers in the Western states now pay 19 cents per head of livestock per month on public rangeland established under the Taylor Grazing Act and administered by the Bureau of Land Management. The Interior Department, under a new formula, would nearly double the present fee.

This would yield a total of

Continued on Page 18, Column 2

U.N. CHIEF INVITES NATIONS TO GIVE CONGO DIRECT AID

Thant Report on Bilateral Help Attributed to World Body's Lack of Funds

By THOMAS J. HAMILTON
Special to The New York Times.

UNITED NATIONS, N. Y., Jan. 29—Secretary General U Thant said today that the United States and other countries were now free to supply bilateral assistance to the Congo, without going through the United Nations.

Mr. Thant's statement seemed to invite such assistance. It appeared to have been prompted by the realization that the United Nations, which is near bankruptcy, cannot provide the large sums needed for the rehabilitation of the Congo.

Harlan Cleveland, Assistant Secretary of State for International Organization Affairs, said yesterday that the Congolese Central Government would have a deficit of $100,000,000 this year.

According to Mr. Thant's statement, the United Nations would have no objection if the Soviet Union resumed direct aid to the Congo, provided it was requested by the Congolese Government.

Soviet Aid Recalled

The Soviet Union provided transport aircraft and supplies for the Congo in the summer of 1960 when the late Patrice Lumumba, a leftist, was in power. Soviet aid stopped, however, after Mr. Lumumba was ousted.

In any case, Mr. Thant's statement apparently foreshadows increased direct United States assistance to the Congo. A mission, headed by Mr. Cleveland, left for Leopoldville today to discuss the Congo's needs with Premier Cyrille Adoula.

Previous United Nations resolutions had requested all states to channel their assistance to the Congo through the organization. Mr. Thant said in his statement, however, that the Congo, like any other independent state, had a right to accept bilateral assistance from any country if it wished to do so.

Military Phase Over

Mr. Thant commented that with the occupation of Elisabethville, Jadotville, and other Katanga centers. "It may be said with reasonable confidence that the phase of active military involvement by United Nations forces in the Congo is about over."

The Secretary General added that the United Nations Congo force, which now has a strength of 19,000, would be reduced to between 12,000 and 13,000 by the end of March. But he indicated that the United Nations force would have to be maintained at reduced strength for some time to help the Central Government cope with tribal disputes and to maintain law and order.

The Secretary General did not reply when a reporter asked

Continued on Page 2, Column 2

BRITON IS BITTER

Heath Says One Man's Will Has Thwarted Hopes of Many

Special to The New York Times.

BRUSSELS, Jan. 29—Edward Heath, Britain's chief negotiator in her effort to join the Common Market, said tonight that the end of negotiations was a "blow to the cause of that wider unity for which we have been striving."

In a bitter reference to President de Gaulle, who blocked British entry, Mr. Heath said at a news conference:

"The high hopes of so many have thus been thwarted for political reasons by the will of one man."

"We entered these negotiations 16 months ago in good faith, and have endeavored strenuously to reach a successful conclusion," Mr. Heath declared. "Five members of the Community and the Commission have said publicly that all the remaining problems were capable of solution. I share that view."

Some Gains Are Seen

Mr. Heath said that, as a result of the negotiations, the countries had a better understanding of one another's problems. He added that there was a "deeper recognition" in Europe of the nature of the British Commonwealth.

"We shall continue to work with all our friends in Europe," to make the Commonwealth "stronger and more prosperous," he said.

British sources of the highest authority disclosed three elements of British policy in the aftermath of the crisis:

¶There will be no policy of reprisal, economic or otherwise, against France.

¶Britain is not contemplating some form of "association" with the Common Market. An offer of association has been made by General de Gaulle but has not been made by the Community as such, which would have to make the offer for it to be valid.

¶There are unlikely to be any dramatic changes in British domestic policy.

A Heavy Blow to London

By SYDNEY GRUSON
Special to The New York Times.

LONDON, Jan. 29—The collapse of Britain's Common Market negotiations, though no surprise, came as a heavy blow here today. But the tenor of British reaction was that the country now must face up to

Continued on Page 3, Column 6

Washington Is Concerned; Moscow Welcomes Split

De Gaulle Aims Studied

By MAX FRANKEL
Special to The New York Times.

WASHINGTON, Jan. 29 — Administration officials declared today that President de Gaulle's veto of British membership in the Common Market had merely postponed the inevitable.

They told reporters and diplomats that history was on the side of allied unity, and that Washington intended to press ahead with economic and military policies to promote such unity.

But also discernible were an attitude of great disappointment and frustration and a foreboding of serious trouble for the Western alliance as a result of the collapse of negotiations at Brussels.

Privately, officials wondered about General de Gaulle's "real" objectives and some foresaw a French drive to cut down United States influence in Europe. They feared open economic and political competition within the alliance and acknowledged some suspicions of

Continued on Page 3, Column 2

Discord Pleases Soviet

Special to The New York Times.

MOSCOW, Jan. 29 — The Soviet Union, plagued by its quarrels with Communist China, welcomed today with unconcealed satisfaction the disarray among the Atlantic alliance.

The rift in the West has come at a time when Moscow has adopted a cautious foreign policy because of the ideological dispute with Peking, the Cuban reversal and internal economic difficulties.

Western diplomatic observers said it was unlikely that the Kremlin would attempt immediately to exploit the Western differences by provoking a crisis because the Soviet leaders have learned that pressure only tends to unify the Western allies. Soviet Government propaganda hailed the "breakdown" of the negotiations at Brussels for the entry of Britain into the Common Market. Wide prominence was given to the differences between President Kennedy and President de Gaulle.

Pravda, the Communist

Continued on Page 3, Column 3

DE GAULLE IS FIRM

Erhard Says Britain's Exclusion Is 'Black Day for Europe'

By EDWIN L. DALE Jr.
Special to The New York Times.

BRUSSELS, Jan. 29 — Sixteen months of negotiations for British entry into the European Common Market ended today in failure and bitterness.

The end came at the demand of France. Britain and France's five Common Market partners wanted the talks continued, but France's right of veto made continuation without her useless. There is no move for a revival.

The end of the talks not only meant the wreckage of the historic move by Britain to cast her lot with continental Europe; it also left a heavy cloud over the future of the Common Market itself. Ludwig Erhard, West German Vice Chancellor and Minister of the Economy, said:

"This is a black day for Europe. The Common Market is now only a mechanism and no longer a living thing."

Kennedy Plan Shattered

Today's collapse also left in ruins, for the foreseeable future, President Kennedy's policy of an "equal partnership" between the United States on one hand and an enlarged Common Market including Britain on the other.

It was widely regarded as the worst political crisis in Europe since World War II, surpassing in its consequences that created by France's rejection in 1954 of the European defense community. All of the leading figures today blamed the crisis squarely on French President de Gaulle.

But General de Gaulle was evidently willing to take the blame in his stride. A French spokesman remarked: "France's shoulders are broad enough to bear the burden of responsibility."

Briton Is Summoned

The final act of the drama was played out today in an atmosphere of deep pessimism. Firm to the end, France's five Common Market partners — West Germany, Italy, Belgium, the Netherlands and Luxembourg — reached agreement on a concrete proposal for keeping negotiations going by giving a special mandate to the Common Market Executive Commission to make a three-week study of the outstanding problems and suggest solutions.

Maurice Couve de Murville, the French Foreign Minister, doggedly persisted in his refusal to accept this proposal because it would imply a continuation of the negotiations. In mid-afternoon, Edward Heath, Lord Privy Seal, the chief British negotiator, was called in to hear the result that he already knew.

Although Mr. Heath met briefly afterward with the foreign ministers of "the five,"

Continued on Page 3, Column 1

BRUSSELS BREAK DEPRESSES BONN

Germans Fear They Will Be Chief Loser From Failure of Britain's Market Bid

By ARTHUR J. OLSEN
Special to The New York Times.

BONN, Jan. 29—News of the breakdown of the Brussels talks was received in West Germany tonight with discouragement and foreboding.

The feeling is general in official and private quarters that Bonn may turn out to be the big loser from the failure of the effort to bring Britain into the European Common Market. The adverse reaction in the United States, West Germany's indispensable ally, represents the dominating worry here.

Government comment was withheld until tomorrow, but a spokesman of Chancellor Adenauer's Christian Democratic party said that the policy of European unity had been thrust into "serious danger."

Comment by Ollenhauer

"The consequences cannot yet be foreseen," said Kurt Schmucker, spokesman of the Christian Democratic parliamentary group.

Erich Ollenhauer, chairman of the Opposition Social Democratic party, said collapse of the Brussels talks had dealt "a heavy blow to European unification and Atlantic solidarity."

Another party chief, Dr. Erich Mende of the Free Democrats, said France's act in Brussels was "bound to affect" West Germany's attitude toward its new treaty of cooperation with France. The treaty, signed last week, will soon be submitted to Parliament for ratification.

The leader of the Free Democrats, who are the junior partners in the governing coalition, said the treaty should not be permitted to become "the end station of European cooperation."

Preventive Action Urged

"A greater Europe without Britain and the Scandinavian countries is impossible in the long run," Dr. Mende said.

West German politicians and press commentators were quick to name President de Gaulle as the villain of the drama and Premier Khrushchev as the clear winner. The Hamburg newspaper Die Welt will sum up this bitter judgment this way in its leading editorial tomorrow:

"De Gaulle is responsible for the breakdown of the talks. This must be stated squarely in the light of attempts at putting the blame on the five other Common Market partners.... The winner of the day, a black day for both Europe and Western cooperation, is Khrushchev.

Continued on Page 3, Column 7

BRITAIN MAY CUT HER NATO FORCE

Reduction in Army of Rhine Likely to Follow Nation's Failure to Enter Market

By DREW MIDDLETON
Special to The New York Times.

PARIS, Jan. 29—The forward strategy of the North Atlantic Alliance in defense of Europe has been seriously threatened by France's exclusion of Britain from the European Economic Community, qualified sources declared tonight.

This strategy depends on the concentration as far east as possible of allied divisions. One consequence of Britain's exclusion from the economic community is expected to be the reduction, for economic reasons, of the British Army of the Rhine, a pivotal force on the northern flank in Europe.

Coupled with the failure of France to assign two badly needed divisions to the forward NATO forces, this is expected to force a re-examination and perhaps a revision of the alliance's forward strategy.

NATO, however, conscious that it is now the last stronghold in Europe of trans-Atlantic unity, intends to intensify its efforts to create a nuclear force.

The gloom that hung over the political and military offices in NATO as a result of the breakdown of the Brussels negotiations is matched by the forebodings of some French politicians.

Some, normally faithful to President de Gaulle's policies,

Continued on Page 3, Column 3

Kennedy to Open Tax Returns Of Foreign Agents to Senate

By TAD SZULC
Special to The New York Times.

WASHINGTON, Jan. 29 — President Kennedy signed an Executive Order today allowing the Senate Foreign Relations Committee to inspect the tax returns of all non-diplomatic representatives of foreign governments in the United States.

The committee is investigating the activities of lobbyists and agents of foreign nations here to determine the extent of violations of the Foreign Agents Registration Act of 1938.

The study, which has the personal attention of Senator J. W. Fulbright, Arkansas Democrat who is committee chairman, is expected to lead to Congressional action tightening the law. This is necessary, he believes, to stop serious abuses and improper attempts to influence the conduct of United States foreign policy.

The committee expects to open formal hearings next week following seven months of inquiries by its investigators.

Under Secretary of State George W. Ball is scheduled to be the first Administration witness in open hearings. Subsequently, the committee plans to concentrate on executive sessions, questioning lobbyists and foreign agents in connection with material gathered here and abroad by its investigators.

The Presidential order provides for inspection by the committee of "any income, excess-profits, estate or gift tax returns for the years 1950 to 1962, inclusive" until next June 30, when the committee's investigation is to be completed.

Involved are returns that may

Continued on Page 4, Column 8

NEWS INDEX

Major Fight on Mental Illness Urged on Congress by Kennedy

By ROBERT C. TOTH
Special to The New York Times.

WASHINGTON, Jan. 29 — President Kennedy will send to Congress within the next few days an ambitious national program to fight mental illnesses that afflict an estimated total of 22,000,000 Americans.

The program of prevention, care and rehabilitation would cost more than $400,000,000 over four to five years, in addition to the $1,000,000,000 annual Federal outlay for mental health today.

About three-fourths of the new funds would be directed at the psychological disorders grouped under mental diseases, while the rest would aim at the intelligence deficiencies that characterize the mentally retarded. This 3-1 ratio reflects the number of Americans institutionalized for these illnesses, roughly 700,000 and 200,000, respectively.

Beyond the Government effort, however, some officials hope the President's message will mobilize a national attack on mental illnesses much as Franklin D. Roosevelt's support of the March of Dimes sparked the fight against polio 25 years ago.

Behind the proposals on mental disease is an exhaustive, 10-volume report by the Joint Commission on Mental Illness and Health, which was set up by Congress. The commission's report, published in 1961 after six years of study, called for radical reforms in the public care of mentally ill at Federal, state and local levels.

It urged that the monolithic, prison-like mental institutions be replaced by intensive treatment hospitals, community clinics and emergency mental wards in general hospitals. It recommended Federal funds for making those changes, and for training specialists in mental health fields.

Political steam to implement the report has been building up, largely through the 80 specialized organizations who helped in the commission study, including the National Association for Mental Health with its 3,000 local chapters.

Mr. Kenedy was expected to propose Federal assistance for building and operating community centers that can treat patients either within the institution or on an out-patient basis. In both cases the ill would be treated as much as

Continued on Page 6, Column 3

Thant Sees a Threat in Borneo That May Require U.N. Action

By ARNOLD H. LUBASCH
Special to The New York Times.

UNITED NATIONS, N. Y., Jan. 29—Secretary General U Thant warned today that the Borneo area in Southeast Asia could become a major trouble spot that would require United Nations action.

Surveying world problems in an hour-long news conference, Mr. Thant singled out the British protectorate of Brunei as posing a potentially "very serious problem." The Secretary General added that he might try to devise a formula to help ease tensions in the Borneo area.

Britain announced yesterday that an infantry brigade had been alerted to go to the Far East because of possible "outside interference" in Brunei, a rich oil-producing enclave on the island of Borneo. British forces there put down a brief rebellion last month.

Reports have circulated in London that 10,000 Soviet-equipped Indonesian troops were massed on the border for an effort to occupy Brunei. The reports were denied yesterday by Indonesia.

The situation in the South China Sea area has been further complicated because of the Philippine's claim to North Borneo. North Borneo and Sarawak are both British colonies and are scheduled to join Malaya and Singapore in forming the federation of Malaysia by Aug. 31.

Brunei, a British-protected sultanate, is also expected to join the federation.

Mr. Thant's warning on Borneo was regarded as implying that the situation there was

Continued on Page 2, Column 3

1963

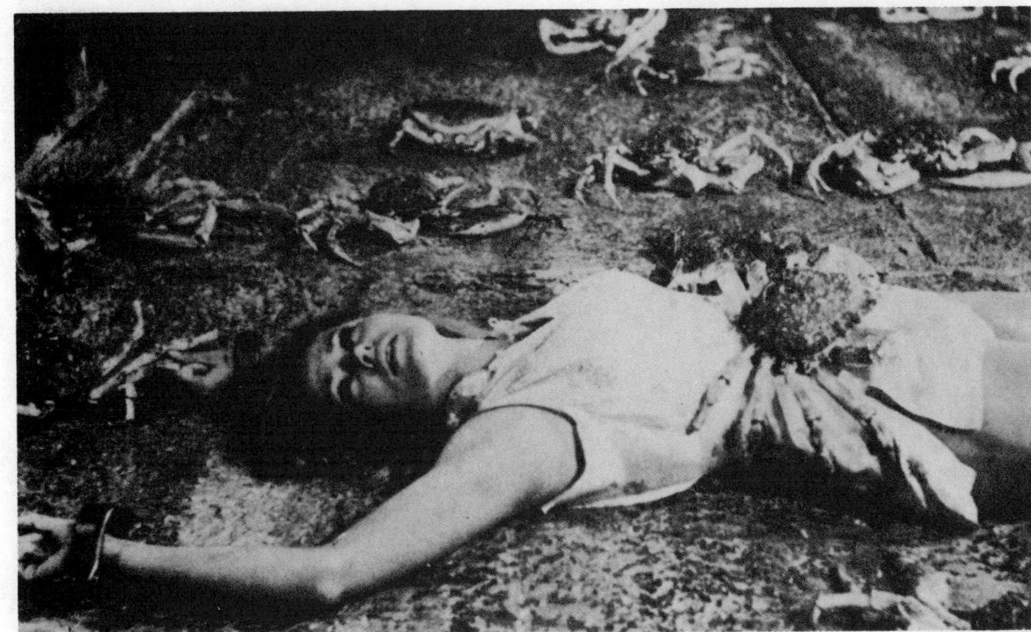

Ursula Andrews shown in a rather uncomfortable position in a scene from *Dr. No*, the first of Ian Fleming's novels made into a film.

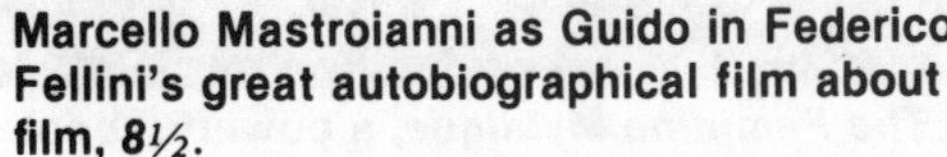

Marcello Mastroianni as Guido in Federico Fellini's great autobiographical film about film, *8½*.

Albert Finney and Diane Cilento shown in a scene from the bawdy comedy, *Tom Jones*.

Battling atheist, Madalyn Murray O'Hair, celebrated with her sons after winning a Supreme Court ruling against recitation of bible verses in public schools.

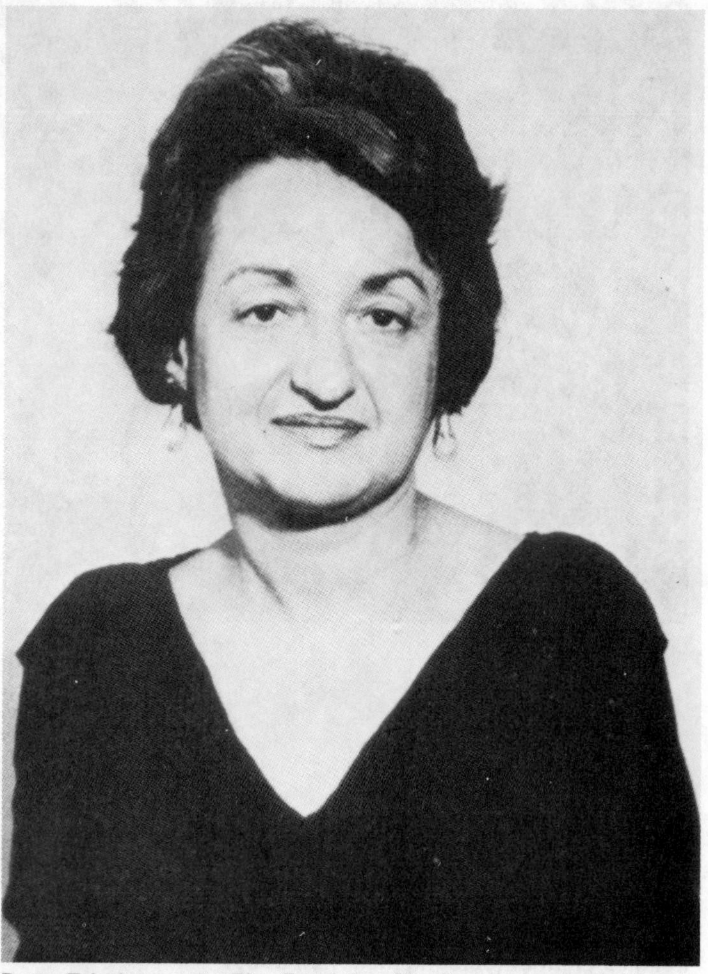
Betty Friedan wrote *The Feminine Mystique,* a powerful book that motivated the women's liberation movement.

The Pan Am building was the latest steel and glass behemoth. It was completed in 1963.

Poet Robert Frost fell asleep while dictating an article about Ezra Pound and never woke up. The four-time Pulitzer Prize winner died at the age of 88.

The Jaguar XK-E was a hot import from Great Britain.

"All the News That's Fit to Print"

The New York Times.

LATE CITY EDITION

U. S. Weather Bureau Report (Page 86) forecasts: Mostly sunny, breezy and cool today; fair and cold tonight. Fair tomorrow. Temp. range: 52—35; yesterday: 48—38.

VOL. CXII. No. 38,428. © 1963 by The New York Times Company. Times Square, New York 36, N. Y. NEW YORK, THURSDAY, APRIL 11, 1963. TEN CENTS

ATOM SUBMARINE WITH 129 LOST IN DEPTHS 220 MILES OFF BOSTON; OIL SLICK SEEN NEAR SITE OF DIVE

Thresher, nuclear-powered attack submarine, commissioned Aug. 3, 1961, at Portsmouth (N. H.) Naval Shipyard

THRESHER HUNTED

Rescue Craft Search Area of Last Test in 8,400-Foot Water

By ROBERT F. WHITNEY
Special to The New York Times

WASHINGTON, April 10 — The Navy said tonight that its atomic submarine Thresher and 129 men aboard "appeared to be lost" in the Atlantic.

An oil slick was reported to have been sighted in the area where the vessel took a deep test dive at about 9 o'clock this morning in water 8,400 feet deep, 220 miles east of Boston.

"At that depth," said Adm. George W. Anderson, Chief of Naval Operations, "rescue would be absolutely out of the question."

Loss of the Thresher and 129 men would be the Navy's worst peacetime submarine disaster.

However, the Navy still clung to the possibility that there had been a communications failure and the $45,000,000 submarine was unable to report by radio or otherwise.

This appeared to be a dim hope after the ship, named for the thresher shark, had not been heard from since early morning.

Radiation Peril Denied

Admiral Anderson announced that the accident would be investigated by a court of inquiry headed by Vice Adm. Bernard Austin, president of the Naval War College.

Admiral Anderson, who was at the Pentagon answering reporters' questions about the disaster, assured them that there was "no chance of nuclear explosion in the submarine" or "radioactive contamination" dangers to shipping.

The Navy chief said quietly: "To those of us who have been brought up in the traditions of the sea it is a sad occasion when a ship is reported lost."

The Navy's first announcement that the Thresher was missing came after reports flooded Newport, R. I., that a submarine was "on the bottom and unable to rise."

Rescue Vessels Sent

With the Thresher missing, the Navy sent destroyers from Newport and aircraft from the Quonset, R. I., Air Station. They are probing for possible radio signals and a fix on the submarine's position.

The 129 men aboard include 96 enlisted men, 16 officers and 17 civilian technicians from the Portsmouth, N. H., Navy Yard.

The Thresher had recently been at Portsmouth for overhaul and had gone out for deep diving tests. With her was the submarine rescue ship Skylark, which lost contact after the Thresher's dive.

The depth at which the Navy thinks the Thresher may be lying would doom the vessel and her crew. Pressures at such a depth would crush the hull, it was said.

Presumably this was the reason why Admiral Anderson said

Continued on Page 14, Column 1

Lieut. Comdr. John Wesley Harvey, skipper of craft. (United Press International)

Thresher reported down in the Atlantic at cross. (The New York Times, April 11, 1963)

NATO TO PROCEED ON ATOMIC FORCE INCLUDING FRENCH

Paris Expected to Contribute Two Squadrons to Carry U.S. Nuclear Weapons

NASSAU PLAN APPROVED

Progress Reported in Effort to Heal Rift Over British Tie to Common Market

By DREW MIDDLETON
Special to The New York Times

PARIS, April 10—The North Atlantic alliance is to establish an allied nuclear force, including French squadrons, informed sources said tonight.

The United States will contribute three Polaris submarines and Britain her V-bomber force while France, West Germany and other European powers will make available planes and missiles capable of delivering nuclear weapons provided by the United States.

The assumption that France will contribute to this force rests on the American conviction that President de Gaulle will agree to the inclusion of two French fighter-bomber squadrons for purposes of strategic coordination, including the assignment of targets.

French Go Part Way

The establishment of the force, which is to be completed at a NATO meeting in Ottawa next month, can thus be represented as the acceptance of the United States-British project for an interallied nuclear force as laid down in last year's Nassau agreement.

The French, qualified sources said, are unlikely to go that far. But they have made known to Secretary of State Dean Rusk and others their willingness to play a role in any cooperative allied nuclear effort.

President de Gaulle rejected the Nassau proposal for an interallied force last December. The present American view apparently is that he will cooperate as long as the nuclear force is not called by that specific term.

The disclosure of French willingness to contribute to the force was made known after a meeting this afternoon of the North Atlantic Council attended by Mr. Rusk and the Foreign Ministers of Britain, France, West Germany and Italy.

Strengthening of Alliance

The North Atlantic alliance, rattled in recent months by France's pursuit of an independent national policy, appears on the surface to be considerably strengthened by the events of the last three days.

Mr. Rusk talked with President de Gaulle and received the French leader's assurances on his belief in the importance of the Atlantic alliance. The Earl of Home, Britain's Foreign Secretary, met Maurice Couve de Murville, the French Foreign Minister, and some degree of cordiality on defense issues was reintroduced into the British-French relationship.

The American and British ministers remained firm in contending that Britain should be a member of the European Economic Community. The initiative for an improvement in

Continued on Page 3, Column 5

SEATO Reaffirms Support for Laos

By HENRY GINIGER
Special to The New York Times

PARIS, April 10—The eight nations of the Southeast Asia Treaty Organization reaffirmed their support today for a neutral and independent Laos in the face of a renewed Communist menace.

In a communiqué capping a three-day meeting, the Council of Ministers of the organization expressed concern over "continued and increased threats weighting on the security" of the area.

There was no question of the intervention of the organization in Laos. As a neutral nation Laos has asked to be no longer a beneficiary of the treaty group's help.

It was strongly hinted, however, that some of SEATO's members would be prepared to take a military stand such as taken in May, 1962, when

Continued on Page 6, Column 3

SOVIET'S CONCERN ON BERLIN GROWS

Moscow Says That NATO's Atomic Program Causes a Special Urgency

By SEYMOUR TOPPING
Special to The New York Times

MOSCOW, April 10—A Soviet diplomatic source said today that the talks between the United States and the Soviet Union on Berlin had acquired a new urgency because of Western plans to establish a nuclear force in the North Atlantic Treaty Organization.

The source asserted that the dangers stemming from West German access to nuclear weapons through such a NATO force would be raised by Anatoly F. Dobrynin, the Soviet Ambassador in Washington, at his next meeting with Secretary of State Dean Rusk.

Mr. Dobrynin and Mr. Rusk are scheduled to meet Friday for their second conversation on Berlin and Germany in the current exploratory talks.

Interruptions Over Cuba

The private talks were resumed on March 26 after having been interrupted by the Cuban crisis last October.

Soviet officials here suddenly are evincing a new interest in the Berlin talks after a period of a month in which they appeared content to accept the status quo. They now say that a renewed effort must be made to achieve an understanding on Germany before any Western arrangement is made that would give West Germany access to nuclear weapons.

The Soviet position on the possible creation of a nuclear force for the Western military alliance was stated in notes to the Western powers published yesterday. The notes dismissed the United States arguments that the proposed nuclear

Continued on Page 2, Column 4

POPE JOHN URGES A WORLD NATION TO GUARD PEACE

His Encyclical on Problems of Atomic Age Proposes Broadening of U.N.

Text of encyclical appears on Pages 17, 18 and 19.

By ARNALDO CORTESI
Special to The New York Times

ROME, April 10—Pope John XXIII proposed in an encyclical today the establishment of a world political community or public authority, a kind of supernation to which all countries should belong. Its aim would be to insure peace.

"The moral order itself," he said, demands that a public authority be established on a worldwide basis.

He made it clear that this new world organization should not be in contrast to or competition with the United Nations, of whose existence the 81-year-old Pontiff took note with satisfaction. He expressed hope that "the day may come when every human being will find therein an effective safeguard for the rights which derive directly from his dignity as a person."

Pope's Eighth Encyclical

The Pope's proposal was contained in an encyclical, or circular letter, dealing with present-day problems of peace. He signed it at the Vatican yesterday. It bears tomorrow's date, Holy Thursday.

The encyclical, the eighth of John XXIII's four-and-a-half-year Pontificate, is known by the first significant words of the Latin text, "Pacem in Terris" ("Peace on Earth"). In a departure from precedent, it was addressed not only to the Roman Catholic episcopacy, clergy and faithful but also to "all men of goodwill."

The Pontiff warned that nuclear warfare could destroy mankind. He noted the "enormous stocks of armaments that have been and still are being made in more economically developed countries" and said that they "should be reduced equally and simultaneously."

Other Principal Points

Other principal points made in the encyclical were these:

¶Governments and men must avoid the frequently committed error of supposing that relationships between men and states are controlled by the same laws as the physical universe.

¶Gains made by the working classes, the participation of women in public life and wider recognition of the equality and dignity of men bespeak progress toward a more just society.

¶Civil authorities must promote as well as protect the rights of individuals.

¶Governments must protect all racial minorities.

The essential part of the en-

Continued on Page 16, Column 1

House Votes Works Plan; Backs President, 228-184

By JOHN D. MORRIS
Special to The New York Times

WASHINGTON, April 10—Administration forces won the first major skirmish today in what promises to be a session-long battle over Federal spending. The House of Representatives overrode Republican opposition and approved an appropriation of $450,000,000 for a public works program designed to create jobs in communities with high rates of unemployment.

The roll-call vote was 228 to 184. This affirmed an earlier count of 202 to 172, taken by tellers.

The majority on the roll-call, which reversed an action taken by the House Appropriations Committee last week, included 208 Democrats and 20 Republicans. Voting against the fund were 151 Republicans and 33 Democrats.

Republican Foes Assailed

The White House issued a statement hailing the action as a victory "in the fight against unemployment." The statement also accused Republicans who voted against the appropriation of "blind opposition."

Republican leaders, who have resolved to cut total requests for new spending authority by at least $10,000,000,000, said they were not disheartened by the outcome.

They noted that they were handicapped today by the fact that the program at issue promised Federal funds for local projects in the districts of many Representatives. It was politically hazardous for members to vote against the appropriation in the face of strong pressure from home.

The pressure rose to a high point before the voting as many telegrams and telephone calls from Governors, Mayors and other public officials were received by House members.

The funds were added to an omnibus bill providing supplementary appropriations for various agencies in the remaining months of the fiscal year 1963, which ends June 30.

The bill, as passed by voice

Continued on Page 34, Column 4

CLAY ADVOCATES FURTHER AID CUT

Declares Additional Savings Won't Be 'Tremendous'—Opposes 'Stroke of Ax'

By FELIX BELAIR Jr.
Special to The New York Times

WASHINGTON, April 10—Gen. Lucius D. Clay called today for a bigger cut in foreign aid spending than the $400,000,000 President Kennedy has pruned from his January budget estimate of $4,900,000,000.

General Clay, head of a Presidential advisory commission on foreign aid, indicated that any additional savings "would not be tremendous," but he declined to estimate the further potential economies.

At a public hearing before the House Foreign Affairs Committee, he said that such an estimate would entail a country - by - country analysis that he would give only behind closed doors.

"But I am sure that a careful analysis would show the possibility of some further savings," General Clay said. "We on the committee were very gratified that the President did cut his original request. The new request contains programs that we have not reviewed, but I would say that his proposals for continuing programs are very closely in agreement with our report."

In its report, the Clay committee proposed tighter administrative criteria and a gradual termination of economic aid programs in some countries. It proposed that military aid be

Continued on Page 6, Column 5

Revival of Saloons, Outlawed Since '34, Is Studied by State

By CHARLES GRUTZNER

The corner saloon may stage a legal comeback in New York State with safeguards against its antisocial features.

The saloon was outlawed by name in the state alcoholic beverage control law adopted in 1934, right after the repeal of Prohibition.

It could be restored to respectability and legality through the elimination of some current restrictions on licensed drinking places. These restrictions will be examined by the Moreland Act Commission, which was appointed by Governor Rockefeller to review and recommend changes in liquor and beer controls.

Rule on Meals a Factor

The main restriction—which is being widely circumvented—is the requirement that any drinking place be operated as part of a bona fide eating place, at which regular meals are available. The law says specifically that sandwiches and salads alone do not fill the bill.

The commission chairman, former Federal Judge Lawrence E. Walsh, said yesterday that the major areas of the inquiry, which will take a year or more, would include the requirements for full-meal facilities and a full view from the street, and the prohibition against swinging doors on drinking places.

Mr. Walsh said the whole subject of liquor control would be reviewed by the commission in the light of social changes since 1934. He said there was a question whether some of the "nuisance" regulations were making it too difficult for conscientious persons to comply with all the rules.

One field of inquiry will involve whether the state's fixing of liquor prices should be abolished.

Continued on Page 36, Column 4

KENNEDY WEIGHS STEEL PRICE MOVE

Puts Off Trip and Confers With His Advisers After Wheeling Concern Acts

By RICHARD E. MOONEY
Special to The New York Times

WASHINGTON, April 10 — President Kennedy maintained a conspicuous silence today on the Wheeling Steel Corporation's price increase.

He postponed overnight his planned departure for a long Easter weekend in Florida. Pierre Salinger, his news secretary, said that this was because "the President has a number of matters here at the White House that he feels he should attend to this afternoon." But it was widely interpreted as a psychological move to make the steel industry apprehensive.

[Most of the nation's major steel producers declined Wednesday to discuss the Wheeling company's announcement.]

Meeting Is Held

The President met in the late morning with a half-dozen members of his Cabinet and top-ranking aides, essentially the same group that drafted the Administration's counterattack on the United States Steel Corporation's price increase a year ago today. There was also one outsider present—Clark M. Clifford, the Washington lawyer who was the President's private agent in dealing with United States Steel last year.

There were two later meetings of the group. One, with Walter W. Heller, chairman of the President's Council of Economic Advisers, followed the morning meeting with the President. Then in the late afternoon the group met with the President again.

There had been no announcement of any meetings, though the word had spread fast. It was evident that at the first meeting the conferees had decided that the Administration should sit tight for the moment and gather facts.

Mr. Salinger said "no comment" to all questions about steel all day, and other officials were told to do the same. At a late hour it was still not known whether the President would make a statement and the White House lobby was jammed with reporters in anticipation.

The Administration was disturbed, though not completely surprised, by Wheeling's move

Continued on Page 54, Column 1

Mississippi Faculty Backs Artist Arrested for Painting Integration Riots

The New York Times (by Claude Sitton)

G. Ray Kerciu, assistant professor of art at University of Mississippi, with his painting "America the Beautiful"

By CLAUDE SITTON
Special to The New York Times

OXFORD, Miss., April 10—Faculty members urged the University of Mississippi today to support an artist under attack for a painting portraying the desegregation riots here last September. In a unanimous resolution, the local chapter of the American Association of University Professors called on the school's administrators to take the following steps: First, to issue a vigorous public statement upholding the right of G. Ray Kerciu, assistant professor of art, to express his convictions through the painting "America the Beautiful." Then, to direct the university attorney to represent Mr. Kerciu in his trial on charges of obscenity and desecration of the Confederate flag. "If this is not done, it is the belief of this body that the individual members of this faculty can only con-

Continued on Page 21, Column 4

Rockefeller Scores U.S. Cuban Policy

By WARREN WEAVER Jr.
Special to The New York Times

WASHINGTON, April 10 — Governor Rockefeller sharply criticized today United States policy on Cuba.

At a news conference the New York Governor said that he found it "very hard to understand" why the Administration was supporting "freedom fighters" in South Vietnam and "holding them back and preventing them from operating in Cuba."

"I hope it is not as a means or an endeavor to placate or to appease the Soviet," he said.

Mr. Rockefeller was asked if he had any evidence that appeasement of the Russians was involved in the attempt to prevent refugee raids on Cuba.

"It is hard to see what other reason there would be, in view

Continued on Page 10, Column 4

Ex-Lefkowitz Aide Is Silent at Inquiry

By JACK ROTH

A former law associate of State Attorney General Louis J. Lefkowitz refused yesterday to sign a waiver of immunity and testify before the grand jury investigating the State Liquor Authority.

The former associate, Hyman D. Siegel, who said he had worked for Mr. Lefkowitz from 1930 until 1957, entered and left the grand jury room in less than five minutes. Outside the room he met with reporters, but let his lawyer, Matthew H. Brandenburg, respond to most of the questions.

Mr. Lefkowitz was asked later to comment on Mr. Siegel's refusal to testify. A spokesman would not go beyond a statement that Mr. Lefkowitz had not practiced law since assuming his state post and that Mr.

Continued on Page 36, Column 1

Belmont Park Shut; Track Held Unsafe

By JOE NICHOLS

Belmont Park, accepted as the finest race course in the world since its founding in 1905, will be closed "for reasons of public safety" for at least two years. This was announced by James Cox Brady, chairman of the board of the New York Racing Association, after a meeting of the board of trustees yesterday.

A state of "progressive deterioration" of the physical properties of the plant, discovered in a spring engineering inspection, prompted the N.Y.R.A. to ask the New York State Racing Commission for permission to keep the park closed. Ashley Trimble Cole, the commission chairman, attended the meet-

Continued on Page 39, Column 1

NEWS INDEX

"All the News That's Fit to Print"

The New York Times.

LATE CITY EDITION

U. S. Weather Bureau Report (Page 56) forecasts: Mostly sunny today; fair tonight. Cloudy, chance of late rain tomorrow. Temp. range: 62—44; yesterday: 64—43.

VOL. CXII . No. 38,460. NEW YORK, MONDAY, MAY 13, 1963. TEN CENTS

U. S. SENDS TROOPS INTO ALABAMA AFTER RIOTS SWEEP BIRMINGHAM; KENNEDY ALERTS STATE'S GUARD

Associated Press Wirephoto

NEGROES' HOMES AFIRE IN BIRMINGHAM: As flames rise behind them, Negro Civil Defense worker leads a woman occupant to safety. Fire occurred early yesterday.

WARNING ISSUED

President Appeals for Peace and Vows to Keep Order

Text of President's statement appears on Page 25.

By ANTHONY LEWIS
Special to The New York Times

WASHINGTON, May 12 — President Kennedy tonight dispatched Federal troops to bases near Birmingham, Ala., for use if racial violence breaks out again.

His action followed three hours of rioting early this morning in which 50 persons were injured. The rioting erupted after two buildings were bombed.

The President also ordered all "necessary preliminary steps" be taken to call the Alabama National Guard into Federal service. The actual call can then be accomplished in minutes if the President decides it is needed.

[Air Force C-47 transports with troops and equipment began arriving at Maxwell Air Base, about 80 miles south of Birmingham, within an hour after the President announced the move, United Press International reported. It said 10 transports had arrived by 12:45 A.M. Monday, New York time, and other troops were moving into Fort McClellan, 40 miles east of Birmingham.]

Confers With McNamara

The President made known these emergency moves at the White House tonight. He appeared before the press and television cameras at 8:48 P. M. to read a grave statement on the Birmingham crisis. The President declared:

"This Government will do whatever must be done to preserve order, to protect the lives of its citizens and to uphold the law of the land. I am certain that the vast majority of the citizens of Birmingham, both white and Negro—particularly those who labored so hard to achieve the peaceful, constructive settlement of last week—can feel nothing but dismay at the efforts of those who would replace conciliation and good will with violence and hate."

The Defense Department would not identify the troop units or indicate their size, except to say that all came from outside Alabama.

Mr. Kennedy acted after conferring for three hours with Secretary of Defense Robert S. McNamara, Attorney General Robert F. Kennedy, Secretary of the Army Cyrus Vance and other officials.

The President's statement made clear the deep concern of the Administration over last night's bombings of Negro residences in Birmingham and the resulting riots and police action.

Concerned Over Police

Government sources said the events of the night gave an entirely new cast to the Birmingham racial crisis. From a protest demonstration, they said, it had become an ugly, violent struggle.

In addition to concern over the bombings and the rioting, officials were disturbed by the police reaction. It was reported that the Birmingham police, behaving efficiently and fairly, had the situation under control when state troopers came in and revived tensions.

The eruption of violence threatened the agreement reached last week, with the help of Federal mediation, to end the Negro protest demonstrations. White business leaders had agreed to

Continued on Page 25, Column 1

50 Hurt in Negro Rioting After Birmingham Blasts

By CLAUDE SITTON
Special to The New York Times

BIRMINGHAM, Ala., May 12—Riots raged out of control for more than three hours early today, after bombings of a motel and an integration leader's home had enraged Negroes. The city police quelled the disturbances shortly after 5 A.M., New York time, with assistance from Negro ministers and civilian defense workers.

About 50 persons were injured, including a policeman and a taxicab driver who were stabbed.

About 2,500 persons joined the crowds that attacked the police and firemen, wrecked scores of police and private automobiles and burned six small stores and a two-story apartment house. Aside from the authorities, only a relative handful of whites became involved.

Troopers Take Control

Some 250 state highway patrolmen under Col. Albert J. Lingo, Director of Public Safety, and 100 irregulars made up of deputy sheriffs and other whites deputized by patrol officials, moved in and appeared to have assumed control. A few of the troopers, along with Jefferson County deputy sheriffs and policemen from suburban cities, helped in putting down the riots.

The first bombing demolished the front half of the home of the Rev. A. D. King. He is the younger brother of the Rev. Dr. Martin Luther King Jr., whose Southern Christian Leadership Conference has led an integration drive here during the past five weeks. Mr. King and his wife and five children escaped injury.

The second bombing rocked the A. G. Gaston Motel, which has served as headquarters for the Negroes' integration campaign. Four persons were injured by the blast, but none seriously enough to require hospitalization. Three house trailers in a lot adjoining the motel

Continued on Page 24, Column 1

WALLACE DECRIES KENNEDY ACTION

Says Birmingham and State Can Cope With Crisis—Doubts Move Is Legal

Statements by Wallace and Boutwell are on Page 24.

By United Press International.

MONTGOMERY, Ala., May 12—Gov. George C. Wallace told President Kennedy tonight that "we have sufficient state and local forces" to handle the situation in Birmingham and asked him to leave the entire matter to the state and local governments.

Governor Wallace, in a telegram to the President, questioned Mr. Kennedy's authority to send Federal troops into Alabama.

The United States Constitution, he said, "states that the Federal Government may send troops to quell domestic violence upon application of the State Legislature or the Governor of a state." He declared:

"The Legislature of this state has made no request, nor have I.

"May I ask by what authority you would send Federal troops into this state?"

In Washington it was said that President Kennedy's order had been issued under a United States law giving the President power to quell civil disturbances.

The law, which dates to 1871

Continued on Page 25, Column 2

CABINET RESIGNS IN BUENOS AIRES; ELECTION PERILED

Interior Minister's Demands for Political Purge Stir New Argentine Crisis

ARMY HEAD BACKS GUIDO

Collapse of Regime Follows Charges That Top Aides Were Guilty of Fraud

Special to The New York Times

BUENOS AIRES, May 12—President José Maria Guido's Cabinet resigned today, leaving Argentina without a government.

The ministers and secretaries stepped down as a result of continued demands by the Interior Minister, Gen. Enrique Rauch, that Dr. Guido permit a political purge of hundreds of persons the general viewed as public enemies.

The three armed forces secretaries resigned first. The rest of the Cabinet followed suit after a conference with Dr. Guido in the presidential residence in suburban Buenos Aires.

General Rauch resigned only after he was persuaded to do so by the army's commander in chief, Gen. Juan Carlos Ongania. General Rauch presented his resignation to General Ongania and not to the President.

Rauch's Successor Named

President Guido immediately named Gen. Osiris Villegas to succeed General Rauch as Interior Minister. He will be sworn in tomorrow.

General Rauch had been named to the Interior Ministry, a key post, to insure that elections called for July 7 would take place. He insisted that a political purge was a prerequisite to any elections.

Late in the evening reliable sources indicated that President Guido was accepting immediately only General Rauch's resignation and that the President planned to make the fewest possible Cabinet changes.

Dr. Guido appeared, at this time, to be surviving another of the major crises that have shaken the government since he took office at the end of March, 1962, after the military had ousted President Arturo Frondizi.

General Villegas was wounded last month when civilian commandos tried to assassinate him in a campaign of terror that marked the beginning of an abortive revolution led by the navy.

The three armed service secretaries who resigned were Gen. Benjamin Rattenbach, War;

Continued on Page 11, Column 4

PEKING CRITICIZES DISCORDS IN BLOC

Liu Shao-chi Tells Reds Not to Harry One Another

By ROBERT TRUMBULL
Special to The New York Times

HONG KONG, May 12—Liu Shao-chi, chief of state of Communist China, urged today that Communist countries "refrain from interfering in each other's internal affairs." In a speech at Hanoi, the North Vietnamese capital, he said that members of the Communist bloc should "cooperate on the basis of mutual benefit and help each other" militarily as well as politically.

Mr. Liu's statement held special significance in view of the prospective meeting of Chinese Communist and Soviet delegates in Moscow next month to iron out their ideological differences.

The Chinese leader's reference to mutual help recalled recent accusations by Communist China that the Soviet Union had reneged on numerous agreements for military and economic assistance to Peking.

Moscow and Peking have disagreed violently on policy toward the West with the Chinese demanding that Communists everywhere adhere to a "hard line." Statements from Peking have repeatedly castigated Premier Khrushchev for conciliatory efforts with the West. The

Continued on Page 12, Column 4

New Approach to Housing Is Weighed in Washington

Subsidies for Rehabilitation of Rundown Buildings and for Rent Proposed—Federal Program Near End Here

By WARREN WEAVER Jr.
Special to The New York Times

WASHINGTON, May 12—President Kennedy's housing advisers are studying two significant departures from past policy in the continuing effort to help needy families find decent homes.

Both proposals represent efforts to produce more shelter for less money and win broader acceptance in Congress.

Legislation embodying the Administration's new look at housing will not be introduced until early next year, for both practical and political reasons. The bill-drafting, it is said, could not be completed early enough for 1963 consideration; moreover, approval appears more likely in an election year.

Although final decisions have not been reached, the President's 1964 housing program is expected to include recommendations for the following:

¶A nationwide subsidy program to encourage the rehabilitation of large, old, rundown housing—particularly for big-family apartments—in preference to building new public housing projects.

¶A system of rent-supplement payments that would permit selected low-income families to move into privately operated apartments that they could not otherwise afford, thereby encouraging private construction and freeing more space in existing public projects.

These new approaches are designed to supplement a substantial extension of the orthodox public-housing program, under which local government agencies borrow private money to build projects and Federal subsidies are granted, in effect, to retire the loans.

The President is expected to ask Congress to authorize the underwriting of about 500,000

Continued on Page 19, Column 2

U.S. Nearing Normal Ties With Communist Hungary

By M. S. HANDLER
Special to The New York Times

WASHINGTON, May 12—The State Department is considering the advisability of restoring normal relations with the Communist regime in Hungary. A firm decision has not yet been made. But the department is convinced that there are sound reasons to warrant a review of its attitude.

Relations were reduced to a minimum after the abortive anti-Communist revolt in Hungary in 1956. Premier Janos Kadar was regarded as a usurper put into power by the Soviet tanks and infantry forces that crushed the uprising.

The State Department's changing attitude was outlined in a memorandum to the Senate and House foreign affairs committees.

Easing of Controls Seen

The burden of the memorandum was that there had been a relaxation of Communist controls in the principal areas of Hungary's national life and that the lot of the people was considerably improved.

The United States position has been that it could not consider a normalization of relations until the Kadar regime restored decent government and humane rule.

The tenor of the memorandum indicated that the State Department believed that Premier Kadar had met these conditions to a certain extent.

The State Department is also being motivated toward a reassessment of its relations with Hungary by a strong belief that there will not be enough votes this year in the United Nations General Assembly to withhold approval of the credentials of the Hungarian delegation.

The presence of the Hungarians at the United Nations was

Continued on Page 2, Column 4

USTINOV APPEARS KOZLOV SUCCESSOR

Listing of Soviet Industrial Head Among Top Leaders Indicates Selection

By THEODORE SHABAD
Special to The New York Times

MOSCOW, May 12—Dmitri F. Ustinov, a First Deputy Premier, appears to have been picked to fill the vacancy in the Presidium of the Soviet Communist party left by Frol R. Kozlov's illness.

Mr. Ustinov, former production coordinator of defense industries, was named in March to be one of the First Deputy Premiers under Premier Khrushchev, and head of the Supreme Council of the National Economy, the country's top management and coordinating agency for industry and construction.

Mr. Ustinov's name appeared today in Pravda, the Communist party newspaper, in the listing of members of the Soviet leadership who attended a dinner in honor of visiting Uruguayan Communists.

The inner circle of the Soviet hierarchy is made up of 12 full members and six alternate members of the party's Presidium and eight national party secretaries who are not Presidium members.

Committee Meeting May 28

Mr. Ustinov, 55 years old, is not a member of either of these bodies, and the listing of his name after the Presidium and Secretariat indicated to qualified observers here that he was going to be elevated into the top ruling group.

A formal election to the Presidium is expected to take place at the plenary meeting of the Central Committee of the party scheduled for May 28. There have been unconfirmed reports that the meeting may be delayed because of an overcrowded calendar.

The naming of Mr. Ustinov to the Presidium would not necessarily mean that the disabled Mr. Kozlov would be dropped. It is believed possible that Mr. Kozlov, who is reported to be partly paralyzed after a stroke, may be retained on the ruling body in an honorary capacity.

Mr. Ustinov's advancement to the Presidium would not come as a surprise. His ranking as one of three First Deputy Premiers and head of the country's highest industrial administrative agency was generally expected to lead to his membership in Presidium.

However, Mr. Ustinov would differ from most other Presidium members, except for another First Deputy Premier,

Continued on Page 2, Column 6

NEW HAVEN GIVEN PLAN FOR LEASE OF 100 NEW CARS

All Air-Conditioned Service by 1965 Urged by State and Port Authority

Special to The New York Times

ALBANY, May 12—A new plan to rehabilitate the New Haven Railroad's commuter cars has been developed by Governor Rockefeller's staff and the Port of New York Authority. It has been submitted to the line's trustees.

The plan calls for leasing 100 new cars by the Port Authority to the New Haven and rehabilitating about 100 older cars for use before delivery of the new equipment.

Completion of the plan would give the New Haven an all-air-conditioned commuter fleet for service to and from New York City. The 100-car lease would be the largest completed with the railroad.

Submission of the plan to the New Haven trustees follows Governor Rockefeller's approval of a bill that the trustees termed "punitive." That bill denies tax relief to a railroad in default on current taxes unless it is leasing commuter cars from the Port Authority.

Earlier Effort Failed

Earlier negotiations with the Port Authority for new cars collapsed last January. They were for the lease of 50 cars.

One of the requirements was that the New Haven would be obligated to maintain New York commuter service without any substantial reduction. The Federal district judge whose court has jurisdiction over the reorganization of the railroad approved the lease provided the maintenance - of - service clause be eliminated. He pointed out that acquisition of 50 cars would leave a substantial number of antiquated cars still on the road, creating doubt that present levels of service could be maintained.

Negotiators for the Governor and the Port Authority expressed hope today that the objection has been overcome in the new plan by basing it on 100 cars.

Advantages Explained

A total of 200 cars are used in the railroad's commuter service to and from New York City. By 1965, if the plan is carried out, the fleet would have 100 cars acquired in 1954 and 100 new cars in place of those bought between 1914 and 1931. The plan also calls for establishment of an "adequate" car maintenance facility at Stamford, Conn., by the railroad.

In a letter to the trustees, Dr. William J. Ronan, secretary to Governor Rockefeller, discussed the plan's anticipated financial advantages.

The trustees have maintained there will never be enough profit in the railroad to support deficits in much of the passenger operation. They have said that without large-scale public subsidy, passenger service would have to be curtailed, tax relief or not.

According to Dr. Ronan's letter, the plan would assure the

Continued on Page 16, Column 6

Stratton Opposes Nomination Of Wagner for Senate in 1964

Representative Says Mayor Is Not State's Leader—Denies Candidacy

By LAYHMOND ROBINSON

Representative Samuel S. Stratton said yesterday that he did not regard Mayor Wagner as the state Democratic party leader.

He also said that the party might make a serious mistake if it chose the Mayor or any other New York City Democrat to run next year against Senator Kenneth B. Keating, Republican of Rochester. Mr. Stratton is from Schenectady.

His statements, made on a television program, fanned speculation that he would make a drive with Kennedy Administration backing for the Democratic Senatorial nomination.

Mr. Stratton, who lost to Robert M. Morgenthau, Mayor Wagner's choice for the nomination for Governor last year, denied that he was a candidate for the 1964 Senate nomination.

"I am not a candidate," he insisted. "I haven't thought about being a candidate and no one has suggested me."

Referring to reports that he was "the White House choice" for the race—instead of Mayor Wagner—Mr. Stratton said:

"The President should not

Continued on Page 21, Column 4

The New York Times

Samuel S. Stratton

NEEDLES ORBITED FOR RADIO RELAY

Radar Confirms Release of Wires From Satellite to Form Belt in Space

By The Associated Press

LEXINGTON, Mass., May 12—Radar contact confirmed today the successful release in space of 400,000,000 tiny copper needles in an Air Force experiment in a new method for worldwide radio communication.

The experiment is being conducted for the Air Force by Lincoln Laboratory of the Massachusetts Institute of Technology.

An announcement from the laboratory late today said that the needles — known as dipoles, three-quarters of an inch long and about one-third the thickness of a human hair — had been successfully ejected from an Air Force satellite in orbit.

Contact Reported

"The first conclusive radar contact with the cloud of fibers was made about 1 P.M., Eastern daylight time, today by the Lincoln Laboratory field station in Westford, Mass.," the announcement said. "Observation has also been made by the West Coast station in Pleasanton, Calif. Tracking operations are continuing, to get more accurate information about the location of the cloud and to observe the formation of the belt."

The fibers are expected to spread along an orbital path 40,000 miles in circumference to form a thin, narrow belt around the earth. The 400,000,000 needles weighed 50 pounds.

Lincoln Laboratory offered this explanation of the experiment:

"Each of the dipole fibers is, in fact, a tiny passive communications satellite, and the orbital belt of fibers will be used to bounce radio signals back to earth over very long distances. A belt of this sort is practically invulnerable to any sort of physical damage and has many other desirable features when used for long-distance microwave communication."

The announcement said that the fibers would have a life of not more than five years.

"By that time, the solar radiation pressure will have forced all the dipole fibers down to lower altitudes where the atmospheric density is greater and they will disappear harmlessly," it said.

A similar experiment was attempted in October, 1961, but it failed, after raising considerable controversy among scientists.

Experiments to Start

A spokesman for the Lincoln Laboratory said that the 1 P. M. observation showed the band of copper fibers to be roughly 300 miles long, 10 miles high and 10 miles wide. It was understood that communications experiments would begin immediately.

U.S. Rescinds Tax Exemption Held by Pacifist Group Since '26

The Internal Revenue Service has revoked the tax-exempt status held since 1926 by the Fellowship of Reconciliation, a pacifist organization. It said that the group's aim, to prevent war by abolishing arms, "can only be obtained by legislation"—a taxable effort.

The action was decried yesterday by 29 churchmen, including two former presidents of the National Council of Churches, the president of the University of Notre Dame, five Protestant bishops and four rabbis.

The clergymen called the Federal move "a challenge to the right of the religious community in America to address itself to peace or indeed to any social issue where some governmental or legislative action may by implied."

A letter urging withdrawal of the revocation was made public yesterday by the American Civil Liberties Union. John de J. Pemberton Jr., executive director, said the Federal move encroached on an area protected by the First Amendment, which guarantees freedom of religion, and put the Internal Revenue Service in the position of "a censor of religion."

Organized in 1915, the fellowship had been tax exempt for 37 years as a religious and educational organization. It reports 13,000 members, including 1,500 clergymen, who endorse a statement that "love.

Continued on Page 17, Column 3

NEWS INDEX

"All the News That's Fit to Print"

The New York Times.

LATE CITY EDITION

U.S. Weather Bureau Report (Page 74) forecasts: Cloudy with occasional rain today and tonight. Fair and warmer tomorrow. Temp. range: 62–51; yesterday: 73–47.

VOL. CXII.. No. 38,475. © 1963 by The New York Times Company. Times Square, New York 36, N. Y. NEW YORK, TUESDAY, MAY 28, 1963. TEN CENTS

SUPREME COURT PROHIBITS ANY UNWARRANTED DELAY IN SCHOOL DESEGREGATION

Associated Press Wirephoto

GOVERNOR IS GUARDED: Gov. George C. Wallace, in light coat, surrounded by Alabama state troopers yesterday. Marshals could not get to him with Federal summons.

RULES ON MEMPHIS

City Told to Abandon Racial Barriers in Parks at Once

Text of the Court's decision appears on Page 24.

By ANTHONY LEWIS
Special to The New York Times

WASHINGTON, May 27 — The Supreme Court made clear today that it would not permit "indefinite delay" in the desegregation of public schools.

"The basic guarantees of our Constitution are warrants for the here and now," Justice Arthur J. Goldberg said, "and unless there is an overwhelmingly compelling reason, they are to be promptly fulfilled."

Justice Goldberg wrote for a unanimous court in a case dealing with segregated parks and playgrounds in Memphis, Tenn. The decision was that Memphis must desegregate all these recreational facilities at once, without delay or gradualism.

Says Delays Must End

But the opinion went beyond the park problem to deal specifically with public-school segregation. What it said amounted to a pointed warning that the days of delay, evasion and token integration are coming to an end.

Nine years have passed, Justice Goldberg noted, since the Supreme Court outlawed public school segregation in the case of Brown v. Board of Education. The next year, 1955, in the second Brown case, the Court permitted implementation not at once but "with all deliberate speed."

In view of "the passage of a substantial period of time," Justice Goldberg said, even the "deliberate speed" standard might not be satisfied today by desegregation plans "which eight years ago might have been deemed sufficient."

Ruling in '55 Explained

The second Brown decision, the opinion continued, "never contemplated that the concept of 'deliberate speed' would countenance indefinite delay in elimination of racial barriers in public schools."

Justice Goldberg said the decision in 1955 allowed delay only for specific administrative problems, such as remapping of school districts. Even then, he said, delay was not to be "tolerated unless it imperatively and compellingly appeared unavoidable."

In two states, Alabama and Mississippi, not one Negro student has been admitted to a public elementary or high school. There is one Negro, James H. Meredith, in the University of Mississippi.

In the deep Southern states that have begun school deseg-

Continued on Page 24, Column 3

Justices Decline to Allow Wallace to Sue on Troops

Special to The New York Times

WASHINGTON, May 27—Gov. George C. Wallace's legal challenge to the posting of Federal troops in Alabama was swiftly rejected today by the Supreme Court.

Nine days ago, on May 18, the Alabama Governor filed a motion for leave to bring an original lawsuit in the Supreme Court.

In a brief order today the Court denied the motion, thus prohibiting a suit, at least at this time.

The Court did not fulfill the Justice Department's desire to have the case decided squarely on its merits. A department brief had asked the justices to "make it clear" that the President may use troops to protect constitutional rights.

Instead, the Court said President Kennedy had taken only "preparatory measures" by posting troops near Birmingham. Thus any challenge to the actual use of troops in a tense racial situation was premature, the Court indicated.

[In Montgomery, Ala., helmeted state troopers surrounded Governor Wallace and prevented two United States deputy marshals from serving papers on the Governor in a Federal Government suit to enjoin Mr. Wallace from interfering with the registration of two Negro students at the University of Alabama on June 10, The Associated Press reported. The papers were later served on the Governor's maid.]

The Court's decision in the case challenging the Federal troops was unanimous. Justice Byron R. White did not participate, presumably because of

Continued on Page 24, Column 6

THEATER MEN GET INTEGRATION PLEA

Robert Kennedy Calls for Voluntary Desegregation by Southern Group

By JOSEPH A. LOFTUS
Special to The New York Times

WASHINGTON, May 27 — The Administration tried today to persuade Southern theater owners to desegregate their theaters voluntarily.

A group of theater owners met for 90 minutes with Attorney General Robert F. Kennedy. Afterward, a spokesman for the owners referred all questions to the Attorney General.

Mr. Kennedy's press officer, Edwin O. Guthman, said there had been a frank and "extremely useful" exchange of views.

The Attorney General also met for the first time James H. Meredith, the Negro student whose admission to the University of Mississippi last September was accompanied by rioting and two deaths. Mr. Meredith said that more effective desegregation laws were needed.

The theater men represented chains or associations of chains that account for about 80 per cent of the South's movie

Continued on Page 25, Column 7

Zeckendorf Arranges to Auction Some Properties to Reduce Debt

By VARTANIG G. VARTAN

Webb & Knapp, Inc., the realty concern headed by William Zeckendorf, said yesterday that it would auction off more than 20 properties in Queens and Manhattan on July 10 to raise cash to cut its debt. The value of the properties is more than $5,000,000.

For Mr. Zeckendorf, the master showman of modern real estate, this move points up the fact that he faces the most critical crisis of his career.

"We are engaged in a broad-scale liquidation program amounting to some $150,000,000, which should virtually eliminate our short-term debt," Mr. Zeckendorf declared.

Much of this property, however, is heavily saddled with mortgage and other debt.

Mr. Zeckendorf told a news conference that the auction, the first of its kind ever undertaken by his company and the only one planned, would liquidate the properties in the most rapid manner. The normal procedure of piecemeal sales through private negotiation would take a long time.

The upset, or starting, prices in the auction will total more than $5,000,000. The sale will be held in the grand ballroom of the Astor Hotel. Joseph P. Day, Inc., will be the auctioneer.

With two exceptions, the properties lie in the heart of the Flushing, Queens, shopping district. Most of the units up for sale are small retail or office buildings. Some of the lots are unimproved.

These properties are in a two-block area at the intersection of Main Street and Roosevelt Avenue in Flushing, across the street from the Long Island

Continued on Page 41, Column 4

34 SENATORS ASK FOR NEW EFFORTS TO LIMIT A-TESTS

Similar Offers Before Were Perfunctory, Dodd Says in Sponsoring Plan

HUMPHREY JOINS MOVE

Explosions Under Water and in Air Would Be Banned by Resolution's Terms

By JOHN W. FINNEY
Special to The New York Times

WASHINGTON, May 27—A move developed in the Senate today to offer the Soviet Union an agreement that would prohibit all nuclear tests in the atmosphere and under water. The aim is to break the stalemate on a test-ban treaty by offering a first-step agreement.

The move was led by two active advocates of progress on the test-ban issue—Senator Thomas J. Dodd, Democrat of Connecticut, and Senator Hubert H. Humphrey, Democrat of Minnesota.

Senator Dodd introduced a resolution calling upon the Administration to offer the Soviet Union an agreement banning all tests that contaminate the atmosphere or the oceans.

The Dodd resolution was cosponsored by Senator Humphrey and 32 other Senators—26 Democrats and six Republicans.

The idea of a partial test ban covering only readily detectable atmospheric tests is not new. It was formally proposed by the Eisenhower Administration in April, 1959, and again by the Kennedy Administration in August, 1962.

U.S. Attitude Criticized

Senator Dodd asserted that on both those occasions the proposal was "submitted to the Soviet Union in a half-hearted and perfunctory manner, and when the Soviet Union said 'no' the proposals were immediately dropped."

The resolution represents the first attempt to place the Senate formally on record as favoring a limited test ban. If passed it would give new backing to the Administration's proposal, which is still pending in the Geneva negotiations.

Should the Soviet Union reject such an agreement, the resolution urges, the United States would refrain from conducting tests in the atmosphere or under water as long as the Soviet Union abstains from such tests.

In a speech accompanying

Continued on Page 5, Column 3

BANKRUPTCY LAID TO GANGSTER PLOT

U.S. Says Company Was Looted of $1,300,000

By EDWARD RANZAL

Six men and a corporation were indicted yesterday by a Federal grand jury on charges of looting a company on the brink of bankruptcy of $1,300,000.

United States Attorney Robert M. Morgenthau described it as the "biggest" and "most audacious" bankruptcy fraud case ever to come before the courts in the Southern District of New York.

The case also underscored a Justice Department contention that racketeers had moved into the bankruptcy field to gain control of distressed businesses to raid their treasuries.

Three of the defendants were said to have connections with notorious racketeers. The three others named were officers of the distressed company. All were charged with conspiring to violate the Bankruptcy Act.

Those indicted were:

Peter Castellana, 45 years old, of 2255 Benson Avenue, Brooklyn, president of the Pride Wholesale Meat and Poultry Corporation, also of Brooklyn. He is a nephew of Paul Castellana, who attended the Apalachin crime convention in 1957, and a partner in the meat business with Paul Gambino, described as a Brooklyn racketeer. He is also associated in a money lending business, the Jo-Ran Realty Trading Corpora-

Continued on Page 22, Column 1

Kenyatta Triumphs In Kenya Elections

United Press International

Jomo Kenyatta

By ROBERT CONLEY
Special to The New York Times

NAIROBI, Kenya, May 27—Jomo Kenyatta, who was sentenced to a seven-year prison term in 1953 as a leader of the Mau Mau African terrorist group, won a victory today in Kenya's national elections.

He will become this British colony's first Prime Minister.

Mr. Kenyatta's Kenya African National Union party easily took a majority of the

Continued on Page 2, Column 4

INDIA IS WARNED BY PEKING AGAIN

Chinese Say 'Provocation' Could Renew Border War—Press Demand for Talks

Special to The New York Times

HONG KONG, May 27—Communist China warned India today that "provocation" by New Delhi's forces along the disputed Himalayan frontier might lead to renewed warfare.

Peking also insisted that India accept Chinese terms for direct negotiation of the frontier issue.

"If the Indian Government, because of domestic or external considerations, is not yet ready to negotiate, the Chinese Government can wait patiently," the Peking statement said.

The statement said that if the Indian Government attempted to regain the territory taken by Chinese forces last year New Delhi would "again pick up a stone to drop on its own feet."

'Favorable Atmosphere' Cited

Peking declared that its repatriation of all Indian prisoners of war, which was completed over the weekend, "created a favorable atmosphere for a peaceful settlement" of the Chinese-Indian boundary question.

"Whether direct negotiations between India and China can be held quickly or not and whether the Chinese-Indian boundary question can be settled peacefully soon or not depends on the attitude of the Indian Government," the Peking statement asserted.

Peking's views were stated in an editorial in Jenmin Jih Pao, the official newspaper of the Chinese Communist party. This daily in Peking reflects Government policy.

Colombo Plan Backed

The newspaper insisted that the basis of any negotiations be Peking's qualified acceptance of proposals last year by the six neutral powers that met in Colombo, Ceylon. The nations were Ceylon, Burma, Cambodia, Indonesia, Ghana and the United Arab Republic.

India accepted the formula devised at Colombo for a withdrawal of opposed forces to lines they had held before hostilities began Sept. 8, 1962. Peking has demanded modifications unacceptable to New Delhi.

Fighting along the border halted when Peking declared a cease-fire Nov. 20 after the Indian forces had been badly beaten. The Chinese then withdrew from part of the territory they had overrun, but they continue to hold about 12,000 square miles claimed by India.

Jenmin Jih Pao said that Communist China's release of all Indian prisoners showed Peking's "reluctance to cross swords" with India.

"Recent repeated intrusions by Indian troops along the Chinese-Indian border show that the Indian side, ignoring repeat-

Continued on Page 3, Column 5

BRITISH QUESTION U.S. ON PROPOSAL FOR ATOM FLEET

Decision on Joining Polaris Missile Force May Depend on Washington Reply

By SYDNEY GRUSON
Special to The New York Times

LONDON, May 27—Britain's decision on whether to participate in a proposed fleet of nuclear-armed surface ships under the North Atlantic Treaty Organization may depend on the answers she gets to a long list of questions submitted to Washington.

The political wisdom of the United States proposal for such a fleet has been accepted reluctantly. The British believe that Washington is exaggerating at least the current urge in West Germany for nuclear parity within the alliance.

The British have not accepted yet what they describe as a mere outline of some of the basic military and cost problems involved in creating the fleet of 25 ships. The fleet would carry Polaris missiles and be manned by mixed crews from the NATO nations.

The questionnaire sent to Washington is designed to get a more precise appraisal of the problems and detailed American answers to them, British sources said today.

Query on Fleet's Defense

The British want to know, for example, whether the ships would carry defensive arms besides Polaris missiles, whether they would need an escort fleet, where they would be based, whether they would patrol singly or in groups, what kind of communications system would be used and which capital the communications would be linked to.

Some preliminary answers to questions such as these have already been given in technical talks between naval representatives of the two countries in Washington.

But the British belittle the information received so far as "computer answers." They want to talk over the problems.

War Damage Recalled

The British are not as convinced as the United States that the fleet could roam the seas undetected, without heavy anti-aircraft armament or escorting warships.

The British recall the damage they inflicted on the Nazi fleet when it was bottled up in German or Norwegian harbors during World War II. They also recall the sinking of two unescorted British capital ships, the Prince of Wales and the Repulse, by Japanese planes.

If the Polaris-armed ships are to carry other weapons and be protected by warships, the British believe, the cost of the project will be considerably greater than the $5,000,000,000 spread over 10 years that was estimated a few months ago.

The British, it is reported, are being asked to pay 10 per cent of the cost. This would make them the third largest

Continued on Page 6, Column 3

Condition of Pope Improves Slightly

By ARNALDO CORTESI
Special to The New York Times

ROME, May 27—The condition of Pope John XXIII, who was brought close to death in the night between Saturday and Sunday by a recurrence of hemorrhaging caused by a stomach ailment, was reported improved today.

He took a slight turn for the better last night after a blood transfusion, and his doctors found that he had passed a "good night." The reports on his condition came from Vatican sources.

An official statement said: "Last evening an improvement was noted in the Pope's general condition and particularly in his subjective condition. His Holiness's doctors found further progress of this improvement this morning."

That the Pope had slept well was indicated by reports

Continued on Page 16, Column 5

SECRET RECORDING IN TRIAL IS UPHELD

Supreme Court Backs Use of Hidden Device to Gain Evidence in Tax Case

By The Associated Press

WASHINGTON, May 27—The Supreme Court upheld today the use as evidence of secret recordings a Federal tax agent made of his conversations with a suspected tax evader.

The tax agent used an electronic device hidden on his person.

The decision was given on an appeal by German S. Lopez, who was convicted of attempted bribery of an agent in a tax case involving the operations of Clauson's Inn at North Falmouth, Mass.

The court was divided, 6 to 3, with Justice John M. Harlan writing for the majority and Justices William J. Brennan Jr., William O. Douglas and Arthur J. Goldberg dissenting. Chief Justice Earl Warren wrote a separate opinion concurring with the majority.

Convicted on 3 Counts

Lopez was convicted on three of four counts in an indictment charging that he tried to bribe the tax agent, Roger S. Davis, in October of 1961. The three counts charged that Lopez gave Mr. Davis $200 and promised him $200 more, as well as an expense-paid weekend for Mr. Davis and his family at the inn. Lopez was acquitted on the fourth count, which charged that he gave Mr. Davis $420.

The purpose of the attempted bribery was allegedly to influence Mr. Davis to conceal sales and receipts and any cabaret tax due on the bar and lounge of the inn. Lopez was sentenced in Federal court in Boston to one year in prison.

Lopez contended that he should have been acquitted on all counts because of illegal entrapment. He said the agent gained entry to his office by misrepresentation and then surreptitiously made a wire recording of the conversation.

In his appeal, Lopez argued

Continued on Page 24, Column 7

Corrupt Use of U.S. Aid Goods Charged in Congo and Morocco

Smugglers in Leopoldville

By J. ANTHONY LUKAS
Special to The New York Times

LEOPOLDVILLE, the Congo, May 27 — The women padded single file past the United States Embassy and down the hill toward the Congo River. From an embassy window one could see the packages of butter rocking in the huge wicker baskets on their heads.

"Sometimes I see all those headloads of butter slipping past and I want to rush out and tell those women to turn around," said Robert L. West, director of United States aid in the Congo.

The butter, which comes here under the $24,000,000-a-year United States surplus food program, was on its way across the river to Brazzaville in the former French Congo, where it commands a high price in hard currency.

This smuggling is one of the most blatant abuses hampering the United States aid program here. Mr. West and his staff are doing all they can to halt the abuses, but their efforts are often frustrated. Tightening

Continued on Page 3, Column 1

Rabat Accused of Abuses

Special to The New York Times

RABAT, Morocco, May 27—Morocco's leading opposition party formally protested to the United States Embassy today against use of American wheat and other commodities during the country's first national legislative elections May 17.

A delegation from the conservative Istiqlal party charged that Moroccan authorities had used the American products to influence the elections in favor of the Government-backed Front for Defense of Constitutional Institutions.

"The Government of the United States is an accomplice of the Moroccan Government in rigging our elections," the Istiqlal newspaper La Nation Africaine declared.

A United States Embassy spokesman told the Istiqlal delegation that the United States Government had not wanted to be involved in any way in the Moroccan political campaign. He stressed that the United States commodity loans and grants were designed for the good of the Moroccan people and

Continued on Page 3, Column 3

SENATE BACKS AID TO MENTALLY ILL BY VOTE OF 72 TO 1

Plan Calls for Treatment in New Local Hospitals and More Help for Retarded

By MARJORIE HUNTER
Special to The New York Times

WASHINGTON, May 27 — The Senate passed the Administration's $840,000,000 mental health bill today by a vote of 72 to 1.

The measure, termed by President Kennedy a "bold new approach" for treating the mentally ill and retarded, calls for Federal help in financing a system of community mental hospitals and new facilities for the retarded.

The community mental hospitals would gradually replace traditional state hospitals and allow patients to be treated in their home environment near friends and relatives.

The bill also calls for more research into the causes of retardation.

The only Senator to vote against the measure on passage was Carl T. Curtis, Republican of Nebraska.

The bill now goes to the House.

The bill was approved after most Democratic liberals teamed up with Southern conservatives to turn back a Republican effort to attach a civil rights rider to the measure. The vote against the amendment was 43 to 27.

Civil Rights Fight

In offering the civil rights amendment, Senator Jacob K. Javits, Republican of New York, said he had hoped to win assurances from the Administration that racial discrimination would not be practiced in the new mental health program.

He said he had tried to get such a commitment from Anthony J. Celebrezze, Secretary of Health, Education and Welfare.

"I have been waiting all day to hear," he said. "Now I have no alternative but to offer, this amendment."

Senator Javits said that the Hill-Burton Hospital Construction Law, adopted some years ago, specifically allows separate facilities as long as they are equal.

"Segregation in hospitals is accepted and practiced in Southern states," he continued. "How can we pass a new program, knowing in advance it will be administered in a segregated way?"

Senator Javits cited two hospital-admission cases now pending in Greensboro, N. C. And he said there had been examples of Negroes actually being denied treatment when they attempted to get into white hospitals.

Keating Another Sponsor

The Javits amendment would have withheld Federal mental health funds from states maintaining segregated state programs.

Joining him in offering the amendment were Senators Kenneth B. Keating of New York, Clifford P. Case of New Jersey, J. Glenn Beall of Maryland and Hugh Scott of Pennsylvania, all Republicans.

The Senate majority leader, Mike Mansfield of Montana, rounded up 41 Democrats to table the amendment. Joining them were two Republicans, Milton R. Young of North Dakota and John J. Williams of Delaware.

Joining 22 Republicans in voting against the tabling motion were five Democrats: Harrison A. Williams Jr. of New Jersey, Jennings Randolph of West Virgina, William Proxmire of Wisconsin, Frank J. Lausche of Ohio, and Philip A. Hart of Michigan.

The bill has been labeled top priority by the Administration.

The bill would provide the following:

¶A four-year program, costing $230,000,000, under which Federal grants would go to states for construction of public or other nonprofit commu-

Continued on Page 21, Column 4

NEWS INDEX

President Kennedy was welcomed by an enthusiastic crowd when he visited West Berlin.

Khrushchev sought to counter Kennedy's impact on West Berlin by visiting the Berlin Wall a few months afterwards. After drawing only a quarter of Kennedy's turnout, he charged the President with inciting the Germans.

John F. Kennedy, America's first Roman Catholic President, met the newly crowned Pope Paul VI, during his European summer tour.

"All the News That's Fit to Print"

The New York Times.

LATE CITY EDITION

U. S. Weather Bureau Report (Page 78) forecasts: Cloudy with chance of showers today; clear tonight. Fair, warm tomorrow. Temp. range: 80—63; yesterday: 67—58. Temp.-Hum. Index: high 60's; yesterday: 67.

VOL. CXII..No. 38,482. © 1963 by The New York Times Company. Times Square, New York 36, N. Y. NEW YORK, TUESDAY, JUNE 4, 1963. TEN CENTS

POPE JOHN XXIII IS DEAD AT 81, ENDING 4½-YEAR REIGN DEVOTED TO PEACE AND CHRISTIAN UNITY

ARIZONA UPHELD OVER CALIFORNIA ON WATER RIGHTS

Supreme Court's 7-1 Ruling Caps 40-Year Fight on Use of the Colorado River

WIDE EFFECT FORESEEN

3 Justices Strongly Oppose Provision Allowing U. S. to Apportion Supplies

By WILLIAM M. BLAIR

Special to The New York Times

WASHINGTON, June 3 — Arizona won in the Supreme Court today its 40-year struggle with California over how much water each state can take from the Colorado River.

The Court, voting 7 to 1, upheld a special master's recommendations on division of the water. The decision is of great economic significance to the Southwest, for the Colorado and its tributaries are the major water sources in that rapidly growing area.

The Court split, 5 to 3, however, on the majority ruling that the Secretary of the Interior had the power to apportion mainstream water among users in the lower basin states, particularly in periods of shortage.

Oppose Federal Role

The dissenters on this issue were Justices John Marshall Harlan, William O. Douglas and Potter Stewart. They sharply challenged the majority view that Congress intended a "single appointed Federal official" to have the authority to apportion mainstream waters, whether in shortage or surplus.

They found this delegation of power "extraordinary." And they argued that state law was intended to control apportionment among users within a single state and that this principle had been established by the Court in earlier water rights cases.

The majority opinion said California was entitled to 4,400,000 acre feet of water annually from the mainstream of the Colorado, Arizona 2,800,000 acre feet and Nevada 300,000 acre feet. An acre foot is the amount of water that will cover one acre to a depth of one foot—about 325,850 gallons.

The division was confined to the area's mainstream. The Court rejected California's effort to include the Colorado's tributaries, principally the Gila in Arizona, in any water allo-

Continued on Page 23, Column 1

Douglas Upbraids Black From Bench

Special to The New York Times

WASHINGTON, June 3 — Justice William O. Douglas made an unusually sharp attack today on a major opinion by his colleague on the Supreme Court, Hugo L. Black.

The tenor of Justice Douglas's extemporaneous remarks from the bench startled those in the courtroom. His strong language was the more surprising because the two men have served together for 24 years and have been regarded as extremely close in judicial philosophy.

Justice Douglas's dissent was in the Colorado River water case. Justice Black wrote the opinion of the court deciding generally against California's claims and in favor of Arizona's.

From the bench Justice

Continued on Page 22, Column 3

PRESIDENT DELAYS RIGHTS MESSAGE

Plans Conferences in Fight on Public Discrimination —G.O.P. Offers a Bill

By E. W. KENWORTHY

Special to The New York Times

WASHINGTON, June 3—President Kennedy decided tonight to delay for a week his civil rights message to Congress proposing legislation to outlaw discrimination in public accommodations.

He had hoped to get new legislative proposals to Congress tomorrow. He leaves on Wednesday for a Western trip and will stay out of Washington the rest of the week.

One factor in tonight's decision was that last-minute tinkering with the draft bills and the accompanying Presidential message was still going on. It was deemed wise not to rush so important a matter.

The President believed also that it would help the legislation to go ahead first with scheduled conferences. He will meet tomorrow, for example, with business executives with large holdings in the South. His brother, Attorney General Robert F. Kennedy, will meet other groups.

Democrats Briefed

The week will also be used to try to create a favorable climate at the Capitol. Democratic Congressional leaders, who were briefed on civil rights by the President today, will discuss the legislation with others in both parties.

The decision to delay the message was especially difficult for the President because 24 House Republicans introduced today their own legislation to bar racial discrimination in public accommodations. They were plainly intent on beating the Administration in offering a measure.

One of two main proposals in the Administration's legislation would deal with racial discrimi-

Continued on Page 27, Column 1

AGENCY SHOP WINS COURT'S APPROVAL

Ruled Permissible by U. S. Law, Optional in States

By JOSEPH A. LOFTUS

Special to The New York Times

WASHINGTON, June 3—A labor contract requiring nonmembers to pay service fees to a union is permissible under Federal law, but may be prohibited by state law, the Supreme Court ruled today.

The agency shop, as this type of contract is called, was reviewed in two decisions. There was no dissent. Associate Justice Arthur J. Goldberg did not participate.

Where the state's prohibition is enforceable—in state courts or before the National Labor Relations Board—was a question reserved for later decision. That point was set for argument in the next term.

In two other labor decisions, the Court reversed damage verdicts won by individuals against unions in the state courts of Texas and Ohio. The vote in each was 6 to 2. Justices William O. Douglas and Tom C. Clark dissented. Justice Goldberg did not participate.

The central point in all four cases was the extent of state jurisdiction in the field of labor-management relations. Under the Court's doctrine of Federal pre-emption, the states have no jurisdiction except where Congress has specifically conceded it, or where the N.L.R.B. can afford no remedy, or where there is an overriding state in-

Continued on Page 24, Column 5

PUPIL TRANSFERS TO DIVIDE RACES VOIDED BY COURT

Supreme Bench Says Plan in Two Tennessee Areas Slows Desegregation

By ANTHONY LEWIS

Special to The New York Times

WASHINGTON, June 3 — The Supreme Court held unconstitutional today a school desegregation plan that allows pupils to transfer out of schools where their race is in the minority.

Justice Tom C. Clark said that the plan was invalid because it based transfers "solely on racial factors" and led to "perpetuation of segregation." He spoke for a unanimous Court.

The transfer plan was at issue in cases from Knoxville, Tenn., and from Davidson County, adjoining Nashville. Similar provisions are in use in Memphis and in some Virginia communities.

Five other Southern states have statutes saying that no child may be compelled to attend a school where he would be in a racial minority. They are Alabama, Arkansas, Florida, Louisiana and North Carolina.

Broad Impact Likely

Thus today's decision can be expected to have a major impact on the South. It will remove the legal basis for a device widely used to cushion the effect of school desegregation.

In practice, the Tennessee provisions — and those in other areas — worked as follows:

School boards, in response to the Supreme Court's desegregation decision, abolished the former separate school maps for whites and Negroes. New school districts were drawn for a single, nonracial system.

But any white student who thereupon found himself in the district of "a school previously serving colored students" could automatically transfer to another school. So could a Negro zoned into a school formerly serving whites.

Transfers Made Easy

The plan also, significantly, permitted automatic transfers "when a student would otherwise be required to attend a school where the majority of students of that school or in his or her grade are of a different race."

A student in such a minority situation had only to ask and he would be transferred. Others who wanted to switch schools had to persuade the school board there was "good cause."

The provision was generally regarded as a way of assuring white families that their children would not be placed in a mostly Negro school. It was defended as necessary to reduce opposition to desegregation.

Negroes, on the other hand, said the transfer provision had made true integration of the schools impossible. They especially criticized the fact that there was no automatic right of a pupil to transfer from a school entirely or mostly of his

Continued on Page 25, Column 3

Army May Release Ft. Tilden for Park

By CHARLES G. BENNETT

There is a "very, very good possibility" that the Army might make Fort Tilden available to the city for the Breezy Point park development, Mayor Wagner said yesterday.

"We learned last week," the Mayor said at an impromptu press conference, "that there is a good possibility that the Army might move its installations and Nike bases from there in the near future, and then we can start negotiations."

An Army spokesman said in Washington last night that the Army had been reviewing the situation but had not made any decision.

Fort Tilden is on 317 acres next to the 236-acre Jacob Riis Park. The city proposes ultimately to have in all 1,362

Continued on Page 43, Column 5

HAITIAN CONTACTS RESUMED BY U. S.

Duvalier Regime Regarded as Firmly in Power Even if Not Constitutional

By TAD SZULC

Special to The New York Times

WASHINGTON, June 3 — The United States resumed "normal diplomatic business" with Haiti today after nearly three weeks of a suspension of contacts intended to underline Washington's disapproval of President François Duvalier.

The decision to return to normal relations and to remove a Navy task force from the vicinity of Haiti appeared to reverse last month's undisguised policy efforts aimed at Dr. Duvalier's removal.

At the peak of the Haiti crisis, the Kennedy Administration is known to have convinced itself that President Duvalier's regime was on the brink of collapse because of mounting United States pressures.

It was then expected that Dr. Duvalier would voluntarily give up office and leave Haiti on May 15. The United States regarded that date as the end of his legal term.

Marine Landing Envisaged

Accordingly, the Administration secretly prepared with at least three Latin-American governments a plan that might have involved a landing in Haiti by United States marines, it has been disclosed. An inter-American "police action" in support of a new regime in Haiti was also envisaged.

The details of this planned operation were disclosed by diplomats who participated in its preparation last month.

The operation was abandoned on May 15, however, after an all-night vigil here by officials of the Organization of American States. It then became clear that Dr. Duvalier did not intend to leave Haiti.

The State Department later that day instructed Ambassador Raymond L. Thurston in Port-au-Prince to suspend immediately his contacts with the Haitian Government. The move was made secretly and the Administration confirmed it indirectly only after it was published in press dispatches from Haiti.

Regime Still Held Illegal

Today, Lincoln White, the State Department spokesman, announced that the United States chargé d'affaires in Port-au-Prince, Glion Curtis Jr., was being instructed "to resume normal diplomatic business with the Government of Haiti."

Administration officials insisted that the lifting of the short-lived diplomatic sanctions did not imply any change in the United States view that the Duvalier regime was unconstitutional. It was made clear, however, that the United States had concluded that the Haitian Government was firmly in power.

Therefore, officials said, a re-

Continued on Page 6, Column 3

DC-7 With 101 Lost in Alaska; 95 Military Men and Kin Aboard

Vast Air-Sea Hunt Pressed for Chartered Craft After Radio Contact Breaks Off

By The Associated Press

JUNEAU, Alaska, June 3—A military-chartered airliner carrying 101 persons—men, women and children — vanished off southeastern Alaska today under circumstances suggesting sudden disaster.

The Northwest Airlines DC-7, a piston-engined aircraft, last radioed 30 to 40 miles at sea off Prince of Wales Island, requesting a change of altitude from 14,000 to 18,000 feet. Air traffic men trying to reply minutes later got no answer.

The last confirmed message from the plane was at 10:06 A.M., about two and a half hours after it left McChord Air Force Base, Wash., with 95 military passengers, including dependents, and a crew of six.

An intensive search by planes and vessels was made in deteriorating weather.

The Coast Guard said later tonight that a Canadian plane had reported sighting what appeared to be wreckage near

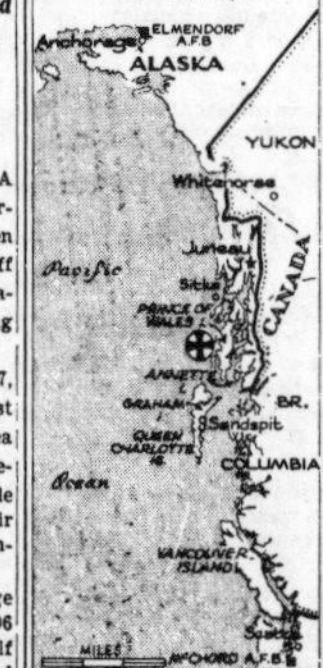

The New York Times June 4, 1963

Cross shows where plane last reported its position.

Graham Island, in northern British Columbia.

The only detailed information concerning the sighting came

Continued on Page 13, Column 1

POST AWAITS VOTE

Archbishop of Milan a Possible Choice as New Pontiff

By PAUL HOFMANN

Special to The New York Times

ROME, June 3—Amid the drama of Pope John XXIII's final hours, Romans speculated whether his successor would be an Italian or a "foreigner."

At the same time, ecclesiastics and laymen debated whether the next Pontiff would show the conciliatory, progressive attitude of Pope John or lead the Roman Catholic Church back to a more conservative position.

An Italian prince of the church, Giovanni Battista Cardinal Montini, 65-year-old Archbishop of Milan, was widely mentioned as the leading candidate.

Cardinal Montini is regarded as a prominent representative of the "progressive" wing of the world episcopacy, which revealed its strength with the manifest encouragement of Pope John during the first session of the Ecumenical Council in the Vatican last autumn.

A Close Aide to Pius XII

As monsignor, the present Cardinal Montini was for many years a close aide to the late Pope Pius XII, Pope John's predecessor, in the Vatican Secretariat of State. The slim, ascetic-looking churchman, who is credited with a prodigious capacity for hard work, became Archbishop of Milan, one of the largest Catholic dioceses in the world, in 1954, but still was not a Cardinal when Pope Pius XII died in 1958.

The Archbishop of Milan then already had such a reputation that some commentators suggested that the Cardinals would depart from a 600-year-old tradition and elect a prelate who was not one of their number.

Instead the Cardinals elevated one of their number, Angelo Giuseppe Cardinal Roncalli, Patriarch of Venice. As Pope John XXIII he conferred on Archbishop Montini the red hat of Cardinal in his first consistory in December, 1958. Cardinal Montini was close to Pope John throughout his pontificate and if he is elected as his successor he is expected to continue his policies.

Cardinals Take Over Rule

Soon after Pope John died tonight, the Cardinals present in the Vatican started taking over the interim government of the church on behalf of the 82 members of the Sacred College of Cardinals. The Cardinals will rule jointly until their vote in conclave results in the election of the new Pope.

Prominent among conservative Italian Cardinals thought to be of papal timber is Giuseppe Cardinal Siri, Archbishop of Genoa. He is 57 years old.

The leader of the conservative wing at the Ecumenical Council, Alfredo Cardinal Ottaviani, a 72-year-old Vatican theologian and guardian of

Continued on Page 18, Column 6

Africans Complain Of Bias in Moscow

By SEYMOUR TOPPING

Special to The New York Times

MOSCOW, June 3 -- A sharp controversy has arisen between Soviet authorities and African students here who have complained of discrimination fostered by a Moscow newspaper article.

The article, published by Komsomolskaya Pravda, the newspaper of the Communist Youth League, purported to tell the experiences of a Russian girl who was sold into a harem by a Moslem student she had married.

African students here interpreted the article as a warning to Russian girls against association with them. It was published on Oct. 27 after a number of Africans had complained of being attacked by Russians because they had appeared publicly in the company

Continued on Page 5, Column 1

POPE JOHN XXIII

Associated Press

Washington Mourns Loss Of Great Force for Peace

By M. S. HANDLER

Special to The New York Times

WASHINGTON, June 3—President Kennedy paid high tribute today to the statesmanship and moral leadership of Pope John XXIII. The President said of the Pontiff: "His compassion and kindly strength have bequeathed humanity a new legacy of purpose and courage for the future."

Mr. Kennedy led official Washington in mourning the passing of Pope John as a great loss to mankind. Members of both houses of Congress and churchmen of various faiths joined in expressing the belief that the Pontiff had made an immense contribution to the reconciliation of all Christian faiths, to the reconciliation of his church with Judaism, and to the preservation of peace.

President Kennedy said the Pope had "brought compassion and understanding drawn from wide experience to the most divisive problems of a tumultuous age."

Statement by President

The President's statement said:

"The highest work of any man is to protect and carry on the deepest spiritual heritage of the race. To Pope John was given the almost unique gift of enriching and enlarging that tradition. Armed with the humility and calm which surrounded his earliest days, he brought compassion and an understanding drawn from wide experience to the most divisive problems of a tumultuous age. He was the chosen leader of world Catholicism, but his concern for the human spirit transcended all boundaries of belief or geography.

"The ennobling precepts of his encyclicals and his actions drew on the accumulated wisdom of an ancient faith for guidance in the most complex and troublesome problems of the modern age. To him the divine spark which unites men would ultimately prove more enduring than the forces which divide. His wisdom, compassion and kindly strength have bequeathed humanity a new legacy of purpose and courage for the future."

The reference to Pope John's encyclicals marked the second time Mr. Kennedy had expressed such praise. At Boston College

Continued on Page 21, Column 7

WAGNER ORDERS FLAGS LOWERED

Leads City in Mourning and Picks 2 Representatives to Attend Pope's Funeral

Mayor Wagner yesterday ordered flags on all city buildings flown at half-staff until the burial of Pope John. The Mayor led the city in mourning the Pope.

"Pope John XXIII symbolized faith, goodness, courage and compassion," Mayor Wagner said, adding, "He appealed always to the best in the human heart and all humanity is uplifted by the noble example which he set."

Mayor Wagner also designated Commissioner of Public Events Richard C. Patterson Jr. and Thomas J. Deegan, chairman of the World's Fair executive committee, as official city representatives at the Pope's funeral.

Both are in Rome on other business.

Washington will not accord the Pope the flag tribute he will receive in New York. The State Department explained that flags in Washington are

Continued on Page 18, Column 4

St. Peter's Throng Silenced by Grief

Special to The New York Times

ROME, June 3—A vast throng in the piazza in front of St. Peter's Basilica heard the news of the death of Pope John this evening in sad and resigned silence.

Many knelt in quiet prayer and crossed themselves as other hundreds surged toward the bronze doors leading into Vatican City to watch as one of the two portals was swung shut as a traditional sign that the Pope was dead.

The Pope's death came only minutes after a choral offering brought to an end a mass celebrated for the Pontiff on the steps of the Basilica by Luigi Cardinal Traglia, pro-vicar of the Diocese of Rome.

More than 35,000 Romans, visitors, pilgrims, nuns and clergymen gathered to hear the mass, which started at 7 P.M. By the time the last sacred

Continued on Page 21, Column 2

A LIBERAL PONTIFF

Church Council and Encyclical on Amity Marked Tenure

By ARNALDO CORTESI

Special to The New York Times

ROME, June 3 — Pope John XXIII, champion of world peace and a tireless fighter for the union of all Christian churches, died in the Vatican tonight while Cardinals and other prelates and several of his relatives prayed around his sickbed. He was 81 years old.

John XXIII was the 261st Pope to sit on the throne that was first occupied by the Apostle Peter.

In the four years, seven months and six days of his reign he conquered the hearts of people throughout the world. Few other Popes before him were so universally admired.

The Pope's death came at 7:49 P.M. (2:49 P.M. Eastern daylight time.)

After a long struggle the Pope developed peritonitis, brought on by a stomach tumor. The tumor was discovered last November.

Doctors Gave Up Hope

His doctors had given up hope at the onset of the peritonitis, an inflammation of the lining of the abdominal cavity. This was given as the cause of his death.

Much of the intervening period was passed in a state of coma or semicoma. The Pope was lucid most of yesterday, however, but in great pain, which he bore with remarkable fortitude. Early yesterday afternoon he suffered a "new crisis."

Before entering his last state of coma, he repeatedly said in Latin: "Into Thy hands, O Lord, I commit my soul."

The Pope had dedicated much of his pontificate to promoting Christian unity and the unity of all men as brothers with a common God.

Pope's Last Words

In his last words, addressed to the assembled Cardinals and prelates around his sickbed, the Pope said:

"Ut unum sint." They are Latin words meaning "That they may be one."

The words were originally spoken by Jesus after the Last Supper.

The night of May 25 the Pope suffered a hemorrhage that brought him close to death. A series of blood transfusions saved his life. He had been improving when peritonitis developed.

John XXIII was elected Pope Oct. 28, 1958. He was born in the village of Sotto il Monte in northern Italy Nov. 25, 1881. He was 81 years, six months and nine days old at his death.

Pope John passed his last days in his bedroom on the top floor of the Vatican Palace. A small crowd of ecclesiastics and laymen had congregated there when they were told that the Pope was near death.

Those at Bedside

Those around the bedside included Eugene Cardinal Tisserant, the bearded French dean of the Sacred College; Benedetto Cardinal Aloisi Masella, who as Cardinal Camerlengo, or Chamberlain, heads the interim administration of the Roman Catholic Church; the Pope's three brothers—Giuseppe, Alfredo and Zaverio Roncalli—and his widowed sister, Assunta; three nephews, several members of the Papal household, such as his sacristan, his confessor and his Master of the Chamber.

A larger crowd, including ambassadors and ministers, waited in an adjacent room.

Swiss guards kept all others out of the Papal apartment.

About 30 minutes before the Pope died it became clear from his labored breathing and his falling pulse rate that he was near death. The Pope's personal physician, Prof. Antonio Gasbarrini, warned Cardinal Aloisi Masella that the Pope had not long to live.

Mass for the Pope was said at an altar in an adjoining room

Continued on Page 18, Column 1

NEWS INDEX

"All the News That's Fit to Print"

The New York Times.

LATE CITY EDITION
U. S. Weather Bureau Report (Page 65) forecasts: Partly cloudy and cool today; clear and cool tonight. Fair tomorrow.
Temp. range: 72—56; yesterday: 74—56. Temp.-Hum. Index: 68; yesterday: 71.

VOL. CXII..No. 38,490. NEW YORK, WEDNESDAY, JUNE 12, 1963. TEN CENTS

ALABAMA ADMITS NEGRO STUDENTS; WALLACE BOWS TO FEDERAL FORCE; KENNEDY SEES 'MORAL CRISIS' IN U.S.

STEEL LABOR PACT IS REPORTED NEAR; TALKS PEACEFUL

McDonald Calls Meetings of Union's 2 Top Boards in Pittsburgh Next Week

NEW APPROACH IS TRIED

Deadline Pressure and Hint of Strike Absent for First Time in 25 Years

By JOHN D. POMFRET
Special to The New York Times

WASHINGTON, June 11—The steel industry and the United Steelworkers of America were understood today to be close to a history-making agreement on contract revisions.

David J. McDonald, union head, set a meeting of the union's executive board for Monday at Pittsburgh and of the rank-and-file wage policy committee for Tuesday. The committee has power to ratify contract settlements and there was a strong likelihood that union officials would have an agreement to report.

A union spokesman, however, denied that an agreement had been reached.

Some Issues Remain

"If there's anything in the bag, McDonald certainly would like to know about it," he said.

Sources close to the talks in Pittsburgh reported that some fundamental issues remained before the agreement could be counted as final.

The principal question is what benefits the industry will concede in exchange for the union's agreement to extend present contracts past the scheduled expiration date of July 1, 1964.

The industry was understood to be willing to agree to an extended vacation plan along the lines of that agreed to by the union and the can manufacturing industry last year.

But steel also was understood to want the term of the present contract lengthened in exchange for assuming the cost of extended vacations.

Concessions Sought

The union was said to be willing to extend the present agreements if the industry made substantial enough concessions in other areas.

Both sides were said to be pleased with the prospect of avoiding contract negotiations in a Presidential election year. They were thinking about extending the agreements well into 1965 or even 1966.

The discussions have not been negotiations in the traditional sense. They have been carried on within the framework of the industry-union human relations committee. For the first time they have been free of deadline pressure or the hint of a strike threat.

The union was free to reopen

Continued on Page 33, Column 7

Greek Premier Out In Clash With King

Special to The New York Times

ATHENS, June 11—Premier Constantine Caramanlis resigned tonight because King Paul had rejected his advice to call off a state visit by the King and Queen to Britain next month.

The King later in a proclamation reaffirmed his belief that he and Queen Frederika should proceed with the visit. He said he would await the recommendation of the new government on this question.

King Paul has accepted British assurances that no repetition of incidents such as marred the Queen's last visit to London would be tolerated. When the Queen attended the wedding of Princess Alexandra last April her hotel was picketed, and at one time she was forced to seek refuge in a private home

Continued on Page 9, Column 3

BRITISH CABINET WILL MEET TODAY IN PROFUMO CRISIS

Macmillan Fate May Hinge on Unity of Ministers on Stand in Scandal

By SYDNEY GRUSON
Special to The New York Times

LONDON, June 11 — Prime Minister Macmillan has summoned his Cabinet to meet tomorrow on the Profumo scandal. The conference could be vital in determining whether he will survive as Britain's leader.

Mr. Macmillan's chances, political observers said today, will be brightened if he gets the unanimous endorsement of his Cabinet. Some Cabinet members are known to be critical of what they regard as the Prime Minister's failure to force John Profumo to resign earlier than he did as Secretary of State for War.

Mr. Profumo resigned last week. With his resignation, it became public knowledge that he had had an affair, which he had previously denied, with Christine Keeler, a 21-year-old party girl.

Miss Keeler was seeing a former Soviet deputy naval attaché in London at the same time that she was involved with Mr. Profumo. The Russian, Capt. Yevgeni E. Ivanov, was said to be a Soviet intelligence agent.

Ministers Hurry Home

The call for a Cabinet meeting tomorrow forced several ministers to change their plans.

Iain Macleod, a co-chairman of the Conservative party and Leader of the House of Commons, interrupted a visit to the United States to fly home tonight. Edward Heath, Lord Privy Seal, postponed a trip to Oslo. The Earl of Home, Britain's Foreign Secretary, returned to London earlier than scheduled from a holiday. So did several other ministers.

Mr. Macmillan will disclose to the Cabinet the results of an investigation by Lord Dilhorne, the Lord Chancellor, into the security aspects of the Profumo case.

Osteopath Accused

Also involved in the scandal is Dr. Stephen Ward, a London society osteopath, who was arrested Saturday and charged with living off the earnings of prostitutes. Dr. Ward introduced Miss Keeler to both Mr. Profumo and Captain Ivanov.

Reliable sources said the report had confirmed the Prime Minister's belief that there was no breach of security. Even the Opposition did not expect to find that Mr. Profumo had been involved directly with Captain Ivanov.

The Opposition argument has been the security danger posed by the involvement of both men with Miss Keeler.

The security question is only one aspect of the scandal. An increasing number of people

Continued on Page 6, Column 4

HARRIMAN TO LEAD TEST-BAN MISSION TO SOVIET IN JULY

Kennedy Envoy Expected to Tell Khrushchev of Hope for Nuclear Breakthrough

By MAX FRANKEL
Special to The New York Times

WASHINGTON, June 11 — President Kennedy has chosen W. Averell Harriman to lead United States efforts to reach a nuclear test-ban agreement at new three-power negotiations in Moscow next month.

Mr. Harriman has long enjoyed special respect among the Russians, who regard him as a symbol of the better East-West relations that prevailed in World War II when he was Ambassador to Moscow. Now 71 years old, he is Under Secretary of State for Political Affairs and Mr. Kennedy's troubleshooter on many foreign assignments.

A breakthrough in the five-year-old talks on a test ban was defined by the President yesterday as the only major opportunity for reducing tensions.

Harriman to Convey Hopes

Mr. Harriman is expected to convey the President's hopes and anxieties not only to the Soviet negotiators but to Premier Khrushchev personally.

The Soviet leader's willingness to schedule new talks with the United States and Britain for mid-July has raised some hopes here for the Harriman mission.

But generally there was not much optimism in official Washington that the President's conciliation address at American University would produce agreement on a test ban treaty or anything else.

In the speech Mr. Kennedy announced the Moscow talks as a first step in a "strategy of peace." He also said that the United States, to make clear its good faith, would refrain from nuclear testing in the atmosphere as long as others did likewise.

Significance Noted

Administration officials read some significance into Mr. Khrushchev's readiness to schedule talks on nuclear testing before his July 5 "peace conference" with Communist China. Peking's opposition to agreements with the West has been one of the central issues in its quarrel with Moscow.

President Kennedy and Prime Minister Macmillan had tried since April to interest Mr. Khrushchev in a private conference on nuclear testing at a reasonably high level. Until last Saturday, the Russians had spurned these offers and called instead for a public debate of the issue at the 17-nation disarmament conference in Geneva.

The slight change in the Soviet position has had to be weighed against Moscow's continuing reiteration of views that

Continued on Page 4, Column 3

PRESIDENT IN PLEA

Asks Help of Citizens to Assure Equality of Rights to All

Text of the President's speech will be found on Page 20.

By TOM WICKER
Special to The New York Times

WASHINGTON, June 11—President Kennedy told the nation tonight that it faced a "moral crisis" as a result of the rising tide of Negro discontent.

"This is a problem which faces us all in every city of the North as well as the South," Mr. Kennedy said in a brief address televised by all three national networks.

It is a time to act, the President said. He promised to send to Congress next week sweeping legislation to speed school desegregation and open public facilities to every American, regardless of color.

Problem 'Must Be Solved'

Above all, Mr. Kennedy solemnly told the millions of citizens watching him speak from the White House, the problem of the Negro's place in American life "must be solved in the homes of every American across the country."

The objective of every citizen, the President said, must be "for every American to enjoy the privilege of being American without regard to his race or color" — to be treated "as one would wish his children to be treated."

This is, he said, "a matter which concerns this country and what it stands for, and in meeting it I ask the support of all our citizens."

He asked it, the President said, because "this nation for all its hopes and all its boasts will not be fully free until its citizens are free."

Makes Broad Appeal

Mr. Kennedy's address, arranged late today, was made in part as the result of the successful desegregation of the University of Alabama. But the President seized the occasion to make a broad appeal that Negroes and liberals of both parties had been urging upon him for weeks.

The Administration had laid plans well in advance for meeting the Alabama crisis. An executive order federalizing the Alabama National Guard was ready for Mr. Kennedy's signature when the White House received word of Gov. George C. Wallace's defiance of court orders not to interfere with desegregation of the university.

Mr. Kennedy's address was one of the most emotional speeches yet delivered by a President who has often been criticized as being too "cool" and intellectual. Near the end of his talk, Mr. Kennedy appeared to be speaking without a text, and there was a fervor in his voice when he talked of the plight of some Americans.

Education Is Cited

"Today there are Negroes unemployed—two or three times as many compared to whites," he said. "Inadequate education, moving into the large cities, unable to find work, young people particularly out of work, without hope, denied equal rights, denied the opportunity to eat at a restaurant or a lunch counter, or go to a movie theater, denied the right to a decent education, denied—almost today—the right to attend a state university even though qualified."

Mr. Kennedy devoted only a few opening sentences of his 15-minute speech to the Alabama events.

"This afternoon," he began, "following a series of threats

Continued on Page 20, Column 5

Associated Press Wirephoto

CONFRONTATION: Gov. George C. Wallace, left, of Alabama blocks the entrance to Foster Auditorium at University of Alabama as Nicholas deB. Katzenbach, Deputy Attorney General, attempts to get two Negroes enrolled.

GOVERNOR LEAVES

But Fulfills Promises to Stand in Door and to Avoid Violence

Text of Wallace proclamation is printed on Page 20.

By CLAUDE SITTON
Special to The New York Times

TUSCALOOSA, Ala., June 11 — Gov. George C. Wallace stepped aside today when confronted by federalized National Guard troops and permitted two Negroes to enroll in the University of Alabama. There was no violence.

The Governor, flanked by state troopers, had staged a carefully planned show of defying a Federal Court desegregation order.

Mr. Wallace refused four requests this morning from a Justice Department official that he allow Miss Vivian Malone and James A. Hood, both 20 years old, to enter Foster Auditorium and register.

This was in keeping with a campaign pledge that he would "stand in the schoolhouse door" to prevent a resumption of desegregation in Alabama's educational system.

Students Go to Dormitories

The official, Nicholas deB. Katzenbach, Deputy Attorney General, did not press the issue by bringing the students from a waiting car to face the Governor. Instead, they were taken to their dormitories.

However, the outcome was foreshadowed even then. Mr. Katzenbach told Mr. Wallace during their confrontation:

"From the outset, Governor, all of us have known that the final chapter of this history will be the admission of these students."

Units of the 31st (Dixie) Division, federalized on orders from President Kennedy, arrived on the campus four and a half hours later under the command of Brig. Gen. Henry V. Graham.

A Birmingham real estate executive in civilian life, General Graham is the former State Adjutant General who enforced modified martial law in Montgomery, the state capital, following the Freedom Rider riots in 1961.

'Sad Duty' Emphasized

In a voice that was scarcely audible, General Graham said that it was his "sad duty" to order the Governor to step aside.

Mr. Wallace then read the second of two statements challenging the constitutionality of court-ordered desegregation and left the auditorium with his aides for Montgomery.

This sequence of events, which took place in a circus atmosphere, appeared to have given the Governor the face-saving exit he apparently wanted.

Whether the courts find that he actually defied the order issued last Wednesday by District Judge Seybourn H. Lynne in Birmingham remained to be seen. Significantly, Edwin O. Guthman, special assistant

Continued on Page 20, Column 1

Courtesy and Curiosity Mark Campus Reception

By HEDRICK SMITH
Special to The New York Times

TUSCALOOSA, Ala., June 11—Vivian J. Malone and James A. Hood, the two Negro students who entered the University of Alabama today, got a courteous reception from intensely curious students.

There were no incidents during the day, even when the two students went to lunch in the university cafeterias. The campus remained under heavy state police guard and security restrictions throughout the day.

Miss Malone was the first to break the ice. Not long after she entered Mary Burke Hall, she became involved in a gabfest with other girls in the dormitory.

"She's very attractive," one coed said afterward, "I don't think we'll have any trouble with her. She was calm. She wasn't nervous or close-mouthed. She acted very mature."

Enjoyed Meeting Her

Another girl said she had been eager to meet Miss Malone, "We enjoyed meeting her and talking to her," she said. "I'm glad she's on our hall."

The reaction of a third coed, from Birmingham, was different. "She has a right to be here," the student said. "But no one can be forced to accept her."

Miss Malone, tall and attractive in a two-piece pink suit and bouffant hairdo, drew a wolf-whistle from one of the men's dormitory windows when she entered Foster Auditorium to register late this afternoon.

Mr. Hood, a 20-year-old transfer student from Clark College

Continued on Page 21, Column 6

PRESIDENT CALLS NEGRO-JOB TALKS

He Will Meet 300 Labor Leaders Tomorrow on Ending Barriers

Special to The New York Times

WASHINGTON, June 11 — President Kennedy today called about 300 of the nation's top national, state and local labor leaders to the White House Thursday to discuss eliminating discrimination against Negroes in employment.

The meeting will be the labor counterpart of sessions the President has held with businessmen, Mayors and Governors. He will have discussions with religious leaders next Monday.

The President today discussed his forthcoming civil rights proposals with both Democratic and Republican Congressional leaders at separate meetings at the White House. The message probably will go to Congress early next week. The Democrats predicted enactment of an "effective" bill.

Acceleration Aim Seen

At the meeting with the labor leaders, Mr. Kennedy is expected to urge an acceleration of efforts to break down barriers to Negroes in employment. He probably will have some specific suggestions about what the labor leaders should do. He may also discuss his civil rights message and ask for comments.

Invitations to the meeting were sent to the presidents of international unions and to members of the executive council of the American Federation of Labor and Congress of Industrial Organizations who are not also international union presidents. Also invited were the heads of the state A.F.L.-C.I.O. central bodies, of major A.F.L.-C.I.O. local central bodies and of state and local building trades and metal trades councils.

The nation's largest labor union — the International Brotherhood of Teamsters — was understood not to have been invited. Its president, James R. Hoffa, is under indictment in Nashville on a charge of trying to influence the jury in his conspiracy trial there last year.

U.S. Troops Leave Mississippi Campus

By The Associated Press

OXFORD, Miss., June 11—Soldiers helping to guard two Negro students were withdrawn from the University of Mississippi campus today.

Col. William R. Lynch said the Government had decided that Federal marshals protecting the Negroes no longer needed Army backing.

However, Colonel Lynch said the 300-man detachment assigned to duty at the university would remain indefinitely at the tent camp adjoining the campus.

When James H. Meredith arrived at the campus last fall, a riot ensued in which two men were killed and many persons were hurt. Later, 22,000 troops were sent to the area. Last week Mr. Meredith and a second Negro, Cleve McDowell, registered for the summer term without incident.

WATCH ON YEMEN APPROVED BY U.N.

Soviet Stands Aside and Council Votes Sanction—Thant Orders Action

By SAM POPE BREWER
Special to The New York Times

UNITED NATIONS, N. Y., June 11 — With the Soviet Union abstaining, the Security Council voted today to go ahead with a peace-keeping operation under which a 200-man observer team would be sent to Yemen.

The resolution approved by the 10 other members of the Council represented a compromise between the view of the Soviet Union and that of the United States. It was drafted by the representatives of Ghana and Morocco.

The Secretary General, U Thant, sent an order immediately to Maj. Gen. Carl Carlsson von Horn to proceed to Yemen with the advance party of the mission. General Von Horn is chief of the United Nations Truce Supervision Organization, with headquarters in Jerusalem. He had already made a preliminary survey of the situation in Yemen.

Financing an Issue

United States sources said the resolution was acceptable because it did not deal with financial questions in the operative paragraphs. The Soviet Union refrained from vetoing it, apparently, because it did mention financing in the preamble.

After the vote the Soviet delegate, Nikolai T. Fedorenko, said he had abstained because he found the resolution inadequate. He said it should have set a time limit on the operation.

Adlai E. Stevenson, United States representative, said there was no reason for a time limit on the operation, and that the delay already caused by the Council meeting was unfortunate. He expressed thanks to Mr. Thant for "his prompt and effective initiative to avoid international conflict in this area."

Delegates in general seemed agreeably surprised by the moderate and conciliatory tone taken by Mr. Fedorenko. It had been widely believed that he would make strenuous efforts to establish the principle that all such operations must be managed by the Security Council.

Obstruction Not Tried

He stated this principle but did not try to block the resolution that was adopted.

Largely to avoid a showdown with the Soviet Union over the competence of the General Assembly to order expenditures for such operations, Mr. Thant had arranged for Saudi Arabia and the United Arab Republic, supporting the two sides in the Yemeni civil war, to pay for the observation team.

Soldiers from the United Arab Republic form most of the armed forces of the Yemeni republicans now in power. Saudi Arabia furnishes arms and supplies to the royalists trying to put Mohamad al-Badr on his throne.

Mr. Fedorenko said he would accept this arrangement since it had been ordered by the Security Council, "the only organ which under the Charter of the United Nations is competent to take decisions relating to United Nations action for the maintenance of international peace and security."

He stipulated, however, that the mission should involve "a limited number" of observers "for a period of two months."

"The facts of recent years

Continued on Page 14, Column 1

ASIAN LANDS BACK ANTI-PEKING PACT

Alliance to Link Philippines, Malaya and Indonesia

By ROBERT TRUMBULL
Special to The New York Times

MANILA, June 11—Indonesia, Malaya and the Philippines announced plans today for a mutual defense pact against subversion "in any form or manifestation." By implication, the agreement is aimed at Communist China.

The accord is regarded as a significant shift in favor of the West in the power alignments of Southeast Asia.

The leading foreign-affairs officials of the three countries also urged that their heads of government, at a subsequent meeting, take the first steps toward joining in a "confederation of nations of Malay origin."

They announced agreement on their dispute over the proposed formation of Malaysia, a union of Malaya with the British dependencies of Singapore, North Borneo, Sarawak and Brunei.

Under the formula worked out in a strenuous four-day conference, U Thant, Secretary General of the United Nations, will be asked to ascertain the

Continued on Page 2, Column 4

U.S. Enlarges Fire Island Plan; Seeks 8,000-Acre Shore Park

The New York Times June 12, 1963

New Udall plan would convert entire waterfront stretch of Long Island between arrows into a national seashore.

By WARREN WEAVER Jr.
Special to The New York Times

WASHINGTON, June 11—The Administration asked Congress today to create an enlarged Fire Island national seashore that would include 20 miles more of beachfront than anyone had previously suggested.

The plan, advanced by Secretary of the Interior Stewart L. Udall, would add about 2,000 more acres of southern Long Island to the original 6,000-acre project, increasing the land acquisition cost of $15,000,000 by $5,000,000.

Secretary Udall said at a briefing session for Congressmen and reporters that the project "should have the highest priority in the country" because it would preserve recreation land for its most crowded population area.

The new proposal got off to a fast start. Representative Leo W. O'Brien of Albany, ranking Democrat on the House Interior Committee, introduced the bill later in the day, together with Representative William Fitts Ryan, Democrat of Manhattan.

Despite increased activity and influential sponsorship, it ap-

Continued on Page 32, Column 5

Provenzano Guilty In Extortion Case

Special to The New York Times

NEWARK, June 11—Anthony (Tony Pro) Provenzano, a vice president of the International Brotherhood of Teamsters, was convicted tonight of having extorted $17,100 from a trucking company.

The 46-year-old union official faces a maximum penalty of 20 years in prison and a $10,000 fine.

A jury of six men and six women brought in its verdict in Federal court here shortly before 8 o'clock on the second day of deliberations.

Most of today was occupied by the reading by Judge Robert Shaw of testimony by the Government's chief witness, Walter A. Dorn, head of the Dorn Transportation Company of Rensselaer, N. Y.

Mr. Dorn testified about pay-

Continued on Page 33, Column 3

NEWS INDEX

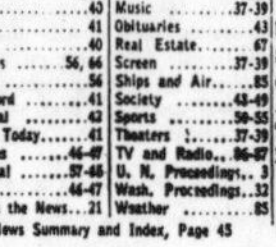

Bull Conner, Sheriff of Birmingham, Alabama, won international notoriety for his violent handling of civil rights demonstrators.

President Kennedy's intervention to force the desegregation of Alabama's public schools was followed by the death of four children in the Birmingham church bombing.

President Kennedy called out the National Guard to enforce integration at the University of Alabama, overcoming the strong objections of Gov. George Wallace.

"All the News That's Fit to Print"

The New York Times.

LATE CITY EDITION

U. S. Weather Bureau Report (Page 66) forecasts: Mostly sunny today; clear tonight. Fair, then cloudy late tomorrow. Temp. range: 71—52; yesterday: 66—56. Temp.-Hum. Index: 65; yesterday: 63.

VOL. CXII..No. 38,491. © 1963 by The New York Times Company. Times Square, New York 36, N. Y. — NEW YORK, THURSDAY, JUNE 13, 1963. — TEN CENTS

BRITAIN'S CABINET IS REPORTED SPLIT ON PROFUMO CASE

Health Chief and 2 Others Said to Weigh Resigning to Protest Scandal

NEW PARLEY SET TODAY

Public Pressures Against Macmillan Are Growing—Moral Issue Stressed

By SYDNEY GRUSON
Special to The New York Times

LONDON, June 12—Three of Prime Minister Macmillan's Cabinet ministers were reliably reported tonight after a Cabinet meeting to be considering resigning over the Profumo scandal.

The leader of the revolt within the Government was said to be Enoch Powell, Minister of Health, who left the Government once before on an issue of principle. He resigned as Secretary to the Treasury in 1958 because the Government refused to make heavier cuts in public spending.

Named by political sources as sharing Mr. Powell's views were Sir Edward Boyle, Minister of Education, and Sir Keith Joseph, Minister of Housing and Local Government.

Henry Brooke, the 60-year-old Home Secretary, was reported to have expressed serious misgivings at the Cabinet session, but he said later he was not planning to resign. Mr. Brooke was reported to be angered because some documents available to Mr. Macmillan had been withheld from him.

'Serious Personal Doubts'

Also the moral issue was said to be weighing heavily with the members of the Cabinet.

The Cabinet met in emergency session for two hours, but the meeting apparently failed to resolve what some observers described as the "serious personal doubts" of the three ministers on supporting Mr. Macmillan.

Another meeting was called by Mr. Macmillan for tomorrow. Whether the revolt breaks into the open by then, according to some politicians, depends on Mr. Powell's decision.

Mr. Macmillan has, in effect, demanded collective responsibility from the Cabinet for his handling of the crisis generated by the involvement of John Profumo, former Secretary of State for War, with Christine Keeler, a 21-year-old party girl who calls herself a model, and who, in turn, was having an affair with the former deputy Soviet naval attaché in London.

The Cabinet was informed that the investigation by the Lord Chancellor, Lord Dilhorne, showed no breach of national

Continued on Page 2, Column 3

United Press International Radiophoto

REPORTS ON PROFUMO INQUIRY: Lord Dilhorne, British Lord Chancellor, as he arrived by auto yesterday at the London residence of Prime Minister Macmillan.

4 Shot as Jagan Escapes Mob in Continuing Riots

Special to The New York Times

GEORGETOWN, British Guiana, June 12—Anti-Government demonstrations continued here today. Four men were shot by policemen who fired into a crowd reported to have been converging on Prime Minister Cheddi B. Jagan's automobile as he was leaving Parliament.

Earlier, ten other persons had been wounded by gunfire.

The incident involving Dr. Jagan touched off a new wave of looting and attacks by Negroes on East Indians in the city.

The police said that someone in the crowd had thrown homemade bombs at the Prime Minister's car. Others in the crowd pelted the automobile.

More than 200 riot policemen tried to chase the demonstrators from the streets. Nine were hit by police bullets. Two businessmen fired on a crowd attempting to enter their establishments, wounding one man.

Use of Force Authorized

The police commissioner said that organizers of the Trades Union Council's passive resistance campaign against the Government had to share the blame for the disturbances and the attacks on the Indians. He said that he had ordered the police to use all force necessary to end the disorders.

Meanwhile, frightened Indians in Georgetown remained indoors and those living in the countryside remained away from the city.

Rahaman Gajraj, Speaker of the Legislative Assembly, summoned a meeting of the Assembly for next Wednesday. It will be the body's first meeting since it suspended Dr. Jagan and three Assemblymen of his Peoples Progressive party May 28 for gross disrespect to the Speaker. The suspended Prime Minister and Assemblymen cannot attend.

In their two-hour battle with rioters in and around Parliament, the police again used tear gas. Yesterday they used tear gas to disperse strikers

Continued on Page 9, Column 1

MOSCOW DISPUTES U.N.'S DUES STAND

Asserts Two-thirds Action Is Needed to Deny Vote to Member in Arrears

By THOMAS J. HAMILTON
Special to The New York Times

UNITED NATIONS, N. Y., June 12 — The Soviet Union challenged today the generally accepted doctrine that a member two years in arrears on its assessments automatically loses its vote in the General Assembly.

The Soviet Union contended that the decision to suspend a member from voting could be taken only by a two-thirds vote of the members present and voting.

A number of Western delegates interpreted the Soviet stand as a sign of growing concern in Moscow over the fact that the Soviet Union's unpaid assessments for the Congo and Middle Eastern forces would amount to the equivalent of two years' assessments next Jan. 1.

The United States and a number of West European members hold that if a member is two years in arrears the President of the Assembly must announce at the start of the session that it has lost its vote.

In that case a simple majority would be required to overrule the President's ruling and allow the member to retain its vote.

If the Soviet position is accepted, however, Moscow would need to muster only one-third

Continued on Page 2, Column 5

RUSSIANS STIRRED BY KENNEDY TALK ABOUT COLD WAR

Soviet Publication of Text Regarded as an Indication of Kremlin's Approval

By SEYMOUR TOPPING
Special to The New York Times

MOSCOW, June 12—Izvestia published tonight the text of President Kennedy's speech on Monday in which he appealed for re-examination of attitudes toward the cold war.

The decision to make the speech available to the Soviet people through the Government newspaper was interpreted here as an indication that the speech had made a favorable impression in the Kremlin.

Critical of Soviet policy and Communism in some sections, the speech was being read eagerly by Muscovites, who receive Izvestia in the evenings. The newspaper, which is reported to have a circulation of more than 4,500,000, is distributed in other major centers of the Soviet Union on the following morning.

Tone of Speech Appreciated

The initial reaction of Soviet citizens in conversation with foreigners was guarded but unmistakably appreciative of the conciliatory tone of the speech.

A Soviet intellectual commented: "The speech and its publication in Izvestia show that there can be mutual understanding."

A young woman worker was overheard to ask a friend: "Have you read the Kennedy speech? It is all about peace."

Premier Khrushchev, in approving the publication of the speech, provided President Kennedy with a rarely afforded opportunity to communicate directly with the Soviet people.

The last occasion was Nov. 28, 1961, when Izvestia published the text of President Kennedy's interview with Alexei I. Adzhubei, the editor of the newspaper and Mr. Khrushchev's son-in-law.

Inaugural Carried

The text of the President's inaugural speech was published in Izvestia Jan. 21, 1961.

In his interview with Mr. Adzhubei, Mr. Kennedy was more sharply critical of Soviet policy than he was Monday in his speech at the commencement exercises of American University in Washington. The commencement address was largely an appeal to Americans to reappraise their attitudes toward the Soviet Union and the cold war.

It was understood that Soviet leaders had become dubious about the wisdom of publishing the Adzhubei interview after assessing the possible impact on the Soviet public. The President had said in the interview that world peace could be consoli-

Continued on Page 4, Column 4

Ex-Aides of Javits Lean to Lewisohn

By CLAYTON KNOWLES

Two strong supporters of Senator Jacob K. Javits were reported yesterday ready to serve on the campaign committee for Richard Lewisohn for Republican Councilman at Large in Manhattan.

They are John Trubin and John A. Wells, both former campaign managers for Mr. Javits.

Mr. Trubin, a law partner of the Senator, acknowledged that he had been invited to serve and was considering accepting. But he stressed that the decision would be a personal one. He insisted that his acceptance should not be construed as indicating that Mr. Javits was lining up with Mr. Lewisohn.

Mr. Lewisohn's principal rival for the nomination is Richard S. Aldrich, a cousin

Continued on Page 34, Column 1

ADMIRAL DECRIES PLANE REVERSAL

Anderson Finds Danger in Rejecting Experts' Views on the V/STOL Aircraft

By JACK RAYMOND
Special to The New York Times

WASHINGTON, June 12 — High Navy officers told the Senate today that they had been overruled in the award of a contract for a new type of vertical or short-takeoff-and-landing airplane. They said they had recommended a cheaper and better plane than the one selected by the Defense Department.

In a statement to the Senate Preparedness subcommittee, Adm. George W. Anderson, retiring Chief of Naval Operations, said the Navy's recommendation had surprised him.

"The philosophy of reversal without adequate and thorough consultation is dangerous," he said.

"It is my personal conviction that reversal of source selection recommendations made on the basis of long-established and widely accepted procedures is improper on two bases," Admiral Anderson went on.

Would Foster Competition

"First," he said, "the professional advice of military and civilian experts charged with the technical evaluation of design proposals should not be overturned except for the most compelling and persuasive reasons.

"Second, such reversals can only be detrimental to the competitive spirit of American industry. For many years, the Navy has attempted to foster and maintain this spirit at a high level in the belief that such will accelerate the technological progress and innovation to insure that we receive the most effective weapons systems and hardware attainable."

The hearings, similar to the TFX (tactical fighter, experimental) airplane hearings, opened this morning. Senator John Stennis, Democrat of Mississippi, chairman of the subcommittee, explained the purpose of the hearings.

He pointed out that the Navy had recommended the Douglas Aircraft Corporation of Santa Monica, Calif., to develop the X-22, a vertical or short takeoff

Continued on Page 11, Column 1

ROCKEFELLER SEES POLITICAL MOTIVE IN LEVITT ATTACK

Says Criticism of Financial Policies May Be Part of a White House Campaign

By DOUGLAS DALES
Special to The New York Times

NEW CITY, N. Y., June 12—Governor Rockefeller charged today that State Controller Arthur Levitt had been politically motivated in his attack Sunday on state financing practices. The Governor suggested that the attack might have been inspired by the White House.

The charge was made at a news conference in Albany just before Mr. Rockefeller left for a Rockland County Republican dinner here and his first political conferences with local party leaders since his remarriage. He repeated the charge at the dinner.

Mr. Levitt, the only elected Democrat in the state administration, had assailed the Governor's financing methods for state construction in a television appearance and in an interview.

He had quoted financial sources in alleging that the methods were jeopardizing the state's triple-A credit rating.

Foresees No Increases

The Governor, replying to a question at his news conference about the possibility that he would call for a higher revenue next year to balance the budget, said, "My best 'guesstimate' at the moment is that I plan to finance the next budget without tax increases or higher fees."

Because of the use of $250,000,000 in non-recurring income to finance the 1963-64 budget and the certainty that school-aid costs will rise $50,000,000 or more, there has been considerable speculation whether new sources of income will have to be found next year to avoid the use of state bonds.

The Governor conferred this afternoon with Republican chairmen from eight lower Hudson Valley counties at the St. George Hotel in Nyack, while Mrs. Rockefeller was the guest of Rockland County Republican women at a tea in another part of the hotel.

Tonight, many of the 600 dinner guests here filed through a reception line to meet Mrs. Rockefeller.

First of 11 Meetings

The meeting with party leaders was the first of 11 planned to help strengthen the party for the local elections this fall. Tomorrow the Governor will confer in Buffalo.

At the news conference, called specifically to rebut the Levitt charges, the Governor read a statement disputing the contention that the interest for financing construction through authorities was more expensive than state-bond interest.

Mr. Rockefeller also denied that his administration was circumventing the constitutional requirement for voter approval of borrowing by giving the special construction agencies bonding authorization.

He declared that the Controller had lent himself to a Democratic propaganda campaign "to discredit the fiscal integrity and soundly solvent fiscal policies of this administration," and added:

"Controller Levitt is a partisan, organization Democrat, not an independent, nonpartisan,

Continued on Page 34, Column 3

N.A.A.C.P. LEADER SLAIN IN JACKSON; PROTESTS MOUNT

WHITES ALARMED

Victim Is Shot From Ambush—158 Negro Marchers Seized

By CLAUDE SITTON
Special to The New York Times

JACKSON, Miss., June 12—A sniper lying in ambush shot and fatally wounded a Negro civil rights leader early today.

The slaying touched off mass protests by Negroes in which 158 were arrested. It also aroused widespread fear of further racial violence in this state capital.

The victim of the shooting was Medgar W. Evers, 37-year-old Mississippi field secretary of the National Association for the Advancement of Colored People. Struck in the back by a bullet from a high-powered rifle as he walked from his automobile to his home, he died less than an hour later—at 1:14 A.M. (3:14 A.M., New York time)—in University Hospital.

Agents of the Federal Bureau of Investigation joined Jackson, Hinds County and state authorities in the search for the killer.

Suspect Is Released

A 51-year-old white man was picked up, questioned for several hours and released. Investigators discovered a .30-06-caliber rifle with a newly attached telescopic sight in a vacant lot near the honeysuckle thicket from which they believed the fatal shot had been fired.

[In New York, the N.A.A.C.P. offered a $10,000 reward for information leading to the arrest and conviction of Mr. Evers's killer. The Rev. Dr. Martin Luther King Jr. mourned Mr. Evers as a "pure patriot."]

The first demonstration today occurred at 11:25 A.M., when 13 ministers left the Pearl Street African Methodist Episcopal Church and walked silently toward the City Hall.

The police, who refused to let them proceed by twos at widely spaced intervals, arrested all 13. The group included many of the Negro leaders who had been working with white officials in efforts to resolve this city's month-old racial crisis.

An hour and a half later, approximately 200 Negro teen-agers marched out of the Masonic Building on Lynch Street, site of Mr. Evers's office. Some

Continued on Page 12, Column 1

Eisenhower Meets Kennedy on Rights

Special to The New York Times

WASHINGTON, June 12 — President Kennedy, continuing to push ahead on the civil rights front, talked with former President Dwight D. Eisenhower today about the turbulent racial situation.

The President sought support for the new package of civil rights legislation he expects to send to Congress next week. The White House gave no details of the conversation and did not indicate what success the President had.

The whole racial issue continued to dominate the capital today. The mood of tension and apprehension was heightened by the murder of a Mississippi Negro leader and by renewed Negro demonstrations in Danville, Va., and Cambridge, Md.

At the Capitol the shooting

Continued on Page 13, Column 1

UNIONS HERE GET WARNING ON BIAS

Screvane Threatens to Halt Work at Harlem Hospital After Picketing There

By SAMUEL KAPLAN

Acting Mayor Paul R. Screvane said yesterday that the city would halt construction of the Harlem Hospital annex if the building trade unions did not act immediately to end any discriminatory practices there.

This warning followed a brief skirmish between the police and civil rights demonstrators at the site of the annex, at 136th Street and Lenox Avenue. About 150 demonstrators protested alleged discrimination in the building trades against Negroes and Puerto Ricans.

Three demonstrators received minor injuries yesterday morning when the police prevented them from reaching an entrance to the construction site. They had attempted to sit down and block the entrance to prevent workers from entering the enclosed site.

44 Workers Enter

Forty-four of the workmen, including two Negroes, eventually entered the site after policemen had formed a corridor for them to pass through. Eight Negro workmen stayed out.

Mr. Screvane and other high city officials met with leaders of the demonstration in the afternoon. The conference, which lasted three hours, was described as a historic one in that it resulted in the strongest pledge of action in this area that has yet come out of City Hall.

At a press conference following the meeting, Mr. Screvane said the Building and Construction Trades Council would meet at 10:30 this morning to discuss

Continued on Page 20, Column 2

NASA LOSES CHIEF OF MOON PROJECT

Eisenhower Hits Space Cost —Mercury Flights End

By JOHN W. FINNEY
Special to The New York Times

WASHINGTON, June 12—A crisis developed in the man-in-space program today as the space agency formally terminated Project Mercury, the nation's first step in manned space flight.

The National Aeronautics and Space Administration announced that D. Brainerd Holmes was resigning as director of the Office of Manned Space Flight. A former executive with the Radio Corporation of America, Mr. Holmes was recruited nearly two years ago to direct the multibillion-dollar effort to land a man on the moon before the end of the decade.

The developing political attack on the Kennedy Adminis-

Continued on Page 10, Column 5

VENEZUELA BALKS ASSASSINS' PLOT

Betancourt, Escaping Bomb, Orders All Reds Jailed

By The Associated Press

CARACAS, Venezuela, June 12 — Three terrorists tried to assassinate President Romulo Betancourt with a time-bomb in the Archbishop's Palace at Ciudad Bolivar, the President announced in a radio-television speech tonight.

Police guards captured two of the terrorists but the third got away shortly before President Betancourt was scheduled to arrive for the inaugural of the new palace of the Archbishop, Msgr. Juan José Bernal Ortiz, the announcement said.

The police said they had seized a high-powered bomb from the captives.

President Betancourt said that he had ordered the arrest of all Communists in Venezuela.

Supporters of Premier Fidel Castro of Cuba and other leftist enemies of the Betancourt regime have been conducting almost daily terrorist attacks in various parts of the country.

President Betancourt, who has escaped several previous attempts on his life, is currently on an extensive tour of the interior of Venezuela inaugurating public works projects.

A special committee of the

Continued on Page 8, Column 1

Jobless Areas Denied More Aid As House Vote Rebuffs Kennedy

By C. P. TRUSSELL
Special to The New York Times

WASHINGTON, June 12—The House of Representatives defeated today an Administration bill to strengthen the two-year-old program for helping economically distressed areas combat unemployment.

The vote was 209 to 204.

Voting for the bill were 189 Democrats and 15 Republicans. Opposing were 152 Republicans and 57 Democrats, the latter mostly from Southern states.

The House action was viewed widely as the sharpest defeat suffered by the Administration in the current Congress. It occurred with the same legislation that had brought President Kennedy his first major victory in Congress, enactment of the Area Redevelopment bill of 1961.

The defeat of the measure, which would have authorized $450,000,000 in new funds for loans and grants, apparently means that the area-redevelopment program will continue at its present pace, at least until next year. The program, which was enacted for a four-year period, is due to terminate in 1965.

The defeat came as a shock to the House's Administration leadership. It had been predicted that the measure would pass by a close margin.

The bill went to the floor accompanied by reports from both the majority and minority members of the Banking and Currency Committee. The minority, led by Representative Clarence E. Kilburn, Republican of upstate New York, said:

"We are impressed by the

Continued on Page 52, Column 3

10 SEIZED BY U.S. AFTER CUBA RAID

Exiles Say the Group Killed 'Many Soldiers' in Attack

By United Press International

MIAMI, June 12—Ten Cuban exiles returning from a raid on their homeland were detained by United States authorities today. Exile sources here said the raiders killed "many soldiers," blew up a refinery and sank a Cuban gunboat.

The sources here said the 10 Cubans, members of an unnamed exile splinter group, left an undisclosed base in the Caribbean five days ago on a converted PT boat.

The raiders said they were forced to commandeer a fishing schooner after the PT boat sank. They were detained in the Florida Keys today along with two captured Cuban militiamen and a refugee.

Joseph Fortier, director of the Miami Customs Office, said that the 10 raiders were being detained pending "further investigation." He added that the two soldiers would probably be allowed to return home.

One of the raiders, identified as Evangelio Rufin Calaro, was taken to a Key West hospital. A bullet was lodged in his back.

Sources in Miami said the PT boat attacked a sugar refinery in Matanzas Province at mid-

Continued on Page 8, Column 3

The New York Times

BUILDING SITE BESIEGED: Police reinforce barricades near Harlem Hospital, where civil rights demonstrators charged discrimination in membership by building unions.

NEWS INDEX

The Black Muslims, led by Mohammad Elijah, rejected racial integration and instead, advocated an independent Negro state in the South or a return to Africa.

Mrs. Shirley Chisholm is being sworn into office by House Speaker John McCormack. She was the first black to be elected to the House.

The assassinated civil rights leader, Medgar Evers, was buried in Arlington National Cemetery.

Two stars that shone in the integration movement were Charlayne Hunter and Hamilton Holmes, the first blacks to attend the University of Georgia.

1963

The fastest human to hit the finish line was Bob Hayes of Florida A&M, who tied the world's record for the 220-yard dash at 20.5

Bob Cousy is seen in a tender moment when the Boston Celtics honored him at the end of his career.

Sandy Koufax seen firing a fast one to clinch the World Series victory for the Los Angeles Dodgers. He pitched two of the Dodgers four straight wins against the New York Yankees.

President Kennedy, amidst a crowd of equally exhuberant fans, threw out the first ball of the season at Washington's opening game.

"All the News That's Fit to Print"

The New York Times.

LATE CITY EDITION
U. S. Weather Bureau Report (Page 74) forecasts: Mostly sunny today; cloudy, chance of showers tonight. Fair tomorrow. Temp. range: 80—60; yesterday: 80—59. Temp.-Hum. Index: low 70's; yesterday: 72.

VOL. CXII..No. 38,496. NEW YORK, TUESDAY, JUNE 18, 1963. TEN CENTS

MACMILLAN WINS IN VOTE OVER PROFUMO SCANDAL; DEBATE WEAKENS HIS GRIP

HOUSE IN UPROAR

Abstentions by Tories Mar Government's 321-252 Victory

Excerpts from the Commons debate are on Page 12.

By SYDNEY GRUSON
Special to The New York Times

LONDON, June 17 — Prime Minister Macmillan's position was shaken, perhaps fatally, tonight when the Government's majority fell to 69 in the House of Commons vote after six and a half hours of dramatic debate on the Profumo scandal.

The Conservatives have an over-all majority of 93.

There were shouts of "Resign!" from the Opposition Labor benches when the vote was announced. It was 321 to 252 in support of the Government's handling of the security aspects of the scandal.

Twenty-seven Conservatives abstained. Up to a short time before the debate began Conservative politicians were predicting that not more than 12 would refuse to support the Government. The abstentions were enough to create doubts that Mr. Macmillan could continue in office long.

Three Laborites Absent

The present state of the parties is: Conservatives 357, Labor 255, Liberals seven and Independents two. Three Labor legislators were absent.

The Prime Minister, clearly shaken, had risen to leave the House after the vote when Harold Wilson, Labor's leader, rose to question him about his intentions. Mr. Macmillan returned to his seat and heard Mr. Wilson say:

"In view of the fact that on a motion of confidence their [the Conservatives] theoretical majority is nearly 40 less . . ." He was halted by the uproar in the House.

Sir Harry Hylton-Foster, the Speaker of the House, refused to allow Mr. Wilson's question. He ruled the Labor leader out of order.

Mr. Macmillan then left the House, to further cries of "Resign!" from the Opposition and to the cheers of most of his own party.

Effects Will Last

It was clear from the fierceness of the debate and from the number of abstentions that the political effects of the scandal would be felt for a long time.

The scandal erupted publicly on June 5 when John Profumo resigned as Secretary of State for War. He admitted having lied to the House of Commons on March 22 when he denied that there was "any impropriety whatsoever" in his relations with Christine Keeler, a 21-year-old party girl and self-styled model.

It then became known that Mr. Profumo had had an affair with Miss Keeler during several months of 1961 while she was also the mistress of Capt. Yevgeni E. Ivanov, who was the Soviet deputy naval attaché in London until last December and presumably served as a military intelligence agent.

Security Data Withheld

Out of Mr. Macmillan's chronological account of events emerged the fact that the security services and the former Secretary of the Cabinet, Sir Norman Brook, (now Lord Normanbrook) had withheld vital reports from the Prime Minister, the man in charge of security.

Acting on the advice of the security services, Lord Normanbrook warned Mr. Profumo in August, 1961, to end his association with Miss Keeler. The security services had even earlier warned Dr. Stephen Ward, the society osteopath who introduced Miss Keeler to Mr. Profumo and to Captain Ivanov, to be cautious in his relations with the Russian.

Dr. Ward, whom Mr. Wilson described as a "tool" of the Russians, is under arrest on

Continued on Page 13, Column 1

United Press International Radiophoto — Associated Press Cablephoto

ON THE WAY TO DEBATE: Prime Minister Macmillan, left, leaving Admiralty House, his official residence. At right, Harold Wilson, Labor leader, leaves Hampstead home.

BYKOVSKY NEARS A FLIGHT RECORD

Approaches Nikolayev Mark of 64 Orbits—Woman Has Some Difficulty

By HENRY TANNER
Special to The New York Times

MOSCOW, Tuesday, June 18—Junior Lieut. Valentina V. Tereshkova, the world's first spacewoman, circled the globe for the second day today, after having experienced some difficult moments during the early part of her flight.

Her male companion, Lieut. Col. Valery F. Bykovsky, traveled in an adjoining orbit and maintained close radio contact with her. He was in the fourth day of his flight.

If Colonel Bykovsky stays in flight until early afternoon today, he will equal the record established by Maj. Andrian G. Nikolayev last August. Major Nikolayev circled the globe 64 times.

[The Russians reported that Colonel Bykovsky lost altitude on Monday, according to The Associated Press. His maximum altitude, originally about 146 miles, dropped to 125.5, and his minimum altitude, originally 112.4 miles, fell to 102.5.]

Three Miles Apart

At the beginning of their joint flight the two Soviet astronauts orbited only five kilometers (three miles) apart, or about nine-tenths of a mile closer than their predecessors traveled last August in the first "group flight" in space.

Group flights are intended eventually to lead to a link-up of several spacecraft, which would then form an orbiting staging platform from which flights to the moon and the planets could be launched.

There were persistent rumors

Continued on Page 3, Column 1

U.S. May Retaliate If Europe Retains Farm Import Curbs

By FELIX BELAIR Jr.
Special to The New York Times

WASHINGTON, June 17—Secretary of State Dean Rusk told the Senate Foreign Relations Committee today that the United States might find it necessary to retaliate against France and other European Common Market countries unless they eased restrictions on American farm products.

The Secretary did not use the word "retaliate." He said it might prove necessary "to withdraw [trade] concessions already given" to such countries.

His statement followed a blistering attack by several Democratic Senators on military aid and financial support for North Atlantic Treaty Organization countries of Western Europe that were discriminating against United States exports, chiefly through tariff duties.

Hostile Questions

The resentment of committee members toward foreign aid appeared to mushroom into hostile questions to the Secretary after Senator Stuart Symington, Democrat of Missouri, had remarked:

"I just can't correlate this multibillion-dollar foreign aid proposal with the increasingly difficult problems we are having with the Common Market countries."

The Missouri Senator noted that the Administration was planning to negotiate tariff reductions of more than 50 per cent on a long list of industrial and agricultural products, although the Common Market countries, under French leadership, were adopting even more restrictive policies against United States exports.

"We are planning to negotiate very vigorously next year for

Continued on Page 14, Column 3

Nenni Ends Support for Moro As Left-Wing Socialists Revolt

By PAUL HOFMANN
Special to The New York Times

ROME, June 17—Pietro Nenni, leader of the Left-wing Socialists, announced tonight that his party had "failed to support" the attempt of Premier-designate Aldo Moro to form a new center-left coalition government.

The announcement followed a rebellion within the Left-wing Socialist party against Mr. Nenni, who had favored support of Mr. Moro. The turmoil over formation of a new Italian government, following the resignation of Premier Amintore Fanfani a month ago, was deepened.

Mr. Moro was scheduled to call on President Antonio Segni tomorow morning to inform him officially of his decision. It was expected that Mr. Moro either would try to form a cabinet consisting only of his own Christian Democrats or would ask Mr. Segni to entrust another Christian Democrat with setting up a government.

Mr. Nenni, a 72-year-old veteran of Italian Socialism, had pleaded vainly for many hours yesterday with the rebels in his party to give Mr. Moro a chance to establish another center-left regime.

Faced with the prospect of being voted out of office as party secretary, Mr. Nenni bowed to the rebels. Reports circulated that he was considering resigning from his long-held post. However, sources close to him explained that he was clinging to the secretaryship to be in a better tactical position at the party's national

Continued on Page 15, Column 1

HOUSE COMMITTEE VOTES A TAX RISE FOR OIL INDUSTRY

50-Million-a-Year Increase Backed to Offset Benefit of Depletion Allowance

By JOHN D. MORRIS
Special to The New York Times

WASHINGTON, June 17 — The House Ways and Means Committee agreed today to raise taxes of oil and gas producers by about $50,000,000 a year.

Reversing an earlier decision, the committee tentatively accepted one of four Administration proposals designed to offset part of the tax benefits available to the oil and gas industry through depletion allowances. It approved a modified version of another.

The actions came as the committee began taking a second look at some of the Administration's tax-reform proposals that it had previously rejected.

Earlier in the day, Secretary of the Treasury Douglas Dillon told the panel, meeting in closed session, that the reforms it had approved so far would net only about $75,000,000 a year in new Federal revenue.

3 Billion Sought

This is only a fraction of the $3,300,000,000 in new revenue sought by President Kennedy as partial compensation for the $13,600,000,000 in revenue losses that would result from approval of his proposals for cuts in individual and corporation income tax rates.

The Administration's four-part package of oil and gas tax revisions was originally calculated to yield $280,000,000 a year. But the Treasury has since reduced the estimate to about $230,000,000.

The proposal accepted without change by the committee today would produce about $30,000,000. It would prohibit oil and gas producers from lumping together high-profit and low-profit operations, regardless of geographical location, for the purpose of increasing the maximum tax allowances they may take for depletion of their mineral resources.

Curb on Use of Gains Tax

The other approved proposal, as modified by the committee, would yield about $20,000,000 in increased taxes. It would require the payment of ordinary income taxes on part of the profits from sales of mineral properties. Under present law these profits are subject to the more favorable capital-gains rate.

The Administration plan, as submitted, called for taxation of a larger part of such profits as ordinary income. This would have netted $50,000,000 a year.

Taxpayers are eligible for depletion allowances of 27½ per cent of their gross income from oil and gas wells. That is, up to 27½ per cent of their gross income is deductible from taxable income. The allowance is subject to a ceiling of 50 per cent of the taxpayer's net income, after deductions for drilling costs and the like.

The Administration's main

Continued on Page 17, Column 1

SUPREME COURT, 8 TO 1, PROHIBITS LORD'S PRAYER AND BIBLE READING AS PUBLIC SCHOOL REQUIREMENTS

Saturday Work Ban By a Church Upheld

Special to The New York Times

WASHINGTON, June 17—A state may not deny unemployment benefits to a person whose religious scruples keep him from working on a particular day, the Supreme Court held today.

The 7 to 2 decision was a victory for Mrs. Adell H. Sherbert, a Seventh-Day Adventist in South Carolina. Her church observes Saturday as the Sabbath and enforces the Biblical command to do no work on that day.

Mrs. Sherbert was employed at Spartan Mills in Beaumont, S. C., when the company went on a six-day week in 1959. She was dismissed for having refused to work Saturdays. Other textile plants were on the same work week, and she could not find a job.

South Carolina law denies unemployment benefits to a

Continued on Page 27, Column 7

WIDE EFFECT DUE

Decision Will Require Change in Majority of State Systems

By FRED M. HECHINGER

The Supreme Court decision that Bible reading and the recitation of the Lord's Prayer are unconstitutional as part of regular public school devotional exercises will affect 41 per cent of the nation's school districts.

The affected districts are in 37 states and the District of Columbia. Among them are a high proportion of large systems and apparently a majority of schools.

In New York City, the ruling has led to a hurried appeal by Dr. Calvin E. Gross, Superintendent of Schools, to Dr. James E. Allen Jr., State Education Commissioner, for immediate instructions concerning Bible reading.

A conflict between practices in New York State and New York City underscores the general confusion over the controversial issue.

Reading Required Here

The state does not permit Bible reading under the currently accepted interpretation of the State Constitution. But the city, under the bylaws of the Board of Education, requires that "the regular assemblies of all schools shall be opened by reading to the pupils a portion of the Bible without comment."

"We shall obey the law of the land, whatever it is," Dr. Gross said. But he added that action must await interpretation of the ruling. He said, however:

"I think the handwriting is on the wall."

The majority of state education officials is expected to support the Supreme Court ruling. Some of the commissioners or superintendents, however, may attempt to find legal substitutes for the outlawed observance.

Pennsylvania Position

Such steps were outlined yesterday by Charles H. Boehm, Pennsylvania's Superintendent of Public Instruction, when he recommended "an inspirational period" and silent meditation as well as readings on the role of religion in history and literature.

Dr. Boehm said the decision would be interpreted in Pennsylvania "to mean the elimination of religious services and ritual, but God and religion will remain in the schools." He said the school authorities there would consult with scholars from the four major religions and others "on important matters relating to religion and the curriculum."

The eventual stand taken by state public school officials may, to some extent, be influenced by their relationship to the political powers and pressures of their states. Twenty-four of these top officials at present are appointed by boards of regents or the equivalent; 21

Continued on Page 27, Column 5

Churches Divided, With Most in Favor

By GEORGE DUGAN

Religious reaction to the Supreme Court decision banning formal Bible reading and the recitation of the Lord's Prayer in public schools was mixed but, in balance, on the favorable side.

Representatives of the "main stream" of Protestant thinking, whose views are reflected in the National Council of Churches, hailed the court ruling. Jewish opinion, too, was largely favorable to it.

For the most part Roman Catholics viewed the ruling with alarm, however, and conservative Protestants, members of small fundamentalist bodies or minority groups in the large denominations, deplored it.

There were many persons of all faiths, however, who took a "so what?" attitude.

Continued on Page 29, Column 6

2 CASES DECIDED

Government Must Be Neutral in Religion, Majority Asserts

Texts of the Supreme Court opinions, Pages 28 and 29.

By ANTHONY LEWIS
Special to The New York Times

WASHINGTON, June 17 — The Supreme Court decided today that no state or locality may require recitation of the Lord's Prayer or Bible verses in public schools.

An 8-to-1 majority wrote what appeared to be a final legal answer to one of the most divisive issues of church and state. The opinion of the Court was by Justice Tom C. Clark.

Even the sole dissenter, Justice Potter Stewart, said that religious ceremonies in public schools could violate the constitutional rights of dissenters. But he found the record in today's cases inadequate and would have sent them back for further hearings.

The prayer cases were among a dozen decided today in what turned out to be the final session of the present Supreme Court term. The Court recessed until October.

Insists on Neutral Stand

Justice Clark sounded the theme that government must be "neutral" in religious matters. His opinion ended with these philosophical phrases:

"The place of religion in our society is an exalted one, achieved through a long tradition of reliance on the home, the church and the inviolable citadel of the individual heart and mind.

"We have come to recognize through bitter experience that it is not within the power of government to invade that citadel, whether its purpose or effect be to aid or oppose, to advance or retard.

"In the relationship between man and religion, the state is firmly committed to a position of neutrality."

Seek to Soften Criticism

Today's decision was a follow-up to last year's ruling against the recitation in New York public schools of a prayer composed by the State Board of Regents. The Justices were evidently concerned to prevent, as best they could, the bitter criticism that greeted the New York case.

In his opinion Justice Clark stressed the importance of religion in this country's tradition. He took care to say that the decision did not affect the right to use the Bible for teaching purposes or did not deal with such other matters as Army chaplains.

Justices William J. Brennan Jr. and Arthur J. Goldberg, in concurring opinions, also sought to disarm potential criticism. The Goldberg opinion was joined by Justice John Marshall Harlan.

Varied Voices Speak

It was particularly noted by courtroom observers that the voices of a Protestant, a Catholic and a Jew on the Court spoke up for the principle of church-state separation.

Justice Clark is a Presbyterian active in the affairs of his church here. Justice Brennan is the Court's only Roman Catholic and Justice Goldberg the only Jewish member.

The Court's decision dealt with two cases, from Maryland and Pennsylvania. Each involved both the reading of Bible verses to the students each morning, and the recitation of the Lord's

Continued on Page 27, Column 1

CITY G.O.P. FACING FIGHT IN PRIMARY

4 Rivals for Manhattan Seat in Council Forcing Test—Leaders Meet Tonight

By LEONARD INGALLS

Vincent F. Albano Jr., the New York County Republican chairman, acknowledged last night that rivalry for the party's nomination for councilman at large in Manhattan would lead to a primary fight.

The Republican leader made his statement after the party's county executive committee had heard 10 candidates state their qualifications for the nomination at a closed meeting.

A battle in the Sept. 5 primary would pit against each other elements of the party supported by Governor Rockefeller and a group that has the backing of Representative John V. Lindsay of Manhattan's 17th Congressional District.

Two of the leading candidates are Richard S. Aldrich, a cousin of the Governor, and Richard Lewisohn, leader of the Ninth Assembly District, who is favored by Representative Lindsay.

Mr. Rockefeller has denied that he sought the nomination for Mr. Aldrich. But Mr. Lindsay has insisted that Mr. Albano told him the Governor had directed that Mr. Aldrich be given the nomination.

The nomination is considered tantamount to election. Two councilmen at large will be chosen, with each party nom-

Continued on Page 31, Column 3

DIRKSEN IMPERILS CIVIL RIGHTS PLAN

Won't Back Part of Kennedy Bill Banning Segregation in Private Facilities

By MARJORIE HUNTER
Special to The New York Times

WASHINGTON, June 17—Senate Minority Leader Everett McKinley Dirksen said today that he would not support any legislation outlawing segregation in private business accommodations, facilities and services.

The Illinois Republican's stand was viewed as a setback for Administration efforts to get bipartisan support for a civil rights bill to require desegregation of motels, hotels, restaurants and theaters throughout the nation.

President Kennedy is expected to send his civil rights proposals to Congress on Wednesday.

Dirksen Sees President

Administration sources said that the President still favored pushing for legislation to prohibit the exclusion of Negroes from theaters and from eating and sleeping facilities.

Southern Senators already have promised to filibuster against the Administration bill. To shut off such a debate, the Administration would need a large bloc of Republican votes.

Capitol Hill sources expressed doubt that Senator Dirksen can now be won over to the Administration stand.

Senator Dirksen had indicated last week that he might go along with an equal accommodations law if it were based on the Constitution's 14th Amendment. The Amendment bars state discrimination because of race.

He said then that he objected to basing the accommodations law on the Federal Govern-

Continued on Page 21, Column 1

City University Asks 80 Million For a Record Building Program

By LEONARD BUDER

A record capital budget request of $80,873,714 for 1964-65 was approved by the Board of Higher Education last night. The request had been submitted by the presidents of the seven colleges of the City University.

The total eventual cost of new or pending projects listed in the budget request was estimated at $222,914,244. This is more than half of the $400,000,000 goal of the Long-Range Plan of the City University adopted by the board last year.

The funds sought for next year, it was explained, would provide a start on projects for which additional money would be sought in future budgets.

Gustave G. Rosenberg, chairman of the board, said that the request—if granted by city and state authorities—would enable the City University to plan or start building projects that would increase senior college capacity by 15,000 students and community college capacity by 6,000.

Mr. Rosenberg said the mounting demand for free and low-cost college education in the city required a vast expansion of the City University. The university, he noted, had 103,000 full-time and part-time students last fall.

The number of high school graduates in the city next year will be 10,000 higher than this year, he added.

The City University consists of four senior and three community colleges. The senior institutions—City, Hunter, Brooklyn and Queens—offer regular undergraduate and graduate programs.

The community colleges—in the Bronx, Richmond and Queens—offer two-year programs. Although community colleges originally were intended for students not suited for or interested in a regular college program, many of their graduates now go on to obtain degrees. These institutions, which charge a moderate tuition, are supported jointly by the city and state.

The budget request, for the fiscal year beginning July 1, 1964, was prepared by the board's administrative council, consisting of the presidents of the seven institutions. It was four times as much as the

Continued on Page 31, Column 1

Negroes Fight Police in Harlem; Several Injured and 27 Arrested

A minor street incident in Harlem set off a series of clashes between angry Negroes and the police last night. Several persons were injured, including two policemen, and at least 27 were arrested.

The area for blocks around the intersection of 125th Street and Seventh Avenue was closely guarded much of the night by hundreds of helmeted policemen posted a few yards apart. Order appeared to have been restored early today.

Witnesses said the trouble began at the intersection about 9:30 P.M., when a white policeman ordered a Negro vender of ices to move on. The vender protested loudly, and a crowd quickly gathered.

Two youths joined the vender and a scuffle followed. Two stones shattered the windows of a jewelry store at the corner, and a flying bottle struck a patrol car.

Police reinforcements took two persons under arrest, to angry shouts from the corner.

One noisy crowd formed a half-block north of the intersection in front of a store that is the headquarters of the African Nationalists, an extremist group. Its windows bear a picture of a police dog biting a Negro, and a sign reading, "Damn white men."

A line of policemen sought to push this crowd away, and was shoved back. Street traffic was halted as the numbers of both demonstrators and policemen grew.

During a lull, a policeman waved a car through, and was knocked down by its fender. As he scrambled to his feet, the car sped off. The policeman

Continued on Page 27, Column 1

NEWS INDEX

"All the News That's Fit to Print"

The New York Times.

LATE CITY EDITION
U. S. Weather Bureau Report (Page 50) forecasts: Sunny and cool today; clear tonight. Sunny and warmer tomorrow.
Temp. range: 74—55; yesterday: 70—55. Temp.-Hum. Index: 70; yesterday: 69.

VOL. CXII...No. 38,500. © 1963 by The New York Times Company. Times Square, New York 36, N. Y. NEW YORK, SATURDAY, JUNE 22, 1963. TEN CENTS

CARDINAL MONTINI ELECTED POPE; LIBERAL, 65, WILL REIGN AS PAUL VI; LIKELY TO CONTINUE JOHN'S WORK

5TH VOTE DECISIVE

New Pontiff Gives His Blessing to Crowd—Coronation June 30

By ARNALDO CORTESI
Special to The New York Times

ROME, June 21 — Giovanni Battista Cardinal Montini, 65-year-old Archbishop of Milan, was elected Supreme Pontiff of the Roman Catholic Church today. He will reign as Pope Paul VI.

The man who had been described as the most likely prince of the church to succeed Pope John XXIII manifested his intention of continuing his predecessor's policies by confirming Amleto Giuseppi Cardinal Cicognani as Apostolic Secretary of State. Cardinal Cicognani held the post under John XXIII.

Pope Paul was elected on the fifth ballot conducted in the Sacred College of Cardinals. He and 79 other Cardinals from 29 nations — both figures were records — went into conclave Wednesday evening.

The news that the more than 500,000,000 Roman Catholics in the world had a new spiritual leader was given at 11:22 A.M. by a white puff of smoke from a stovepipe on the roof of the Sistine Chapel in Vatican City.

262d on Papal Throne

The new Pope, a native of the Lombardy region, who was 65 last Sept. 26, will be, according to Catholic tradition, the 262d occupant of the throne of St. Peter.

The coronation of Paul VI will take place in St. Peter's Basilica early in the morning of June 30, the day President Kennedy is to arrive in Rome during his 10-day tour of Europe. In the Western church the day is the Feast of St. Paul, the apostle who was the first in the church to bear the name. The last Pope to use it, Paul V, a Borghese, died in 1621.

An hour after his election, Pope Paul appeared on a balcony of St. Peter's Basilica to impart an apostolic benediction to a huge crowd. There were emotional scenes as most people dropped to their knees to receive the blessing. Some women wept and others held infants toward the Pope.

Acceptance at 11:15 A.M.

The conclave that elected Pope Paul lasted 41 hours. It ranks as the sixth shortest in the last four centuries. In the last century there have been only two that were shorter, the one that elected Pius XII in 1939, which lasted 30 hours, and the one that elected Leo XIII in 1878, which lasted 36 hours. Pope John was elected in 1958 on the 11th ballot on the third day.

Paul VI assumed all papal prerogatives and rights at 11:15 A.M. (6:15 A.M., Eastern daylight time) when, after protesting that he felt unworthy, he gave his acceptance to the dean of the Sacred College, Eugene Cardinal Tisserant. The coronation is a formality and the reign

Continued on Page 2, Column 1

United Press International Radiophoto
POPE PAUL VI in his first public appearance gives his blessing to the crowd that had gathered outside St. Peter's Basilica. Holding missal is Msgr. Salvatore Capoferri.

18 UNION CHIEFS ACT TO END BIAS IN CONSTRUCTION

Bld Locals Admit Qualified Negroes as Apprentices and as Members

PROGRAM NOT BINDING

N.A.A.C.P. Aide Says Plan Sounds Good, but Notes It Must Be Implemented

Special to The New York Times

WASHINGTON, June 21—The presidents of the 18 building trades unions adopted today a program to eliminate racial discrimination in apprenticeship, union membership and assignment to job openings.

At the same time, they warned that they would fight any effort by the Government to determine qualifications necessary for admission into the industry and into union membership.

The building trades unions have been the most criticized segment of the labor movement on discrimination. The National Association for the Advancement of Colored People has long contended that most building trades locals practice systematic exclusion of Negroes. Recently, the association picketed construction projects in New York and Philadelphia.

Government Pressure

This activity and increased pressure on them by the Government to eliminate discriminatory practices prompted the building trades presidents to discuss the situation. Today's statement, adopted unanimously, was the result.

The union leaders said they recognized the Government's interest and its duty to correct economic injustice and pledged their "good faith to work toward the goal."

The program consists of the following points:

¶Local unions are urged to accept any applicant for membership who meets the required qualifications regardless of his race, creed, color or national origin.

¶If a local operates an exclusive hiring hall or a work referral system, applicants for employment are to be referred to work without discrimination as to race, creed, color or national origin.

¶Locals shall also accept and refer applicants for apprenticeship without discrimination.

Adoption of the statement does not automatically bind the local unions to abide by it.

A spokesman for the Building

Continued on Page 8, Column 1

STATE DEMOCRATS MAY SHIFT POWER

Change in Rules Proposed to Move Control Upstate

By RICHARD P. HUNT

State Democratic leaders are considering a reorganization plan that would for the first time give upstate Democrats a major, if not dominant, role in party affairs.

The plan, which is contained in a proposed set of rules of the state committee, implies that the traditional control of the party machinery by New York City Democrats will be limited or ended.

The rules have been proposed after a year of study by a nine-member committee appointed by William H. McKeon, the Democratic state chairman. They will be submitted for ratification at a state committee meeting in Albany on Tuesday.

The most important change proposed is the creation of a 38-member executive committee, which would be empowered to carry on the party's business in behalf of the full 300-member state committee.

Democrats from the 57 coun-

Continued on Page 24, Column 5

NEWS INDEX

Lawyers Promise Kennedy Aid in Easing Race Unrest

Leaders of Bar Agree to Form Working Group Across Nation—President to See Negro Officials Today

By MARJORIE HUNTER
Special to The New York Times

WASHINGTON, June 21—Many of the nation's leading lawyers promised President Kennedy at a conference today that they would help open the lines of communication between the races. But they were told by a participant at the conference that they faced "a long hot summer."

At a meeting in the White House, the lawyers acceded to a Presidential request that they set up a committee that would try to ease racial tensions and provide national and local leadership.

Today's meeting was one in a series that the President has held in recent weeks with religious leaders, businessmen, Governors and labor leaders. So far, the President has conferred with several thousand persons on civil-rights matters.

Heading the lawyers' racial communications committee will be Harrison Tweed of New York and Bernard G. Segal of Philadelphia. All of the 244 lawyers attending today's meeting were invited to serve on the committee.

Another committee, also dealing with racial communications, will be established by the American Bar Association. This was announced during the White House meeting by Sylvester C. Smith Jr. of Newark, N. J., the association's president.

Joining the President in meeting the lawyers in the East Room were Vice President Johnson and Attorney General Robert F. Kennedy. Of the lawyers present, 66 were from Southern states. There were 23

Continued on Page 8, Column 3

Wagner to Help Negroes Get More Building Jobs

By CHARLES G. BENNETT

Mayor Wagner said yesterday that he would appoint "in a day or two" a panel of three qualified persons to induce construction unions to take in more Negroes. The panel will be given a week to examine employment records, talk with all groups concerned and make recommendations.

At the same time the Mayor said he had been assured by Peter Brennan, president of the Building Trades and Construction Council, that "technically qualified" members of minority groups would be put to work "right away" if job opportunities existed.

The Mayor spoke at a news conference in City Hall a few hours after his return from two weeks in Hawaii and Tokyo. Beforehand he had conferred at Gracie Mansion with Mr. Brennan and with Harry Van Arsdale Jr., president of the Central Labor Council.

Asks Special Session

Mr. Wagner dashed from the City Hall news interview back to Idlewild Airport, where he had landed early in the morning, to fly to Lake Placid, N.Y., to attend the New York State Conference of Mayors.

At the Lake Placid conference last night, Mayor Wagner called on Mayors throughout the state to join him in a request to Governor Rockefeller and the legislative leaders to summon a special session to deal with racial discrimination.

New state laws, Mr. Wagner proposed, should include financial aid to municipalities to speed desegregation in jobs, housing, education and other fields.

At City Hall the Mayor said of Mr. Brennan's promise to bring more Negroes into construction jobs as fast as possible:

"During the week the panel is preparing its recommendations, my office staff will be

Continued on Page 9, Column 2

MAYOR TO OPPOSE RACE BY DE SAPIO

Indicates He May Campaign in 'Village' in an Effort to Block Comeback Drive

Mayor Wagner made it clear yesterday that he would actively oppose Carmine G. De Sapio's attempted political comeback.

The Mayor was asked at a wide-ranging City Hall news conference about Mr. De Sapio's announcement Wednesday that he would be a candidate for the Democratic leadership of the First Assembly District South. This Greenwich Village area was the base of his former statewide political power.

"This is a free country," the Mayor replied. Then he added grimly, "My position on Mr. De Sapio has not changed."

Pressed as to whether he would actually go into Greenwich Village to oppose a De Sapio comeback, Mr. Wagner said a Mayor did not generally have time to go into the districts in district campaigns. But he conceded that he had done so, and indicated he might do so again.

He was asked, "No one should expect any encouragement from you for Mr. De Sapio?"

"That is the understatement of the year," the Mayor shot back.

Then the Mayor said: "I'll wait until the campaign begins

Continued on Page 24, Column 3

JUDICIAL INQUIRY ON PROFUMO SET; LABOR ASSAILS IT

Macmillan Announces Study of Security Aspects, but Foes Call It 'Cover-Up'

By SYDNEY GRUSON
Special to The New York Times

LONDON, June 21 — Prime Minister Macmillan announced today that a judicial inquiry would be held into the security aspects of the Profumo scandal. The form of the inquiry was immediately criticized by the Opposition Labor party as a "cover-up."

Mr. Macmillan told the House of Commons that Lord Denning, as Master of the Rolls, the third-highest judicial official in Britain, would conduct the inquiry. The Prime Minister also gravely took note of continuing rumors about the involvement of "all sorts of people" in the affair.

Asked by Harold Wilson, Labor's leader, whether he was satisfied that nothing more remained to be disclosed, Mr. Macmillan replied:

"I know of no things which I have not told the House, but I have heard these terrible things being said now of all sorts of people which, if allowed to go on, will destroy not only one side of the House of Commons but the other side of the House of Commons."

Chamber Is Crowded

To a chamber unusually crowded for a Friday session Mr. Macmillan said that the rumors "affect the honor and integrity of public life" in Britain "and if they were true such a situation might point to a security risk."

Pressing for the appointment of a select committee of Members of Parliament to conduct the inquiry, Mr. Wilson said that Lord Denning would have no power to compel the attendance of witnesses or compel proof.

"Is the Prime Minister aware that some of the evidence required will be collected from some of the most unmitigated liars in this country?" Mr. Wilson asked.

He also referred to the rumors. In a judicial inquiry, he said, they "cannot be dissipated and the men concerned enabled to clear their names, as they have every right to do."

Blackmail Linked to Case

The rumors are boundless on Fleet Street, the home of the British press, and in Westminster, the home of Parliament. Not even the royal family has escaped.

One of the rumors has linked blackmail to the case of Dr. Stephen Ward, 50-year-old society osteopath. Dr. Ward is in custody on charges of living off the earnings of prostitution. He introduced Christine Keeler, 21-year-old self-styled model, to John Profumo when Mr. Profumo was Secretary of State for War and to Capt. Yevgeni E. Ivanov, a Soviet deputy naval attaché until his recall last December. Miss Keeler had simultaneous affairs with the two men.

Another rumor involves the identity of a man said to be

Continued on Page 7, Column 1

The New York Times
PROMISES ACTION: Mayor Wagner at City Hall news conference where he announced plans to eliminate racial discrimination in the city's construction-industry unions.

FRENCH NAVY ENDS NATO ATLANTIC TIE

Paris Announces Resuming of Unrestrained Control of Virtually Whole Fleet

By DREW MIDDLETON
Special to The New York Times

PARIS, June 21—France announced today that she would resume unrestrained control of virtually the whole of the nation's naval fighting force.

A curt bulletin issued by the semiofficial French Press Agency said that "the French Government has decided to withdraw from the NATO Fleet in the North Atlantic." The bulletin cited official sources.

The Government's decision was described here as a logical consequence of France's action in 1959. In that year she withdrew her Mediterranean fleet from the alliance's control.

Effect of New Move

Earlier this year the squadrons of that fleet were transferred from the Mediterranean base of Toulon to the North Atlantic base of Brest in Brittany.

As a consequence of today's announcement, the bulk of the powerful French forces hitherto earmarked for training and planning under the ultimate command of the Supreme Allied Commander Atlantic have now been withdrawn.

[In Washington officials were distressed by the French action. The Administration was embarrassed by its timing on the eve of President Kennedy's departure for Europe.]

Allied diplomats almost universally deplored the psychological shock that the action

Continued on Page 20, Column 5

World Labor Parley Bars South African

Special to The New York Times

GENEVA, June 21 — United States Government and American worker delegates voted today for the expulsion of a South African from the International Labor Organization conference.

The credentials of the South African, a worker delegate, were rejected by a vote of 135 to 3, with 57 abstentions. His credentials had been issued by his Government.

The member states of the 108-nation organization, a United Nations specialized agency, are represented by two government delegates, a representative of employer groups and a trade unionist. Each has separate voting rights. The worker repre

Continued on Page 4, Column 5

Rome Believes New Pope Will Press for Reforms

Clear-cut Decision Seen

By PAUL HOFMANN
Special to The New York Times

ROME, June 21 — Pope Paul VI began his pontificate today amid general forecasts that it would bring an energetic continuation of the progressive course charted by Pope John XXIII.

The consensus in Rome was that the conclave, by elevating the 65-year-old Archbishop of Milan to the papacy, had made a clear decision for a liberal pontificate—and one hopefully expected to last a long time.

First responses from world centers showed international agreement with this evaluation.

The general belief here was that Pope Paul had been elected with the understanding that he would soon reopen the church's Ecumenical Council in the Vatican, suspended by the death of his predecessor. Ecclesiastics who had served in the past with the new Pontiff predicted that he would press for enactment

Continued on Page 3, Column 5

Choice Widely Hailed

By GEORGE DUGAN

The election of Giovanni Battista Cardinal Montini to succeed Pope John XXIII has met with worldwide acclaim.

Both Protestant and Jewish leaders said yesterday that the election of Pope Paul VI showed that the reform and renewal so close to the heart of Pope John would be emphasized in the days to come.

The new Pope, who was given the red hat of a cardinal by his predecessor, was deeply involved in the Ecumenical Council, which had been scheduled to reconvene on Sept. 8.

The election of Pope Paul aroused great interest in Washington, which is curious about the political effects the choice of a liberal will have on the European left. President Kennedy, who will visit the new Pope July 2, sent the Pontiff his "heartiest congratulations."

J. Irwin Miller, president of

Continued on Page 3, Column 3

HOUSE UNIT VOTES DEFENSE FUND CUT

Reduction of 1.9 Billion Is Protested by McNamara

By JACK RAYMOND
Special to The New York Times

WASHINGTON, June 21 — The House Appropriations Committee approved a $47,092,209,000 defense fund measure today, with only relatively small changes in the Administration's original request.

But even these changes drew an immediate protest from Secretary of Defense Robert S. McNamara. He said the cuts in airplane procurement money "would deny us necessary tactical support for our combat-ready Army divisions."

He charged also that other cuts would force a reduction in military personnel by some 60,000 men.

President Kennedy last January requested $49,014,237,000 in defense appropriations for the fiscal year 1964, beginning July 1. The committee cut the total by $1,922,028,000.

The committee noted that more than $500,000,000 of the cut represented bookkeeping shifts.

"The accompanying bill," the committee said in its report, based on four months of closed hearings, "will support programs which will promote the security of the United States and assure the continuation of a policy of military supremacy."

According to the report, the bill would provide armed forces totaling 2,695,000 officers and

Continued on Page 20, Column 3

TAX DISCLOSURE AROUSES OTTAWA

Minister Admits Plan Was Known to 3 Businessmen

By HOMER BIGART
Special to The New York Times

OTTAWA, June 21—Walter L. Gordon, the harassed Minister of Finance in the minority Liberal Government, gave fresh ammunition to his critics in Parliament today.

He admitted that the three Toronto businessmen who helped write his budget knew in advance of the withdrawal Wednesday of a controversial tax proposal. The tax had been aimed at halting the take-over of Canadian companies by foreigners.

The admission brought astonished gasps from Opposition benches in the House of Commons. Mr. Gordon had told the House yesterday that only Prime Minister Lester B. Pearson and the Cabinet knew of his decision to withdraw the tax.

The proposal would have placed a 30 per cent tax on the seller of a large block of shares in a Canadian company to a foreigner. Its withdrawal was announced while the stock markets of Canada were still open, and caused frenzied speculation. Members of the Opposition have demanded an investigation to determine whether the leakage of budget secrets permitted "insiders" to make windfall profits on the markets.

Mr. Gordon had been under fire all week for employing three financial experts from Toronto, two of whom had re-

Continued on Page 14, Column 7

Brezhnev Advances As Khrushchev Heir

By SEYMOUR TOPPING
Special to The New York Times

MOSCOW, June 21—Leonid I. Brezhnev, a member of the ruling Presidium of the Soviet Communist Party, emerged tonight after plenary meetings of the Central Committee as a likely political heir of Premier Khrushchev.

Mr. Brezhnev, who is 57 years old and a protégé of Mr. Khrushchev, has been appointed to the Secretariat of the Central Committee. The Secretariat is the chief executive body of the party.

Western analysts note that Mr. Brezhnev now holds an array of party and Government positions that make it appear that he is being groomed to assume the roles of Frol R.

Continued on Page 5, Column 3

"All the News That's Fit to Print"

The New York Times.

LATE CITY EDITION

U.S. Weather Bureau Report (Page 66) forecast: Sunny, hot and more humid today; clear tonight. Fair, warm tomorrow. Temp. range: 92—69; yesterday: 96—69. Temp.-Hum. Index: high 70's; yesterday: 79.

VOL. CXII..No. 38,505. © 1963 by The New York Times Company. Times Square, New York 36, N. Y. NEW YORK, THURSDAY, JUNE 27, 1963. TEN CENTS

ROBERT KENNEDY OFFERS TO MODIFY CIVIL RIGHTS BILL

Would Exempt Small Stores and Tourist Homes From Public Facilities Clause

HOUSE HEARING OPENED

Attorney General Says That Ending of Discrimination Is Up to Congress

Excerpts from Robert Kennedy's testimony are on Page 18.

By E. W. KENWORTHY
Special to The New York Times

WASHINGTON, June 26—Attorney General Robert F. Kennedy said today that the Administration would be willing to exempt small stores and tourist homes from its proposed ban on discrimination in privately owned public accommodations.

Appearing as the initial witness on President Kennedy's civil rights bill, the Attorney General told the antitrust subcommittee of the House Judiciary Committee that if Congress wanted more explicit language, "we would be happy to work out some cut-off line."

Presumably this would be based on an annual dollar volume of business.

The public accommodations section of the bill is the most controversial. The Attorney General's concession was regarded as greatly improving the chances that the House committee would report a relatively strong bill.

Senate Doubts Noted

In the Senate, however, the doubts of many key members, including the minority leader, Everett McKinley Dirksen of Illinois, go beyond the issue of a cut-off point to the question of whether any ban on public accommodations is not an impairment of property rights.

As the Attorney General was testifying today, Mr. Dirksen predicted that the final bill would contain no ban and would provide simply for voluntary community action with the help of the President's proposed Community Relations Service.

The committee room in the Old House Office Building was jammed, with spectators lining the walls three and four deep, when the Attorney General appeared promptly at 10:30 A.M. He was accompanied by

Continued on Page 18, Column 1

Space Science Fund Cut by House Panel

By JOHN W. FINNEY
Special to The New York Times

WASHINGTON, June 26—The House Science and Astronautics Committee cut back the scientific portion of the space program today, eliminating $134,248,600 in funds for research and exploration.

With the $259,122,000 cut made yesterday in funds for manned space flight, the committee has now cut $393,370,600 from the $5,700,000,000 budget submitted by the National Aeronautics and Space Administration.

Tomorrow, the committee is expected to cut $90,000,000 more from the fund request for the coming year. This would bring the total reduction in the budget authorization bill to $483,000,000.

The committee acted today on two major divisions of the space program—the scientific

Continued on Page 13, Column 7

KENTUCKY FORBIDS BIAS IN BUSINESSES

Governor's Order Affects All Licensed Activities—He Prods School Districts

Special to The New York Times

FRANKFORT, Ky., June 26—Gov. Bert T. Combs signed an executive order today forbidding racial discrimination in all businesses licensed by the state.

The order, which went into effect immediately, covers such businesses as taverns, restaurants, barber shops, beauty parlors, funeral homes and real estate concerns.

The Governor warned that school districts, which need accreditation by the State Department of Education, would be in danger of losing state and Federal funds if they did not integrate.

His order directed those state agencies empowered to license businesses to prepare reports within 60 days on how they planned to enforce the order.

Mr. Combs suggested that enforcement could be patterned after the procedures of the State Alcoholic Beverage Control Board.

Could Lose License

After an illegal act has been charged, the board cites a licensee and orders him to appear for a hearing to show cause why he should not have his license suspended or revoked.

Hence, the Governor noted, "the penalty under this executive order also would go to a man's pocketbook."

Mr. Combs acted as a special session of the General Assembly, the legislature, met here. Civil rights groups and Mayor William O. Cowger of Louisville had urged the Governor to extend the special session to include consideration of a state anti-discrimination law.

The session had been called to provide state aid for four eastern Kentucky hospitals owned and operated by the United Mine Workers of America. The union plans to close the hospitals this summer because of economic reasons.

Governor Combs said he had declined to place a civil rights bill before the legislators because many had come un-

Continued on Page 19, Column 2

United Press International Radiophoto

EAST GERMAN CHALLENGE CONFRONTS KENNEDY: President, indicated by arrow, looks across Berlin wall toward sign near the Brandenburg Gate. The sign says: "In the agreements of Yalta and Potsdam U.S. Presidents Roosevelt and Truman undertook: ¶To uproot German militarism and Nazism. ¶To arrest war criminals and bring them to judgment. ¶To prevent the rebirth of German militarism. ¶To ban all militarists and Nazi propaganda. ¶To ensure that Germany never again menaces her neighbors of world peace. These pledges have been fulfilled in the German Democratic Republic. When will these pledges be fulfilled in West Germany and West Berlin, President Kennedy?" East German officials had had red cloths hung between pillars of gate, blocking off the view for the President's party and East Berliners.

CITY GETS U.S. AID IN COMMUTER TEST

$3,185,000 Granted to Seek New Types of Service

By WARREN WEAVER Jr.
Special to The New York Times

WASHINGTON, June 26—The Federal Government gave New York City $3,185,000 today to try to improve commuter service from Queens and Nassau Counties to the city.

The money, together with $1,593,000 from the city and $1,860,000 in anticipated fare revenue, will be used to finance experiments on transportation by bus, subway and the Long Island Rail Road.

Basically, the program will underwrite the cost of providing more service at somewhat lower fares for selected routes to determine whether the changes will attract enough new passengers to make the service self-supporting.

Very little, if any, of the money is to be spent on new equipment or facilities. It is to be used to find out how the equipment now in use can be used more productively.

The grant was one of the largest for transit demonstrations made by the Federal Housing and Home Finance Agency, and the air was heavy with Democratic politics at the presentation ceremony.

Mayor Wagner flew down from New York for the occasion, bringing with him Borough President Mario J. Cariello of Queens and Eugene A. Nickerson, the Nassau County Execu-

Continued on Page 41, Column 4

City Swelters in 96°; Heat Wave to Linger

The temperature rose to 96 degrees at 3:10 P.M. yesterday, making it the hottest day here since last July 9. More of the same was forecast for today.

The temperature edged above Tuesday's high of 95, giving New Yorkers a foretaste of the summer ahead. The temperature, however, stayed below the record of 100 for a June 26, reached in 1952.

A third rail on the New York Central's Harlem Division was buckled by the heat at 6:10 P.M. The rerouting of trains to the single open track delayed 10,000 commuters as much as two hours.

The breakdown occurred just south of Tuckahoe. By midnight, with repairs in progress, more than 25 trains in both directions had been delayed by the trouble.

The railroad said it expected

Continued on Page 67, Column 1

Aid for Distressed Areas Revived by Senate, 65-30

By C. P. TRUSSELL
Special to The New York Times

WASHINGTON, June 26—The Senate passed and sent to the House today its own bill to strengthen the program for aid to economically distressed areas. The vote was 65 to 30.

The House, which rejected a similar bill two weeks ago by only five votes, is now expected to reverse itself and approve the job-stimulating program.

The measure is a major item on President Kennedy's legislative agenda.

Providing $455,000,000 to expand the current development program; it agrees substantially with the bill defeated in the House. It would:

¶Increase from $100,000,000 to $250,000,000 the amount authorized at any one time for industrial or commercial loans to create jobs through urban projects.

¶Increase from $100,000,000 to $250,000,000 the authorization for industrial or commercial loans in rural areas.

¶Increase from $75,000,000 to $175,000,000 the authorization for appropriations for public facility grants.

¶Increase from $100,000,000 to $150,000,000 the amount authorized for public facility loans.

The legislation would also permit states or communities to pay the 10 per cent contributions required for the projects at the same time they repaid funds extended by the

Continued on Page 15, Column 4

PAN AM PROPOSES $160 LONDON FARE

Plans Coast-Hawaii Rate of $100 in New Thrift Class Without Liquor or Food

By JOSEPH CARTER

Pan American World Airways proposed a new class of service to Europe and Hawaii yesterday that would radically reduce fares and eliminate meals and liquor aboard the plane.

Under the new year-round thrift class, the one-way New York-London fare would be $160, a reduction of $103, or 39 per cent, compared with the economy-class rate that becomes effective July 16. There would be no round-trip discount as at present.

Thrift-class service would be provided between California and Hawaii at a one-way fare of $100, compared with the current economy-class rate of $133.

The airline would introduce the service to Hawaii next Nov. 1, subject to approval of the Civil Aeronautics Board. The service to Europe would start next April if the foreign carriers and Governments concerned and the C.A.B. approve.

Submitted for Study

Juan T. Trippe, Pan American president, announced the new thrift-class rates a month after the trans-Atlantic airlines reached a compromise agreement on fares following a long and bitter dispute.

Airline observers here said his proposal would provide fuel for further heated debate when the International Air Transport Association, the world airlines organization, meets in Europe next fall to set rates and fares.

To become effective, they must be agreed upon unanimously. The meeting is tentatively scheduled to open in early September at Salzburg, Austria.

Mr. Trippe said the plans for the new North Atlantic service had been announced at this time "to give all the other airlines concerned time for study" before the meeting at which "future trans-Atlantic fares to become effective next April will be considered and recommended by the airlines to their respective Governments for approval."

Trans World Airlines, Pan

Continued on Page 67, Column 2

47 BILLION VOTED IN HOUSE FOR ARMS

Second Biggest Peacetime Allocation Backed 410 to 1 and Sent to the Senate

Special to The New York Times

WASHINGTON, June 26—The House passed and sent to the Senate today a bill appropriating $47,082,009,000 for defense.

If it is approved by the Senate, it will be the second highest annual military appropriation in peacetime. The $48,350,082,500 allocated last year is the highest thus far.

The House passed the measure, which provides funds for the fiscal year 1964, starting July 1, with one dissent. Representative Thomas B. Curtis, Republican of Missouri, said he had voted "No" because "we haven't got the money."

"I hope by this vote to call to the people's attention the seriousness of deficit spending," he said.

He said he had no specific objections to the bill, but believed that something should have been cut for economy's sake.

The roll-call vote on the measure was 410 to 1.

The final vote came after two days of discussion but no major debate.

The House did not restore a cut of $1,900,000,000 made in the Administration's appropriations

Continued on Page 13, Column 5

Dublin Acclaims Kennedy As One Returning Home

By SYDNEY GRUSON
Special to The New York Times

DUBLIN, June 26—President Kennedy arrived in Dublin this evening and in a sense, he said, it was like coming "home." That was the way the Irish felt about it, too. Mr. Kennedy was hailed by President Eamon de Valera as the "first citizen" of the United States but also by the people

Speeches by de Valera and Kennedy are on Page 13.

of Dublin as the local boy—three generations removed—who made good.

All the Dubliners seemed to be at the airport or lining the road of the 12-mile route to the United States Embassy in Phoenix Park.

If the President was tired after his grueling three days in West Germany, or by the vast emotional outpouring of the West Berliners earlier in the day, he did not show it.

It had rained off and on during the day in and around Dublin, and hailstones had fallen, covering the green fields with a short-lasting unseasonable blanket of white.

But the sky was blue and the last of the day's sun was shining when the President's plane landed and for most of the drive to the embassy.

Then the rain came down again, hard. President Kennedy, riding in an open car beside the 80-year-old Mr. de Valera,

Continued on Page 13, Column 1

MOSCOW WAVERS ON CURBING ARTS

Resistance of Intellectuals Said to Cause Indecision in Party Leadership

By SEYMOUR TOPPING
Special to The New York Times

MOSCOW, June 26 — The Kremlin is wavering in its drive to impose strict ideological curbs on liberal writers and artists.

Western analysts have detected signs of indecision in statements published after the plenary session of the Central Committee of the Soviet Communist party.

The closed four-day plenum, which ended Friday, had been convened to reinforce internal ideological discipline and to find means of insulating the Soviet people against the influx of Western ideas.

The plenum was the first to be called to deal specifically with ideological questions. Its published results hardly support earlier Soviet statements that the plenum would be a monumental event.

No New Curbs Announced

Statements issued about the meeting have not contained anything substantially new. No further measures were announced that would subject liberal intellectuals to severe organizational controls.

Available evidence, in fact, has indicated to Western analysts that the Soviet leadership has retreated from its announced plan to compel abandonment of all liberal and avant-garde tendencies in literature and art.

In a speech on March 8 Premier Khrushchev asserted that unswerving conformity with the Communist party line would be demanded of literature, fine arts, music, theater, cinema and the press. He de-

Continued on Page 5, Column 3

Annapolis Gets First Academic Dean, a Civilian

Dr. Drought of Marquette Appointed for a Year

By JACK RAYMOND
Special to The New York Times

WASHINGTON, June 26—The Navy appointed a civilian academic dean for the Naval Academy at Annapolis today as part of a major program to improve general education standards for midshipmen.

Dr. Arthur B. Drought, dean of engineering at Marquette University, Milwaukee, was named by Secretary of the Navy Fred Korth for one year.

The 48-year-old educator, who has had wide experience in teaching, research and college administration, will be the 118-year-old Naval Academy's first academic dean.

The United States Military Academy at West Point has an officer as dean of the academic board and he has two civilian advisers. The Air Force Academy at Colorado Springs, Colo., has a brigadier general as dean of faculty.

Heretofore at the Naval Academy, the Superintendent, an officer, was responsible for all courses. The secretary of the academic board, also an officer, functioned in a capacity similar to that of academic dean.

Rear Admiral Charles C. Kirkpatrick, the present superintendent at Annapolis, said:

"I am delighted to have such a distinguished educator and administrator accept this appointment."

Dean Drought's appointment

Associated Press

Dr. Arthur B. Drought

Action Follows Settlement of Dispute With Officers

came after a dispute that developed two years ago but was settled last year. The dispute was precipitated by efforts on the part of Secretary Korth to have civilian educators assume virtually all of the nonprofessional instructional positions.

The Navy several years ago had proposed having an academic dean. However, uniformed officers resisted Secretary Korth's sweeping proposals.

If these were carried out, it was said, Navy officers at the academy would be limited to disciplinary and administrative positions. The academy, it was stressed, was a military institution in which habits of command and other military considerations were of considerable importance, more than in an ordinary academic institution.

Secretary Korth subsequently withdrew his proposals for sweeping civilianization of the teaching staff at Annapolis. Meantime officials at the Naval Academy succeeded in obtaining not only an academic dean

Continued on Page 11, Column 1

NEWS INDEX

PRESIDENT HAILED BY OVER A MILLION IN VISIT TO BERLIN

He Salutes the Divided City as Front Line in World's Struggle for Freedom

LOOKS OVER THE WALL

Says Berliners' Experience Shows Hazard in Trying to Work With Communists

Texts of President's speeches in Berlin, Page 12.

By ARTHUR J. OLSEN
Special to The New York Times

BERLIN, June 26—President Kennedy, inspired by a tumultuous welcome from more than a million of the inhabitants of this isolated and divided city, declared today he was proud to be "a Berliner."

He said his claim to being a Berliner was based on the fact that "all free men, wherever they may live, are citizens of Berlin."

In a rousing speech to 150,000 West Berliners crowded before the City Hall, the President said anyone who thought "we can work with the Communists" should come to Berlin.

However, three hours later, in a less emotional setting, he reaffirmed his belief that the great powers must work together "to preserve the human race."

Warning on Communism

His earlier rejection of dealing with the Communists was a warning against trying to "ride the tiger" of popular fronts that unite democratic and Communist forces, Mr. Kennedy explained in an interpolation in a prepared speech.

The President's City Hall speech was the emotional high point of a spectacular welcome accorded the President by West Berlin. He saluted the city as the front line and shining example of humanity's struggle for freedom.

Those who profess not to understand the great issues between the free world and the Communist world or who think Communism is the wave of the future should come to Berlin, he said.

In his later speech, at the Free University of Berlin, President Kennedy returned firmly to the theme of his address at American University in Washington June 10 in which he called for an attempt to end the cold war.

'Wounds to Heal'

"When the possibilities of reconciliation appear, we in the West will make it clear that we are not hostile to any people or system, provided that they choose their own destiny without interfering with the free choice of others," he said.

"There will be wounds to heal and suspicions to be eased on both sides," he added. "The difference in living standards will have to be reduced—by leveling up, not down. Fair and effective agreements to end the arms race must be reached."

The changes might not come tomorrow, but "our efforts for a real settlement must continue," he said.

Then the President introduced an extemporaneous paragraph into his prepared text.

"As I said this morning, I

Continued on Page 12, Column 1

Berliners' Welcome Filled With Emotion

By TOM WICKER
Special to The New York Times

BERLIN, June 26 — President Kennedy saw the miracle and the tragedy of West Berlin today as the city turned out to greet him and applaud his country.

The reception was one of the largest and most emotional Mr. Kennedy has ever received.

The West Berliners leaped and screamed along the curbs, waved their handkerchiefs and a variety of flags, threw flowers and broke through police barriers to run beside Mr. Kennedy's car. Some succeeded in shaking his hand. Twice he caught bouquets.

A hand-painted ungrammatical but heartfelt placard spoke the city's heart, reading: "John. You our best friend." In the Rudolph Wilde Plaza, where the President spoke shortly after

Continued on Page 12, Column 6

"All the News That's Fit to Print"

The New York Times.

LATE CITY EDITION

U. S. Weather Bureau Report (Page 53) forecasts: Sunny, hot and humid today and tomorrow. Clear tonight.
Temp. range: 94—72; yesterday: 91—70.
Temp.-Hum. Index: low 80's; yesterday: 80.

VOL. CXII . No. 38,534. NEW YORK, FRIDAY, JULY 26, 1963. TEN CENTS

U.S., SOVIET AND BRITAIN REACH ATOM ACCORD THAT BARS ALL BUT UNDERGROUND TESTS; SEE MAJOR STEP TOWARD EASING TENSION

TREATY INITIALED

Rusk and Lord Home Will Go to Moscow to Sign Pact

Communiqué and the proposed treaty are on Page 8.

By SEYMOUR TOPPING
Special to The New York Times

MOSCOW, July 25 — The United States, the Soviet Union and Britain concluded today a treaty to prohibit nuclear tes'ing in the atmosphere, in space and under water.

The historic document was initialed at 7:15 P.M., Moscow time, by W. Averell Harriman, Under Secretary of State for Political Affairs; Soviet Foreign Minister Andrei A. Gromyko, and Viscount Hailsham, British Minister for Science.

A communiqué on the initialing said:

"The heads of the three delegations agreed that the test ban treaty constituted an important first step toward the reduction of international tension and the strengthening of peace, and they look forward to further progress in this direction."

Austrian Treaty Recalled

It was noted in the diplomatic community here that the treaty represented the first major East-West accord since the conclusion of the Austrian State Treaty on May 15, 1955. That agreement ended the postwar four-power occupation of Austria.

The United States and Britain agreed at the test-ban talks to further discussion of the Soviet proposal relating to a pact of nonaggression between the North Atlantic Treaty Organization and the Soviet-bloc's Warsaw Pact alliance. The communiqué said this would be done in consultation with the NATO allies "with the purpose of achieving agreement satisfactory to all participants."

Mr. Harriman, who appeared tired but happy after 10 days of intensive negotiations, said the test-ban treaty would relieve the fears of people all over the world about nuclear contamination of the atmosphere.

Others Urged to Join

He expressed the hope that other nations would adhere to the test ban treaty, which provides for the accession of other members.

Mr. Harriman also announced that Secretary of State Dean Rusk and the Earl of Home, the British Foreign Secretary, would come to Moscow in the near future for the ceremonial signing of the treaty. Foreign Minister Gromyko presumably will sign for the Soviet Union.

Mr. Harriman has requested an appointment with Premier Khrushchev for tomorrow to discuss the results of the conference and to take up the question of civil strife in Laos. He has arranged to leave by air Saturday for Washington to report to President Kennedy and to brief members of Congress on the treaty.

The treaty, after signing, would be subject to parliamentary ratification by the United States Senate, the Supreme Soviet and the British Parliament.

The Western delegates to the three-power talks were unable to persuade Mr. Gromyko to accept international on-site inspection to verify the nature of seismic disturbances. The treaty, therefore, does not cover underground nuclear testing.

The preamble to the treaty pledges the three nations to con-

Continued on Page 8, Column 1

United Press International Radiophoto

MOSCOW ACCORD: Negotiators after initialing nuclear test ban treaty. In foreground, back to camera, are Andrei A. Gromyko, center, and Valerian A. Zorin, right, of the Soviet Union. In background are Viscount Hailsham, far left, Britain; Foy D. Kohler, at right center, hands folded, and W. Averell Harriman, at the far right, of the U.S.

3 Envoys Jovial as Treaty Emerges

By HENRY TANNER
Special to The New York Times

MOSCOW, July 25—Six letters scrawled at the bottom of a typewritten page sealed today one of the most important East-West agreements since World War II. They contained the promise of the world's three most powerful governments to refrain from further contaminating the air and the ocean with nuclear explosions.

The letters were W.A.H., for W. Averell Harriman, the United States Under Secretary of State for Political Affairs, on the left side of the page; a carefully drawn A.G. in Russian script for Andrei A. Gromyko, the Soviet Foreign Minister, on the far right, and a single H. for Viscount Hailsham, British Minister for Science, in the middle.

The three, in jovial mood, initialed a treaty for a partial ban on nuclear testing at 7:15 tonight in the conference room of the Spiridonovka Palace, a 19th-century mansion built by a Russian merchant family.

The beige-colored imitation-gothic mansion is occasionally used by the Foreign Ministry for conferences and receptions. Its first owners were the Morozovs, a family that grew rich introducing the textile industry to czarist Russia.

When reporters and photographers were admitted to the conference room a few mo-

Continued on Page 8, Column 8

Rail Crisis Off a Month

ROADS BACK DELAY

Congress Hails Move Providing Time to Study Peace Plan

By JOHN D. POMFRET
Special to The New York Times

WASHINGTON, July 25 — The nation's railroads postponed today until Aug. 29 work rules changes that would set off a national railroad strike.

They hope that by then Congress will act to block a strike and provide a way to resolve the dispute.

Congress has before it a request from President Kennedy to refer the bitter four-year dispute over the size of train crews to the Interstate Commerce Commission for an interim decision.

The railroads have given the plan their qualified approval. The heads of three of the five unions involved in the dispute have opposed the President's plan; the two others have been silent.

Under Pressure to Delay

The railroads had been under intense Congressional pressure to postpone the work-rules changes, which had been set for 12:01 A.M. next Tuesday.

Congress received the President's message on Monday, a week before the strike deadline. A week was not enough time for intelligent action, the legislators said.

By accepting the delay, the railroads kept intact their record of cooperating with every Government request.

During the dispute, they have agreed to the recommendations of two Presidential boards that have looked into the controversy. They have agreed to every Government suggestion that the dispute be submitted to arbitration.

On six previous occasions, in response to Administration requests or court order, they have postponed instituting the work-rules changes that would allow them to eliminate thousands of jobs that they contend are unnecessary.

Although the railroads made it clear that another postpone-

Continued on Page 26, Column 1

U.S. Denies Reds Lead Integrationists

By E. W. KENWORTHY
Special to The New York Times

WASHINGTON, July 25—Attorney General Robert F. Kennedy said today the Justice Department had no evidence that the Rev. Dr. Martin Luther King Jr. and other leaders of the civil rights movement were "Communists or Communist-controlled."

Mr. Kennedy made the statement in a letter to Senator A. S. Mike Monroney, which the Oklahoma Democrat read to colleagues on the Senate Commerce Committee today.

Govs. Ross R. Barnett of Mississippi and George C. Wallace of Alabama charged in testimony before the committee two weeks ago that the civil rights movement and recent demonstrations had been "Communist-inspired" and "Communist-controlled."

Continued on Page 11, Column 2

ROCKEFELLER BARS NEGRO JOB QUOTA; HAILS UNION PLAN

84 More in Sit-Downs Are Seized—14 Chain Wrists, Block Brooklyn Street

By PETER KIHSS

Governor Rockefeller declared yesterday that it was "realistically not possible" to meet Negro demands to put large numbers of Negroes on skilled construction jobs here "overnight."

The Governor, warning against proposals for job quotas as both unlawful and counter to American principles, said:

"We can't abandon our concepts of equal opportunity for all by giving special privilege to some."

In a news conference here, the Governor praised Peter J. Brennan, leader of the city and state construction unions, for his recent proposal to set up a panel to review and recommend applications of Negroes for membership in construction unions.

Mr. Rockefeller said he could understand the impatience of demonstrators, but he stressed that recruitment and training were necessary to fill jobs.

New Contracts Planned

Mr. Rockefeller announced that $400,000,000 in new contracts for state construction would be awarded in the next 18 months as part of an effort to provide more jobs.

Eighty-four more arrests were made yesterday in the continuing Brooklyn civil rights demonstrations.

Meanwhile, the five Manhattan defendants who received 30-day and 60-day workhouse sentences were released in $1 bail apiece, pending appeals. They had spent a night in prison after being sentenced Wednesday for a sit-down demonstration at the Rutgers Housing project July 11.

The five were granted their release by Supreme Court Justice Joseph A. Sarafite following a motion by George Shiffer, defense lawyer, for a certificate of reasonable doubt to appeal to the Appellate Division.

In yesterday's Brooklyn demonstrations, 14 Negroes and whites manacled themselves together with a long chain, each locking it to his wrists. They then sat down in the roadway at the Downstate Medical Center project in Brooklyn.

The police had to send for

Continued on Page 12, Column 4

CITY'S UNIVERSITY PICKS CHANCELLOR

Bowker, Graduate Dean at Stanford, to Start Oct. 1—Salary to Be $40,000

By LEONARD BUDER

The Board of Higher Education appointed Dr. Albert H. Bowker of Stanford University as chancellor of the City University yesterday. He will take office Oct. 1.

Dr. Bowker, who is 43 years old, has been dean of the Graduate Division of Stanford since 1958. The California institution has 4,262 graduate students.

In his new post, he will be the top administrative officer of a university with seven colleges, two others in the planning stages and a total enrollment of more than 104,000 students.

The board's action culminated a nationwide search for a chancellor that started 14 months ago when Dr. John R. Everett announced he would resign from the post on Aug. 31, 1962, to become senior vice president of Encyclopaedia Britannica Films, Inc.

Dr. Everett had been appointed chancellor on June 8, 1960, after a three-year search for a man to coordinate the city college system and to oversee its expansion. He was the first

Continued on Page 23, Column 2

HOUSE UNIT VOTES JAKARTA AID CURB

Moves, 17-12, to Require Presidential Finding That U.S. Security Is Affected

By FELIX BELAIR Jr.
Special to The New York Times

WASHINGTON, July 25 — The House Foreign Affairs Committee voted today to ban further economic and military aid to Indonesia unless the President made a public finding that it was vital to United States security interests.

The committee voted 17 to 12 to reverse the stand it took on this same amendment to the foreign aid bill last week. In approving the censure of the Jakarta government, some members switched their earlier position in the belief that the committee action would prevent an even more stringent limitation on the House floor.

The amendment, proposed by Representative William S. Broomfield, Republican of Michigan, was opposed by the Administration on the ground that Indonesian resentment would push that country into closer association with the Soviet Union. The Agency for International Development was planning to step up aid to Indonesia after the country's recent move toward economic stabilization.

After committee approval of

Continued on Page 3, Column 2

DAY QUITS CABINET TO JOIN LAW FIRM

Smith, Kennedy Successor in Senate, May Get Job

Special to The New York Times

WASHINGTON, July 25 — Postmaster General J. Edward Day has submitted his resignation and it has been accepted by President Kennedy.

In a letter to the President dated July 19, Mr. Day said he felt he could no longer postpone his return to private life because of "an unusual opportunity" for private employment as head of the Washington office of a Chicago law firm.

The third of President Kennedy's original Cabinet appointments to leave, Mr. Day said it was "with deep personal regret" that he had decided to resign from the Federal service.

Associates of the Postmaster General said he first talked to the President about resigning just before Mr. Kennedy left for Europe in June. It was agreed at the time that the resignation would take effect at the President's convenience.

Associates of Mr. Day said he expected the President to name former Democratic Senator Benjamin Smith of Massachusetts to fill the vacancy. A former roommate of the President's when they attended Harvard, Mr. Smith was appointed to fill the Senate seat left vacant by Mr. Kennedy when he was elected President. In his letter,

Continued on Page 30, Column 7

The New York Times (by Neal Boenzi)

BROOKLYN DEMONSTRATION: Police use wire cutters to separate civil rights demonstrators who manacled themselves together at the site of the Downstate Medical Center.

PRESIDENT HOPES PARIS JOINS PACT

Sends de Gaulle Report on Test Parley — Qualified Refusal by General Due

By DREW MIDDLETON
Special to The New York Times

PARIS, July 25—President Kennedy today expressed the hope that President de Gaulle would adhere to the nuclear test ban treaty initialed in Moscow.

Qualified sources said the wish was part of a report from Mr. Kennedy on the Moscow negotiations delivered to the French President. A similar report, also including hope for French agreement, was sent by Prime Minister Macmillan.

The reports were delivered to the Elysée Palace, General de Gaulle's Paris residence, and transmitted to the President's country home at Colombey-les-Deux-Eglises, where he is preparing a statement to be delivered to a news conference Monday afternoon.

No message has yet been received from Premier Khrushchev, the sources reported.

Comment by Foreign Chief

The sources thought that President de Gaulle's reaction would probably be a qualified refusal in which he would cling to his familiar position that the test ban is only a superficial gesture with no connection with serious disarmament.

Before the Kennedy message was delivered, Foreign Minister Maurice Couve de Murville had declared that France would not be bound by the treaty.

The ban on nuclear testing, Mr. Couve de Murville told the Foreign Affairs Committee of the National Assembly, is simply a device to "crystallize the differences" between the nuclear haves and have-nots. The expectation in official circles is that France will continue her program for establishing an independent nuclear force.

This may be altered by Gen-

Continued on Page 8, Column 3

Senate Democrats Seek Big Majority For Atomic Treaty

By JOHN D. MORRIS
Special to The New York Times

WASHINGTON, July 25 — Democratic leaders set out today to muster a near-unanimous Senate vote for the treaty providing for a limited ban on nuclear tests.

There was little doubt that the treaty would be supported by the required two-thirds majority. But the size of the majority above the minimum requirement apparently will depend on the position finally taken by a number of Republicans and Southern Democrats who will not commit themselves at this time.

Among these is Senator Richard B. Russell of Georgia, chairman of the Armed Services Committee and leader of the Southern Democratic bloc in the Senate.

Others reserving judgment pending full committee hearings include Senators Bourke B. Hickenlooper of Iowa, senior Republican member of the Foreign Relations Committee, and

Continued on Page 9, Column 2

French Offer Terms For NATO Inquiry

Special to The New York Times

PARIS, July 25 — France is prepared to agree to a compromise plan for establishing an inquiry into the North Atlantic alliance's strategy and resources, informed sources reported tonight. However, President de Gaulle's Government would insist on two conditions, one of which might stall the inquiry at the starting line.

This is French insistence that the inquiry deal first with NATO's strategic concepts. Since there is a wide difference between French and United States thinking on how, where and when the alliance's strategy is to be enforced, this condition appeared to condemn the investigation to endless debate.

The other French stipulation

Continued on Page 7, Column 1

KENNEDY TO VOICE CAUTION TONIGHT

Will Warn on TV and Radio Against Expecting Too Much From Test Ban

By TOM WICKER
Special to The New York Times

WASHINGTON, July 25—In a radio and television address tomorrow night President Kennedy will caution the nation against expecting too much to result from the initialing of a treaty for a limited nuclear test ban.

The White House announced today that Mr. Kennedy would appear on the four national networks at 7 P.M. Eastern Daylight time tomorrow to discuss the treaty and its effects.

Mr. Kennedy will take the position, informed sources said, that was briefly stated in the communiqué issued today by the United States, Britain and the Soviet Union.

'Important' First Step

That is, he will say that the treaty is "an important first step toward the reduction of international tension and the strengthening of peace" and that all parties to it "look forward to further progress in this direction."

But he is expected to warn that the treaty is only a first step.

The speech is expected to be partly aimed at domestic critics of too much coexistence with Communism, and to be calculated to marshal Congressional support for ratification of the treaty.

President Kennedy's address will be broadcast and televised on the networks of the American Broadcasting Company, the National Broadcasting Company and the Columbia Broadcasting System. It also will be carried on the radio network of the Mutual Broadcasting System.

Americans in the Eastern time zone can see or hear Mr. Kennedy on any of these networks at 7 P.M. daylight time.

Continued on Page 8, Column 4

NEWS INDEX

"All the News That's Fit to Print"

The New York Times.

LATE CITY EDITION
U. S. Weather Bureau Report (Page 66) forecasts:
Warm, early and late showers today.
Clearing tonight, fair tomorrow.
Temp. range: 82—67; yesterday: 81—63.
Temp.-Hum. Index: mid-70's; yesterday: 76.

VOL. CXII..No. 38,560. © 1963 by The New York Times Company. Times Square, New York 36, N. Y. NEW YORK, WEDNESDAY, AUGUST 21, 1963. TEN CENTS

CRISIS IN SOUTH VIETNAM DEEPENS AS DIEM'S FORCES RAID PAGODAS; U.S. SEES ITS TROOPS ENDANGERED

KENNEDY OPPOSES QUOTAS FOR JOBS ON BASIS OF RACE

Says Education Is Greatest Need of Negroes—Doubts U.S. Can 'Repair Past'

RIGHTS BILLS PRESSED

Congress Urged to Act This Session—Election Year Pressure in '64 Cited

Transcript of news conference and summary, Page 14.

By CABELL PHILLIPS
Special to The New York Times

WASHINGTON, Aug. 20 — President Kennedy said today that he disapproved of employment quotas based on race.

This device has been proposed as a means of correcting the effects of past discrimination against Negroes in hiring. The theory is that Negroes should be given jobs in rough proportion to their representation in the population.

The President told his news conference this afternoon, however, that he felt such a solution would lead to a "good deal of trouble." The American society, he said, is too complex and too mixed to make such a practice feasible. [Question 11, Page 14.]

Mr. Kennedy said that Negroes had suffered a long accumulation of injustices. But he doubted that the nation could repair the past through any scheme of special or preferential compensation.

Calls Education Vital

The greatest need of the Negro both in redressing his grievances of the past and improving his lot in the present, the President said, is education.

Negroes would like to see their children well educated, he said, "so that they could hold jobs" and become "accepted as equal members of the community."

"I don't think we can undo the past," Mr. Kennedy asserted. "I don't think quotas are a good idea. I think we'd get into a good deal of trouble."

The President was emphatic in saying that he saw no good reason that Congress should put over action on his civil rights bill until next year.

His comment came in response to a question suggesting that this probably would be the result of the crowding of the legislative calendar.

The Senate majority leader, Mike Mansfield of Montana, said yesterday that it might be Christmas before the civil rights bill was taken up.

Mr. Kennedy said that he could see no advantage in putting the bill over until next year.

He said there would be as many excuses by Congress "to

Continued on Page 23, Column 1

Khrushchev Is Welcomed by Tito

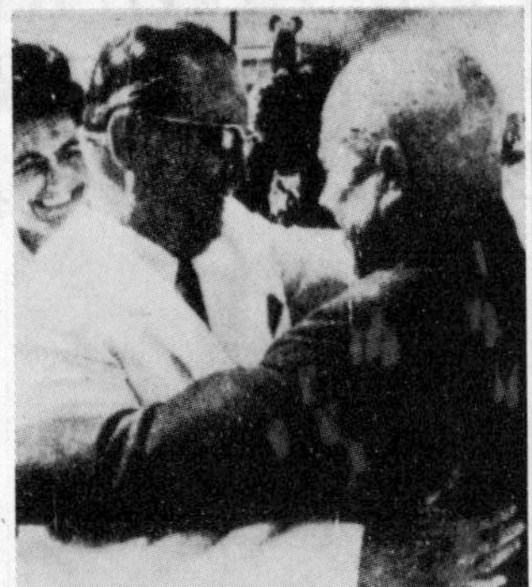

The Soviet Premier, right, with President and Mrs. Tito

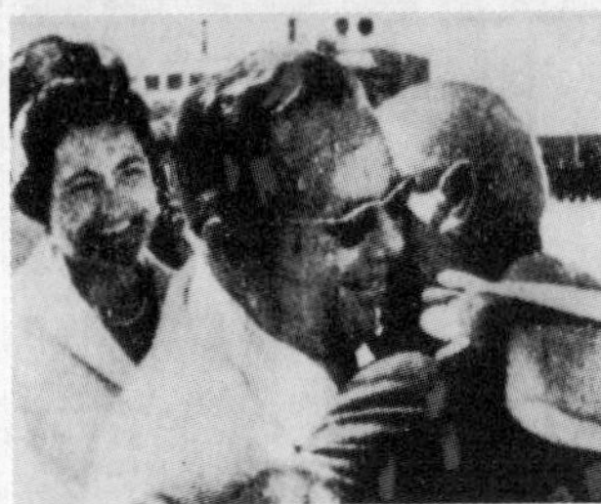

Associated Press
Soviet and Yugoslav leaders embrace at Belgrade Airport

MAYOR INDICATES TAX GAP IS LIKELY

In Annual Message, He Says City May Need New Levies —Pledges Economies

By CHARLES G. BENNETT

Mayor Wagner indicated yesterday that new or increased taxes would be required to meet the city's needs in the fiscal year beginning July 1, 1964.

In his annual message to the City Council, the Mayor said: "I cannot give assurance that our present tax resources will be sufficient to meet next year's needs."

Just before the Mayor spoke, his address was amended to include a promise to economize, to "maximize" available revenues and to avoid new taxes if possible.

Bill Is Before Council

The addition to the text apparently resulted from a feeling by the Mayor and his aides that the afternoon newspapers, TV and radio were unduly emphasizing the possibility of added taxes in 1964-65.

Speaking to an audience that included not only the City Councilmen, but also about 30 city commissioners, agency heads, deputies and aides, the Mayor asked the Council to establish a citizens' commission "to consider our entire fiscal picture in the light of our expanding budgetary needs."

Such a commission would review the city's sources of revenue and study "other possible sources." Bills calling for a commission of this nature are now pending before the City Council. If the group is to be

Continued on Page 21, Column 2

Khrushchev Begins Visit to Yugoslavia; Lauds Tito Regime

By DAVID BINDER
Special to The New York Times

BELGRADE, Yugoslavia, Aug. 20—Premier Khrushchev opened a 15-day visit to Yugoslavia today by declaring that the Soviet Union regarded the country as "Socialist" and "fraternal."

Although not a blanket endorsement of the type of socialism practiced by the independent Communist Government of President Tito, Mr. Khrushchev's remarks, made at the Belgrade Airport, appeared to be a direct rebuke to the Chinese Communist leadership.

The Peking regime, which was represented at the airport ceremony by a second secretary instead of its embassy's chargé d'affaires, has vehemently insisted for the last five years that Yugoslavia has been practicing heresy to Marxism-Leninism.

Premier Khrushchev, his face still pink from a holiday on the shores of the Black Sea, spoke with great warmth about Yugoslavia. He added that Moscow would continue to strive for closer relations with Belgrade as a matter of ideological principle.

"The Communst party of the Soviet Union and the Soviet Government," Mr. Khrushchev said, "are building relations with Socialist Yugoslavia, led by the Leninist principles of foreign policy, the principles of Socialist internationalism."

"There is no doubt," he added, "that the present visit will serve the cause of further strengthening friendship and cooperation between our countries and peoples." For his part,

Continued on Page 9, Column 1

PRESIDENT VOWS U.S. WILL STEP UP ATOMIC READINESS

Disputes Teller on Danger to Security in Test Ban —Schriever Against Pact

By E. W. KENWORTHY
Special to The New York Times

WASHINGTON, Aug. 20—President Kennedy assured Congress and the country today that a program of safeguards would be vigorously carried out to insure that national security would not be jeopardized by any Soviet abrogation of the treaty to limit nuclear tests.

At his news conference, the President was asked to comment on fears expressed by some Senators during the hearings on the treaty that the safeguards proposed by the Joint Chiefs of Staff might not be diligently carried out.

"We are just as anxious," he said, "we appreciate the concern of the members of Congress, but this matter is of concern to us also and I can assure them we will do the job." [Question 1, Page 14.]

Commenting also in relation to the treaty, the President said that the United States was still "a good, long way" from formulating its final position on a possible agreement with the Soviet Union on safeguards against surprise attack. [Question 10.]

Rejects Teller View

He rejected the arguments of Dr. Edward Teller, the physicist, who continued his opposition to the treaty at a Senate hearing.

The President said "it would be very difficult, I think, to satisfy Dr. Teller in this field."

He said the physicist had "made it very clear that he is opposed" to the treaty, noting: "He opposed it all last week and this week." [Questions 3 and 16.]

There were these other developments on the treaty today:

¶In what appeared to be a gathering Air Force offensive, Gen. Bernard A. Schriever, chief of military space development, told the Senate Preparedness Subcommittee, that he could carry out his mission better without the treaty. Yesterday Gen. Thomas S. Power, head of the Strategic Air Command, opposed the treaty as inimical to the nation's interests in testimony before the same subcommittee.

¶Roswell L. Gilpatric, Deputy Secretary of Defense, told the Senate Appropriations Committee that the treaty "does not alter our assessment of the military threat confronting us now or likely to face us in the future." It was, he said, but "a small first step albeit a very important one."

¶Mike Mansfield of Montana, Senate Democratic leader, said that hearings were going well and floor debate should begin the first week in September.

Mr. Kennedy ticked off the

Continued on Page 15, Column 1

Red Force Overruns Hamlet in Vietnam

Special to The New York Times

SAIGON, Vietnam, Aug. 20 — A show-place strategic hamlet 30 miles north of here was overrun by Vietcong guerrillas yesterday morning and many of the homes were burned, military sources said today.

The hamlet, called Ben Tuong, is situated in a Communist-controlled region among rubber plantations. It was the first project of "Operation Sunrise," the plan for the organization of armed villages in the heart of the Vietcong area. The project was begun in March, 1962.

Critics of the operation say that the strategic hamlets are overextended and are neither

Continued on Page 3, Column 8

SOVIET TROOP CUT IN CUBA REPORTED

Kennedy Says Combat Units Are Departing—Others Train Castro Forces

By TAD SZULC
Special to The New York Times

WASHINGTON, Aug. 20—A decline in the number of Soviet troops in Cuba, possibly bringing the total down to about 10,000 men, was reported today by President Kennedy.

The Russians maintain a sizable program for training troops of the regime of Fidel Castro. The program concentrates on ground-to-air and coastal defense missiles, on operations of the Cuban Air Force, which is equipped with MIG jet fighters, and on other modern equipment.

The President said at his news conference that it was difficult to discuss the precise rate of the Soviet withdrawals, but his comments, combined with information from other Government quarters, seemed to indicate the Russians had removed most of their combat units from the island.

These units were estimated last June at between 4,000 and 5,000 out of a total of 12,500 men. The President said that in the opinion of the intelligence services the "primary emphasis" of the Soviet troops remaining in Cuba was "in training, and not in concentrated military units." [Questions 15 and 21, Page 14.]

Although this apparent dis-

Continued on Page 7, Column 3

BUDDHISTS SEIZED

Police Hurl Tear Gas and Grenades During Saigon Attacks

By United Press International

SAIGON, Vietnam, Wednesday, Aug. 21 — Hundreds of heavily armed policemen and soldiers, firing pistols and using tear-gas bombs and hand grenades, swarmed into the Xa Loi pagoda early today and arrested more than 100 Buddhist monks.

The big pagoda has been the scene of frequent clashes between Buddhists, demonstrating against what they call religious persecution by the Government, and Government troops.

Policemen and soldiers also stormed into three other pagodas in Saigon, but the Xa Loi pagoda is the main cathedral of the Buddhists, who have been embroiled in a religious and political crisis with the Government.

Grenade explosions were heard and tear-gas smoke could be seen rising from inside the walls of the main pagoda.

Outspoken Opponent

On Sunday more than 15,000 Buddhists held an all-day sit-down hunger strike in front of the pagoda to protest the policies of President Ngo Dinh Diem and of his sister-in-law, Mrs. Ngo Dinh Nhu, both Roman Catholics.

Mrs. Nhu, one of the most outspoken opponents of the Buddhists, has accused them of treason, murder and Communist tactics and has ridiculed the Buddhist suicides by fire.

Violence has also been reported in Hue and other Buddhist centers. Martial law was imposed yesterday in the coastal city of Danang after demonstrators clashed with soldiers during a Buddhist mass march.

Danang, about 380 miles northeast of Saigon, is headquarters for the Vietnamese First Army Corps and is a major military base on the northeast coast.

Regime Cites Protests

The Government press agency said officials imposed martial law after a Vietnamese soldier was wounded and a Government vehicle damaged during protests Sunday by about 1,000 demonstrators.

A Buddhist protest letter to President Ngo Dinh Diem said that 36 demonstrators were injured, 18 seriously, and that 200 Buddhists were arrested in Danang. It said eight priests and nuns were among those seriously injured.

Tinh Khiet, Vietnam's supreme Buddhist priest, charged that Government troops were too harsh in putting down the demonstrations.

Other sources in Saigon reported that the demonstrators in Danang numbered about 3,000. They said the trouble began when a Vietnamese Army captain and two soldiers riding in a jeep became entangled in a

Continued on Page 3, Column 6

The New York Times
RESORTING TO FORCE: President Ngo Dinh Diem of South Vietnam. His troops attacked pagodas in Saigon.

AID BILL IS 'VITAL', KENNEDY ASSERTS

In Plea to House Members for Passage, He Terms It Necessary to Security

By FELIX BELAIR Jr.
Special to The New York Times

WASHINGTON, Aug. 20—House members of both political parties were asked by President Kennedy today to support the $4,087,750,000 foreign aid authorization bill. He said it was "vital to the security and well-being of the United States and the free world."

"No party or group should call for a dynamic foreign policy and then seek to cripple this program," the President said in a statement opening his news conference.

As he was citing the fact that the legislation carries $850,000,000 less than his budget estimate of last January, Republican speakers were urging the House to cut deeper into the amount recommended by its Foreign Affairs Committee.

House Debate Limited

Debate in the House was limited to opening speeches for the record. It will be late tomorrow before the bill is read for amendment.

But an indication of the fireworks yet to come was supplied by Representative H. R. Gross, Republican of Iowa, who demanded that the Secretaries of State and Defense be prosecuted for the "lobbying" letter they sent to all House members yesterday. The letter urged support of the bill.

Nobody on either side of the aisle took Mr. Gross's proposal seriously. Wayne Hayes, Democrat of Ohio, called it "stupid."

The exchange served only as a demonstration that nothing so arouses members like the annual battle over foreign aid.

Even President Kennedy — although he read from a prepared statement — sounded impatient as he reached words anticipating efforts to "cripple"

Continued on Page 14, Column 6

PHONE LINKS CUT

Threat of Martial Law Reported—U.S. Aide Protects Monks

By JAMES RESTON
Special to The New York Times

WASHINGTON, Wednesday, Aug. 21 — The United States is convinced that a major crisis is developing in South Vietnam.

Official reports reaching here indicated this morning that the conflict between the Government of President Ngo Dinh Diem and the Buddhists had created a situation that threatened the security of the Diem Government and of the United States forces in Vietnam.

Normal communications between Saigon, the South Vietnamese capital, and the United States were cut off yesterday afternoon. At that time, according to official reports reaching here, Vietnamese Government troops occupied the headquarters of the telephone and telegraph offices in Saigon.

Strict censorship was imposed on all outgoing cables and telephone calls after Government troops raided a Buddhist temple serving as the headquarters of the religious opposition to the Government.

Several Persons Hurt

It is understood that several persons were killed and several more injured in that raid.

William C. Trueheart, the United States chargé d'affaires in Saigon, is known to have reported to Washington that in the course of the Government's attack on Buddhist headquarters several monks fled into the headquarters of the United States mission. The mission has been supplying aid to the South Vietnamese Government.

Mr. Trueheart reported that Vietnamese soldiers demanded the right to enter the mission headquarters and take custody of the monks. On his own authority, Mr. Trueheart refused entry to the soldiers.

The South Vietnamese Defense Minister, Nguyen Dinh Thuan, thereupon informed Mr. Trueheart that the Diem Government would declare martial law in Saigon at 2 A.M. Saigon time (2 P.M. Tuesday, Eastern daylight time.)

But while this was reported to Washington, there was no subsequent message from Saigon to confirm that martial law had actually gone into effect.

The correspondent of The New York Times in Saigon, David Halberstam, could not be

Continued on Page 3, Column 2

COUNCIL APPROVES BET REFERENDUM

Voters to Be Asked to Back a Study Commission

By CHARLES GRUTZNER

The City Council ordered yesterday a referendum in the November election to let New York City voters indicate whether they favored off-track betting.

An emergency message of necessity from Mayor Wagner permitted the Council to vote the same day the measure was introduced, dispensing with a public hearing. The vote was 20 in favor, 3 against and 1 abstention.

The referendum, described privately by an aide of the Mayor as a "gimmick," can have no legal standing; off-track betting can be legalized only by the Legislature, whose Republican leadership has for the last 10 years turned a deaf ear on the city's plea for such action.

A strongly favorable vote, however, could bring pressure on Governor Rockefeller and the Republican legislative leaders to support permissive legislation.

The opposition in the Council made up for the scarcity of its numbers in the vehemence of its attack. The minority leader,

Continued on Page 20, Column 3

Court Backs Reform Democrats In Bid to List Slates in Primary

By RICHARD P. HUNT

A State Supreme Court justice ordered the Board of Elections yesterday to list candidates by slates on the primary election ballots, as a group of reform Democrats had urged.

Justice John J. Flynn said in a brief opinion that there was "ample" legal authority for putting slates on the ballot and that it would be "far less confusing for the average voter."

The Board of Elections immediately asked the Appellate Division of the Supreme Court to reverse Justice Flynn's decision. The Appellate justices will hear the case at 2 P.M. today, and the Court of Appeals will review it in Albany tomorrow.

This will enable the Court of Appeals, which is the state's highest court, to consider the ballot case on the same day it will review one to decide whether councilmen at large will be elected this year. The Appellate Division heard arguments in that case yesterday and reserved decision.

The Board of Elections had planned to use the form of the old paper ballot, which was used in the primary elections here until 1959, in listing candidates on the city's 2,750 new Shoup voting machines.

But four reform Democrats, acting with the support of the Committee for Democratic Voters, contended that the board's plan would make it difficult for the voters in the Sept. 5 primary to determine which candidates were running together as a team. Edward Greenfield, who

Continued on Page 20, Column 4

State of Economy Called 'Good'; White House Presses for Tax Cut

Special to The New York Times

WASHINGTON, Aug. 20—The state of the economy was characterized today by President Kennedy as "good." But he indicated he would be worried about the future if Congress did not enact his tax reduction bill this year.

The President told his news conference that the upturn in business activity this year had been "slightly better, although not much better," than the Administration foresaw in January.

Favorable Congressional action on taxes this year, even though the actual reduction would not go into effect until January, 1964, could give a lift to economic activity in the final months of this year, he said. [Questions 6 and 14, Page 14.]

If hopes for a tax cut are disappointed and Congress takes until the middle of next year before voting tax reduction, "what would happen to the economy in the meanwhile?" the President asked.

"Right now," the President said, "I would say the state of the economy is good."

He noted in particular the rise in industrial production, which has increased from 119 per cent of its 1957-59 base in January to 127 per cent in July.

Statistics made public by the Commerce Department today bolstered the President's generally optimistic assessment. One key indicator of future business activity, the volume of new orders received by manufacturers of durable goods, rose in July. The rise followed a decline in June, which had caused some pessimism about the business outlook.

Personal income set a record in July, for the fifth straight month, although the wages received by factory workers failed to increase for the first time since January.

Housing starts were down, but this is a business indicator that has been notoriously erratic.

An increase in orders for industrial machinery was considered the most hopeful sign in the new orders statistics. Orders for this type of equipment, which fell in June, provide a clue to the future trend of business capital investment.

Government economists have

Continued on Page 16, Column 4

NEWS INDEX

Butts Gets 3-Million Libel Award For Saturday Evening Post Story

By JOHN SIBLEY
Special to The New York Times

ATLANTA, Aug. 20—A Federal jury awarded $3,060,000 today to Wally Butts, the former football coach and athletic director at the University of Georgia, in his libel suit against the publishers of The Saturday Evening Post.

The magazine, in an article March 23, had accused Mr. Butts of divulging the Georgia team's secret formations and plays to the University of Alabama coach before last season's Georgia-Alabama game in Birmingham.

The jury of 12 men announced its verdict after deliberating 7 hours 20 minutes. The jurors were closeted for slightly less than two hours this morning, after having been excused and sent to a hotel at 10:45 P.M., New York time, yesterday.

The Alabama coach, Paul (Bear) Bryant, has filed a separate libel suit against The Post in Federal Court at Birmingham. Mr. Bryant is demanding $10,000,000 damages, as did the 58-year-old Mr. Butts in this suit.

The award to Mr. Butts consisted of $60,000 in general damages to compensate him for loss of earnings and damage to his reputation, plus $3,000,000 in punitive damages. A jury may assess punitive damages only when it finds malice and "callous disregard" for the injured party.

This was the second-highest sum awarded in a libel action. In July, 1962, a New York Supreme Court jury awarded $3,500,000 to John Henry Faulk, a television entertainer who had been branded a Communist sym-

Continued on Page 41, Column 1

ISRAEL ASKS U.N. TO MEET ON SYRIA

Appeals to Council to Curb 'Aggression' on Border

By W. GRANGER BLAIR
Special to The New York Times

JERUSALEM (Israeli Sector), Aug. 20—Israel accused Syria of aggression today and asked the United Nations Security Council to meet in urgent session.

Syrian and Israeli forces exchanged fire throughout the afternoon in the area of Ashmura, a border farm settlement in the demilitarized zone 10 miles north of the Sea of Galilee.

The army announced that two Israeli Mirage Jet fighters had attacked and damaged one of at least six Syrian MIG-17 jets that entered Israeli airspace over the demilitarized zone on the southeast shore of the Sea of Galilee. It was the first time the Mirages, recently acquired from France, had seen combat.

The Cabinet met to consider "a grave threat to peace" in the area. Haim Yahil, director general of the Foreign Ministry, said at a news conference tonight: "We feel there is a real danger to peace if the Syrian actions do not stop."

The Government acted after two Israelis were killed yesterday by Syrian armed forces

Continued on Page 2, Column 5

"All the News That's Fit to Print"

The New York Times.

LATE CITY EDITION

U. S. Weather Bureau Report (Page 58) forecasts: Cloudy with scattered showers today; partly cloudy tonight and tomorrow. Temp. range: 77—62; yesterday: 81—61. Temp.-Hum. Index: 70 to 75; yesterday: 72.

VOL. CXII. No. 38,568. | NEW YORK, THURSDAY, AUGUST 29, 1963. | TEN CENTS

200,000 MARCH FOR CIVIL RIGHTS IN ORDERLY WASHINGTON RALLY; PRESIDENT SEES GAIN FOR NEGRO

ACTION ASKED NOW

10 Leaders of Protest Urge Laws to End Racial Inequity

Excerpts from talks at rally are printed on Page 21.

By E. W. KENWORTHY
Special to The New York Times

WASHINGTON, Aug. 28—More than 200,000 Americans, most of them black but many of them white, demonstrated here today for a full and speedy program of civil rights and equal job opportunities.

It was the greatest assembly for a redress of grievances that this capital has ever seen.

One hundred years and 240 days after Abraham Lincoln enjoined the emancipated slaves to "abstain from all violence" and "labor faithfully for reasonable wages," this vast throng proclaimed in march and song and through the speeches of their leaders that they were still waiting for the freedom and the jobs.

Children Clap and Sing

There was no violence to mar the demonstration. In fact, at times there was an air of hootenanny about it as groups of schoolchildren clapped hands and swung into the familiar freedom songs.

But if the crowd was good-natured, the underlying tone was one of dead seriousness. The emphasis was on "freedom" and "now." At the same time the leaders emphasized, paradoxically but realistically, that the struggle was just beginning.

On Capitol Hill, opinion was divided about the impact of the demonstration in stimulating Congressional action on civil rights legislation. But at the White House, President Kennedy declared that the cause of 20,000,000 Negroes had been advanced by the march.

The march leaders went from the shadows of the Lincoln Memorial to the White House to meet with the President for 75 minutes. Afterward, Mr. Kennedy issued a 400-word statement praising the marchers for the "deep fervor and the quiet dignity" that had characterized the demonstration.

Says Nation Can Be Proud

The nation, the President said, "can properly be proud of the demonstration that has occurred here today."

The main target of the demonstration was Congress, where committees are now considering the Administration's civil rights bill.

At the Lincoln Memorial this afternoon, some speakers, knowing little of the ways of Congress, assumed that the passage of a strengthened civil rights bill had been assured by the moving events of the day.

But from statements by Congressional leaders, after they had met with the march committee this morning, this did not seem certain at all. These statements came before the demonstration.

Senator Mike Mansfield of Montana, the Senate Democratic leader, said he could not say whether the mass protest

Continued on Page 16, Column 1

Associated Press

VIEW FROM THE LINCOLN MEMORIAL: The scene during the march looking toward the Washington Monument

United Press International Telephoto

VIEW FROM THE WASHINGTON MONUMENT: Marchers assembling around Reflecting Pool at the Lincoln Memorial

KENNEDY SIGNS BILL AVERTING A RAIL STRIKE

PRECEDENT IS SET

Arbitration Imposed by Congress—Vote in House 286-66

Text of Kennedy's statement will be found on Page 13.

By JOHN D. POMFRET
Special to The New York Times

WASHINGTON, Aug. 28—Congress passed today a bill that prevented a national railroad strike scheduled for midnight. President Kennedy signed it immediately.

The House completed the Congressional action. It adopted by a standing vote of 286 to 66 the same joint resolution passed yesterday by the Senate. The measure provides for arbitration of the two principal issues in the railroad work rules dispute and bars a strike for 180 days.

The action was without Federal precedent. Never before in the history of peacetime labor relations has Congress imposed arbitration in a labor-management dispute.

The failure of the railroads and the five train operating unions to resolve their dispute, and the Congressional action this made necessary, is considered by many to represent a major failure for the collective bargaining system.

Many Are Reluctant

Even many Congressmen who voted for the measure, convinced that the economic consequences of a national railroad strike made action to head it off essential, did so with great reluctance. They said they feared that their action might set a precedent detrimental to collective bargaining.

An arbitration board was created by Congress to consider the two key issues. These are whether diesel locomotive firemen are necessary in freight and yard service and the size of train-service crews.

Congress ord[illegible] negotiations on the remaining issues on the theory that with the two main issues disposed of, the presumably less important matters could be settled by traditional collective bargaining.

But some well-informed Government sources do not believe the remaining issues will be

Continued on Page 13, Column 1

LODI KILLER SLAIN; 2D MAN GIVES UP

Ex-Convict Is Shot 7 Times in a Midtown Hotel

One of the killers of two New Jersey policemen was shot to death early yesterday by New York detectives during a violent struggle in his midtown hotel room. Sixteen hours later, the second man wanted in the slayings quietly surrendered.

The slain killer, 25-year-old Frank Falco, was asleep in his underwear when the police, using a passkey, entered his room at the Manhattan Hotel, Eighth Avenue and 44th Street. Although awakened with a revolver pressed to his throat, he fought desperately before being killed by seven bullets. He died snarling at the police and cursing them.

Thomas (Rabbi Tom) Trantino, 27, the second man, walked into the East 22d Street station house at 9:10 P.M., accompanied by a lawyer. He was neatly dressed and clean-shaven.

The men, both ex-convicts, had been the object of a grim police hunt since Detective Sgt. Peter Voto and Gary Tedesco, a police appointee, were gunned down early Monday morning in the Angel Lounge on Route 46 in Lodi, N. J. Mr. Tedesco was to have officially joined the Lodi force today.

A tip led the New York detectives to the hotel, where Falco had checked in at 8 P.M. Tuesday under the name of J. Rello of Newport, R. I.

Lieut. Thomas Quinn, a 53-year-old police veteran with 16 citations for bravery, entered Falco's 23d-floor room first, his

Continued on Page 35, Column 2

8 Dead in Utah Mine; Fate of 15 Unknown

Special to The New York Times

MOAB, Utah, Aug. 28—Eight men were known dead today and 15 were trapped a half-mile underground in a potash mine rocked yesterday by a severe explosion.

Two survivors hoisted to the surface today reported that three men were dead, at least five were alive and the fate of 15 was unknown. Later, however, rescue workers deep in the mine spotted five more bodies that officials said might be the men whom the survivors first believed alive.

Rescuers were being hampered by deadly gas, extreme heat, water and mechanical failures. A communications breakdown added to their frustrations.

Donald Hanna, 27 years old, of Price and Paul McKinney,

Continued on Page 14, Column 3

U.S. SPURNS DENIAL BY DIEM ON CRISIS

Absolves the Army Again in Vietnam Pagoda Raids and Points Toward Nhu

By TAD SZULC
Special to The New York Times

WASHINGTON, Aug. 28.—The United States reaffirmed today its belief that the South Vietnamese Government had violated pledges on the Buddhist crisis and that Vietnamese military chiefs were innocent of responsibility for assaults on pagodas.

This was the reaction of the Administration to communiqués issued in Saigon in the last 24 hours by the Government of President Ngo Dinh Diem in the name of the Vietnamese Joint General Staff.

The communiqués charged that Washington's public statements on the crisis reflected "totally erroneous information."

[In Saigon, youths loyal to the secret police were reported to be warning the population against anti-Government demonstrations.].

Change Is Held Vital

With the Vietnam crisis already regarded by the United States as extremely grave, this public dispute seemed to push it toward an unpredictable showdown.

The quarrel over who smashed pagodas and who arrested leaders of the Buddhist protest movement is understood to affect deeply the Kennedy Administration's evolving policy of encouraging Vietnamese military chiefs to reach for power.

This policy, still tentative, is that a fundamental change is required in the structure of the Saigon Government, Washington sources explain. They say the goal is national harmony that would let Vietnam concentrate again on the war against the Communist guerrillas of the Vietcong.

Specifically, Washington is said to deem internal peace out of the question as long as Ngo Dinh Nhu, chief of secret police and brother of the President, retains his vast power.

Mr. Nhu is considered almost a symbol of the friction between Vietnam's Buddhists and the Roman Catholic Ngo family, which dominates the Government.

It is reported that in searching for an alternative to the regime—a course that was unthinkable here before the Buddhist crisis—the United States has almost openly been ad-

Continued on Page 3, Column 4

NEWS INDEX

U.S. PRESSES U.N. TO CONDEMN SYRIA ON ISRAELI DEATHS

Stevenson Deplores Killing of Youths—Thant Assures Council on Cease-Fire

Text of Stevenson statement appears on Page 2.

By KATHLEEN TELTSCH
Special to The New York Times

UNITED NATIONS, N. Y., Aug. 28—Adlai E. Stevenson declared today that the recent slaying of two Israeli farmers by Syrians was "wanton murder" deserving the strongest condemnation by the Security Council.

The United States delegate, followed by the British representative, gave forceful support to Israel's charges arising from the Aug. 20 ambush killing of two 19-year-old Israelis at the Almagor farm settlement.

Mr. Stevenson rejected Syria's countercharges against Israel as "not corroborated" by United Nations investigations.

The United States policy statement drew a favorable reaction from Michael S. Comay of Israel, who said it encouraged him to expect the Council to take "firm and vigorous action."

Syrian Disapproves

However, there was disapproval from Dr. Salah el-Tarazi of Syria, who criticized Mr. Stevenson as "not particularly objective." He added that Mr. Stevenson in past years had not deplored Syrian losses with equal feeling.

The Council, resuming its airing of the new crisis, was told by the Secretary General, U Thant, that United Nations inspection showed "no evidence of a military build-up on either side" of the armistice line.

Mr. Thant reported that both parties were heeding the United Nations cease-fire achieved last Friday after the ambush and subsequent exchanges of shooting greatly increased tension in the area. Bullets collected at one shooting site were on exhibit in the Council chamber.

Both Mr. Stevenson and Roger W. Jackling of Britain urged Syria and Israel to accept the suggestion by the United Nations truce chief, Lieut. Gen. Odd Bull, for avoiding new eruptions along their border, including an exchange of prisoners. Mr. Comay indicated a favorable Israeli reaction.

Evidence Questioned

Dr. Tarazi, in his turn, insisted that Israel's allegations remained unproved and that some evidence could have been faked. He noted photographs of footgear found at the ambush scene and said Syrian soldiers did not wear such shoes.

He was supported by Sidi Baba of Morocco, who accused Israel of making a "great superficial fuss" over the Almagor incident to create a climate for pressuring the Arabs into signing a peace treaty.

The United States and Britain are understood to be drafting a resolution that would condemn the killings and rebuke Syria by implication, rather than by outright condemnation, as Israel has been asking. Similar formulas have been used in the past.

Such an indirect condemnation might be blocked by a veto from the Soviet Union, however, which in the past has rejected resolutions opposed by the Arabs.

Mr. Stevenson told the 11-nation Council that General Bull's information was admit-

Continued on Page 2, Column 3

2 Girls Murdered In E. 88th St. Flat

Two young women, one the daughter of a writer and the other of a prominent surgeon, were bound and stabbed to death yesterday in their apartment at 57 East 88th Street.

The victims, Janice Wylie, 21 years old, and Emily Hoffert, 23, had been slashed repeatedly. Three bloodstained kitchen knives were found in the five-room apartment, which the girls shared with another young woman. The suite had been ransacked.

The bodies were found on a bedroom floor by Janice's father, the writer Max Wylie, and by Patricia Tolles, 23, the third roommate.

Mr. Wylie, who lives nearby, at 55 East 86th Street, is a

Continued on Page 35, Column 5

CONGRESS CORDIAL BUT NOT SWAYED

Leaders of March Pay Calls of Courtesy at Capitol

By WARREN WEAVER Jr.
Special to The New York Times

WASHINGTON, Aug. 28—The civil rights demonstration that swept more than 200,000 people through the capital today appeared to have left much of Congress untouched — physically, emotionally and politically.

In the morning, 13 demonstration leaders drove quietly up Capitol Hill and paid courtesy calls on Congressional leaders of both parties. The atmosphere was cordial, but there were no conversions.

In the afternoon, about 75 Senators and Representatives went from Capitol Hill to the Lincoln Memorial to be introduced, sit on the steps and listen to Gospel singing and speeches on civil rights.

A few demonstrators violated marching orders and went up to the Capitol to visit legislators in their offices. A few Senators welcomed trainloads and busfuls of constituents in person.

Otherwise, there was really very little contact between the marchers and the group they were working hardest to impress. And there was very little evidence that the demonstration, however large and fervent, would play a material role in advancing civil rights legislation.

Senator Hubert H. Humphrey, one of the most enthusiastic of

Continued on Page 17, Column 1

'I Have a Dream . . .'

Peroration by Dr. King Sums Up A Day the Capital Will Remember

By JAMES RESTON
Special to The New York Times

News Analysis

WASHINGTON, Aug. 28—Abraham Lincoln, who presided in his stone temple today above the children of the slaves he emancipated, may have used just the right words to sum up the general reaction to the Negro's massive march on Washington. "I think," he wrote to Gov. Andrew G. Curtin of Pennsylvania in 1861, "the necessity of being ready increases. Look to it." Washington may not have changed a vote today, but it is a little more conscious tonight of the necessity of being ready for freedom. It may not "look to it" at once, since it is looking to so many things, but it will be a long time before it forgets the melodious and melancholy voice of the Rev. Dr. Martin Luther King Jr. crying out his dreams to the multitude.

It was Dr. King who, near the end of the day, touched the vast audience. Until then the pilgrimage was merely a great spectacle. Only those marchers from the embattled towns in the Old Confederacy had anything like the old crusading zeal. For many the day seemed an adventure, a long outing in the late summer sun—part liberation from home, part Sunday School picnic, part political convention, and part fish-fry.

But Dr. King brought them alive in the late afternoon with a peroration that was an anguished echo from all the old American reformers. Roger Williams calling for religious liberty, Sam Adams calling for political liberty, old man Thoreau denouncing coercion, William Lloyd Garrison demanding emancipation, and Eugene V. Debs crying for economic equality—Dr. King echoed them all.

"I have a dream," he cried again and again. And each time the dream was a promise out of our ancient articles of faith: phrases from the Constitution, lines from the great anthem of the nation, guarantees from the Bill of Rights, all ending with a vision that they might one day all come true.

Find Journey Worthwhile

Dr. King touched all the themes of the day, only better than anybody else. He was full of the symbolism of Lincoln and Gandhi, and the cadences of the Bible. He was both militant and sad, and he sent the crowd away feeling that the long journey had been worthwhile.

This demonstration impressed political Washington because it combined a number of things no politician can ignore. It had the force of numbers. It had the melodies of both the church and the theater. And it was able to invoke the principles of the founding fathers to rebuke the inequalities and hypocrisies of modern American life.

There was a paradox in the day's performance. The Ne-

Continued on Page 17, Column 6

PRESIDENT MEETS MARCH LEADERS

Says Bipartisan Support Is Needed for Rights Bill

Rights statement and Labor Day proclamation, Page 16.

By TOM WICKER
Special to The New York Times

WASHINGTON, Aug. 28—President Kennedy served tea and sympathy and blunt political advice late today to the tired but proud leaders of the march on Washington.

In an hour-long conference, the President told the 10 leaders that "very strong bipartisan support" would be needed to get civil rights legislation enacted this year.

In a statement issued immediately after the conference, Mr. Kennedy said that "the cause of 20,000,000 Negroes has been advanced" by the orderly demonstration, "conducted so appropriately before the nation's shrine to the Great Emancipator."

Earlier, in a Labor Day statement released in advance of the holiday, the President called on the nation to speed up its efforts to achieve equal rights for all in jobs, education and voting.

The main discussion between the march leaders and the President concerned prospects for civil rights legislation, the leaders said after the White House meeting. They talked with Mr. Kennedy around the long table in the Cabinet Room, where the leaders were served tea, coffee,

Continued on Page 16, Column 7

Capital Is Occupied By a Gentle Army

By RUSSELL BAKER
Special to The New York Times

WASHINGTON, Aug. 28—No one could remember an invading army quite as gentle as the 200,000 civil rights marchers who occupied Washington today.

For the most part, they came silently during the night and early morning, occupied the great shaded boulevards along the Mall, and spread through the parklands between the Washington Monument and the Potomac.

But instead of the emotional horde of angry militants that many had feared, what Washington saw was a vast army of quiet, middle-class Americans

Continued on Page 17, Column 7

Dr. Martin Luther King's "I Have a Dream" speech influenced a great number of people, both black and white, in the struggle for racial equality.

Throngs of protesters gathered together to demand equal rights and an end to segregation.

180,000 blacks and 30,000 others filled up every inch of ground from the Lincoln Memorial to the Washington Monument in a peaceful demonstration that came down to two words—*Freedom Now.*

"All the News That's Fit to Print"

The New York Times.

LATE CITY EDITION
U. S. Weather Bureau Report (Page 85) forecasts: Sunny today; clear tonight. Mostly sunny tomorrow.
Temp. range: 78—60; yesterday: 83—61. Temp.-Hum. Index: high 60's; yesterday: 73.

VOL. CXII...No. 38,581. NEW YORK, WEDNESDAY, SEPTEMBER 11, 1963. TEN CENTS

WALLACE ENDS RESISTANCE AS GUARD IS FEDERALIZED; MORE SCHOOLS INTEGRATE

BILL TO CUT TAXES 11 BILLION VOTED BY HOUSE PANEL

Modified Kennedy Measure Approved, 17 to 8—Faces Floor Action Next Week

G.O.P. PLAN IS DEFEATED

President Appeals for His Proposal Reducing Levies Over Two-Year Period

Summary of the tax bill's provisions is on Page 26.

By JOHN D. MORRIS
Special to The New York Times

WASHINGTON, Sept. 10—A modified version of President Kennedy's tax program emerged from the House Ways and Means Committee today. The vote was 17 to 8.

The bill, providing for cuts in income tax rates for individuals and corporations in all brackets, was tentatively scheduled for consideration by the House next week. Senate hearings are expected to begin soon after the House acts.

The prospects of House passage of the bill are regarded as good. The Senate outlook for completion of action this year is less certain, although Administration leaders continue to express confidence that the bill will become law before Congress adjourns.

Corporations Affected

If enacted in its present form, the measure would give individuals and corporations $11,060,000,000 in annual tax relief when its provisions became fully effective in 1965. Reductions in rates would be partly offset by revenue-raising revisions, or reforms, of the tax structure. The reductions would take effect in two steps starting next January.

The House committee's action coincided with a new plea by President Kennedy for enactment of the bill this year as "recession insurance."

The combined effect of the rate reductions and structural revisions under the bill would be $8,750,000,000 in annual tax relief for individuals and $2,310,000,000 for corporations.

A typical married couple with two children and an income from wages or salaries of $5,500 would get a tax cut of $77 in 1965. The reduction for such a couple with an income of $7,500 would be $144. At $10,-

Continued on Page 26, Column 1

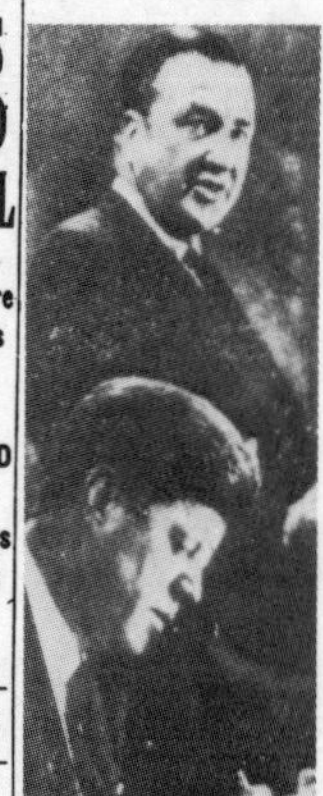

Associated Press

PUSHES TAX CUT: President Kennedy makes last-minute changes in speech as Henry Ford 2d introduces him to business group.

AID FOR RETARDED IS VOTED BY HOUSE

Program Cut to 238 Million and Sent Back to Senate, Which May Restore Funds

By C. P. TRUSSELL
Special to The New York Times

WASHINGTON, Sept. 10 — The House of Representatives approved today a $238,000,000 program to combat mental retardation. The vote was 335 to 18.

The legislation was sent back to the Senate, which on May 27 approved an $850,000,000 program that was closer to Administration recommendations.

The House reduction reflects principally the elimination of $427,000,000 in grants to help finance the staffing of community mental health centers. The remainder resulted largely from a shortening of the program from five to three years.

There was no opposition to the program itself in debate. The Committee on Interstate and Foreign Commerce had voted against the grants for staffing the health centers.

It held that Federal aid should not infringe on the traditional responsibility of the states, localities and the medical profession for the care and treatment of the mentally ill. The House vote supported this position.

Some Administration supporters still hope that at least some of the cut will be restored by the Senate and retained in a compromise between the two houses.

As passed by the House, the measure would authorize:

¶$20,000,000 over three years for grants for up to 75 per cent of costs, for the construction of

Continued on Page 23, Column 4

KENNEDY ORDERS HALT IN DRAFTING OF MARRIED MEN

Status of 340,000 Affected —Inductees to Be Called Up at an Earlier Age

By TOM WICKER
Special to The New York Times

WASHINGTON, Sept. 10—President Kennedy signed an Executive order today that had the effect of halting the draft of married men into the armed forces. The order affects the draft status of 340,000 men.

The Selective Service System has been drafting an average of about 6,000 men for the armed forces each month. About one-third of them have been married men without children.

The order Mr. Kennedy signed today places married men, 19 to 26 years old, in the lowest pool of men classified 1-A, or available for the draft. The order is effective immediately.

The 1-A pool now contains about 1,700,000 men. Lieut. Gen. Lewis B. Hershey, the Selective Service Director, estimated that about 20 per cent of that total were now married.

Enough Bachelors Available

Since the remaining unmarried youths are considered numerous enough to fill monthly quotas for the foreseeable future, the effect of the President's action was to halt the draft of married men.

A previous order signed by Mr. Kennedy last March halted the induction of fathers.

When the signing of the new Executive order was announced, Pierre Salinger, the White House press secretary, was asked why so many married men had been drafted each month when plenty of unmarried men were available to fill quotas.

"That," Mr. Salinger said, "is exactly the question the President asked."

The President apparently got no satisfactory answer and the order today resulted.

Three Receive Pens

Mr. Kennedy signed the order in his office this morning in the presence of General Hershey, Deputy Secretary of Defense Roswell L. Gilpatric and Assistant Secretary of Defense Norman S. Paul. The President gave each of them a pen used in the signing.

One effect of the order, the White House said, will be to lower the age of men inducted each month. The average induction age is about 23 years.

Thus, the White House said, young unmarried men will know what their induction status is at an earlier age than they now do.

The pool of single men is now considered adequate because the total pool of men 19 to 26 years old has been growing rapidly in recent years as the World War II "war babies" have come of draft age.

The order issued today will apply only to men who are married before they receive an induction notice. It described married men as those "who have a wife with whom they maintain

Continued on Page 16, Column 4

Washington Divided Over Aid to Vietnam

By TAD SZULC
Special to The New York Times

WASHINGTON, Sept. 10—President Kennedy's policy on South Vietnam, ruling out a reduction in aid "at this time," was described today as intentionally flexible.

Officials said the door was still open to cuts if President Ngo Dinh Diem resisted Washington's pressure to reform his Government and to seek popular support. This was their interpretation of the President's remarks in a television interview yesterday.

At the same time, it was widely reported that the Administration's policy in the three-week-old South Vietnamese crisis remained fluid and that the President faced divided counsel.

It was known that an influential group of advisers had favored "selective" cuts

Continued on Page 14, Column 8

PARIS DRAWS PLAN TO HALT INFLATION

Proposes Wage and Price Restraint—Living Costs Up 16% in 3 Years

By DREW MIDDLETON
Special to The New York Times

PARIS, Sept. 10—Premier Georges Pompidou outlined today the Government's "stabilization plan" intended to check the inflation that is weakening the French economy.

The main points of the plan include a drastic effort to cut some Government spending, tightening of credit, agreements with shopkeepers to maintain prices at present levels and ultimately to reduce them, and an attempt to keep wage increases within reasonable bounds.

The Premier also disclosed that in an effort to increase France's labor force many young men would be exempted from military service on Nov. 1.

Details of these and other measures in the campaign against inflation will be announced Thursday. Mr. Pompidou's outline of policy appeared in the Paris weekly Paris-Match.

Legislation to Be Offered

Valéry Giscard d'Estaing, Minister of Finance and Economic Affairs, said the Government program included legislative measures that would be submitted to the National Assembly.

The steady rise in prices, and the demand for wage increases to meet them, are regarded by the Government as serious dangers to France's continued prosperity and the greatest source of political discontent.

The extent of the inflation in France is indicated by the rise in consumer prices of 6 per cent over last year. In the same period consumer prices in the United States rose 1.5 per cent.

In the last three years in France consumer prices have risen more than 16 per cent. Increases in food prices have put an especial strain on the people.

Wage Increases Lag

Wage increases, particularly in the nationalized industries, have lagged behind rises in living costs.

The Government believes in tying wage increases to advances in productivity. But management and employe antipathy to such a policy has prevented its development in many industries.

The connection between stable prices and continued prosperity has not been understood by a large section of the population.

Statements in the last two days by agricultural and industrial unions emphasized the resistance that would be made to the stabilization plan.

Agricultural unions criticized the Government's rejection of increased farm prices. The farm-

Continued on Page 4, Column 3

VIETNAM CLOSES 5 MORE SCHOOLS; 100 ARE ARRESTED

2,400 Now Held in Saigon —Regime Presents Two Girls as Red Agents

Special to The New York Times

SAIGON, South Vietnam, Sept. 10—Troops removed the students from five more Saigon high schools today in an attempt to prevent new protests. Some of the schools were occupied by the soldiers.

About 100 students, most of them leaders at the schools, were believed to have been arrested.

Most of the students were ordered out and sent home. It is reported that eight high schools in the city are now temporarily shut.

At two large high schools, students who had been planning demonstrations for today arrived to find soldiers and policemen inside the schools. The Government appeared to be moving to head off the protests before they gained further momentum.

The students, many of them from middle-class and upper-class homes, started their protests against the Government on Saturday. About 800 were arrested then.

Protests Are Weaker

The demonstrations today, not so strong as yesterday's, consisted mostly of anti-Government squealing and yelling by girls.

In the demonstrations yesterday, at a school in the Cholon district of Saigon and a school in central Saigon, secret policemen reinforced by soldiers were reported to have arrested about 1,500 students. At a boys' school in the Cholon district, the students hurled desks at the police and troops and attempted to prevent them from entering.

The number of students arrested in the last four days is believed to be about 2,400. Few have been released. The protests have been mainly against the Government of President Ngo Dinh Diem, but some students have displayed banners criticizing the United States for supporting the Government through aid programs.

Some of the student leaders are being taken to the main police station in Saigon for questioning; others are being taken to detention camps outside of Saigon.

Angered by Charges

At a girls' school today the students yelled denunciations of the Government and appeared to be particularly angered over the Government's charge that the student movement had been infiltrated by the Vietcong, the Communist agents operating in South Vietnam.

At a news conference today, the Government presented two girls and said they were examples of the Vietcong agents responsible for the student protests.

One of the girls, 17 years old, said her orders were "very clear-cut." She said, "When there is a struggle against the regime I am to participate actively in it."

The other, who is 16, said she had helped to lead a demonstration in her school. She said that she had paint and "slogan-making material."

Asked whether the two girls were leaders of the entire student-protest movement, Pham Van Tao, Director General of Information, said they were typical of the leadership. He maintained that the demonstrations

Continued on Page 15, Column 1

Associated Press

DEMONSTRATOR ARRESTED: Policemen subdue man protesting admission of Negroes to West End High School, Birmingham. Twelve white demonstrators were arrested there.

United Press International Telephoto

AFTER INTEGRATION: Weeping girls leave the West End school, where attendance dropped almost 90 per cent.

20 NEGROES ENTER

12 Whites Arrested in Birmingham—Other Cities Are Peaceful

By CLAUDE SITTON
Special to The New York Times

BIRMINGHAM, Ala., Sept. 10 — Twenty Negroes attended previously white schools in three Alabama cities today after President Kennedy's federalization of the state's National Guardsmen ended the defiance of Gov. George C. Wallace.

The police here arrested 12 whites in a rowdy, two-hour demonstration over the admission of two Negro girls to West End High School under a Federal court order. This, coupled with already existing racial tension, raised a threat of further disorder.

No major incidents marred the desegregation of two other schools here, four in Huntsville — where classes began yesterday—and one each in Tuskegee and Mobile. The 425 Guardsmen ordered to active duty by Federal officials remained in their armories.

Combined school attendance here at West End and Graymont elementary school, where two Negroes enrolled, dropped by almost 90 per cent. But Ramsay High School, which accepted one Negro, showed a slight increase.

Wallace Concedes Defeat

Only some 165 of an expected total of 550 students appeared for classes at the Tuskegee public school, which 13 Negroes are attending. Attendance figures at four Huntsville schools that have one Negro pupil each and at Murphy High School in Mobile, which has two, were near normal.

Governor Wallace conceded at a news conference in the state Capitol in Montgomery that for the second time in three months he had been forced to retreat from a posture of massive resistance to desegregation in education. "I can't fight bayonets with my bare hands," he said.

A legal battle directed by Mrs. Constance Baker Motley of New York, associate counsel of the N.A.A.C.P. Legal Defense and Educational Fund, was largely responsible for the Governor's predicament. To preserve the right of admission this effort had won for the 20 students, Justice Department attorneys obtained a sweeping court order against Mr. Wallace last night.

The temporary restraining order, signed by all five of Alabama's Federal District judges, prohibited him and state troopers from any further interference with desegregation.

The Governor then ordered

Continued on Page 30, Column 1

Soviet Offers Aid To British Guiana Against 'Blockade'

Special to The New York Times

WASHINGTON, Sept. 10 — The Soviet Union has announced an offer of "ample" economic aid to British Guiana to break "the imperialist blockade" against the regime of Premier Cheddi B. Jagan.

A Moscow radio broadcast in Spanish to South America last Friday said that "a few days ago" the Soviet Ministry of Foreign Trade offered to sell British Guiana "agricultural chemicals at half price" and to supply "a long-term loan for agricultural equipment."

[An aide of Premier Jagan said in New York Tuesday that negotiations were pending between a Soviet trade organization and the British Guiana Rice Marketing Board for the purchase by the Guianese of fertilizer valued at $588,000.]

Earlier, the Moscow radio added, the Soviet Union sent British Guiana two ships with petroleum products and other material at Dr. Jagan's request.

"This aid," the broadcast continued, "will contribute to the termination of the imperialist

Continued on Page 2, Column 3

PRESIDENT AVOIDS A SHOW OF FORCE

His Strategists Feel They Outwitted Wallace at His Own Game in Crisis

Texts of proclamation and Executive order, Page 31.

By CABELL PHILLIPS
Special to The New York Times

WASHINGTON Sept. 10—A strategy hastily devised at the White House between 10 o'clock last night and dawn led to the successful integration of several Alabama schools today without reliance upon "a Federal presence."

This was a solution toward which the Kennedy Administration had worked during the last hectic week in the face of defiance from Gov. George C. Wallace. Government officials had sought means of avoiding the use of force to carry out Federal court orders to admit Negro pupils to the schools.

Their success, in the view of the strategists themselves, obliterates—for the time being at least — the basis of Governor Wallace's complaint today that "I can't fight bayonets with my bare hands." For there were no bayonets in evidence today as the Negro pupils entered previously all-white schools in Birmingham, Mobile and Tuskegee.

National Guardsmen with bayonets, acting under the Governor's orders to keep the Negro children out, had taken up their posts at the beleaguered schools before dawn.

But before the school bells rang, President Kennedy had federalized the Guardsmen and they had been whisked back to their armories, where they stayed, "awaiting orders."

The only display of legal force at the schools this morning was by the local police, who escorted some of the Negro pupils to the door to see

Continued on Page 31, Column 1

RES GET 6 MONTHS IN STOCK SWINDLE

Father and Son Also Must Pay Fines of $15,000

By DAVID ANDERSON

Gerardo A. (Jerry) Re and his son, Gerard F., were sentenced yesterday in United States District Court to serve six months in prison and to pay $15,000 fines in a multimillion-dollar stock swindle.

Judge Dudley B. Bonsal imposed three-year sentences on the former specialists on the American Stock Exchange, but ordered that the rest of the imprisonment be suspended. The Res will be on parole, however, for three years after their release.

They will remain free now on $40,000 bail each, pending an appeal.

They were convicted with three co-defendants on July 11 on charges of having rigged the market to facilitate the high-pressure sale of $10,000,000 worth of Swan-Finch Oil Corporation common stock from 1954 to 1957.

The Res, as specialists charged with maintaining a stable and orderly market in assigned stocks, held positions of unusual responsibility. The disclosure of their rigging activities led to the 1962 reorganization of the American Stock Exchange, and prompted Congress to appropriate nearly $1,000,000 for a two-year special study of the nation's securities markets.

The court sentenced Ely Batkin, a broker, to the same prison

Continued on Page 64, Column 4

State Liquor Investigators Study Controls on Habits of Drinkers

Moreland Panel to Examine Foreign Systems Providing for Individual Permits

By CHARLES GRUTZNER

Possible state controls over the drinking habits of individuals are being studied by the Moreland Act Commission.

The commission, headed by Lawrence E. Walsh, will open hearings here next month on proposed revisions of the Alcoholic Beverage Control Law.

Among the systems to be examined is that in use in Finland, where the individual receives a liquor purchase permit that can be suspended or revoked when his drinking leads him into trouble. In Poland and Czechoslovakia drunks are taken to treatment centers, where, after being sobered up, they are examined to learn if there is a deep-seated reason for their excessive tippling.

In Canada, where liquor controls vary among the provinces, some provinces ration liquor sales to individuals. A person's card may be canceled for certain offenses, including the carrying of liquor in a passenger car. In Norway and

The New York Times

Lawrence E. Walsh

Sweden the police periodically halt cars at unannounced checkpoints and examine drivers for whisky breath. Because offenders are jailed rather than fined, it has become the custom at social gatherings for the driver to abstain while his passengers make merry with aquavit,

Continued on Page 23, Column 1

Pain Drug Found Nonaddictive But as Powerful as Morphine

By ROBERT K. PLUMB

A drug that promises new freedom to physicians in the treatment of chronic pain was described here yesterday to the American Chemical Society.

The drug, developed by the Sterling-Winthrop Research Institute, was reported to be as potent as morphine; but it is nonaddictive.

An evaluation of the compound has been carried out by the Baylor University School of Medicine in Houston under a grant made through the National Academy of Sciences and National Research Council, with funds supplied by pharmaceutical manufacturers.

The evaluation was made by Dr. Arthur S. Keats, chairman of the Baylor department of anesthesiology.

Up to this time, Dr. Keats pointed out in his report, physicians have faced a difficult problem in using morphine for chronic pain. The problem is that a patient may become addicted.

"With this drug," Dr. Keats reported, "the fear of addiction in chronic pain will be eliminated. Physicians will have new freedom to treat patients with chronic pain."

The drug is called pentazocine. Dr. Keats said that it was the first highly potent, nonaddicting pain killer to be available to physicians. It is not a

Continued on Page 22, Column 3

NEWS INDEX

1963

Elizabeth Taylor starred in *Cleopatra.*

Jack Lemmon and Shirley MacLaine starred in Billy Wilder's *Irma La Douce.*

Peter Sellers in one of his more charming moments in *The Pink Panther.*

Prisoners seen leaving the Alcatraz cell block.
The toughest federal prison (known as "The Rock") was closed on March 21, after 29 years of serving as a maximum security federal penitentiary.

Marked mobster, Joseph Valachi just scratched the surface when he testified against organized crime before the Senate.

"All the News That's Fit to Print"

The New York Times.

LATE CITY EDITION
U. S. Weather Bureau Report (Page 68) forecasts: Windy, cool with rain today; clearing late tonight. Warmer tomorrow.
Temp. range: 64—56; yesterday: 62—48.

VOL. CXII..No. 38,586. | NEW YORK, MONDAY, SEPTEMBER 16, 1963. | TEN CENTS

BIRMINGHAM BOMB KILLS 4 NEGRO GIRLS IN CHURCH; RIOTS FLARE; 2 BOYS SLAIN

Associated Press Wirephoto

AFTER BLAST: Rescue workers examine debris outside Negro church in Birmingham

GUARD SUMMONED

Wallace Acts on City Plea for Help as 20 Are Injured

By CLAUDE SITTON
Special to The New York Times

BIRMINGHAM, Ala., Sept. 15—A bomb severely damaged a Negro church today during Sunday school services, killing four Negro girls and setting off racial rioting and other violence in which two Negro boys were shot to death.

Fourteen Negroes were injured in the explosion. One Negro and five whites were hurt in the disorders that followed.

Some 500 National Guardsmen in battle dress stood by at armories here tonight, on orders of Gov. George C. Wallace. And 300 state troopers joined the Birmingham police, Jefferson County sheriff's deputies and other law-enforcement units in efforts to restore peace.

Governor Wallace sent the guardsmen and the troopers in response to requests from local authorities.

Sporadic gunfire sounded in Negro neighborhoods tonight, and small bands of residents roamed the streets. Aside from the patrols that cruised the city armed with riot guns, carbines and shotguns, few whites were seen.

Fire Bomb Hurled

At one point, three fires burned simultaneously in Negro sections, one at a broom and mop factory, one at a roofing company and a third in another building. An incendiary bomb was tossed into a supermarket, but the flames were extinguished swiftly. Fire marshals investigated blazes at two vacant houses to see if arson was involved.

Mayor Albert Boutwell and other city officials and civic leaders appeared on television station WAPI late tonight and urged residents to cooperate in ending "this senseless reign of terror."

Sheriff Melvin Bailey referred to the day as "the most distressing in the history of Birmingham."

The explosion at the 16th Street Baptist Church this

Continued on Page 26, Column 1

Full-Scale F.B.I. Hunt On In Birmingham Bombing

Special to The New York Times

WASHINGTON, Sept. 15—The Federal Government responded today to the church bombing at Birmingham, Ala., in which four girls were killed, by rushing to the scene 25 agents of the Federal Bureau of Investigation, including bomb experts.

Burke Marshall, Assistant Attorney General in charge of civil rights, headed the investigators sent to augment those already there.

With Mr. Marshall were Joseph Dolan, Assistant Deputy Attorney General, and John Nolan, administrative assistant to Robert F. Kennedy, the Attorney General.

Mr. Marshall's primary mission, according to a spokesman for the department, will be to keep the Attorney General fully and quickly informed of developments.

Full Inquiry Ordered

The spokesman said that, while the F.B.I. automatically assists in investigations of all bombings such as the one today in Birmingham, in this case the department had specifically ordered a full-scale investigation.

President Kennedy, relaxing at Newport, R. I. when the bombing occurred, has since returned to the White House. He is being kept informed of developments by the Justice Department.

Mr. Marshall, who was called back from his West Virginia farm, played a leading role in achieving a compromise between white and Negro leaders of Birmingham earlier this year. The agreement, which dealt with such issues as desegregation of public accommodations, followed a series of disorders that attracted worldwide attention.

A Justice Department spokesman said there was "a presumption" that a Federal crime had been committed under a section of the Civil Rights Act of 1960. The section outlaws the trans-

Continued on Page 26, Column 5

SIGNALS RELAYED BY WIRES IN ORBIT

Successful Test Finds No Evidence of Interference With Radio Astronomy

By HAROLD M. SCHMECK Jr.

Experiments with the earth-girdling belt of fine copper wires put into orbit by the United States in May were pronounced successful yesterday.

The 400,000,000 wires, each as thin as a human hair and less than an inch long, were put into a polar orbit about 2,000 miles above the earth to test the possibilities of such belts for a worldwide communications network.

Just two such belts, one orbiting from pole to pole and the other ringing the equator, could provide a global communications system that would be inexpensive to launch, difficult to jam and impossible to shoot down, according to calculations made several years ago.

The present belt was put into orbit as a feasibility study called Project West Ford, supported by the Air Force and conducted by the Massachusetts Institute of Technology's Lincoln Laboratory. A report made public by the laboratory yesterday said the major objectives of the study had been fulfilled.

The two prime points were that the belt gave a "significant communication capacity" and that this was achieved "without

Continued on Page 15, Column 3

Dakota Quintuplets Doing Fine; Respond Well to First Feedings

By DONALD JANSON
Special to The New York Times

ABERDEEN, S.D., Sept. 15—The Fischer quintuplets are "getting along fine," their physician said tonight.

The boy and four girls, born to Mrs. Andrew Fischer early yesterday, received their first feeding, two cubic centimeters of glucose water each, at 9:30 A.M. today.

Dr. James Berbos, who delivered them, said they had been fed at two-hour intervals since.

All five tolerated the fluid well, he said, and the amount was doubled at the fourth feeding this afternoon.

"There have been no complications so far," he said at a news conference in the crowded basement cafeteria of St. Luke's Hospital. "The babies are moving around well and squalling normally."

He said they would be "fairly well out of danger" if they lived until Tuesday morning.

No other quintuplets born in the United States have survived infancy.

The Fischer babies have not been weighed yet, but range from about 2½ to 4 pounds. They arrived two months prematurely.

"All their systems are immature," Dr. Berbos said. "They

Continued on Page 41, Column 1

GROMYKO ARRIVES FOR U.N. SESSION AND OTHER TALKS

Soviet Minister Will Also Meet Rusk and Home on Outstanding Issues

POSITIVE ATTITUDE SEEN

He Is Expected to Show Restraint on Subject of Nonaggression Pact

Text of provisional agenda for the U.N., Page 16.

Foreign Minister Andrei A. Gromyko of the Soviet Union arrived in New York yesterday to attend the 18th session of the United Nations General Assembly, opening tomorrow.

Mr. Gromyko, who landed at Idlewild Airport at 6:40 P.M. in a Soviet turboprop Il-18, said he expected to confer with Secretary of State Dean Rusk before the Assembly opens. He declined to speculate on the subject or results of the meeting.

The Foreign Minister was accompanied by his wife and 48 Soviet officials, including Mikhail A. Menshikov, former Ambassador to the United States. He was greeted by, among others, Carlos M. Lechuga, the Cuban representative at the United Nations.

Fourteen Hungarian exiles picketed the International Arrivals Building.

Negotiations to Continue

By HENRY TANNER
Special to The New York Times

MOSCOW, Sept. 15—Andrei A. Gromyko, the Soviet Foreign Minister, left for the United States today in what Western observers expect to be a "positive" frame of mind toward negotiations with the West.

While in the United States, Mr. Gromyko will confer with President Kennedy, Secretary of State Dean Rusk, and the Earl of Home, the British Foreign Secretary. He will also attend the opening of the 18th annual session of the United Nations General Assembly on Tuesday.

The meetings of Mr. Gromyko, Mr. Rusk and Lord Home will continue the talks held by the three men after the signing of the treaty for a limited ban on nuclear testing. The treaty was signed in Moscow Aug. 5.

At that time, the treaty was called a "first step" by all

Continued on Page 16, Column 2

ALGERIA TO SEIZE SETTLERS' LANDS

Ben Bella, Now President, Will Speed Socialism

By Reuters

ALGIERS, Sept. 15—Ahmed Ben Bella, elected today as President of Algeria, said in a radio broadcast tonight that he planned to "nationalize all the lands of the settlers and of the traitors as well."

Mr. Ben Bella, who became the country's first President only a few hours before in voting in which he was the only candidate, said he would reshuffle his cabinet "within the next two days.

"True militants will take part in the Government," he said.

Speaking in Arabic, he said that in the coming year he would move fast toward Socialism and the new Government would "reflect the Algerian people."

The French translation of President Ben Bella's speech, made public by the Algerian National News Agency, quoted him as saying, "The principal enterprises will be nationalized. We shall nationalize all the lands of the settlers and the lands of the traitors as well."

"In 1964," he added, "important stages will be reached on the road toward Socialism and in particular by the creation of cooperatives and the radical elimination of go-betweens."

Before the election Mr. Ben Bella announced that the Government would take over 2,500,-

Continued on Page 8, Column 4

Anti-Castro Crowds Disrupt Times Sq.; Police Escort 1,400 at Rally to Safety

The New York Times

ON ALERT: Mounted police seek to contain the demonstrators massing along 43d Street

Exiles Mass to Denounce Group Protesting Ban on Travel to Cuba

By PETER KIHSS

Thousands of anti-Castro demonstrators swarmed in and around the Times Square area yesterday protesting a Town Hall rally by American students who had traveled to Cuba.

The rally, from which two groups of anti-Castro demonstrators were forcibly ejected, wound up with the police escorting 1,400 participants in the meeting along 43d Street to the Times Square subway station.

One anti-Castro Cuban was cut above the eye; five persons were arrested in scuffles waged at various points in the area; a police inspector and a newspaper reporter were hit by an egg, and a police horse was gashed when thrust against a car.

'Repression' Charged

But the meeting went off as scheduled from 2:15 to 4:45 P.M. Phillip Abbott Luce, one of the leaders, said the Student Committee for Travel to Cuba would sponsor another trip to Cuba—perhaps next January or June—to uphold its claim to freedom of travel, despite a State Department ban.

At the rally, Conrad J. Lynn, panel moderator, asserted that "we are making a demonstration here this afternoon not so much for Cuba as for America."

"There will be no peaceful solution to American problems if we are going to have repression of expression," he said.

The Times Square area has been ruled out for mass demonstrations by an order of Police Commissioner Michael J. Murphy since last Oct. 24. The ban covers the area between 40th and 59th Streets and Fifth and Ninth Avenues.

But before yesterday's gathering at Town Hall, 113 West 43d Street, between the Avenue of the Americas and Seventh

Continued on Page 39, Column 1

MALAYSIA'S BIRTH MARKED IN 4 LANDS

Southeast Asian Federation Asks Peace but Confronts Boycott by 2 Neighbors

By SETH S. KING
Special to The New York Times

KUALA LUMPUR, Malaysia, Monday, Sept. 16—The country of Malaysia came into being this morning with the raising of her new flag and the release of 101 white pigeons.

In a ceremony in the huge Merdeka (Freedom) Stadium, the federation of Malaya, Singapore, Sarawak and Sabah—formerly North Borneo—was completed.

Similar ceremonies were held in the three other states.

In Southeast Asia, where the British flag once flew over vast territories, Britain now retains only the colony of Hong Kong, a few islands in the Indian Ocean, and Brunei, a protectorate.

Malaysia, an anti-Communist, pro-Western grouping of 10 million people, is one of the smaller countries, in population, in this part of the world. Her armed forces are small.

Britain Pledged to Defense

But Britain, which will retain bases in Singapore and Malacca, is bound by treaty to defend Malaysia Australia and New Zealand are also committed to come to Malaysia's aid if needed.

The releasing of the 101 pigeons—101 is considered to be an auspicious number by Malaysians—was a gesture to emphasize Malaysia's desire for peace with her neighbors, some of whom are hostile to the federation.

Indonesia, for instance, announced yesterday that she could not approve of the federation until the United Nations made certain unspecified "corrections."

Last weekend, more special forces of the Indonesian Army were flown into Kalimantan (Indonesian Borneo) to reinforce units along the Sarawak border, across which there were raids this summer by Indonesian-based "rebels."

The Philippines, which still claims North Borneo, has withheld her judgment on the fed-

Continued on Page 3, Column 1

20 in Haiti Receive Safe-Exit Permits

By HENRY RAYMONT

The Haitian Government has granted safe-conduct passes to 20 of the 40 remaining political refugees who sought asylum in Latin-American embassies in Port-au-Prince.

This was disclosed yesterday by diplomats who have just returned from Haiti, which is embroiled in a bitter dispute with the Dominican Republic over the question of political asylum.

Haiti acted, the diplomats said, in response to an appeal by a special committee of the Organization of American States. The committee returned from Port-au-Prince earlier this

Continued on Page 14, Column 3

ROCKEFELLER PLANS '64 DECISION SOON

May Announce Intentions in November — He Prefers Goldwater to Kennedy

By LEONARD INGALLS

Governor Rockefeller said last night that he would announce before the end of the year, possibly in November, whether he will seek the Republican nomination for President next year.

Mr. Rockefeller was interviewed on "Meet the Press" over the television and radio networks of the National Broadcasting Company.

A questioner noted that Senator Barry Goldwater of Arizona had promised to let the country know by Jan. 1 whether he would be a candidate for the nomination.

'November, Maybe'

"I'd do it before that," Mr. Rockefeller replied when asked when he would tell his plans. Pressed as to whether it would be in a matter of weeks, he said, "No, I would think November, maybe."

Friends of Mr. Rockefeller were understood last night to have organized to enter his name in the New Hampshire preferential primary. Hugh Gregg, a former Governor of that state, was reported to have been selected to direct the Rockefeller primary campaign.

Rockefeller aides have indicated that the Governor will run in both the New Hampshire and California primaries.

Mr. Rockefeller ranged over a variety of subjects in response to questions. He repeated criticisms of President Kennedy for his economic and tax programs, warned again about

Continued on Page 29, Column 3

AMERICA CANCELS SAILING IN DISPUTE ON RACIAL CHARGE

2 Unions and Line Disagree on Engineer Accused of Being a Segregationist

By ROBERT C. DOTY

The sailing of the liner America with 945 passengers was canceled yesterday as a result of labor difficulties. Blame for the tie-up was tossed back and forth between the United States Lines and two crew members' unions.

The sailing of the 33,961-gross-ton liner—second largest in the United States merchant fleet—for British and continental ports, scheduled for noon Saturday, was first delayed, then canceled when crew members refused to sail with a senior engineer officer. They accused him of discriminating against Negroes, Puerto Ricans and Jews.

The National Maritime Union which represents most of the 680 unlicensed crew members, demanded that the officer be removed, and then struck. The line refused to remove the accused officer without a full hearing.

Some Passengers Angry

The Marine Engineers' Beneficial Association refused to accept any solution involving even the temporary removal of the accused engineer.

As a result, the passengers, in moods ranging from disappointment to anger, milled through the ship at Pier 86, West 46th Street and the Hudson River, seeking alternate transportation, by sea or air, with the help of the line.

The maritime union said its national officers would meet today to decide whether to extend the tie-up to any of 53 other United States Lines ships currently in United States ports.

The tie-up followed the signing last month by the union and the American Merchant Marine Institute—the ship operators' bargaining unit—of a contract hailed by Joseph Curran, president of the union, as a no-strike contract running through 1969. The contract provided for mandatory arbitration, but it failed to halt the walkout.

No Rebuttal Made

Crew members, in statements given to N.M.U. officials, accused Louis Neurohr, the first assistant engineer, of having made declarations and committed acts indicative of prejudice against Negroes, Puerto Ricans and Jews.

These remained officially unanswered because Mr. Neurohr was being kept away from reporters. Officials of the line declined to comment "without affording him a full and fair hearing."

Spokesmen for the line said the engineer was "resting." There were apparently well-founded reports, however, that he had left the ship under guard.

Yesterday, when the dispute flared into the open, he was

Continued on Page 38, Column 3

The New York Times (by Neal Boenzi)

FINDING A WAY: Tourist-class passengers confer with company officials on the liner America after sailing was canceled. The United States Lines, operator of ship, offered disappointed travelers refunds or transfer of their tickets to airlines or other ships.

NEWS INDEX

"All the News That's Fit to Print"

The New York Times.

LATE CITY EDITION

U. S. Weather Bureau Report (Page 96) forecast: Partly cloudy and cold today; clear tonight. Fair and milder tomorrow. Temp. range: 50—36; yesterday: 48—40.

SECTION ONE

NEWS SUMMARY AND INDEX, PAGE 95

VOL. CXIII. No. 38,634. NEW YORK, SUNDAY, NOVEMBER 3, 1963. THIRTY CENTS

40c beyond 50-mile zone from New York City, except on Long Island. 50c beyond 200-mile zone from New York City, higher in air delivery cities.

DIEM AND NHU ARE REPORTED SLAIN; ARMY RULING SAIGON AFTER COUP; KENNEDY REVIEWS VIETNAM POLICY

AFTER COUP: Crowd jeers as head of a demolished statue is carted through Saigon. The head was part of a monument that was destroyed by a mob because it was thought to bear a resemblance to Mrs. Ngo Dinh Nhu. *Associated Press*

U.S. GIVES SOVIET COMPROMISE PLAN FOR WHEAT RATES

Suggests Providing Vessels for 20 to 30% of Grain at a Cost of $18 a Ton

RUSSIANS WEIGH OFFER

Approval Will End Deadlock —Bulgaria May Purchase 8 Million in Tobacco

By WILLIAM M. BLAIR

Special to The New York Times

WASHINGTON, Nov. 2—The United States has moved to break the impasse on its shipping rates that has held up sales of wheat to the Soviet Union.

A new proposal, which the Russians are understood to be considering over the weekend, would involve concessions by both sides. It includes a lowered United States cargo rate and a division of $250 million worth of wheat between American and foreign-flag vessels.

A spokesman for the Department of State denied tonight that the United States had suggested such a formula to the Russians.

The sale of up to four million tons of wheat has been blocked because United States cargo schedules have been $10 to $13 or more higher than foreign charter charges for shipments to Black Sea and Baltic ports.

Stipulation by Kennedy

President Kennedy stipulated that wheat sold to the Soviet Union and its satellites should be carried in American vessels, as available, supplemented by foreign ships.

It is understood that the United States is willing to provide a cargo rate of $18 a ton if 20 to 30 per cent of the wheat is carried in American vessels. Payment for this amount would be in dollars or gold.

The $18-a-ton rate compares with the $21 a ton recently offered by a group of tramp-ship owners to move wheat to the Soviet Union. The tramp-ship operators, whose unscheduled vessels ply between any ports where cargo is available, recently reduced their rate by $5 from $26 a ton.

Foreign Ships Would Be Used

Presumably, the remainder of the wheat purchase, 70 to 80 per cent, would be carried by foreign vessels at the world charter rate of about $12.50 a ton. This amount of wheat would be paid for through normal commercial credits of about 18 months.

The $18-a-ton figure was said to have been worked out with American tramp-ship owners, whose vessels are regarded as most suitable by wheat shippers, at an unannounced meeting earlier this week in New York. It was understood that ship representatives and officials of the Commerce Department had

Continued on Page 31, Column 1

Sports News

FOOTBALL

Army beat the Air Force yesterday before 76,660 fans at Soldier Field, Chicago.

Scores of major games:

Alabama	20	Miss St.	19
Army	14	Air Force	10
Auburn	19	Florida	0
Baylor	32	T. C. U.	13
Boston Coll.	19	Vanderbilt	6
Colgate	20	Lehigh	6
Cornell	18	Columbia	17
Georgia T.	30	Duke	6
Illinois	41	Purdue	21
Indiana	24	Minnesota	6
Miami (Fla.)	20	Kentucky	14
Michigan	27	N'western	6
Mich. St.	30	Wisconsin	13
Mississippi	37	L. S. U.	3
Navy	35	N. Dame	14
Nebraska	13	Missouri	12
N. Carolina	28	Georgia	7
N. C. St.	15	Virginia	9
Ohio St.	7	Iowa	3
Oklahoma	35	Colorado	0
Oregon St.	10	Stanford	7
Penn	7	Harvard	2
Penn St.	17	Maryland	15
Pittsburgh	35	Syracuse	27
Princeton	34	Brown	13
Rutgers	21	Boston Univ.	6
Texas	17	S. M. U.	12
Villanova	22	Holy Cross	14
Washington	22	So. Calif.	7
West Va.	20	G. Wash.	16
Yale	10	Dartmouth	6

HORSE RACING

The Axe II won the $113,700 Man o' War Stakes at Aqueduct by five lengths.

Details in Section 5.

Vatican Decides to Invite 5 Women to the Council

They Will Join Laymen's Panel Viewing Ecumenical Meeting for First Time— May Participate in This Session

By MILTON BRACKER

Special to The New York Times

ROME, Nov. 2—The Vatican has decided in principle to add five women to the list of delegates who are attending an ecumenical council for the first time.

Pope Paul VI announced Sept. 14 that qualified laymen would be permitted to attend the resumed session of Ecumenical Council Vatican II. The day after it opened, Sept. 29, the names of 10 laymen from six nations were listed.

Among them was James J. Norris of Rumson, N. J., assistant to the Most Rev. Edward E. Swanstrom, Auxiliary Bishop of New York and executive director of relief services of the National Catholic Welfare Conference. Mr. Norris has returned to the United States after having attended several Council meetings.

The precedent of adding women to the group may still be set during the present session, which is due to end Dec. 4.

Two references to the important part played by women in the organized Roman Catholic laity, and one specific demand that they be invited not only to listen but to be heard, have been made at the Council.

On Oct. 24 the Most Rev. Georges Hakim, Melchite Archbishop of Nazareth, criticized the chapter on the laity in the schema on the church for being "so silent as to the place of women in the church as to give the impression that they do not exist."

On Thursday the Right Rev. Giocondo Grotti, Prelate of Acre and Purus, Brazil, asserted that if laywomen were to be invited to the Council, they should be given an active role.

"They should be asked to talk

Continued on Page 4, Column 3

GOLDWATER WINS WIDE LEAD IN POLL

Backed in 85% of Replies by G.O.P. Leaders—Nixon and Rockefeller Far Behind

Senator Barry Goldwater of Arizona is the runaway choice in a nationwide poll of Republican Presidential preferences for 1964, taken by The Associated Press among Republican state and county leaders.

Of the 1,404 who answered a questionnaire, 1,194, or 85.1 per cent, voted Senator Goldwater the party's "strongest candidate" against President Kennedy as of today.

Fewer, however, believe that Mr. Goldwater will be nominated. Here his vote was 901, or 64.2 per cent of those who replied.

Governor Rockefeller received 56 votes as the "strongest candidate" and former Vice President Richard M. Nixon received 44.

See Nixon as Compromise

On the outlook for the nomination, Mr. Nixon had 72 votes to 65 for Mr. Rockefeller. Moreover, a sizable number of those who favor Mr. Goldwater for the nomination predicted that, if a deadlock should develop in the nominating convention, Mr. Nixon would emerge again as the candidate.

The convention, scheduled to open in San Francisco July 13, has a tentative apportionment of 1,308 delegate votes.

The survey was started early last month.

Correspondents in every state polled by mail and telephone 2,961 Republicans, including some city and town leaders. In Alaska, which has no counties, the national committeeman and committeewoman participated in the poll.

More than 47 per cent of those questioned replied. Republicans in New Jersey and Hawaii declined to participate.

The questionnaire asked opinions on two points:

"Who is the strongest potential G.O.P. candidate against

Continued on Page 46, Column 1

Last Hunting Curb Lifted by Governor

By RICHARD P. HUNT

Governor Rockefeller ended the state's forest-fire emergency yesterday by reopening the last of the woodlands and fields that had been closed because of a long autumn drought.

Sportsmen had been complaining about the ban on recreational use of open spaces in the hunting and fishing areas close to New York City. The drought was relieved by rain yesterday and Friday.

The Governor signed an order restoring the hunting season in seven Hudson Valley counties shortly after he had left a bridge-opening ceremony in Newburgh with the explanation that "a development has come up in the state."

Robert T. McManus, the Gov-

Continued on Page 55, Column 1

7 Feared Drowned As an Auto Plunges Into Harlem River

At least seven persons, including several children, were believed to have drowned early today when the car in which they were riding plunged into the Harlem River in the Bronx.

The police said there was a possibility that eight persons had died.

The only survivor was a man identified at Isias Martinez, of 366 South Second Street, Brooklyn. He apparently climbed out of the submerged car, scrambled up the pilings and walked two blocks to a tavern to telephone the police.

Mr. Martinez was taken to Lincoln Hospital and was treated for shock and submersion. The police said he was incoherent.

The accident occurred at the foot of Lincoln Avenue just south of East 132d Street in the Mott Haven section. There were no witnesses.

Grappling Is Begun

Police launches and a Coast Guard rescue craft rushed to the scene and began grappling operations.

A police helicopter hovered in the darkness over the scene. The area was lit by floodlights on shore and on the rescue vessels.

Mr. Martinez told the police that all the passengers had been returning from a wedding in the Bronx. He said the passengers had included his wife, Judith, 27 years old, and their two children, David, 9, and Dadala, 7.

He identified the other passengers as Robinson Aponte, whose address he did not know and who apparently owned the

Continued on Page 60, Column 1

TRUCE IN SAHARA REMAINS IN DOUBT AFTER NEW CLASH

Moroccans and Algerians Exchange Accusations on Breach in Figuig Area

By PETER GROSE

Special to The New York Times

FIGUIG, Morocco, Nov. 2— An Algerian artillery barrage at this border town early today appeared to have erased the cease-fire agreement between Algeria and Morocco that was to have taken effect at midnight last night.

[On the Algerian side, the cease-fire breach was laid to Morocco. After having expressed the hope that the cease-fire would be successful, Algerian officials announced that all firing along the border area near Figuig had ceased.]

Algerian forces launched the attack on Figuig, an ancient Moroccan frontier fortress, at dawn. Heavy Moroccan artillery replied from hills around the town.

Attack and Counterattack

The bombardments followed a day of attack and counterattack yesterday, during which King Hassan II of Morocco announced at one point that his forces had withdrawn from the town of 8,000.

Diplomatic observers were flown to the scene from Rabat to confirm the attack described by the King yesterday. They listened in silence to this morning's battle reports, which revive the border crisis that flared into open fighting Oct. 8.

Included in the diplomatic party at Figuig was Ya Doumbouia, Ambassador of Mali, in whose capital, Bamako, King Hassan and President Ahmed Ben Bella of Algeria signed the truce. It was then heralded as a victory for African mediation and statesmanship under the aegis of King Haile Selassie of Ethiopia. The Ambassador declined to comment on the new situation.

Algerian Tells of Attack

An Algerian captured on the outskirts of Figuig last night told interrogators that his unit had been moved into position at 11 P.M. Thursday on the heights at the edge of Algerian territory overlooking the border fort. The first Algerian attack came early yesterday.

"We were told we would occupy Figuig," the prisoner said in the presence of newsmen.

He said no orders had been issued to cease fire at the time agreed upon.

Moroccan officers and men interviewed yesterday confirmed that they had received orders to stop firing at midnight. At 11 P.M. King Hassan sent personal instructions that the truce should be observed unless the front-line units had to defend themselves.

The first technical rupture of the cease-fire came only minutes after midnight. The artillery batteries of both sides had been

Continued on Page 18, Column 3

Kennan Says Congress Impeded His Work as Envoy in Belgrade

Asserts That U.S. Must Keep Foreign Policy Separated From Domestic Politics

By MAX FRANKEL

Special to The New York Times

WASHINGTON, Nov. 2 — George F. Kennan has told Congress that he would not have become Ambassador to Yugoslavia had he known how little value the legislators would assign to his judgment.

Reflecting, for a Senate subcommittee, upon his "recent ambassadorial experience," Mr. Kennan said Congressional actions had been the "main impediments" to his performance.

He also said that he had lacked access to information about Yugoslavia in the files in Washington, and he deplored what he called the general tendency to make foreign policy "a function of domestic political convenience."

The nation has a foreign service "second to no other," he said, "and better than it has a right to expect, given the lack of appreciation and respect exhibited by the public at large for its tasks and its achievements."

Mr. Kennan, who has served the State Department and Foreign Service for more than 25 years, returned this autumn to Princeton, N. J., where he is a permanent professor in the School of Historical Studies at the Institute for Advanced Study.

A former director of the State Department's policy planning

Continued on Page 55, Column 1

Associated Press

George F. Kennan

Polish Army Drafts Priesthood Students

By PAUL UNDERWOOD

Special to The New York Times

WARSAW, Nov. 2—Poland's Communist regime has ordered students of four of the country's largest Roman Catholic seminaries to report for military service, church sources said today.

Seminarians have previously been exempt from army duty. The action was the latest in a series of moves by the Government that have soured church-state relations and threatened the uneasy truce between these two powerful forces in Polish life.

The church sources said news of the order, which affected seminaries in Warsaw, Poznan,

Continued on Page 7, Column 1

MRS. NHU SAYS U.S. WILL BEAR STIGMA

Calls Americans Responsible for Fate of Her Family— Rules Out Suicide

Text of Mrs. Nhu's statement appears on Page 24.

By JACK LANGGUTH

Special to The New York Times

BEVERLY HILLS, Calif., Nov. 2—Mrs. Ngo Dinh Nhu, pausing to wipe away tears, said today that "no one can seriously believe in the disclaimer" that the United States Government had nothing to do with the military revolt in South Vietnam.

She said that "whatever happens to my family will be an indelible stigma against the United States."

Mrs. Ngo Dinh Nhu rejected the possibility that her husband and his brother, the deposed President of South Vietnam, had committed suicide. Her husband was the President's political adviser.

She Affirms Faith

In a brief news conference on her way to an All Souls' Day mass, Mrs. Ngo Dinh Nhu read a statement that did not accept as final the reports that Ngo Dinh Nhu and Ngo Dinh Diem were dead.

But she added: "If the news is true, if really my family has been treacherously killed with either the official or unofficial blessing of the American Government, I can predict to you all that the story in Vietnam is only at its beginning."

"Any crime against the Nhu family cannot be hidden under the label of suicide," she said, noting that suicide was incompatible with the family's religion. The Nhus are Roman Catholic.

Reliable military sources in

Continued on Page 24, Column 7

Washington Expects Ties With Saigon Within Week

By HEDRICK SMITH

Special to The New York Times

WASHINGTON, Nov. 2—President Kennedy met twice today with his top national-security advisers to formulate a United States policy on establishing relations with the Provisional Government of South Vietnam.

The President canceled plans to attend the Army-Air Force football game in Chicago so he could conduct a full policy review. Officials said the action did not indicate any new crisis in Saigon.

Washington was expected to extend recognition, probably early in the week, as soon as the revolutionary rulers of South Vietnam listed a cabinet and declared their policies.

The United States Ambassador, Henry Cabot Lodge, was reported to be in contact with the military leaders who overthrew President Ngo Dinh Diem this morning, but the White House and the State Department have not officially characterized Washington's reaction to the coup.

The Administration also made no official comment on reports of the deaths of Ngo Dinh Diem and his brother, Ngo Dinh Nhu. Although some members of Congress expressed regret at this news, the Administration maintained silence.

Officials accepted reports that the Ngo brothers had died in the wake of the coup, but Washington was unable to confirm reports that they had been assassinated. It was disclosed,

Continued on Page 25, Column 1

IZVESTIA DERIDES REVOLT LEADERS

Sees U.S. Behind Coup— Asserts New Chiefs Will Be Repressive as Diem

By THEODORE SHABAD

Special to The New York Times

MOSCOW, Nov. 2—The leaders of the South Vietnamese coup d'état were derided here today as puppets of the United States.

The Soviet press was evidently pleased with what Izvestia, the Government newspaper, called the "ignoble" end of President Ngo Dinh Diem. But it foresaw no fundamental changes in the struggle between the Communist guerrillas of the Vietcong and the Government forces backed by the United States.

"Judging from Saigon dispatches and from Washington's reaction, new American puppets have come to power," Izvestia's Washington correspondent wrote.

Anti-Red Stand Scored

"They came to power because the old ones compromised themselves to such an extent in the eyes of the Vietnamese people that they no longer suited their American masters. Leaders of the coup made clear their anti-popular program in their first appeal to the armed forces, calling for continued struggle against 'Communists,' meaning the patriotic forces seeking genuine progress for their country."

A commentator of Tass, the official Soviet press agency, said that Washington had undoubtedly engineered the coup and that the decision had probably been taken soon after the return of President Kennedy's fact finders, Secretary of Defense Robert S. McNamara and Gen. Maxwell D. Taylor, chairman of the Joint Chiefs of Staff.

"But the change of scenery," said the Tass commentator, Igor Oriov, "will not slow, let alone end, the dragging and deepening crisis in South Vietnam."

Echoing a point of view expressed repeatedly in the past by the Soviet Government, he added that only a withdrawal by the United States could

Continued on Page 27, Column 2

SUICIDES DOUBTED

Deposed Chiefs Fled, Then Were Seized— Throngs Exult

By DAVID HALBERSTAM

Special to The New York Times

SAIGON, South Vietnam, Nov. 2 — President Ngo Dinh Diem and his brother, Ngo Dinh Nhu, are dead in the wake of the military uprising that ended their regime.

While the Saigon radio announced that they had committed suicide, reliable private military sources said that they had been assassinated.

With Saigon under military rule, crowds of jubilant youths set fire to the homes of government security officials, offices of government-controlled newspapers and police stations.

[The military leaders set up a Buddhist-led provisional Government with Nguyen Ngoc Tho, former Vice President, as Premier, The Associated Press reported. The recently elected National Assembly was dissolved.]

Reports on Death Conflict

The military sources that reported that the brothers had been killed said they had escaped from the palace by a tunnel shortly before marines overran it.

Later, Ngo Dinh Diem was seen in a small Roman Catholic church in Cholon, a suburb of Saigon, it was reported. The military leaders sent troops and armored cars and both men were taken prisoner.

They were placed inside an armored personnel carrier and were guarded by several soldiers, according to this account. On the way to military headquarters, an informed source said, an order was given to kill both. When the armored car arrived at headquarters both men were dead.

Military men said that both men shot themselves while in transit.

Captured After Escape

The reports that the President and his brother, considered the most powerful man in his regime, had committed suicide were received skeptically in some quarters since both were Roman Catholics. The President was considered particularly devout.

The military, denouncing what it termed the Diem Government's despotism and corruption, suspended the Constitution and ended the presidential system. Imprisoned Buddhist monks were freed.

The military coup d'état ended nine years of Ngo Dinh Diem's rule shortly before 7 A.M. when the palace was stormed by marines. Moments before this, both Ngo Dinh Diem and Ngo Dinh Nhu had told the military they were surrendering.

Continued on Page 24, Column 1

Today's Sections

Index to Subjects

Bill Bixby was visited by Ray Walston, an alien from another planet, in *My Favorite Martian.*

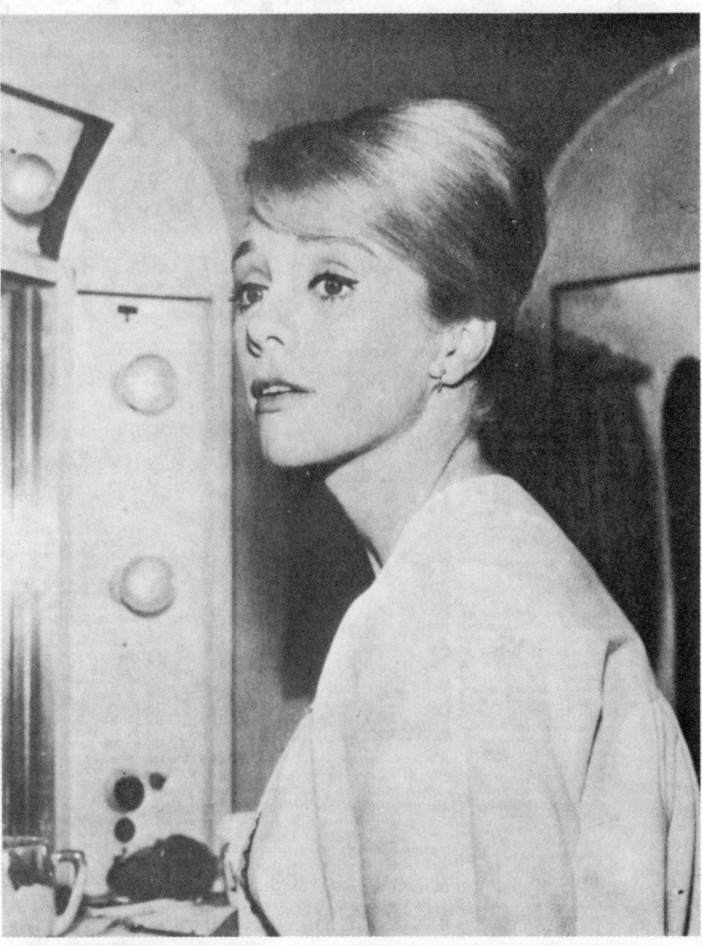

Inger Stevens starred as a Swedish farm girl who marries a Congressman in *The Farmer's Daughter.*

David Janssen was relentlessly pursued each week as the unjustly accused Dr. Richard Kimble in *The Fugitive.*

After allowing TV cameras into the Kremlin, the Soviet government protested against certain aspects of this dramatic documentary.

"All the News That's Fit to Print"

The New York Times.

LATE CITY EDITION
U. S. Weather Bureau Report (Page 58) forecasts: Cloudy, windy, chance of showers today and tonight. Cold tomorrow.
Temp. Range: 62—54; yesterday: 64—51.

VOL. CXIII..No. 38,654. NEW YORK, SATURDAY, NOVEMBER 23, 1963. TEN CENTS

KENNEDY IS KILLED BY SNIPER AS HE RIDES IN CAR IN DALLAS; JOHNSON SWORN IN ON PLANE

TEXAN ASKS UNITY

Congressional Chiefs of 2 Parties Give Promise of Aid

By FELIX BELAIR Jr.
Special to The New York Times

WASHINGTON, Nov. 22—Lyndon B. Johnson returned to a stunned capital this evening to assume the duties of the Presidency.

The new President asked for and received from Congressional leaders of both parties their "united support in the face of the tragedy which has befallen our country." He said it was "more essential than ever before that this country be united."

Partisan differences disappeared in the chorus of assurances with which the Congressional leaders responded.

Mr. Johnson was described by those who talked with him as "stunned and shaken" by the assassination of President Kennedy.

Discusses U.S. Security

But he moved quickly from problems of national security and foreign policy to funeral arrangements for Mr. Kennedy.

Across the street from the West Wing of the White House, the President conferred with officials in his old Vice Presidential offices in the Executive Office Building.

Senator George A. Smathers, Democrat of Florida, a personal friend of the dead President, was one of those who described Mr. Johnson as shaken.

"Everyone is," he added. "But the President is the more so because he was right there when the tragedy occurred."

While flying to Washington aboard the Presidential plane, Mr. Johnson arranged for a meeting with Cabinet members to ask that they remain at their posts. He made the same request of staff members in the executive office.

Meets With Harriman

"Calm and contained" was the way Senator J. W. Fulbright described the President's manner during a discussion of foreign-policy matters with Under Secretary of State W. Averell Harriman. The Arkansas Senator said the President had been working on "what looked like a statement"—presumably an assurance of continuity of the nation's foreign policy.

The new President's first conference was aboard the helicopter that flew him the 15 miles from Andrews Air Force Base

Continued on Page 11, Column 3

Henry Grossman

"This is a sad time for all people. We have suffered a loss that cannot be weighed. For me it is a deep personal tragedy. I know the world shares the sorrow that Mrs. Kennedy and her family bear. I will do my best. That is all I can do. I ask for your help —and God's."—President Lyndon Baines Johnson.

PRESIDENT'S BODY WILL LIE IN STATE

Funeral Mass to Be Monday in Capital After Homage Is Paid by the Public

By JACK RAYMOND
Special to The New York Times

WASHINGTON, Saturday, Nov. 23—The body of John F. Kennedy will lie in state in the rotunda of the Capitol tomorrow and then will be borne to St. Matthew's Roman Catholic Cathedral for a pontifical requiem mass at noon Monday.

The President's body was returned to Washington yesterday in the same Air Force jet that carried him to Texas Thursday.

The plane, with Mrs. Kennedy, the new President, Lyndon B. Johnson, and Mrs. Johnson aboard, arrived at Andrews Air Force Base at about 6 P.M.

It was announced later that Mr. Kennedy's body would lie in the East Room of the White House today from 10 A.M. to 6 P.M., during which time Government and diplomatic officials will pay their respects.

The coffin will be taken from the White House to the Capitol rotunda tomorrow morning,

Continued on Page 9, Column 3

PARTIES' OUTLOOK FOR '64 CONFUSED

Republican Prospects Rise —Johnson Faces Possible Fight Against Liberals

By WARREN WEAVER Jr.
Special to The New York Times

WASHINGTON, Nov. 22 — President Kennedy's assassination threw the American political scene into turmoil today.

It removed at a single blow the man who would have been nominated for a second term in the White House by acclamation nine months from now.

It elevated into the Presidency and the leadership of the Democratic party an older, more conservative man still emerging from his Southern heritage.

It increased immeasurably for the leaders of the Republican party prospects of electing a President next November.

The shock of the President's death stilled the official voices of politics in the capital. But so profound was the potential effect on the Government and leadership that private consideration could not be silenced.

Before, there had been facts and strong probabilities on the

Continued on Page 6, Column 3

LEFTIST ACCUSED

Figure in a Pro-Castro Group Is Charged—Policeman Slain

By GLADWIN HILL
Special to The New York Times

DALLAS, Saturday, Nov. 23—Lee Harvey Oswald, a 24-year-old warehouse worker who once lived in the Soviet Union, was charged late last night with assassinating President Kennedy.

Oswald was arrested at 2:15 yesterday afternoon, nearly two hours after the assassination of the President, as the suspected killer of a policeman on the street in the Oak Cliff district, three miles from where the President was shot.

Chief of Police Jesse Curry announced that Oswald had been formally arraigned at 1:40 A.M., Central standard time, today on a charge of murder in the President's death. The arraignment was made before a justice of the peace in the homicide bureau at Police Headquarters.

Capt. Will Fritz, head of the homicide bureau, identified Oswald as an adherent of the left-wing "Fair Play for Cuba Committee." But there were also reports that Oswald, apparently politically erratic, had once tried to join anti-Castro forces.

Worked in Warehouse

Oswald was employed in the Texas School Book Depository, the warehouse from which the fatal shots were fired at the President's car.

The police said at least six witnesses placed Oswald in the building at the time of the assassination.

One was quoted as saying that Oswald had stayed behind on an upper floor when other employes went down to the street to see Mr. Kennedy pass by.

The defendant's only comment, shouted at reporters as he was led handcuffed through a police building corridor to be questioned, was "I haven't shot anybody." "He has not con-

Continued on Page 4, Column 1

Henry Grossman

John Fitzgerald Kennedy
1917-1963

Why America Weeps

Kennedy Victim of Violent Streak He Sought to Curb in the Nation

By JAMES RESTON
Special to The New York Times

WASHINGTON, Nov. 22—America wept tonight, not alone for its dead young President, but for itself. The grief was general, for somehow the worst in the nation had prevailed over the best. The indictment extended beyond the assassin, for something in the nation itself, some strain of madness and violence, had destroyed the highest symbol of law and order.

Speaker John McCormack, now 71 and, by the peculiarities of our politics, next in line of succession after the Vice President, expressed this sense of national dismay and self-criticism:

"My God! My God! What are we coming to?"

The irony of the President's death is that his short Administration was devoted almost entirely to various attempts to curb this very streak of violence in the American character.

When the historians get around to assessing his three years in office, it is very likely that they will be impressed with just this: his efforts to restrain those who wanted to be more violent in the cold war overseas

Continued on Page 7, Column 6

City Goes Dark

By ROBERT C. DOTY

Shock and sorrow for the murdered President darkened and silenced midtown Manhattan last night.

In early afternoon, when the first radio and television bulletins carried the news, the city began its mourning. By nightfall, the normal quick Friday night pace had slowed as near to a halt as it ever comes.

Many of the city's normal weekend commercial, social and sporting activities were canceled. Decisions for closings by many stores and other businesses were being debated.

Courts closed in the middle of hearings yesterday. Hundreds of public and private social functions and sporting events were interrupted or postponed. Most midtown legitimate and motion picture theaters, night clubs and dance halls locked

Continued on Page 5, Column 2

Gov. Connally Shot; Mrs. Kennedy Safe

President Is Struck Down by a Rifle Shot From Building on Motorcade Route—Johnson, Riding Behind, Is Unhurt

By TOM WICKER
Special to The New York Times

DALLAS, Nov. 22—President John Fitzgerald Kennedy was shot and killed by an assassin today.

He died of a wound in the brain caused by a rifle bullet that was fired at him as he was riding through downtown Dallas in a motorcade.

Vice President Lyndon Baines Johnson, who was riding in the third car behind Mr. Kennedy's, was sworn in as the 36th President of the United States 99 minutes after Mr. Kennedy's death.

Mr. Johnson is 55 years old; Mr. Kennedy was 46.

Shortly after the assassination, Lee H. Oswald, who once defected to the Soviet Union and who has been active in the Fair Play for Cuba Committee, was arrested by the Dallas police. Tonight he was accused of the killing.

Suspect Captured After Scuffle

Oswald, 24 years old, was also accused of slaying a policeman who had approached him in the street. Oswald was subdued after a scuffle with a second policeman in a nearby theater.

President Kennedy was shot at 12:30 P.M., Central standard time (1:30 P.M., New York time). He was pronounced dead at 1 P.M. and Mr. Johnson was sworn in at 2:39 P.M.

Mr. Johnson, who was uninjured in the shooting, took his oath in the Presidential jet plane as it stood on the runway at Love Field. The body of Mr. Kennedy was aboard. Immediately after the oath-taking, the plane took off for Washington.

Standing beside the new President as Mr. Johnson took the oath of office was Mrs. John F. Kennedy. Her stockings were spattered with her husband's blood.

Gov. John B. Connally Jr. of Texas, who was riding in the same car with Mr. Kennedy, was severely wounded in the chest, ribs and arm. His condition was serious, but not critical.

The killer fired the rifle from a building just off the motorcade route. Mr. Kennedy,

Continued on Page 2

Capt. Cecil Stoughton via United Press International

THE NEW PRESIDENT: Lyndon B. Johnson takes oath before Judge Sarah T. Hughes in plane at Dallas. Mrs. Kennedy and Representative Jack Brooks are at right. To left are Mrs. Johnson and Representative Albert Thomas.

Associated Press

WHEN THE BULLETS STRUCK: Mrs. Kennedy moving to the aid of the President after he was hit by a sniper yesterday in Dallas. A guard mounts rear bumper. Gov. John B. Connally Jr. of Texas, also in the car, was wounded.

Jack Ruby seen firing the fatal shot into Lee Harvey Oswald, accused assassin of President Kennedy.

The surviving brothers of John Kennedy escorted his widow at the funeral.

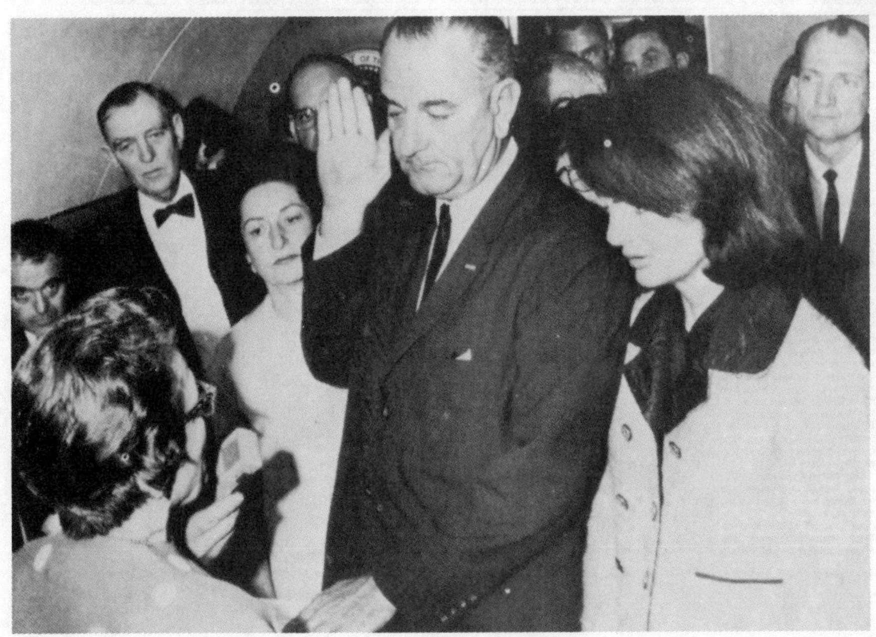

Lyndon Johnson took his oath of office from District Judge Sarah Hughes on *Air Force One.* He is seen here with Lady Bird on his right and Jacqueline Kennedy at his left.

"All the News That's Fit to Print"

The New York Times.

LATE CITY EDITION
U. S. Weather Bureau Report (Page 38) forecasts: Sunny and cool today; fair, milder tonight. Cloudy, milder tomorrow.
Temp. Range: 46–32; yesterday: 53–37.

VOL. CXIII..No. 38,656. NEW YORK, MONDAY, NOVEMBER 25, 1963. + TEN CENTS

PRESIDENT'S ASSASSIN SHOT TO DEATH IN JAIL CORRIDOR BY A DALLAS CITIZEN; GRIEVING THRONGS VIEW KENNEDY BIER

Associated Press Wirephoto

FAREWELL: Kneeling with her mother at John Fitzgerald Kennedy's coffin in the Capitol, Caroline touches the flag

CROWD IS HUSHED

Mourners at Capitol File Past the Coffin Far Into the Night

Texts of eulogies spoken in Washington, Page 4.

By TOM WICKER
Special to The New York Times

WASHINGTON, Monday, Nov. 25—Thousands of sorrowing Americans filed past John Fitzgerald Kennedy's bier in the Great Rotunda of the United States Capitol yesterday and early today.

Mr. Kennedy's body lay in state in the center of the vast, stone-floored chamber. Long after midnight the silent procession of mourners continued.

Some wept. All were hushed. As the two lines moved in a large circle around either side of the flag-covered coffin, almost the only sounds were the shuffle of feet and the quiet voices of policemen urging the people to "keep moving, keep moving right along."

By 2:45 A. M. today 115,000 persons had passed the bier.

Yesterday afternoon a crowd estimated at 300,000 lined Pennsylvania and Constitution Avenues to watch the passage of the caisson bearing the body of the 35th President of the United States, slain in the 47th year of his life by an assassin's bullet.

A Riderless Horse

Behind the caisson, following military tradition, came a riderless bay gelding, with a pair of military boots reversed in the silver stirrups.

The horse was Sardar, the thoroughbred that belongs to Mrs. John F. Kennedy.

Mrs. Kennedy, her two children, President and Mrs. Johnson and Mr. Kennedy's brother, Attorney General Robert F. Kennedy, rode in the first car of a 10-car procession that followed the caisson.

The procession moved at a funeral pace, to the sound of muffled drums, from the White House to Pennsylvania Avenue. It was a journey Mr. Kennedy had made formally four times.

At the Capitol, brief ceremonies of eulogy were held in the Rotunda before the admission of the waiting thousands who swarmed over the plaza and stretched in a long line up East Capitol Street.

At the conclusion of the cere-

Continued on Page 2, Column 1

World's Leaders to Attend Requiem Today in Capital

Mrs. Kennedy Will Walk Behind the Caisson to Mass at Cathedral

By JACK RAYMOND
Special to The New York Times

WASHINGTON, Nov. 24 — Mrs. John F. Kennedy, joined by world and national leaders, will walk behind the horse-drawn caisson that bears her husband's body from the White House to St. Matthew's Roman Catholic Cathedral tomorrow.

Following a requiem mass, John Fitzgerald Kennedy, the 35th President of the United States, will be escorted in a solemn state procession to Arlington National Cemetery to be buried with military honors.

The gravesite, on a beautiful grassy knoll, provides a sweeping view of the capital city and it is itself easily in view from the Memorial Bridge approach to the national burial ground.

The state funeral procession will begin at 10:30 A.M. at the Capitol, where the closed, flag-draped coffin of the President

Continued on Page 6, Column 8

Officials of Nearly 100 Lands in U.S.—They Will Meet Johnson

By MAX FRANKEL
Special to The New York Times

WASHINGTON, Nov. 24 — An emperor, a king, a queen, princes, presidents, premiers and ministers from every continent converged on Washington this evening to pay final tribute to

List of leaders expected at the funeral, Page 6.

President Kennedy and to make the acquaintance of President Johnson.

Representing nearly 100 nations, the foreign dignitaries will include the largest assembly of ruling statesmen ever gathered in the United States for any event.

Their arrival here, through the night, virtually overwhelmed an already tense and overburdened capital. Nonetheless, each visitor received the protocol deference and police protection of more normal

Continued on Page 6, Column 1

ONE BULLET FIRED

Night-Club Man Who Admired Kennedy Is Oswald's Slayer

By GLADWIN HILL
Special to The New York Times

DALLAS, Nov. 24 — President Kennedy's assassin, Lee Harvey Oswald, was fatally shot by a Dallas night-club operator today as the police started to move him from the city jail to the county jail.

The shooting occurred in the basement of the municipal building at about 11:20 A.M. central standard time (12:20 P.M. New York time).

The assailant, Jack Rubenstein, known as Jack Ruby, lunged from a cluster of newsmen observing the transfer of Oswald from the jail to an armored truck.

Millions of viewers saw the shooting on television.

As the shot rang out, a police detective suddenly recognized Ruby and exclaimed: "Jack, you son of a bitch!"

A murder charge was filed against Ruby by Assistant District Attorney William F. Alexander. Justice of the Peace Pierce McBride ordered him held without bail.

Detectives Flank Him

Oswald was arrested Friday after Mr. Kennedy was shot dead while riding through Dallas in an open car. He was charged with murdering the President and a policeman who was shot a short time later while trying to question Oswald.

As the 24-year-old prisoner, flanked by two detectives, stepped onto a basement garage ramp, Ruby thrust a .38-caliber, snub-nose revolver into Oswald's left side and fired a single shot.

The 52-year-old night-club operator, an ardent admirer of President Kennedy and his family, was described as having been distraught.

[District Attorney Henry Wade said he understood that the police were looking into the possibility that Oswald had been slain to prevent him from talking, The Associated Press reported. Mr. Wade said that so far no connection between Oswald and Ruby had been established.]

Oswald slumped to the concrete paving, wordlessly clutching his side and writhing with pain.

Oswald apparently lost con-

Continued on Page 10, Column 1

Mrs. Kennedy Leads Public Mourning

By MARJORIE HUNTER
Special to The New York Times

WASHINGTON, Nov. 24 — Mrs. John F. Kennedy, firmly holding the hands of her two children, followed the coffin bearing the body of her husband as it left the White House today for the last time.

Her eyes swollen, she moved quietly to the edge of the steps of the North Portico and paused to watch the coffin placed in the caisson by military bearers.

Her son, John Jr., tugged at her hand and pointed to a black, riderless horse, part of the ceremonial procession. She leaned down and spoke to him.

Mrs. Kennedy wore a simple black suit and black lace mantilla. John Jr., who will be 3 years old tomorrow, and Caroline, who will be 6 on Wednesday, wore similar pale blue coats, white anklets and red shoes.

As the three stood there, framed against the black-draped doorway, there was an eerie silence. It was broken only by the occasional sound of hoofs of the restless gray horses that were to pull the caisson up Pennsylvania Avenue to the Capitol.

Mrs. Kennedy was composed, but appeared to be on the verge of tears as she and the children stepped into a black limousine for the slow ride to the Capitol. In the car, too, were President and Mrs. Johnson and Attorney General Robert F. Kennedy.

Still holding the hands of her children, Mrs. Kennedy followed the flag-draped coffin into the Capitol Rotunda. She stared straight ahead as the coffin was placed on the catafalque, a simple funeral bier draped in black broadcloth.

John Jr., wide-eyed and bewildered, was restless. Clutching a tiny flag, he was led away by a military aide.

Later, after the tributes had been spoken, Mrs. Kennedy walked slowly to the coffin, touched it with her fingertips, knelt and kissed it. Caroline was by her side. They were rejoined by John Jr. at the door.

Shortly after 9 o'clock tonight Mrs. Kennedy returned to the Capitol and again kneeled before the coffin and kissed it.

Mrs. Kennedy walked into the Rotunda on the arm of her husband's brother, Robert, who stopped at the rope holding

Continued on Page 2, Column 3

JOHNSON AFFIRMS AIMS IN VIETNAM

Retains Kennedy's Policy of Aiding War on Reds—Lodge Briefs President

By E. W. KENWORTHY
Special to The New York Times

WASHINGTON, Nov. 24 — President Johnson reaffirmed today the policy objectives of his predecessor regarding South Vietnam. He called upon all Government agencies to support that policy with full unity of purpose.

This was disclosed by White House sources after a meeting between President Johnson and Henry Cabot Lodge, United States Ambassador to South Vietnam.

The meeting lasted nearly an hour. It was described as being devoted to a full review of the conclusions reached by participants in a strategy conference on South Vietnam held in Honolulu last Wednesday.

In another move today that emphasized the President's desire to convey at home and abroad the impression of continuity, Mr. Johnson asked all members of the White House staff to remain at their jobs.

This was announced by Pierre Salinger, White House press secretary.

Some Expected to Leave

Mr. Salinger said the President would leave up to the officials involved how long they wished to serve him.

Inevitably some of these officials — especially those from the universities and foundations — will decide to leave their posts after an interval.

But the President's request today would seem to insure that during the difficult days of adjustment and transition he would continue to have the benefit of the experience of key policy figures.

Attending the meeting between the President and Ambassador Lodge today were Secretary of State Dean Rusk, Secretary of Defense Robert S. McNamara, Under Secretary of State George W. Ball, John A. McCone, director of the Central Intelligence Agency, and McGeorge Bundy, special assistant to the President for national security affairs.

Secretaries Rusk and McNamara, Ambassador Lodge and Mr. Bundy all took part in the Honolulu conference.

As a result of the meeting, White House informants said, President Johnson laid down a

Continued on Page 5, Column 1

Millions of Viewers See Oswald Killing On 2 TV Networks

By JACK GOULD

The fatal shooting of Lee H. Oswald, who was held as the assassin of President Kennedy, was seen as it occurred yesterday by millions of television viewers.

The National Broadcasting Company telecast the dramatic happening live. Less than a minute later the Columbia Broadcasting System telecast it by means of tape, made as the shooting occurred.

C. B. S. headquarters recorded the pictures from Dallas as they were received here over a closed circuit. Officials, upon seeing the contents of the Dallas relay, put the tape out over the network instantly.

The incident marked the first time in 15 years of television around the globe that a real-life homicide had occurred in front of live cameras. The closest parallel occurred in October, 1960, when Inejiro Asanuma, Japanese political leader, was knifed on a public stage in

Continued on Page 10, Column 8

JOHNSON SPURS OSWALD INQUIRY

President Orders F. B. I. to Check Death—Handling of Case Worries Capital

By ANTHONY LEWIS
Special to The New York Times

WASHINGTON, Nov. 24—President Johnson directed the Federal Bureau of Investigation tonight to look into "every aspect" of the murder of Lee H. Oswald.

He spoke with the director of the F.B.I., J. Edgar Hoover, and ordered the redoubled investigation.

The action came as official Washington was showing increasing concern about the entire handling of the aftermath of President Kennedy's assassination.

Officials were convinced that Oswald was the assassin. But their concern was over the public impression of the criminal proceedings.

Tonight they were consider-

Continued on Page 11, Column 3

BUSINESS OF CITY WILL HALT TODAY

Mayor Says Only Essential Services Will Be Provided

Changes in events here are listed on Page 9.

By LEONARD INGALLS

Normal public, business and social activity in the city will be almost completely suspended today out of respect for President Kennedy.

Mayor Wagner announced yesterday that the city would continue in full mourning throughout the day. Only essential city services will be maintained, he said.

"Those city employes not engaged in activities imperative to the health, safety and welfare of our citizens are to be released from duty and their offices closed through Monday," Mr. Wagner said at City Hall.

Proclamation of the day as a legal holiday by Governor Rockefeller in observance of Mr. Kennedy's funeral permits banks and other institutions to close.

Classes at schools and colleges will be suspended. Department stores and specialty shops will be shut. Securities exchanges and commodity markets will not operate. Most places of entertainment will be closed. There will be no deliveries of mail and post offices will be shut.

Special memorial services for the murdered President have been scheduled at churches and synagogues.

At St. Patrick's Cathedral

Continued on Page 9, Column 1

Pope Paul Warns That Hate and Evil Imperil Civil Order

Special to The New York Times

ROME, Nov. 24 — Pope Paul VI, alluding to the assassination of President Kennedy, said today that it showed how much "capacity for hatred and evil still remains in the world."

Without mentioning Mr. Kennedy by name, the Pontiff spoke of "the crime that has aroused in these days the deploration of the whole world." He said it illustrated "how great the threat to civil order and peace still is."

The Pope was addressing thousands of people gathered in St. Peter's Square for his usual Sunday-noon benediction.

"We cannot, at this moment of prayer together, take our thoughts from the crime that has aroused in these days the deploration of the whole world," he said.

"After dwelling upon the man who is no longer with us and after comforting those who still live in mourning and grief, our thoughts show us how much the capacity for hatred and evil yet remains in the world, how great the threat to civil order and peace still is, and how great is the need for the grace

Continued on Page 4, Column 7

NEWS INDEX

News Summary and Index, Page 21

JOHNSON SCORED BY CHINESE REDS

Views Called 'Reactionary' —Taiwan Aid Attacked

By United Press International

TOKYO, Nov. 24—Communist China bitterly criticized President Johnson today and termed him a supporter of the late President Kennedy's "trickery policy."

"Since the emergence of the Kennedy regime," the Chinese Communist press agency Hsinhua said, "Johnson has positively supported various reactionary policies of the Kennedy Administration and participated in formulating and promoting such policies.

"Johnson has supported Kennedy's trickery policy and has called for the maintenance of such a policy in a series of his speeches."

The Chinese Communists reported the assassination of President Kennedy in a four-paragraph dispatch eight hours after it occurred. But they made no comment.

Hsinhua said Mr. Johnson "was one of the central figures in the Kennedy Government and has made frequent trips abroad."

The Chinese statement added that Mr. Johnson believed "the United States, in making two-faced antirevolutionary plots, must maintain a strong position on the basis of strong force."

"He also looks toward Cuba with animosity and has called for the elimination of the Cuban revolutionary Government," it

Continued on Page 7, Column 8

Copyright 1963—Dallas Times-Herald and Photographer Bob Jackson, from United Press International Telephoto

OSWALD IS SHOT: Lee Harvey Oswald cringes as Jack Ruby attacks him at Dallas jail. Policeman is J. R. Leavelle.

1964

1964

Paul McCartney in a scene from *A Hard Day's Night*, the Beatles' first film.

Julie Andrews with Dick Van Dyke, Karen Dotrice and Matthew Garber in Walt Disney's *Mary Poppins.*

Rex Harrison and Audrey Hepburn in an early scene from *My Fair Lady.*

"All the News That's Fit to Print"

NEWS SUMMARY AND INDEX, PAGE 95

The New York Times.

LATE CITY EDITION

U. S. Weather Bureau Report (Page 96) forecasts: Sunny today. Fair tonight and tomorrow. Temp. Range: 47–33; yesterday: 46–37.

SECTION ONE

VOL. CXIII—No. 38,697. NEW YORK, SUNDAY, JANUARY 5, 1964. THIRTY CENTS

50c beyond 50-mile zone from New York City, except on Long Island. Higher in air delivery cities.

POPE ACCLAIMED IN HOLY LAND; SURGING CROWDS SURROUND HIM AS HE FOLLOWS PATH OF JESUS

CITY RIGHTS UNITS TO START BOYCOTT OF SCHOOLS FEB. 3

N.A.A.C.P. Charges Board Has Failed to Produce a Plan for Integration

GROSS CALLS MEETING

But Negro Leader Asserts Discussion Tomorrow Will Not Affect Protest

By GENE CURRIVAN

A boycott of the New York City school system will be started Feb. 3—the day the new term begins—by civil rights groups that are dissatisfied with the Board of Education's integration efforts.

This was announced yesterday by representatives of the National Association for the Advancement of Colored People, who charged that the board had broken an agreement under which a boycott was suspended last September.

At a press conference at the Henry Hudson Hotel, 353 West 57th Street, Frederick Jones, education chairman of the State Conference of N.A.A.C.P. Branches, said the boycott would be carried out with the cooperation of the Citywide Committee for School Integration, which includes the N.A.A.C.P., the Congress of Racial Equality and two large parents' groups.

He said "freedom schools" would be set up in churches to take care of the children.

Will Attend Meeting

Mr. Jones said he would attend a meeting called for tomorrow in the offices of Dr. Calvin E. Gross, the Superintendent of Schools, to discuss the school integration plan. But, he added, this will not alter the boycott plans.

The Rev. Milton A. Galamison, chairman of the citywide committee, a coordinating agency for the independent groups, said he would not attend the meeting but he left individual members free to make their own decisions.

Miss June Shagaloff, special assistant for education for the N.A.A.C.P., said the organization's position was that the board had made no commitment on integration and was attempting to shift the responsibility to the Negro parents.

This was an allusion to the board's free-choice transfer plan, under which parents elect

Continued on Page 66, Column 1

AUBURN U. CALM AS NEGRO ENTERS

Troopers Provide Protection at School in Alabama

By JOHN HERBERS
Special to The New York Times

AUBURN, Ala., Jan. 4—Auburn University peacefully enrolled its first Negro student today.

Harold Alonzo Franklin, 31 years old, registered for graduate school and was assigned a room in Magnolia Hall, where he will live among some of the 10,000 white students who attend the university.

State troopers, who had previously been a symbol of Gov. George C. Wallace's defiance of the Federal courts, provided protection for the court-ordered registration.

The troopers, wearing felt hats instead of the riot helmets they wore at Birmingham and Tuscaloosa, were stationed at all entrances to the campus. They admitted only students, faculty and employes who showed identification cards.

Mr. Franklin was driven to the campus by a university official at 2:20 P.M. Central standard time and walked to the library to register.

A light rain was falling and about 200 students lined the sidewalk in front of the building, many of them under umbrellas. Troopers stood at all entrances.

A number of students jeered and laughed as Mr. Franklin approached, bare-headed and wearing a dark gray raincoat.

"Boo, nigger!" one of them shouted.

"I bet the nigger won't have

Continued on Page 64, Column 3

Schools Here Draft A 'Saturation' Plan For Negro Areas

By FRED M. HECHINGER

Dr. Calvin E. Gross, Superintendent of the city's schools, is evolving plans for a "saturation program" to overcome educational deficiencies in areas of slums and racial imbalance.

The program has been the subject of a series of unpublicized high-level staff meetings since Dr. Gross's appointment to his post almost a year ago. It will incorporate the nation's most successful educational experiments, including the use of team-teaching, team mothers and small-group instruction.

Those who have been discussing the program are fully aware that it may be attacked by some civil rights groups as an attempt to create a Northern version of the "separate but equal" doctrine.

Dr. Gross, however, insists that a saturation approach would offer superior schooling to children in the non-white slums and would be the

Continued on Page 67, Column 1

DRAFT PHYSICALS TO BE GIVEN AT 18

Johnson Orders Program to Correct Defects in Youths Registering for Service

By The Associated Press

JOHNSON CITY, Tex., Jan. 4—President Johnson ordered a new effort today to correct physical and mental flaws found among young men eligible for military service.

He directed, starting July 1, that most men reaching the draft-registration age of 18 be given physical and mental tests. He said that those who fail would be allowed to enter new, voluntary rehabilitation programs.

Such examinations of potential draftees are not given now until the age of 22 or 23.

The President acted because of the high percentage of rejections of draftees because of health and mental and educational incapacity.

"This will be the most important human salvage program in the history of our country," Secretary of Labor W. Willard Wirtz said.

Report on Manpower

The President released a report on manpower conservation with the comment that it disclosed "a situation more serious and more extensive than has been our understanding."

[In New York, a separate report showed that the rate of draftees rejected in the city for psychiatric reasons was three times greater than the national rate.]

The national report estimated that one-third of all young men in the United States reaching 18 years of age would be found unqualified for induction into the armed forces, about half being rejected for medical reasons and the remainder failing mental tests.

The report said that the majority of those disqualified appeared to be the victims of inadequate education and insufficient health services.

Congress to Get Plea

"The findings of the task force are dramatic evidence that poverty is still with us, still exacting its price in spoiled lives and failed examinations," the President said in a statement accompanying the report. "For entirely too many Americans the promise of American life is not being kept. In a nation as rich and productive as ours this is an intolerable situation."

Mr. Johnson said that he would shortly present to Congress a program designed "to attack the roots of poverty in our cities and rural areas."

Meanwhile, the President gave two orders, effective July 1, designed to discover job training and education deficiencies as soon as possible and correct many of them.

The Department of Defense and the Selective Service System were directed to give physical and mental examinations to most youths reaching 18, as soon as possible after registration for the draft. Most youths eligible for military service are not examined now until they are 22 or 23 years of age. The President stressed that early

Continued on Page 42, Column 3

PENTAGON PLANS TO SLOW BUILD-UP OF ATOM WEAPONS

New Budget to Reflect Cut—Step Seen as Concession to Theory of 'Overkill'

By JACK RAYMOND
Special to The New York Times

WASHINGTON, Jan. 4—The Administration is cutting back the pace of this country's build-up of strategic nuclear weapons. The move is viewed as a significant concession to the controversial "overkill" theory.

According to this theory, the United States, at unnecessarily high cost, has been building an arsenal of long-range nuclear weapons that could be used only by hitting the same targets several times over.

The Administration in the past has tended to reject this claim. But official sources made clear today that the next defense budget would reveal a slackened pace in strategic weapons investment.

Secretary of Defense Robert S. McNamara has come to the conclusion that any further investment would bring diminishing returns and would not significantly alter the defense picture.

$51 Billion in Spending

The defense spending budget for the next fiscal year, beginning July 1, will total about $51 billion, Administration officials have said. They point out that this would be a billion-dollar reduction from current spending.

More significantly, it is said, the Administration plans to ask Congress for about $51 billion in new appropriations, about $3 billion less than asked last year.

The effect of this lower request will make itself felt in years to come. It is the result largely of limits placed on planned strategic weapons systems.

For example, when President Kennedy took office in 1961, he and Secretary McNamara accelerated the installation of intercontinental ballistic missiles and the construction of Polaris missile submarines.

Estimates Are Cut

This was in the period immediately following widely publicized charges that there was a "missile gap" with the United States behind the Soviet Union. The gap never developed.

The change in attitude was reflected in a decision in recent weeks to add 50 Minuteman missiles, for a total of 1,000 in the coming fiscal period, instead of 150 as the Air Force requested.

Mr. McNamara believes an eventual total of 1,200 Minuteman missiles will be enough. The Air Force has recommended 1,850.

Similarly, the Navy's request for money for more than the six Polaris submarines scheduled this year was also turned down.

In decelerating the invest-

Continued on Page 45, Column 1

HISTORIC MEETING

Patriarchs Greet Paul, Ending 500 Years of East-West Coolness

Texts of Pope's discourses to Orthodox leaders, Page 27.

By The Associated Press

JERUSALEM (Jordanian sector), Jan. 4—The first encounter in five centuries between a Roman Catholic Pope and a Patriarch of the Eastern Orthodox Church took place tonight on the Mount of Olives—not far from the Garden of Gethsemane, where Christ prayed before His crucifixion.

Pope Paul VI, wearied after his tumultuous reception in the Holy City, first received Orthodox Patriarch Benedictos of Jerusalem. It was the first contact at this level since all formal relations between the two churches broke down in the 15th century after hundreds of years of schisms and feuding.

The Pope also received His Beatitude Yeguishe Derderian, Armenian Orthodox Patriarch of Jerusalem.

New Listing of Churches

"Our meeting," said the Pontiff, "has a particular significance because of the friendly ties which have developed between us and the Armenian Church through the delegated observers who participated in the work of the Second Vatican Council."

He urged Orthodox leaders and faithful to "forget what is past and push on to what lies ahead."

Praising united care of the holy places, he said, "We salute these expressions of Christian charity which already exist, and we express the earnest desire that they may multiply and expand into every area of our common Christian endeavor."

His first meeting was with Patriarch Benedictos. The Pontiff and the bearded, slenderly built Patriarch met for half an hour in the papal quarters at the headquarters of the Roman Catholic delegation. Later the Pope returned the visit at Galalia, the Patriarch's summer residence, 500 yards away across the Mount of Olives.

The meeting preceded by 24 hours a call scheduled to be paid on the Pope tomorrow by Ecumenical Patriarch Athenagoras I of Constantinople (Istanbul), spiritual leader of the Eastern Orthodox Church. The Ecumenical Patriarch will fly

Continued on Page 27, Column 1

Rockefeller Rebuts Goldwater; Senator Scorns Call to Debate

Governor Presses Drive

By WARREN WEAVER Jr.
Special to The New York Times

CONCORD, N. H., Jan. 4—Governor Rockefeller rejected today Senator Barry Goldwater's assertion that he would be politically indistinguishable from a Democrat in the Presidential election.

The Governor was asked at a news conference here whether the Senator was not attempting to depict him as a "me too" candidate for President. Mr. Goldwater, who announced yesterday that he would seek the Republican nomination, contends that his own candidacy would offer the voters in November "a choice, not an echo."

Mr. Rockefeller, who will face the Senator March 10 in the Republican Presidential primary in New Hampshire, told his news conference:

"I don't think that 'me too' label has any application, either to the Democratic party here or on the national level. There are fundamental differences between my views and their [the Democrats'] views.

"I think that was just a political statement on his [Mr. Goldwater's] part, and I have complete confidence that the Ameri-

Continued on Page 47, Column 1

Arizonan Attacks Again

By The Associated Press

LOS ANGELES, Jan. 4—Senator Barry Goldwater said today that Governor Rockefeller was more a Democrat than a Republican.

The conservative Arizona Senator, stopping here on his way back to Washington from Phoenix, Ariz., said he saw no sense in the face-to-face debates proposed by the New York Governor, the only other announced candidate for the Republican Presidential nomination.

"I'd rather take on President Johnson on the weaknesses of his Administration," Mr. Goldwater said.

He said in an interview at the airport here that Mr. Rockefeller advocated policies more in keeping with the Democratic platform than with Republican principles.

Mr. Goldwater, who entered the race for the Republican nomination yesterday, said the nation should have a clear choice of philosophies. But he said of Governor Rockefeller: "Debating him would be more like debating a member of the New Frontier than like debating another Republican."

Mr. Goldwater said that if he

Continued on Page 46, Column 4

Associated Press Radiophoto

VISIT TO SHRINE: Pope Paul VI, surrounded by Orthodox and Roman Catholic prelates, leaves tomb at Church of the Sepulcher, where, according to tradition, Jesus was buried.

WEST BERLIN ASKS NEW PASS ACCORD

East Germany Is Expected to Close Border Today as 18 Days of Visits End

By ARTHUR J. OLSEN
Special to The New York Times

BERLIN, Jan. 4—The West Berlin Government proposed to East Germany today a liberalized agreement for movement of Berliners across the Communist-built wall that divides the city.

Egon Bahr, a spokesman for Mayor Willy Brandt, said prospects for a new agreement were "about 50-50."

It appears definite now that the wall will be closed against West Berliners at midnight tomorrow, at least for some weeks.

While it remains possible that the East German authorities may extend the expiration date past Jan. 5, there is no sign of such a move.

The proposal for a new accord was delivered to East Germany's Deputy Minister of Culture, Erich Wendt, by Horst Korber, an official of the West Berlin government.

New Flood of Crossings

These two middle-level officials negotiated the Dec. 17 agreement for Christmas visits by West Berliners to relatives in the East.

Today West Berliners, taking last-minute advantage of this breach in the 29-month-old wall, streamed into East Berlin in record numbers on foot, by automobile and by elevated railway.

The total of visitors today approached 250,000. Another 300,000 are expected to cross tomorrow, bringing the total of crossings to 1.2 million in the 18 days of the pass agreement.

The number greatly exceeds the expectations of the East Germans, who have struggled earnestly and in general effectively to speed the processing of huge numbers of West Berliners at the crossing points.

Today, faced with nearly twice as many visitors as on any previous day, East German border guards rushed West Berliners past the wall in the

Continued on Page 8, Column 5

Pontiff, in Tears, Offers Prayers at Jesus' Tomb

By The Associated Press

JERUSALEM (Jordanian Sector), Jan. 4—Pope Paul VI, with crowds around him, prayed in tears today in the Church of the Holy Sepulcher. The church stands above the traditional site of the tomb of Jesus.

Once disaster threatened. Fire broke out high in the church as the Pope was saying mass. The flames were soon extinguished, and he went on, unheeding. But earlier, tears showed on his cheeks in the course of his first mass of the Holy Land pilgrimage.

The blaze was in two connected cables supplying power for television lights and cameras recording the historic moment.

Foot-long tongues of flame licked out for a few minutes 30 feet up scaffolding erected for restoration of the church.

A man climbed the scaffolding and a soldier handed up his Bedouin headdress for an attempt to beat out the flames. That was unsuccessful. Lights went out, then a soldier handed the man a stick and he poked the cables apart, extinguishing the blaze.

Those close to the altar said Pope Paul never interrupted the mass during the episode, although the crowd of worshipers murmured and looked up. Only

Continued on Page 27, Column 2

Rise in Red Arms To Vietnam Is Seen

By HEDRICK SMITH
Special to The New York Times

SAIGON, South Vietnam, Jan. 4—A high-level United States military spokesman reported today a "measurable increase" in Communist-bloc arms shipments into South Vietnam during the last six months.

Other well-informed military sources estimated that roughly three-quarters of these contraband shipments were moving through normal commercial channels into neighboring Cambodia and then down the Mekong River into South Vietnam.

These sources said weapons, ammunition and explosives were being shipped in Communist-bloc vessels from Chinese or North Vietnamese ports to Si-

Continued on Page 3, Column 1

PAUL VI CROSSES BORDER TO ISRAEL

Leaves Jordan After Drive of 67 Miles to Frontier Under Heavy Guard

By The Associated Press

JERUSALEM (Jordanian Sector), Sunday, Jan. 5—Pope Paul VI crossed into Israel from Jordan this morning on the second day of his historic three-day pilgrimage to the Holy Land.

He arrived at the border at 8:25 A.M. (1:25 A.M. Eastern standard time) and crossed into Israel at 8:56 A.M.

The Pontiff, scheduled to arrive at Megiddo, three miles from the border, for a welcoming ceremony at 8:40 A.M., was running 16 minutes behind schedule when he crossed the frontier.

Delayed at Frontier

He arrived at the border accompanied by a heavy Jordanian guard after a 67-mile drive from Jerusalem that took one hour and 23 minutes.

There was a delay at the border while journalists accompanying the Pope transferred to Israeli vehicles. The Pontiff remained in his limousine.

Part of the delay was caused by customs and immigration formalities, which had been cut to a minimum for the Pope and his entourage.

The Pontiff was greeted at the border by the Israeli Chief of Protocol and the Christian Affairs Chief of the Foreign Ministry.

The papal convoy pulled away from the Pope's quarters in the Apostolic delegation on the Mount of Olives at 7:02 A.M. (two minutes past midnight, Eastern standard time).

A radio jeep and two motorcycle outriders preceded the papal motorcade on its drive northward to Jenin, the point

Continued on Page 26, Column 6

PONTIFF FATIGUED

Jordanians Guard Him in Jerusalem Crush at Damascus Gate

Texts of Pope's messages on his visit are on Page 26.

By MILTON BRACKER
Special to The New York Times

JERUSALEM (Jordanian Sector), Sunday, Jan. 5—Pope Paul VI arrived in the Holy Land yesterday on his historic pilgrimage and was engulfed by hysterical crowds near the Damascus Gate to Jerusalem.

Excited policemen in his security guard virtually carried him through the throngs to the walled city, where he followed the traditional path that Jesus followed bearing the Cross. Soldiers used rifle butts and fists in an effort to protect Pope Paul, who was swept past many of the Stations of the Cross without a chance to pray.

At times the 66-year-old Pontiff's smiling serenity faded and he appeared worried.

Jordan military authorities announced a tightening of security measures. The Pope's program was somewhat curtailed because of the strain and fatigue that resulted from the crush.

He Celebrates Mass

After the chaotic scene outside the Damascus Gate, the spiritual leader of 500 million Roman Catholics celebrated mass in the Church of the Holy Sepulcher, the most sacred shrine of Christendom. Beneath it is the place where, according to Christian tradition, Jesus was entombed before the Resurrection.

The Pope passed the night in the quarters of the Apostolic delegation on the Mount of Olives. He left there at 7:02 A.M. today in a motorcade that proceeded north to Jenin, on the Jordanian-Israeli border.

About two hours later, the Pope crossed into Israel for his visit to Nazareth, where Jesus spent his boyhood.

Through today the papal party, exempted from the barriers imposed by Jordan because of her state of war with Israel, will tour sacred Christian sites in Israel, returning to Jordanian soil later in the day. The Pope will go back to Rome tomorrow.

Pope Paul and an entourage of about 30 prelates left Rome early yesterday by jet plane on a pilgrimage without precedent in nearly 2,000 years of Christian history to further world peace and brotherhood and Christian unity. The plane

Continued on Page 26, Column 1

Today's Sections

Index to Subjects

*Included in all copies in the New York metropolitan area and adjacent territory.

"All the News That's Fit to Print"

NEWS SUMMARY AND INDEX, PAGE 95

The New York Times.

LATE CITY EDITION

U.S. Weather Bureau Report (Page 95) forecasts: Snow, chance of sleet or rain today, tonight, then clearing tomorrow. Temp. Range: 37-28; yesterday: 36-23.

SECTION ONE

VOL. CXIII . No. 38,704. | NEW YORK, SUNDAY, JANUARY 12, 1964. | THIRTY CENTS

CIGARETTES PERIL HEALTH, U.S. REPORT CONCLUDES; 'REMEDIAL ACTION' URGED

CANCER LINK CITED

Smoking Is Also Found 'Important' Cause of Chronic Bronchitis

Committee's summary of its findings, Pages 64 and 65.

By WALTER SULLIVAN

Special to The New York Times

WASHINGTON, Jan. 11—The long-awaited Federal report on the effects of smoking found today that the use of cigarettes contributed so substantially to the American death rate that "appropriate remedial action" was called for.

The committee that made the report gave no specific recommendations for action. But health officials said that possible steps might include educational campaigns, the requirement that cigarette packages carry warnings and control of advertising.

The report dealt a severe blow to the rear-guard action fought in recent years by the tobacco industry. It dismissed, one by one, the arguments raised to question the validity of earlier studies.

Role of Smoking in Cancer

Combining the results of many surveys, the study panel found no doubt about the role of cigarette smoking in causing cancer of the lungs.

In men who smoke cigarettes, the death rate from that disease is almost 1,000 per cent higher than in nonsmokers, it said. Lung cancer has become the most frequent form of cancer in men.

Such smoking was also found to be "the most important" cause of chronic bronchitis, increasing the risk of death from that disease and from emphysema, a swelling of the lungs due to the presence of air in the connective tissues. Emphysema is a disease of increasing incidence.

As to coronary artery disease, a frequent cause of heart failure and the leading cause of death in this country, mortality is 70 per cent higher for cigarette smokers than for nonsmokers, the report said.

Relationship Assumed

The role of smoking as a cause of the disease, it said, "is not proved." However, it said, the study committee considers it "prudent" from the public health viewpoint to assume such a cause-and-effect relationship rather than wait until such a relationship has been established beyond doubt.

[The Tobacco Institute rejected the report, saying it was not the last word on smoking and health. The three major broadcasting networks said they would review their policies on tobacco advertising in the light of the report.]

The report was prepared on the initiative of President Kennedy to help the Government decide what to do about the smoking question. The committee was formed by Dr. Luther L.

Continued on Page 65, Column 6

DISCUSSES SMOKING REPORT: Dr. Luther Terry, the Surgeon General, at news conference held in Washington.

Associated Press Wirephoto

Johnson Chides the G.O.P. For Opposing His Budget

By WARREN WEAVER JR.

Special to The New York Times

WASHINGTON, Jan. 11—President Johnson made his first frankly partisan speech tonight to the first purely political group he has invited to the White House. Standing under a picture of Abraham Lincoln in the State Dining Room, the President grinned as he told members of the Democratic National Committee he could not understand why his budget had not gotten a warmer Republican reception.

"I always thought there could be nothing more satisfying to economy-minded Republicans than the reduction of the budget," he declared.

Then he quoted critical budget comments by such Republicans as Senator Thruston B. Morton of Kentucky, Governor Rockefeller of New York, Representative Charles A. Halleck of Indiana and Senator Everett McKinley Dirksen of Illinois.

Notes Arends Remark

He recalled that Representative Leslie C. Arends of Illinois had accused him of providing "something for everyone."

"He sounds kind of sorry, doesn't he?" Mr. Johnson asked, and his guests laughed.

The President quoted Senator Barry Goldwater as saying that the Johnson budget "out-Roosevelts Roosevelt, out-Kennedys Kennedy and makes Truman look like a piker."

"What finer compliment could anyone have?" Mr. Johnson inquired, and the Democratic leaders cheered.

These critical Republicans,

Continued on Page 55, Column 3

ATLANTA HOTELS DROP COLOR LINE

14 Leading Establishments Agree to Admit Negroes in Bid to Avert Protests

Special to The New York Times

ATLANTA, Jan. 11—Fourteen major Atlanta hotels and motels have publicly pledged to accept reservations regardless of race "in accordance with usual hotel practices."

Antisegregation demonstrations have appeared imminent in Atlanta. The hotels' announcement, made from the office of Mayor Ivan Allen Jr., was seen as an effort to forestall the protests.

The establishments in the agreement represent most of the city's main downtown hostelries and several on the fringes of the city. Six have been regarded as desegregated for some time. Others have been pledged to operate under the "Dallas plan," accepting some Negroes for conventions, but recently there had been word that they were quietly honoring Negro reservations.

The practices of most Atlanta hotels have been vague since last fall. The announcement today, listing the 14 participants, seemed to pin down their commitments more clearly and represented a liberalizing of policy for most.

A group of civil rights leaders, meanwhile, voted today to organize massive demonstrations against segregation in Atlanta. Immediately after the

Continued on Page 62, Column 5

SIX-PHASE INQUIRY ON ASSASSINATION CHARTED BY PANEL

Aides Chosen for Detailed Study of Kennedy Slaying and Security Agencies

By ANTHONY LEWIS

Special to The New York Times

WASHINGTON, Jan. 11—The staff of the commission investigating President Kennedy's assassination has divided its job into six broad areas of inquiry.

One covers every detail of Lee Oswald's activities on the day of the assassination, Nov. 22. Oswald was charged with the crime.

A second topic is the life and background of Oswald—an attempt to reconstruct his associations and ideas and psychology.

Oswald's career in the Marine Corps and his stay in the Soviet Union will be handled separately as a third.

His murder in the Dallas police station will be the fourth subject, including all the controversial questions of how it was allowed to happen.

Fifth will be the story of Jack Ruby, the nightclub operator who slipped into the police station and shot Oswald. This will be a particularly delicate subject because of possible conflict with Ruby's trial.

Study of Agencies

Finally, the staff will inquire exhaustively into the procedures used to protect President Kennedy. This will involve a scrutiny of the performances of the Secret Service, the Federal Bureau of Investigation and the Dallas police, as well as the influence, if any, of hate movements in the Dallas community.

The commission's counsel, J. Lee Rankin, outlined the plan in an interview.

He said it was clear to him now that the job could not be done in a matter of weeks, but he still hoped the inquiry could be finished three to six months from now. He recognized the importance of not letting it drag on.

"The commission realizes that the country wants to be sure of the facts," Mr. Rankin said. "The first thing is to do the job right. The second is to do it as quickly as possible."

New Name to Be Added

A senior lawyer assisted by a younger man will handle each of the six inquiry subjects. Mr. Rankin himself will have charge of one topic, and a group of distinguished lawyers from around the country has been gathered for the other senior posts.

The commission announced four of these senior appointments today, and a fifth is expected to follow shortly. The four named today, all men in active practice, are:

Francis W. H. Adams of New York, 59 years old. He was Police Commissioner in New York City in 1954-55.

Joseph A. Ball of Los Angeles, 61 years old, a leading criminal lawyer, a member of the Supreme Court's Advisory Committee on the Federal Rules

Continued on Page 46, Column 3

U.S. AND PANAMA AGREE TO CLEAR BORDERS IN STEP TO EASE TENSION; PLEDGE ON FLAG ISSUE IS OFFERED

FUNERAL PROCESSION IN PANAMA CITY: Thousands following the coffin yesterday bearing the body of a Panamanian student killed in Thursday's rioting near Canal Zone.

Associated Press Wirephoto

TROOPS CURB RIOTS

Chiari's Regime Finds Reds Infiltrating—Arms Search On

By HENRY RAYMONT

Special to The New York Times

PANAMA, Sunday, Jan. 12—The United States and Panama have agreed to take practical steps to ease the tensions along the borders of the Canal Zone.

After consultations with Assistant Secretary of State Thomas C. Mann and Secretary of the Army Cyrus R. Vance, the Canal Zone authorities agreed last night to remove troops that had been stationed along the border since the outbreak of violence Thursday.

For its part, the Panamanian National Guard undertook to clear its side of the border of snipers and those suspected of planning to provoke incidents.

In addition, the United States, in a conciliatory gesture, promised to make sure that the flags of both nations would henceforth fly side by side in the Canal Zone.

Link to Castro Alleged

The Government of President Roberto F. Chiari charged that the demonstrations had been infiltrated by Communists and supporters of Premier Fidel Castro of Cuba. It was stressed, however, that the majority of the demonstrators were engaged in a "purely civic movement."

During the night, cars in the city were being stopped and searched for arms.

Late last night, fighting between jeering Panamanians and United States soldiers with fixed bayonets erupted again on the Canal Zone border. Rioters stormed the barricade at the Tivoli guest house, and were forced back by the soldiers.

Bands Roam City

Bands of youth roamed the city, screaming anti-American slogans and hurling bottles and other missiles toward the border. One group praised President Chiari in the same slogans used by Castro sympathizers.

The pledges to ease the tensions were made at all-day meetings among Panamanian officials, the high-level United States mission, and the Inter-American Peace Committee, representing the Organization of American States.

The three-way talks began yesterday morning after the O.A.S. group arrived from Washington and moved to conciliate the deepening United States-Panamanian crisis.

The United States and Panama each each named a permanent

Continued on Page 25, Column 1

MORRISON BEATEN IN LOUISIANA VOTE

Former Diplomat Loses to McKeithen in Democratic Gubernatorial Primary

By CLAUDE SITTON

Special to The New York Times

NEW ORLEANS, Jan. 11—John J. McKeithen, a militant segregationist, today won the Democratic gubernatorial nomination in Louisiana and almost certain election by upsetting deLesseps S. Morrison.

Unofficial returns from 2,187 of the state's 2,219 precincts showed these totals:

McKeithen	484,179
Morrison	437,994

The victory of the rural northern Louisiana lawyer may spell trouble in this state for the Democratic Presidential nominee in the November election, even if, as expected, it is President Johnson. Mr. McKeithen has refused to commit himself to support the party's choice.

Scattered rains that cut the turnout of voters in the populous southern section, a Morrison stronghold, helped to account for the margin for Mr. McKeithen, 45-year-old State Public Service Commissioner.

Far more important, however,

Continued on Page 59, Column 3

Long Panama Negotiation Expected by Washington

By TAD SZULC

Special to The New York Times

WASHINGTON, Jan. 11—The United States searched today for steps that it hoped could lead to a mutually acceptable political solution of the Panama crisis. But the Administration was aware that, in the highly charged emotional atmosphere of Panama, it might be difficult for the Government of President Roberto F. Chiari to enter immediately into what is considered here a reasonable basis for negotiations on the fundamental issues.

The United States, therefore, was preparing for what may be a prolonged and complicated negotiating process that may have to be conducted in part without formal diplomatic relations. Diplomatic ties were broken by Panama yesterday.

Mann Reports to Johnson

President Johnson received a written report from Thomas C. Mann, Assistant Secretary of State for Inter-American Affairs, who flew to Panama yesterday at the head of a high-level United States mission to try to resolve the crisis.

The crisis developed Thursday night in a battle between Panamanian and United States forces on the border of the Canal Zone, culminating a dispute over the flying of the Panamanian flag.

The report covered mainly Mr. Mann's 90-minute meeting last night with President Chiari. It is understood that Mr. Mann limited himself for the most part to listening to the Panamanian President's exposition of the situation.

The White House said later that, on the basis of the first report and of a telephone con-

Continued on Page 25, Column 3

SENATORS SCORE BALL'S AID PLAN

2 Democratic Chiefs Oppose State Department Control Urged by Rusk Aide

By FELIX BELAIR Jr.

Special to The New York Times

WASHINGTON, Jan. 11—Senate Democratic leaders rejected today a proposal that the State Department take over direction and control of the foreign aid program in place of the Agency for International Development.

The proposal, submitted by Under Secretary of State George W. Ball, was sharply criticized by the Senate majority leader, Mike Mansfield of Montana, and the assistant majority leader, Hubert H. Humphrey of Minnesota.

They said that President Johnson's interdepartmental committee now studying the aid program was "wasting its time" if it was seriously considering turning over A.I.D. to the State Department or scattering its functions among six or seven other departments and agencies.

"I can think of nothing that would foul up the foreign aid program more completely and effectively than to turn it over to a bunch of Foreign Service officers," Senator Humphrey declared.

'Scramble and Hide'

"And the 'scatteration' scheme," he continued, "is nothing more than a transparent attempt to scramble and hide the aid appropriation by breaking it down into its components and assigning a part of it to various agency budgets. It would only mean that the Senate and House Appropriations Committees would have to unscramble the items and put them back together in a single money bill again."

President Johnson has given the study group, which is headed by Mr. Ball, until next Wednesday to make recommendations for overhauling the aid program.

In his instructions to the eight-member panel, the President stressed the criterion of Congressional acceptance. For this reason, the position of the Senate Democratic leadership was viewed as spiking any

Continued on Page 31, Column 3

Today's Sections

City Democrats to Restore Clubs As Job Centers for Minorities

By LEONARD INGALLS

The Democratic party in New York County is moving on a broad scale to restore to its neighborhood clubhouses some of their functions of the past in helping people find jobs and better housing.

Edward N. Costikyan, the Democratic county leader, has proposed that the county organization embark on such a program that also would include a special effort to improve public education in Harlem.

He has recommended to the county executive committee, made up of district leaders, that the party's 300,000 enrolled members and 35 district clubs in Manhattan be enlisted in an intensive effort to obtain pledges of nondiscrimination and to help members of minority groups find work.

He proposed that every Democratic district club solicit every Democrat and local businesses, labor unions and institutions like hospitals to obtain pledges that they would hire any person who met the qualifications for a job.

They also would be asked to agree to advise the Democratic county organization of vacancies and job qualifications. A full-time employment expert would be kept at Democratic county headquarters in the Chatham Hotel, 33 East 48th Street.

In submitting his proposals recently, Mr. Costikyan noted that many enrolled Democrats in Manhattan owned their own businesses and that others played key roles in labor unions. The committee is scheduled to

Continued on Page 22, Column 1

Mrs. Johnson Cheered in 'Poverty Pocket' Coal Towns

Mrs. Lyndon B. Johnson greets youngster who turned out to welcome her to Wilkes-Barre

United Press International Telephoto

By NAN ROBERTSON

Special to The New York Times

WILKES-BARRE, Pa., Jan. 11—Mrs. Lyndon B. Johnson visited today one of the "pockets of poverty" that President Johnson has declared war on the Wilkes-Barre and Scranton area of Pennsylvania. It is part of that impoverished 10-state strip known as Appalachia. Here, in the anthracite mine area, the jobless rate is nearly double the nation's average. On the way from Washington, Mrs. Johnson was briefed on the region, its problems and some of the solutions that have been found by two Pennsylvania Representatives. They were Daniel

Continued on Page 42, Column 4

West Berlin Offered Emergency Passes

By United Press International

BERLIN, Jan. 11—East Germany has offered to permit West Berliners through the Communist-built wall to visit relatives in East Berlin in certain hardship cases, it was disclosed today.

The offer was made public as the East German Communist leader, Walter Ulbricht, returned from a two-day visit to Moscow and meetings with Premier Khrushchev.

West Berlin officials said that they were convinced that Mr. Ulbricht and Mr. Khrushchev had conferred on plans to revive the system of passes through the wall as a wedge to gain recognition for East Germany.

Under the terms of the hardship plan, passes would be issued to West Berliners in the event of the death or sickness

Continued on Page 9, Column 3

"All the News That's Fit to Print"

The New York Times.

LATE CITY EDITION
U. S. Weather Bureau Report (Page 66) forecasts: Heavy showers, then clearing today. Fair, colder tonight and tomorrow.
Temp. Range: 55—41; yesterday: 54—42.

VOL. CXIII . No. 38,757. NEW YORK, THURSDAY, MARCH 5, 1964. TEN CENTS

U.N. ACTS TO SEND FORCE TO CYPRUS WITH A MEDIATOR

Thant Asks Troops From 5 Nations After Unanimous Approval by Council

LEADERS PRAISE ACTION

French, Russian and Czech Delegates Voice Objection but Vote for Resolution

By SAM POPE BREWER
Special to The New York Times

UNITED NATIONS, N. Y., March 4 — The Security Council unanimously approved a resolution on Cyprus today that provides for an international peace-keeping force and a mediator reporting to the Secretary General, U Thant.

Mr. Thant in turn is to report periodically to the Security Council. This satisfies demands of some members for Security Council authority.

Mr. Thant immediately began consultations on troop contingents for the force. A spokesman announced that the Secretary General had made formal requests to Brazil, Canada, Finland, Ireland and Sweden.

In accepting the assignment Mr. Thant told the Council that the problem of setting up the force was "delicate and difficult" because of limitations on choice, but that he believed he could organize it. He has said it would be limited to units of Commonwealth and nonaligned member countries and some of the British troops now there.

Thant Sees Leaders

Mr. Thant had meetings this afternoon and evening with the Cypriote Foreign Minister, Spyros Achilles Kyprianou, Turgut Menemencioglu of Turkey, Dmitri S. Bitsios of Greece and Sir Patrick Dean of Britain.

The spokesman said there would be no information on the identity of the mediator or of the commander of the international force until Mr. Thant received replies to his request for troops, made immediately after passage of the resolution.

Reliable sources have said the commander is to be Lieut. Gen. Prem Singh Gyani of India, who has been Mr. Thant's personal observer in Cyprus. There has been widespread speculation on the identity of the mediator. The name most heard has been that of C. W. A. Schurmann of the Netherlands.

Mr. Schurmann has represented his country here for nine years and has just been named Ambassador to Washington. His delegation says he has not been approached on the Cyprus question.

Neither has anyone else. Mr.

Continued on Page 2, Column 3

Associated Press

VOTE ON CYPRUS PROPOSALS: Nikolai T. Fedorenko, left, of the Soviet Union, joins Sir Patrick Dean of Britain and Adlai E. Stevenson, chief U.S. delegate, in the unanimous vote for U.N. moves to restore peace to Cyprus.

U. S. Cautions Vietnamese Against Split With Paris

By PETER GROSE
Special to The New York Times

SAIGON, South Vietnam, March 4—United States diplomats were reported today to have cautioned the South Vietnamese Government against a break in relations with France that would end French economic and cultural assistance.

Although high United States officials express strong resentment and concern over France's advocacy of neutralism for Vietnam, they say they have no concrete evidence of any plotting against the regime of Maj. Gen. Nguyen Khanh.

Premier Khanh has been advised, qualified sources said, that the United States is in no position to replace the extensive French participation in South Vietnam's agriculture and industrial projects and educational system.

The issue arose in connection with Premier Khanh's charges that the French were plotting to have him assassinated because of his opposition to a proposal for the neutralization of Vietnam.

Influence Hinders Struggle

Many Americans here feel that General Khanh went too far with these charges, which he has yet to document publicly. They agree, however, that current French political influence is unhealthy for the anti-Communist struggle being pursued by the Saigon regime with American assistance.

The officials who express these views say it is not specific French activities in Vietnam they fear.

"We hear a dozen rumors a week that such and such a person is plotting for neutralism or is acting as go-between for French agents and disgruntled Vietnamese officers or politicians," an American official said. "When investigated every one of these slips through our fingers."

The increasingly anti-French feeling of highly placed Americans here is a result of President de Gaulle's continuing pronouncements for neutrality, which they feel are undercutting the United States effort to resist Communist advances in Southeast Asia.

Observers here feel that if one puts aside rumors and un-

Continued on Page 7, Column 1

PEKING BIDS REDS IMITATE VIETCONG

Says Defeats of U.S. Show What Revolutionaries Can Do Against Imperialists

By SEYMOUR TOPPING
Special to The New York Times

HONG KONG, March 4 — The Chinese Communist party said today that United States reverses in South Vietnam had encouraged revolutionary action in other countries of Asia and in Africa and Latin America.

Peking said that defeats of the tactics used by the United States advisers in South Vietnam proved that revolutionary forces could overcome the superior military strength of the United States.

The call to other left-wing movements to emulate the Vietcong was part of a long editorial in Jenmin Jih Pao, the Chinese Communist party organ. It commented on lessons to be learned from the war in South Vietnam.

'Confusion' Is Seen

Analysts here said the editorial demonstrated that Peking viewed the struggle in South Vietnam as a pivotal one whose outcome would affect the East-West struggle.

The party organ cited the fact that Secretary of Defense Robert S. McNamara is due in Saigon Sunday and recent statements by President Johnson as signs of "shock and confusion" among United States leaders.

Deriding setbacks suffered by South Vietnamese troops backed by United States power, Jenmin Jih Pao asserted that the "U.S. paper tiger had been punctured and exposed."

"The people of any country or region subjected to U.S. aggression can win victory if only they are not overawed by its apparent strength, and dare

Continued on Page 6, Column 4

JERSEY CITY SHUTS SCHOOLS IN STRIKE

607 of 1,500 Teachers Hold One-Day Walkout Over City's Cut in Budget

By MARTIN GANSBERG
Special to The New York Times

JERSEY CITY, March 4—A strike by more than 40 per cent of this city's teachers today forced the Board of Education to close the schools at 12:30 P.M.

Dr. Robert A. Coyle, Superintendent of Schools, decided at 10:45 A.M. to close the city's four high schools and 30 elementary schools, after reports from principals showed that 607 of the system's 1,500 teachers were absent. There are 34,500 students in the schools.

The strike was called by two groups, the Jersey City Education Association and the Jersey City Federation of Teachers, who objected to a $700,000 cut in the education budget for 1964-65 ordered by Mayor Thomas J. Whelan.

There were no demonstrations or picketing. The teachers stayed at home or met at designated sites to discuss their position. Hardest hit by absences were the city's four high schools, Lincoln, Dickinson, Ferris and Snyder, where almost 65 per cent of the teachers were absent.

At Dickinson High School, where 60 of 151 teachers were absent, Mayor Whelan took over a class in civics. He pointed out that he had no certification as a teacher, but he said: "If there is one subject I know, it's civics."

He had no comment on the strike, but did remark that it was up to the Board of Educa-

Continued on Page 27, Column 2

33-Day Tug Strike Ended on Terms Set By Splinter Group

By WERNER BAMBERGER

The port's 33-day-old tugboat strike, the second longest in harbor history, ended yesterday.

Within hours of the union's acceptance of a management proposal for a three-year contract, some of the 350 idle tugs, tankers and barges returned to service.

However, most of the idle fleet was not to resume operating until today under an agreement between Local 333, United Marine Division of the National Maritime Union, and the Marine Towing and Transportation Employers Association.

The tugs that started to move yesterday afternoon are owned by five companies that broke away from the 65-member association last Friday. The splinter group offered the 3,000 striking tugboatmen a contract settlement in excess of what the association's majority was then willing to propose.

Association Concedes

However, late Monday night negotiators for the association acceded to union demands that all 65 companies agree to identical terms before the union returned to work.

These terms—a three-year-contract calling for a wage-and-benefit package increase of 68¾ cents — were accepted unanimously by 3,000 union members at a ratification meeting at Manhattan Center, 311 West 34th Street.

Capt. Joseph O'Hare, union president, told his men at the end of the meeting: "Call your dispatchers and go back to work."

The new contract calls for a wage increase of 50 cents for

Continued on Page 44, Column 2

STATE SAYS UNION BARRED NEGROES FOR LAST 76 YEARS

Sheet Metal Workers Found Guilty by Rights Agency —'Breakthrough' Seen

By SYDNEY H. SCHANBERG

A key construction union has been found guilty by the state of having systematically barred Negroes from its ranks.

In a decision announced yesterday, the State Commission for Human Rights ruled that Local 28 of the Sheet Metal Workers International Association had "automatically excluded" Negroes over the entire 76 years of the union's existence. Such exclusion is a violation of state law.

John Mulhearn, the union's recording secretary, said: "They are all wrong; anyone who heard the evidence would know they're all wrong." An official statement will be issued later in the week, he said.

The union has about 3,300 members, none of whom are Negroes.

A spokesman for the commission said that an order would be given to the union to "cease and desist" discriminatory practices. He said this would be followed by an "affirmative action," the details of which have not yet been set by the commission.

Guarantee To Be Ordered

Such action, it was said, would involve a further order to guarantee and facilitate the end of discrimination against any minority groups.

The commission chairman, George H. Fowler, called the decision "revolutionary in that it takes into account a historical pattern of exclusion and not merely a specific complaint."

Observers viewed the ruling as a key harvest of the seeds planted by the massive civil rights protests at construction sites here last year. Local 28 has been a prime target of the rights groups.

Herbert Hill, labor secretary of the National Association for the Advancement of Colored People, said it was "a significant breakthrough for Negro workers in New York."

"It is earnestly hoped," he said, "that the state commission will now invoke its full authority against other lily-white A.F.L.-C.I.O. building trade unions in the state."

Wide Inquiry Urged

Earlier, Mr. Hill, speaking at a news conference, had called for a statewide investigation into "broad violations" of anti-discrimination laws by private employment agencies.

Citing the "crisis in Negro unemployment," Mr. Hill demanded "fines, punishment and suspension of licenses."

The decision on the sheet metal workers, which was unanimous, was based on public hearings conducted last fall by three commissioners of the human rights agency. Bernard Katzen, the presiding commissioner, wrote the 22-page opinion.

The hearings were called to investigate a charge brought by the State Attorney General's office that the union and a union-contractor committee for selecting apprentices had discriminated against Negroes.

It was also charged in the complaint that the apprenticeship committee had refused admission to a qualified Negro,

Continued on Page 27, Column 2

HOFFA IS GUILTY OF TRYING TO FIX A FEDERAL JURY

Associated Press Wirephoto

AFTER VERDICT: James R. Hoffa leaving the court yesterday in Chattanooga.

HE FACES 10 YEARS

Teamster Chief Plans Appeal—3 Others Also Convicted

By JOHN D. POMFRET
Special to The New York Times

CHATTANOOGA, March 4—James R. Hoffa, president of the International Brotherhood of Teamsters, was convicted today of tampering with a Federal jury in 1962.

A jury of four women and eight men found the 51-year-old head of the nation's largest labor union guilty on two counts and acquitted him on a third. The jurors got the case yesterday.

Hoffa faces a maximum sentence of 10 years in prison and a $10,000 fine—five years and $5,000 on each count.

Hoffa and the other defendants were charged with trying corruptly to influence the jury in Hoffa's trial in Nashville in 1962 on charges of accepting illegal payments from an employer.

Convicted with Hoffa on one count each of jury-tampering were Ewing King, 50, recently defeated as president of Teamsters Local 327 in Nashville; Larry Campbell, 39, a business agent with Hoffa's home local in Detroit, and Thomas E. Parks, 50, Campbell's uncle, a Nashville funeral home employe.

Two Are Acquitted

Two defendants were acquitted. They were Allen Dorfman, 41, a Chicago insurance broker with close personal and business ties to Hoffa, and Nicholas J. Tweel, a Huntington, W. Va., businessman who has done business with Mr. Dorfman.

Hoffa's conviction was not expected to start a revolt against him within the union. Although there have been rumblings of discontent with his leadership, he has tight control of the union and no one was expected to come forward immediately to lead an attempt to unseat him unless he is put in prison.

Hoffa will appeal all the way to the Supreme Court, if necessary. This is expected to take at least two years. He called today's verdict unfair.

United States District Judge Frank W. Wilson, who presided at the trial, was expected to delay sentencing until after the defense lawyers argue motions for a new trial and until a

Continued on Page 22, Column 1

SENATE SUPPORTS TOBACCO SUBSIDY

Rejects, 63-26, Move to Kill Federal Price Aid During Wheat-Cotton Bill Debate

By WILLIAM M. BLAIR
Special to The New York Times

WASHINGTON, March 4 — The Senate almost staged a full-dress debate today on whether smoking caused cancer but cut it off by refusing to kill Federal price supports on tobacco.

On a roll-call vote of 63 to 26, the Senate rejected an amendment to the pending farm bill that would have wiped out tobacco subsidies on the ground that tobacco was an evil or that the Federal support program was too costly. Tobacco subsidies have been in effect 30 years.

Tobacco-state Senators argued that elimination of price supports on the rich crop would bring uncontrolled production of cheap tobacco rather than a curb on cigarette smoking, which has been cited as a health menace in a Government report.

Amendments Opposed

The vote was in line with the Administration's fight to keep the wheat-cotton farm bill free of amendments. Democratic leaders regard this as necessary to assure approval by the House of Representatives and to avoid any threat of a Presidential veto.

Lobbying activities by wheat and cotton interests have been unusually noticeable, as have efforts by cattle producers to gain a limit on meat imports and by packing and storage interests to block a Congressional limit on meat imports.

The Senate will vote tomorrow on an amendment by Senator Roman L. Hruska, Republi-

Continued on Page 16, Column 3

MALAYSIA TAKING ISSUE TO THE U.N.

Bangkok Parley Founders on Cease-Fire Differences

By The Associated Press

BANGKOK, Thailand, March 4—A conference on the Malaysian crisis foundered here today and Prince Abdul Rahman announced that Malaysia would take the dispute with Indonesia to the United Nations.

The talks between Indonesia, the Philippines and Malaysia bogged down over differences of opinion about the cease-fire arranged in January by Attorney General Robert F. Kennedy. A statement issued by the Malaysians appeared to be a warning that they considered the cease-fire to be void.

[A Philippines spokesman in Bangkok said early Thursday he still expected the talks to continue there, Reuters reported.]

The Malaysian Prime Minister called on his people to give their lives if necessary in defense of the country. He charged that the Indonesians had never carried out their side of the bargain.

"To them a cease-fire means that we cease but not they, with the result that many of our men were taken unaware and shot down in cold blood," he said.

Malaysia, represented at the

Continued on Page 8, Column 3

Cogen Says Attacks by Pupils On Teachers Average One a Day

By MICHAEL T. KAUFMAN

Charles Cogen, president of the United Federation of Teachers, said yesterday that attacks by pupils on teachers in the city schools averaged one a day.

Commenting on recent attacks, Mr. Cogen said he believed that "in many cases incidents are not reported, the teachers are intimidated and the principals are likewise discouraged from making reports."

A spokesman for the Board of Education refused to comment on these charges, but said that they would be discussed today at a previously scheduled meeting between Mr. Cogen and Dr. Calvin E. Gross, the Superintendent of Schools.

Mr. Cogen said he would recommend that "principals be given freedom of action in suspending unruly pupils."

Earlier in the day another incident was reported and one that occurred on Tuesday came to light.

The first took place at Public School 17, Roebling Street and North Fifth Street in Brooklyn, when a former student kicked and struck a teacher. School officials gave this account:

During the lunch period, William L. Schulster, a shop teacher, noticed that a boy was trying to take away a pupil's free-lunch pass. Mr. Schulster learned that the boy did not attend the school and asked him to leave.

The youngster then kicked

Continued on Page 27, Column 5

The New York Times

NEW FACE IN CLASSROOM: Mayor Thomas J. Whelan of Jersey City takes over civics class at Dickinson High School after strike by 607 of the city's 1,500 teachers.

Ex-Page in Senate Says He Paid $50-a-Month Kickback to Baker

A former Senate page said last night that he had paid Robert G. Baker $50 a month from his Federal salary before the then Vice President Johnson intervened and ordered a halt to the payments.

The youth, Boyd Ritchie, said the former secretary of the Senate Democratic majority had told him his pay was being cut back "because I was young and inexperienced in the job."

Mr. Ritchie, now a student at the University of the South in Sewanee, Tenn., told of the payments in a televised interview with Stanley Levey of the Columbia Broadcasting System.

The former page said his salary at the time the alleged kickbacks were made was $403 a month. He asserted that the payments had continued for "two or three months."

Mr. Baker, whose business affairs are being investigated by the Senate Rules Committee, refused to answer a committee question about the alleged payments when he testified in Washington on Feb. 25. Mr. Baker is himself a former page.

Mr. Ritchie, asked what reason had been given by Mr. Baker for withholding the money, said the former secretary had told him "that I was young and had just started on the job and that later on he [Mr. Baker] would up it back to its original amount."

The youth said he had told Mr. Baker the cutback "would be fine."

"I was making a good sal-

Continued on Page 14, Column 1

PRESIDENT GIVES JOBS TO 10 WOMEN

Jerseyan Will Be Envoy—Mrs. Kross Gets Award

By MARJORIE HUNTER
Special to The New York Times

WASHINGTON, March 4—President Johnson appointed a woman as Ambassador and named nine other women to Government posts tonight as part of his pledge to end a "stag Government."

At a dinner at which the first Eleanor Roosevelt Memorial Award was presented to Mrs. Anna M. Kross, Commissioner of Corrections in New York City, the President said:

"Our determination to enlist women in this Administration is no sporadic, election-year objective. It will be a continuing aim not because it is politic but because it is sound."

He chose Mrs. Leon Keyserling of Washington, an economist, to be director of the Women's Bureau in the Labor Department. She is the wife of

Continued on Page 25, Column 5

NEWS INDEX

"All the News That's Fit to Print"

The New York Times.

LATE CITY EDITION
U. S. Weather Bureau Report (Page 77) forecasts: Mostly sunny and warmer today; fair tonight and tomorrow.
Temp. Range: 66—44; yesterday: 47—41.

VOL. CXIII..No. 38,806. © 1964 by The New York Times Company. Times Square, New York, N. Y. 10036 NEW YORK, THURSDAY, APRIL 23, 1964. TEN CENTS

5-YEAR RAIL DISPUTE ENDS; PRESIDENT WINS ACCORD HE TERMS 'JUST AND FAIR'

STRIKE IS AVERTED

Settlement Viewed as Personal Triumph for Johnson

Transcript of statements on rail accord, Page 25.

By JOHN D. POMFRET
Special to The New York Times

WASHINGTON, April 22 — The five-year-old railroad work rules dispute was settled today, ending the threat of a nationwide rail strike at midnight Friday.

The agreement, which provides for a raise for about 100,000 workers along with other benefits and gives the railroads additional flexibility in assigning work crews, was announced by President Johnson over nationwide television about 6:45 P.M.

The President said the terms of the accord "are just and are fair."

The settlement was a great personal triumph for Mr. Johnson. He intervened forcefully in the dispute on April 9 to persuade the five operating rail unions and the railroads to call off a national rail shutdown set for midnight that day.

And Mr. Johnson clinched the settlement personally today by persuading the railroads to accept it.

Throughout the talks, the President had kept in close contact with the negotiators, dropping in on them almost daily.

Half to Get Raise

The agreement by itself appeared to be a victory for the unions. They won a pay raise for about half of the 200,000 employes they represent and got the carriers to drop several important demands.

The total settlement, however, including the earlier arbitration award covering the two main issues in the original dispute, represents a substantial gain for the railroads. This results from eliminating thousands of workers the roads contend are no longer needed.

An informed source estimated that the railroads would save $317 million a year from the manpower reductions permitted by the arbitration award, once it is fully in effect. The cost to the railroads of today's settlement was put at $64 million. The eventual net saving to the railroads was thus estimated at $253 million a year.

That an agreement emerged

Continued on Page 25, Column 1

Southerners Gain Support On Juries for Rights Cases

Bill's Managers in Senate Are Willing to Have Panels for Criminal Contempt Arising Out of Injunction Suits

By E. W. KENWORTHY
Special to The New York Times

WASHINGTON, April 22 — Southern Senators were savoring in advance today their first taste of victory in the civil rights battle. But it was only a partial victory in a relatively small skirmish.

The leaders of the civil rights coalition said they were willing to meet part way a Southern demand for jury trials in all cases of criminal contempt arising out of injunction suits provided for in the civil rights bill.

Last night Senator Herman E. Talmadge, Democrat of Georgia, suddenly offered an amendment to change the Federal Criminal Code to provide a jury trial in all criminal contempt of court cases, not just those involving civil rights.

This was identical with an amendment that the Senate appended to the Civil Rights Bill of 1957, but that the House refused to accept.

After a snarl lasting two weeks, House and Senate leaders of both parties finally agreed that, in voting-rights cases only, a person held in criminal contempt could have a jury trial if the judge fined him more than $300 or sentenced him to more than 45 days in jail.

The bill now before the Senate extends this 1957 formula to criminal contempt cases arising out of Title II, the section banning discrimination in public accommodations.

Today Senator Hubert H. Humphrey of Minnesota, Democratic floor manager of the bill, said he would be willing to have the same limited right of jury trial for all titles of the bill that authorize injunction proceedings.

In addition to Title II on

Continued on Page 32, Column 2

Brooklyn Navy Yard Faces '64 Closing, House Is Told

By JACK RAYMOND
Special to The New York Times

WASHINGTON, April 22—The House heard a warning from one of its leading members today that the New York, Boston and Philadelphia naval shipyards might be ordered closed before the end of 1964.

The warning, by Representative Carl Vinson, chairman of the House Armed Services Committee, highlighted a furious debate as the House unanimously passed a $46,785,867,000 defense appropriations bill for the fiscal year 1965, beginning next July 1.

At one point members shouted at each other, declaring that the naval shipyards—or private shipyards, as the case might be—in their districts would suffer if the present system of contract allocations were changed or not changed, depending on the point of view.

Ratio Retained

The debate involved a provision of the bill that calls for dividing contracts for naval repair, alteration and conversion on the basis of 65 per cent for Government naval yards and 35 per cent for private shipyards.

The provision, originally established two years ago to give more work to the navy yards, was retained today after defeat of an amendment submitted by Representative L. Mendel Rivers, Democrat of South Carolina.

Mr. Rivers proposed eliminating the 65-35 provision and substituting language that would give the Navy discretion to place more work with the Government yards. The vote

Continued on Page 15, Column 1

U.S.-SOVIET LINKS STIR BONN UNREST

American Troop Reduction Decried by Erhard Aide—Tacit Accords Feared

By ARTHUR J. OLSEN
Special to The New York Times

BONN, April 22—A senior Cabinet member spoke out sharply today against "détente talk" and the new reduction of United States forces in West Germany.

The critical comments from Dr. Heinrich Krone, chairman of the National Defense Council, were expressive of a sense of uneasiness evident in political quarters here over multiplying signs of Soviet-United States undertakings to reduce tensions.

Chancellor Ludwig Erhard and his ministers have no quarrel with moves such as the parallel decisions in Moscow and Washington to cut back production of fissionable materials. The Chancellor specifically hailed the twin announcements as a step toward general and controlled disarmament.

Coordinated Moves Noted

The uneasiness stems from the technique of coordinated moves, which are thought to be based on private consultations between the Soviet and United States Governments. It is speculated that the time might come for a tacit agreement on matters affecting vital German interests.

It is widely believed in informed West German quarters that such an agreement is already in existence between the Soviet Union and the United States with respect to Berlin. It is believed that there is an understanding to "freeze" existing relationships and procedures affecting the Western presence in and access to the former German capital.

There have been no significant "incidents" involving the exercise of Western or Soviet rights in the Berlin area for six months.

Last week the allied commandants overruled the West Berlin authorities in favor of Communist diplomats on a procedural question concerning credentials. The United States commandant in Berlin, Maj.

Continued on Page 8, Column 4

BIRRELL FLYING HERE FOR TRIAL

Fugitive Leaves Brazil to Face Swindling Charges

By The Associated Press

RIO DE JANEIRO, Thursday, April 23—Lowell M. Birrell, American financier who fled to Brazil five years ago, left for New York early today by plane in the company of a Brazilian police officer.

Birrell, 57 years old, was on a nonstop Varig flight scheduled to reach Kennedy International Airport at 7:30 A.M.

The fugitive was understood to be returning voluntarily to face stock swindle charges in New York, Pennsylvania, New Jersey and California in addition to Federal charges of income tax evasion. He once was reputed to have manipulated a $60 million paper empire.

Birrell was reported virtually penniless.

He came to Brazil in 1959 and was charged with entering the country illegally with a false Canadian passport. This charge had prevented him from leaving Brazil earlier.

The charge was understood to have been dropped by the new Brazilian Government in an action that some interpreted as a warning that the new regime would not continue to give

Continued on Page 56, Column 5

LAOS JUNTA ASKS SOUVANNA TO HEAD A NEW COALITION

Western and Soviet Envoys Press King and Vientiane to Restore Regime

By SEYMOUR TOPPING
Special to The New York Times

VIENTIANE, Laos, April 22—The Western Powers and the Soviet Union appealed to King Savang Vatthana of Laos today to preserve the coalition Government of the neutralist Premier, Prince Souvanna Phouma.

Prince Souvanna Phouma and the diplomats of the powers, including Ambassador Leonard Unger of the United States, conferred during the day with the King at Luang Prabang, the royal capital 130 miles north of this administrative capital of the country.

The military junta that seized power here Sunday is asking that Prince Souvanna Phouma continue as Premier. But the junta expects him to resign and then form a new Government, it was indicated.

The envoys, who returned during the afternoon from Luang Prabang, were told by the King that he condemned the military coup d'état and that he wanted Prince Souvanna Phouma to stay as Premier.

Prince Is Noncommittal

Mr. Unger said that he had delivered to King Savang Vatthana a message from W. Averell Harriman, the United States Under Secretary of State for Political Affairs, urging that the King help in restoring the coalition.

[Prince Souvanna Phouma also returned to Vientiane late Wednesday, evidently to confer again with the military coup leaders, said The Associated Press. He was noncommittal on developments, saying only that he was "continuing to look for a reasonable solution" of the national crisis.]

Gen. Siho Lamphouthacoul, the 29-year-old right-wing security chief who is emerging as a dominant personality of the military junta, was reported opposed to restoration of the coalition Government as it stood.

Set Up Under Geneva Pact

Under the Geneva agreement of June, 1962, the coalition under Prince Souvanna Phouma, a neutralist, included the rightists, headed by Gen. Phoumi Nosavan (who was not involved in Sunday's coup) as Deputy Premier and Prince Souphanouvong, leftist and head of the pro-Communist Pathet Lao, also as Deputy Premier. Ministries were divided among the three factions.

General Siho and Gen. Kouprasith Abhay, nominal head of the Revolutionary Committee, the junta, have kept Prince Souvanna Phouma under close surveillance since their unsuccessful attempt Sunday to compel his resignation.

The danger overshadowing the political confusion in Vientiane was that the pro-Communist Pathet Lao forces would exploit the apparently developing rifts in the ranks of the rightist forces and mount a strong military offensive.

The envoys of the United States, Britain, France, the Soviet Union, India and Australia flew this morning to Luang Prabang to lodge their appeal with the King. They were insist-

Continued on Page 2, Column 4

Miss Taylor and Burton Sued For $50 Million on 'Cleopatra'

By EDWARD RANZAL

Elizabeth Taylor and Richard Burton were sued yesterday for $50 million in damages in connection with the motion picture "Cleopatra."

Miss Taylor and Mr. Burton, who were married recently, were charged with breach of contract and with depreciating the commercial value of the movie by their "scandalous" conduct before and during the filming.

The suit was filed in Federal Court by the producers and distributors of the film, 20th Century-Fox Film Corporation and 20th Century-Fox Productions, Ltd.

Under the terms of her contract, Miss Taylor was guaranteed a salary of $750,000 against 10 per cent of the gross receipts.

The film company said that the actress had received in excess of $2 million.

In the first part of the suit, Fox seeks $20 million in damages from Miss Taylor.

She was charged with breaching her contract in the following manner:

"By not reporting for work; by not reporting for work on time; by not performing her services with due diligence, care or attention; by reporting for work in a condition which did not permit her to perform her services by suffering herself by her own acts and fault to become disabled, incapacitated, or unphotographable, and unable to perform her services.

"By conspiring with and inducing others to breach their agreements faithfully to perform their services in the pro-

Continued on Page 33, Column 1

FAIR OPENS, RIGHTS STALL-IN FAILS; PROTESTERS DROWN OUT JOHNSON; 300 ARRESTED IN DEMONSTRATIONS

The New York Times (by Meyer Liebowitz)

SPEAKER: President Johnson dedicates Federal Pavilion. Others are Franklin D. Roosevelt Jr., left, Under Secretary of Commerce, and Fair Commissioner Norman Winston.

The New York Times

PROTEST: Police removing civil rights demonstrators after the President spoke.

Associated Press

SCUFFLE: Demonstrators and the police clash at Jackson Heights subway station.

RAIN SOAKS CROWD

Sit-Ins Mar Festivities at Some Pavilions —Attendance Cut

Text of speech by President will be found on Page 26.

By HOMER BIGART

The New York World's Fair was opened by President Johnson on schedule yesterday, despite the double obstacle of foul weather and civil disobedience.

Massive demonstrations that had been threatened by civil rights groups outside and inside the fair failed to materialize. A few hundred Negro and white activists did, however, distract and disturb the crowds during the colorful premiere of the great exposition.

A band of youthful pickets and sit-ins assailed President Johnson with rude shouts when he dedicated the Federal Pavilion.

It rained most of the morning, and it was cloudy and chilly the rest of the day. The grim, November-like weather, combined with the fear that integration activists might block access to the fair, undoubtedly kept thousands away. Attendance was 92,646, with 63,791 paid.

An attendance of at least 250,000 had been forecast.

Wide publication of a threat to pull emergency cords on subway trains apparently had alarmed many. Yet there was only one serious attempt to stop a train.

Traffic Flows Smoothly

Similarly the forecast of a paralyzing stall-in evaporated: traffic moved smoothly.

By evening about 300 persons had been taken into custody outside and inside the fair grounds.

Among those arrested were leaders of the demonstration. James Farmer, national director of the Congress of Racial Equality, and Bayard Rustin, organizer of last summer's March on Washington, were taken into custody as the police dispersed a sit-in at the New York State Pavilion.

The militant integrationists were unable to disrupt the opening ceremonies, of which the climax was the President's speech to 10,000 rain-soaked spectators in Singer Bowl. Entrance to the bowl was by invitation only.

But when the President moved to the Federal Pavilion for the dedication there, groups of demonstrators sat in clumps of freshly planted shrubbery at either side of the building. The President spoke from under the shelter of the huge structure, which resembles a giant ice cream sandwich balanced on a small pyramid.

Shouts of 'Freedom Now!'

Another group of teen-age militants marched in a circle 100 yards away, surrounded by the police. They brandished placards, and their shouts of "Freedom Now!" sometimes drowned out the strong voice of the President.

"We do not try to mask our national problems," said the President. "We do not try to disguise our imperfections or cover up our failures. No other nation in history has done so much to correct its flaws."

The President's forecast of "a world in which all men are equal" drew loud derisive laughter from the pickets.

As soon as the President had left, police wagons drove up, and the sit-ins were flushed from the shrubbery. They had to be dragged into the wagons.

The opening-day crowd tried to ignore the pickets, but they seemed to be all over the fair.

Continued on Page 26, Column 1

SHUTTLE SERVICE DUE THIS MORNING

One Track to Be Opened for Rush Hour as Repairs Go On After 42d St. IRT Fire

By CHARLES GRUTZNER

Service was expected to resume by rush hour this morning on at least one track of the Grand Central-Times Square subway shuttle, which was closed by a six-alarm fire early Tuesday.

Joseph E. O'Grady, the Transit Authority chairman, made the announcement last night and said he was hopeful that a second track could also be put in service today, probably after the 7-9 A.M. rush. The third track was still blocked by the heat twisted wreckage of a four-car train.

Surface traffic, which had been tied up by detours after the underground fire caused the 42d Street pavement to buckle and to develop cracks, was eased with the reopening of sections of Vanderbilt and Madison Avenues that had been closed.

The only section still barricaded last night was 42d Street between Fifth Avenue and Vanderbilt Avenue. John T. Carroll, Commissioner of Highways, said it would take 24 to 48 hours to strengthen and repave this heavily traveled section, where the paving dropped as much as two feet in spots.

The resumption of shuttle service is expected half a day sooner than originally estimated as a result of round-the-clock efforts above and below ground by more than 300 workers employed by the Transit Authority and two private contractors, Spencer White & Prentis, Inc.,

Continued on Page 33, Column 3

7 Injured in IRT Station; New Picketing Is Planned

By PETER KIHSS

Demonstrators for Negro rights failed yesterday to produce their threatened stall-ins to tie up traffic going to the opening of the World's Fair. But four demonstrators and three policemen were injured when a crowd tried to stop one morning subway train and there were a number of other incidents.

In demonstrations pegged to the start of the fair, whose slogan is "Peace Through Understanding," 299 persons were arrested. Three youngsters under 16 years old also were held but were not technically arrested. Thirty-four of the arrests were made outside the fairgrounds in Flushing Meadow.

A leader of the demonstrations inside the grounds said more protests were planned in an effort to "awaken the American conscience."

Thousands on Guard

Thousands of city, transit and World's Fair policemen had mobilized to resist the threatened demonstrations. Police cars and tow trucks waited sometimes as close as every half mile along Grand Central Parkway near the fair and every 50 to 100 yards apart on the Triborough Bridge.

The Transit Authority had at least one man to each car to guard emergency cords on its IRT Flushing subway line to the fair, pressing into duty maintenance workers and others as well as its entire police force.

Traffic Commissioner Henry A. Barnes spent an hour and a half flying in a helicopter until 10:15 A.M. and found traffic less than normal in the drizzle.

Leaders of local Congress of Racial Equality chapters turned out only a dozen cars—instead of a threatened 2,000—and decided against even attempting to carry out their stall-in threat.

They contended their would-be followers had been intimi-

Continued on Page 28, Column 1

STALL-IN LEADERS ERRED ON BACKING

Admit They Overestimated Pledges to Supply Cars

By JUNIUS GRIFFIN

Supporters of the planned stall-in of 2,000 automobiles said yesterday that it had failed to materialize because its leaders drastically overestimated their ability to win support—in the city and from out of town.

Confidants of Isiah Bronson, the chairman of the rebel Brooklyn chapter of the Congress of Racial Equality, said he believed he could deliver. But they said they relied on new leaders on the civil rights scene who promised much and delivered nothing.

Mr. Bronson, a 22-year-old Negro automobile factory worker from South Carolina who has suddenly become an integration personality in New York, could not be reached for comment. One of his close friends said he was deeply upset at the failure of the stall-in and had gone off by himself in his unhappiness and bitterness.

Earlier yesterday a bench warrant was issued against him in Brooklyn Criminal Court when he failed to appear at 11 A.M. for trial on a charge of disorderly conduct in connection with a sit-down demonstration at the Downstate Medical Center construction site last summer. The trial was recessed Tuesday after he gave assurances that he would be there yesterday. A bench warrant

Continued on Page 29, Column 1

NEWS INDEX

The 250-ton stainless steel Unisphere symbolized the 1964 World's Fair theme, "Peace Through Understanding." About 20 million people visited the exposition in New York.

Mario Salvo was at the center of the Free Speech Movement at the Berkeley campus of UCLA, where massive political protests occurred.

"All the News That's Fit to Print"

The New York Times.

LATE CITY EDITION
U. S. Weather Bureau Report (Page 78) forecasts: Mostly sunny, windy and cooler today; Fair and cool tonight and tomorrow.
Temp. Range: 75—62; yesterday: 82—66.
Temp.-Hum. Index: 60's; yesterday: 72.

VOL. CXIII..No. 38,860. NEW YORK, TUESDAY, JUNE 16, 1964. TEN CENTS

SUPREME COURT HOLDS STATES MUST APPORTION LEGISLATURES ON BASIS OF EQUAL POPULATION

ROCKEFELLER GIVES UP RACE; AIDS SCRANTON

VOWS FULL HELP

Terms Pennsylvanian 'in the Mainstream' of Political Thought

Text of Governor's statement is printed on Page 25.

By JOSEPH LELYVELD

Governor Rockefeller, the first candidate to enter the Republican Presidential race, withdrew yesterday in favor of Gov. William W. Scranton of Pennsylvania.

In a brief statement released at his New York office, Mr. Rockefeller urged moderates in the party to unite behind Governor Scranton as "a candidate in the mainstream of American political thought and action."

This was the closest the statement came to mentioning Senator Barry Goldwater of Arizona, the leading candidate for the nomination. After he lost the California primary on June 2, Mr. Rockefeller remarked that if Senator Goldwater was in the mainstream "we've got a meandering stream."

85 to 88 New York Votes

The Governor's campaign aides estimated that he would be able to deliver 85 to 88 votes from the 92-member New York delegation to Governor Scranton at the Republican Convention in San Francisco next month. These delegates are not legally bound to the Governor, but since they are from his home state he is confident of his political control.

In addition, Governor Rockefeller will attempt to give Governor Scranton the 18 delegates he won in Oregon in his only victory in a contested primary. These delegates will be legally free after he releases them and for that reason the Governor's statement stopped short of a release.

There are 20 to 25 more delegates pledged to Governor Rockefeller. It is considered likely that they will follow his lead into the Scranton camp.

Meeting With Aides Set

The Governor scheduled a meeting for today with his representatives from across the country and a news conference for this afternoon.

Mr. Rockefeller was at his Pocantico Hills estate when the curtain fell on a campaign that began officially last Nov. 7 and unofficially as soon as the votes were counted in the 1960 election.

For more than two years, it was widely assumed that he would be the party's nominee in 1964. All this changed overnight when he remarried on May 4, 1963, after his divorce earlier. From then on, his campaign was under a cloud.

In his statement yesterday, he stressed that he had become an active candidate in November "to fight for the basic principles of progress and moderation on which the Republican party was founded and has prospered."

Now, he said, if that fight is to be won, it will be won under the Scranton banner.

"Accordingly," the statement

Continued on Page 25, Column 1

Lodge Denies Plan To Quit as Envoy

By PETER GROSE
Special to The New York Times

SAIGON, South Vietnam, June 15—Henry Cabot Lodge firmly denied today a Washington report that he had resigned as United States Ambassador to South Vietnam for health reasons. The report, he said, is "totally false."

Mr. Lodge underwent a thorough medical checkup only a few days ago, sources said, and was reported to be in good health. At 61, he continues to go for energetic swims nearly every day during his lunch hour.

The question plaguing Ambassador Lodge today is whether he should resign for other reasons—political reasons. It is a question that remains unanswered.

As a liberal Republican and a possible though undeclared contender for the Republican

Continued on Page 24, Column 3

SCRANTON BEGINS DRIVE IN MIDWEST

Governor Is Critical of Both 'Dime-Store Feudalism' and Foreign Policy

By JOSEPH A. LOFTUS
Special to The New York Times

DES MOINES, Iowa, June 15—Gov. William W. Scranton of Pennsylvania opened a fighting campaign for convention delegates in the Midwest tonight, swinging to the right at Senator Barry Goldwater of Arizona and to the left at President Johnson.

With one hand he struck at "dime-store feudalism" and "extreme reactionaries." With the other he aimed blows at an Administration that he said had "put together a short-order foreign policy, serving up each day's hash from the leavings of yesterday's mistakes."

The Governor received two rousing receptions, although Goldwater enthusiasts infiltrated both and interrupted speeches with yells for the Senator.

Response Is Warm

A two-floor auditorium that seats more than 4,000 was nearly filled. The crowd responded to the Governor's speech with deafening approval time after time. Goldwater fans chose the quiet moments of the speech to yell, "We want Barry."

The Goldwater claque hooted the Governor's remarks that "this is not the hour for us to join those extreme reactionaries who are anything but conservative."

More than 500 persons, with a band, met the Governor at the airport.

A late starter in the race for the Republican Presidential nomination, delighted rather than dismayed by his underdog role, the Governor set out to tap in the next four weeks every state with uncommitted

Continued on Page 25, Column 5

PEKING WARNS U.S. RISKS RETALIATION WITH LAOS FLIGHTS

Says Southeast Asia Peace 'Is Hanging by Thread'—Renews Parley Call

By SEYMOUR TOPPING
Special to The New York Times

HONG KONG, June 15—Communist China asserted today that United States air operations in Laos were inviting retaliatory action.

Warning that "peace in Indochina and Southeast Asia is hanging by a thread," Peking pressed its demand for the prompt reconvening of the 1962 Geneva conference on Laos.

Jenmin Jih Pao, official organ of the Chinese Communist party, said in a lengthy editorial that the United States bore responsibility for the bombing Thursday of Peking's mission at the headquarters of the Communist-led Pathet Lao at Khang Khay, in north-central Laos. One Chinese was reported to have been killed and five staff members to have been injured.

Provocation Charged

Rejecting denials by the United States Embassy at Vientiane, Laos, that United States planes were involved in the attack Thursday, the editorial charged that the bombing had been planned by the Johnson Administration as a premeditated and deliberate provocation against Communist China.

According to information received here, the raid was carried out by T-28 trainer aircraft converted to fighter-bombers that were supplied to the right-wing Laotian Air Force by the United States. Strikes by the Laotian Air Force and reconnaissance flights by United States Navy planes began last month after Pathet Lao troops had attacked neutralist forces on the Plaine des Jarres.

Reliable sources in Washington reported last weekend that United States Air Force jets bombed Communist gun positions in Laos last Tuesday after two Navy planes had been downed. But there were no reports that United States planes were involved in the raid Thursday.

Pressure Held Aim

Western analysts here said the editorial had apparently been intended to exert pressure for acceptance of Peking's demand for reconvening the Geneva conference without delay. This demand was put forward in notes sent to Britain and the Soviet Union, co-chairmen of the Geneva conference, which guaranteed Laotian independence and neutrality.

The notes strongly protested the Khang Khay bombing.

However, analysts also noted that the editorial had hinted more strongly than any previous statement that Chinese Communist forces might become directly involved in the Laotian conflict.

"Having reconnoitered inten-

Continued on Page 3, Column 1

Rights Groups, in Switch, Back Schools' Racial Plan

7 Organizations Drop Opposition After Gross Changes Setup on Transfers—Taxpayer Group Continues Fight

By LEONARD BUDER

Representatives of seven civil rights and community organizations switched their positions yesterday and said they would urge their members to support the Board of Education's integration plan.

The representatives acted after Dr. Calvin E. Gross, the Superintendent of Schools, agreed, as they put it, to eliminate "a number of objectionable features" in the plan, which is scheduled to go into effect in September. Dr. Gross described the changes as "refinements."

A key change will allow Negro children who were scheduled to attend sixth-grade classes in specified junior high schools next fall to transfer to specified integrated or white elementary schools. The groups had previously charged that the Negro pupils were merely being transferred from segregated elementary schools to segregated junior high schools.

Yesterday's development, which came as a surprise, ended for the time being the long controversy between civil rights groups and the school system.

All of the groups had previously denounced the board's integration plan because, they said, it did not substantially correct racial imbalance in the schools. Several had indicated that they might sponsor new demonstrations in the fall, including possibly a prolonged boycott by Negro pupils.

The organizations that an-

Continued on Page 18, Column 5

GOMULKA ASSAILS CHINESE LEADERS

Polish Chief Says They Are 'Dangerous'—Proposes World Red Conference

By DAVID BINDER
Special to The New York Times

WARSAW, June 15—Wladyslaw Gomulka condemned the Chinese Communist leadership today in sharp terms.

The First Secretary of the Polish United Workers (Communist) party, who was addressing the opening session of the party's fourth congress, called the Peking leaders "shortsighted and dangerous."

In a speech lasting six and a half hours he said that the Chinese, in their pursuit of "great-power ambitions," had indulged in policies "that have nothing to do with Marxism-Leninism or proletarian internationalism."

Mr. Gomulka then urged preparation of a world conference "of all parties to participate" in seeking to re-establish Communist unity. The split is over methods of achieving world Communism, with Peking advocating revolutionary tactics and Moscow favoring the coexistence approach. The Polish

Continued on Page 5, Column 1

GREECE'S PREMIER TO VISIT JOHNSON

Coming to U.S. for Cyprus Talks June 24-25, After President Sees Turk

By TAD SZULC
Special to The New York Times

WASHINGTON, June 15—President Johnson announced tonight that Premier George Papandreou of Greece would confer with him here on the Cyprus crisis immediately after a similar meeting with Premier Ismet Inonu of Turkey.

Mr. Inonu will meet with President Johnson next Monday. According to tonight's announcement, Mr. Papandreou will be in Washington June 24 and 25.

The Presidential invitations to the two Premiers were issued last week. This coincided with hastily arranged visits to the Greek and Turkish capitals by Under Secretary of State George W. Ball.

The Ball mission reflected the mounting concern here over the situation on the Mediterranean island, where fighting has raged between the majority Greek Cypriotes and the Turkish Cypriotes. Clashes broke out in December after the Government

Continued on Page 7, Column 2

PRIVILEGE RULING

Justices Widen Scope of Fifth Amendment in State Actions

Special to The New York Times

WASHINGTON, June 15—In two landmark criminal-law decisions, the Supreme Court extended today the protections of the Fifth Amendment's privilege against compelled self-incrimination.

Overruling a 56-year-old precedent, the Court held that the privilege applied in state as well as Federal proceedings. The vote was 5 to 4, but two of the Justices dissented on the facts of this case and did not necessarily disagree with the constitutional ruling.

The Court also held, again overturning a prior decision, that if a state granted a man immunity and then forced him to testify, the testimony could not be used in a Federal prosecution. This result was reached unanimously, but on diverse grounds.

The first case involved William Malloy of Windsor, Conn., who was convicted on a betting charge in Hartford in 1959. He drew a 90-day jail sentence and a $500 fine.

Queried About Arrest

In 1961 he was called to testify before an inquiry into gambling and other illegality in Hartford County. He was asked questions about his arrest in 1959 and about whether he knew a John Bergoti, apparently a suspect of some kind.

Mr. Malloy refused to answer, invoking the Fifth Amendment. He did not explain how answers to those questions might incriminate him. He persisted in silence even after he was told that the statute of limitations had run out on any gambling activities as early as 1959.

At the time, Mr. Malloy's invocation of the Fifth Amendment was in error. The Supreme Court had held for more than a century that the protections of the first 10 amendments to the Federal Constitution applied only to the Federal Government, not the states.

Bill of Rights Applied

In this century the Court has gradually applied some of the Bill of Rights protections to the states. It has found these protections encompassed in the 14th Amendment, which prohibits the states from denying any person the "due process" of law.

But in 1908 the Court specifically held that the Fifth Amendment privilege against being forced to testify against oneself was not applicable in state proceedings. It reiterated that view in a 5-to-4 decision in 1947.

Connecticut, however, like all other states, has its own protections against compulsory self-incrimination. The Connecticut Supreme Court of Errors therefore, went ahead and considered whether Mr. Malloy had come within the privilege.

The Connecticut court found

Continued on Page 32, Column 1

The New York Times

PRESENTS DECISION: Chief Justice Earl Warren, who announced Supreme Court ruling on apportionment of state legislatures.

DEMOCRATIC GAIN IN STATE IS SEEN

Court Ruling Is Expected to Liberalize Legislature by Shift of Influence

By DOUGLAS DALES
Special to The New York Times

ALBANY, June 15—The decision of the United States Supreme Court declaring New York's legislative apportionment formula unconstitutional is expected to have two major long-range effects upon the Legislature.

First, it will require a major political realignment of the Republican and Democratic forces. While not assuring the Democrats of majorities in the Legislature, historically dominated by Republicans, a formula based on population will put control by the Democrats within their grasp.

Second, by increasing the relative influence of the cities and suburban areas in the Legislature at the expense of upstate rural counties, the decision is almost certain to change the character of the Legislature, giving it a more liberal point of view.

Two Questions Open

The decision in Washington left unanswered the question when the change in districting formulas must be put into effect. And it also left open for interpretation the meaning of reapportionment based "substantially" on population.

In mandating the case back to the three-member statutory court that originally dismissed the suit, the Supreme Court gave the lower court authority to decide when the changes must go into effect.

Should the lower court order the changes effective for the 1964 elections, it could create a vast assortment of technical problems in view of the relatively short time remaining until the general election Nov. 3.

Candidates for the 150 Assembly seats and the 58 Senate seats were nominated by the political parties in the primary election June 2.

In view of the time that would be required for the statutory court to make its findings, the time required for a special session of the Legislature and the weeks required for the circulation of nominating petitions by candidates, the view here was that the implementation of today's decision probably would be put off until the 1966 legislative election.

Among those subscribing to this expectation was Assembly Speaker Joseph F. Carlino, who

Continued on Page 31, Column 1

HISTORIC DECISION

Both Houses Affected —Ruling Upsets 6 States' Districts

Excerpts from decision are on Pages 28 to 31.

By ANTHONY LEWIS
Special to The New York Times

WASHINGTON, June 15—The Supreme Court held today that the districts in both houses of state legislatures must be "substantially equal" in population.

It was a decision of historic importance. Not since the school segregation cases 10 years ago had the Court interpreted the Constitution to require so fundamental a change in this country's institutions.

A 6-to-3 majority laid down the broad rule that both houses of state legislatures "must be apportioned on a population basis."

Only a handful of states meet that standard now. While the opinions gave no specific guide, it would not be surprising if 40 of the 50 states found their districts upset.

Suburbs Also Gain

The big gainers from redistricting will be the cities and especially now the fast-growing suburbs. Rural areas have long had many more seats in most state legislatures than their population would indicate.

The Court said there was no valid analogy between state legislatures and the Federal Congress, in which the Senate is based not on population but on two members for each state. Today's decision does not affect the United States Senate.

The specific provision in the Constitution for the Senate, the Court said, resulted from a compromise among the sovereign states that formed the Union. But counties and other subdivisions of states have never been sovereign, and states are subject to the Constitution's overriding requirement of equality.

Opinion by Warren

Chief Justice Earl Warren wrote for the majority. He was joined by Justices Hugo L. Black, William O. Douglas, William J. Brennan Jr., Byron R. White and Arthur J. Goldberg.

Justice John Marshall Harlan delivered an impassioned dissent. Extemporizing from the bench, he spoke of the "solemnity of this occasion" and warned against the Court's damaging itself by so sweeping a decision.

Justices Tom C. Clark and Potter Stewart did not accept the majority's reasoning. But they did agree, on narrower grounds, that some of the state legislative apportionments before the Court were unconstitutional.

The Court passed on six cases from Alabama, New York, Colorado, Maryland, Virginia and Delaware. It found the existing districts in all six legislatures unconstitutional.

Suits are pending in almost 40 states. Cases are awaiting

Continued on Page 28, Column 2

Goldwater Joins in Futile Effort To Kill Key Part of Rights Bill

By E. W. KENWORTHY
Special to The New York Times

WASHINGTON, June 15—Senator Barry Goldwater and four of his stanchest supporters joined with the Southern bloc in the Senate today in a futile attempt to kill the public accommodations section of the civil rights bill.

The vote by which the Senate repulsed the effort to strike out what Negroes regard as the vital core of the measure was 63 to 23.

Seventeen Southerners, five Republicans and one Northern Democrat voted for the amendment. The other Republicans were Norris Cotton of New Hampshire, who was Mr. Goldwater's campaign manager in that state's Presidential primary last March; Wallace F. Bennett of Utah, Edwin L. Mechem of New Mexico and Milward L. Simpson of Wyoming.

The Northern Democrat voting for the amendment was its sponsor, Robert C. Byrd of West Virginia.

The public accommodations section, called Title II, bans discrimination or segregation in hotels, motels, restaurants, theaters and sports arenas.

Mr. Goldwater's vote for the motion to eliminate the title was expected. He has always taken the position that he deplores discrimination in public accommodations but opposes any attempt to outlaw it as

Continued on Page 17, Column 1

After 134 Years, Soldiers of France Leave Algiers

United Press International Radiophoto

Trucks, carrying detachment of French troops sailing for home, roll onto Algiers pier

By PETER BRAESTRUP
Special to The New York Times

ALGIERS, June 15—For the first time since 1830, the French Tricolor did not fly over the port of Algiers today. The last French troops here—2,000 of them—quietly boarded transports and headed home across the Mediterranean. Few Algerians seemed to notice. Two years after independence, the French military presence, which dominated this city's life during the bitter 1954-62 war for independence, had ceased to matter. Apparently fearful of incidents, Paris decreed that the waterfront embarkation ceremonies on the Quai Gabès be brief and closed to the press and the public. Shortly after 8 P.M., a 300-man rear guard in combat dress marched across the quai behind a band. It consisted of troops of the First Spahi

Continued on Page 5, Column 4

Moseley Gets Chair; Verdict Is Cheered

By DAVID ANDERSON

Applause broke out in State Supreme Court yesterday after a jury had voted to send Winston Moseley to the electric chair for the murder of Catherine Genovese in Kew Gardens.

The sudden hand-clapping and a few cheers, all from women, in the Queens County Criminal Courthouse, caused Justice J. Irwin Shapiro to pound his desk angrily for order.

After the courtroom had quieted, however, Justice Shapiro told the jurors:

"I don't believe in capital punishment, but I must say I feel this may be improper when I see this monster. I wouldn't hesitate to pull the switch on him myself." Moseley himself

Continued on Page 53, Column 2

Jersey Labor Split By Power Struggle

By DAMON STETSON
Special to The New York Times

NEWARK, June 15—New Jersey's merged labor organization fell apart today, broken by a power struggle between the former leaders of the Congress of Industrial Organizations and the American Federation of Labor.

The former C.I.O. unions, which formed their own Industrial Union Council last winter, said they would hold a separate convention in Atlantic City on June 26-28. At that convention, they said, they will decide whether to go it alone in the future.

The bitter division at the opening of the state A.F.L.-C.I.O. convention here today made it clear that there would

Continued on Page 20, Column 1

NEWS INDEX

"All the News That's Fit to Print"

The New York Times.

LATE CITY EDITION

U. S. Weather Bureau Report (Page 53) forecasts: Fair and hot today and tomorrow. Chance of late showers each day.

Temp. Range: 91—71; yesterday: 80—65. Temp.-Hum. Index: 80 to 85; yesterday: 74.

VOL. CXIII . No. 38,864. NEW YORK, SATURDAY, JUNE 20, 1964. TEN CENTS

CIVIL RIGHTS BILL PASSED, 73-27; JOHNSON URGES ALL TO COMPLY; DIRKSEN BERATES GOLDWATER

U.S. STRESSING IT WOULD FIGHT TO DEFEND ASIA

WARNING TO REDS

Commitment to Laos and South Vietnam Called Unlimited

By MAX FRANKEL

Special to The New York Times

WASHINGTON, June 19—The Administration is saying more emphatically each day that North Vietnam and its closest ally, Communist China, must leave their neighbors alone or face a war with the United States.

In the minds of officials here the United States commitment to the security of Southeast Asia is now unlimited and comparable with the commitment to West Berlin.

In diplomatic terms this means the officials find themselves unable to negotiate with anything except the threat of force to persuade the Asian Communists to stop the efforts to "liberate" South Vietnam and Laos.

Thus far, the Administration is not sure that the Asian Communists have accurately interpreted the warning signals from Washington. It is not sure that its allies in Europe appreciate the gravity of the United States commitment. And it is not sure that the American people understand the reasons for it.

Decision Publicized

Accordingly, the word is being passed with increasing vigor to the Congress, to the Washington press corps and to the Western allies.

These official assertions suggest that the decision to deny Southeast Asia to Communism was, in effect, taken a long time ago through circumstance and a cumulative series of lesser decisions.

The view that Laos can somehow be handled separately from South Vietnam has been abandoned. The earlier emphasis on limited involvement in South Vietnam's guerrilla war has been replaced by unlimited pledges of support for the whole region.

The hope here is that Hanoi and Peking are alert to this hardening of attitudes and that they have been properly forewarned by the less direct as well as public utterances of Administration leaders and, particularly, by the recent involvement of United States military planes in Laos.

Compromise Doubted

The subtleties of the situation have made the Administration reticent to discuss future military moves beyond hints that every violation of past agreements in Southeast Asia and every change in the forms of contest will draw a firm response.

All the comments here stress that the choice between war and peace lies in the hands of the Asian Communists because Washington sees no way of negotiating a compromise. It will not sit down with Peking and Hanoi until recent violations of past agreements for Laos are redressed because it could have no confidence in any new agreement.

To some extent, the Adminis-

Continued on Page 7, Column 1

JOHNSON IS FIRM

Vows in California to Oppose Violators of Freedom in World

By TOM WICKER

Special to The New York Times

SAN FRANCISCO, June 19—President Johnson promised tonight to open an "offensive in the pursuit of peace" based on an overwhelming military power that "makes it possible to seek agreement without fearing loss of liberty."

The President, addressing an audience of nearly 2,500 at a Democratic party fund-raising dinner, also pledged stern American opposition to "those who believe they can violate their neighbor's borders and steal their neighbor's freedom."

At the end of a day in California during which he gave several indications that he expected to be President for at least four more years, Mr. Johnson said he wanted to double the size of the Peace Corps, pursue what he called the "great society" with "the vision and valor of pioneers" and achieve "full equality for all our people."

Earlier in the day, after an enthusiastic welcome from more than 300,000 San Franciscans who lined Market Street to see his motorcade, the President came as near as he ever has to predicting his election in November.

Predicts the Good Life

"A Government which can get things done and knows where it is going," he said, is "the kind of Government you have had for the past four years—and that is the kind of Government you are going to get for the next four years."

Mr. Johnson's remarks were made at the dedication of a new Federal office building in downtown San Francisco. Before coming here, he also spoke at Edwards Air Force Base in the Mojave Desert and broke ground for a new Oakland Bay area rapid transit system at ceremonies in Concord.

It was not until tonight, when he attended the $100-a-plate fund-raising dinner, that Mr. Johnson played an openly political role.

At every stop he voiced his prophecies of the good life for every American, promising Californians the lion's share.

At the party dinner, he shifted his emphasis somewhat, detailing the increases since 1960 in American military might. He declared:

"We have used that strength not to intimidate others, but to

Continued on Page 6, Column 4

SENATOR KENNEDY HURT IN AIR CRASH; BAYH INJURED, TOO

Both Are in Fair Condition in Massachusetts Hospital —Pilot of Plane Killed

By The Associated Press

SOUTHAMPTON, Mass., Saturday, June 20—Senator Edward M. Kennedy, younger brother of President Kennedy, and Senator Birch Bayh were injured in the crash of a private plane last night while on the way to the Massachusetts Democratic Convention.

The pilot was killed and two other persons were injured. Mr. Kennedy was semiconscious.

Both Senators were reported in fair condition at Cooley Dickinson Hospital in nearby Northampton.

Also injured were Mrs. Bayh, reported in good condition, and Edward Moss of Andover, administrative aide to Mr. Kennedy, who was reported in critical condition.

Associated Press

Senator Edward M. Kennedy

The pilot was identified as Edwin J. Zimny, 48 years old, of Lawrence, a last-minute substitute for the regular Kennedy pilot.

Senator Kennedy, Democrat of Massachusetts, was treated in an emergency room for back and chest injuries. His wife, Joan, visited him after he was transferred to an intensive-care unit.

Senator Bayh, Democrat of Indiana, suffered a hip injury. Mrs. Bayh was reported suffering from shock.

Mr. Kennedy's parents, Mr. and Mrs. Joseph P. Kennedy, who were vacationing at their summer home in Hyannis Port, were not told of the plane crash.

Attorney General Robert F. Kennedy, brother of the Senator, boarded the family plane with an aide and was reported on the way to Boston.

Two Civil Aeronautics Board investigators were sent from

Continued on Page 54, Column 1

PRESIDENT'S PLEA

He Declares the Task Now Is to Change Law Into Custom

Special to The New York Times

SAN FRANCISCO, June 19—President Johnson called the Senate passage of his civil rights bill today a "challenge to men of good will in every part of the country to transform the commands of our law into the customs of our land."

Mr. Johnson said it was now the nation's task "to reach beyond the content of the bill to conquer the barriers of poor education, poverty, and squalid housing which are an inheritance of past injustice and an impediment to future advance."

He said that he did not "underestimate the depth of the passions involved in the struggle for racial equality."

But he also spoke of "a large reservoir of goodwill and compassion, of decency and fair play which seeks a vision of justice without violence in the streets."

Johnson Statement

If these forces, the President said, "do not desert the field, if they can be brought to the battle, then the years of trial will be a prelude to the final triumph of a land 'with liberty and justice for all.'"

The President issued his statement on the rights bill here, while he was beginning a two-day tour of California. The full text of the statement follows:

"Senate passage of the civil rights bill is a major step toward equal opportunities for all Americans. I congratulate Senators of both parties who worked to make passage possible.

"I look forward to the day, which will not be long forthcoming, when the bill becomes law. That will be a milestone in America's progress toward full justice for all her citizens.

"No single act of Congress can, by itself, eliminate discrimination and prejudice, hatred and injustice.

Broad National Consensus

"But this bill goes further to invest the rights of man with the protection of law than any legislation in this century.

"First, it will provide a carefully designed code to test and enforce the right of every American to go to school, to get a job, to vote, and to pursue his life unhampered by the barriers of racial discrimination.

"Second, it will, in itself, help educate all Americans to their responsibility to give equal treatment to their fellow citizens.

"Third, it will enlist one of the most powerful moral forces of American society on the side of civil rights—the moral obligation to respect and obey the law of the land.

"Fourth, and perhaps most important, this bill is a renewal and a re-enforcement, a symbol and a strengthening of that abiding commitment to human dignity and the equality of man which has been the guid-

Continued on Page 11, Column 8

United Press International Telephoto

ON HAND FOR THE VOTE: Visitors waiting outside the Capitol yesterday for admittance to the Senate Chamber, before the vote on the civil rights bill was registered.

ARIZONAN TARGET OF G.O.P. LEADER

Illinoisan, in Speech on the Senate Floor, Scores View Bill Is Unconstitutional

By ANTHONY LEWIS

Special to The New York Times

WASHINGTON, June 19 — The Republican leader in the Senate, Everett McKinley Dirksen of Illinois, closed the civil rights debate tonight with a biting attack on his party's leading Presidential prospect, Senator Barry Goldwater.

Senator Goldwater's announced opposition to the bill brought on the attack. He said yesterday that he could not "in good conscience" vote for the bill because he thought it was "unconstitutional" and would lead to a "police state."

Earlier, it was reported that former President Dwight D. Eisenhower had indicated to Mr Goldwater that the general would not hold a negative vote on the bill against the Arizonan.

On the floor of the Senate, Mr. Dirksen ridiculed the Goldwater constitutional argument and moral position.

Looking often at Senator Goldwater, though never mentioning him by name, Mr. Dirksen in effect challenged the likely nominee of his party on what may be the chief issue at the Republican National Convention next month.

Dirksen Cites Legislation

First, Senator Dirksen mentioned many past pieces of legislation that had first been denounced as "unconstitutional." He listed the child labor prohibition, the Pure Food and Drug Act, the Minimum Wage Law and Social Security.

"It required no constitutional amendment," Senator Dirksen said, "to bring about all these forward thrusts in the interests of the people.

"It leads me to one conclusion: in the history of mankind, there is an inexorable moral force that moves us forward.

"No matter the resistance of people who do not fully understand, it will not be denied."

At this point, Senator Dirksen turned and looked directly at Senator Goldwater, who sat at his desk at the side of the chamber. Thrusting his right arm in Senator Goldwater's direction, he said:

"Utter all the extreme opin-

Continued on Page 11, Column 6

Rights Bill Roll-Call Vote

By The Associated Press

WASHINGTON, June 19—Following is the 73-27 vote by which the Senate passed the civil rights bill tonight:

FOR PASSAGE—73

Democrats—46

Anderson (N.M.)	Hayden (Ariz.)	Monroney (Okla.)
Bartlett (Alaska)	Humphrey (Minn.)	Morse (Ore.)
Bayh (Ind.)	Inouye (Hawaii)	Moss (Utah)
Brewster (Md.)	Jackson (Wash.)	Muskie (Me.)
Bible (Nev.)	Kennedy (Mass.)	Nelson (Wis.)
Burdick (N.D.)	Lausche (Ohio)	Neuberger (Ore.)
Cannon (Nev.)	Long (Mo.)	Pastore (R. I.)
Church (Idaho)	Magnuson (Wash.)	Pell (R. I.)
Clark (Pa.)	Mansfield (Mont.)	Proxmire (Wis.)
Dodd (Conn.)	McCarthy (Minn.)	Randolph (W. Va.)
Douglas (Ill.)	McGee (Wyo.)	Ribicoff (Conn.)
Edmondson (Okla.)	McGovern (S. D.)	Symington (Mo.)
Engle (Calif.)	McIntyre (N.H.)	Williams (N. J.)
Gruening (Alaska)	McNamara (Mich.)	Yarborough (Tex.)
Hart (Mich.)	Metcalf (Mont.)	Young (Ohio)
Hartke (Ind.)		

Republicans—27

Aiken (Vt.)	Dirksen (Ill.)	Morton (Ky.)
Allott (Colo.)	Dominick (Colo.)	Mundt (S. D.)
Beall (Md.)	Fong (Hawaii)	Pearson (Kan.)
Bennett (Utah)	Hruska (Neb.)	Prouty (Vt.)
Boggs (Del.)	Javits (N. Y.)	Saltonstall (Mass.)
Carlson (Kan.)	Jordan (Idaho)	Scott (Pa.)
Case (N. J.)	Keating (N. Y.)	Smith (Me.)
Cooper (Ky.)	Kuchel (Calif.)	Williams (Del.)
Curtis (Neb.)	Miller (Iowa)	Young (N. D.)

AGAINST PASSAGE—27

Democrats—21

Byrd (Va.)	Hill (Ala.)	Russell (Ga.)
Byrd (W. Va.)	Holland (Fla.)	Smathers (Fla.)
Eastland (Miss.)	Johnston (S. C.)	Sparkman (Ala.)
Ellender (La.)	Jordan (N. C.)	Stennis (Miss.)
Ervin (N. C.)	Long (La.)	Talmadge (Ga.)
Fulbright (Ark.)	McClellan (Ark.)	Thurmond (S. C.)
Gore (Tenn.)	Robertson (Va.)	Walters (Tenn.)

Republicans—6

Cotton (N. H.)	Hickenlooper (Iowa)	Simpson (Wyo.)
Goldwater (Ariz.)	Mechem (N. M.)	Tower (Tex.)

Negro Leaders Hail Passage; Some Southerners Voice Anger

CORE Plans Tests

By MARTIN ARNOLD

Leaders of national civil rights groups last night hailed the Senate passage of the civil rights bill, and vowed that the measure would be quickly tested.

There was little indication that the Senate's action would reduce the number of demonstrations in the immediate future.

James L. Farmer, national director of the Congress of Racial Equality, said that CORE would press for implementation and enforcement of the bill's provisions.

"There will be no breathing spell on demonstrations," Mr. Farmer said. "We breathe easiest when the pressure is on."

"The passage of the civil rights bill may well be the single most important act of our Congress in several decades," Mr. Farmer said. "It gives hope to Negroes that the American people and Government mean to redeem the promise of the Declaration of Independence and the Emancipation Proclamation."

Mr. Farmer also saw the bill

Continued on Page 10, Column 4

Region's Reaction Varied

By United Press International

ATLANTA, June 19 — Deep South politicians and businessmen lashed out angrily at passage of the civil rights bill today and an elderly Negro said, "I'll believe it when I see it."

Gov. George C. Wallace of Alabama declared that "this is a sad day for individual freedom and liberty," but a Chattanooga housewife said, "I firmly believe in it."

Reaction differed sharply between stanchly segregationist areas and areas where there has been desegregation.

Many Negroes approached on the streets in the South had little, if any comment.

"I just don't know much about it. I'm afraid to say," said a Negro in Nashville.

"It is good. I am glad," said George Thomson, a 40-year-old Negro cab driver in Montgomery, Ala.

Jefferson Johnson, an elderly Negro selling ice cream on a street in Birmingham, Ala., said:

"I'll believe it when I see it. I hope it'll do good, but—well,

Continued on Page 12, Column 6

ACTION BY SENATE

Revised Measure Now Goes Back to House for Concurrence

By E. W. KENWORTHY

Special to The New York Times

WASHINGTON, June 19 — The Senate passed the civil rights bill today by a vote of 73 to 27.

The final roll-call came at 7:40 P.M. on the 83d day of debate, nine days after closure was invoked.

Voting for the bill were 46 Democrats and 27 Republicans. Voting against it were 21 Democrats and six Republicans.

Except for Senator Robert C. Byrd of West Virginia, all the Democratic votes against the bill came from Southerners.

Senator Barry Goldwater of Arizona voted against the bill, as he said yesterday he would. The five other Republicans opposing it all support Mr. Goldwater's candidacy for the Republican Presidential nomination.

They were Bourke B. Hickenlooper of Iowa, chairman of the Senate Republican Policy Committee; Norris Cotton of New Hampshire, Edwin L. Mechem of New Mexico, Milward L. Simpson of Wyoming and John G. Tower of Texas.

2 Pledge Acceptance

The bill will now go back to the House for concurrence in the changes that the Senate made in the measure the House passed last Feb. 10 by a vote of 290 to 130.

Tonight, Representatives Emanuel Celler, Democrat of New York, and William M. McCulloch, Republican of Ohio, who are the chairman and ranking minority member of the House Judiciary Committee, said that they would accept the Senate version of the bill.

"We believe that the House membership will take the same position," they said.

With the support of these two men, who were responsible for the House bill, acceptance of the Senate bill in the House is assured.

President Johnson hopes to have the bill on his desk by July 3 at the latest so that he can sign it on the Fourth of July.

Powers of the Bill

The bill passed by the Senate outlaws discrimination in places of public accommodation, publicly owned facilities, employment and union membership and Federally aided programs. It gives the Attorney General new powers to speed school desegregation and enforce the Negro's right to vote.

The Senate bill differs from the House measure chiefly in giving states and local communities more scope and time to deal with complaints of discrimination in hiring and public accommodations. It allows the Attorney General to initiate suits in these areas where he finds a "pattern" of discrimination, but does not permit him, as did the House bill, to file suits on behalf of individuals.

After the roll-call, several thousand people gathered in the plaza before the floodlit Capitol to applaud the Senate Democratic leader, Mike Mansfield of Montana, and the Republican leader, Everett McKinley Dirksen of Illinois. Mr. Dirksen was instrumental in shaping the compromise that the Senate passed.

Burke Marshall, the Justice Department's civil rights chief, said after the bill was passed tonight that the department would move promptly to enforce the measure.

"I think there is going to be compliance with this bill," Mr. Marshall said. "That's the first thing."

"But where there is a pattern

Continued on Page 10, Column 1

NEWS INDEX

North Katanga City Is Seized By Rebels, the Congo Reports

Europeans Flee Albertville, Crossing Lake Tanganyika to Nearby Burundi

By J. ANTHONY LUKAS

Special to The New York Times

LEOPOLDVILLE, the Congo, June 19—Albertville, the capital of North Katanga Province, was reported today to have fallen to anti-Government rebels.

According to messages reaching here, rebels striking south along the shore of Lake Tanganyika entered the city about midday. It is not known here whether there was any resistance from Congolese soldiers there.

Many of the city's Europeans have fled in steamers across the lake. At least 150 women and children left on two steamers last night for Bujumbura, the capital of Burundi.

Another steamer, with 350 persons aboard, was scheduled to leave early this afternoon, but it was not whether it got away.

Meanwhile, the United States Embassy here said that two American civilian pilots who had been flying combat missions for the Congolese Army had voluntarily decided to cease the flights. An embassy official said the pilots made their decision after they learned that they might be subject to penalties under United States law.

CENTRAL AFRICAN REPUBLIC — SUDAN — CONGO REP. — RWANDA — BURUNDI — REPUBLIC OF THE CONGO — Leopoldville — Albertville — L. Tanganyika — ANGOLA — Elisabethville — NORTHERN RHODESIA

The New York Times June 20, 1964

Rebels were said to have seized Albertville (cross).

The embassy spokesman adhered to the official United States position tht the two men were "individual Americans on contract to the Congolese Government."

He said the United States Government had neither authorized their contract nor directed their activities here.

The Americans, Ed Dearborn and Don Coney, also insisted in an interview here, as they had previously, that they were civilians under contract to the Congolese Government.

Mr. Dearborn said he had hepatitis and planned to return to the United States soon. However, he and Mr. Coney would answer no other questions.

Continued on Page 4, Column 3

Yanks Woo Cabbies With 20,000 Tickets

By ROBERT LIPSYTE

The New York Yankees, long lordly and aloof atop baseball's corporate standings, have gone down to the street to wage promotional warfare.

They have given away more than 10,000 reserved tickets worth $25,000 to more than 5,000 city cab drivers on the sidewalk along Broadway between 60th and 61st Streets in the last two days. Today, they expect to give away 10,000 more.

The Yankees' first mass giveaway program is the latest in a series of gimmicks to raise lagging attendance and combat the Mets at the box office.

"The idea," said Robert O. Fishel, the Yankees' public relations director, "Is to make

Continued on Page 18, Column 2

Erhard Bars Visit To the Soviet Union

Special to The New York Times

BONN, June 19 — Chancellor Ludwig Erhard turned down today an unofficial but urgent Soviet invitation to go to Moscow for an attempt at improving Soviet-West German relations.

He suggested instead that the Soviet Premier ask for an official invitation to Bonn if he thought the trip would be worthwhile.

At his first news conference here in six months, Dr. Erhard carefully held open the door for an eventual encounter with Premier Khrushchev while dashing cold water on the prospects of settling soon any of the fundamental questions that divide Bonn and Moscow.

As he spoke, Bonn's Western allies were putting the final

Continued on Page 2, Column 4

"All the News That's Fit to Print"

The New York Times.

LATE CITY EDITION
U. S. Weather Bureau Report (Page .3) forecasts:
Showers, then fair and warm today; fair and cooler tonight, tomorrow.
Temp. Range: 90—68; yesterday: 78—68.
Temp.-Hum. Index: low 80's; yesterday: 73.

VOL. CXIII..No. 38,868. NEW YORK, WEDNESDAY, JUNE 24, 1964. TEN CENTS

LODGE IS LEAVING VIETNAM TO HELP SCRANTON'S DRIVE; GEN. TAYLOR TO BE ENVOY

POLICY UNCHANGED

A Diplomat Also Sent to Saigon—Wheeler Heads Joint Chiefs

Transcript of news conference and summary, Page 12.

By MAX FRANKEL
Special to The New York Times

WASHINGTON, June 23 — Henry Cabot Lodge is hurrying back from South Vietnam to help Gov. William W. Scranton's bid for the Republican Presidential nomination.

President Johnson accepted today the resignation of his Ambassador in Saigon and assigned Gen. Maxwell D. Taylor to replace him.

In a highly unusual move, the President also appointed a prominent career diplomat, U. Alexis Johnson, to the specially created job of Deputy Ambassador to South Vietnam.

Gen. Earle G. Wheeler will succeed General Taylor as chairman of the Joint Chiefs of Staff. No replacement has been chosen for General Wheeler as Army Chief of Staff.

Thompson to Fill In

Ambassador at Large Llewellyn Thompson will fill in on an acting basis for Mr. Johnson, the Deputy Under Secretary of State for Political Affairs. Mr. Thompson, a senior career diplomat and a former Ambassador to the Soviet Union, is a top adviser on United States-Soviet affairs.

Mr. Lodge, whose wish to return home before the Republican National Convention in San Francisco July 13 was reported by The New York Times last week, said in Saigon that he intended to support Mr. Scranton for his party's Presidential nomination.

President Johnson announced the changes at a news conference in his office. His demeanor and his choice of men were intended to reassure the Government and people of South Vietnam that Mr. Lodge's departure would not affect Washington's commitment to the fight against Communist guerrillas or result in any other significant policy changes.

The objective of reassuring the Vietnamese was said to have been taken so seriously by President Johnson and his top aides that volunteers to replace

Continued on Page 12, Column 2

United Press International Telephoto

GETTING NEW ROLE: Gen. Maxwell D. Taylor, who is to be Ambassador to South Vietnam, signing autographs as he left Senate Foreign Relations Committee hearing.

U.S. REORGANIZES VIETNAM MISSION

Military to Direct Civilian Activity in Three Critical Areas Around Saigon

By PETER GROSE
Special to The New York Times

SAIGON, June 23—The United States Military Assistance Command is assuming greatly increased responsibilities in a reorganization of the American military and civilian advisory mission to Vietnam.

As a first step, Lieut. Gen. William C. Westmoreland, the new United States commander in Vietnam, has been named an "executive agent" to supervise civil as well as military pacification measures by Americans in three provinces around Saigon.

The principle of a unified command of the American effort at the province level is later to be extended to the whole country, according to a classified plan. This plan was drawn up and approved last week after many weeks of discussions between General Westmoreland and heads of American civilian agencies operating in Vietnam.

No change in the relationship between American field advisers and their Vietnamese counterparts is envisaged under the plan except that the Vietnamese will be dealing with a more tightly coordinated American team.

At a meeting today with the deputy heads of civilian agencies, including the Agency for International Development and

Continued on Page 11, Column 2

Johnson and Inonu End Cyprus Talks, Reaffirm '59 Pacts

By TAD SZULC
Special to The New York Times

WASHINGTON, June 23 — President Johnson and Premier Ismet Inonu of Turkey ended two days of conferences on the Cyprus crisis today with a brief communiqué stressing the validity of the 1959 treaties that led to the island's independence.

The otherwise noncommittal communiqué announced that Mr. Johnson and Mr. Inonu had "covered ways in which present difficulties might be adjusted by negotiation and agreement," and underlined the "urgent necessity" for such accords aimed at a permanent solution of the Cyprus problem.

Beyond this, however, there were no indications that the meetings had produced any formula to solve the crisis that has threatened armed conflict between Greece and Turkey, both members of the North Atlantic Treaty Organization.

Tomorrow President Johnson will embark upon the second phase of his diplomatic intervention when he opens two days of consultations with Premier George Papandreou of Greece.

The communiqué on the Johnson-Inonu discussions said:

"Prime Minister Inonu of Turkey and President Johnson have discussed all aspects of the problem of Cyprus. Both leaders welcomed the opportunity presented by the Prime Minister's visit at the President's invitation for a full exchange of views.

"The discussion, proceeding from the present binding effects of existing treaties, covered ways in which present difficulties might be adjusted by

Continued on Page 10, Column 4

ROBERT KENNEDY RULES OUT RACE FOR SENATE SEAT

Brother's Injury Influenced Final Decision—Field in State Is Wide Open

By ANTHONY LEWIS
Special to The New York Times

WASHINGTON, June 23 — Attorney General Robert F. Kennedy removed himself today as a potential candidate for the United States Senate from New York this fall.

In a brief statement he ended speculation that he might seek the Democratic nomination by saying: "I will not be a candidate." He gave no reasons and did not indicate his long-range plans.

Mr. Kennedy said in his statement:

"Over the last several weeks, Democratic leaders and friends in New York and elsewhere have contacted me urging that I seek the Democratic nomination for United States Senator for New York.

"Representing the state of New York in the United States Senate is a challenging and important opportunity for public service. I deeply appreciate the loyalty and friendship of those who have urged me to run and who believe I could perform a service for the people of New York.

"However, in fairness to them, and to end speculation, I wish to state that I will not be a candidate for United States Senator for New York."

Sends Word to Johnson

Mr. Kennedy sent word of his decision to President Johnson but did not discuss it with him before the announcement this afternoon.

The Attorney General is scheduled to leave tomorrow on a one-week trip to West Germany, Berlin and Poland. He had a meeting with the President tonight to discuss the trip, but the subject instead turned out to be the civil rights crisis in Mississippi.

Mr. Kennedy's announcement left the choice of a Democratic nominee wide open. Many party leaders in New York had been urging Mr. Kennedy to make the Senate race, believing he would be the strongest possible opponent for the Republican incumbent, Senator Kenneth B. Keating.

Polls being taken by Democratic state leaders have not yet been completed. The results already in, from New York City, were said to look very good for Mr. Kennedy, but associates said these did not figure in his mind when he decided against the Senate race.

The idea of a Senate race appealed to Mr. Kennedy at first, despite the difficulty it would

Continued on Page 14, Column 2

HOUSE UNIT VOTES $3.3 BILLION IN AID, DEFYING PASSMAN

Chairman Assails President as He Storms From Closed Subcommittee Session

By FELIX BELAIR Jr.
Special to The New York Times

WASHINGTON, June 23 — President Johnson scored a personal triumph today in his fight for a $3.5 billion foreign aid money bill.

By a 7-5 vote, the House Appropriations Subcommittee on Foreign Aid decided during a hard-fought five-hour session to recommend an appropriation of $3,316,700,000 for economic and military aid during the fiscal year beginning July 1.

This was just $200 million less than the President's asking figure.

But it was the first time in 10 years that a President had won over the subcommittee chairman, Otto E. Passman of Louisiana, who had defied the parent committee's chairman, George E. Mahon of Texas, in his demand for a combined cut of $519.4 million in the Administration's asking figure.

Storms From Meeting

The implacable foe of foreign aid programs stormed out of the meeting when it was clear that he was beaten and told reporters that he would not "be used as a rubber stamp for the Administration" and would not be dissuaded from his fight by offers of "airplane rides and sniffling at the roses."

Mr. Passman had planned to make a trip to South Vietnam in mid-June along with several of his anti-aid supporters. But the new Appropriations Committee chairman, Mr. Mahon, notified him that he would agree to the trip only if Mr. Passman obtained affirming signatures of all members of his subcommittee.

He was invited also to attend a recent White House meeting as a member of the appropriations group, which included an informal talk by President Johnson in the Rose Garden on the south lawn of the White House. He did not attend.

Mr. Passman's face was flushed and his manner highly agitated as he told newsmen after the hearing that "no one can ever get in trouble doing what is right," and declared: "God forbid that I ever would be weak enough to capitulate to political pressure and flattery."

The Louisiana Democrat went on to suggest that if President Johnson was "so infallible" on foreign aid, "let's give him a life term," and shouted:

"I am not a political prostitute!"

Mr. Passman's direct refer-

Continued on Page 16, Column 5

RIGHTS TEAM'S BURNED CAR FOUND IN MISSISSIPPI BOG; DULLES TO AID HUNT FOR 3

United Press International Telephoto

Charred station wagon of civil rights workers was found in a swamp by F.B.I. agents

PRESIDENT ACTS

Sends Ex-C.I.A. Head to South After Seeing Parents of Youths

Special to The New York Times

WASHINGTON, June 23 — President Johnson decided tonight to send Allen W. Dulles to Mississippi to assist in the search for three missing civil rights workers.

Mr. Dulles, former director of the Central Intelligence Agency, will leave tomorrow. He will consult with state and Federal officials in Mississippi on the disappearance case and on the broader question of observance of law there.

The President's decision was announced in a White House statement tonight after he had held a lengthy meeting with top officials of the Justice Department. Attorney General Robert F. Kennedy was there with his deputy, Nicholas DeB. Katzenbach, and his civil rights chief, Burke Marshall.

Talks With Governor

The statement disclosed that the President had talked on the telephone today with Gov. Paul B. Johnson Jr. of Mississippi. It said that Governor Johnson had pledged the state's law enforcement facilities to prevent acts of violence.

"By arrangement with Governor Johnson," the statement said, "the President has asked Allen W. Dulles to go to Mississippi to meet with the Governor, other officials of the state, the F.B.I. and others who have information on the law observance problems that exist there and are a matter of such great concern."

The "law observance problems" referred to were evidently the announced determination of various white groups in Mississippi to use any means to preserve racial segregation. Among other things, an upsurge of Ku Klux Klan activity has been reported.

"We are basically law-abiding nation," the White House

Continued on Page 21, Column 3

0 MILES 150
TENN.
ARKANSAS
Oxford
Greenville
Philadelphia
Meridian
Jackson
MISSISSIPPI
Hattiesburg
ALABAMA
Mississippi R.
LA.
Baton Rouge
Mobile
Biloxi
New Orleans
Gulf of Mexico

The New York Times June 24, 1964

Cross shows where rights workers' car was discovered.

HARLEM PROGRAM GETS $3.4 MILLION

Mayor Names Screvane to Disburse City Antipoverty Funds Through Haryou

By MARTIN ARNOLD

Mayor Wagner announced yesterday that the city would provide $3.4 million in the 1964-1965 budget for the antipoverty program in Harlem.

He also named City Council President Paul R. Screvane to disburse the funds through Haryou-Act, the newly created social agency that will operate the program in Harlem.

Haryou-Act, which has been involved in a controversy over its leadership, seeks to spend more than $110 million over the next three years in its antipoverty and youth program.

The $3.4 million includes $600,000 that was set aside in last year's city budget for Haryou-Act but was never used because Haryou-Act had not yet come into being.

Part of $15 Million Rise

The money is part of the $15 million increase put into the 1964-65 budget for antipoverty and welfare funds. That budget goes into effect July 1. In last year's budget, $800 million was earmarked for city welfare and social agencies and programs.

The funds for the Haryou-Act program will come from Federal, state and city governments and from private foundations.

The program already has been promised $1 million by President Johnson's Committee on Juvenile Delinquency and Youth Crime, headed by Attorney General Robert F. Kennedy.

In addition to that, Haryou-

Continued on Page 23, Column 6

TIP LEADS TO AUTO

Wreckage Raises New Fears Over Fate of the Missing Men

By CLAUDE SITTON
Special to The New York Times

PHILADELPHIA, Miss., June 23—The automobile of three missing civil rights workers was found burned today 15 miles northeast of this town in east-central Mississippi.

Discovery of the 1964 Ford station wagon aroused deep concern over the fate of the men and brought an intensified search by agents of the Federal Bureau of Investigation and by state highway patrolmen.

The three men have not been heard from since Sunday night, when they were released from the Neshoba County jail here. They had been arrested four hours earlier, shortly after they began work in a two-month civil rights campaign in Mississippi.

[In Washington an F.B.I. spokesman said it had been determined that the car had been burned Monday, United Press International reported.]

Two Are New Yorkers

The missing men are Michael Schwerner, a 24-year-old member of the Congress of Racial Equality and former settlement house worker from Brooklyn; James E. Cheney, 21, a plasterer from Meridian, Miss., also a CORE member, and Andrew Goodman, 20, a Queens College student from New York. Mr. Schwerner and Mr. Goodman are white. Mr. Cheney is a Negro.

F.B.I. agents, acting on a tip, found the station wagon wreckage in a swamp on Bogue Chitto Creek, about 50 feet off State Highway 21, in the county's northeastern corner.

The F.B.I. will examine the charred auto, which was brought to Philadelphia and locked in a garage.

H. G. Maynor, special agent

Continued on Page 20, Column 3

U.S.-SOVIET TALKS ON DESALTING SET

Parley in July to Discuss Possibility of Joint Effort

By JOHN W. FINNEY
Special to The New York Times

WASHINGTON, June 23 — The United States and the Soviet Union have agreed to explore the possibility of cooperative development of methods for desalting sea water, President Johnson announced today.

As an initial step, representatives of the two nations will meet here in mid-July to discuss possible areas of cooperation, including the use of nuclear power for running desalination plants.

In announcing the meeting at his news conference, President Johnson expressed hope that the exploratory discussions would lead to "effective scientific cooperation" in "what could become a very important activity of great economic significance to many areas of the world." [Opening statement Page 12.]

As outlined by the President, the meeting will have three purposes: To discuss the general problem of desalting, to review the present activities and plans of the two countries, and to consider areas of cooperation.

White House officials said the initiative for the cooperative discussions had come from the Soviet Union. For more

Continued on Page 14, Column 4

Pope Says Church Is Making 'Profound' Birth Control Study

Special to The New York Times

ROME, June 23 — Pope Paul VI said today that the Roman Catholic Church was giving "wide and profound" study to the problem of birth control.

Pope Paul's remarks on birth control are on Page 3.

But the Pontiff cautioned against public statements deviating from the church's opposition to the practice of birth control by artificial means.

The directives "given by Pope Pius XII in this regard . . . must be considered valid, at least until we feel obliged in conscience to change them," the Pope said. He recommended that "no one for the present," should take "it on himself to make pronouncements in terms different from the prevailing norm."

His remarks, the first official Vatican acknowledgment of the current dispute in Catholic circles over the use of birth control pills, came in a speech to about 26 Cardinals of the Roman Curia, the Vatican's central administrative body.

They had gathered in the Pope's library to pay their respects upon the eve of his name day, the Feast of St. John the Baptist. Paul was Giovanni Battista (John the Baptist) Montini before becoming Pope.

In his address, the Pope said the question of birth control "is being subjected to study, as wide and profound as possible, as grave and honest as it must be on a subject of such importance."

Interest in birth control has been renewed with the growing

Continued on Page 3, Column 1

Fireworks on Barge Kill 2 Here; Explosion at Armory Injures 18

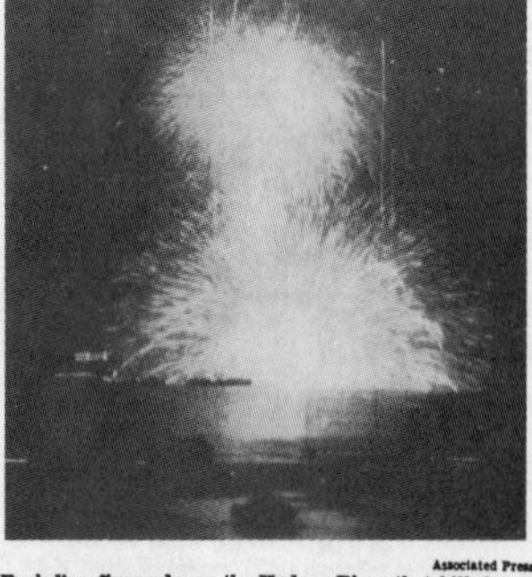

Associated Press

Exploding fireworks on the Hudson River that killed two men last night. The view is from the Manhattan shore.

500,000 View Accident

Two men were killed and four injured by an explosion last night on a barge carrying fireworks 10 minutes after Macy's annual Hudson River pre-Fourth of July display began last night.

The barge, the last of four to leave the 72d Street area bound for 120th Street, was about 1,200 feet offshore when the blast occurred.

A crowd of about 500,000 applauded the tragedy unknowingly. They accepted the blinding blast as the climax of the

Continued on Page 30, Column 2

Park Ave. Building Shaken

Eighteen National Guard reservists were injured last night in an explosion that demolished the ammunition room of a Manhattan armory. About 385 other reservists attending a weekly drill escaped unharmed.

The blast occurred shortly before 9 P.M. in the subbasement of the 71st Infantry Regiment Armory on Park Avenue between 33d and 34th Streets.

Two of the injured were hospitalized and reported in serious condition. All of the injured

Continued on Page 30, Column 1

Alex Rose Resigns At Fair Over Mural

By WALTER CARLSON

Alex Rose, vice chairman of the Liberal party, resigned in anger yesterday from the World's Fair board of directors over the fair's refusal to act against the controversial mural in the Jordan Pavilion.

In a letter mailed yesterday to Robert Moses, the president of the World's Fair Corporation, Mr. Rose said he regarded the mural as "sheer war propaganda — offensive to a sovereign people, and to millions of American citizens, Jews and non-Jews alike."

Meanwhile, at City Hall, the City Council unanimously adopted a resolution yesterday calling for immediate removal of the mural "as a source of insult to millions of people in

Continued on Page 24, Column 1

NEWS INDEX

Wilkins Denounces Negro 'Hoodlums'

Roy Wilkins has denounced "teen-age Negro hoodlums" who by their violence "are undercutting and wrecking gains made by hundreds of Negro and white youngsters who went to jail for human rights."

Mr. Wilkins, executive secretary of the National Association for the Advancement of Colored People, expressed his view in a recent column in The Amsterdam News, a Negro weekly newspaper published here.

He writes the column, "Along This Way," every other week for the paper. The Rev. Martin Luther King Jr., chairman of the Southern Christian Leadership Conference, writes the column on the alternate weeks.

In May and earlier this month

Continued on Page 23, Column 3

Three faces that spread across the nation's front pages were (left to right) Michael Schwerner, James Chaney, and Andrew Goodman. The three civil-rights workers were victims of a triple lynching.

Surgeon General Luther Terry displayed government reports on the perils of smoking.

The manager of a Florida motel is pouring muriatic acid into his pool to prevent integration.

The blast of smoke over the western area of mainland China signalled China's entry into the nuclear club.

"All the News That's Fit to Print"

The New York Times.

LATE CITY EDITION

U. S. Weather Bureau Report (Page 63) forecasts: Sunny, hot and humid today; fair, hot and humid tonight and tomorrow.

Temp. Range: 94—70; yesterday: 89—67. Temp.-Hum. Index: about 80; yesterday: 77.

VOL. CXIII..No. 38,890. © 1964 by The New York Times Company. Times Square, New York, N. Y. 10036 NEW YORK, THURSDAY, JULY 16, 1964. TEN CENTS

GOLDWATER IS NOMINATED ON FIRST BALLOT; HE CALLS JOHNSON 'BIGGEST FAKER IN U.S.'; SELECTS REP. MILLER AS HIS RUNNING MATE

MIKOYAN IS NAMED SOVIET PRESIDENT; BREZHNEV SHIFTED

Former Chief to Serve Full Time as Khrushchev Aide —His Position Enhanced

By HENRY TANNER

Special to The New York Times

MOSCOW, July 15—Anastas I. Mikoyan became President of the Soviet Union today.

Leonid I. Brezhnev, who had held the post since 1960, stepped aside to devote himself full-time to his duties as Premier Khrushchev's deputy in the Secretariat of the Communist party, the center of power in the Soviet Union.

Western analysts drew the following conclusions from the change:

¶Mr. Brezhnev's chances of becoming Mr. Khrushchev's eventual successor have been substantially enhanced.

¶Mr. Khrushchev's own power has been increased, since his two closest associates now occupy the key posts of titular head of state and deputy party leader.

¶The Presidency — technically the post is the chairmanship of the Presidium of the Supreme Soviet (Parliament)—is likely to gain in importance. Mr. Mikoyan, while assuming the representative functions of his new post, is expected to continue many of his activities in the field of foreign relations.

Step in Long-Range Plan

Some analysts saw today's move as the first step in a long-range program to assure an orderly transition from Mr. Khrushchev to Mr. Brezhnev.

The analysts thought that the change raised a possibility that Mr. Khrushchev, when he felt the time had come, might decide to turn over the party leadership to Mr. Brezhnev and take over the Presidency from Mr. Mikoyan.

Mr. Mikoyan's rise to the Presidency came at a short and surprisingly matter-of-fact meeting of the Supreme Soviet.

Mr. Khrushchev rose and in the name of the Central Committee of the Communist party nominated Mr. Mikoyan.

He praised Mr. Mikoyan as a "true Leninist" and a "fighter for peace" and declared that the Central Committee felt he de-

Continued on Page 8, Column 1

Associated Press Cablephoto

SOVIET HIERARCHY: Premier Khrushchev with Leonid I. Brezhnev, center, and Anastas I. Mikoyan before Supreme Soviet. Mr. Mikoyan succeeded to the Presidency.

SOVIET SAYS CHINA FEARS RED PARLEY

Peking Told in Sharp Letter That It Would Get Rebuff at Conference of Parties

Special to The New York Times

MOSCOW, July 15 — The Soviet Union made public today a letter to Communist China harsher in tone than any other published Soviet document about their ideological dispute.

The long letter, sent to Peking June 15, charged that the Chinese leaders opposed a Soviet call for a world conference of Communist parties because they were "afraid" of facing the other parties at a meeting.

"You have never seriously thought of a conference . . . because you could not count on the support for your ideological and political platform on the part of a world Communist forum," the letter said.

Tone of Letter Caustic

The letter, though pale compared with some of the accusations made by Soviet and Chinese newspapers, was more caustic than any Soviet message sent to the Chinese and made public so far. It gave an insight into the tone the Russians and Chinese have been using in the private exchanges in their ideological dispute.

The Russians asserted that only two parties in the world —the Chinese and Albanian—were against a world conference.

The "overwhelming majority" of the other parties, the letter continued, are actively supporting the idea and a number of parties are for it in principle but have "reservations" about the timing.

The Soviet plan for a conference will be discussed again next week when Premier Khru-

Continued on Page 7, Column 1

Britain Now Backs Independence Talk For South Rhodesia

By LAWRENCE FELLOWS

Special to The New York Times

LONDON, July 15 — Britain agreed tonight to call a conference of Southern Rhodesians, black and white, to discuss terms on which the self-governing colony would achieve independence.

Up until now Britain has resisted proposing such a conference, fearing that the Rhodesian Government, if pressed too hard, might unilaterally declare the colony independent.

Sir Alec Douglas-Home, the British Prime Minister, also undertook to approach Ian D. Smith, the Southern Rhodesian Prime Minister, to try to persuade him to release African nationalists now detained.

Sir Alex was supported in this by a unanimous declaration of the Prime Ministers of the British Commonwealth that none of them would recognize a declaration of independence by the Southern Rhodesian regime.

The Commonwealth Prime Ministers' conference here was supposed to have ended at noon today. The agreement on a Rhodesian conference was reached nine hours later. It helped to relieve the tension that resulted when a young white man assaulted Jomo Kenyatta, Prime

Continued on Page 5, Column 1

STATEN ISLAND HIT BY A FERRY STRIKE

City Employes Defy Court Order—35,000 Daily Commuters Affected

Ferry workers walked off the job early today, tying up service between Manhattan and Staten Island that is used by more than 35,000 persons a day.

The strike, in addition to halting ferries on the Whitehall Street-St. George, S.I., run, also affects ferry service to North Brother Island, Riker's Island, City Island and Hart Island.

The walkout started at 12:20 A.M. when employes of the ferryboat Verrazano refused to open the entrance gates to the ferry at the Battery. About 150 ferry employes cheered when the gates stayed closed.

Leo Brown, Commissioner of the Department of Marine and Aviation, immediately had copies of a temporary strike injunction given to the employes of the Verrazano. The employes still refused to open the gates.

The injunction was issued Monday by Supreme Court Justice George Tilzer several hours after members of Local 333 of the United Marine Division of the National Maritime

Continued on Page 62, Column 6

SCORNFUL ATTACK

Senator Charges That President Changed Civil Rights Stand

By CHARLES MOHR

Special to The New York Times

SAN FRANCISCO, July 15—Senator Barry Goldwater accused President Johnson today of being "the biggest faker in the United States" and the "phoniest individual who ever came around."

The Arizona Republican made his extemporaneous remarks on his way to a service elevator in a back hall of the Mark Hopkins Hotel after addressing a "captive nations" rally.

A reporter asked him if the Republican National Convention's refusal to strengthen its civil rights plank would not give the Democrats a good issue in November.

The Senator's head snapped around. With an edge of scorn in his voice, he said:

"After Lyndon Johnson—the biggest faker in the United States? He opposed civil rights until this year. Let them make an issue of it. I'll recite the thousands of words he has spoken down the years against abolishing the poll tax and F.E.P.C. [Fair Employment Practices Commission]. He's the phoniest individual who ever came around."

Plans 'Vigorous Campaign'

Later in the day, after his nomination, Senator Goldwater told a news conference that he intended to wage a "vigorous campaign" but assumed that it would not be a campaign of personal attack.

He added that he expected President Johnson also to wage a vigorous campaign.

The Senator said he hoped the campaign would give the American people "time to think, and I hope that I'm the better salesman."

Senator Goldwater said that the differences within the Republican party were "rather minor" and that, "with some exceptions, we could almost overlook them."

"I can't find words to express the feeling that is in my heart," Mr. Goldwater said. "No greater honor can come to any Republican."

Mr. Goldwater said that he knew Mr. Johnson's campaign would be conducted like his own, on the issues and not on personalities.

Mr. Goldwater said he would attempt to withdraw as a candidate to succeed himself in the Senate. But he said that a "dis-

Continued on Page 17, Column 1

Associated Press Wirephoto

AFTER NOMINATION: Senator and Mrs. Barry Goldwater embrace during news conference in San Francisco.

G.O.P. Chairman Picked For No. 2 Spot on Ticket

Special to The New York Times

SAN FRANCISCO, July 15—Senator Barry Goldwater today selected Representative William E. Miller of upstate New York as his Vice-Presidential running mate. Mr. Goldwater was reported to have asked Mr. Miller to run with him in a phone call about noon, many hours before the Arizonan was formally chosen as the Republican standard-bearer.

Reliable sources made known Mr. Goldwater's choice. Asked after his nomination whether he had phoned Mr. Miller to offer him the No. 2 position on the Republican ticket, the Senator said "No." But he added that he was "favorably inclined" toward the New Yorker.

"I didn't think it would be fair to ask him, if that was my intention, until he was through with his official duties at the convention," Mr. Goldwater said.

Mr. Miller is the Republican national chairman.

Mr. Miller, interviewed later, said he would be "delighted" to run with the Senator.

Before he made his choice, Mr. Goldwater also had been

Continued on Page 18, Column 3

EISENHOWER CHIDES SENATOR'S FORCES

Says Rejection of Changes in the Platform Violated Democratic Method

By FELIX BELAIR Jr.

Special to The New York Times

SAN FRANCISCO, July 15—Former President Dwight D. Eisenhower condemned today the tactics of Goldwater delegates to the Republican National Convention in rejecting efforts to strengthen a platform declaration on civil rights and to add one on "extremism."

His comment concerned two proposals by Gov. George Romney of Michigan. These, as well as others, were overwhelmingly defeated by the convention in a dramatic demonstration of the support that a majority of the delegates were giving Senator Barry Goldwater.

In a television appearance as a political consultant for the American Broadcasting Company, General Eisenhower said that he was "unhappy" about the defeat of the proposals, but even more about the way in which this was accomplished.

His earlier disappointment apparently forgotten, General

Continued on Page 18, Column 5

U.S. Judge Orders Sheppard's Release

Special to The New York Times

DAYTON, Ohio, July 15—Dr. Samuel H. Sheppard, convicted of slaying his wife in 1954, today was ordered released from prison.

Federal District Judge Carl A. Weinman ruled that Sheppard had been denied his constitutional rights in his trial 10 years ago in Cleveland. He declared Sheppard's custody void and ordered his release in $10,000 bond.

The judge said Sheppard's trial had been "a mockery of justice." Sheppard is expected to be released from Ohio Penitentiary in Columbus tomorrow.

If Cuyahoga County (Cleve-

Continued on Page 32, Column 1

VOTE IS 883 TO 214

Scranton Plea to Make It Unanimous Is Then Approved

By TOM WICKER

Special to The New York Times

SAN FRANCISCO, July 15—Barry Morris Goldwater, the champion of a new American conservatism, was nominated for President tonight by the 28th Republican National Convention.

The Arizona Senator, the 20th man in the line of Republican nominees that began with John C. Frémont and Abraham Lincoln, needed only one ballot to win the nomination and crush the moderate forces that had controlled his party for a quarter-century.

The only serious challenger was Gov. William W. Scranton of Pennsylvania.

At the conclusion of the ballot he appeared on the platform to move for the unanimous nomination of Senator Goldwater. The convention then adopted by acclamation a resolution making it so.

The count of the first ballot stood as follows for the two leading contenders:

Goldwater 883

Scranton 214

Will Accept Today

Senator Goldwater did not appear at the convention, which adjourned at 11:11 P.M. Pacific daylight time (2:11 A.M., Thursday, New York time). He will accept the nomination tomorrow, after his choice for Vice President, Representative William E. Miller of New York, is duly nominated.

There was never any contest from the moment Senator Everett McKinley Dirksen concluded his nominating speech for Senator Goldwater and set off a wild demonstration that thundered through the Cow Palace for 29 minutes.

Governor Scranton, who entered the race only a few weeks ago, nevertheless refused to withdraw before the ballot was taken. He was on the Cow Palace grounds with his wife, waiting in a trailer for the results.

As soon as the ballot was completed, however, Governor Scranton came striding briskly down the long wooden ramp to the platform, his wife just behind him, with his campaign

Continued on Page 16, Column 1

COURT OPENS WAY ON REDISTRICTING

U.S. Judges Give State Until July 27 to Offer Plan

By THOMAS P. RONAN

A three-judge Federal Court cleared the way yesterday for reapportionment of the New York Legislature in time for the November election, but it did not specifically order the change.

After formally declaring the present system of apportionment unconstitutional, the court recessed until July 27 "to await action, if any, by the duly constituted authorities of the State of New York in the light of this declaration."

On that date it will hear "representations" by the parties involved in the suit on how its judgment of unconstitutionality can be implemented. The representations will include suggested reapportionment plans,

Continued on Page 20, Column 3

CONGO TO BOYCOTT AFRICAN MEETING

Tshombe Also Says Regime Has Released Gizenga

By J. ANTHONY LUKAS

Special to The New York Times

LEOPOLDVILLE, the Congo, July 15 — Premier Moise Tshombe announced tonight that the Congo would boycott the conference of African leaders opening Friday in Cairo.

Mr. Tshombe also said that his Government had released Antoine Gizenga, the leftist leader who was held on an island in the mouth of the Congo River for the last two and a half years.

The announcements were made in a seven-paragraph declaration after a day of frantic meetings in Mr. Tshombe's home.

The decision to boycott the Cairo conference followed declarations by several African leaders that they would not sit at the conference table with Mr. Tshombe.

Among those who made statements sharply critical of Mr. Tshombe were President Ahmed Ben Bella of Algeria and President Kwame Nkrumah of Ghana.

Mr. Tshombe, who was named last week as the Congo's fourth Premier, is considered by many African leaders to be a pawn

Continued on Page 4, Column 3

2 More Policemen Ousted in Inquiry

By EDITH EVANS ASBURY

A police lieutenant and a patrolman were dismissed yesterday for refusing to cooperate in the investigation into alleged collusion between policemen and gamblers.

Both men had served in plainclothes in strategic posts.

Police Commissioner Michael J. Murphy, who announced the dismissals, said earlier in the day that changes had been made in his department and "there will be others" as a result of the investigation. Three grand juries in Manhattan and one in Brooklyn are questioning policemen and gamblers.

Yesterday's dismissals brought

Continued on Page 14, Column 3

Prime Minister of Kenya Is Attacked by a British Fascist in London

Associated Press Cablephoto

Prime Minister Jomo Kenyatta, left, of Kenya, braces against attack by member of British National Socialist Movement, in London. Mr. Kenyatta announced that he was unhurt.

United Press International Radiophoto

Mr. Kenyatta leaving conference later in the day.

NEWS INDEX

Haight-Ashbury in San Francisco was at the heart of the "hippie" movement. Its popular slogan, "Haight is Love", expressed the culture's prevalent theme.

The suggestive bathing suit above exhibits the essence of the sexual revolution of the Sixties.

Hemlines rose a handspan above the knees for the first time in history when the mini-skirt made its debut.

Jackie Kennedy, seen here with her sister, Princess Lee Radziwill, wearing the year's hottest fashion trend, the mini-skirt.

In *Bewitched* Agnes Moorehead played the mother of TV's beautiful witch, Samantha, played by Elizabeth Montgomery.

The debut of *The Man from U.N.C.L.E.* in 1964 stirred a great deal of audience interest. Robert Vaughn starred as Napoleon Solo but co-star David McCallum as Ilya Kuryakin drew more attention, especially from teen-aged girls.

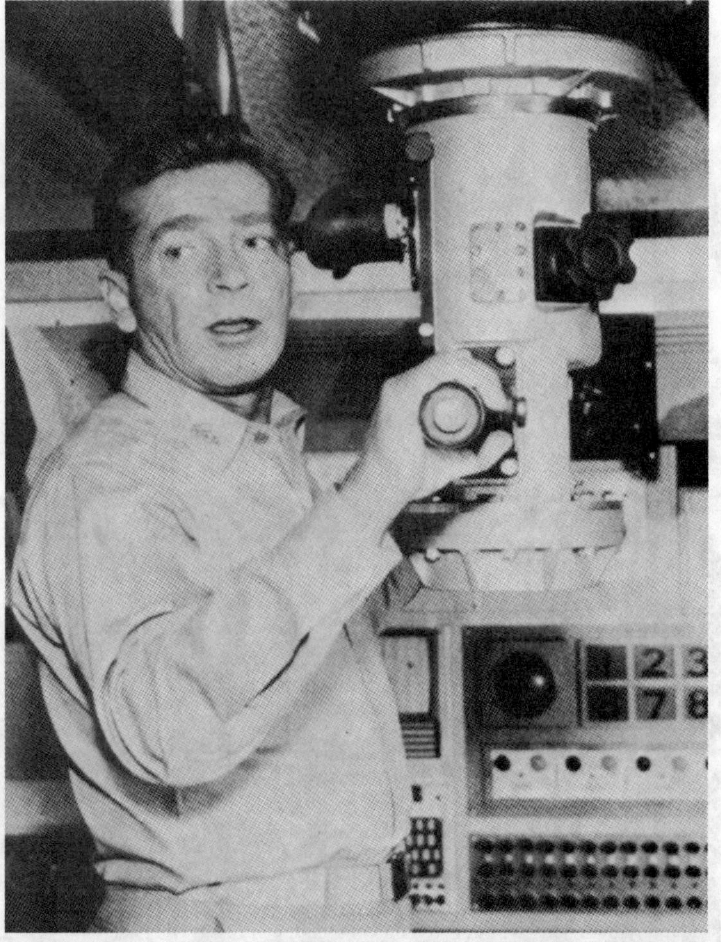

Richard Basehart starred in *Voyage to the Bottom of the Sea,* a futuristic series.

"All the News That's Fit to Print"

The New York Times.

LATE CITY EDITION

U.S. Weather Bureau Report (Page 58) forecasts: Sunny and hot today. Fair tonight. Chance of showers late tomorrow.
Temp. Range: 96—73; yesterday: 89—69. Temp.-Hum. Index: about 80; yesterday: 80.

VOL. CXIII..No. 38,902. NEW YORK, TUESDAY, JULY 28, 1964. TEN CENTS

COURT SAYS STATE MUST REDISTRICT BEFORE APRIL '65

U.S. Judges Set One-Year Terms for Legislators to Be Elected This Fall

SPECIAL SESSION LIKELY

December Meeting Expected —Plan for Connecticut Is Termed Unworkable

By R. W. APPLE Jr.

A Federal Court ordered the New York Legislature yesterday to pass a reapportionment measure by April 1, 1965.

The court directed that Assemblymen and Senators be elected Nov. 3 on the basis of the legislative districts now in effect. But it ruled that the legislators elected on that date could serve only one year instead of two.

By its actions, the three-judge court set the first definite timetable for the implementation of the United States Supreme Court's decision of June 15, which declared the state's formula for legislative apportionment unconstitutional.

The state must now hold three legislative elections in three years—the one in November; a special election in November, 1965, based on new districts, for one-year terms; and a regular election in November, 1966, also based on new districts, for two-year terms.

Democrats' Plea Denied

By ordering the short terms, the court advanced the effective date of the Supreme Court's reapportionment ruling by a full year — from November, 1966, to November, 1965.

The decision yesterday was a defeat for the Democrats, who had asked the court to order immediate redistricting. However, it was not an unqualified victory for the Republicans, who had hoped to delay the impact of reapportionment for two years.

In another development growing out of the Supreme Court's ruling, Gov. John N. Dempsey of Connecticut rejected a Federal Court's plan for redistricting in that state and asked permission to present a proposal of his own.

Mr. Dempsey described the court's plan as unworkable. It calls for a special session of the General Assembly by next week to begin preparations for a constitutional convention.

Sources in Albany reported that Governor Rockefeller was

Continued on Page 26, Column 4

FIELD INSPECTION: Governor Rockefeller chats with members of mess detail at National Guard encampment in Rochester, where troops are on hand to prevent rioting. Associated Press Wirephoto

Police Inspector Demoted In Gambling Graft Inquiry

By EDITH EVANS ASBURY

Police Commissioner Michael J. Murphy demoted a deputy police inspector to captain yesterday on a charge of permitting gambling operations "in an open and notorious manner" in Brooklyn. The officer, Deputy Inspector Anthony Obremsky, also came under fire from District Attorney Frank H. Hogan's office.

The Commissioner charged that the officer had failed to perform his duties properly as supervisor of plainclothes men in the Greenpoint-Williamsburg section of Brooklyn. He had been assigned to that post in the 14th Inspection Division last Jan. 29.

The Commissioner said charges would be brought against the officer, who is on vacation and whose whereabouts were not immediately known yesterday.

Two Charges Made

Mr. Hogan's office cited the manner in which the officer had answered grand jury questions about his activities while stationed in midtown Manhattan, and took note of his seeking retirement July 17 after a third appearance before the grand jury.

Two specific charges were made against Captain Obremsky.

The first alleged that he "failed and neglected to properly perform his duties between June 26 and July 14, 1964, between 7 and 10 P.M., and that within the area of his responsibility at Union Avenue and Withers Street, Brooklyn, during these times, a gambling operation took place in an open and notorious manner."

The second charge asserted that Captain Obremsky's alleged failure to perform his duties "did bring or tend to bring adverse criticism of this department and a loss of confidence and respect of the people."

12 Others Face Charges

The announcement, made by Deputy Commissioner Walter Arm, said that 12 other policemen stationed in the 14th Division would be served with similar charges.

Previously Captain Obremsky served as deputy inspector on plainclothes patrol duty in the Third Division of Manhattan, which handles vice and gambling cases in midtown.

The officer's appearance before the special New York County grand jury investigating allgeed links between the police and gamblers was disclosed yesterday when Assistant District Attorney Peter D. Andreoli applied to Supreme Court Justice Charles Marks for the release of testimony.

Mr. Andreoli stated, in an affidavit for the court, that the

Continued on Page 60, Column 1

GOVERNOR DENIES VOTING-LAW PLEA

Rejects Wagner Demand for Special Session to Revise Literacy Requirement

By DOUGLAS DALES
Special to The New York Times

ALBANY, July 27 — Governor Rockefeller rejected today Mayor Wagner's request for a special session of the Legislature to revise the state's literacy requirements for voting.

Mr. Wagner had said the state should act to make its literacy requirements conform with the Federal Civil Rights Act of 1964. However, Mr. Rockefeller said today that the Mayor's request had been based on a "misunderstanding" of the 1964 statute.

The New York law since 1923 has permitted literacy to be established by proof of an eighth-grade education.

Provisions of Law

The literacy provision in the new Federal law applies to suits in which the United States Attorney General alleges that discrimination exists in the voting process. It makes a sixth-grade education presumptive evidence of literacy. It does not intend to supersede state voting requirements, the Governor said.

[In New York, Mayor Wagner said he had not seen the Governor's statement and did not know what the basis for the Governor's decision was. But he added: "Of course, I disagree completely on the issue."]

In a letter to the Mayor, Mr. Rockefeller buttressed his position on the intent of the 1964 law with an opinion from the Department of Justice and by reference to statements by Senators Kenneth B. Keating, Republican of New York, and Hubert H. Humphrey, Democrat of Minnesota, during the debate on the 1964 law.

Confusion Feared

Mayor Wagner, in requesting the special session last July 8, expressed fear that the differences in the educational standards for literacy would create a chaotic situation, with some voters eligible to vote in national but not state elections.

Mr. Rockefeller said that there was no inconsistency between the Federal and state literacy requirements and that the state's requirements continue to apply to Federal and state elections alike.

"The Civil Rights Act of 1964," the Governor wrote, "is concerned with voter literacy

Continued on Page 26, Column 2

HARLEM KILLINGS REPORTED URGED

Police Testify That Leftist Called on Negroes There to Slay Patrolmen

By PETER KIHSS

A left-wing Harlem Negro was said yesterday to have urged Negroes to kill policemen and judges.

Testimony by police witnesses in Supreme Court ascribed the actions to William Epton, leader of the Harlem Defense Council and a top member of the Progressive Labor Movement. He was also said to have urged Negroes to lure policemen into side streets where they could be bombarded with bottles and other missiles.

Justice Gerald P. Culkin continued a restraining order against demonstrations in Harlem by Mr. Epton's group and by Jesse Gray's Community Council on Housing. The restraining orders have been sought by the city to avert further racial disorders.

5 Negroes Transferred

There were these other developments in the city's race problems:

¶Police Commissioner Michael J. Murphy transferred five Negro sergeants into the three Harlem precincts to replace five whites.

¶The Rev. Dr. Martin Luther King Jr., president of the Southern Christian Leadership Conference, flew here at the invitation of Mayor Wagner and met with the Mayor at Gracie Mansion late last night.

¶A Harlem unity committee held a press conference last night at which Dr. King's presence in the city was denounced. A spokesman said Harlem leaders were "mad as hell at Mayor Wagner for importing Dr. King from Atlanta to discuss problems of Harlem."

¶The City Council, in a move endorsed by Mayor Wagner, ar-

Continued on Page 15, Column 1

SENATE BARS PLAN TO LIST FINANCES

Then Clears Way to Set Up a Federal Ethics Panel

By CABELL PHILLIPS
Special to The New York Times

WASHINGTON, July 27—The Senate rejected all efforts tonight to require members to disclose details of their finances.

It then paved the way for the creation of a special commission to study ethical practices in every branch of the Federal Government.

Final action will be taken tomorrow on a resolution sponsored by the minority leader, Everett McKinley Dirksen, that in effect sidetracks efforts by the Rules Committee to require Senators and Senate employes to make periodic disclosures of their outside financial holdings.

The Rules Committee disclosure plan, rejected by a vote of 48 to 39, was the outgrowth of the committee's eight-month investigation of the outside business activities of Robert G. Baker, former secretary to the Democratic majority.

The proposal would have required all members of the Senate, and all Senate employes earning more than $10,000 annually, to identify periodically the sources of outside income exceeding 50 per cent of their Senate pay.

This proposal was vigorously opposed throughout a day of debate by Senator Dirksen and many other Senators of both parties.

Efforts to stiffen the Rules Committee's plan were defeated

Continued on Page 18, Column 1

GOVERNOR TOURS ROCHESTER AREA, DENOUNCES RIOTS

He Finds 'Clear Evidence of Extremism'—Visits Troops and Meets Officials

By FRED POWLEDGE
Special to The New York Times

ROCHESTER, July 27—Governor Rockefeller flew here unannounced today and inspected the scene of three nights of racial rioting. He said he was saddened and shocked by what he saw.

The Governor toured the riot area in an automobile, and visited with the National Guardsmen he called out yesterday and congratulated them and the state policemen on their work.

He met with city, county and state officials for about an hour, and then returned to New York City.

Quiet prevailed throughout Rochester tonight. The police radio buzzed with routine traffic. In areas where violence had occurred earlier, the loudest noise came from television sets in houses and apartment buildings.

Governor Cites Extremism

The Governor was asked at a news conference late in the afternoon whether the racial violence here was the kind of extremism he had had in mind when he appealed to the Republican National Convention to adopt a platform plank condemning all forms of extremism.

Mr. Rockefeller replied: "Have you been downtown through the streets where these riots took place and seen the boarded-up stores? I think that's clear evidence of extremism, that anyone who had seen it would not hesitate to call it extremism.

"As Governor, and as a citizen, I deplore this kind of violence. Regardless of the objectives, it cannot be justified."

Question of Agitation

He said he saw no direct connection between the rioting here and the recent outbreaks in New York City. "There is no indication that I have from any source of outside agitators," he added.

Mr. Rockefeller said he had come here "because the state has committed some 450 police, and because I've called out the National Guard."

He said his reaction to the situation was "the same reaction that everyone has—a reaction of shock, a reaction of sadness."

Declaring that the state would take "all steps necessary" to preserve peace, he said he hoped it would not be

Continued on Page 14, Column 1

JOHNSON STRESSES ECONOMIC ISSUES AS CAMPAIGN KEY

He Counsels Party Leaders to 'Talk Jobs' in Dealing With 'White Backlash'

By EARL MAZO

President Johnson has sent word to Democratic leaders that "bread and butter" issues should be stressed in the coming political campaign to overshadow the possible adverse effect in some places of racial issues.

Mr. Johnson's message has been conveyed to top-rank party figures in New York and elsewhere by members of the Cabinet.

They revealed that the President lectured the Cabinet for more than an hour last week on campaign strategy and techniques. The President reportedly emphasized that the best way to deal with the "white backlash" vote was to "talk jobs, prosperity, opportunity . . . a good future."

Voter Trend Reported

One Cabinet member quoted Mr. Johnson as stating:

"When the people know how good things are and are going to be, they'll stop worrying about who is going to move next door."

His reference was to reports that some voters in overwhelmingly Democratic communities of the North and West believed that the Civil Rights Act might cause them to lose jobs to Negroes and accelerate the integration of their neighborhoods.

Mr. Johnson instructed his Democratic colleagues to talk "prosperity, people and peace" in the campaign.

Appearances Limited

The President also indicated that he was inclined to schedule relatively few barnstorming tours during the campaign. That chore would fall to his Vice-Presidential running mate, he implied. His own public appearances would be restricted to normal Presidential activities, such as news conferences, with major addresses to the nation on television.

Mr. Johnson reviewed in detail the campaign strategies of President Franklin D. Roosevelt in 1936 and 1940 and President Dwight D. Eisenhower in 1956. Mr. Johnson said he considered these campaigns models for an incumbent seeking reelection.

At one point, according to a Cabinet member, the President asked if anyone in the room realized that Mr. Roosevelt had

Continued on Page 9, Column 4

U. S. TO ENLARGE VIETNAM FORCE BY 5,000 ADVISERS

TOTAL TO BE 21,000

More Materiel Also Will Be Provided to Counter Reds

By EDWIN L. DALE Jr.
Special to The New York Times

WASHINGTON, July 27 —The United States will add about 5,000 men to its 16,000-man military mission in South Vietnam, it was reliably reported tonight.

The Vietnamese Government announced in Saigon earlier today that the United States would increase its military assistance, but the magnitude was not disclosed. Officials in Washington said tonight that it would be "in the order" of 5,000 men.

It is understood that the additional troops will work mainly in the field, accompanying and advising Vietnamese units down to the battalion level. The Saigon announcement said that, in addition, the United States would send more military equipment to bolster the critical struggle against the Communist forces.

Evidence of Concern

The announcement of the step-up of about 30 per cent was viewed as further evidence of the deep concern in Washington about the trend of the war. However, there was still no sign of a United States decision to carry the war into North Vietnam or to throw American units into combat.

The 5,000 men will be sent to South Vietnam the next few months. The first contingent is expected to be a 600-man unit from Okinawa. Plans for the shipment of this unit had been announced before today's action.

The disclosure of a major increase in the United States mission illustrates a complete change from the more hopeful atmosphere of last year. In October, the White House announced that its goal was the withdrawal of all United States forces by the end of 1965.

Reduction Abandoned

This policy was changed before the year was out as the Vietcong guerrillas stepped up their military activity. The plan to reduce the United States forces was abandoned in December. Now, seven months later, comes the announcement of a major increase.

Already 158 American servicemen have lost their lives in the war even though they have not been serving as members of United States combat units.

The basic United States policy remains unchanged. This is to help the South Vietnamese fight the war on their own territory and gradually wear down the guerrilla forces.

There have been recent reports from Saigon that the Vietcong, now sometimes attacking in organized strength, may be preparing for a major military campaign in central Vietnam. One objective that has been mentioned is capture of the former capital city of

Continued on Page 5, Column 1

Makarios Proposes U.N. Assembly Step

By W. GRANGER BLAIR
Special to The New York Times

NICOSIA, Cyprus, July 27 —Archbishop Makarios, President of Cyprus, said today that the Cyprus question should be taken "soon" to the United Nations General Assembly.

He prefaced the statement with the remark that he did not believe an "agreed solution" of the crisis was "possible."

The President expressed his views at the airport before leaving for Athens to consult with the Greek Government on the political and military situation relating to Cyprus.

Archbishop Makarios is expected back Wednesday after

Continued on Page 2, Column 6

GOLDWATER PLANS G.O.P. UNITY TALKS

Will Invite Party's Leaders and All Its Governors— Eisenhower Expected

By E. W. KENWORTHY
Special to The New York Times

WASHINGTON, July 27 — Senator Barry Goldwater announced today that he intended to call a meeting of all Republican Governors and other leading party figures in the interest of party unity.

The Republican Presidential nominee did not set a date for the meeting. He said it would come after two breakfast conferences to which he and Representative William E. Miller of upstate New York, the Vice-Presidential nominee, have invited Republican members of the House and Senate on Aug. 6 and 7.

At these breakfast sessions, Mr. Goldwater said, "we will discuss what we will have made by then for our campaign, and we will find out what is on their minds." Because of the number of Republicans in Congress—33 in the Senate and 178 in the House—it will be

Continued on Page 10, Column 2

Churchill Pays Last Visit to Commons

50-Minute Stay Ends 64-Year Service of Wartime Leader

By JAMES FERON
Special to The New York Times

LONDON, July 27 — Sir Winston Churchill, looking fit, spent what was probably his final hour in the House of Commons today.

Tomorrow the chamber he has served for 64 years will record, in an official tribute, its "unbounded admiration and gratitude for his services," but Sir Winston is not expected to be there.

The frail health of the 89-year-old former Prime Minister, his colleagues feel, would not permit the response he would feel obliged to give if he were present.

Instead, a written reply will be read to the House later in the week. Parliament will adjourn Friday and Sir Winston, who still represents the Woodford constituency, has said he intends to retire.

Today there was nothing to keep Sir Winston from a final visit to the House he has frequented for so long.

He entered the chamber shortly after 3 P.M. supported by two fellow Conservative members, Capt. Lawrence P. S. Orr and Sir Dudley Williams, and leaning on a cane.

Foreign Secretary R. A. Butler was answering questions as Sir Winston's colleagues guided him to his usual place on a front bench at the foot of the gangway. There were no cheers, no interruption, at his arrival.

He wore a dark bow tie

Continued on Page 7, Column 1

Sir Winston Churchill being escorted from London home for trip to Parliament. In foreground is one of his cats. Associated Press Cablephoto

Teamsters Cut Off Liquor for Harlem

By EMANUEL PERLMUTTER

The teamsters' union placed a temporary embargo yesterday on liquor deliveries to Harlem and the Bedford-Stuyvesant section of Brooklyn.

Lester Connell, secretary-treasurer of Local 816 of the International Brotherhood of Teamsters, said the action had been taken primarily to protect the drivers and their helpers from assault and robbery.

He added that withholding liquor from the two areas might also reduce a cause of violence and disorder.

The embargo was imposed as the men returned from a two-week vacation during which wholesale liquor dealers observed their annual summer shutdown.

About 200 union members and several hundred bars and liquor

Continued on Page 14, Column 6

India Acts to Stop Grain Speculation

By JACQUES NEVARD
Special to The New York Times

NEW DELHI, July 27—India acted vigorously today to increase food supplies at prices her masses can afford to pay.

In a move aimed at forcing speculators to unload hoarded stocks, the Government announced the imposition of strict controls on the purchase, sale, storage and transportation of grains.

Prime Minister Lal Bahadur Shastri has called the shortage and high prices of food the "most formidable problem" facing India.

[The police in Bombay arrested about 700 persons during a demonstration over soaring prices, Reuters reported.]

The announcement of controls was made by Coimbatore

Continued on Page 5, Column 5

NEWS INDEX

"All the News That's Fit to Print"

The New York Times.

LATE CITY EDITION
U. S. Weather Bureau Report (Page 48) forecasts: Sunny and pleasant today; clear, cool tonight. Sunny tomorrow.
Temp. Range: 82—62; yesterday: 81—62.
Temp.-Hum. Index: high 60's; yesterday: 71.

VOL. CXIII..No. 38,986. | NEW YORK, SATURDAY, AUGUST 1, 1964. | TEN CENTS

RANGER TAKES CLOSE-UP MOON PHOTOS REVEALING CRATERS ONLY 3 FEET WIDE; DATA GAINED ON LANDING SITE FOR MAN

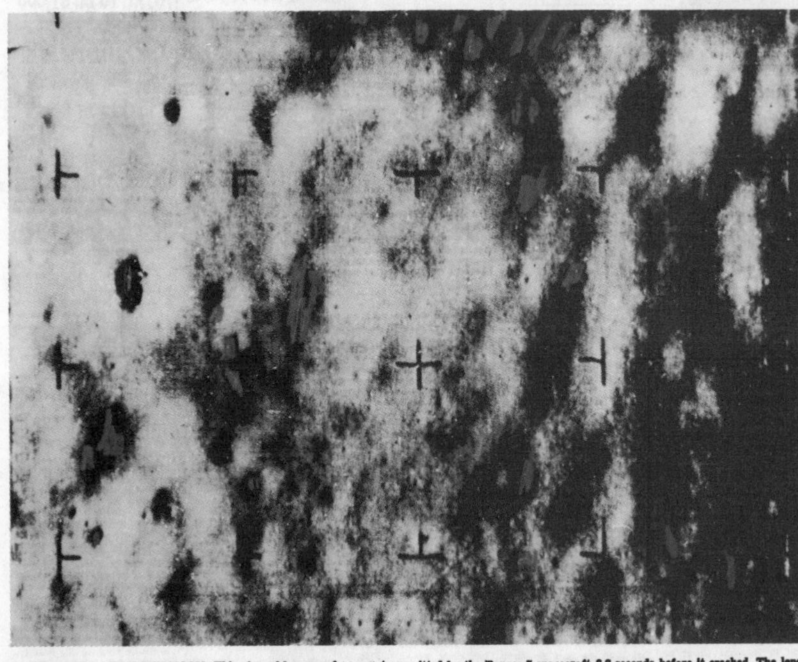

THREE MILES FROM THE MOON: This view of lunar surface was transmitted by the Ranger 7 spacecraft 3.2 seconds before it crashed. The lens gridmarks are scale references to calibrate amount of distortion. Smallest craters shown are about 30 feet in diameter and about 10 feet in depth.

Associated Press Wirephotos

1,000 FEET FROM THE MOON: Upper photo was the last. At right it merges into blur caused by static after the Ranger 7 crashed. Below, photo taken from 3,000 feet.

U.S. STEEL WEIGHS MIDTOWN PROJECT

$100 Million Industrial and Housing Complex May Be Built Above Rail Yard

By ROBERT E. BEDINGFIELD

The United States Steel Corporation has acquired the air rights over a 40-acre railroad yard in mid-Manhattan and is considering erecting a $100 million housing and industrial complex over the site.

U.S. Steel's board of directors has approved the purchase of Webb & Knapp's lease of the air rights over the New York Central Railroad's freight yard that lies between West 30th and West 37th Streets and extends from 10th to 12th Avenue.

Webb & Knapp realized about $7 million on the deal.

It is understood that the plan being considered calls for the construction of nine apartment buildings of about 30 stories each that would provide middle-income housing for 12,000 families. The project also envisages numerous adjoining industrial buildings of several stories each.

Plan Still Studied

Last night a spokesman for U.S. Steel confirmed that the directors had authorized the acquisition of the air rights from Webb & Knapp.

He said, however, that no definite plan had yet been decided for utilization of the area. If the corporation decides to go ahead with the proposed housing development, he added, it would be for the purpose of demonstrating the company's contention that steel is useful as a prime material in middle-income housing.

Webb & Knapp since Dec. 15, 1961, has held a leasehold on the air rights to the part of the Central yard that lies between West 30th and West 37th Streets and extends from 11th to 12th Avenue and from West 30th to West 33d Street between 10th and 11th Avenues.

Webb & Knapp will net $3 million on the deal since $4 million of the proceeds will be applied to the repayment of a note of that amount owed the steel company.

The proposed U.S. Steel plans

Continued on Page 34, Column 3

Wagner Rejects Demands For Civilian Police Board

By R. W. APPLE Jr.

Mayor Wagner refused yesterday to appoint an independent civilian police review board sought by civil rights leaders.

In a long statement released at City Hall, the Mayor omitted any mention of another key demand of Negro leaders—the suspension of Police Lieut. Thomas R. Gilligan, who shot and killed a 15-year-old Negro on the East Side on July 16.

Instead, Mr. Wagner proposed a seven-point program whose main thrust was economic, calling for the creation of about 1,500 temporary and permanent city jobs for unemployed young people.

Text of Wagner's statement is printed on Page 11.

The Mayor also set up a committee to review the findings of Deputy Mayor Edward F. Cavanagh Jr., who had been directed earlier to review the actions of the Police Department's review board.

King Voices Regret

Mr. Wagner's statement was his first since he began last Monday a series of conversations with the Rev. Dr. Martin Luther King Jr., president of the Southern Christian Leadership Conference, following racial riots here two weeks ago.

Dr. King said in a telephone interview from Atlanta that he was "very sorry" the Mayor had not ordered the creation of an independent board to evaluate allegations of police brutality. He said he had pressed the issue again and again during his talks with Mr. Wagner.

L. Joseph Overton, president of the Unity Council of Harlem Organizations, condemned the Mayor's actions and demanded again the creation of a review board composed of persons associated with neither the city government nor the police.

"I believe the Mayor has made my position untenable," Mr. Overton said. "He has made it virtually impossible for me to guarantee continued peace on the streets of Harlem."

Mr. Overton's organization was set up in an attempt to restore order in Harlem after the riots touched off by the Gilligan incident. The council has insisted that only the creation of a review board would solve the city's racial crisis.

Police Commissioner Michael

Continued on Page 11, Column 5

M'KESSON TO CUT ANTIBIOTIC PRICE

Plans to Sell Tetracycline at Third of Present Cost—Pfizer Says It Will Sue

By MARTIN ARNOLD

The nation's largest wholesale drug distributor announced yesterday that it would manufacture and sell tetracycline at about one-third the price at which it is sold by other manufacturers in the United States.

Tetracycline is a broad-spectrum antibiotic that is effective against a variety of bacterial infections. Yearly sales in the country total about $100 million, or about a third of the total sale of antibiotics.

The announcement was made by McKesson & Robbins, which said that it would offer pills for about 6 cents each wholesale, or about $6 for 100 250-miligram tablets. A spokesman for the company said that other drug concerns that manufacture tetracycline in the United States sell it for "slightly more than $17 a hundred tablets wholesale."

Chas. Pfizer & Co., one of the discoverers of tetracycline, immediately announced that it would file suit against McKesson & Robbins for patent infringement.

There are a number of small distributing concerns that buy tetracycline abroad, notably in Italy, and sell it for a low price here.

The importance of the McKesson & Robbins move, observers point out, is that the company's product will be American made and therefore, justifiably or not, druggists and doctors will be less hesitant

Continued on Page 34, Column 6

PAKISTAN ACCEPTS LOAN FROM CHINA

$60 Million, Interest Free, to Be Used for Imports of Industrial Goods

Special to The New York Times

KARACHI, Pakistan, July 31—Pakistan announced today that she would accept a "generous offer" by Communist China of a $60 million long-term, interest-free loan.

It is the first loan offered by Peking to Pakistan, which is allied with the West in the Central Treaty Organization and the Southeast Asia Treaty Organization, both aimed at preventing Communist aggression.

Commerce Minister Wahid-uz-Zaman, who recently returned from a tour of Communist China, said at a news conference in Rawalpindi that the loan would be used to pay for imports of machinery, cement and sugar mills.

Mr. Zaman said the Chinese Government would not even place a service charge on the loan.

United States loans offered to Pakistan are repayable in United States dollars in 40 years, including a 10-year grace period during which no payment is

Continued on Page 3, Column 2

Attitude on Soviet Is Upheld by Rusk In Policy Warning

By MAX FRANKEL
Special to The New York Times

WASHINGTON, July 31—Secretary of State Dean Rusk, in an oblique jab at Senator Barry Goldwater, said today that it was "unrealistic" to think the Soviet Union would "roll over and play dead" if its vital interests were threatened by the United States.

In answering several political questions at a news conference, Mr. Rusk said the Administration had "eminently demonstrated" that it was "just as tough and just as stubborn as is necessary" to protect its vital interests and those of the Western allies.

But he cautioned that the Soviet Union, too, would be stubborn in defending its interests. Therefore, he said, conflicts of interest must be approached with care and persistence to find ways in which the Communist and Western parts of the world can live together.

Mr. Rusk did not refer directly to Mr. Goldwater, the Republican candidate for President, or his views, but the Secretary's questioners did, leaving no doubt about the meaning of their inquiries.

Secretary Rusk said he

Continued on Page 2, Column 3

Johnson Is Said to Have Asked Kennedy to Manage Campaign

Offer Being Considered

By The Associated Press

WASHINGTON, Saturday, Aug. 1—President Johnson has asked Attorney General Robert F. Kennedy to manage his Presidential campaign, informed sources said today.

They said the offer was made Wednesday at the same time Mr. Johnson told Mr. Kennedy he was eliminating him from consideration as a Vice-Presidential candidate.

The offer reportedly is under consideration.

"I don't want to get into that," Mr. Kennedy said yesterday when asked about reports of the offer before he left for Hyannis Port, Mass., for the weekend. And Kennedy

Continued on Page 6, Column 2

Rusk Post Desired

By CABELL PHILLIPS
Special to The New York Times

WASHINGTON, July 31 —Attorney General Robert F. Kennedy would like to be Secretary of State now that the Vice-Presidency has been foreclosed to him.

This is the consensus of several close friends and associates of Mr. Kennedy after President Johnson's statement yesterday that the Attorney General and others of Cabinet rank had been eliminated from consideration for the second spot on the Democratic ticket.

Mr. Kennedy, his friends say, is exerting no pressure to obtain the State Department post. But they say he has let it be

Continued on Page 6, Column 5

PRESIDENT HAILS NEW LUNAR FEAT

Calls Ranger Flight 'Basic Step' to Manned Landing —Praises Scientists

By JOHN D. POMFRET
Special to The New York Times

WASHINGTON, July 31—President Johnson congratulated today the scientists and technicians responsible for the successful flight of Ranger 7 to the moon.

The President was in the White House living quarters when Dr. William H. Pickering, director of the Jet Propulsion Laboratory at Pasadena, Calif., telephoned to inform him that the shot was a success.

The President felicitated Dr. Pickering and Dr. Homer E. Newell, assistant administrator for space science and application of the space agency, then had the White House issue a statement praising those who participated in the flight.

Mr. Johnson called the flight "a basic step forward in our orderly program to assemble the scientific knowledge necessary for man's trip to the moon."

Guide in Planning Trip

"The pictures obtained of the lunar surface should prove extremely useful," the President said, continuing:

"They will be a guide in constructing the lunar excursion module and in planning the trip.

"We shall now be able to better map out our descent route. We'll be able to build our lunar landing equipment with greater certainty and knowledge of the conditions which our astronauts will encounter on the moon.

"I recognize that this great success has come only after a number of failures and partial failures in our efforts to send probes to the moon. This success should spur us on to added effort in the future.

"The fact that our Soviet competitors have had many unpublicized failures to the moon and the planets also confirms the complexity of today's success.

"On behalf of a grateful nation, let me again congratu-

Continued on Page 8, Column 3

Craft Hits Target Area; 4,000 Pictures Sent Back

Details of Lunar Region Seen Thousand Times Clearer Than Before—Feat Hailed as Leap in Knowledge

By RICHARD WITKIN
Special to The New York Times

PASEDENA, Calif., July 31—Ranger 7 radioed to earth today the first close-up pictures of the moon—a historic collection of 4,000 pictures one thousand times as clear as anything ever seen through earth-bound telescopes.

Scientists here were hailing the achievement, which exceeded all expectations, as by far the greatest advance in lunar astronomy since Galileo.

Text of the news conference will be found on Page 10.

They said the pictures not only represented a great leap in man's knowledge of the moon, but also, on a more practical level, lent encouragement that the lunar surface was suitable for Project Apollo's manned lunar landings.

Taken in 17 Minutes

The still pictures were snapped and transmitted in the last 17 minutes before the spacecraft crashed into an area northwest of the Sea of Clouds.

They meant in effect that the 240,000 mile distance to the moon had been shrunk by man's ingenuity to a mere half-mile in terms of what he could see of its topography. They showed craters three feet in diameter and a foot to a foot and a half deep.

The best earthbound telescopes, handicapped by the shimmering mantle of the atmosphere, can shrink the lunar distance only to 500 miles and reveal features no smaller than about one-mile across.

The startling disclosures of what Ranger 7 had wrought were made at a packed news conference here by a team of scientists headed by Dr. Gerard P. Kuiper of the University of Arizona.

The conference, televised nationally, was held in the auditorium of the Jet Propulsion Laboratory of the National Aeronautics Space Administration.

"This is a great day for science," the eminent astronomer said at the start, "and a great day for the United States.

"What has been achieved is truly remarkable. We have made progress in resolution [clarity of pictures] not by a factor of 10 . . . not by a factor of 100, which would have been remarkable, but by a factor of 1,000."

As a series of ten samples of the Ranger 7 photographs were flashed on a screen, Dr. Kuiper pointed out some of the more interesting features. Among the highlights of his recital and of answers both he and another member of the scientific panel made were these:

¶A few hours' quick study of Ranger 7's massive output had not revealed that there were any totally unforeseen problems on the moon. But the numberless new details opened a region of knowledge that would keep scientists in deep study for three or four years or more.

¶There was evidence that the white rays around some major craters were caused not by light fluffy material tossed up from the moon but by sizable rocks thrown off in the formation of these large craters. The rocks made numerous secondary craters deep enough to represent an extreme hazard for a manned lunar landing in the area. Such areas were to be avoided like poison, Dr. Kuiper said.

¶The tentative impression of the scientific team was that the lunar surface dust or other substance was not thick enough to swallow an astronaut landing craft. Dr. Eugene Shoemaker

Continued on Page 8, Column 1

NEWS INDEX

"All the News That's Fit to Print"

The New York Times.

LATE CITY EDITION
U.S. Weather Bureau Report (Page 66) forecasts: Variable cloudiness today; clear tonight. Fair and cool tomorrow.
Temp. Range: 86—65; yesterday: 81—57. Temp.-Hum. Index: low 70's; yesterday: 73.

VOL. CXIII—No. 38,910. © 1964 by The New York Times Company. Times Square, New York, N. Y. 10036 NEW YORK, WEDNESDAY, AUGUST 5, 1964. TEN CENTS

U.S. PLANES ATTACK NORTH VIETNAM BASES; PRESIDENT ORDERS 'LIMITED' RETALIATION AFTER COMMUNISTS' PT BOATS RENEW RAIDS

F. B. I. Finds 3 Bodies Believed to Be Rights Workers'

GRAVES AT A DAM

Discovery Is Made in New Earth Mound in Mississippi

By CLAUDE SITTON
Special to The New York Times

JACKSON, Miss., Aug. 4—Bodies believed to be those of three civil rights workers missing since June 21 were found early tonight near Philadelphia, Miss.

Federal Bureau of Investigation agents recovered the bodies from a newly erected earthen dam in a thickly wooded area about six miles southwest of Philadelphia, in east-central Mississippi.

The dam is several hundred yards off State Highway 21, near the Neshoba County fairgrounds.

Fulton Jackson, the county coroner, made a preliminary examination at the scene. The bodies were then sealed in plastic bags and brought by ambulance to the University of Mississippi Medical Center in Jackson, 70 miles to the southwest.

Pledge by Governor

Roy K. Moore, special agent in charge of the Jackson F.B.I. office, said physicians and fingerprint experts would seek to make positive identification and establish the cause of death.

[In Washington, authoritative sources said that President Johnson had telephoned Gov. Paul B. Johnson Jr. of Mississippi after having learned of the discovery of the bodies. However, this could not be confirmed immediately.]

Governor Johnson said in a statement:

"If these are the bodies of the three civil rights workers who have been missing several weeks, the investigative forces of the State of Mississippi will exert every effort to apprehend those who may have been responsible."

Area Searched Earlier

Mr. Johnson said he understood F.B.I. agents had searched the area once before and had noticed the new dam. Later, when they saw that the dam had collected no water despite heavy showers, they returned for a further investigation.

Excavation uncovered the bodies in the fill of the dam, the Governor said.

Sheriff L. A. Rainey, who had just returned from a vacation, visited the scene a short while after the discovery.

The missing men were Michael H. Schwerner, 24 years old, and Andrew Goodman, 20, both white and both from New York City, and James E. Chaney, 21, a Negro of Meridian, Miss.

All three had been taking part in the Mississippi Summer Project, a state-wide civil rights drive, which began on the week-

Continued on Page 37, Column 2

Scattered Violence Keeps Jersey City Tense 3d Night

400 Policemen Confine Most of Rioters to 2 Sections—Crowds Watch in Streets Despite Danger

By FRED POWLEDGE
Special to The New York Times

JERSEY CITY, Aug. 4—Scattered violence broke out again here tonight as roving groups of Negroes hurled crude Molotov cocktails in the streets. There was some gunfire but no injuries were reported.

About 400 city policemen contained most of the young rioters to two predominantly Negro neighborhoods. There were at least [illegible] arrests.

Text of Whelan's statement will be found on Page 36.

Although it was dangerous to be on the streets on this third night of violence, many people watched from sidewalks and front porches as police cars, their red lights flashing, sped from one pocket of violence to another.

On Ocean Avenue the police trained spotlights on the roof of a three-story block of apartments. A man had been seen on the roof, and it was feared that he was armed with a rifle, fire bombs, or both. Yet on the sidewalk below, a woman walked her dog, apparently without concern, through throngs of helmeted policemen. From a front porch across the street, a baby cried.

Since the rioting started Sunday night, more than 30 persons have been injured, two of them with gunshot wounds. None of the wounds was critical. More than three dozen persons have been arrested.

Five hundred more Jersey City policemen stood ready to

Continued on Page 36, Column 1

REDS DRIVEN OFF

Two Torpedo Vessels Believed Sunk in Gulf of Tonkin

By ARNOLD H. LUBASCH
Special to The New York Times

WASHINGTON, Aug. 4—The Defense Department announced tonight that North Vietnamese PT boats made a "deliberate attack" today on two United States destroyers patrolling international waters in the Gulf of Tonkin off North Vietnam.

The attack came two days after North Vietnamese torpedo boats attacked the Maddox, one of the destroyers in today's incident.

The destroyers and covering carrier-based aircraft fired on the vessels in today's attack, drove them off and apparently sank at least two of them, according to the announcement. The Pentagon said there were no United States casualties or damage.

The attack was made by an "undetermined number of North Vietnamese PT boats" during darkness about 65 miles from the nearest land, the Pentagon reported. It said the attack came at 10:30 P. M., North Vietnamese time, or 10:30 A. M., Washington time.

'Fabrication,' Reds Say

[The North Vietnamese regime said Wednesday that the report of another attack on United States ships was a "fabrication."]

The second attack was described in Washington as much fiercer than the first one, which was said to have lasted half an hour. The second battle was understood to have lasted about three hours in rough sea, with bad weather and low visibility.

"We are in a very serious situation," a Government official said.

The attack came shortly before the State Department made public a stern protest about the North Vietnamese attack Sunday on the Maddox, which was then patrolling about 30 miles off North Vietnam, also in international waters in the Gulf of Tonkin.

The protest over the first incident was announced shortly after noon here, when the

Continued on Page 3, Column 1

2 CARRIERS USED

McNamara Reports on Aerial Strikes and Reinforcements

By JACK RAYMOND
Special to The New York Times

WASHINGTON, Wednesday, Aug. 5—Secretary of Defense Robert S. McNamara said at a postmidnight news conference that the United States planes that attacked North Vietnam yesterday and today had come from the carriers Constellation and Ticonderoga in the Gulf of Tonkin.

He said that the attacks had been directed against the bases used by the North Vietnamese PT boats that attacked two United States destroyers in international waters yesterday.

The Secretary added that the naval planes, believed to have included propeller-driven as well as jet-powered craft, had also conducted strikes against "certain other targets directly supporting the operation of the PT boats."

The United States planes used conventional weapons.

Separate Targets

Mr. McNamara, who held his news conference shortly after President Johnson had addressed the nation on television, emphasized in his report that the PT boat bases and the supporting facilities in North Vietnam had been separate targets.

He offered a guess, based on incomplete reports, that in the exchange of fire between the attacking PT boats and the United States destroyers and aircraft in international waters, at least two and possibly four of the North Vietnamese Soviet-made PT boats had been sunk.

The Defense Secretary disclosed that at one point in the Vietnamese PT boat attack, the Maddox observed an unidentified aircraft on radar, but that there was no air attack and the radar image was soon lost.

The hostilities that provoked United States retaliation began Sunday with an attack by North Vietnamese PT boats on the United States destroyer Maddox in the Gulf of Tonkin.

Hanoi Not Attacked

The first United States reaction was a note of protest and warning. But, as announced by the President and the Secretary of Defense, the second PT boat attack on the destroyers Maddox and C. Turner Joy yesterday precipitated the counter-action.

The Secretary of Defense said at the news conference that the retaliatory strikes were still under way at that time.

He made clear, in response to questions, that no targets outside North Vietnam had been attacked by the United States warplanes. He specifically ex-

Continued on Page 4, Column 3

Associated Press Wirephoto

DECISION: President Johnson, in a nationwide broadcast, tells of action he ordered taken against North Vietnam.

The President's Address

Following is the text of the President's address on Vietnam last night, as recorded by The New York Times:

My fellow Americans:

As President and Commander in Chief, it is my duty to the American people to report that renewed hostile actions against United States ships on the high seas in the Gulf of Tonkin have today required me to order the military forces of the United States to take action in reply.

The initial attack on the destroyer Maddox on Aug. 2 was repeated today by a number of hostile vessels attacking two U.S. destroyers with torpedoes.

The destroyers and supporting aircraft acted at once on the orders I gave after the initial act of aggression.

We believe at least two of the attacking boats were sunk. There were no U.S. losses.

The performance of commanders and crews in this engagement is in the highest tradition of the United States Navy.

But repeated acts of violence against the armed forces of the United States must be met not only with alert defense but with positive reply.

Action 'Now in Execution'

That reply is being given, as I speak to you tonight. Air action is now in execution against gunboats and certain supporting facilities in North Vietnam which have been used in these hostile operations.

In the larger sense, this new act of aggression aimed directly at our own forces again brings home to all of us in the United States the importance of the struggle for peace and security in Southeast Asia.

Aggression by terror against the peaceful villages of South Vietnam has now been joined by open aggression on the high seas against the United States of America.

The determination of all Americans to carry out our full commitment to the people and to the Government of South Vietnam will be redoubled by this outrage. Yet our response for the present will be limited and fitting.

We Americans know—although others appear to forget—the risk of spreading conflict. We still seek no wider war. I have instructed the Secretary of State to make this position totally clear to friends and to adversaries and, indeed, to all.

I have instructed Ambassador Stevenson to raise this matter immediately and urgently before the Security Council of the United Nations.

Congressional Resolution Asked

Finally, I have today met with the leaders of both parties in the Congress of the United States and I have informed them that I shall immediately request the Congress to pass a resolution making it clear that our Government is united in its determination to take all necessary measures in support of freedom and in defense of peace in Southeast Asia.

I have been given encouraging assurance by these leaders of both parties that such a resolution will be promptly introduced, freely and expeditiously debated, and passed with overwhelming support.

And just a few minutes ago I was able to reach Senator Goldwater and I am glad to say that he has expressed his support of the statement that I am making to you tonight.

It is a solemn responsibility to have to order even limited military action by forces whose over-all strength is as vast and as awesome as those of the United States of America.

But it is my considered conviction, shared throughout your Government, that firmness in the right is indispensable today for peace.

That firmness will always be measured. Its mission is peace.

FORCES ENLARGED

Stevenson to Appeal for Action by U.N. on 'Open Aggression'

By TOM WICKER
Special to The New York Times

WASHINGTON, Aug. 4—President Johnson has ordered retaliatory action against gunboats and "certain supporting facilities in North Vietnam" after renewed attacks against American destroyers in the Gulf of Tonkin.

In a television address tonight, Mr. Johnson said air attacks on the North Vietnamese ships and facilities were taking place as he spoke, shortly after 11:30 P.M.

State Department sources said the attacks were being carried out with conventional weapons on a number of shore bases in North Vietnam, with the objective of destroying them and the 30 to 40 gunboats they served.

The aim, they explained, was to destroy North Vietnam's gunboat capability. They said more air strikes might come later, if needed. Carrier-based aircraft were used in tonight's strike.

2 Boats Believed Sunk

Administration officials also announced that substantial additional units, primarily air and sea forces, were being sent to Southeast Asia.

This "positive reply," as the President called it, followed a naval battle in which a number of North Vietnamese PT boats attacked two United States destroyers with torpedoes. Two of the boats were believed to have been sunk. The United States forces suffered no damage and no loss of lives.

Mr. Johnson termed the North Vietnamese attacks "open aggression on the high seas."

Washington's response is "limited and fitting," the President said, and his Administration seeks no general extension of the guerrilla war in South Vietnam.

Goldwater Approves

"We Americans know," he said, "although others appear to forget, the risks of spreading conflict."

Mr. Johnson said Secretary of State Dean Rusk had been instructed to make this American attitude clear to all nations. He added that Adlai E. Stevenson, chief United States delegate, would raise the matter immediately in the United Nations Security Council. [The Council was expected to meet at 10:30 A.M. Wednesday.]

The President said he had informed his Republican Presidential rival, Senator Barry Goldwater, of his action and

Continued on Page 2, Column 3

JOHNSON SEEKING EXTREMISM PLANK

Favors a Stand Against Far Left and Right Without Naming Any Groups

Special to The New York Times

WASHINGTON, Aug. 4—President Johnson wants the Democratic platform to take a stand against extremism of the right and the left, without naming any particular organization.

Mr. Johnson, at the moment, plans to attend the party's national convention in Atlantic City only on Thursday night, Aug. 27, when he is scheduled to make his acceptance speech. But his wish on the platform is likely to be enough to make his views effective.

As yet, however, he has had no detailed discussions with the platform drafters.

The President is also planning to follow a somewhat unusual procedure in having himself placed in nomination. This is to be done by "co-nominators" — Governors Edmund G. Brown of California and John B. Connally Jr. of Texas.

These and other fairly well-advanced plans of the President have been learned from high Democratic sources.

However, on the question of most current interest, Mr. Johnson's choice for a Vice-Presidential candidate, no decision has yet been made.

Senator Hubert H. Humphrey

Continued on Page 14, Column 6

Rockefeller to Join Goldwater's Parley On Campaign Unity

Special to The New York Times

ALBANY, Aug. 4—Governor Rockefeller has accepted the invitation of Senator Goldwater to attend a meeting of Republican Governors at Hershey, Pa., on Aug. 12.

The invitation was extended by the Republican Presidential nominee in telegrams last Saturday to the 16 Republican Governors.

Mr. Rockefeller, who was a candidate for the Presidential nomination until after his defeat in the California primary, June 2, was one of Senator Goldwater's severest critics through the Republican National Convention last month in San Francisco.

Mr. Goldwater has called the Hershey gathering in an effort to promote unity within the Republican party behind his candidacy.

The prospects for success of

Continued on Page 16, Column 1

Salinger Appointed to the Senate

United Press International Telephoto

Pierre Salinger, left, with Gov. Edmund G. Brown of California after the announcement yesterday in Sacramento.

By WALLACE TURNER
Special to The New York Times

SAN FRANCISCO, Aug. 4—Pierre Salinger was appointed to the Senate today by Gov. Edmund G. Brown of California to fill the remaining five months of the term of the late Senator Clair Engle. Mr. Salinger is scheduled to be sworn in tomorrow about noon. He will be escorted to the rostrum by Senator Thomas H. Kuchel of California, the assistant Senate Republican leader. Governor Brown is to head a party of about 160 Democratic leaders who will be present in the Senate galleries when the new Senator takes his oath. Mr. Salinger, who was White House press

Continued on Page 16, Column 2

Auto Collision Insurance Rates In State Increased 4.3 to 25%

By JOSEPH C. INGRAHAM

Higher auto damage insurance rates — with increases from 4.3 to 25 per cent—will go into effect today for private passenger car owners in the state.

The increases were disclosed yesterday by the National Automobile Underwriters Association, which said that sharp rises in auto thefts and in the cost of repairs had made them necessary.

The association said that although the statewide rise would be the lesser amount, the rates in most of the metropolitan areas had been increased as much as 25 per cent.

Physical damage insurance, which reimburses a car owner for loss of or damage to his own car, is optional. The rate revisions apply to collision insurance and to comprehensive coverage, which protects motorists against loss due to theft, fire, windstorm, glass breakage and other hazards.

While each of these coverages can be bought separately, the National Automobile Underwriters Association, rating organization for more than 400 companies here, lumps the vari-

Continued on Page 67, Column 2

Congolese Battling Inside Stanleyville

By J. ANTHONY LUKAS
Special to The New York Times

LEOPOLDVILLE, the Congo, Aug. 4—Rebels of the "Popular Army" and Government troops battled tonight in the streets of Stanleyville, the chief city in the northern Congo.

Messages from the United States consul there said heavy fighting was going on early this evening in front of the consulate, about half a mile from the center of the city.

At 6:15 P. M. Stanleyville time, the consul, Michael P. E. Hoyt, telegraphed that the army was "advancing across front lawn of consulate" and seemed to be "pushing rebels back."

Eight minutes later he wired that the army troops were "advancing rapidly and in numbers beyond consulate on road to Wanie Rukula." He said that

Continued on Page 5, Column 4

Khanh Is Fighting Threat of a Coup

By SEYMOUR TOPPING
Special to The New York Times

SAIGON, South Vietnam, Aug. 4—Premier Nguyen Khanh struggled today to strengthen the political stability of his Government as his aides privately warned of plots to drive him from office. United States officials were concerned about the political deterioration in Saigon.

The malaise in the capital was attributed more to a clash of rival political and military personalities than to pressure from the Vietcong insurgents.

United States sources said reports from provinces indicated that conditions there were generally better than in Saigon.

Once again, rumors of a coup d'état were circulating in Sai-

Continued on Page 4, Column 7

Joe Garagiola was the new "Voice of the Yankees." He injected a greater degree of humor into baseball commentary than had previous sportscasters.

Although Mel Allen stepped down in 1964 as the announcer for the New York Yankees, he continued on as one of that baseball team's most exhuberant fans.

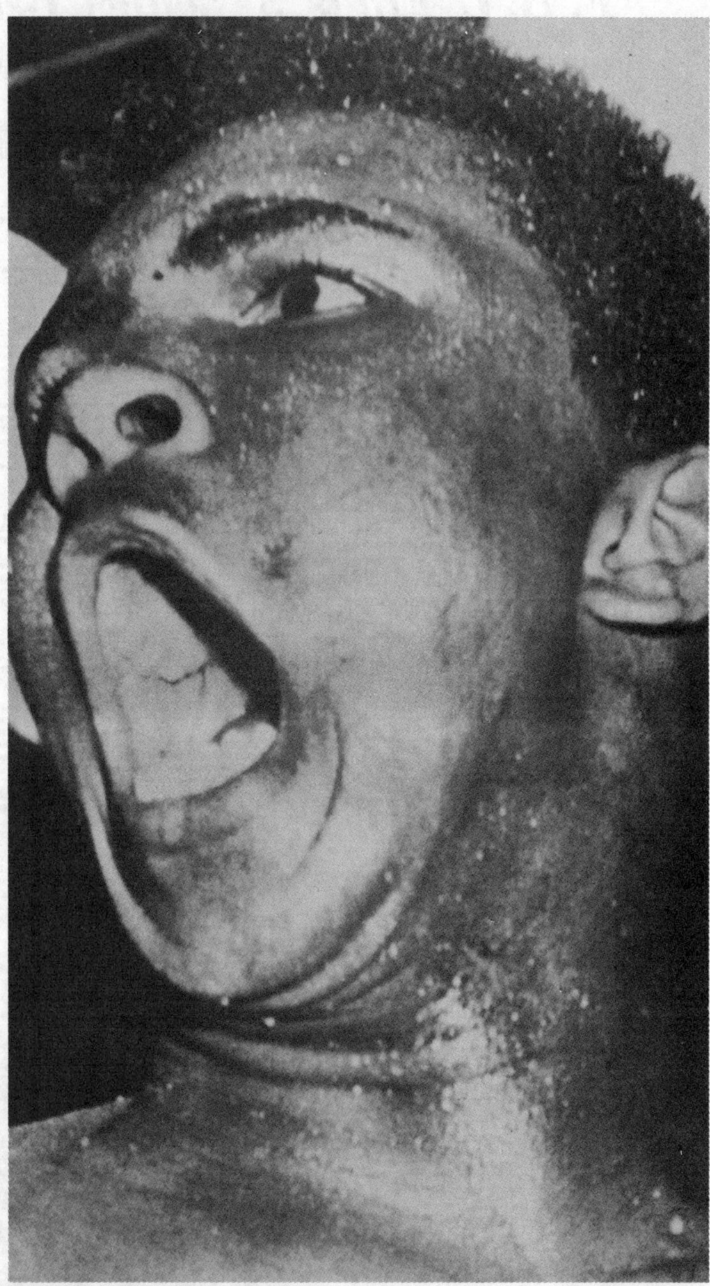

Cassius Clay changed his name to Muhammad Ali, shortly after he emerged as the heavyweight champ over Sonny Liston.

"All the News That's Fit to Print"

The New York Times.

LATE CITY EDITION
U. S. Weather Bureau Report (Page 44) forecasts: Mostly sunny with chance of showers late today; fair tonight, tomorrow.
Temp. Range: 85—67; yesterday: 84—61. Temp.-Hum. Index: 75 to 70; yesterday: 75.

VOL. CXIII..No. 38,913. NEW YORK, SATURDAY, AUGUST 8, 1964. TEN CENTS

CONGRESS BACKS PRESIDENT ON SOUTHEAST ASIA MOVES; KHANH SETS STATE OF SIEGE

RESOLUTION WINS

Senate Vote Is 88 to 2 After House Adopts Measure, 416-0

By E. W. KENWORTHY
Special to The New York Times

WASHINGTON, Aug. 7—The House of Representatives and the Senate approved today the resolution requested by President Johnson to strengthen his hand in dealing with Communist aggression in Southeast Asia.

After a 40-minute debate, the House passed the resolution, 416 to 0. Shortly afterward the Senate approved it, 88 to 2. Senate debate, which began yesterday afternoon, lasted nine hours.

The resolution gives prior Congressional approval of "all necessary measures" that the President may take "to repel any armed attack" against United States forces and "to prevent further aggression."

The resolution, the text of which was printed in The New York Times Thursday, also gives advance sanction for "all necessary steps" taken by the President to help any nation covered by the Southeast Asia collective defense treaty that requests assistance "in defense of its freedom."

Johnson Hails Action

President Johnson said the Congressional action was "a demonstration to all the world of the unity of all Americans."

"The votes prove our determination to defend our forces, to prevent aggression and to work firmly and steadily for peace and security in the area," he said.

"I am sure the American people join me in expressing the deepest appreciation to the leaders and members of both parties in both houses of Congress for their patriotic, resolute and rapid action."

The debates in both houses, but particularly in the Senate, made clear, however, that the near-unanimous vote did not reflect a unanimity of opinion on the necessity or advisability of the resolution.

Except for Senators Wayne L. Morse, Democrat of Oregon, and Ernest Gruening, Democrat

Continued on Page 2, Column 1

Associated Press Wirephoto

TO TOUR ALLIED CAPITALS: Henry Cabot Lodge with President Johnson on White House steps yesterday.

SAIGON DECREES EMERGENCY RULE

Khanh Says Chinese Army Threatens Nation—Urges People of North to Rebel

By PETER GROSE
Special to The New York Times

SAIGON, South Vietnam, Aug. 7—Premier Nguyen Khanh decreed a state of emergency throughout South Vietnam today and urged the people of North Vietnam to "stand up and overthrow the dictatorial party rule" of their Communist Government.

The Premier also ordered stringent measures to tighten his Government's control over the population and to safeguard the country against the threat of large-scale Communist attacks.

"The coming weeks will decide the destiny of our entire people," General Khanh said. "We will not accept becoming a minor province of Red China."

Quotes Intelligence Reports

According to intelligence reports, General Khanh said, Chinese Communist troops are massed along China's southern frontier and are "stationed—not infiltrated but stationed—in North Vietnam itself."

Emergency measures, to be put into effect immediately, include controls on travel and food distribution, regional curfews where dictated by security requirements, enlarged authority for detention and house arrest, unlimited search rights in private homes and a ban on strikes and meetings "considered harmful to public order."

The press and all public-information media are to be censored. [This apparently will not extend to foreign news dispatches and other communications leaving the country, The Associated Press said.]

For anyone taking part in

Continued on Page 2, Column 2

Lodge to See Allies Of U.S. to Explain Vietnam Situation

By TOM WICKER
Special to The New York Times

WASHINGTON, Aug. 7—Henry Cabot Lodge, only a few months ago a leading Republican Presidential possibility, will tour allied capitals for President Johnson to explain the situation in South Vietnam.

Speaking in front of the White House today, Mr. Lodge said he had Gen. Dwight D. Eisenhower's approval for the mission. He will leave within a week.

Mr. Lodge was the United States Ambassador to South Vietnam for 10 months until he resigned in late June to return and work against the nomination of Senator Barry Goldwater by the Republicans.

He did not elaborate on what he would tell officials he would talk with during his trip, except to say that it would be "in support of our national policy." Presumably a large part of his mission will be to explain the reasons for and the intent of the retaliatory action taken this week against North Vietnam for attacks on American naval vessels.

Politics Not Discussed

Mr. Lodge's announcement vibrated with domestic political overtones. However, he would not discuss politics, even whether he would support Senator Goldwater against Mr. Johnson in the fall campaign.

Asked if he would, he replied: "I do not think this is the time or the place to discuss partisan politics."

The domestic political significance of today's announcement was twofold:

One of the nation's leading Republicans, that party's Vice-Presidential nominee in 1960, agreed to a diplomatic assignment from the Democratic President, against whom Senator Goldwater is running.

By lending his support to the Administration's policy on South Vietnam, as he has con-

Continued on Page 2, Column 8

TURKS SEND JETS TO WARN CYPRUS; STRAFING ALLEGED

But Ankara Denies Nicosia Accusation of an Attack—U.S. Aides Distressed

By The Associated Press

ANKARA, Turkey, Saturday, Aug. 8—Turkey reported early today that she was sending jet aircraft on warning and surveillance flights over Cyprus.

After an emergency Cabinet meeting, Deputy Premier Kemal Satir also warned that the island could be bombed if American conciliation efforts failed to ease the tension between Greek and Turkish Cypriotes.

Mr. Satir denied, however, a Greek Cypriote charge that four Turkish Air Force Sabrejets had already strafed the northwestern coastal town of Polis and had hit an Italian cargo vessel in the harbor.

[In Washington, high State Department officials described the Cyprus situation as "very serious." Other high officials said they had had some forewarning that the Turks "would probably try something like this."]

U.S. Envoy at Meeting

The Cabinet met under Premier Ismet Inonu. The session was attended by the United States Ambassador, Raymond A. Hare, and the chief of the Turkish general staff, Gen. Cevdet Sunay.

Mr. Satir said afterward that Ambassador Hare had "promised to do everything in his power to ameliorate the tense situation in Cyprus."

In denying Cypriote charges of strafing and machine-gun fire by Turkish jets, Mr. Satir said, "They must have mistaken the planes' noise for machine-gun fire."

After the Cabinet meeting, Minister of Information Ali Hassan Gogush issued this statement:

"The Government is closely watching the latest developments in Cyprus. The Greek Cypriote Administration has increased its aggression against the Turkish Cypriote community. The Turkish Government is taking defensive precautions and making political contacts."

Nicosia Plans Protest

NICOSIA, Cyprus, Aug. 7 (AP)—The Cypriote Government said tonight that four Turkish Air Force jet fighters had strafed the northwestern coastal town of Polis and hit an Italian cargo vessel in the harbor.

The Government said the planes, identified as United States-made Sabrejets, attacked a few minutes after 6 P.M. (11 A.M., Eastern daylight time). Witnesses said the four planes had made several low runs from

Continued on Page 5, Column 3

KENNEDY WEIGHS RACE FOR SENATE; HE SEES WAGNER

Attorney General's Backers Seeking Support Among Top State Democrats

By R. W. APPLE Jr.

Attorney General Robert F. Kennedy is once again seriously considering running for Senator from New York State this fall.

Authoritative sources disclosed yesterday that relatives and political allies of the Attorney General had begun tentative discussions with a number of important Democrats in the state, seeking a broad base of support for his candidacy.

Stephen Smith, Mr. Kennedy's brother-in-law, has told people eager to work for the Attorney General to expect a go-ahead signal by this weekend, barring unforeseen developments.

However, other intimates of Mr. Kennedy, while confirming that he has expressed a definite interest in a Senate campaign, said they expected no final decision for two weeks.

Talks to Wagner

Mr. Kennedy was in New York yesterday for a meeting with Mayor Wagner, the state's most powerful Democrat. They had breakfast together at Gracie Mansion and discussed the Senate situation as well as the recent racial riots in Harlem.

After studying the idea of making a race for the Senate for several weeks, Mr. Kennedy said on June 23 that he would not be a candidate. At that time he was hopeful that President Johnson would choose him as his running mate.

When Mr. Johnson eliminated the Attorney General and other Cabinet members from the list of potential Vice-Presidential candidates on July 30, Mr. Kennedy was "immediately urged by influential New York Democrats to reconsider. He has now done so.

Strong Support in Sight

Mr. Kennedy is known to have the support of a powerful group of Democratic leaders, including Peter Crotty of Erie County (Buffalo), Stanley Steingut of Brooklyn, Charles A. Buckley of the Bronx and John F. English of Nassau County.

With the exception of Mr. English, each of these men is a political opponent of the Mayor. They will control close to 400 votes at the state Democratic convention on Sept. 1, with a total of 573 votes needed to win nomination.

While it is conceivable that Mr. Kennedy could win the nomination without the open endorsement of Mr. Wagner, it is not thought likely that he would attempt to do so.

Mr. Wagner is considered re-

Continued on Page 8, Column 8

JOHNSON ANTIPOVERTY BILL APPROVED IN HOUSE, 228-190, BUT FOES BALK FINAL VOTE

CRITICS REPULSED

Size of Victory Margin Surprises Backers—Action Due Today

By MARJORIE HUNTER
Special to The New York Times

WASHINGTON, Aug. 7 — President Johnson's antipoverty bill won an all-but-final victory in the House tonight by a surprisingly wide margin of 38 votes.

However, opponents succeeded in delaying final action until tomorrow.

Tentative approval came on adoption of the Administration-sponsored substitute bill, embodying all the changes made by both the Senate and the House. The vote was 228 to 190.

Even sponsors of the bill were surprised at the wide margin of support. They had expected to get the votes of only six to ten Republicans.

Twenty Republicans joined 208 Democrats in voting for the measure. Voting against it were 153 Republicans and 37 Democrats, most of them conservative Southerners.

Thus, after a day of bitter wrangling and one close brush with defeat, the $947.5-million antipoverty program was on the verge of passage.

Engrossed Bill Demanded

But opponents delayed a final vote by demanding an engrossed bill—a printed copy of the measure and all its amendments. This demand automatically put off final action until the printers could prepare the document.

The delaying maneuver was viewed as a temporary setback for the Administration, which had pressed for quick passage while the votes were in hand.

Many members usually go home for the weekend. It could prove difficult to keep the supporters, particularly those who reluctantly backed the Administration, in town for the final vote scheduled for tomorrow. The House will meet at noon.

However, the tentative approval represented a major victory for President Johnson.

The antipoverty bill, one of

Continued on Page 6, Column 7

Goldwater Sees a Victory If He Takes 5 Big States

Asserts California, Texas, Illinois, Ohio and Indiana and Smaller 'States Already for Me' Could Beat Johnson

By CHARLES MOHR
Special to The New York Times

WASHINGTON, Aug. 7—Senator Barry Goldwater has told Republican Congressmen that he could assure his election by carrying California, Texas, Illinois, Indiana and Ohio.

The Republican Presidential nominee was reported to have told the Congressmen that if he could win the 130 electoral votes of those major states and add them to the "states that are already for me" it would be possible to defeat President Johnson.

His reference to states already for him was understood to cover many smaller Western, Midwestern and Southern states he believes he will carry.

Mr. Goldwater expressed these views, and others on several important subjects, in two closed breakfast meetings with about 200 Republican members of the Senate and House. The meetings were held yesterday and today.

Mr. Goldwater's statements and views were reported by Congressmen who attended the breakfasts as guests.

James H. Doolittle, retired Air Force General, and Mrs. Clare Boothe Luce have been asked to become co-chairmen of the Citizens for Goldwater Committee, Mr. Goldwater was reported to have said. The committee will muster volunteer support for the Senator.

F. Clifton White, a seasoned political professional who helped Mr. Goldwater win the

Continued on Page 8, Column 2

Rockefeller Denies That He Will Stump For National Ticket

By DOUGLAS DALES
Special to The New York Times

ALBANY, Aug. 7 — Governor Rockefeller's office said today that he had no intention of stumping for the Goldwater ticket either inside or outside New York State.

The Governor's press secretary, Robert McManus, made the statement as a result of a prediction yesterday by Fred A. Young, Republican State Chairman, that Mr. Rockefeller would stump for the national ticket.

[In New York, Representative Seymour Halpern of Queens was reported ready to disavow Mr. Goldwater and run as an independent Republican.]

While Governor Rockefeller was distressed at the action of the Republican National Convention in selecting Senator Barry Goldwater as the party standard-bearer, he had said before the convention that he would support any nominee.

He renewed his pledge of support at a meeting of Republican county chairmen and vice chairmen here yesterday.

However, as the Governor's

Continued on Page 8, Column 5

HARLEM LEFTISTS CURBED BY COURT

Three Barred From Staging Protests — Epton Freed on Bail Put Up by Texan

By FRED POWLEDGE

A state judge granted a temporary injunction yesterday against continued "illegal demonstrations" by three individuals and organizations in Harlem.

Supreme Court Justice Gerald P. Culkin said the "conduct" of Milton Rosen, William Epton Jr. and Jesse Gray "creates a clear and present danger of irreparable injury to life and property."

The three men and their organizations, the Progressive Labor Movement, the Harlem Defense Council and the Community Council on Housing, had been accused by the city and state of fomenting tensions during the recent period of racial violence in Harlem.

Mr. Rosen is chairman of the Progressive Labor Movement; Mr. Epton, head of the Harlem Defense Council, and Mr. Gray head of the Community Council on Housing.

The city obtained a restraining order on July 25 to prohibit a demonstration by the Harlem Defense Council, scheduled for that day. The order, and a show-cause order, were argued during the next week. Justice Culkin's injunction was the result of that hearing.

Mr. Epton, meantime, was freed in $10,000 bond yesterday in another action and told that he could not leave the city limits of New York. The son of a wealthy Texas oilman posted collateral for Mr. Epton, a professed Communist.

Mr. Epton was indicted

Continued on Page 7, Column 4

PHONE AIDE CITED IN POLICE INQUIRY

Investigator Implicated in Gambling Conspiracy

By JACK ROTH

A suspended chief investigator for the New York Telephone Company was identified yesterday as the man who allegedly sold information to two police officers about gamblers' telephone numbers. The gamblers were reportedly shaken down by the policemen.

The telephone employe, Harold A. McElroy, was named by Victor Herwitz, a lawyer, who represents one of the police officers—Capt. Anthony Obremski—in a departmental trial on conspiracy charges that began yesterday.

Captain Obremski is accused of conspiring to get information about the gamblers' telephones with Mr. McElroy, Lieut. James J. Sullivan, the other police officer, and Seymour Freedman, a plainclothesman who left the force five years ago.

Mr. McElroy was scheduled to be the first prosecution witness against Captain Obremski when Trial Commissioner Aloysius J. Melia adjourned the trial to Monday at 10 A.M. to permit Mr. Herwitz time to examine Mr. McElroy's recent testimony

Continued on Page 8, Column 6

MOSCOW ASSURES HANOI OF BACKING

Gromyko Says U.S. Actions Risk Grave Consequences

By United Press International

MOSCOW, Aug. 7—Foreign Minister Andrei A. Gromyko said tonight that the United States military action against North Vietnam could "entail dangerous consequences."

Mr. Gromyko, in a telegram to the North Vietnamese Foreign Minister, Suan Tui, accused the United States of "flagrant violation of international law" and an attempt to introduce "piratical arbitrariness" in foreign relations.

The text of the message was published by Tass, the Soviet press agency.

Mr. Gromyko gave North Vietnam assurances of Soviet diplomatic backing against the United States.

"Such actions, generating a threat to the security of the people of other countries, can entail dangerous consequences, the scope of which it is now hard to foresee," the message said.

"The Soviet Government has demanded that the United States should immediately stop military operations against the Democratic Republic of Vietnam [North Vietnam]."

Mr. Gromyko said the presence of United States ships in the Gulf of Tonkin was an "openly hostile challenge" to the nations whose shores are "washed by the waters" of the gulf—which would include Communist China.

"This armed demonstration, of course, cannot be justified by

Continued on Page 3, Column 4

Hanoi Invited by U.N. Council To Testify on Clashes With U.S.

By SAM POPE BREWER
Special to The New York Times

UNITED NATIONS, N. Y., Aug. 7—The Security Council invited North Vietnam today to appear before it to testify on the recent armed clashes with United States naval forces in the Gulf of Tonkin.

The Council also asked South Vietnam to appear or to present pertinent information on the situation.

The Council adjourned without further action. It was agreed that the members would set the date for the next meeting, which presumably depends on the replies to the invitations.

Adlai E. Stevenson, the United States representative, rejected an assertion by Czechoslovakia's delegate, Jiri Hajek, that United States ships violated North Vietnamese territorial waters on July 30, three days before the first Vietnamese attack on the U.S.S. Maddox, and had fired on Vietnamese territory.

Mr. Stevenson said there had been no attack on North Vietnam and no incursion into its territorial waters before the retaliatory attack of Aug. 5. United States ships were attacked on the high seas 65 miles from Vietnamese territory, he said.

It was not known here whether North Vietnam was interested in appearing. South Vietnam was invited because, although it was not directly involved in the clashes this week, the incidents grew out of the conflict with the North.

No vote was taken on today's decision. This month's Council President, Sivert A. Nielsen of

Continued on Page 2, Column 7

U.S. and Belgium Plan Increased Aid to Bolster Congo

United Press International Radiophoto

At meeting in Brussels are, from left: Under Secretary of State W. Averell Harriman, Foreign Minister Paul-Henri Spaak of Belgium and Ambassador Douglas MacArthur 2d.

By EDWARD T. O'TOOLE
Special to The New York Times

BRUSSELS, Aug. 7 — Belgium and the United States are ready to increase technical aid to shore up Premier Moise Tshombe's Government in the Congo, but neither country will provide military personnel for combat, informed sources indicated here tonight. W. Averell Harriman, United States Under Secretary of State for Political Affairs, arrived here from Washington today and conferred for five hours with Belgium's Foreign Minister, Paul-Henri Spaak. They refused to comment later on their discussions beyond saying that they had had a "useful exchange of views." A Belgian official said the visit of Mr. Harriman had been initiated by the State Department after Premier Tshombe had requested more United States aid to combat Communist-guided rebels in the Congo. Other sources disclosed that Mr. Harriman and Mr. Spaak had apparently reached a working agreement on a program under which the United States would provide matériel to the Tshombe Government and Belgium would supply experts to teach the Congolese troops how to

Continued on Page 4, Column 3

Nuclear Test Blast Set for Mississippi

Special to The New York Times

WASHINGTON, Aug. 7 — The Government announced today arrangements for evacuating residents in an area 28 miles southwest of Hattiesburg, Miss., next Sept. 22 when it touches off an underground nuclear detonation.

The blast will be the first of three in a series known as Project Dribble.

The project is part of the Department of Defense's Vela program, which is designed to develop techniques for detecting and locating underground nuclear explosions.

Earlier investigations in the Vela series contributed to the United States decision to press for the exclusion of underground tests in the treaty with the Soviet Union that prohibited nuclear explosions in the at-

Continued on Page 6, Column 6

NEWS INDEX

Barry Goldwater had much attention during the 1964 presidential campaign but Lyndon Johnson had more of the votes at the polls.

Prime Minister Nehru, India's most astute politician, had inspired his people for 47 years before his death in 1964.

Premier Khrushchev's conflict with Mao Tse-Tung and within the Russian Communist Party were strong factors in Khrushchev's ouster.

President Johnson and Vice President Hubert Humphrey sating their hunger at the LBJ ranch. Their hearty appetites were worked up by their smashing victory over Goldwater and Miller.

"All the News That's Fit to Print"

The New York Times.

LATE CITY EDITION
U.S. Weather Bureau Report (Page 66) forecasts: Mostly sunny today; fair tonight. Fair and warmer tomorrow.
Temp. Range: 81—62; yesterday: 89—70. Temp.-Hum. Index: low 70's; yesterday: 78.

VOL. CXIII. No. 38,932. © 1964 by The New York Times Company. Times Square, New York, N. Y. 10036 NEW YORK, THURSDAY, AUGUST 27, 1964. TEN CENTS

DEMOCRATIC TICKET: JOHNSON AND HUMPHREY; BOTH NOMINATED BY ROARING ACCLAMATION; PRESIDENT AT SCENE, BREAKING A TRADITION

RULERS IN SAIGON UNABLE TO AGREE ON A NEW REGIME

Khanh and Colleagues Split —U.S. Being Consulted on Shift—Riots in Danang

By PETER GROSE
Special to The New York Times

SAIGON, South Vietnam, Aug. 26 — South Vietnam's political crisis deepened today with the failure of its military rulers to agree on a new head of state and a new form of government.

"The situation is very serious," said Major General Nguyen Khanh after emerging from protracted talks with members of the Military Revolutionary Council — talks that were supposed to formulate a new framework to supplant General Khanh's seven-month-old regime.

General Khanh was Premier until he became President Aug. 16 on the basis of a new Constitution. He and leaders of the armed forces agreed yesterday to step aside under the pressure of Buddhist and student protests against the dictatorial aspects of the Government.

Council to Meet Again

Today's meetings made it clear that the generals and colonels could not agree on how much power they were preparing to relinquish or to whom they would relinquish it. The council has controlled the country since the ouster and assassination of President Ngo Dinh Diem last November.

Another meeting of the council is scheduled tomorrow.

[In Washington, authoritative sources said that the crucial steps taken by the Khanh Government to deal with the political situation were made known in advance to the United States.]

Meanwhile, religious strife continued in the central Vietnamese city of Danang, where Buddhist-Roman Catholic violence has resulted in 70 casualties, including at least a dozen deaths, in the last three days.

Taylor to Fly to U. S.

Grim and weary after a virtually sleepless night and day of bargaining, General Khanh said, "We military men have to consider things thoroughly before offering a solution to the people."

The President's intention of achieving re-election with new support from Buddhist groups and the political parties had clearly been blocked by the leaders of the armed forces.

The crisis, which flared into violence Sunday, showed how fragile is the political structure on which the United States has based its efforts to defeat the Communist Vietcong.

An American spokesman said Ambassador Maxwell D. Taylor was adhering to plans to return to the United States by air for

Continued on Page 3, Column 5

Pontiff Says Some Tenets Of Peace Are 'Crumbling'

He Is Reported to Have South Vietnam, Cyprus and the Congo in Mind in Talk Deploring the Divisions Among Men

Special to The New York Times

CASTEL GANDOLFO, Italy, Aug. 26—Pope Paul VI, in a vibrant appeal for peace, said today that some of the basic principles of peace were crumbling.

The Pontiff said there were new symptoms of the reappearance of divisions among peoples, races and cultures. "This spirit of division is guided by nationalistic pride, by prestige politics, the armaments race, social and economic antagonisms," he said.

He called on all "men of goodwill" to "listen to our humble voice" and place above "every other interest" the values of human dignity and fraternal accord.

The Pontiff's appeal was made to pilgrims attending a general audience at his summer residence. It was motivated, he said, not only by the anniversary at this time of year of the start of both world wars, but also by the "acute disagreements" that he said existed between various countries today.

The Pope did not specify any areas or countries, but L'Osservatore Romano, the Vatican newspaper, remarked in commenting on the speech that "to name islands or peninsulas or near and far hinterlands in which there is fighting" was superfluous.

Vatican sources commented that there was no doubt the Pope had Cyprus, the Congo and South Vietnam in mind.

The speech amounted to another step in a peace effort that the Pope started Aug. 10 with his encyclical "Ecclesiam Suam" ("His Church"). In that encyclical he said he was willing to intervene in disputes between nations to help find solu-

Continued on Page 12, Column 3

SENATOR PRAISED

'Best Man in America for the Job,' Johnson Tells Convention

By EARL MAZO
Special to The New York Times

ATLANTIC CITY, Thursday, Aug. 27—Senator Hubert H. Humphrey was nominated for Vice President by acclamation at the Democratic National Convention early today.

Mr. Humphrey's name was placed in nomination by Senator Eugene J. McCarthy, his colleague from Minnesota, after President Johnson had appeared before the convention to name Mr. Humphrey as his choice and describe him as "the best man in America for the job."

In the seats of honor at Convention Hall for the long series of speeches supporting the nomination of Mr. Humphrey were the President and the Johnson and Humphrey families.

After the voice vote by which Mr. Humphrey was unanimously nominated, the Vice-Presidential candidate joined the President in the box of honor.

Because of the late hour—about 12:30 A.M.—and the fact that most of the audience and many of the delegates had left Convention Hall, Mr. Humphrey's acceptance speech was postponed until the final convention session tonight.

Triple Announcement

The process by which President Johnson let out the secret of his choice for Vice President was highly unusual.

All told, he announced it three times last night.

He did so at 8:30 at Andrews Air Force Base, near Washington, before leaving for Atlantic City. He presented Mr. Humphrey to newspapermen as "the next Vice President."

On his arrival here an hour later, Mr. Johnson told newsmen at Bader Airport that Mr. Humphrey was his man. At that impromptu news conference he delivered what amounted to a preliminary nominating address, speaking at length of his high regard for Mr. Humphrey.

The Minnesotan, standing beside the President, smiled broadly and declared he was honored and proud.

The third announcement came before the convention itself.

Mr. Humphrey had gotten a glimpse, yesterday morning, of what lay ahead later in the day. And in midafternoon he had been summoned from Atlantic City to Washington by the White House.

When he returned last night at 9:30, he came to Convention

Continued on Page 21, Column 8

Associated Press Wirephoto

NOMINEE PRESENTS RUNNING MATE: President Johnson as he introduced Senator Hubert H. Humphrey to the Democratic convention. Mrs. Humphrey is at the left.

JOYOUS WELCOME

Hall Erupts in Sound as Suspense Over Ticket Is Ended

Texts of Johnson speech and airport conference, Page 20.

By TOM WICKER
Special to The New York Times

ATLANTIC CITY, Thursday, Aug. 27—Lyndon Baines Johnson of Texas, the man who took over the Presidency last Nov. 22 in the shattering hour of John F. Kennedy's assassination, was nominated for a term of his own last night by the 34th Democratic National Convention.

Then Mr. Johnson did what he loves to do. He smashed precedent by going before a turbulent and happy gathering of more than 5,000 delegates and alternates to name Senator Hubert H. Humphrey of Minnesota as his choice for the Vice-Presidential nomination.

The happy Democrats, and thousands of spectators jammed into Convention Hall, cheered wildly for both Mr. Johnson and Mr. Humphrey.

Speech Put Off

Late in the program, after Senator Humphrey had been nominated by acclamation, it was announced that he would put off his acceptance speech until tonight. The convention then adjourned, at 12:37 A.M.

After lingering for an hour and chatting with the Texas delegation, the President finally left for Washington.

The President's nomination was also by acclamation. The motion to suspend the rules and dispense with the call of the states was offered by Mrs. Lloyd Danzig of Florida. It came after the remnants of the Alabama delegation yielded to Texas, so that Gov. John B. Connally Jr. could place the Johnson name in nomination.

It also was Governor Connally who nominated Mr. Johnson in his first abortive bid for the Presidency, at the Chicago convention in 1956.

Gov. Edmund G. Brown of California shared the nominating process, and was followed by seven seconding speakers.

Roared Into Effect

The delegates whooped the nomination into effect with a roar. Speaker of the House John W. McCormack of Massachusetts, the permanent chairman, confirmed it with a bang of his huge gavel.

The nomination set off an enthusiastic demonstration. All over the hall banners waved, balloons soared toward the lofty curved ceiling, bands played in an ear-splitting cacophony, the great organ bellowed and men struggled through the jammed aisles, screaming at the top of their lungs.

When it was quieted with much gaveling, Mr. Johnson came to the platform and sat

Continued on Page 20, Column 1

The Choice of Humphrey, Step by Step

Special to The New York Times

WASHINGTON, Aug. 26—President Johnson's long delay in picking Senator Hubert H. Humphrey for the Vice-Presidency was carefully planned and for a specific purpose.

He had no doubts about Senator Humphrey's qualifications, but he wanted to get the widest possible support for Mr. Humphrey within the Democratic party, and he got it before making his decision at 3 o'clock this afternoon.

Also, the President wanted to make sure at the end that he and Senator Humphrey agreed on their concept of the Vice-Presidency. When Mr. Humphrey flew in here this afternoon, they had a long talk and agreed on the following things:

¶The Vice-Presidency, if the Democrats win in November, should have important executive responsibilities.

This special report on how President Johnson picked his Vice-Presidential running mate was prepared by Tom Wicker, James Reston, Anthony Lewis, Earl Mazo and E. W. Kenworthy of The New York Times staff.

¶The Vice President should supervise the Johnson Administration's policies on space, disarmament, the antipoverty program, health, education and welfare and other fields within Mr. Humphrey's special competence.

¶The Vice President should take on a great deal of responsibility in the field of foreign affairs. He should represent the President abroad on special missions and assume many of the ceremonial duties that President Johnson has had to carry alone in the last nine months. For this purpose, the President intends to ask the Congress to provide an official residence for the Vice President in Washington.

"I think in all my life," the President said tonight before going to the Convention Hall, "that I have never taken any decision more seriously than picking Humphrey. I have had one thing in mind above all others, that is that when fellows like you come to write the history of this period they will say that we paid attention to the main thing.

"I picked Humphrey because, in my judgment, and after checking with leaders all over the country, I was convinced that he would be the best man to be President if anything happened to me."

Having reached a decision on the principle of picking a possible President, Mr. John-

Continued on Page 22, Column 1

PRISONERS FREED BY EAST GERMANY

Accord With Bonn Reported for Thousands Detained on Political Charges

Special to The New York Times

BERLIN, Aug. 26—Communist East Germany has quietly begun to release a large number of political prisoners, the majority of them West Germans and West Berliners, official sources said here today.

They declined to confirm or deny that the release was an outcome of secret talks between East and West German justice officials. Observers said there was evidence that West German authorities had been informed and consulted.

On Monday, West German authorities freed Günther Hofe, an East Berlin publisher. He had been held in pretrial detention for almost 11 months on charges of having acted as a Soviet and East German agent. Bonn refused to explain the release.

Informed sources said several thousand persons were involved in the East German release.

The West German news

Continued on Page 10, Column 1

Saks Fire Forces 5,500 Into Streets, Shuts Store a Day

By THEODORE JONES

High-fashion models and beauty salon patrons with their hair in curlers were among 5,500 persons forced into the streets from Saks Fifth Avenue by a smoky fire yesterday morning.

The fire, which broke out in a subbasement shortly after 11 A.M., sent clouds of dense smoke up through elevator shafts and air-conditioning ducts, and forced the store to close for the rest of the day.

Two firemen were injured in fighting the blaze, which was brought under control an hour after it had started. An employe of the store inhaled smoke and was given oxygen at the scene.

Allen Johnson, vice president and general manager of the store, said that damage to merchandise had been slight and that the fire had been confined to the basement. He also said he could not estimate the revenue lost through the closing of the store.

Adam Gimbel, president of the store, said that Saks would open on schedule at 9:30 A.M. even "if we have to work all

Continued on Page 37, Column 5

NEW LAW ENDING ATOMIC MONOPOLY

Johnson Signs Bill to Allow Private Ownership of Fuel

By JOHN W. FINNEY
Special to The New York Times

WASHINGTON, Aug. 26 — President Johnson signed legislation today that ends an 18-year government monopoly of atomic fuels. Under the law, by June 30, 1973, the nuclear power business will be on its own within the framework of the free-enterprise system.

The amendment is the most far-reaching change in atomic legislation since the postwar McMahon Act was supplanted in 1954.

The 1954 law took the first step toward ending the government monopoly, created in a postwar concern over the awesome and little understood new force that had been unleashed, by permitting private possession of nuclear fuels and private ownership and operation of atomic power plants.

Reflecting a holdover of the postwar caution, however, the 1954 law still required Government ownership of the fissionable materials, such as enriched uranium, used as fuels in atomic reactors.

The government-owned and government-produced materials were leased, or in some cases given, to the private owners of atomic power plants.

Under the new amendment, unexpectedly approved by the Joint Congressional Committee on Atomic Energy this month after two years of deliberation, the commission after 1970 will be required to sell the nuclear fuels.

After mid-1973 all nuclear

Continued on Page 19, Column 3

Keating Declares Some Democrats Are Offering Help

By WARREN WEAVER Jr.
Special to The New York Times

ONEONTA, N.Y., Aug. 26—Senator Kenneth B. Keating said today that he had received promises of personal and political support from a number of New York Democrats in the 24 hours since Robert F. Kennedy announced his Senate candidacy.

The list of those who telephoned or sent personal messages, Mr. Keating reported, includes "some Democratic officeholders and at least two party officials," as well as others prominent in Democratic circles in New York City and upstate.

The Senator declined to identify any of the Democratic supporters, but he said their comments "certainly showed a resentment against this invasion from outside the state."

His reference was to the fact that Attorney General Kennedy is moving into New York State for the purpose of seeking the Democratic nomination for the Senate and running against Mr. Keating. For a number of years Mr. Kennedy has lived in Virginia and voted in Massachusetts.

Mr. Keating made his claims of Democratic support in an informal press conference in the office of The Oneonta Star. He said later that some of his Democratic friends had sug-

Continued on Page 25, Column 4

ALABAMIANS QUIT OVER PARTY OATH

Mississippi Delegates Begin Leaving Atlantic City

By CLAUDE SITTON
Special to The New York Times

ATLANTIC CITY, Aug. 26—The Alabama delegation to the Democratic National Convention followed the Mississippi delegation today in withdrawing rather than signing pledges of loyalty to President Johnson for the coming election.

They left behind only token groups of loyalists—nine from Alabama and three from Mississippi—to take part in the President's nomination by acclamation.

Eugene Connor, Alabama's national committeeman, was turned away by sergeants-at-arms when he sought to take his seat. Mr. Connor, former Birmingham police commissioner, predicted that the action would hurt President Johnson politically in the South.

The refusals by the two delegations to participate in the proceedings came after the convention's adoption yesterday of a recommendation by the Credentials Committee that the Mississippians take the loyalty pledge. The convention had earlier approved a similar requirement for the Alabamians.

Many of the Mississippians, who had made known their intention last night to quit the convention, left Atlantic City earlier today.

Mayor Jess Lanier of Bessemer, chairman of the unpledged group in the Alabama delegation, and its other leaders said tonight before the convention opened that they would suffer no further "insults" and that they were returning to Alabama.

Seymore Trammell, Ala-

Continued on Page 24, Column 3

Goldwater Favors Some Peking Talks

By CHARLES MOHR
Special to The New York Times

AVALON, Calif., Aug. 26—Senator Barry Goldwater said today that he had long believed "talks with Red China might be profitable" to end the war in South Vietnam.

If he were elected President, he indicated, he would be willing to permit negotiations with Peking.

He also expressed a qualified belief that the Johnson Administration was working for a negotiated settlement of the war in South Vietnam.

A little later, however, Mr. Goldwater appeared to modify his remarks to indicate that he had in mind some form of ultimatum rather than negotiations in the usual sense.

Mr. Goldwater interrupted a five-day Pacific cruise to hold

Continued on Page 2, Column 3

Associated Press

BUSINESS AS USUAL—MORE OR LESS: Saks Fifth Avenue hairdresser continuing work on patron's coiffure after smoky fire in the store's basement forced evacuation of the building. Women who had been in the beauty salon wear robes provided by store.

Hurricane's Gusts Sweep Into Miami

By The Associated Press

MIAMI, Thursday, Aug. 27—A hurricane struck Miami early today with winds of 75 miles an hour.

After toying with the city for hours, the hurricane, named Cleo, sent gusts across Miami's Key Biscayne that reached hurricane intensity.

Sustained gales—winds 25 to 75 miles an hour—battered the rest of the city as the storm's center churned just 25 miles to the southeast.

Forecasters warned that the storm center might go ashore north of the city and subject the coast from Fort Lauderdale to West Palm Beach to winds of 60 to 80 miles an hour.

The island of Bimini, about 35 miles offshore, also was struck

Continued on Page 17, Column 3

NEWS INDEX

"All the News That's Fit to Print"

The New York Times.

LATE CITY EDITION
U. S. Weather Bureau Report (Page 45) forecasts. Cloudy, then fair today; fair and cooler tonight. Fair tomorrow. Temp. Range: 70—55; yesterday: 73—59.

VOL. CXIV . No. 38,964. | NEW YORK, MONDAY, SEPTEMBER 28, 1964. | Today's Issue Contains 96 Pages in Two Sections | TEN CENTS

WARREN COMMISSION FINDS OSWALD GUILTY AND SAYS ASSASSIN AND RUBY ACTED ALONE; REBUKES SECRET SERVICE, ASKS REVAMPING

F.B.I. IS CRITICIZED

Security Steps Taken by Secret Service Held Inadequate

By FELIX BELAIR Jr.
Special to The New York Times

WASHINGTON, Sept. 27—A sweeping revision of the organization and basic operating practices of the United States Secret Service was recommended today by the Warren Commission.

The commission sharply rebuked the Secret Service for failure to make adequate preparation for the visit of President Kennedy to Dallas last November. It reprimanded the Federal Bureau of Investigation for failure to supply the Secret Service with information concerning the presence of Lee Harvey Oswald in Dallas.

The commission deplored the fact that "there was no fully adequate liaison" between the F.B.I. and the Secret Service before the Dallas trip. It noted that some improvements had occurred since then but it insisted that, ultimately, Presidential protection required improvement in working arrangements of all Federal agencies concerned, including the Central Intelligence Agency, the State Department and the military intelligence branches.

Scrutiny Is Urged

The State Department was admonished to scrutinize more carefully requests for return to the United States of defectors

The report's appendix on Presidential protection will be printed in tomorrow's Times.

like Oswald "who have evidenced disloyalty or hostility to this country or who have expressed a desire to renounce their citizenship."

The brunt of the commission's indictment was directed at the century-old agency responsible for the safety of the President and his family. Its chief charge was that the Secret Service had not checked buildings along the route of the Presidential motorcade in Dallas nor asked the local police to do so.

The commission called for the appointment of a new special assistant to the Secretary of the Treasury with general supervisory authority over the Secret Service.

The commission found, however, that the conduct of the Secret Service agents in the Presidential motorcade "demonstrates that the President and the nation can expect courage and devotion to duty from agents of the Secret Service."

It acknowledged that whatever the human and material resources at the command of the Secret Service, a President can only be made as safe as he wants to be.

The report declared that its recommendations were "compelled by the facts disclosed in this investigation." It noted that

Continued on Page 15, Column 1

Harris & Ewing

THE WARREN COMMISSION: President's Commission on the Assassination of President Kennedy at commission offices at Veterans of Foreign Wars Building, Washington. From left: Representative Gerald R. Ford, Representative Hale Boggs, Senator Richard B. Russell, Chief Justice Earl Warren, Senator John Sherman Cooper, John J. McCloy, Allen W. Dulles, and J. Lee Rankin, commission counsel. Portraits are of President Johnson, President Kennedy and Joseph J. Lombardo, head of Veterans of Foreign Wars.

JOHNSON NAMES 4 TO ACT ON REPORT

Commission Calls for Action to Increase the Security of the Presidency

By The Associated Press

JOHNSON CITY, Tex., Sept. 27—President Johnson appointed a four-man committee today to advise him "on the execution of the recommendations of the Warren Commission."

The commission, which investigated the assassination of President Kennedy, recommended action to tighten the protection of Presidents and to make the killing of a President or a Vice President a Federal crime.

[Mike Mansfield of Montana, the Senate majority leader, said in Washington that Congress, which has been aiming at adjournment at the end of this week, "should stay here and act, if the President sends us any recommendations."]

Members of the committee are Secretary of the Treasury Douglas Dillon, Acting Attorney General Nicholas deB. Katzenbach, John A. McCone, director of the Central Intelligence Agency, and McGeorge Bundy, Special Assistant to the President for National Security Affairs.

The President named no chairman for the committee, but it was understood that Secretary Dillon, as ranking member, would have general supervision over the group.

The group will presumably

Continued on Page 17, Column 3

A New Chapter Unfolds in the Kennedy Legend

By JAMES RESTON
Special to The New York Times

News Analysis

WASHINGTON, Sept. 27—The Warren Commission has fulfilled its primary assignment. It has tried, as a servant of history, to discover truth. But the assassination of President Kennedy was so symbolic of human irony and tragedy, and so involved in the complicated and elemental conflicts of the age, that many vital questions remain, and the philosophers, novelists and dramatists will have to take it from here.

The commission has not concluded the Kennedy mystery so much as it has opened up a whole new chapter in the Kennedy legend.

It has provided the greatest repository of Presidential political history, drama and fiction since the murder of Mr. Lincoln and since legend is often more powerful than history, this may be the commission's most significant achievement.

Now the central mystery of who killed the President has been answered by the commission only in the process of raising a new catalogue of mysteries. Now the main characters in the play have been surrounded by a host of new characters, each of whom appears briefly at a critical moment with some vital testimony, only to disappear without our really knowing much about who they are.

The whole story is full of the mystery of life. Lee Harvey Oswald's motive for murdering the President remains obscure. The distinguished members of the commission and their staff obviously gave up on it.

The "might-have-beens" are maddening. If only he had been given that visa to go to Cuba and thence to the Soviet Union just before the assassination! If he had not been allowed to come back from there in the first place! Who was "the neighbor" who got him the job in the Texas Book Depository, from where he shot the President? And what were the details of Oswald's attempted suicide in Moscow?

The wild accidents are equally intriguing. There is, for example, the case of Mrs. Bledsoe, who rented Oswald a room in Dallas and then, on a 10,000-to-1 chance, just happened to be on the bus he boarded when he was running away from the crime.

Then there are the consoling yearnings and kindnesses in the midst of tragedy: Ruth Paine, who was also "alienated" and "isolated," and frustrated like Oswald, but who nevertheless "befriended" Marina Oswald in her time of

Continued on Page 15, Column 6

'MYTHS' OF CASE DENIED IN DETAIL

Panel Says Misinformation on the Assassination Led to 'Distorted' Views

By PETER KIHSS

The Warren Commission rejected in detail yesterday a number of charges suggesting that Lee Harvey Oswald had not acted alone in the assassination of President Kennedy.

The commission said that "publicizing of unchecked information" had led to "myths" and "distorted" interpretations. While each inaccuracy could be explained, it went on, "the number and variety of misstatements issued by the police" in Dallas would have "greatly assisted a skillful defense attorney."

On the other hand, Mark Lane, chairman of a Citizens Committee of Inquiry here, contended that if the report contained all the available evidence, "Oswald would have been acquitted" of both the President's assassination and the murder of the Dallas patrolman, J. D. Tippit.

In a news conference, Mr. Lane, a former Assemblyman, said his group would continue its efforts to "answer the unanswered questions." He said it had more than 250 workers here, with other committees in England, France and Denmark, and interested groups on 20 college campuses. His group estimated that it had raised and

Continued on Page 16, Column 4

PANEL UNANIMOUS

Theory of Conspiracy by Left or Right Is Rejected

The text of the report begins on the first page of the second section.

By ANTHONY LEWIS
Special to The New York Times

WASHINGTON, Sept. 27—The assassination of President Kennedy was the work of one man, Lee Harvey Oswald. There was no conspiracy, foreign or domestic.

That was the central finding in the Warren Commission report, made public this evening. Chief Justice Earl Warren and the six other members of the President's Commission on the Assassination of President John F. Kennedy were unanimous on this and all questions.

The commission found that Jack Ruby was on his own in killing Oswald. It rejected all theories that the two men were in some way connected. It said that neither rightists nor Communists bore responsibility for the murder of the President in Dallas last Nov. 22.

Why did Oswald do it? To this most important and most mysterious question the commission had no certain answer. It suggested that Oswald had no rational purpose, no motive adequate if "judged by the standards of reasonable men."

A Product of His Life

Rather, the commission saw Oswald's terrible act as the product of his entire life—a life "characterized by isolation, frustration and failure." He was just 24 years old at the time of the assassination.

"Oswald was profoundly alienated from the world in which he lived," the report said. "He had very few, if any, close relationships with other people and he appeared to have had great difficulty in finding a meaningful place in the world.

"He was never satisfied with anything.

"When he was in the United States, he resented the capitalist system. When he was in the Soviet Union, he apparently resented the Communist party members, who were accorded special privileges and who he thought were betraying Communism, and he spoke well of the United States."

The commission found that Oswald shot at former Maj. Gen. Edwin A. Walker in Dallas on April 10, 1963, narrowly missing him. It cited this as evidence of his capacity for violence.

It listed as factors that might have led Oswald to the assassination "his deep-rooted resentment of all authority, which was expressed in a hostility toward every society in which he lived," his "urge to try to find a place in history" and his "avowed commitment to Marx-

Continued on Page 14, Column 1

High Clerics to Ask Stronger Statement By Council on Jews

Special to The New York Times

ROME, Sept. 27—A powerful array of Roman Catholic prelates, including at least three American Cardinals, are preparing to speak out for a strong statement by the Ecumenical Council on the Jews, clerical sources said today.

The sources said that Richard James Cardinal Cushing, Archbishop of Boston, is known to have prepared an address to be given at the Council when the issue is debated.

The draft of the declaration was introduced last Friday by Augustin Cardinal Bea, the German Jesuit, who heads the Council's Secretariat for the Promotion of Christian Unity. It is considered by many Council Fathers—the voting prelates—and observers to be a "watered down" version of an earlier draft.

Other Cardinals Named

The earlier statement, among other things, made plain that the Jews of Christ's time and of today bore no responsibility for the Crucifixion. The weakened declaration declares only that Jews of today cannot be blamed.

Among those expected to attack the newer version are two other American Cardinals—Joseph Elmer Ritter, Archbishop of St. Louis, and Albert Gregory Meyer, Archbishop of Chicago.

Cardinal Spellman of New York has also said that he favors the more forceful state-

Continued on Page 7, Column 1

2 CITIES DENY REIN ON POLICE IN RIOTS

Civilian Review Units Hold F.B.I. Criticism Unfounded

By FRED POWLEDGE

Officials of civilian police advisory boards in Rochester and Philadelphia disagreed yesterday with a statement by the Federal Bureau of Investigation that boards such as theirs had "virtually paralyzed" the police during the summer riots.

The Rev. William H. Gray Jr., executive secretary of Philadelphia's eight-member review board, said: "It's over-simplifying the situation to say that the board has an effect on the rioting or the police behavior."

Ross J. Guglielmino, the executive director and legal counsel of the Rochester board, said he did not feel the F.B.I. criticism applied to Rochester.

What the F.B.I. Found

The two men commented in telephone interviews on a report released Saturday by President Johnson. The President had asked the F.B.I. to collect its investigations of summer riots in New York City, Rochester, Dixmoor, Ill.; Philadelphia, Seaside, Ore., Hampton Beach, N. H., and Jersey City, Paterson, and Elizabeth, N. J., and advise him if there were any pattern in the outbreaks.

The report, submitted by F.B.I. Director J. Edgar Hoover, concluded that the riots were not basically racial, although large numbers of Negroes took part; that they were not organized on a national basis, and that none of them was planned by any one group or individual.

Among the several points

Continued on Page 48, Column 1

Congress Will Act On Appalachia Aid And Medical Care

Special to The New York Times

WASHINGTON, Sept. 27—The fate of two key Administration programs—health insurance for the aged and aid to Appalachia—may be decided this week as Congress pushes toward adjournment.

"We could finish up Saturday; that's my most optimistic guess," Senator Mike Mansfield of Montana, the majority leader, said today. "But I have my fingers crossed."

The health insurance issue, currently in House-Senate conference, could delay adjournment until the following week, some legislative leaders believe.

Prospects for conference approval of some form of health insurance for the aged under Social Security have ranged from bright to gloomy in recent days.

The House passed a bill this summer to increase Social Security taxes as well as cash

Continued on Page 18, Column 4

CAMPAIGN IMPACT BELIEVED LIKELY

'Kennedy Legacy' Could Aid Democrats at the Polls

By TOM WICKER
Special to The New York Times

WASHINGTON, Sept. 27—The effects of the Warren Commission's report are sure to extend far beyond its conclusion that Lee Harvey Oswald, acting alone, killed President Kennedy last Nov. 22.

The massive document could have repercussions in the 1964 elections, on the present conduct of President Johnson, and ultimately on the availability to the public of Mr. Johnson and future Presidents.

It may produce major changes for the Secret Service, the agency now assigned to protect the President.

Other Agencies Affected

The assignments and powers of other agencies such as the Federal Bureau of Investigation and even the Central Intelligence Agency might be revamped and independent review of their activities and efficiency might be increased.

In the field of legislation, the report might produce—as recommended by the commission—a law making it a Federal crime to kill or attempt to kill a President, a Vice President or any officer next in line to the Presidency and the President-elect and Vice President-elect. Other legislation, particularly relating to security and investigative agencies and to the protection of Presidents, could also grow from the report.

Although the State Department was generally cleared of

Continued on Page 15, Column 5

G.I.'s Rescue Vietnam Captives; Uprising Stirs Mistrust of U.S.

By PETER GROSE
Special to The New York Times

SAIGON, South Vietnam, Sept. 27 — United States Army helicopters rescued 60 Vietnamese hostages today from a camp of rebel tribesmen in the central highlands.

The release of the prisoners met a Government condition for negotiations with the armed mountain tribesmen. It appeared to reduce the danger of a violent clash.

Nevertheless the revolt is having serious political consequences, involving growing suspicion between the United States mission and the Premier, Maj. Gen. Nguyen Khanh. The rebellion has intensified Saigon's feeling that the United States, which has supported General Khanh, is undergoing a change of policy.

[About five persons were reported shot dead when security forces fired on a crowd in Quinhon, 270 miles northeast of Saigon. Later a mob stormed a radio station and troops were called in to evict the demonstrators, Reuters reported.]

Officials around General Khanh say he no longer believes he can count on American help to stay in power and he feels he must seek firmer support from

Continued on Page 2, Column 1

NEWS INDEX

In this issue editorials appear on Page 28, obituaries on Page 29, TV and radio news on Page 47, and the News Summary and Index on Page 2.

Scientific Police Work Traced Bullets to Rifle Oswald Owned

By JOHN W. FINNEY
Special to The New York Times

WASHINGTON, Sept. 27—The Warren Commission's conclusion that Lee Harvey Oswald killed President Kennedy rests in large part on scientific evidence painstakingly established through modern technology.

On the basis of the scientific evidence alone it was possible to establish that the shots were fired by a rifle owned and possessed by Oswald, that the shots were fired from the sixth-floor window of a building in which Oswald worked, and that the fatal wound could have been caused by the bullets from the high-powered rifle.

These crucial points were established through scientific detective work that combined the techniques of handwriting, ballistics, and fiber and wounds analysis. Among the devices used were microscopes, spectroscopes, X-rays, surveying instruments and skulls filled with gelatin.

Even nuclear science was employed. Paraffin casts from Oswald's hands and face were put into a nuclear reactor at the Oak Ridge (Tenn.) National Laboratory in an unsuccessful attempt to see if radiation would show up traces of gunpowder. One major question left

Continued on Page 16, Column 5

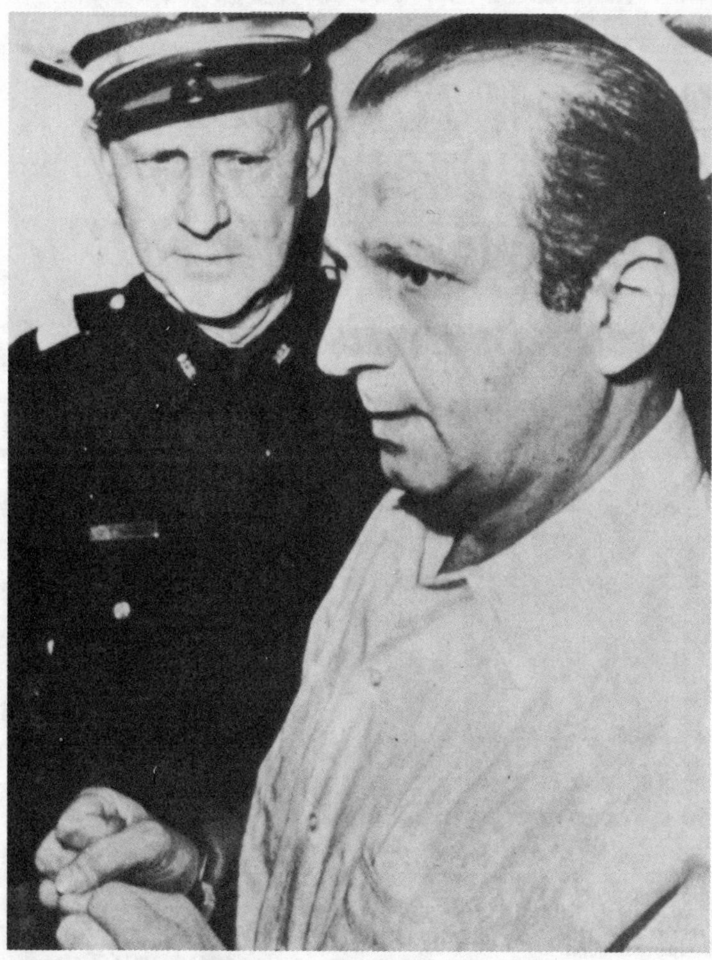

Jack Ruby handcuffed in the Dallas city jail just after his arraignment for the murder of the Presidential assassin, Lee Harvey Oswald.

Chief Justice Earl Warren (left) chaired the panel for the President's Commission on the Assassination of President Kennedy. He is seen here with J. Lee Rankin, Commission member, leaving Dallas where they inspected the scene.

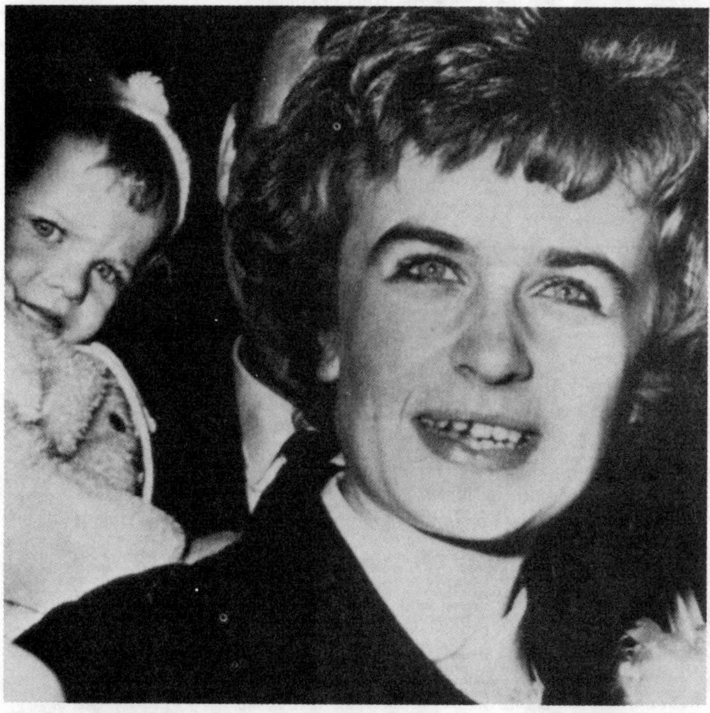

Marina Oswald arrived with her two-year-old daughter to go before the Warren Commission. Nothing in her testimony shook the Commission findings of 1964.

Douglas MacArthur is seen here with President Truman in 1950. MacArthur, the controversial hero, died in 1964.

"All the News That's Fit to Print"

The New York Times.

LATE CITY EDITION
U.S. Weather Bureau Report (Page 76) forecasts: Cloudy and cooler today; chance of rain tonight and tomorrow.
Temp. Range: 68—53; yesterday: 66—48.

VOL. CXIV..No. 38,982. NEW YORK, FRIDAY, OCTOBER 16, 1964. TEN CENTS

KHRUSHCHEV OUSTED FROM TOP POSTS; BREZHNEV GETS CHIEF PARTY POSITION AND KOSYGIN IS NAMED NEW PREMIER

Labor Party Is the Apparent Victor in British Election

JOHNSON DENIES JENKINS COVER-UP; SETS F.B.I. INQUIRY

Praises His Aide's Service, but Says He Requested Resignation From Post

By TOM WICKER
Special to The New York Times

WASHINGTON, Oct. 15—President Johnson said tonight that until late yesterday he had had no information of any kind that "had ever raised a question" about the personal conduct of Walter W. Jenkins, his friend and special assistant.

The President made the statement, his first public comment on the Jenkins case, as he flew back here from a day of campaigning in New York.

In effect, he was denying Republican allegations that he had covered up knowledge of Mr. Jenkins's two arrests on morals charges. The disclosure of these arrests yesterday has shaken the Johnson Administration and the Democratic Presidential campaign.

Mr. Jenkins's resignation as special assistant to the President was announced in New York last night after the disclosure of his police record.

Mr. Johnson also disclosed in his statement tonight that he had requested the resignation of Mr. Jenkins.

'Dedication' Is Cited

The text of Mr. Johnson's statement follows:

"Walter Jenkins has worked with me faithfully for 25 years. No man I know has given more personal dedication, devotion and tireless labor.

"Until late yesterday no information or report of any kind to me had ever raised a question with respect to his personal conduct. Mr. Jenkins is now in the care of his physician and his many friends will join in praying for his early recovery. For myself and Mrs. Johnson I want to say that our hearts go out with the deepest compassion for him and for his wife and six children—and they have our love and prayers.

"On this case as on any such case, the public interest comes before all personal feelings. I have requested and received Mr. Jenkins's resignation.

"Within moments after being notified last night, I ordered Director J. Edgar Hoover of the F.B.I. to make an immediate and comprehensive inquiry and report promptly to me and the American people."

The incident apparently is regarded by the Republicans as a major development in their

Continued on Page 20, Column 1

G.O.P. Hopes Rise, But Jenkins Effect On Race Is Cloudy

By EARL MAZO

The Walter W. Jenkins case inspired high hopes in the camp of Senator Barry Goldwater yesterday and dismay among supporters of President Johnson.

But by nightfall, reports from Moscow that Premier Khrushchev has been replaced led many political observers to speculate that the possible anti-Johnson impact of the Jenkins disclosure might be nullified by the effect of an international crisis upon the voters.

A leading Republican put it this way:

"That Lyndon Johnson is lucky. The arrest of his man Jenkins accented the whole Bobby Baker corruption mess, which is Barry Goldwater's strongest issue. But then comes this Khrushchev thing, taking the headlines and accenting Barry's greatest weak-

Continued on Page 21, Column 1

JOHNSON HAILED AT LIBERAL RALLY

Asserts 'Great Society' Is a Practical Goal—He Is Acclaimed Upstate

By HOMER BIGART

President Johnson received a frenzied ovation last night from 20,000 persons who packed Madison Square Garden for a Liberal party rally.

The President expounded to the Garden audience his vision of the "Great Society" and insisted it was a practical goal —"not some vague, dreamlike utopia."

He said he would present a series of proposals dealing with the total needs of a metropolitan area.

These proposals, he said, would be built on the cooperation of government with industry—"the same sort of cooperation that has built our national defense and allowed us to explore the stars."

Campaigns With Kennedy

The President went to the Garden after stumping the state with Robert F. Kennedy, the Democratic-Liberal candidate for the Senate, and receiving tumultuous welcomes from huge crowds on a 22-mile tour of Brooklyn.

Despite the Walter Jenkins scandal, no lessening of enthusiasm was apparent in the throngs that greeted the President in Brooklyn or jammed the Garden for the Liberal party's climactic demonstration.

Roaring applause greeted the President and Mrs. Johnson when they entered the Garden at 8:20 P.M.

The President read his speech in a matter-of-fact voice and the subject matter—the "Great Society"—inspired no cheers.

Interest Stimulated

But when he turned to the day's dramatic developments in the Soviet Union, the crowd's interest was stimulated. A crescendo of applause followed his remark: "We do not intend to bury anyone anywhere and we do not intend to be buried ourselves."

The President warned that this was no time for impulsive leadership. He said "an impulsive thumb can move up toward a button," resulting in the destruction of millions of lives in a matter of moments.

Recalling the Cuban missile crisis, he declared that President Kennedy "had the steadiest thumb, the greatest heart and

Continued on Page 22, Column 1

SLIM EDGE LIKELY

Wilson Aide Defeated in Campaign Marred by a Racial Issue

By SYDNEY GRUSON
Special to The New York Times

LONDON, Friday, Oct. 16—Britain apparently elected a Labor Government in yesterday's general election and sent the Conservatives, who have governed for 13 years, into opposition.

However, all indications pointed to the closest result since the Conservatives won with a majority of 17 in 1951. There is still a chance that Labor will not get a working majority.

With counting finished for the night, the standing of the parties from the results in 430 of the 630 constituencies was:

Labor—247
Conservative—181
Liberal—2

But this Labor lead of 66 House of Commons seats was misleading. Most of the results were from urban areas and the Conservatives are expected to cut deeply into the lead when counting in the rural Conservative strongholds resumes later this morning.

Labor Gains 52 Seats

The computers of the British Broadcasting Corporation and of Press Association, the cooperative news-gathering agency, both forecast an ultimate Labor majority over the Conservatives of 17.

Labor gained 52 seats, two from the Liberals and the rest from the Conservatives. The Conservatives lost 50 seats and took four from Labor.

Sir Alec Douglas-Home, the Conservative leader and Prime Minister, would not concede. He did not emerge from 10 Downing Street, his London office and residence, where he watched the election results on television.

So long as he did not concede, Harold Wilson, Labor's leader, refused to claim victory. Mr. Wilson would be Prime Minister in a Labor Government.

Patrick Gordon Walker, slated to be Foreign Secretary in a Labor Cabinet, lost the Smethwick constituency of industrial Birmingham to Peter Griffiths, a Conservative.

It was at Smethwick that a bitter campaign had been waged

Continued on Page 18, Column 1

Nikita S. Khrushchev
Relieved of political posts

Leonid I. Brezhnev
Named as the leader of the party

Aleksei N. Kosygin
Appointed as the Soviet Premier

Associated Press

MOSCOW IS QUIET

Pravda Says Change Won't Bring Return of Harsh Policies

By HENRY TANNER
Special to The New York Times

MOSCOW, Friday, Oct. 16—Premier Khrushchev has been deprived of political power in the Soviet Union.

He was replaced by Leonid I. Brezhnev, 57 years old, as First Secretary of the Communist party and by Aleksei N. Kosygin, 60, as Premier.

Mr. Khrushchev, who is 70, even lost his seat in the Presidium of the Central Committee of the party, the third most important position he held in the leadership.

This indicated that he had fallen into disgrace.

[Dispatches did not mention if Mr. Khrushchev had been removed from the Central Committee itself. Under normal procedure such action would come at a meeting of the Soviet Communist party Congress.]

Adzhubei Reported Ousted

The changes were announced by Tass, the Soviet press agency, a few minutes after midnight. The Tass statement did not contain a single word of praise for the ousted leader.

Unofficial but reliable sources later reported that Aleksei I. Adzhubei, Mr. Khrushchev's son-in-law, had been deposed as chief editor of the Government newspaper Izvestia.

Mr. Khrushchev's whereabouts was not known. Nor was it known whether he was at liberty or under surveillance. Western diplomats assumed, however, that the changeover had been made peacefully.

Diplomats Voice Assurance

Moscow's streets were quiet. There were no signs of movements by either the army or police. Some of the smaller Western embassies, which had been without a police guard for the last several months, reported yesterday that the policemen were back in front of the gates.

Western diplomats said they did not expect the new leaders to change basic Soviet policy toward the West.

Mr. Brezhnev and Mr. Kosygin can be expected to continue Mr. Khrushchev's policy of "peaceful coexistence" with the United States, the diplomats said.

The Soviet Communist party newspaper Pravda indicated today that the party would continue to carry out policies of de-Stalinization and economic improvements under its new leadership.

The paper printed the same bare announcement that had been carried in the English-

Continued on Page 14, Column 1

Cholesterol Studies Bring Nobel Award To Two Biochemists

By The Associated Press

STOCKHOLM, Oct. 15—The 1964 Nobel Prize in Physiology or Medicine was awarded jointly today to Prof. Konrad E. Bloch of Harvard University and Prof. Feodor Lynen of the University of Munich.

The two were honored for their discoveries concerning the mechanism and regulation of cholesterol and fatty acid metabolism. They will share prize money equivalent to about $54,000.

In its citation, the prize-awarding body, the Royal Caroline Institute, said the therapy against circulatory diseases and related disturbances in steroid hormone metabolism would in the future rest upon the work of today's Nobel Prize winners.

Dr. Bloch, a 52-year-old naturalized American born in Germany, is Higgins Professor of Biochemistry at Harvard. He was credited with "brilliant investigations" showing how cholesterol is built up from acetic acid.

Cholesterol, a fatty substance

Continued on Page 3, Column 1

THREATENED SUIT HALTS STATE LOAN

Deals to Borrow $17 Million Delayed by Challenge to Rockefeller Financing

By PETER KIHSS

Two state agencies have had to postpone the closing of deals to borrow $17.3 million because of a threatened court suit by Teamsters Joint Council 16 against financing methods of the Rockefeller administration.

The Governor's office declined yesterday to say why the closing had been held up. But a high state official said the purchasers of bond-anticipation notes required standard certificates assuring that they would not become involved in litigation, and he said that such statements could not be given because of the threatened teamsters suit.

Governor Rockefeller was reported to have sought through intermediaries to get the union council president, John J. O'Rourke, to drop the threatened suit. The Governor's view was said to have been that "thousands" of jobs of currently employed construction workers would be endangered if the financing were held up.

But Nicholas M. Kisburg, legislative and research director of the teamsters' council, said last night that the state could use $806 million to carry on construction through bond issues already approved by the voters but not yet invoked by the Governor.

Governor Rockefeller's office said that $13.8 million in bond-anticipation notes of the State Housing Finance Agency had first been sold to five buyers Oct. 8, with delivery scheduled for yesterday. Yesterday, the agency "postponed delivery of the notes," the Governor's office said.

Similarly, it said, $3.5 million in bond-anticipation notes of the State Dormitory Authority had been sold Oct. 8, but delivery had to be "postponed" on Wednesday.

The purchasers of the Housing Finance Agency notes were

Continued on Page 31, Column 1

U.S. Surprised but Expects No Radical Shift in Policy

By MAX FRANKEL
Special to The New York Times

WASHINGTON, Oct. 15—The Administration was surprised but not alarmed by the change of leadership in Moscow today. Analysts of Soviet affairs were almost unanimous in the view that Premier Khrushchev had suddenly been forced to step down for reasons of personality and policy, not merely age and health.

But the survival and promotion of prominent Khrushchev lieutenants, officials said, seemed to preclude any radical policy changes in the near future, at least in East-West relations.

In New York, President Johnson said that the shift in the Kremlin "may or may not be a sign of deep turmoil or a sign of changes to come." He commented at the end of his prepared remarks at a Liberal party rally.

Peace Is the Mission

"For ourselves, the need is clear—we should keep steady on our goals," he said. "Peace is the mission of the American people and we are not about to be deterred. We will be firm and restrained. We can meet any test but our quest is always for peace."

In Milwaukee, Senator Hubert H. Humphrey expressed doubt that the Soviet change would bring about a "quick" meeting of Soviet and United States leaders. Talking to newsmen

Continued on Page 15, Column 1

STOCKS PLUMMET IN HECTIC TRADING

Changes in Kremlin Set Off Sharpest Drop in Prices Since Kennedy's Death

By RICHARD PHALON

Rumors of impending changes in the Kremlin swept Wall Street yesterday. By 1:30 P.M. a rolling tide of uneasiness had driven prices on the New York Stock Exchange to their deepest loss since the assassination of President Kennedy last Nov. 22.

Trading volume ran to 6.5 million shares, well below the record of 14.7 million shares churned up in the big market break of May 29, 1962, but much of it came in a concentrated burst after the noon hour. By 2:30 P.M. the tape lagged 27 minutes behind activity on the floor of the stock exchange.

Many brokers felt yesterday's market break followed a classic pattern. As one diagnosed it, the small investors were doing much of the selling. "They can't see anything, they can't touch anything and they're nervous. They're selling and the professionals are bargain-hunting," he observed.

Losses Cut in Half

The first tangible sign that bargain hunters were on the move came at 2:30 P.M. when market losses were cut in half. By 3 P.M. reports that Premier Khrushchev was retiring were confirmed and the news spread rapidly across the floor of the stock exchange.

At the close of trading, the stock market was down 6.74 points as measured by the Dow-Jones industrial average. The New York Times combined average of 50 stocks closed with a loss of 5.79 points.

Despite the late rally, it was the biggest loss since Aug. 4 when the stock prices plummeted after the Gulf of Tonkin naval action.

Boardroom habitués at midtown brokerage houses glared at the dancing symbols on the big Trans-Lux tapes with a frown—in, concentration usually re-

Continued on Page 55, Column 7

Cards Win World Series, Defeating Yankees, 7 to 5

By JOSEPH DURSO
Special to The New York Times

ST. LOUIS, Oct. 15—The St. Louis Cardinals completed their melodramatic climb from the depths of the National League to baseball's pinnacle today when they defeated the New York Yankees, 7—5, and captured the World Series.

They won it in the seventh and final game before a roaring crowd of 30,346 persons in Busch Stadium after they had won the National League pennant in the final game of the regular season. And they won it in the same way—behind the fast-ball pitching of 28-year-old Bob Gibson, who struck out nine Yankees and survived three late home runs that knocked in all the Yankees' runs.

Five pitchers struggled against Gibson to withstand the Cardinals. But the Redbirds scored three runs in the fourth inning, three in the fifth and one in the seventh to bring St. Louis its first championship in 18 years and send the Yankees to their second straight loss of the World Series.

The Yankees had not lost two years in a row since 1921 and 1922, the first two times they played in the World Series. Since then, they had appeared in 25 Series in 40 years and won 20 of them until the Los Angeles Dodgers defeated them in four games last year.

Today they threatened until the last out to overpower the Cardinals in the winner-take-all game. Five home runs were struck, two by the Cardinals and three by the Yankees. Two were hit by the Boyer brothers—Ken of the Cards and Clete of the Yanks—while Lou Brock hit one for St. Louis and Mickey Mantle and Phil Linz for New York in the late innings.

But when Gibson got the Yankees' hitting star of the Series, Bobby Richardson, on a high pop-up to Dal Maxvill at second base in the ninth, the titanic struggle was over.

Busch Stadium erupted into shouting, chanting, singing, bugle-blaring and fireworks as fans emptied the grandstand

Continued on Page 44, Column 3

Cole Porter Is Dead; Songwriter Was 72

By The Associated Press

SANTA MONICA, Calif., Oct. 15 — Cole Porter, the world-famed composer and lyricist, died at 11:05 P.M. today at a Santa Monica hospital, where he underwent kidney surgery last Tuesday. He was 72 years old.

Mr. Porter wrote the lyrics and music for his songs, and to both he brought such an individuality of style that a genre known as "the Cole Porter song" became recognized.

The hallmarks of a typical Porter song were lyrics that were urbane or witty and a melody with a sinuous, brooding quality. Some of his best-known songs in this vein were "What

Continued on Page 29, Column 1

American Motors Struck by U.A.W.

By DAVID R. JONES
Special to The New York Times

DETROIT, Friday, Oct. 16—The United Automobile Workers struck the American Motors Corporation this morning after failure to reach a new labor agreement.

Edward L. Cushman, American Motors vice president and top labor negotiator, announced at 1:05 A.M. today that the parties had agreed to retain a profit-sharing plan in a new contract. But he said the strike deadline arrived before they could resolve other differences.

The strike affects about 23,000 workers at four plants in two Wisconsin cities. The company makes Rambler automobiles.

The walkout widened labor strife in the industry, where nearly 300,000 workers already have been made idle by an auto

Continued on Page 40, Column 1

The TFX Unveiled; McNamara Hails It

By RICHARD WITKIN
Special to The New York Times

FORT WORTH, Tex., Oct. 15—The TFX, the plane that launched 3,000 pages of Congressional inquiry, was rolled out the factory door into public view today.

The twin-jet plane, which has revolutionary movable wings and now is called the F-111, is scheduled to make its first flight by the end of the year.

The rollout ceremony was attended by a dais full of civilian and military dignitaries, headed by Secretary of Defense Robert S. McNamara.

Mr. McNamara has been at the center of the political storm that has enveloped the F-111 program since his office overruled the unanimous judgment

Continued on Page 11, Column 1

NEWS INDEX

1964

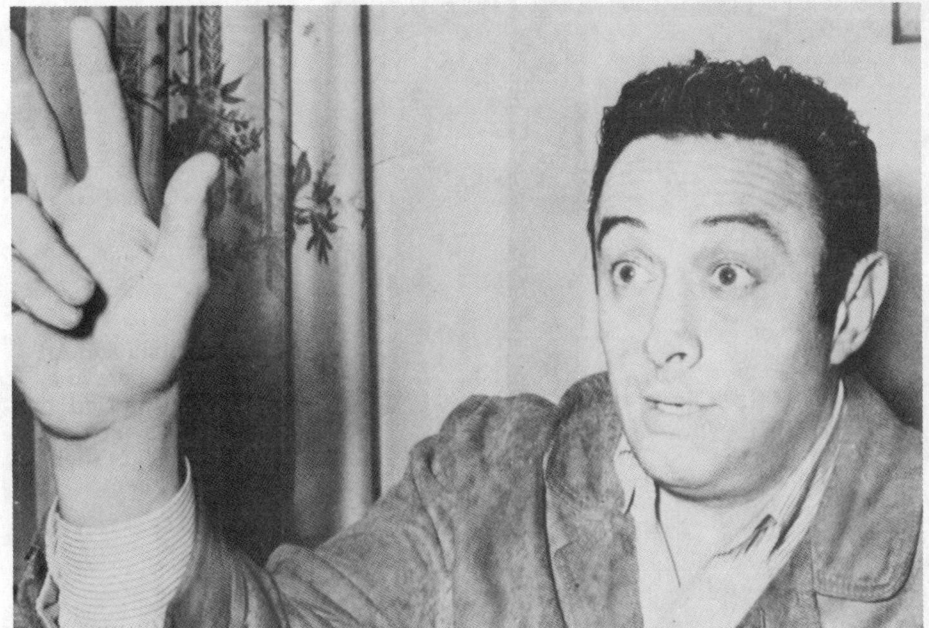

The law viewed Lenny Bruce, the controversial entertainer, as a distasteful component of society. Drug addiction caused his early death.

Throngs of feverish fans had to be controlled whenever the Beatles appeared.

Ed Sullivan received the highest ratings in history for one Sunday night show when four shaggy British musicians appeared as his guest stars. It was the Beatles' first appearance in this country.

Walter Matthau and Art Carney, seen here in a scene from *The Odd Couple,* drove each other "up the walls" of their shared apartment.

Carol Channing starred with David Burns in *Hello Dolly!* The hit musical was a box-office sell-out in 1964.

"All the News That's Fit to Print"

The New York Times.

LATE CITY EDITION
U. S. Weather Bureau Report (Page 55) forecasts:
Cloudy and windy with rain today;
fair tonight and tomorrow.
Temp. Range: 71—58; yesterday: 76—54.

VOL. CXIV..No. 38,983. NEW YORK, SATURDAY, OCTOBER 17, 1964. TEN CENTS

PRAVDA SAYS KHRUSHCHEV IS HAREBRAINED SCHEMER; GIVES WEST PEACE PLEDGE

POLICIES OUTLINED

New Chiefs Promise to Continue Efforts for 'Coexistence'

Text of the Pravda editorial is printed on Page 12.

By HENRY TANNER
Special to The New York Times

MOSCOW, Saturday, Oct. 17—Without naming the deposed Soviet leader, Nikita S. Khrushchev, the new regime accused him today of "harebrained scheming," "bragging and phrase-mongering" and "armchair methods."

In its first declaration of a program the Soviet leadership at the same time pledged to continue its policy of peaceful coexistence with the West.

The new leadership, headed by Leonid I. Brezhnev and Aleksei N. Kosygin, said that it would press for a conference of world Communist parties next year to deal with the ideological challenge of the Chinese Communists.

In the ouster of Mr. Khrushchev, announced yesterday, Mr. Brezhnev took over the post of party First Secretary and Mr. Kosygin became Premier.

The program was defined in an editorial in Pravda, the party newspaper. A text of the editorial was made public by Tass, the Soviet press agency.

The Pravda editorial was clearly a devastating attack on Mr. Khrushchev by his former associates.

Pretenses Removed

Western observers felt that it did away with any pretense that Mr. Khrushchev's departure might have been voluntary on the grounds of old age and health, as yesterday's official announcement said.

The charges against Mr. Khrushchev seemed to center on his domestic economic policies.

This was contrary to the expectations of Western diplomats who had been convinced that the Soviet-Chinese conflict was the pivotal issue in his downfall. They still did not rule out the possibility that Mr. Khrushchev would be castigated on this issue later.

The editorial said:

"The Leninist party is an enemy of subjectivism and drifting in Communist construction.

"Harebrained scheming, immature conclusions and hasty decisions and actions divorced from reality, bragging and phrase-mongering, commandism, unwillingness to take into account the achievements of

Continued on Page 12, Column 1

Brezhnev Urged End of China Rift

Special to The New York Times

BERLIN, Oct. 16 — When Leonid I. Brezhnev was in East Berlin 10 days ago, he underlined the Soviet Union's wish to overcome the split with Communist China and to maintain a state of "peaceful coexistence" with the West.

Experts at the United States mission here considered it likely that the leadership change in Moscow had been prepared well in advance of Mr. Brezhnev's trip to East Germany since only three days elapsed between his return home and his take-over of the top Communist party post from Nikita S. Khrushchev yesterday.

There were no hints in what Mr. Brezhnev said in public in East Germany that changes were imminent. In his East Berlin speech he quoted Mr.

Continued on Page 13, Column 3

JOHNSON BRIEFED

Exchanges Messages With New Leaders —Sees Dobrynin

By MAX FRANKEL
Special to The New York Times

WASHINGTON, Oct. 16 — President Johnson and the new leaders of the Soviet Government exchanged messages today pledging further efforts to promote world peace.

This first contact after the ouster of Premier Khrushchev was made at Moscow's initiative.

Anatoly F. Dobrynin, the Soviet Ambassador here, called on President Johnson to deliver assurances that his Government would continue, as he put it, to work for better relations with the West. Mr. Johnson welcomed that message and sent word to Moscow that the United States wanted only peace and international understanding.

Officials here felt that the meeting had more symbolic than practical significance. It yielded no clues to the reasons for yesterday's shake-up in Moscow. It demonstrated, however, that Mr. Khrushchev's successors were willing to reassert at once — and in Washington — the goals of coexistence and negotiation with the West that have outraged the Chinese Communists.

Many Questions Posed

President Johnson received Mr. Dobrynin with great cordiality after an Administration policy conference to review the Soviet shake-up, China's detonation of a nuclear device and the Labor party's narrow election victory in Britain.

All three developments posed many more questions for United States diplomacy than they answered. But officials decided that they required no major Washington moves at this time.

The significance of the changes in Moscow remained a subject of speculation. The Chinese nuclear test had been expected and required only a continuation of efforts to prevent panic among other Asian nations, officials said. Relations with the new British Government, it was thought, could develop without too much friction.

In their only important shift of attitude, State Department officials passed the word that they would now support a postponement of the opening of the United Nations General Assembly from Nov. 10 until some-

Continued on Page 13, Column 1

United Press International Cablephoto

NEW MAN AT 10 DOWNING STREET: Harold Wilson, leader of the victorious Labor party, arriving yesterday as the Prime Minister at his official London residence.

Wilson Is Prime Minister; Labor Has 4-Seat Margin

New Leader Sees a Complete Mandate Despite Narrow Majority—He Names Defeated Aide Foreign Secretary

By SYDNEY GRUSON
Special to The New York Times

LONDON, Oct. 16—Harold Wilson became Britain's Prime Minister today. He immediately made it known that the new Labor Government felt it had a complete mandate despite the slender majority it won in yesterday's election.

When the last vote is counted tomorrow from Argyll in Scotland, a safe Conservative constituency, Labor's majority will be only four seats in the 630-seat House of Commons. The standing of the parties tonight, with only the Argyll result still to come, was:

Labor 317
Conservative 303
Liberal 9

After a swift and smooth transition of the Prime Ministership from Sir Alec Douglas-Home, the Conservative leader, to Mr. Wilson, the Labor leader moved quickly to squelch talk that his Government would be paralyzed by its razor-thin victory.

In a brief television address to the nation, Mr. Wilson said the electorate had given Labor a mandate for "many changes" over all of government.

"We intend to fulfill that mandate and we are concerned to insure that there should be a true partnership between the Government and the people," he went on. The Government, he added, will not hesitate to do what it thinks fit.

"Nothing could be worse than failing both at home and abroad because of the Parliamentary balance of power," Mr. Wilson said.

Shortly afterward he announced his first Cabinet appointments. He named Patrick Gordon Walker as Foreign Secretary. The posts of First Secretary of State and Minister for Economic Affairs went to George Brown, deputy party leader, who becomes, in effect, Deputy Prime Minister.

Mr. Wilson named Herbert Bowden as Lord President of the Council and Leader of the House of Commons; James Callaghan as Chancellor of the Exchequer; Denis Healey as Minister of Defense, and Lord Gardiner as Lord Chancellor.

He also named Edward Short as Chief Whip, a parliamentary post. The Chief Whip, although not technically a member of the Cabinet, attends Cabinet meetings.

Mr. Gordon Walker lost his

Continued on Page 8, Column 2

CHINA TESTS ATOMIC BOMB, ASKS SUMMIT TALK ON BAN; JOHNSON MINIMIZES PERIL

HE SEES 'TRAGEDY'

Calls Costs Too Great for Chinese, Though Weapon Is Crude

Text of Johnson's statement will be found on Page 10.

By JOHN W. FINNEY
Special to The New York Times

WASHINGTON, Oct. 16 — President Johnson said today that Communist China's first nuclear test was more a "tragedy for the Chinese people" because of their poverty than a threat to world peace.

While the test is a reflection of policies that do not serve "the cause of peace," the President said, "there is no reason to fear that it will lead to immediate dangers of war."

The President gave his views at the White House in confirming that Peking had exploded what he described as a crude nuclear device.

While the President's announcement said only that the explosion took place in "western China," it was learned that the test site was in Sinkiang Province, which borders on the Soviet Union.

The explosion was above ground and thus was the first test in the atmosphere since the signing a year ago of the treaty forbidding all but underground nuclear tests. Communist China did not sign the treaty.

U.S. Assesses Device

State Department officials dismissed as a "grandstand play" a Chinese proposal for a meeting of world leaders to discuss the prohibition of nuclear weapons.

Based on their monitoring observations, United States detection experts estimated the explosion had a yield of 10 to 20 kilotons—the equivalent of 10,000 to 20,000 tons of TNT.

This was a little less than had been expected by United States experts, some of whom had feared that Communist China would try for a larger nuclear explosion or perhaps set off a thermonuclear device on its first test.

The test was believed to have had a slightly smaller yield than the first atomic explosion by the United States in July, 1945, and the first two atomic bombs dropped on Japan—all of which were around 20 kilotons.

The Chinese test was no surprise to the Administration. As the President pointed out, Secretary of State Dean Rusk an-

Continued on Page 10, Column 5

U.N. Session Delay Is Believed Certain

By THOMAS J. HAMILTON
Special to The New York Times

UNITED NATIONS, N. Y., Oct. 16—The 1964 session of the General Assembly, scheduled to begin Nov. 10, will almost certainly be postponed to give delegates time to appraise the impact of developments in Moscow, London and Peking in the last 24 hours.

Adlai E. Stevenson, the United States Representative, said today that "while no one has proposed the postponement of the General Assembly, in view of recent developments the United States is open-minded."

According to reliable sources Communist China's successful atomic test had nothing to do with the United States decision to agree to the postponement of the Assembly session. But it was

Continued on Page 13, Column 5

U.S. IS DENOUNCED

Peking Says Purpose of Test Is to Defend Peace of World

The text of Peking statement is printed on Page 10.

By SEYMOUR TOPPING
Special to The New York Times

HONG KONG, Oct. 16 -- Communist China announced tonight that it had exploded its first atom bomb. Peking pledged that it would never be the first to use nuclear weapons in the future.

A communiqué stated that a nuclear test was successfully conducted at 3 P.M. Peking time (3 A.M., Eastern daylight time) in the western region of China. No details were disclosed. [In Washington, the test site was reported to be in Sinkiang, a province bordering the Soviet Union.].

"The success of China's nuclear test is a major achievement of the Chinese people in the strengthening of their national defense and the safeguarding of their motherland as well as a major contribution by the Chinese people to the cause of the defense of world peace," the communiqué asserted.

An accompanying Government statement declared that the purpose of developing nuclear weapons was to protect the Chinese people "from the danger of the United States' launching a nuclear war."

Excesses Ruled Out

"On the question of nuclear weapons, China will commit neither the error of adventurism nor the error of capitulation," the statement said. "The Chinese people can be trusted."

The Peking statement formally proposed to the governments of the world that a universal summit conference be convened to discuss the question of a complete prohibition on and the thorough destruction of nuclear weapons.

It said that as a first step the summit conference "should reach agreement to the effect that the nuclear powers and those countries which will soon become nuclear powers undertake not to use nuclear weapons, neither to use them against nonnuclear countries and nuclear-free zones nor against each other."

The proposal was dismissed by Western observers here as propaganda. The terms do not allow for practical negotiations

Continued on Page 10, Column 1

SECRET SERVICE HAD JENKINS FILE

Knew in 1961 of His First Arrest but Told No One—Johnson Orders Inquiry

By TOM WICKER
Special to The New York Times

WASHINGTON, Oct. 16—The Secret Service knew in 1961 that Walter W. Jenkins had been arrested in 1959 but did not report it to anyone, the agency informed the White House today.

President Johnson immediately directed Secretary of the Treasury Douglas Dillon to investigate the agency's procedures to learn if they needed strengthening or changing.

Mr. Jenkins was arrested in 1959 and again last week on morals charges. After the facts became known, he resigned Wednesday night from his post as special assistant to the President, touching off a political storm that has shaken the Democratic Presidential campaign.

Dillon to Head Inquiry

Republicans have charged—and Mr. Johnson has denied—that the President covered up Mr. Jenkins's 1959 arrest. Secret Service officials reported to the White House today that they did not inform anyone of the arrest when they learned of it in 1961 because it was not considered important and because Mr. Jenkins already had a "Q" clearance, dating from 1958, for access to top-secret information.

The Secret Service did not know, because of the wording of the report, that the arrest involved a morals charge.

Mr. Dillon will conduct the investigation of these procedures separately from a study of the Secret Service and other agencies already undertaken by a special committee he heads.

That committee was named by the President to follow up on the recommendations of the

Continued on Page 17, Column 3

ROME AUTHORIZES CHANGES IN MASS

Under Revisions Advanced by Council, Priests Are to Face the Congregation

By ROBERT C. DOTY
Special to The New York Times

ROME, Oct. 16—Beginning March 7, Catholics throughout the world will see the priest's face, instead of his back, when he celebrates the mass—the central sacramental mystery of the church.

This change was one of many authorized today by an instruction distributed in St. Peter's Basilica to the more than 2,000 bishops and higher prelates at today's session of Ecumenical Council Vatican II.

It represented the first major change applicable to the entire church resulting from the labors of the Fathers of the Council in the 1962 and 1963 sessions on liturgical revision. Announcement of the distribution of the instruction, approved finally on Sept. 26 by Pope Paul VI, was greeted by applause and cheers.

Use of the Vernacular

The liturgical constitution, setting forth general standards for the introduction of vernacular tongues into the sacraments in place of Latin and giving national conferences of bishops authority to propose other modifications of rites consistent with national needs, was the first major work completed by the Council in two annual sessions.

The applications of these principles were worked out by a commission of 40 members, including Joseph Cardinal Ritter, Archbishop of St. Louis, and Archbishop Paul J. Hallinan of Atlanta, reviewed by the Vatican's Sacred Congregation of Rites and approved by Pope Paul.

Other changes include elimination of the last gospel of the mass, abbreviation of the introduction by elimination of the

Continued on Page 3, Column 5

BLUE CROSS FOUND NEAR BANKRUPTCY

Court Upholds Rate Rise to Help Bar Its Collapse

By ROBERT E. TOMASSON

A State Supreme Court justice described the Blue Cross hospital plan in New York yesterday as being on the verge of bankruptcy. He gave the description in upholding the recent rate increase.

Justice Gerald P. Culkin indicated that the increase, which went into effect July 1, was necessary to help stave off the collapse of Blue Cross's coverage of 7,500,000 subscribers in the metropolitan area.

The decision was critical of the organization's administrative policies and of Henry Root Stern Jr., the State Superintendent of Insurance, who oversees the program. The justice said:

"Both the Associated Hospital Service of New York (Blue Cross) and the superintendent seem intent on adopting the notion that no matter how costly operations become, for whatever reasons, eventually and inevitably, subscribers will shoulder the load.

"Small wonder that subscriber rates have increased 124 per cent in the past five years."

The new rate increases average 32.92 per cent. The last

Continued on Page 7, Column 1

Wagner Backs Plan For Improving Port

By JOSEPH LELYVELD

Mayor Wagner announced yesterday that he had accepted the City Planning Commission's recommendations for developing the port.

The recommendations, sent to the Mayor last month, call for a luxury passenger terminal for superliners, a shift of new pier development to Staten Island and Brooklyn, and more living space at the edge of Manhattan where old piers are now rotting away.

This last feature—"opening windows on the waterfront," the Mayor said at a Planning Commission luncheon, had particularly attracted him.

Under the plan, the bank of the Hudson River for five blocks south of 42d Street and alongside Greenwich Village

Continued on Page 58, Column 3

Berra Out as Manager; Keane Quits Cards

Yogi Gets New Post --Yanks Consider Keane and Dark

Lawrence Peter (Yogi) Berra was dismissed yesterday as manager of the New York Yankees just one day after losing the World Series.

Berra immediately accepted a two-year contract to remain as a "special field consultant," a loosely defined, newly created position dealing with scouting and player evaluation.

Ralph Houk, general manager of the Yankees and Berra's predecessor as field manager, made the announcement at a hastily arranged press conference in the same hotel ballroom used less than a year ago to announce the promotion of Houk and the installation of Berra as manager.

Upon hearing of Berra's release, Sargent Shriver—who had been sworn in earlier in the day as director of the Government's war on poverty—sought Berra for a top-level position with the bureau's youth program. An aide to the poverty drive chief said Berra turned down the job, with regret.

Berra's Yankees, who won the American League pennant by one game, lost the seventh and deciding game of the World Series to the St. Louis Cardinals on Thursday. Less than two hours before Houk's announcement yesterday, Johnny Keane, manager of the Cardinals, resigned in St. Louis.

Keane immediately developed into a leading contender for the Yankee job. Another is Alvin Dark, recently deposed manager of the San Francisco Giants.

Houk declined to discuss any of the reasons for Berra's dismissal beyond his prepared statement that "it was better for all concerned." Then he was asked about possible successors.

"A decision will be made within a week," he said. "We have two or three men under consideration."

Was Dark one of them?

Houk hesitated only a fraction of an instant.

"Yes," he said.

"What about Keane?" someone asked.

"He's not available, is he?" said Houk.

"He resigned this morning," the interviewers told Houk.

"I didn't know that when I came into this room," said Houk, "but if that's so, then

Continued on Page 22, Column 1

Yogi Berra

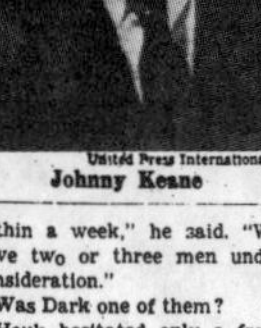

United Press International

Johnny Keane

St. Louis Manager Turns In Notice Dated Sept. 28

By JOSEPH DURSO
Special to The New York Times

ST. LOUIS, Oct. 16 -- Johnny Keane resigned as manager of the St. Louis Cardinals today, less than a day after the team had won the World Series from the New York Yankees.

The 53-year-old native of St. Louis ended 35 years in the Cardinal organization with a letter he had written on Sept. 28, at the beginning of the final week of the season, when his team was a game and a half out of first place.

Keane handed the letter to August A. Busch Jr., the owner of the Cardinals, half an hour before a news conference Busch had called in the expectation of announcing Keane's return to the job he had taken over three years ago last July.

The letter had been discussed "very quietly" by Keane and his wife Lela, had been typewritten by her 12 days ago and had been kept secret, he said, because "we didn't want to upset the players during the pennant race."

It caught the Cardinal owner, the players and the baseball world by surprise, a few hours after the team had celebrated

Continued on Page 22, Column 4

Signs About Jenkins Draw Ire of Johnson

By FENDALL W. YERXA
Special to The New York Times

DAYTON, Ohio, Oct. 16 — President Johnson, his voice edged, struck back from the speaker's platform tonight at political use of the Walter W. Jenkins case.

The President, addressing a huge crowd under floodlights in downtown Dayton, was confronted by several crudely lettered signs that alluded to the White House aide who resigned Wednesday after his arrest on a morals charge had been made public.

Mr. Johnson took note of the signs, and said he was not on hand to indulge in "muckraking or mudslinging," since "those are always weapons of desperation and of fearful, frightened men." He added:

"You can always tell them by

Continued on Page 16, Column 4

PAY PACTS SCORED BY TREASURY AIDE

Accords 'Probably Too Big' This Year, Roosa Says

By EILEEN SHANAHAN
Special to The New York Times

HOT SPRINGS, Va., Oct. 16—A high official of the Johnson Administration said today that some of this year's union wage-contract settlements had "probably been too big."

Robert V. Roosa, Under Secretary of the Treasury, told the Business Council that the wage settlements threatened the continuation of the recent improvement in the United States balance of international payments.

"It has me worried," he said.

He said he believed that the only real solution to the balance of payments deficit was an increase in American export sales, and that this required American products to be competitively priced. The balance

Continued on Page 5, Column 4

NEWS INDEX

1964

Martin Luther King was congratulated by Sweden's Crown Prince Harald and King Olav for winning the Nobel Peace Prize. The smiling Coretta King looked on.

Contralto Marian Anderson was the first black to sing at the Metropolitan Opera.

Military Police often were used to control the frequent outbursts of angry protest from black Americans.

"All the News That's Fit to Print"

The New York Times.

LATE CITY EDITION
U. S. Weather Bureau Report (Page 78) forecasts: Sunny today; clear tonight. Fair and milder tomorrow.
Temp. Range: 63—48; yesterday: 60—49.

VOL. CXIV.... No. 39,001. NEW YORK, WEDNESDAY, NOVEMBER 4, 1964. TEN CENTS

JOHNSON SWAMPS GOLDWATER AND KENNEDY BEATS KEATING; DEMOCRATS WIN LEGISLATURE

KENNEDY EDGE 6-5

Keating's Defeat Is Termed a 'Tragedy' by Rockefeller

New York Vote

PRESIDENT
Johnson, Dem. 4,509,514
Goldwater, Rep. 2,089,113
11,330 of 12,439 E.D.'s rptg.

SENATOR
Kennedy, Dem. 3,479,976
Keating, Rep. 2,857,023
11,318 of 12,439 E.D.'s rptg.

By R. W. APPLE Jr.

Robert F. Kennedy was elected to the United States Senate from New York yesterday in his first bid for elective office, overwhelming Republican Senator Kenneth B. Keating.

With more than 80 per cent of the vote counted, Mr. Kennedy held a 6-to-5 lead. Because most of the untallied vote was in heavily Democratic New York City, it appeared that the former Attorney General's plurality might reach 650,000.

Mr. Keating conceded defeat at 11:39 P.M. with the announcement at the Roosevelt Hotel that he had sent a congratulatory telegram to Mr. Kennedy.

Governor Rockefeller, standing beside the white-haired Rochester legislator, said Mr. Keating's defeat was "a tragedy for the state and nation."

Runs Behind Johnson

"Senator Keating, one of the great Senators in the history of New York, has been rolled under by a national landslide," the Governor added. "He waged a magnificent campaign."

Mr. Kennedy ran well behind President Johnson, who seemed to be headed for a record margin of 2.5 million votes or more in the state. The President won all of the state's 62 counties.

It thus appeared that about a million New York voters had split their ticket to cast votes for Mr. Johnson and Mr. Keating — but even this wasn't enough to make the Senate contest close.

A major surprise was the showing of the Liberal party, which had expected to deliver

Continued on Page 27, Column 4

The Election at a Glance

President

	Number of States*	Electoral Votes
Johnson	45	486
Goldwater	6	52

*Includes Dist. of Columbia

President—New York

Johnson	4,509,514	
Goldwater	2,089,113	Incomplete

Senator—New York

Kennedy	3,479,976	
Keating	2,857,023	Incomplete

The Senate

Newly Elected Senators		Make-up of New Senate	
Democrats	25	Democrats	65
Republicans	5	Republicans	30
In doubt	5	In doubt	5

The House

Democrats elected	261
Republicans elected	127
In doubt	47

UPSET AT ALBANY

Carlino and Mahoney Defeated—Special Session Expected

By LAYHMOND ROBINSON

A surge of Democratic votes swept the Republicans from control of the State Legislature yesterday for the first time in more than a quarter of a century.

The massive victory gave the Democrats a probable working majority of a dozen seats in the Assembly and a half dozen in the Senate.

Not since 1935, in the sweep of Franklin D. Roosevelt's New Deal, had the Democrats had control of both the houses. Not since 1938 had they held control of the Senate.

Toppled from their powerful posts in stunning upsets were Assembly Speaker Joseph F. Carlino of Long Beach, L. I., and Senate Majority Leader Walter J. Mahoney of Buffalo.

Beaten by Outsiders

Both suffered defeat at the hands of virtually unknown Democrats.

Mr. Carlino, the top Republican figure in the lower house for six years and an Assemblyman representing Nassau's Second Assembly District for 20 years, was beaten by Jerome R. McDougal Jr., a car salesman making his first race for public office.

Senator Mahoney, often called the most powerful man in the Legislature, was unseated by John H. Doerr of Buffalo in Erie County's 55th Senate District.

Another high-ranking Republican who lost was Senator MacNeil Mitchell of Manhattan, the most influential New York City member of the two houses.

In some districts in the suburbs and in upstate counties, Democrats captured Assembly and Senate seats for the first time in this century.

Districting Fight Due

At the last session, the G.O.P. had a 10-vote edge over the Democrats in the Assembly, holding 85 seats to 65 for the Democrats. In the Senate they had a 33-25 edge.

Although the Democrats ended this G.O.P. domination, the battle for control could be resumed again in December.

The Governor is expected to call a special session of the Legislature then to adopt a new plan for reapportioning seats in the two houses.

This reapportionment session will be controlled by the present members, with the Republicans in control.

Members elected yesterday do not take their seats until the

Continued on Page 33, Column 3

LYNDON BAINES JOHNSON — HUBERT HORATIO HUMPHREY

The New York Times

TURNOUT IS HEAVY

President Expected to Get 60% of Vote, With 44 States

By TOM WICKER

Lyndon Baines Johnson of Texas compiled one of the greatest landslide victories in American history yesterday to win a four-year term of his own as the 36th President of the United States.

Senator Hubert H. Humphrey of Minnesota, Mr. Johnson's running mate on the Democratic ticket, was carried into office as Vice President.

Mr. Johnson's triumph, giving him the "loud and clear" national mandate he had said he wanted, brought 44 states and the district of Columbia, with 486 electoral votes, into the Democratic column.

Senator Barry Goldwater, the Republican candidate, who sought to offer the people "a choice, not an echo" with a strongly conservative campaign, won only five states in the Deep South and gained a narrow victory in his home state of Arizona. Carrying it gave him a total of 52 electoral votes.

Senator Plans Statement

A heavy voter turnout favored the more numerous Democrats.

In Austin, Tex., Mr. Johnson appeared in the Municipal Auditorium to say that his victory was "a tribute to men and women of all parties."

"It is a mandate for unity, for a Government that serves no special interest," he said.

The election meant, he said, that "our nation should forget our petty differences and stand united before all the world."

Mr. Goldwater did not concede. A spokesman announced that the Senator would make no statement until 10 A.M. today in Phoenix.

Johnson Carries Texas

But the totals were not the only marks of the massive Democratic victory. Traditionally Republican states were bowled over like tenpins—Vermont, Indiana, Kansas, Nebraska, Wyoming, among others.

In New York, both houses of the Legislature were headed for Democratic control for the first time in years. Heralded Republicans like Charles H. Percy, the gubernatorial candidate in Illinois, went down to defeat.

Former Attorney General Robert F. Kennedy, riding Mr. Johnson's long coattails, overwhelmed Senator Kenneth B. Keating in New York.

But ticket splitting was widespread. And in the South, Georgia went Republican; never

Continued on Page 22, Column 1

JOHNSON CRUSHES RIVAL IN JERSEY

Lead Near 900,000, Topping Eisenhower's Record—Williams Re-elected

New Jersey Vote

PRESIDENT
Johnson, Dem. 1,645,844
Goldwater, Rep. 853,708
4,001 of 4,603 E.D.'s rptg.

SENATOR
Williams, Dem. 1,474,523
Shanley, Rep. 891,425
4,001 of 4,603 E.D.'s rptg.

By GEORGE CABLE WRIGHT

President Johnson won New Jersey's 17 electoral votes yesterday in the biggest political victory ever scored in the state.

With 91 per cent of the vote tallied, the President held a record lead of nearly 900,000 votes over his Republican opponent, Senator Barry Goldwater.

Until yesterday, the record plurality for a Presidential candidate in New Jersey was the 756,605-vote margin rolled up by President Eisenhower, a Republican, in 1956.

In sweeping at least 19, and possibly all of the state's 21 counties, Mr. Johnson carried to victory with him incumbent Democratic Senator Harrison A. Williams Jr. Democrats also captured a majority of the state's 15 seats in the House of Representatives for the first time since 1912.

In the present Congress, Republicans hold eight of the seats. On the basis of incomplete returns from yesterday's balloting, Democrats won at least 10 seats.

The Democratic candidate James J. Howard also held a narrow lead over his Republican opponent, Marcus Daly, in an

Continued on Page 32, Column 4

Connecticut Votes 2-1 for President; All Democrats Win

Connecticut Vote

PRESIDENT (Complete)
Johnson, D. 825,416
Goldwater, R. 392,556

SENATOR
Dodd, D. 779,252
Lodge, R. 425,376

By RICHARD H. PARKE

President Johnson led a sweeping Democratic victory in Connecticut yesterday.

His better than 2-to-1 margin over Senator Barry Goldwater eclipsed the previous record plurality in a Presidential race in the state. Mr. Johnson's plurality was 432,860. The earlier record had been set by President Dwight D. Eisenhower in 1956 when he defeated Adlai E. Stevenson by 306,758 votes.

Senator Thomas J. Dodd, the Democratic incumbent, also triumphed easily over his Republican opponent, former Gov. John Davis Lodge. But the 57-year-old Senator ran about 45,000 votes behind the President.

One result of President Johnson's landslide was the defeat of the state's only Republican Congressman, Representative Abner W. Sibal of the Fourth (Fairfield County) District. Mr. Sibal lost the normally Republican district to former Representative Donald J. Irwin, a

Continued on Page 32, Column 1

SOUTH REVERSES VOTING PATTERNS

Goldwater Makes Inroads, but More Electoral Votes Go to the President

By JOHN HERBERS

Special to The New York Times

ATLANTA, Nov. 3—President Johnson carried a majority of Southern states tonight by turning the normal voting patterns inside out.

The rural Deep South, solidly Democratic in the past, voted for Senator Barry Goldwater of Arizona on the Republican ticket. The states on the border of the region, which had gone Republican in recent Presidential elections, returned to the Democrats.

But so strong was the Goldwater tide in the Deep South that seven Republican Congressional candidates rode to victory on the Senator's coattails from districts that had been Democratic since Reconstruction.

The Republicans made their biggest gains in Alabama, where five candidates for Congress defeated Democratic opponents.

President Johnson carried Virginia, North Carolina, Florida, Tennessee, Arkansas and Texas with a total of 81 electorial votes. Senator Goldwater carried Louisiana, Mississippi, Alabama, Georgia and South Carolina with a total of 47 electorial votes.

South Carolina and Mississippi had not voted for Repub-

Continued on Page 24, Column 2

Democrats Are Assured Of Majorities in Congress

House Gain for Democrats

By JOHN D. MORRIS

Democrats strengthened their control of the House of Representatives in yesterday's elections, scoring substantial gains in all regions except the South.

With returns from Congressional races still incomplete early this morning, the trend indicated a Democratic pickup of at least 20 seats and possibly 30 or more.

The Republicans nevertheless scored spectacular breakthroughs in the South, winning five of Alabama's eight seats, one of Mississippi's five and at least one of Georgia's 10.

Those gains were more than offset, however, by the loss of both of their Texas seats and by heavy Democratic gains in other parts of the country.

The House division in the expiring 88th Congress is 257 Democrats and 178 Republicans. This credits five vacancies to the parties last holding the seats. Three were occupied by Democrats and two by Republicans.

With 218 needed for a major-

Continued on Page 21, Column 1

3 G.O.P. Senators Lose

By E. W. KENWORTHY

The Democrats appeared virtually certain today of maintaining a nearly 2-to-1 majority in the United States Senate.

At 3 A.M. the Democrats had won 25 of the 35 contests in yesterday's elections. These, added to their 40 holdovers, assured them of 65 seats when the Eighty-ninth Congress convenes in January.

The Republicans, at the same hour, had won only five seats—in Vermont, Nebraska, Delaware, Arizona and Hawaii—all of which were won by incumbent Senators. These, added to 25 holdovers, assured the Republicans of at least 30 seats.

The party line-up when Congress adjourned last month was 66 Democrats and 34 Republicans.

By 3 A.M the Democrats had captured three seats from the Republicans.

In New York, Robert F. Kennedy, former Attorney General, a brother of President Kennedy,

Continued on Page 20, Column 1

STATE DEMOCRATS GAIN SIX IN HOUSE

Lindsay and Other Liberal Republicans Keep Seats

By WARREN WEAVER Jr.

Democrats swept through the New York Congressional delegation in yesterday's election, unseating six Republican Representatives and threatening the House seat of a seventh.

In the wake of the Johnson victory, the Democrats increased their strength in the delegation from 20 to 26 while the number of Republicans dropped from 21 to 14, with one district in doubt.

Although they failed to dislodge any of the three New York City Republican Congressmen, Democratic candidates scored victories elsewhere across the state. They took two seats in Nassau County, one in Westchester, one in the Hudson Valley and two in Western New York.

Among the chief Republican survivors was Representative John V. Lindsay of Manhattan, who won by a 65,000-vote margin in his East Side district.

Other Republicans to retain their seats were Representative Seymour Halpern of Queens, who like Mr. Lindsay had opposed Senator Barry Goldwater, and, Representative Ogden R.

Continued on Page 24, Column 5

G.O.P. Grip Broken In Suburban Voting

By JOHN SIBLEY

Traditional Republican bastions in the suburbs crumbled before the Johnson onslaught yesterday, and the President carried with him many local Democratic candidates in nearby New York and New Jersey communities.

Widespread ticket-splitting showed, however, that Republican suburbanites were not forsaking their party so much as they were renouncing its Presidential nominee, Senator Barry Goldwater.

Westchester County, for the first time since 1912, gave a plurality to a Democratic Presidential candidate. Rockland County went Democratic for the first time since Franklin D. Roosevelt carried the county in 1936 and for only the fourth time in 100 years.

Long Island's suburbs, too, went to the President. Mr. Johnson became the first Democratic Presidential candidate in modern

Continued on Page 33, Column 2

ROMNEY IS VICTOR; PERCY'S BID FAILS

Democrats Likely to Achieve Gain in Governorships

By JOSEPH A. LOFTUS

Democrats gave a good account of themselves in 25 contests for Governor yesterday, but it was a Republican who produced the spectacular.

Gov. George Romney, running aloof from Senator Barry Goldwater, set off a Michigan ticket-splitting spree to win re-election and thereby planted himself firmly in the thin front ranks of 1968 Presidential possibilities.

While Senator Goldwater gathered barely a third of Michigan's votes, the Governor defeated Neil Staebler with more than 55 per cent of the tally.

Strong Goldwater supporters "cut" Governor Romney, but the latter improved on his own 1962 vote totals in the labor-Democratic areas of Detroit and Flint-Saginaw.

The Republicans failed to capture a major prize, the Illinois governorship. The defeated nominee, Charles H. Percy, had figured in Presidential talk for the future.

Gov. Otto J. Kerner won a second term in Illinois despite the failure of Mayor Richard Daley's organization to deliver Chicago majorities as big as those Mr. Kerner won there four years ago.

Nationally the Democrats seemed likely to score a net

Continued on Page 24, Column 4

Summary of International News: Wilson Acts to Nationalize Steel

Following is a summary of foreign news. A full report begins on the first page of the second part.

Labor Offers Program

Britain's new Labor Government offered a program of controversial legislation to Parliament. Headed by a demand for renationalization of the steel industry, the proposals indicate one of the bitterest sessions in parliamentary history.

French Explain Aim

Foreign Minister Maurice Couve de Murville told the French Parliament that the United States and Europe should develop separate, but not necessarily hostile, policies. In Washington, officials predicted that a major crisis for Atlantic unity would arise at a NATO meeting in December.

Bolivian Troops Revolt

A military revolt broke out in Bolivia and appeared to be spreading across the country. A truce designed to open the way for efforts "to resolve the present crisis" facing the Government of President Victor Paz Estenssoro was announced. In neighboring Chile, Eduardo Frei Montalva was inaugurated as the country's 28th President. In Cuba workers will vote Dec. 2 for worker councils.

Soviet Voices Concern

The Soviet Union expressed concern to the United States over the situation along the Cambodian-South Vietnamese border. In Pnompenh, Prince Norodom Sihanouk said his nation was ready to retaliate against any further border incursions by South Vietnamese forces. In Saigon, United States officials raised the casualty toll in Sunday's bombardment of the Bienhoa air base to 76 Americans, of whom four were dead.

WHITE BACKLASH DOESN'T DEVELOP

Vote in Suburbs in North Is Strong for President

By ANTHONY LEWIS

Rich and poor, Protestant and Roman Catholic and Jew, farmer and city-dweller and suburbanite—all showed marked shifts toward President Johnson in yesterday's extraordinary election.

Only in the Deep South did Senator Barry Goldwater score any significant gains for the Republican ticket over four years ago. Riding the crest of the racial issue there, he swung Mississippi, Alabama, Georgia, South Carolina and Louisiana to his party.

The white backlash, on which Mr. Goldwater had counted so strongly, failed to materialize in most parts of the North. Only among voters of Polish and other East European origins were there signs of this resentment toward Negroes, and even this phenomenon was scattered

Continued on Page 28, Column 1

NEWS INDEX

PRESIDENT SEES A UNITY MANDATE

In Victory Talk, He Pays Tribute to Predecessor

The text of Johnson's talk will be found on Page 22.

By CHARLES MOHR

Special to The New York Times

AUSTIN, Tex., Wednesday, Nov. 4—President Johnson said early this morning that his election was a "mandate for unity" and for a "government that provides equal opportunity for all and special privilege for none."

Mr. Johnson, obviously deeply moved by his landslide victory, told a crowd at the Municipal Auditorium here that it was a tribute to "the program begun by our beloved President John F. Kennedy."

Of the returns, Mr. Johnson said, "I doubt there have ever been so many people seeing so many things alike" on an Election Day.

Earlier, Mr. Johnson had said of Senator Barry Goldwater's refusal to concede that it was "purely a matter for the individual involved—whatever reasons he may have, I don't know."

He also said that the election was going "about as we expected."

Mr. Johnson appeared on the Municipal Auditorium stage with his wife and two daughters to a long ovation.

He said that "no words are

Continued on Page 22, Column 6

Salinger Is Losing; Johnson Wins State

By LAWRENCE E. DAVIES

Special to The New York Times

SAN FRANCISCO, Wednesday, Nov. 4—President Johnson captured California's 40 electoral votes in his triumph over Senator Barry Goldwater in yesterday's election.

On the basis of the incomplete count of ballots, however, the President's former press secretary, Senator Pierre Salinger, apparently lost his Senatorial battle to George Murphy, the Republican nominee.

Mr. Salinger late last night refused to concede defeat but said he "would be less than candid if I didn't say the vote doesn't look good." Some of his campaign strategists agreed that the results "looked bad" but declared they would await developments for a few hours before having anything definite to say.

Mr. Salinger, who has been

Continued on Page 34, Column 4

Fred Gwynne (shown here with Paul Lynde) played television's most lovable monster in *The Munsters.* Yvonne DeCarlo was his wife Lily and the mother of the family.

Hullabalo celebrated the arrival of the discotheque. Lada Edmund, Jr. (far left), was the "Girl in the Cage" and a favorite of many viewers.

Johnathan Winters captured television audiences in a series of comedy specials in 1964.

Mia Farrow, then a young actress of unknown ability, played in *Peyton Place*, the nighttime soap-opera that enthralled viewers all over the world.

1965

Stripes and dots, paisleys and plaids, and unexpected color combos all paired off to fit the style of the times.

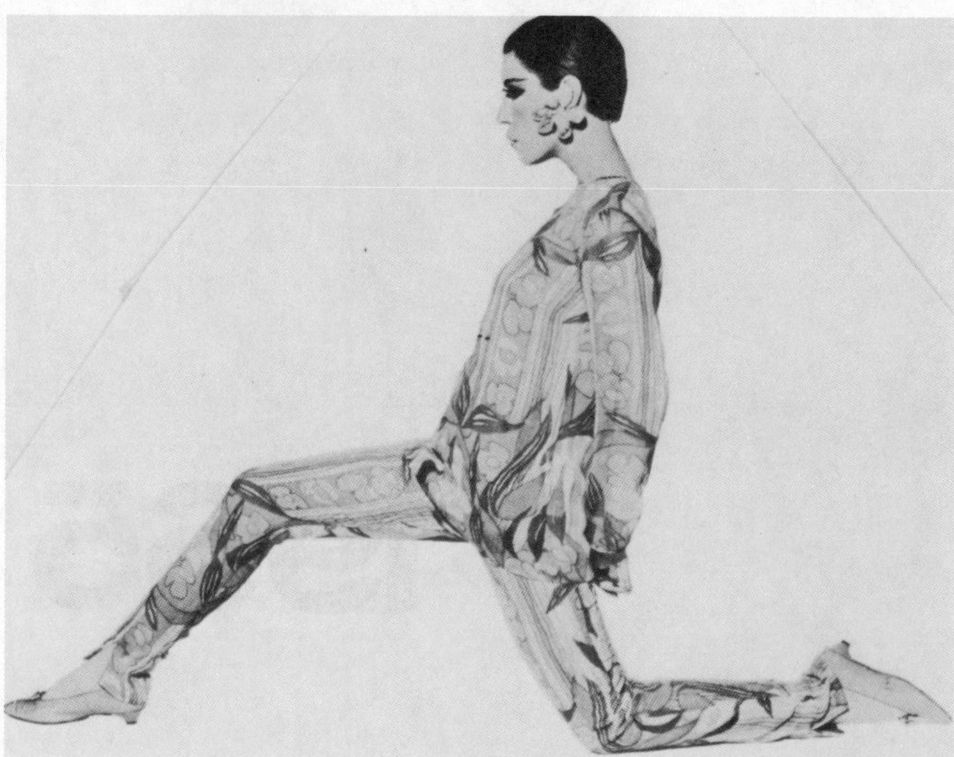

This "Gauguin" print pants suit is an example of at-home elegance created by increased leisure time.

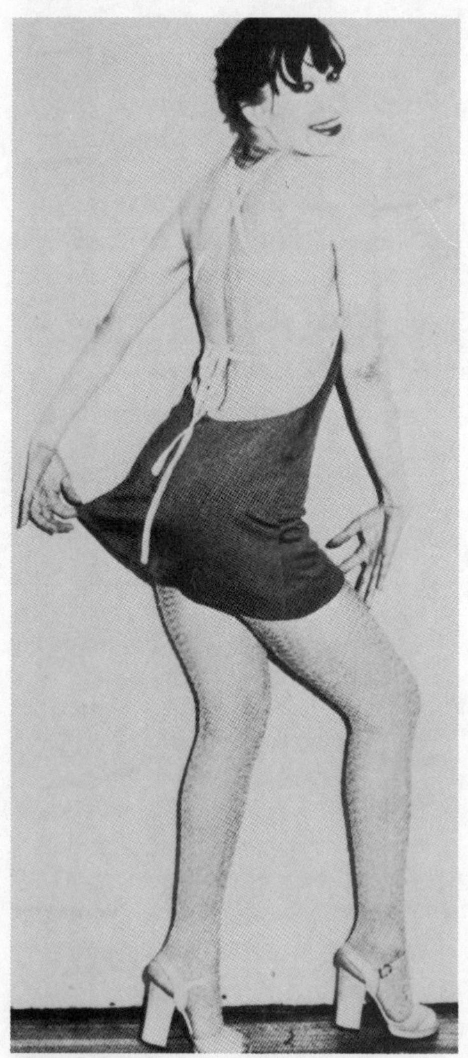

The *mod* scene's quest for freedom of expression and movement found an outlet in this backless outfit.

The popularity of op-art was an expression of the year's craze for *mod* style as seen in fashion. Bridget Riley's "Current" was an example of the art community's experimentation.

"All the News That's Fit to Print"

The New York Times.

LATE CITY EDITION
U. S. Weather Bureau Report (Page 66) forecasts: Fair, then partly cloudy today and tonight; fair tomorrow.
Temp. range: 46—28; yesterday: 39—26.

VOL. CXIV..No. 39,063. | © 1965 by The New York Times Company. Times Square, New York, N. Y. 10036 | NEW YORK, TUESDAY, JANUARY 5, 1965. | TEN CENTS

PRESIDENT BIDS SOVIET LEADERS VISIT U.S., ACCEPT TV EXCHANGE; OUTLINES 'GREAT SOCIETY' PLAN

WILL GO ABROAD

Stresses Education in Message at Capitol on State of Union

The text of State of Union Message is on Page 16.

By TOM WICKER
Special to The New York Times

WASHINGTON, Jan. 4 — President Johnson expressed the hope tonight that the new leaders of the Soviet Union could visit the United States and that they and American leaders could exchange television appearances in their respective countries.

In his second State of the Union Message, Mr. Johnson also disclosed plans to visit Europe and Latin America this year. Then he moved on to outline a sweeping program for improved education and for moving the nation "toward the Great Society."

The bid for a visit by the Soviet leaders was the major surprise of a 50-minute address. Government sources said diplomatic approaches to the Soviet Government had been going forward for some time and that Soviet officials had been informed today of what Mr. Johnson would say.

Domestic Program

Mr. Johnson set forth a domestic program that swept almost literally from the Potomac to the Pedernales in his native Texas.

He addressed a joint session of the House and Senate from the rostrum of the House of Representatives nine hours after Congress convened at noon.

Mr. Johnson spoke in a packed chamber and before jammed galleries. Mrs. Johnson and her two daughters, Lynda Bird and Luci Baines, sat in a box to his left.

Members of the Cabinet, the Supreme Court Justices, the diplomatic corps and most of the members of the 89th Congress were in a semicircle before him. Chief Justice Earl Warren was absent from the row of black-robed Justices.

A Somber Speech

The President read his message from an electrically operated prompter—the first time such a device has been used for a State of the Union Message. He read slowly, pausing long to make many of his points, and a planned 30-minute speech gradually stretched out to about 50 minutes.

Mr. Johnson occasionally glanced at a reading script. In a generally somber speech, he evoked one laugh by asserting that a President's hardest job was not "meeting daily troubles, large and small—or even working with the Congress."

He was interrupted for applause 57 times—a slight drop from the more than 80 interruptions recorded for his first State of the Union address last year.

Government sources said the

Continued on Page 17, Column 1

Associated Press Wirephoto

JOHNSON SPEAKS: The President addressing Congress at the House rostrum. Behind him are Speaker John W. McCormack, left, and Carl Hayden, President pro tem of Senate.

WELFARE HELP IN CITY CURBED BY A WALKOUT

9 CENTERS CLOSED

8,000 Strikers Facing Penalties—Accord Sought by Judge

By EMANUEL PERLMUTTER

About 8,000 Welfare Department workers went on strike yesterday, curtailing the city's public-assistance services to 500,000 persons.

Approximately 4,500 nonstriking employes crossed picket lines to maintain most services. But the strike by two unions for higher pay and better working conditions forced the closing of nine of the department's 25 welfare centers. Only emergency service was given at the 16 other centers.

Although the employes walked out in defiance of both a court antistrike order and of the Condon-Wadlin Act, which prohibits strikes by public employes, punitive action against them was being withheld for the present.

Court Conferences Held

Supreme Court Justice Irving H. Saypol, who had continued a restraining order last Thursday pending argument on the city's request for a temporary strike injunction, conferred with both sides through most of yesterday in an effort to resolve the dispute.

At 1 A.M. today, after nearly 14 hours of mediation efforts, Justice Saypol announced that he was reserving decision until this afternoon on the application for a temporary injunction.

In making the announcement Justice Saypol declared: "I think these employes ought to go back to work."

During the day the employes—members of the Social Service Employes Union and of Local 371 of the American Federation of State, County and Municipal Employes—maintained noisy but peaceful picket lines at welfare centers in the five boroughs. However, 12 telephone lines were cut at the Melrose Welfare Center, 266 East 161st Street, the Bronx.

"This is an act of sabotage," Welfare Commissioner James R. Dumpson said angrily when he heard of the incident. He notified the police. The wires were repaired.

Picketing Starts at 7 A.M.

Although the welfare offices did not open until 9 A.M., the strikers began picketing them at 7 o'clock.

As they walked in freezing weather, wearing heavy sweaters, coats and mufflers, they made bitter comments about Mayor Wagner and Commissioner Dumpson. Chill winds buffeted picket signs that read: "Our Families Have To Eat" and "Support Your Staff."

At the Harlem Welfare Center, Park Avenue and 131st Street, a score of welfare applicants, including a woman with a baby in her arms, waited for the doors to open. They seemed impervious to the pickets and the cold.

Despite the strike, Commissioner Dumpson indicated that no substantial hardships had been suffered by relief recipi-

Continued on Page 21, Column 2

Saigon's Generals Insisting on Control

By JACK LANGGUTH
Special to The New York Times

SAIGON, South Vietnam, Jan. 4—The young generals of South Vietnam have proposed the setting up of a military commission that would oversee the civilian government, reliable sources said today.

The commission, a so-called organization of control, would be headed by Air Vice Marshal Nguyen Cao Ky, the sources added.

[East of Saigon the Vietcong have renewed their fight for Binh Gia, according to The Associated Press. Page 3.]

The proposal of the generals was believed to be unsatisfactory to the American officials who have insisted on a clearer line of responsibility for the Vietnamese Government.

By persisting with policies that the United States has

Continued on Page 5, Column 2

2 U.S. COMPANIES WILL AID RUMANIA

Americans to Build 2 Plants—Breakthrough on Ties With East Europe Seen

By TAD SZULC
Special to The New York Times

WASHINGTON, Jan. 4—The Rumanian Government initialed preliminary agreements with two American corporations last month for the construction of a synthetic rubber plant and a catalytic petroleum cracking unit in Rumania. The cost of the two plants may exceed $50 million.

The companies involved are the Firestone Tire and Rubber Company of Akron, Ohio, and the Universal Oil Products Corporation, Des Plaines, Ill.

These preliminary agreements marked a major breakthrough in the development of relations between the United States and Eastern Europe. They represented the first direct entry by American private industry into a Communist nation since World War II and, also, a deliberate policy by the Administration to make this possible.

While American companies have been seeking to negotiate the sale of equipment for a synthetic fiber plant in East Germany, no agreements have been reached. Furthermore, no official support from Washing-

Continued on Page 10, Column 4

MALAYSIA READY FOR 'HOT PURSUIT' OF INDONESIAN FOE

Rahman Tells U.N. Situation Grows Worse—Landing by Guerrillas Balked

By United Press International.

KUALA LUMPUR, Malaysia, Jan. 4—Prince Abdul Rahman, the Prime Minister, said today Malaysia was ready for "hot pursuit" retaliation against attacks by Indonesia.

The Prime Minister held an emergency Cabinet meeting hours after an Indonesian guerrilla landing party, the third in three weeks, was captured in Malaysian waters and disarmed.

He said that Malaysia's existence was threatened by continuing Indonesian attacks and that the danger was greater since Indonesia decided to quit the United Nations.

[Indonesia's representative at the United Nations said he would return to Jakarta for consultations, and reliable sources said Indonesia would not submit formal notice of her withdrawal from the world organization until the consultations were completed. Page 3.]

Plea for Reinforcements

Prince Abdul Rahman asked Britain and Malaysia's other allies to send reinforcements if necessary and informed the United Nations of the deteriorating situation with a view to appealing for help if needed.

Britain moved to bolster the defenses of the new federation, formed in 1963 of the British territories of Malaya, Singapore, Sarawak and Sabah, which was formerly North Borneo.

The first 50 of 1,000 British paratroops arrived today. [Authorities in London ordered the 44,000-ton aircraft carrier Eagle to sail urgently from the East African port of Mombasa for Singapore. The Naval Minister, Christopher Mayhew, said before leaving London for talks in Washington that Britain was also flying crews to Malaysia to man reactivated ships.]

Abdul Rahman said Indonesian actions defied world opinion, the United Nations and the rule of international law.

Guerrillas Taken on Island

The latest moves in President Sukarno's campaign to crush Malaysia, he said, threatened the existence of the federation. President Sukarno has opposed the federation, a member of the Commonwealth, from the start, calling it a new form of British colonialism designed to encircle Indonesia.

The Prince said the Cabinet decided to prepare for retaliation if attacked, "under the rule of hot pursuit, when and if forced to do so for our own existence."

The Indonesian guerrillas were

Continued on Page 2, Column 3

CONGRESS BEGINS

Ford Replaces Halleck as G.O.P. Leader—Rules Changed

By JOHN D. MORRIS
Special to The New York Times

WASHINGTON, Jan. 4—Republicans chose a new leader and Administration Democrats won the adoption of major rules changes today as both parties executed strategic maneuvers in the House of Representatives.

Representative Gerald R. Ford Jr. of Michigan, a 51-year-old former football star, deposed Representative Charles A. Halleck of Indiana as minority leader in a move to give the party a fresher and younger but no less conservative look in the new 89th Congress, which convened today.

Mr. Halleck, who is 64, had held the job since 1959. He was the victim of a power play that gave comparatively junior insurgents control of the party's machinery in the House.

Aid for Johnson Program

New rules swiftly steered through the House by dominant Administration forces are designed to ease the way for President Johnson's legislative program.

One effect was to curtail the authority of the House Rules Committee to obstruct legislation favored by Administration leaders. Another was a significant increase in the powers of the House Speaker for the first time this century.

The House also seated the Mississippi delegation of five members today in the face of a challenge by the Mississippi Freedom Democratic party, which contended that the state's regular Democrats had excluded Negroes from voting. The test vote on the issue was 276 to 148.

Representative Ford defeated Representative Halleck in the struggle for leadership of the 140-member Republican minority on a secret ballot of 73 to 67. The vote was taken at a closed caucus just before the House met for the opening-day session.

Representative Melvin R. Laird of Wisconsin was elected to succeed Mr. Ford as chairman of the House Republican Conference, or caucus. He defeated Representative Peter H. B. Frelinghuysen of New Jersey, 75 to 62.

Representative John W.

Continued on Page 17, Column 7

PARTY PICKS LONG AS SENATE WHIP

Louisianian Pledges He Will Not Obstruct Johnson—Mansfield Re-elected

By E. W. KENWORTHY
Special to The New York Times

WASHINGTON, Jan. 4 — Russell B. Long of Louisiana was chosen by his party colleagues today to succeed Vice President-elect Hubert H. Humphrey as assistant Democratic leader of the Senate.

Mr. Long, who is serving his third term although he is only 46 years old, beat out John O. Pastore of Rhode Island and A. S. Mike Monroney of Oklahoma.

Senator Long won on the second ballot under a procedure that eliminated the low man if no candidate got a majority of the 68 Democrats in the Senate.

On the first ballot, Mr. Long received 34 votes, one short of the needed 35; Mr. Pastore got 20 and Mr. Monroney 14. The Oklahoman was thus eliminated.

On the second ballot, Mr. Long received 41, Mr. Pastore

Continued on Page 18, Column 1

Steingut Offers Program Of 'Minimum' Legislation

By R. W. APPLE Jr.
Special to The New York Times

ALBANY, Jan. 4 — Assemblyman Stanley Steingut issued his own "State of the State" message this afternoon, 48 hours before Governor Rockefeller was to deliver the official message. The Brooklyn legislator, who appears all but certain of election as Speaker of the Assembly when the Legislature convenes here on Wednesday, proposed what he called a "minimum program" to correct the failures of New York State.

Most of Mr. Steingut's proposals were contained in a memorandum he drew up late in November, when he was campaigning for the Speaker's post. But his statement today included many more details.

Among the new items were proposals for a state division of narcotics control, a state commission on urban and suburban affairs, a recodification of civil rights legislation, and a call for a constitutional convention.

The timing of the statement indicated that it was designed in part to divert public attention from Mr. Rockefeller.

Mr. Steingut backed away from at least one recommendation he had made in November, a recommendation for "a new public housing bond issue."

He suggested, instead, that the state subsidize the interest payments of nonprofit and limited-profit builders of housing for families with incomes below $6,000 a year.

"This proposal," he said, "would require no new state bond issue in an economy-minded year."

Mr. Steingut said "the new

Continued on Page 14, Column 1

REVENUE SERVICE WILL REMAIN HERE

Robert Kennedy Is Victor Over Brother as Boston Loses Bid for Offices

By EILEEN SHANAHAN
Special to The New York Times

WASHINGTON, Jan. 4—Which Senator Kennedy can do more for his home state?

Today's award may go to the elder brother, the newer Senator and the one with the recently adopted state, Robert F. Kennedy of New York.

The Internal Revenue Service, in any event, announced today that it has decided to go ahead with its controversial plan to consolidate its New England and New York State regional offices, but to locate the new regional headquarters in New York.

The decision is a reversal of one made two years ago—and subsequently withdrawn—to locate the headquarters in Boston.

Outcry From New York

Members of Congress from New York, whose outcry killed the 1963 plan, charged that the plan for the headquarters to be in Boston had been dictated by a desire to help Senator Edward M. Kennedy, then newly elected, make good on his campaign promise that he could "do more for Massachusetts."

The Internal Revenue Service and the Treasury Department denied the charge, but also held up the consolidation plan.

The Treasury Department said today that the decision to put the headquarters in New York had been based, in part, on the need to give closer supervision to the Manhattan and Brooklyn Internal Revenue offices, where widespread corruption has recently been uncovered.

The Treasury also said that

Continued on Page 18, Column 5

T. S. Eliot, the Poet, Is Dead in London at 76

Writer, Born in U.S., Gained Fame With 'The Waste Land'

Special to The New York Times

LONDON, Jan. 4—T. S. Eliot, the quiet, gray figure who gave new meaning to English-language poetry, died today at his home in London. He was 76 years old.

Eliot was an American, born in St. Louis. He moved to England at the beginning of World War I and became wholly identified with Britain, even becoming naturalized in 1927.

Nevertheless, when President Johnson recently awarded the Medal of Freedom to leaders in American literature and public life, Eliot was among those honored. He did not make the trip to the United States, however, to receive the award.

The influence of Eliot began with the publication in 1917 of his poem "The Love Song of J. Alfred Prufrock." Perhaps his most significant contribution came five years later in the lengthy poem "The Waste Land."

From time to time Eliot would give readings of his poetry in public. He read softly, but when he ended "The Waste Land" in a quick rush of words audiences were always moved.

Eliot was a convert to Anglo-Catholicism and his religious belief showed up strongly in his later works.

Eliot won the Nobel Prize for Literature in 1948 and was awarded the Order of Merit by Britain in the same year.

R. Thorne McKenna

T. S. Eliot reading in the study of his home in London

His Verse Reflected Spiritual Despair After First War

By THOMAS LASK

An Appraisal

It is very likely that when the literary history of our time comes to be written, it will be characterized as the Age of Eliot, just as we speak now of the Age of Pope or Tennyson.

For no man in the period between the two World Wars so dominated his time as critic and creator as did T. S. Eliot. And no man did more to help shape the standards by which he was judged. For this expatriate American caught and expressed in his verse the sense of a doomed world, of fragmentation, of a wasteland of the spirit that moved the generation after the war.

It was a generation that felt tricked by the politicians, felt that the enormous bloodletting of World War I had been a fraud and saw in the disintegrating Europe of their time the symbol of their own lives. Their mood of spiritual despair was exquisitely rendered in Eliot's poetry.

It is said that he resented being spoken of as the poet of a wasteland, and yet the dry tone, the arid physical and spiritual landscape of his early poems are also the essence of Eliot as he established his reputation as a poet of post-World War I disillusion and despair.

This is the way the world ends
This is the way the world ends
This is the way the world ends
Not with a bang but a whimper.

These four lines by Thomas Stearns Eliot, written as the conclusion to "The Hollow Men" in 1925, are probably the most quoted lines of any 20th-century poet writing in English. They are also the essence of Eliot as ... They were written by an expatriate from St. Louis, a graduate of Harvard College, who had chosen to live in London and who was working as a bank clerk.

The "bang and the whimper," together with "The Waste Land"

Continued on Page 30, Column 1

Continued on Page 30, Column 3

Murph the Surf Held On a Third Charge

By PHILIP H. DOUGHERTY

Jack Roland (Murph the Surf) Murphy, one of three men charged with the $410,000 jewelry burglary at the American Museum of Natural History, stepped out of a quiet courtroom here yesterday and into more trouble.

He was arrested on charges of taking part in a $250 armed robbery and assault at the Algonquin Hotel on July 10. Detectives pushed the 27-year-old defendant across the courthouse corridor into a narrow hall, where he was searched, handcuffed and then led away.

Allen Dale Kuhn, 26, and Roger Frederick Clark, 29, the two other men under indictment for the museum robbery, in

Continued on Page 15, Column 3

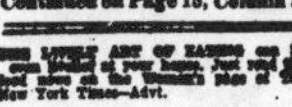

$400,000 in Heroin Found on Ship Here

By MARTIN ARNOLD

About four pounds of uncut heroin enough to supply at least 100,000 shots to addicts—was discovered yesterday by a young crew member among a cluster of pipes in the boiler room of the liner France.

Diluted and sold to addicts the narcotic would bring about $400,000, customs agents estimated. Wholesale, the heroin would sell for about $40,000.

There were no arrests.

The customs agents said that the heroin had apparently been placed aboard the liner in Le Havre, France, before she left there on her last trans-Atlantic run before sailing on a West Indies cruise.

They speculated that the heroin had been left aboard until after the cruise in the belief that the agents would make a

Continued on Page 26, Column 1

N.A.A.C.P. to Hoid Citizenship Clinics

By FRED POWLEDGE

The National Association for the Advancement of Colored People announced yesterday a nationwide program of "citizenship clinics" designed to strengthen the Negro community from within.

Roy Wilkins, N.A.A.C.P. executive director, said the clinics would not confine their duties to combating discrimination. The "broad goal," he said, "will be the assumption of full citizenship responsibilities along with utilization of full citizenship rights."

The announcement of the clinics, which will be a significant departure from the programs developed by the civil rights movement in recent years, was made at the N.A.A.C.P.'s annual membership meeting at the national

Continued on Page 20, Column 3

NEWS INDEX

"All the News That's Fit to Print"

The New York Times.

LATE CITY EDITION
U. S. Weather Bureau Report (Page 50) forecast: Rain, then partly cloudy, mild today, tonight. Showers likely tomorrow.
Temp. range: 60—50; yesterday: 52—37.

VOL. CXIV..No. 39,097.

NEW YORK, MONDAY, FEBRUARY 8, 1965. TEN CENTS

U.S. JETS ATTACK NORTH VIETNAM IN REPRISAL FOR VIETCONG RAIDS; JOHNSON ORDERS FAMILIES HOME

ALBANY LEADERS PROMISE TO SLASH 'LULUS' AND JOBS

$1 Million Cut in Costs of Legislature Is Pledged by Zaretzki and Travia

AUDITS ARE SUGGESTED

Bronston to Seek Reforms —Fairness Assured on Top Committee Jobs

By PETER KIHSS

An overhaul of the Legislature's "lulu" system and trimming of the patronage plum tree were pledged yesterday by Democratic leaders.

Senator Joseph Zaretzki of Manhattan, the newly elected temporary president of the Senate, and Anthony J. Travia of Brooklyn, the new Speaker of the Assembly, promised a $1 million cut in the legislative budget.

The two, who were elected with Republican support, said they were "determined to cut out all superfluous and no-show jobs."

Senator Jack E. Bronston of Queens, a Democrat who was defeated by Mr. Zaretzki in last week's voting at Albany, announced he would fight for the "elimination of the lulu system," by which lump sum expense funds are given to legislators in lieu of detailed accounts.

Periodic Audits Favored

Mr. Bronston declared that he and Controller Arthur Levitt had agreed there should be complete periodic audits of the legislative budget by the Controller, including the "evaluation" of jobs. Last year the Legislature appropriated $12 million for its operation.

Mr. Levitt, the only elected Democratic state executive, said the Legislature had "some pretty big lulus, $16,000 in some cases," and he favored a careful study. But he said a lulu could "avoid red tape" and be proper when expenses could be reasonably and regularly anticipated.

Each of the 208 legislators gets a $1,000 lulu in addition to his $10,000 salary. Mayor Wagner precipitated an outcry last month when he charged that extra lulus for certain committee chairmanships had been offered in the leadership struggle, offers which he said were in effect attempted bribes.

Senator Zaretzki said yester-

Continued on Page 12, Column 3

A.M.A. MOBILIZES TO BEAT MEDICARE

Votes Own 'Eldercare' Plan and an Educational Drive

Special to The New York Times

CHICAGO, Feb. 7 — The American Medical Association's House of Delegates set the stage today for a campaign to defeat the Johnson Administration's medicare bill with its own "eldercare" plan.

The House passed a resolution endorsing and "enthusiastically" supporting the A. M. A. proposal, which will be promoted by a large-scale national "educational program."

The eldercare bill would expand the present Kerr-Mills state - administered plans by subsidizing private health insurance plans with Federal and state funds for the poor of age 65 and older.

The medicare bill would provide hospital and nursing home benefits under Social Security for persons 65 and older.

Adoption of the eldercare program today marked a change from the last House of Delegates meeting in Miami Beach in December. At that time—before eldercare had been proposed—the House reiterated its support of the Kerr-Mills Act.

The Board of Trustees, which runs the A.M.A. between House sessions, announced the eldercare plan last Jan. 10.

Today's voice vote by the 234-member House came on the final day of a two-day special session in the Pick-Congress Hotel. The decision not only endorsed eldercare but also reaffirmed opposition to medicare and empowered the trustees to conduct a "vigorous" campaign for the A.M.A. plan.

Two standing committees and

Continued on Page 9, Column 2

5-Union Pact Ends Last Rail Dispute

By JOHN D. POMFRET
Special to The New York Times

WASHINGTON, Feb. 7 — Five nonoperating rail unions and the nation's railroads reached final agreement tonight on a contract of major importance. The agreement protects most of the members of the unions against layoff and gives the carriers new flexibility to transfer workers.

For the first time in more than five years, the railroads now have no major national collective bargaining dispute pending with any union or group of unions. Tonight's was the 15th major labor settlement reached by the railroads since last spring.

The new agreement extends the attrition principle to about 290,000 railroad workers. This is the largest single group inside or outside of the rail industry to be covered by such

Continued on Page 11, Column 1

LEADING LAWYERS JOIN RIGHTS DRIVE

150 Will Be Recruited to Go to Mississippi in Summer —Jackson Office Planned

By FRED P. GRAHAM
Special to The New York Times

NEW ORLEANS, Feb. 7—Plans were announced today to recruit 150 volunteers from the leading law firms of the nation to represent civil rights workers in Mississippi.

The plan has the approval of the Mississippi Bar Association.

Bernard G. Segal, a corporate lawyer of Philadelphia, Pa., who is co-chairman of the Lawyers Committee for Civil Rights Under Law, announced that the committee would establish a law office in Jackson, Miss., before the expected influx of civil rights workers occurs this summer. Efforts are under way to raise $200,000 to cover expenses for the first year of operation.

The office in Jackson is expected to consist of three full-time staff attorneys, secretarial help and a law library. A second office in another Mississippi city may be opened later, Mr. Segal said.

Training Course Planned

Leading law firms across the nation will make available the services of experienced lawyers for periods of at least one month. The committee will pay expenses, and will provide a training course in Mississippi law and procedure. Lawyers will be available for duty in Mississippi on a year-round basis, although most of them will be used in the summer.

Last month the committee sent 15 volunteer lawyers to Mississippi to represent members of the National Council of Churches.

Mississippi law allows out-of-state lawyers to practice unless they are challenged by two members of the local bar. Pending a decision by the State Bar Association's Admissions Committee, the challenged lawyers cannot practice in the state courts.

Mr. Segal said he had been assured that the Mississippi Committee on Admissions

Continued on Page 17, Column 3

ACCORD REACHED ON DOCK CONTRACT IN PHILADELPHIA

Agreement Could Pave Way for Return to Work in All North Atlantic Ports

Striking longshoremen and shipping employers agreed to a new contract for the Port of Philadelphia last night in an action that could pave the way for the return to work of 60,000 dockworkers on the North Atlantic Coast.

Philadelphia had been the major holdout port in the Northeast in the strike that has halted work in ports from Maine to Texas since Jan. 11.

Thomas W. Gleason, the president of the International Longshoremen's Association, said here in a telephone interview that he would call a meeting of his executive council shortly to work out union policy.

He added that the 22-man council would give "special consideration" to the question of getting the men in the North Atlantic ports back on the job.

Other Pacts Pending

The convening of the meeting, Mr. Gleason said, hinges on negotiations in Philadelphia involving four craft locals representing such workers as coopers, carpenters and clerical employes. These locals are expected to follow the lead of the longshoremen and settle quickly.

Mr. Gleason said his council's meeting, to be held in New York, might come as early as tonight or tomorrow.

The longshoremen's union has traditionally refused to work until all ports under its jurisdiction have settled, but it now has a plan to send its men back to the piers from Searsport, Me., to Hampton Roads, Va. However, the executive council must approve such action.

Pressure for an end to the long tie-up on the Atlantic and Gulf Coasts has been mounting for days. President Johnson appealed more than a week ago through the Department of Labor for a return to work in ports that had reached contracts, and there have been fears among some union leaders that Congress may take action.

The strike has tied up 775 ships and cost nearly $1.7 billion to the nation's economy.

Similar to Pact Here

The announcement of the Philadelphia longshoremen's pact was made just before 11 P.M., after 33 hours of almost continuous negotiations. Assistant Secretary of Labor James J. Reynolds, needing a shave but otherwise looking fresh, emerged from the meeting and said "a complete and final settlement" had been achieved.

The terms still have to be ratified by the 2,500 members of the union's Local 1291, who are expected to vote either Tuesday night or Wednesday.

As described by negotiators, the agreement is similar to the one reached in New York on Jan. 21. It provides an 80-cent-an-hour wage and welfare increase spread over the four-year life of the contract.

The longshoremen would be

Continued on Page 60, Column 5

REDS CLAIM TOLL

'Barbarous' Attackers Lost Four Planes, Hanoi Declares

Special to The New York Times

HONG KONG, Feb. 7—Communist North Vietnam asserted today that four United States jets were shot down as they made retaliatory raids against North Vietnamese targets.

In a statement by the Defense Ministry, North Vietnam also declared that the attack "constituted a new and extremely serious act of aggression."

The North Vietnam press agency said in a report received here that United States jets "coming in several waves from the sea" strafed and bombed villages around Donghoi, the capital of Quangbinh Province, in two strikes.

[Communist China said the air strikes were an "extremely serious provocation." A Moscow radio broadcast called them a "large - scale provocation." Page 16.]

Time of Attack

The press agency said that the first strike began at 2 P.M. local time (1 A.M. Sunday, New York time) and lasted about 20 minutes.

It said that the "United States imperialists were so barbarous and brazen" as to strafe the Donghoi hospital and an area in front of the office of the International Control Commission.

This is the three-nation body established in 1954 to supervise the execution of the Geneva cease-fire agreement that ended the fight between French and Communist forces in Indochina. Its members are India, Canada and Poland.

The agency said that at 2:35 P.M. United States jet planes returned and strafed the same localities for 10 more minutes.

The Defense Ministry statement said the fact that the "brazen aggressive act" had taken place while McGeorge Bundy was in Saigon further exposed the "sinister designs of United States imperialists" to expand the war in South Vietnam.

U.S. 'Severely' Warned

It added: "The Ministry of National Defense of the Democratic Republic of Vietnam severely warns United States imperialists and their henchmen they must bear full responsibility for the extremely serious consequences of aggressive acts provoked by them."

Before today's air strikes, Premier Aleksei N. Kosygin of the Soviet Union, who is visiting Hanoi, renewed Moscow's pledge to help North Vietnam should it be attacked.

Speaking at a rally in the North Vietnamese capital this morning, he said: "We sternly

Continued on Page 16, Column 2

United Press International Telephoto

EXPLAINS TACTICAL PROBLEMS: Secretary of Defense Robert S. McNamara during news conference yesterday. He shows point in North Vietnam where attacks on the South (arrows) are believed to have started, as well as situation of carriers off the coast.

Associated Press Radiophoto

RESULT OF VIETCONG ATTACK: Wreckage of U.S. helicopter at Camp Holloway air base, which was shelled early yesterday by mortars in a surprise attack by guerrillas.

TAYLOR CONSULTS WITH SAIGON CHIEF

Bundy, Back From Saigon, Reports to Johnson— Vietcong in New Raid

By SEYMOUR TOPPING
Special to The New York Times

SAIGON, South Vietnam, Monday Feb. 8 — Ambassador Maxwell D. Taylor conferred twice yesterday with Acting Premier Nguyen Xuan Oanh. The Ambassador had been in touch with President Johnson through the highspeed communications of the United States Military Assistance Command here since the Vietcong attacks on the air base at Pleiku.

Three hours before a joint statement was issued by South Vietnam and the United States, announcing that action had been taken against military installations in North Vietnam, McGeorge Bundy, special assistant to President Johnson on security affairs, left Saigon hurriedly to report to the White House.

[Mr. Bundy returned home Sunday night and promptly went to see the President, The Associated Press reported.]

Communist guerrillas made another hit-and-run attack on a United States installation last night. They staged a 15-minute assault on an American air base at Soctrang, 90 miles south of Saigon, with mortar and small-arms fire. There were no casualties or damage as the Communist fire fell north of the runway.

Soctrang is the main center for helicopter operations in the Mekong delta area.

A United States spokesman said that about 30 aircraft at the base went aloft when the raid began. Except for two medical evacuation helicopters and four armed helicopters, all aircraft were diverted to a base at Cantho.

The Soctrang attack came less than 24 hours after the Pleiku assault.

Mr. Bundy had been sched-

Continued on Page 14, Column 6

Vietnamese Guard Was Half Strength When Reds Struck

By United Press International

PLEIKU, South Vietnam, Feb. 7—Only 44 of the 100 available Vietnamese security guards were on duty when Communist guerrillas attacked the airfield and billet area here today. Eight Americans were killed and 108 wounded.

Col. Joseph Ulatoski, 37 years old, of Stamford, Conn., adviser to the II Vietnamese Corps, estimated the infiltrating Vietcong force at Camp Holloway at about two squads and one platoon. It is estimated that this would be about 300 men.

The colonel said there were 12 Vietnamese guards in a pillbox near the United States billets. "Apparently they did not see much of anything," the colonel added.

Lieut. Col. John C. Hughes, 42, of Herrin, Ill., commanding officer of the 52d United States Army Aviation Battalion, told President Johnson's special assistant, McGeorge Bundy, who toured the damaged area before leaving for the United States, that the Americans and the Vietnamese share

Continued on Page 14, Column 2

Strike in Bermuda Perils Food Supply

By MURRAY SCHUMACH
Special to The New York Times

HAMILTON, Bermuda, Feb. 7—The armed forces of Bermuda will unload a grain ship tomorrow because dock workers, in sympathy with a strike by electric company employes, have refused to do it. The effects of the strike have spread steadily since the labor dispute began Jan. 19.

This is the first time since World War II that the army and navy have done such work. They have been called to dock duty now because Bermuda, a British crown colony, is largely dependent upon imports for its food supplies.

The use of troops to unload the grain is also an indication

Continued on Page 17, Column 1

U.S. VIEWED RAIDS AS A TEST OF WILL

Administration Retaliated in Belief That Inaction Would Be Seen as Defeatist

By MAX FRANKEL
Special to The New York Times

WASHINGTON, Feb. 7—The Administration ordered the strike against North Vietnam today in the belief that it faced the most serious test so far of its will to help resist aggression in South Vietnam.

Informed sources said the United States had acted on the assumption that North Vietnam's Communist Government organized that test without warning Soviet Premier Aleksei N. Kosygin, its guest in Hanoi at the moment.

Sensing that the Soviet leader might find himself in an awkward position there, the Administration sent a special message to Moscow to explain its raid as an act of retaliation rather than as a move to expand the war in Southeast Asia.

Sense of Challenge

President Johnson and his leading advisers were said to have had no doubt they were being tested. They were described as confident that a failure to respond would have been interpreted as a defeatist position in several Communist capitals.

Their sense of challenge as they met at the White House last night to plan the response was said to have been based on the following factors:

¶The severity of the Vietcong attack on a United States military compound in South Vietnam, in which eight Americans died. That attack, presumably coordinated with two other major Vietcong strikes, was interpreted here as an effort to demonstrate American vulnerability.

¶Secret but "clear" evidence that North Vietnam not only knew of this test but also participated in its planning. The

Continued on Page 15, Column 4

CAPITAL IS TENSE

But President Asserts Nation Still Opposes Widening of War

Text of the McNamara-Ball news conference, Page 15.

By TOM WICKER
Special to The New York Times

WASHINGTON, Feb. 7 — United States aircraft struck at North Vietnam early today in response to what President Johnson called "provocations ordered and directed by the Hanoi regime."

Mr. Johnson made it clear, however, that the air strike was a limited response rather than a signal for a general expansion of the guerrilla warfare in South Vietnam.

In what appeared to be the most threatening crisis in Southeast Asia since the Gulf of Tonkin clash last August, Washington replied to severe Vietcong attacks.

The guerrillas had struck without warning against major American installations at Pleiku in the central plateau of South Vietnam, at an airstrip in Tuyhoa and at villages near Nhatrang.

49 Aircraft in Action

At the President's order, 49 carrier-based fighter planes bombed and strafed barracks and staging areas of the Vietcong guerrillas in the vicinity of Donghoi, just north of the border between North and South Vietnam.

The raid occurred swiftly about 2 P.M. Sunday, Vietnamese time (1 A.M., Eastern standard time). Secretary of Defense Robert S. McNamara said one American plane had gone down in the South China Sea. The Hanoi radio in the North Vietnamese capital said four aircraft had been knocked out.

Today, amid tension, President Johnson ordered the evacuation of about 1,800 dependents of United States military and civilian personnel stationed in South Vietnam.

Missile Unit Dispatched

He also ordered into the Danang area of South Vietnam an air-defense battalion equipped with Hawk ground-to-air missiles.

In the Vietcong attack at Pleiku, 8 Americans were killed and 108 wounded, but first reports did not indicate American casualties in the two other attacks.

Tension in Washington was heightened, and the United States response appeared conditioned to some extent by the Hanoi visit of Premier Aleksei N. Kosygin of the Soviet Union. Mr. Kosygin said in a speech to a Hanoi group that Moscow would assist North Vietnam against any nation that encroached on its territory.

Johnson Repeats Pledge

Administration officials insisted that the air attack had been carried out without regard to Mr. Kosygin's visit to Hanoi and would have been staged even if he had not been there.

In a White House statement announcing the retaliatory attack, Mr. Johnson repeated the pledge, given at the time of the Tonkin incident, that "we seek no wider war."

But the President cautioned that "whether or not this course can be maintained lies with the North Vietnamese aggressors."

The response to the Vietcong attacks, he said, "was carefully limited to military areas which are supplying men and arms for attacks in South Vietnam." Thus, he said, "the response is appropriate and fitting."

Mr. McNamara, at a news conference with George Ball,

Continued on Page 14, Column 1

Visitors to Museum Hall See Man Slay Ex-Wife

Violin Maker, 72, Shoots His Former Mate After Talk

A 72-year-old master violin maker shot and killed his former wife in the main hall of the American Museum of Natural History yesterday afternoon.

About 30 people, including the couple's 12-year-old daughter, were in the cavernous, marble-pillared hall when the shooting occurred. The five shots, three of which struck the 43-year-old woman, transformed the normally hushed lobby into a bedlam. Youngsters screamed and parents ran to protect their children as museum guards grappled with the slayer.

The embittered violin maker was identified by the police as Dmytro Didchenko, who had worked at his craft on two continents since leaving his native Russia after the 1917 Revolution. He and his wife, Gertrude, a German immigrant, had been battling in court for most of their marriage of 13 years. Last Thursday the marriage was annulled.

Associated Press

Dmytro Didchenko leaving 68th Street police station.

A few hours after the 1:15 P.M. shooting, Mrs. Didchenko's lawyer, former State Senator Bernard Tompkins, collapsed and died on the steps inside the West 68th Street station house while being interviewed.

The day's events apparently began when Didchenko, who

Lawyer in Marital Case Dies at Police Station House

lives at 101 West 85th Street, made an appointment with his former wife to discuss the visitation rights of their daughter, Susan. The dark-haired girl lived with her mother at 63-15 110th Street, Rego Park, Queens.

The couple were married in 1952. In 1956 a court case involving the two—by then separated—received some attention because Mrs. Didchenko said she was afraid her husband would kill her if she took her daughter for the visits stipulated by the judge.

Neighbors of Didchenko said yesterday that he had become an embittered and lonely man during the long round of court appearances. They said they had finally avoided him because he seemed obsessed with discussing his marital troubles, and they had difficulty understanding him.

Before he died, Mr. Tompkins had said that the marriage was finally annulled on the ground that Didchenko had had an-

Continued on Page 19, Column 2

NEWS INDEX

1965

Pope Paul VI delivered his theme, *"Jamais plus la guerre!"* ("No more war, never again!") in a speech to the huge crowd of people at Yankee Stadium.

Sir Winston Churchill shown riding to Parliament for his last appearance in the venerable chamber. The aging leader had been a member of Parliament for 64 years before his death in 1965.

Despite talks of peace initiatives by world leaders, use of the word "escalation" became common. The reality of the situation is shown on the faces of these men on a search-and-destroy mission patrol in Phuc Tuy Province.

Barbara Eden (shown here with Sammy Davis, Jr.) starred as Larry Hagman's live-in genie in *I Dream of Jeannie*.

Robert Culp and Bill Cosby starred in I Spy. **The white and black camaraderie provoked little or no protest in the South or elsewhere.**

"All the News That's Fit to Print"

The New York Times.

LATE CITY EDITION

U. S. Weather Bureau Report (Page 82) forecasts: Fair and cooler today; clear, cold tonight and tomorrow. Temp. range: 40—37; yesterday: 53—40.

VOL. CXIV..No. 39,127. NEW YORK, WEDNESDAY, MARCH 10, 1965. TEN CENTS

DR. KING LEADS MARCH AT SELMA; STATE POLICE END IT PEACEABLY UNDER A U.S.-ARRANGED ACCORD

Associated Press Wirephoto

SELMA MARCH BEGINS: In the front row at yesterday's demonstration are, from the left: James Farmer, Bishop John Wesley Lord, the Rev. Andrew Young, foreground, the Rev. Dr. Martin Luther King Jr. and James Foreman.

United Press International Telephoto

CONFRONTATION: Column of marchers approaches line of state troopers outside town. Marchers turned back.

Associated Press Wirephoto

AND A PRAYER: Demonstrators, many of them clergymen, kneel in prayer after being stopped outside Selma

1,500 TURNED BACK

Protest Begun Despite Court—3 Ministers Attacked Later

Text of Federal court order will be found on Page 22.

By ROY REED

Special to The New York Times

SELMA, Ala., March 9—The Rev. Dr. Martin Luther King Jr. led 1,500 Negroes and whites on a second attempted protest march today. State troopers turned them back on the outskirts of Selma, after they had gone one mile.

But this time there was no violence—unlike a similar confrontation at the same spot on Sunday. Then, troopers and Dallas County sheriff's officers broke up an attempted march to Montgomery, the state capital, 50 miles away, with clubs and tear gas.

"We had the greatest demonstration for freedom today that we've ever had in the South," Dr. King said as he disbanded the brief march today.

Tonight, three Unitarian ministers who had participated in the march were beaten by whites on a downtown street corner. The ministers are white.

One of them, the Rev. James J. Reeb, 38 years old, of Boston, was taken to University Hospital in Birmingham with a serious head injury and later underwent surgery. The police said he had been knocked unconscious with a club.

Ate in Negro Restaurant

The Rev. Clark B. Olsen, 32, of Berkeley, Calif., and the Rev. Orloff W. Miller, 33, of Boston, were less seriously injured.

They told the police they had been attacked by five men in sports clothes after they had eaten dinner in a Negro restaurant.

The meeting of troopers and demonstrators had been awaited here with dread following the Sunday clash, in which 84 marchers were hurt.

Its peaceful resolution resulted from an arrangement between leaders of the march and the troopers worked out beforehand, with the Federal Government as mediator. The arrangement had face-saving features for both sides.

The demonstrators began their march in the face of a Federal Court injunction prohibiting the march and in spite

Continued on Page 22, Column 1

PRESIDENT'S PLEA CURTAILS MARCH

Johnson Scores 'Brutality' Against Selma Negroes

Text of President's statement is printed on Page 23.

By CHARLES MOHR

Special to The New York Times

WASHINGTON, March 9—President Johnson and his representatives successfully urged the Rev. Dr. Martin Luther King Jr. today not to carry out a protest march from Selma, Ala., to Montgomery, the state capital.

Mr. Johnson and Attorney General Nicholas deB. Katzenbach believed, on the basis of Justice Department conversations with Federal District Judge Frank M. Johnson Jr., that the judge would permit the march on Thursday and enjoin Alabama officials from blocking it then.

Judge Johnson issued an order prohibiting the march today. The marchers went a mile and were turned back.

The President strongly deplored in a statement today what he called "brutality" against Negroes in Selma, where a similar march was broken up by the police on Sunday. He asked the Negro demonstrators, as well as state officials, to respect law and order.

Dr. King, leader of the civil

Continued on Page 23, Column 5

Thousands Across Nation Hold Sympathy Marches

Romney Leads a Protest

Thousands of Negroes and whites demonstrated in major cities yesterday to show their sympathy with Negroes whose voter registration march in Selma, Ala., was broken up by the Alabama police Sunday.

Gov. George Romney of Michigan led 10,000 persons in a 10-block march in Detroit. He was joined in the quiet demonstration by Mayor Jerome P. Cavanagh. The march, organized by religious leaders, was allowed by the police even though a parade permit had not been issued.

Government policemen hauled a group of singing demonstrators away from the Washington office of Attorney General Nicholas deB. Katzenbach, but no one was arrested. Nearly 1,000 persons demonstrated at the White House.

There were similar demonstrations in support of the Alabama Negroes in Chicago, Los Angeles, Berkeley, Calif., Hartford, Syracuse, Springfield, Ohio, Beloit, Wis., and Boston.

Eight hundred persons participated in a noisy but peaceful march along Fifth Avenue in New York. It involved clergymen, college students and professional men as well as civil rights workers.

In most of the cities, interracial groups appeared at Federal buildings and in public places, carrying signs asking for Federal intervention in Alabama.

Some of the demonstrations were small street marches designed to demonstrate sympathy for the Selma group.

Following are reports from various cities:

10,000 March in Detroit

By DAVID R. JONES

Special to The New York Times

DETROIT, March 9—Governor Romney and Mayor Jerome P. Cavanagh led thousands of persons today in a 10-block march through downtown Detroit to protest events in Selma, Ala.

The Detroit police estimated that about 10,000 people had

Continued on Page 23, Column 1

The Walk Through Selma

By GAY TALESE

Special to The New York Times

SELMA, Ala., March 9—There were young blondes in polo coats and hipsters with beards, and the wives of Senators; there were white faces and black faces, ministers' collars and turtlenecked sweaters.

There were about 1,500 such people here today. They differed in age and religion, but they shared a unity of purpose. They had come to march through the streets of Selma and they were hoping to be heard, if not seen, in the state capital at Montgomery, 50 miles away.

Many had come from California, Chicago, Texas, New York, Mississippi. Some, unable to book space on regular flights, had chartered planes.

Several, after landing at the Montgomery Airport, were unable to rent cars to complete the journey to Selma. But they got here by bus or by getting lifts.

One group, unable to do either, met a farmer on the road with a tow truck. For an undisclosed but not exorbitant fee, he drove them the 50 miles west to Selma.

Once in Selma, the visitors, who included an estimated 450 clergymen—about half of them white—were welcomed into the homes of Negroes. Many who did not leave Selma after the march spent the night as guests of the Negroes. Others were accommodated in the two Negro motels here or in the clergymen's residences of three Negro churches.

All those who were interviewed after the march said they were happy they had come. They said they had found the experience moving and inspiring and unforgettable. It was a perfect day for such a march.

Among the marchers were Mrs. Paul H. Douglas, the wife of the Democratic Senator from Illinois; Mrs. Charles W. Tobey, the widow of the Republican Senator from New Hampshire, and Mrs. Harold L. Ickes, the

Continued on Page 22, Column 3

U.S. TURNS DOWN THANT PROPOSAL ON TRUCE PARLEY

Says It Can Accept No Bid for a Vietnam Discussion Until 'Aggression' Ends

CHANNELS REMAIN OPEN

Hope Voiced for a Peaceful Solution—Saigon Troops Score Major Victory

By MAX FRANKEL

Special to The New York Times

WASHINGTON, March 9—The United States has told U Thant, the Secretary General of the United Nations, that it cannot accept his or any other invitation to a conference on Vietnam until North Vietnam indicates a readiness to halt its "aggression."

The rejection of Mr. Thant's proposal for a seven-nation "preliminary" discussion was disclosed today by the State Department. It was accompanied by a word of thanks for his efforts and expressions of hope that diplomatic channels would be held open for a peaceful solution.

[In South Vietnam, Government forces achieved a major victory Monday in the repulse of a Vietcong assault on a Special Forces camp 270 miles northeast of Saigon. The guerrillas left at least 100 dead. According to The Associated Press, one United States Marine was killed and one was wounded Tuesday in a clash with the Vietcong. Page 3.]

After issuing its statement replying to Mr. Thant, the State Department hastily altered some of the language it used to describe Washington's condition for negotiations. But in either form, the statement marked no change in the Administration's positions.

Raids Are Warnings

In fact, officials here are beginning to suspect that the Soviet Union, Communist China and North Vietnam, like Washington, are temporarily frozen in their diplomatic positions. If such a freeze persists, the Administration will soon face another major decision about how much additional military pressure on North Vietnam it wishes to risk.

By raiding a few military installations in North Vietnam in the last month, the United States has tried to warn the Hanoi Government that it faces continuing and intensified punishment unless it halts the infiltration of men and arms into South Vietnam.

These raids have raised fears in many places of a wider war in Southeast Asia and they have evoked pressures from

Continued on Page 2, Column 3

RED PARTIES HINT FAILURE OF TALKS

Sought Ways to Avert Wider Soviet-Chinese Split

By HENRY TANNER

Special to The New York Times

MOSCOW, Wednesday, March 10—The Soviet-sponsored conference of 19 Communist parties that met here last week failed to produce any plan of action that might prevent further fragmentation of the international Communist movement.

A final communiqué published early today made it clear, Western specialists said, that the Soviet leaders had failed in yet another effort to meet the challenge of the Chinese Communists and to restore the Kremlin's position as the leader of world Communism.

The communiqué indicated that even the pro-Soviet parties were unable to agree on a meaningful joint course.

On the crucial question whether a conference of all Communist parties should be

Continued on Page 6, Column 3

NEWS INDEX

Kerr Is Resigning At U. of California; Aide Also Leaving

Clark Kerr

By WALLACE TURNER

Special to The New York Times

BERKELEY, Calif., March 9—Clark Kerr announced today his intention to resign as president of the University of California. Martin Meyerson announced that he would resign as acting chancellor of the Berkeley campus.

Neither man would answer questions beyond the brief statements handed out at a hurriedly convened news conference in University Hall, where Mr. Kerr has his offices.

Mr. Kerr, 53 years old, is responsible for the entire seven-campus university system; Mr. Meyerson, 42, for the 27,500-student Berkeley

Continued on Page 25, Column 1

ARABS PUSH DRIVE TO PENALIZE BONN

League Meets in Cairo to Consider Retaliation for Move Toward Israel

By HEDRICK SMITH

Special to The New York Times

CAIRO, March 9—Pressures mounted among Arab states today for concerted and sharp retaliation against West Germany for its decision to seek diplomatic relations with Israel.

In a speech tonight, President Gamal Abdel Nasser hailed the Kuwaiti National Assembly for favoring an immediate break with West Germany, establishment of relations with East Germany and a pan-Arab boycott of West Germany.

While he was speaking, representatives of 13 Arab countries held their second urgent session of the day to reach a unified strategy against West Germany.

Adoption Unanimous

It was announced after the first meeting that the Arab League delegates had unanimously adopted resolutions and were referring them to the 13 Arab Governments. The communiqué said the Arab foreign ministers would meet here Sunday to ratify the resolutions, which were not described.

President Nasser, apparently encouraged by the progress, said at a rally at Menya, 150 miles south of here, that on the basis of what he knew, the Arabs would win "this political showdown" with Israel and West Germany. He did not elaborate.

"If the Jews win this battle then the Arabs' word is valueless, and Arabs had better go and bury their faces in the

Continued on Page 8, Column 4

Appalachia Aid Bill Is Signed by Johnson

By MARJORIE HUNTER

Special to The New York Times

WASHINGTON, March 9—A program to invigorate the lagging economy of Appalachia became law today in the sunny Rose Garden of the White House.

"The dole is dead, the pork barrel is gone," President Johnson said as he prepared to sign into law the first of his Great Society legislation this year.

The $1.1 billion measure cleared Congress last week. The Federal-state program of economic aid will move into action immediately. About 78 per cent of the funds will be used to build highways and access roads. The groundwork has been laid. A staff is being as-

Continued on Page 27, Column 1

F.P.C., 3-1, GRANTS CON ED A LICENSE FOR HUDSON PLANT

Damage to Scenic Values Is Discounted—Rep. Ottinger Sees a Court Challenge

By WARREN WEAVER Jr.

Special to The New York Times

WASHINGTON, March 9—The Federal Power Commission today granted the Consolidated Edison Company a license to build the world's largest pumped-storage hydroelectric power plant on the banks of the Hudson River near Cornwall.

Conservation groups had strongly opposed giving the utility permission for the $162 million project, maintaining that it would spoil the beauty of the Hudson highlands.

One of the power plant's chief opponents, Representative Richard L. Ottinger of Westchester County, said today he was sure that there would be a court challenge of the commission decision.

Ross the Dissenter

The commission divided 3 to 1 on the issue, with Commissioner Charles R. Ross dissenting. He called for further hearings on aspects of the controversy and no decision before March 1, 1966.

[Residents of Cornwall-on-Hudson were pleased by the decision, and Consolidated Edison officials were relieved, but conservationists vowed to keep fighting the project. Page 28.]

In a single concession to the opposition, the F.P.C. agreed to hold further hearings on the route that the overhead power lines from the Cornwall project will follow on the 24-mile course between Nelsonville and Millwood. It refused to order the lines underground, however.

The additional hearings, to open in Washington on May 4, will also deal with equipment to prevent injury to fish in the area around the power plant.

Impact Held 'Minimal'

The 17,000-word majority opinion was written by the commission chairman, Joseph C. Swidler. Joining him were L. J. O'Connor Jr. and David S. Black.

"We find that the impact of the project upon scenic resources will be minimal; that it will create additional recreational opportunities, and that its advantages for power-supply purposes far outweigh any negative considerations," the commission majority declared.

"In these circumstances and viewing sympathetically the case made by the Scenic Hudson [Preservation Conference], we cannot conclude that the Cornwall powerhouse substantially impairs the scenic, historic or recreational values in the area.

"Whatever may be the negative aspect of adding this

Continued on Page 28, Column 7

PUBLIC BUYS OUT ANILINE OFFERING

U.S. Ends Its Ownership of Concern Seized in 1942

By JOHN H. ALLAN

A $341 million block of General Aniline and Film Corporation common stock, the largest asset seized by the Government as enemy property during World War II, was sold out quickly to the public yesterday.

The stock was priced by the underwriters at $30.60 a share, and it subsequently traded as high as $36. At the close of trading yesterday afternoon, the price had settled down to about $32.

The shares were sold by the Attorney General for the Federal Government in what was the largest sale of stock at competitive bidding in Wall Street history. Public excitement over the sale was the most prevalent since the Communications Satellite Corporation sold $200 million of stock last June.

A nationwide syndicate of about 225 investment banking firms headed by Blyth & Co., Inc., and the First Boston Corporation submitted the winning bid of $29.476 a share for the Aniline stock.

The Blyth-First Boston bid topped a bid of $28.2677 a share that was submitted by a group

Continued on Page 58, Column 1

"All the News That's Fit to Print"

The New York Times.

LATE CITY EDITION

U.S. Weather Bureau Report (Page 69) forecast: Rain with chance of snow today; rain tonight and tomorrow. Temp. range: 40—32; yesterday: 42—36.

VOL. CXIV..No. 39,143. NEW YORK, FRIDAY, MARCH 26, 1965. TEN CENTS

25,000 GO TO ALABAMA'S CAPITOL; WALLACE REBUFFS PETITIONERS; WHITE RIGHTS WORKER IS SLAIN

JOHNSON HINTS AT AID FOR ASIA IF STRIFE ENDS

A 'MARSHALL PLAN'

Indirect Offer to Hanoi Holds Out Prospect of Regional Growth

Text of Johnson statement is printed on Page 5.

By CHARLES MOHR
Special to The New York Times

WASHINGTON, March 25—President Johnson indirectly offered to North Vietnam today the prospect of "economic and social cooperation" if peace was restored in Southeast Asia.

Qualified sources said Mr. Johnson was not thinking of direct aid to Hanoi but was opening the door to vast regional development plans in Asia from which Communist nations like North Vietnam would not be excluded.

The sources said that the President believes that even if the war in South Vietnam is won and American troops come home, the United States would not want to abandon the area but would give it maximum help. It may be necessary, he believes, to develop a broader and more coherent aid plan for the area—a sort of Marshall Plan for Asia.

Statement Read to Cabinet

Mr. Johnson's action did not represent any softening of American support for the war in South Vietnam. However, Administration sources said it was the "carrot" to go along with the stick of aerial bombardment of North Vietnam.

A statement on Vietnam policy was read by the President at a two-hour Cabinet meeting and then was made public. The statement appeared to be intended in part to reassert that American policy was reasonable in view of the international furor over the use of nonlethal gases in the South Vietnamese guerrilla war.

Mr. Johnson's statement said that "the United States looks forward to the day when the people and governments of all Southeast Asia may be free from terror, subversion and assassination — when they will need no military support and assistance against aggression, but only economic and social cooperation for progress in peace."

Regional Growth the Aim

It added that "wider and broader" development programs "can be expected in the future from Asian leaders and Asian councils—and in such programs we would want to help."

It became known later that Mr. Johnson had in mind American participation in regional development programs.

The statement was described as not so much a proposal as an expression of receptiveness to possible proposals from Asian leaders and Asian political groupings. The idea goes back to Mr. Johnson's trip to Southeast Asia in 1961, when he was Vice President and suggested large-scale regional development plans to President Kennedy.

The purpose of the statement, the sources said, was to

Continued on Page 5, Column 1

President Kennedy Balked C.I.A. Plot On Russian Sugar

By MAX FRANKEL
Special to The New York Times

WASHINGTON, March 25—Discussions here about the use of nausea-inducing gas in Vietnam have brought to light the story of an ingenious scheme by which the White House once nullified the use of a totally different kind of chemical agent on some sugar bound for the Soviet Union.

It is the story of how former President John F. Kennedy outraged the Soviet Government by conspiring in the detention of a British ship with cargo from Cuba so as to undo a successful sabotage operation of the Central Intelligence Agency.

It is a Caribbean melodrama involving mysterious shipboard fires and hijacked sacks of sugar, bitter court battles and angry diplomatic messages, all against the background of the Cuban missile crisis of 1962.

The story is 30 months old but not completely ended. At

Continued on Page 2, Column 3

'70 TRIAL CUTOFF FOR NAZIS VOTED

Bundestag Enacts Shortest of Suggested Extensions —Justice Minister Quits

By ARTHUR J. OLSEN
Special to The New York Times

BONN, March 25 — The West German Parliament voted today the shortest suggested extension of the legal deadline for new prosecutions of Nazi war criminals.

The Bundestag, or lower house, voted overwhelmingly to prolong the expiration of the statute of limitations for murder during the Hitler regime by four years and eight months to Dec. 31, 1969.

After Dec. 31, 1969 — just 20 years after the fledgling West German republic was granted its first measure of sovereignty by the Allied occupation powers—no new charges may be laid against persons suspected of having committed murder during the Nazi era.

But 14,000 suspects now charged and others discovered during the four years and eight months will remain subject to trial, even after 1969.

Immediately after the parlia-

Continued on Page 14, Column 3

JUDGE QUESTIONS VOTE ALLOCATION IN ESTIMATE BODY

Refuses to Dismiss Suit on Apportioning — Deadline for State Extended

By PETER KIHSS

Federal Judge Lloyd F. McMahon has indicated that the present distribution of votes in the city's Board of Estimate might be unconstitutional under the United States Supreme Court's "one-man, one-vote" ruling.

In a decision filed yesterday rejecting a city motion to dismiss a challenge to the board's constitutionality, Judge MacMahon said each citizen must be "afforded equal representation" in a governmental body.

Robert R. McMillan, 1964 Republican Queens candidate for the City Council, who had brought the suit, said he was studying whether to seek a summary judgment. Corporations Counsel Leo A. Larkin said the city would reply to Mr. McMillan's suit, probably within 10 days, anticipating a trial.

The Board of Estimate consists of the five borough presidents, each with two votes, and the Mayor, Council President and Controller, each accorded four votes.

Vote Formula Offered

On the basis of 1964 population estimates, Mr. McMillan said yesterday that a formula giving the borough president of Staten Island a single vote might call for 6 votes for the Bronx, 7 for Manhattan, 8 for Queens and 11 for Brooklyn. His own informal suggestion would give the three citywide officials 11 votes each, or a total equal to that of the borough presidents.

Meanwhile, a three-judge Federal court extended the deadline for reapportioning the State Legislature under the one-man, one-vote principle from April 1 to May 5, acting on a proposal by radio station WMCA.

The three-judge court had upheld a Republican plan last Jan. 26 as valid under the Federal Constitution, only to have State Supreme Court Justice Matthew M. Levy on March 15 rule in another WMCA suit that the plan violated the State Constitution.

The State Court of Appeals is to hear an appeal Tuesday by the Rockefeller administration on Justice Levy's decision. Notice of appeal from the Federal court's January decision, which had invalidated three other plans preferred by the Republicans, had been filed by the state with the United States Supreme Court Feb. 23. The law firm of former Gov. Thomas E. Dewey, who will be special counsel, said yesterday a jurisdictional statement would be filed about April 26.

Mr. McMillan's taxpayer's

Continued on Page 20, Column 7

Associated Press Wirephoto

CLIMAX OF FREEDOM MARCH: Thousands of civil rights demonstrators gather in front of Alabama State Capitol, at left, in Montgomery, at end of five-day, 54-mile march from Selma. At right is Dexter Avenue Baptist Church, where the Rev. Dr. Martin Luther King Jr. had first pastorate.

2 Who 'Confessed' In Hammer Slaying Cleared by Hogan

By SIDNEY E. ZION

District Attorney Frank S. Hogan has dropped first-degree murder charges against two drifters who were indicted last March after confessing to the hammer-slaying of a derelict.

The dismissal, signed last week by State Supreme Court Justice Mitchell D. Schweitzer, is expected to rock the Police Department, which is still reeling from the collapse of its case against George Whitmore Jr. for the murders of Janice Wylie and Emily Hoffert in August, 1963. Whitmore was cleared of the charges last January, when his 61-page confession was discredited.

Mr. Hogan's office has not announced the dismissals, which is contrary to its usual procedure in matters of significance.

The New York Times learned of the case when one of the defendants appeared at its office recently after his discharge but before his formal dismissal. At that time, James C. Mosley, one of the Assistant District Attorneys handling the case, told

Continued on Page 25, Column 1

JOHNSON ASKS AID FOR NEEDY AREAS

Regional Development Plan Would Give $510 Million in Annual Assistance

By EILEEN SHANAHAN
Special to The New York Times

WASHINGTON, March 25—A revised program of economic assistance to depressed areas, with emphasis on regional development rather than on individual cities or counties, was proposed today by President Johnson.

In a special message to Congress, the President asked that the Federal Government be authorized to make loans and grants totaling $510 million annually to help areas of high unemployment and low income. The program would be a permanent one.

The area and regional development program should be supported by everyone, Mr. Johnson said, because "the distress or under-development of any part of the country holds back the progress of the entire nation."

The amount of money proposed to be spent on the new program is about double the annual outlays of the present area redevelopment program plus the more recent accelerated public works program, which would also be replaced by the new plan.

The Johnson program would establish an economic development administration as part of the Commerce Department, as the Area Redevelopment Administration has been. The administrator of the Area Rede-

Continued on Page 16, Column 4

Woman Is Shot to Death On Lowndes County Road

By PAUL L. MONTGOMERY
Special to The New York Times

MONTGOMERY, Ala., March 25—A white woman worker for the Southern Christian Leadership Conference was shot to death tonight while returning to Montgomery from Selma, Ala., where she had delivered a carload of civil rights workers who took part in the Freedom March that ended here today.

The victim, Mrs. Viola Gregg Liuzzo, 38 years old, was a member of the transportation committee of the civil rights march and was completing her third day as a transport driver.

She was shot on U.S. Highway 80 a mile from Lowndesboro in Lowndes County. The small village is about half way between Selma and Montgomery. The only witness to the slaying was a Negro youth, Leroy Moten, about 17, who was in the front seat of the 1963 sedan that Mrs. Liuzzo was driving.

Mr. Moten said Mrs. Liuzzo had been shot through the head or neck by a high-powered rifle. He said he ducked to the floorboards immediately.

Mr. Moten said Mrs. Liuzzo was shot by a group of unidentified men in another car.

The car from which the shot or shots were fired then turned back, Mr. Moten said. The intention, he said, seemed to be to fire again.

He said he kept his head down and could not identify the killers or their vehicle. He was being held as a material witness and agents of the Federal Bureau of Investigation said they would continue to work on the case throughout the night.

Mrs. Liuzzo, the mother of five children, lived at 19375 Marlow Street, Detroit. She was reported to have been attending Wayne State University there.

Her husband was identified as Anthony J. Liuzzo, an official of the teamsters' union.

Mrs. Liuzzo lost control of her car when she was shot and it traveled several hundred feet along the shoulder of the road before it stopped. Mr. Moten was unhurt.

Tonight's killing was the third since the start of the voter

Continued on Page 23, Column 4

DR. KING CHEERED

He Says 'No Wave of Racism Can Stop Us Now'

Excerpts from King speech and text of petition, Page 22.

By ROY REED
Special to The New York Times

MONTGOMERY, Ala., March 25—The Rev. Dr. Martin Luther King Jr. led 25,000 Negroes and whites to the shadow of the State Capitol here today and challenged Alabama to put an end to racial discrimination.

Gov. George C. Wallace sent word about 2 P.M. that he would receive a delegation from the marchers after the rally, but the delegation met twice with rebuffs when it tried to see him. State policemen stopped the group the first time at the edge of the Capitol grounds and said no one was to be let through.

The delegation was later admitted to the Capitol, but was told that the Governor had closed his office for the day. The group left without giving its petition to anyone.

At Steps of Capitol

The Alabama Freedom March from Selma to Montgomery ended shortly after noon at the foot of the Capitol steps, and as people from all over the nation stood facing the white-columned statehouse, Dr. King assured them:

"We are not about to turn around. We are on the move now. Yes, we are on the move and no wave of racism can stop us."

The throng let out a mighty cheer, so loud that it was easily audible 75 yards away in the office of Governor Wallace, where the Governor was seen several times parting the venetian blinds of a window overlooking the rally.

Even though the 54-mile march from Selma was a dramatization of a grievance, its windup at the steps of the Capitol carried the trappings of triumph.

The march was hailed by several speakers as the greatest demonstration in the history of the civil rights movement. The caravan that followed Dr. King up Dexter Avenue, up the broad slope that once accommodated the inaugural parade of the President of the Con-

Continued on Page 22, Column 1

Astronauts Call Flight Almost Perfect

Associated Press Wirephoto

Maj. Virgil I. Grissom uses model at news conference to describe maneuvers in space. At left is Lieut. Comdr. John W. Young, his co-pilot during the three-orbit flight.

By EVERT CLARK
Special to The New York Times

COCOA BEACH, Fla., March 25—The two quietest men in space turned out to be two of the funniest on the ground today as Lieut. Comdr. Virgil I. Grissom and Maj. John W. Young told of their flight in the Gemini 3 spacecraft, Molly Brown. They described the three-orbit flight of two days ago as busy, exhilarating, near-perfect and short on surprises.

They also said it was highly significant for future flight in space. It proved that a spacecraft can be maneuvered precisely and at will more independently of the ground than before.

And it proved that men can eat and can safely dispose of wastes as they will need to do on long flights, the astronauts said.

At a news conference here

Continued on Page 13, Column 1

Chou Says Russians Would Be War Ally

By DREW MIDDLETON
Special to The New York Times

PARIS, March 25—Premier Chou En-lai of China has predicted that "the Chinese and Russian people will close ranks" should the United States provoke a wider conflict in Asia.

For this reason, the Premier said, President Johnson, "who is dancing on the tightrope of war and doesn't know how to turn around, is risking some surprises."

Mr. Chou's statements were made to K. S. Karol in an interview published here today in the weekly Nouvel Observateur. The interview took place in Peking.

Although the tone of Mr. Chou's remarks was belligerent, diplomats noted that he cast China in the role of a supporter of North Vietnam and of "the South Vietnamese National Lib-

Continued on Page 4, Column 4

Printers' Stoppage Delays The Times

By DAMON STETSON

The first edition of The New York Times was delayed for more than an hour last night when the newspaper's printers left their jobs to attend a union meeting in the composing room.

The stoppage lasted for an hour, with the printers returning to work at 9:17 P.M. But the first edition, normally out at 9:35 P. M., was not published until 10:43 P.M.

A printers' union meeting was also held at The Daily News, after the first edition had gone to press. But a spokesman for The News said that the meeting there had not interfered with publication schedules.

The Times issued this statement:

"We had a work stoppage tonight in our composing room that lasted for one hour. The stoppage took the form of an

Continued on Page 24, Column 1

ALBANY PUTS OFF BLUE CROSS VOTE

Democrats in Senate Spurn Request by Rockefeller

By MURRAY SCHUMACH
Special to The New York Times

ALBANY, March 25—After a debate that became acrimonious at times, Senate Democrats rejected a plea by Governor Rockefeller for prompt action on his Blue Cross plans today and tossed the entire matter into public legislative hearings that will begin here next Tuesday.

The plans espoused by the Governor would permit Blue Cross to cut its reserves from 15 to 5 per cent. The Governor contended this would make a rate increase unnecessary for two years. Blue Cross said yesterday that it would not.

By a straight party vote of 32 to 15, the Democrats refused to allow the bills urged by the Governor to leave the Public Health Committee. The Assembly had passed the same bills yesterday with many Democrats joining Republicans.

During the debate a Democrat accused a Republican of fearing public hearings on the subject. A Republican derided the Democrat, and the suggestion was raised that the state might have to grant a partial subsidy to Blue Cross to prevent repeated rate increases.

The Senate action came after a plea from the Governor that

Continued on Page 20, Column 4

ZARETZKI ADMITS BUDGET FAILURE

Says Governor Must Supply Votes Needed for Passage

By SYDNEY H. SCHANBERG
Special to The New York Times

ALBANY, March 25—The political impasse over the state's next budget persisted today as Senate Majority Leader Joseph Zaretzki tried and failed to get the budget bills reported out of the Senate Finance Committee.

Mr. Zaretzki emerged wearily at 6 P.M. from a brief committee meeting and told reporters that Governor Rockefeller would have to round up Republican votes if he wanted his budget—and in particular his proposed state sales tax — passed by the Democratic-controlled Legislature.

[In New York, Mayor Wagner spoke out strongly in a speech against legislative proposals for state budget cuts that would reduce state payments to the city.]

Mr. Zaretzki said he recognized how critical the situation was, with only six days to go for the passage of a budget. But he repeated his admission of last night that he had not been able to muster enough votes within his own party to put the Rockefeller budget through.

"It's the Governor's program" he said. "It's his duty to get

Continued on Page 20, Column 1

NEWS INDEX

1965

Casey Stengel retired as the Mets manager in 1965.

Muhammad Ali felled Sonny Liston (nicknamed the Bear) in less than two minutes of the first round in their return heavyweight title bout.

Princeton star Bill Bradley led his team into the NCAA semifinals, averaging more than 30 points a game.

Jets coach Weeb Ewbank and Sonny Werblin are full of smiles—they just signed Joe Namath to a 4-year contract.

"All the News That's Fit to Print"

The New York Times.

LATE CITY EDITION
U. S. Weather Bureau Report (Page 61) forecasts:
Sunny and mild today; fair tonight.
Increasing cloudiness tomorrow.
Temp. range: 58—38; yesterday: 57—34.

VOL. CXIV..No. 39,153.

NEW YORK, MONDAY, APRIL 5, 1965. TEN CENTS

CONGRESS NEARS TEST ON MEDICARE AND SCHOOL BILL

Senate Is Expected to Begin Floor Debate Wednesday on Aid to Education

JOHNSON PUSHES PLANS

House Committee Is Likely to Clear Medical Proposal for Action Same Day

By MARJORIE HUNTER
Special to The New York Times

WASHINGTON, April 4 — Congress moves tomorrow into what could be the single most important week of the session, with action scheduled on medical care for the aged and aid to the nation's schools.

Seldom have two such major bills come up for floor action in a single week. Both are being pushed vigorously by President Johnson.

The $1.3 billion school-aid bill, already passed by the House, is expected to reach the Senate floor on Wednesday and could become law before the end of the week.

The House is expected to begin debate Wednesday on a bill to provide medical care for the aged and increases in Social Security benefits.

Waiting in the wings, once the Senate completes action on the school bill, will be the Administration's voting-rights legislation.

A Friday Deadline

The Senate Judiciary Committee faces a Friday deadline for reporting the voting-rights bill to the floor. It is possible, but not likely, that Senate action on the school legislation will be completed in time for floor debate to begin Friday on voting rights.

Mike Mansfield of Montana, the Senate majority leader, said today that he thought the school bill "will take us at least through Friday, maybe even Saturday."

Senator Mansfield and other Democratic leaders hope to steer the school-aid bill through the Senate without change. This would avoid having to send the bill to conference to work out differences with the House.

The school bill cleared a Senate Education subcommittee Thursday in exactly the same form in which it passed the House. The full Senate Labor and Public Welfare Committee is scheduled to act Tuesday, in time for floor action Wednesday.

Long-Standing Battle

Its passage would mark the end of a series of Congressional battles, dating back many years, over providing Federal aid to the nation's elementary and secondary schools.

The money would go only to public schools, but there would be aid to parochial-school students in the form of library materials, textbooks and such special services as shared-time classes.

The bill would focus on largely impoverished neighborhoods. Supplementary educational centers, open to both adults and youths, also would be established.

While the Senate debates school aid, the House will be involved with another Congres-

Continued on Page 20, Column 4

The Car and Smog: A Growing Controversy

Auto Industry Says Evidence Does Not Warrant Controls

By DAVID R. JONES
Special to The New York Times

DETROIT, April 4—A little-noticed controversy involving the family car, which seems destined to have significant influence on the welfare and pocketbooks of millions of Americans in the years ahead, is raging throughout the nation.

The controversy centers on the question of how much the automobile contributes to the nation's air-pollution problem, in which the major metropolitan areas, such as Los Angeles, face the prospect of eventually choking on their own exhaust.

What should be done to control the gases vehicles spew into the air? The question is pitting the automobile industry against Federal, state and local authorities.

This debate over automotive air pollution will be in the spotlight this week as the Senate Public Works Committee's subcommittee on air and water pollution begins three days of hearings Tuesday in Washington. Senator Edmund S. Muskie,

Continued on Page 27, Column 1

Smog enveloping a section of downtown Los Angeles. Motor vehicle exhaust is said to be a major contributing factor to the condition, but industry sources question this theory.

BRANDT IS HALTED BY EAST GERMANS ON ROAD TO BERLIN

Mayor Forced to Fly to City as Harassment Continues —Reds to Bar Deputies

By PHILIP SHABECOFF
Special to The New York Times

BONN, April 4—Mayor Willy Brandt of West Berlin was barred by the East German police from traveling on the autobahn to his own city today.

The Mayor's car was turned back at a control point near the town of Lauenburg, 174 miles from Berlin, as the Communist regime stepped up its harassing tactics in reprisal for a scheduled meeting of the Bundestag in West Berlin Wednesday. The Bundestag is the lower house of the West German Parliament.

Tonight the East German Government announced that Bundestag Deputies and "other persons" who planned to take part in the meeting would be barred from the land corridors to West Berlin.

The announcement, made by the East German press agency A.D.N., made no mention of barring air traffic.

Mayor Assails 'Impudence'

Mayor Brandt said the East German officials had acted with "boundless impudence" in turning him back at the border. It was the first time a governing Mayor of West Berlin had been prevented from passing through East Germany to the city.

The Mayor had been returning from the northern city of Lübeck in West Germany, where he visited his mother, who is ill. Later in the day he arrived in Berlin from Hamburg by plane.

[The Allied commandants in Berlin formally protested Monday on the action against Mr. Brandt, Reuters said.]

Mayor Brandt was not the only motorist left fuming by the East German tactics. At the Helmstedt-Marienborn control point farther south, hundreds of autos were kept waiting in a line stretching back two miles.

The Communist authorities saw to it that only 10 cars an hour passed into East German territory for the trip to Berlin.

Baggage Is Inspected

Waiting time to get through the Helmstedt check point exceeded three hours. The East German guards forced motorists to get out of their cars and open their baggage for inspection. At one point last night the waiting time was about seven hours.

The East German Government has acknowledged that its harassment techniques on the Berlin autobahns are a direct reprisal for the scheduled Bundestag meeting. East Germany contends that West Berlin is not a part of West Germany and that the Bundestag has no right to assemble there.

The East German authorities had indicated before the weekend that they would not permit members of the West German Parliament to drive through their territory. Last Thursday the wife and secretary of a Deputy were denied passage on the autobahn.

The West German Parliament last held an official assembly in Berlin in 1958. This year, after repeated urging by West German officials, the Western

Continued on Page 4, Column 4

HANOI MIG'S DOWN 2 AMERICAN JETS IN FIRST AIR CLASH

The New York Times April 5, 1965

MIG jets downed two U.S. planes near Thanhhoa (1) during a raid on bridges. Another target was a span just south of Donghoi (2).

U.S. RAIDS 4 SITES

Red Planes Appear During a Bombing Attack on Bridge

By JACK LANGGUTH
Special to The New York Times

SAIGON, South Vietnam, Monday, April 5—North Vietnamese MIG fighter planes shot down two United States Air Force jets that were taking part in a bombing attack on a bridge yesterday.

The MIG's appeared during one of four attacks by planes of the United States Air Force and Navy and the South Vietnamese Air Force on bridges and roads in North Vietnam.

The assault by the MIG's marked the first clash between Communist and American planes in Vietnam.

The drowned body of one American pilot was later found at sea. Search operations were continuing for the second American flier, military sources said.

One Vietnamese A-1H Skyraider, piloted by an American, was downed by fire from a Communist vessel. The pilot has been given up as dead. Other aircraft were known to have been destroyed by ground fire, but details were withheld while the search continued.

F-105's Are Faster

The supersonic jet interceptor aircraft that accompanied the American bombers did not appear in time to head off the four MIG-15 and MIG-17 jets that downed the two American F-105 fighter-bombers. The F-105 is about twice as fast as the old MIG's.

Maj. Gen. Joseph H. Moore, commander of the Second Air Division, said United States planes had returned the fire of the MIG's, which he said bore North Vietnamese markings. But he added, "We didn't knock down any."

The general said the attacks by the MIG's were "not unexpected." He added, "We have felt that at some point they would feel bold enough to try out their aim."

An American mission spokesman said, however: "We have obviously entered a new phase."

Asked why the American jet bombers, with their greater

Continued on Page 15, Column 1

Wagner Urges New Talks To Avert Strike on Papers

By DAMON STETSON

Mayor Wagner urged the printers and publishers last night to continue to make "every conceivable effort" to settle their dispute and avoid a strike that might affect seven of the city's daily newspapers.

The Mayor made his plea after receiving a report from Theodore W. Kheel, his labor adviser who has been attempting to mediate the controversy.

The possibility of a strike, starting as early as today, arose when negotiations collapsed at 3 A.M. yesterday after more than 12 hours of bargaining on economic issues. These issues have been the major block to a settlement.

Mayor Is Notified

After the talks broke up, Bertram A. Powers, president of New York Typographical Union No. 6, said he had notified the Mayor through Mr. Kheel that he had been unable to reach agreement with the publishers. This notification, he said, fulfilled the union's promise to give at least 24 hours' notice before calling a strike and left the printers free to strike after 3 A.M. today.

Mr. Powers emphasized last night that the union was reserving the right to strike any time after that hour.

"It could be tomorrow [Monday], Tuesday or Wednesday," he said. "A time and a day will be set. We may or may not give advance notice."

Mr. Powers said he saw no purpose in further meetings with the publishers.

"We've now met 30 times and we have not been able to resolve the situation," he said. "We are prepared to strike at

Continued on Page 24, Column 3

HUGHES PROPOSES JERSEY RAIL PLAN

$5.8 Million, 16-Month Trial Seeks More Revenue and Riders for the Lines

By WALTER H. WAGGONER
Special to The New York Times

TRENTON, April 4 — Gov. Richard J. Hughes made public today a plan for preserving and improving commuter service of the Erie-Lackawanna Railroad and other rail lines in the state.

The plan would first establish a $5.8 million, 16-month Demonstration Project for putting in effect recommended schedule and service changes designed to attract passengers and increase revenues for the Erie-Lackawanna.

Beyond that, it would utilize a $50 million fund, half state and half Federal, for a two-year capital improvement program to reduce the operating costs of both the Erie-Lackawanna and other passenger lines in the state.

The plan is set forth in a comprehensive 75-page study of the state's railroad problems by State Highway Commissioner Dwight R. G. Palmer, whose department has a Division of Railroad Transportation.

The objectives of the plan, Mr. Palmer said, are two-fold:

1. "Preserve and improve essential rail passenger service" while ending the present year-to-year subsidy program.

2. "Preserve the railroads themselves, and strengthen their ability to operate in a competitive atmosphere, so that

Continued on Page 26, Column 3

U.S. AND INDONESIA BACK AMITY MOVE

Sukarno and Bunker Agree to Try to Ease Irritants —No Real Gain Seen

By NEIL SHEEHAN
Special to The New York Times

JAKARTA, Indonesia, April 4— President Sukarno and Ellsworth Bunker agreed today that the United States and Indonesia should try to minimize some of the irritants that have resulted in a grave deterioration in their relations.

Mr. Bunker, a former ambassador who is here as a special envoy of President Johnson, met with the Indonesian President and Dr. Subandrio, the Foreign Minister, for two hours and 45 minutes at the Merdeka (Freedom) Presidential Palace.

It was Mr. Bunker's second meeting with Mr. Sukarno since his arrival last Wednesday.

Sides Agree 'to Disagree'

Dr. Subandrio said after the meeting that the talks had brought "an agreement to disagree" on specific issues, but that this "should not mar the relationship between both sides."

"Even if we cannot reach an agreement on all specific issues," he said, "then at least we should minimize irritations on both sides."

Despite the optimistic tone of these statements, diplomats did not believe the Bunker-Sukarno talks would lead to any real improvement in relations.

It was felt that differences between the two countries were so great that they could not be

Continued on Page 11, Column 1

Guantanamo Plant Helping Base End Reliance on Cuba

By HANSON W. BALDWIN
Special to The New York Times

UNITED STATES NAVAL BASE, Guantánamo Bay, Cuba, April 4—The largest plant in the world that both produces electric power and removes the salt from sea water will be formally turned over to the United States Navy in a few days.

The ceremony will mark a definitive milestone in making the United States naval base here completely independent of Fidel Castro's Cuba.

The base now generates all its own electricity and processes all its fresh water from the sea. The Cuban "commuters" working on the base, who once numbered thousands, have been reduced to 861.

Jamaican laborers under 120-day contracts have been imported to replace the Cubans. All food and other supplies — much of them once bought in Cuba — now come to the base by ship or plane.

Likened to a U.S. City

Rear Adm. John D. Bulkeley, the base commander, has likened the base to a small American city of 8,300 people. But unlike most American cities, the 45-square-mile enclave is virtually self-contained.

The $10 million desalting and generating plant was constructed in record time by the Westinghouse Electric Corporation and the Burns & Roe Construction Corporation.

The base was formerly supplied with water by pipelines from the Yateras River, five miles outside the naval reservation. The United States Government paid Cuba about $14,000 a month for about two million gallons a day used at the base.

The Yateras River lines were closed and then cut by the removal of a section of pipe on Feb. 17, 1964. This action by Mr. Castro caused the construction of the desalting plant and the other measures that have

Continued on Page 8, Column 3

U.S. SAYS BOMBING CUT VITAL ROUTES

Stresses Effect of Attacks on Bridges Linking North Vietnam With South

By TAD SZULC
Special to The New York Times

WASHINGTON, April 4—The Defense Department announced today that United States air strikes in the last two days had made "impassable" three bridges that were "vital links in the North Vietnamese transportation system supporting Communist guerrilla operations in South Vietnam and Laos."

A department statement said that "the vital importance of these bridges to the North Vietnamese was indicated by the heavy antiaircraft defense and the fact that the MIG interceptor aircraft were employed for the first time."

The statement, which acknowledged that six United States aircraft were lost in the attacks between Friday and last night, said two Air Force fighter planes "were shot down in a hit-and-run attack by Communist MIG aircraft."

The MIG's, which first appeared during the early Saturday strikes, came back to attack the United States planes in the second attack on the Thamhhoa railroad-and-highway bridge over the Ma River.

The 540 foot-long, two-span, steel and concrete bridge is 76 miles south of Hanoi, the North Vietnamese capital, and is one of the farthest points of penetration in the North by United States aircraft in the now daily raids.

Officials observed that the MIG's appeared only in this area, close to Hanoi, though the weekend strikes ranged along the North Vietnam coast from the Ma River, about 65 miles south of Hanoi, to as far south as a bridge on a coastal highway near Donghoi, just above the 17th Parallel, the dividing

Continued on Page 14, Column 4

PANEL TO STUDY TRADE WITH REDS

Johnson Picks 12-Man Unit on Expansion Possibilities

Special to The New York Times

WASHINGTON, April 4—President Johnson named today a 12-man special Presidential committee to study the possibilities and implications of expanding United States trade with Eastern Europe and the Soviet Union.

The panel, composed of outstanding business and industrial leaders, educators and foreign policy specialists, is headed by J. Irwin Miller, board chairman of the Cummins Engine Company, Inc., of Columbus, Ind., and a member of the executive committee of the World Council of Churches.

It includes a representative of organized labor, which on occasion has expressed doubts about expanding trade with Communist nations. He is Nathaniel Goldfinger, director of research for the American Federation of Labor and Congress of Industrial Organizations.

The White House announcement said that "on completion of its investigations, the committee will report its findings and recommendations to the President."

In his State of the Union

Continued on Page 18, Column 4

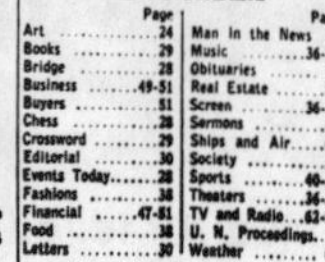

NEWS INDEX

Integration of Harlem by 1975 Is Aim of Area Planning Group

A neighborhood planning group is drawing up guidelines to transform Harlem into a quality, integrated community in 10 years.

District Planning Board No. 10, an advisory body on Central Harlem to the Borough President's office, which is in charge of the project, is gathering information on the problems and needs of the area and possible solutions.

The study covers all of Harlem and small parts of adjoining communities—from 110th to 165th Street and from the Hudson to the East and Harlem Rivers. Most of the area's 500,000 residents are Negroes and Puerto Ricans.

Among the proposals already suggested are the transformation of 125th Street into a new commercial area, the establishment of a community college, new transportation facilities to bring commercial and commuter traffic into Harlem, and the construction of a television center.

To further integration, the shifting of large blocs of Negroes and Puerto Ricans both within the area under study and to outside communities has been suggested.

Undertaken with the cooperation of Columbia University, the study is intended to provide for "a substantially integrated Harlem based on excellence by 1975," according to George Gregory Jr., chairman of the planning board.

Mr. Gregory, a tall, lanky Negro who is a City Civil Service Commissioner, explained in a recent interview that his group hoped to avoid the pit-

Continued on Page 22, Column 4

A Prince Can't Drop In at a Pub, Philip Notes With Some Regret

By The Associated Press

LONDON, April 4—Prince Philip said today his role as husband of Queen Elizabeth II prevented him from indulging in small pleasures like visiting a pub or catching a movie.

"These are things that I miss, but on the other hand I've got a lot of advantages which compensate for it," Philip told a British radio audience.

The Prince was on an unrehearsed question-and-answer radio show with a panel of four young people. The British Broadcasting Corporation taped the program a few days ago and put it on the air today.

Philip was asked what he would like to do but could not because of his position.

"There are a lot of things," Philip replied: "Just being able to walk into a cinema or go out to a nightclub or go to a pub, or something like that.

"I can do it, but it isn't always particularly enjoyable because if you're recognized, the atmosphere changes and people nudge each other and conversation stops and somebody asks you for your autograph or something."

"Do you ever wish you could go off to a desert island, or do you feel that you're better when you're under tremendous pressure?" Susan Bucknell, a student at Oxford University, asked.

"No, I think the essence of the exercise is to vary it, you know, if you can," Philip replied.

He said his travels abroad brought Britain to the minds of other peoples. "It makes them realize that we're still living in the same world," he said.

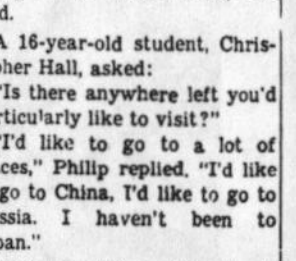

A 16-year-old student, Christopher Hall, asked:

"Is there anywhere left you'd particularly like to visit?"

"I'd like to go to a lot of places," Philip replied. "I'd like to go to China, I'd like to go to Russia. I haven't been to Japan."

Vivienne Barton, 18, who is training to be a reporter on a Brighton newspaper, asked: "Does the decision lie solely with you? If you want to go to China next week, can you do it?"

"No, not really," Philip replied, "because as you can imagine people would say it would — it would attract a certain amount of political attention

Continued on Page 4, Column 5

Associated Press Cablephoto

HIGHWAY INCIDENT: Mayor Willy Brandt of West Berlin with West German customs officers at Lauenburg. Later, East Germans forbade him to continue to Berlin on autobahn.

Pianist Vladimir Horowitz performed his first public concert in 12 years at Carnegie Hall on May 9 and received cheering ovations.

Dame Margot Fonteyn and the famous Russian defector, Rudolph Nureyev, shown amidst bouquets of flowers in the Metropolitan Opera House. Their performance of Romeo and Juliet was followed by 33 curtain calls.

Although he had no history of heart trouble, Adlai Ewing Stevenson fell dead suddenly while walking in the sun on a London street. Two days before his death he had told Eric Sevareid of CBS he was thinking of retiring from public life.

Ralph Nader, one of the first consumer advocates, published *Unsafe at Any Speed*, declaring GM cars as deathtraps. The book influenced a large task force of volunteers, which demonstrated the abuse of large industries and bureaucracies.

Senator Robert Kennedy climbed a 13,900 ft. peak in the Yukon in honor of his brother's memory.

Stan Laurel, the sad part of comedy team Laurel and Hardy died of a heart attack in California.

"All the News That's Fit to Print"

The New York Times.

LATE CITY EDITION
U. S. Weather Bureau Report (Page 60) forecasts:
Sunny and cool today, tomorrow.
Fair and cool tonight.
Temp. range: 66—52; yesterday: 70—52.

VOL. CXIV..No. 39,213. | NEW YORK, FRIDAY, JUNE 4, 1965. | TEN CENTS

AMERICAN FLOATS IN SPACE FOR 20 MINUTES AS HE AND PARTNER START 4 DAYS IN ORBIT; FUEL SHORTAGE BARS BOOSTER RENDEZVOUS

ASSEMBLY PASSES A TOTAL REVISION OF THE PENAL LAW

Homosexual Acts Remain as Crimes Under Amendment —Adultery Issue Open

By JOHN SIBLEY
Special to The New York Times

ALBANY, June 3—The Assembly voted approval today of a complete revision of the Penal Law, which lawyers agree has become a bewildering morass since its last major overhaul in 1881.

After intricate parliamentary maneuvering, however, the Assembly left uncertain the outcome of the most controversial issues in today's debate: whether adultery and homosexuality should be treated as matters of law or of morality.

As put forward by a special commission that worked four years to redraft the law, neither adultery nor homosexual acts between consenting adults would be treated as crimes.

From both sides of the aisle today there were applause and lavish praise for the commission chairman, Republican Assemblyman Richard J. Bartlett of Glens Falls. Though there was criticism of specific provisions of the proposed new law, virtually every speaker credited the Bartlett Commission with a brilliant job of tightening and clarifying the penal law as well as bringing it into conformity with current judicial and social thinking.

Churchmen's Fears Cited

From the beginning, there was no doubt that the commission's version would be overwhelmingly approved. After its adoption, the House turned to two bills that would retain adultery and homosexuality in the criminal law.

These measures were introduced by Assemblyman Julius Volker, an Erie County Republican who is a member of the Bartlett Commission. Mr. Volker said his bills were "inspired by the entreaties of churchmen who fear we would be appearing to give passive approval to deviant sexual practices."

The Volker amendment to retain homosexual acts as crimes was passed by a vote of 115 to 16.

Then the Assembly voted, 73

Continued on Page 20, Column 5

SENATORS TIGHTEN STATE ETHICS CODE

But Reject Assembly's Plan for Stricter Control

By RONALD SULLIVAN
Special to The New York Times

ALBANY, June 3 — The Senate voted overwhelmingly late today to strengthen the legislative code of ethics after engaging in the longest and one of the most vigorous debates of the session.

The bill, which was passed 47 to 9, made these changes in and additions to the existing ethics code:

¶Legislators who are lawyers are prohibited from representing clients in actions against the state in the Court of Claims for a fee.

¶Former legislators are forbidden to become lobbyists until they have been out of office at least two years.

¶Former state commissioners and their deputies are barred from appearing before their former agencies on a contingency-fee basis for two years after their resignations.

¶Legislators are required not only to disclose their direct or indirect financial interests in state-regulated companies, but also to identify the companies involved.

Approval of the bill followed the rejection by a close vote of a highly controversial amendment that would have restricted legislators' appearances before state agencies for a fee. This

Continued on Page 20, Column 2

President Asks Quarters And Dimes Without Silver

Half Dollar Content Would Be Reduced —Shortage of Silver Underlies Request for Greater Use of Nickel and Copper

By EDWIN L. DALE Jr.
Special to The New York Times

WASHINGTON, June 3—President Johnson asked Congress today to approve the first major change in United States coinage since 1792.

The change would eliminate silver from dimes and quarters and sharply reduce it in half dollars. The penny and the nickel, neither of which contains silver, would be unchanged.

The sole reason for the change is a growing world shortage of silver.

The first of the new coins, almost certainly dimes, are expected to go into circulation early next year. Quarters would be next.

If Congress approves, as expected, the new dime and quarter would become the world's first "sandwich" coins, with a cupro-nickel exterior and a copper interior. They would be of the same size and design as at present, but they would weigh slightly less than the present coins. Their surface would look and feel like that of the present nickel and their edges would reveal their copper interior.

The text of Johnson's message will be found on Page 18.

Suited to Coin Devices

Of major importance, the new coins would work in the nation's 12 million coin-operated devices, ranging from vending machines to pay telephones. Modification of the machines to adapt to alternate choices for coinage would have cost at least $100 million and would have put machines out of action for many months.

The new half dollar would also be a sandwich coin, but its appearance would be almost the same as at present. Its outside would be a silver-copper alloy with a high silver content and its inside an alloy with a low silver content, making an overall silver content of 40 per cent, compared with 90 per cent at present.

The half dollar has a low priority in production plans. There is already an acute shortage of the half dollar, but it is far less essential to commerce than are dimes and quarters. The new half dollars, when they eventually appear, will continue to bear the likeness of President Kennedy. The new

Continued on Page 18, Column 7

RATE OF JOBLESS LOWEST SINCE '57

Unemployment in May Down to 4.6 Per Cent—Total at Work Rose 1.3 Million

By JOHN D. POMFRET
Special to The New York Times

WASHINGTON, June 3 — President Johnson announced today that the nation's unemployment rate fell in May to 4.6 per cent, the lowest level since October, 1957, when the rate was 4.5 per cent.

The President reported that unemployment fell between April and May by 220,000, to 3.3 million. The decline, he said, was about triple the seasonal drop expected.

Employment rose by 1.3 million, to 72.4 million, in May. The gain was about 200,000 more than the seasonal expectation.

The drop in unemployment and the rise in employment combined to reduce the jobless rate from the 4.9 per cent level of April.

51st Month of Growth

The President announced the figures at a White House meeting of businessmen active in his program for promoting summer jobs for teen-agers. He made the announcement about an hour and a half before the regular announcement of the figures by the Bureau of Labor Statistics.

The President said that May was the 51st month of the longest peacetime economic expansion in the nation's history.

Since the start of the expansion in February, 1961, he said, unemployment declined by 1.4 million and the unemployment rate dropped from 6.9 to 4.6 per cent. Every worker group showed a marked improvement during the 51-month period except teen-agers, he said.

The President announced that the number of long-term unemployed—those out of work for 15 or more weeks—dropped

Continued on Page 22, Column 2

Johnson Asks Peace In Plea to Russians

By ROBERT B. SEMPLE Jr.
Special to The New York Times

CHICAGO, June 3—President Johnson issued an unusually strong and direct appeal to the people of the Soviet Union tonight to seek new initiatives for world peace.

"There is no American interest," the President declared, "in conflict with the Soviet people anywhere."

He made the appeal in a speech at a Jefferson-Jackson Day dinner sponsored by the Cook County Democratic organization. At the same time he announced that he had ordered the withdrawal of all the remaining United States marines in the Dominican Republic.

The $100-a-plate dinner, attended by approximately 5,000 people, was held in McCormick

Continued on Page 3, Column 5

SOVIET BOMBERS SEEN NEAR HANOI

Russian-Built IL-28 Jets Observed, Pentagon Says

By JACK RAYMOND
Special to The New York Times

WASHINGTON, June 3 — The Defense Department announced today that a "small number" of Soviet jet bombers of an old type had been sighted near Hanoi, the capital of North Vietnam.

The announcement follows reports that six or eight Ilyushin-28 twin-jet bombers had been seen in North Vietnam, but that there was no indication whether they were being flown by Soviet pilots.

The Pentagon's confirmation was made in a brief sentence: "A small number of IL-28 type aircraft have been observed on the ground in the Hanoi area."

A Pentagon source declared that estimates of the number of such planes might change from day to day, presumably as a result of aerial reconnaissance.

The same source also emphasized that the IL-28 warplanes were of comparatively old design and not highly regarded as a military threat, although their range made them capable of use against South Vietnam.

The IL-28 was first tested in 1947. It was used by North Korean and Chinese Communist pilots in the Korean war.

The planes have a range of 1,500 miles. With extra tanks

Continued on Page 3, Column 4

NASA via United Press International Telephoto

TWO MEN FOR SPACE: Maj. James A. McDivitt, commander of the Gemini 4 flight, precedes Maj. Edward H. White 2d to elevator that will take them to top of erector holding capsule. They carry portable air-conditioners.

VIETCONG AMBUSH BATTALION TWICE

Most of 300 Believed Lost in Attacks Near Pleiku—U. S. Marines Balk Foe

By JACK LANGGUTH
Special to The New York Times

SAIGON, South Vietnam, June 3—Two ambushes by the Vietcong 50 miles southeast of Pleiku wiped out another South Vietnamese Army battalion today. The setback raised Government losses in ambushes to 1,000 men during the last week.

[United States marines defending the Danang Air Base repulsed a sharp Vietcong attack early Friday against key bridges near the base, Reuters reported. Page 3.]

Final casualty reports from the two ambush sites in Phou-bon have not yet been received. But all but about 80 of the 300-man battalion were said to be dead or missing.

The senior American adviser to the battalion, slightly wounded by enemy fire, called for a helicopter to lift him and two American enlisted men out of the trap.

A United States military spokesman noted that the American officer had been "charged with the safety of his men." When their lives were threatened, he said, "of course it was proper for him to call for evacuation."

Smaller Attacks Made

Smaller Vietcong ambushes in Kontum and Darlac Provinces cost the Government at least 50 more men.

A high-ranking United States officer in Pleiku described the situation as "very serious" and said the American advisers in the II Army Corps had requested more troops.

"The VC are coming out of the bloody hills," the officer said. "We're barely holding our own."

The force of the Vietcong units has caused so[illegible] in the American mission to question official intelligence estimates of Communist strength.

United States military intelligence now lists 64,200 "main force" or full-time professional enemy soldiers, plus 80,000 to 100,000 part-time guerrillas.

Of the "main force" troops, 46,600 men are considered to be field soldiers and 17,600 to be officials in province and district commands and control officials.

These figures represent an increase in the main force's

Continued on Page 3, Column 2

NASA via Associated Press Wirephoto

IN PLACE FOR FLIGHT: Major McDivitt, left, and Major White wait in their seats for technicians to make final adjustments. Exit in space was made through door, right.

Banter in Space: A Textual Account

Excerpts from the conversations of Maj. James A. McDivitt, Maj. Edward H. White 2d, Maj. Virgil I. Grissom, mission control communicator, and ground control crews as gathered by The Associated Press, United Press International and The New York Times:

MAJOR McDIVITT—I am turning around to watch the second stage booster. The second stage looks pretty. It is tumbling about 400 to 500 feet away.

GUAYMAS STATION (in Mexico)—Guaymas, Gemini 4.

MAJOR McDIVITT—Roger, Guaymas. We still have the booster. We're out quite a ways from it now. It's taken a little more fuel than we'd anticipated. We appear right now to be about holding our own with it. Of course we should start to close with it, but it's out farther than we'd hoped to let it get right now.

GUAYMAS STATION — Roger, I copy.

MAJOR McDIVITT—Guaymas, this is Gemini 4. We're going to have to get resolution right away on whether we really make a major effort to close the thing or to save the fuel.

GUAYMAS STATION—I think we should save the fuel.

MAJOR McDIVITT — I guess we've probably expended about 100 feet per second.

GUAYMAS STATION — You've expended 100 feet per second?

MAJOR McDIVITT — I don't think it is worth it.

HOUSTON TO GUAYMAS —You might tell him as far as we're concerned, we want to save the fuel. We're concerned about the lifeline more than we are catching that booster.

GUAYMAS STATION — Gemini 4, Flight advises they'd like to save the fuel. You'll be advised over the Cape.

MAJOR McDIVITT — I just can't wait until I get to the Cape. I guess we're just going to have to watch it go away.

GUAYMAS STATION — Forget it.

HOUSTON—Okay, I guess we'll scrub it.

MAJOR McDIVITT (as the spacecraft neared the East African Coast and as Major White began preparing his equipment to leave the capsule)—It is a bit crowded in here, Gus.

MAJOR GRISSOM—You bet . . . Hey, Jim, you don't have to go upside down unless you want to. Whatever is best for you.

MAJOR McDIVITT—We're running late on the flight plan. . . . We'll wait until next pass around. I don't think we want to try it [floating in space] this time.

GROUND CONTROL—Roger, Gemini 4, we're happy with that.

MAJOR McDIVITT—We just couldn't try that.

GROUND CONTROL—We understand.

MAJOR McDIVITT (an hour and a half later)—It's go.

GROUND CONTROL — We're ready for him to go out whenever he is.

HAWAII STATION — We think he said, "I'm getting out."

MAJOR McDIVITT (to Major White, who is now out of the capsule)—Tell us what you think.

MAJOR WHITE—The maneuvering unit is good. The only problem I have is that I haven't got enough fuel. I've exhausted the fuel now and I was able to maneuver myself down to the bottom of the spacecraft and I was right up on top of the adapter, Jim, and came back into view. The only thing I am . . . over my head and I'm looking right down and it looks like we're coming up on the coast of California. And I'm going in slow rotation to the right. There is absolutely no disorientation association.

MAJOR McDIVITT—One

Continued on Page 14, Column 6

JOKES IN THE VOID

Talk of 2 Astronauts Is Heard by Millions on Radio and TV

By WALTER SULLIVAN
Special to The New York Times

CAPE KENNEDY, Friday, June 4—For 20 minutes yesterday afternoon Maj. Edward H. White 2d of the Air Force was a human satellite of the earth as he floated across North America from the Pacific to the Atlantic.

Tethered to the Gemini 4 spacecraft, he chatted good-humoredly and snapped pictures as he darted about in raw space with the aid of a gas-firing jet gun. Asked how he was doing by Maj. James A. McDivitt of the Air Force, the spaceship commander, Major White replied to his partner in the capsule:

"I'm doing great. This is fun."

When he was told to re-enter the capsule, Major White laughed and said: "I'm not coming in." But later, after more banter, he followed through on orders to return.

Both in 'Great Shape'

At 3 A.M., Eastern daylight time, the spaceship was in its 11th orbit and the astronauts reported that they were in "real great shape." They spent the night taking turns napping and checking radiation levels both in the spacecraft and on its outside surface. The space control center at Houston cut off voice contact with them for more than an hour at a time in order not to disturb them.

Major White's floating venture came after earlier difficulties had forced cancellation of the plan for two close approaches by the spacecraft to the final stage of the rocket that had placed the capsule in orbit.

Attempts to draw near to the rocket during the first orbit had expended roughly half the fuel allocated to such maneuvering. It appeared that the reason for this high fuel consumption would not be known until after analysis of the flight records following the four-day mission.

The mastery of rendezvous techniques is the central goal of the Gemini program, since such operations are essential for landing men on the moon and bringing them home again.

62 Orbits Scheduled

If the two-man vehicle flies its 62 scheduled orbits it should come down about 10 A.M. Monday.

Unlike the Soviet cosmonaut, Lieut. Col. Aleksei A. Leonov, who ventured outside his spaceship in March, Major White apparently suffered no disorientation. During his period in space he pushed himself to various sides of the Gemini craft with his jet gun.

The vehicle's radio circuit was open so that his colleagues on earth could hear the talk between him and Major McDivitt.

Major McDivitt, operating a camera from inside the vehicle, called to his free-floating companion outside:

"Get out in front where I can see you again!"

Major White explained that he could see the California coast. Then he came close enough to brush the ship commander's window.

"You smeared up my windshield, you dirty dog!" called Major McDivitt. His voice traveled by wire to the helmet of his floating companion over the 25-foot tether and also to earth by radio.

The launching from Cape Kennedy had been delayed an hour and a quarter by an electrical failure in the "overspeed regulator" of the erector. The erector is a 130-ton tower,

Continued on Page 14, Column 1

NEWS INDEX

"All the News That's Fit to Print"

The New York Times.

LATE CITY EDITION

U. S. Weather Bureau Report (Page 70) forecasts: Cool with a few showers today and tonight; clearing tomorrow.

Temp. Range: 70—54; yesterday: 73—53. Temp.-Hum. Index: mid-60's; yesterday: 66.

VOL. CXIV..No. 39,227. © 1965 by The New York Times Company. Times Square, New York, N. Y. 10036 NEW YORK, FRIDAY, JUNE 18, 1965. TEN CENTS

27 HEAVY BOMBERS FROM GUAM HIT VIETCONG FORCE IN SOUTH VIETNAM; WILSON WILL LEAD PEACE MISSION

United Press International Radiophoto

DESCRIBES CLASH: Comdr. Louis C. Page, right, relates details of duel over North Vietnam. With him are, from left: Lieut. Comdr. Robert C. Doremus; Lieut. Jack E. Batson Jr., his radar operator, and Lieut. John C. Smith Jr., radarman for Commander Page.

2 B-52'S ARE LOST

Missiles of Navy Jets Down 2 MIG-17's Close to Hanoi

By JOHN W. FINNEY

Special to The New York Times

WASHINGTON, June 17—Twenty-seven B-52's based on Guam carried out today—early Friday in Vietnam—the first attack by these heavy bombers in the war in Vietnam, the Defense Department announced tonight.

Thirty planes started out on the raid against a Vietcong concentration north of Bencat in Binhduong province, 30 miles north of Saigon. One B-52 went down about 100 miles northwest of Luzon Island in the Philippines after a collision with another B-52.

There was radio silence during the flight, and the fall of the second plane was not observed, so its fate was not known. But it was missing and was believed to have fallen into the sea.

One survivor from the first plane was rescued and others were sighted, the Pentagon said. The B-52's usually have crews of six men.

A third plane reached the target area but because of mechanical difficulties was unable to release its bomb load.

First Combat Use

The attack by the big, jet-powered bombers was the first mass bombing raid in Vietnam on World War II tactics. The action also marked the first use of the planes in combat.

[The Pentagon reported early Friday that the two B-52's that had collided on the way to Vietnam crashed; 27 of the bombers returned to the Guam base, and the plane that had mechanical trouble was diverted to Clark Air Base in the Philippines, The Associated Press said.

[Over North Vietnam, United States Navy jet fighters, using air-to-air missiles, downed two Communist MIG-17 fighters 40 miles south of Hanoi. Page 2.]

There was no immediate information on the effectiveness of the B-52 attack, which was carried out at the request of the Vietnamese Government.

In the bombing raids in Vietnam up to now, the United States has used tactical

Continued on Page 2, Column 5

JOHNSON REPORTS DEFICIT REDUCED TO $3.8 BILLION

Figure Is $2.5 Billion Less Than January Estimate—Tax Cut Impact Cited

JOBLESS AREAS FEWER

President, at News Parley, Discloses Reclassification of 16 Manpower Centers

Transcript of news conference is on Pages 14 and 15.

By JOHN D. POMFRET

Special to The New York Times

WASHINGTON, June 17—President Johnson said today that the Federal budget deficit for the year ending June 30 would be about $3.8 billion, or $2.5 billion less than his estimate of last January.

The announcement was the third since April of a drop in the estimated deficit. It came at a rapid-fire 80-minute news conference in the President's White House office. [Opening statement, Page 14.]

Mr. Johnson commented on a wide variety of foreign and domestic issues, told some favorite stories and jokingly accused reporters crowded around his desk of stirring up trouble for him by writing that no one was opposing him.

Employment Gain

He also announced these further developments on the economic front:

¶The Labor Department has reclassified 16 major manpower centers to categories denoting lower unemployment. This reduced the number of major areas classified as having substantial unemployment to 22, the lowest figure since May of 1957 and 17 below the number thus classified a year ago.

¶A new report from the Budget Bureau shows that the Administration's program to cut the dollar drain of Government programs abroad has reduced the net balance-of-payments costs of these programs by 23 per cent, or $635 million, in the two years ending this June 30.

The President also congratulated Congress on passing the measure reducing excise taxes. He indicated that he would sign it soon.

Mr. Johnson said that the excise reductions would release about $1.75 billion in extra purchasing power into the economy during the rest of 1965 and another $1.75 billion next January.

The excise tax reduction, Mr. Johnson said, "will help maintain the steady growth of jobs

Continued on Page 15, Column 5

CONGRESS PASSES EXCISE TAX CUTS

Johnson Indicates He'll Sign $4.6 Billion Bill Quickly

Special to The New York Times

WASHINGTON, June 17—Congress approved today the final text of legislation for $4.6 billion in reductions on excise taxes on a wide variety of consumer goods.

Both the House and Senate acted by voice vote after brief discussions, sending the Administration-backed bill to the White House. President Johnson thus could sign it in time for shoppers to benefit this weekend.

The first big batch of cuts will take effect the day after the President signs the bill. He indicated at his news conference this afternoon that he would sign it quickly. [Opening statement, Page 14.]

If he signs tomorrow, about $1.75 billion annually in taxes on sales that occur after midnight tomorrow would be eliminated.

The bill, a compromise between versions passed June 2 by the House and two days ago by the Senate, provides for additional cuts of about $1.6 billion next Jan. 1, with other reductions scheduled for Jan. 1 in 1967, 1968 and 1969.

Under the bill, the reduction of the tax on passenger automobiles, which will fall from 10 per cent to 7 per cent, and the repeal of the 10 per cent levy on air-conditioners are

Continued on Page 32, Column 1

Goldwater Forms Group For Political Education

Asserts New Unit Will Not Be a 3d Party but Will Try to Guide Conservative Voters Away From Extremism

By TOM WICKER

Special to The New York Times

WASHINGTON, June 17—Barry M. Goldwater formally announced today a new "crusade of political education" designed to give the millions who supported him for President last year a "focus" for their political activities.

Mr. Goldwater insisted at a news conference here that the Free Society Association of which he will be honorary chairman, was not the nucleus of a new political party and that he would not participate in any such movement.

Sources close to him said that a major purpose of the new "educational organization" would be to channel conservative voters and political action into a more moderate and acceptable force than the John Birch Society or other right-wing groups.

"I wish to make it crystal clear," Mr. Goldwater said in a prepared statement, "that the Free Society Association will perform no organizational tasks—no precinct, district, or other political subdivision task. It will back no candidates nor raise any money other than that needed for its research and educational efforts."

Nevertheless, there were reports of some dismay at the Republican National Committee's headquarters and in some organizations such as the American Conservative Union. Their officials were said to regard the Free Society Association as a

Continued on Page 20, Column 1

Lindsay Urges Computers To Raise Police Efficiency

By RICHARD L. MADDEN

Representative John V. Lindsay proposed yesterday that the Police Department be "computerized" to increase its efficiency by as much as 20 per cent. "It is time we realized that the two-way radio is no longer the hottest innovation in law-enforcement circles," the Republican candidate for Mayor said.

To combat what he called "the crisis in crime," Mr. Lindsay said that the Police Department should employ, "on a top priority basis, the resources offered by planning and modern technology in communications and electronic data-processing systems."

Excerpts from Lindsay speech will be found on Page 21.

Second Police Proposal

Mr. Lindsay's proposal, called a major policy statement, was made in a luncheon speech to about 100 persons at a meeting of the Idlewild Lions Club in the International Arrivals Building at Kennedy International Airport.

It was the second of a series of Lindsay statements on law enforcement. On May 20 he proposed the addition of four civilians to the Police Department's board of three deputy commissioners for reviewing complaints of police brutality.

A spokesman for Police Commissioner Vincent L. Broderick said there would be no comment on Mr. Lindsay's latest proposals.

Talking with reporters after

Continued on Page 21, Column 6

MEDICARE REVISED TO HELP THE POOR

Senate Committee Rewrites Measure in Major Upset for the Administration

By JOHN D. MORRIS

Special to The New York Times

WASHINGTON, June 17—The Administration program of medical care for the aged was radically revamped by the Senate Finance Committee today to shift a greater share of the benefits to persons with low income.

The surprise action was a major upset for the Administration. If sustained by the Senate and House, it would have the effect of converting the program's basic concept from one of limited benefits for everyone over 65 years old to one of unrestricted benefits mainly to those in low-income brackets.

Patient Would Pay More

The committee adopted two fundamental amendments to the hospitalization and nursing-care provisions of the House-approved medicare bill. Both were sponsored by Russell B. Long of Louisiana, the Democratic whip, or assistant leader, of the Senate.

The first would remove all restrictions on the length of time a beneficiary could stay in a hospital or nursing home and on the number of home-nursing visits to which he would be entitled after discharge.

To offset the added cost to the Social Security insurance system, the second amendment would require the patient to pay a larger part of his hospital bill. The higher his income, the more he would have to pay.

The vote was 8 to 6 on the first amendment and 10 to 3

Continued on Page 18, Column 5

New Yorkers Face Record Realty Tax

By LAWRENCE O'KANE

The city's property owners can expect to pay a record basic tax of $4.54 for each $100 of assessed valuation next year.

The new basic tax, an increase of 13 cents above the current rate of $4.41, was indicated yesterday when figures for the taxable value of city property were released. In addition, property owners also will pay varying borough taxes.

William E. Boyland, president of the City Tax Commission, reported to Mayor Wagner that the total assessed value of taxable city property, beginning on July 1, would be $30,901,763,159.

This total is an increase of $1,149,023,050 above the 1964-65 figure. As usual, the total was less than the tentative estimate released in February, which was $31,377,694,465 this

Continued on Page 21, Column 7

LAWN SPRINKLING IS BARRED IN CITY; SUMMONSES DUE

350 Inspectors to Enforce Rules on Saving Water—The Problem Worsens

By WILLIAM E. FARRELL

The watering of lawns, gardens, tennis courts, sidewalks and other surfaces was banned entirely yesterday by the Department of Water Supply, Gas and Electricity as part of an intensified campaign to conserve the city's dwindling water supply.

In a directive superseding one issued on April 19, Commissioner Armand D'Angelo prohibited the use of city water in sprinklers and other lawn devices and barred the use of hoses for any purpose other than fighting fires, unless special permission is obtained from him.

The earlier directive permitted the watering of lawns and gardens on Saturdays from 6 to 9 A.M. and 8 to 11 P.M.

Ban Is Immediate

The new order takes effect at once. The department said studies had shown that 200 million gallons of water were used every Saturday on lawns and gardens.

Mr. D'Angelo declared that it was "absolutely necessary to impose this restriction" because "the storage in our reservoirs is dropping daily and the water supply is growing progressively worse."

The latest figures from the department show that the city's reservoirs contain 256.4 billion gallons, or 53.8 per cent of capacity. Last year at this time there were 412.9 billion gallons in storage, or 86.7 per cent of capacity.

The Commissioner also announced that beginning Monday 350 inspectors would no longer give warnings to those who "willfully waste water."

Summonses to Be Given

Instead, summonses will be issued calling for a fine of up to $50 or 30 days in jail or both. A spokesman for the department said that it was expected that the police would aid the inspectors in issuing the summonses.

Mr. D'Angelo was interviewed as he ate lunch at his desk in his office in the Municipal Building. He said many owners of the 50,000 private swimming pools in the city "have indicated their displeasure" at his order barring the filling of ponds. "We are now in the pools dropped below the reach of recirculating equipment."

"We're talking about hundreds of millions of gallons of water here," he said, explaining his reason for the order.

Continued on Page 36, Column 2

JOHNSON ACCUSES DOMINICAN REBELS

Charges Them With Seeking to Block Political Accord—Plan Expected Today

By RICHARD EDER

Special to The New York Times

WASHINGTON, June 17—President Johnson today accused the rebel side in the Dominican conflict of "flagrant violation" of the cease-fire that had been established in Santo Domingo.

Displaying considerable emotion, the President said at a news conference that elements on the rebel side had engaged in what appeared to be "premeditated" attacks on the inter-American peace-keeping force for the purpose of obstructing efforts toward a political settlement.

[In Santo Domingo it was expected that an inter-American peace plan calling for elections this year would be presented to both factions Friday. Page 10.]

As Mr. Johnson made his statement, the State Department moved to quell a report that had gathered considerable momentum among diplomatic circles here.

This report attributes to the

Continued on Page 10, Column 3

5 Commonwealth Nations To Seek Peace in Vietnam

By CLYDE H. FARNSWORTH

Special to The New York Times

LONDON, June 17—Leaders of the British Commonwealth decided today to take an initiative toward bringing the war in Vietnam to an end. Prime Minister Wilson of Britain and leaders of four other Commonwealth countries will visit the Governments principally concerned to try to lay the groundwork for a peace conference.

The mission will try to go to Peking and Hanoi as well as to Moscow, Washington and Saigon. There was no indication whether it would be received in Peking or Hanoi.

The Chinese Communists have rebuffed earlier initiatives toward a peace conference. In addition, Peking and Hanoi refused to give visas to former Foreign Secretary Patrick Gordon Walker, who undertook a peace mission on behalf of Britain earlier this year.

21 Nations at Conference

The decision to send the new mission was taken at the first day of the Commonwealth Prime Ministers' Conference in London, at which 21 countries, mostly in Asia and Africa, are represented. It was announced before President Johnson held a news conference at which the Vietnam issue was discussed.

The Prime Minister, as chairman of the Commonwealth conference, would head the mission. Those invited to participate are: President Kwame Nkrumah of Ghana, Prime Minister Sir Abubakar Tafawa Balewa of Nigeria, Prime Minister Eric E. Williams of Trinidad and Tobago, and Prime Minister Dudley Senanayake of Ceylon.

It was not yet clear whether all four would be able to accept. Mr. Senanayake is not at the conference, his country being represented by Minister of Justice A. F. Wijemanne.

The suggestion to send the mission came from Mr. Wilson, who opened the afternoon ses-

Continued on Page 3, Column 2

PRESIDENT SAYS HANOI BARS TALKS

Calls Reds Unresponsive—Reiterates Stand Against Dealing With Vietcong

By MAX FRANKEL

Special to The New York Times

WASHINGTON, June 17—President Johnson said today that North Vietnam had shown itself opposed to any kind of negotiations now and reiterated his stand against diplomatic dealings with the Vietcong in the south.

Expressing a strong wish to settle the war through discussions, the President said his Administration had found the Communist side wholly unresponsive. He predicted that its next move would be to try to force the United States to deal directly with the rebels.

He said that idea had been carefully studied here and rejected on the ground that negotiations were proper only with a recognized government. The Administration has condemned the hard core of the Vietcong as intruders from North Vietnam and therefore as mere agents of that country.

If the Vietcong have anything to offer or to negotiate, Mr. Johnson said at a news conference in his office, they would have no difficulty in finding a government with which to discuss it.

Mr. Johnson warmly endorsed

Continued on Page 2, Column 2

AILES RESIGNING AS HEAD OF ARMY

President Names Resor as Secretary's Successor

By MARJORIE HUNTER

Special to The New York Times

WASHINGTON, June 17—President Johnson announced today the resignation of Secretary of the Army Stephen Ailes and the choice of Stanley R. Resor as his successor.

Mr. Resor, a New York lawyer, has been Under Secretary of the Army since April 5 of this year. He is 47 years old.

Mr. Ailes is scheduled to testify tomorrow before a House Banking subcommittee that is investigating his connection with a concern that makes loans to servicemen.

The shift in the Army's top civilian post, effective July 1, was one of several personnel changes at the Pentagon and the White House announced today by the President at his news conference. [Opening statement, Page 14.]

Mr. Johnson disclosed the resignation of Kenneth E. BeLieu as Under Secretary of the Navy, effective July 1, and the choice of Robert H. B. Baldwin of New Jersey as his successor.

The President said that David E. McGiffert, now assistant to the Secretary of Defense for legislative matters, would replace Mr. Resor as Under Secretary of the Army.

The President also announced that two of his personal White House assistants, Horace Busby

Continued on Page 15, Column 2

Astronauts Leave Today for Goodwill Trip Abroad

Associated Press Wirephoto

President Johnson receives flag carried on Gemini 4 flight from Maj. James A. McDivitt, left, and Maj. Edward H. White 2d. Vice President Humphrey is at center. President Johnson cited astronauts and Charles W. Mathews, right, manager of Gemini program office.

By ROBERT B. SEMPLE Jr.

Special to The New York Times

WASHINGTON, June 17—President Johnson said tonight that he was sending the Gemini 4 astronauts on another trip at 4 A.M. tomorrow, starting with the Paris Air Show. The President's announcement, made in the presence of the pair, was a climax to their 12-hour triumphal orbit of Washington today. This began with ceremonies in the White House Rose Garden this morning and ended—after a sudden change in flight plans—in the guest rooms three flights up. Along the way, Maj. James A. McDivitt and Maj. Edward H. White 2d received medals from the President, applause from a crowd lining Pennsylvania Avenue and the unabashed praise of Congressmen and diplomats. Charles W. Mathews, the manager of

Continued on Page 18, Column 1

Colleges Face U.S. Aid Cutoff If They Permit Fraternity Bias

By WALLACE TURNER

Special to The New York Times

DENVER, June 17 — The terms of the Civil Rights Act of 1964 require individual colleges to make certain that fraternities do not discriminate on racial grounds, Francis Keppel, Commissioner of Education, declared today.

Under the legislation, Mr. Keppel could cut off all Federal funds to the colleges if they allowed the fraternities to continue discriminating.

His statement was in a letter to Senator Lee Metcalf, Democrat of Montana, who had asked about the situation involved in the suspension last April of the Sigma Chi chapter at Stanford University.

The suspension came in a letter from the national fraternity dated four days after a Negro student had accepted a bid to pledge the Stanford chapter.

The issue touches on the entire system of Federal grants to colleges and universities.

If Mr. Keppel found that a fraternity was practicing racial discrimination, he would then question the "assurances of compliance" filed by the schools under Title VI of the Civil Rights Act, which empowers Federal agencies to withhold funds from any recipients practicing discrimination. The

Continued on Page 24, Column 1

NEWS INDEX

Representatives of the *Women's Strike for Peace*, demonstrated across the street from the UN, demanding admission of Red China to the world organization.

After being treated brutally on their march to Selma, Martin Luther King's followers enjoyed protection on the road to Montgomery.

Among the increasing protests that were sweeping the nation, were the university "teach ins" protesting the Administration's policy in Vietnam.

"All the News That's Fit to Print"

The New York Times.

LATE CITY EDITION

U.S. Weather Bureau Report (Page 54) forecasts: Sunny and warm today; fair, mild tonight. Sunny, hot tomorrow.

Temp. Range: 85—67; yesterday: 87—73. Temp.-Hum. Index: low 70's; yesterday: 77.

VOL. CXIV..No. 39,255.

NEW YORK, FRIDAY, JULY 16, 1965.

TEN CENTS

FIRST MARS PHOTO IS TRANSMITTED; MARINER SIGNALS INDICATE PLANET LACKS A LIQUID CORE LIKE EARTH'S

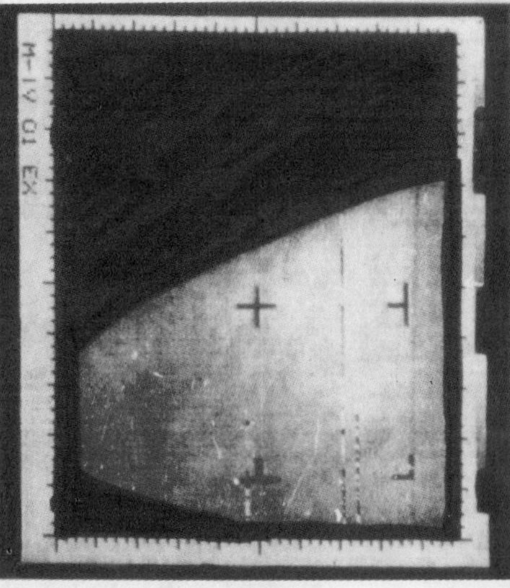

United Press International Telephoto

FIRST CLOSE-UP OF MARS: Photograph made by Mariner 4 of the planet and sent back to earth. The area covered along edge of planet is about 200 miles. Shot was taken at about 10,500 miles. It is expected to add greatly to scientists' knowledge of Mars.

HARRIMAN MEETS KOSYGIN IN SOVIET; TALK 'SIGNIFICANT'

Conference, Arranged After Moscow Rebuffs, Deals With Vietnam Issues

BID BY HANOI REPORTED

Nkrumah, Member of Peace Group, Said to Be Asked to Northern Capital

By PETER GROSE

Special to The New York Times

MOSCOW, July 15 — W. Averell Harriman, President Johnson's Ambassador at Large, conferred for more than three hours today with Premier Aleksei N. Kosygin in what Mr. Harriman called a "significant" discussion of Soviet-American relations.

Neither side was willing to disclose the precise subjects discussed. Vietnam figured as a major topic and reliable sources said Mr. Harriman had given a full explanation of the policy behind the continued bombing raids on North Vietnam.

[According to reports in London, President Kwame Nkrumah of Ghana, a member of the Commonwealth peace mission, has been invited to Hanoi. Page 3.]

Meeting a Hopeful Sign

The Kosygin-Harriman meeting seemed a hopeful sign in the relations between Moscow and Washington. This was the highest personal contact between a member of the Johnson Administration and the Soviet leadership since the overthrow of Nikita S. Khrushchev in Moscow last October.

Mr. Harriman indicated that the conference was not the end of his present activity in Moscow. "I have no other engagements yet," he said, "but I expect to see other officials before I leave."

The former Ambassador to the Soviet Union arrived Monday for what was called a private visit. Originally scheduled to remain five or six days, Mr. Harriman said tonight that he would stay through the middle of next week, possibly longer.

Americans Seen Relieved

Both Mr. Harriman and the United States Ambassador, Foy D. Kohler, seemed relieved that the meeting had been arranged.

When Mr. Harriman arrived, qualified Soviet officials insisted that discussions would not take place and said the diplomat would probably not even be officially received.

As late as last night, Mr. Harriman said he did not know whether his requests for meetings would be granted.

The most optimistic American diplomat predicted only that "courtesy calls" were probable. Instead, Mr. Harriman and the Soviet Premier sat in conference from 10 A.M. until 1:15 P.M.

At Mr. Kosygin's side was Mikhail N. Smirnovsky, head of the United States desk of the Soviet Foreign Ministry. With Mr. Harriman were Ambassador Kohler and Marshall Brement, an American political officer dealing with Chinese and Southeast Asian affairs.

Mr. Harriman's mission has not been disclosed. He has denied that he brought any specific message for the Soviet leaders from Washington.

The lengthy conference was the most significant between the United States and the So-

Continued on Page 3, Column 2

Johnson Policy Next Year Will Seek to Prolong Boom

Administration Commits Itself to Spur Economy by Tax Cut or New Spending —Course of Action Still Uncertain

By EDWIN L. DALE Jr.

Special to The New York Times

WASHINGTON, July 15—The Johnson Administration committed itself today to an expansionary economic policy again next year with the aim of keeping the record boom going indefinitely.

At the same time, President Johnson himself disclosed the prospect of a huge increase in expenditures in the next budget unless major new efforts at savings were successful.

The commitment to an expansionary policy came in two forms.

Gardner Ackley, chairman of the President's Council of Economic Advisers, told a luncheon meeting here that the Government had begun to prepare its next budget and economic program. He said:

"I can assure you that we have the means, and I believe the will, to adjust either or both sides of the budget, if that should be necessary, in a way which will contribute to the steady and adequate expansion of private purchasing power in the economy."

This was a reference to either cuts in taxes or increases in spending. Both have been used in the last four years. The result has been a purposeful, though relatively small, deficit in the budget.

The Administration message was also conveyed in remarks by authoritative White House sources. They said that the President was shaping his program with the aim of "expanding purchasing power in line with the nation's capacity to produce."

No choices have yet been made as to which course of expansionary policy to follow, other high Administration officials said. One major reason is

Continued on Page 6, Column 4

SENATE APPROVES HOUSING MEASURE WITH RENT SUBSIDY

Administration Forces Beat a Republican-Led Effort to Kill 'Renticare'

By MARJORIE HUNTER

Special to The New York Times

WASHINGTON, July 15 — Administration forces narrowly rescued a rent subsidy plan as a $7.3 billion housing bill passed the Senate tonight.

The bill now goes to conference for the reconciling of differences with a measure passed by the House two weeks ago. The differences are regarded as relatively minor.

The final House vote for passage was 54 to 30. Voting for the bill were 47 Democrats and seven Republicans; against it were 11 Democrats and 19 Republicans.

Republican-led efforts to kill the rent subsidy plan—called "renticare" by one critic—provided the only drama of two days of generally low-key debate.

A Seven-Vote Margin

The Republican move was defeated, 47 to 40, as Democratic leaders nervously tallied the votes. The rent subsidy plan had cleared the House two weeks ago by six votes.

Voting to retain rent subsidies were 13 Democrats and five Republicans—Jacob K. Javits of New York, Clifford P. Case of New Jersey, George Aiken of Vermont, Hugh Scott of Pennsylvania and Margaret Chase Smith of Maine.

Joining 26 Republicans in voting to kill rent subsidies were 16 Democrats, including such usually strong Administration supporters as Clinton P. Anderson of New Mexico, Albert Gore of Tennessee and Stuart Symington of Missouri.

A second Republican move to slash the four-year program from $50 million in new contracts each year to $10 million in each year also was defeated, 45 to 38.

Smaller Cut Approved

Minutes later, however, Administration leaders guided through a smaller cut of their own, reducing the program to $150 million over the four-year period.

An identical reduction in rent subsidy funds was made on the House floor two weeks ago, with Administration blessings.

Largely ignored in debate, both in the House and Senate, were a wide range of new and expanded housing and urban renewal programs provided under the bill.

The attention focused on rent subsidies, which Republican critics said "smacked of socialism."

Under the subsidy plan, a lower-income family would pay 25 per cent of its total income

Continued on Page 6, Column 6

M'NAMARA, LODGE ARRIVE IN VIETNAM

Will Survey Need for More G.I.'s—Vietcong Cut Off Unit Close to Saigon

Special to The New York Times

SAIGON, South Vietnam, Friday, July 16—Secretary of Defense Robert S. McNamara and Henry Cabot Lodge, who is taking over as Ambassador to South Vietnam, arrived today for a survey of the need for more American combat troops in Vietnam.

Mr. McNamara, accompanied by Gen. Earle G. Wheeler, Chairman of the Joint Chiefs of Staff, retiring Ambassador Maxwell D. Taylor, and Mr. Lodge, said at a news conference at Tansonhut Airport that he had not yet received any recommendations from the Joint Chiefs as to the size of the increase of American forces here.

It had been reported in Washington that the chiefs had unanimously recommended an increase to 179,000 men, a rise of more than 100,000 above the 75,000 troops now scheduled for Vietnam duty.

On the military front, the Saigon Government reported attacks in two regions.

Military headquarters in Saigon lost contact yesterday with a large force of Government troops that had come under heavy Vietcong attacks only 35 miles from the capital. In

Continued on Page 2, Column 2

C.A.B. to End Limit On Weight of Bags For Flights in U.S.

By FREDRIC C. APPEL

Domestic airline passengers will soon be allowed to carry free as much weight as they can get into two pieces of luggage, according to a change in regulations announced yesterday by the Civil Aeronautics Board.

Under the new regulations, which were proposed by American Airlines and are expected to go into effect within the next month, a passenger will be able to take with him two pieces of luggage, neither larger than 62 by 43 inches. It will make no difference what the luggage weighs.

This compares with the previous free luggage allowance of 40 pounds. A passenger will still be allowed to carry a small bag to his seat.

The board noted that the 40-pound limit was set in 1938 and was based on the space available in DC-3 aircraft, commonly used by the domestic air carriers at that time.

"With the introduction of jet aircraft," the board said, "weight is no longer the critical factor limiting aircraft capacity and the baggage allowance based on the 40-pound weight has since become obsolete."

One expected result of the change, the board said, will be to speed the check-in process at the air terminals, since most passengers' luggage will not have to be weighed.

"One of the important prob-

Continued on Page 54, Column 2

Stevenson's Body Is Flown to Capital

Associated Press Wirephoto

Mourners filing past catafalque of Adlai E. Stevenson in National Cathedral in Washington

By ROBERT B. SEMPLE Jr.

Special to The New York Times

WASHINGTON, July 15—Adlai E. Stevenson returned tonight to a nation that mourned him in death as deeply as it had admired him in life. The Presidential plane bearing his body touched down at 6:35 P.M. Eastern daylight time at Andrews Air Force Base, 15 miles from Washington. The body had been flown from London, where Mr. Stevenson collapsed and died of a heart attack yesterday at the age of 65 on a street 50 yards from the American Embassy. President Johnson led a delegation of Government dignitaries to meet the plane and pay homage to the man who had spent most of his life in the public service of his country, who was twice the Democratic candidate for President, and who, at his death, was serving as this country's representative to the United Nations. Afterwards, the coffin containing Mr. Stevenson's body was taken to the capital's National Cathedral, where it lay in repose in the cathedral's Bethlehem Chapel. Tonight, thousands of mourners — young and old, Democrats and Republicans, public officials and private citizens—filed by to pay their final respects. There was perhaps some irony in the fact that Mr. Stevenson had last appeared at the cathedral as the principal American spokesman at memorial services for

Continued on Page 8, Column 1

Jews See Russians On Forming Agency

By HENRY KAMM

Special to The New York Times

STRASBOURG, France, July 15—World Jewish leaders are holding quiet talks with Russian diplomats to bring about the formation of a central body to represent the Jews of the Soviet Union and to participate in international Jewish affairs.

While stressing that no definite results have yet been achieved, participants in the discussions declare themselves encouraged by the Russian willingness to talk and by indications that the issue is being discussed within the Soviet Government.

According to Dr. Nahum Goldmann, president of the World Jewish Congress, Russian

Continued on Page 4, Column 4

TRIAL OF MARTINIS ENDS IN HUNG JURY

Panel Reported 8 to 4 for an Acquittal—Prosecutor Asks September Retrial

By EDITH EVANS ASBURY

The jury that had been deliberating the fate of Gareth Martinis reached a "hopeless deadlock" yesterday and was discharged.

Jurors said afterward they had become deadlocked on a vote of 8 to 4 for acquittal.

"It is always regrettable when a jury is unable to reach a verdict," Supreme Court Justice Samuel J. Silverman told the jurors, "but that does not alter the fact that you have worked long and hard."

The 11 men and one woman had deliberated past midnight for two days, after listening to tstimony for four weeks in a small sweltering courtroom of the Bronx County Courthouse.

Divided From the Start

At the beginning of the deliberations at noon Tuesday, nearly half of the jury had been in favor of acquitting Mr. Martinis, it was learned from jurors afterward.

The vote shifted somewhat during deliberations. However, in the opinion of one juror, Bernard J. McGarry, "We were hung from the start, because one particular juror had his mind all made up less than one second after we got into the jury room."

Assistant District Attorney Andrew J. McCarthy, who had presented the prosecution's case, moved immediately to set

Continued on Page 11, Column 3

Marshall Regarded As Johnson Choice For Supreme Court

By JOHN D. POMFRET

Special to The New York Times

WASHINGTON, July 15—President Johnson wants to name Thurgood Marshall to be the first Negro on the Supreme Court, according to informed comment on the President's selection of Judge Marshall to be Solicitor General.

Mr. Johnson announced the selection at his news conference Tuesday. Yesterday he sent the nomination to the Senate for approval.

In agreeing to accept the new post, Judge Marshall is surrendering his lifetime position as a member of the United States Court of Appeals for the Second Circuit, in New York. He is also taking a pay cut from $30,000 to $28,500 a year.

Many in Washington believe that the main reason the President would ask Judge Marshall to make these sacrifices is to improve the judge's position as an eventual nominee to the Supreme Court.

President Johnson has not spelled this out to Judge Marshall, according to informed comment, but the judge's selection as Solicitor General points

Continued on Page 24, Column 4

M'KEON RESIGNING DEMOCRATIC POST

State Chairman Decides to Quit on July 27

By CLAYTON KNOWLES

William H. McKeon, a controversial figure for two of his three years as Democratic State Chairman, announced yesterday he would submit his resignation to the Democratic State Committee at a meeting called for July 27.

He said he had just reached a "private, personal decision" to step down, "after long and heavy reflection and consultation with many friends I have made over the years throughout this great state."

"This was a decision I made quite voluntarily," he asserted in recalling Democratic successes in 1964, when the state party gave the Johnson-Humphrey ticket a record plurality, elected a United States Senator for the first time in eight years and a Democratic Legislature for the first time in 30 years.

Nowhere in his statement was there any mention that Mayor Wagner called for his resignation on Jan. 16, contending that he had offered induce-

Continued on Page 9, Column 1

Sister of Lindsay Found Dead in Pool

By RICHARD L. MADDEN

Mrs. Cooper Schieffelin, the only sister of Representative John V. Lindsay, Republican-Liberal designee for Mayor, was found dead early yesterday in the swimming pool on her 11-acre estate in Laurel Hollow, L. I.

The Nassau County police listed the death of the 47-year-old Mrs. Schieffelin as an apparently accidental drowning.

Mr. Lindsay, who learned of his sister's death about 5 A.M., canceled all campaigning at least through tomorrow. He borrowed a car and drove to the Schieffelin home with his wife, two brothers and two of his sister's children, who had been working as volunteers in his

Continued on Page 9, Column 3

JAVITS IS PRESSED TO STOP GOVERNOR

Senator's Allies Seeking to Head Off Re-election Bid for Fear of Defeat

By RICHARD WITKIN

Close political allies of Senator Jacob K. Javits are convinced he has the power to end Governor Rockefeller's reign in Albany in 1966 and are urging him to use it.

They are confident that at the proper moment in the pre-election maneuvering early next year, Mr. Javits could persuade the Governor not to run again.

They want him to vow to fight the Governor, if necessary, at the nominating convention, reasoning that the threat of such a fight will convince the Governor to pull out if all other arguments fail.

Mr. Javits's allies say their main motive is to prevent possible Republican defeat in the state in 1966 by giving the gubernatorial nomination to Mr. Javits, whom they consider a much stronger candidate than Mr. Rockefeller. Mr. Javits is also widely believed to view the Governorship as a possible jumping off place for a Vice-Presidential nomination in 1968.

Best Vote-Getter

Mr. Javits's power is that of a man who has demonstrated that he is the Republicans' best vote-getter in the state. He outpolled Mr. Rockefeller by almost 200,000 votes in the 1962 election.

It is also the power of a man who has already drawn pledges from many upstate and suburban party leaders that they will back him in an oust-Rockefeller effort, even though many of these leaders are much more conservative ideologically than the Senator.

"It's a problem dealing with such a high-voltage politician as Rockefeller," one Javits supporter said. "But the Senator can handle it, if anyone can."

Rockefeller backers are making no secret of their concern over the anti-Rockefeller movement. They are convinced that the Governor's prestige is on the way back, particularly after what they regard as a success-

Continued on Page 11, Column 4

NEWS INDEX

OTHER DATA SENT

Sensors Find Scant Radiation Belt and Thin Atmosphere

By WALTER SULLIVAN

Special to The New York Times

PASADENA, July 15—Mariner 4 has sent to earth the first close-up photograph of Mars.

The picture, transmitted today in an eight-hour broadcast over a distance of 134 million miles, shows the "limb," or rounded edge of Mars, including a vast, desert-like region.

It does not show any of the controversial canals. But this is not necessarily significant, since the view is extremely oblique and covers a region under the noonday sun. Such lighting makes for little contrast.

The picture, the first ever taken of another planet at close range, covers a region between the areas of Mars known as Cebrenia, Arcadia and Amazonis

Part of the second picture, which should overlap the first, has already been transmitted to earth and it is possible that as many as 22 pictures of the planet will be delivered in the next 10 days.

Officials here at the Jet Propulsion Laboratory, which is in charge of the project for the National Aeronautics and Space Administration, were jubilant.

No Magnetic Field

Meanwhile, scientists associated with the project reported some of their initial findings. These include:

¶Mars has virtually no magnetic field and hence, presumably, no liquid core. This means the planet may differ fundamentally from earth in terrain and the chemical composition of its surface. The radioactivity of its air must be comparatively high, as well as the exposure of its surface to space radiation.

¶Mars has no significant radiation belt. This is good news for those planning the exploration of Mars. Vehicles will be able to orbit the planet for long periods without radiation hazard to their passengers or instruments.

¶The atmosphere of Mars is extremely thin—probably too much so for the use of parachutes or other conventional devices in the gentle landing of instruments and, ultimately, astronauts on its surface.

¶Mars, like the earth, has swept its orbit clear of much of the cosmic dust that would otherwise be adrift there. Since the orbit is elliptical, the distance of the planet from the sun varies from 128 to 155 million miles. It is this region that

Continued on Page 10, Column 1

POLICEMAN KILLS BROOKLYN NEGRO

CORE Disputes Police on Shooting of Ex-Convict

By HOMER BIGART

A Negro ex-convict was fatally shot by a rookie policeman in a fight yesterday at the busy intersection of Nostrand Avenue and Fulton Street in the Bedford-Stuyvesant section of Brooklyn.

At least 100 persons saw the battle, in which the policeman was shot in the arm.

Forty members of the Tactical Patrol Force were rushed to the scene to forestall any violence. The Congress of Racial Equality quickly demanded an investigation. The Kings County District Attorney urged the sprawling Negro community to remain calm and began interviewing some of those who had seen the shooting.

The police said the dead man had a record of 12 arrests and two felonious assault convictions, including a 1958 attack on a policeman.

The District Attorney, Aaron E. Koota, in his remarks ad-

Continued on Page 15, Column 2

"All the News That's Fit to Print"

The New York Times.

LATE CITY EDITION
U. S. Weather Bureau Report (Page 56) forecasts: Cloudy with showers today, tonight; sunny tomorrow.
Temp. Range: 78—67; yesterday: 83—62. Temp.-Hum. Index: 72—61; yesterday: 74.

VOL. CXIV..No. 39,268. NEW YORK, THURSDAY, JULY 29, 1965. TEN CENTS

JOHNSON ORDERS 50,000 MORE MEN TO VIETNAM AND DOUBLES DRAFT; AGAIN URGES U.N. TO SEEK PEACE

FORTAS TAKING GOLDBERG SEAT ON HIGH COURT

LIBERAL IS NAMED

Lawyer First Refused Post, Then Acceded to President's Plea

By ROBERT B. SEMPLE Jr.
Special to The New York Times

WASHINGTON, July 28—President Johnson today named his long-time friend Abe Fortas, the Washington lawyer, to succeed Arthur J. Goldberg on the Supreme Court.

Mr. Fortas's appointment, in the view of students of the Court, means that there probably will be no appreciable change in the liberal course charted by the Court since 1962, when Mr. Goldberg replaced Justice Felix Frankfurter.

It also keeps alive the tradition of a Jewish seat on the Court. Justice Louis D. Brandeis was appointed in 1916, and Justice Benjamin Cardozo was appointed in 1932. Justice Cardozo was succeeded by Justice Frankfurter, who was Mr. Goldberg's predecessor.

Mr. Goldberg resigned from the Court last week to become, at Mr. Johnson's request, the United States representative at the United Nations. There was immediate and widespread speculation that Mr. Fortas would be named to replace him, particularly in view of his close relationship with the President and his immense prestige in the legal profession.

First Choice for Post

However, officials here, including at least one Cabinet member and the President's press secretary, Bill D. Moyers, tried hard to dampen this speculation. Thus, until yesterday it was generally assumed that, despite the earlier rumors, Mr. Fortas had either withdrawn himself from consideration or had not been considered at all.

Today informed sources said that Mr. Fortas was not only the President's first choice, as Mr. Johnson disclosed at his news conference, but was also the only man to whom he had offered the job.

The President, in announcing his first appointment to the Supreme Court, said, "In this instance, the job has sought the man." [Opening statement, Page 12.]

Mr. Johnson made his first overture to Mr. Fortas Monday evening, July 19, the same night that he asked Mr. Goldberg to take the United Nations assignment. At that time the offer was conditional on Mr. Goldberg's taking his new post.

When Mr. Goldberg agreed to the President's request the

Continued on Page 13, Column 1

Associated Press Wirephoto
Abe Fortas as he appeared yesterday at White House.

HOUSE VOTES END OF UNION SHOP BAN

Acts, 221 to 203, to Repeal Part of Taft-Hartley Law —Labor Is Jubilant

By MARJORIE HUNTER
Special to The New York Times

WASHINGTON, July 28—The House handed organized labor its biggest victory in years by voting today to outlaw state "right to work" laws. The vote was 221 to 203.

The bill now goes to the Senate, where passage is expected.

The measure seeks repeal of Section 14(b) of the Taft-Hartley Act of 1947. Under this 44-word section, states are permitted to pass laws that forbid labor contracts making union membership a condition for keeping a job.

Nineteen states, most of them in the South and Midwest, now have such "right to work" laws.

The House action marked another in a long string of Administration victories. President Johnson had pledged he would seek repeal of 14(b) this year.

Forecast Off by One Vote

The final vote closely tallied with an informal count made months ago by union lobbyists. They said then that they could count on 222 votes for repeal—just one more than today's tally.

Voting for repeal were 200 Democrats and 21 Republicans. Voting against were 117 Republicans and 86 Democrats.

Labor leaders were jubilant at the outcome, for it was the first pro-labor legislation involving the internal affairs of unions to clear the House since World War II.

During that period, two major labor laws have been enacted over bitter protests of organized labor. The Taft-Hartley Act of 1947 created categories of unfair labor practices by unions for the first time. The Landrum-Griffin Act of 1959 imposed internal controls on union operations.

Amendments Rejected

Administration forces held firm against a barrage of amendments offered by Republicans and a lone Democrat, Representative Edith Green of Oregon.

The amendments were held as "not germane" by the presiding officer, Representative Leo W. O'Brien, Democrat of upstate New York.

Discovering that avenue closed, the House minority leader, Gerald R. Ford of Michigan, asked that the bill be sent back to the House Education and Labor Committee.

"This body today is precluded from working its will," he protested. "The people are not having their day in court."

The Ford motion for recommittal was defeated, 223 to 200.

"We're being paralyzed," rep-

Continued on Page 14, Column 6

U. S. RULE DEFIED BY JERSEY COURT

Weintraub Is Supported on Admitting Confessions

By SIDNEY E. ZION

The New Jersey Supreme Court, in a unanimous decision, has supported its Chief Justice's defiance of a Federal court ruling on confessions.

The decision upheld the murder convictions of two youths who had confessed without having been advised of their constitutional rights.

The ruling, which was handed down July 12 but which has not yet been published in official court reports, creates a Federal-state judicial conflict that will be appealed to the United States Supreme Court—the only court that can finally resolve the dispute.

The conflict arose May 20 when the United States Court of Appeals for the Third Circuit, covering New Jersey, Pennsylvania and Delaware, reversed two New Jersey murder convictions because the police had not advised the defendants, before taking their confessions, of their right to counsel and their right to remain silent.

Two weeks later, Chief Justice Joseph Weintraub of the New Jersey Supreme Court sent

Continued on Page 17, Column 1

NEWS INDEX

U.S. AIRLINES TOLD TO PUT PROSPERITY INTO LOWER FARES

C.A.B. Also Tells Carriers to Add Coach Seats and Allow Free Stopovers

By FREDRIC C. APPEL

The Civil Aeronautics Board told the nation's airlines yesterday that they were making too much money and should start passing some of it on to the consumer in the form of lower fares and better service.

The board said it thought the following improvements could be made:

¶Lower fares on short trips. The board noted that the new short-range jets now coming into use had lower operating costs that could make possible lower fares over routes such as that between New York and Washington.

¶More coach seats. The board suggested a higher ratio of coach seats to first-class seats to reflect the public's desire. Last year 76 per cent of domestic air passengers flew coach, according to the Air Transport Association. The board also called for more coach service into more communities.

¶More coach service to smaller cities. This suggestion was apparently a reaction to a hearing, ended two weeks ago, by the Senate Aviation subcommittee, in which the airlines were severely criticized for neglecting the less profitable service to smaller cities.

¶Additional economy services on highly traveled routes.

¶Free stopover privileges. With such privileges, a man flying from New York to Los Angeles might stop in Chicago for a few days at no extra cost.

The board, which abolished these privileges in 1958 when the airlines were having financial problems, said that now that the airlines' finances had improved, they should be revived as a method of stimulating vacation travel in the United States and from abroad.

No Reaction Yet

There has been no official reaction from the airlines yet, but one industry source privately predicted "a very strong" one.

Addressing itself to air fares, the board virtually told the airlines to forget about any increases and concentrate on reductions.

After first noting that the rate of return of the 11 domestic trunk carriers had risen to 10.6 per cent in the 12 months ended March 31, 1965, the board said:

"In this setting, the board believes it is difficult to find justification for fare increases. Rather, the C.A.B. feels, the present favorable earnings position of the airlines offers an excellent opportunity for carriers themselves to consider reductions in fares or improvements in service without fare

Continued on Page 56, Column 5

LETTER TO THANT

Goldberg Delivers It—U.S. Would Discuss Hanoi's 4 Points

Johnson's letter to U Thant is printed on Page 10.

By TOM WICKER
Special to The New York Times

WASHINGTON, July 28—The United States has asked the United Nations to employ its "resources, energy and immense prestige" in finding ways "to halt aggression and to bring peace in Vietnam," President Johnson said today.

The President conveyed this request to U Thant, the Secretary General of the United Nations, in a letter delivered by Arthur Goldberg, the new United States representative.

The letter contained Mr. Johnson's "hope that the members of the United Nations, individually and collectively, will use their influence to bring to the negotiating table all governments involved in an attempt to halt all aggression and evolve a peaceful solution."

The President described the action in a statement at his news conference. [Opening statement, Page 12.]

Opportunity Is Seized

High Government sources expressed no great confidence that the United Nations, acting as a body, could find a way to bring the Vietnamese question to the conference table.

They said, however, that the President wished to seize the opportunity of Mr. Goldberg's arrival at the United Nations to emphasize that the United States would welcome any possible initiatives and to give him a chance to work on the matter with strong backing from the White House.

In addition, the sources said, the possibility was not discounted that new emphasis on the United Nations might lead to "corridor talk" or informal meetings between delegates that would be useful in working toward negotiations.

For months Mr. Thant has been trying behind the scenes to initiate negotiations but has met with rebuffs from Hanoi and Peking.

Mr. Johnson emphasized again that the United States' objective in Vietnam still was a negotiated settlement, not the military defeat of North Vietnam. That settlement, he again made plain, could include elec-

Continued on Page 10, Column 1

Associated Press
PRESENTS CREDENTIALS AT U.N.: Arthur J. Goldberg, right, the new United States representative at the United Nations, with U Thant, the Secretary General.

NO RESERVE CALL

Additional Troops Will Be Sent as Needed, President Says

Transcript of news conference and summary, Page 12.

By JOHN D. POMFRET
Special to The New York Times

WASHINGTON, July 28—President Johnson announced today that United States military strength in South Vietnam would be increased from the present 75,000 men to 125,000 "almost immediately."

Draft calls, Mr. Johnson said, will be gradually raised to 35,000 men a month from the current rate of 17,000 and the campaign for voluntary enlistments will be stepped up.

However, the President said at a nationally televised news conference at the White House that he had concluded it was not necessary now to order reserve units into active duty. [Opening statement, Page 12.]

The purpose of Mr. Johnson's announcement was twofold: to disclose the military measures being taken in the Vietnam war and to emphasize the desire of the United States for negotiations on ending the conflict.

The President opened his statement by quoting a letter received recently from "a woman in the Midwest." She wrote that she had a son in Vietnam and that her husband had served in World War II, and she concluded: "Our country was at war, but now, this time, it is just something that I don't understand. Why."

He Tries to Meet Question

The President said he had tried to answer that question dozens of times. "Let me again now discuss it," he said, and continued with his statement.

Mr. Johnson announced that the United States was asking the United Nations to make a major effort to bring peace to Vietnam. He also said that the United States was prepared to discuss the peace proposals put forward by the Government of North Vietnam.

The 50,000-man increase in United States forces in Vietnam is considerably smaller than some Congressional and military sources had expected. It apparently does not involve military units beyond those already alerted for service in South Vietnam.

The President said that additional forces would be needed later and would be sent as requested. He did not specify how many more troops would be sent. Qualified sources said it was impossible to estimate the number because it would depend on the extent of the fighting.

The President said that he ordered the First Cavalry Division (Airmobile) to Vietnam today, as well as other forces. The Airmobile Division, which had been tentatively marked for Vietnam service, began

Continued on Page 11, Column 1

ECONOMIC IMPACT IS CALLED SLIGHT

Prosperity Cited by Johnson in Rejecting Declaration of National Emergency

By EDWIN L. DALE Jr.
Special to The New York Times

WASHINGTON, July 28—The moderate increase in the war effort in Vietnam announced today by President Johnson will impose no noticeable strain on the national economy, high economic officials said today.

In answer to a question on this point at his news conference, Mr. Johnson said he was certain the American people would face "whatever it is necessary to face." [Question 4, Page 12.] But he cited the current prosperity and added:

"I see no reason for declaring a national emergency and I rejected that course of action earlier today when I made my decision."

War Days Recalled

Mr. Johnson had been asked whether he believed the nation would face the choice of "guns or butter." The exchange brought to mind the days of World War II when rationing was in effect and some materials, such as butter, gasoline, food and clothing, were in short supply.

The economic impact of the Vietnam war so far has been minimal. Today's modest increases in defense spending and military manpower will leave it minimal, officials believe, though a few defense industries will be affected.

The extra effort is not expected to put any notable strain on the nation's supply of labor, its plant capacity for production or its budgetary resources, top officials said after the President's announcement.

Several measures of the relatively small impact of the expanded war effort were cited.

Revenues Are Growing

The increase of 17,000 in monthly draft calls compares with an expected growth of the labor force this year of 1,250,000. It also compares with a regular monthly turnover of about 115,000 workers in the nation's manufacturing industries alone and at least five times that for the economy as a whole. And it compares with a currently unemployed total of 3.5 million.

The prospective increase in defense spending is generally put in the range of $3 billion to $5 billion during the fiscal year that has just begun, and almost certainly no more than $5 billion. The Government's revenues, with no change in tax rates, now grow by $7 billion a year with an expanding economy, or more than enough to accommodate the defense increases.

The moderate rise in defense outlays will probably enlarge somewhat the prospective small

Continued on Page 13, Column 4

Most in Congress Relieved By the President's Course

By E. W. KENWORTHY
Special to The New York Times

WASHINGTON, July 28—Most members of Congress received President Johnson's statement on the Vietnam crisis today with a sense of relief. First, there was general satisfaction that the President had decided to increase the draft and postpone a decision on calling up reserve units. Second, there was approval of his avowal to seek an honorable resolution of the conflict through the United Nations.

These feelings were especially keen in those members who have circumspectly voiced doubts and reservations about the course of Administration policy since last February, when the President made the decision to bomb selected military installations in North Vietnam.

'Honorable Settlement'

Mike Mansfield of Montana, the Senate Democratic leader, spoke the sentiments of many of these members when he said the President had spoken in a "calm and deliberately measured manner" and was plainly desirous of "seeking an honorable settlement."

Even before Secretary of Defense Robert S. McNamara went to Saigon two weeks ago, there had been an expectation that the President would call up some Army and Marine Corps reserve units. This belief became firmer during the first days of intense review of military needs following the Secretary's return.

Consequently, it was widely believed on Capitol Hill today that the President had "backed off" this decision in the last few days.

Some of the leaders who attended one or both of the meetings with the President last night and this morning thought there were three reasons be-

Continued on Page 11, Column 2

HANOI PREPARES PEOPLE FOR WAR

Defense Minister Says U.S. May Invade North—Soviet Scores Johnson Speech

By SEYMOUR TOPPING
Special to The New York Times

SAIGON, South Vietnam, July 28—North Vietnam has begun to prepare its people for possible involvement in a full-scale war with the United States.

The Hanoi leadership, in its statements and in domestic propaganda, is demonstrating growing concern about the build-up of United States troop strength in South Vietnam. Gen. Vo Nguyen Giap, the Defense Minister, has warned that these troops might be used in an invasion of North Vietnam.

These North Vietnamese developments preceded President Johnson's announcement today that United States forces in Vietnam would be enlarged.

[The Moscow radio said President Johnson was taking a "colossal risk" in increasing American armed strength in Vietnam, The Associated Press reported. Page 9.]

No Big Expansion Noted

Apart from a decision taken by Hanoi in April to extend the tour of duty of conscripts indefinitely, no reports have been received here by United States officials of any rapid expansion of the North Vietnamese Army to meet a United States invasion. North Vietnamese men are normally drafted into the 250,000-man army for three-year terms and subsequently enrolled in the militia of 1.5 million.

A Youth Volunteer Brigade made up of men between 17 and 30 years old was founded on July 7 for defense duty. Detachments have been identified in connection with work on such projects as road-building, repair of bridges and other emergency tasks.

Since the systematic United States bombings of North Vietnam began on Feb. 19, Hanoi has been gradually mobilizing the population. Women have been organized to do the work of men called away for defense duty.

General Giap, writing in the current issue of Hoc Tap, the theoretical journal of the Lao Dong, or Communist, party, declared: "We need to make every preparation to defeat the United States aggressors in case

Continued on Page 9, Column 2

John Chancellor of N.B.C. Named Director of the Voice of America

Johnson Selects White House Reporter as First Working Newsman in the Post

By LLOYD GARRISON
Special to The New York Times

WASHINGTON, July 28—John W. Chancellor, White House correspondent for the National Broadcasting Company, was named by President Johnson today to head the Voice of America.

The 38-year-old reporter and broadcaster succeeds Henry Loomis, the long-time director of the Government's overseas radio, who resigned last March with a charge that the Voice was losing credibility because of an overdose of propaganda.

This controversy was discussed in connection with Mr. Chancellor's appointment. Reliable sources said that he and President Johnson had talked at length on the role of the Voice and that Mr. Chancellor would be free to emphasize the bad as well as the good in the treatment of United States affairs.

In a farewell address to Voice employes, Mr. Loomis contended that the Voice's reputation for objectivity was being undercut because the United States Information Agency, which has over-all responsibility for overseas broadcasts, was insisting

United Press International Telephoto
John W. Chancellor after his appointment yesterday.

that news commentaries reflect and reinforce Administration policies and de-emphasize dissenting opinion.

Carl T. Rowan, the head of U.S.I.A., countered that news reports of the Voice had the same "judicial balance" of the favorable and unfavorable "that a responsible newspaper gives."

Mr. Rowan later resigned as U.S.I.A. director and on July 13 Mr. Johnson named Leonard H. Marks, a Washington communications lawyer, to succeed him.

In announcing Mr. Chancel-

Continued on Page 18, Column 6

City Faces 'Order' To Meter Water

By HOMER BIGART
Special to The New York Times

PHILADELPHIA, July 28—New York City may be forced to adopt universal metering as a condition of its further use of Delaware River water.

The Delaware River Basin Commission accepted today a report by its advisory committee recommending that universal metering be "ordered" by the commission throughout the basin and its service area.

That report, according to one committee member, was designed to prod Mayor Wagner into an early decision to impose metering on New Yorkers regardless of political consequences.

The Mayor has been reluctant to sponsor universal metering. At present New York compels water meters only for business, which accounts for

Continued on Page 37, Column 1

White Youth Is Shot Near Georgia Rally

By GENE ROBERTS
Special to The New York Times

AMERICUS, Ga., Thursday, July 29—A white teen-ager was shot in the head from a car early today three blocks from a night-long civil rights protest rally in the rain.

Police officers and witnesses said that a Negro was the assailant.

The shooting took place near a street corner where only an hour before a group of about 20 white youths had been yelling "nigger, nigger," and hurling stones and bottles at passing Negroes.

Wounded in the shooting was Andy Whatley, 19 years old, a projectionist at an Americus drive-in theater.

Dr. R. A. Collins, an Americus surgeon, called his condition "critical—very bad," and transferred him to an Albany hospital, 40 miles away. Dr. Collins

Continued on Page 15, Column 2

The famous musical quartet, the Beatles, in a scene from *Help!*

Omar Sharif and Julie Christie in *Dr. Zhivago.*

Julie Andrews shown inspiring the youngsters in a scene from *The Sound of Music.*

"All the News That's Fit to Print"

The New York Times.

LATE CITY EDITION
U.S. Weather Bureau Report (Page 46) forecasts: Sunny, hot, humid today, fair tonight. Partly cloudy and hot tomorrow.
Temp. Range: 92—70; yesterday: 82—64.
Temp.-Hum. Index: near 80; yesterday: 77.

VOL. CXIV...No. 39,277.

NEW YORK, SATURDAY, AUGUST 7, 1965.

TEN CENTS

JOHNSON SIGNS VOTING RIGHTS BILL, ORDERS IMMEDIATE ENFORCEMENT; 4 SUITS WILL CHALLENGE POLL TAX

United Press International Telephoto

IN THE ROTUNDA: President Johnson speaks at Capitol before signing Voting Rights Act. To left are daughter Luci Baines, Vice President Humphrey and members of Congress. "Surrender of Cornwallis" by John Trumbull is on wall.

VIETCONG APPEAL TO NORTH VIETNAM FOR MEN AND AID

Political Front of Guerrillas Urges Open Assistance to Intensify the War

PEACE TERMS RESTATED

Insurgents Bar Negotiation Unless They Participate With 'Decisive Voice'

Text of Vietcong statement will be found on Page 2.

By The Associated Press

TOKYO, Saturday, Aug. 7 -- The political front of the Vietcong guerrillas in South Vietnam has asked North Vietnam for active assistance against United States forces in the South and for preparations to send men into battle, the Hanoi radio reported today.

Hanoi, which has said it would send volunteers if asked, quoted a Vietcong statement as having said that the guerrillas wanted help "to increase our forces and step up the resistance of the war 10 times more vigorously."

The significance of the statement, and its timing, immediately aroused speculation. United States officials report that the Vietcong guerrillas have suffered heavy losses recently, raising a possibility that the insurgents are experiencing a shortage of men.

Bargaining Move Considered

It also seemed possible that the statement was part of a preparation for Hanoi itself to take new action, or for bargaining should there be some sort of new approach to the conference table.

The statement was issued by the Vietcong Tuesday but was not broadcast until last night by the Vietcong radio, the Hanoi broadcast said.

[The Hanoi announcement coincided with a new statement from Moscow saying that the United States decision to send 50,000 more troops was an attempt to "break the will of the people of Vietnam." It said the United States leaders "should have no delusions that American aggression would go unpunished." Page 3.]

Up to now, Communist North Vietnam has disclaimed a direct involvement in the war, although United States officials say that units of the North's regular army have been identified in the South and that there has been a steady infiltration.

A month ago, the National Liberation Front for South Vietnam, the Vietcong's political organization, noted that the

Continued on Page 2, Column 2

Associated Press Wirephoto

CONFER ON ASIA: Alex Quaison-Sackey, Foreign Minister of Ghana, hands a letter from President Kwame Nkrumah to President Johnson in White House. Mr. Quaison-Sackey said message should promote peace in Vietnam.

Nkrumah Note on Vietnam Is Delivered to President

By RICHARD EDER
Special to The New York Times

WASHINGTON, Aug. 6 — President Johnson saw Ghana's Foreign Minister, Alex Quaison-Sackey, for 15 minutes today—long enough to receive a letter from President Kwame Nkrumah and to assure Mr. Quaison-Sackey that the Ghanaian President would be safe from United States bombs if he decided to visit Hanoi.

There was nothing in the White House reports or in the reactions of other officials to indicate that Mr. Nkrumah's letter—which reflected recent conversations of a Ghanaian diplomat with Hanoi officials—had opened the way for negotiations in Vietnam.

[Arthur J. Goldberg, United States representative to the United Nations, discussed the Vietnam situation with delegates of the six elected members of the Security Council. Page 3. Saigon said that former Premier Nguyen Khanh, who has been in the United States, was being ousted as roving Ambassador and called home for investigation. Page 2.]

Nkrumah Reply Likely Soon

According to one official source, the Nkrumah letter did not refer to the matter of negotiations with Hanoi. The source described it as a general appeal for peace, with no clear indication of any willingness on the part of Hanoi to take any new steps.

A White House spokesman indicated that the contents of Mr. Nkrumah's letter would be divulged once Mr. Quaison-Sackey had returned to Ghana with President Johnson's answer. He said that the reply would be made promptly.

The spokesman, Bill D. Moyers, said that the brief conversation between the Ghanaian Foreign Minister and President Johnson did not take up the question of negotiations with Hanoi. Mr. Moyers described

Continued on Page 2, Column 6

VIETCONG'S LOSSES IN JULY SET HIGH

U.S. Says More Than 3,000 Guerrillas Were Killed — Communist Attacks Drop

By JACK LANGGUTH
Special to The New York Times

SAIGON, South Vietnam, Aug. 6—The United States command reported today that more than 3,000 Vietcong were killed in July, the highest number of casualties the Communist guerrillas have yet lost in a month.

The figure of 3,050 represented only bodies counted on the ground, a spokesman said.

Vietnamese and American pilots and forward air controllers, who fly light observation planes, estimated that 8,000 Vietcong were killed in July, but that figure was discounted.

However, by including half the pilots' total and by estimating the number of Vietcong wounded during the month at 6,000, the United States command calculated that the Communists lost the equivalent of a full division, almost 15,000 men, during July.

Number of Battles Drops

In the same period, the Government losses were 3,850. Of these, 1,335 were killed, 1,765 were wounded and 750 were missing.

The most significant figure of the month might have been the number of battles waged by the Vietcong. There were 54 battles in May. The number rose to 80 in June and dropped back to 46 attacks in July. The Government has always been able to point to more favorable statistics in the periods that the Vietcong are not active, when they are regrouping and retraining after a series of sustained and successful offensives.

Defectors from the Vietcong during the month totaled 4,130, including 775 Government soldiers who had previously gone over to the Vietcong, the spokesman said.

The heaviest recent ground action has centered on the Ducco Special Forces camp, 30 miles southwest of Pleiku. The Communists have been battering the small installation.

The United States spokesman said that the Vietcong had been tenacious in their attempt to take the post. He speculated that they wanted control of nearby Route 19, an important road in the Central Highlands.

In the heavy fighting between the Communist forces and Vietnamese airborne units that have gone into the area as a relief

Continued on Page 2, Column 7

ENGINEER WARNS CITY CAN RUN OUT OF WATER IN 1966

Commission Told of Danger in Measures to Protect Philadelphia Supply

By McCANDLISH PHILLIPS
Special to The New York Times

PHILADELPHIA, Aug. 6 — New York City told the Delaware River Basin Commission today that the city could "run out of water by the middle of February, 1966," if adverse conditions continued.

Demands now being placed upon the city's diminishing water supplies constitute what is "actually not safe operation," Edward J. Clark, the city's chief water engineer, declared at a special emergency meeting of the commission here today.

But Mr. Clark acknowledged that for the city to come within the margin of safe operation, it would have to take actions that would endanger the water supplies of Philadelphia and Camden.

Holding Back Salt Water

Sea water driven by tides is threatening to invade a Philadelphia water intake on the river that supplies half this city.

A Philadelphia water official said that some industries would have to shut down if too much salt were washed into the city's supply.

New York City has been releasing about 200 million gallons of stored water a day into the Delaware from two of its reservoirs. This has kept the flow of fresh water strong enough to hold back the salt advance.

New York spokesmen also said that, at the present rate of use, the city's Delaware River basin reservoirs—Neversink and Pepacton—will be empty on Nov. 25.

Armand D'Angelo, New York's Commissioner of Water Supply, received the thanks of the commission for measures that have reduced daily water consumption by 20 per cent. The city is using about 1 billion gallons of water a day, and somewhat more on the hottest days.

Meets the Commission

Mr. D'Angelo introduced Mr. Clark to the commission, which met on the top floor of Philadelphia's new Municipal Services Building opposite City Hall. Mr. Clark, a man with a ruddy and friendly countenance under brush-cut white hair, said:

"Should water supply conditions not improve in the next 30 days, it will then be disastrous for New York City to make further releases from storage."

Afterward, Mr. Clark remarked, "We're leaning over backward. We're gambling in the interest of Philadelphia."

He saw the possibility of a water disaster for New York City—if the drought continues, if present rates of discharge from the reservoirs continue, and if a cold winter prevents snow and ice from melting before spring thaws, thereby preventing early runoffs into the reservoirs.

The city has been taking 335

Continued on Page 24, Column 2

NEW VOTING LAW ATTACKED IN SUIT

Brooklyn Couple Say Wider Puerto Rican Franchise 'Dilutes' Others' Rights

By BEN A. FRANKLIN
Special to The New York Times

WASHINGTON, Aug. 6—The constitutionality of the new voting rights law was challenged here today by a Brooklyn couple who complained that the new statute "dilutes" their voting power by permitting Puerto Ricans who cannot read or write English to vote.

The Federal law invalidates the state's English-language literacy test.

The suit plainly had political implications in New York City, which will elect a Mayor on Nov. 2. Puerto Ricans constitute a major voting bloc in the city.

Alfred Avins, a lawyer, filed the complaint in the name of John P. and Christine Morgan, whom he identified only as "citizen objectors" from Brooklyn. He declined to disclose the "principal party" behind the suit. But he said it was "obvious that Mr. and Mrs. Morgan do not have the wherewithal to hire a lawyer and send him to Washington."

In an interview, Mr. Avins, a professor of law at Memphis State University in Tennessee, who practices in New York during the summer, described the challenged section of the voting law as "Bobby Kennedy's personal contribution."

New York State's two United States Senators, Robert F. Ken-

Continued on Page 9, Column 2

Americus Names Negroes To Jobs as Polling Clerks

By GENE ROBERTS
Special to The New York Times

AMERICUS, Ga., Aug. 6—County officials named three Negro voting clerks in a surprise move today and registered more than 300 Negro voters.

Benjamin V. Clarke, field secretary for the Southern Christian Leadership Conference, called the appointments a "major step" toward ending a 17-day series of civil rights demonstrations here. The appointments were announced by Joe Daniels, chairman of the County Board of Registrars.

He declined to give reasons for the sudden appointment of Mrs. Dorothy Bozeman, Mrs. Gwendolyn Pace and Mrs. Thelma Walker as deputy clerks.

However, some white leaders here said privately that the new Federal voting law was a major factor, as was "the desire to get this thing [the city's racial crisis] over."

March on Courthouse

After the registration office opened here at 10 A.M., 37 Negroes and 27 white supporters marched to the Sumter County Courthouse. Nearly half crowded into the corridors to wait their turn at the registration office. Civil rights workers went out to round up other Negroes during the morning to register.

At 1:30 P.M., the registrars temporarily suspended registration tests until they could determine whether the new voting law, signed by President Johnson today, voided Georgia literacy tests. Before the suspension, 97 Negroes were registered.

When the registrars learned that the new law would not take effect until its publication next week they began registration again, using a test.

The exact number of Negroes registered was not certain. A total of 351 persons, a few of them white, applied today and

Continued on Page 9, Column 1

U.S. VOTING AIDES DEPART FOR SOUTH

They Will Start to Register Negroes Next Week in 'Hard Core' Counties

By JOHN HERBERS
Special to The New York Times

WASHINGTON, Aug. 6—About 45 Federal examiners, carrying bundles of registration forms, were dispatched to the South today to begin registering Negroes under the new Voting Rights Act.

The examiners, all Southern employes of the Civil Service Commission, will move Monday or Tuesday into the counties where they will be assigned by the Justice Department.

In signing the law today, President Johnson said:

"I have requested the Department of Justice to work all through this weekend so that on Monday morning they can designate many counties where past experience clearly shows that Federal action is necessary and required. And by Tuesday morning, trained Federal examiners will be at work registering eligible men and women in 10 to 15 counties."

Work in Teams of Two

The examiners have completed a three-day training session at Civil Service Commission headquarters. Although the counties where they will work were not immediately designated, it was learned that they were prepared to go to work in "hard core" sections of Louisiana, Mississippi, Alabama, Georgia and South Carolina.

Apparently no examiners will be used immediately in Virginia and North Carolina, parts of which are covered by the new law.

The examiners will work in teams, two to a county, in offices rented in the county seats by the Civil Service Commission. Their offices will be open six days a week to anyone who believes he has been denied the right to register with the local voting registrar.

John W. Macy Jr., chairman of the Civil Service Commission, said that 75 commission employes, all volunteers, were trained this week as examiners. Those who left for the South today were employes in the Atlanta and Dallas regions.

They have been serving as personnel officers, investigators, supervisors and clerks in the states where they will be

Continued on Page 8, Column 7

CAPITOL IS SCENE

Room in Which Lincoln Freed Some Slaves in 1861 Is Used

Text of Johnson's speech is printed on Page 8.

By E. W. KENWORTHY
Special to The New York Times

WASHINGTON, Aug. 6 — President Johnson signed today the Voting Rights Act of 1965 and announced steps to bring about its quick and vigorous enforcement.

Tomorrow, he said, the Justice Department will officially certify the states where discrimination exists under the definition of the act.

On Monday morning, the President continued, the Justice Department will designate the counties in those states "where past experience" had shown that Federal action was needed to register Negroes.

On Tuesday, he said, Federal examiners will begin registering Negroes "in 10 to 15 counties."

Poll Tax Challenged

The President also announced that tomorrow at 1 P.M., Attorney General Nicholas deB. Katzenbach would file suit challenging the poll tax of the state of Mississippi on the ground that it is used to abridge the right of Negroes to vote in violation of the 15th Amendment to the Constitution.

Next Tuesday, the President went on, additional suits will be filed against the three other states — Alabama, Texas and Virginia—that require payment of a poll tax as a prerequisite to voting in state and local elections.

The signing took place in the President's Room of the Capitol, just off the Senate chamber. There, 104 years ago today, President Lincoln signed a bill freeing slaves impressed into the service of the Confederacy.

Will Act Quickly

Gathered in the small, ornate room, dominated by a great gilt chandelier, were Vice President Humphrey, the Cabinet, Congressional leaders, members of the Senate and House Judiciary Committees who had refined and strengthened the bill, and Negro and white leaders of the civil rights movement.

Earlier, in the Rotunda of the Capitol, the President said that Congress had acted swiftly in passing the bill and that he intended to act "with equal dispatch" in enforcing it.

In his speech, which was broadcast and televised nationally, the President compressed into three sentences the history, the meaning and the hope of the occasion. He said:

"Today is a triumph for free-dom as huge as any victory won on any battlefield.

"Today we strike away the last major shackle of those fierce and ancient bonds.

"Today the Negro story and

Continued on Page 8, Column 1

INDIA WILL RATION GRAIN IN CITIES

Sets a 12-Ounce Daily Limit to Counter Shortages

By J. ANTHONY LUKAS
Special to The New York Times

NEW DELHI, Aug. 6—India decided today to impose food rationing on her city dwellers.

In a major move to meet the country's chronic food shortage, the Government will limit men, women and children in urban areas to 12 ounces of wheat or rice a day.

Twelve ounces of wheat will make six chappatis, the large slabs of unleavened bread that are the staple of the North Indian diet.

In South India, where rice is the staple, 12 ounces covered with boiled vegetables, curd or curry will provide about two meals.

The national average consumption of food grains is now about 14.4 ounces a day, according to Government statistics.

The rationing system, which is expected to begin in about two weeks, will put city dwellers under more controls than at any time since World War II, when nationwide rationing was in effect.

Initially, the new rationing will affect only the eight cities with more than a million residents and certain highly industrialized areas.

However, it will eventually

Continued on Page 23, Column 1

NEWS INDEX

East River Pier Urged as Site for U.N. School

City Is Said to Favor Use of Dock at 25th Street

By KATHLEEN TELTSCH
Special to The New York Times

UNITED NATIONS, N. Y., Aug. 6—City officials proposed today that the United Nations International School be erected on a platform to be built 550 feet into the East River.

The site is at Pier 73, where former Soviet Premier Nikita S. Khrushchev's liner Baltika docked when he arrived here in 1960.

The proposal to use the 25th Street pier site was made today during a meeting of Arthur J. Goldberg, the United States representative to the United Nations; Laurance S. Rockefeller; Eleanor Clark French, City Commissioner to the United Nations, and others. The Board of Estimate will consider the proposal Aug. 26.

The pier was suggested as an alternative to using property at the northern end of the United Nations' 16-acre enclave at 48th Street. The use of that site was approved in March by the General Assembly when it sanctioned a new school. The Ford Foundation agreed to give up to $7.5 million for the building and equipment.

The New York Times — Aug. 7, 1965

Proposed site of school (cross)

Soon after the Assembly decision, second thoughts about the use of headquarters property were expressed by city officials and others, including Mr. Rockefeller, whose family had given the East Side tract to the United Nations. Some objected to the use of the park-like area for another building

4-Story Building Would Be Erected on Piles or Fill

and others contended that the expanding United Nations should reserve the location for possible future needs.

The search for alternatives began with a proposal to use Welfare Island, which brought protests from parents about the inaccessibility of the island.

Any change in plans now would have to be approved by the General Assembly. The Ford Foundation also would review its financial offer and take into account such matters as the wishes of United Nations members, the school officials and the parents, it was explained here.

The school at present is housed in an 84-year-old building of grimy red brick at 71st Street and First Avenue, which the city would like to repossess and raze. The 550 pupils come from the families of delegations and the international staff as well as the local community.

Mayor Wagner and other city officials were said to be enthusiastic about the suggestion to use Pier 73. Mr. Rockefeller is said to have offered $1 million to finance the plat-

Continued on Page 10, Column 3

Youth's Death Laid To Police Beating

By SIDNEY E. ZION

The Brooklyn District Attorney's office and the Police Department ordered investigations yesterday into the death of a 20-year old grocery clerk last week, allegedly caused by a policeman at Coney Island with a billy club.

The investigations had been sought by the New York Civil Liberties Union, which asserted that the case underscored the need for a civilian review board to judge complaints of police brutality.

The Police Department would not comment on the case, except to say that a thorough investigation was beginning immediately. Hearings into the death of the youth, Theodore Jones of Brooklyn, on July 26 had been scheduled for Monday but have been postponed. The dead youth was a Negro, as is the police-

Continued on Page 9, Column 3

Simone Signoret and Oscar Werner in *Ship of Fools.*

Peter Sellers starred in *What's New Pussycat?*, one of the best examples of free-wheeling farces of the period. Woody Allen made his film debut in a small part in this 1965 comedy.

"All the News That's Fit to Print"

The New York Times.

LATE CITY EDITION

U. S. Weather Bureau Report (Page 95) forecasts: Mostly sunny, hot and humid today; fair, warm tonight and tomorrow.
Temp. Range: 92—68; yesterday: 87—63.
Temp.-Hum. Index: high 77; yesterday: 77.

NEWS SUMMARY AND INDEX, PAGE 95

SECTION ONE

VOL. CXIV—No. 39,285. © 1965 by The New York Times Company. Times Square, New York, N. Y. 10036 THE NEW YORK TIMES, SUNDAY, AUGUST 15, 1965. 50c beyond 50-mile zone from New York City, except on Long Island. higher in air delivery cities THIRTY CENTS

21 DEAD IN LOS ANGELES RIOTS; 600 HURT; 20,000 TROOPS CALLED; PRESIDENT CONDEMNS VIOLENCE

U.S. ADDING 6,400 TO MARINE FORCE IN SOUTH VIETNAM

Step Goes Beyond Increase Announced by Johnson—Advance Units Arrive

DANANG STRENGTHENED

Company There Carries Out Attack by Copter Against Vietcong-Held Village

By CHARLES MOHR
Special to The New York Times

SAIGON, South Vietnam, Sunday, Aug. 15—A few thousand more United States marines landed in South Vietnam today as advance elements for a total of 6,400 Marine Corps reinforcements expected within days.

A military spokesman said that headquarters units of the Seventh Regimental Landing Team of the First Marine Division, with a battalion of troops, had come ashore in landing craft at Chulai, 350 miles north of Saigon, yesterday. Another regiment of marines has been stationed there for several months.

The spokesman did not disclose the size of the newly arrived group, but a battalion landing team numbers 1,500 to 1,800 men.

Another Battalion Lands

This morning another battalion of marines began landing at Danang, north of Chulai. Danang is the main headquarters of the Marine forces in South Vietnam.

The spokesman said the full regimental strength of 6,400 would soon be on hand.

The Marine landings were not part of the planned increase of 50,000 American troops announced by President Johnson on July 28, the spokesman added. Instead, he said, they represent a "supplement."

As of Aug. 8, there were 82,400 American servicemen in South Vietnam, 25,700 of them marines. Mr. Johnson has said that the total will soon reach at least 125,000.

In the Danang area before dawn, United States marines engaged in an unorthodox night helicopter-assault operation. A rifle company was landed near the village of Phoan under the illumination of aerial flares of 1.5 million candlepower dropped

Continued on Page 2, Column 3

Earl Brown Rejects Spot on Beame Slate

The New York Times
Earl Brown

By RICHARD L. MADDEN

Earl Brown, chairman of the city's Commission on Human Rights, declined yesterday to run for Manhattan Borough President on the slate of Controller Abraham D. Beame in the Democratic primary.

Mr. Brown said that "overriding personal considerations have left me no choice." He did not elaborate.

The Beame forces circulated petitions to put Mr.

Continued on Page 43, Column 1

MOSCOW REPORTS NEW MOON PHOTOS

Pictures of Far Side Said to Fill In the Gap of Earlier Survey by Spacecraft

By PETER GROSE
Special to The New York Times

MOSCOW, Aug. 14—An unmanned spacecraft has transmitted high-definition television pictures of hitherto unphotographed areas on the side of the moon opposite the earth, Tass, the Soviet press agency, said today.

The pictures were not made public.

Combined with the first photographs ever of the far side of the moon, taken in October, 1959, the new pictures give the Russians a complete pictorial record of the side of the moon that is never turned toward the earth, Tass said.

The pictures announced today were taken July 20 from a point much closer to the moon than the earlier series, less than 7,000 miles above the surface against about 40,000 in 1959.

The new pictures show surface features three miles or less across, according to Grigory Leikin, a senior researcher of the Astronomical Society at the Soviet Academy of Sciences.

A complete atlas of the

Continued on Page 41, Column 1

PAPANDREOU BLOC SPLIT BY WALKOUT IN HIS OWN PARTY

Two of Ex-Premier's Aides Claim Enough Support to Form New Greek Regime

Special to The New York Times

ATHENS, Aug. 14—Two of former Premier George Papandreou's principal aides announced today that they had decided to break away from his majority Center Union party at the head of an undisclosed number of Members of Parliament.

The declaration by Stephanos Stephanopoulos, Deputy Premier in the Papandreou Government ousted July 15, and Elias Tsirimokos, its Interior Minister, raised hopes that a Greek Government would be formed Monday.

A spokesman for the two leaders said they had "the support of more Center Union Deputies than is needed to swing a parliamentary majority in their favor."

Third Aide May Defect

A third Papandreou aide, Savros Papapolitis, who heads a group of 10 Center Union Deputies, asserted that he was reconsidering his allegiance to the former Premier and might join the defectors.

The spokesman for Mr. Stephanopoulos and Mr. Tsirimokos, both of whom were expected to be candidates for Premier, said a formal declaration of secession from the Papandreou party would be sent to Parliament Monday.

Today's development was a direct result of former Premier Papandreou's stiffening attitude in his conflict with King Constantine, who forced him out of power July 15 in a clash over political influence in the Greek army. The King was opposed to a Papandreou plan to replace the Defense Minister and to purge right-wing army officers.

Novas Cabinet Failed

Constantine promptly appointed a Papandreou aide, George Athanasiadis-Novas, Speaker of Parliament, to form a new government. But Mr. Athanasiadis-Novas managed to get the support of only 25 Center Union deputies.

He was overthrown in a stormy session of Parliament early on Aug. 5 by the combined Papandreou forces and 22 pro-Communist Deputies while Athens was in the grip of riots and street fighting between Papandreou supporters and the police.

A week ago, King Constantine asked another Papandreou aide, Mr. Stephanopoulos, to form a government. But the Premier-designate gave up the attempt after having been rebuffed at a Center Union caucus by a majority still loyal to Mr. Papandreou.

At a 90-minute audience at the palace Friday, Mr. Papan-

Continued on Page 42, Column 1

JOHNSON SHOCKED

He Calls Disturbances 'Tragic' and Appeals for Order on Coast

By ROBERT B. SEMPLE Jr.
Special to The New York Times

AUSTIN, Tex., Aug. 14—President Johnson described the Los Angeles riots today as "tragic and shocking." He warned the rioters that their rights could not be won and their grievances remedied "through violence."

The President appealed to "every person in a position of leadership" in Los Angeles to make "every effort to restore order."

He also instructed two high Administration officials to meet with Gov. Edmund G. Brown of California in New York and to place themselves at the Governor's disposal in an effort to stop the riots. Mr. Brown stopped in New York before returning to California from an interrupted overseas vacation.

The two officials were Lee C. White, special counsel to the President, and LeRoy Collins, Under Secretary of Commerce. Mr. Collins is former director of the Community Relations Service, which is charged with encouraging voluntary compliance with the Civil Rights Act of 1964.

Report on Troops Denied

A report from California said that the Administration had also promised to provide Federal troops if necessary to quell the disturbance. This report was quickly denied by a Presidential aide, Joseph A. Califano Jr.

Reached in Washington, Mr. Califano pointed out that California had 21,000 National Guardsmen on whom it could call and said that there was no need to involve Regular Army troops.

Mr. Johnson's appeal for speedy restoration of order was read to reporters by his press secretary, Bill D. Moyers. The President, spending the weekend at his ranch 65 miles west of Austin, has been keeping in close touch with the situation through the Justice Department and members of his staff in Washington.

The President's statement did not speculate on the causes of the disturbances and White House aides here were reluctant to do so. One aide said that the riots had happened so quickly there had been little opportunity to examine the reasons for them. He said that the

Continued on Page 77, Column 3

GUARDSMEN SWEEP AREA: Mobilized National Guardsmen move in convoy formation through Negro section of Los Angeles where looting and arson continued into fourth day.

United Press International Telephotos

SCENE OF DESTRUCTION: Deserted after another night of violence in the city, 103d Street is littered with debris. Estimates of damage ranged up to $100 million.

CURFEW ORDERED

Outbursts Spread to New Areas—Disaster Zone Is Proclaimed

By GLADWIN HILL
Special to The New York Times

LOS ANGELES, Aug. 14—Rioting, looting and burning spread today for the fourth day in the Negro district of southwestern Los Angeles. The disorders continued despite the rifle fire of National Guard troops and local peace forces.

The death toll from the hoodlum-instigated lawlessness rose tonight to 21. Nineteen of the victims were rioters, one was a sheriff's deputy and one a fireman. The last two were white men, as was one of the victims officially classed as a rioter.

The number of injured reached about 600, most of them rioters. Arrests totaled 1,400. Estimates of property damage ranged from $30 million to $100 million.

The number of California guardsmen called up rose to 20,000, according to Lieut. Gen. Roderick Hill, the state's National Guard adjutant. Some 4,000 were on patrol today. More than 1,000 policemen and deputies were in the area.

Curfew Hours

Tonight Lieut. Gov. Glenn Anderson proclaimed a curfew in a 35-square-mile area where the rioting has centered. From 8 P.M. to sunrise, he decreed, anyone on the streets except law-enforcement officers and newsmen will be seized.

Mr. Anderson, serving as acting Governor until Gov. Edmund G. Brown returned tonight from a European vacation, also proclaimed the riot zone a disaster area. This permitted policemen to be brought in as needed from surrounding cities in four counties.

Local authorities said help might have to be sought from the Federal Government.

"It's a mess, and it's getting progressively worse," General Hill said. "It started with a few square blocks, and today it was spreading over 21 square miles."

Sniping Increases

There were signs late tonight of some diminution in the disorders. Reports of new outbreaks of looting and fires were less frequent. But there was an increase in sniping from roofs and buildings.

Two sheriff's deputies were wounded in one exchange with snipers.

The depredations in the four-day rampage, triggered by the arrest last Wednesday night of a Negro on charges of drunken driving, spread despite a massive sweep operation. Block by block, the troops and civilian officers removed everyone from the streets who could give no

Continued on Page 79, Column 1

2,000 GUARDSMEN ON CHICAGO ALERT

Kerner Notifies Units After 2d Night of Racial Riots—Negroes Get Appeal

By DONALD JANSON
Special to The New York Times

CHICAGO, Aug. 14—Gov. Otto Kerner placed 2,000 National Guardsmen on stand-by alert at armories here today in the wake of two nights of Chicago's worst racial rioting in 13 years.

The action was taken at the request of Orlando W. Wilson, Chicago's superintendent of police, to forestall any resumption of the bottle-throwing violence that injured 60 persons last night.

Mr. Wilson warned residents of the largely Negro West Side neighborhood where the rioting occurred that unless they did "all in their power" to help the police prevent lawlessness the situation could deteriorate into uncontrolled strife such as Los Angeles has suffered the last few days.

He spoke at a solemn news conference in the office of Mayor Richard J. Daley. The Mayor, by his side, appealed to Chicagoans to stay off the street in the West Side neighborhood so that the police could isolate troublemakers and prevent any recurrence of last night's eight-hour riot.

The area, 40 blocks west of downtown Chicago, was quiet tonight. Taverns that ordinarily would have been jammed on a Saturday night were closed. Pulaski Road between Madison Street and the Eisenhower expressway was littered with broken glass, and store windows hit by rocks and bottles were boarded up to prevent looting.

By the time the police restored order shortly before dawn today 104 persons had been arrested, primarily on charges of disorderly conduct and resisting arrest. Most of

Continued on Page 76, Column 1

Discontent and Hate Viewed as Factors In Coast Violence

By WALLACE TURNER
Special to The New York Times

LOS ANGELES, Aug. 14—Negroes in a depressed area of Los Angeles were swept up into an emotional tide of hate and bitterness that caused them to beat and burn, observers said here today.

One worker for the Congress of Racial Equality, Cornell Henderson, a Negro, declared, "There were a lot of young hoods and agitators. But there were a lot of others who were just discontented and took advantage of the situation for emotional release."

There also was a heavy overlay of hate preaching, said Mr. Henderson.

"I saw the Black Muslims in the area," he said. "They were preaching resistance and 'down with the police brutality' and the usual thing that they talk about. They wanted to have the white men driven away. They chanted 'go away, whitey' at any white people they saw."

Psychiatrists, examining and

Continued on Page 80, Column 1

Policeman Kills One, Shoots 2d in Beating

By THEODORE JONES

A 23-year old Brooklyn laborer was fatally shot and a 15-year-old youth was wounded early yesterday by an off-duty patrolman who went to the aid of a man being beaten and robbed by six youths.

The police said both the youth and the laborer had attacked the patrolman with knives after he had identified himself and sought to help the beaten man in front of a five-story apartment house at the corner of Nostrand and Vernon Avenues. The policeman and all others involved were Negroes.

However, a witness to the shooting gave a different version. He said the slain man, identified as Willie James

Continued on Page 77, Column 1

GOV. BROWN VOWS TO RESTORE ORDER

Arrives in Los Angeles Aboard White House Plane—Cut Short Holiday in Greece

Special to The New York Times

LOS ANGELES, Aug. 14—Gov. Edmund G. Brown returned to California tonight and pledged "to restore law and order in Los Angeles."

In a news conference alongside the White House jet that flew him from New York, he said that he did not plan to accept President Johnson's offer of Federal help now.

"I don't want to federalize the National Guard—that's a major step—unless I have to," Governor Brown said.

"But if I have to, I will. I intend to restore law and order to Los Angeles."

"I will go down to the area as soon as I can," he said.

In a brief stopover in New York, the Governor referred to the Negro rioting here as "a state of insurrection."

Governor Brown arrived at the Los Angeles international airport just before 10 P.M. Pacific daylight time (1 A.M. Sunday, Eastern daylight time.) He was met by Lieut. Gov. Glenn Anderson, who ordered the National Guard to riot control duty Friday afternoon.

The Governor appeared on the steps of the Air Force Jetstar after a four-minute conference inside the cabin. Other participants were the state Attorney General, Thomas Lynch; Hale Champion, the State Director of Finance, one of the Governor's chief advisers, and Jack Burby, the Governor's press secretary.

Mrs. Brown accompanied her husband.

The Governor said he had returned to California to "give what aid the Governor can give to the Mayor and police officials of Los Angeles."

He said: "I want to see this catastrophe ended."

The Governor sidestepped

Continued on Page 81, Column 3

Sports News

GOLF

Dave Marr shot a one-under-par 70 yesterday to tie Tommy Aaron for first place in the Professional Golfers Association tournament in Ligonier, Pa. Each has 209 for 54 holes. Gardner Dickinson shot a 69 for 210 and Jack Nicklaus and Bill Casper shared fourth place at 211.

BASEBALL

Hector Lopez's single with the bases loaded in the ninth inning yesterday gave the New York Yankees a 3-2 victory over the Kansas City Athletics in the second Bat Day at the Stadium. The victory gave the Yanks a 59-59 won-lost mark, the first time they have been at .500 since they were 7-7. The Cleveland Indians beat the league-leading Minnesota Twins, 3-1, behind the three-hit pitching of Sam McDowell, who struck out 11 to run his total to 227, best in the league.

The New York Mets beat the Astros, 1-0, in 10 innings at Houston and ended an 11-game losing streak. The victory was the Mets' first in the Astrodome. The Los Angeles Dodgers beat the Pittsburgh Pirates, 1-0, in the 10th inning for Sandy Koufax's 21st victory.

FOOTBALL

The New York Giants opened their exhibition season by absorbing a 44-7 trouncing from the Packers at Green Bay.

HORSE RACING

What a Treat scored a neck victory in the 85th Alabama Stakes for 3-year-old fillies at Saratoga. Discipline was second and Terentia third in the $63,200 race, but their order was reversed after a foul claim by Larry Adams, Terentia's jockey. Eighteen fillies started. Mister Judge, $21, won the $22,950 Longport Handicap at Atlantic City by a neck.

Details in Section 5

164-Year-Old Brooklyn Navy Yard Launches Last Ship

The New York Times (by Jack Manning)

Mrs. Bruce Solomonson, daughter of Vice President and Mrs. Humphrey, christens the amphibious transport Duluth, the last ship to be launched at the Brooklyn Navy Yard.

By DOUGLAS ROBINSON

The 164-year-old Brooklyn Navy Yard launched its last ship yesterday amid the blare of martial music, the boom of cannon and the fluttering of flags. The installation, formally known as the New York Naval Shipyard, was one of 95 bases and facilities ordered closed last year by Defense Secretary Robert S. McNamara as part of an economy move. Despite the gay trappings of the launching, an air of sadness hung over the assembled workers and their families who joined Navy officers and officials to watch the amphibious transport Duluth float into the East River. "It's not a happy day, especially for the younger workers," commented Vincent DiNovi, who has been a machinist at the yard for 25 years. "It's not a happy launching and it's the last

Continued on Page 47, Column 4

Today's Sections

Index to Subjects

1965

The Ku Klux Klan captured headlines as a major political force, terrorizing much of the South with its anti-Negro campaign.

Disastrous rebellion in the black ghetto of Watts (downtown Los Angeles) was the most violent to occur that year.

Malcolm X, passionately dedicated to the Muslim cause was fatally wounded at the Audubon Ballroom while making his Sunday address. He had preached to his followers that "there can be no revolution without bloodshed."

"All the News That's Fit to Print"

The New York Times.

INTERNATIONAL EDITION

Algeria	DI. 0.70	Israel	Agoroth 80
Austria	Sch. 5	Italy	Lire 180
Belgium	B.Fr. 7	Lebanon	Piastres 60
Canary Isl.	Pts 12.00	Libya	Piastres 6
Cyprus	Mils 70	Luxembourg	L.Fr. 7
Denmark	D.Kr. 1.25	Netherlands	G. 0.60
Egypt	Piastres 10	Norway	N.Kr. 1.25
Finland	F.M. .70	Poland	Zlotys 3
France	F. 0.60	Portugal	Esc. 5
Germany	D.M. 0.60	Spain (SGEL)	Pts. 8
Great Britain	1s	Sweden	Sw. Kr. 1
Greece	Dr. 6	Switzerland	S.Fr. 0.60
India	Rps. 1.25	Turkey	Kurus 1.75
Iran	Rials 20	U.S. Mil-Europe	$0.10
Ireland	1s	Yugoslavia	DI. 80

VOL. CXV .... No. 39,336 © 1965 by The New York Times Company. + PARIS, TUESDAY, OCTOBER 5, 1965.

TODAY'S WEATHER—PARIS: Clear. LONDON: Partly cloudy. BERLIN: Clear. ROME: Clear. NEW YORK: Sunny. CHANNEL: Calm. Details, Page 3.

POPE CALLS FOR 'NO MORE WAR' AS U.N. GOAL AND URGES EFFORT TO ADMIT ALL NATIONS; SEES JOHNSON; N.Y. MILLIONS HAIL PONTIFF

OFFICERS OF RIGHT SEEN DIMINISHING SUKARNO'S POWER

Jakarta Chief Contradicted on Air Force Role in Coup —6 Generals Dead

Special to The New York Times.

SINGAPORE, Oct. 4—President Sukarno appeared today to have lost some of his power to right-wing generals after three days of military upheaval in Indonesia.

Western sources in Singapore, which is only three miles from Indonesia's outlying islands, said diplomatic reports from Jakarta had indicated the Army was in control, militarily and politically, and that President Sukarno was striving to restore his position.

[Communist China's leaders were reported Monday to have sent their regards to President Sukarno. No mention of the attempted coup was made.]

These sources feel President Sukarno has an even chance to recover full power if he still has his health. This has been in doubt since last Friday when palace guards staged a coup that was quickly crushed by Army troops under Major General Suharto and the Defense Minister, Gen. Abdul Haris Nasution. These two appear to be on top at present.

[Rebel forces were heading for a major clash with loyalist troops in Central Java. Reuters reported the Malaysian radio as saying Monday.]

Martial law and an all-night curfew continued but no fighting was reported in Jakarta today. The rebel battalion of Lieutenant Colonel Untung was retreating toward Serang, 75 miles west of the capital.

Rebel Chief in Java

Colonel Untung flew to Central Java, sources said, to try to fan the revolt and link with dissident Colonel Suherman, who has been relieved of his command in the Diponegoro Division. Units of the crack Siliwangi Division were reported moving in that direction from Jakarta in case of trouble.

Indonesian Communists have given full oral support to Colonel Untung's rebellion, but the extent of their activity remained unclear. Unconfirmed reports said about 3,000 Communists had been armed and had joined the revolt.

The Indonesian radio announced tonight that the bodies of the Army Chief of Staff, Lieut. Gen. Achmad Yani, and five other generals who were kidnapped and murdered early in the revolt, were found today in a common grave at a spot called Crocodile Hole near Halim Airbase 15 miles from Jakarta.

Punishment Promised

The other victims, all anti-Communists like General Yani, were Major Generals Harjono, Suparma and Suprapto and Brigadier Generals Sutayo, Dikorko and Panjaitan. Their bodies are lying in state in Jakarta. A military funeral for them is planned for tomorrow.

General Suharto, 50 years old, the new top man in the Army along with Major General Pranoto, went on the air tonight and contradicted President Sukarno—an extremely rare occurrence in Indonesia—in accusing Air Force officers of killing the six generals.

Though President Sukarno has said the Air Force was not involved, "I, as a member of the Army condemn these Air Force officers and will see that they are dealt with firmly," General Suharto said.

A statement attributed to Vice Marshal Omar Dani, the Air Force commander and Communist sympathizer who dropped from sight after lending vocal support to Colonel Untung's attempted coup, was read over the Indonesian radio tonight. It said some Air Force men had taken part in the coup and would be punished.

President Sukarno said on the radio he had gone to Halim

Continued on Page 3, Column 1

India Said to Ask Soviet and U.S. Aid On Kashmir Issue

By J. ANTHONY LUKAS
Special to The New York Times.

NEW DELHI, Oct. 4—India has suggested that the United States and the Soviet Union might jointly help resolve political aspects of her dispute with Pakistan.

An authoritative source in the Indian Government said today that the idea had been tentatively broached as a substitute for the four-nation subcommittee suggested last week by U Thant, the United Nations Secretary General.

The proposal for the four-nation subcommittee—Britain, France, the United States and the Soviet Union—has been rejected by India.

The sources said today that Britain's attitude on the present conflict had been "very adverse" and France's had been "not very favorable." Therefore, he said, it would not serve India's interests to have these two nations on the committee.

However, he said the United States had been much

Continued on Page 3, Column 8

VIETCONG REPEAT BRIDGE AMBUSH

Hanoi Troops Said to Join in Battles—Reds Seek Control of Province

By R. W. APPLE Jr.
Special to The New York Times.

SAIGON, Oct. 4—The drawn-out struggle for control of Binhdinh province was reopened today when Vietcong guerrillas fell upon Government troops defending a bridge.

The bridge, on Highway 1 25 miles north of Quinhon, was cut by the Vietcong during a double ambush 10 days ago. An engineer unit was sent to repair the span last week, together with a South Vietnamese infantry battalion that was to act as a screening force.

Early today, an enemy unit of unknown size launched an attack on the infantrymen with mortars and automatic weapons. Flare planes and artillery were called in, and a relief column started from the north.

When the reinforcements reached the bridge six hours later, the defenders were hard pressed and had suffered heavy casualties. One American adviser attached to the infantry battalion was killed, according to reports from the battlefield.

At about the same time, American Skyraiders began strafing and bombing runs in the area, and within 40 minutes the fighting began to taper off. Helicopters were able to land to begin the evacuation of wounded troops.

No Vietcong casualties were listed in the initial reports.

Government troops have now

Continued on Page 3, Column 3

GUEVARA HAS QUIT CUBA AND REGIME, CASTRO REVEALS

Major Fights Imperialism on 'New Fields'—Red Cross Refugee Role Barred

HAVANA, Oct. 4 (Reuters)—Maj. Ernesto Che Guevara left Cuba earlier this year for "a new field of battle in the struggle against imperialism," Premier Fidel Castro announced last night.

Before leaving, the Argentine-born Minister of Industry gave up his Cuban citizenship and all posts he held in the country.

Premier Castro made the disclosure, after months of mystery over Major Guevara's whereabouts, at a public presentation of the Central Committee of the country's Communist party.

Letter Is Read

Mr. Castro also rejected a suggestion by President Johnson yesterday that the International Red Cross assist in the departure of Cuban refugees for the United States. The Premier said that diplomatic channels through the Swiss Embassy, which represents American interests in Cuba, were sufficient.

Mr. Castro read a letter from Major Guevara that had been given to him on April 1. At the end of the letter the whole committee and audience of party delegates gave a two-minute ovation.

Mr. Castro gave no hint of where Major Guevara was. At the beginning of the ceremony special applause was given to Major Guevara's wife.

Throughout the ovation she stood with head bowed and looking sad.

Major Guevara was once considered Cuba's No. 3 leader after Mr. Castro and his brother Raul.

He was one of the architects of the revolution that ousted the dictator Fulgencio Batista and brought Mr. Castro to power.

Posts Are Abandoned

Two days ago it was announced that he had been dropped from the leadership of the country's United Socialist Revolutionary Party.

Mr. Castro announced last night that the party had been renamed the Cuban Communist party.

In his letter, datelined Havana, Major Guevara declared: "I feel I have completed the duty which the Cuban revolution gave me. I say farewell to you. I give up all my posts as minister in the party, as a major and as a Cuban citizen."

The letter continued: "My only fault has been that I did not understand more fully your great qualities. I am proud of having followed you. . ."

"Other nations require my services and I must leave you. I leave behind my dearest me-

Continued on Page 3, Column 2

2 LEADERS MEET

Paul and President Confer 46 Minutes on World Issues

By TOM WICKER
Special to The New York Times.

NEW YORK, Oct. 4—President Johnson and Pope Paul VI met today for 46 minutes of what the President later called "stimulating and inspiring convers 'ion' about world peace and man's welfare.

Mr. Johnson said he believed the first visit of the Pope to the New World, together with his address to the United Nations, "may be just what the world needs to get us thinking on how to achieve peace and getting us to make progress in that area."

The scene of the fourth meeting in history between a President and a Pope was a room in Suite 35-H, high above sunlit Manhattan in the Waldorf-Astoria Hotel.

The two men talked alone, except for their interpreters, and Bill D. Moyers, the President's press secretary.

Mr. Moyers took notes on the long and friendly exchange, which centered on repeated expressions of hopes for peace.

Pose for Photographs

Later, the President and the Pope posed for photographs in a sitting room of the suite, and each delivered a brief statement to the press. Then Mr. Johnson presented his wife and his daughter Luci, who converted to Roman Catholicism, to the Pope.

Each man also introduced members of their official parties to the other. Then Mr. Johnson accompanied Pope Paul to the East 50th Street entrance of the Waldorf, where thousands of spectators were able to catch a brief glimpse of the two.

Millions more saw their parting on television.

Mr. Johnson, smiling broadly, shook hands three times with the Pope, the last time taking Paul's hand in both of his.

No Specific Proposals

As the Pope's limousine pulled away, Mr. Johnson—who towered above the glass roof of the auto—held out his hand directly above the Pope's head, almost as though extending his own blessing to the spiritual leader of millions of Roman Catholics.

Mr. Moyers account of the private conversation, as well as the personal statements by the Pope and Mr. Johnson, made it clear that they exchanged no specific proposals.

The Pope expressed the gratitude of the church for Mr. Johnson's domestic programs concerning health and education.

As Mr. Johnson put it "His Holiness expressed his pleasure at our not only talking about education and health but our acting on it in this country."

The two men also gave strong praise to the United Nations, where the Pope addressed the General Assembly later in the afternoon. They laid special stress on a "resurgence" of the

Continued on Page 2, Column 2

HISTORIC MEETING: Pope Paul VI gestures to an interpreter as he talks with President Johnson. Their conversation took place in apartment at Waldorf-Astoria Hotel.

United Press International

NEW YORKERS GREET POPE: Crowds line the route as the Pontiff's motorcade moves through streets of Queens County en route to Manhattan from Kennedy Airport.

KENNEDY QUOTED

World Urged to Ban Offensive Arms—2,000 Hear Talk

U. N. talk highlights, Page 2; Related articles, 4 and 5.

By DREW MIDDLETON
Special to The New York Times.

UNITED NATIONS, N.Y., Oct. 4—Pope Paul VI fervently asked the United Nations today to do away with offensive weapons.

The Pontiff, a slim figure in white, stood at the green marble rostrum of the General Assembly and cried, "No more war, never again war!"

"Drop your weapons," the Pope exhorted, "one cannot love with offensive weapons in hand." But the Pontiff noted that man, weak and "even wicked," must "unfortunately" retain defensive arms.

Before him in the great green, gold and blue Assembly hall were the representatives of 116 of the United Nations' 117 members. Only tiny Albania, Communist China's spokesman in Eastern Europe, boycotted the papal address.

Millions Line Route

The Pope addressed the world just a few hours after his arrival for a 13½-hour visit. He received a tumultuous welcome from millions of New Yorkers and ivsitors who lined the route of his triumphal procession through the city.

Two thousand delegates and special guests filled the hall. The Pontiff received a standing ovation when he entered the hall and at the conclusion of his 35-minute address.

Peace was the highest theme of Pope Paul's message. But he also asked the Assembly to "bring back among you" those that have left and to study methods of "uniting in your brotherhood, in honor and loyalty those who do not share in it."

"Advance always," was the slogan the Pontiff offered.

Notes Kennedy's Words

Citing the words of the "great, departed" President Kennedy, that mankind must put an end to war or war would put an end to mankind, Pope Paul appealed for "no more war, never again."

There must not be, the Pontiff emphasized, "the ones against the others, never again, never more."

"Peace, it is peace, which must guide the destinies of peoples and of all mankind," Pope Paul declared.

To this end, the Pontiff asked the nations to "let the arms fall from your hands."

While man remains "weak, changeable and wicked," defensive arms "unfortunately will be necessary," the Pope said. But if the United Nations continues to study ways to guarantee international security, the aim will be secured, the Pope predicted.

Warns on Birth Control

Pope Paul asked the nations to insure "that there is enough bread on the tables of mankind" rather than "encourage an artificial birth control, which would be irrational, in order to diminish the number of guests at the banquet of life."

The Pontiff put the authority of the Catholic Church and his own convictions behind the world organization, which he called "the last hope of peace."

But he went on from there to stress "the necessity of a world authority, able to act effectively at the juridicial and political levels."

The Pontiff's address, with its emphasis on universality, disarmament and the development of a world authority, went far beyond the simple plea for peace expected by most delegates. The plea was there, but it was clothed in lambent phrases and insistent logic that elevated it to a level not often heard in the Assembly.

Pope Paul's reference to widening the membership of the United Nations went straight to one of the most bitterly debated issues of this General Assembly.

Those countries that do not

Continued on Page 2, Column 4

Thousands Guard Paul on Trip

He Sees Harlem and Glitter of 5th Ave. From Closed Car

BY ROBERT ALDEN
Special to The New York Times.

NEW YORK, Oct. 4—Pope Paul VI arrived in New York this morning on a historic mission in behalf of peace.

Millions of New Yorkers and visitors gave a warmhearted welcome to the first Pontiff to visit the Western Hemisphere in the 20 centuries since the Christian Church was founded.

The Pope came to speak at the United Nations to dramatize the urgency of the need for peace in the atomic age. Before his address he met President Johnson and the President's family at the Waldorf-Astoria Hotel.

The Pope was greeted at the door of his airplane by U Thant, Secretary General of the United Nations. They shook hands warmly and the Pope, smiling, gave his blessing to the large crowd gathered to greet him at Kennedy International Airport. He appeared rested after the longest journey any Pope has ever made.

Before he greeted the scores of dignitaries who had gathered at the apron of the airfield to meet him, the Pontiff stepped before a battery of microphones at the foot of the ramp.

He Blesses America

"Greetings to you, America," he declared. "The first Pope to set foot upon your land blesses you with all his heart.

"He renews, as it were, the gesture of your discoverer, Christopher Columbus, when he planted the Cross of Christ in this blessed soil. May the cross of blessing, which we now trace over your skies and your land, preserve those gifts, which Christ gave you, and guarantee you:

"Peace, concord, freedom, justice—and above all the vision of life in the hope of immortality.

"God bless this land of yours."

The Pope spoke in English marked by a soft Italian accent.

Immediately after concluding his message, the Pontiff, wearing a gleaming white robe and a red cape and a gold embroidered red cape, greeted the cardinals of the Roman Catholic church in the United States and a score of official guests, including Amintore Fanfani, President of the United Nations General Assembly and former Italian Premier; Secretary of State Dean Rusk; Gov. Nelson A. Rockefeller of New York; Mayor Robert F. Wagner, and Senator Robert F. Kennedy.

Then, smiling and waving greetings to invited guests massed on an observation deck, the Pope, with Cardinal Spellman of the Archdiocese of New York at his side, mounted a specially constructed open limousine.

The Pope then began a 25-mile procession through the streets of New York. Millions of New Yorkers and others who had streamed into the city lined the thoroughfares to receive his blessing.

The Pope, with the Cardinal at his side, changed to a closed, bubble-top limousine early in the procession because of a brisk, chill wind that blew under sunny skies.

Security Is Strong

Security precautions were without precedent in New York's history.

Eighteen thousand of the city's 26,000-man police force were stationed along the route of the papal procession and at points where Pope Paul was to make his stops.

The journey through the city, at the Pope's request, took him through contrasting areas of the city — Spanish Harlem, where many of the impoverished Puerto Ricans newly arrived in New York live; Harlem, the festering Negro ghetto; Central Park, cleaned and pruned by an army of workers, and Fifth Avenue, the luxurious showcase of the city.

Traveling at 15 miles an hour through a brisk, chill wind, the Pontiff was cheered

Continued on Page 2, Column 1

South Africa Crash Kills at Least 60

DURBAN, South Africa, Oct. 4 (Reuters)—At least 100 Africans were feared killed and several hundred injured tonight when three coaches of a crowded passenger train were derailed 10 miles northwest of Durban, the police reported.

A white signalman was battered to death by an incensed crowd of Africans who attacked him and another white man minutes after the disaster, the police said.

In Johannesburg, early reports reaching railway headquarters said 60 to 70 Africans were believed to have been killed. It appeared to have been the worst rail disaster in South Africa's history.

The train was taking about 1,500 persons home to the African township of Kwa Mashu when it was derailed at Effingham Junction station, about two miles from its destination.

U.S. Accuses Saigon Colonel of Misusing Aid Funds

Alleged Fraud May Involve $250,000—Officer Has Friends in Regime

By NEIL SHEEHAN
Special to The New York Times.

SAIGON, Oct. 4—A serious case of alleged corruption by South Vietnamese provincial officials has become a source of considerable political embarrassment to both the Vietnamese and United States Governments.

The case allegedly involves large-scale misuse of United States aid funds—possibly as much as $250,000—by a Vietnamese Army lieutenant colonel who is chief of Binhtuy province, 175 miles northeast of Saigon, and an army major who is his deputy.

It finally came to head 12 days ago when, after several fruitless attempts by the United States mission here to rectify the situation, two American aid officials assigned to the province were withdrawn and American aid to Binhtuy was suspended.

Informed sources said the United States mission has handed Air Vice-Marshal Nguyen Cao Ky, the Premier, a dossier containing a lengthy list of charges against the Vietnamese officials. The mission reportedly has made clear to him that aid to the province will not be resumed until the province chief and his assistant are removed.

On the basis of the American charges, the Premier has, according to sources, started an investigation of his own but has so far taken no action against the Vietnamese officials.

Since the investigation began a week ago the province chief, a Lieutenant Colonel Chi has made countercharges of an unspecified nature against the two American aid officials.

The major problem and source of embarrassment, however, is that the province chief has reportedly been enjoying the patronage of Brig. Gen. Nguyen Huu Co, the Deputy Premier, and one of the most powerful men in the country.

The Premier is thus finding it extremely difficult to take abrupt action against the province chief for fear of alienating one of his principal colleagues and upsetting the delicate political balance within the ruling military junta.

United States officials are fully aware of the delicacy of the issue and are, according to sources, attempting to avoid placing extreme pressure on the Premier. They have attempted to avoid giving the case any publicity and have declined to discuss details with correspondents.

The United States mission has, nevertheless, decided to make an issue of the case because of a growing belief that suspected widespread corruption within Vietnamese Government ranks is having a

Continued on Page 3, Column 4

"All the News That's Fit to Print"

The New York Times.

LATE CITY EDITION
U. S. Weather Bureau Report forecasts: Mostly sunny, cool today; increasing cloudiness tonight and tomorrow.
Temp. Range: 45—30; yesterday: 57—45.

VOL. CXV....No. 39,372. © 1965 by The New York Times Company, Times Square, New York, N. Y. 10036 NEW YORK, WEDNESDAY, NOVEMBER 10, 1965. TEN CENTS

POWER FAILURE SNARLS NORTHEAST; 800,000 ARE CAUGHT IN SUBWAYS HERE; AUTOS TIED UP, CITY GROPES IN DARK

To Our Readers

Because of the power blackout, the mechanical facilities of The New York Times were put out of operation last night and early today. Through the courtesy of The Newark Evening News this issue of The Times was set into type and printed in The Evening News's plant from The Times's own news reports. The financial tables are those of The Evening News.

Johnson Restates Goals in Vietnam

By The Associated Press

JOHNSON CITY, Tex., Nov. 9—President Johnson has restated broad American goals in Viet Nam and proclaimed Nov. 28 as "a day of dedication and prayer" for all members of the anti-Communist forces there.

The United States Government, he said, "remains ready without condition for the international discussions that can lead to lasting peace."

Mr. Johnson's proclamation, which followed a cue from Congress, was made public today though he actually signed it three days ago.

The Presidential document sidestepped one potential source of direct friction between Americans who support and oppose the Vietnam war.

Nov. 27 Suggested

Congress had suggested Nov. 27 as the day of prayer. However, a series of antiwar demonstrations, including a march on Washington, had been planned for that day.

Mr. Johnson, who had authority to fix the timing of the tribute to fighting forces in Vietnam, decided on the following day, a Sunday. In so doing, he is reported to have wanted to avoid a direct confrontation between backers and critics of American policy in Vietnam.

As the President has said on many occasions, he believes the great majority of Americans support his policy on Vietnam.

'Honored Tradition' Cited

The President proclaimed Nov. 28 "as a day of dedication and prayer, honoring the men and women of South Vietnam, of the United States, and of all other countries, who are risking their lives to bring about a just peace in South Vietnam."

He had this to say about American war aims:

"In assisting the people of South Vietnam to resist unprovoked aggression, the United States and other nations are carrying on the honored tradition of defending a people's right to freedom ... the purpose of the United States in Vietnam is to help open the way for social justice in place of unprovoked aggression and peace instead of war."

Mr. Johnson noted that both the Senate and the House had passed resolutions saying "it would be fitting for the President to set aside a national day of remembrance dedicated to those Americans who are committing their lives, blood and energies in the defense of world peace."

Miss Liberty Shines Through Blackout

The Statue of Liberty maintained its illumination throughout last night's long blackout.

Residents of lower Manhattan saw clearly the floodlit base of the statue on Liberty Island and the lighted torch. Except for an occasional passing river craft, the statue appeared to be the only beacon of light in the harbor.

Power for statue's lights was supplied by the New Jersey Public Service Company.

G.I.'s Score Big Victory

Vietcong Force Almost Wiped Out by U.S. Airborne Unit

By R. W. APPLE JR.
Special to The New York Times

BIEN HOA, South Vietnam, Nov. 9—The toll of almost 400 Vietcong killed in a battle 30 miles northeast of Saigon yesterday marked a decisive victory for troops of the US 173d Airborne Brigade.

The American paratroopers, members of one battalion, fired into waves of enemy troops at point-blank range in the eight-hour battle.

The United States troops suffered substantial casualties in the battle in a dense tropical thicket, but only at the battle of Chulay had an American unit inflicted heavier losses on the Vietcong.

Most of the fighting took place at such close range that American M-79 grenades, which explode only after they have traveled 12 yards, bounced harmlessly off the guerrillas.

Assaults Thrown Back

The Americans were surrounded several times, but each time they threw back enemy assaults and held their positions. The Vietcong, using flame throwers and molten-metal thermite grenades for the first time in the war, attacked until they were almost wiped out.

This afternoon, with the battle over, the United States troops were returned by helicopter to their base camp at the sprawling installation here.

Sunday night, two platoons from the 173d, moving through the underbrush on patrol in the jungle area where they had been operating since Nov. 5, found fresh footprints and heard the frightened cackling of chickens.

At 7:30 A.M. yesterday the two platoons moved out again, clawing their way through the brush in the jungle gloom, and began climbing a pair of rocky hills. Both platoons were from C Company of the First Battalion, 503d Infantry.

'Right on Their Patio'

Suddenly the platoon on the right, about 50 men, found itself in a circle of mud and thatch huts. The huts were invisible from the air because of the palmetto trees arching overhead and almost invisible from the ground because of the underbrush.

The company's commanding officer, Capt. Henry B. Tucker of Columbus, Miss., said later:

(Continued Page 5, Column 3)

CITY IN DARKNESS: Except for scattered independent lighting this is how the city looked from the Jersey side.

The New York Times

ON A TRAIN GOING NOWHERE: Commuters waiting on subway in Times Square area. Picture was made in ——

Snarl at Rush Hour Spreads Into 9 States

10,000 in the National Guard and 5,000 Off-Duty Policemen Are Called to Service in New York

By PETER KIHSS

The largest power failure in history blacked out nearly all of New York City, parts of nine Northeastern states and two provinces of southeastern Canada last night. Some 80,000 square miles, in which perhaps 25 million people live and work, were affected.

It was more than three hours before the first lights came back on in any part of the New York City area. When they came on in Nassau and Suffolk Counties at 9 P.M., overloads plunged the area into darkness again in 10 minutes.

Striking at the evening rush hour, the power failure trapped 800,000 riders on New York City's subways. Railroads halted. Traffic was jammed. Airplanes found themselves circling, unable to land. But the Defense Department reported that the Strategic Air Command and other defense installations functioned without a halt.

National Guard Called Out

Five thousand off-duty policemen were summoned to duty here. Ten thousand National Guardsmen were called up in New York City alone. Other militiamen were alerted in Rhode Island and Massachusetts, as well as upstate New York.

The lights and the power went out first at 5:17 P.M. somewhere along the Niagara frontier of New York state. Nobody could tell why for hours afterward.

The tripping of automatic switches hurtled the blackout eastward across the state—to Buffalo, Rochester, Syracuse, Utica, Schenectady, Troy and Albany.

Within four minutes the line of darkness had plunged across Massachusetts all the way to Boston. It was like a pattern of falling dominoes—darkness sped southward through Connecticut, northward into Vermont, New Hampshire, Maine and Canada.

Sputtering at 5:27

At 5:27 P.M. the lights began sputtering in New York City, and within seconds the giant Consolidated Edison system blacked out in Manhattan, the Bronx, Queens and most of Brooklyn—but not in Staten Island and parts of Brooklyn that were interconnected with the Public Service Electric and Gas Company of New Jersey.

The darkness probed outward into northern New Jersey, up into Westchester and Rockland Counties, eastward into Long Island.

As far south as Washington, a Potomac Electric Power Company spokesman reported a power "dip" at 5:30 P.M., lasting less than a minute and virtually unnoticed in the nation's capital.

In Pennsylvania, the blackout spread through Pittsburgh and Reading into parts of Philadelphia and then into New Jersey along the coast above Atlantic City.

President Johnson, in Austin, Tex., ordered the full resources of the Federal Government thrown into an investigation by the Federal Power Commission. The Federal Bureau of Investigation, the Defense Department and other agencies were ordered to report "at the earliest possible moment."

Some Fear Sabotage

Asked whether there was any belief that sabotage might have been involved, Bill D. Moyers, the President's Press Secretary, would say only that "all of the resources of the Government" were being invoked in the investigation.

Later Mr. Johnson was advised that utility officials were "pretty well agreed upon the belief that there is substantially no chance of sabotage." Mr. Moyers said one theory was that the failure had been in automatic frequency control equipment.

Power companies, stripped of the protection of interconnected grids that would guard against minor failures, moved to isolate their areas to restore energy on their own. This was how the Ontario Hydro Electric Commission, a Government-owned utility, cut away after loss of power for six million persons. It began bringing power back at 6:15 P.M.

In New York City, the Ravenswood plant in Queens, which provides 1.8 million kilowatts out of the 7.6 million produced by the city's Consolidated Edison plants, began sending smoke up from its stacks, as auxiliary steam power began to build up for its generators.

At 7:15 P.M. smoke began curling up also from the Hudson Avenue station in Brooklyn. It was from Hudson Avenue that the first power was restored here: Five feeder cables of 27,000 volts each sent light back into Coney Island at 8:42 P.M.

An hour later Consolidated Edison reported 17 of the

(Continued on Page 2, Column 1 and 2)

U.S. Orders An Inquiry

President Calls for a Study of Power Failure in East

By JOHN D. POMFRET
Special to The New York Times

AUSTIN, Tex., Nov. 9—President Johnson ordered today an immediate and complete investigation of the power failure that blacked out a large section of the East.

The President issued the order in a memorandum to Joseph C. Swidler, chairman of the Federal Power Commission.

Within minutes after the investigation was ordered, Mr. Swidler sent telegrams to all power companies in the affected areas, requesting their assistance. He also telephoned Defense Secretary Robert S. McNamara and Attorney General Nicholas de B. Katzenbach, telling them to coordinate the inquiry with them.

During the evening Mr. Johnson talked by telephone with Governor Rockefeller and Mayor

(Continued Page 3, Column 3)

City's Glitter Goes But Not Its Poise

By FRED POWLEDGE

Broadway, Manhattan and the rest of the city lost their glitter last night. Yet New Yorkers, who are used to living in crises, seemed to take the blackout in stride.

By the thousands they calmly filed out of office buildings and stores soon after the blackout started.

They grabbed every taxicab in sight. Some cab drivers turned on their "off duty" signs and headed for home themselves. Then the New Yorkers grabbed every bus in sight.

Although many merchants feared looting and violence, the police reported little such trouble. Many New Yorkers even seemed merry. There was the same air of revelry that often accompanies a heavy snowstorm.

Time to Admire Skyline

Commuters stuck in Manhattan with the prospect of a long wait before getting to their homes found time to admire the unexpected sight of a moonlit Manhattan skyline, with stars, clouds and no neon.

Below ground, subway riders who waited in stalled trains sat quietly, resigned and good-humored.

At the Piccadilly Hotel on 45th Street in the heart of the theater district, a guest sat behind the desk helping the management dispense candles. No one seemed panicky, although a woman at the cigarette counter refused to sell anything to anyone who didn't have the correct change. Her cash register would not open.

Huckster Sells Flashlights

A huckster on Broadway sold flashlights, complete with batteries, for $1 apiece. A few doors away, in one of the shops that specializes in imported transistor radios and tape recorders a salesman got rid of dozens of flahlights at $3 each.

"It's a good quality flashlight," he said to someone who objected to the price. "It'll be working long after the current emergency is over."

After an initial period of darkness, little lights started appearing in windows. They were candles, retrieved from dusty desk drawers and kitchen cabinets, from the Bronx to Staten Island.

On street corners, New Yorkers gathered to listen to portable radios and wait for some form of transportation home.

Some did not wait. Thousands walked across the Queensboro and Brooklyn Bridges, where the stunning night views of the city were strangely missing. The Brooklyn Bridge has a pedestrian walkway, above the automobile roadway, but the Queensboro does not. The Queens bound pedestrians walked across the south lane of the auto roadway four and five abreast. Cars crawled along behind them.

Cross Streets Jammed

Although many offices and stores closed immediately after the blackout began, some essential services stayed open.

Hospitals, using emergency generator power supplies, stayed lighted. Newspapers did too, but the light came from candles.

Manhattan's crosstown streets became unbroken ribbons of white light as automobiles, the brightest sources of light, jammed the narrow roadways.

Police cars turned on their red blinking lights. Buses crawled down the streets, their interior lamps lighting the faces of crowded passengers.

A Woolworth's store on Lexington Avenue reported a "land-office business" in candles. People stood in lines that stretched into the street, waiting for a chance to buy a candle.

A street repair crew worked on, filling a hole in the pavement as their supervisor held a flashlight.

Bars filled quickly. The Astor Bar in Times Square, always a popular place, was more popular than ever. The candles planted in ashtrays seemed to produce more than enough light for drinkers.

Another bar in Times Square locked its doors, leaving contented drinkers with a good excuse to remain inside, but angering those who wanted to get in.

Brief Thought of Disaster

A young actress who lives in Greenwich Village was taking a bath when the lights went out. She said that her first thoughts were that "we were under attack," but that she quickly dismissed such an idea and poured herself a drink.

In Times Square, pedestrians

(Continued Page 3, Column 6)

Food Is Sent To Subways

10,000 Are Stranded Long After Most Are Led Out

By SAMUEL KAPLAN

Subway trains sputtered to a halt in tunnels, on elevated tracks and in stations yesterday, stranding about 800,000 rush hour riders—10,000 of whom were still stuck at midnight.

The Transit Authority and the Police Department worked into the early hours of the morning attempting to remove passengers from crowded, stalled cars.

At midnight, food was sent to the passengers who were still waiting to be escorted out along the narrow catwalks in dark tunnels and high above rivers and streets.

Despite the anxious condition, no panic was reported, although there was confusion and fear in some of the 600 trains when they first stalled on the city's tracks.

The most difficult evacuation took place on the Williamsburg

(Continued Page 2, Column 8)

Man, 22, Immolates Himself In Antiwar Protest at U.N.

By THOMAS BUCKLEY

A 21-year-old former seminarian soaked himself with gasoline and then set himself aflame in front of the United Nations at dawn yesterday, as a protest against "war, all war."

Guards from the world organization and city patrolmen beat out the flames that enveloped him as he sat cross-legged on First Avenue and then rushed him to Bellevue Hospital.

He was drifting near death in the emergency ward last night, with second and third-degree burns covering 95 per cent of his body. The hospital staff said he had almost no chance of surviving.

The youth, Roger Allen LaPorte, was a member of the Catholic Worker movement, a charitable and pacifist organization with headquarters at 175 Chrystie Street on the Lower East Side. He lived in a tenement apartment leased by the organization at 58 Kenmare Street, a few blocks away.

Mr. LaPorte's self-immolation was the second in seven days attributable, at least in part, to continued United States' involvement in the war in Vietnam. Last Monday, Norman R. Morrison, a 32-year-old Quaker from Baltimore, burned himself to death in front of the Pentagon in Washington.

U Thant, the Secretary General of the United Nations, which has been seeking a solution to the Asian conflict, and Arthur Goldberg, the chief United States delegate to the world body, reacted with shock and horror to Mr. LaPorte's action.

Questioned at a city reception, Mr. Goldberg said that while the youth had undoubtedly been impelled by "the highest principles and motives," his action was "terribly unfortunate and terribly unnecessary."

"Perhaps there has been a failure on our part," he went on. "Perhaps we are not sufficiently communicating to the people of the world our dedication, our attachment and complete commitment to the idea that peace is the only way for mankind in the nuclear age."

A spokesman said that Mr. Thant was "deeply grieved over this human tragedy, whatever the motivation might be. U Thant regards human life as very sacred."

Attended Union Sq. Protest

Friends of Mr. LaPorte said that he had been melancholy but not obviously emotionally disturbed since Saturday, when he attended the demonstration at Union Square at which five other youths burned their draft cards.

Robert Steed, a fellow member of the Catholic Workers, said that Mr. LaPorte had been unable to make up his mind to

(Continued Page 5, Column 1)

How City Met the Emergency: Off-Duty Men Are Mobilized

The city's emergency services were mobilized last night to deal with the sudden power blackout.

Five thousand off-duty policemen were summoned by a message broadcast over WNYC, the city's radio station. They joined the 7,000 who were on duty when the lights went out and who were held on for the emergency.

The Fire Department, too, brought in off-duty firemen because their overloaded telephone and telegraphic communications made it difficult to keep contact with scattered fire apparatus in the field.

The Fire Department radio was out of service from 5:30 p.m. to 8:30 p.m. and the dispatchers had to keep in touch with the firehouses and vehicles by telephone. They had the radio system back in operation at 8:30 and were able to communicate with men in the field from that hour.

Hospitals were generally able to carry on with the generating systems that they have for such emergencies. Operations were performed in some of them by lights provided by these auxiliary systems.

The switchboard in the Communications Bureau at Police Headquarters was swamped by calls from puzzled and frightened persons. So many calls came in for radio cars to help persons trapped in stalled elevators, in the subways and to deal with fires and other emergencies that no count was kept of their errands or destinations.

Looting Is Reported

Detectives were sent to West 123d Street in Harlem where they were told there had been looting. When they got there, they found one store window broken.

At Bellevue Hospital, the 2,300 patients were treated by several hundred nurses and doctors in candlelight. Although the city hospital has an auxiliary generating system, it is too small to service the massive enclave of buildings and was not used. However, in the operating and emergency rooms, the Fire Department set up emergency lights powered by small generators. One operation was finished just before the blackout occurred.

The major problems at Bellevue involved reassuring mentally disturbed patients and mixing medicines in dimly lighted pharmacies. Quantities of dry ice was obtained to keep blood plasma from spoiling.

Louis Lobo, who has been in an iron lung at Bellevue since 1962, was transferred to a Bird Resperator, which is operated by compressed air. No ill effects were reported.

Car Battery Used

One Bellevue employe brought in his car battery, set it up on a wheelchair and powered emer-

(Continued Page 2, Column 7)

Many stranded commuters were forced to use the lobby steps of the Hotel Commodore in New York City. Vacancies were nonexistent shortly after the blackout set in.

Delacroix Island (east of New Orleans) shown in the wake of Hurricane Betsy. One of the most devastating disasters of the decade, Betsy had a 15-mile-thick band of 129-140-mile-an-hour winds encircling her eye.

The televising of controversial trials such as in the case of Billy Sol Estes (right) was ruled improper by the Supreme Court. This was another extension of the areas being designed by the Court to extend personal freedom.

Television audiences found it easy to laugh about a difficult situation during World War II in *Hogan's Heroes.* Featured were Werner Klemperer as Commander Klink, John Banner as Schultz and Bob Crane as Hogan.

Larry Storch and Forrest Tucker were cavalrymen and Edward Everett Horton played an Indian in *F Troop,* the television series that was a slapstick portrayal of army life.

Barbra Streisand's one-hour special was the most generously praised special of the 1964-65 season. Just having conquered Broadway (in *Funny Girl*), television was just one more item to her list of accomplishments.

Jeffrey Hunter, Dina Merrill and series' star Efrem Zimbalist, Jr. (left to right), shown in *The FBI.*

"All the News That's Fit to Print"

The New York Times.

LATE CITY EDITION

U. S. Weather Bureau Report (Page 94) forecasts: Cloudy today and tonight. Rain likely tomorrow.

Temp. Range: 53—40; yesterday: 49—44.

VOL. CXV..No. 39,374. © 1965 by The New York Times Company. Times Square, New York, N. Y. 10036 NEW YORK, FRIDAY, NOVEMBER 12, 1965. TEN CENTS

RHODESIA ASSERTS INDEPENDENCE; BRITAIN DECRIES ACT AS TREASON AND APPLIES ECONOMIC SANCTIONS

EMERGENCY OVER, WAGNER RESCINDS SAVE-POWER PLEA

Con Edison Reports Ample Reserve—Mayor Calls His Appeal Successful

FAILURE STILL MYSTERY

U.S., State, Local Officials Seek Answer—Subway Service Now Normal

By PETER KIHSS

New Yorkers were told yesterday by Mayor Wagner that they no longer needed to maintain voluntary restrictions on electrical power.

The Consolidated Edison Company reported that it had restored an ample reserve for its system serving the metropolitan area, with 5.1 million kilowatts of capacity on hand as against yesterday's peak demand of 4,333,000 between 5 P.M. and 6 P.M. The city's record use was 5,710,000 kilowatts last June 23.

The Mayor's earlier appeals for conservation had followed a blackout that plunged nearly the entire city into darkness at 5:27 P.M. Tuesday along with parts of eight states and one Canadian province. It affected 30 million persons.

Cause Still Mystery

Federal, state, local and utility investigators were still trying to unravel the mystery of why 80,000 square miles in the Northeast power grid territory went black.

Joseph C. Swidler, chairman of the Federal Power Commission, and other officials conferred all day and into the night with utility leaders, at the request of President Johnson.

"The fault was not, so far as we now know, in the failure of any specific piece of equipment," Mr. Swidler said at one point. "It is somewhere in the complexities of the system operation."

Only one day earlier, Mayor Wagner had called on New Yorkers to save power as they have been holding down on use of water in the current drought.

Plea Gets Response

But at 11:40 A.M. yesterday, the Mayor issued a statement saying he had been advised by the Consolidated Edison Company and Armand D'Angelo, Commissioner of Water Supply, Gas and Electricity, that "emergency power conservation measures are no longer necessary."

The Mayor said use of electricity went down sharply Wednesday night after his earlier appeal, and he asserted that "the people of New York City once again responded magnificently in the face of anxiety and possible crisis."

"Now that the immediate

Continued on Page 36, Column 1

41 on Jet Believed Dead In Salt Lake City Crash

48 Survivors Reported—Accident Is Third for the Boeing 727

By United Press International

SALT LAKE CITY, Nov. 11—A Boeing 727 jet with 89 persons aboard crashed and burst into a ball of flame while landing at Salt Lake City Municipal Airport tonight. Authorities tentatively set the death toll at 41.

Salt Lake County authorities said 48 of the United Air Lines plane's passengers and crew members had been accounted for, leaving the 41 presumed dead.

The survivors pushed through emergency exits and leaped from the wings of the flaming jet.

The plane was going from New York to San Francisco and was landing for its fourth and final intermediate stop at 5:50 P.M. mountain standard time, 7:50 New York time, when it suddenly burst into flames.

It was the third crash of a

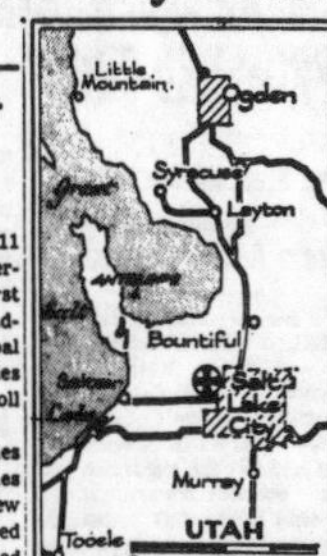

The New York Times Nov. 12, 1965

Site of accident (cross)

Boeing 727 in the last 87 days. The Civil Aeronautics Board in Washington said no decision on grounding the three-engine planes would be made until the cause of the latest crash was determined. An investigator for the board, George R. Baker,

Continued on Page 43, Column 1

MORE U.S. TROOPS AND PLANES DUE TO GO TO VIETNAM

McNamara Sees Johnson—Says Enemy Force Grows Despite Heavy Losses

By JOHN D. POMFRET

Special to The New York Times

AUSTIN, Tex., Nov. 11—Secretary of Defense Robert S. McNamara said today that the United States would send more troops to Vietnam.

He made the announcement after a day-long conference with President Johnson, Secretary of State Dean Rusk and other top Presidential foreign policy advisers at Mr. Johnson's ranch 65 miles west of here.

[In Saigon, authoritative sources reported that the United States intended to double the number of American tactical warplanes in South Vietnam by early next year. Page 2.]

Despite heavy Vietcong casualties, Mr. McNamara said, the Communist force in Vietnam continues to increase.

160,000 Men in U.S. Force

"We believe it will be necessary to add further to the strength of the United States combat forces now deployed in Vietnam," he declared.

"The President instructed me to meet the requirements of our military commanders as they are received."

Mr. McNamara noted that United States military forces in Vietnam now totaled 160,000 men, but he would not say how many more troops would be sent.

President Johnson on July 28 announced an increasing commitment. It has been authoritatively estimated that the force will be up to 200,000 by the end of the year.

Mr. McNamara said he did not wish to give "our opponents" information about the "deployments" before they actually happened.

The Defense Secretary reported that he had received requests for more forces from United States military commanders in Vietnam in the last four weeks.

No Call-Ups Planned

These requests will have to be approved for movement and will move when they are ready, he said. He added that he expected further requests for men.

Mr. McNamara said there were no plans to call up Reserve or National Guard personnel or to extend the duty terms of those now in service.

The increased manpower requirements will be met through voluntary enlistments and draft calls, he explained.

Mr. McNamara said that he did not expect it would be necessary "any time in the near future" to raise draft calls above the 40,000-to-42,000 level of December.

The Defense Secretary said

Continued on Page 2, Column 4

SIGNS DECLARATION OF INDEPENDENCE: Prime Minister Ian D. Smith of Rhodesia proclaims the country's separation from Britain in a ceremony in Salisbury.

United Press International Cablephoto

SMITH IS DEFIANT

He Rejects Final Plea for Talks and Enacts Emergency Rules

Texts of Smith's proclamation and remarks, Page 16.

By LAWRENCE FELLOWS

Special to The New York Times

SALISBURY, Rhodesia, Nov. 11 — The Government of Rhodesia declared its independence from Britain today.

Prime Minister Ian D. Smith read an independence proclamation to the nation on the radio at 1:15 P.M., after a series of dramatic exchanges in which Britain sought to stave off the long-threatened step.

The self-governing colony's break with the mother country came on an issue that had defied solution in more than two years of negotiations.

Britain had refused to grant the colony independence unless its Government, firmly in the hands of 220,000 whites, took steps to assure eventual majority rule by the colony's four million blacks.

Queen Suspends Smith

Even before Prime Minister Smith finished his 20-minute broadcast, the British Governor of Rhodesia, Sir Humphrey Gibbs, announced as the representative of Queen Elizabeth, that he had suspended Mr. Smith and his ministers from office on the Queen's instruction.

The British message never reached the citizens of Rhodesia, for as soon as Mr. Smith issued his proclamation of independence, a set of emergency regulations, including censorship, went into effect.

After the declaration of independence, some Rhodesians were taken into detention. No details have been made available by the Government, but Leo Baron, a white lawyer who advises Joshua Nkomo, the black nationalist leader, was taken from his home in Bulawayo by the police.

Troop Convoy Moves Out

There was also no official information about troop movements, but a convoy of troops left Salisbury in the morning on a northbound road, possibly to reinforce the contingent of light infantry at the Zambezi River, on the Zambian border.

After reading the independence proclamation, Prime Minister Smith declared: "We Rhodesians have rejected the doctrinaire philosophy of appeasement and surrender. We have struck a blow for the preservation of justice, civilization and Christianity, and in the spirit of this belief, we have this day assumed our sovereign independence."

"God bless you all," he added.

White Rhodesians seemed to take the news calmly, many with an air of pride and satisfaction. "Jolly good" was a typical reaction on the street.

Black men sat about in the warm sun or loafed against shop windows, talking among themselves. Their conversations

Continued on Page 16, Column 1

Byrd of Virginia Resigns After 32 Years in Senate

By BEN A. FRANKLIN

Special to The New York Times

RICHMOND, Va., Nov. 11—United States Senator Harry Flood Byrd, the 78-year-old conservative patriarch of Virginia politics, resigned today, citing his failing health.

His departure opened the way for what is expected to be a bitter struggle for control of the Virginia Democratic party, already showing signs of progressivism after nearly half a century of tight conservative control by the Senator's organization.

The battle is expected to center on a succession attempt by Senator Byrd's oldest son, Harry F. Byrd Jr.

[Under the seniority system, Senator Byrd, an opponent of the Administration's fiscal and economic policies, will be succeeded as chairman of the Senate Finance Committee by Senator Russell B. Long, Democrat of Louisiana, an Administration supporter. The committee has jurisdiction over tax legislation. Page 32.]

Serving Sixth Term

The influential Senator Byrd, in his sixth term and suffering from painful arthritis, submitted his resignation in a letter to Gov. Albertis S. Harrison Jr.

Mr. Harrison, who has held virtually unswerving loyalty to Senator Byrd's declining organization, frequently called "the Byrd machine," announced at a news conference here this morning that he had accepted the resignation today. It had been a tightly held secret.

The two-page letter of resignation, dated Nov. 6 on the stationery of the Senate Finance Committee, which Senator Byrd headed for nearly 11 years, was delivered to the Governor's Mansion here last night, Mr. Harrison said.

Mr. Harrison read the letter to the newsmen but declined to answer most questions. He said he was certain that he could not have dissuaded Senator Byrd from resigning.

In his letter, Senator Byrd noted that he was first elected to the Virginia Senate 50 years ago this month. Later, from 1926 to 1930, he served as one

Continued on Page 33, Column 3

BUSINESS CRITICAL OF ALUMINUM CUT

But Market Takes Rollback of Prices in Its Stride—Pressure Is Assailed

By VARTANIG G. VARTAN

Bankers and business leaders across the nation criticized yesterday the methods used by the Johnson Administration in achieving the rollback of aluminum price increases.

The consensus of many executives was that the honeymoon between the President and the business community had reached its rockiest stage since Mr. Johnson took office nearly two years ago.

On Wall Street the stock market shrugged off the controversy to post its first general advance—a token one—in the past five trading sessions. Several aluminum stocks even made gains of a point or better.

Lawrence Harvey, president of Harvey Aluminum Company, a large integrated producer, said in Los Angeles:

"I feel very bad about the Administration's action. Aluminum prices are lower than they were in 1961 and would have been even with the increase."

Also in Los Angeles, R. E. Radcliffe, manager of the Hico Company of America, dealer in construction beams and panels, declared:

"It was none of the Government's business to interfere."

In Minneapolis, Philip R. Harris, senior vice president of the Northwestern National Bank, said:

"It looks like it certainly was a forced deal."

Eliot Janeway, an economist and author as well as a friend

Continued on Page 28, Column 3

U.N. ASKS BRITAIN TO HALT RHODESIA

Assembly Votes Resolution Urging All Needed Steps to Block Independence

By RAYMOND DANIELL

Special to The New York Times

UNITED NATIONS, N. Y., Nov. 11 — The General Assembly adopted a resolution tonight calling on Britain to take all necessary steps to end the rebellion by Rhodesia's white minority Government.

The vote was 102 to 2, with only South Africa and Portugal dissenting and France abstaining.

The Assembly acted on the insistence of 36 African states unwilling to wait until tomorrow's meeting of the Security Council, requested by Lord Caradon of Britain immediately after learning that Rhodesia had declared its independence.

Move for Meeting Fails

The permanent representative of Britain urged patience until tomorrow, when his Foreign Minister, Michael Stewart, could report on action the British Government had taken or would take to meet the challenge of Prime Minister Ian D. Smith's Government in Salisbury.

The Africans, joined by some representatives of the Asian group, sought unsuccessfully to force a meeting of the Security Council tonight. They held that the situation resulting from the action of the Rhodesian Government was too explosive for the exercise of patience, as Lord Caradon had counseled.

Chafing for some kind of action, 36 African states took their case to the Trusteeship Committee, which after brief debate adopted the resolution that it sent to the Assembly.

In the debate preceding the

Continued on Page 17, Column 6

Wilson Denounces Smith; Commonwealth Tie Is Cut

By ANTHONY LEWIS

Special to The New York Times

LONDON, Nov. 11—The British Government, denouncing Rhodesia's unilateral declaration of independence as rebellion and treason, today took the first counter-measures.

Rhodesia was expelled from the sterling area. Her preferential tariff treatment as a Commonwealth land was

Excerpts from Wilson's speech are printed on Page 17.

suspended. Controls were imposed on all trade and exchanges of currency. Purchases of tobacco and sugar, the main Rhodesian crops, were banned.

Prime Minister Wilson announced these moves to a House of Commons that had about it a sense of occasion, of history.

Mr. Wilson spoke quietly, almost sadly, but his words were not soft as he traced the last few desperate days of negotiations.

Act Called Treasonable

"The British Government condemn the purported declaration of independence by the former Government of Rhodesia as an illegal act and one which is ineffective in law," Mr. Wilson declared. "Action taken to give effect to it will be treasonable."

At 6 o'clock this morning, he disclosed, he talked with Rhodesia's Prime Minister, Ian D. Smith, on the telephone to try again to head off the "illegal act."

"I ended the conversation," Mr. Wilson said, "with a heavy heart, feeling that reason had fled the scene and that emotions, unreasoning racialist emotions at that, had taken command regardless of the consequences for Rhodesia, for Africa and for the world."

The Prime Minister called the white Rhodesians' decision a

Continued on Page 17, Column 1

UNILATERAL MOVE DEPLORED BY U.S.

Washington Recalls Consul General—Ends Activities of Information Agency

Special to The New York Times

AUSTIN, Tex., Nov. 11—Secretary of State Dean Rusk said today that the United States Government "deplores" the "unilateral action of the white minority Government of Rhodesia in illegally seizing power."

He announced that the United States was recalling its Consul General in Rhodesia, Roswell D. McClelland, and terminating the activities of the United States Information Service there.

He said also that Arthur J. Goldberg, the chief United States representative at the United Nations, would state the Government's position on Rhodesia tomorrow. Until then and until "we see what Britain does," further sanctions will be withheld, Mr. Rusk declared.

The Secretary made his statement after about six hours of discussions with President Johnson at the President's ranch 65 miles west of here.

Advisers Return to Capital

Other participants in the talks were Secretary of Defense Robert S. McNamara, Under Secretary of State George W. Ball; McGeorge Bundy, Special Assistant to the President for National Security Affairs, and Walt W. Rostow, Assistant Secretary of State for Planning.

The President's advisers flew here from Washington today for the conference and returned there early this evening.

It was the first full-scale foreign-policy review that Mr. Johnson had held with his advisers since he entered the hospital Oct. 7 for surgery the next day to remove his gall bladder.

Mr. Johnson is convalescing at his ranch and is expected to return to Washington early next week to entertain Princess Margaret of Britain and her husband, the Earl of Snowdon.

The President also conferred

Continued on Page 17, Column 5

EISENHOWER AIDES TAKE GRAVER VIEW

Physicians Say New Heart Attack Is Always Threat

By FELIX BELAIR Jr.

Special to The New York Times

AUGUSTA, Ga., Nov. 11—The heart specialists attending former President Dwight D. Eisenhower acknowledged for the first time today that his recurring attacks of "coronary insufficiency" could develop into what they called "a full-blown heart attack."

A medical bulletin at noon also disclosed for the first time that General Eisenhower's treatment and therapy were the same "as if he had suffered a heart attack." It said that this was only the accepted preventive procedure and that there was still no evidence of any recent heart muscle damage. The 75-year-old former President remained under an oxygen tent through much of the day.

A 5 P.M. statement said that "General Eisenhower spent a comfortable day reading and visiting with Mrs. Eisenhower, Dr. Milton S. Eisenhower, his younger brother, and members of his staff."

A note of optimism was sounded by the former President's brother, president of Johns Hopkins University at Baltimore, who was asked how the General looked to him.

"Wonderful," was the reply. "I hope I look as good at age

Continued on Page 34, Column 3

Nobel Winner Is Named by State To $45,000 University Position

By FRANCIS X. CLINES

Special to The New York Times

STONY BROOK, L. I., Nov. 11—The fledgling division of the State University here announced a major step in its development today in the appointment of Dr. C. N. Yang, physicist and Nobel laureate, to the Albert Einstein Chair in Science.

The chair is one of 10 teaching and research positions set up by the Legislature two years ago that carry an annual endowment of $100,000. Dr. Yang will be paid a salary of $45,000, or $5,000 more than Dr. Samuel B. Gould, president of the university, to make him the highest paid professor in the university.

The remaining $55,000 will be used for staff salaries and research as Dr. Yang chooses.

Dr. Yang, who is 43 years old, was born in Anwei, China. He is a theoretical physicist

Dr. C. N. Yang

and an authority on elementary particles.

The appointment was praised by Dr. Maurice Goldhaber, director of the Brookhaven National Laboratory in nearby

Continued on Page 46, Column 3

WHITE CONVICTED OF RAPING NEGRO

Mississippi Jury Sentences Youth to Life in Prison

By United Press International

HATTIESBURG, Miss., Nov. 11—A Mississippi jury, in an unusual action, found a young white man guilty today of the rape of a Negro girl.

The all-white jury convicted Norman Cannon, 19 years old, of nearby Sumrall, after deliberating five and a half hours.

Rape is a capital offense, but the jury exercised an option and fixed punishment for the slim, bushy-haired youth at life in prison.

Defense attorneys immediately told Circuit Judge Stanton Hall they would file a motion for a new trial and would appeal the case to the State Supreme Court if necessary.

Cannon allegedly picked up the girl at her home on the pretense he sought a baby sitter, drove her to a logging road and attacked her at the point of a yellow-handled knife. The girl was 15 years old.

Lawyers and court sources here and at the State Capitol in Jackson said that this was apparently the first time in modern times in Mississippi that a white man had been convicted of raping a Negro.

Civil rights leaders here have long said that no white men had ever been convicted of assaulting Negroes, but that

Continued on Page 19, Column 1

Macapagal Apparently Defeated By Marcos in Philippines Vote

By SEYMOUR TOPPING

Special to The New York Times

MANILA, Friday, Nov. 12—Senator Ferdinand E. Marcos claimed victory last night in the Philippines presidential election as his lead over the incumbent President, Diosdado Macapagal, increased to a seemingly unbeatable 665,000 votes.

Mr. Marcos, the Nationalist party's candidate, outlined his program at a news conference and told his Liberal party opponents that "there shall be no vindictiveness" despite the turbulent election campaign.

With more than 65 per cent of the vote reported, Senator Marcos's lead already exceeds the margin of 650,000 by which President Macapagal defeated Carlos Garcia in 1961.

Liberal party leaders privately were conceding Senator Marcos's election, although a statement by President Macapagal last night described Senator Marcos's claims as "quite premature."

Senator Marcos said there would be "no serious changes" in foreign policy. But he added that he would adopt a more flexible attitude toward the question of sending combat troops to Vietnam.

Upon assuming office, the Senator said, he will ask Congress for authority to send troops to Vietnam if this becomes necessary and it will help to compel North Vietnam to open peace talks. He said this categorically, but his remarks were later qualified in a summary issued by his press office.

Senator Marcos's party earlier had blocked approval of a Macapagal proposal that a combat engineer battalion and security

Continued on Page 20, Column 4

Rhodesians Borrow Phrases From 1776

By DANA ADAMS SCHMIDT

Special to The New York Times

LONDON, Nov. 11—Today's declaration by Rhodesia was the first unilateral declaration of independence from Britain since that of the American colonies in 1776.

In his pronouncement, Prime Minister Ian D. Smith borrowed the phraseology of the American declaration if not its ideals.

Paraphrasing the American text, "When in the course of human events . . ." the Rhodesian one opens: "Whereas in the course of human affairs . . ."

But the Rhodesian document then omits the ideas that have influenced much subsequent American political thought: "We hold these truths to be self-evident, that all men are created equal, that they are endowed by their Creator with

Continued on Page 11, Column 3

NEWS INDEX

"All the News That's Fit to Print"

The New York Times.

LATE CITY EDITION

U. S. Weather Bureau Report (Page 90) Forecast: Mostly sunny, cooler today; cold tonight. Milder tomorrow. Temp. Range: 50—40; yesterday: 63—46.

NEWS SUMMARY AND INDEX, PAGE 95

SECTION ONE

VOL. CXV. No. 39,390. © 1965 by The New York Times Company. Times Square, New York, N. Y. 10036 NEW YORK, SUNDAY, NOVEMBER 28, 1965. 30c beyond 50-mile zone from New York City, except on Long Island, higher in air delivery cities THIRTY CENTS

7 BILLION DEFICIT SEEN AS SPENDING NEARS 105 BILLION

U.S. Aides Say Outlay Will Exceed $100 Billion Mark for First Time in History

DEFENSE IS MAIN FACTOR

War in Vietnam Accounts for Most of the $5 Billion Rise in Expenditure Estimate

By ROBERT B. SEMPLE Jr.
Special to The New York Times

AUSTIN, Tex., Nov. 27 — White House sources disclosed today that Federal spending in the current fiscal year—now nearly half over—would rise to a high of between $105 billion and $107 billion.

This means that Federal outlays will exceed by from $5 billion to $7 billion the original estimate of $99.7 billion made by the Administration last January.

It also means that for the first time in history, Federal expenditures will exceed $100 billion. This had been widely expected in Washington.

The extraordinary increase in expenditures, according to officials here, will be offset in part by an increase in revenues amounting to about $2 billion and possibly more. The January budget predicted receipts of $94.4 billion. The new revised estimates call for receipts of $96.5 billion or more.

$10 Billion Gap Possible

Accordingly, the budget deficit for the fiscal year 1966, which ends next June 30, will be substantially larger than the January estimate of $5.3 billion. If expenditures reach the top predicted figure of $107 billion, and receipts are $96.5 billion, the deficit will exceed $10 billion.

However, sources here said that they had been conservative in figuring receipts, and that in their view the deficit would probably turn out to be somewhere between $7 billion and $8 billion, although it could go higher. They also emphasized that these figures were preliminary, rough and susceptible to change.

These sources said that much of the increase in expenditures—but by no means all—was attributable to the war in Vietnam and the accompanying rise in defense expenditures.

Unless the pace of the war in Vietnam shows unexpected increases, the deficit does not appear likely to exceed the $12.4 billion deficit of the fiscal year 1959. It will, however, be well above last fiscal year's deficit of $3.5 billion. The deficit in the

Continued on Page 65, Column 1

United Press International Telephoto

OUTSIDE THE WHITE HOUSE: Marchers demonstrating yesterday their opposition to U.S. action in Vietnam

U.S. BOMBERS CUT HANOI'S RAIL LINE FROM RED CHINA

Also Blast Missile Center—Vietcong Maul Saigon Unit at a Rubber Plantation

Special to The New York Times

SAIGON, South Vietnam, Nov. 27 — United States planes bombed an assembly and maintenance center for surface-to-air missiles in North Vietnam today and cut the important railroad between Hanoi and the Chinese Communist border, according to military spokesmen.

To the south, Vietcong guerrillas staged a series of attacks.

The guerrillas made an attack in more than regimental strength against a somewhat smaller South Vietnamese force at an abandoned French rubber plantation about 40 miles northwest of Saigon.

[The Vietcong, reinforced by North Vietnamese regulars to a total of perhaps 2,000 men, mauled a Saigon regiment in the fight at the rubber plantation and machine-gunned South Vietnamese who surrendered, The Associated Press reported Sunday. Page 3.]

Yesterday other guerrillas inflicted serious casualties in attacks on four Government outposts 15 miles southwest of the capital in an area regarded as relatively secure.

The attack on the North Vietnamese missile center occurred at Dongem, 22 miles from Hanoi. Flights of F-105 Thunderchief jets dropped 57 tons of 750-pound and 3,000-pound bombs, destroying 17 buildings and damaging three.

No U.S. Planes Lost

Despite what was called moderate antiaircraft fire, no American planes were lost.

The Dongem center, which assembles and maintains missiles for at least three launching sites nearby, was bombed Nov. 7 in what has become a drive to knock out the 30-odd known missile sites in North Vietnam.

Other American jets damaged six bridges on the main railroad line 105 miles northwest of Hanoi and cut the track in two other places. The rail line is believed to be used to move military and other supplies south from China to Hanoi. Some of the supplies are then infiltrated to Vietcong and North Vietnamese troops in South Vietnam.

The regimental-size Vietcong attack occurred in the area of a rubber plantation owned by the Michelin Rubber Company of France. The company abandoned the plantation last month rather than yield to political and military demands by Vietcong guerrillas who had infil-

Continued on Page 3, Column 6

Rising War Worries Vietnamese in South But They Stay Loyal

By CHARLES MOHR
Special to The New York Times

SAIGON, South Vietnam, Nov. 27—A recent survey by a group of American civilian officials here has reported signs of increasing anxiety among South Vietnamese over the growing intensity of the warfare and its effects on civilians.

The study could find no evidence, however, that the population had begun to go over to the political control of the Vietcong in protest against artillery and air strikes by South Vietnamese and United States forces.

Fears that such political shifts might take place have been frequently aired and discussed in the American mission here and in United States reports. It is probable that no single question has received more attention.

The study indicated that Buddhist religious leaders were critical of the increas-

Continued on Page 2, Column 3

5,000 A-WARHEADS STORED FOR NATO, M'NAMARA SAYS

Stockpile in Europe Will Be Increased by 20 Per Cent in the Next Six Months

U.S. ALSO HOLDS 5,000

10 Allied Defense Ministers Meet in Paris on How to Share Nuclear Planning

By HENRY TANNER
Special to The New York Times

PARIS, Nov. 27—Secretary of Defense Robert S. McNamara declared here today that more than 5,000 United States nuclear warheads were currently stored on European soil in support of Atlantic alliance forces.

He announced that this nuclear arsenal would be increased by 20 per cent during the next six months.

"This will represent a doubling of nuclear weapons strength in Europe over the past five years," the Secretary declared.

The warheads are under United States control but have been supplied to the North Atlantic Treaty Organization for the delivery systems of alliance members. Mr. McNamara called the warheads "the nuclear component of the NATO deterrent forces."

The Defense Secretary said that, in addition to the nuclear weapons at the disposal of NATO, the United States strategic forces, including its Polaris submarines, American-based Minuteman missiles and B-52 bombers, had an arsenal of more than 5,000 warheads of their own.

Ministers Form Special Unit

Mr. McNamara made his statement at a one-day conference of Defense Ministers of 10 of the 15 NATO countries.

He and the Defense Ministers of Britain, Canada, West Germany, Italy, Belgium, the Netherlands, Denmark, Greece and Turkey met as a Special Committee on Nuclear Consultation.

The purpose of the committee, which Mr. McNamara proposed last May, is to give European members of the alliance greater influence on decisions involving nuclear planning and the use of nuclear weapons.

But American officials repeated today that the committee was not intended as a substitute for any projects of nuclear sharing such as the allied nuclear-armed force proposed by the United States or the Atlantic force suggested by Britain. These and other projects are still under discussion, the officials said.

Mr. McNamara did not give a reason for the planned increase in the nuclear arsenal, which, he said, included artillery shells, missile warheads and bombs. But observers speculated that his emphasis on the warheads backing NATO was meant to discourage pressure from non-nuclear member countries for access to nuclear weapons.

The West German delegation, whose Government is pressing for a greater nuclear role, was

Continued on Page 5, Column 1

LINDSAY DELAYING ON HEAD OF POLICE

Says He Seeks Man Sensitive to Minority Problems—Other Selections Due

By RICHARD L. MADDEN
Special to The New York Times

DORADO, P. R., Nov. 27—Mayor-elect John V. Lindsay said today that he was searching for a Police Commissioner who would be "very sensitive" to the problems of minority groups.

The Commissioner, Mr. Lindsay added, will have to be a "Renaissance man"—a man of many talents—who also understands the problem of the policeman on the beat.

Mr. Lindsay made the comments as he described the "well-rounded" man he wanted to head the city's 26,000-man police force. Of all his appointments, Mr. Lindsay said, the selection of a Police Commissioner will be the hardest one to decide.

"I think you have to have someone who has an understanding about minority group problems," he explained. "The people would have to believe that he has an understanding of those problems."

Decision Still Pending

The Mayor-elect said he had not yet made his choice for Police Commissioner. "I don't want to feel rushed about it," he said.

Asked if Vincent L. Broderick, who was appointed Police Commissioner last June by Mayor Wagner, would fit his description, Mr. Lindsay say: "He could." He added later that "Mr. Broderick is a very good man."

Mr. Lindsay, who is scheduled to return to New York tomorrow night after a five-day visit in Puerto Rico, said he planned to announce the appointment of two commissioners and his press secretary next week.

He refused to identify the appointees or the departments the new commissioners would head. He did say that the Police Commissioner would not be among the next round of appointments.

Mr. Lindsay sketched the word outline of his Police Commissioner as he had breakfast, pineapple juice, one fried egg

Continued on Page 75, Column 3

Thousands Walk in Capital To Protest War in Vietnam

Demonstrators Decorous—3 White House Aides Meet With Leaders

By MAX FRANKEL
Special to The New York Times

WASHINGTON, Nov. 27—A great throng of young and middle-aged Americans from all parts of the country strolled decorously around the White House today to protest the war in Vietnam and urge negotiations to end it.

Variously estimated by the police to number from 15,000 to 25,000, and by their own leaders as high as 50,000, the demonstrators joined in what they called a March on Washington for Peace in Vietnam.

For two hours, they carried placards that for the most part bore cautiously phrased slogans, such as "Stop the Bombing" or "Supervised Cease-Fire," around three sides of the White House.

Then they went to the Washington Monument and sat under a cloudless sunny sky to hear a series of moderate appeals for United States peace initiatives.

There were small clusters of fired-up youths in the crowd, some of whom carried the flags of the Vietcong.

More Babies Than Beatniks

There were the organized forces of Youth Against War and Fascism pressing upon the marchers signs that called for an immediate American withdrawal from Vietnam. The organizers of the march had tried to keep out such placards.

But most of the crowd would not have been out of place at the Army-Navy game. There were more babies than beatniks, more family groups than folk-song quartets.

Among the marchers there appeared to be as many differences of opinion, even about Vietnam, as in any large assembly. Some praised President Johnson's desire for peace and objected only to his "over-reliance" on military advisers, as one woman put it. Others condemned him as a hypocrite.

The President remained at his Texas ranch today and let three White House aides meet the leaders of the protest. Through

Continued on Page 86, Column 3

Asian Communists Sure Public Opinion in U.S. Will Force War's End

By SEYMOUR TOPPING
Special to The New York Times

HONG KONG, Nov. 27—Asian Communists declared today that they were sure the United States war effort in Vietnam would collapse under the pressure of adverse American public opinion.

Demonstrators in the United States opposing the war were commended by the Communist Vietcong and Peking for joining in the common struggle against what were described as imperialist policies of the Johnson Administration.

[The Vietcong radio said Saturday that two American captives had been freed after two years in prison camps. The action was taken, the broadcast said, in honor of protest demonstrations against the war in Vietnam. Page 87.]

Nguyen Huu Tho, president of the South Vietnam Liberation Front, the political organization of the Vietcong, sent his best wishes for the "brilliant success" of the March on Washington for Peace in Vietnam. In a radio message to Frank Emspak, president of the National Coordinating Committee to End the War in Vietnam, he said:

"With sympathy and support of all strata of American people and progressive people the

Continued on Page 87, Column 3

NEW BOARD ASKED ON CITY COLLEGES

Public Education Association Wants Governor to Name Five Members of Panel

By LEONARD BUDER

The Public Education Association asked yesterday the removal of the Board of Higher Education by the state and the appointment of a new reform board to govern the City University.

The organization, composed of influential citizens interested in education here, said the Governor should be given the power to appoint one-third of the proposed new board, which would have 15 members. At present the Mayor appoints the entire 21-member board.

Although the association's proposal would give the state its first direct voice in the operation of the municipal college system, the group said it foresaw "no threat to the integrity of the City University."

William B. Nichols, the association's president, announced that it would make the request this week at a public hearing to be conducted by the Joint Legislative Committee on Higher Education. He said the state committee would be asked to "initiate" appropriate action at the next session of the Legislature, which begins in January.

The organization sharply criticized the present board as an "unwieldy body" that had failed to provide "leadership in financ-

Continued on Page 48, Column 3

DEVELOPMENT AID IS PLEDGED AT RIO

19 Nations in O.A.S. Agree to Joint Effort for Social and Economic Growth

By ARTHUR J. OLSEN
Special to The New York Times

RIO DE JANEIRO, Nov. 27—The Special Inter-American Conference approved today in committee a pledge of joint efforts for the well-being of the 400 million people embraced in the Organization of American States.

The pledge of the 19 nations meeting here to assist one another in the economic and social development of the hemisphere is summed up in a 3,000-word document.

It will become a key part of a protocol entitled "The Act of Rio de Janeiro" to be formally adopted early next week.

The declaration on development policy is one of the principal fruits of this two-week assembly of the Western Hemisphere alliance due to conclude Tuesday. The other is a program of revitalization and reform of the Organization of American States, a sprawling group of councils and agencies that constitutes the inter-American system.

Session Planned in 1966

Representatives at this meeting have agreed to convene another Special Inter-American Conference next year—probably in Lima, Peru, in July—at which the reforms and the new commitment to economic development will be written into the O.A.S. Charter.

The declaration on development essentially affirms in solemn form and in more specific detail the undertakings of the hemispheric community when it inaugurated the Alliance for Progress at Punta del Este, Uruguay, in 1961.

United States officials here are confident that it will lend new impetus and direction to the 10-year Alliance development program, which is acknowledged to have progressed with disappointing slowness.

The document incorporates the offer made by Secretary of State Dean Rusk at the outset of this conference to extend United States support of the Alliance for Progress beyond

Continued on Page 36, Column 1

ARMY-NAVY GAME ENDS IN 7-TO-7 TIE

102,000 Attend Classic—Choker Wins at Aqueduct

Army and Navy played to an undistinguished 7-7 tie yesterday in the 66th football meeting between the service academies.

Before a crowd of 102,000 in Philadelphia's John F. Kennedy Stadium, the Cadets scored early in the first period following a fumble recovery. Navy tied the game with 63 seconds left in the first half.

Results of other games:

Alabama	30	Auburn	3
Baylor	17	Rice	13
Boston Coll.	35	Holy Cross	0
Brig. Young	42	New Mexico	8
Florida	30	Florida St.	17
Georgia	17	Georgia Tech	7
Miami (Fla.)	0	Notre Dame	0
Mississippi	21	Miss'sippi St.	0
Southern Cal.	56	Wyoming	6
Tennessee	21	Vanderbilt	3
Texas Christ.	10	So. Methodist	7
Texas West.	38	W. Texas St.	21

HORSE RACING

The Hobeau Farm's Choker, paying $13 for $2 to win, captured the $57,100 Gallant Fox Handicap at Aqueduct.

HOCKEY

Ken Wharram's shot with less than six minutes remaining lifted the Chicago Black Hawks to a 1-0 victory over the New York Rangers. The game, at Madison Square Garden was the first National Hockey League contest to be televised in color.

Details in Section 5

Wagner Says 15c Fare Issue Is Lindsay's Alone to Resolve

By EMANUEL PERLMUTTER

Mayor Wagner put the retention of the 15-cent fare squarely up to Mayor-elect John V. Lindsay yesterday.

"Its future depends on how willing the next administration is to give money to preserve it," Mr. Wagner asserted after a conference in Gracie Mansion with Daniel T. Scannell, a member of the three-man Transit Authority.

The Mayor had conferred with Mr. Scannell on the progress of the authority's negotiations with the Transport Workers Union for a new two-year contract. The authority has estimated that the union's demands would cost it $680 million.

Mr. Lindsay said both before and after his election that he considered the 15-cent fare essential to the city and that he would do all in his power to preserve it. However, with the city already in a financial squeeze, doubts have arisen as to whether it could give the Transit Authority more money.

The Transit Authority already faces a deficit of many millions of dollars in its current fiscal operations. In past contract settlements, Mr. Wagner has always received permission of the Legislature to grant the authority financial aid. In placing the responsibility for future grants with Mr. Lindsay, the Mayor apparently sought to divorce himself from the problem.

John J. Gilhooley, the only

Continued on Page 46, Column 1

Manuscripts Stolen in Vatican Found

United Press International Cablephoto

Vatican manuscripts of Petrarch, open, and Tasso after they and crown were recovered

By ROBERT C. DOTY
Special to The New York Times

ROME, Nov. 27 — Major items stolen from the Vatican Library, including precious manuscripts by the Italian poets Petrarch and Tasso, were recovered yesterday only minutes after the first public announcement of the burglary, the police disclosed today.

However, for about 18 hours the police and Vatican authorities withheld the news of the recovery in the hope that the thief or thieves would make a slip that would trap them. Meanwhile the world press headlined the search for documents that were already in police hands. The theft was discovered yesterday morning.

One or more persons had either secreted themselves in the Vatican Museum, of which the library forms a part, when it was locked for the night or scaled a wall to gain entry to the Sistine Hall, where many of the thousands of documents and art objects in the Vatican collection are displayed. A showcase was forced open and the 72-page parchment "Canzoniere" of the 14th-century Italian poet Francesco Petrarch, most of it in his own handwriting, and a 152-page book of poems by Torquato Tasso of the 16th century, with many corrections in the poet's hand, were stolen. From another cabinet in the Borgia apartments a replica of the crown of St. Stephen, 11th-century

Continued on Page 30, Column 4

Iowa's Amish Fight 'Worldly' Schooling

By WALTER RUGABER
Special to The New York Times

HAZLETON, Iowa, Nov. 24—Local officials who tried to force 36 Amish children into a "worldly" public school here this week ran into the same stiff resistance that has frustrated educators in several states.

The Amish say they have no formal religious objection either to public education generally or to state-controlled teachers in their own schools.

But some parents in this fertile farm country oppose both on somewhat different grounds. They fear a school or a teacher that might prove "too worldly" for the simple, 17th-century life they prefer.

These parents have been fined

Continued on Page 35, Column 2

Today's Sections

Index to Subjects

Many stranded commuters were forced to use the lobby steps of the Hotel Commodore in New York City. Vacancies were nonexistent shortly after the blackout set in.

Delacroix Island (east of New Orleans) shown in the wake of Hurricane Betsy. One of the most devastating disasters of the decade, Betsy had a 15-mile-thick band of 129-140-mile-an-hour winds encircling her eye.

The televising of controversial trials such as in the case of Billy Sol Estes (right) was ruled improper by the Supreme Court. This was another extension of the areas being designed by the Court to extend personal freedom.

Television audiences found it easy to laugh about a difficult situation during World War II in *Hogan's Heroes.* Featured were Werner Klemperer as Commander Klink, John Banner as Schultz and Bob Crane as Hogan.

Barbra Streisand's one-hour special was the most generously praised special of the 1964-65 season. Just having conquered Broadway (in *Funny Girl*), television was just one more item to her list of accomplishments.

Larry Storch and Forrest Tucker were cavalrymen and Edward Everett Horton played an Indian in *F Troop,* the television series that was a slapstick portrayal of army life.

Jeffrey Hunter, Dina Merrill and series' star Efrem Zimbalist, Jr. (left to right), shown in *The FBI.*

Don Adams played the most inefficient secret agent in *Get Smart!* With the assistance of Barbara Feldon, Agent 99, the show was the ultimate spoofery of all international agents à la James Bond.

Patrick McGoohan starred as Drake in *Secret Agent*, a popular spy series among the many in the mid-sixties.

Roger Smith starred in *Mr. Roberts.*

"All the News That's Fit to Print"

The New York Times.

LATE CITY EDITION

U.S. Weather Bureau Report (Page 94) forecasts: Light rain and snow, then clearing today; becoming cloudy tomorrow. Temp. range: 46—37; yesterday: 48—42.

VOL. CXV..No. 39,408.

NEW YORK, THURSDAY, DECEMBER 16, 1965. TEN CENTS

TWO GEMINIS FLY 6 TO 10 FEET APART IN MAN'S FIRST SPACE RENDEZVOUS; CREWS, FACE TO FACE, TALK BY RADIO

U.S. JETS SMASH BIG POWER PLANT OUTSIDE HAIPHONG

Cut Nation's Current 15%—Generators Supported Industries in Hanoi

By NEIL SHEEHAN
Special to The New York Times

SAIGON, South Vietnam, Dec. 15—United States jet fighter-bombers destroyed a large power plant today 14 miles from Haiphong, North Vietnam's chief port, in the first American air strike against a North Vietnamese target of major industrial importance.

A military spokesman said the planes, flown by Air Force pilots, had struck the Uongbi thermal power plant, northeast of Haiphong. The plant has a capacity of 24,000 kilowatts, about 15 per cent of North Vietnam's total electric-power output. It supplies some of the power needs of both Hanoi and Haiphong.

The center of the plant, housing steam turbines, generators and other sensitive equipment, was smashed at 11 A.M. with 12 tons of 3,000-pound bombs. A single flight of F-105 Thunderchief fighter-bombers—apparently four to six craft—made the raid.

Secondary Blasts Sighted

A spokesman said that the pilots had encountered bad weather and heavy antiaircraft fire but reported having destroyed the plant. Several secondary explosions—detonations of explosives on the ground—were observed during the raid.

This was the first time United States aircraft had struck so close to North Vietnam's two major cities—Hanoi and Haiphong. The closest previous strike was a recent raid against a firing site for Soviet-made surface-to-air missiles, 22 miles from Hanoi.

[Secretary of Defense McNamara, who arrived back in Washington shortly after midnight from the North Atlantic Alliance meeting in Paris, said the bombing of the power plant near Haiphong "is representative of the type of attack we have carried out and will continue to carry out," The Associated Press reported Thursday. Page 3.]

Many Homes Darkened

According to military spokesmen here, the destruction of the power plant was certain to affect North Vietnamese civilians much more directly than have previous strikes, almost all of which have been aimed at road, rail and river networks and military installations.

The power-station raid will probably cut off electricity in large numbers of civilian homes as well as significantly reduce the amount of power available for industries in the Hai-

Continued on Page 3, Column 1

Gemini 7 Crew

Lieut. Col. Frank Borman

Lieut. Col. Frank Borman

Comdr. James A. Lovell Jr.

Major Steps From Launching to Rendezvous

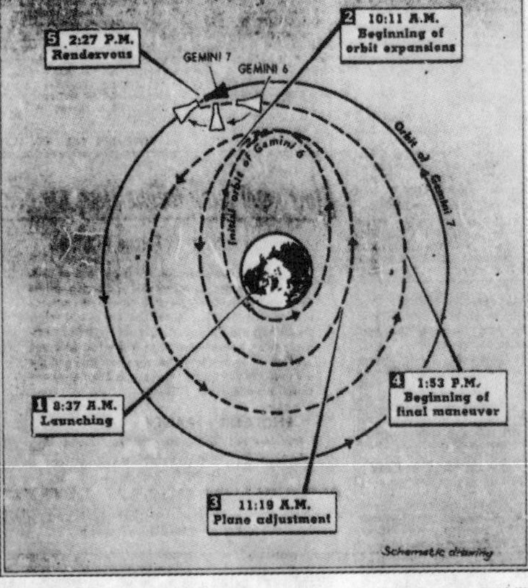

The New York Times Dec. 16, 1965

Major steps of yesterday's rendezvous of the Gemini 6 and Gemini 7 spacecraft are shown from the launching of Gemini 6 to its meeting with Gemini 7, orbiting about 185 miles above the earth. At rendezvous two craft were nose to nose within 10 feet of each other.

Gemini 6 Crew

Capt. Walter M. Schirra Jr.

Capt. Walter M. Schirra Jr.

Maj. Thomas P. Stafford

Craft in Formation Orbit 185 Miles Up

Officials of Space Agency Are Jubilant at Success—Maneuver Is Vital to a Manned Landing on Moon

By JOHN NOBLE WILFORD
Special to The New York Times

HOUSTON, Dec. 15—Four American astronauts steered Gemini 6 and Gemini 7 today to man's first rendezvous in the vastness of outer space.

In a spectacular performance of space navigation, the astronauts brought their craft within six to ten feet of each other about 185 miles above the earth. The two capsules then circled the earth nearly two times on a four-hour formation flight before Gemini 6 broke away to a lower orbit.

The pilots of the pursuing Gemini 6 were Capt. Walter M. Schirra Jr. of the Navy and Maj. Thomas P. Stafford of the Air Force. Pilots of the Gemini 7 target ship were Lieut. Col. Frank Borman of the Air Force and Comdr. James A. Lovell Jr. of the Navy.

The crews came close enough to see into each other's cabins, trade gibes and inspect details on the exteriors of their funnel-shaped spacecraft. The Gemini 6 astronauts could see Commander Lovell's beard and could tell that Colonel Borman was chewing gum.

"We have company tonight!" radioed Colonel Borman from Gemini 7, which has been in orbit 11 days of its record 14-day mission. Gemini 6, launched from Cape Kennedy at 8:37 A.M., Eastern standard time, today, is expected to splash down near the Bahamas at 10:29 A.M. tomorrow.

Officials Jubilant

The success of the mission brought jubilation at the space center here.

"It's the biggest milestone since the flight of John Glenn," Christopher C. Kraft Jr., the flight director, said.

Colonel Glenn's Mercury flight, on Feb. 20, 1962, was the first orbital mission by an American.

The two Geminis today proved that two spacecraft can find each other, rendezvous and presumably link up.

Such a maneuver is necessary if astronauts are to land on the moon and then return to their mother ship, which would be circling in a lunar orbit. Space officials are aiming for such a manned landing in 1969.

Today's rendezvous also opens the way to operations in which men and supplies can be ferried out to orbiting stations, such as the Air Force's planned Manned Orbiting Laboratory.

'Made It Look Easy'

"These crews made it look easy," said Dr. Robert Gilruth, director of the Manned Spacecraft Center here, praising all those who had made the mission a success.

Just before final rendezvous, there was an anxious moment of silence. Radio contact between the craft and the ground was lost. Then a relay tracking station off Hawaii reported in. The two Gemini had drawn within 120 feet of each other.

"There just seems to be a lot of traffic up here," Captain Schirra commented.

"Call a policeman," Colonel

Continued on Page 28, Column 1

AT LAST, GEMINI 6 HAS A PERFECT DAY

Even Sun Comes Out in Time to Dispel Last Doubt of Jubilant Ground Staff

By EVERT CLARK
Special to The New York Times

CAPE KENNEDY, Fla., Dec. 15—After twice having had its wings clipped by failure, the Gemini 6 finally climbed to its space rendezvous today in a most spectacular way.

For 15 years, missiles have flown from this sandy point of land. But no one today could recall a flight of greater beauty.

It left behind a sense of exhilaration missing since Mercury capsules took the first American astronauts into space four years ago.

On top of the triumph, plans were quickly made to have Gemini 6 splash down about 800 miles east of here at 10:29 o'clock tomorrow morning. The pilots will return here on Friday for the first of many days of debriefings.

A splendid sunrise had created the perfect backdrop and set the mood for the day. It dispelled a worrisome ground fog that had clung to the scrubby palmetto like the doubts that had hung over Gemini 6 in recent days.

Attitude Was Cautious

Through last night the memory of two recent false starts was so fresh that the attitude was one of caution and crossed fingers.

Yet today, from the beginning, a cockiness and almost a jubilance seemed to run through the pilots, the overworked ground crews and official observers.

It was typified by the reaction of James S. McDonnell, the 67-year-old engineer whose factory in Missouri makes the Gemini capsules.

He overslept. Awakened at 6:30 A.M., as the sun began to turn the high, scattered clouds the color of a tea rose, he looked at the sky and cried out:

"You see! I told them I'd bring them good weather from St. Louis!"

It became a day for enthusiasm.

"She looks like a dream," Navy Capt. Walter M. Schirra

Continued on Page 28, Column 8

McNamara Warns NATO Of Chinese Atom Threat

By PETER BRAESTRUP
Special to The New York Times

PARIS, Dec. 15—Defense Secretary Robert S. McNamara urged the United States' Western European allies today to start worrying now about the threat posed by Communist China's growing nuclear strength.

At the same time, he pledged that the mounting United States effort in Vietnam would not require the withdrawal of "major combat units" from American forces in Western Europe.

Mr. McNamara addressed ministers of the 15-nation North Atlantic Treaty Organization in their year-end meeting, which began yesterday.

Behind Closed Doors

The Defense Secretary spoke behind closed doors. His remarks, like those of other speakers, were summarized by a delegation spokesman.

Mr. McNamara said that the Chinese Communists, having already detonated two test nuclear devices, would produce enough fissionable material in the next two years to start a small stockpile of atomic weapons.

Moreover, he continued, the Chinese, despite a "near-famine" economy, are spending 10 per cent of their gross national product on defense.

He said Peking's new mili-

Continued on Page 8, Column 3

JOHNSON AND AYUB CALL PEACE VITAL

Say Dispute With India Must Cease So Efforts Can Be Turned to Key Problems

By JOHN D. POMFRET
Special to The New York Times

WASHINGTON, Dec. 15 — President Johnson and President Mohammad Ayub Khan of Pakistan said today that they agreed on the need for a peaceful resolution of all outstanding differences between India and Pakistan.

This is necessary, they said, "so that the energies and resources of the peoples of the subcontinent would not be wastefully diverted from their efforts to meet their vitally important social and economic problems."

The two leaders issued a joint communiqué at the conclusion of two days of meetings at the White House. It described the discussions as "frank, wide-ranging and productive."

Kashmir Main Issue

The main dispute between India and Pakistan is over Kashmir. This dispute led to a short war last summer.

There was no expressed agreement between the two Presidents on the specific lines along which the dispute over Kashmir should be settled.

They both were said to believe that the working out of such specific arrangements must await the outcome of further conferences that already have been scheduled.

President Ayub and India's Prime Minister, Lal Bahadur Shastri, are to meet Jan. 4 at the invitation of the Soviet Union to discuss their differences. They will confer at the Soviet Central Asian city of Tashkent.

Prime Minister Shastri and President Johnson will meet in Washington Feb. 1 and 2.

The United States cut off military aid and new economic

Continued on Page 6, Column 3

47-CENT FARE SEEN IN QUILL DEMANDS

Transit Authority Warns It Would Be Needed to Meet Union Pay Proposals

By EMANUEL PERLMUTTER

The Transit Authority said yesterday that if it granted the contract demands of its unions it would have to raise the 15-cent fare to 47 cents.

It asserted that a fare increase that great would lead to such a loss of riders that "the reduced use of the system would be financially catastrophic."

The authority has estimated that demands of the Transport Workers Union would cost it $680 million in a two-year contract.

"Adding an increased labor cost of $340 million annually to the T.A. budget would, in the absence of other sources of revenue, increase the present 3-cent deficit incurred for each passenger carried by 19 cents, creating a 22-cent operating deficit per ride," the authority asserted. "The fare would have to be increased to not less than 47 cents."

The authority said that granting the demands would also result in increasing the "basic wage rate per hour alone

Continued on Page 58, Column 4

Staggered Working Hours Urged to Cut Transit Jam

By JOSEPH C. INGRAHAM

The chronic morning and evening subway crushes can be eliminated by staggering working hours, according to a plan made public by Mayor Wagner yesterday. The success of the proposal hinges on whether employers and employes can be persuaded to alter their traditional 9-to-5 work pattern, the Mayor said.

Only the conclusions of the eight-volume, 200,000-word report, based on a six-year study that cost $200,000, were released by the Mayor. The study was directed by Prof. Lawrence B. Cohen of the department of industrial engineering of Columbia University.

Principal Finding

The principal finding was that "work staggering is a feasible way of relieving subway congestion into and out of Manhattan's central business district during the rush hours so that standing passengers might be reasonably comfortable."

Professor Cohen held that the idea was technically and economically feasible and, within limits, which he defined very generally, was sociologically acceptable to management and labor.

In Professor Cohen's view, rush-hour crowding would be markedly alleviated if a 25 per cent spread of the peak loads

Continued on Page 58, Column 3

NASA CUTS BACK SCIENCE PROGRAM

Orbiting Solar Observatory Canceled in Move to Hold Down Expanding Budget

Special to The New York Times

WASHINGTON, Dec. 15—The National Aeronautics and Space Administration, caught in a tight budgetary squeeze, canceled today one of its most ambitious scientific projects.

"Budgetary considerations" were cited by the agency in explaining a halt in further work on the Advanced Orbiting Solar Observatory. The observatory, capable of making detailed observations of the sun, had been planned for launching in 1969.

Behind the cryptic explanation was the deliberately unpublicized fact that the agency was faced with a budgetary dilemma. It has been attempting to finance its expanding program and still heed White House directives to hold down nonmilitary spending.

Some Delays Foreseen

The present expectation is that the civilian space budget for the fiscal year 1967, beginning next July 1, will be held by the White House to about $5.17 billion, equal to the appropriation for this year, and perhaps even less. This would be about $500 million less than the space agency considered necessary to maintain the momentum of its expanding program and sought from the White House.

Enough money will be provided in the budget next year to keep Project Apollo on its schedule of landing a manned expedition on the moon before 1970. But to keep within the budgetary confines imposed by the White House, there will have to be some curtailment in the

Continued on Page 30, Column 4

U.S. Said to Caution Latins on Moscow

By HENRY RAYMONT
Special to The New York Times

MONTEVIDEO, Uruguay, Dec. 15—The United States is warning Uruguay and other Latin - American countries against underestimating the continued aggressiveness and subversive potential of Soviet Communism, qualified sources said today.

The diplomatic initiative is directed against what United States authorities consider to be undue complacency among Latin-American leaders.

These authorities think that the split between Moscow and Peking has led to the assumption among Latins that pro-Soviet Communists no longer threaten republican institutions in the Western Hemisphere.

According to United States officials, this assumption ignores the deterioration in East-West

Continued on Page 17, Column 1

Somerset Maugham Is Dead at 91

Novelist, Short Story Writer, Playwright Succumbs in Nice

By The Associated Press

NICE, France, Thursday, Dec. 16—W. Somerset Maugham died early today at his Riviera villa, La Mauresque. The world-famous novelist, playwright and short-story writer was 91 years old.

Maugham fell last Friday and then suffered a stroke. He was taken to the British-American Hospital Saturday. After a medical consultation on Sunday, physicians gave him only hours to live.

He rallied slightly but weakened yesterday. When all hope was gone, he was taken from the hospital to die in his Moorish-style villa at nearby Cap Ferrat, his secretary and companion of many years, Alan

Pictorial Parade

W. Somerset Maugham

Searle, said in announcing Maugham's death.

A prolific author, Maugham turned out 30 plays, 21 novels and 120 short stories. His masterpiece was "Of Human Bondage," published in 1915 when he was 41 years old. It centered

Continued on Page 50, Column 1

Johnson Calls Feat Step Toward Moon

By JACK RAYMOND
Special to The New York Times

WASHINGTON, Dec. 15 — President Johnson hailed the Gemini satellite rendezvous today as a step toward the moon.

The President congratulated the astronauts and all those who had anything to do with the space feat.

"You have all moved us one step higher on the stairway to the moon," he said exuberantly.

The President conveyed his feelings in a message to James E. Webb, administrator of the National Aeronautics and Space Administration. He had watched the progress of the launching and flight anxiously throughout the day.

Bill D. Moyers, the President's press secretary, said Mr. Johnson watched the Gemini 6 launching over his bedroom television set. Then, throughout the

Continued on Page 29, Column 4

NEWS INDEX

1966

Mississippi state troopers used tear gas on Meredith marchers in their tent colonies.

Floyd McKissick of CORE was among the civil rights leaders who encouraged the "Meredith March Against Fear."

Police and firemen fought off "open city" demonstrators in Chicago.

The black effort to assert the doctrines of Black Power were met with equally angry supporters of white supremacy.

"All the News That's Fit to Print"

The New York Times.

LATE CITY EDITION

U. S. Weather Bureau Report (Page 35) Forecast: Cloudy, windy and cold today; fair, cold tonight and tomorrow.
Temp. Range: 17—14; yesterday: 38—19.

VOL. CXV..No. 39,454.

NEW YORK, MONDAY, JANUARY 31, 1966.

TEN CENTS

RAIDS ON NORTH VIETNAM RESUMED BY U.S. PLANES AS 37-DAY PAUSE IS ENDED

Associated Press Radiophoto

A MISSION OF MERCY: Although he had been hit in eye by enemy fire, Pfc. Thomas Cole, medical corpsman from Richmond, administers first aid to First Cavalry Division (Airmobile) comrade in trench in landing zone near Anthai during bitter fighting there.

JOHNSON TO TALK

Saigon Reports Strike by Navy and Air Force Bombers

By CHARLES MOHR

Special to The New York Times

SAIGON, Monday, Jan. 31 — United States war planes resumed bombing attacks on North Vietnam today.

The bombing raids on that Communist country had been suspended for 37 days from 6 P.M. on Christmas Eve, Dec. 24, until today as one step to encourage Hanoi to negotiate a peaceful settlement of the Vietnam war.

[The White House said that President Johnson would make a statement at 10 A.M. on the renewed bombing of North Vietnam.]

Today's raids apparently signaled the end of the so-called Washington peace offensive and marked a return to a hard military line toward the North Vietnamese.

Embassy Announcement

Barry Zorthian, Minister Counselor for Information for the United States Embassy here, summoned reporters to a press briefing at 3 P.M. (2 A.M., Monday, New York time) and read the following announcement:

"The Prime Minister of the Republic of Vietnam (South Vietnam) and the American Ambassador to Vietnam announce that United States aircraft today attacked targets in designated areas of North Vietnam."

Mr. Zorthian added that the raids today had already been completed and that full details would be made available later at the regular daily military briefing.

He turned aside other questions.

It was not stated whether the planes that struck North Vietnam today followed the same rules of engagement which had governed air strikes before the long pause. These prohibited pilots from striking the population center of Hanoi or Haiphong.

Efforts at Negotiation

The United States has twice ordered cessation of bombing in the North to encourage negotiations. The first pause was for a period of five days last May.

Air raids against North Vietnam began almost a year ago, on Feb. 7, 1965 after Vietcong guerrillas raided an American compound at Pleiku and caused a number of American deaths.

It was noted that the resumption of bombing came at a time when military activity in general was being elevated by the United States. A series of large scale military operations, involving United States Army and Marine Corps troops along the Central Vietnam coast, amounted to a general offensive in that area.

Other large scale operations

Continued on Page 8, Column 3

BLIZZARD BRINGS 7-INCH SNOW HERE, SNARLING TRAVEL

Bitter Cold and High Winds Likely to Continue Today —Emergency Declared

EAST COAST IS BATTERED

Pennsylvania Turnpike Shut —Albany Cancels Session —9 Deaths Laid to Storm

By PETER KIHSS

A Sunday blizzard whistled through the city and the East Coast states yesterday, dumping seven inches of snow here and causing the second declaration of a snow emergency in eight days.

The bitter cold weather, with west winds gusting to 40 and 50 miles an hour, was expected to continue into today.

At least nine deaths in the metropolitan area were attributed to the storm. Among the deaths was that of an 18-month-old baby in Harlem who was the 11th child killed by fire in the city since last Thursday.

Road travel was hazardous and the New York Thruway was ordered closed at 5 P. M. from Albany to Buffalo. The entire Pennsylvania Turnpike was closed and Governor Mills Godwin of Virginia declared that in his state "no one can be assured of safe travel to any given destination."

Legislative Session Postponed

For the first time in many years, the New York State Legislature called off its session in Albany for today because snow tie-ups would have prevented many members from getting back to the capital. This week's meetings were rescheduled for tomorrow and Wednesday.

John F. Kennedy International Airport was closed from 2 P.M. to 6:18 P.M. Most airports from Charleston, S. C., north were reported closed earlier in the day. Newark Airport kept operating.

La Guardia Airport was closed to passenger traffic at 2 P.M. and remained closed through the night. The airport was open to freight traffic.

The Pennsylvania Railroad said it was unable to run trains between Baltimore and Washington because of switch trouble, and for 11 hours southbound trains were halted at Baltimore.

The New York Central's 20th Century Limited from Chicago encountered so much storm trouble that it reached Grand Central Terminal at 2:09 P.M., four hours and 39 minutes late.

5,218 Complain

Buildings Commissioner Charles Moerdler reported 5,218 telephone calls to his central complaint bureau at WOrth 4-3000 most of them dealing with lack of heat during the 24 hours ended at 4 P.M.

More than 100 volunteers, including Republican and Democratic political figures, responded to appeals to man 30 telephones for incoming calls and 10 for outgoing calls at the complaint bureau, 53 Chambers Street.

Commissioner Moerdler said a number of buildings had been ordered vacated during the weekend, and armory and hotel space remained available for

Continued on Page 20, Column 1

The Plow's the Thing, So to Speak

Plow dumping snow into a Sanitation Department truck on Fifth Avenue yesterday north of St. Patrick's Cathedral.

The New York Times (by Allyn Baum and Ernest Sisto)

In the suburbs it was often worse. This man uses small snow blower at Fairfield Street in Valley Stream, L. I.

BRODERICK URGES $50 PARKING FINES IN MIDTOWN AREA

Barnes Backs Idea, but Notes Scofflaw Problem—Mayor Says Cleanup Is Needed

By ROBERT E. DALLOS

Police Commissioner Vincent L. Broderick urged yesterday that fines for illegal parking in midtown Manhattan be raised to $50. Traffic Commissioner Henry A. Barnes immediately supported the idea.

The increase from the present $15 fine, Mr. Broderick said, "would be a deterrent" to illegal parking and would be "more realistic."

The Commissioner, who was interviewed on "Direct Line" over WNBC, said that the plan must be worked out with the traffic commissioner and with the courts.

In a telephone interview after Mr. Broderick's radio and television appearance, Commissioner Barnes said: "I think the idea is good. The $15 fine hasn't in any way been a deterrent to parking in midtown Manhattan."

Scofflaw Problem Cited

But Mr. Barnes added: "Even a $50 fine or a $100 fine isn't going to deter anyone unless means can be developed to apprehend scofflaws.

"I can put in all the signals, all the systems, all the signs and all the regulations but if people don't pay attention to them, we can save the money."

He suggested the registration and driver license files of scofflaws be flagged at the Department of Motor Vehicles and that renewal of these documents be denied to such persons.

A spokesman for Mayor Lindsay said that Mr. Lindsay agreed that traffic in Manhattan "must be cleaned up." But the spokesman added that Mr. Lindsay could not comment on whether or by how much fines should be raised since he had not talked with either of his commissioners.

Mayor Has Started Drive

On Friday Mr. Lindsay had announced a drive on illegal parkers. He said cars double parked would be ticketed and towed from congested midtown areas.

The Automobile Club of New York said it would be difficult to oppose higher fines for people who "flout the law" but it decried the sweeping nature of Commissioner Broderick's proposal. Gilbert B. Phillips, the club's president, said the city "should stop dragging its feet on providing of off-street parking space."

Final authority for higher parking fines must come from the First and Second Departments of the Appellate Division of the State Supreme Court.

Presiding Justice Bernard Botein of the First Department said in a telephone interview last night that it would be "unrealistic" to think that such action would be taken unless the police and traffic commissioners requested it.

Although he refused to speculate on any action the court might take, he said a request to raise parking fines "would engage our serious consideration."

These courts used their jurisdiction during the transit strike by temporarily raising $15 parking fines to $35 at the request

Continued on Page 20, Column 5

500 City Tenants Will Get New Homes With U.S. Aid

By SAMUEL KAPLAN

Five hundred low-income families here will receive Federal subsidies so they can move into privately owned middle-income apartments under a new public housing program.

The program will be carried out by the City Housing Authority, which announced yesterday that it planned to lease about 500 middle-income apartments in private buildings and then sublease them at lower rents to families eligible for public housing.

The leasing agreement will be known only to the landlord, the authority and the tenant to avoid any possible social ostracism of the tenant by other residents of the building.

The authority explained that it would charge the low-income family the same rent it would pay if it moved into a comparable apartment in a public housing project.

Program Explained

For example, a four-bedroom apartment in a Federally aided low-income project rents for about $76 a month. If a four-bedroom apartment is found in a middle-income development renting for $190 a month, the authority would pay the landlord $114 a month. The tenant would pay $76.

The cost of the program, which was not disclosed, will be borne by the Federal Department of Housing and Urban Development under the rent-subsidy section of the 1965 Housing Act.

The experimental program was developed to provide needed

Continued on Page 17, Column 3

COURT APPORTIONS SHUBERT ESTATES

Partnership's Value Is Put at $33.5-Million, Divided in 2 Parts by State Justice

By MILTON ESTEROW

A State Supreme Court justice has ruled that the estate of Lee Shubert is entitled to receive about $28-million from the estate of his brother, J. J. Shubert.

Justice John L. Flynn said that the partnership of the brothers who built Broadway's most powerful theatrical dynasty was worth $33.5-million when Lee Shubert died in 1953. J. J. Shubert died in 1963.

Justice Flynn, in a decision handed down Friday, held that the Lee Shubert estate was entitled to half of the value of the partnership, or $16.7-million, plus 6 per cent interest for every year since 1953—more than $11-million.

The ruling supported every recommendation made several months ago by Edwin L. Weisl Sr., who has been serving as a court referee in the dispute, which began in 1954.

The decision by Justice Flynn may be appealed by both estates as well as by the Federal Government. The Government intervened in the case to protect tax claims of $15.7 million made in 1963 against the Lee Shubert estate. There are no tax claims against the J. J. Shubert estate.

Theatrical sources said yesterday that the case could ultimately force a reorganization of the Shubert enterprises.

No agreement has yet been

Continued on Page 22, Column 1

BRITAIN TIGHTENS CURB ON RHODESIA

Blocks Remainder of Imports —Treasury Warns Against Loans to Smith Regime

By W. GRANGER BLAIR

Special to The New York Times

LONDON, Jan. 30—The Government announced today a ban on the relatively small amount of Rhodesian imports that had still been permitted to enter Britain.

Effective next Wednesday, the 5 per cent of imports that had not been covered by earlier British economic sanctions against the rebellious regime in Rhodesia will be barred from Britain.

The Board of Trade, making public the new measures, said licenses for British exports to Rhodesia would "in general" be refused from Wednesday on, thus virtually halting all trade between the two countries.

The Treasury issued a warning that anyone who extended credit to Rhodesia risked losing his money when constitutional government was restored.

The Rhodesian regime, which is controlled by the territory's

Continued on Page 6, Column 5

Troops From North Fight First Cavalry In Binhdinh Province

Special to The New York Times

SAIGON, Jan. 30—Military developments this weekend laid to rest a feeling that the war in South Vietnam might be gradually "fading away."

Troops of the 18th North Vietnamese Army Regiment have been identified as among those in battle against the United States First Cavalry Division in Binhdinh Province 300 miles northeast of Saigon, an American military spokesman said today.

Four major United States military operations were under way in various parts of the country tonight and all of them had encountered at least some resistance.

A South Vietnamese military spokesman said the South Vietnamese were conducting 42 military operations that each involved a battalion or more of troops.

This represents about 40 per cent of Saigon's combat battalions.

The enemy forces also were active. In addition to doggedly fighting the First Cavalry troops near Bongson in Binhdinh Province, they harassed a

Continued on Page 8, Column 1

GOLDBERG STATES PEACE BID STANDS

Says Ho Chi Minh, in Letter 'Plainly' Spurning Talks, Is Now on Defensive

By IRVING SPIEGEL

Arthur J. Goldberg declared last night that despite the "intransigent" position taken by President Ho Chi Minh of North Vietnam, the United States would continue to press for peace in Vietnam.

In a speech delivered here, the chief United States delegate to the United Nations directly rebutted remarks by the North Vietnamese leader.

Last week, writing to the leaders of Communist and some other countries, President Ho Chi Minh sharply denounced United States offers of unconditional peace talks as an "effort to fool public opinion."

Peace Wish Unaltered

Mr. Goldberg asserted that the letters "plainly" spurned the peace offer. Voicing regret over this, he added: "In no way, however, does it change or diminish our desire for peace. In no way does it change or diminish our effort to seek an honorable settlement. It will continue."

Mr. Goldberg was the principal guest at a dinner session of the 53d annual meeting of the Anti-Defamation League of B'nai B'rith, at the New York Hilton Hotel. He accepted the league's America's Democratic Legacy Award for "distinguished contributions to the enrichment of our democratic heritage."

Dore Schary, national chairman of the league, made the presentation and cited Mr. Goldberg for "lifelong dedication and commitment to assuring constitutional principles of freedom and dignity to all Americans."

President Johnson sent a message describing Mr. Goldberg as "a man who epitomizes the highest qualities of public life."

In his address Mr. Goldberg noted the requests addressed to the United States "by individuals and nations of many ideologies" for a pause in bombing attacks on North Vietnam "for a reasonable period of time" so that

Continued on Page 10, Column 3

Fund Goal Passed By Lincoln Center

By RICHARD F. SHEPARD

The fund drive to build and launch Lincoln Center for the Performing Arts has reached its goal — one of the largest ever set for this purpose — and brought in several millions extra.

The campaign has reaped $165.4-million, well above the $160.7-million set in 1963 as its objective. However, unforeseen expenses incurred since 1963 have absorbed the difference, and an additional $1.4-million not included in the fund drive target must now be raised to complete the Juilliard School. The total cost of the center is now $166.8-million.

Four of the six buildings on the 14 West Side acres are in

Continued on Page 22, Column 4

NEWS INDEX

The News Summary and Index will be found on Page 2 today.

'Arty' Therapy Is Criticized by Scholar

By RAYMOND H. ANDERSON

A growing abuse of the term "creativity" in occupational therapy, entertainment and business is vulgarizing original thought in modern society, according to Dr. Michael Wyschogrod, an assistant professor of philosophy at City College.

Creativity must be served for its own sake, not for psychological needs, he said yesterday at a meeting of the American Association of Existential Psychology and Psychiatry.

"We cannot pretend that dabbling with creativity is the solution to the problem of the housewife and the salesman who find their lives empty," the professor added. "The only result we will achieve is to cheapen creativity without solving their problems."

Fred Stein

Prof. Michael Wyschogrod

The true artist, Professor Wyschogrod said, must work solely "to improve his story or his picture, his poem or his song." If this is not done, he added, the result is "a form of occupational therapy that is destructive of the dignity of labor, particularly creative labor."

"The person who attempts to create in order to find a meaning in his life, to convert a pointless existence into one that is no longer pointless is using creativity to his own end and that cannot be done," he declared.

The theme of the association's two-day meeting at the Barbizon-Plaza Hotel was "Imagination and Existence." Among the participants were Ben Shahn, the artist; Saul Bellow, the writer; Dr.

Continued on Page 14, Column 3

Wyszynski Defies Regime in Poland

By HENRY KAMM

Special to The New York Times

CZESTOCHOWA, Poland, Jan. 30—Stefan Cardinal Wyszynski defiantly declared today that the Roman Catholic Church of Poland could not be vanquished by any temporal power.

His stern sermon, delivered at an occasion of special significance in Poland's holiest shrine, was a clear reply to the Government's present campaign against the church.

It was the Cardinal's strongest statement of the dispute since he was refused a passport to visit the Vatican early this month.

It was well understood as such by a densely packed crowd of worshipers at the Basilica of

Continued on Page 3, Column 4

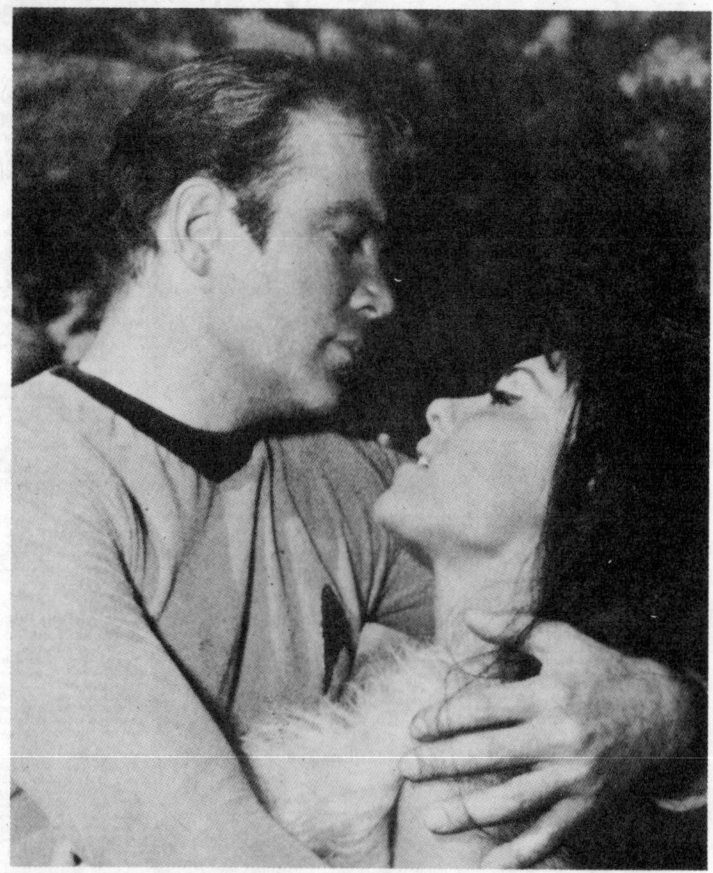

William Shatner starred as Captain Kirk of the Starship Enterprise. His mission was to seek out new worlds and restore universal peace and goodwill, not necessarily as shown above.

Tony Franciosa and Jill St. John in a scene from the feature-length TV pilot, *Fame is the Name of the Game.* Ratings inspired a later series, *The Name of the Game* which rotated Franciosa, Gene Barry and Robert Stack in three 90-minute shows.

Leonard Nimoy was a logical being named Mr. Spock on *Star Trek.* His Vulcan nature helped guide the more impassioned crew of the Enterprise.

"All the News That's Fit to Print"

The New York Times.

LATE CITY EDITION

U. S. Weather Bureau Report (Page 63) Forecast: Partly cloudy and cold today, tonight. Cloudy, colder tomorrow. Temp. range: 37—26; yesterday: 37—30.

VOL. CXV..No. 39,458. NEW YORK, FRIDAY, FEBRUARY 4, 1966. TEN CENTS

SOVIET ACHIEVES A SOFT LANDING ON MOON; BRITISH SAY CRAFT IS SENDING TV PICTURES

U.S., IN U.N. TALKS, TRIES TO PROMOTE APPEALS TO HANOI

Seeks Peace Move Through Council, Pope, Allies and Nonaligned Nations

By DREW MIDDLETON
Special to The New York Times

UNITED NATIONS, N. Y., Feb. 3 — The United States opened consultations today with other members of the Security Council aimed at stimulating new approaches to North Vietnam on a negotiated peace.

Reliable sources said the United States hoped that by stressing to the Council its desire for a settlement through a draft resolution, it would encourage new proposals to Hanoi from groups within the Security Council, from Pope Paul VI and from allied and nonaligned governments.

Arthur J. Goldberg, the United States representative, conferred, among others, with Akira Matsui, of Japan, President of the Council this month, and Chief S. O. Adebo, the Nigerian member.

African Delegations Confer

Earlier Chief Adebo met with a number of African delegations, including those from Uganda and Mali, which also are nonpermanent members of the Council.

Thinking on an African initiative is in the formative stage, the sources said. The drafting of peace proposals by the African members of the United Nations based on the Geneva accords of 1954 is one step under consideration. The proposals would be transmitted to Hanoi through French or Algerian diplomatic channels.

Should these approaches fail, the African delegations would consider drafting a resolution of their own paralleling in some respects the United States' draft, which was inscribed on the agenda of the Security Council yesterday. Hanoi, it is thought, might be more responsive to a Security Council resolution originating among nonaligned delegations than to one sponsored by the United States.

African Views Diverge

These views were put forward by one influential African delegate. They are not accepted by all the African delegations. Some of them believe that any approach to Hanoi under the aegis of the United Nations is doomed to failure. But there is a desire on the part of many Africans to play a responsible peace-making role.

On one point they all agree: the National Liberation Front, the parent organization of the Vietcong, must be a party to any negotiations.

The American draft resolution asks for discussions leading to a conference of interested powers dealing with the application of the Geneva accords of 1954 and 1962. A cease-fire in Vietnam would be the first business of the conference.

The United States, the draft says, would assist in a provision for arbitrators or mediators should they be necessary to a settlement.

The United States, reliable sources said, is prepared to set-

Continued on Page 2, Column 2

Senate Panel Will Conduct Broad Inquiry on Vietnam

Foreign Relations Unit Hears David Bell at Session Today—Fulbright Inviting Critics and Backers of U.S. Policy

By E. W. KENWORTHY
Special to The New York Times

WASHINGTON, Feb. 3—The Senate Foreign Relations Committee, intent on reasserting the Senate's constitutional prerogatives in foreign affairs, decided today to conduct a broad inquiry into Vietnam policy.

At a meeting attended by 16 of the 19 members, the committee agreed to hold public hearings beginning tomorrow and probably extending over several days.

The genesis of this decision was a growing feeling among many Senators, including J. W. Fulbright, the committee chairman, that while President Johnson wants their "consent" on any moves he may decide to make, he does not want their "advice."

This feeling reached the boiling point last week after Senators had urged that the pause in the bombing of North Vietnam be continued and had questioned the increasing involvement of United States ground forces.

In reply to the Senators, Mr. Johnson and Secretary of State Dean Rusk both cited the Tonkin Gulf Resolution of 1964.

Although that resolution gave prior approval to "all necessary measures" for preventing aggression in Southeast Asia, many Senators said they did not regard their vote for it as a blank check.

The first hearing will be at 8:30 A.M. tomorrow with David E. Bell, administrator of the Agency for International Development, as the witness.

Mr. Bell will be the first witness because the vehicle for the

Continued on Page 2, Column 5

JONES DENOUNCES BROWN ON CHARGE OF HOUSING RICHES

Testifies 'Archenemy' Came to Home to Ask Aid on Project for Scheuer

By EDITH EVANS ASBURY

Councilman J. Raymond Jones denied yesterday that he had suggested to Earl Brown, a former Harlem Councilman, that housing projects offered an opportunity for anyone to "get rich—in or out of office."

"I more than deny it, sir," Councilman Jones declared at a hearing of the State Investigations Commission. "Earl Brown is known to be my archenemy. He is malicious and vindictive."

Mr. Brown, who recently resigned as City Human Rights Commissioner and was a member of the Housing and Redevelopment Board at the time of the alleged remark, had attributed the statement to Mr. Jones at the Wednesday session of the hearing held by the S.I.C.

Inquiry On for 2 Weeks

The bipartisan commission has been holding hearings for two weeks into alleged political interference and influence peddling in the Mitchell-Lama housing program.

The Mitchell-Lama law, passed in 1955, was designed to provide limited-profit housing for middle-income families with the help of 90 per cent, low-interest mortgages from the state or city.

Jackie Robinson, the former baseball star, also appeared at yesterday's session. He told the commission that he had filed an application to build Esplanade Gardens Sept. 1, 1960, nearly three weeks before the one filed by Mr. Seavey on behalf of another sponsor.

Mr. Robinson said he made several telephone inquiries, one of which brought the response, from a person he could not identify, that the site had been reserved "for Powell and Jones."

After that, Mr. Robinson said, he dropped the matter, because "You don't fight City Hall."

In his testimony Wednesday, Mr. Brown had said that the Jones statement was made during a conversation at Mr. Jones's home at 270 Convent Avenue early in 1962 at which they discussed the proposed Esplanade Gardens middle-income housing project.

Denies He Invited Brown

Councilman Jones acknowledged that they had met at his home, but he gave an entirely different version of what occurred.

According to Councilman Jones, who is the New York County Democratic leader, he did not invite Mr. Brown to his home.

Instead, he said, Mr. Brown asked to come to see him. And instead of his asking Mr. Brown's support for a friend's application for Esplanade Gardens, Mr. Brown asked his support, Councilman Jones said, for another applicant for the project.

Mr. Jones was at first reluctant to identify the friend on whose behalf Mr. Brown spoke. Pressed for the name, he said it was James Scheuer, then

Continued on Page 36, Column 2

The New York Times Feb. 4, 1966

ON THE MOON: Crosses indicate where the Soviet Union's Luna 9 spacecraft soft-landed yesterday in the Ocean of the Storms. Numbers (white for the United States and black for the Soviet Union) indicate the earlier vehicles that made crash landings on the moon:

1. Luna 2, Sept. 13, 1959	4. Ranger 7, July 31, 1964	7. Luna 5, May 12, 1965
2. Ranger 4, April 23, 1962	5. Ranger 8, Feb. 20, 1965	8. Luna 7, Oct. 8, 1965
3. Ranger 6, Feb. 2, 1964	6. Ranger 9, March 24, 1965	9. Luna 8, Dec. 7, 1965

MOSCOW JUBILANT

Scientific Reports Are Relayed to Earth by Unmanned Ship

By PETER GROSE
Special to The New York Times

MOSCOW, Feb. 3—An unmanned Soviet spaceship made a successful soft landing on the moon tonight and immediately began transmitting telemetric signals, possibly including television pictures, back to the earth. The landing was the first of its kind.

The soft landing occurred at 9:45 P.M. Moscow time (1:45 P.M., Eastern standard time). It was announced one hour later by the official press agency, Tass. The Moscow radio interrupted its regular programs to read the announcement and followed the brief statement with martial music.

The spaceship, Luna 9, was launched from earth Monday. It followed four unsuccessful attempts by Soviet space scientists to bring down an experimental station intact on the moon.

[In Britain, scientists said that two 15-minute transmissions of television signals from Luna 9 had been received at the Jodrell Bank radio telescope. The scientists said it would take considerable time to convert the signals into pictures, presumably of the lunar surface.]

Confirmation Lacking

There was no confirmation from Soviet sources of a report from Britain that Luna 9 was sending back television pictures.

The Moscow radio announced that one communication contact had been made with the landed vehicle, and that more would be made later.

The first news flashes gave no details of the landing procedure or of the initial information obtained from man's first direct observations of the earth's satellite and closest neighbor in space.

Measuring instruments on board Luna 9 are expected to supply data on the composition of the moon's surface, its temperature and heat-conducting characteristics and its strength for supporting heavy objects such as manned spaceships.

Soviet scientists also hoped to assemble data on the extent of meteorite bombardment of the moon and the frequency of moon quakes.

First Details Scanty

Tass gave no indication of how often communications contacts would be made or of how long the transmitter of Luna 9 was expected to continue beaming its signals to the earth.

The soft landing is clearly a major turning point in space exploration, comparable to the successful launching of Russia's first Sputnik on Oct. 4, 1957, and the first Soviet space vehicle to hit the moon, on Sept. 13, 1959.

Space experts believe that it gives the Soviet Union a major lead over the United States in the program to land a man on the moon.

The first hint of the imminent announcement came when the Moscow radio program was interrupted and the musical call signal of the station was put on the air, repeated over and over.

Then an announcer said: "Moscow speaking. Here is a Tass announcement:

"An outstanding achievement of Soviet science and technology: At 21:45 Luna 9 achieved a soft landing in the Ocean of Storms. A communication link has been established with the earth."

The Tass announcement distributed on the agency's teleprinters said that the landing had occurred to the west of the

Continued on Page 37, Column 1

THAIS EXPANDING ARMED STRENGTH

U.S. Assists Them and They Help Train Laotians to Fight the Pathet Lao

By HANSON W. BALDWIN

Thailand, threatened by Communist subversion within her borders and by the North Vietnamese and Laotian Communists across the Mekong River, is strengthening her armed forces and police and assisting anti-Communist factions in Laos.

Thailand has been acquiring military strength with United States help, and in turn has helped to train some Laotian fliers and ground troops.

The Bangkok Government has denied a recent newspaper report that Thai armed forces "invaded" Laos. But it did not deny a report published last October in Fortune magazine that Thai pilots and artillerymen in Laotian uniforms had been supporting Laotian forces against attacks by the pro-Communist Pathet Lao.

Thai experts, along with experts from the United States and other countries, are also said to have participated in organizing the Meos and other

Continued on Page 4, Column 3

Cold-War G.I. Bill Unanimously Voted In House Committee

By JOHN D. MORRIS
Special to The New York Times

WASHINGTON, Feb. 3—The House Committee on Veterans Affairs approved today a "cold-war G.I. bill" providing educational and other benefits for veterans of the armed services.

A unanimous voice vote sent the measure to the House for consideration next Monday under a procedure that will limit debate to 40 minutes and prohibit any amendments. Passage under this procedure requires a two-thirds majority vote, but Democratic leaders were confident of favorable action by a more than ample margin.

The bill calls for a permanent program of benefits, available to all men and women serving as many as 180 days in the armed forces after Jan. 31, 1955, when the Korean War G.I. bill expired.

It does not cover the six-month training period required for volunteers entering reserves or the two weeks of active training duty that reservists must serve each year.

Eligible veterans would be entitled to one month of college education or vocational training for each month of service but not more than 36 months

Continued on Page 6, Column 3

Taylor Rejects 'Enclave' Plan; Gavin Says It Is Misunderstood

United Press International — Associated Press Wirephoto

Gen. Maxwell D. Taylor, at left, speaking here yesterday and Lieut. Gen. James M. Gavin at Boston news conference.

Gen. Maxwell D. Taylor rejected yesterday the "enclave strategy" for Vietnam recommended by his former paratroop colleague, Lieut. Gen. James M. Gavin.

General Taylor told the City Club of New York that the Gavin strategy would amount to "a crushing defeat of international proportions" for the United States and a victory for Hanoi and Peking. He did not mention General Gavin by name.

In Boston, General Gavin said his views on Vietnam had been misunderstood. He said he had not suggested that United States forces "withdraw" to coastal enclaves, but that they hold the enclaves they now occupied while weighing alternative strategies.

General Taylor, a former Ambassador to South Vietnam and now a special adviser to President Johnson, said he believed the United States and its allies could achieve their objective in Vietnam: "To give the people of South Vietnam their choice of government."

General Gavin, a former Ambassador to France, has proposed that United States forces

Continued on Page 3, Column 5

Soviet Said to Offer Cairo Atom Defense

By HEDRICK SMITH
Special to The New York Times

CAIRO, Feb. 3—The Soviet Union recently refused to sell weapons to the United Arab Republic but promised to give President Gamal Abdel Nasser a guarantee of nuclear protection if Israel developed or obtained such weapons, according to reports received by Western embassies here.

These reports, still not officially confirmed, apparently mean that the Russians are prepared to use their own nuclear arms as a deterrent to safeguard the United Arab Republic, much as the United States nuclear umbrella shields a large part of Western Europe.

According to diplomatic cir-

Continued on Page 12, Column 3

BANK-CITY TEAM TO AID BUSINESS

'Intelligence' Unit Planned to Help Lindsay Council Curb Trade Exodus

By MURRAY ILLSON

Four of the city's largest banks have agreed to provide an intelligence network to help Mayor Lindsay combat the exodus of distressed businesses from the city.

The program involves the formation of an "Economic Intelligence Service" that will enlist the officers of the more than 550 branches of the four banks. When the officers of a local branch bank learn that a business is in distress or is considering leaving the city, they will notify the city administration to determine what can be done to prevent the departure.

Donald F. Shaughnessy, assistant to the Mayor, said last night that the city was losing about 15,000 jobs a year in manufacturing fields alone. These jobs, he observed, are normally filled by Negro and Puerto Rican workers, who are largely unskilled, and it is in these categories that the city faces one of its most serious employment problems.

In Planning Stage

Mr. Shaughnessy said the four banks participating in the program were the Chase Manhattan, the First National City, the Chemical Bank-New York Trust Company and the Manufacturers Hanover Trust.

The special service, Mr. Shaughnessy said, is still in the planning stage and is not expected to get under way for about a month. But when it does, he said, it will function in the following manner:

A local bank manager, learning that a business in his district is in distress or planning to leave the city for whatever reason, will pass the information along to the city Economic Development Council, which has headquarters at 230 Park Avenue.

The council was formed last

Continued on Page 14, Column 5

Landing Is Viewed As Signaling Start Of New Space Era

By WALTER SULLIVAN

The landing of Luna 9 intact on the moon marks the beginning of on-the-surface exploration of the solar system.

Not only does it open a new era in this respect, but also its success implies that manned vehicles will be able to touch down on the moon without vanishing into a choking sea of dust.

To date it has been as though the early navigators had sighted the coast of the New World and speculated on what it was like, but had never set foot there. Landing should provide incomparably more information—first through the good offices of automation, then through the observational skill of astronauts.

The most detailed information on the lunar surface heretofore was that furnished by the Ranger spacecraft sent to the moon by the United States in 1964 and 1965. The television images that they sent as they crashed into the surface revealed small, dimple-like craters, a few rocks and other features.

However they did not answer

Continued on Page 37, Column 2

President Praises Soviet on Success

By The Associated Press

WASHINGTON, Feb. 3 — President Johnson sent a personal message to the Soviet Union today saying "all mankind applauds" the landing of the Soviet Luna 9 spaceship on the moon.

The White House made public this text of a cable of congratulations sent by the President to Nikolai V. Podgorny, President of the Soviet Union:

"You and the people of the Union of Soviet Socialist Republics are to be congratulated for the great success of Luna 9. Your accomplishment is one that can benefit all mankind and all mankind applauds it. Your scientists have made a major contribution to man's

Continued on Page 37, Column 4

U.S. HOPES SOVIET WILL SHARE DATA

Space Officials Praise Feat but Are Disappointed at Not Beating Russians

American scientists and space experts greeted the Soviet Union's successful soft landing on the moon with strong praise, a trace of wounded pride and high hopes that the Russians would share their new knowledge of the moon's surface.

Officials of the National Aeronautics and Space Administration called the landing "a fine technological achievement." A spokesman said that officials were "eagerly awaiting whatever is found by way of scientific information."

But the first reaction of an official of Jet Propulsion Laboratory in Pasadena, Calif., which is in charge of the Surveyor soft landing program of the United States, was one of wry disappointment.

Echoing a well-advertised runner-up in the auto rental business, Frank Colella, chief of public information, said: "Now I know how Avis feels."

Look at Bright Side

Generally, space experts looked at the bright side. If the Russians can do it, they said, so can the United States.

Dr. William H. Pickering, director of the Jet Propulsion Laboratory, said:

"The success of this mission has already added to our knowledge of the lunar surface. We now await with interest the scientific data which will be received in the next few days."

Reporting that the Surveyor project is "progressing well," he continued:

"It is to be hoped that scientific data from Surveyor will complement that received from the Soviet spacecraft and provide us with not only a detailed description of the surface of the moon, but also a far better picture of the evolution of our solar system."

American scientists believe that the Russians will release at least some television pic-

Continued on Page 37, Column 6

Divorce Bill Backed By Catholic Group

By NATALIE JAFFE

Eighteen prominent Roman Catholic laymen urged the Legislature yesterday "to support significant revisions" in New York's 18th-century divorce laws this year.

Their 250-word statement was in direct opposition to a request for delay and further study issued to the Legislature Monday by a spokesman for Roman Catholic bishops in the state. The request, made by Charles J. Tobin, secretary of the state Catholic Welfare Committee was widely interpreted as opposition to reform.

The sponsors of a divorce reform bill now before the Legislature say that sentiment among their colleagues in the

Continued on Page 36, Column 4

NEWS INDEX

"All the News That's Fit to Print"

The New York Times.

LATE CITY EDITION

U.S. Weather Bureau Report (Page 86) forecasts: Fair and milder today; cool tonight. Fair and warmer tomorrow.
Temp. range: 74–53; yesterday: 70–52.

VOL. CXV..No. 39,576. © 1966 by The New York Times Company. Times Square, New York, N.Y. 10036 NEW YORK, THURSDAY, JUNE 2, 1966. TEN CENTS

SURVEYOR MAKES A SOFT LANDING ON MOON AND SENDS BACK PHOTOGRAPHS OF SURFACE

ALBANY DEFEATS MEASURE TO SAVE 15-CENT CITY FARE

3 Senate Democrats Join Republicans in Barring $69-Million for Transit

By RICHARD L. MADDEN
Special to The New York Times

ALBANY, June 1—Upstate legislators moved tonight to force New York City to raise its 15-cent transit fare.

By a vote of 35 to 27 the Republican-controlled Senate defeated a bill that would have permitted the city to transfer $69-million to the deficit-ridden Transit Authority.

Without the $69-million, Transit Authority officials have said, they will be forced to raise the fare on July 1.

When the vote was called after a two-hour debate, three upstate Democrats joined the Republican majority against the bill. Four New York City Republicans sided with the Democratic minority in supporting the measure, which had been sought by Mayor Lindsay.

[In New York, City Council President Frank D. O'Connor and Council Majority Leader David Ross, the two top Democrats at City Hall, declared Mayor Lindsay, Governor Rockefeller and upstate Republicans must assume the blame for any increase in the city's transit fare.]

Move Is Unusual

Senate Majority Leader Earl W. Brydges, made the unusual move of bringing the transit-aid bill out of committee to defeat it on the Senate floor to emphasize his demand for a fare increase in the city. Normally, the legislative leaders dispose of unwanted bills simply by burying them in committee.

The effort by the upstate lawmakers to kill the transit-aid bill was another strategic move in the jockeying by the politically divided Legislature over Mayor Lindsay's request for $520-million in new taxing power for the city.

Senator Brydges and other Republican legislators have insisted that the city should raise the transit fare to ease its financial troubles and to make the Mayor's tax program more palatable to the Legislature.

At the request of Governor Rockefeller, the Legislature voted last January to advance $100-million in state aid to the city to ease the impact of setting the transit strike.

Tonight's vote was on a companion bill that was required before the city could actually transfer part of the money from its treasury to the independent authority.

The bill was sought because the law now requires the transit agency to meet its operating expenses out of its revenues or raise the fare.

On Sunday, Joseph P. O'Grady, chairman of the authority, said the transit agency would be broke by July 1 unless the city got permission to transfer the $69-million to cover the transit deficit. On Tuesday he said the fare would have to be raised a nickel on July 1 if financial

Continued on Page 34, Column 4

Rights Conference to Vote On Criticism of U.S. Policy

Leaders Yield to Militants on Resolutions —Johnson Warns Against Expecting Miracles to Undo Old Injustices

By JOHN HERBERS
Special to The New York Times

WASHINGTON, June 1—Leaders of the White House Conference on Civil Rights yielded today to militant delegates and reluctantly agreed to permit a vote on resolutions that could embarrass the Administration.

As a result, resolutions criticizing the Johnson Administration's role in Vietnam and its enforcement of civil rights are likely to be approved in some sessions of the conference.

The development was a clear victory for Floyd McKissick, national director of the Congress of Racial Equality, and other delegates who opposed the White House plan to have no parliamentary procedures in the two-day conference.

"Our request has been granted," Mr. McKissick said triumphantly as delegates aligned with him began working on resolutions for presentation tomorrow.

President Johnson made an unscheduled appearance in the evening and asked the delegates not to expect one man or one Administration to undo the injustice of centuries.

"Do not expect from me, or any man, a miracle," he said. "Do not expect us, even together, to put right in one year or four all that took centuries to make wrong."

Nonetheless, he brought the delegates to their feet in an ovation when he said:

"I do pledge this—to give my days, and such talents as I have been given, to the pursuit of justice and opportunity for those so long denied them."

Mr. Johnson said some citi-

Continued on Page 21, Column 4

KY JUNTA AGREES TO TAKE CIVILIANS INTO LEADERSHIP

Buddhists Look to Election of New Chief of State and Premier Under Pact

By CHARLES MOHR
Special to The New York Times

SAIGON, South Vietnam, June 1—South Vietnam's ruling junta, which consists of 10 generals, agreed today to add 10 civilian members, but the accord failed to stop Buddhist violence in Saigon.

Buddhists who have opposed the junta said that it had agreed to allow the expanded group, whose formal name is to be the National Leadership Committee, to vote on whether to replace the present Chief of State, Lieut. Gen. Nguyen Van Thieu, and to allow the Chief of State to name a Premier.

Such an arrangement would offer the Buddhists some hope of achieving their goal of driving General Thieu and Premier Nguyen Cao Ky from office.

[Premier Ky ordered the Mayor of Hue, rebel-controlled northern city, to quell Buddhist-led anti-Government forces there. All semblance of governmental authority vanished from the city's streets as Hue drifted into a state of anarchy. Page 2.]

Election Not Mentioned

A Government communiqué announcing the planned expansion of the ruling group did not mention the question of an election of a new Chief of State or the possible replacement of Air Vice Marshal Ky.

It said the junta had decided "to make an effort to establish a people's armed forces council" to advise the Premier and the Cabinet.

The new leadership committee is to come into being next Monday and the advisory council June 19.

Whether the steps announced today could end the political crisis remained questionable. Political passions were still high and some factions seemed in no mood to compromise.

Thich Ho Giac, a monk of the Unified Buddhist Church, defended the new plan and the need to cooperate with the junta in a speech tonight to a huge crowd at the compound of the church's Institute of Secular Affairs, the Vien Hoa Dao.

He was followed by another monk, Thich Phap Sieu, who shouted that compromise with the Ky Government was unthinkable.

Thich Phap Sieu then threatened to burn himself to death and announced that 20 other

Continued on Page 3, Column 1

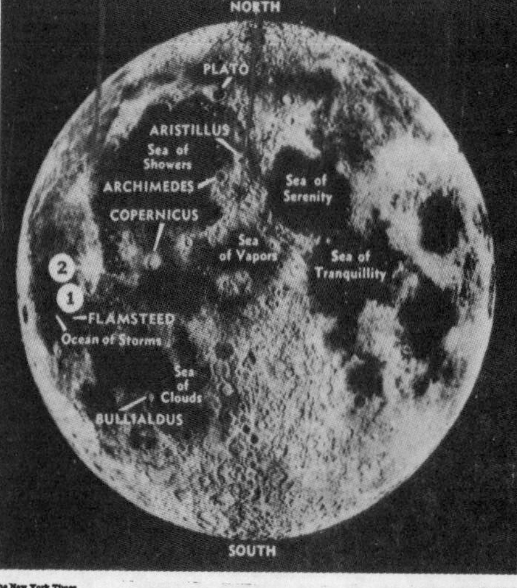

The New York Times June 2, 1966

SOFT LANDING ON MOON: Surveyor spacecraft accomplished a soft landing in the Ocean of Storms at (1). Last Feb. 3 Soviet Union's Luna 9 spaceship made landing at (2).

A 63-HOUR VOYAGE

Long Odds Overcome by U.S. Spaceship—Officials Delighted

By EVERT CLARK
Special to The New York Times

PASADENA, Calif., June 1—The Surveyor 1 spacecraft made a triumphant soft-landing on the moon late today and was hailed as the first man-made vehicle ever to settle gently onto another celestial body.

The spaceship landed at 11:17 P.M. (2:17 A.M. Thursday, Eastern daylight time).

Thirty-six minutes later Surveyor topped this feat by sending back photographs of the moon's surface and one of its own crushable, aluminum honeycombed "feet," or landing pads. The first picture also showed part of the leg to which the footpad was attached.

Surveyor landed in the Ocean of Storms just south of the lunar equator on the western side of the moon at a site where Apollo astronauts may land within two or three years.

Scientists at the Jet Propulsion Laboratory here, who developed the Surveyor and commanded its flight, were jubilant.

They had been through all the successes and failures of the Ranger moon craft and the Mariner vehicles that have flown past Venus and Mars. But tonight's victory was particularly sweet.

More Important Goal

The six-year-old Surveyor program is now running three years late and costing 10 times the original estimate. It has had more than its share of technical problems, and to do what it did on its very first flight defied all the odds of space technology.

The controllers announced that the engineering data radioed back "indicates a soft touchdown," a goal more important in many ways than the pictures because it proves Surveyor's design. The engineers had not expected to get this proof until several flights had been made.

Surveyor, an advance scout for the men who will land on the moon, was launched at 10:41 A.M., Eastern daylight time, last Monday from Cape Kennedy, Fla., aboard an Atlas-Centaur rocket. Throughout its 63½-hour, 248,000-mile journey its performance had exceeded all expectations.

The Descent to the Moon

The final approach and descent to the moon began 41 minutes before the actual touchdown. Surveyor was then a little over 2,000 miles from the moon and traveling at about 5,000 miles an hour. A series of commands from the earth caused Surveyor to roll 90 degrees then yaw itself around by 60 degrees and then roll another 94 degrees.

The first two maneuvers pointed the braking rocket in Surveyor's tail almost directly downward at the moon. The third turned one of its two conical antennas toward the earth.

Then, with the control center calling out precise times, speeds and altitudes, the braking rocket fired and Surveyor settled downward, losing speed and altitude rapidly.

From this point on, the spacecraft was commanding its own flight and the earthmen could do nothing. As the braking rocket fired, applause broke out in the hot, crowded auditorium where space officials and newsmen were following the flight.

Twice more at crucial points in the descent, applause broke out, and again at touchdown.

The American Ranger moon craft and the Soviet Union's lunar and Venus probes have all made hard landings, including the Luna 9 that sent back pho-

Continued on Page 28, Column 4

ALBANY GETS BILL FOR SCHOOL BONDS

Tax-Exempt Issues Outside City's Debt Limit Proposed for Dual-Use Buildings

By SYDNEY H. SCHANBERG
Special to The New York Times

ALBANY, June 1 — Mayor Lindsay and Governor Rockefeller today sent the Legislature a bill that would make available to New York City the hundreds of millions of dollars it needs to catch up with its long-postponed public school construction.

The legislation would permit construction of elementary and secondary schools with apartment or office floors above them.

Funds for such structures would come from the sale of special tax-exempt bonds that would be available to the public. The bill would create a New York City Educational Construction Fund to float such bonds, on an unlimited basis, outside the city's debt limit.

The debt limit, which restricts the city's borrowing ability, and the high cost of many school sites have been the key snags in the school construction program.

Under the Rockefeller-Lindsay bill, the new bond money would be used exclusively for

Continued on Page 35, Column 3

Dominicans Vote; Race for President Seems to Be Close

By PAUL L. MONTGOMERY
Special to The New York Times

SANTO DOMINGO, Dominican Republic, June 1—The Dominican people voted in an atmosphere of tranquility today in the country's third free election of this century. The election came about a year after a four-month civil war that was halted by the intervention of United States and other American troops.

Early returns in the contest for President between Juan Bosch and Dr. Joaquín Balaguer indicated that it would be an extremely close race. With 50 districts out of 3,421 reporting in an unofficial tally, the count was Mr. Bosch 13,194 and Dr. Balaguer 8,300. Dr. Rafael Bonnelly, the third candidate, had 448.

Balaguer Shows Strength

All the polling places reporting were from the Federal District, where Mr. Bosch captured 75 per cent of the vote when he won in 1962 with 58.7 per cent of the national total. His margin this time for the preliminary returns was 60 per cent.

A check of individual polling places in the city showed that Dr. Balaguer was showing considerable strength in some areas where Mr. Bosch was considered the favorite. The margins in the country districts, where Dr. Balaguer is strong, were ex-

Continued on Page 13, Column 1

JOHNSON HOPEFUL ON VIETNAM VOTE

Says Progress of Election's Planners Encourages Him —He Appears Relaxed

Text of the news conference appears on Page 20.

By JOHN D. POMFRET
Special to The New York Times

WASHINGTON, June 1 — President Johnson expressed confidence today that representative government would be achieved in South Vietnam.

Without fixing a date, Mr. Johnson said at a news conference: "We are hopeful that it can be done as early as possible. We solicit the support, the counsel and assistance of everybody concerned in helping us attain it." [Question 4, Page 20.]

The President answered questions in the Cabinet Room at the White House after a Cabinet meeting at which a wide range of foreign and domestic issues were discussed.

Sees No Need for Panic

Although a number of Cabinet members remained behind at Mr. Johnson's request to answer questions, they never had the chance. After Mr. Johnson finished, the reporters rushed from the room to file their accounts.

Mr. Johnson seemed relaxed and a bit philosophical about the problems he confronts.

Leaning back in his big black leather swivel chair, fingers interlaced behind his head, the President said:

"I don't think we should panic because we have some problems. Politics is never easy in our country—even with

Continued on Page 4, Column 4

War's Biggest Raid By U.S. Jets Wrecks Arms Plant in North

By NEIL SHEEHAN
Special to The New York Times

SAIGON, South Vietnam, June 1—United States Air Force fighter-bombers have reduced much of North Vietnam's extensive Yenbay arsenal and munitions storage area to flaming rubble in the largest single raid of the war, Air Force officers said today.

The Yenbay complex, one of the most important military installations in the north, is in a horseshoe bend of the Red River about 75 miles northwest of Hanoi.

Air Force officers said that 71 of the estimated 120 wood and masonry buildings that make up the arsenal were destroyed and 44 others damaged in an hour and a half raid yesterday afternoon. Twenty-five of the 30 antiaircraft batteries defending the installation were also silenced. Each battery contained 10 to 18 radar-controlled guns.

Secondary Blasts Observed

Informed sources attributed the unusually effective suppression of the flak batteries to the use of a highly improved version of an antipersonnel bomb. Details about the weapon and how it functions are secret.

The weapon is specially designed to kill and wound the antiaircraft gun crews.

Pilots said the square-mile area had been enveloped in a sheet of flames. Two large secondary explosions from munitions detonated by the bombs were observed. Flames from one group of burning buildings shot 50 feet into the air and a column of smoke rose to 8,000 feet.

It was 16 hours before the flames and smoke subsided

Continued on Page 5, Column 3

GEMINI 9 DELAYED UNTIL TOMORROW

Launching Is Halted at Last Minute by a Malfunction —Target Put in Orbit

By JOHN NOBLE WILFORD
Special to The New York Times

CAPE KENNEDY, Fla., June 1 — Once again, the hard-luck astronauts of Gemini 9 sat in their spacecraft on the launching pad here today, waited through most of the countdown —and went nowhere.

A last-minute electronic hitch forced flight controllers to call off the launching of the three-day space mission of Lieut. Col. Thomas P. Stafford of the Air Force and Lieut. Comdr. Eugene A. Cernan of the Navy. The launching was rescheduled for Friday morning.

The trouble spot was traced this morning to two units in the inertial guidance system that processed computer data on their way by radio to the spacecraft.

"The exact cause of the malfunction has not yet been determined.

Christopher C. Kraft, the National Aeronautics and Space Administration's director for flight operations, said that the two-day postponement would not change the objectives of the mission but would result in some revisions in the timing of events.

The three-day mission is to include several rendezvous and docking exercises and an astronaut's two-and-a-half-hour excursion outside the cabin.

The Gemini 9 troubles developed after a clockwork liftoff earlier of the Atlas rocket that hurled a stubby, 11-foot-

Continued on Page 30, Column 5

Cox Says He Made DiFalco Selection

By ROBERT E. TOMASSON

Surrogate Joseph A. Cox said yesterday that he had decided to designate the son of the other Manhattan surrogate, S. Samuel DiFalco, as special guardian of 35 minors involved in an estate estimated at $5-million.

Judge Cox's statement came in response to an article in Sunday's New York Times that said Judge DiFalco had appointed his son, Anthony, and would determine his fee. The two judges have been handling separate aspects of the case.

The two Manhattan surrogates, both Democrats, process wills totaling almost $1-billion a year. Last year they appointed 438 lawyers to act as

Continued on Page 36, Column 1

Associated Press Radiophoto

VOTING ON A NEW GOVERNMENT: One of the many lines that formed outside polling places in Santo Domingo yesterday. There were no reports of major incidents at the polls.

France Expected to Pull Troops Out of Germany

U.S. and Britain Foresee Action — Allies Propose Talks on NATO Issue

By ANTHONY LEWIS
Special to The New York Times

LONDON, June 1—The British and United States Governments are acting on the belief that, in the end, President de Gaulle of France is likely to pull French troops out of West Germany.

This view was reported today as France's allies in the North Atlantic Treaty Organization proposed to negotiate with her over the troop issue. Britain and the United States, it was said, would regret a French withdrawal but are quite prepared for it.

The experts trying to read General de Gaulle's mind do not believe that he will accept the minimum degree of military coordination that the allies regard as essential.

The critical issue is likely to be the allies' call for an arrangement that would assure the automatic commitment of French troops to some kind of joint command in the event of an attack on West Germany.

General de Gaulle has announced that France is leaving the NATO command because military integration is unacceptable. The feeling is that he cannot be expected to approve what amounts to another kind of integration, even though it would be conditioned on an emergency.

Trying to divine the general's plans has often proved an unprofitable game. But in this situation, the experts feel, the views he has so often and so publicly proclaimed about the preservation of French sovereignty look in one direction.

The feeling is that, given those views, it would be surprising if General de Gaulle were now to agree to let command of French troops pass out of French hands on the basis of an automatic trigger in an emergency.

The West German Government is now said to be coming around to the view that the general would rather withdraw his troops than give ground on the issue of integration. This poses very hard questions for the West Germans.

Chancellor Ludwig Erhard of West Germany will be under heavy domestic pressure to make concessions to the French that would keep their troops

Continued on Page 16, Column 1

NEWS INDEX

Vivien Merchant and Michael Caine in *Alfie.*

Raquel Welch starred in *One Million Years B.C.* .

Richard Burton, Elizabeth Taylor, George Segal and Sandy Dennis shown in a scene from *Who's Afraid of Virginia Woolf?* This powerful film was a landmark in on-the-screen use of vulgar language.

"All the News That's Fit to Print"

The New York Times.

LATE CITY EDITION

U.S. Weather Bureau Report (Page 93) forecasts: Showers, thundershowers and warm today, tonight. Fair tomorrow. Temp. Range: 88—74; yesterday: 90—73. Temp.-Hum. Index: about 80; yesterday: 78.

VOL. CXV. No. 39,581. NEW YORK, TUESDAY, JUNE 7, 1966. TEN CENTS

SAIGON GENERALS ADD 10 CIVILIANS TO RULING JUNTA

Act to Placate Opponents but Vote to Keep Ky and Thieu as Leaders

BUDDHISTS UNSATISFIED

Still Press for New Regime—Monks Seem Confused and Split on Tactics

Special to The New York Times

SAIGON, South Vietnam, June 6—The junta of 10 generals that has ruled South Vietnam for almost a year added 10 civilians to its ranks today.

However, a conclave of senior army officers voted overwhelmingly that the military should continue to lead the country for the time being and that the Premier, Air Vice Marshal Nguyen Cao Ky, and the Chief of State, Lieut. Gen. Nguyen Van Thieu, should remain in office.

The Unified Buddhist Church, the leading opposition to the military Government, said the addition of civilians to the junta would "not solve any problem" unless Marshal Ky and General Thieu were removed from office.

Since early March the Buddhists have won a number of important tactical victories over the generals, forcing them to promise elections this fall and to admit civilians into the Government.

Buddhists Seem Confused

But it appeared that the Buddhists were now confused and split on how hard to press a continuing campaign for the removal of Marshal Ky and General Thieu.

The two leaders had retreated a long distance, but now appeared to be on high, defensible ground in their fight to keep their dignity and to stay in power for a few more months until an elected civilian Government takes over in orderly fashion.

The Armed Forces Congress, a body of about 30 generals and 15 other important troop commanders, met for more than four hours and approved the addition of 10 civilians to the National Leadership Committee, the supreme ruling body of the nation.

The National Leadership Committee is more commonly referred to as the directorate. It already included 10 officers, including Marshal Ky and General Thieu.

The 10 civilians added did not include any representative of the Unified Buddhist Church's Institute of Secular Affairs, partly because the organized Buddhists had refused to join.

Some Represent Faiths

However, it did include at least two nominal, lay Buddhists as well as two Roman Catholics, two members of the Cao Dai religious sect and two members of the Hoa Hao sect. Two other members were not chosen for any religious ties.

The group as a whole could loosely be described as aging "intellectual politicians," a body of generally conservative, earnest men who had come and gone often in public life, leaving behind no great personal following or reputation.

Some observers thought, however, that the civilians might be harder to control than the

Continued on Page 2, Column 3

Gemini 9 Lands Safely Near Bullseye

Lieut. Comdr. Eugene A. Cernan, left, and Lieut. Col. Thomas P. Stafford after landing in Atlantic yesterday

Associated Press Radiophoto

NATO POSTPONES ACTION 4 MONTHS

Ministers to Act in October on Shifting Headquarters of Council From France

By HENRY TANNER

Special to The New York Times

BRUSSELS, June 6—The foreign ministers of 14 of the 15 members of the Atlantic alliance today deferred until October a decision on whether the political headquarters of the alliance should be moved from France along with the military headquarters.

The four-month postponement was described as a "face-saving formula."

Secretary of State Dean Rusk had said the United States felt strongly that French politics made it mandatory, for efficiency and other reasons, to move the headquarters of the alliance's council of permanent civilian representatives from France.

France Is Absent

The American position was opposed by the Canadian Secretary of State for External Affairs, Paul Martin, who declared that a shift of the council would unnecessarily deepen the rift between France and the other allies. He was supported by Foreign Minister Per Haekkerup of Denmark and, to a lesser extent, by Foreign Minister Amintore Fanfani of Italy, who, in the end, proposed the face-saving delay.

The 14 invited the Benelux countries—Belgium, the Netherlands and Luxembourg—to provide a new site for Supreme Headquarters Allied Powers Europe, or SHAPE, the military headquarters of the alliance.

France was absent from today's one-day meeting. The French Foreign Minister, Maurice Couve de Murville, will join the others tomorrow for a two-day ministerial meeting of the 15-member council. The pur-

Continued on Page 8, Column 3

Astronauts Flown to Cape For Debriefing on Mission

By JOHN NOBLE WILFORD

Special to The New York Times

CAPE KENNEDY, Fla., June 6—In a near-perfect climax to an often-troubled flight, the Gemini 9 astronauts steered their spacecraft to a safe splashdown in the Atlantic Ocean today.

Lieut. Col. Thomas P. Stafford of the Air Force and Lieut. Comdr. Eugene A. Cernan of the Navy set their craft down into choppy waters 345 miles east of here at 10 A.M., Eastern daylight time, after 44 complete trips around the world since their launching on Friday.

Their aim, as space flight controllers say, was "right down the pickle barrel"—within three miles of the aircraft carrier Wasp and within a half-mile of their target point. If it had been any closer, Navy officers said, it might have been too close.

Such precision enabled television cameras for the first time to record a Gemini descent for a nationwide audience and transmit it instantaneously by way of the communications satellite Early Bird.

Within an hour, Colonel Stafford and Commander Cernan stepped aboard the Wasp, smiling and showing none of the strain from the excitement, fatiguing maneuvers, frustrating problems, ever-present danger and tough decisions of their three days in space.

At 6:40 P.M., they arrived here by plane from the carrier to begin several days of medical examination and debriefings. A preliminary examination showed the astronauts to be in good physical condition.

On their flight the Gemini 9 astronauts achieved a difficult triple rendezvous with an orbiting target vehicle. And Commander Cernan set a record by spending more than two hours outside the spacecraft cabin.

But they failed to link their spacecraft with the orbiting target vehicle when they found that its docking apparatus was blocked by the "angry alligator" jaws of a stuck nose cover.

President Johnson, telephoning from his Texas ranch to the carrier, told the astronauts:

"You have made us all aware of what performance under pressure is all about."

Dr. George E. Mueller, the

Continued on Page 34, Column 1

EAST BLOC AIDES MEET IN MOSCOW

Foreign Ministers Confer on European Detente

By PETER GROSE

Special to The New York Times

MOSCOW, June 6—The foreign ministers of the Eastern European Communist countries assembled today to coordinate, according to reliable sources, a joint bargaining stand for an attempt to loosen the stalemate in political relations between Eastern and Western Europe.

With the Soviet Foreign Minister, Andrei A. Gromyko, as host, the seven nations of the Warsaw Pact opened what is expected to be a two- or three-day ministerial conference.

Soviet sources said it was a coincidence that the Communist diplomats were meeting at the same time as the foreign ministers of the North Atlantic Treaty Organization.

But the concurrent meetings seemed to demonstrate a search in both East and West for new attitudes toward the long deadlocked European security problem.

The Communist foreign ministers are meeting just 10 days after a conference of defense ministers of the Warsaw pact. Both gatherings are viewed as part of preliminary discussions building toward a meeting of East European party and Government leaders scheduled for early July.

Western diplomats expect the Communists to press a concerted initiative in the summer months to reap maximum advantage from the West's apparent disarray brought about

Continued on Page 9, Column 2

RACIAL PATTERNS SHIFT IN SCHOOLS

Non-Negro and Non-Puerto Rican Exodus Rises

By LEONARD BUDER

The exodus of non-Negro and non-Puerto Rican children from the city's public schools gained momentum last year.

The loss—nearly 25,000—was the greatest of any year since the Board of Education began taking an annual ethnic census of the city system in 1957.

At the same time, the number of Negro and Puerto Rican pupils rose 36,500. Since 1957, the system has gained 212,000 Negro and Puerto Rican children, while losing 98,750 "others."

These findings are contained in a report on the 1965 census. Although the report has not yet been made public, a copy was obtained yesterday by The New York Times.

Questioned about the report, Dr. Bernard E. Donovan, the Superintendent of Schools, said there was "no clear picture of all the causes" of the decline in the white enrollment.

"One of the greatest factors is the changing composition of the population of the city," he said in an interview. "Other factors might be the great num-

Continued on Page 36, Column 3

NEWS INDEX

News Summary and Index, Page 49

GOVERNOR FAVORS CITY REALTY LEVY OVER INCOME TAX

Indicates He Backs Senate's Ban on Personal Impost—Fare Issue Left Open

By RICHARD L. MADDEN

Special to The New York Times

ALBANY, June 6—Governor Rockefeller, breaking his silence in the legislative deadlock over New York City's tax package, gave an implied endorsement tonight to the program of the Senate Republicans who favor increases in the transit fare and real estate tax instead of a city personal income tax.

"The Senate has acted," Mr. Rockefeller said in a statement. "It is now up to the Assembly to act promptly to pass these measures or to come foward with any alternatives or additions."

"The time for action is now," he declared.

The Governor did not say specifically, however, whether he favored killing the proposed city income tax or increasing the 15-cent transit fare.

But the Governor did include in his statement a list of most of the proposed tax revenues and other sources of money for the city that were part of the Senate Republican plan to eliminate a city income tax and force a fare increase.

Water Rate Rise Included

Among the items were the $130-million yield of the real estate tax increase, $84-million for the "elimination of subway subsidy," $33-million for increased water rates, $6-million from increased enforcement of the cigarette tax, and $10-million from increased state aid under new legislation.

Mr. Rockefeller issued his statement after Mayor Lindsay spent the day in Albany trying to rescue his embattled tax program. The Mayor went away looking downcast and saying that things were "at an impasse—a very serious impasse."

After spending the day meeting and waiting to meet with the leaders of the politically divided Legislature and Governor Rockefeller, the Mayor slumped in a chair in the Capitol press room, sipped a soft drink and told reporters:

"The impasse is there. I've done everything in my power to break it—to press, to push, to fight. They remain immobile. I've done everything that I can do in Albany today."

Huge Budget Cut Feared

Unless the Legislature acts to provide new sources of revenue by the end of this month, Mr. Lindsay said, the proposed city budget for the fiscal year starting July 1 will have to be "slashed by $420-million—that's approximately 10 per cent right across the board."

The Republican-Liberal Mayor said it was up to "the Albany scene," including the legislative leadership aided by the Republican Governor, to resolve the deadlock over the city's tax package.

Did he hold Mr. Rockefeller responsible for the impasse?

"I'll judge by the results," Mr. Lindsay replied. At another point he said: "When the Legislature is finished staring at each other, then we'll judge the results."

Mr. Rockefeller, who heretofore has declined to endorse any part of the Mayor's tax re-

Continued on Page 33, Column 2

HIGH COURT VOIDS SHEPPARD VERDICT

Asserts 'Virulent Publicity' Denied Fair Murder Trial to Osteopath in Ohio

Excerpts from court opinion appear on Page 43.

By FRED P. GRAHAM

Special to The New York Times

WASHINGTON, June 6—The Supreme Court threw out today the conviction of Dr. Samuel H. Sheppard on charges of murdering his pregnant wife. It ruled that "virulent publicity" had denied him a fair trial.

In an 8-to-1 decision that could become a milestone in the effort to reconcile the constitutional rights of a free press with the guarantee of a fair trial, the Court placed the responsibility for preventing "trial by newspaper" on public officials, not the press.

Under the decision, the Cuyahoga County prosecutor in Cleveland, John T. Corrigan, must try Dr. Sheppard again "within a reasonable time" or drop the case. Mr. Corrigan said today he would not decide about a retrial until he had studied the Court's opinion.

Married After Release

The opinion by Justice Tom C. Clark placed most of the blame for the "carnival atmosphere" of Dr. Sheppard's trial in 1954 on Circuit Judge A. Edward Blythin, now dead, who presided at the Cleveland trial.

Dr. Sheppard, an osteopath, who has steadfastly denied his guilt, was convicted of second degree murder and given a life sentence. After serving more than nine years in prison, he was granted a writ of habeas corpus and released in 1964 by Federal District Judge Carl Weinman of Dayton, Ohio.

Dr. Sheppard married a German divorcee who had corresponded with him in prison. When

Continued on Page 43, Column 1

Kennedy Denounces Apartheid as Evil

Excerpts from Kennedy's talk will be found on Page 10.

By Reuters

CAPETOWN, South Africa, June 6—Senator Robert F. Kennedy branded apartheid tonight as one of the evils of the world.

Mr. Kennedy, a New York Democrat, listed as other evils discrimination in New York, serfdom in Peru, starvation in India, mass slaughter in Indonesia and the jailing of intellectuals in the Soviet Union.

"These are differing evils. But they are the common works of man," he said.

Mr. Kennedy addressed the multiracial National Union of South African Students at the University of Capetown. The students had invited him to South Africa.

Many observers believed

Continued on Page 10, Column 1

MAY JOBLESS RATE UP SHARPLY TO 4%

Rise, the Biggest in 2 Years, Is Seen as Indication That the Boom Is Tapering Off

By DAVID R. JONES

Special to The New York Times

WASHINGTON, June 6—The nation's booming economy showed further signs today of cooling off as the Government reported that the unemployment rate last month had made its sharpest rise in 23 months, to 4 per cent of the civilian labor force.

Arthur M. Ross, Commissioner of Labor Statistics, said in a news conference that the seasonally adjusted jobless rate's climb to that level from 3.7 per cent in April was added evidence that "economic growth has tapered off." Much of the May increase reflected a flood of students into the labor market.

The official emphasized that nonfarm employment, while growing less rapidly than earlier, had continued to rise more than seasonally last month. And he predicted that the jobless rate would resume its general decline, probably around September or October, and fall below 3.7 per cent by the end of the year.

Summer Jobs Scarce

The rise in the unemployment rate to 4 per cent put the figure back where it was in January, and was another indication that the need for a tax increase to head off inflation was easing. The jobless rate, which has been running between 3.7 per cent and 4 per cent for five months, last rose by 0.3 point in June, 1964.

Another anti-inflationary sign was a drop in the average factory work week to 41.4 hours last month from 41.5 hours in April and 41.6 hours in February. Mr. Ross said this indicated "that employers have been able to catch up with their manpower requirements."

Mr. Ross attributed most of last month's 140,000 increase in unemployment to the inability of women and students entering the summer job market to find work.

Although the "rate of economic growth has decelerated" in April and May, he said, this

Continued on Page 26, Column 3

MEREDITH IS SHOT IN BACK ON WALK INTO MISSISSIPPI

Ambushed Negro Reported in Satisfactory Condition—Johnson Denounces Act

WHITE SUSPECT IS HELD

CORE Plans to Finish March to Spur Voter Registration and End Fear of Racists

By ROY REED

Special to The New York Times

HERNANDO, Miss., June 6—James H. Meredith, the Negro who desegregated the University of Mississippi in 1962, was shot in the back from ambush today as he walked along United States Highway 51 two miles south of here.

Mr. Meredith suffered what a hospital official called superficial wounds of the head, neck, shoulder, back and legs. He was reported to be in satisfactory condition after surgery to remove 60 to 70 pellets at a hospital at Memphis, 26 miles north of here.

Immediately after the shooting, which occurred at 4:15 P.M. Central standard time (6 P.M. Eastern daylight time), the police arrested a white man with an automatic 16-gauge shotgun. He was identified as Aubrey James Norvell, 40 years old, an unemployed former hardware contractor of Memphis.

Sheriff Lee Meredith of De-Soto County, said the suspect had admitted the shooting but had told him he did not know why he had done it. The sheriff said the man had been drinking.

[At his Texas ranch, President Johnson deplored the shooting as an "awful act of violence" and ordered a Justice Department investigation. Page 29.

[In New York City, the Congress of Racial Equality declared that it planned to take up his march from the site of the shooting to Jackson, the state capital. Page 28.]

Object of Hatred

Mr. Meredith, 32 years old, now a Columbia University law school student and a resident of New York, became an object of hatred among white Mississippians after he enrolled in their all-white, tradition-shrouded "Ole Miss."

He had already marched 28 miles of a 220-mile projected walk from Memphis to Jackson when he was shot today. The walk was a homecoming and a pilgrimage aimed at promoting Negro voter registration. It also was a personal test for Mr. Meredith to learn whether he and other Negroes in Mississippi had reason to fear whites in Mississippi.

"The tension is high," Mr. Meredith had said this morning. "I can tell from the way the Negroes are acting along the way."

Sherwood Ross, a New York and Washington radioman acting as Mr. Meredith's press coordinator, was one of six men walking with him when the shooting occurred.

Mr. Ross, a white man, said he had heard a voice shout "James Meredith" twice from the woods at the roadside. He said he saw a white man standing in the brush.

The man raised a gun, he said, and Mr. Ross warned Mr.

Continued on Page 29, Column 1

Cambodian Villagers Describe April Shelling by U.S. Forces

By HARRISON E. SALISBURY

Special to The New York Times

PNOMPENH, Cambodia, June 5—Outside the Governor's house in Svayrieng, red, blue and green light bulbs turned the mango grove into a fairyland. Inside, wine glasses tinkled gently on the flower-strewn dinner table.

"It is the bombing," said Gov. Ou Tong Hao quietly. "Do you hear it? For more than a year now we have heard it almost every night. Do you wonder that we sometimes fear the bombs will fall on us?"

Governor Hao's fear is shared by most Cambodians these days.

Svayrieng Province, on the border of South Vietnam, provides a case study of the perils overhanging officially neutral Cambodia. Americans accuse Cambodia of helping the Vietcong, and Cambodians accuse the Americans of a plot to drag Cambodia into the Vietnamese war.

Prince Norodom Sihanouk, Cambodian Chief of State, has proposed bolstering the International Control Commission, composed of India, Canada and Poland, to provide better policing of the frontiers. An attempt to establish what happened in the Caibac River incident April 29 and 30 provides support for Prince Sihanouk's thesis.

In mid-April the United States First Infantry Division launched an operation to clean out so-called War Zone C, northwest of Saigon. It was the American bombing of this area that rattled the wine glasses on Governor Hao's table at Svayrieng, five miles from the frontier.

The American operation start-

Continued on Page 4, Column 3

SHOT WHILE MARCHING: James H. Meredith on U.S. Highway 51 after he was wounded near Hernando, Miss.

Jim Ryun was a 19-year-old Kansas boy who ran a 3:51.3 mile in Berkeley and lopped 2.3 seconds off the world record.

At the height of his career, injuries forced Sandy Koufax to retire as the Dodgers' star pitcher.

Red Auerbach collected his 1,000th win and turned his Boston Celtics over to Bill Russell, the first black head coach of a major professional team.

Helen Gurley Brown, author of *Sex and the Single Girl*, turned the formerly lagging *Cosmopolitan* magazine into the bible for single girls of the sixties.

Jacqueline Susann dominated the American fiction scene of the sixties as mistress of the sex novel. Despite harsh reviews from critics, she pulled in over one million dollars on her first novel, *Valley of the Dolls.*

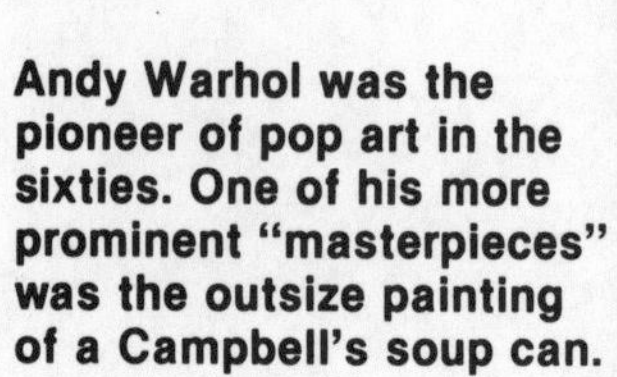

Andy Warhol was the pioneer of pop art in the sixties. One of his more prominent "masterpieces" was the outsize painting of a Campbell's soup can.

"All the News That's Fit to Print"

The New York Times.

LATE CITY EDITION

U.S. Weather Bureau Report (Page 77) forecasts: Fair, hot, less humid today; cooler tonight. Fair, seasonable tomorrow.
Temp. Range: 90—73; yesterday: 92—73.
Temp.-Hum. Index: about 70; yesterday: 80.

VOL. CXV..No. 39,604. NEW YORK, THURSDAY, JUNE 30, 1966. TEN CENTS

U.S., EXTENDING BOMBING, RAIDS HANOI AND HAIPHONG OUTSKIRTS; CITES REDS' DISPERSAL OF FUEL

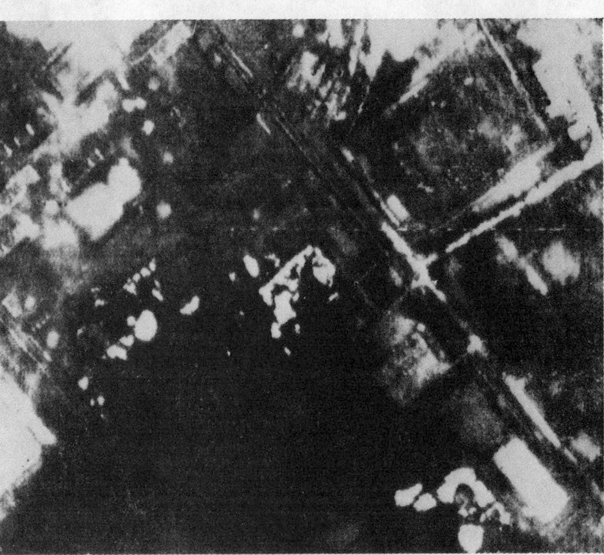

U.S. TARGET: Burning fuel storage facilities three-and-a-half miles northeast of Hanoi are shown in photograph taken from American plane after raid yesterday. Flames rose 12,000 feet. Bomb craters are visible at upper left.

U.S. Air Force photo, via Associated Press

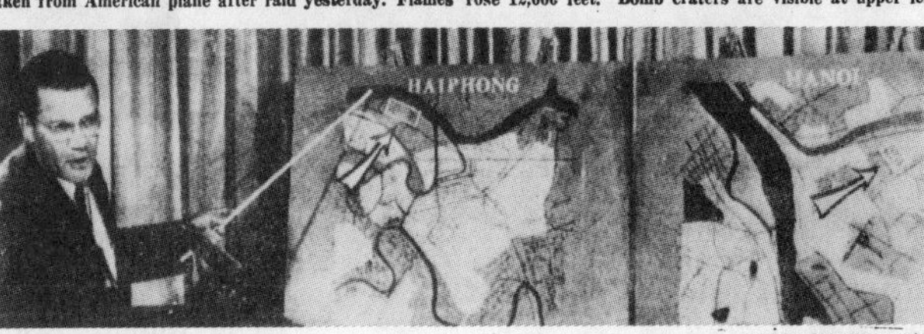

DESCRIBING THE TARGETS: Defense Secretary Robert S. McNamara uses maps of Haiphong and Hanoi as he tells reporters about U.S. strikes against oil facilities. Arrows, which have been added to photograph, show raided areas.

United Press International Telephoto

HEAVY LOSS SEEN

Oil-Storage Capacity Is Reduced by 50%, Pilots Indicate

By CHARLES MOHR
Special to The New York Times

SAIGON, South Vietnam, June 29—United States bombers struck close to the heart of Hanoi and Haiphong today in raids that military informants said had damaged the gasoline and oil supplies of North Vietnam severely.

The raids marked a change from restrictions that had kept American planes well away from the two major cities since they began hitting the North in February, 1965. It also marked an important escalation of the United States effort against the North Vietnamese-backed guerrillas in South Vietnam.

Whether the restrictions will now be further altered to allow raids on manufacturing plants, military airfields and other targets around Hanoi and Haiphong was unclear, but some informed sources believed that such targets would soon be hit. The decision, like that to carry out today's raids, must be made in Washington.

Air Force Joins Attack

Navy A-4 and A-6 jet fighter-bombers attacked a large tank farm for petroleum products at the very edge of Haiphong, two miles northwest of the center of the city.

The complex, which represents 40 per cent of the fuel-storage capacity of North Vietnam and 95 per cent of the facilities for unloading tanker ships, was 80 per cent destroyed, according to preliminary damage reports by returning pilots.

Air Force F-105 jet fighter-bombers struck another large tank farm 3½ miles from the center of Hanoi that contained 20 per cent of the nation's storage facilities. The pilots estimated that they had destroyed 90 per cent of the target area.

Haiphong, the port for Hanoi, is about 60 miles from the capital.

In a Single Stroke

If the assessments are correct, the raids, in a single stroke, destroyed 50 per cent of North Vietnam's fuel-storage capacity as well as most of its ability to unload petroleum products from ships efficiently and expeditiously.

Another petroleum facility at Doson, 12 miles southeast of Haiphong, was also bombed, but there was no damage assessment.

The United States command made it clear that it had staged the raids because previously restricted air action had failed to deal with the major problem of North Vietnamese infiltration of troops and supplies to the Vietcong.

The Hanoi radio claimed seven United States planes shot down, three near Haiphong and four near Hanoi. Such reports have been exaggerated and there was no reason to doubt the accuracy of an American statement that only one plane, an F-105, had been lost.

The nearest previous strike in relation to Haiphong was a

Continued on Page 14, Column 1

PRIME LOAN RATE IS RAISED TO 5¾% BY MAJOR BANKS

Chemical Initiates Increase on Business Borrowings —Others Due to Join

AIDES AT RESERVE WARY

Action Sets Off Speculation That Upturn in Discount Charge May Follow

By H. ERICH HEINEMANN

The cost of business borrowing at the nation's banks started to move up another notch yesterday.

Late in the afternoon, the Chemical Bank New York Trust Company, the fourth largest commercial bank in New York City and the fifth largest in the United States, announced that, effective immediately, its prime or minimum rate on loans to businesses would be raised to 5¾ per cent from 5½ per cent.

Almost at once, the First National Bank of Chicago announced a similar increase in the prime rate, the interest charged by banks on short-term loans to large depositors with the highest credit rating.

In Los Angeles, the Union Bank, which specializes in corporate banking, also increased its prime rate to 5¾ per cent.

[In Washington, Federal Reserve Board officials reacted cautiously to the Chemical Bank's increase in the prime rate, noting that it was "not out of line" with the general pressures on banks and money-market conditions.]

Reaction at Other Banks

The move to a higher business-lending rate came against the background of mounting demands for bank credit, selective rate increases by banks on some types of loans, and an increasingly restrictive credit policy by the Federal Reserve.

Some bankers speculate that the Federal Reserve might follow by increasing its discount rate.

The action came too late in the day for other major banks in New York City and elsewhere to react formally. However, there were strong indications from several of the country's largest banks—in New York, Chicago, San Francisco, and Boston—that they would join in today.

If the increase does become general, it will be the third time since last December that

Continued on Page 61, Column 1

City Tax Program Mired as Senators Fail to Rally Votes

By RICHARD L. MADDEN
Special to The New York Times

ALBANY, June 29—Senate leaders struggled again today to round up enough votes to pass New York City's tax program, and again they failed.

After a day of huddles and whispered conversations in the red-carpeted Senate chamber, the members recessed until tomorrow without having acted on the tax package, which the city is counting on for the fiscal year starting at 12:01 A.M. Friday.

The Democratic-controlled Assembly is not scheduled to act on the city tax bills until the Senate moves. The Assembly spent much of today wrangling over Republican efforts to soften the impact of the state's controversial new medical assistance program.

The Senate leaders appeared to be in about the same position they were in last week when they first postponed action on the tax

Continued on Page 17, Column 1

G.O.P. RELUCTANT ON OPEN SUPPORT FOR KLEIN IN FALL

Javits 'Not Enthusiastic' and Price Cool to Backing Democrat for Surrogate

By RICHARD WITKIN

Republican Senator Jacob K. Javits said yesterday that he deplored "very much" the fact that "we now have a candidate for Surrogate who has been rejected by his own party."

In an interview here in which he commented on the results of Tuesday's Democratic primary, Mr. Javits said it was "now essential for me to maintain a much closer eye on my own party and the details of its internal operations."

In the Surrogate primary, State Supreme Court Justice Arthur G. Klein, an old-line Democrat, was roundly defeated by Justice Samuel J. Silverman, who was backed by a coalition led by Senator Robert F. Kennedy.

But because Justice Klein also had been designated, unopposed, by the Republican regulars, he will be the Republican candidate in November against Justice Silverman.

Support in Doubt

Mr. Javits, asked if he would support Justice Klein in the fall, said:

"I am not very enthusiastic about the prospect, but I'll consider it."

Mr. Javits's comments reflected the wide Republican embarrassment over seeing the party maneuvered into being the only backer of an Old Guard Democrat.

"The general odor of a deal seems to have been pervasive enough," the Senator said, "to move a majority of the Democratic voters to reject Justice Klein in favor of Justice Silverman. I don't know what the deal was or even if there was one. I propose to keep a much closer eye on my own party than heretofore because of what has happened."

Governor Rockefeller, whose chances of winning re-election could suffer from having Justice Klein on his ticket, refused comment on the situation.

So did Mayor Lindsay, who said after the Republicans had picked Justice Klein that he had tried to stop it and was not happy.

Focus on Governorship

Sources close to Deputy Mayor Robert Price indicated that he would vote for Justice Klein but that he would campaign actively only for Governor Rockefeller and for Representative Theodore R. Kupferman, his former law partner.

Mr. Javits was interviewed at the offices of the First National City Bank, 399 Park Avenue, near 54th Street, just before addressing a group of business executives seeking to have the Federal Government add a huge new accelerator to the Brookhaven National Laboratory in Suffolk County.

Politicians everywhere yesterday were turning their attention again to the scramble for the Democratic nomination for Governor.

It was almost universally agreed that Mr. Kennedy could have a dominant voice in picking the candidate, if he wanted to. The guessing game over whom he might prefer picked up momentum.

There was some feeling that, among the active candidates, Franklin D. Roosevelt Jr. and Nassau County Executive Eugene H. Nickerson had been

Continued on Page 24, Column 1

A.M.A. FOR POLICY OF DIRECT BILLING

Urges All Members to Act Under Medicare Provision —Choice Is Retained

By AUSTIN C. WEHRWEIN
Special to The New York Times

CHICAGO, June 29 — The House of Delegates of the American Medical Association adopted today a resolution that recommended direct billing of patients by every member under Medicare.

Under direct billing, doctors would be enabled to ignore the machinery of Medicare, which goes into effect Friday. But in its zeal to encourage use of the method, the 238-member policy-making house went beyond the wishes of its leadership.

But later the delegates, by reinterpreting the resolution, apparently accepted the leadership view of how doctors should act under the new plan.

The leadership also favors direct billing, but in a carefully worded form to avoid any possible antitrust action. In their short-lived revolt, the delegates were seeking doubly to emphasize that they favored "individual responsibility" on the part of the patients and their conviction that they were protecting the doctor-patient relationship.

Picked by Acclamation

The development was seen as indicative of the dominant conservative sentiment in the House of Delegates, most of whose members are unreconciled to the whole Medicare law and intend to employ direct billing as one means of demonstrating this to patients, the public, Congress and the Johnson Administration.

Although the dispute over how hard to push doctors toward direct billing was smoothed over, it left the A.M.A. sharply split. There was no immediate explanation from the leaders on exactly what the policy was after the revolt.

Also, the A.M.A. was split over the question of discrimination against Negro doctors, especially in the South, although a debate on the floor on this issue was avoided.

By acclamation, the delegates

Continued on Page 19, Column 3

WILSON DEPLORES LATEST ATTACKS

Backs General U.S. Policy —Thant Scores Raids on 'Populated Areas'

Text of Wilson's statement is printed on Page 14.

By DANA ADAMS SCHMIDT
Special to The New York Times

LONDON, June 29 — Prime Minister Wilson reaffirmed general British support of the United States policy in Vietnam today but declared that "we must dissociate ourselves" from the American bombing of oil storage installations at Hanoi and Haiphong.

The Conservative leader, Edward Heath, expressed full understanding and support of the American action.

Before a gravely silent House of Commons, Mr. Wilson expressed guarded disapproval for the first time of a major United States move in the war.

[At the United Nations, Secretary General Thant voiced "deep regret" over the bombings of what he termed "the heavily populated areas." In Moscow, there was no hint of an intensified Soviet commitment in Vietnam, although the raids were sharply criticized.]

Mr. Wilson explained that Britain had "made it clear on many occasions that we could not support an extension of the bombing to such areas, even though we were confident that

Continued on Page 14, Column 6

Bombing Evokes Criticism And Praise in Both Parties

By E. W. KENWORTHY
Special to The New York Times

WASHINGTON, June 29—On Capitol Hill today, President Johnson's decision to bomb oil depots at Hanoi and Haiphong was regretted, praised, denounced and accepted with resignation.

Those who have been urging expansion of the bombings endorsed the decision, as might be expected, and those who have counseled against stepping up the war were deeply dejected and despondent.

The reactions cut across party lines, with influential Senators lined up on opposite sides.

Mike Mansfield of Montana, the Senate Democratic leader, who has steadily urged the President not to extend the bombing, was described as angry by those close to him.

In his customary exchange with reporters just before the Senate session, Mr. Mansfield was reluctant to comment. When pressed, he said, "I think it indicates a new stage in the war. I think it will also bring about a greater amount of aid from the Soviet Union and Peking.

"The destruction of petrol facilities won't deter infiltration. It may slow it down for the time being, but the end result may be increased infiltration that will make the road to the negotiating table that much more difficult."

Senator Richard B. Russell, Democrat of Georgia, chairman of the Armed Services Committee, said of the bombing:

"I approve of it. It seems to me we have exhausted every effort to arrive at negotiations. Any further delay in drying up the sources of supply for the Vietcong and the North Vietnamese troops in the South could only increase the casualty lists of American dead and wounded."

Senator Leverett Saltonstall

Continued on Page 14, Column 4

M'NAMARA GIVES REASON FOR RAIDS

Rise in Infiltration and Move by North to Camouflage Depots Are Mentioned

Transcript of news conference appears on Page 15.

By BENJAMIN WELLES
Special to The New York Times

WASHINGTON, June 29 — Defense Secretary Robert S. McNamara today attributed the timing of the United States bombing attacks near Hanoi and Haiphong to increasing infiltration into South Vietnam and recent moves to camouflage the North Vietnamese oil storage and distribution system.

The "perishable" nature of the vital petroleum targets, he said at a news conference, made an attack now "much more desirable" than it might have been earlier in the year.

Crisp and alert, despite his all-night vigil waiting in the Pentagon for reports on the raid, Secretary McNamara looked as if a weight had been lifted from his shoulders. Mounting speculation that the United States would strike at North Vietnam's remaining oil supplies had reached fever pitch.

Policy Aims Underlined

While he declined to speculate on future United States air attacks or on reactions by Communist China, he emphasized the following points:

¶The United States will continue a policy of military "restraint," hitting only "military" and not civilian targets.

¶American objectives in Vietnam remain "limited." These objectives are not to destroy the Communist Government in the North; not to destroy or damage the North Vietnamese people; not to make South Vietnam a military ally nor even to develop permanent military bases in the South.

¶The United States aims are

Continued on Page 15, Column 1

HOUSE UNIT EASES HOUSING BIAS BAN

Exempts Individual Sales—Bill Cleared for Floor

By JOHN HERBERS
Special to The New York Times

WASHINGTON, June 29—The House Judiciary Committee approved President Johnson's civil rights bill today after accepting a compromise amendment to the open housing section that would exempt the vast majority of individual home sales.

By a vote of 21 to 13, the committee adopted the amendment sponsored by Representative Charles McC. Mathias Jr., Republican of Maryland.

This broke a two-day deadlock over the controversial section that would ban discrimination in the sale or rental of all types of housing.

The committee then approved the entire bill by a vote of 24 to 9 and asked that it be brought to a vote by the full House as soon as possible.

However, the committee also accepted an amendment sponsored by civil rights groups and offered by Representative John Conyers Jr., Democrat of Michigan, to establish an enforcement agency for open housing with power to issue cease-and-desist orders.

The vote on this amendment was 13 to 4, and there were indications that some members were not aware of how strong it was, although Mr. Conyers announced that it would give the agency powers beyond conciliation, similar to those of the National Labor Relations Board.

It was the Mathias amendment that made the housing

Continued on Page 23, Column 4

Reading Standards Are Raised For Promotion in City Schools

By LEONARD BUDER

Higher standards for promotion have been put into effect in the city school system in an effort to improve academic performance.

The new policy emphasizes higher requirements in reading as a condition for promotion of pupils to the next grade.

Its impact will be felt for the first time today when the city's school year ends and pupils receive their report cards, which will tell them whether they have been promoted or "left back."

For the first time in nearly two decades, pupils will be retained in the first grade if they fail to meet minimum requirements in reading. Until now the policy has been to promote all first-graders, regardless of academic performance, so that they would not be discouraged by failure.

In most of the upper grades, two months have been added to the reading scores required for promotion.

This means that youngsters who previously could have lagged two years behind in reading and still be promoted, will now be retained in the same grade if they are more than a year and eight months behind in reading. (There are 10 months in the school year.)

An even more dramatic change will take effect in June, 1968, when students will be re-

Continued on Page 42, Column 3

NEWS INDEX

British Ship Strike Called Off One Year for Study of Industry

By W. GRANGER BLAIR
Special to The New York Times

LONDON, June 29—The leaders of Britain's National Union of Seamen decided today to end the 45-day-old maritime strike.

By a vote of 29 to 16, the union's executive council, which Prime Minister Wilson said yesterday had a "lack of guts," ordered the seamen back to work as of midnight Friday.

After a four-hour meeting at its headquarters in South London, the council voted to "adjourn strike action" for a year to permit the special committee of inquiry headed by Lord Pearson to conclude its scheduled study of seagoing employment and the shipping industry.

When a spokesman for the union came out to announce the decision, a group of placard-carrying seamen broke into boos and catcalls. The placards read, "Don't Let Us Down."

One seaman shouted, "You will have to get somebody else to sail your ships." Another, referring to the union leaders, cried, "None of you lads will be here in 12 months' time."

While some of the seamen were smashing their placards on the entrance steps to the headquarters, another wrote "Judas Hogarth" in red chalk on the steps, a reference to William Hogarth, head of the union.

There were also reports of

Continued on Page 6, Column 4

U.S. Sounds Latins On Argentine Ties

By RICHARD EDER
Special to The New York Times

WASHINGTON, June 29—The United States has begun, with a deliberate lack of haste, to consult other nations in the Western hemisphere about the question of resuming relations with Argentina's new military government.

Although ultimate United States policy toward the regime of Lieut. Gen. Juan Carlos Onganía, the new President, is still undetermined, it was evident that no quick move would be made to reverse Washington's initial coldness towards the coup d'état.

The consultations, which are being conducted in the Latin-American capitals, are expected to take three or four weeks. It

Continued on Page 5, Column 3

Adam West brought *Batman*, the famous comic-strip character, to life on the small screen.

Lyndon Johnson conducted a tour of his Texas ranch on a televised special, *The Hill Country: Lyndon Johnson's Texas.*

Alvin Childress, Tim Moore and Spencer Williams (left to right) starred, in *Amos 'n' Andy.* CBS withdrew the program in 1966 due to protest from several civil-rights groups who felt the show stereotyped blacks.

"All the News That's Fit to Print"

The New York Times.

LATE CITY EDITION

U.S. Weather Bureau Report (Page 69) forecasts: Mostly sunny today; fair tonight and tomorrow.

Temp. Range: 92—67; yesterday: 95—63. Temp.-Hum. Index: 68; yesterday: 80.

VOL. CXV..No. 39,605. © 1966 by The New York Times Company Times Square, New York, N.Y. 10036 NEW YORK, FRIDAY, JULY 1, 1966. TEN CENTS

PRESIDENT VOWS TO PRESS PUNISHING OF AGGRESSORS; HANOI AREA BOMBED AGAIN

Associated Press Wirephoto

DISCUSSING WAR AND PEACE: President Johnson stressing a point during his speech yesterday in Omaha.

TALKS IN MIDWEST

Johnson Again Urges Foe to Set a Time for Peace Parley

The text of Johnson speech is printed on Page 11.

By JOHN D. POMFRET

Special to The New York Times

OMAHA, June 30—President Johnson said today that United States air strikes on military targets in North Vietnam "will continue to impose a growing burden and a high price on those who wage war against the freedom of their neighbors."

The resolute tone of Mr. Johnson's remarks, made in a speech, indicated no wavering in his decision to step up the tempo of the war to convince North Vietnam that it cannot win and should seek to negotiate a settlement.

It was the President's first pronouncement alluding to the important escalation of the war signaled by the United States bombing raids yesterday on fuel dumps close to Hanoi and Haiphong. The tenor of the President's remarks made it plain that he was unswayed by criticism of the raids in Congress and abroad.

Support for Policy Urged

In a broad-ranging speech, Mr. Johnson emphasized the perils posed by developing world food shortages and his hope that nations, no matter what their ideologies, could cooperate to end poverty, ignorance and disease.

He also urged Americans to stand fast behind his policy in Vietnam.

"If you are too busy and not inclined to help, please count 10 before you hurt," the President asked.

[In a later speech in Des Moines, Mr. Johnson said that if the leaders of North Vietnam "will only let me know when and where they would like to ask us directly what can be done to bring peace to South Vietnam, I will have my closest and most trusted associates there in a matter of hours." He said there need be no agenda or commitments, Page 11.]

The President chose for his earlier speech a site calculated to underscore the peaceful intentions of the United States: The Omaha Municipal Dock on the Missouri River.

Tied up there was a barge

Continued on Page 10, Column 3

3 More Oil Storage Sites Are Raided by U.S. Planes

By CHARLES MOHR

Special to The New York Times

SAIGON, June 30—American bombers hit three more fuel storage areas in the Hanoi area today, following the raids yesterday on the two major North Vietnamese storage facilities for gasoline and oil on the outskirts of Haiphong and Hanoi.

In the ground war in South Vietnam, a unit of the United States First Infantry Division engaged in heavy combat for most of the day with a Vietcong unit that attempted an ambush 60 miles northwest of Saigon.

Military spokesmen said that 140 guerrillas were killed in the fight, but had no description of American casualties.

In another ground battle near the 17th Parallel, which divides North and South Vietnam, a South Vietnamese marine battalion suffered "heavy" casualties. But the Vietnamese marines, reinforcing companies of United States marines and fighter pilots, said they had killed 202 enemy soldiers.

Concentration on Oil

The initial raids on fuel depots struck the two main petroleum storage centers of North Vietnam—two miles from Haiphong and three and one-half miles from Hanoi—apparently destroying 50 per cent or more of the nation's fuel storage capacity.

The follow-up raids, aimed at smaller facilities, were intended to increase North Vietnam's fuel problems.

Navy jets struck the Bacgiang storage center 25 miles northeast of Hanoi, which can store 6,000 metric tons of fuel, or 4 per cent of the national storage capacity.

Returning pilots said they saw "billowing smoke and immense fireballs." They added that "fire extended throughout the area and smoke could be seen 70 miles away."

Air Force jet fighter bombers struck the Viettri storage area on the banks of the Red River 28 miles northwest of Hanoi, an area also containing eight main storage tanks.

The pilots, who dropped 1,000-

Continued on Page 3, Column 1

PARIS AND MOSCOW MAP COOPERATION

De Gaulle and Podgorny Sign a Declaration of Principle —General Leaves Today

Soviet-French declaration will be found on Page 14.

By PETER GROSE

Special to The New York Times

MOSCOW, June 30—France and the Soviet Union declared today their intent to collaborate with each other as a catalyst around which all Europe would refashion itself in confidence and peace.

A declaration of principle, drawn as a design for evolution over years or even decades, was solemnly signed at the Kremlin by President de Gaulle and the Soviet chief of state, Nikolai V. Podgorny.

Sealing of the declaration, a title used deliberately to elevate the joint statement above the level of a routine communiqué, was the highlight of the twelve-day state visit of General de Gaulle to the Soviet Union. The French President will return to Paris tomorrow.

Space Accord Signed

At the practical level the two countries signed a 10-year agreement on space research providing, in principle, for the launching of a French instrumented satellite by a Soviet rocket.

As the Soviet and French speakers toasted their future cooperation at a daylong Kremlin reception, General de Gaulle in a prerecorded television statement told the Soviet people of his vision of Europe.

Speaking in French, which was subsequently translated, General de Gaulle praised the reconstruction and renovation under way in both the Soviet Union and France after the destruction of World War II.

"Certainly we do not accomplish all this along the same lines and the measures that we employ are often different," he told Soviet viewers. "But in sum, your destiny and ours are similar. The Russians and the French can go hand in hand."

Then, in exuberant Russian,

Continued on Page 14, Column 5

THANT IS DISPUTED BY U.S. ON VIETNAM

Goldberg Says Raiding Halt Would Not End War

Text of the Goldberg letter appears on Page 8.

By DREW MIDDLETON

Special to The New York Times

UNITED NATIONS, N. Y., June 30—Arthur J. Goldberg told the Security Council and Secretary General Thant tonight that a halt in the bombing of North Vietnam would not end the war.

This was a direct rejection of the first of the three steps toward peace proposed by Mr. Thant on June 20.

The chief United States representative also answered the Secretary General's complaint yesterday about the United States bombing of what Mr. Thant had termed heavily populated areas in the Haiphong-Hanoi area. Mr. Goldberg emphasized the care taken to hit only military targets.

No such discrimination has been shown by the Vietcong in their terrorism and assassination of innocent civilians in South Vietnam, Mr. Goldberg noted.

He declared that a peaceful solution could be found through the reconvening of the Geneva conference in order "to reaffirm and revitalize" the Geneva agreements of 1954 and 1962

Continued on Page 8, Column 4

CITY INCOME TAX VOTED BY SENATE; ASSEMBLY WAITS

Levy on Commuters Also Passes by 37-27 Margin —Budget Action Delayed

COUNCIL IS STANDING BY

Republicans in Lower House Holding Back, Travia Says —Adjournment Put Off

By RICHARD L. MADDEN

Special to The New York Times

ALBANY, June 30—The Senate voted tonight for a New York City income tax on residents and a levy on the earnings of commuters. But the tax package bogged down again in the Democratic-controlled Assembly.

In the Republican-controlled Senate the vote, which crossed party lines, was 37 to 27 on both measures. In the Assembly, after three hours of conferences and waiting, action was postponed on the city tax package until tomorrow.

The latest snag was that Republican Assemblymen were reluctant to provide enough votes to pass the city tax bills until the Democratic majority agreed on Republican efforts to tone down the state's new medical assistance program.

The new taxes, which are scheduled to take effect tomorrow after the Assembly gives final approval and the City Council imposes them, mean that a family of four with a $10,000 annual income would pay about $38.40 a year to the city under the tax on residents and $17.50 under the levy on commuters.

Three-Month Deadlock

The Assembly delay means that the city will start its fiscal year at 12:01 A.M. tomorrow without the final legislative authorization of the new taxes it had been counting on to balance its budget.

The Senate completed action on the tax bills after a strenuous effort by Governor Rockefeller and the legislative leaders to round up the votes. In the expectation that the Assembly would also move tonight to end the three-month deadlock over city taxes, the Senate also passed a resolution calling for adjournment of the legislative session — already the longest since 1911—by 4 P.M. tomorrow.

Adjournment prospects soon dimmed, however. Shortly after he adjourned the Assembly about 10:30 P.M., Speaker Anthony J. Travia, Brooklyn Democrat, told reporters:

"Nobody had better talk to me about adjournment. We've got a lot of work to do and I'm prepared to stay until November."

Mr. Travia said he wanted

Continued on Page 20, Column 1

STATE BUDGET DUE TO PASS $4-BILLION

Additional Outlays Expected to Be About $300-Million

By SYDNEY H. SCHANBERG

Special to The New York Times

ALBANY, June 30—The state's supplemental budget, which picks up the expenses not anticipated when the main budget is passed early in the legislative session, will reportedly be in the vicinity of $300-million this year.

This would be the largest in the state's history.

It would push the total state budget for fiscal 1966-67 well over $4-billion for the first time. Governor Rockefeller went to great pains in maneuvering his expense figures to avoid having to present a $4-billion budget in an election year. He came up just short of that record figure with a budget of $3.98-billion.

Before passing the Rockefeller budget in March the Legislature pared it back by about $93-million to $3.89-billion. The $300-million supplemental budget would thus put the total state budget at about $4.2-billion.

Many legislators contend that the Governor, to stay under the $4-billion figure, deliberately kept several essential items out of the main budget so that he could slip them quietly into the supplemental budget.

Little attention is paid to the supplemental budget by rank-and-file legislators. The public almost never gets a peek at it until after it is passed.

Unlike the main budget,

Continued on Page 19, Column 5

A Kennedy Choice On Governor Seen Before Convention

By WARREN WEAVER Jr.

Fresh from directing a major political victory, Senator Robert F. Kennedy is expected to endorse one of the Democratic candidates for Governor before the party's nominating convention in early September.

John J. Burns, the Democratic State Chairman, predicted yesterday that Senator Kennedy would drop a position of neutrality "after he analyzes how the candidates appear to be doing as to popularity within the Democratic party."

Mr. Burns, a trusted Kennedy political lieutenant, said also he believed the candidate would be one of the four current major competitors "unless there is some sort of an impasse or a real problem."

These competitors are Eugene H. Nickerson, the Nassau County Executive; Frank D. O'Connor, president of the New York City Council; Franklin D. Roosevelt Jr., former Representative and

Continued on Page 15, Column 1

CITY FISCAL PANEL ASKS MORE TAXES

Schwulst Group Calls New Program Only 'Stopgap' for Huge Income Need

Excerpts from the Schwulst report are on Page 21.

By ROBERT ALDEN

The Temporary Commission on City Finances declared yesterday that the compromise tax program was only "a brief stopgap" measure that would have to be supplemented "at the earliest possible time, perhaps in a special session of the Legislature after the November election."

The commission called the tax program, though inadequate, "absolutely essential." Earl B. Schwulst, chairman of the commission, said: "God knows, we need at least that. But very soon we're going to need fuller and more realistic authorizations of additional city revenues."

The commission, in a comprehensive third report touching on all city departments, said that New York would have to re-establish its tradition of educational excellence to stem the flight of the middle class from the city.

To that end it suggested "revolutionary" changes that would place the Mayor's office in more direct control in establishing educational policies and that would de-emphasize the role of the Board of Education.

The commission recommended a 5-cent increase in the transit fare, higher meter rates for parking, tolls on the East River bridges, a $25 annual auto-use tax, a tax on taxi rides, a city tax on liquor and legalized off-track betting in the city if a statewide lottery is not approved.

At a news conference at which the report was presented, Mr. Schwulst said that despite all that New York might be able

Continued on Page 21, Column 1

MEDICARE STARTS COVERAGE TODAY; 17 MILLION SIGNED

Smooth Beginning Expected —Hospitals With 92% of Beds Are Qualified

By HAROLD M. SCHMECK Jr.

Special to The New York Times

WASHINGTON, June 30 — The Medicare program begins tomorrow amid predictions of a smooth start for the most extensive expansion of Social Security since the first law was passed in 1935.

President Johnson announced that more than 92 per cent of the nation's general hospital beds were in hospitals that already complied with the law.

"Since I signed the historic Medicare Act last summer, we have made more extensive preparation to launch this program than for any other peaceful undertaking in our nation's history," the President said.

A Government health official said compliance with civil rights laws had been better than had been hoped, although there were still gaps. He also said that even the hospitals of the roughly 100 counties where crowding is already serious had generally said they would take Medicare's opening in stride.

19 Million Covered

Virtually all of the nation's 19 million citizens over 65 will be eligible to have part of their hospital costs paid. More than 17 million of them have signed up for the voluntary program, which provides for payment of part of their medical bills.

Aside from the patients, Medicare is certain to have a great impact on the nation's hospitals and doctors. Although Medicare does not create shortages of hospital beds, nurses, medical technicians and others, it will make these shortages more "visible" and may hasten remedies, experts predict.

Although it is generally believed that some persons have delayed elective surgery to take advantage of their rights under Medicare, there was little evidence that hospital admissions would take a sudden upward jump after July 1.

Pressures are considered more likely to develop gradually than suddenly. Furthermore the summer and particularly the beginning of a summer holiday weekend is a time of ordinarily low hospital occupancy.

No Early Crowding

A spot check of hospitals at various places in the country revealed no trend toward immediate crowding. Since reservations are customarily made in advance for anything but emergency care, it seemed unlikely that pressure on hospitals could develop rapidly.

In St. Petersburg, Fla., where many elderly men and women live, Mound Park Hospital reported it was not crowded now and, from the list of reservations, did not expect to be in July. Hospital occupancy in that city is greatest in the winter, a spokesman for Mound Park said.

The 649-bed hospital, second in size only to Jackson Memorial in Miami among the state's general hospitals, has been planning for Medicare for some time and is expanding its facilities substantially. While

Continued on Page 16, Column 1

Travia, in Reversal, To Ask Tightening Of Medicaid Rules

By RICHARD REEVES

Special to The New York Times

ALBANY, June 30—Democrats and Republicans in the Assembly agreed today to reduce the scope and cost of the state's controversial new medical-care law. But party leaders disagreed on how much the two-month-old law should be changed.

Under continuing pressure from upstate legislators of both parties, Speaker Anthony J. Travia reluctantly ended his opposition to amending the law, known commonly as Medicaid.

But Republican Minority Leader Perry B. Duryea, after six hours of sporadic conferences with the Democratic Speaker, held out for more modifications than Mr. Travia was willing to accept.

Mr. Travia announced early in the day that he would introduce four amendments, the most important of which would require all families with annual gross incomes of more

Continued on Page 17, Column 1

U.S. BUDGET GAP MAY BE REDUCED

Both Spending and Receipts Exceed $100-Billion as Fiscal Year Is Ended

By EDWIN L. DALE Jr.

Special to The New York Times

WASHINGTON, June 30 — The Government wound up its fiscal year today, having spent more and collected more than in any other year, including those of World War II.

With receipts running above the estimates made as recently as May, the chances are good that the budget deficit will be the lowest since the fiscal year 1960, the last year when there was a surplus. Since then, the smallest deficit was $3.4-billion in the last fiscal year, 1965.

In the fiscal year 1966, ended today, expenditures in the regular or "administrative" budget exceeded $100-billion for the first time. The exact total will not be known for about three weeks, but it will be in the vicinity of $106-billion.

Estimates Topped

Receipts now seem likely to turn out between $103-billion and $104-billion, also the first time that collections have surpassed the $100-billion level. Despite massive tax cuts, receipts have grown by some $25-billion in five years, thanks to the expanding economy.

Total expenditures and receipts in the fiscal year ended today, including the operations of the Government's trust funds for Social Security and highway building, were far higher than the figures in the administrative budget.

Payments and collections both exceeded $135-billion, with the exact totals still not known.

When the budget for the fiscal year 1966 was presented to Congress by President Johnson nearly 18 months ago, the estimate of administrative budget expenditures was $99.7-billion and that of receipts was $94.4-billion. The war in Vietnam has

Continued on Page 39, Column 3

PENTAGON URGES YOUTHS 19 TO 20 BE DRAFTED FIRST

Would Revise System, After Build-Up in Vietnam, to Spare Most Older Men

The text of report on draft will be found on Page 12.

By BENJAMIN WELLES

Special to The New York Times

WASHINGTON, June 30—The Defense Department told Congress today that it favored changing the draft system so that men 19 or 20 would be taken ahead of older men.

Thomas D. Morris, Assistant Defense Secretary for Manpower, told the House Armed Services Committee that this plan "reverses" the present Selective Service System of calling the oldest men first. In three of the four orders of call-up in use today the oldest men are called first.

Mr. Morris also recommended that men up to 35 years old who had received college deferments be subject to call-up upon completion or termination of their education.

Under the proposed plan, which would become effective when the Vietnam build-up ends, Mr. Morris said, men who reach 19, or 20, as the case may be, plus students leaving school would be placed in a "priority" 1-A draft category.

Drop to Bottom of List

Those who were not drafted by the year's end would drop automatically to the bottom of the following year's list, below the new class of 19- or 20-year-olds and the newly available former students.

Mr. Morris told newsmen later that it would be highly improbable that men passed over in their "priority" year would be called again short of a national emergency. Thus, he implied, the new system would help end the current uncertainty among 19- to 26-year-olds that has generated so much national criticism.

With a steadily growing manpower pool, Mr. Morris explained, the number of 18-year-olds who must register for the draft is expected to reach 2.1 million by 1974 and the problem for the armed services will be how to select the minority needed to supplement the volunteers, who now outnumber draftees 2 to 1.

6,000-Word Summary

Mr. Morris presented a 6,000-word summary of an exhaustive manpower study that has been more than two years in preparation by the Pentagon and other Government agencies.

A major objective of the study was to assess the possibility of meeting the military manpower requirements on an entirely voluntary basis in the coming decade.

The study, which was ordered by President Johnson, remains classified in the Pentagon's files. It was prepared jointly by the Selective Service System, the military departments, the Census Bureau, the Labor Department and the Public Health Service, and was based on the "experience and attitudes" of several hundred thousand men, Mr. Morris said.

The Pentagon official, who addressed the House Committee

Continued on Page 13, Column 1

Medicare: How the Elderly Patient Gets Benefits

By NAN ROBERTSON

Special to The New York Times

WASHINGTON, June 30—The passport to Medicare benefits is a red, white and blue card. Social Security offices around the country are being swamped with questions about how to use the card.

Handbooks explaining the program have been mailed to the 19 million Americans 65 years of age and older holding the cards. As persons covered by Social Security reach 65, they will receive the handbooks, which are available at all Social Security offices.

But Arthur E. Hess, director of the Bureau of Health Insurance of the Social Security Administration, concedes that a "communications gap" exists. Many doctors and hospital administrators, as well as patients, do not understand the program, he says.

What does a patient have to do to make sure he gets the benefits he is entitled to? Take the case of a retired engineer, a 66-year-old widower.

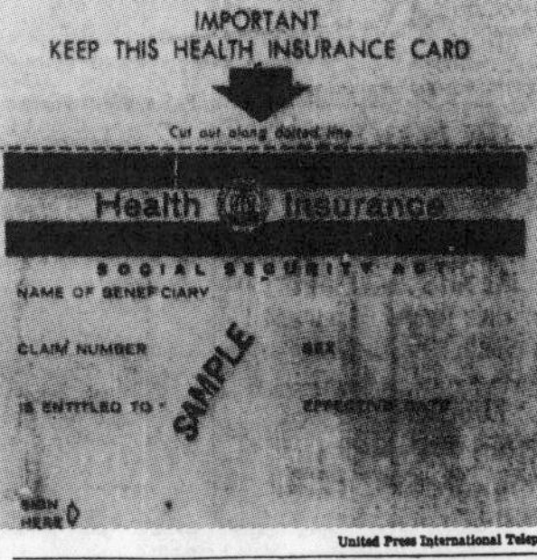

United Press International Telephoto

He had been feeling a sharp pain in his abdomen. Remembering his Medicare card, he pulled it from his wallet to see what he should do. All it said at the top was "Health Insurance." Below, it gave his name, his claim number and said he was entitled to "Hospital Insurance." This is an automatic benefit for him and virtually all others 65 and older to help pay hospital bills.

Below this were the words "Medical Insurance," which meant that he, like nine of 10 persons now eligible for Medicare, had enrolled in the voluntary second part of the program to help cover his doctor bills.

For doctors' services, he paid $3 a month, deducted from his Social Security check; for hospital care, there was no premium.

The widower telephoned his doctor. Like anybody eligible for Medicare, he could have called any physician, but not a chiropractor, naturopath, Christian Science practitioner or any unlicensed "healer."

Medicare card in hand, the stricken man went to his doctor's office. An aide recorded the claim number on his card, plus the information it contained that he was covered for both hospital and doctors' bills. Hospital insurance is called Part A in the Medicare

Continued on Page 15, Column 2

Lewis Quits S.N.C.C.; Shuns 'Black Power'

Special to The New York Times

ATLANTA, June 30—John Lewis, who was regarded as a militant figure in the civil rights movement during his three years as chairman of the Student Nonviolent Coordinating Committee, has resigned from the organization and taken issue with its new concept of "black power."

Mr. Lewis, 26 years old, was defeated by Stokely Carmichael in an election in May. Mr. Carmichael is a civil rights activist who strongly advocates third-party politics for Southern Negroes and is considered more militant than Mr. Lewis. Mr. Carmichael also is a prominent figure in the new S.N.C.C. emphasis on "black power."

Mr. Lewis has continued to

Continued on Page 15, Column 5

NEWS INDEX

"All the News That's Fit to Print"

The New York Times.

LATE CITY EDITION
U.S. Weather Bureau Report (Page 62) forecasts: Fair and pleasant today, tonight and tomorrow.
Temp. Range: 85—68; yesterday: 95—77. Temp.-Hum. Index: 74; yesterday: 79.

VOL. CXV..No. 39,619. NEW YORK, FRIDAY, JULY 15, 1966. TEN CENTS

8 Student Nurses Slain in Chicago Dormitory

Killer Ties 9th, but She Hides and Escapes

By AUSTIN C. WEHRWEIN
Special to The New York Times

CHICAGO, July 14 — Eight student nurses were killed here early this morning in one of the most savage multiple murders in the history of crime.

Another nurse, 23-year-old Corazon Amurao, escaped death by rolling under a bed in the row house that served as a dormitory for the South Chicago Community Hospital on the Far South Side.

Wriggling free of her bonds after she had fought down her terror, she groped her way to a second-floor window ledge minutes after 6 A.M., sat there and screamed:

"They are all dead! They are all dead! My friends are all dead! Oh, God, I'm the only one alive."

Describes Murderer

Miss Amurao, a Filipino here under an exchange program, was taken to the hospital, seven blocks north on 93d Street, to be given sedatives. She told the police that the murderer was a white man, about 25 years old, six feet tall, weighing 170 pounds, his dark hair cut short. She said he was wearing a black suit jacket.

The Chicago police force started on a massive manhunt. Specifically 40 men, with 100 more to back them up, were given definite assignments on the case.

All other law enforcement bodies in the area, including the Federal Bureau of Investigation, offered their full resources and laboratory facilities.

Several men were picked up as suspects within a few hours after the discovery of the murders. All were released after it had been determined that they had not been near the town-house, one of a row of garden apartment buildings.

Miss Amurao lay under the bunk bed while the killer first assured his victims that he meant them no harm, then led them one by one to their deaths in other rooms.

Preliminary examinations showed that three had their throats slashed or stabbed. One of these three also was stabbed elsewhere. In addition four were strangled. And of the four who were strangled, two also were stabbed.

"It is the crime of the cen-

Continued on Page 14, Column 1

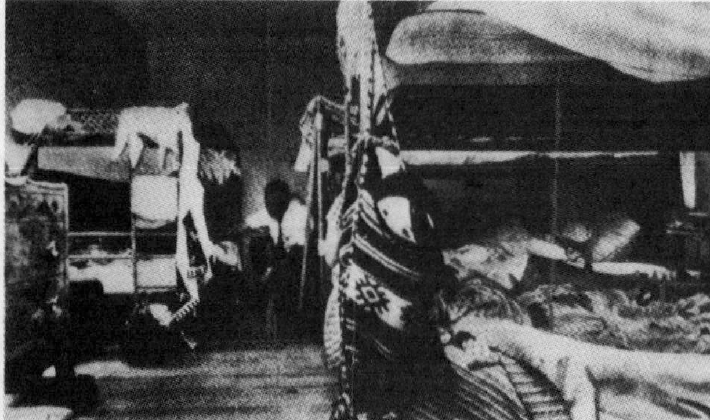

Associated Press Wirephoto
Detective inspects area under bed where lone survivor hid as slayer took bound victims from this room one at a time

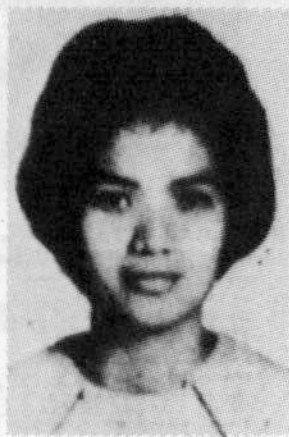

United Press International
Corazon Amurao, survivor

United Press International Telephoto
A broken screen is visible at upper left window of structure in which slayings took place

BRITAIN TIGHTENS CREDIT SQUEEZE; RAISES BANK RATE

London, Lifting Loan Cost to 7%, Warns of Further Restraints to Aid Pound

WILSON FEARS A CRISIS

Promises Tough Measures to Curb Spending—Banks' Reserve Level Increased

By ANTHONY LEWIS
Special to The New York Times

LONDON, July 14—The Government clamped down today the tightest credit restrictions in recent memory and warned that further stern measures would follow to rescue the beleaguered pound.

Britain's principal lending rate, known as the bank rate, was raised to 7 per cent from 6 per cent. The Government also removed £100-million ($280-million) of liquid assets from banks, severely restricting their lending ability.

[In Washington, the Federal Reserve Board took no action to raise the United States discount rate in the wake of Britain's increase in her bank rate. The Treasury, in a brief statement, said, "We regard this as an appropriate action for the British to take." Page 39.]

These assets, or deposits, are withdrawn for lending purposes from the banking system. The effect of this tough new squeeze, bankers said, may well be the calling in of some loans.

New Measures Urged

The Bank of England said the increase in its bank rate and special deposit call were aimed at relieving "pressure (on sterling) on the exchanges" by reinforcing the policy of credit restraint at home and by counteracting higher interest rates and tight money abroad.

Unless novel new control measures such as a wage freeze are undertaken now, a massive dose of deflation would seem the only choice available for Britain, observers said. That is, the Government would have to take money out of the economy by taxation, doubtless causing some unemployment.

The other alternative would be devaluation of the pound. Though many newspaper and other commentators have renewed talk about devaluation, Government officials insist that it is not under consideration.

Drain on Reserves Cited

Today's increase in the bank rate follows interest-rate increases in other countries recently.

Ordinarily bank-rate increases are expected to attract confidence in the pound. Today, the reaction was disappointing. The pound closed at $2.78 13 16, up 1/16 from yesterday. But no support from the Bank of England was needed.

In addition to the deposit calls substantially reducing the amount available for loans, most bankers still felt that direct measures against consumption would be needed.

Prime Minister Wilson acknowledged officially that Britain faced a renewed financial crisis. In a statement to the House of Commons he spoke of the drain on British monetary reserves that had caused growing concern here and abroad in recent weeks.

Mr. Wilson said that he

Continued on Page 39, Column 2

ARMED NEGROES FIGHT THE POLICE IN CHICAGO RIOTS

3D DAY OF STRIFE

Dozens Are Injured, Including Captain—5,000 Jam Streets

By DONALD JANSON
Special to The New York Times

CHICAGO, Friday, July 15—Roving gangs and snipers in the predominantly Negro West Side exchanged gunfire last night and early this morning with heavily reinforced police patrols.

Dozens of persons were injured, including a police captain who was shot in the back. He was reported in good condition.

More than 1,000 policemen tried to contain 5,000 Negroes in the streets, but could not do so despite the help of the Rev. Dr. Martin Luther King Jr. and other clergymen.

A total of 157 marauders were arrested by 1 A.M. on the third successive night of violence. The police called for tear gas to repel armed Negroes at Lake and Wood Streets. Bus service in that area was discontinued.

Squad cars and passing automobiles and buses were peppered with bricks, rocks and flying bottles.

Car Turned Over

A gang turned over a car at 16th Street and Lawndale Avenue.

Gangs of Negroes moved from street to street and doorway to doorway along Roosevelt Road, smashing windows in stores, looting, tossing fire bombs and retreating to side streets when the police rushed in.

Roosevelt Road was strewn with glass. Some residents were shooting from windows and roofs. Some were throwing fragments of brick and other objects at the police.

The wounded police captain was Francis Nolan, 43 years old. A rifle bullet fired from a roof entered his back near his shoulder and came out in front. Patrolman James Castellano, 41, was hit in the eye by an object and hospitalized and a Negro boy was reported shot in the leg.

Captain Nolan was treated at Mt. Sinai Hospital. So were six other policemen who were wounded by the gunfire.

As the violence mounted, the police brought machine guns and rifles into the area. At 1 A.M., 10,000 more rounds of ammunition were delivered to the embattled police. Shortly before, marauders had shattered the windows of a fire station.

Too Busy for Stores

The police were kept too busy to guard all the stores where windows were broken. In some areas looters smashed and grabbed merchandise freely.

In the gun fight at Lake and Wood, the police had to radio for 200 more rounds of ammunition.

Superintendent of Police Orlando W. Wilson had assigned 1,500 policemen to the West Side in an attempt to prevent a new outbreak of violence. Sixty Negro policemen in plain-clothes also circulated in the heart of the troubled area to seek out and arrest ringleaders.

In the early part of the evening, Dr. King met with 100 clergymen at the Shiloh Baptist Church. They decided to go into

Continued on Page 28, Column 5

House Unit Asserts Powell Is Evading It

By MARJORIE HUNTER
Special to The New York Times

WASHINGTON, July 14 — The House Rules Committee, in a rare move, issued a report today accusing Representative Adam Clayton Powell of dodging committee efforts to question him about a $250,000 anti-poverty investigation made under his jurisdiction.

The Manhattan Democrat is chairman of the House Education and Labor Committee, which has jurisdiction over antipoverty legislation.

Mr. Powell has not made public the results of the antipoverty investigation conducted last year by one of his special subcommittees. He has also not disclosed how the

Continued on Page 12, Column 1

SENATE REJECTS C.I.A. PANEL PLAN

Fulbright's Merger Proposal Beaten in Rare Session Behind Locked Doors

By E. W. KENWORTHY
Special to The New York Times

WASHINGTON, July 14 — After an extraordinary closed session, the Senate turned aside today an attempt to enlarge the committee supervising the activities of the Central Intelligence Agency. The vote was 61 to 28.

The outcome was a signal victory for Senator Richard B. Russell of Georgia, who, as chairman of both the Armed Services Committee and the present C.I.A. "watchdog" subcommittee, strenuously opposed any change.

By the same token, the vote was a setback for Senator J. W. Fulbright of Arkansas, who, as chairman of the Foreign Relations Committee, had argued that his committee should be represented on legislative oversight of the C.I.A. His argument was that the supersecret spy agency obviously influenced foreign policy decisions.

Doors Locked and Guarded

The vote came after an hour of intense and sometimes sharp exchanges between Mr. Russell and Mr. Fulbright, followed by three and a half hours of debate behind locked and guarded doors.

At one point Mr. Russell said the "self-serving, self-seeking" resolution offered by Mr. Fulbright would "destroy the normal procedures of the Senate."

Mr. Fulbright replied hastily that there was something "peculiar" also about the charter of the present watchdog committee since it assumed jurisdiction simply because the Armed Services Committee handled the original C.I.A. legislation and the Senate had never formally created it.

Following the initial statements of Mr. Fulbright and Mr. Russell, Senator Mike Mansfield of Montana, the majority leader, moved to go into closed session on the ground that "things might be said that aren't particularly true and could be

Continued on Page 10, Column 1

House Votes Aid Measure, Rejecting Curb by 2 Votes

By FELIX BELAIR Jr.
Special to The New York Times

WASHINGTON, July 14—By a margin of only two votes, the House of Representatives averted today a crippling blow to the $4.1-billion foreign aid authorization bill. The vote was 193 to 191 on a Republican-sponsored motion to reduce the two-year authorization to a single year and to trim $250-million from the $1-billion ceiling on long-term loans for economic development.

The deftly contrived counterattack came just before the 237-to-146 vote for final passage and after a smoothly functioning Democratic majority had cut down a series of efforts by individual Republican members to scrap the multi-year features of the bill and to cut major economic aid categories.

'Blank Check' Opposed

The Administration had asked for a five-year authorization of "such amounts as may be necessary" for both economic and military assistance programs.

It proposed an actual appropriation for the current fiscal year of $3.4-billion, including $2.4-billion for economic aid and $917-million for military assistance.

The Foreign Affairs Committee balked at the "blank check" approach and wrote into the bill specific ceilings for all aid categories. All categories

Continued on Page 7, Column 1

KOSYGIN REBUFFS PEACE OVERTURES

Russian, at Fete for India, Assails U.S. 'Barbarism'—Stresses Aid to Hanoi

By RAYMOND H. ANDERSON
Special to The New York Times

MOSCOW, July 14 — Premier Aleksei N. Kosygin charged tonight that the United States was guilty of "vandalism and barbarism on an international scale" in Vietnam.

The Soviet leader, abandoning his usual dry tone to speak with emotional force, reiterated the readiness of the Soviet Union and its allies in the Warsaw Pact to allow "volunteers" to fight in Vietnam if the Communist regime in Hanoi called for their help.

He also emphasized moves to increase the supply of military equipment to North Vietnam.

Mr. Kosygin, speaking in the Kremlin at a Soviet-Indian friendship meeting, appeared to give a conclusive rebuff to a Vietnam peace plan brought to Moscow by the Indian Prime Minister, Mrs. Indira Gandhi.

Soviet Stand Adamant

Mrs. Gandhi arrived Tuesday to urge the Soviet leadership to relent in its opposition to taking steps to reconvene the 1954 Geneva conference, which ended the French Indochina war and led to the division of Vietnam.

Moscow, in the words of a senior Western diplomat here, is "refusing to budge on reconvening the Geneva conference unless it gets a green light from Hanoi."

The Soviet Union, as a cochairman with Britain of the Geneva conference, has continuing responsibilities for developments falling within the

Continued on Page 2, Column 2

AIR TALKS REACH 'SERIOUS IMPASSE'

Mediator Asks Both Sides to Reassess Their Positions as Parleys Bog Down

By DAVID R. JONES
Special to The New York Times

WASHINGTON, July 14 — The negotiations to end the week-long airline strike have reached "a serious impasse on a number of issues," a Federal mediator said today.

James J. Reynolds, Assistant Secretary of Labor, gave that assessment at the end of a full day of bargaining between the striking International Association of Machinists and five major airlines.

Mr. Reynolds said that "some progress" had been made since yesterday in the negotiations. But he emphasized that "I don't want to give any impression that we're out of the woods by a long shot."

Reassessment Sought

The mediator's comments coincided with statements by the top negotiators for the union and management, who said that they were as far apart on basic issues today as when the strike began.

Mr. Reynolds recessed the talks until tomorrow, and asked the parties to reassess their positions overnight.

The Post Office Department, meantime, said that the strike had delayed mail deliveries by as much as 24 hours and that the situation threatened to get worse.

The walkout by 35,400 mechanics and ground service workers against Eastern, National, Northwest, Trans World and United airlines continued to snarl the nation's transportation.

The first progress in the ne-

Continued on Page 12, Column 4

City Due for Relief Today After Nine Days Over 90°

By MURRAY SCHUMACH

The most intense July heat wave in the city's history sent the temperature to 95 degrees yesterday, but the Weather Bureau promised substantial relief today with the arrival of cool air from Canada. The high for today should be in the middle or low eighties, the bureau said.

The torrid temperatures have produced abnormal death rates, power failures and suffering that was particularly acute in the slums.

In some sections, for instance, the poor were spending food money to buy electric fans that they kept turned on fire escapes where they slept. Air-conditioning units are not allowed in low-cost housing projects because the wiring is inadequate.

9th Straight Day

Yesterday was the ninth consecutive day of above-90-degree readings, thus equaling the city's record for this century, established in July, 1944. The record heat wave here is 10 successive 90-degree days, but that was set in August of 1896.

The mercury soared to 101 on Wednesday, smashing the previous high for the date by 5 degrees. And the day before that, a reading of 99 set a high for July 12 by 3 degrees.

A thermometer carried in subways at Grand Central and Times Square stations during

Continued on Page 17, Column 5

MAYOR SEEKS END OF HOSPITAL TIE-UP

He Asks That Union Accept Arbitration—Stoppages Affect 4 Institutions

By RALPH BLUMENTHAL

Mayor Lindsay appealed last night to members of the Drug and Hospital Employes Union for an immediate end to their work stoppages, which spread yesterday to four voluntary hospitals.

There was no indication that the stoppages would cease. In fact, more were expected today to back up demands for higher wages.

According to a key hospital official, Mayor Lindsay's appeal came after Senator Robert F. Kennedy told him about 6 P.M. that if City Hall did not immediately call for action, Mr. Kennedy would.

The official reported that Senator Kennedy had sent aides to talk to hospital representatives after they had appealed in vain to several city, state and national figures for help in settling the dispute.

Kennedy Reluctant

Mr. Kennedy was ready to issue a statement Wednesday night but was reluctant to intrude in city affairs, the official said, without giving the Mayor a chance to act first.

The Mayor's appeal, in a telegram to Leon Davis, president of Local 1199 of the union, was sent out about 6:30 P.M., during the 14-hour stoppage at Montefiore in the Bronx. Earlier in the day there had been stoppages at Long Island Jewish, Queens General and Mount Sinai Hospitals.

Montefiore, which had discharged or transferred 170 of its 620 patients on Wednesday to minimize the effects of the expected stoppage, evacuated

Continued on Page 17, Column 3

Popovic Replaces Ousted Aide to Tito

By DAVID BINDER
Special to The New York Times

BELGRADE, Yugoslavia, July 14—Koca Popovic, a rich man's son who became a Communist, was unanimously acclaimed as Vice President of Yugoslavia today by the 670 members of the Federal Assembly.

Mr. Popovic replaces Aleksandar Rankovic, the second-ranking man in the Communist party until his ouster by President Tito July 1 on charges of having participated in a "factional struggle for power."

Mr. Rankovic, vacationing at Dubrovnik, sent in his resignation from his Government post pleading that "for well-known reasons" he was unable to re-

Continued on Page 8, Column 1

Rusk Warns Hanoi Not to Try Captives

By MAX FRANKEL
Special to The New York Times

WASHINGTON, July 14—Secretary of State Dean Rusk warned North Vietnam today that the trial and punishment of captured American pilots as "war criminals" would be regarded as "a very, very grave development indeed."

Publicly hinting at vigorous private diplomacy by American officials to prevent such trials, Mr. Rusk told a Senate judiciary subcommittee that he still hoped that "sober judgment" would prevail in the Government in Hanoi. He said he did not yet know whether the trials would be held or, if held, whether special punishment would result.

Continued on Page 3, Column 1

Israeli Jets Blast Syrian River Work

Special to The New York Times

TEL AVIV, July 14—Israeli jet planes attacked an earth-moving equipment eight miles inside Syria today in what the Israelis said was a reprisal for Arab incursions.

The Israelis also said they had shot down a Syrian MIG-21 east of the Sea of Galilee.

Maj. Gen. Itzhak Rabin, the Israeli Chief of Staff, derided a Syrian report that Israel had lost two planes in the operations. He said all Israeli planes had returned to their bases.

The Israelis said they had destroyed five to eight tractors and excavators engaged in diverting the Baniyas River, a

Continued on Page 4, Column 3

City and Port Authority Mired In Deadlock on Trade Center

By TERENCE SMITH

A bitter disagreement between the Lindsay administration and the Port of New York Authority broke into the open yesterday as their negotiations over the World Trade Center reached a serious deadlock.

Top administration officials charged that the authority had not "given one inch on any single item under discussion" during the five months of negotiations.

In reply, the Port Authority disclosed a set of letters that charged Mayor Lindsay had reneged on his word to permit the agency to begin a preliminary step in the construction of the $525-million project. The authority asserted in the letters that Mr. Lindsay had "plainly stated" in private conversations that he would grant such permission, and that he had failed to do so.

The agency further charged that the Mayor had said repeatedly he was personally in favor of granting the permission, but that he could not do so because it would "pull the rug out from under" the members of the city's negotiating committee.

The members of the committee, all appointed by the Mayor, had voted not to grant the authority permission to close a section of West Street to per-

Continued on Page 16, Column 5

NEWS INDEX

William Manchester's authorized version of John Kennedy's assassination was hotly contested by Jackie and Bob Kennedy.

Rudy Gernreich's dresses were the "new look" for the year.

Angela Lansbury starred on Broadway in *Mame* with Bea Arthur (right).

TV cameras awaited celebrities who attended the opening of the Metropolitan Opera Company at Lincoln Center in Manhattan.

"All the News That's Fit to Print"

The New York Times.

LATE CITY EDITION
U. S. Weather Bureau Report (Page 66) forecasts: Cloudy today, showers likely late today, tonight. Fair tomorrow.
Temp. Range: 90—70; yesterday: 93—65. Temp.-Hum. Index: near 70; yesterday: 78.

VOL. CXV..No. 39,637. NEW YORK, TUESDAY, AUGUST 2, 1966. TEN CENTS

Sniper in Texas U. Tower Kills 12, Hits 33; Wife, Mother Also Slain; Police Kill Him

Dust kicked up by policemen's bullets as they returned the sniper's fire rises before clock at University of Texas.

By United Press International

AUSTIN, Tex., Aug. 1—An architectural honor student carried an arsenal of weapons to the top of the 27-story tower on the University of Texas campus today and shot 12 persons to death and wounded at least 33 others before the police killed him.

Later, the student's wife and mother were found dead in their homes in Austin. The police said he had killed them during the night.

The sniper was identified as Charles J. Whitman, 25 years old, a former altar boy and Eagle Scout — who was an architectural engineering student from Lake Worth, Fla. He crouched on an observation ledge far above the campus and sprayed the area with bullets for 80 minutes.

Students, professors and visitors ran for cover. A student on a bicycle was shot and toppled off. Passers-by ran to help him, and began to fall. A small boy was shot. Three bodies lay on the campus for nearly an hour in the 98-degree heat. Rescuers could not reach them until an armored car was brought up.

An off-duty policeman, Romero Martinez, who had responded to a call on his radio, inched his way around a wall at the top of the tower and fired six bullets into the sniper with his service revolver after the sniper shot at him.

Fifteen persons, including Whitman, his wife and mother, died in all. Eleven victims were killed at the campus or died soon after. The 12th, Edna Townsley, about 51, of Austin, died later at a hospital.

A pregnant woman, Mrs. Claire Wilson, was shot in the abdomen. When she was admitted to the hospital she gave birth to a stillborn baby.

Police Chief R. A. Miles said a long, rambling, letter found

Continued on Page 14, Column 1

United Press International Telephoto

A girl takes cover from the shooting behind a flagpole base while a man wounded by the sniper lies unaided at left

FORD FUND URGES F.C.C. TO CONSIDER NEW TV SATELLITE

Bundy Suggests Commercial Relay Income Be Used to Aid Educational Video

PROPOSAL CHALLENGED

Comsat and A.T.&T. Say Agency Lacks Authority to Approve System

The text of Bundy's letter will be found on Page 18.

By JACK GOULD

A revolutionary nationwide satellite television system that would use profits from the relay of commercial TV shows to finance noncommercial video was proposed yesterday by the Ford Foundation.

The country's largest philanthropic organization, through its new president, McGeorge Bundy, asked the Federal Communications Commission to consider creation of a nonprofit corporation to distribute TV programs across the country by satellite.

The step brought the foundation into immediate conflict with the Communications Satellite Corporation (Comsat) and the American Telephone and Telegraph Company. Both declared the commercial carriers should operate domestic satellites.

Social Usefulness Stressed

The Ford Foundation plan envisaged using the income derived from the national distribution of such shows as "Batman" and "Bonanza" to support a coast-to-coast live network of information and culture for home viewers, at least four channels of instructional TV for colleges and schools and six commercial channels.

Four satellites—one in each time zone—could each carry the 11 channels.

Mr. Bundy, president of the foundation since March 1, said the long-range social usefulness of the home screen should take priority over the possible loss of a "microscopic portion" of the total profitability of commercial communication carriers.

Mr. Bundy urged the F.C.C. to delay any thought of making an exclusive award of TV satellites to commercial carriers until the regulatory agency could explore other systems.

Originated With Friendly

The basic idea of tapping program relay income to expand national educational TV originated chiefly with Fred W. Friendly, former president of the news division of the Columbia Broadcasting System. Mr. Friendly is now television adviser to Mr. Bundy.

The foundation contended that the F.C.C. already has the power to authorize such a satellite system and that the act creating Comsat anticipated additional systems to meet unique national needs.

Comsat, in a brief that did not refer to the Ford plan, told the F.C.C. that it was sole chosen instrument of Congress to operate satellite systems and that the commission lacked authority to authorize a rival.

A.T.&T. submitted a brief arguing that it would be against

Continued on Page 18, Column 1

ARMY AIDE TAKES POWER IN NIGERIA

Chief of Staff Announces He Heads Regime—Fate of Ironsi Still Uncertain

Special to The New York Times

LAGOS, Nigeria, Aug. 1—The Chief of Staff of Nigeria's Army announced today that he had taken over the Government after an army mutiny and the kidnapping of the chief of state.

The new leader is Lieut. Col. Yakubu Gowon, 32 years old. He is a Hausa tribesman from Nigeria's Moslem North, as are the soldiers who started the mutiny. He was third in command of the junta that took over power after the coup d'état Jan. 15.

Colonel Gowon told Nigeria's 55 million people in a broadcast that the head of state, Maj. Gen. Johnson T. U. Aguiyi-Ironsi, had been kidnapped by mutineers during a visit to the town of Ibadan. He said his whereabouts and fate were not known.

The broadcast signaled success for the mutineers' aim—the end of the policy pursued by General Ironsi to convert Nigeria into a unified country under a strong central government.

Policy Aroused Suspicions

His policy aroused the suspicions of the Hausas in the North and of the Yoruba tribes from the West, who feared domination by the more advanced Ibo people.

At least 600 people were reported killed in fighting in the North earlier after General Ironsi, an Ibo, announced the abolition of the federal system, in which the country was divided into regions, each with a powerful government.

In last week's mutiny the Governor of the Western province, Lieut. Col. Adekunle Fajuyi, also was kidnapped. His whereabouts, too, is unknown, according to the broadcast.

It made no mention of the second in command to General Ironsi in the deposed junta, Brig. Babafemi A. O. Ogundipe, chief of staff of the army supreme headquarters, but he is believed to be alive.

Colonel Gowon said he was assuming control of the military Government with the support of a majority of the Supreme Military Council.

"All is now quiet," he said.

Continued on Page 6, Column 1

Argentina Facing Teacher Migration Following Attacks

By H. J. MAIDENBERG
Special to The New York Times

BUENOS AIRES, Aug. 1—A mass departure of teachers from the University of Buenos Aires was being organized today. Many said they planned to leave Argentina.

The move followed the beating of scores of professors and students by the police Friday night after the military regime decreed the seizure of Argentina's eight nationally chartered universities.

At the Faculty of Exact Sciences of the huge university here, more than two-thirds of the teaching staff of 350 told Assistant Dean Manuel Sadosky that they had resigned.

[The State Department summoned the chief Argentine representative in Washington and expressed concern over the beating of an American professor, Warren Arthur Ambrose, by the police at the University of Buenos Aires. Page 10.]

Most of the teachers who said they had resigned also said they planned to leave Argentina. Leading teachers at other faculties indicated that they had similar intentions.

"If we cannot keep them

Continued on Page 10, Column 3

G.O.P. UNIT SCORES HOUSING BIAS BAN

House Policy Group Asserts Proposal in Rights Bill Is Unrealistic and Divisive

By JOHN HERBERS
Special to The New York Times

WASHINGTON, Aug. 1—The House Republican Policy Committee announced today that it was opposed to the open housing section of the Johnson Administration's civil rights bill. The committee said the provision was politically motivated, unrealistic and divisive.

A committee statement asserted that since its inception Title IV of the bill "has created confusion and bitterness."

"It has divided the country and fostered discord and animosity when calmness and a unified approach to the civil rights problems are desperately needed," the committee added.

The action was another blow to the embattled housing section of the civil rights bill, now under debate on the House floor. The committee is composed of 27 Republican leaders and key members, and its pronouncements are usually interpreted as the views of the minority party in the House.

Position Not Binding

At the same time, the committee's position is not binding on the 139 Republicans in the House, and today's announcement did not completely rule out the possibility of Republicans' supporting some kind of open occupancy legislation.

Rather, the committee's action reflected the division and confusion that exists among Southerners, Northern liberals and the two parties over the provision that is intended to ban racial discrimination in the sale or rental of housing.

The committee rejected not only the Johnson Administration's draft of Title IV but also a Republican compromise worked out in the Judiciary Committee to exempt private homeowners and owner-occupied apartments of up to four units.

Representative Charles McC. Mathias Jr., Maryland Republican who is the author of that amendment, is not a member of the policy committee. Neither is Representative William M. McCulloch of Ohio, ranking Republican on the Judiciary Com-

Continued on Page 13, Column 2

'Bewildered' Speck Pleads Not Guilty In 8 Nurses' Deaths

By AUSTIN C. WEHRWEIN
Special to The New York Times

CHICAGO, Aug. 1 — Under heavy guard, Richard Speck pleaded not guilty today to eight indictments charging him with the murder of eight student nurses on July 14.

Speck, his pockmarked face chalky, his pale blue eyes downcast, appeared in public for the first time since his capture 15 days ago. At the hearing in the Criminal Courts Building, he did not himself speak the words "not guilty." That was done by his lawyer, Gerald Getty, public defender for Cook County.

The not guilty plea, Mr. Getty explained outside court, is routine in cases involving indigent defendants. Mr. Getty said this after he had been appointed by Judge Alexander J. Napoli to represent Speck from now on at his trial.

He also told reporters that Speck, "to me, as a layman, seemed to be bewildered."

Felony Judge Daniel J. Ryan had previously appointed Mr.

Continued on Page 66, Column 6

REGULARS SWEEP DEMOCRATIC VOTE ON JUDGES' SLATE

Reform Faction Is Defeated for Manhattan and Bronx Supreme Court Posts

By PETER KIHSS

Senator Robert F. Kennedy and Reform Democrats appeared squeezed out last night when Manhattan and Bronx regulars got together behind four candidates for Supreme Court justice at the First District judicial nominating convention.

The regulars, riding hard over Reform opponents, nominated Francis J. Bloustein of the Bronx, who is vice chairman of the City Planning Commission, and Civil Court Judges Alfred M. Ascione and Samuel A. Spiegel, both of Manhattan.

Then a fight broke out shortly before 11 P.M. over the regulars' fourth candidate — Administrative Judge John M. Murtagh of Criminal Court.

One after another opposing candidates were put up—Civil Court Judge Jawn A. Sandifer and Criminal Court Judge Kenneth M. Phipps, both Negroes; Criminal Court Judge Manuel A. Gomez, of Puerto Rican extraction, and Civil Court Judge Arnold L. Fein, backed by the Reform group.

Murtagh Is Chosen

But Judge Murtagh won the nomination, with 124 votes. Judge Fein polled 72; Judge Sandifer, 16; Judge Gomez, 5, and Judge Phipps, 4. Civil Court Judge Sidney Asch of the Bronx had also been nominated in the flurry, but he failed to receive a vote.

Senator Kennedy had sought to blend both regular and Reform factions in the two boroughs with a proposal to nominate Robert L. Carter, general counsel for the National Association for the Advancement of Colored People. But Mr. Carter, a Negro, whose name the Senator advanced privately last week and again yesterday, was rebuffed even by the Harlem regulars.

The Reform delegates were still in caucus at 7:30 P.M. at the Concourse Plaza Hotel—a half-hour before the scheduled start of the convention at the Park Terrace Caterers, 880 River Avenue, at 161st Street—when they learned that the regulars under J. Raymond Jones, New York County leader, and Charles A. Buckley, Bronx County leader, were moving to freeze them out.

2 Reform Candidates

The Reform group, with 77 votes out of the convention's 221, had been trying to decide between Civil Court Judge Edward J. Greenfield of Manhattan and Murray Gordon, a Bronx lawyer prominent in Jewish affairs, for a nomination. This would have been in a package involving Mr. Carter, Mr. Bloustein and Judge Ascione.

But after a telephone call, Richard S. Lane, Reform district leader on the East Side, stormed back, exclaiming: "No go!"

Ot the convention's 221 votes, Mr. Buckley's Bronx organization controlled 76. The Reform group counted 77—a total of 33

Continued on Page 19, Column 2

SENATE UNIT ACTS TO LET PRESIDENT END AIR WALKOUT

FIGHT IN PROSPECT

Rival Measure Giving Power to Congress Is Gaining Support

By DAVID R. JONES
Special to The New York Times

WASHINGTON, Aug. 1—A Senate committee approved today legislation that would authorize President Johnson to order an end to the airline strike for any period up to 180 days.

The Senate Labor and Public Welfare Committee reported out the bill by a vote of 10 to 6. Mike Mansfield of Montana, the Senate Democratic leader, said that the bill, which is not favored by the Johnson Administration, would be taken up by the Senate tomorrow.

The bill, proposed by Senator Joseph S. Clark, Democrat of Pennsylvania, would authorize the President to sign an executive order ending the strike for 180 days, or any shorter period or periods totaling 180 days. This means he could issue orders ranging from one stopping the strike for 180 days to 180 orders stopping it for one day each.

While the walkout was in abeyance, efforts would be made to mediate the strike.

The committee bill appeared headed for trouble on the Senate floor, however. Forces there were already coalescing behind a bill that would have Congress, rather than the President, order an end to the strike.

Course Johnson Favors

This is the course that President Johnson would prefer if legislation was going to be enacted in an election year.

The bill behind which these forces were uniting will be introduced tomorrow by Senator Wayne Morse, Democrat of Oregon. Under it, Congress would order an end to the strike for 180 days while further efforts were made to settle the dispute.

Senator Mansfield disclosed tonight that he met today with Everett McKinley Dirksen of Illinois, the Senate Republican leader; Carl Albert of Oklahoma, the House Democratic leader, and Representative Gerald R. Ford of Michigan, the House Republican leader. They all agreed that a bill of the type Senator Morse proposes was preferable, he said.

[Prices of airline stocks declined sharply in trading on the New York Stock Exchange, where a general price retreat carried leading market indicators to new lows for the year. Airline stocks declined by $2 to $4 a share, losing gains they made on Friday when a settlement of the strike seemed imminent. Page 39.]

Action Weighed in House

Harley O. Staggers, chairman of the House Interstate and Foreign Commerce Committee, said that the House leadership had asked him to call a meeting promptly after the Senate sent over legislation to end the strike. The West Virginia Democrat said that a session could be held tomorrow.

The Senate committee's swift action on legislation to end the 25-day-old strike by 35,400 members of the International Association of Machinists came a day after the union membership overwhelmingly rejected a settlement that was endorsed by its leaders and President Johnson.

The strike by mechanics and ground service workers against five major airlines—Eastern, National, Northwest, Trans World and United—has disrupted 60 per cent of the na-

Continued on Page 30, Column 2

City to Add Nurses To Medical Boards

By RICHARD REEVES

Dr. Howard J. Brown, the City Health Services Administrator, announced yesterday that registered nurses would be added to the boards that supervise the medical affairs of municipal hospitals.

"The appointment of nurses to our medical boards signifies a revolutionary reorganization of our hospitals that is the only answer to our critical nursing shortage," Dr. Brown said.

"New York nurses are going to be recognized professionals; they will no longer be a doctor's handmaiden, but will be his professional partner."

Dr. Brown, a 42-year old physician, said that the first appointment of a nurse to a medical board would be made at Bellevue Hospital and that

Continued on Page 17, Column 1

FREEMAN TO HELP FOOD PRICE STUDY

Agriculture Chief Due Here This Week to Seek Cause of Increase in Costs

By ROBERT E. DALLOS

Secretary of Agriculture Orville L. Freeman will come to New York this week to help look into the cause of a rise in food prices here.

Mr. Freeman was invited by City Council President Frank D. O'Connor, who said yesterday that he would present a resolution to the City Council today calling for a "full investigation" into the rise in the cost of eggs, butter, milk and other staple foods.

In Washington, Representative Graham Purcell, a Texas Democrat who is chairman of the wheat subcommittee of the Agriculture Committee in the House, announced that he would begin hearings on Monday into the recent increases in bread prices across the country.

Situation Being Surveyed

An aide of Mr. Freeman said that the Secretary, who will be accompanied by a number of other Agriculture Department officials, would come to New York probably Wednesday or Thursday. He said he expected to testify before the City Council hearings on the O'Connor resolution.

"The Secretary has been watching the New York situation for the last two days," the aide said. "His attention has been drawn to the problems by

Continued on Page 37, Column 1

Army Chief Ousted In Red China Purge

Special to The New York Times

HONG KONG, Aug. 1—Lo Jui-ching, Chief of the Army's General Staff, has been replaced in another major development of the purge sweeping Communist China.

His downfall was disclosed tonight when the Peking radio announced that an Army Day reception in the capital had been addressed by Yang Cheng-wu, who was described as Acting Chief of the General Staff. Mr. Yang, a Korean War veteran, is an alternate member of the Communist party's Central Committee and a former Peking garrison commander.

Mr. Lo, a Deputy Premier, has not been seen in public or mentioned in Communist China's press since last November. Tonight's broadcast appears to confirm speculation that he was a victim of the purge.

Peking indicated, meanwhile,

Continued on Page 2, Column 3

G.I.'s Find No Foe After Raid by B-52's

Special to The New York Times

SAIGON, South Vietnam, Tuesday, Aug. 2—United States infantrymen swept through a jungle area that was torn up and charred in an attack by B-52 bombers yesterday, but they found no enemy bodies.

They said, however, that they found a cache of 90,000 rounds of small-arms ammunition, an assortment of mines and booby traps and two submachine guns.

Today a United States military spokesman reported that two Air Force F-104 Starfighters were shot down yesterday over North Vietnam and that an RF-100 Voodoo reconnaissance plane had been missing over North Vietnam since Sunday. All three pilots are listed as missing.

In the B-52 raid yesterday the bombers flew in from Andersen Air Force Base an Guam at 7 A.M. to pound the jungle area

Continued on Page 3, Column 1

Associated Press Wirephoto

AFTER ARRAIGNMENT IN CHICAGO: Richard Speck, who is accused of killing eight student nurses, back in hospital at Cook County's jail after pleading not guilty.

NEWS INDEX

1967

Astronauts Ed White, Gus Grissom and Roger Chaffee (left to right) were killed in a preflight test for their Apollo flight when their command module went ablaze.

Bart Starr of the Green Bay Packers completed seven out of eight passes against the Kansas City Chiefs, the losing team, in the first Superbowl.

The "flower children" abandoned all societal dictates, recruiting thousands of angry young people who found solace in their "dropped-out, tuned-in" community.

Muhammad Ali refused to enter the army on the grounds that it violated his Muslim faith. The champion is seen just after his indictment.

"All the News That's Fit to Print"

The New York Times.

LATE CITY EDITION

U. S. Weather Bureau Report (Page 54) forecast: Partly cloudy and cold today; fair, cold tonight. Fair, warmer tomorrow. Temp. Range: 39—32; yesterday: 44—37.

VOL. CXVI . No. 39,816. NEW YORK, SATURDAY, JANUARY 28, 1967. 10 CENTS

3 APOLLO ASTRONAUTS DIE IN FIRE; GRISSOM, WHITE, CHAFFEE CAUGHT IN CAPSULE DURING A TEST ON PAD

United Press International

BEFORE AN EARLIER TEST: Lieut. Col. Virgil I. Grissom, left, Air Force Lieut. Col. Edward H. White 2d, center, and Navy Lieut. Comdr. Roger B. Chaffee in front of the launching pad. Photograph was released Tuesday.

NASA, via Associated Press Wirephoto

HOURS BEFORE THE TRAGEDY: Colonel Grissom walking to the Apollo spacecraft ahead of Commander Chaffee, yesterday, some 5½ hours before the fire broke out. The capsule was atop a Saturn 1-B rocket, 218 feet above pad.

TRAGEDY AT CAPE

Rescuers Are Blocked by Dense Smoke—Cause Is Studied

Excerpts from news parley on accident, Page 10.

By The Associated Press

CAPE KENNEDY, Fla., Jan. 27—The three-man crew of astronauts for the Apollo 1 mission were killed tonight in a flash fire aboard the huge spacecraft designed to take man to the moon.

Those killed in the blaze on a launching pad were:

VIRGIL I. GRISSOM, 40 years old, Air Force lieutenant colonel, one of the seven original Mercury astronauts.

EDWARD H. WHITE 2d, 36, a lieutenant colonel in the Air Force, the first American to "walk" in space.

ROGER B. CHAFFEE, 31, a Navy lieutenant commander, who had been awaiting his first space flight.

The astronauts were the first American spacemen to be killed on the job and, ironically, died while on the ground. The bodies were removed hours later and a space agency spokesman said death was "instantaneous."

Three other astronauts died in airplane crashes, in the line of duty, but today's tragedy involved the first "on premises" deaths in the American space program—the first time anyone was killed while in space hardware.

Simulation Under Way

The fire broke out at 6:31 P.M. while the three men were taking part in a full-scale simulation of the scheduled Feb. 21 launching that was to take them into the heavens for 14 days of orbiting the earth.

They were trapped behind closed hatches, according to the National Aeronautics and Space Administration.

[Officials said an electrical spark must have ignited the pure oxygen inside the cabin, United Press International reported.]

Paul Haney, spokesman for America's astronauts, said he understood there had been a fire in the cockpit. He said monitors had received no word from the astronauts during the fire.

Mr. Haney said 26 members of the launching pad crew were treated for smoke inhalation. He said 24 were released and two were hospitalized in good condition.

Space agency officials were alerted by someone on the ground that the fire had broken out, Mr. Haney reported. He said emergency crews tried to reach the astronauts but were blocked by the dense smoke that rolled out of the cockpit.

Officials at Cape Kennedy said that the three astronauts were seated abreast in the rocket in the exercise, just as they would be in actual

Continued on Page 10, Column 1

Fire on Spacecraft Captured on Film

By MARTIN WALDRON

Special to The New York Times

HOUSTON, Jan. 27—The flash fire that killed three astronauts in a spacecraft at Cape Kennedy tonight was filmed, an official of the National Aeronautics and Space Administration said today.

However, the film and recordings made of the astronauts' voices, which were being monitored at Cape Kennedy and at Houston during the test, were sealed immediately after the accident.

Paul P. Haney, director of public affairs for the Manned Spacecraft Center here, said the film and the recordings would be turned over to a board of inquiry that has been given the task of finding out exactly what happened.

The board of inquiry, which will include top officials of the space program, will be appointed tomorrow, Mr. Haney said.

Space officials from Houston

Continued on Page 10, Column 5

500,000 IN THE CITY GO WITHOUT HEAT IN HOUSING STRIKE

Elderly Are the Hardest Hit in Public Developments Affected by Dispute

6,000 EMPLOYES ARE OUT

'Real Progress' Is Reported by Union as Negotiations With Officials Resume

By DAMON STETSON

Nearly all of the 500,000 residents in public housing developments here were left without heat or hot water yesterday by a strike of 6,000 employes of the City Housing Authority.

Elderly persons, mothers and small children huddled around gas stoves in their kitchens in an effort to keep warm. School children and workers returning home through the drenching rain and wind found their apartments cold and cheerless.

A housewife at Riis Houses on East 10th Street summed up her feelings with the comment, "Got no heat, no hot water—they don't get my rent."

The temperature during the day remained close to 40 degrees but dropped to the mid-30's last night.

Governor Rockefeller, taking note of the plight of the thousands of dwellers in public housing in the city, ordered all state armories in the city opened last night to accommodate residents without heat.

'Cold and Damp'

"We've got no hot water or nothing," said Mrs. Ruth Bradley, an elderly tenant in Red Hook Houses in Brooklyn. "It's cold and damp in here anyway, but now it's really cold, and it hurts my arthritis."

The strike by members of Local 237 of the International Brotherhood of Teamsters began officially at 11 P.M. Thursday, but most tenants didn't feel its impact until they got up yesterday morning and found they had no hot water and that their apartments were becoming increasingly chilly.

A spokesman for the authority said that the fuel tanks had been filled to capacity and that the strikers had been requested to set boilers on automatic controls. But Barry Feinstein, vice president of Local 237, said that the union had instructed its members to avoid a possibly dangerous situation that might result from untended boilers and to shut them down.

The authority said that the automatic controls were equipped with safety devices and could have operated for several days without attention. But an official conceded that in 90 per cent of the authority's 147 developments, the boilers had been shut down and that tenants were without heat or hot water.

Negotiations aimed at ending the strike were resumed yesterday afternoon by Mr. Feinstein and his committee and by Walter E. Washington, the chairman, and other officials of the authority. The talks were continuing early this morning.

A union spokesman said that

Continued on Page 24, Column 4

Chicago Is Crippled By a 23-Inch Snow; Police Kill Looter

By DONALD JANSON

Special to The New York Times

CHICAGO, Jan. 27—A city accustomed to snowstorms succumbed to one today.

Chicago is not easy to fell. The nation's third largest city takes in stride weather that makes winter hurt.

But this time wind and snow combined with paralyzing fury in a two-day onslaught that brought Chicago to its knees. It was the worst storm in history here, dumping more than 23 inches of snow on the city and 26 inches on its southern suburbs.

[The Chicago police shot and killed a 10-year-old girl who they said was helping loot a store in the snow-filled streets of the West Side Friday, according to The Associated Press. The storm thundered toward the East during the day and snow warnings were posted as far east as Maine, Vermont and New York.]

Chicagoans trooped to work yesterday, ignoring the heavy

Continued on Page 16, Column 1

LINDSAY ORDERS O'DWYER OUSTED

But Procaccino Says Board Counsel Will Stay On in Transit Subsidy Suit

By SETH S. KING

Mayor Lindsay dismissed Paul O'Dwyer yesterday as a special corporation counsel.

He acted after Mr. O'Dwyer had summoned the Mayor and the Transit Authority to court to explain why they refused to use $84.3-million to subsidize the transit system.

Controller Mario A. Procaccino immediately declared that Mr. O'Dwyer would go right on representing the Board of Estimate in the case.

The board is trying to force the Republican Mayor to use the $84.3-million for a transit subsidy as the Democratic-controlled City Council had directed.

Mr. Procaccino said the dismissal of Mr. O'Dwyer was "an incredible step" in a politically inspired move to thwart the board, which the Democrats also control.

"The Mayor really wants to use $84-million of the taxpayers' money for other purposes," the controller declared. "That money was specifically appropriated to keep the subway fare where it is and not to help the Mayor balance his budget."

The latest phase in the battle over the proposed transit subsidy began Thursday when the board overruled the Mayor and directed Mr. O'Dwyer to go into court for a ruling on whether the city had the right to subsidize the transit system.

Last November, at the insistence of the board, Mr. O'Dwyer, a brother of former Mayor William O'Dwyer and a former Democratic City Councilman, had been appointed by Corporation Counsel J. Lee Rankin to pursue the question

Continued on Page 25, Column 6

NATION'S BANKS SET 5¾% RATE; REBUKING CHASE

Prime Borrowing Cost Falls From 6% but Not to Level of 5½%, Kept by Leader

By H. ERICH HEINEMANN

Business borrowing costs dropped yesterday as banks across the country reduced their prime interest rate to 5¾ per cent from 6 per cent.

The reduction contrasted with the drop to 5½ per cent announced on Thursday by the Chase Manhattan Bank. The question immediately arose whether Chase would adjust its rate to conform to the new industry standard. Late yesterday, a spokesman for Chase said the bank had "no present intention" of doing so.

Meanwhile, it was learned yesterday that there had been discussions between the Chase Bank and the Johnson Administration prior to the bank's announcement of the reduction to 5½ per cent.

Well-informed sources in Washington said last night that the Government "was not taken by surprise" by Chase's action.

Prime Rate Defined

A spokesman for Chase confirmed last night that "as a matter of courtesy" both the Federal Reserve Bank of New York and the Treasury Department had been notified of the decision to lower the rate shortly before the bank's public announcement.

The prime rate, or minimum business-lending rate, according to one major New York bank, "applies to short-term loans to substantial depositors with the highest credit ratings."

[The Bank of Canada announced a reduction in its lending rate to 5 per cent from 5¼ per cent, effective Monday. The rate had remained unchanged since last March 14 when it was raised to 5¼ per cent from 5 per cent.]

A Conspicuous Exception

The general reduction in the prime rate by banks in the United States was the first since Aug. 23, 1960, when it dropped to 4½ per cent from 5 per cent. The new reduction is only the fifth decline since the custom of a prime rate was established in the nineteen-thirties.

The rate reduction was interpreted by bankers and economists as further evidence of the trend toward lower interest rates that started last fall. In time, they said, credit should become more plentiful and its cost should continue to decline—not only for business but for consumers as well, particularly on home mortgages.

The move to 5¾ per cent was led by the First National City Bank of New York. The bank announced its decision about 11 A.M. By the end of the day practically every other large bank in the country had joined in the decision to post a 5¾ per cent rate.

Chase, of course, stayed at 5½ per cent.

Other bankers, though, voiced the opinion that sooner or later

Continued on Page 32, Column 1

TOWAWAY POLICY IS EASED FOR U.N.

City to Extend Parking Area for Diplomats and Chase Other Motorists Out

The city joined with United Nations officials yesterday in an effort to meet the complaints of diplomats about the towaway crackdown on cars illegally parked in midtown.

The program worked out at a private meeting seeks to reduce the towing away of diplomatic vehicles by the police and provides for various cooperative measures. Specific measures include plans to supply the diplomats with more on-street parking spaces and to chase "squatters" out of parking areas already reserved for the diplomats.

The move to provide more space for diplomats' cars followed similar action regarding handicapped drivers and physicians. On Thursday, the city said that it would designate as many as 700 new special parking places for invalids. A study was also ordered to provide similar spaces for physicians.

The city, however, reserved the right to tow away illegally parked diplomatic vehicles that create a hazard.

Henry A. Barnes, city Traffic Commissioner, said that the city hoped to supply 100 or more reserved on-street parking places—designated by blue traffic signs—for the diplomats. That would raise their midtown total to about 700.

Diplomats have not been carried away by Mayor Lindsay's "no exceptions" towaway program against illegal midtown parking—but a number of their cars have been.

Since the tough policy went into effect Monday—and up to 11:30 P.M. yesterday—998 vehicles have been towed to the "pound" on Pier 74 at the Hudson River and 34th Street. This number includes 22 diplomatic or foreign consular cars.

About a dozen foreign delegations have been affected. Although the diplomats are exempt from the $40 fee—$25 for towing and the $15 fine—they

Continued on Page 28, Column 1

62 Nations Sign Treaty To Curb Arms in Space

By MAX FRANKEL

Special to The New York Times

WASHINGTON, Jan. 27—President Johnson presided today over a White House ceremony at which the United States, the Soviet Union and 60 other countries signed a treaty to limit military activities in outer space.

Mr. Johnson hailed it as an "inspiring moment in the history of the human race" and described the treaty as a "first, firm step toward keeping outer space free forever from the implements of war."

The ceremony took place before the accident at Cape Kennedy, Fla., in which three American astronauts lost their lives.

Treaty-signing ceremonies were held earlier today in Moscow and London, but the pact will not take effect until it is ratified by the United States, the Soviet Union, Britain and two other countries.

For most nations, that is a mere formality, but in the United States, the Senate must give its consent by a two-thirds vote.

Eventual ratification here is expected, because the treaty does not prohibit any present or planned American military activities in space.

It prohibits the placing of nuclear weapons or other weapons of mass destruction in orbit, on the moon or on other celestial bodies. It also bars all military installations and maneuvers from the moon and other planets.

It does not, however, prohibit the orbiting of military spacecraft without large weapons or the use of unmanned satellites for military purposes, such as reconnaissance.

Some opposition here may focus on the difficulties of inspecting Soviet satellites for the presence of nuclear weapons. But American officials expressed confidence that the treaty posed no threat to national security.

They predicted that the Joint

Continued on Page 6, Column 2

NEWS INDEX

ARMY OPPOSITION TO MAO REPORTED

Troops in 2 Regions Said to Resist Orders to Help in Ousting Party Officials

By CHARLES MOHR

Special to The New York Times

HONG KONG, Jan. 27—Disunity and confusion in the Chinese Army seemed apparent to some political analysts here today in the wake of an order to the army to stamp out resistance to Mao Tse-tung's political purge.

There was no immediate confirmation of Peking wall posters reporting that troops in the far western autonomous region of Sinkiang and in Inner Mongolia were opposing orders by Mr. Mao, who is Chairman of the Chinese Communist party, to help oust entrenched party officials.

[Reacting to clashes in Moscow in which Chinese students were hurt, Peking declared that the Soviet Union's leaders were "swine" in the same category as the last Czar, Hitler and the Ku Klux Klan. Page 2.]

The analysts here noted that the troop commander in the Sinkiang military region, Wang En-mao, was concurrently the head of the Communist party's Provincial Committee there. He could hardly be expected to use his troops to oust himself and his comrades from office, the analysts said.

A similar situation prevailed in Inner Mongolia, where Ulanfu, a Mongol, was both military commander and head of the party committee. Whether he is in

Continued on Page 2, Column 4

APOLLO PROGRAM DEALT HARD BLOW

The Slim Margin for Failure Believed Jeopardizing a Moon Landing by '70

By EVERT CLARK

Special to The New York Times

WASHINGTON, Jan. 27—Tonight's accident at Cape Kennedy is expected to deal a serious blow to the Apollo program, which has struggled hard to stay on schedule in the face of annual budget cuts.

Space officials have warned for several years that their margin of operation was thin, that continual economy by the Administration and Congress had left no room for failures if the moon was to be reached by 1970.

Since they first raised this cry, the mishaps have gradually accumulated.

Although it will be some time before the full impact of the accident can be assessed, it means more than the loss of a carefully selected, highly competent crew.

It probably means the loss of a spacecraft and possibly parts of the launching rocket. It also may mean damage to the launching pad that could delay a flight using the backup crew. A backup crew flew the Gemini 9 after the original Gemini 9 pilots were killed in a plane crash.

Last March, President Johnson reaffirmed the goal laid down by President Kennedy when he announced the Apollo program in May of 1961. The United States, Mr. Johnson said, still intends "to land the first man on the surface of the moon" by 1970.

Mr. Johnson's words were interpreted at the time as an answer—and a bit of a reprimand—to the National Aeronautics and Space Administration, which had been complaining to Congress about budget cuts made within the Administration.

On the same day, Vice President Humphrey reminded the space leaders that their program "cannot be exempt" from tight budgetary discipline.

Following the ceremony at

Continued on Page 10, Column 2

Einstein Relativity Theory Challenged

By WALTER SULLIVAN

A leading physicist reported yesterday an observation that, if true and correctly interpreted, would invalidate Albert Einstein's theory of relativity.

Dr. Robert H. Dicke, professor of physics at Princeton University, told a conference on astrophysics here that his observations of the sun last summer showed that its shape was flattened at the poles.

The effect of this flattening, or oblateness, is sufficient, he said, to explain a significant portion of the orbital behavior of Mercury, the planet closest to the sun, without recourse to relativity. It was the precise conformity of Mercury's orbit to Dr. Einstein's predictions that was the chief pillar of his theory.

If Dr. Dicke is correct, this pillar has been undermined.

However, he struck a cautious note in his report to the astrophysical conference. "It wouldn't surprise me," he said, "if general relativity is just plain wrong."

General relativity deals with gravity and its manifestations

Continued on Page 12, Column 4

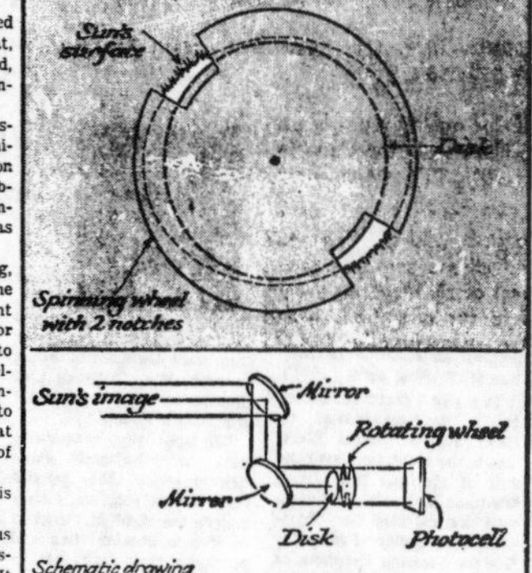

The New York Times (Daniel Brownstein) Jan. 28, 1967

Instrument used by Dr. Robert H. Dicke to determine the sun's shape was based on notched spinning wheel, as shown in upper schematic diagram. As the wheel spun, light of sun passing through notches varied with sun's shape. Light variations during each spin were detected by photocell.

"All the News That's Fit to Print"

The New York Times

LATE CITY EDITION

Weather: Snow ending this afternoon; partly cloudy through tomorrow. Temp. range: today 36-30; Mon. 38-33. Full U.S. report on Page 82.

VOL. CXVI..No. 39,854 | © 1967 The New York Times Company. | NEW YORK, TUESDAY, MARCH 7, 1967 | 10 CENTS

JOHNSON PLANS DRAFT BY LOTTERY, WITH 19-YEAR-OLDS CALLED FIRST; WOULD CUT DEFERMENTS SHARPLY

1969 DEADLINE SET

Message to Congress Calls for Debate on Students' Status

Text of Johnson's message is printed on Page 32.

By MAX FRANKEL
Special to The New York Times

SAN ANTONIO, Tex., March 6—President Johnson announced today in a special message to Congress that he intended to establish by Jan. 1, 1969, a kind of lottery that would determine which young men were drafted for military service.

By the same date, the White House said, and possibly sooner—unless Congress inhibits his present freedom of action—the President also plans to decree by Executive order:

¶That 19-year-old men be the first exposed to the random call-up each year, along with older men whose deferments had expired.

¶That deferments for all graduate students, except those preparing to be physicians, dentists or ministers, be abolished.

¶That all deferments for fathers and men in so-called essential occupations be abolished, and that rules governing deferments in other categories be tightened and made uniform.

Undergraduate Deferments

Mr. Johnson left undecided for the time being the question whether undergraduates should be deferred until they obtain a bachelor's degree.

He invited the nation to debate the issue of college deferments, noting that his expert advisers could not agree. Officials expect him to make up his mind before the end of the year.

In no event, however, will he permit college students "to pile deferment on deferment" to evade the risk of call-up, the President said.

Even if student deferments are continued under stricter rules, he indicated, each year's eligible graduates will be entered in the next lottery pool.

Disruption Doubted

Mr. Johnson's principal request of Congress was for a four-year extension of the draft law, which expires next June 30. If Congress agrees and adds no inhibiting amendments, the President will be able to make the changes he wants by Executive order, without further legislative action.

Mr. Johnson was aware that the idea of a lottery and other changes would meet strong resistance in Congress, especially among Southern delegations. By revealing his intentions many months before he would be ready to act, he apparently hoped to stimulate public support for his plans.

The problems posed by transition to the new system have not yet been thought through, officials said, but the chances are that the new rules will not be used to disrupt the plans of

Continued on Page 33, Column 1

CRITICISM VOICED

Some Democrats Seek a Change in Laws to Bar Random Choice

By NEIL SHEEHAN
Special to The New York Times

WASHINGTON, March 6—Democratic leaders of the House Armed Services Committee said today they would attempt to block President Johnson's decision to create a lottery system for drafting young men.

In his special message on the draft sent to Congress today, Mr. Johnson announced that he was ordering the creation of a system of random selection, or lottery, for eligible 19-year-olds. It would be put into operation by Jan. 1, 1969.

The President has the discretionary power under the Selective Service Act to set up such a lottery on his own authority. Crucial portions of the act are due to expire June 30, but Mr. Johnson asked Congress today to renew the act for four more years.

In a telephone interview today, Representative L. Mendel Rivers, Democrat of South Carolina, who is chairman of the House committee, said: "I do not favor a lottery."

Change in Law Predicted

Mr. Rivers indicated he would work for legislation to prevent the President from setting up a lottery.

"I suspect we'll change the law, as far as I'm concerned," he said.

Representative F. Edward Hébert, Democrat of Louisiana, who is senior Democratic member of the committee, said he also "will certainly work toward the end of preventing a national lottery."

"While I appreciate the President's interest and desire to extend the law," Mr. Hébert said, "the Congress has a responsibility under the Constitution to raise and maintain the Army and Navy, and certainly the Congress should discharge this responsibility to the fullest."

The attitude of Representatives Rivers and Hébert toward the President's draft message was considered by observers as the most significant Congres-

Continued on Page 33, Column 5

KOSYGIN DECLARES U.S. STEP-UP SPURS MORE AID TO HANOI

Soviet Leader Also Assails Rejection of North's Peace Offer Based on Bomb Halt

IT IS CALLED VITAL MOVE

Americans Are Accused of Hiding Aggressive Intention Behind New Ultimatums

By RAYMOND H. ANDERSON
Special to The New York Times

MOSCOW, March 6—Premier Aleksei N. Kosygin declared today that United States escalation of the Vietnamese war would bring retaliatory increases in Communist aid to North Vietnam.

The Soviet leader denounced Washington's rejection of Hanoi's offer of peace talks in exchange for an unconditional halt in the United States bombing raids.

Hanoi's gesture, made Jan. 28 by Foreign Minister Nguyen Duy Trinh, was described by Premier Kosygin as "an extremely important peace initiative."

The United States refused to respond to the proposal unless Hanoi indicated that it would reciprocate for a bombing halt by a curtailment of military operations against South Vietnam.

Opportunity Called Genuine

Mr. Kosygin, speaking at a rally for candidates in the election Sunday of members of the Supreme Soviet (parliament) of the Russian Republic, reiterated Moscow's insistence that Foreign Minister Trinh's proposal had opened a genuine opportunity for settling the conflict.

"The American Government, however, did not avail itself of this opportunity," he said. "On the contrary, trying to camouflage its aggressive intentions, it hastened to set forth ultimatums that were absolutely unacceptable to the Vietnamese people."

Instead of responding to the peace overtures, Mr. Kosygin declared, the United States violated the lunar new year truce last month by redeploying troops and preparing to step up the war.

The escalation followed, he continued, with the resumption of bombing raids on North Vietnam, artillery attacks on the demilitarized zone between North Vietnam and South Vietnam, naval bombardment of the North Vietnamese coastline and the mining of rivers in North Vietnam.

Continued on Page 16, Column 1

Tass, via United Press International Cablephoto

CONDEMNS U.S. AT RALLY: Premier Aleksei N. Kosygin speaking at an election rally yesterday in Moscow. He said that U.S. escalation of the war in Vietnam would bring increased Communist aid to the Hanoi regime.

Lodge Reported Seeking To Leave Post in Vietnam

By R. W. APPLE Jr.
Special to The New York Times

SAIGON, South Vietnam, March 6—Ambassador Henry Cabot Lodge has asked to be relieved of his duties in Saigon late in the spring or early in the summer, according to friends. Mr. Lodge has declined to discuss his plans publicly.

Informed sources said that the White House was conducting an intensive search for a successor. The search has proved more difficult than expected, the sources indicated, so the Ambassador's departure date has not yet been set.

In any case, observers believe that Mr. Lodge would not want to leave until after the promulgation of the new South Vietnamese constitution, which he considers a major step forward not only for South Vietnam but also for American policy here.

Charter by March 27

The Constituent Assembly is scheduled to complete a draft of the document by March 27, after which the governing military junta will have 30 days to evaluate it and to propose any changes before making the text public.

It is unlikely, then, that Mr. Lodge would depart before May. His departure could be delayed—possibly until after the scheduled Vietnamese elections in July, August or September—if a replacement cannot be found.

A tall, elegant New England Brahmin, Mr. Lodge is 65 years old. He has served two terms as Ambassador in Saigon, the first from August, 1963, to June, 1964, the second beginning on Aug. 19, 1965.

If he leaves when he hopes to, his departure will coincide roughly with those of two advisers.

Philip C. Habib, the embassy's chief political officer, is to depart next Tuesday. Barry Zorthian, who had headed public information and propaganda operations for three years, is

Continued on Page 16, Column 3

U.S. GUNS SHELLED; 5 MARINES KILLED

Attacks on Artillery Position Near Border Wound 11—Weapons Undamaged

By The Associated Press

SAIGON, South Vietnam, March 7 — North Vietnamese forces staged two mortar attacks early today against long-range United States artillery that fires across the demilitarized zone into North Vietnam, the United States command reported.

Five United States marines were killed and 11 were wounded in the two shellings, headquarters said. The bombardments were directed against the United States Army's 175-mm. guns on the artillery plateau at Camp Carroll, about eight-and-a-half miles south of the demilitarized zone.

These guns, the biggest in Vietnam with a 20-mile range, only recently began a campaign of bombardments into the demilitarized zone and beyond the zone into North Vietnam.

The United States headquarters said 150 rounds of enemy mortar fire struck the camp perimeter shortly after last midnight and 35 more rounds hit the camp just before daybreak. Spokesmen said there was no damage to the big guns or to other equipment.

Only a few miles south of the demilitarized zone, outnumbered United States marines clashed

Continued on Page 15, Column 1

CHOU SAID TO TAKE THE HELM IN CHINA; SOFTER LINE SEEN

East Europeans in Peking Say He and 4 Top Aides Run Nation's Affairs

By Agence France-Presse

PEKING, March 6—Informed East European sources said today that Premier Chou En-lai, assisted by a small "working group," had assumed control of China's governmental, Communist party and military affairs, as well as the guidance of the Cultural Revolution.

It is not yet clear whether the present pre-eminence of Mr. Chou signifies a permanent shift in the direction of the Cultural Revolution, or merely masks a "tactical withdrawal" by Mao Tse-tung, the party chairman, and his followers, the sources said.

They said that Mr. Mao and his group remained as militant and intransigent as ever. The chief members of the group are Mr. Mao's apparent successor, Defense Minister Lin Piao; a Politburo member, Kang Sheng; the Cultural Revolution leader, Chen Po-ta, and Chairman Mao's wife, Chiang Ching.

Soviet Break Favored

The "toughest" members of this group, including Mr. Kang, favor a break with the Soviet Union and more active Chinese intervention in Vietnam, the sources said.

Other members, including Mr. Lin, are more cautious concerning Vietnam. However, they envisage a long period of isolation for China, which in their view must become a fortress prepared to fight on two fronts—against "imperialism" in the east and south, and against Soviet "revisionism" in the west.

The working group assisting Premier Chou includes Li Fu-chun, chairman of the Planning Commission; Hsieh Fu-chih, Minister of Public Security; Liu Po-chang, a deputy chairman of the Defense Commission, and Foreign Minister Chen Yi.

Concerned With Theory

While this group handles the practical running of the country, Mr. Mao and Mr. Lin are devoting themselves mainly to theoretical and ideological aspects of the Cultural Revolution, the sources said.

Mr. Lin, whose activities have not been mentioned officially since last November, rarely leaves his Peking residence except to confer with Mr. Mao or to attend meetings of the Central Committee's Military Commission, of which he is chairman.

The East European sources were pessimistic about the durability of the new softer line of the Cultural Revolution, the inauguration of which was heralded in a speech by Premier Chou.

The new line was marked by the halting last Feb. 11 of demonstrations outside the Soviet Embassy here, the dissolution of the Red Guards and other Maoist organizations, and a call

Continued on Page 7, Column 1

Election for Powell's Seat Set by State for April 11

Harlem Leader Expected to Run Again and Win Even Without a Campaign—Liberals Will Not Enter Contest

By SYDNEY H. SCHANBERG
Special to The New York Times

ALBANY, March 6—Governor Rockefeller today called a special election for Tuesday, April 11, to fill the Congressional seat of Adam Clayton Powell.

The Harlem Democrat, excluded from his place in the House by a 307-to-116 vote of its members last Wednesday, is considered a sure winner if he runs for the seat again.

Mr. Powell, who is still at his vacation retreat on the island of Bimini in the Bahamas, has said that if necessary he will run for the seat again, "and win."

The necessity may arise, since most observers believe that two lawsuits being prepared by Mr. Powell's lawyers in an attempt to overturn the exclusion vote will probably not be decided before the April 11 election date.

Both suits will be filed in Federal courts—one in Washington against the House Speaker, John W. McCormack, charging that the House exceeded its authority, and the other in New York against Governor Rockefeller, seeking to enjoin him from calling a special election.

Some of the Governor's advisers are concerned that, by acknowledging that the Powell seat is vacant and calling such an election, he may antagonize many Harlem voters.

The Governor is said to be-

Continued on Page 35, Column 1

Hoffa Goes to Jail Today After Losing New Appeal

By DAVID R. JONES
Special to The New York Times

WASHINGTON, March 6—James R. Hoffa today lost a crucial court appeal in his long battle to stay out of prison and was due to begin an eight-year sentence for jury tampering tomorrow. Imprisonment was assured for the president of the International Brotherhood of Teamsters after the Federal Court of Appeals here rejected his plea.

Hoffa can carry his case to Chief Justice Earl Warren, and there were indications that he would do so. But the Supreme Court head is traveling in South America, and Hoffa's lawyers apparently decided not to appeal to him until he returns here later this week.

Hoffa is to appear at the United States marshal's office in the Federal Courthouse here at 9 A.M. tomorrow to be put under arrest. He is then to be taken to the Federal penitentiary at Lewisburg, Pa.

10-Year Struggle

The 54-year-old head of the nation's largest labor union—1.7 million members—approached the end of the legal road 10 years to the month after the Justice Department began to pursue him on what turned out to be a variety of charges. The conviction under which he will be jailed came in 1964.

Hoffa still has two motions for a new trial pending in the Court of Appeals for the Sixth Circuit, in Cincinnati. He also has filed with the Federal District Court in Chattanooga what he contends is new evidence that the Government illegally eavesdropped on him and the jurors in his trial there for jury tampering in 1964.

The teamster leader's lawyers apparently hoped that Chief Justice Warren would take their appeal and perhaps free Hoffa while his motions were pending, because he was the only Justice

Continued on Page 28, Column 4

CAR SAFETY RULE TERMED ILLEGAL

Companies Tell U.S. They Can't Meet Standard on 'Interior Impact' by '68

By United Press International

DETROIT, March 6—The nation's leading auto makers told the Federal Government today that its safety rule governing passenger protection from crash injury was impossible to meet in time to include on 1968 models.

Two of them, the General Motors Corporation and the Chrysler Corporation, said that the so-called "interior impact" rule was illegal. Chrysler warned that it would take the issue to court unless the rule was changed.

The complaints came in separate replies to 20 Federal car safety standards proposed by Dr. William Haddon Jr., administrator of the new National Traffic Safety Agency.

The Ford Motor Company had a few minor complaints about other rules.

The American Motors Corporation said only that it did not have time to finish the engineering and test work needed, and doubted that it could meet the deadline even if all the testing was finished.

But the industry threw up a united front against the rule that would outlaw protruding knobs

Continued on Page 28, Column 3

BONN IS OPTIMISTIC ON U.S. TROOP PLAN

Says Talks Cleared Way to Solve Problem of Costs

Special to The New York Times

BONN, March 6 — A West German spokesman said today that the way had been cleared for a solution of problems related to meeting the foreign exchange costs of the 225,000 American troops in Germany.

Conrad Ahlers, deputy spokesman for the Government, said that talks held by John J. McCloy, President Johnson's special envoy, with Chancellor Kurt Georg Kiesinger in Stuttgart Saturday and Foreign Minister Willy Brandt here yesterday had proceeded "smoothly." They produced "a clarification and strengthening of German-American relations," according to Mr. Ahlers.

These talks, following the announcement Friday by the State Department that the United States would no longer insist on West Germany's buying exclusively military equipment in the United States to offset the local costs of maintaining

Continued on Page 3, Column 3

U.S. to Arm Observer Craft in Vietnam

Twin-engine Cessna Super Skymaster. With minor modifications, this commercial craft is being turned into a plane, with machine guns and rockets, for air patrol in Vietnam.

By WILLIAM BEECHER
Special to The New York Times

WASHINGTON, March 6—The Pentagon has decided to provide new planes armed with machine guns and rockets for the few hundred Air Force pilots in Vietnam who now fly reconnaissance missions over guerrilla positions in unarmed, single-engine Cessnas.

These forward air controllers are assigned to American and South Vietnamese combat units. They spend hours each day winging low over jungles, marshes and mountains looking for signs of enemy activity.

Black-shirted figures suddenly diving into the underbrush on hearing the plane's approach, a hut appearing overnight in a "deserted" hamlet, a herd of water buffalo grazing where they have not appeared before, fires at dusk in a strange place—any of these signs can alert the air controller to new guerrilla activity. He then calls in a jet strike or a ground patrol to check the sighting.

Often the first inkling of untoward activity is the sight of small red-yellow flashes and wisps of smoke as enemy sharp-shooters fire at a controller.

For the most part, the only armament on the Cessna observer plane today is a rifle

Continued on Page 14, Column 6

U.S. RANKED LOW IN MATH TEACHING

12-Nation Study Says Japan Does Best Job in Subject

By FRED M. HECHINGER

American public schools have been found to rank low in an international comparison of pupils' achievements in mathematics, and Japan's schools to be doing "the best over-all job" in that field.

But although American schools were found to be doing poorly in cultivating mathematical talent among young teen-agers, they recouped some of the losses by enrolling relatively large numbers of students in mathematics courses in the upper years of high school.

These findings are the result of a 12-nation educational endeavor, sponsored by the International Project for the Evaluation of Educational Achievement, which had the support of the participating countries' top-level education authorities.

Of the Japanese 13-year-olds tested, 76 per cent scored in the upper half, 31 per cent in the upper tenth, and 5 per cent in the upper 1 per cent on the internationally devised test scale.

By contrast, of the American 13-year-olds, only 43 per cent were in the upper half, 4 per cent in the upper tenth and only one-third of 1 per cent in the upper 1 per cent.

However, they lagged only slightly behind Scottish, English and French youngsters.

A comparison of accomplish-

Continued on Page 18, Column 4

Doctors Upheld in Barring an Abortion

By RONALD SULLIVAN
Special to The New York Times

TRENTON, March 6—The State Supreme Court held today that a defective child's right to life was greater than the wish of his parents to employ an abortion to keep him from being born.

In a 4-to-3 decision, marked by a vigorous dissent by Chief Justice Joseph Weintraub, the court dismissed the suit of Mr. and Mrs. Irwin Gleitman of North Arlington, who charged that two physicians were guilty of malpractice for allowing the birth of their 7-year-old son, Jeffrey, who is blind, deaf, dumb and mentally retarded.

Jeffrey was born at Margaret Hague Hospital in Jersey City after Mrs. Gleitman, who is now 27 years old, had contracted German measles during the early months of her pregnancy.

The parents alleged in their suit that two obstetricians, Dr. Robert Cosgrove Jr. and Dr. Jerome Dolan of Jersey City, were negligent in failing to warn Mrs. Gleitman that German measles could result in a defective child.

"Though we sympathize with the unfortunate situation in which these parents find themselves, we firmly believe the right of the child to live is greater than and precludes their right not to endure emotional and financial injury," Justice Haydn Proctor wrote for the majority.

In a 15-page dissent, Chief Justice Weintraub warned of the effects of today's ruling so far as it affected abortion.

"When the highest court of the state even intimates the practice may be criminal, I would doubt that a reputable doctor or reputable institution would take the risk [of permitting an abortion]. Rather the question will likely be presented by some back-alley abortionist with all the diversion from the merits that a character of that kind can induce.

"Meanwhile, we can be sure, the pregnant woman who up until now has had the services of the highest run of medical men and the safety of a hospital will deliver herself to dirty hands, if she can afford it, for a woman unwilling to

Continued on Page 35, Column 3

NEWS INDEX

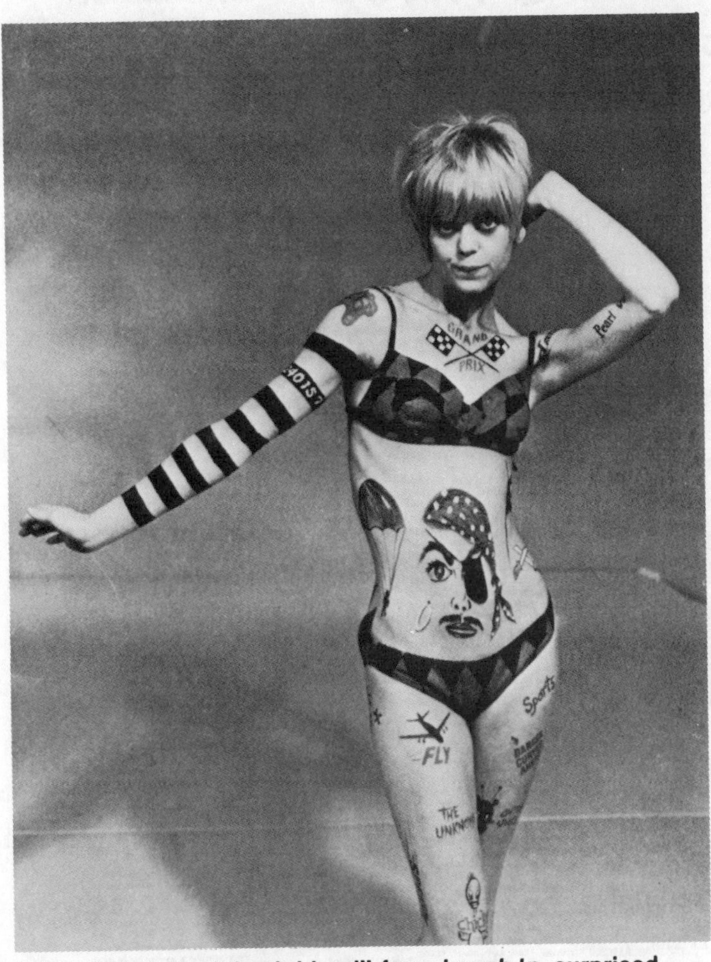

Goldie Hawn, the "dumb blond" from *Laugh-In,* surprised critics when she emerged later in sensitive roles on the big screen.

Dan Rowen (left) and Dick Martin (right) were the comedy team of *Rowan and Martin's Laugh-In.* This daring satirical series became a top-rated program for NBC.

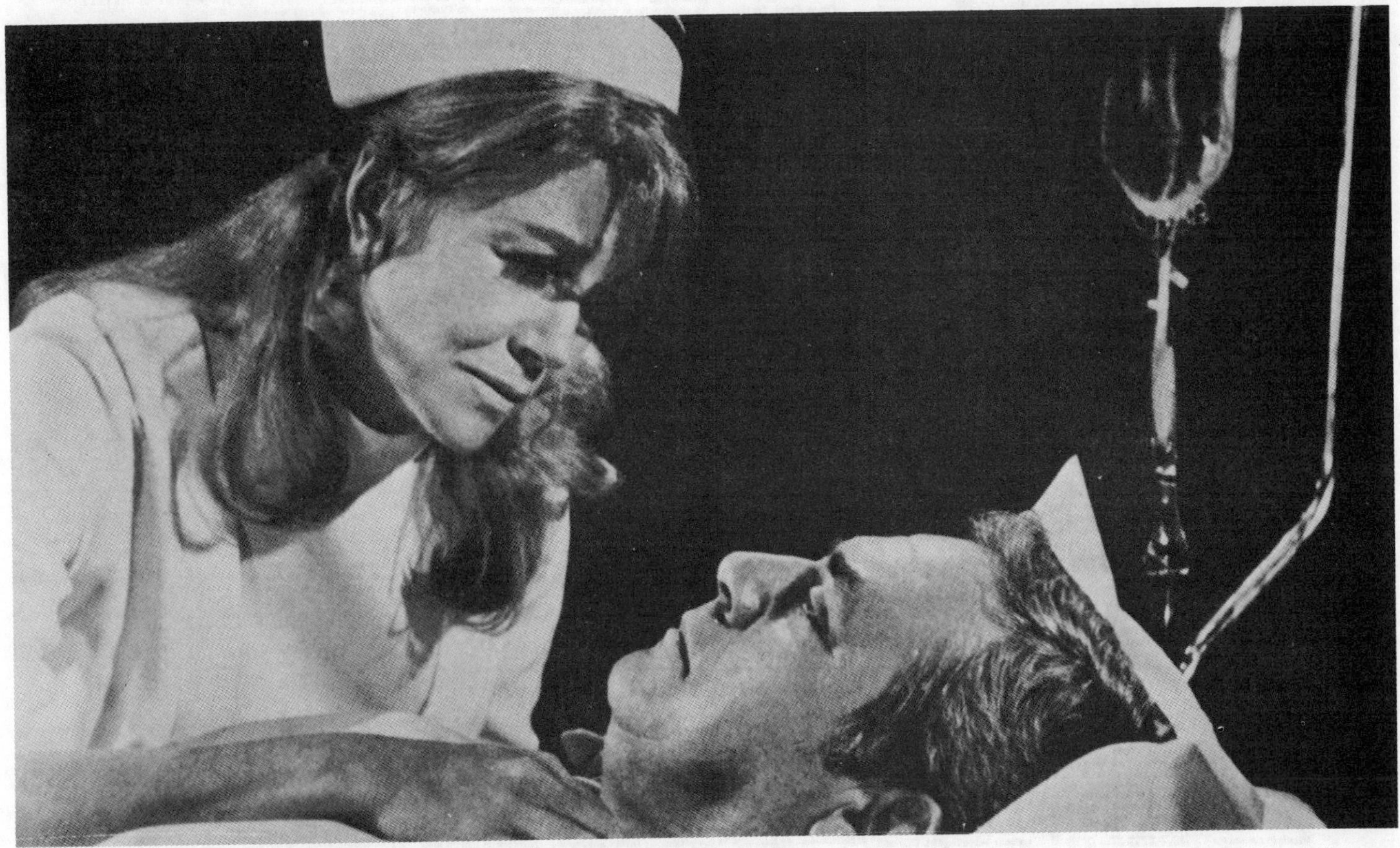

Raymond Burr and guest star, Dorothy Malone, in a scene from *Ironside.*

"All the News That's Fit to Print"

The New York Times

LATE CITY EDITION

Weather: Mostly sunny and mild today; fair tonight and tomorrow. Temp. range: today 69-40; Saturday 56-41. Full U.S. report on Page 91.

SECTION ONE

VOL. CXVI..No. 39,894 NEW YORK, SUNDAY, APRIL 16, 1967

80c beyond 50-mile zone from New York City, except Long Island. Higher in air delivery cities. 35 CENTS

F.B.I. IS WATCHING 'ANTIWAR' EFFORT, PRESIDENT SAYS

Press Aide Refuses to Tell if Hoover Is Checking on the Vietnam Protests

LODGE SENDS WAR DATA

Copter Plant in Connecticut Struck—Johnson Moves to Prevent Long Tie-Up

By MAX FRANKEL

Special to The New York Times

SAN ANTONIO, Tex., April 15—President Johnson's attention was turned again to the war in Vietnam today only a few hours after he returned to his Texas ranch from the conference with Latin American leaders in Uruguay.

His preoccupation was evident as he received reports from J. Edgar Hoover on "antiwar activity" and from Ambassador Henry Cabot Lodge on progress in the war and as he moved to prevent a long tie-up at a helicopter plant in Connecticut that produces engines for Vietnam.

[A strike began at the plant, the Lycoming Division of the Avco Corporation in Stratford, Conn., early Sunday after expiration of the contract at midnight. A spokesman at the plant said the strike's major effect would not be felt until Monday.]

F.B.I. Work Disclosed

The President reached the ranch shortly after midnight this morning, after a 14-hour flight from Punta del Este, Uruguay, with a refueling stop in Surinam (Dutch Guiana).

Mrs. Johnson had come here earlier this week from Washington, and the President apparently planned to spend a few days here to catch up on accumulated paper work.

With major demonstrations being held against the Vietnam war today, Mr. Johnson let it be known that the Federal Bureau of Investigation was keeping an eye on "antiwar activity." The President's spokesman refused, however, to make any connection between this disclosure and the demonstrations.

The disclosure was made by George Christian, White House press secretary, in listing a series of reports that were awaiting the President when he awoke at 6:30 A.M.

Mr. Christian was asked if the "antiwar activity" referred

Continued on Page 8, Column 1

100,000 Rally at U.N. Against Vietnam War

The Rev. Dr. Martin Luther King Jr. addresses antiwar rally outside United Nations. He praised march and rally. The New York Times

LINDSAY PROMISES AID FOR PROGRAMS OF PUERTO RICANS

Key Officials Told to Work With Representatives of All Levels of Community

By PETER KIHSS

Mayor Lindsay yesterday ordered every key city agency to designate a top-level representative to work with Puerto Ricans on proposals to better their life here.

The proposals will come out of the city's first conference with representatives of all segments of the Puerto Rican community, which started yesterday.

The Mayor declared, for example, that there was a need for a fundamental review of the teaching methods and curriculum for the more than 200,000 Puerto Ricans among the one-million youngsters in public schools. This 20 per cent proportion, he said, "calls for a greater voice of the Puerto Rican community on all levels of the educational structure."

About 1,000 persons started the two-day conference, called by the Mayor, at the High School of Art and Design, Second Avenue at East 57th Street.

Wide Range of Leaders

The conference, in preparation for four months, brought together the whole wide range of leaders of the 700,000 Puerto Ricans here.

At least 15 commissioners and deputies were on hand to attend a dozen panels. A panel headed by Nick Ortiz, manager of the Banco Popular, said the city had 10,000 Hispanic-owned businesses, but said they were marginal and in ghetto areas, victimized in many ways.

On the social side, Dr. Efrén Ramirez, the city's Narcotics Coordinator, said addiction was growing faster among Puerto Ricans than any other ethnic group here. He estimated that they made up 24.2 per cent of the city's addicts in 1964 while at the same time totaling only 8 per cent of the over-all population.

Progress Is Cited

Nevertheless, Borough President Herman Badillo of the Bronx noted that "when all of us came here from Puerto Rico, we were all living below the poverty level" — as was he on his arrival at the age of 12. Now, he said, half had climbed above that median despite society's demands for more and more education — as against only 3 per cent of New Yorkers having had high school training in 1860.

Under the administrations of former Mayors Vincent R. Impellitteri and Robert F. Wagner, the city had held three conferences in San Juan and one here on migration problems—but on an intergovernmental level. When another such San Juan session was set for last December, objections from New York Puerto Ricans led to its replacement by yesterday's self-help effort here instead.

Mayor Lindsay had assigned

Continued on Page 45, Column 1

School Board Gets Mayor's Assurance Of Budget Freedom

By THOMAS P. RONAN

The Lindsay administration told the Board of Education yesterday that it intended to exercise only limited control over how the board spent its funds.

For the last five years the city has given the board a lump-sum appropriation and complete freedom to shift funds within its budget without getting approval from City Hall. But on Friday an aide to Mr. Lindsay said the Mayor felt this freedom should be ended. The board quickly complained that this would hamper the flexibility of its operations.

Yesterday, one of the Mayor's budget experts said that the board would have the power to transfer certain funds, but not all. He said that the board would be given appropriations for broadly stated programs, and that it could switch funds within each of these programs. However, it will not be allowed to

Continued on Page 79, Column 6

SPECK IS GUILTY AND FACES DEATH

But the Judge Can Soften Jury's Recommendation With Prison Sentence

By EDWARD C. BURKS

Special to The New York Times

PEORIA, Ill., April 15—Richard Speck was found guilty here this afternoon of the murder of eight young nurses in Chicago last July.

The jury of seven men and five women recommended that his punishment be death in the electric chair. Under Illinois law the jury alone can fix the death penalty. But the judge in imposing sentence can give the convicted man a prison term. This term cannot be less than 14 years.

Judge Herbert C. Paschen, in leaving the courtroom today, said that it would be "better than 50 days probably" before sentencing.

The jurors deliberated only 49 minutes.

As the verdicts were read out, the 25-year-old pockmarked native of Monmouth, Ill., appeared to be chewing on a piece of gum. He stopped and turned his furrowed brow aside, closed his eyes for a second, but showed no emotion. There was no sound in the courtroom.

Seems Resigned

As George Weiman, a steel and wire company foreman, continued reading the verdicts, Speck seemed resigned to his fate. But he did not flinch or lower his head. When the public defender, Gerald Getty, asked for a polling of the jury, Speck turned his somewhat lopsided gaze on them, then for a moment he looked at the 100 spectators packed into the small courtroom.

Opposing attorneys will meet with Judge Paschen here Monday morning to discuss defense motions.

Parents of four of the slain nurses, whose ages ranged from 20 to 24, were in the courtroom this afternoon. The evidence showed that five of the girls were strangled and three stabbed to death. Altogether there were 32 stab wounds.

Family Not in Court

Speck's mother and six brothers and sisters had testified during the trial, giving a picture of a ninth-grade dropout who was borrowing money from a sister just a few days before the crime. None of them appeared in court today.

During the final summations by the two sides this morning, Speck was flushed and attentive. As the jury filed out at 2 P.M. to begin its deliberations he turned to smile broadly at others at the defense table.

The prosecutor, William Martin, had presented his case, buttressed by 42 witnesses, in an even-toned methodical way. But today his voice alternated between a whisper and a shout as he reminded the jury of the way in which the girls were killed.

He used repetition to drive home his argument. Speaking of one of the girls, the prosecu-

Continued on Page 56, Column 3

12% RISE PROPOSED IN CITY SPENDING, WITHOUT NEW TAX

Lindsay Asks $5.18-Billion, With Biggest Shares for Schools and Welfare

GAP IN REVENUE CLOSED

$803-Million Allotted Health Services — $502-Million Goes to Fight on Crime

Digest of the budget message will be found on Page 78.

By SETH S. KING

New York City will provide for the governmental needs of its eight million people in the coming fiscal year by spending more money than ever before without asking for new taxes.

This was shown yesterday in the executive budget Mayor Lindsay gave to the Board of Estimate and City Council calling for expenditures of $5,183,508,877. This was an increase of $584.8-million, or 12.7 per cent, over the current year's budget, making it the largest budget in the city's more than 300-year history.

The money for the increased expenditures will come in part from the normal growth of revenue in the city's existing taxes, from the new educational lotteries and from increased State and Federal aid.

The budget covers the expenditure of all funds for the day-to-day operating expenses of the city for the year beginning July 1. A capital budget of $1.059-billion was approved Tuesday by the board and the Council to pay for permanent improvements. It is financed by borrowing, with the debt service on the loans provided for in yesterday's executive budget.

Schools Head List

Again, education leads the list of expenditures in the executive budget, with a total appropriation of $1.093-billion. Among other large allocations are those for welfare and community development, which will total $1.015-billion. Health and hospital programs will take $803.2-million.

Police, court and prison costs total $502.2-million. Collection of garbage and air and water pollution control are given $216.1-million.

Appropriations for transportation (not including direct subway operating costs) total $177.3-million. Parks and recreation get $114.8-million. Finally, the payment of interest and principal on the city's debts will cost $648.3-million.

There has been virtually no change in the city's population in the last year. But in the coming year the cost for each man, woman, and child will reach $650, compared with $591 in the current year. Ten years ago it was $237.

In presenting his budget, Mayor Lindsay said that it had been formulated in a time of

Continued on Page 79, Column 1

NAVY'S NEW PLANE UNDERGOES A TEST

Flown in Rain to Determine if Jet Engine Will Stall in Vietnam-Like Squalls

By HANSON W. BALDWIN

The Navy's newest aircraft, the A-7A Corsair 2, is hunting thunderstorms in Florida to find out whether or not its jet engine will lose power or stall in rain squalls.

The basic engine in the A-7A is the same as that in the swept-wing General Dynamics F-111, a fighter-bomber that has also experienced engine problems, though of a different nature.

The Florida tests for the Ling-Temco-Vought A-7A are part of a "quick-fix" program that the Navy and Pratt & Whitney Aircraft Division of the United Aircraft Corporation, makers of the engine, are pushing to insure deployment of the new plane in Vietnam by November.

The Navy attack plane, meant to supplement and ultimately replace the Navy's Douglas A-4 Skyhawk, has been ordered in quantity, and the Navy has been counting on the aircraft to help replace Vietnam combat losses and losses from accidents.

Sees Quick Resolution

Production models of the plane are now being delivered to the Navy and two development squadrons have flown hundreds of hours.

High Navy spokesmen insist that the plane will meet its November deployment date unless the Florida tests show a more serious deficiency than is expected.

One naval aviator admiral said last week that in his experience he had never seen "an airplane program that has gone as fast or as well as the A-7", and he predicted that the engine problems would be resolved quickly. He added that the Navy was planning to fly one of the planes nonstop—and without air refueling—to the Paris air show in late May.

But the same admiral, as well as other Defense Department and naval sources, said that the A-7A had encountered a number of technical and other problems.

At the least, the officials said, the problems might delay for a considerable period the capability of the plane to meet its design specifications. At the worst, they might result in an

Continued on Page 60, Column 1

Many Draft Cards Burned — Eggs Tossed at Parade

By DOUGLAS ROBINSON

Thousands of antiwar demonstrators marched through the streets of Manhattan yesterday and then massed in front of the United Nations building to hear United States policy in Vietnam denounced.

The Police Department's Office of Community Relations said that police officers at the scene estimated the number of demonstrators outside the United Nations at "between 100,000 and 125,000."

It was difficult to make any precise count because people were continually leaving and entering the rally area. It was also almost impossible to distinguish the demonstrators from passersby and spectators.

On Friday the police had announced that they were preparing for a crowd of 100,000 to 400,000.

Leaders of Parade

It was the largest peace demonstration staged in New York since the Vietnam war began. It took four hours for all the marchers to leave Central Park for the United Nations Plaza.

The parade was led by the Rev. Dr. Martin Luther King Jr., Dr. Benjamin Spock, the pediatrician, and Harry Belafonte, the singer, as well as several other civil rights and religious figures, all of whom linked arms as they moved out of the park at the head of the line.

The marchers — who had poured into New York on chartered buses, trains and cars from cities as far away as Pittsburgh, Cleveland and Chicago—included housewives from Westchester, students and poets from the Lower East Side, priests and nuns, doctors, businessmen and teachers.

Chant From Youths

As they began trooping out of Central Park toward Fifth Avenue, some of the younger demonstrators chanted: "Hell no, we won't go," and "Hey, Hey, L. B. J., How Many Kids Did You Kill Today."

Most of the demonstrators, however, marched silently as they passed equally silent crowds of onlookers. At several points—notably Central Park South from the Avenue of the Americas to Fifth Avenue—the sidewalks were swarming with onlookers. Other blocks were almost deserted.

Some of the marchers were hit with eggs and red paint. At 47th Street and Park Avenue, several demonstrators were struck by steel rods from a building under construction. Some plastic cups filled with

Continued on Page 2, Column 3

OPTIMISM VOICED ON BIRTH CONTROL

World Population Assembly Ends With Plea to All Lands to Promote Programs

By JUAN de ONIS

Special to The New York Times

SANTIAGO, Chile, April 15—The World Planned Parenthood assembly adjourned today with a call on all governments to adopt national programs that would help their people utilize birth control.

Sir Colville Deverell of Britain, Secretary General of the International Planned Parenthood Federation, said family planning of the number and spacing of children was "a contemporary human right" that governments and international bodies such as the United Nations must support.

The eighth international conference of the federation, which attracted official and private delegates from 87 countries and international organizations, closed at the municipal theater with a basically optimistic assessment by delegates of the possibilities of controlling the world "population explosion" in this century.

But, summing up the general

Continued on Page 35, Column 4

DR. FAGER VICTOR IN GOTHAM STAKES

Damascus Finishes Second in Feature at Aqueduct

Dr. Fager, making his first start of the season, became a strong pre-Kentucky Derby favorite yesterday by capturing the $57,800 Gotham at Aqueduct.

The crowd of 50,522 saw Manuel Ycaza ride the 3-year-old, who outran Damascus, with Willie Shoemaker riding, in the stretch to win the mile race and return $4.60 for $2.

At Pimlico in Baltimore, Dawn Glory broke the track record for 1⅛ miles, winning the $31,150 Survivor Stakes. Ridden by Gilberto Vasquez, Dawn Glory was timed in 1:49 4/5 and paid $10.

BASEBALL

Mel Stottlemyre pitched his second consecutive shutout, defeating the Boston Red Sox, 1-0, at the Stadium. Horace Clarke drove in the Yankee run.

The Mets became the victims of Tony Gonzalez's first major league home run with the bases filled and dropped a 6-2 decision to the Phillies at Philadelphia.

ROWING

Princeton's varsity crew, starting at a fast 44 strokes a minute, went on to defeat Navy by almost two lengths in a 1¾-mile race on Lake Carnegie. The Tigers were timed in 9 minutes 19.3 seconds.

HOCKEY

The Toronto Maple Leafs took a 3-2 lead in their four-of-seven-game semi-final Stanley Cup series with the Black Hawks by scoring a 4-2 victory at Chicago.

Details in Section 5.

O'Brien Prices Modern Postal Service at $5-Billion

Special to The New York Times

WASHINGTON, April 15 — Postmaster General Lawrence F. O'Brien believes that it will take annual expenditures of a billion dollars for five years to equip the postal service to handle efficiently the increasing volume of mail.

This is the first time that the Postmaster General has publicly put a price tag on his department's over-all need for modernizing post offices, for new post offices, and for new equipment, including computers and mail-sorting machinery.

In addition, the Postmaster General remains convinced that his own Cabinet-level post must be abolished and the functions of his department turned over to a non-profit corporation.

Mr. O'Brien believes that both the commission named by President Johnson to investigate the postal system and Congress should review the present postal rate structure, which gives a wide variety of preferential rates to certain senders of mail.

He says, however, that the postal system must continue to subsidize some categories of mail for "public service" reasons.

These and other views—in-

Continued on Page 66, Column 3

The New York Times (by George Tames)

Postmaster General Lawrence F. O'Brien as he discussed the problems and plans of his department at an interview in his office. He favors nonprofit corporation to handle mail.

Today's Sections

*Included in all copies in the New York metropolitan area and adjacent territory.
**Section 11—Limited Distribution—New York City and its Suburban Area, and States of New York, New Jersey and Connecticut.

Index to Subjects

Clint Eastwood starred in *For a Few Dollars More.*

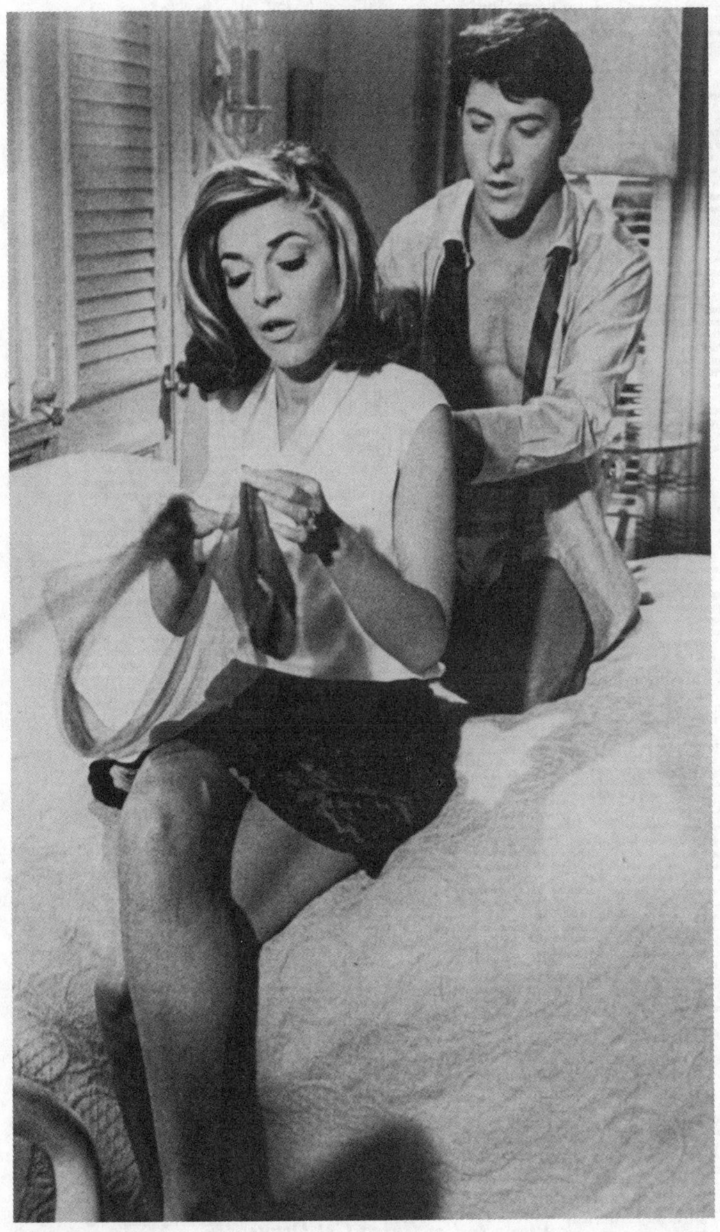

Dustin Hoffman shown as Anne Bancroft's awkward lover in a scene from *The Graduate.*

Some rather graphic love scenes in *I Am Curious (Yellow)* stirred the censors and became a major censorship testcase.

"All the News That's Fit to Print"

The New York Times

LATE CITY EDITION

Weather: Sunny today, cloudy tonight; chance of showers tomorrow. Temp. range: today 63-44; Thurs. 65-43. Full U. S. report on Page 76.

VOL. CXVI..No. 39,899 — NEW YORK, FRIDAY, APRIL 21, 1967 — 10 CENTS

U.S. JETS BOMB HAIPHONG; FIRST ATTACK INSIDE CITY KNOCKS OUT POWER PLANT

2D UNIT ALSO HIT

Port Area Is Spared —One Residential Section Damaged

By R. W. APPLE Jr.

Special to The New York Times

SAIGON, South Vietnam, April 20—United States planes struck targets in Haiphong today for the first time.

Dozens of fighter bombers from the aircraft carrier Kitty Hawk pounded a power plant a mile from the center of the port city's business district. At the same time, planes from the carrier Ticonderoga hit a second power plant on the northeastern fringe of the city, two miles from downtown.

Rear Adm. David C. Richardson of Meridian, Miss., commander of the carrier task force operating in the Gulf of Tonkin, conceded that some damage had been inflicted on a residential district in the attack on the plant a mile from the center of the city.

On board the Kitty Hawk, the admiral said: "Between the power plant and a small canal to the east of it, there is a little street. There was some destruction in there but very few places. We saw no evidence of damage to any significant number of houses in our photographs."

Admiral Richardson emphasized that all possible precautions against extensive civilian casualties had been taken.

No U. S. Plane Losses

Despite heavy antiaircraft fire, no United States planes were reported lost.

Both targets were well removed from the docks, where ships of the Soviet Union and, occasionally, non-Communist nations are moored. The presence of these ships has often been cited as a reason for avoiding attacks on Haiphong.

One senior American official, who was unwilling to permit the use of his name, described the strike on Haiphong as a "tremendously important intensification — escalation, if you will—of the air war."

He said it was part of a series of steps ordered by the White House to penalize North Vietnam for refusing to agree to negotiations.

Other power plants have been struck in the past, including a number substantially larger than either of those hit today. But the symbolic significance of bombing Haiphong itself for the first time outweighed this fact, diplomats here said.

A pilot who took part in the

Continued on Page 6, Column 1

The New York Times — April 21, 1967

PORT CITY RAIDED: A power plant (1) in the city and another (2) northeast of downtown section were hit. The built-up areas of Haiphong are indicated by shading.

SENATE STALLED ON TAX INCENTIVE AND CAMPAIGN AID

Mansfield Moves to Strip Bill on Investment Credit of Unrelated Riders

FILIBUSTER IS PROMISED

Long Objects to Proposal to Repeal Contribution Plan, Restored by 46-42 Vote

By EILEEN SHANAHAN

Special to The New York Times

WASHINGTON, April 20—The Senate worked itself into an angry stalemate today over legislation that would restore the 7 per cent tax bonus for business investment and also modify the new law permitting taxpayers to contribute $1 to finance Presidential campaigns.

The controversial campaign financing proposal, which the Senate voted to repeal only a week ago, was reinstated in the bill early this afternoon by a vote of 46 to 42.

Immediately after the vote on the campaign funds issue, Senator Mike Mansfield of Montana, the Democratic leader, moved that the bill be returned to the Senate Finance Committee, there to be stripped of the campaign financing proposal and other amendments unrelated to the restoration of the investment tax credit.

Seeks Quick Action

Mr. Mansfield's motion also provided that the new stripped-down measure, to be reported "forthwith" by the Finance Committee, contain a provision repealing the campaign financing law next July 31.

In the House, meanwhile, Representative Wilbur D. Mills, chairman of the Ways and Means Committee, rejected the view of the Administration's chief economist that frequent tax changes were necessary to keep the economy prosperous and growing.

Mr. Mansfield, explaining his motion on the tax bill in the Senate, said that he did not wish the campaign financing law to be permanently repealed. He said, however, that he thought every member of the Senate agreed that the law needed amendment.

He proposed the July 31 date for expiration of the present law, he said, so that the Senate Finance Committee and the Senate as a whole would face a deadline in rewriting the meas-

Continued on Page 20, Column 3

Associated Press Wirephoto

PROTEST TEACHER'S DISMISSAL: Students of Catholic University of America in Washington, demonstrating for reinstatement of the Rev. Charles E. Curran, who was dismissed as instructor effective Aug. 31. In background is Immaculate Conception shrine.

ARMY IS REPORTED RULING IN GREECE ON KING'S ORDER

Military Radio Asserts Step Was Taken to Keep Peace —Curbs Announced

By The Associated Press

LONDON, Friday, April 21—An army radio station in Athens said today that the military had taken control of Greece under a royal proclamation signed by King Constantine, Premier Panayotis Kanellopoulos and his Cabinet.

The broadcast, monitored in London, said the army took over at midnight last night to preserve public order.

Vehicles were ordered off city streets and the public was warned against hoarding food.

Monitors said the broadcast was made by the Athens army radio.

Telephone service to Athens was not obtainable. Early yesterday, Greek telecommunications personnel went on a 24-hour strike for higher pay.

First word of the army takeover did not make it clear which side in Greece's political crisis the army had taken. There was immediate speculation in London, however, that the army action was a move to strengthen 26-year-old King Constantine in his long struggle with the 80-year-old former Premier, George Papandreou, leader of the powerful Center Union party. Observers believed that if the army had taken over, it had done so to strengthen the King's position by disbanding political parties.

Origins of Crisis

The speculation seemed to be borne out by the army broadcast.

There was no immediate word on what had happened to the country's political leaders.

Mr. Papandreou and his son Andreas have been outspoken critics of the monarchy, accusing it of meddling in politics, while many of the top army officers are known partisans of the throne.

Greece's latest political crisis began last month when the interim Government of Premier Ioannis Paraskevopoulos resigned after three months in office.

King Constantine summoned a meeting of all parliamentary leaders to try to form a coalition Government, but the meeting was boycotted by the elder Papandreou, whose Center Union held 172 of the 300 seats in Parliament.

New Government Falls

King Constantine then asked the National Radical Union leader, Panayotis Kanellopoulos, to form a Government pending new elections. Premier Kanellopoulos took over on April 3, but his Government was unable to function. Last Friday he dissolved Parliament and ordered elections for May 28.

His Government was to stay in power during the campaign

Continued on Page 17, Column 3

7 Vietnam Allies Confer; Troop Needs Are Studied

By HEDRICK SMITH

Special to The New York Times

WASHINGTON, April 20—The United States and its six allies in the Vietnam war held their first high-level strategy conference in six months today amid private talk of the need for more troops for the war effort.

An authorized conference source said that American and Asian spokesmen mentioned the increasing Communist "aggressiveness" in the northern provinces of South Vietnam, but said they did not deal directly with the question of new troop commitments in their formal discussions.

Excerpts from communiqué are printed on Page 6.

Some participants indicated privately, however, that rising tensions near the demilitarized zone dividing north and south had increased the need for sizable new American forces in Vietnam.

Reds' Propaganda Noted

Two themes dominated today's session, conference sources reported. One was the allies' concern that a worldwide Communist propaganda campaign had put them on the defensive. The other was the caution expressed by some delegations over the dangers of being lured into false cease-fires or sham peace talks by the Communists.

The seven allies, who held their first strategy meeting last October in Manila, met behind closed doors this afternoon after the conclusion of a three-day ministerial meeting of the Southeast Asia Treaty Organization.

In a final communiqué, the SEATO group indirectly endorsed continued American bombing of North Vietnam until Hanoi agreed to scale down its own military activities. "It is agreed that reciprocity is an essential element of any acceptable proposal for reduction in the fighting" the declaration by the treaty group's council declared.

The treaty organization and the seven-nation Manila group largely overlap. Australia, New Zealand, the Phillippines, Thailand and the United States are members of both groups. Britain and Pakistan are members

Continued on Page 7, Column 1

TOLL OF CIVILIANS RISING IN VIETNAM

First Official U.S. Figures on Wounded in the South Show a 3-Year Climb

By JONATHAN RANDAL

Special to The New York Times

SAIGON, South Vietnam, April 20—United States officials have disclosed that the number of civilian casualties in South Vietnam is rising as the tempo of the war increases.

About 50,000 civilians may be treated for war-related injuries in Government hospitals this year, according to an estimate by Maj. Gen. James W. Humphreys, director of the United States aid mission's Office of Public Health.

In an interview, the Air Force general disclosed the first major American statistical effort to keep track of civilian casualties in South Vietnam.

Critics' Role Cited

Before the survey, no reliable statistics were kept by either South Vietnamese or United States authorities. Civilian casualties were not distinguished from other hospital cases. The change is generally attributed to criticism from opponents of the Johnson Administration's position in Vietnam.

General Humphreys disclosed his estimate at a time when American military and civilian officials were voicing concern over such criticism. In particular, there is bitter resentment of an article in the January issue of Ramparts magazine, which asserted that allied weapons had caused "at least a million child casualties since 1961."

Barry Zorthian, director of the United States public-affairs office here, has called the article "a fantasia of numbers"

Continued on Page 8, Column 1

PARENTS WILL GET CITY SCHOOL VOICE

East Harlem and West Side to Choose Administrators in Experimental Plan

By GENE CURRIVAN

For the first time the Board of Education is planning to give parents and community representatives an authoritative role in administering schools.

The experiment will be conducted in East Harlem and the upper West Side where each of two communities will elect its own board and choose an administrator who will share "the full administration of the schools." If successful, the plan would be extended to other schools.

The plan, announced yesterday at a news conference at the board's headquarters, 110 Livingston Street, Brooklyn, is part of a decentralization program providing for greater community involvement and the delegation of authority to school districts.

Under the plan, which will not be put into effect until parents, local boards and community representatives help work out details, there will be two groups of schools, each with its own elected board and administrator. No deadline was set for implementation.

One of the groups will include Intermediate School 201, in East Harlem, where the parents conducted boycotts and demonstrations last September demanding "control" of the school and the right to select the principal. The dispute was never resolved inasmuch as the board refused to abdicate its rights.

I.S. 201 is in District 4, which includes its feeders,

Continued on Page 26, Column 2

Catholic U. Classes Stopped as Protest Spreads in Faculty

By JOHN D. MORRIS

Special to The New York Times

WASHINGTON, April 20—Nearly all classes were suspended today in a spreading strike of students and teachers at the Catholic University of America.

Protests against the threatened dismissal of the Rev. Charles E. Curran, 33-year-old assistant professor of moral theology, took on aspects of a full-scale revolt against the Cardinals and Bishops who govern the institution.

Father Curran, who is known for his liberal views on birth control and other doctrinal issues, was notified Monday that his two-year contract would not be renewed after it expired Aug. 31. No reason was given.

It is generally assumed on the campus that the action was prompted by Father Curran's written and spoken theological views, particularly those in favor of relaxing the church's stand against the use of contraceptives by Catholics.

Faculty Votes

The decision against renewing Father Curran's contract was taken at a recent secret meeting of the university's board of trustees, which consists of 33 Cardinals, Archbishops and Bishops and 11 laymen. The board, which governs the university on behalf of the Pope, is headed by Cardinal Spellman of New York.

With almost all of the 6,600 students boycotting classes since the start of the day, faculty members from the university's 11 schools voted at a mass meeting this afternoon to go on strike.

"We cannot and will not function as members of our respec-

Continued on Page 50, Column 2

RIGHTS PROGRESS URGED BY ROMNEY

Legislation on All Levels Is Sought in Speech Here at A.J.C. Banquet

Gov. George Romney said yesterday that "more is needed" in Federal civil rights legislation. It was the second major message of his undeclared campaign for the Republican nomination for President.

In his address he did not spell out precisely what legislation he had in mind.

Addressing a banquet of the American Jewish Committee in the Americana hotel, Mr. Romney declared: "The elimination of social injustice depends not only on Federal action, but on state action, local action and private, personal action. All four are needed."

With a grin, the Michigan Governor began his 15-minute speech by alluding to the public fund-raising effort at the dinner. It produced $1-million in pledges. "As my contribution," he said, "I've discarded my script."

He then skipped in and out of his five-page text, interpolating a long reference to his Mormon sect, which he had mentioned only briefly in his prepared remarks.

The Mormons, he said, con-

Continued on Page 26, Column 2

CITY IS CHECKING ON COST OF BOOKS

Rankin Charges Conspiracy on Works for Children

By HENRY RAYMONT

An investigation has been started by the Lindsay administration to determine whether New York City's schools and public libraries have been paying artificially high prices for children's books for years.

Corporation Counsel J. Lee Rankin said yesterday that although the data from the inquiry were not complete, he was convinced that the city had been overcharged by major book publishers.

Mr. Rankin disclosed in an interview that he was planning to file an antitrust suit against publishing houses, possibly as an adjunct to litigation already initiated in Philadelphia and by several other cities, including Rochester, Los Angeles and Madison, Wis. A Federal suit against children's book publishers has also been filed.

"There's no question in my mind that conspiracy is involved in the sale of library editions of children's books," the Corporation Counsel declared. "We are now trying to assess to what extent this has damaged New York City schools and public libraries."

He added that he expected the city's claim to be "very substantial."

In the lawsuit that was started last June by the public libraries of Philadelphia, 14 publishers and three wholesale distributors were charged with conspiracy to fix prices of library editions. The plaintiffs asked the Eastern District Court of Pennsylvania to award

Continued on Page 36, Column 4

40,000 Rubber Workers Strike Three Big Tire Manufacturers

By BEN A. FRANKLIN

Special to The New York Times

AKRON, Ohio, Friday, April 21—The United Rubber Workers union struck three of the Big Four tire manufacturers early today.

The union struck all plants of the Firestone Tire and Rubber Company, the B. F. Goodrich Company and UniRoyal, Inc., in a deadlocked dispute mainly over a proposal for a guaranteed annual wage.

It was the biggest strike in the union's 32-year history.

The strike was not the first simultaneous walkout against three of the Big Four tire companies. In 1959, the union pulled workers out of plants of the same three companies for a brief time and continued the strike against two of them—Firestone and Goodrich—for eight weeks.

The issue this time were regarded as far more complex.

The strike called early today affects more than 40,000 workers at 39 plants in Ohio and 15 other states. The struck companies were expected to resume meetings with union negotiators later today.

The talks had been under way for a month, against a strike deadline of midnight last night. The Firestone sessions, which were broken off by the union late last night, were held in Cleveland. Bargaining with Goodrich was in Columbus and with UniRoyal in Cincinnati.

The union said it would continue negotiations on a "day-to-day basis" with the Goodyear Tire and Rubber Company. But midnight shift workers at the

Continued on Page 50, Column 5

Word 'Idiot' in Paris Assembly Raises Passions to Dueling Point

By HENRY TANNER

Special to The New York Times

PARIS, April 20—Premier Georges Pompidou was shouted down for several minutes in the National Assembly today as he refused to yield the floor while defending his Government against Opposition criticism.

Feelings became so heated and the language so strong that Gaston Defferre, Mayor of Marseilles and one of the four leading figures of the non-Communist left, was challenged to a duel by a Gaullist deputy.

The Gaullist, René Ribière, asserted that Mr. Defferre had called him an "idiot." Afterward, when Mr. Defferre confirmed that this was so, Mr. Ribière sent him his two seconds.

The duel, which is not likely to draw much blood, is scheduled for tomorrow morning. Since dueling is against the law, the place must be kept secret or the police will be there.

"I want to get this over quickly, I have to be back in Marseilles tomorrow afternoon," Mr. Defferre said. He, too, named two seconds, and the four seconds conferred after the close of the session. Nobody, so far as could be found out, was slapped with a glove.

The angry scene came toward the end of a three-day debate in which the Assembly demonstrated its new unruly spirit. The unruliness results from last month's legislative election in which the Gaullists lost more than 40 seats to the parties of the left.

The Gaullists retain a narrow working majority in the Assembly, but the debate showed that the Opposition is determined to keep Mr. Pompidou under strong and constant pressure.

Mr. Pompidou, early during his rebuttal speech, had yielded the floor to François Mitterrand, the leader of the non-Communist Federation of the Left. Mr. Mitterrand, his voice nearly drowned out by Gaullist voices and banging of desk covers, repeated earlier charges of large-scale election frauds in overseas territories.

Later Mr. Pompidou refused to yield to Guy Mollet, the Socialist leader and former Premier.

Mr. Mollet felt insulted by Mr. Pompidou's assertion that the Mollet Government, which was in power shortly before General de Gaulle's return, had brought the country to the brink of bankruptcy.

The Assembly President, Jacques Chaban-Delmas, a Gaullist, told the Assembly that he

Continued on Page 4, Column 1

U.S. Guarantees Aid to Thais; Plans to Let China Get Drugs

Spur to Private Capital

By FELIX BELAIR Jr.

Special to The New York Times

WASHINGTON, April 20 — The United States began blazing a new trail today to induce private capital to help increase agricultural production in developing countries.

In a radical departure from its usual government-to-government loans and technical assistance grants, the Agency for International Development issued an "extended risk" guarantee of a $3-million bank loan by the Chemical Bank New York Trust Company to modernize agriculture in Thailand.

The bank loan goes to the Thailand subsidiary of Calabrian Company of New York. The effect of the arrangement is that the New York trading concern is guaranteed against

Continued on Page 18, Column 1

New Gesture to Peking

By B. DRUMMOND AYRES Jr.

Special to The New York Times

WASHINGTON, April 20—The United States is prepared to relax its strict trade embargo of Communist China so that American drugs may be sold or donated to thousands of Chinese suffering from cholera, meningitis and infectious hepatitis, Government officials said tonight.

The relaxation of the embargo was described by the officials as a humanitarian gesture motivated by reports that parts of China are being swept by various epidemics that the Chinese Government is having difficulty controlling because of drug shortages.

But the move also was seen as another step by Washington to improve relations with

Continued on Page 18, Column 2

U.S. GETS GO-AHEAD ON NUCLEAR PACT

NATO Backs Reopening of Talks With Soviet on Text

By RICHARD E. MOONEY

Special to The New York Times

PARIS, April 20 — United States officials said today that they had received "a green light" from the Atlantic allies to resume negotiations with Moscow for a treaty to prevent the spread of nuclear weapons. They declared that the talks would be reopened soon.

A West German official, reflecting the fact that his Government and others still objected to some fundamental aspects of the proposed treaty, said: "It looks more like a yellow light to us."

These comments followed a two-hour meeting of the permanent council of the North Atlantic Treaty Organization. For

Continued on Page 3, Column 1

NEWS INDEX

"All the News That's Fit to Print"

The New York Times

LATE CITY EDITION

Weather: Fair and warm today and tonight. Partly cloudy tomorrow. Temp. range: today 85-63; Wed. 81-62. Temp.-Hum. Index: mid-70's; Wed. 72. Full report on Page 93.

VOL. CXVI . No. 39,947 NEW YORK, THURSDAY, JUNE 8, 1967 10 CENTS

ISRAELIS ROUT THE ARABS, APPROACH SUEZ, BREAK BLOCKADE, OCCUPY OLD JERUSALEM; AGREE TO U.N. CEASE-FIRE; U.A.R. REJECTS IT

JOHNSON WILL USE CABINET TO COURT STATES' OFFICIALS

Aides Will Seek to Tighten Ties Between Governors and the White House

By WARREN WEAVER Jr.
Special to The New York Times

WASHINGTON, June 7—President Johnson has decided to use the members of his Cabinet as diplomatic agents in his campaign to improve relations between the Administration and state governments.

The President has approved a plan under which each member of the Cabinet would be assigned four or five states as his personal responsibility, with instructions to maintain personal contact between the Governors and the White House.

As part of the same effort, each of the 50 states will be given a "day" in Washington next fall and winter, when a planeload of its key officials will fly here to hold conferences all over the capital, capped by a meeting of the Governors with the President.

Bryant's Work Continued

Both projects reflect Mr. Johnson's continuing determination to build domestic as well as foreign bridges by working to sort out the tangled Federal-state relations that have been increasingly complicated by the administration of the Great Society programs.

Both are attempts to give some permanency to the contacts established during the last four months by Farris Bryant, the President's envoy to the states, on visits to 40 capitals with a squad of Federal experts.

Mr. Bryant, a former Governor of Florida who is now the director of the Office of Emergency Planning, plans to leave his White House post this summer, possibly to return to politics in his home state, and he is eager to help establish more permanent lines of communication before his departure.

As now envisioned, each Cabinet officer would visit all of

Continued on Page 29, Column 2

Rise in Debt Ceiling Rejected in House; Johnson Rebuffed

Special to The New York Times

WASHINGTON, June 7—The House of Representatives dealt the Johnson Administration a sharp setback today by rejecting a bill to increase the ceiling on the national debt $29-billion, to $365-billion.

The vote against passage was 210 to 197, with Republicans voting solidly to kill the bill. Enough Democrats, mostly Southerners, voted with them to turn the tide.

About six Northern Democratic "doves"—opponents of the war in Vietnam—also joined the opposition.

In all, 34 Democrats joined with 176 Republicans to defeat the measure.

Today's action raised the possibility—though a slim one—of financial chaos after June 30. At that time the debt limit reverts to its "permanent" ceiling of $285-billion, though the debt, at $330-billion, is already far above that level. The legal authority of the Treasury to pay its bills would be in doubt.

However, the Ways and

Continued on Page 30, Column 4

U.S. VOWS TO SEEK A DURABLE PEACE

Johnson Recalls Bundy for New Mideast Planning Unit —'Real Chance' Is Seen

By MAX FRANKEL
Special to The New York Times

WASHINGTON, June 7—President Johnson pledged today to do his best to help translate the new Middle Eastern situation into a more lasting settlement between Israel and her Arab neighbors.

Apparently hoping to exploit Israel's lightning military success—which has surprised but not displeased the White House—Mr. Johnson ordered the drafting of special policies for a "new peace" and set up new machinery to deal with the situation.

The President said that the United States, which had worked hard to avoid the war, felt that "there is now a real chance" to turn from "the frustrations of the past to the hopes of a peaceful future."

But Mr. Johnson said the handling of the crisis and the preparations for a lasting settlement would require the most careful consideration in the United States Government. To organize that effort he recalled McGeorge Bundy to temporary duty at the White House as executive secretary to a special subcommittee of the National Security Council.

Mr. Bundy will seek a temporary leave from the presidency of the Ford Foundation, which he assumed last year after serving as special assistant for

Continued on Page 19, Column 1

CONFEREES BLOCK A DRAFT LOTTERY

Compromise Bill Continues Deferment of Students

By United Press International

WASHINGTON, June 7—Senate and House negotiators reached agreement today on a new military draft bill that rules out, for the present, any lottery-like random selection system to determine the order of induction.

The bill was a compromise of differing bills that the Senate and House had passed. It would guarantee the continuance of educational deferments for college undergraduates and students enrolled in apprentice and job training programs.

Senator Richard B. Russell, Democrat of Georgia, who is chairman of the Senate conferees, said the Senate might act on the four-year draft extension bill tomorrow. House action must await approval by the Senate.

Congressional action will clear the way for President Johnson, under current discretionary powers, to reverse the order of induction and take 19-year-olds first from the Selec-

Continued on Page 3, Column 1

Dorothy Parker, 73, Literary Wit, Dies

By ALDEN WHITMAN

Dorothy Parker, the sardonic humorist who purveyed her wit in conversation, short stories, verse and criticism, died of a heart attack yesterday afternoon in her suite at the Volney Hotel, 23 East 74th Street. She was 73 years old and had been in frail health in recent years.

In print and in person, Miss Parker sparkled with a word or a phrase, for she honed her humor to its most economical size. Her rapier wit, much of it spontaneous, gained its early renown from her membership in the Algonquin Round Table, an informal luncheon club at the Algonquin Hotel in the nineteen-twenties, where some of

Continued on Page 38, Column 1

NEWS INDEX

EBAN SEES THANT

Says Acceptance Is Based on Enemy's Reciprocal Action

Excerpts from debate at U.N. are printed on Page 18.

By DREW MIDDLETON
Special to The New York Times

UNITED NATIONS, N. Y., June 7—The Security Council unanimously adopted a Soviet resolution today calling on the combatants in the Middle East to "cease fire and all military activities" at 4 P.M., New York time today.

The Government of Israel shortly thereafter announced that she had accepted the call of the Council for a cease-fire, provided her Arab foes agreed.

In the evening, reports from the Middle East indicated rejection of the call by the United Arab Republic, Syria, Iraq, Saudi Arabia, Algeria and Kuwait. Jordan told Secretary General Thant that she would abide by the cease-fire, except in self-defense.

Says It's in Effect

Abba Eban, the Foreign Minister of Israel, told the Secretary General that a cease-fire was already in effect between Jordan and Israel.

In presenting the resolution, the Soviet delegate, Nikolai T. Fedorenko, made it clear that if Israel failed to heed the Security Council's demands, Moscow would consider severing diplomatic relations. The original Security Council resolution, adopted yesterday, simply called for a cease-fire.

But the reports from the Arab capitals indicate, diplomatic sources here said, that military operations will continue.

According to diplomats, the best hope lies in a draft resolution presented by George Ignatieff, the Canadian delegate. This proposes that the President of the Security Council and the Secretary General take measures to insure compliance with the resolutions.

Today's resolution demanded that the combatants "cease fire and all military activities on 7 June 1967 by 2000 hours Greenwich mean time." The resolution was adopted less than an hour before this time, which is 4 P.M. New York time, 10 P.M. in Jordan and Israel and 11 P.M. in the United Arab Republic and Syria.

The Council adjourned without voting on the Canadian draft largely because Milko Ta-

Continued on Page 18, Column 2

United Press International Radiophoto

OLD JERUSALEM IS NOW IN ISRAELI HANDS: Israeli soldiers in prayer at the Wailing Wall yesterday

Major Mideast Developments

On the Battlefronts

Israel claimed victory in the Sinai Desert after three days of fighting. Sharm el Sheik, guarding the entrance to the Gulf of Aqaba, fell after a paratroop attack, and the Israelis said the blockade of the gulf was broken. Other Israeli units were within 20 miles of the Suez Canal, and one Israeli report placed them in the eastern section of Ismailia, on the canal itself.

In Jerusalem, for the first time in 19 years, Israeli Jews prayed at the Wailing Wall as their troops occupied the Old City. Israeli troops captured Jericho, in Jordan, and sped northward to take Nablus, giving them control of the west bank of the Jordan.

The Egyptian High Command reported that its forces had fallen back from first-line positions in the Sinai Peninsula and were fighting fiercely from unspecified secondary positions. It announced that Egyptian troops had pulled back from Sharm el Sheik to join main defense units.

In the Capitals

In the United Nations, Israel accepted the call for a cease-fire, provided the Arabs complied. Jordan announced that she would accept and ordered her troops to fire only in self-defense. But Baghdad declared that Iraq had refused. There were indications that Syria, Algeria and Kuwait were also opposed.

In Cairo, an Egyptian official said the United Arab Republic would fight on.

In Moscow, the Soviet Union threatened to break diplomatic relations with Israel if she did not observe the cease-fire.

In Paris, the French proposed an international agreement for free passage in the Gulf of Aqaba similar to the one governing the Dardanelles in Turkey.

In Washington, President Johnson promised to seek a settlement that would assure lasting peace in the Mideast.

In London, the British urged the Israelis to halt before they aroused more turmoil in the Arab world and diminished the chances for a settlement.

Continued on Page 18, Column 2

Israelis Weep and Pray Beside the Wailing Wall

By TERENCE SMITH
Special to The New York Times

JERUSALEM, June 7—Israeli troops wept and prayed today at the foot of the Wailing Wall—the last remnant of Solomon's Second Temple and the object of pilgrimage by Jews through the centuries.

In battle dress and still carrying their weapons, they gathered at the base of the sand-colored wall and sang Hallel, a series of prayers reserved for occasions of great joy.

They were repeating a tradition that goes back 2,000 years but has been denied Israeli Jews since 1948, when the first of three wars with the Arabs ended in this area.

The wall is all that remains of the Second Temple, built in the 10th century before Christ and destroyed by the Romans in A.D. 70.

The Israelis, trembling with emotion, bowed vigorously from the waist as they chanted psalms in a lusty chorus. Most had submachine guns slung over their shoulders and several held bazookas as they prayed.

Among the leaders to pray at the wall was Maj. Gen. Moshe Dayan, the new Defense Minister. He told the troops:

"We have returned to the holiest of our holy places, never to depart from it again."

General Dayan, who was ap-

Continued on Page 17, Column 1

CAIRO ANNOUNCES A SINAI PULLBACK

Blames Foreign Aid to Foe, but Says Troops Fight On in Secondary Positions

By ERIC PACE
Special to The New York Times

CAIRO, June 7—An Egyptian military communiqué reported today that forces of the United Arab Republic had fallen back from some first-line positions on the Sinai Peninsula and were engaged in fierce fighting against Israeli troops from secondary positions.

Another statement of the High Command, broadcast four hours later by the Cairo radio, said Egyptian troops at Sharm el Sheik, guarding the entrance to the Gulf of Aqaba, had joined other Egyptian forces "now concentrated in the Sinai Peninsula."

There was no elaboration, but the communiqué, broadcast about 5:30 P.M., appeared to confirm Israeli reports that the Egyptians had been forced to retreat from Sharm el Sheik.

At night, the High Command reported that Israeli paratroops had dropped over the "second-line Egyptian front" but had been "completely wiped out."

The communiqué also said the Israelis had tried another drop at Sharm el Sheik after the

Continued on Page 17, Column 6

AQABA GULF OPEN

Dayan Asserts Israel Does Not Intend to Capture the Canal

By The Associated Press

TEL AVIV, June 7—Israel proclaimed victory tonight in the Sinai Peninsula campaign against the United Arab Republic. On the eastern front, both the Old City of Jerusalem and Bethlehem were captured from the Jordanians.

"The Egyptians are defeated," said Maj. Gen. Itzhak Rabin, the Israeli Chief of Staff. "All their efforts are aimed at withdrawing behind the Suez Canal, and we are taking care of that. The whole area is in our hands. The main effort of the Egyptians is to save themselves."

Israel Losses 'Not Great'

Describing the developments through the third day of this third Arab-Israeli war in 19 years, General Rabin made these claims:

¶Sinai, the Egyptian territory between Israel's Negev Desert and the Suez Canal, is taken.

¶Most of the Jordanian territory on the west bank of the Jordan River, including Jericho, is in Israeli hands, and most of Jordan's army has been captured.

¶Relative to what was done, the number of Israelis casualties was "not great."

The Israelis were reported to have swept to the Suez Canal.

[An Israeli delegation source at the United Nations said Israeli troops had seized that part of the canal city of Ismailia that is on the eastern side of the waterway. But this was denied by an army source in Tel Aviv, who said, according to Reuters, that the Israelis had not taken any point along the canal.

[Maj. Gen. Moshe Dayan, the Israeli Defense Minister, declared that there was "no intention" of taking the canal, United Press International reported.]

'Never to Depart'

After the fall of the Old City of Jerusalem, Defense Minister Moshe Dayan said there that the Israelis had reunited their capital and would never "depart from it again."

Israel reported that paratroops aided by naval units had captured Sharm el Sheik, commanding the entrance to the Gulf of Aqaba, and said the blockade that the Egyptians had mounted from that position had been broken.

"The Strait of Tiran is now open," General Rabin said.

Israel's chief of staff said his men had taken on the United Arab Republic, Jordan, Syria and Iraq, knocked out their air forces and overrun their armor and infantry.

"All this the armed forces of Israel did alone," he declared.

The general then turned over the briefing to Brig. Mordechai Hod, commander of the air force, who announced 441 Arab

Continued on Page 16, Column 1

The New York Times June 8, 1967

CONQUEST IN THE MIDEAST: Israeli troops took Sharm el Sheik (1), drove on to the Suez Canal (2) and seized control of the Old City in Jerusalem (3). Photo was taken in September, 1966, during the flight of Gemini II.

Pentagon Believes Israeli Jets Struck From Sea, Eluded Radar

By WILLIAM BEECHER
Special to The New York Times

WASHINGTON, June 7—At least a part of the Israeli Air Force that caught large numbers of Egyptian aircraft on the ground in the early hours of the war may have slipped through gaps in the United Arab Republic's radar net by flying in over the Mediterranean.

This possibility was raised today by Pentagon analysts. If correct, it would help to explain how Israeli pilots were able to surprise so many Egyptian jets before they could get into the air.

It might also serve to provide part of the explanation behind insistent Arab assertions that carrier-based United States and British jets participated in the raids.

The early blows to Arab, and especially Egyptian, air strength is credited by most military analysts as having been a decisive factor in the Israeli successes on land that followed.

"We know that some of the Israeli planes returned to their bases by way of the sea," one ranking officer said, "and we assume they may have approached from the seaward too."

The officer said it was obvious that Israel had excellent intelligence on weaknesses in the Egyptian radar system and exploited them.

Shortly after the raids, he went on, the Jordanian radio charged that Jordanian radar

Continued on Page 18, Column 8

"All the News That's Fit to Print"

The New York Times

LATE CITY EDITION

Weather: Fair and warm today, tonight and tomorrow. Temp. range: today 85-63; Thurs. 85-64. Temp.-Hum. Index: today 70 to 75; Thurs. 77. Full U.S. report on Page 89.

VOL. CXVI..No. 39,948 NEW YORK, FRIDAY, JUNE 9, 1967 10 CENTS

EGYPT AND SYRIA AGREE TO U.N. CEASE-FIRE; ISRAEL REPORTS TROOPS REACH SUEZ CANAL; JOHNSON, KOSYGIN USED HOT LINE IN CRISIS

SENATE APPROVES A TIGHTENED RULE ON REDISTRICTING

33 States Ordered to Bring Population Variant Down to 10% by 1968 Election

By JAMES F. CLARITY
Special to The New York Times

WASHINGTON, June 8—The Senate approved today a bill requiring that by the 1968 election no state have a population variance of more than 10 cent between its largest and smallest Congressional districts.

The approval, which came in a surprise vote of 57 to 25, was a result of a fight by Senator Edward M. Kennedy, Democrat of Massachusetts, to amend a measure that would have permitted a variance of 35 per cent until the 1972 election.

The Kennedy amendment, which was soundly defeated in committee two weeks ago, is intended, according to the Senator, to make Congressional redistricting conform with the Supreme Court's one-man, one-vote ruling of 1964. The amendment also deleted language giving the states power to determine when the compactness of a district was "practicable."

An Altered Version

The measure, before it was amended today, was an altered version of a bill already passed by the House. The House bill provided for a population variance of 30 per cent, and was amended by the Senate Judiciary Committee to cover four additional states.

The version passed today, which now goes to a Senate-House conference, would apply to 33 states having variances of more than 10 per cent. Nine of these states are under Federal court orders to redistrict. The 17 states not covered by today's Senate action either elect Representatives at large or have variances lower than 10 per cent.

Mr. Kennedy's proposal was approved, first in a crucial 44-to-39 vote as an amendment, then in the final vote on the bill as amended, 57 to 25.

"We knew it would be close.

Continued on Page 26, Column 1

Arms Cost Stress Scored by Rickover

By EVERT CLARK
Special to The New York Times

WASHINGTON, June 8—Vice Adm. Hyman G. Rickover has denounced the cost-effectiveness approach to weapons development as an "ism," a "new religion" and a "fog bomb" that is keeping the nation from gaining technology that would save lives.

In Congressional testimony released today, the head of the nuclear-powered ship program attacked present management techniques in the Pentagon.

By Presidential order, many of these techniques—including the mathematical analysis of cost vs. effectiveness—are now being spread throughout the executive branch of

Continued on Page 2, Column 4

JURY FINDS LAXITY IN BUILDINGS UNIT

Graft, Shirking and Lack of Personnel Training Are Cited—Moerdler Agrees

By JACK ROTH

A New York County grand jury criticized yesterday long-standing conditions in the Buildings Department that it said had resulted in corruption among housing inspectors and landlords.

The jury also said the situation permitted some inspectors and their supervisors to quit work as early as 10:30 A.M. and go to bars and racetracks for the rest of the day.

The jury, in a presentment handed up to Supreme Court Justice Mitchell D. Schweitzer, charged that the department suffered from lack of financial and manpower resources.

It asserted that inspectors were not properly trained for their jobs, that they were unaware of their department's rules and regulations, that there was duplication in inspections, that electronic processing equipment was failing to do its job and that unauthorized persons had access to file rooms and private departmental offices.

The Buildings Commissioner,

Continued on Page 31, Column 1

ALL SINAI IS HELD

U.A.R. Loses 50 Tanks in Actions Termed Fiercest of War

By Reuters

TEL AVIV, Friday, June 9—Israeli troops have reached the bank of the Suez Canal and have taken control of the entire Sinai Peninsula, the Israeli radio reported this morning.

The radio broadcast the text of a message from the commander in the southern front, to the Chief of Staff, Gen. Yitzhak Rabin. The message said:

"Happy to inform you that our forces are stationed on the bank of the Suez Canal and the Red Sea. The Sinai Peninsula is in our hands. Greetings to you and to the whole defense forces of Israel."

Battle reports yesterday indicated that the remnants of two Egyptian armored divisions and four infantry divisions were trapped in the western part of that Sinai Desert.

50 Tanks Reported Wrecked

The news of Cairo's acceptance of the United Nations cease-fire coincided with an announcement by an Israeli spokesman that three battles in the desert yesterday had been "the fiercest in this war."

The Israelis said they had shot down eight Egyptian planes and destroyed at least 50 Egyptian tanks during the fighting.

Other tanks were wrecked and left on the road to Qanbara, about 30 miles north of Ismailia, about midway along the 100-mile Suez Canal.

Among the Egyptian planes downed were a Soviet-made Ilyushin bomber and several Soviet-built Sukhoi-7's. Israeli planes also struck Soviet-made missile sites in the Suez Canal zone during daylight raids, the spokesman added.

Despite the continuation of heavy fighting, the Israeli spokesman said that all escape routes for Egyptian armored units had been closed.

He added that Israeli forces had captured oilfields at Ras Sudar, south of the port of Taufiq on the western coast of the Sinai Peninsula. Israeli soldiers said the wells were afire

Continued on Page 17, Column 6

United Press International Cablephoto

AFTER THE BATTLE: Egyptian prisoners, prone on the sand, their hands behind their heads, are guarded in a compound by Israeli troops at El Arish in the northern Sinai Peninsula. El Arish was taken by Israel Tuesday.

A SHIFT BY CAIRO

Thant Notifies Council in Middle of Debate on Resolutions

Excerpts from the U.N. debate are printed on Page 16.

By DREW MIDDLETON
Special to The New York Times

UNITED NATIONS, N. Y., June 8—The United Arab Republic, the leader of the anti-Israel coalition, today accepted the Security Council's demand for a cease-fire in the Middle East provided Israel did the same.

Yesterday, the delegate of Israel said his country accepted the cease-fire provided Israel's foes agreed to it. Reports here yesterday indicated rejection by Cairo.

Syria gave notice tonight that she would also comply, informing the Secretary General after the Security Council recessed.

This afternoon, in his dry, precise voice Secretary General Thant read to the Council a brief letter from Mohamed Awad el-Kony, the Egyptian delegate, disclosing that President Gamal Abdel Nasser's Government had "decided to accept the cease-fire" called for in the two Council resolutions "on the condition that the other party ceases fire."

He Scraps Long Speech

Mr. el-Kony wrote the letter after a long telephone conversation with Cairo shortly before the Council meeting began. After the call, he scrapped a 20-page speech he had prepared and wrote the note to Mr. Thant.

The Israeli Foreign Minister, Abba Eban, hailed "the immediate prospect" of a cease-fire as "a notable step" and called on other Arab governments to follow the Egyptian lead.

Cairo's acceptance of the Council resolutions adopted unanimously on Tuesday and Wednesday raised rather than lowered the heat of the debate between the United States and the Soviet Union over the resolutions each submitted to the Council.

Arthur J. Goldberg, the United States delegate, saying he hoped for a peace "stable and just to all concerned," submitted a draft of a resolution calling for the "withdrawal and disengagement of armed personnel," the renunciation of force, "the maintenance of vital international rights" and the establishment of a durable peace in the area.

The Administration was said

Continued on Page 17, Column 1

EGYPTIANS TOLD OF TRUCE DECISION

Cairo Broadcast Is Terse —Syrians Also Announce Approval of Cease-Fire

By ERIC PACE
Special to The New York Times

CAIRO, Friday, June 9—The Government told the Egyptian people this morning that it had conditionally accepted a cease-fire in the war with Israel.

There was no immediate popular reaction because the Cairo radio waited until early morning before announcing, more than three hours after the fact, that the United Arab Republic had told Secretary General Thant of the United Nations that it would agree to a truce if Israel did so.

[The Damascus radio announced that Syria, too, had accepted the cease-fire, Reuters reported. Page 17.]

Cairo was blacked out as protection against possible Israeli air raids when the news came, but nocturnal strollers reported that policemen were already taking down at least some of the anti-Israeli banners that have festooned the city for the last few weeks.

An early edition of a popular Cairo newspaper, Al Akhbar, put the news on the front page but made no comment. There was also no elaboration from the radio, which broadcast a military communiqué saying that the battle against Israel was continuing at all points along the Egyptian front.

The terse announcement of the cease-fire contrasted with

Continued on Page 17, Column 2

Major Mideast Developments

In the Capitals

The United Arab Republic accepted a United Nations cease-fire. Israel had previously agreed to stop hostilities if her enemies were willing to go along.

In Damascus, after a series of militant vows to fight on, the Syrians announced that they would also accept the cease-fire.

President Johnson welcomed the cease-fire agreement and urged prompt action to solve the "many more fundamental" questions in the Middle East.

An emergency declaration on oil was being considered by the Johnson Administration after major oil companies reported that a worldwide transportation problem had resulted from the war.

The hot line between Washington and Moscow was used this week for the first time during a crisis.

On the Battlefronts

Before the cease-fire went into effect, Israeli planes and torpedo boats mistakenly attacked a United States communications ship about 15 miles off Sinai. The Pentagon reported that 10 Americans had been killed and 100 wounded. Israel sent an apology.

Israel reported that her troops had reached the bank of the Suez Canal and that the entire Sinai Peninsula was under her control. Earlier Israel reported three fierce desert battles in which at least 50 Egyptian tanks had been destroyed.

The United Arab Republic announced that its air force had inflicted heavy damage on Israeli armored columns trying to advance westward from El Arish in the Sinai Peninsula.

At the Strait of Tiran, a Soviet freighter bound for the Jordanian port of Aqaba was the first ship to pass since Israel declared the waterway open to shipping on Wednesday. Two Israeli ships prepared to follow.

JOHNSON PLEASED BY GAINS ON TRUCE

Looks to a Stable Peace—White House Discloses Use of the Hot Line

Texts of the Mansfield letter and Johnson reply, Page 18.

By MAX FRANKEL
Special to The New York Times

WASHINGTON, June 8—President Johnson welcomed spreading acceptance of a cease-fire agreement in the Middle East today, but urged all parties to move promptly toward the "many more fundamental questions" bearing on a stable peace.

While thus pressing for more than merely another frail armistice, the While House also disclosed that its hot-line connection with Moscow had been used for the first time this week in an international crisis.

The United States used the teletype link this morning when it heard of an attack on an American communications ship off the Sinai Peninsula. At the time, the source of the attack was not known.

The Soviet Government, whose warships have been observing the movements of the United States Sixth Fleet in the eastern Mediterranean, was advised that the carrier-based American planes were scrambling into action for the sole purpose of assisting the distressed vessel.

It was later learned that Israeli forces had attacked the American ship in error.

The announcement of quick exchanges to prevent misunder-

Continued on Page 18, Column 1

The New York Times June 9, 1967

CRUSHING OFFENSIVES: Israelis thrust westward across northern Sinai (1) to the Suez Canal after sharp fighting at Bir Gifgafa and Mitla Pass, and routed Egyptians at Nakhl and Thamed in drive farther south (2). Soviet ship passed through Strait of Tiran (3), now under Israeli control. Mistaken Israeli attack on U.S. ship in Mediterranean (4) killed 10 men. Israelis held west bank of the River Jordan as far north as Jenin (5).

U.S. Planes Batter MIG Base in North

Special to The New York Times

SAIGON, South Vietnam, June 8 — American fighter-bombers knocked out a MIG base near Hanoi yesterday and wrecked a surface-to-air missile storage area 50 miles southwest of the capital, the United States Command reported today.

At the same time, new fighting broke out just south of the demilitarized zone at the border between North Vietnam and South Vietnam, where a fierce battle raged for control of three hills last month.

Navy carrier pilots attacked the Kep Airfield, 37 miles northeast of Hanoi, for the seventh time since April 24. A headquarters spokesman said the airfield is "closed tempo-

Continued on Page 3, Column 4

DONATIONS POUR IN FOR ISRAELI FUND

Many Give All They Have—Some Gifts in Millions

By M. S. HANDLER

"You have got it all now," said a brief letter containing a check for $25,000.

The message was from a professor at the Jewish Theological Seminary who said he had gladly stripped himself of his worldly goods and sent the proceeds to the United Jewish Appeal for the Israel Emergency Fund.

The owner of two gas stations arrived at the appeal's offices and turned over the deeds to the stations as his contribution to the multimillion fund drive.

Other Jews walked in with the cash-surrender values of their life insurance policies. Still others, deeply moved by the Arab-Israeli war, sold real estate and securities and sent the money to the fund's headquarters, on the Avenue of the Americas at 51st street.

These were some examples of the dramas being played out in the Jewish communities across the United States, U.J.A. officials said yesterday.

The contributions, appeal of-

Continued on Page 11, Column 1

ISRAEL, IN ERROR, ATTACKS U.S. SHIP

10 Navy Men Die, 100 Hurt in Raids North of Sinai

By WILLIAM BEECHER
Special to The New York Times

WASHINGTON, June 8—An American naval vessel was mistakenly attacked by Israeli planes and torpedo boats today in international waters about 15 miles north of the Sinai Peninsula. Reports tonight listed the toll as 10 dead and 100 wounded. Twenty of the wounded were hurt critically.

The vessel, the Liberty, was on a peaceful, though war-related mission. Pentagon sources said she had been dispatched from Spain to the war zone to provide additional communications to facilitate the evacuation of American citizens from the Middle East and North Africa.

Pentagon officials said it was too early to tell whether indemnification would be asked from Israel for the loss of life and the damage to the Navy ship.

President Johnson, in a letter to the Senate majority leader, **Mike Mansfield,** noted that the

Continued on Page 19, Column 1

Russians Continue To Harass 6th Fleet

By NEIL SHEEHAN
Special to The New York Times

ABOARD U. S. S. AMERICA, in the Eastern Mediterranean, June 8—Two Soviet warships, a destroyer and a small, highly maneuverable patrol craft, moved into the formation of this Sixth Fleet carrier task force group this morning and began systematically harassing the American ships.

The harassment was undertaken despite a warning to another Soviet destroyer yesterday from Vice Adm. William I. Martin, the Sixth Fleet commander. Admiral Martin warned the Soviet vessel to withdraw from the area of the American formation. He said the Soviet ship, while following the carrier

Continued on Page 15, Column 1

SOVIET SHIP SAILS INTO AQABA GULF

Passage Is First Since Israel Lifted Arab Blockade

By Reuters

ELATH, Israel, June 8—A Soviet freighter bound for the Jordanian port of Aqaba passed through the Strait of Tiran today, the first ship to do so since Israel declared the passage an international waterway yesterday.

Two outgoing Israeli freighters were preparing to be the first Israeli ships to pass through the strait since the Egyptians blockaded the Gulf of Aqaba on May 23.

A report from Sharm el Sheik, which dominates the strait, dis-

Continued on Page 17, Column 7

NEWS INDEX

A Vietnamese mother and her children were forced to flee when a government attack on Vietcong outposts burned their village.

Carl Stokes of Cleveland became the first black mayor of a major U.S. city.

President Johnson and his daughter Lynda Bird with Soviet Premier Kosygin on his visit to the U.S.

Black Panther leader H. Rap Brown addressed a rally in Jacksonville, Florida. After a previous flare-up in Maryland he told his followers: "Burn this town down."

A National Guardsman amidst the blaze started by rioters incited by Black Power forces in Michigan.

Detroit was devastated by a racial outbreak. Forty-three people died before the Army restored peace to what was left of the motor city.

Military Police hurled back anti-war demonstrators who stormed the Pentagon.

"All the News That's Fit to Print"

The New York Times

LATE CITY EDITION

Weather: Cloudy in morning and tonight, fair in afternoon. Temp. range: today 80-58; Tues. 77-64. Temp.-Hum. Index in 70's. Tues. 72. Complete U.S. report on page 94.

VOL. CXVI . No. 39,953 NEW YORK, WEDNESDAY, JUNE 14, 1967 10 CENTS

SOVIET ASKS SHIFT OF MIDEAST ISSUE TO U.N. ASSEMBLY

Facing Veto in the Council, Moscow Seeks New Forum for Vote Against Israel

GROMYKO WRITES THANT

Asserts It Is Essential That U.N. Erase War's Results —He May Join Debate

By DREW MIDDLETON
Special to The New York Times

UNITED NATIONS, N. Y., June 13—The Soviet Government asked today for an emergency session of the General Assembly to enforce the withdrawal of Israeli forces from the Arab states.

Foreign Minister Andrei A. Gromyko, in a letter to Secretary General Thant, proposed that the session be convened within 24 hours. Mr. Gromyko, Soviet sources said, will be a member of the Soviet delegation, which will also include other "leading statesmen."

Reports circulated here that Premier Aleksei N. Kosygin would lead the delegation, but the reports could not be confirmed among Soviet officials.

The Soviet Union, Mr. Gromyko wrote, considers it essential that the General Assembly consider the situation in the Middle East and "adopt a decision designed to bring about the liquidation of the consequences of aggression and the immediate withdrawal of Israel forces behind the armistice lines."

Defeat Looms in Council

Mr. Gromyko's move to transfer the Soviet campaign for the withdrawal of Israeli forces from the Security Council to the General Assembly apparently reflected a realization that a proposal made by the Soviet Union today for a resolution on a pullback would be defeated in the 15-member Council. The Council meeting was called by the Soviet Union.

Nikolai T. Fedorenko, the Soviet delegate, demanded that the Council adopt the Soviet resolution today. He also challenged Arthur J. Goldberg to fulfill the United States pledge to maintain political independence and territorial integrity throughout the Middle East.

Ambassador Goldberg called the Soviet draft "a prescription for renewed hostilities."

Quotes May 24 Speech

Mr. Fedorenko quoted from the United States Ambassador's speech of May 24, in which Mr. Goldberg said that the United States "was firmly bound by the obligation to maintain political independence and territorial integrity of all—and I stress all—states in this area."

"We would like to ask," the Soviet delegate said, "if this statement of the distinguished representative of the United States is still valid and, if so, is the United States prepared to affirm it against the territorial claims of Tel Aviv?"

Despite the support for the Soviet draft in the Council by Bulgaria, India and Mali—who are members of the Council—

Continued on Page 16, Column 1

United Press International Cablephoto

ARABS RETURN TO WEST BANK OF THE JORDAN: People who had fled to the river's east bank, under pressure of the advancing Israeli Army, using ropes to help them cross back. King Hussein Bridge had been wrecked.

Arabs at U.N. Charge Israel Drove Out Thousands

By JUAN de ONIS
Special to The New York Times

UNITED NATIONS, N. Y., June 13—Jordan and Syria, backed by the Soviet Union, accused Israel today of having driven thousands of Arabs out of occupied territory in what the Jordanian delegate called a "pattern embarked upon in 1948," when Israel was established.

Dr. Muhammad H. el-Farra, Jordan's representative, called on Secretary General Thant for a report to the Security Council "on the security of the people living in the illegally occupied areas" and on the "exodus" from western Jordan that he said was under way.

George J. Tomeh, the Syrian delegate, said that "mass evictions and crimes against civilians" were being committed in territory occupied by Israel while the Security Council remained "silent and impotent."

Speaking for Israel, Mordecai R. Kidron said that some civilians had moved out of western Jordan during the fighting, but that a "large-scale return movement from east to west had now begun."

"Israeli authorities are doing nothing to prevent this," said Mr Kidron, who is Israel's representative at United Nations headquarters in Geneva. He is substituting here for Gideon Rafael, Israel's permanent representative, who has returned to Jerusalem for consultations.

Mr. Thant reported to the Council that he had requested assurances from the Israeli representative on the safety and well-being of civilians in the occupied territories and the protection of their rights.

Information reaching here on the civilian situation in those areas is sketchy because of difficulties in communica-

Continued on Page 16, Column 3

Johnson Avoids Specifics On U.S. Policy in Mideast

By JOHN W. FINNEY
Special to The New York Times

WASHINGTON, June 13—President Johnson affirmed today an American commitment to protect the territorial integrity of all nations in the Middle East and expressed the hope that a peace could be achieved to protect the interests of both Israel and the Arab states.

The President said at a news conference that the ways of achieving peace would "depend a good deal" on the nations directly involved in the conflict rather than on any peace formulas advanced by the United States [Question 1, Page 18.]

In what appeared to be an attempt to place the burden on Israel and her Arab neighbors for finding a settlement, the President left the United States attitude vague.

Israeli Stand Cited

The noncommittal character of the United States attitude is best illustrated by the problem raised by Israel's warning that she will not relinquish all the Arab territory she has occupied.

In a statement on May 23, before the fighting broke out, President Johnson said the United States was "firmly committed to the support of the political independence and territorial integrity of all nations of the area."

This commitment dates back to a declaration issued by the

Continued on Page 18, Column 2

CHOU DENOUNCES RED GUARDS' ACTS

Wall Posters Report Harsh Speech Declaring Youths' Excesses Buoy Enemies

By United Press International

TOKYO, Wednesday, June 14—Wall posters in Peking disclosed today a scathing attack by Premier Chou En-lai against China's youthful Red Guards, whom he accused of giving "great pleasure and an advantage to enemy countries."

The posters, as reported by Japanese correspondents in Peking, contained the harshest words so far used publicly by a ranking Chinese official against the unruly protégés of the Communist party chairman, Mao Tse-tung.

"Is China under the dictatorship of you or under Chairman Mao?" Chou was said to have asked Red Guards who called to demand the expulsion of one of his own aides, Deputy Premier Li Hsien-nien.

Mr. Chou was then said to have burst out angrily:

"You have often broken into Government offices in your attempts to drag out anti-Mao elements and you have taken away many important documents of the party and of the Government.

"But such thoughtless acts have given nothing but a great pleasure and advantage to enemy countries."

Mr. Li, who also serves as Finance Minister, has long been subjected to Red Guard diatribes charging him with backing President Liu Shao-chi. Mr. Liu is regarded by the Maoists as Public Enemy No. 1 in the Proletarian Cultural Revolution, the name given to the purge of Mr. Mao's opponents.

Hassan Is Reported Planning U.S. Trip

By ERIC PACE
Special to The New York Times

CAIRO, June 13—Informed Egyptian sources said today that King Hassan II of Morocco would probably visit the United States in the next few days in an Arab campaign to persuade the West to get Israel to relinquish her war gains.

The sources, who declined to be identified, said that King Hassan would have the support of the Egyptian President, Gamal Abdel Nasser, and of other Arab leaders in his mission, which is considered a parallel to the visit of the Algerian President, Houari Boumedienne, to Moscow.

There was no immediate official confirmation of the report, but the sources said King Hassan was expected to ask Washington to use its influence to get Israel to relinquish the territory in the United Arab Republic, Syria and Jordan that she seized during the fighting last week. It is not known

Continued on Page 16, Column 5

NEWS INDEX

$70-BILLION VOTED FOR DEFENSE IN '68

House, 407-1, Sends Bill to Senate—$20-Billion Provided for Vietnam

By MARJORIE HUNTER
Special to The New York Times

WASHINGTON, June 13—The House passed today a $70.3-billion defense money bill described by Congressional leaders as the largest single legislative appropriation in world history.

The vote was 407 to 1, sending the bill to the Senate. The single vote against was cast by George E. Brown Jr., Democrat of California.

Included is $20.3-billion attributable to the war in Vietnam. However, both Democrats and Republicans predicted that additional billions of dollars would have to be appropriated later to finance the war. The bill covers the 1968 fiscal year, starting July 1.

5% Trim Rejected

The House shouted down an effort by Mr. Brown, a war "dove," to trim the over-all bill by 5 per cent.

The House Appropriations Committee had earlier cut $1.3-billion from the Administration's $71.6-billion request, but none of this was for war-related programs.

The so-called war "hawks" had their say, too, demanding a sharp escalation of the war.

If necessary, the United States should drop the atomic bomb on North Vietnam, said George Andrews, Democrat of Alabama.

"Why, North Vietnam isn't as big as the State of New Jersey," he said. "If we can't

Continued on Page 5, Column 3

Gasoline Explodes In Bronx, Burning 19

By MICHAEL T. KAUFMAN

A sheet of flame streaked out of a Bronx taxi garage after an explosion last evening and burned 19 persons, seven of them critically.

Most of the victims were children who were playing at dusk in front of the Classy Cab Company's garage, just across Cypress Avenue from the city's Mill Brook housing project, near East 137th Street.

A taxi with a ruptured gasoline tank had just pulled into the garage past the youngsters, leaving a trail of spilled fuel. Then, according to a driver who was in the garage, a youth deliberately threw a match into a puddle of gas on the sidewalk.

The flames raced along the trail of gasoline as if it were a fuse leading to the damaged cab. The explosion followed and a jet-like flame shot back more than 20 feet to the street and the children.

"Kids on fire were running in

Continued on Page 29, Column 1

Lindsay Defeated In Fight to Prevent Cuts in His Budget

By SETH S. KING

The Board of Estimate and the City Council, with their large Democratic majorities, overrode 18 vetoes by Mayor Lindsay yesterday and cut nearly $6-million from his executive budget.

In doing so the Democrats accused the Republican Mayor of shedding false tears with the intention of preparing the taxpayers for more tax increases next year.

The City Council president, Frank D. O'Connor, said the Mayor's original budget was "dishonest on its face."

"While accusing us of political motivation he is trying to fix the blame on us for tax increases he will want next year," Mr. O'Connor said when he talked with reporters on the steps of City Hall before the Council session began.

Last Action on Budget

As a result of yesterday's legislative action — the last to be taken on the 1967-68 expense budget — the Mayor will have a record $5,177,513,877 to spend during the fiscal year beginning July 1.

He had requested $5,183,508,877. The Council and Board of Estimate added $19.3-million of their own appropriations and cut $25.2-million from those of the Mayor, for a net reduction of $5.9-million.

The two legislative bodies overrode the Mayor's vetoes of these changes with more than the required two-thirds majorities. Their net reduction was less than one-half of 1 per cent of the Mayor's original total.

Mr. Lindsay, now in Honolulu, quickly issued a statement denouncing their action as "one

Continued on Page 25, Column 1

The New York Times (by Carl T. Gossett Jr.)

OUTLINES POSITION: City Council President Frank D. O'Connor on the steps of City Hall yesterday explaining to newsmen his opposition to the Mayor's executive budget.

GUARD IS CALLED INTO CINCINNATI AS RIOTS SPREAD

47 Are Arrested and 13 Hurt as Negro Teen-Agers Loot in 3 Sections of City

By EARL CALDWELL
Special to The New York Times

CINCINNATI, June 14—Ohio National Guardsmen with fixed bayonets were ordered into Cincinnati to join 900 policemen battling intense rioting that continued to sweep a large part of the city early today and spread to at least one suburban town.

Forty-seven persons were reported arrested and at least 13 were injured in the second night of violence in Ohio's second largest urban center.

One of the injured was reportedly a Negro man who was shot in the neck while sitting on his porch in the Mount Auburn section. Neither his condition nor his assailant was known immediately.

Police officials said that the rioting was spreading throughout the city, and late last night violence flared in Lockland, a suburban community about 18 miles northeast of Cincinnati.

Molotov Cocktails Hurled

The guardsmen were mobilized by Gov. James A. Rhodes of Ohio after Mayor Walton S. Bachrach of Cincinnati asked for their help in putting down racial violence in the city.

Police Chief Jacob Schott estimated that "thousands" of teen-agers and young adults were storming through three of the city's sections, hurling Molotov cocktails, smashing store windows, looting and setting fires.

"There are so many marauding gangs now we just can't contain them," Chief Schott said.

More than 800 members of the Ohio National Guard were called out for riot duty in Cincinnati. The men were issued rifles with fixed bayonets, gas masks and helmets, and some drove jeeps armed with mounted machine guns.

Called to Restore Order

The guardsmen are members of the First Battalion of the 147th Infantry of the Ohio National Guard.

"The guard is going in with our men to restore law and order," Col. Edward T. Darmody, an assistant police chief, said.

[In Tampa, Fla., National Guardsmen withdrew from the riot area after Negro leaders said they could restore peace. And in Montgomery, Ala., Stokely Carmichael led a march after being released from jail at nearby Prattville.]

The police patrolled the area with shotguns, riot sticks and police dogs. They drove through the strife-torn neighborhoods in cars equipped with loudspeakers reading the Ohio riot law, which warned that anyone who failed to get off the streets or obey police orders would be subject to insurrection charges.

Weather Is Muggy

The weather was hot and muggy, maintaining without relief a heat wave that has gripped the city for more than a week.

The rioting erupted at 7 P.M. yesterday in the heavily Negro Avondale section of the city, about two miles northeast of the downtown area.

As the violence grew more intense, it spilled into the Evanston and Walnut Hills sections, both integrated residential neighborhoods.

By midnight, some of the vio-

Continued on Page 34, Column 3

MARSHALL NAMED FOR HIGH COURT, ITS FIRST NEGRO

United Press International Telephoto

President Johnson with Thurgood Marshall at White House

Johnson Calls Nominee 'Best Qualified,' and Rights Leaders Are Jubilant—Southerners Silent on Confirmation

By ROY REED
Special to The New York Times

WASHINGTON, June 13 — President Johnson named Solicitor General Thurgood Marshall to the Supreme Court today.

Mr. Marshall, the great-grandson of a slave, will be the first Negro to serve on the Court if the Senate confirms him.

He is the best-known Negro lawyer of the century because of his battles against segrega-

Johnson statement and news conference text, Page 18.

tion. Southerners in the Senate once delayed his appointment to the Federal judiciary for several months. But judging from initial reaction in the Senate today, his confirmation to the Court seems likely.

Non-Southern Senators applauded the appointment and Southerners accepted it, at least for the moment, in silence.

Hailed by Negro Leaders

Negro leaders were jubilant. Floyd B. McKissick, the militant chairman of the Congress of Racial Equality, said the appointment had stirred "pride in the breast of every black American."

Mr. Marshall, 58 years old, is to succeed Associate Justice Tom C. Clark, who retired yesterday.

It had been expected for years that Mr. Marshall would eventually become the first Negro justice, but recent speculation had given him no special edge over other prospective nominees at this time.

The President, as is his custom, gave no advance hint of his selection. Reporters were unexpectedly called into the White House Rose Garden outside his office shortly before noon.

Blinking in the sun, Mr. Johnson stepped in front of the microphones and matter-of-factly announced what may be the most dramatic appointment of his Presidency.

'A Place in History'

Mr. Marshall stood by with his hands in his pockets, his usually mobile face solemn, as the President told of his nomination.

"I believe he has already earned his place in history," Mr. Johnson said. "But I think it will be greatly enhanced by his service on the Court."

Mr. Johnson declared that Mr. Marshall had earned the appointment by his "distinguished record" in the law. He added:

"He is best qualified by training and by very valuable service to the country. I believe it is the right thing to do, the right time to do it, the right man and the right place."

Mr. Marshall's official selection was chiefly the work of

Continued on Page 32, Column 3

Dodd Accused by Stennis; Asks Justice, Not Mercy

By E. W. KENWORTHY
Special to The New York Times

WASHINGTON, June 13—Senator John Stennis, chairman of the ethics committee, told the Senate today that it could not afford to ignore or condone the conduct of Senator Thomas J. Dodd.

Mr. Dodd, in reply, denied the charges of misuse of funds on which a resolution of censure

Excerpts from Stennis speech, Dodd statement, Page 30

against him is based. "I do not ask for mercy," he said in a prepared text. "I ask for justice."

Although his speech was released to the press, he put off reading it in the Senate until tomorrow.

Approved on April 27

The Senate opened debate this morning on the resolution, which was recommended by the ethics committee last April 27 after 14 months of investigation.

Mr. Stennis was the opening speaker, and in the course of retracing the committee's findings he bluntly accused the Connecticut Democrat of diverting to his own use at least $116,000 of political campaign funds and proceeds from testimonial dinners.

At the close of his two-hour speech, Mr. Stennis said:

"As an act of generosity, as an act of feeling of compassion, I would like to be more gener-ous than this resolution is, but that is really not the question. There is no Constitutional question involved, as I said in the beginning. There is not much dispute about the essential facts.

"The matter comes down to the question: What is the Senate going to do about it? The question rests right in the lap of everyone."

Mr. Stennis said he did not believe the Senate could regard Mr. Dodd's alleged conduct as "proper conduct for a sitting member."

Speeches Scheduled

The Senate leadership had announced that following the opening speech by Senator Wallace F. Bennett, Republican of Utah, the ethics committee's vice chairman, Senator Dodd would be given the floor to reply to the charges.

This schedule was thrown awry, however, when Senator Russell B. Long of Louisiana, the Democratic whip, who has undertaken to be Mr. Dodd's floor counsel, pre-empted much of Mr. Dodd's time with an arm-waving denunciation of the columnists Drew Pearson and Jack Anderson and four former

Continued on Page 30, Column 6

"All the News That's Fit to Print"

The New York Times

LATE CITY EDITION
Weather: Partly cloudy, warm today, Sun. Chance showers late both days. Temp. range: today 86-68. Fri. 81-76. Temp.-Hum. Index: 74. Fri. 77. Full U. S. report on page 56.

VOL. CXVI.. No. 39,963 | © 1967 The New York Times Company. | NEW YORK, SATURDAY, JUNE 24, 1967 | 10 CENTS

JOHNSON, KOSYGIN TALK 5 HOURS ABOUT MIDEAST, VIETNAM, ARMS, AND AGREE TO MEET TOMORROW

The New York Times (by Patrick A. Burns)
AFTER THE MEETING: Premier Kosygin takes leave of President Johnson. Between them is Secretary of State Rusk.

A CORDIAL SESSION

But There Is No Sign of Substantive Gains on Major Issues

Texts of Johnson and Kosygin remarks are on Page 8.

By MAX FRANKEL
Special to The New York Times

GLASSBORO, N. J., June 23—President Johnson and Premier Aleksei N. Kosygin talked for five and a half hours here today about the Middle East, Vietnam and arms control, and ran out of time before they ran out of things to say.

Emerging arm in arm and with broad smiles, the two leaders announced that they had agreed to meet here again at 1:30 P.M. on Sunday.

They appeared to have gotten along extremely well on a personal level but it appeared doubtful that they had made any significant progress on the most troublesome issues in the Middle East and in Vietnam.

Mr. Johnson, characterizing the meeting as "very good and very useful," placed particular emphasis on his agreement with the Soviet leader that it was "now" very important to reach international accord on a treaty to prevent the spread of nuclear weapons.

'Very Correctly Drawn Up'

Mr. Kosygin, expressing warm appreciation for the meeting, said he had nothing essential to add to Mr. Johnson's statement, "which was very correctly drawn up."

The two leaders summarized their views for the news media after their conversations, held at the residence of Dr. Thomas E. Robinson on the campus of Glassboro State College, of which he is president. The meeting was arranged unexpectedly yesterday after several days of pulling and hauling between the two sides on acceptable conditions.

United States officials said afterward that aside from noting the obvious fact that "Israel does exist," the two delegations had familiar and divergent views on the causes of and possible solutions to the problems between Israel and her Arab neighbors.

Hope for Some Consensus

The Russians have accused Israel of aggression in the six-day war early this month and have pledged full support to the Arab cause — a position that they apparently reiterated today.

Secretary of State Dean Rusk was said to have concluded at the meeting that "serious problems" remained in the Middle East but he also passed along an expression of hope that some consensus might yet be reached between Moscow and Washington on at least some policy objectives in that region.

Before the conference, President Johnson proposed a limitation on arms shipments to the Middle East, direct nego-

Continued on Page 6, Column 1

DODD CENSURED BY SENATE, 92-5, ON FUND COUNT

2D CHARGE KILLED

Democrat Exonerated of Double Billing in 51-to-45 Vote

United Press International Telephoto
FUND USE CRITICIZED: Thomas J. Dodd, Democrat of Connecticut, yesterday.

By E. W. KENWORTHY
Special to The New York Times

WASHINGTON, June 23 — The Senate voted 92 to 5 today to censure Senator Thomas J. Dodd for using campaign and testimonial funds "for his personal benefit," then exonerated him, 51 to 45, of intentionally seeking double reimbursement on air travel.

The vote on the double-billing charge came not on the resolution itself but on a motion to strike the words of the charge, namely that Mr. Dodd had used his influence "to request and accept reimbursements for expenses from both the Senate and private organizations for the same travel."

This motion was offered by Senator Allen J. Ellender, Democrat of Louisiana.

After the vote exonerating Mr. Dodd on the double-billing charge, the Senate, again by 92 to 5, formally adopted the resolution minus the stricken second count. This was simply a procedural step confirming the earlier action on censure.

Seniority Retained

Thus, on the ninth day of debate, did Senator Dodd, 60 years old, become the sixth Senator in the history of the United States to be censured or condemned by his colleagues.

A censure resolution carries no penalties. Mr. Dodd will not lose his seniority, his chairmanship of the Subcommittee on Juvenile Delinquency or his vice chairmanship of the Subcommittee on Internal Security.

Nevertheless, censure is regarded as a most serious chastisement and has never been resorted to except when the misconduct was judged to affect the Senate as an institution and to subject it to diminution of public confidence.

As a result of the Dodd case, there is a general recognition within the Senate of the need for a code of ethics, and many members during the course of the debate—including Senator Dodd himself—asked the ethics committee to move quickly to propose such a code.

The last member to vote on

Continued on Page 14, Column 1

MAYOR CONDEMNS WELFARE WORK-IN

Says Union 'Uses' Clients—Calls Tactics Contemptible

By DAMON STETSON

Mayor Lindsay assailed the Social Service Employes Union yesterday and called the tactics of its members in the welfare dispute "irresponsible" and "contemptible."

In his first news conference since his return from the conference of Mayors in Honolulu, Mr. Lindsay charged that the union was attempting to take over the Welfare Department. He said that refusal of caseworkers to perform their regular duties and their harassment of others trying to work constituted a "callous exploitation" of welfare clients.

"To use people as pawns in this fashion is contemptible," the Mayor declared.

Mr. Lindsay's attack on the union was made on the fifth day of its so-called work-in, which the Mayor described as a work stoppage. During the day tempers flared, welfare clients complained of inadequate service and caseworkers scuffled with the police at several locations.

The Welfare Department re-

Continued on Page 26, Column 4

NEWS INDEX

POPE REAFFIRMS RULE OF CELIBACY FOR PRIESTHOOD

Encyclical Calls for Greater Use of Psychological Tests in Preparing Candidates

Excerpts from Pope's letter appear on Page 10.

By EDWARD B. FISKE
Special to The New York Times

ROME, June 23 — Pope Paul VI responded today to growing pressures in the church to permit priests to marry with a long encyclical strongly reaffirming the traditional Roman Catholic rule on clerical celibacy.

The Pope also called for reforms in the preparation of young candidates for the celibate life, including the increased use of medical and psychological tests.

The Pontiff described the celibate state as a "brilliant jewel" that had been guarded by the church for centuries and that would continue to be "firmly linked to the ecclesiastical ministry."

Decline Acknowledged

He acknowledged that the church had experienced a "disquieting decline" in the ranks of the priesthood, but he stated: "It is simply not possible to believe that the abolition of ecclesiastical celibacy would considerably increase the number of priestly vocations."

The Pontiff said that poor judgment on the fitness of candidates for the priesthood, not the celibacy requirement, was at the root of defections.

He also rejected the argument that celibacy is an unnatural condition for healthy and mature human beings.

"Man, created to God's image and likeness, is not just flesh and blood," he said. "The sexual instinct is not all that he has; man is also, and pre-eminently, understanding, choice, freedom, and, thanks to these powers, he is and must remain superior to the rest of creation. They give him mastery over his physical, psychological and affective appetites."

Mandatory Since 1139

The requirement that priests not marry is a rule, rather than a matter of doctrine or dogma, in the Catholic Church, and it could be changed by the Pope. It was written into law by the Council of Elvira in A.D. 306, but the law was not universally followed. The Second Lateran Council of 1139 made celibacy mandatory.

In Eastern Orthodox Churches and in the Eastern Rite of the Roman Catholic Church, priests are permitted to marry before ordination, but bishops are chosen from the celibate clergy.

The encyclical made only passing reference to proposals for the creation of a married diaconate, whose members would be permitted to perform most priestly duties other than celebrating mass and hearing confessions.

Pope Paul has yet to act on the married diaconate, which was approved by the recent Ecumenical Council, but Vati-

Continued on Page 10, Column 2

JET CRASH KILLS 34 IN PENNSYLVANIA

President of Mohawk Line Suggests Plane Going to Capital Was Sabotaged

Special to The New York Times

BLOSSBURG, Pa., June 23—Thirty passengers and a crew of four were killed today when a twin-jet Mohawk Airlines plane crashed near here in an area ringed by storms.

The BAC-111, manufactured by the British Aircraft Corporation, took off 13 minutes before the crash from Elmira, N. Y., on a flight to Washington.

Late tonight Robert E. Peach, president of Mohawk, demanded an investigation by the Federal Bureau of Investigation.

In a telegram to J. Edgar Hoover, director of the F.B.I., Mr. Peach said: "Evidence has developed in the course of notification of next of kin of crash victims which leads to strong suggestion of sabotage. Mohawk Airlines formally demands that the F.B.I. investigate the possibility of sabotage."

Mr. Peach would not make public the nature of the "evidence."

Fell in Wooded Area

The police said that the plane had plunged into a heavily wooded area served only by dirt roads. They reported no survivors.

The crew members included two stewardesses.

Among the passengers were two priests high in the Roman Catholic Society of the Atonement. They were the Very Rev. Alexander Beaton, newly elected head of the order's Graymoor Friars, and the Rev. De Sales Standerwick, rector of Graymoor's St. John's Seminary at Montour Falls, near Elmira.

The plane gouged a strip through the woods about 100 yards wide and 500 yards long. The tail section was thrown 400 yards from the impact site of the crash.

Some of the witnesses were workmen at a coal strip mine who immediately took a bulldozer and plowed two roads through to the site a mile and a half away. Rescue workers

Continued on Page 28, Column 2

Rochester Negroes Gain Pact at Kodak

Special to The New York Times

ROCHESTER, N. Y., June 23—The Eastman Kodak Company reached an agreement today with a militant civil rights organization to cooperate in finding jobs and developing training programs for this city's nonskilled Negroes.

The agreement came after six months of bitter infighting between the company and FIGHT (an acronym for Freedom, Integration, God, Honor—Today). The dispute was over an agreement for a job-training program for 600 Negroes that was signed by a Kodak assistant vice president last Dec. 20 and repudiated by the company two days later.

The agreement came in a telegram from Dr. Louis K. Eilers,

Continued on Page 17, Column 3

JOHNSON, IN WEST, TELLS OF SUMMIT

Says He and Kosygin Agree on Need for Peace—51 Protesters Arrested

By GLADWIN HILL
Special to The New York Times

LOS ANGELES, June 23—President Johnson flew to Los Angeles tonight after his meeting with Premier Aleksei N. Kosygin and told California Democrats at a fund-raising dinner that he and the Soviet leader had "agreed that we wanted a world of peace for our grandchildren."

While the President spoke in the ballroom of the Century Plaza Hotel in West Los Angeles, 1,300 policemen massed to restrain several thousand Vietnam peace demonstrators. The gathering was declared unlawful and 51 arrests were made. Most of those arrested were charged with unlawful assembly or refusal to disperse.

"I was glad to meet with Chairman Kosygin," Mr. Johnson told the 1,000 Democrats at the $500-a-plate dinner, "and to talk quietly and straightforwardly with him, and I found that he came to our meeting in the same spirit. He has been a grandfather longer than I have, and he and I agreed that

Continued on Page 9, Column 1

Big Day in Glassboro

Movie Shows 'Russians Are Coming,' And Flower Shop Sends Red Roses

By MAURICE CARROLL
Special to The New York Times

GLASSBORO, N. J., June 23—The folks from Dorothy's Flower Shop sent red roses. The Glassboro Theater shifted tonight's show to "The Russians Are Coming the Russians Are Coming."

The weekly newspaper prepared to put out a picture-filled extra on Monday. With polite neighborliness that seemed natural, and with a practiced worldliness that could hardly have been expected, this South Jersey community of 11,000 served as host to the summit conference.

The Talk of Glassboro

Glassboro was interested. Crowds turned out to watch. But Glassboro was not rocked by its sudden importance. The summit meeting had not much more of an impact on the tenor of local life than would a big strawberry festival.

At about 10 o'clock this morning, Mr. and Mrs. Paul Lisa and Mr. and Mrs. John Silvestri, who run Dorothy's Flower Shop, put together a bouquet of 25 red roses.

They marked it "Best wishes for peace" and sent it to the joint attention of President Johnson and Premier Aleksei N. Kosygin.

On a wobbly rust-red scaffold next to the Glassboro Theater stood Charles Tower and Joe Vacc.

They took down the block letters proclaiming tonight's show "Hot Rods to Hell" and "Easy Come, Easy Go." They put up the letters for the replacement show, "Cast a Giant Shadow," about Israel's war for independence, and "The Russians Are Coming the Russians Are Coming!"

Clayton Platt, the theater owner, painted the same letters on a big piece of poster board out on the lobby floor. "I decided to swap this morning," he said. "It seemed like a good idea."

•

At 5:45 yesterday morning William Schwoebel, publisher of The Glassboro Enterprise, learned that Mayor Joseph L. Bowe had died.

Mr. Schwoebel told the printers to stop the press, which had run off half of the scheduled 3,600 copies. He quickly rearranged the front page to include the Mayor's

Continued on Page 8, Column 2

TOWN'S RESIDENTS APPLAUD KOSYGIN

Premier, Turned Ebullient, Tells Them Soviet Wants 'Nothing but Peace'

By PETER GROSE
Special to The New York Times

GLASSBORO, N. J., June 23—The crowd cheered, the Premier of the Soviet Union was ebullient and his words to the residents of Glassboro were full of encouragement.

Premier Aleksei N. Kosygin probably could not resist the greetings as he started driving off from his meeting with President Johnson. He stopped the car, jumped out and, with Ambassador Anatoly F. Dobrynin as his interpreter, he said:

"I want friendship with the American people and I can assure you we want nothing but peace with the American people."

The crowd cheered again, and one Glassboro resident shouted, "Tovarishch Kosygin, shake my hand." The Premier responded, and in a sort of afterthought reference to the hours of discussion just concluded, he said: "There are many beautiful and wonderful things to be done."

Mr. Dobrynin's translation could hardly be heard across the street crowded with several hundred bystanders who had waited since midmorning. Gesticulating and beaming, Mr. Kosygin showed more enthusiasm than usual.

This was his first encounter

Continued on Page 6, Column 6

The New York Times (by Neal Boenzi)
IN THE LIMELIGHT: A view of Glassboro, N. J., where U.S. and Soviet leaders met. Road leads to site of talks.

Rumania, Differing With Soviet, Calls at U.N. for Mideast Talks

By DREW MIDDLETON
Special to The New York Times

UNITED NATIONS, N. Y., June 23—Premier Ion Gheorghe Maurer of Rumania deviated today from the stand of other Communist countries by calling for negotiations and agreements to establish a lasting settlement in the Middle East.

Foreign Minister Abba Eban of Israel has advocated negotiations between his Government and the Arab states as the means of making peace. The United States seeks "negotiated agreements."

Excerpts from U.N. speeches will be found on Page 4.

Premier Maurer said at the emergency session of the General Assembly that "due regard" for the independence and sovereign existence of each Middle Eastern state was an "essential element" for an effective solution.

Later, authoritative Rumanian sources indicated uncertainty about Rumanian support for the Soviet draft resolution before the Assembly.

Although the Rumanian delegation asked that Israel withdraw from seized territory of the United Arab Republic, Syria and Jordan, it will apparently not vote for any resolution that serves only to condemn Israel or for one that does not recognize her existence.

Rumania's disagreement with the Soviet bloc in the United Nations was foreshadowed at a Moscow meeting of Communist leaders on June 9. Rumania's delegate, alone among those

Continued on Page 4, Column 4

The Dirty Dozen, with Lee Marvin, set the standard for graphic war scenes.

Sidney Poitier and Lee Grant starred in *In the Heat of the Night.*

Katharine Hepburn and Spencer Tracy starred as the bewildered parents in *Guess Who's Coming to Dinner.*

The outlaws of the 30s were glorified by Warren Beatty and Faye Dunaway in Arthur Penn's *Bonnie and Clyde.*

"All the News That's Fit to Print"

The New York Times

LATE CITY EDITION

Weather: Mostly cloudy, showers today and tonight. Fair tomorrow. Temp. range: today 78-68; Sat. 78-68. Temp.-Hum. Index 73; Sat. 75. Complete U.S. report on Page 67.

SECTION ONE

VOL. CXVI . . . . No. 39,985

NEW YORK, SUNDAY, JULY 16, 1967

50c beyond 50-mile zone from New York City, except Long Island. Higher in air delivery cities. 40 CENTS

NEWARK RIOT DEATHS AT 21 AS NEGRO SNIPING WIDENS; HUGHES MAY SEEK U.S. AID

ISRAELIS REPORT DOWNING 6 PLANES IN SUEZ CLASHES

Cairo Also Claims 6 Enemy Aircraft Destroyed in Day of Heavy Fighting

NEW CEASE-FIRE CALLED

U.N. Says Both Sides Have Halted Hostilities Under Terms Set by Gen. Bull

By TERENCE SMITH
Special to The New York Times

TEL AVIV, July 15—Israeli and Egyptian jet fighters clashed over the Suez Canal today in the fiercest fighting in the area since the cease-fire became effective on June 9.

The Israelis said that five Egyptian MIG jet fighter planes and a Sukhoi-7 fighter-bomber were downed during dogfights over the canal and that one of their jets had been hit. The Israeli pilot was reported to have parachuted safely before his plane crashed in the central Sinai.

[At the United Nations an official spokesman announced that a new cease-fire between Egyptian and Israeli forces in the Suez Canal area went into effect at 6 P.M. New York time. Arrangements were made by Lieut. Gen. Odd Bull, head of the United Nations truce organization in Cairo Page 2.]

Pilot Reported Seized

The Israelis said the Egyptian pilot of the Soviet-supplied Sukhoi fighter-bomber bailed out and came down in Sinai, where he was captured. [Cairo reported that six Israeli aircraft had been downed in the Suez area while Egypt lost one plane and three tanks.]

The Israeli military spokesman here also reported the first fighting along the Jordanian front since the cease-fire. He said the Jordanians had opened machine-gun fire from two places along the east bank of the Jordan River.

The fire was returned and silenced, without Israeli casualties, the spokesman added. [In Amman, the Jordanian Government charged that Israeli forces had opened exchanges of fire three times.]

Military sources here saw no immediate connection between the Egyptian and Jordanian actions, though they said the firing in the Jordan River area came as a surprise. They said they still regarded the Egyptian attacks as primarily political maneuvers intended to influence the discussions at the

Continued on Page 2, Column 3

DE VICENZO'S 278 WINS BRITISH OPEN

Nicklaus Is Second, 2 Shots Behind the Argentine

Roberto de Vicenzo of Argentina won the British Open golf championship yesterday with a 278 total for 72 holes at Hoylake, England. De Vicenzo carded a final round of 70 to stave off a closing challenge by Jack Nicklaus, the defending champion, whose 69 earned him second place with a 280 total.

THOROUGHBRED RACING

Mrs. Edith Bancroft's Damascus, ridden by Willie Shoemaker, rallied from last place to win the $83,350 Dwyer Handicap by three-quarters of a length at Aqueduct.

Tartan Stable's Dr. Fager, with Braulio Baeza up, scored a 4¼-length triumph in the Rockingham Special at Salem, N. H. In the mutuel betting, restricted to the win pool, Dr. Fager returned $2.20, lowest win price in Rockingham Park history.

BASEBALL

Steve Barber notched his first triumph for the Yankees, downing the Cleveland Indians, 4-1. Mel Queen pitched a six-hitter as the Cincinnati Reds topped the Mets, 6-1. The Minnesota Twins won and the Chicago White Sox lost to tighten the close American League race.

Details in Section 5

Associated Press Radiophoto

DAWN ATTACK: Cargo planes burning on a parking ramp of the Danang base after enemy rocket barrage yesterday

U.S. Offers Gold for Aid To Pilots Down in North

Special to The New York Times

SAIGON, South Vietnam, July 15—Any Vietnamese who helps a downed American pilot to escape from North Vietnam will receive a reward of gold worth $1,060, a United States spokesman announced here today. The reward was set at 50 taels of gold, a quantity approximating 50 troy ounces.

About 16 million leaflets offering the reward have been dropped over the southern part of North Vietnam, the spokesman said.

Meanwhile, the Danang air base was back in operation after a rocket barrage early this morning that killed eight Americans and wounded 173 and destroyed 11 planes.

The leaflets dropped in North Vietnam said:

"Helping American pilots and other U. S. military personnel escape to freedom can bring you 50 taels of gold.

'Do Not Be Afraid'

"If you see an American who has parachuted to the ground or who has escaped capture do not be afraid. Approach him. Make him understand you wish him no harm by raising your hands.

"Help him in any way you can. Hide him from hostile authorities. Cooperate with him in finding his way to safety. You may escape to freedom with him or return home just as you choose.

"You will be paid the 50 taels of gold at the time the American is rescued or at any other time you choose. You may collect the reward in gold bullion or in the equivalent amount of any currency you choose, payable in any free world country you wish."

The leaflets were signed by the United States Ambassador

Continued on Page 7, Column 1

POPE PAUL WILL GO TO TURKEY JULY 25

Will Confer on Jerusalem With Patriarch and Make Pilgrimage to Shrines

By TAD SZULC
Special to The New York Times

ROME, July 15—Pope Paul VI announced today that he would fly to Turkey on July 25 for a two-day visit designed to strengthen the bonds between the Roman Catholic and Eastern Orthodox Churches and to seek ways of assuring the protection of the holy sites in Jerusalem.

The Pope announced the trip at a Vatican ceremony at which he gave rings to three new Cardinals.

He said that he would visit Istanbul—the historic Constantinople of the eastern Roman Empire—and the shrines of Ephesus, where, according to tradition, the Virgin Mary died, and where St. John the Apostle was martyred.

Pope Paul said that he would confer with Archbishop Athenagoras, the Ecumenical Patriarch, in Istanbul, and with President Cevdet Sunay of Turkey. President Sunay is expected to go to Istanbul. The Pope, who does not visit national capitals, will not stop in Ankara.

Statement by Pope

The Pontiff said that he would meet with the 81-year-old Patriarch "to discuss with him the best manner for promoting the theological and canonic studies for the purpose of smoothing the way towards the re-establishment of a perfect communion between the Catholic Church and the Orthodox Church, and to examine together in what form and through what means it may be possible, with solid sentiment, to protect, in the present situation, not only the safety but the sacred and special character of the holy places in the land that was the motherland of Christ."

The Roman Catholic and Eastern Orthodox churches are the principal guardians of the holy sites in Jerusalem, all of which has been under Israel's control since the Arab-Israeli conflict last month.

While it was believed here that, in talks earlier this month, the Vatican and Israel had agreed in principle on an extraterritorial status for the holy places, the Pope evidently wanted to hear other views on the subject.

Since Patriarch Athenagoras

Continued on Page 14, Column 3

8,000 APARTMENTS IN SLUMS PLANNED

Program Intended to Show New York Is Deserving of Model Cities Aid

By STEVEN V. ROBERTS

New York City will build 8,000 low- and middle-income apartments in its three most deteriorated ghettos in an effort to show the Federal Government that it can use money from the Federal model cities program effectively.

Mayor Lindsay announced yesterday that the housing would be built in Harlem, the South Bronx and Central Brooklyn.

The city is starting its program even though it has not yet been selected to receive model cities aid from the Federal Government. It is using about $150-million from other Federal programs and its own capital budget to get a head start.

Model cities is a Johnson Administration program designed to encourage the physical, economic and social rejuvenation of selected slum neighborhoods. New York has applied for about $400-million in planning funds for the three ghettos but Washington has yet to act on any applications.

The Mayor also announced plans to spend $60-million for

Continued on Page 32, Column 1

City Will Recruit Professors to Help Solve Its Problems

By M. A. FARBER

Mayor Lindsay's administration will recruit faculty experts from major educational institutions here to advise him on such problems as pollution, traffic, health and housing.

In return for the professors' help, the administration will give the institutions a hand in planning their physical growth by helping them to find sites and speeding their applications for construction permits.

As part of the new arrangement, Mayor Lindsay will, starting in the fall, schedule the usual Friday morning cabinet meetings on campuses so as to acquaint city officials with the university staffs. The sessions now rotate among the headquarters of the city departments.

Joint action by the universities and the city to obtain federally funded research programs may be another result of the liaison.

The institutions that already have agreed to participate are Columbia, New York, Fordham, City, Rockefeller and Yeshiva universities, the Polytechnic Institute of Brooklyn and the New School for Social Research.

Mr. Lindsay, who suggested

Continued on Page 27, Column 1

Today's Sections

Index to Subjects

U.S. Acts to Speed Tenant Integration In Public Housing

By ROBERT B. SEMPLE Jr.
Special to The New York Times

WASHINGTON, July 15—The Administration has taken its most significant step so far to end discrimination in its public housing program.

In a 10-page memorandum mailed last Tuesday, the Department of Housing and Urban Development ordered local housing authorities to replace the "free choice" rule governing the selection of tenants with regulations designed to promote desegregation.

The "free choice" rule gave applicants for public housing unlimited time in which to choose a place to live. In practice, white applicants regularly turned down vacancies in predominantly Negro projects while waiting for vacancies in white projects.

'Separate but Equal'

The rule had tended to reinforce a pattern of segregation that began when public housing was authorized by Congress in 1937. Civil rights groups have called it a "separate but equal" system of public housing.

About 700,000 dwelling units have been built under the public housing program. Some 35,000 to 50,000 units are built annually.

Under the new requirements, cities will choose one of three alternative plans to produce desegregation.

First, the local authority may order public housing applicants to accept whatever vacancy is offered or be moved immediately to the bottom of the waiting list. This is the most stringent of the three alternatives.

Or, the local authority may

Continued on Page 29, Column 1

Strike Hits Two Railroads; Nationwide Tie-up Feared

Special to The New York Times

WASHINGTON, Sunday, July 16—The railroad industry said that the International Association of Machinists had struck two railroads early this morning and that it expected a nationwide walkout.

James E. Wolfe, the industry's chief negotiator, said the union had struck the Chesapeake & Ohio Railway at Grand Rapids, Mich., and the Atchison, Topeka & Santa Fe Railway at Kansas City, Kan.

Mr. Wolfe said he had indications that there would be further stoppages as the morning progressed. He predicted that the entire nation would be tied up by rail strikes before long.

He said he believed that Congress had a responsibility to step in and stop the strikes because of the danger he said they posed to the Vietnam war effort.

The union's no-strike pledge to Congress expired at midnight last night.

H. L. Nesbitt, recording secretary of the Cumberland, Md., local, said that a strike against the Baltimore & Ohio and Western Maryland railroads had been set for today.

In Spokane, Wash., the local union chairman, Richard L. Siekerman, said that he had been told by his general chairman in St. Paul that a strike had been ordered against the Great Northern; Northern Pacific; Union Pacific; the Chicago, Burlington & Quincy, and the Spokane, Portland & Seattle Railroads.

Industry sources said they had also been told of planned strikes against the Reading and the Southern Pacific.

There also were reports that the New York Central and the Pennsylvania Railroad would be struck, which would have a severe impact on New York City and its commuter traffic. But industry sources said they were not clear on that point.

The Johnson Administration, lacking any legislative means of

Continued on Page 28, Column 1

Newark Rioting Assailed By Meeting of N.A.A.C.P.

By M. S. HANDLER
Special to The New York Times

BOSTON, July 15—The 58th annual N.A.A.C.P. convention unanimously condemned today the riots in Newark.

A resolution prepared by Roy Wilkins, executive director, and read by William H. Booth, New York City's Commissioner for Human Rights, called upon "all law-abiding citizens of both races to act promptly and sternly to put down such violence."

The resolution, however, placed much of the blame for the outbreak in Newark upon the city's administration "for its failure to take corrective action to meet any of the grave social ills of the Negro community."

Meanwhile, a potential revolt against the board of directors of the National Association for the Advancement of Colored People collapsed as all resolutions submitted to the Resolutions Committee were approved by a bloc voice vote.

The vote was taken without any discussion. No substantive issue reached the floor for discussion. The only arguments that developed in the final plenary session concerned procedural matters.

Eleven sets of detailed resolutions were submitted by the Resolutions Committee to the 2,140 registered delegates at the Sheraton-Boston Hotel ballroom. Most of the resolutions covered civil rights in such areas as labor and industry, education and politics.

Two resolutions introduced by the Wichita Kan., branch and the New York State Conference of Branches to enlarge youth and regional representation on the board and open the way to a revision of the constitution were not admitted to the floor for discussion.

Reaffirmed was a resolution voted by the national board of directors last April 10 opposing involvement in foreign policy or merging with any Vietnam peace groups.

While neither endorsing nor opposing the war in Vietnam, the resolution of reaffirmation emphasized a determination to keep out of the controversy over the war and bar the use of the N.A.A.C.P.'s organizational strength in support of peace movements.

The resolution condemning the Newark riots read as follows:

"This convention of the N.A.A.C.P. can understand, but not condone, quick violence which occurs to express mass

Continued on Page 55, Column 2

NEW BLAZES FLARE

Fire Captain Is Killed—Governor Scores 'Insurrection'

By HOMER BIGART
Special to The New York Times

NEWARK, Sunday, July 16—The Negro districts of Newark erupted again last night and early this morning. Four persons were killed during the night, bringing the total to 21 as the fighting went into its fifth day.

Incensed by the slaying of a white fire captain by Negro snipers, Gov. Richard J. Hughes said he was considering an appeal for Federal help in capturing the terrorists.

Two Negro women were killed in clashes between snipers and the National Guard and the police, and a looter was killed as he ran from a store. Terrorists ranged outside the ghetto and gunfire—including bursts from machine guns—resounded in downtown Newark. There was a renewed outbreak of arson. A guardsman was critically wounded.

Although most of the firing was concentrated in Negro areas, the police reported sniping in every section of the city.

The police used so much ammunition that 20 cases of rifle cartridges were borrowed from nearby Union City.

'Criminal Insurrection'

Governor Hughes, who earlier said that the thousands of militia and policemen appeared to be gaining control of the streets after three days of turmoil, took a more pessimistic view in a midnight press conference. He indicated that he would ask for Federal marshals.

The marshals are better trained than the guardsmen in riot duty and the Governor indicated he wanted men who would go into the ghetto and bring the snipers out alive.

The Governor, red with anger, said shortly before midnight that it was time that the people of Newark chose between the terrorists and law and order.

"This is a criminal insurrection by people who say they hate the white man but who really hate America," Governor Hughes charged.

The number of injured increased to 1,100. The police said 1,600 had been arrested, and the Chamber of Commerce estimated that damage from arson and looting was "well up in the millions."

The Governor threatened to impose stronger sanctions to throttle the violence. Half the city was under curfew that

Continued on Page 54, Column 1

Associated Press

SEARCHING FOR WEAPONS: A National Guard man moving a civilian toward a wall as a policeman searches others last night in Newark. None were arrested. White blur, upper right, is light reflected through car window.

"All the News That's Fit to Print"

The New York Times

LATE CITY EDITION

Weather: Partly cloudy, showers, today and tonight. Partly sunny tomorrow. Temp. range: today 87-76, Mon. 90-75. Temp.-Hum. Index 80. Mon. 82. Full U.S. report Page 69.

VOL. CXVI. No. 39,994 NEW YORK, TUESDAY, JULY 25, 1967 — 10 CENTS

U. S. TROOPS SENT INTO DETROIT; 19 DEAD; JOHNSON DECRIES RIOTS; NEW OUTBREAK IN EAST HARLEM

LEADER IN HOUSE ACTS TO COMPEL ARMS SALE STUDY

Widnall Seeks to Bar Rise in Latin Aid and Force a Weapons Review

SYMINGTON JOINS FIGHT

Says He Will Support Move to Drop Pentagon's Fund That Helped Purchases

Excerpts from Senate hearing will be found on Page 2.

By NEIL SHEEHAN
Special to The New York Times

WASHINGTON, July 24—The minority leader of the House Banking and Currency Committee sought today to force a Congressional review of United States arms sales by attempting to delay an Administration bill to increase economic aid to Latin America.

The move in the House came as Senator Stuart Symington announced his support for abolition of a $383-million revolving credit fund that the Defense Department has been using to guarantee loans for the purchase of American arms by underdeveloped countries.

Mr. Symington is chairman of the Senate Foreign Relations Subcommittee on Near Eastern and South Asian Affairs. Yesterday the subcommittee released testimony by Administration officials and the world's leading private arms merchant. It disclosed that United States controls over surplus American weapons in the hands of European nations were breaking down.

The minority leader of the House committee, William B. Widnall, Republican of New Jersey, said the bill to increase the contribution to the Inter-American Bank from $760-million to $900-million over the next three years should be postponed until the Administration clarified its arm sales policies.

Action Due Tomorrow

The House is scheduled to act on the bill Wednesday.

President Johnson wants the increase to support a pledge made at the Punta del Este Conference in April that he would seek more American aid to help in forming a Latin-American common market.

Mr. Widnall noted statements Senator Symington made at a news conference this morning that the Administration might have used "backdoor" financing to circumvent Congressional limitations on arms shipments to Latin America.

"Unless final House floor debate on the Inter-American Bank bill is delayed pending

Continued on Page 2, Column 3

'Vive Quebec Libre!' De Gaulle Cries Out To Montreal Crowd

By JAY WALZ
Special to The New York Times

MONTREAL, July 24—President de Gaulle shouted a call for a "free Quebec" tonight before a cheering, chanting crowd dominated by French-Canadian extremists.

Speaking from a balcony at City Hall on his arrival in the city, the general told the crowd of about 10,000 that he sensed "liberation" in the air. In the context of his remarks, his only allusion could be to the separation of French-speaking Quebec from English-speaking Canada.

"Vive le Quebec!" the 76-year-old French leader called out at the climax of the headiest reception he has received since arriving in Canada yesterday for a five-day visit. Then he added: "Vive Quebec libre! Vive le Canada Français! Vive la France!"

In Ottawa, Prime Minister Lester B. Pearson was reported to be considering whether the Government should ask

Continued on Page 3, Column 2

RUSSIAN WEAPONS OFFERED BY ISRAEL

She Lists Up-to-Date Arms, Seized in Sinai, for Barter Deals With the West

By DAVID BINDER
Special to The New York Times

BONN, July 24—The Israeli military authorities are offering to sell or barter examples of up-to-date Soviet weapons captured in the Sinai Desert to Western countries in return for tanks and planes.

In addition to outright barter, the Israelis are presumably seeking to use the Soviet weapons as an inducement to obtain purchasing rights for Western equipment, but this could not be confirmed.

Informed sources said Israeli officers had been circulating lists of the captured Soviet weapons to the intelligence services of Britain, the United States and West Germany. The lists include artillery, electronic gear, rockets, tanks and planes. Some of the items have not yet been distributed to the Eastern European nations, members of the Warsaw Pact, according to the sources.

Among devices said to have been unknown in the West heretofore is a tracked vehicle that "plants" bundles of contact mines called deadly moles. The mines, it is said, dig themselves into the ground automatically.

Another mine-laying device is said to be a 50-ton tracked vehicle resembling a plow that "sows" an area about 150 by

Continued on Page 2, Column 7

RUMANIA AFFIRMS CLOSE SOVIET TIES AS A BASIC POLICY

But Ceausescu Also Notes Differences of Views on Mideast and Atom Pact

By RICHARD EDER
Special to The New York Times

BUCHAREST, July 24—Rumania, whose independence in international affairs has been voiced increasingly in recent months, stressed today that close cooperation with the Soviet Union and other Communist nations was still the keystone of her foreign policy.

Upsetting some predictions that he was about to pull further away from Moscow, the Rumanian leader, Nicolae Ceausescu called for more consultation among Communists.

But he also expressed views on the Middle East and on the proposed treaty to bar the proliferation of nuclear weapons that were contrary to those of the Soviet Union.

Reaffirms Pact Adherence

He reaffirmed Rumanian adherence to the Warsaw pact, suggested new forms of Eastern European economic cooperation, and paid a rarely heard tribute to the role of Soviet troops in driving the Germans from Rumania in World War II.

Mr. Ceausescu went so far as to endorse a Soviet-backed proposal, to which Rumania has been cool, for a pooling of Communist efforts to provide material aid to North Vietnam. What form such pooling would take was not made clear.

Mr. Ceausescu, who is General Secretary of the Communist party, gave his views in a two-and-a-half-hour speech at the opening of a foreign policy review by the National Assembly.

Speech Widely Heralded

Because Rumanian diplomats and officials have let it be known for the last two months that important declarations would be forthcoming, and because events in the Middle East have made more emphatic the differences between Rumania and the other Communist countries, there was considerable curiosity about what he would say.

The reaction of diplomats and other observers was that Mr. Ceausescu was attempting to present his policy in terms as acceptable as possible to the Soviet Union, without abandoning in any respect his independent position.

The Rumanian leader's cordial words about the Soviet Union some harsh language about American imperialism, his reaffirmation of Rumania's adherence to the Warsaw pact, were balanced by two sharp reminders of divergence from Soviet policy.

In speaking of the Middle

Continued on Page 4, Column 3

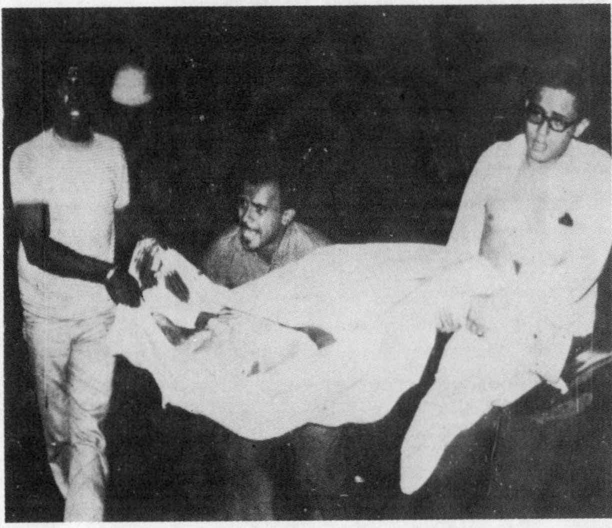

Associated Press

VICTIM IN EAST HARLEM: A Puerto Rican youth is carried by bystanders on 112th Street between Second and Third Avenues. He was found on the sidewalk after shooting between police and snipers. He died of a broken neck.

TANKS IN DETROIT

800 Are Injured and 2,000 Arrested—Business at Halt

By GENE ROBERTS
Special to The New York Times

DETROIT, Tuesday, July 25—President Johnson rushed 4,700 Army paratroopers into Detroit at midnight last night as Negro snipers besieged two police stations in rioting that brought near-paralysis to the nation's fifth largest city.

The death toll stood at 19, and damage from fire and looting — estimated by police at $150 million—was worse than in any riot in the country's history.

Tanks rumbled into the city's East Side to rescue more than 100 policemen and National Guardsmen who were trapped inside the precinct houses. Negro snipers fired into windows and doors, and policemen and Guardsmen fought back with machineguns, shotguns and high-velocity rifles.

"It looks like Berlin in 1945," said Mayor Jerome P. Cavanagh, who along with Gov. George Romney had met with resistance from the White House in trying to have the Federal troops put into action here immediately.

He and Gov. George Romney had pleaded with Cyrus H. Vance, the President's personal representative here, until just before midnight when a reluctant White House finally agreed to send the paratroopers into action.

Vance Held Back

Although the President had ordered the air lifting of the troops to nearby Selfridge Air Force Base from Fort Campbell, Ky, and Fort Bragg, N. C., Mr. Vance declined for hours to commit the men in the hope that the city and state could bring the situation under control.

Federal troops have been used in recent years to enforce Federal desegregation laws, but have not been used in a riot situation since Detroit's racial riot in 1943.

Before the President announced on nationwide television his decision to use the soldiers, Mayor Cavanagh, a Democrat, had taken strong exception to the hesitancy shown by the White House, but he said that he "understood the traditional Federal desire not to get involved in this type of dispute."

"With more and more cities getting involved in riots," he said, "the Government is asking: 'How involved can we get?'"

Hundreds of new fires were reported, bringing the total in two days of violence to more than 731. Large areas of the city were blanketed in smoke.

Thousands of workers stayed away from their jobs, scores of

Continued on Page 19, Column 1

Welfare Workers Reject Settlement; Stoppage to Go On

By EMANUEL PERLMUTTER

Members of the Social Service Employes Union early this morning voted down a settlement of a dispute that has resulted in a work stoppage by welfare caseworkers. The rejection came after city officials and union leaders had agreed earlier on a settlement formula.

After three hours of tumultuous debate, union members voted 800 to 438 to reject the formula and continue the stoppage, which began June 19.

The proposed settlement, which was announced earlier yesterday by Herbert L. Haber, director of the city's labor relations, provided that the caseworkers would begin work at 9 o'clock this morning and negotiations between the city and union on disputed issues would begin at the same hour.

But, after noisy delegates, gathered at the National Maritime Hall at Seventh Avenue and 12th Street, had voted, Mrs. Judith Mage, the union presi-

Continued on Page 27, Column 3

2 KILLED, 12 HURT IN VIOLENCE HERE

Disturbance Is Worst Since 1964—Rioters Set Cars Afire and Loot Stores

By HOMER BIGART

Thousands of Puerto Rican youths swept through East Harlem Streets last night and early today in renewed anti-police demonstrations that left two dead and at least 12 injured.

The police fought several gun battles with snipers in the city's worst disorders since the race riots in Harlem and Bedford-Stuyvesant in 1964.

Mobs overturned automobiles and set them afire, looted stores, pulled fire alarms and pelted firemen and policemen with bricks and bottles.

The fighting extended along Third Avenue from 119th to 103d Streets and from Park Avenue to Second Avenue before 1,000 police reinforcements contained the violence early today. But sporadic outbursts continued.

In the Mott Haven section of the Bronx, across the Harlem River from the disturbance in Manhattan, throngs of Puerto Ricans ran through the streets and broke some windows.

Leary Goes to the Bronx

Eighteen - year - old Carlemo Cordero of 605 East 138th Street was shot in the left arm at 139th Street and St. Anne's Avenue, a block from where firemen had put out a rubbish fire started by rampaging youths.

About 70 extra policemen were sent into the Bronx precinct along with a dozen taxicabs that the police used to make unobtrusive patrols.

Police Commissioner Howard R. Leary and Chief Inspector Sanford D. Garelik left East Harlem and arrived in the troubled Bronx neighborhood at 2:15 A.M. after trouble had been reported in two stores.

In East Harlem a teen-aged youth and a 44-year-old woman were killed last night. Three policemen were listed among the injured.

The police came under sniper fire from roofs for the first time since the disorder flared early Sunday morning. The first shooting incident came in mid-evening on 112d Street between Second and Third Avenues. When the police ceased firing.

Continued on Page 18, Column 1

President Calls on Nation To Combat Lawlessness

By MAX FRANKEL
Special to The New York Times

WASHINGTON, Tuesday, July 25—President Johnson, in the wake of new racial outbreaks, called upon the entire nation early today to condemn and combat lawlessness in all its forms. Mr. Johnson made an unscheduled television appearance after reluctantly yielding to the Michigan authorities late last night and authorizing the use of Federal troops against rioters in Detroit.

President's speech and text of proclamation, Page 20.

"We will not tolerate lawlessness," he declared. "We will not endure violence. It matters not by whom it is done, or under what slogan or banner. It will not be tolerated."

Asserting that the "vast majority of Negroes and whites are shocked and outraged" by rioting, the President said, "This nation will do whatever is necessary to do to suppress and to punish those who engage in it."

"Pillage, looting, murder and arson have nothing to do with civil rights," the President declared. "They are criminal conduct. The Federal Government in the circumstances here presented had no alternative but to respond since it was called upon by the Governor of the state and presented with proof of his inability to restore order."

The President, noting that the

Continued on Page 20, Column 1

JOHNSON ACCUSED BY G.O.P. IN RIOTING

Coordinating Group Asserts He Failed to Recognize Approach of 'Anarchy'

Text of G.O.P. statement is printed on Page 20.

By JOHN HERBERS
Special to The New York Times

WASHINGTON, July 24—The Republican Coordinating Committee said today that the United States was "rapidly approaching a state of anarchy" because of racial rioting and that President Johnson must share in the blame.

"The President has totally failed to recognize the problem," the committee said in a statement. "Worse, he has vetoed legislation and opposed other legislation designed to re-establish peace and order within the country." It added:

"We call upon the President to face the reality of the condition which in three years has grown to crisis. Pleasant platitudes and statements of good intentions can no longer conceal the critical state of the nation."

House Speaker John W. McCormack, after conferring with Mr. Johnson, reported that the President repeated to party leaders what he had said on many occasions before, that "public order is the first business of government." The disregard for law and order "cannot be tolerated," the Speaker added.

Mr. Johnson himself made no personal reply, but he authorized Democratic Congressional leaders to give his opinion that

Continued on Page 20, Column 5

Castro's Havana Cleaner Than the Old, but Shabby

Lee Lockwood from Black Star

Cuban workmen pasting up a propaganda poster. The beard, a trademark of Fidel Castro and his fellow revolutionaries, has not been adopted by the young men of the country.

By JAMES RESTON
Special to The New York Times

HAVANA, July 24 — Havana has lost its old prerevolution opulence, but it has also lost its old revolting slums. The city is cleaner but shabbier than it was seven years ago, and somehow it seems younger.

There are more than 100,000 students here this summer, most of them Cubans, but many from other parts of Latin America and from the Communist world. They stop you on the street and ask whether you are a Russian or Czech. When you say "American," they look surprised, but they are courteous and never hostile.

Incidentally, Premier Fidel Castro's beard has apparently not caught on with the young. Razor blades are a prize on the black market, which is remarkably inactive for a country so long on rationing, but there are probably more smooth young faces at the University of Havana than in Berkeley.

Even the young, however, seem a little old-fashioned. They are neatly but prudently dressed. Trousers for women are accepted as a practical necessity; miniskirts are rare and seem to be regarded as

Continued on Page 11, Column 1

Englewood Police Clash With Snipers

By MARTIN GANSBERG
Special to The New York Times

ENGLEWOOD, N. J., Tuesday, July 25—The police exchanged fire with snipers in the predominantly Negro Fourth Ward here last night in the fourth successive night of racial disorders.

Shortly before midnight, the police in the Fourth Ward requested that headquarters rush in barricades to be set up around a six-block area running from Linden Street north to Jay Street and over to School Street and Englewood Avenue.

Three arrests were reported, one of a juvenile.

There were reports that a Cadillac was cruising around the area, with someone in it taking potshots at policemen.

The city's 65-man force has

Continued on Page 21, Column 1

NEWS INDEX

S.N.C.C. Chief Shot In Cambridge, Md.

By BEN A. FRANKLIN
Special to The New York Times

CAMBRIDGE, Md., Tuesday, July 25—H. Rap Brown, national chairman of the Student Nonviolent Coordinating Committee, was slightly wounded by shotgun fire here last night after urging a crowd of about 400 Negroes in a this frequently troubled Eastern Shore Maryland city to 'burn this town down if this town don't turn around" and grant militant Negro demands.

The Negro leader was struck in the left forehead by a single pellet from one of more than a dozen sudden shotgun blasts on Pine Street in the Negro section of Cambridge about an hour after his fiery speech.

A few hours later, a white city policeman, Patrolman Russell Wroten, riding through

Continued on Page 20, Column 6

Judy Collins was among the folksingers who swept the country with songs for the peace movement.

When *Hair* opened in New York it charmed and shocked audiences with its explicit portrayal of the Sixties generation.

"All the News That's Fit to Print"

The New York Times

LATE CITY EDITION

Weather: Cloudy, warm, humid, chance of showers today, tonight. Temp. range: today 83-71. Thurs. 81-69. Temp.-Hum. Index 78. Thurs. 77. Full U.S. report on Page 58.

VOL. CXVI..No. 40,004 NEW YORK, FRIDAY, AUGUST 4, 1967 10 CENTS

JOHNSON ASKS FOR 10% SURCHARGE ON PERSONAL AND BUSINESS TAXES; 45,000 MORE MEN TO GO TO VIETNAM

LINDSAY FORMING GROUP TO ASSIST SLUM BUSINESSES

Leaders of Corporations and Unions Are Recruited as Members of a Coalition

LOAN NEEDS STRESSED

Mayor Says Banks Are Not Sufficiently Involved in Negro Sections Here

By RICHARD REEVES

Mayor Lindsay is recruiting civic leaders to become members of a new organization—the New York Coalition—designed to unite corporations, unions, churches and other private organizations in an attack on the problems of the city's slums.

The city group, which is similar to the national Urban Coalition formed in Washington last Monday, would attempt to handle such problems as persuading city banks to grant more loans to Negro and Puerto Rican small-business men.

The Mayor, who hopes to announce the formation of the local coalition within two weeks, said yesterday that large banks were not sufficiently involved in helping solve the problems of New York's slums.

Banks 'Better Equipped'

"The banks know the problem—each day they have a greater awareness of the need for ghetto investment," Mr. Lindsay said at a press conference. "But I would like to remind the banks that there is great gain for themselves in vigorous investment in ghetto areas [with] valuable land that isn't being used and great talent that isn't being tapped."

Large banks and insurance companies "are better equipped than the city" to finance small-business men in slum areas, the Mayor continued. He then added that his goal was to help the residents of Harlem and Bedford-Stuyvesant become "their own butchers, bakers and candlestick makers—help them own the haberdasheries and delicatessens."

In an interview after the press conference, Mr. Lindsay said a local organization parallel to the Urban Coalition could help persuade bankers to invest in slum businesses. Other city officials later revealed that a parallel organization, the New York Coalition, was already being recruited by the Mayor and Andrew Heiskell, chairman of Time, Inc.

The mayor and Mr. Heiskell were among 22 leaders in government, business, labor, civil rights and religion who formed the Urban Coalition in Washington earlier this week.

A statement issued by the na-

Continued on Page 13, Column 1

Halo Stolen From Statue of Mary in Jerusalem Shrine

The Rev. Kevin Mooney points to the statue of the Virgin Mary in the Church of the Holy Sepulcher, Jerusalem, from which a golden halo was stolen. Earrings were also removed.

By JAMES FERON

Special to The New York Times

JERUSALEM, Aug. 3—A golden halo studded with precious stones was stolen last night from a statue of the Virgin Mary in the Church of the Holy Sepulcher, one of Christendom's holiest sites.

The church is in the former Jordanian sector of Jerusalem, which was seized by the Israelis during the war in June.

Platinum earrings, similarly studded, and a row of ornamental hearts also were removed from the three-foot-high statue inside the church's Franciscan Chapel.

Neither church officials nor the Israeli police could estimate the value of the missing items, which are among many thousands of precious and historic offerings in the ancient church.

The carved wooden statue, a gift of Queen Maria of Portugal in 1624, was in a glass case before the altar on a balcony in the southwest side of the church.

The balcony, just inside the main entrance, is revered

Continued on Page 8, Column 7

Associated Press Cablephotos

Statue, a gift from Queen Maria of Portugal, before theft

GOAL NOW 525,000

Troop Action Reflects Compromise—Rise in Spending Seen

By WILLIAM BEECHER

Special to The New York Times

WASHINGTON, Aug. 3 — President Johnson announced plans today to dispatch 45,000 to 50,000 more American troops to Vietnam, beyond the number already committed. This will bring the total to 525,000 by June 30, he said.

The decision, disclosed in Mr. Johnson's budget and tax message to Congress, represents a compromise between the 70,000 men sought by Gen William C. Westmoreland and the 15,000 to 30,000 men suggested by Secretary of Defense Robert S. McNamara.

[South Korea's President, Chung Hee Park, proposed to send 3,000 military reservists to Vietnam to free Korean and American support troops for combat duty. Page 2.]

President Johnson also declared that military spending for the fiscal year ending next June might rise as much as $4-billion over the $73.1-billion that was foreseen in January, when he presented his budget request. But he asked Mr. McNamara to defer as many nonessential military expenditures as possible to absorb some of this increase, he said.

Plane Purchases Deferred

It is understood that Secretary McNamara has already pressed the services to eliminate or postpone at least $3-billion in spending. Pentagon sources say, for example, that because aircraft losses in Vietnam have been lower than expected, purchases of replacements will probably be slowed.

Mr. Johnson's action countered any suggestion that he was seriously thinking of reverting to a holding position while seeking a quick solution that would allow him to liquidate the burdensome war effort.

His intentions were indicated by the size of the troop increase, by the reports that he had assured the military that he was not foreclosing further reinforcements and by the language used in justifying the increase in troops.

Mr. Johnson repeated a passage from his State of the Union address conceding that the end of the war was not in

Continued on Page 2, Column 3

Congress Likely to Delay Effective Date of Tax Rise

By JOHN D. MORRIS

Special to The New York Times

WASHINGTON, Aug. 3—Congress scrutinized President Johnson's tax-increase program today with a mixture of resignation, pain and hostility.

Despite the unfavorable tone of many public statements, especially by Republicans, few members of either party expressed outright opposition.

This, coupled with private assessments of the outlook by key legislators, indicated that a bill patterned on the President's recommendations would be reluctantly enacted.

It was highly doubtful, however, whether action would be completed in time to put the 10 per cent surcharge on individual income taxes into effect on Oct. 1 as is proposed.

It was also uncertain whether the full 10 per cent asked by the President for corporations as well as individuals would be approved.

The House Ways and Means Committee scheduled public hearings starting Aug. 14 with Henry H. Fowler, Secretary of the Treasury, as the opening witness.

The chairman, Representative Wilbur D. Mills, Democrat of Arkansas, declined to estimate how long the hearings would continue. But other members expressed doubt that a bill would reach the House floor before Labor Day, at the earliest.

With the Senate following the usual practice of waiting for the House to act before starting work on a tax bill, it

Continued on Page 10, Column 1

INFLATION FEARED

Message to Congress Seeks Withholding Increase Oct. 1

Text of Johnson's message is printed on Page 10.

By EDWIN L. DALE Jr.

Special to The New York Times

WASHINGTON, Aug. 3 —President Johnson asked Congress today for a 10 per cent surcharge on personal and corporate income taxes, excepting only those individuals with the lowest incomes.

Mr. Johnson said the increase was needed to head off "an unsafe and unmanageable deficit" in the Federal budget, which he said might exceed $28-billion without the tax increase. Such a deficit, he continued, could bring these results:

¶"A ruinous spiral of inflation."

¶"Brutally higher interest rates."

¶"An unequal and unjust distribution of the cost of supporting our men in Vietnam."

¶"A deterioration in our balance of payments by increasing imports and decreasing exports."

[Stock prices fell sharply in an initial reaction to the President's tax proposals, but a strong afternoon rally trimmed many of the earlier losses. Volume of 13.44 million shares was the third highest of the year.]

Affects Withholding

If enacted as proposed, the 10 per cent surcharge would take effect for individuals Oct. 1 and be reflected at once in withholding from paychecks. The present amount withheld each week or month will rise 10 per cent.

Next April, the individual taxpayer will calculate his tax as usual on income for the year as a whole and then add 2.5 per cent, because the surcharge would be in effect for only one quarter of 1967. Some or all of this extra payment due will already have been covered by withholding in the case of most wage earners.

A similar 10 per cent surcharge would be applied to corporate profits taxes, but retroactive to July 1. Thus in the case of taxes on 1967 incomes, corporations would be hit a little harder than individuals, though the burden would be equal in later years.

The President asked that the tax remain on the books until mid-1969 "or continue for so long as the unusual expenditures associated with our efforts in Vietnam require higher revenues."

There would be no surcharge on the tax of a family of four with an income up to $5,000, on a married couple with income up to $3,600 or on a

Continued on Page 11, Column 1

U.S. Combat Loss In Vietnam Drops To Six-Month Low

Special to The New York Times

SAIGON, South Vietnam, Aug. 3—American combat casualties dropped last week to their lowest level in six months, a United States command spokesman said today.

During the week, 114 soldiers were killed and 893 wounded, the spokesman said. The week before, United States losses were 164 killed and 1,442 wounded.

Enemy casualties dropped to 1,399 killed, from 1,780 the previous week, but with the low allied losses the announced ratio of allied to enemy deaths was 6.8 to 1, the largest of the year.

Vietnamese Losses at 61

South Vietnamese losses were listed by the United States command at 61 dead for the week, which equaled the figure for the first week in May. A South Vietnamese military spokesman said Government losses were 76 killed and 368 wounded, with 14 missing, equaling the losses of the last week in April.

Other allies suffered 30 killed during the week. The United States command does not break down the losses by country, but South Korean and Australian troops have seen the most recent action.

The spokesman said military activity for the period ranged

Continued on Page 2, Column 7

2 IN VIETNAM RACE URGE PEACE TALKS

Presidential Campaign On —'We Must De-escalate,' One Candidate Says

By R. W. APPLE Jr.

Special to The New York Times

SAIGON, South Vietnam, Aug. 3—The South Vietnamese presidential campaign opened today with pledges from two civilian tickets that they would try to open immediate negotiations with North Vietnam if they were elected.

Dr. Phan Quang Dan, a Harvard-educated physician seeking the vice-presidency on a slate headed by Phan Khac Suu, Speaker of the Constituent Assembly, issued a ringing call for radical change in Government policy.

"It is impossible to fight the Communists the way we are now," he said at a news conference in a smoke-filled restaurant this morning. "It would be better to have a shouting war rather than a shooting war. We must de-escalate."

Speaking in English, he said he favored negotiations "at all levels, including the Vietcong." But his running mate, Mr. Suu, replied to the question in Vietnamese and said he would "deal with Hanoi," not with the Vietcong guerrillas of the South.

The Suu-Dan slate is one of

Continued on Page 3, Column 1

U.S.-AIDED SCHOOL HELD ANTIWHITE

Police Official Says Negroes in Nashville Teach Hatred in Name of Liberation

By JOHN HERBERS

Special to The New York Times

WASHINGTON Aug. 3 — A Nashville police captain testified today that the Federal Government was subsidizing a "liberation school" in his city that taught "unadulterated hatred" of whites and was run by an official of the Student Nonviolent Coordinating Committee.

The captain, John A. Sorace, told the Senate Judiciary Committee that the school director was Fred Brooks, whom he identified as the Nashville chairman of the student committee and who he said was receiving funds from the Office of Economic Opportunity.

Captain Sorace charged that national leaders of the student committee had fomented riots in Nashville last April and that Mr. Brooks was at the scene of the violence.

Later in the day, Senator James O. Eastland of Mississippi read a memorandum from the poverty agency denying that Mr. Brooks was on the Federal payroll. Whereupon, Mr. Sorace whipped out a "list" showing Mr. Brooks to be on the payroll for $300 a month.

Edward M. Kennedy, Democrat of Massachusetts, demanded that Mr. Sorace disclose the source of his "list." The police captain refused to do so publicly.

Senator Eastland, the committee chairman, who had charged that Communist influences were at work in the Negro movement in Nashville, broke off this exchange by saying he would demand that a poverty agency official appear before the panel for questioning.

So ended the second day of

Continued on Page 12, Column 1

Saudis Are Believed Receptive to Offer By Cairo on Yemen

By ERIC PACE

Special to The New York Times

KHARTOUM, the Sudan, Aug. 3—Authoritative sources reported that Saudi Arabia reacted favorably to an Egyptian offer made formally today, to end the struggle for power between the two countries in Yemen.

The sources, who declined to be identified for publication, said the Saudis' reaction made it probable that an Arab summit meeting would be held, most likely later this month, here in Khartoum.

It would be the first gathering of Arab leaders since the 1965 meeting in Casablanca and its purpose would be to close ranks in the wake of the Israeli military victory in June.

Ten of the 13 nations represented at the Arab foreign ministers' conference here have made it known that they favor holding a summit meeting. The exceptions were Saudi Arabia, Algeria and Syria, but these three countries are now expected to agree if the Yemen issue is resolved.

At today's session, the sources reported, the Saudi delegate, Omar Saqqaf, gave a warm initial response to the Egyptian offer, saying all differences between the two countries should be resolved. The Saudis de-

Continued on Page 7, Column 2

DUVALIER FAMILY IN HAITI DIVIDED

Dictator's Struggle to Keep Control Has Caused Open Conflict With His Kin

By HENRY GINIGER

Special to The New York Times

PORT-AU-PRINCE, Haiti, Aug. 2 — President François Duvalier's struggle to maintain his 10-year dictatorship has caused open conflict within his own family.

The family quarrel adds to a growing picture of desperation in the regime.

The latest target of the President's ceaseless hunt for "traitors" among Haiti's mostly black population of 4,660,000 was his son-in-law, Lieut. Col. Max Dominique, now abroad. Last Saturday he was dismissed from the army "for the good of the service" and has been ordered to return within 30 days to face trial on a charge of conspiracy against the President.

Colonel Dominique, the husband of the eldest of the three Duvalier daughters, Marie-Denise, left for Europe late in June, taking his wife and the youngest of the sisters, Simone, with him.

As soon as they left, Colonel

Continued on Page 6, Column 6

NEWARK COLLEGE TO HELP NEGROES

Willing to Set Aside Site for a Slum Area Complex

By RONALD SULLIVAN

Special to The New York Times

TRENTON, Aug. 3—The Newark College of Medicine and Dentistry has agreed in principle to use a major part of its proposed Newark campus for an urban welfare center in the Negro slums.

The complex that is envisioned would contain low-income housing, child care and health centers and facilities for employment and welfare.

After a three-hour meeting here between Gov. Richard J. Hughes and his aides and leaders of the college, John V. Spinale, special assistant to the Governor, reported that everyone had agreed that there "must be full participation of the Negro community" in the development of a 66-acre tract that the college has set aside for future development.

The tract is near the heart of the area that was torn by

Continued on Page 12, Column 6

New York Air Pollution Worst Of Nation's Major Urban Areas

By HAROLD M. SCHMECK Jr.

Special to The New York Times

WASHINGTON, Aug. 3—New York has the most severe air pollution problem of any major metropolitan area in the nation, the Public Health Service reported today.

Chicago was ranked second, Philadelphia third, the Los Angeles-Long Beach area fourth and Cleveland fifth. The report named 65 areas and cautioned against complacency by those that appeared low on the list.

"In all the large urban areas covered in our report the public health and welfare are threatened by air pollution," said Dr. John T. Middleton, director of the Public Health Service's National Center for Air Pollution Control.

The center ranked each of the 65 urban centers on the basis of air pollution measurement and on information on fuel use supplied by the Bureau of Census.

The ratings were based on the following factors:

The average total of air pollution particles in the atmosphere; the average number of particles defined as benzene-soluble particles, mostly associated with man-made pollution; the frequency and severity of excessive air pollution episodes; the area's total gasoline consumption; the population density of automobiles in the area; the average concentration of sulphur dioxide in the atmosphere; the area's total emissions of sulphur dioxide; the density of sulphur

Continued on Page 34, Column 1

NEWS INDEX

United Press International Radiophoto

ACCIDENT IN SOUTH VIETNAM: A U.S. transport, shot down by American gunners, plummeting to earth in Haphan, about 15 miles west of Quangngai, yesterday. Plane, loaded with ammunition, was about to land at a Special Forces camp when a single round of artillery from the ground cut it in half. All three crewmen died in the mishap.

Levitt Finds Taxes Trail State Estimate

By RICHARD L. MADDEN

Special to The New York Times

ALBANY, Aug. 3—Tax collections in the first one-third of the state's fiscal year lagged behind Governor Rockefeller's budget estimates, State Controller Arthur Levitt indicated today.

The Controller reported that tax collections for the first four months of the current fiscal year increased less than 1 per cent over the comparable period last year.

Mr. Levitt, a Democrat and frequent critic of the Republican Governor's budget policies, noted in his brief statement that the current state budget of nearly $4.7-billion is based on the forecast of an 8 per cent increase in revenue during the full fiscal year to stay in balance.

The Controller's report did

Continued on Page 32, Column 3

"All the News That's Fit to Print"

The New York Times

LATE CITY EDITION

Weather: Fair and pleasant today, tonight and tomorrow. Temperature range: today 81-57. Sunday 80-52. Temp.-Hum. Index 73; Sunday 72. Complete U.S. report on Page 42.

VOL. CXVI..No. 40,035 © 1967 The New York Times Company. NEW YORK, MONDAY, SEPTEMBER 4, 1967 10 CENTS

THIEU AND KY ARE VICTORS IN SOUTH VIETNAM BALLOT; 83% OF ELECTORATE VOTES

Associated Press Radiophoto

BABY SITTERS ARE SCARCE: A South Vietnamese woman balloting near Saigon

TWO GENERALS WIN

Their Goal Was 40% but They Get Only 27% of Total

By R. W. APPLE Jr.
Special to The New York Times

SAIGON, South Vietnam, Monday, Sept. 4—Lieut. Gen. Nguyen Van Thieu, the candidate of the armed forces, won a four-year term as President of South Vietnam yesterday in the country's momentous national election.

General Thieu, the incumbent chief of state, and his vice-presidential running mate, Premier Nguyen Cao Ky, built their victory on two strongpoints — the 700,000-man army and the minority groups whose support they had sought: hill tribes, Roman Catholic refugees, ethnic Cambodians and Chinese, and religious splinter sects.

But the military candidates, in a field of 11 slates, fell far short of the 40 per cent of the vote that their supporters had hoped for. With the count nearing completion, the generals had only 27 per cent of the vote, even though they outpolled their closest rival by better than two to one.

Lawyer Finishes Second

In a major surprise, Truong Dinh Dzu, a wealthy Saigon lawyer, finished in second place, running well ahead of both Tran Van Huong, a former Premier, and Phan Khac Suu, the Speaker of the Constituent Assembly. Mr. Suu, although his campaign had appeared to gain momentum in the last week, was a badly beaten fourth.

At 2:30 P.M. today (2:30 A.M. New York time), with 90 per cent of the vote counted, a New York Times tabulation showed:

Nguyen Van Thieu. 1,398,581
Truong Dinh Dzu.... 651,745
Tran Van Huong .. 428,680
Phan Khac Suu.... 425,341

A total of 4,868,266 persons—51 per cent of the 8.5 million persons of voting age and 83 per cent of the 5,853,384 registered voters—marched to the polls on a brilliant, cloudless Sunday.

About 2,650,000 persons of voting age were not registered, most of them because they live in Vietcong-controlled or contested areas. Parts of nearly every province, including some places within 15 miles of Saigon, were on the list of nonvoting localities.

The turnout exceeded the expectations of the Government. It was slightly larger

Continued on Page 2, Column 1

Consensus of U.S. Team Is That Voting Was Fair

By TOM BUCKLEY
Special to The New York Times

SAIGON, South Vietnam, Sept. 3—The consensus today among the 22 American observers of the South Vietnamese election was that, as far as they could see, it had been conducted fairly. Several of those active in politics at home shared a view expressed by Gov. William L. Guy of North Dakota, a Democrat.

He said that, while instances of fraud might come to light, the election "as far as I can see has been carried out with greater detail and checks and balances than many of our own."

[Officials in Washington were surprised and encouraged by the size of the turnout in the election and by the Vietcong's inability to destroy the election machinery through terrorism. Page 3.]

John S. Knight publisher of the Knight Newspapers and the only member of the team who has expressed sharp public criticism of the Johnson Administration's Vietnam policy, implied reservations.

Field Trips Included

"I could see no evidence of wrongdoing," he said, "but we're observers, not inspectors of elections. If I were an inspector, I'd have brought Dick Daley and Ray Bliss along."

Richard J. Daley, Mayor of Chicago and chairman of the Cook County Democratic organization, and Mr. Bliss, chairman of the Republican National Committee, are regarded as among the most astute political organizers of their parties.

The Americans did their observing in Saigon and on field

Continued on Page 2, Column 4

TERRORISTS KILL 26 DURING VOTING

Vietcong Incidents Reported in 21 of 43 Provinces—Polling Places Blasted

Special to The New York Times

SAIGON, South Vietnam, Sept. 3—The Vietcong staged a series of election day terrorist attacks and shellings today in which at least 26 South Vietnamese were killed and 82 wounded.

A South Vietnamese military spokesman said 54 incidents were reported today and 80 in the 24 hours preceding the opening of the polls at 7 A.M. It will be two or three days before all the incidents are reported.

The spokesman said there were incidents or shellings in 21 of South Vietnam's 43 provinces.

Despite the widespread attacks, a United States Embassy spokesman said the Vietcong had prevented voting in only three villages, all in Quangtri Province, the northernmost in South Vietnam. The spokesman said balloting was held at 8,821 polling places in the country.

The most serious incidents were reported in or near Sai-

Continued on Page 4, Column 1

EDUCATION'S COST IN SUBURBS STIRS GROWING CONCERN

Taxpayers Are Scrutinizing Budgets as Area Spending Increases 11 Per Cent

13 COUNTIES SURVEYED

Free-Busing Law in Jersey Poses Obstacles—Broader Curriculums Scheduled

By LEONARD BUDER

Taxpayers' revolts against rising school costs have cast a shadow over many suburban school systems as they prepare to reopen this week.

"There's a fiscal crisis at our heels," said Dr. Carroll F. Johnson, Superintendent of Schools in White Plains, where taxpayers approved an increase in school spending powers last spring after twice voting it down.

"We're in for rougher times ahead," added a Nassau County school board member. On Long Island, 43 school budgets for 1967-68 were initially voted down last spring, compared with 18 the year before.

"The voters are carefully scrutinizing the budgets," the board member continued. "We'll salvage the basic programs, but the extras will suffer. This will probably mean cutbacks in recreation, adult education and special programs."

Free Busing in Jersey

Adding to the concern of school officials in New Jersey is the effect of a new state law requiring districts to provide free bus transportation to children attending private and parochial schools if they generally do so for public-school pupils.

The state will reimburse the districts for 75 per cent of the cost, but the remaining 25 per cent has many officials worried.

"We adopted our budget before we knew how many kids would apply under this law," one superintendent said. "What are we going to do for our share of the cost?"

Implementation of the law is also causing a logistical headache. Districts in some counties, such as Bergen, have joined under what they consider to be a feasible arrangement. But other districts, working on their own, admit

Continued on Page 22, Column 1

Labor Day

Today is Labor Day. Following are services affected:

Parking—Sunday regulations in effect.
Post Offices—Closed except for special delivery.
Stores—Department and most retail stores closed.
Banks and Stock Exchanges—Closed.
Sanitation—No regular refuse collection.
Central Park Drives—Closed to autos, 6 A.M. to 6 P.M.

All Goes Right as Sweden Shifts Her Traffic Pattern

Associated Press Cablephoto

Swedish motorists on King Street in Stockholm turned out at 5 A.M. to participate in change to right-hand driving. There had been a ban on traffic since midnight Saturday.

By The Associated Press

STOCKHOLM, Sept. 3—Swedes took to the highways by the tens of thousands today to test their country's new right-hand driving regulations. The resulting traffic jams had a holiday flavor. Despite the switch from driving on the left, the first hours of the traffic revolution were almost bloodless. No serious accidents were reported. Most city drivers seemed to enjoy the early chaos on the streets. Smaller cities and towns changed over at 6 A.M. after a five-hour prohibition on all traffic. Bystanders cheered as cars moved into right-hand traffic lanes. Townspeople on foot, bicycles and horseback joined the throngs in the roadways. Policemen and soldiers assigned to traffic duty were presented with bunches of flowers. In Stock-

Continued on Page 26, Column 1

REUTHER BLAMES FORD FOR IMPASSE IN NEGOTIATIONS

U.A.W. Chief Says Failure of Company to Supply Data Could Force Walkout

By JERRY M. FLINT
Special to The New York Times

DETROIT, Sept. 3—Walter P. Reuther, president of the United Automobile Workers, said today that unless the Ford Motor Company changes its bargaining approach, "there will be a strike, but they will have called it."

The union president demanded that Ford produce figures on company productivity for use in the bargaining on wages. He said that Ford refused this request today. Mr. Reuther said that he also was rebuffed when he sought to discuss higher wages in terms of company profits.

"If the company isn't prepared to talk about economic facts," Mr. Reuther told newsmen after a bargaining session, then the union has "no recourse but to strike."

In another development, Mr. Reuther announced tonight that William E. Simkin, Director of the Federal Mediation and Conciliation Service, would sit in on tomorrow's talks. Mr. Reuther emphasized that the invitation was extended because the union wanted a Government official to see firsthand what some of the problems are.

Calls Data Essential

The union leader made it clear that he believed Ford's productivity increase was at least 6 per cent a year and that he wanted wages and benefits to equal the productivity gains. This translates into 90 cents an hour over a three-year contract. Ford has offered a three-year contract with wage and fringe benefit increases of close to 4 per cent a year, or 55 to 60 cents an hour over three years.

Mr. Reuther called the company's refusal to talk in terms of productivity and profits the equivalent of saying: "Let's lay the facts aside." Without this information, he said, the only way to decide the size of the wage and benefit increases in a new contract is a strike.

Malcolm L. Denise, Ford's chief negotiator, who is a company vice president, said wages did not change as plant productivity "jiggles up or down."

"They haven't in the past," he said.

Mr. Denise said the amount of wage and benefit increases was determined by collective bargaining.

Federal Mediator Arrives

"If you want to call that a jungle battle, you can call it that," he said, but added, "we've reasoned together in the past."

Mr. Reuther always asks the car manufacturers to produce their productivity figures. The companies always refuse and even decline to say if such figures exist.

Although the strike deadline was only three days away, Ford and union negotiators appeared to be marking time.

Today's bargaining sessions at Ford's headquarters building in Dearborn, west of Detroit, began at 11:25 A.M., adjourned for lunch at 1:30 P.M., and resumed at 4:05 P.M.

Both sides made it clear that

Continued on Page 14, Column 1

A 'BILL OF RIGHTS' DUE FOR TENANTS

City Will Order It Printed on New Leases in Both English and Spanish

By EARL CALDWELL

The City Rent Administrator said yesterday that landlords would be required to print a "tenants' bill of rights" on the back of every lease as a means of reducing abuses of the rent control law.

The Administrator, Frederic S. Berman, said the document would "advise tenants of what their rights are under the rent control law," and would be printed in both Spanish and English.

Mr. Berman said that a number of other major forms used by his department would also be printed in Spanish and English.

The first of these, one used by tenants in applying for rent reductions, is to become available in both languages this week.

The changes, Mr. Berman said, are designed to cope with the "small handful" of landlords who take advantage of their tenants by overcharging, harassment and illegal eviction.

He said the city had found that "a good deal of this" took place in areas where there was a language problem, "where the tenants are not as aware of their rights."

The Administrator also an-

Continued on Page 15, Column 4

New-Politics Group Gives Equal Votes To Negro Minority

By WARREN WEAVER Jr.
Special to The New York Times

CHICAGO, Sept. 3—The National New Politics Convention agreed tonight to demands from its Negro minority for equal voting power.

Supporters of the move called it a gesture of reparation and an earnest of good faith. Opponents said it was a violation of democratic principle and "a farce."

The convention of American radicals, in which white delegates outnumbered Negroes by about 1,500 to 600, thus met in full the second major demand submitted in two days by the convention's Black Caucus as the price of continued racial unity.

In practical terms, the move increased the number of votes that can be cast by the militant all-Negro group from 5,341 to 28,498. All other delegates combined, some representing white groups and some integrated, will retain their collective voting power of 28,498.

Originally, the votes represented the membership of the anti-Vietnam war, civil rights and other local groups that sent delegates to the six-day convention called by the National Conference on New Politics. With tonight's action, this relationship ceased.

Yesterday the convention accepted a controversial 13-point policy statement dictated by the Black Caucus. If the white

Continued on Page 15, Column 2

PARTY IS ACCUSED BY CZECH WRITERS

300 Intellectuals Reported to Implore West to Rescue Their 'Spiritual Freedom'

Special to The New York Times

LONDON, Sept. 3—More than 300 Czechoslovak intellectuals have accused the Communist party in their country of conducting "a witchhunt of a pronounced fascist character" against "the entire Czechoslovak writers' community."

The accusation was made, The Sunday Times of London reported today, by Czechoslovak writers, artists, scientists, publicists and other intellectuals in a "writers' manifesto."

The 1,000-word statement appealed to writers in the West, particularly those of "leftist" sympathies, to join in a protest campaign against restrictions on the freedom of expression of Czechoslovak writers, The Sunday Times said.

The newspaper said it had obtained a copy of the document but was withholding the names of the signers "to reduce the risk of instant reprisals by the regime."

Positions Said to Be Denied

As published by The Sunday Times, the manifesto accused party representatives of having "expressly ordered the crossing-off at first of 12 and later of 4 of the names of the most courageous colleagues from the list of candidates" for the Writers Union's Governing Committee.

The party representatives "threatened to silence" the candidates, the statement said. It contended that the candidates had been "put under police surveillance and prohibited from publishing their works" and were "being subjected to persecution that is endangering their livelihood and personal freedom."

The manifesto said the events occurred during and after the Fourth Congress of Czechoslovak Writers held in Prague June 27 to 29.

Czechoslovakia's acting chargé d'affaires in London, Jan Pátek, said: "I very much doubt whether this document is true. It has all the appearances of being fabricated."

The manifesto said that participants in the congress and

Continued on Page 12, Column 7

Foreclosed Homes Sought for Poor

By MAURICE CARROLL

Some of the people living in city slums should be moved into houses already standing in the suburbs, the chairman of President Johnson's Commission on Urban Problems suggested yesterday.

The chairman, former Senator Paul H. Douglas, said Federal Housing Administration mortgages on 43,000 single-family houses, many of them in the suburbs, were foreclosed each year.

"Why not use some of them, discreetly, for public-housing clients?" he asked.

Mr. Douglas, a former Democratic Senator from Illinois, emphasized that he spoke for himself, not for the commission, which will open hearings here on Wednesday.

The commission was set up to make "a penetrating review of zoning, housing and building codes, taxation and development standards" and to report to the President and the Congress on "ways in which the efforts of

Associated Press

Paul H. Douglas

the Federal Government, private industry and local communities can be marshaled to increase the supply of low-cost decent housing."

On Friday, Robert Moses is scheduled to appear before the group at a hearing at the Community Church of New York, 40 East 35th Street.

Mr. Douglas said the erection of 500,000 public-housing units a year—"we've been building 31,000," he said—seemed a reasonable goal to ease the pressures of the nation's slums.

He suggested four sources of public-housing sites or dwellings: urban vacant lots, dilapidated urban buildings, pockets of Federally owned land and the houses on which the F.H.A. has foreclosed mortgages.

When the mortgage is foreclosed, the Senator said, the house could be turned over to a public-housing agency rather than put on the market.

Mr. Douglas indicated there would not be legal obstacles to this sort of transfer. "My staff is working on it," he said.

Mr. Douglas said that in the committee hearings so far, the clear belief had emerged that "units of local govern-

Continued on Page 15, Column 7

NEWS INDEX

In Leningrad, Three Rubles for a Job

By HENRY KAMM
Special to The New York Times

MOSCOW, Sept. 3—A tale of graft and corruption reminiscent of the most damning Soviet recitals of the evils of capitalism was unfolded this weekend in Leningrad, the birthplace of the Bolshevik Revolution.

Leningradskaya Pravda, the newspaper of the city's government and Communist party organization, told of a chauffeur's vain efforts to make an honest living in a business whose wheels appeared to turn only on bribery and cheating.

The article was viewed here with considerable interest because of muffled reports of dissatisfaction with the party leadership in Leningrad and of an article published last July 21 in Pravda, the Communist party paper. In the Pravda article, party leaders in Leningrad were warned against brushing aside "justified criticism voiced by workers."

The Leningrad paper described Nikolai Nikolayevich Ipatov as a first-class driver with an unblemished record and as a former paratrooper to whom all the highest socialist virtues were attributed.

Presumably, his criticisms are therefore to be taken as justified and not to be brushed aside.

Nikolai Nikolayevich's passport contains stamps indicating that he has been accepted for work 20 times and 11 stamps showing his resignation. The editors of Leningradskaya Pravda said he had dropped in on them on his day off, prompted by righteous indignation. They said he was thinking of going to work in a factory, far from garages and those who run them.

He told them that whenever he quit a job in despair over the prevalence of graft, no one would ever look at his immaculate working papers when he went to apply elsewhere. He got action only when he put on the table three rubles, about $3.30, for a half-liter of vodka.

Then, he said, they would

Continued on Page 12, Column 5

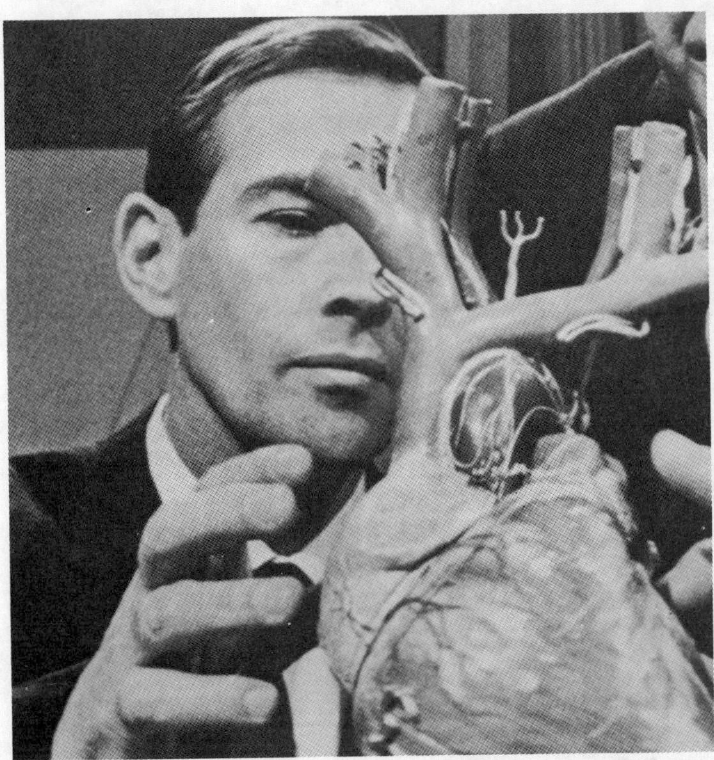

Dr. Christian N. Barnard performed the first human heart transplant.

Bobbie Gentry hit the pop scene with her mournful ballad, *Ode to Billy Joe.*

Pulitzer Prize winner Carl Sandburg spent his last years with his family in North Carolina, treasuring the land he loved and wrote about, until his death in 1967.

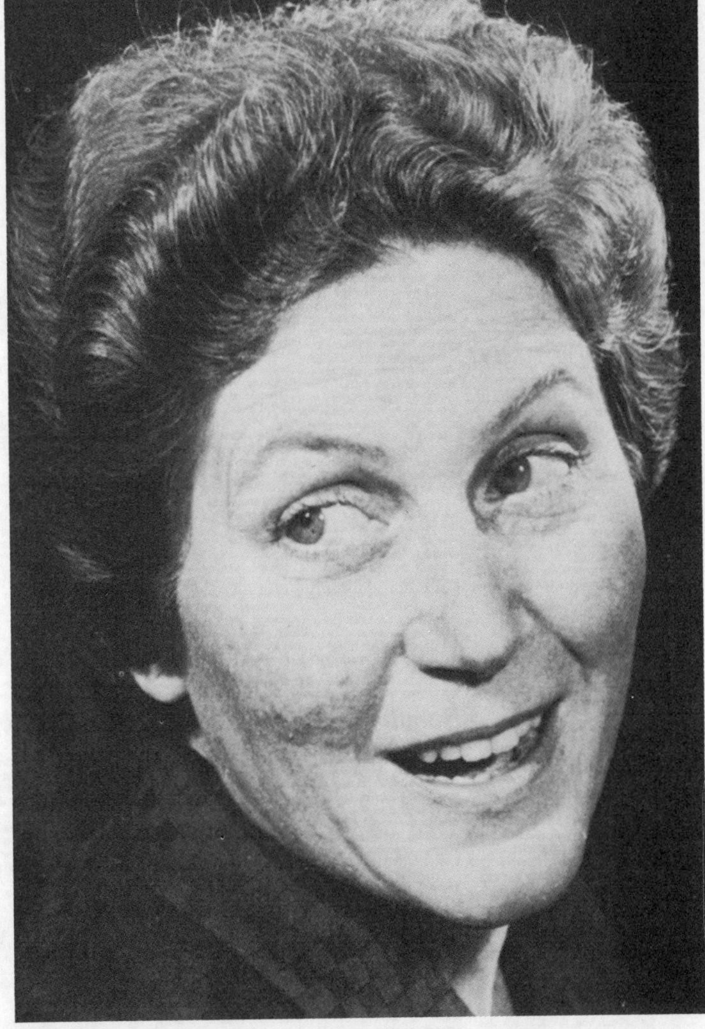

The late Joseph Stalin's daughter, Svetland Alliluyana, settled in New York to escape Soviet censorship. Her quest for self-expression resulted in two best-sellers and over one million dollars for her.

"All the News That's Fit to Print"

The New York Times

LATE CITY EDITION

Weather: Sunny and pleasant today; sunny and milder tomorrow. Temp. range: today 64-43; Saturday 66-48. Full U.S. report on Page 95.

SECTION ONE

VOL. CXVII....No. 40,083

NEW YORK, SUNDAY, OCTOBER 22, 1967

60c beyond 50-mile zone from New York City, except Long Island. Higher in air delivery cities.

40 CENTS

HOUSE PANEL HITS U.S. HEALTH UNITS FOR BUDGET ROLE

Public Health Service and National Institutes Scored on Administering Grants

EXTRAVAGANCE CHARGED

But Operations Committee Study Finds No Fault With the Quality of Research

By HAROLD M. SCHMECK Jr.
Special to The New York Times

WASHINGTON, Oct. 21 — The House Committee on Government Operations issued a report today criticizing severely the performance of the United States Public Health Service and the National Institutes of Health in administering the large research budgets they control.

The report used such terms as "inadequate" and "inept" in describing some of the specifics of the research administration.

"Our nation is presently facing a financial crisis," said Representative L. H. Fountain in a statement that was issued with the report.

"Strong inflationary pressures have developed and will continue to mount as we head toward one of the largest Federal budget deficits in history. In view of the budget situation and the heavy costs of our Vietnam commitment, we can ill afford to subsidize waste and extravagance in any Federal program."

Drafted By Subcommittee

Mr. Fountain, Democrat of North Carolina, is chairman of the Inter-Governmental Relations Subcommittee which drafted the report.

Representative William L. Dawson, Democrat of Illinois, is chairman of the full Committee on Government Operations.

The subcommittee estimates that the Federal Government's contribution to health research amounts to two-thirds of all the money spent for this purpose in the nation. In 1966, the Federal share was $1.6-billion, of which the Public Health Service accounted for $900-million. The National Institutes of Health, the chief research arm of the Public Health Service, spent $808-million of this.

Generally, the committee re-

Continued on Page 28, Column 1

Talks at Ford Push Conclusion of Pact

By JERRY M. FLINT
Special to The New York Times

DETROIT, Oct. 21—Negotiators for the Ford Motor Company and the striking United Automobile Workers went back to the bargaining table this morning in hopes of putting the finishing touches on a new contract agreement.

The major provisions of the proposed pact have been agreed upon, but already there were signs of dissatisfaction among some union men.

The dissatisfaction centered on these areas:

¶A special pay increase of 30 cents an hour a year for

Continued on Page 37, Column 1

HOSPITAL REPORT LISTS NEW CURBS

Progress Study by Terenzio Finds Better Supervision of Voluntary Institutions

By EMANUEL PERLMUTTER

The city reported yesterday that it had tightened its controls over voluntary hospitals and medical schools affiliated with municipal hospitals.

They must now submit monthly expense reports to the city, and physicians they assign to municipal hospitals are strictly limited in the amount of time they spend in outside teaching.

These changes in the hospital affiliation program are among the highlights of a 28-point progress report that has been submitted by Hospitals Commissioner Joseph V. Terenzio to the State Investigation Commission.

Its contents were disclosed yesterday by Mr. Terenzio, one day after City Controller Mario A. Procaccino asked six voluntary hospitals to return $1.5-million to the city that he said had been spent improperly.

Public Hearings Planned

Under the affiliation program, the city pays the private, nonprofit voluntary hospitals and medical schools to provide equipment and personnel and to perform medical, surgical and other professional services at 19 municipal hospitals.

In general, yesterday's report cites in detail improved supervision and control of financial, personnel and professional programing in the affiliation contracts that were signed in July. Many of the improvements were made public previously. These contracts replace agreements drawn up in 1962, which had caused much criticism.

Myles J. Lane, chairman of the Investigation Commission, said yesterday, "We want to study this report before we can comment on its achievements."

"But we intend to continue the investigation of the affiliation program that we started a year ago," he added. "Our accountants have checked the books of the hospitals and we plan to hold public hearings on the whole subject in the next several weeks."

Mr. Procaccino had charged that some hospital directors had improperly certified that physicians were working in

Continued on Page 30, Column 3

Scuffles at the Pentagon Follow Rally and March by Opponents of Policy on Vietnam

U.S. marshals clubbing antiwar demonstrators who tried to storm the Pentagon yesterday

Associated Press Wirephotos

Demonstrators shouting at a military policeman at barrier

GUARDS REPULSE WAR PROTESTERS AT THE PENTAGON

6 Break Through Line Into Building — Mailer and Dellinger Are Arrested

THOUSANDS HEAR TALK

Spock Tells Demonstrators at Lincoln Memorial That Johnson Is Real 'Enemy'

By JOSEPH A. LOFTUS
Special to The New York Times

WASHINGTON, Oct. 21—Thousands of demonstrators stormed the Pentagon today after a calm rally and march by some 50,000 persons opposed to the war in Vietnam.

The protesters twice breached the lines of deputy Federal marshals backed by soldiers armed with bayonet-tipped rifles. But they were quickly driven back by the rifle butts of the soldiers and the marshals' nightsticks.

Six demonstrators succeeded in entering a side door at the main Mall entrance of the building but were pushed out immediately by marshals.

There were no reports of serious injuries but the Pentagon steps were spattered with blood.

128 Held at Pentagon

Soldiers and marshals arrested at least 128 persons at the Pentagon, including David Dellinger, Chairman of the National Mobilization Committee to End the War in Vietnam, which organized the rally and march.

Also arrestted were Norman Mailer, the novelist, who was seized for technical violation of a police line, and the Rev. John Boyles, the Episcopal chaplain at Yale University.

The surging disorderly crowd that milled about the vast Pentagon shouted obscenities and taunted the forces on guard there. Some threw eggs and bottles as darkness fell, built bonfires and waved what they said were burning draft cards.

They clashed with the guards several times

Use of Tear Gas Denied

Several tear gas canisters exploded outside the building at various times. The Defense Department announced that the Army had not used tear gas at any time and charged that the demonstrators had.

Two soldiers were reported to have been injured, one by tear gas and one by a missile that struck him in the eye.

At the Lincoln Memorial and elsewhere, the police reported ten persons arrested, most of them for demonstrations against the demonstrators.

A police and military consensus put the size of the crowd at the Lincoln Memorial, where the demonstrators first

Continued on Page 58, Column 1

112 Major Concerns Would Build in Slum If Decay Is Halted

By STEVEN V. ROBERTS

More than 100 of 700 major corporations questioned by a leading consulting company have indicated a willingness to build new plants in or near slum areas. But not one of them said it would make such a move under current conditions.

The 112 corporations responding favorably to the survey listed a set of stiff conditions, ranging from the elimination of surrounding decay to the presence of "responsible" leadership, that would have to be met before they would consider relocating in rundown neighborhoods.

The survey was made by the Fantus Company, a subsidiary of Dun and Bradstreet, which specializes in finding new locations for industry.

Response Called 'Amazing'

Leonard C. Yaseen, Fantus's chairman, acknowledged that the conditions laid down by the companies do not exist in any city today. But he insisted they might be met "five years from now" if municipal governments went to work immediately.

The response to the survey was "amazing in view of what's been going on in the cities these days," Mr. Yaseen said. The business executive declined to say whether he thought the conditions set by the company were realistic.

"I want to concentrate on the positive side," he said.

Mayor Lindsay, Senator Robert F. Kennedy and other political figures have stressed the importance of attracting industry to poor neighborhoods, both to provide jobs and bolster the city's tax base.

However, such critics as

Continued on Page 46, Column 3

THANT SUGGESTS STAFF RESHUFFLE

Urges Reduction in Number of Top Secretariat Posts to Increase Efficiency

By JOHN M. TAYLOR
Special to The New York Times

UNITED NATIONS, N. Y., Oct. 21 — Secretary General Thant proposed today that the United Nations Secretariat be reorganized. It is expected that the General Assembly's Committee on Budget and Administration will accept the proposals without serious objection.

In his report to the committee, Mr. Thant urged that the top echelon of the Secretariat be divided into two levels, "with proper geographical distribution at both levels."

"While the placement of serving officers at either of the two levels will not prove an easy task," Mr. Thant said, "I believe that in the long-term interests of the organization this has to be undertaken."

Growth of U.N. Is Cited

He explained that the continuous growth of the United Nations and the expansion of its activities made reorganization necessary.

At present, there are 14 Under Secretaries in secretariat headquarters and five at regional offices abroad. Altogether the senior staff numbers 36, all of whom report directly to the Secretary General.

In the interests of efficiency, Mr. Thant wishes to reduce this number to 11, with the rank of Under Secretary General. The lower level of the topmost echelon would hold the rank of Assistant Secretary General.

This is the first time the

Continued on Page 10, Column 1

Israeli Destroyer Is Sunk By Missiles of Egyptians

By JAMES FERON
Special to The New York Times

JERUSALEM, Sunday, Oct. 22—An Israeli destroyer, the 2,500-ton Elath, was sunk by Egyptian missiles last night off the northern coast of Sinai.

An Israeli announcement said the ship had been on routine patrol 14 miles outside Egyptian territorial waters when she was apparently attacked by an Egyptian missile boat.

According to the Cairo radio, the Elath entered Egyptian territorial waters north of Port Said, a coastal town at the northern end of the Suez Canal. "Our naval units engaged and sank it," the Cairo announcement said.

The Israelis said the attack occurred at 5:30 P.M. opposite the village of El Rumana. They conceded that the missiles might have been launched from Port Said.

The vessel was abandoned about 8 P. M. when it became apparent that she would sink, the Israelis said.

There were no immediate reports of casualties, but Israeli Air Force and Navy units were sent to the scene to assist in rescue work, the Israelis said. The 362-foot ship would have carried between 180 and 220 men, according to estimates here. The Central Negev Hospital in Beersheba was alerted to handle any casualties.

Later reports of the incident came from the Cairo radio, which announced the ship's sinking. At first the Israelis confirmed that a destroyer had been hit but declined to say much more.

They did say, however, that

Continued on Page 4, Column 2

1,000 AT VIGIL HERE TO SUPPORT G.I.'S

Battery Park Rally Will Last 31 Hours—Motorists Turn Lights on During Daylight

By PAUL HOFMANN

Almost 1,000 persons attended a vigil in Battery Park yesterday in support of American fighting men in Vietnam.

The 31-hour rally, in which war veterans and youths of draft age are participating, began at noon with speeches and ceremonies.

The vigil, scheduled to end at sundown today, is part of a nationwide series of demonstrations organized by the National Committee for Responsible Patriotism, which comprises organizations of former servicemen and other patriotic groups.

Bus and Taxi Lights On

The events sponsored by the committee for this weekend are also designed to stress respect for law and order. The organizers have said that the demonstrations were planned before yesterday's antiwar march in Washington was announced.

The committee had urged motorists to keep their headlights burning while driving in the daytime during the weekend, and had called on householders to leave a light burning in their homes all night from yesterday to today. Both actions were aimed at displaying backing for the soldiers in Vietnam.

Thousands of autos in the metropolitan area yesterday had their headlights or parking lights on. Conspicuous was the participation of bus drivers and tax drivers in the silent demonstration.

Signatures Collected

Yesterday morning many police patrol cars also had their headlights burning. Later, the more than 1,000 patrol cars on duty were ordered by the chief inspector's office to turn their lights off during the daytime.

"All units will operate on the normal daylight procedures," the directive said.

The order was prompted by complaints from citizens about what they termed a display of the policemen's feelings by driving around neighborhoods with headlights burning. Later yesterday, the police vehicles circulated again with turned-off lights.

In the metropolitan area, five parades in support of the armed forces in Vietnam are scheduled for today—in the Bronx, Brooklyn, Hempstead, L. I., Newark and Waterbury, Conn. The demonstrations, called Opera-

Continued on Page 35, Column 1

PURDUE, ALABAMA AND NAVY UPSET

Oregon St., Tennessee and William and Mary Victors

Purdue, Alabama and Navy were defeated in major college football upsets yesterday. Oregon State dumped the second-ranked Boilermakers, 22-14, Tennessee trounced the Crimson Tide, 24-13. William & Mary rallied to sink the Middies, 27-16.

Scores of other leading games:

Army	14	Rutgers	3
Auburn	28	Ga. Tech	10
Bucknell	28	Penn	27
Clemson	13	Duke	7
Colorado	21	Nebraska	16
Dartmouth	41	Brown	6
Georgia	56	V. M. I.	6
Harvard	14	Cornell	12
Houston	43	Miss. St.	6
Indiana	27	Michigan	20
Miami (Fla.)	58	Pitt	0
Minnesota	21	Mich. St.	0
N. Dame	47	Illinois	7
Penn St.	21	West Va.	14
Princeton	28	Colgate	0
Syracuse	20	Calif.	14
Texas	21	Arkansas	12
U. S. C.	23	Washington	6
U. C. L. A.	21	Stanford	16
Wyoming	30	Wichita St.	7
Yale	21	Columbia	7

THOROUGHBRED RACING

Tartan Stable's Ruffled Feathers, ridden by Dave Hidalgo, scored a dramatic upset in the $116,100 Man o' War Stakes at Aqueduct. The long shot scored by a head over Fort Marcy and paid $82.40, $31.60 and $19.80 for $2 across the board.

Dr. Fager, the odds-on favorite, won the $121,360 Hawthorne Gold Cup in Chicago and returned $2.60 for $2 to win.

Details in Section 5

Beauty Is Now in Fashion in Soviet

By HENRY KAMM
Special to The New York Times

MOSCOW, Oct. 21—An article in the current issue of the influential weekly Literaturnaya Gazeta demands that the Soviet Union break the Western monopoly on beauty contests.

The author, Dr. S. P. Letunov, a specialist in the medical aspects of sports, said Soviet beauty competitions should not imitate the advertising and commercial features that mar Western contests but should be held in the spirit of Socialist competitions.

Russians should acquire beauty by working for it, with physical exercises 30 minutes a day, Dr. Letunov urged. The exercises should be designed to develop grace and reduce weight rather than add muscle.

Beauty would thus be created by man's own hand and not by "God," Dr. Letunov declared. The quotation marks are his. The beauty-through-work theme appeared to make the idea of beauty contests ideologically acceptable.

This ideological approach to beauty was also reflected in the doctor's affirmation of the perfectibility of man by man. We cannot control the physical beauty of a face now, Dr. Letunov said, although cosmetic surgeons have done much to correct the grossest defects. But he added that it would probably be possible to do much more about creating personal beauty through science in the future.

The article was marked by a spirited defense of beauty for beauty's sake, a new idea in a country where social utility remains the ultimate criterion of value. While inner beauty is of principal importance, the doctor said, people have never despised mere outward beauty.

"Everything must be beautiful in a human being—face, clothes, soul and thought," Dr. Letunov said, quoting Chekhov. "We must cultivate, from childhood on, a taste for beauty and must not be ashamed to speak of it."

The kind of athletic training practiced in the Soviet Union today results in great, but unharmoniously devel-

Continued on Page 13, Column 1

School Board Ends Racial Attitude Test After Protest Here

By MALCOLM W. BROWNE

A Board of Education test designed to measure the racial attitudes of pupils toward each other has brought on a controversy between parents and school officials on Manhattan's West Side.

As a result, the test has been canceled and "another wedge has been driven between the community and the teaching professionals," according to Dr. Nathan Jacobson, assistant superintendent for District 5, in which the test was administered.

The test consisted of 18 stories, with each one containing a hero or villain. The pupils were supposed to mark an answer sheet indicating whether they thought the hero or villain was "Negro, white or 'Spanish-speaking.' " They also indicated their own races or linguistic backgrounds. A typical test question was:

"One day the teacher said, 'I have to go out of the room for a few minutes. If everyone is very good while I am gone, we will have a surprise when I come back.'

"When the teacher came back, everyone was working very quietly and good. Everyone except one child. That child was running around the room and shouting. The teacher said: 'Well, I'm very sorry. Now we cannot have our surprise.'

"Put an X on the child (Negro, white or 'Spanish-speaking') who spoiled the surprise

Continued on Page 44, Column 3

WAR COMPROMISE RULED OUT BY GIAP

Hanoi General Says U.S. Bombs Won't Force Talks

By RAYMOND H. ANDERSON
Special to The New York Times

MOSCOW, Oct. 21 — Any form of compromise with the United States in the Vietnam war was ruled out today by Gen. Vo Nguyen Giap, Defense Minister of North Vietnam.

The general asserted that United States bombing attacks on North Vietnam would never break the will of its people to help the Vietcong in South Vietnam achieve victory. The Vietnamese, he added, are ready to pay "any price" for victory.

[Two United States planes bombed six North Vietnamese torpedo boats in the Gulf of Tonkin and reported that four had been sunk. Page 3.]

General Giap outlined Hanoi's stand in an article in Krasnaya Zvezda, newspaper of the Soviet Ministry of Defense.

His assertion that bombing would never force Hanoi to submit to negotiations came amid reports from Washington that President Johnson was believed to be weighing the pros and cons of a bombing halt in response to widening demands for such a step.

The North Vietnamese military leader praised Moscow's expanding assistance, but he carefully balanced the praise of the Russians with appropriate acknowledgments of help from the Chinese Communists.

General Giap reiterated Hanoi's insistence that the only

Continued on Page 3, Column 5

Today's Sections

*Included in all copies in the New York metropolitan area and adjacent territory.
**Limited distribution—Rockland County, New York and nearby New Jersey.

Index to Subjects

1968

Runners Tommie Smith (left) and John Carlos (right) raised their fists in the Black Power salute at the rather discordant Olympics in Mexico.

Peggy Fleming won a gold medal for the U.S. in the women's skating event at the Winter Olympics in France.

Arthur Ashe gets ready to slam the ball at the first United States Open Tennis Championship.

"All the News
That's Fit to Print"

The New York Times

LATE CITY EDITION

Weather: Snow likely today, tonight. Partly cloudy tomorrow. Temp. range: Today 35-31; Tuesday 41-32. Full U.S. report on Page 90.

VOL. CXVII . No. 40,177 NEW YORK, WEDNESDAY, JANUARY 24, 1968 10 CENTS

NORTH KOREA SEIZES NAVY SHIP, HOLDS 83 ON BOARD AS U.S. SPIES; ENTERPRISE IS ORDERED TO AREA

Associated Press

Pueblo, seized off North Korea and taken to Wonsan, is an intelligence collection vessel of the United States Navy

4 CREWMEN HURT

Rusk Says Efforts Are Under Way to Obtain Vessel's Release

U.S. statement and Pyongyang broadcast are on Page 15.

By NEIL SHEEHAN
Special to The New York Times

WASHINGTON, Jan. 23 — North Korean patrol boats seized a United States Navy intelligence ship off Wonsan today and took the vessel and her 83 crew members into the North Korean port.

The Defense Department, reporting the incident, said the ship had been in international waters about 25 miles off the eastern coast of North Korea when she was boarded by armed North Korean sailors at 1:45 P.M. (11:45 P.M. Monday, Eastern Standard time).

But North Korea, in a Pyongyang radio broadcast, asserted that the Pueblo had "intruded into the territorial waters of the republic and was carrying out hostile activities." The broadcast called the Pueblo "an armed spy boat of the United States imperialist aggressor force."

Matter of 'Utmost Gravity'

Secretary of State Dean Rusk called the seizure of the Pueblo "a matter of the utmost gravity." He said the United States was negotiating with North Korea "through the channels that are available to us to obtain the immediate release of the vessel and her crew."

The incident forced a sudden confrontation between the United States and an Asian Communist government that has long been calling for diversionary assaults against "United States imperialism" to distract American energies from the war in Vietnam.

The Defense Department said four crewmen of the Pueblo had been wounded, one critically. One report said a crew member had lost a leg. The Pentagon declined to say how the men had been wounded.

North Korean Report

Later—on Wednesday morning, Korean time—the North Vietnamese said at an armistice meeting in Panmunjom that several of the Pueblo's crew were "killed or wounded" in the incident, and a North Vietnamese broadcast monitored in Tokyo said the vessel resisted seizure. The Pentagon declined to comment.

The Pueblo carried 6 officers, 75 enlisted men and 2 civilians, whom the Defense Department identified as Navy civilian hydrographers performing oceanographic research.

Military sources said that the nuclear-powered aircraft carrier Enterprise and two destroyers

Continued on Page 14, Column 5

MILLS TURNS DOWN AIDES OF JOHNSON ON TAX SURCHARGE

Says They Did Not Convince Him They Had Done Their Best to Cut Spending

'ANOTHER LOOK' URGED

House Leader's Stand Hints at Delay Until March in Acting on New Levy

By EILEEN SHANAHAN
Special to The New York Times

WASHINGTON, Jan. 23 — Representative Wilbur D. Mills told the Administration "no" again today on the tax increase.

At the end of two days of hearings before the House Ways and Means Committee, of which he is chairman, the Arkansas Democrat told Administration officials that they had "not yet established" to his satisfaction that "you've done the best you can" to hold down Government spending.

Mr. Mills asked the officials to "take another look" at next year's planned Government spending of $147.4-billion, on the basis of the traditional administrative budget, while the committee turns its attention to another issue. That is the Administration's proposals to reduce the deficit in the United States' balance of international payments.

Date Left Undecided

Just how long the committee might take with the balance-of-payments program and when it might get back to the tax bill, Mr. Mills did not say. It seemed unlikely that the committee could resume consideration of the proposed 10 per cent tax surcharge before early March, at the soonest.

Meanwhile, the Gallup Poll reported that President Johnson faces a difficult task in trying to sell American voters on a tax increase at this time, and that the opposition comes as much from the rank and file of his own party as from others.

In addition to dealing with the balance-of-payments problem, Mr. Mills indicated that the committee ight also consider, ahead of any new look at the tax surcharge, both the extension of excise taxes on automobiles and telephone service and a further step up in corporate tax collections.

Excise Action Favored

He said that an extension of the excise taxes "has to be done." Under present law they would go down on April 1 from 7 to 2 per cent on automobiles and from 10 to 1 per cent on telephone service.

In addition, he said it "might be possible, without a great deal of argument, to do some part" of what the Administration has asked to bring corporations closer to a pay-as-you-go tax basis.

Mr. Mills's reference to approval of only "part" of the corporate tax collection speed-up reflected his belief that the smallest corporations — those with tax liabilities of $25,000 or less — should probably not be put on a full pay-as-you-go

Continued on Page 25, Column 1

City Council Votes A One-Year Trial Of Group Cab Rides

By SETH S. KING

A year-long experiment in group taxi riding was approved yesterday by the City Council.

As soon as Mayor Lindsay signs the bill his task force on taxis will be allowed to organize and supervise such rides from the Eastern Airlines Shuttle Terminal at La Guardia Airport to four zones in Manhattan.

The Council also passed a bill eliminating a requirement that cab drivers be residents of the city.

It also adopted a resolution calling upon the Police Department's Hack Bureau to require each taxi to be equipped with an exterior switch, or similar device, instead of an interior switch, to operate its off-duty sign.

This was aimed at preventing a driver from suddenly turning on his off-duty sign with an interior switch when he saw a fare he did not want to pick up. The

Continued on Page 35, Column 1

JOHNSON PROGRAM INDICTED BY G.O.P.

In TV Reply, Party Charges His Policies Led to Riots, Crime Rise and Inflation

Excerpts from the statements will be found on Page 28.

By JOHN HERBERS
Special to The New York Times

WASHINGTON, Jan. 23—Republicans in Congress told the American people tonight that President Johnson's policies had led to riots, crime and inflation at home and loss of influence and prestige abroad.

In a one-hour telecast over the Columbia Broadcasting System from the auditorium of the new Senate Office Building, eight Senators and nine Representatives delivered a harsh indictment of the Administration's record and said that President Johnson had vastly underestimated the extent of discontent in the country.

America, they said, needs a new leader who would seek a military victory in Vietnam, take a strong stand against worldwide Communism, move decisively to stamp out crime and violence at home and hold down Government spending.

The broadcast, entitled "The State of the Union—the Republican Appraisal," was a reply to President Johnson's State of

Continued on Page 28, Column 3

PRESIDENT OFFERS PROJECT TO SPUR HIRING OF JOBLESS

$2-Billion Manpower Plea Stresses Industrial Effort to Assist 'Hard Core'

Text of President's message is printed on Page 24.

By MAX FRANKEL
Special to The New York Times

WASHINGTON, Jan. 23 — President Johnson asked Congress today for quick action to help him mount the first large-scale effort to induce private industry to train and hire the hard-core cases among the urban unemployed.

In the first of more than a dozen special messages covering his major legislative proposals for the year, the President urged the expansion of all Government manpower efforts by 25 per cent, from a budget of $1.65-billion in the current fiscal year, ending June 30, to $2.09-billion in the year starting July 1.

Total Is Expanding

He suggested spending the bulk of the $442-million increase on programs to find, train and employ the most disadvantaged citizens, most of whom have given up the search for work because of inadequate training, discrimination, discouragement and a general despair.

There are more than a million such persons, the Administration believes, including a still expanding total of 500,000 in 50 major cities. The President would try to place 100,000 of these in jobs in the next 18 months and aim for a target of 500,000 by mid-1971.

"It is a waste that an enlightened nation should not tolerate," Mr. Johnson said in his message. "It is a waste that a nation concerned by disorders in its city streets cannot tolerate."

National Organization

Existing manpower programs have not reached the hard-core jobless effectively, Mr. Johnson reported. Therefore he proposed the expansion of promising experiments with direct subsidies to private employers who incur the extra costs of training and making jobs available to hitherto unqualified persons.

He said he was creating a national organization of leading businessmen, headed by Henry Ford 2d, chairman of the Ford Motor Company, to enlist the cooperation of industry and to work with Government officials in the regions and cities.

At the same time, the President proposed a significant expansion of the year-old Government program to train the

Continued on Page 24, Column 1

Danish Socialists Beaten in Election; Krag Will Resign

By ALVIN SHUSTER
Special to The New York Times

COPENHAGEN, Denmark, Jan. 23—The Social Democratic party, in power for the last 15 years, was defeated tonight in a huge protest vote.

The Danes, upset over rising prices and taxes, turned to the right in their national elections. Three non-Socialist parties won enough seats in Parliament to enable them to form a new government.

Premier Jens Otto Krag, the Social Democratic Premier, said he would resign tomorrow.

Emerging as victors today were the Radical Liberals, the Conservatives and the Agrarian Liberals. The three parties had indicated strongly before the election that if they won a parliamentary majority they would form a government.

Social Democrats Largest

Between them, with about 95 per cent of the votes counted, they had 101 seats, the Radical Liberals going from 13 to 28, the Conservatives from 34 to 38 and the Agrarian Liberals remaining unchanged at 35.

The Social Democrats will remain the largest single party in Parliament with 63 seats, a loss of six. The extreme leftist Socialist People's party, which had won 20 seats in the last elections in 1966, dropped to 11.

The voting was heavy. The final count may show that 90 per cent of the 3.3 million eligible voters cast ballots.

Mr. Krag appeared on television tonight and made a last-minute appeal to save his

Continued on Page 7, Column 1

RADIATION FOUND WHERE B-52 FELL

It Suggests Hydrogen Bombs Did Not Go Through Ice Off Greenland Base

By JOHN W. FINNEY
Special to The New York Times

WASHINGTON, Jan. 23—Air Force search teams were reported today to have detected small amounts of radiation from some or all of the four hydrogen bombs missing after a B-52 bomber crashed on the ice off northwest Greenland.

After two days of hunting with dog sleds and helicopters, teams from the Thule Air Force Base in Greenland still had not found the unarmed thermonuclear weapons. But the detection of the radiation was taken as an encouraging sign that the bombs were scattered across the surface and had not plunged through the ice with parts of the bomber into about 800 feet of water.

If the bombs are still on the surface, recovery operations will be easier. It was first thought that the bombs had sunk to the bottom of North Star Bay, about seven miles southwest of the Thule base, raising the problem of underwater recovery operations through the sea ice.

The radiation suggested that some of the bombs might have broken apart in the impact of the crash and during the subsequent explosion in the bomber as it careened several hundred feet across the ice. If the bombs have split and

Continued on Page 6, Column 4

The New York Times Jan. 24, 1968

The American vessel was seized off Wonsan (cross)

5,000 MEN MASSED AT KHESANH BY U.S.

Marines Rushed In as Foe Builds Up Force in Area—Supply Planes Fired On

By CHARLES MOHR
Special to The New York Times

KHESANH, South Vietnam, Jan. 23 — More than 5,000 United States marines have been concentrated at Khesanh amid indications that one of the major battles of the Vietnam war may be in the offing.

The marines were rushed in because of an increasingly obvious concentration of North Vietnamese troops in the area.

[Sixty-one enemy soldiers were reported killed by air strikes and artillery fire on Tuesday near Khesanh. In a battle on the Bongson plain, 128 Vietcong troops were reported killed by United States infantrymen.]

The nearness of the enemy forces made itself evident when the unmistakable sound of a bullet striking a fuselage rang out as a transport plane glided in to land at the Marine base here. The fat-bellied C-123 Loadmaster landed, safe despite the bullet hole.

The crew pushed pallets of 155-mm. artillery ammunition off the plane and then turned to four large wooden crates addressed to "Fifth Graves

Continued on Page 3, Column 1

RETURN OF PUEBLO ASKED BY U.S. AIDE

Immediate Action Sought at Meeting in Panmunjom of Armistice Group

By Reuters

PANMUNJOM, Korea, Wednesday, Jan. 24—The American commander of the United Nations Command demanded at a meeting of the Mixed Armistice Commission today that the Pueblo and her crew of 83 be returned immediately by North Korea.

Rear Adm. John V. Smith also told the chief North Korean delegate, Maj. Gen. Chung Kook Pak, that the United States reserved the right to demand compensation for the capture of the vessel by the North Korean Navy yesterday.

[The North Koreans said the ship "will remain in our hands," United Press International reported.]

General Pak said North Korean naval vessels fired at the Pueblo yesterday and "several of her crew members were killed or wounded." The Defense Department in Washington had said no one was killed.

Admiral Smith also protested what he said was an intrusion by a band of 31 North Korean agents into Seoul, the South Korean capital, Sunday night. The intrusion resulted in the death of 11 persons.

The meeting today in the demilitarized zone between North and South Korea was called by the United Nations Command Monday, before the Pueblo was taken, because of the infiltration incident.

The United Nations had asked that the meeting take place yesterday, but the North Koreans wanted it held today and

Continued on Page 14, Column 5

Seizure of Vessel Scored in Capital

By United Press International

WASHINGTON, Jan. 23 — North Korea's seizure of the United States intelligence-gathering ship Pueblo was condemned in Congress today as an act of war. Some lawmakers demanded a quick military response.

Senator Richard B. Russell, chairman of the Senate Armed Services Committee, said that the action was "a breach of international law amounting to an act of war."

The Georgia Democrat added that "it certainly behooves our Government to take a very strong position in demanding release of the ship and return of the men."

Representative Bob Wilson, Republican of California, said that the United States must re-

Continued on Page 14, Column 7

3,600 Drugs Facing Relabeling To List Ailments They Combat

By United Press International

WASHINGTON, Jan. 23 — Virtually every drug originally manufactured in America between 1938 and 1962 will have to be relabeled to tell exactly what ailments it is effective against, the Government told the drug industry today.

Some of the 3,600 drugs — sold in as many as 18,000 different combinations — are going to be ordered off the market, and the advertising of nearly all the drugs will have to be changed, William W. Goodrich, assistant general counsel for the Food and Drug Administration, said.

He spoke at a two-hour conference of drug manufacturers called to explain the agency's study of the effectiveness of all prescription and nonprescription drugs marketed in that 24-year period.

The review had been ordered under the Kefauver-Harris Act of 1962, which requires that all drugs sold domestically be proved effective as well as safe for their intended uses. Prior to the new rules, the drugs had only to be found safe.

The first step toward removal from the market of a group of drugs was taken today with publication by the drug agency of a notice in The Federal Register that there was no evidence that the drugs rutin, quercetin, hesperidin or bioflavonoids "are effective for use in man for any conditions."

The listed drugs have been promoted for years as agents for the control of hemorrhage and in dietary food supplements.

Manufacturers of such drugs licensed by the drug agency and manufacturers of similar products — called "me too" products—were invited by the agency to a hearing Jan. 31 to discuss the ruling.

Robert Giles, a member of the Pharmaceutical Manufacturers Association, rose at the meeting to criticize Mr. Goodrich and other officials of the drug agency for public estimates that 10 per cent of the drugs under study would be found totally ineffective and ruled off the market.

In New York last month, Dr. James L. Goddard, Food and Drug Commissioner, estimated that 10 per cent of prescription and over-the-counter drugs would have to be withdrawn from the market because of the efficacy reviews.

Officials of the agency said

Continued on Page 22, Column 1

Jersey Sues State On Price for PATH

By FRED P. GRAHAM
Special to The New York Times

WASHINGTON, Jan. 23 — New Jersey sued New York in the Supreme Court today in an unusual legal move designed to bar New York courts from approving an excessive land condemnation judgment against the Port of New York Authority.

In a suit filed directly in the Court, Attorney General Arthur J. Sills of New Jersey contended that the New York Court of Appeals violated an agreement between the two states when it ruled that the Port Authority should pay $30-million for the assets of the Hudson Rapid Tubes Corporation.

The assets, consisting of the Hudson & Manhattan Railroad

Continued on Page 30, Column 3

U.S. Resumes Normal Relations With Greece's Military Regime

By PETER GROSE
Special to The New York Times

WASHINGTON, Jan. 23—The United States resumed "normal" diplomatic relations with Greece today, six weeks after King Constantine failed in his attempt to oust the military regime.

The State Department said that Ambassador Phillips Talbot had been instructed to make an official call on the Greek Foreign Minister, Panayotis Pipinelis, and thus signal the resumption of formal contacts between the two governments.

Shipments of large-scale military supplies from the United States remain embargoed, the department added, as they have been since last April when the junta seized power.

This is causing concern among Administration officials on a pragmatic basis, for they fear that the Greek forces in the North Atlantic Treaty Organization are being weakened by lack of heavy matériel.

Small arms, ammunition, spare parts and other maintenance stocks continue to be supplied to the Greek forces by the United States. This kind of military aid was not suspended after the April coup.

The department spokesman, Robert J. McCloskey, swept aside a maze of protocol and political considerations by stating, "The United States Government continues to regard King Constantine as the Greek chief of state—relations between the King and the Government in Athens are an in-

Continued on Page 8, Column 1

NEWS INDEX

1968

Richard M. Nixon won the Republican nomination on the first ballot at the Miami convention.

President Johnson looked weary as he worked on his speech to decline the presidential nomination.

Hubert Humphrey, Ed Muskie, and their wives on the podium at Chicago.

"All the News That's Fit to Print"

The New York Times

LATE CITY EDITION

Weather: Partial clearing today; fair, cool tonight and tomorrow. Temp. range: today 62-53; Sunday 66-48. Full U. S. report on Page 90.

VOL. CXVII..No. 40,245 NEW YORK, MONDAY, APRIL 1, 1968 10 CENTS

JOHNSON SAYS HE WON'T RUN; HALTS NORTH VIETNAM RAIDS; BIDS HANOI JOIN PEACE MOVES

ROCKEFELLER URGES ALBANY LEADERS TO SPEED BUDGET

Ready to Work With Them to Provide Funds as Fiscal Year Opens Today

By PETER KIHSS

Governor Rockefeller urged Republican and Democratic legislative leaders yesterday to agree quickly on a new budget as the state moved into the 1968-69 fiscal year today without a budget.

The Republican-controlled Senate has passed one version of the budget, but the Democratic-controlled Assembly is pondering a counter-version. The Governor said in a statement he was "ready to work with the leadership in both houses" for "a budget that meets the needs of the people of our state and provides the revenues necessary to finance it."

After the Legislature does act, the Governor will presumably seek a supplemental appropriation to restore some of the spending cuts that both parties' legislative fiscal committees make in his proposed school, urban, crime and construction programs. This is a traditional technique.

Assembly May Act Today

Fiscal aides to Assembly Speaker Anthony J. Travia analyzed the Senate proposals through the night. Mr. Travia himself said he was considering two interim moves. One would have the Assembly approve the budget appropriations and cuts already agreed on; the other would seek a temporary authorization for state spending at the rate for the last quarter of the fiscal year just ended.

Joseph Zaretzki, Senate Democratic minority leader, charged here yesterday that the budget bills rammed through the Senate early Saturday by the Republican leader, Earl Brydges, and his party followers aimed only "to get by next November's election."

Senator Zaretzki asserted that two of its key elements—

Continued on Page 38, Column 3

Liberals Designate Javits; Nickerson Race Confused

Baron May Enter Race

By CLAYTON KNOWLES

The Liberal party State Committee designated Senator Jacob K. Javits for re-election late yesterday, but under conditions that confronted him with the prospect of waging a primary fight to gain the extra line on the voting machines.

A bloc of unionists in the party, contending that an endorsement of Mr. Javits would aid Richard M. Nixon in his Presidential bid, put up Murray Baron, a long-time Liberal leader. Although Mr. Baron lost, he rolled up enough votes to qualify to run in the June 18 primary.

The Liberals acted several hours before President Johnson's withdrawal. Mr. Baron came under heavy attack in the prevote debate as "more

Continued on Page 50, Column 1

Johnson Causes Upset

The contest for the Democratic Senate nomination in New York was thrown into confusion last night by President Johnson's announcement that he would not seek the party's nomination for re-election.

Eugene H. Nickerson, the organization's candidate for the nomination and a supporter of Senator Robert F. Kennedy, said of the Johnson announcement: "I was very surprised. It just comes as such a complete surprise to me that I think we have to sleep on it."

Representative Joseph Y. Resnick of Ellenville, a Senate candidate who supports President Johnson, sent a telegram to the President urging the President to reconsider his decision.

"Mr. President," the Resnick

Continued on Page 50, Column 5

TAX RISE PUSHED

Increase in War Costs Cited—No Specific Cuts Suggested

By EILEEN SHANAHAN
Special to The New York Times

WASHINGTON, March 31—President Johnson called on Congress tonight to "move from debate to action, from talking to voting" on a tax increase.

He pledged himself to accept any appropriate reductions in Federal spending that Congress voted, but he proposed nothing specific in the way of economy moves.

He announced, in fact, that there would be an increase in Government outlays because of the war. These, he said, would amount to $2.5-billion in the current fiscal year, which ends June 30, and $2.6-billion in the next fiscal year.

What effect the President's decision not to run for re-election might have on the long fight over the tax increase and Government spending was not immediately clear. A lame duck President is usually considered to have greatly diminished power to influence Congress, but the President's removal of himself from the campaign could also remove some of the partisanship from the tax and spending issue.

Deficit to Increase

The increases the President announced in defense spending would raise the deficit for the current year to $22.3-billion and for next year to $20.5-billion, if the 10 per cent tax surcharge is not enacted, and assuming that there are no other changes in spending from the official January estimates.

If the tax increase is enacted, with April 1 the effective date for individuals and Jan. 1 for corporations, as the President has asked, this year's deficit would be $20.4-billion and next year's, $10.6-billion.

"Enactment of a tax increase now, together with expenditure control, is necessary to protect our security, continue our prosperity and meet the needs of our people," Mr. Johnson said.

He said he believed there

Continued on Page 30, Column 3

DMZ IS EXEMPTED

Johnson Sets No Time Limit on Halting of Air and Sea Blows

By MAX FRANKEL
Special to The New York Times

WASHINGTON, March 31—President Johnson announced tonight that he had ordered a halt in the air and naval bombardment of most of North Vietnam and invited the Hanoi Government to join him in a "series of mutual moves toward peace."

The President said:

"Tonight, in the hope that this action will lead to early talks, I am taking the first step to de-escalate the conflict. We are reducing—substantially reducing—the present level of hostilities. And we are doing so unilaterally and at once."

The President said that attacks would continue only in the area just north of the demilitarized zone, which separates North Vietnam from South Vietnam, and where, he said, the "continuing enemy build-up directly threatens allied forward positions and where movements of troops and supplies are clearly related to that threat."

Hanoi's Stand Recalled

The President set no time limit for his restraint order. Until now, North Vietnam has demanded an "unconditional"—apparently meaning permanent—halt in the bombing of all its territory and all other acts of war against it.

North Vietnam's restraint and other unspecified events, the President indicated, can make possible an early end of "even this limited bombing."

The areas to be spared, he said, include almost 90 per cent of North Vietnam's population and "most of its territory."

The White House refused to give a more specific geographical delineation.

[In Saigon, the United States command said that the order went into effect at 9 P.M. Sunday, New York time, when President Johnson began his address, The Associated Press reported. Page 15.]

At the same time, Mr. Johnson used a televised address to the nation to urge the Soviet Union and Britain to do everything possible to move from his "unilateral act of de-escalation" toward a genuine peace.

He designated Ambassador at Large W. Averell Harriman and the American Ambassador to Moscow, Llewellyn Thomp-

Continued on Page 28, Column 1

Associated Press

ADDRESSES THE NATION: President Johnson last night

SURPRISE DECISION

President Steps Aside in Unity Bid—Says 'House' Is Divided

Text of Johnson's address will be found on Page 26.

By TOM WICKER
Special to The New York Times

WASHINGTON, March 31—Lyndon Baines Johnson announced tonight: "I shall not seek and I will not accept the nomination of my party as your President."

Later, at a White House news conference, he said his decision was "completely irrevocable."

The President told his nationwide television audience:

"What we have won when all our people were united must not be lost in partisanship. I have concluded that I should not permit the Presidency to become involved in partisan decisions."

Mr. Johnson, acknowledging that there was "division in the American house," withdrew in the name of national unity, which he said was "the ultimate strength of our country."

"With American sons in the field far away," he said, "with the American future under challenge right here at home, with our hopes and the world's hopes for peace in the balance every day, I do not believe that I should devote an hour or a day of my time to any personal partisan causes or to any duties other than the awesome duties of this office, the Presidency of your country."

Humphrey Race Possible

Mr. Johnson left Senator Robert F. Kennedy of New York and Senator Eugene J. McCarthy of Minnesota as the only two declared candidates for the Democratic Presidential nomination.

Vice President Humphrey, however, will be widely expected to seek the nomination now that his friend and political benefactor, Mr. Johnson, is out of the field. Mr. Humphrey indicated that he would have a statement on his plans tomorrow.

The President informed Mr. Humphrey of his decision during a conference at the latter's apartment in southwest Washington today before the Vice President flew to Mexico City. There, he will represent the United States at the signing of a treaty for a Latin-American nuclear-free zone.

Surprise to Aides

If Mr. Humphrey should become a candidate, he would find most of the primaries foreclosed to him. Only those in the District of Columbia, New Jersey and South Dakota remain open.

Therefore, he would have to rely on collecting delegates in states without primaries and on White House support if he were to head off Mr. Kennedy and Mr. McCarthy.

Former Vice President Richard M. Nixon is the only announced major candidate for the Republican nomination, although Governor Rockefeller has said that he would accept the nomination if drafted.

Mr. Johnson's announcement tonight came as a stunning surprise even to close associates. His main political strategists, James H. Rowe of Washington, White House Special Assistant Marvin W. Watson, and Postmaster General Lawrence F. O'Brien, spent much of today conferring on campaign plans.

They were informed of what was coming just before Mr.

Continued on Page 27, Column 1

Political Chiefs Stunned; Kennedy Sets News Parley

By SYLVAN FOX

Political leaders across the country reacted with shock, surprise and—in some cases—admiration to President Johnson's announcement last night that he would not seek re-election in November. Some political leaders immediately focused attention on Vice President Humphrey as a possible contender for the Democratic Presidential nomination.

Others suggested that Mr. Johnson's withdrawal could alter the position of Governor Rockefeller, who pulled out of contention for the Republican Presidential nomination on March 21.

Neither Mr. Humphrey nor Mr. Rockefeller was commenting immediately on his political plans in the light of Mr. Johnson's withdrawal.

Senator Robert F. Kennedy, like many others, was left almost speechless by the President's announcement.

"I don't know quite what to say," Senator Kennedy commented when he got the word of the President's decision. The Senator, a leading contender for the Democratic Presidential nomination, scheduled a news conference for 10 A.M. today.

Continued on Page 27, Column 4

WISCONSIN WEIGHS IMPACT ON VOTING

Primary Excitement Turns to Surprise—McCarthy and Nixon Wind Up Campaign

By DONALD JANSON
Special to The New York Times

MILWAUKEE, March 31—Excitement over a spirited contest between Senator Eugene J. McCarthy and President Johnson in the Wisconsin Democratic Presidential primary turned to surprise tonight with the President's announcement that he was not a candidate for re-election.

Thousands of Wisconsin voters, who had expected to choose between the two on Tuesday, saw and heard the President on television take himself out of the contest.

The announcement ended speculation that the Wisconsin primary, the first in the nation to have the President's name on the ballot, would produce a record vote.

It left only Senator McCarthy as an active candidate on the Democratic ballot and only former Vice President Richard M. Nixon as a major candidate on the Republican side. It eliminated the urgency that thousands of Republicans had felt to cross over to the Democratic contest to vote against the

Continued on Page 48, Column 1

3 Beachfront Hotels Destroyed by Fire In Rockaway Park

By LAWRENCE VAN GELDER

Flames spurred by howling ocean winds raged through the Rockaway Park section of Queens yesterday, destroying three beachfront hotels, damaging small stores and bungalows, charring police and fire equipment and forcing the evacuation of hundreds of residents.

As the number of alarms climbed swiftly to eight, more than 400 firemen and 60 pieces of equipment were pitted against the intense blaze, which sent up a column of gray smoke visible for more than a dozen miles in the afternoon sky.

Despite the fury of the fire and the menacing wind-whipped embers that flew through the neighborhood around Beach 116th Street and Ocean Promenade, no serious injuries were reported from the blaze, which was attributed by officials to three small children. Four firemen, however, were reported

Continued on Page 36, Column 4

HOUSE PLAN SPURS INVESTING ABROAD

Committee Asks Creation of Quasi-Public Corporation to Attract Private Capital

By FELIX BELAIR Jr.
By The Associated Press

WASHINGTON, March 31—The House Foreign Affairs Committee urged in a report today that the Federal Government consider creating a quasi-public corporation to promote private American investments in underdeveloped countries.

The report, originated by Representative Leonard Farbstein, Democrat of Manhattan, won the unanimous approval of the committee.

The gist of the report was that the investment guarantee program of the Agency for International Development was no longer able to attract sufficient private capital to spur economic growth in the poor countries of Latin America,

Continued on Page 8, Column 1

The New York Times (by William E. Sauro)

AT ROCKAWAY PARK BLAZE: More than 400 firemen were called out to fight eight-alarm fire that raged on Beach 116th Street in the Rockaway Park section of Queens. Jamaica Bay is in rear. Four firemen were slightly hurt.

Top Saigon Officials Confused By Refusal of Johnson to Run

By GENE ROBERTS
Special to The New York Times

SAIGON, South Vietnam, Monday, April 1—President Johnson's refusal to seek re-election plunged the top level of the South Vietnamese Government into confusion today and touched off a meeting of key American officials.

It was apparent, according to Americans who were at the presidential palace at the time, that President Johnson's announcement caught the South Vietnamese by surprise.

"Top advisers and officeholders began rushing toward the Vice President's office in obvious states of agitation," said one American who was waiting for a conference with Vice President Nguyen Cao Ky. "A few minutes later, Ky's military aide appeared and said all appointments had been canceled."

There was similar excitement at the United States Embassy. A receptionist said that no high officials were available for comment and explained that they were all in a top-level meeting.

There was also a rash of meetings at the headquarters of the military command here.

While many military officers and virtually all South Vietnamese officials are op-

Continued on Page 28, Column 5

NEWS INDEX

The dying Martin Luther King on the motel balcony where he was shot down by James Earl Ray. Aides are seen pointing toward the area from which the shot was fired.

A mule-drawn farm wagon carried the slain minister through the Atlanta streets.

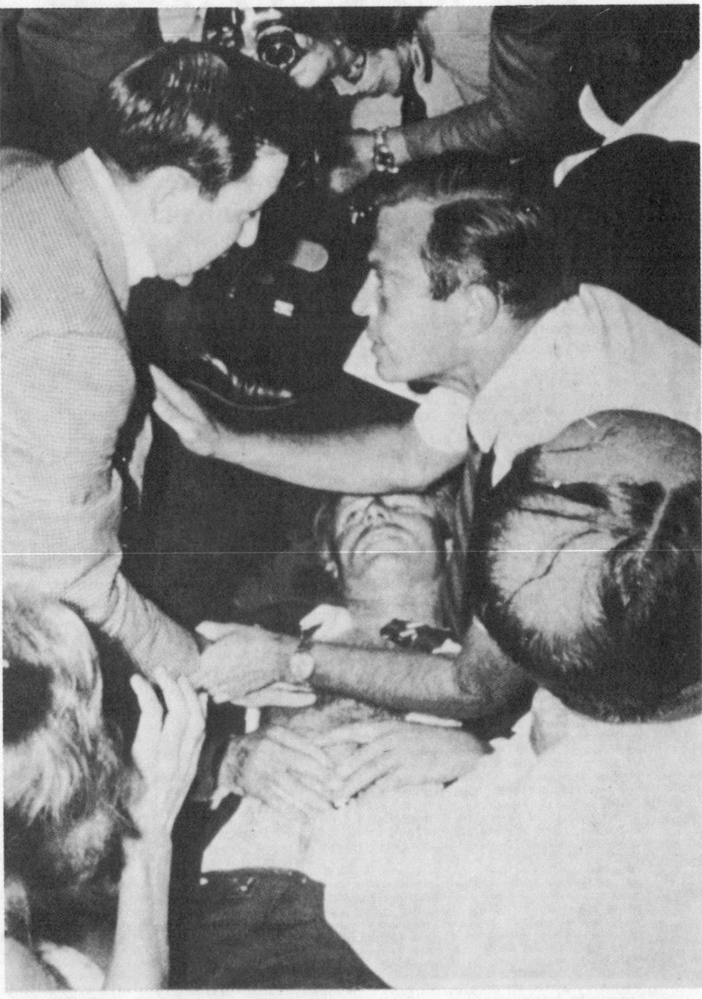

Robert Kennedy lies mortally wounded on the pantry floor of the Ambassador Hotel, only minutes after celebrating his Democratic primary win.

Suspect Sirhan Sirhan was carried away following Robert Kennedy's assassination.

"All the News That's Fit to Print"

The New York Times

LATE CITY EDITION

Weather: Clearing today, turning cold tonight. Fair, cool tomorrow. Temp. range: today 62-44; Thurs. 73-52. Full U.S. report on Page 92.

VOL. CXVII . No. 40,249 NEW YORK, FRIDAY, APRIL 5, 1968 10 CENTS

MARTIN LUTHER KING IS SLAIN IN MEMPHIS; A WHITE IS SUSPECTED; JOHNSON URGES CALM

JOHNSON DELAYS TRIP TO HAWAII; MAY LEAVE TODAY

President Spends a Hectic Day Here and in Capital —Sees Thant at the U.N.

By MAX FRANKEL

Special to The New York Times

WASHINGTON, April 4 — President Johnson postponed his trip to Hawaii at least until tomorrow after he heard of the death of the Rev. Dr. Martin Luther King Jr. tonight.

The news, which visibly shocked the President, came at the end of one of the most extraordinary days in perhaps the most extraordinary week of his Administration.

Mr. Johnson was to have flown from Washington at about midnight for a weekend of strategy conferences with his military and diplomatic leaders stationed in South Vietnam. On the way, he had planned a breakfast meeting in California with former President Dwight D. Eisenhower.

Instead, the President telephoned Mrs. King in Atlanta, made a brief appeal for calm on television and went to his office to follow the reports of unrest and disturbance given him periodically by Attorney General Ramsey Clark.

Cancels Dinner Appearance

Mr. Johnson also canceled an appearance before a Democratic party fund-raising dinner here —the final event of a hectic schedule that became ever more hectic as the day unfolded.

The President began the day by making final arrangements for the Hawaii meeting. It had been tentatively planned before his order Sunday to curtail the bombing of North Vietnam and the news yesterday that Hanoi was interested in establishing direct contact.

[The new United States peace moves are producing a quiet but bitter reaction in the South Vietnamese Government that is causing increasing concern among United States officials in Saigon. Page 14.]

But the diplomatic development, though not the principal subject of the Honolulu meetings, added special weight to his conversations with Gen. Wiliam C. Westmoreland, the American commander in South Vietnam, and other officials.

Mr. Johnson was careful not to arouse false hopes of peace, but he appeared encouraged and in buoyant spirt as he decided before noon to fly first to New York to attend the investiture of the Most Rev. Terence J. Cooke as Archbishop of New York.

Then, while in New York,

Continued on Page 12, Column 1

Hanoi Charges U.S. Raid Far North of 20th Parallel

By EVERT CLARK

Special to The New York Times

WASHINGTON, April 4 — North Vietnam charged in a broadcast today that United States planes had bombed a "populated area" in northwestern Vietnam far north of the 20th parallel. The Defense Department said it knew of no such raid but was investigating.

President Johnson has ordered that there be no attacks on North Vietnam north of the 20th Parallel as a step toward de-escalating the war.

[In South Vietnam, United States marines beat off an attack by about 400 North Vietnamese soldiers charging up a hill near Khesanh, killing 93, The Associated Press reported. Meanwhile, an American relief column was nearing the besieged base. Page 15.]

The Hanoi radio, in a broadcast monitored and translated here, said three waves of United States planes dropped more than 50 bombs on a "populated area" about 30 miles west of Laichau, capital of Laichau Province, this morning.

The nearest village to that

Continued on Page 15, Column 1

The New York Times April 5, 1968

Hanoi said that area near Laichau (cross) was target.

HUMPHREY HINTS HE'LL ENTER RACE

Tells Unionists in Pittsburgh He Will Act Soon—Abel and Wirtz Back Him

By ROY REED

Special to The New York Times

PITTSBURGH, April 4—Two thousand labor representatives, including the head of the United Steel Workers union, clamorously urged Vice President Humphrey today to run for President.

The Vice President left little doubt that he would oblige them, but he indicated that he would wait until President Johnson returned from his Hawaii conference before making an announcement.

"I know what your request is, and I know what your thoughts are," he told the delegates to the Pennsylvania A.F.L.-C.I.O. convention. "I am most grateful. I am not one to walk away from a decision, and a decision will come in due time."

But nothing he does should interfere with President Johnson's peace mission, he said.

Several other political leaders urged Mr. Humphrey today to enter the race for the Democratic Presidential nomination. The most prominent among them was Secretary of Labor W. Willard Wirtz, who was addressing a union convention at Miami Beach.

I. W. Abel, president of the steelworkers Union, rose as Mr.

Continued on Page 32, Column 1

Johnson Shuns Role Of '68 'Lame Duck,' Kennedy Was Told

By JOHN HERBERS

Special to The New York Times

WASHINGTON, April 4—In his meeting with Senator Robert F. Kennedy yesterday President Johnson said he would remain out of the political fight this year because he did not believe it was appropriate for a "lame duck" President to try to pick his successor.

This and other details of the Johnson-Kennedy meeting were learned today from knowledgeable sources.

The meeting, which Senator Kennedy had requested in the interest of "national unity," was described as an extraordinarily friendly one, with both the Senator and the President speaking in a conciliatory manner.

President Johnson was pictured as the "elder statesman" of the party who had decided to remain aloof from this year's scramble for the Presidency in an effort to keep the party as strong as possible and retain his own dignity and effectiveness as President.

At one point, it was reported, the President said he did not want to make a spectacle of himself as a lame duck President attempting to dictate to the party who should be nominated at the national convention.

In this regard, he pointed out that in 1956 former President Harry S. Truman went to the

Continued on Page 31, Column 4

DISMAY IN NATION

Negroes Urge Others to Carry on Spirit of Nonviolence

By LAWRENCE VAN GELDER

Dismay, shame, anger and foreboding marked the nation's reaction last night to the Rev. Dr. Martin Luther King Jr.'s murder.

From the high offices of state to the man in the street, news of the moderate civil rights leader's violent death in Memphis yesterday drew, for the most part, stunned and sober statements.

Most major Negro organizations and Negro leaders, lamenting Dr. King's death, expressed hope that it serve as a spur to others to carry on in his spirit of nonviolence. But some Negro militants responded with bitterness and anger.

Roy Wilkins, executive director of the National Association for the Advancement of Colored People, said his organization was "shocked and deeply grieved by the dastardly murder of Dr. Martin Luther King."

"His murderer or murderers must be promptly apprehended and brought to justice," Mr. Wilkins said.

'A Man of Peace'

"Dr. King was a symbol of the nonviolent civil rights protest movement. He was a man of peace, of dedication, of great courage. His senseless assassination solves nothing. It will not stay the civil rights movement; it will instead spur it to greater activity."

Whitney M. Young Jr., executive director of the National Urban League, said:

"We are unspeakably shocked by the murder of Martin Luther King, one of the greatest leaders of our time. This is a bitter reflection on America. We fear for our country.

"The only possible answer now is for the nation to act immediately on what Dr. King has been fighting for—passage of the civil rights and anti-poverty bills and a true and just equality for all men. Those of us who have remained loyal to his concept of nonviolence have been dealt a mortal blow."

Mayor Richard G. Hatcher of Gary, Ind., a Negro, termed the death of Dr. King "every man's loss."

"Men who care for humankind and struggle for its salvation through reason and faith have lost a leader of monumental stature," he said. "A man of his magnitude will not soon pass this way again."

At his home in Stamford, Conn., the former baseball star Jackie Robinson called the

Continued on Page 26, Column 1

PRESIDENT'S PLEA

On TV, He Deplores 'Brutal' Murder of Negro Leader

Statements by Johnson and Humphrey are on Page 24.

Special to The New York Times

WASHINGTON, April 4—President Johnson deplored tonight in a brief television address to the nation the "brutal slaying" of the Rev. Dr. Martin Luther King Jr.

He asked "every citizen to reject the blind violence that has struck Dr. King, who lived by nonviolence."

Mr. Johnson said he was postponing his scheduled departure tonight for a Honolulu conference on Vietnam and that instead he would leave tomorrow.

The President spoke from the White House. At the Washington Hilton Hotel, where Democratic members of Congress had gathered to honor the President and the Vice President, Mr. Humphrey, his voice strained with emotion, said:

"Martin Luther King stands with our other American martyrs in the cause of freedom and justice. His death is a terrible tragedy."

The dinner was canceled 10 to 15 minutes after the Vice President spoke. Mr. Johnson, who was scheduled to appear at the dinner, canceled his plans to attend.

F.B.I. Inquiry Ordered

Attorney General Ramsey Clark ordered an immediate inquiry by the Federal Bureau of Investigation into the shooting of Dr. King in Memphis.

He said the purpose of the investigation would be to determine whether any Federal law had been violated.

One provision of the law that could be invoked makes it a crime to engage in a conspiracy to deprive a person of his civil rights.

In addition to F.B.I. agents, Department of Justice civil rights representatives were on the scene in Memphis and were in touch with the Attorney General.

Military sources said that no National Guard units had yet been Federalized and no Regular Army troops had been alerted yet for possible movement to cities where violence had broken out.

National Guard troops, such as the 4,000 men who have been called into Memphis, remain under state control until the responsible Governor requests help and the President

Continued on Page 24, Column 7

Associated Press

THE REV. DR. MARTIN LUTHER KING Jr.

Scattered Violence Occurs In Harlem and Brooklyn

12 Are Arrested Here

By THOMAS A. JOHNSON

Sporadic violence erupted in Harlem and Brooklyn's Bedford-Stuyvesant section last night after news of Dr. Martin Luther King's assassination spread in the two predominantly Negro communities.

Mayor Lindsay, who went to Harlem in an effort to quiet the outbreaks, was caught in the midst of an unruly crowd and had to be hustled into a limousine by bodyguards.

Police reinforcements, including elements of the riot-trained Tactical Patrol Force, were rushed into both communities.

Two arrests were reported in Brooklyn and 10 in Harlem. A television crewman was said to have been injured by flying glass.

There were numerous instances of rock-throwing, looting and arson reported both in Brooklyn and in Harlem, starting around 11 P.M. and continuing early today.

Gangs of youth in both areas were reported roaming through the streets, now and then taunting policemen and firemen on duty.

The police fired several volleys of shots in the air to disperse crowds along Brooklyn's Fulton Street and Harlem's

Continued on Page 26, Column 2

Widespread Disorders

Disorders broke out in scattered parts of the nation last night after the slaying of the Rev. Dr. Martin Luther King Jr. The National Guard was called out or alerted in several cities.

In Washington, scattered but persistent looting and vandalism erupted, led for a time by Stokely Carmichael, former head of the Student Nonviolent Coordinating Committee. All available policemen were being called to duty.

About 4,000 Tennessee National Guardsmen were ordered to duty in Nashville because of disorders.

In North Carolina, Gov. Dan K. Moore alerted the Guard in Greensboro at the request of Mayor Carson Bain. State Highway patrolmen were dispatched to Raleigh.

There were riotous outbursts

Continued on Page 26, Column 5

NEWS INDEX

GUARD CALLED OUT

Curfew Is Ordered in Memphis, but Fires and Looting Erupt

By EARL CALDWELL

Special to The New York Times

MEMPHIS, Friday, April 5—The Rev. Dr. Martin Luther King Jr., who preached nonviolence and racial brotherhood, was fatally shot here last night by a distant gunman who then raced away and escaped.

Four thousand National Guard troops were ordered into Memphis by Gov. Buford Ellington after the 39-year-old Nobel Prize-winning civil rights leader died.

A curfew was imposed on the shocked city of 550,000 inhabitants, 40 per cent of whom are Negro.

But the police said the tragedy had been followed by incidents that included sporadic shooting, fires, bricks and bottles thrown at policemen, and looting that started in Negro districts and then spread over the city.

White Car Sought

Police Director Frank Holloman said the assassin might have been a white man who was "50 to 100 yards away in a flophouse."

Chief of Detectives W. P. Huston said a late model white Mustang was believed to have been the killer's getaway car. Its occupant was described as a bareheaded white man in his 30's, wearing a black suit and black tie.

The detective chief said the police had chased two cars near the motel where Dr. King was shot and had halted one that had two out-of-town men as occupants. The men were questioned but seemed to have nothing to do with the killing, he said.

Rifle Found Nearby

A high-powered 30.06-caliber rifle was found about a block from the scene of the shooting, on South Main Street. "We think it's the gun," Chief Huston said, reporting it would be turned over to the Federal Bureau of Investigation.

Dr. King was shot while he leaned over a second-floor railing outside his room at the Lorraine Motel. He was chatting with two friends just before starting for dinner.

One of the friends was a musician, and Dr. King had just asked him to play a Negro spiritual, "Precious Lord, Take My Hand," at a rally that was to have been held two hours later in support of striking Memphis sanitationmen.

Paul Hess, assistant adminis-

Continued on Page 24, Column 1

Archbishop Cooke Installed; President Looks On

By EDWARD B. FISKE

The Most Rev. Terence J. Cooke was installed as the seventh Roman Catholic Archbishop of New York yesterday in a historic pageant attended by the President of the United States and highlighted by prayers for the success of his peace efforts in Vietnam.

"Let us pray with all our hearts that God will inspire our President," the 47-year-old Archbishop said in his homily at St. Patrick's Cathedral.

"In the last few days, we have all admired his heroic efforts in the search for peace in Vietnam. We ask God to bless his efforts with success. May God inspire not only our President, but also other leaders and the leaders of all nations of the world to find a way to peace."

Then the Archbishop, speaking from a white marble pulpit and surrounded by a blaze of purple, gold and scarlet robes, addressed himself directly to Mr. Johnson, who sat below him in a front pew.

The President, sitting with his hands clasped and his legs crossed, listened with obvious intensity to the Archbishop's words.

"Mr. President," he said, "our hearts, our hopes, our continued prayers go with you."

Mr. Johnson, accompanied by his daughter, Mrs. Patrick J. Nugent, led a festive congregation of about 5,000 cardinals, bishops, priests, laymen, nuns, civic leaders

Continued on Page 38, Column 1

The New York Times (by Neal Boenzi)

President Johnson and his daughter, Mrs. Patrick J. Nugent, right, listening during yesterday's ceremonies. At left are Mrs. John F. Kennedy and Lieut. Gov. Malcolm Wilson. Security personnel are in the row between them.

Archbishop Luigi Raimondi, Apostolic Delegate to the U.S., speaking after Archbishop Terence J. Cooke was enthroned

Mayor Daley's armed police units fought the anti-war, pro-McCarthy demonstrators outside the Democratic National Convention site in Chicago. It is believed that this battle is what ultimately cost Humphrey the election.

Stokely Carmichael, who called for action after the assassination of Martin Luther King, incited riots and violence as a means to Black Power.

Mark Rudd was a leader of student protesters at Columbia University who actively challenged establishment policies.

"All the News That's Fit to Print"

The New York Times

LATE CITY EDITION

Weather: Sunny and mild today; fair tonight. Sunny, mild tomorrow. Temp. range: today 50-35. Friday 62-46. Full U. S. report on Page 78.

VOL. CXVII..No. 40,250 · © 1968 The New York Times Company. · NEW YORK, SATURDAY, APRIL 6, 1968 · 10 CENTS

ARMY TROOPS IN CAPITAL AS NEGROES RIOT; GUARD SENT INTO CHICAGO, DETROIT, BOSTON; JOHNSON ASKS A JOINT SESSION OF CONGRESS

SIEGE OF KHESANH DECLARED LIFTED; TROOPS HUNT FOE

Relief Column, Within Mile of Base, Presses Search —Helicopters Kill 50

By The Associated Press

KHESANH, South Vietnam, Saturday, April 6—The 76-day North Vietnamese siege of the Marine base at Khesanh was officially declared lifted yesterday.

United States marines and helicopter-borne Army troops today pushed toward what was described as North Vietnamese regimental headquarters south of the base.

The 20,000-man relief column reached the base and then fanned out on three sides in search of the vanishing enemy soldiers. Army helicopter units entered the base.

The sweep could take the Americans all the way to the Laotian border, less than 10 miles away, in the effort to root out the 7,000 men said to remain in an enemy force once estimated at 20,000. North Vietnam uses Laos as a staging area for attacks along South Vietnam's borders.

Gunships Attack Near Town

The United States command said that helicopter gunships of the First Cavalry Division (Airmobile), crisscrossing the skies ahead of the ground troops, killed 50 North Vietnamese late yesterday near the town of Khesanh, which is two miles south of the base.

Earlier, United States troops fought about 150 enemy soldiers four miles east of the town. Nine enemy soldiers and one American were reported killed.

The town was made an enemy command post after South Vietnamese troops and a small unit of United States marines abandoned it in January after a heavy siege.

Ten thousand civilians, mostly montagnard tribesmen, fled the town when fighting broke out. Many are in refugee camps in the coastal lowlands.

The relief column made no immediate attempt to enter the Khesanh base. Enemy gunners zeroed in on the outpost with 110 rounds of artillery and mortar fire.

Before the pressure on the

Continued on Page 2, Column 4

Hanoi Voices Doubt Over U.S. Sincerity

By Agence France-Presse

HANOI, North Vietnam, April 5—Hanoi protested today against what it called "savage bombings" of North Vietnam and "intensification of the war in South Vietnam" since President Johnson's announcement Sunday of restriction on attacks on the North.

Under the signature "Commentator," a pseudonym customarily indicating official authorship, an editorial in the party newspaper, Nhan Dan, questioned the sincerity of Mr. Johnson's avowed desire for peace.

[Despite the tone of the Hanoi editorial, Administration officials saw no indication that North Vietnam was backing away from talks with the United States. Page 5.]

The Nhan Dan editorial said: "The decision of the United

Continued on Page 3, Column 1

SOVIET ENDORSES ASSENT BY HANOI

Moscow Mentioned as Site of Talks With U.S.—China Urges Continued War

By RAYMOND H. ANDERSON
Special to The New York Times

MOSCOW, April 5 — The Soviet Government today endorsed the agreement by North Vietnam with the United States toward a complete halt of bombing to open the door to full-scale negotiations.

The statement came amid speculation that Moscow might be the site for a meeting between United States and North Vietnamese representatives.

Premier Aleksei N. Kosygin is cutting short his trip to Iran and will return to Moscow Sunday, one day early.

[Communist China, however, termed President Johnson's peace overture a smokescreen and urged the North Vietnamese and the Vietcong to continue fighting.]

The United States Embassy denied that it had any knowledge of arrangements for a meeting here. The United States, it was understood,

Continued on Page 4, Column 3

PRESIDENT GRAVE

Sets Day of Mourning for Dr. King—Meets Rights Leaders

President's statement and his proclamation, Page 23.

By MAX FRANKEL
Special to The New York Times

WASHINGTON, April 5 — President Johnson asked today to address a joint session of Congress no later than Monday evening so that he could propose "constructive action instead of destructive action in this hour of national need."

Gravely imploring Americans to "stand their ground to deny violence its victory" in the reaction to the slaying of the Rev. Dr. Martin Luther King Jr., the President set out to arouse the nation's conscience and to win quick action on the long-stalled major items in his domestic program.

He proclaimed Sunday a national day of mourning for Dr. King, who was shot yesterday in Memphis and died later in a hospital.

Meanwhile, Congressional leaders said that Dr. King's murder could assure passage next week of a landmark civil rights bill.

Conference Canceled

To deal with the divisiveness that he said was "tearing this nation apart," Mr. Johnson canceled the already delayed conference he had planned for this weekend in Hawaii with American military and diplomatic officials stationed in South Vietnam.

Gen. William C. Westmoreland, the American commander in the war zone, was flying to Washington instead and will probably see Mr. Johnson tomorrow morning.

The President spent almost the entire day working "to avoid catastrophe." He met with moderate Negro leaders and members of Congress and of his Administration to find ways of containing the violence, arson and looting that threatened many big cities and that spread here to within a few blocks of the White House.

He also conferred all day with officials of the District of Columbia and gave them Federal troops this evening to help restore order.

Mr. Johnson's demeanor all

Continued on Page 23, Column 1

Associated Press

ON DUTY IN WASHINGTON: A soldier with a machine gun and another with a rifle, left, stand guard on the steps outside the Senate chamber. Flag was lowered to half-staff in tribute to the Rev. Dr. Martin Luther King Jr.

New York Volatile As Anger and Fear Set a Tense Mood

By MICHAEL STERN

A volatile mood of deep sorrow, fist-shaking anger and undefined fear settled on the city yesterday as it absorbed the impact of the death of the Rev. Dr. Martin Luther King Jr.

Many schools, colleges, offices and shops closed early partly out of respect for the memory of the slain civil rights leader, and partly because of reports that new outbreaks of violence would erupt.

The city's bustling waterfront grew still at noon as seamen and longshoremen stopped work as a tribute to Dr. King. The stoppage was announced by the International Longshoremen's Association and the National Maritime Union.

Seven thousand to eight thousand high school and college students released from classes assembled at a memorial rally for Dr. King at the

Continued on Page 26, Column 5

OUTBREAKS HERE RELATIVELY MILD

Negro Areas Are Quiet, but Bands of Young Vandals Roam Midtown Streets

By SYLVAN FOX

The streets of Harlem and Bedford-Stuyvesant were generally calm last night after a burst of violence and looting early yesterday in the wake of the assassination of the Rev. Dr. Martin Luther King Jr. in Memphis.

Mayor Lindsay, appearing on television at 11:30 P.M., praised New Yorkers for keeping the peace and said: "We can work together again for progress and for peace in this city and in this nation."

Earlier in the evening, bands of youths—mostly Negro teen-agers—swarmed into mid-Manhattan, engaged in scattered violence and some looting and were dispersed by a massive show of police force.

The police arrested 27 adults in the Times Square area, most on minor charges, and nine youths were charged with juvenile delinquency. Two persons were reported seized at Columbus Circle, where seven shop windows were smashed and

Continued on Page 27, Column 1

7 Die as Fires and Looting Spread in Chicago Rioting

By DONALD JANSON
Special to The New York Times

CHICAGO, Saturday, April 6—Six thousand National Guard troops were called up yesterday as rioters pillaged stores along a two-mile stretch of Madison Street in the Negro West Side. Seven Negroes were killed and about 350 arrested, the police reported, as the violence and ransacking tapered off late last night.

Half of the armed guardsmen, in fatigues and riot helmets, began patrolling glass-littered West Side streets about 10 P.M. The rest stood by in armories.

About 100 city buses were damaged by bricks and rocks. Drivers, passengers, policemen, firemen, motorists and pedestrians were among at least 75 persons injured.

Mother Beaten

Mrs. Bernadine Laskow, mother of three children, was pulled from her car by Negro youths and beaten. Some white pedestrians who were in the Negro slum suffered the same treatment.

Dozens of automobiles that entered the 12-square-mile riot zone emerged with smashed windows and dented hoods. In some blocks all store windows were boarded or broken.

Cab drivers refused to enter

Continued on Page 23, Column 8

EUROPE DISMAYED; FEARFUL FOR U.S.

Murder of Dr. King Evokes Doubts Over Stability of the American Society

By ANTHONY LEWIS
Special to The New York Times

LONDON, April 5—The murder of the Rev. Dr. Martin Luther King Jr. evoked in Europe today a reaction of intense horror at the deed and of fear for the stability of American society.

In governments, in the press and among the public, there were expressions of sympathy that went beyond formalities. Dr. King was deeply admired in Europe and held up as a symbol of hope for America.

'A Common, Tragic Link'

All the concerns about the United States and its leadership that have grown here in recent years—concerns especially about the war in Vietnam and the violence in America—were fed by the killing of the civil rights leader in Memphis last night.

Everywhere in Europe, people linked Dr. King's death with the assassination of President Kennedy in 1963. That two men so admired here could so similarly be killed intensified doubts about the character of America today.

"From John Fitzgerald Kennedy to Martin Luther King."

Continued on Page 28, Column 3

MANY FIRES SET

White House Guarded by G.I.'s—14 Dead in U.S. Outbreaks

Text of proclamation and Executive order, Page 22.

By BEN A. FRANKLIN
Special to The New York Times

WASHINGTON, April 5—President Johnson ordered 4,000 regular Army and National Guard troops into the nation's capital tonight to try to end riotous looting, burglarizing and burning by roving bands of Negro youths. The arson and looting began yesterday after the murder of the Rev. Dr. Martin Luther King Jr. in Memphis.

The White House announced at 5 P.M. that because the President had determined that "a condition of domestic violence and disorder" existed, he had issued a proclamation and an Executive order mobilizing combat-equipped troops in Washington. Some of the troops were sent to guard the Capitol and the White House.

Reinforcements numbering 2,500 riot-trained soldiers — a brigade of the 82d Airborne Division from Ft. Bragg, N. C.—were airlifted to nearby Andrews Air Force Base, to be held in reserve this weekend.

Guard Called In Other Cities

The National Guard also was called out in a half-dozen other cities in an effort to stem disorders or guard against them—Chicago, Detroit, Boston, Jackson, Miss., Raleigh, N. C., and Tallahassee, Fla.

The death toll from the violence stemming from Dr. King's assassination stood at a total of 14 tonight. Besides five deaths in Washington, they included seven in Chicago, one in Detroit and one in Tallahassee.

Mayor Walter E. Washington, who is a Negro, declared a 13-hour curfew, from 5:30 P.M. to 6:30 A.M. The Mayor's emergency order halted the sale of liquor and forbade the sale, transportation or possession of firearms, explosives or flammable liquids.

At midnight, the police reported five dead, all but one of them Negroes, in 28 hours of disorders in this city of about 800,000, 63 per cent of them Negroes. Four Negroes were killed today, including two suspected looters, one of them 14 years old, who were shot to death by policemen in separate isolated encounters across the Anacostia River, far from the areas of general disorders. The two other Negro deaths today were described as apparently the result of accidents.

The white man, George Fletcher, 28, of suburban Wood-

Continued on Page 22, Column 1

Clark Is Sure Killer Will Soon Be Seized

By MARTIN WALDRON
Special to The New York Times

MEMPHIS, Tenn., April 5—Attorney General Ramsey Clark said today that he was "confident" of a quick solution to the assassination here yesterday of the Rev. Dr. Martin Luther King Jr.

A source close to the intensive manhunt said that agents of the Federal Bureau of Investigation were close to making an arrest.

The Attorney General, who flew here this morning at the order of President Johnson with other top officials of the Justice Department, told a news conference that the F.B.I. was searching for the killer in several states.

He said that the killer, who was believed to have escaped in a white Mustang automobile,

Continued on Page 24, Column 1

The New York Times (by Barton Silverman)

MARCHING DOWN BROADWAY: Demonstrators protesting the slaying of the Rev. Dr. Martin Luther King Jr. crossing 23d Street on the way to City Hall yesterday. The march began after a memorial ceremony in Central Park.

Negroes Strive to Ease Tensions; False Rumors Raise City's Fears

Militants Join Effort

By THOMAS A. JOHNSON

At the height of the violence in Harlem early yesterday morning, about 30 young Negro militants fanned out from Jay's Bar and Grill on 125th Street near Eighth Avenue and tried to persuade other Negroes to stop breaking windows, looting and setting fires.

This particular group was made up of members of Harlem CORE, and they were only a part of the many hundreds of Negroes living in the violence-torn areas of Harlem and Brooklyn who worked actively to stop the disorders.

The volunteer peace-keepers tried to end the violence by a variety of methods and for a variety of reasons.

Some are church groups.

Continued on Page 26, Column 1

Racial Unrest Exaggerated

By MURRAY SCHUMACH

The city was flooded yesterday with wild and unfounded rumors that exceeded the amount of violence and heightened widespread fears of racial riots.

In some instances, the reports became so persistent that corporations allowed employes, particularly women, to leave for home early in the afternoon.

The untrue reports included subway disruptions, bombings, mass assaults and imposition of a citywide curfew. Almost any kind of holdup, apparently, was associated in the minds of some rumor-mongers with racial disturbances and was then exaggerated.

Barry H. Gottehrer, the head

Continued on Page 26, Column 6

NEWS INDEX

"All the News That's Fit to Print"

The New York Times

LATE CITY EDITION

Weather: Sunny, warm today; fair, continued warm tonight, tomorrow. Temp. range: today 88-62; Wed. 83-59. Temp.-Hum. Index 75; Wed. 74. Full U.S. report on Page 94.

VOL. CXVII..No. 40,311 NEW YORK, THURSDAY, JUNE 6, 1968 — 10 CENTS

KENNEDY IS DEAD, VICTIM OF ASSASSIN; SUSPECT, ARAB IMMIGRANT, ARRAIGNED; JOHNSON APPOINTS PANEL ON VIOLENCE

MARCUS TESTIFIES DE SAPIO HAD ROLE IN A CON ED DEAL

Says Itkin Sought Delay of Permit to Aid Own Scheme With Ex-Tammany Head

By BARNARD L. COLLIER

Former Water Commissioner James L. Marcus testified yesterday that he had been asked to delay approval of a permit to Consolidated Edison while the former Tammany Hall leader, Carmine G. De Sapio, was trying to make a deal with the utility company.

Marcus testified that the request came last September from his business partner, Herbert Itkin, who was in turn trying to negotiate a deal with Mr. De Sapio.

The testimony was elicited from Marcus under cross-examination on the third day of a Federal bribery conspiracy trial that has been marked by the mention in Marcus's testimony of several prominent members of both the Republican and Democratic parties.

Marcus was asked if there was a time when he, as Commissioner of Water Supply, Gas and Electricity, had "done business" with Con Edison. His answer was yes.

Says Itkin Asked Delay

"Itkin came to me," he said, "and said that Con Ed wanted a permit to increase the voltage on one of their power lines for 20 miles." He added that his approval as Commissioner was needed.

"Itkin said I should hold up for a while because he was negotiating with Carmine De Sapio, who was negotiating with Con Ed."

Marcus said that Mr. Itkin asked him to delay the approval for "a few weeks."

At that point in the trial, which came at about 4:40 P.M., Herman Zoloto, a lawyer representing Henry Fried, a contractor, and Mr. Fried's company, S. T. Grand, Inc., shouted:

"You're way ahead of your story, Mr. Marcus!"

Judge Edward Weinfeld broke in and scolded Mr. Zoloto for "a highly improper re-

Continued on Page 41, Column 1

TRANSIT PACKAGE SUBMITTED TO CITY

M.T.A. Seeks Approval of 8 New Subway Routes

By EMANUEL PERLMUTTER

A $1.27-billion package of subway and commuter railroad additions and improvements was submitted to the Board of Estimate and Mayor Lindsay yesterday.

The program was presented by the Metropolitan Transportation Authority and the New York City Transit Authority with a request for speedy city agreement on the new routes and engineering designs.

The over-all plan, which would take 10 years to complete, consists of eight new subway routes, including a Second Avenue subway, and Long Island Rail Road connections to the East Side of Manhattan and to Kennedy International Airport.

City approval of the routes and designs is a first step before application can be made for $60-million set aside by the Legislature for the engineering design of the mass transportation program presented by the Metropolitan Transportation

Continued on Page 53, Column 1

France Will Meet Tariff Deadline; Strikes Dwindling

By HENRY TANNER
Special to The New York Times

PARIS, June 5 — Maurice Couve de Murville told France's partners in the Common Market today that despite the nationwide strike now coming to a close, the Government would honor the July 1 deadline for the abolition of remaining tariffs in the European trade bloc.

Today workers in the nationalized railroad company, the Paris transit system, the post and telegraph offices and other public administrations voted to go back to work. Trains are expected to start running tomorrow on several major national lines and the Paris subways.

By the end of the week, it is expected, the nationwide strike, now in its 18th day, will be all but ended.

Mr. Couve de Murville, who is the new Minister of Economy and Finance, also reassured his countrymen

Continued on Page 15, Column 1

JERUSALEM POLICE CLASH WITH ARABS

Israelis Halt Procession on Anniversary of War—U.N. Council Meets on Fighting

Special to The New York Times

JERUSALEM, June 5—A silent Arab procession commemorating the first anniversary of the Arab-Israeli war erupted into a violent clash today when Israeli policemen intercepted the marchers at the edge of the walled Old City of Jerusalem.

The clash was the most violent aspect of a widespread protest in which Arabs shuttered shops and other businesses here and elsewhere on the west bank of the Jordan and in the occupied Gaza Strip. It came after a day-long battle yesterday across the Jordan between the Israelis and Jordanians, in which aircraft and artillery were used.

[The United Nations Security Council met Wednesday at the urgent request of Israel and Jordan to consider recurrent hostilities along their cease-fire line. It postponed debate, probably until Thursday. Page 3.]

In the west-bank towns of Nablus, Jenin and Tulkarm, all centers of Arab nationalism, the general strike was 100 per cent effective. All stores, cafes and offices were closed, public transportation ceased and the streets were virtually devoid of traffic and pedestrians.

Schools throughout the west bank and Gaza Strip had no

Continued on Page 2, Column 4

Italy's Cabinet Quits As Parliament Opens

By ROBERT C. DOTY
Special to The New York Times

ROME, June 5—Premier Aldo Moro and his center-left coalition Government, which has ruled Italy for four and a half years, resigned tonight with the convening of the new parliament, the fifth since World War II.

President Giuseppe Saragat asked Mr. Moro and his ministers to remain in office as a caretaker government while the search for a new government, which may be arduous, goes on.

Resignation of the government with the convening of a new parliament is automatic. But any hope that the Moro

Continued on Page 14, Column 3

6 IN RACE GUARDED

Secret Service Given Campaign Security Task by President

Text of the Johnson speech is printed on Page 23.

By MAX FRANKEL
Special to The New York Times

WASHINGTON, June 5—For the second time in five years, Lyndon B. Johnson undertook today, amid national shock and outrage, to offer protection, prayer, comfort and assistance to his political rivals in the Kennedy family and then to try to heal the country's political and psychological wounds.

The President's first reaction to the shooting of Senator Robert F. Kennedy this morning was that "there are no words equal to the horror of this tragedy."

But tonight, in an emotional and at times even angry statement on television, he pleaded with all Americans to end the violence in their midst once and for all, to tolerate neither hatred nor the preaching of violence and to resolve to live under the law.

A Guard for Candidates

Mr. Johnson said he was appointing a commission of distinguished citizens to investigate both the circumstances and the causes of physical violence of all kinds in the United States, in the hope that the nation can learn "how we can stop it".

Earlier he had moved swiftly to provide protective Secret Service details to the six announced Presidential candidates of major parties, other than Vice President Humphrey, who already has such protection because of his office.

Meanwhile, in the House of Representatives, a vote of 317 to 60 cleared the way for the House to accept the Senate version of an anticrime bill, including controls over the interstate sale of hand guns. The vote rejected a move to send the legislation to a Senate-House conference.

Members of Commission

To the commission Mr. Johnson named Milton Eisenhower, former president of Johns Hopkins University; Archbishop Terence J. Cooke of New York; Albert Jenner, Chicago lawyer who worked for the commission that investigated the assassination of President Kennedy; former Ambassador Patricia Harris; Eric Hoffer, the longshoreman-turned-philosopher; Senators Philip Hart, Democrat of Michigan, and Roman L. Hruska, Republican of Nebraska; Representative Hale Boggs, Democrat of Louisiana, majority whip in the House; Representative William M. McCulloch, Republican of Ohio, and Federal Judge Leon Higginbotham of Philadelphia.

The President described himself as shocked, dismayed and deeply disturbed, as he knew all Americans were, by the shooting, which he described as the "latest spectacular example" of lawlessness and violence.

"So let us, for God's sake, re-

Continued on Page 23, Column 1

NEWS INDEX

AFTER THE SHOOTING: Senator Kennedy's wife, Ethel, bends over him as a man checks pulse to determine condition

HANOI INSISTS U.S. HALT ITS BOMBING

Aides Call Talks Response to Johnson—Suspicion Voiced of a Plot Against Kennedy

By HEDRICK SMITH
Special to The New York Times

PARIS, June 5—North Vietnamese negotiators contended today that Hanoi had responded to President Johnson's restriction of American air attacks on the north by entering official talks here. They asserted that the next move, a total halt in bombing, was up to the United States.

The North Vietnamese argument, put forward in the seventh negotiating session between the two sides since May 13, produced one of the sharpest exchanges since the Vietnam talks began here.

The North Vietnamese made no direct comment on the shooting of Senator Robert F. Kennedy, but circles close to the delegation voiced suspicions in private, asking if the attack was not part of a conspiracy by the Johnson Administration. [Page 33.]

Near the end of today's session at the former Majestic Hotel, Hanoi's chief representative, Xuan Thuy, leaned across the negotiating table and asked the American delegates bluntly:

"When will the United States unconditionally cease the bombing and all other acts of war against the Democratic Republic of Vietnam so that other questions can be discussed?"

In response, W. Averell Har-

Continued on Page 8, Column 4

Big Board Weighs 4 Special Closings

By VARTANIG G. VARTAN

A securities industry panel recommended yesterday that the New York Stock Exchange, the American Stock Exchange and the over-the-counter market close down for four days over the next month to cope with the deluge of paperwork in brokerage offices.

The panel proposed closing the securities markets for three Wednesdays—June 12, 19 and 26—as well as Friday, July 5.

The board of governors of the New York Stock Exchange will meet this afternoon to consider the proposal. Wall Street sources said that in view of the critical situation the governors are expected to accept the pro-

Continued on Page 73, Column 1

The New York Times (by George Tames)

ROBERT F. KENNEDY

A Pall Over Politics

Murder Raises Grave Questions for Presidency Races Now and in Future

By TOM WICKER
Special to The New York Times

News Analysis

WASHINGTON, Thursday, June 6—The murder of Robert F. Kennedy shattered the 1968 Presidential campaign and lowered a pall of uncertainty over American politics now and in the years to come. For the immediate future, it may well have assured the nominations by the Democrats and Republicans of the present front-running candidates — Vice President Humphrey and Richard Nixon. It raised grave questions, however, about the personal dangers of political campaigning in the United States. It added a tragic new dimension to the near-martyrdom of the Kennedy family, which has now lost two sons to assassins' bullets.

It removed forever one of the most promising young political leaders in recent American history, one with particular appeal for the poor, the downtrodden and the alienated inhabitants of the Negro slums. That appeal had been proved in all of Robert Kennedy's primary victories this year.

These elements of society also revered the Senator's brother President Kennedy, who was assassinated on Nov. 22, 1963. How they would react to Robert Kennedy's murder—both in the immediate future and for the long political pull—was a crucial question.

The murder added sorrowful emphasis to one of Robert Kennedy's major political themes—the necessity for orderly and just redress of grievances, in place of violent action.

Ultimately, Mr. Kennedy's death—the first assassination of an American Presidential candidate—might lead to changes in campaigning practices, even to the fundamental manner in which the nation chooses its President.

The most immediate effect, however, was that for the third—and most harrowing—time a shock wave of unexpected events had completely altered the shape of the 1968 campaign.

The first came on March 12 when Senator Eugene J. McCarthy of Minnesota won 42 per cent of the Democratic vote in the New Hampshire primary, and Mr. Kennedy immediately thereafter became an active candidate.

The second transformation

Continued on Page 25, Column 6

NOTES ON KENNEDY IN SUSPECT'S HOME

Cite 'Necessity' to Murder Senator Before June 5, Anniversary of War

By PETER KIHSS

A notebook found in the Pasadena home of Sirhan Bishara Sirhan had "a direct reference to the necessity to assassinate Senator Kennedy before June 5, 1968." Mayor Samuel W. Yorty of Los Angeles said last night.

The date was the first anniversary of the six-day war, in which Israeli forces smashed those of the United Arab Republic, Syria and Jordan.

Sirhan, a 24-year-old Christian Arab, who has described himself as a Jerusalem-born Jordanian, is being held in the shooting of the New York Senator.

Justice Department records indicated that Sirhan came to the United States with his family in January of 1957 as immigrants, less than three months after the Suez war in 1956. Sirhan was 12 at the time.

The family quickly broke up in discord, the father staying in New York to work as a plumber and then going back to their former Palestine home, the mother taking five children to California, where a sixth child immigrated later.

Sirhan was described yesterday by Police Chief Thomas Reddin of Los Angeles as "very cool, very calm, very stable and quite lucid."

He was quoted as having said,

Continued on Page 21, Column 6

Father of Suspect 'Sickened' by News

By TERENCE SMITH
Special to The New York Times

ET TAIYIBA, Israeli-Occupied Jordan, Thursday, June 6—Bishara Sirhan's hands trembled as he talked about his son Sirhan Bishara Sirhan, the accused assailant of Senator Robert F. Kennedy.

Mr. Sirhan dwelled on the tragedy of the shooting. He became angry as he talked, and finally said: "This news made me sick when I heard it. If my son has done this dirty thing, then let them hang him."

Mr. Sirhan's memories of his five sons are those of 10 years ago, when he last saw them and their mother. After years of fierce family quarrels, Bishara

Continued on Page 21, Column 4

SURGERY IN VAIN

President Calls Death Tragedy, Proclaims a Day of Mourning

Texts of the medical reports appear on Page 22.

By GLADWIN HILL
Special to The New York Times

LOS ANGELES, Thursday, June 6—Senator Robert F. Kennedy, the brother of a murdered President, died at 1:44 A.M. today of an assassin's shots.

The New York Senator was wounded more than 20 hours earlier, moments after he had made his victory statement in the California primary.

At his side when he died today in Good Samaritan Hospital were his wife, Ethel; his sisters, Mrs. Stephen Smith and Mrs. Patricia Lawford; his brother-in-law, Stephen Smith; and his sister-in-law, Mrs. John F. Kennedy, whose husband was assassinated 4½ years ago in Dallas.

In Washington, President Johnson issued a statement calling the death a tragedy. He proclaimed next Sunday a national day of mourning.

The Final Report

Hopes had risen slightly when more than eight hours went by without a new medical bulletin on the stricken Senator, but the grimness of the final announcement was signaled when Frank Mankiewicz, Mr. Kennedy's press secretary, walked slowly down the street in front of the hospital toward the littered gymnasium that served as press headquarters.

Mr. Mankiewicz bit his lip. His shoulders slumped.

He stepped to a lectern in front of a green-tinted chalkboard and bowed his head for a moment while the television lights snapped on.

Then, at one minute before 2 A.M., he told of the death of Mr. Kennedy.

Following is the text of the statement from Mr. Mankiewicz:

"I have a short announcement to read which I will read at this time. Senator Robert Francis Kennedy died at 1:44 A.M. today, June 6, 1968. With

Continued on Page 20, Column 1

KUCHEL UNSEATED AS RAFFERTY WINS

Conservative Beats Senator in California's Primary

By LAWRENCE E. DAVIES
Special to The New York Times

LOS ANGELES, June 5—Dr. Max Rafferty, State Superintendent of Public Instruction, defeated Senator Thomas H. Kuchel in the Republican Senatorial primary in California yesterday, cutting short Mr. Kuchel's 15-year career in the Senate.

Returns from 20,714 of 21,301 precincts gave:

Rafferty	1,056,038	50%
Kuchel	985,097	47%

As the vote count continued today, it became apparent that the conservative Republicanism of Southern California had carried Dr. Rafferty to victory over the heretofore unbeatable Republican whip in the Senate.

Mr. Kuchel, an outspoken liberal-moderate who had made political extremists such as John Birch Society members his targets in recent years, was beaten by the voters in Los Angeles, San Diego and Orange Counties, after having led Dr. Rafferty last night and early today.

Dr. Rafferty, who has become

Continued on Page 28, Column 3

"All the News That's Fit to Print"

The New York Times

LATE CITY EDITION

Weather: Partly sunny, cool today. Fair tonight. Fair, warm tomorrow. Temp. range: today 72-60; Wed. 74-61. Temp.-Hum. Index 60; Wed. 70. U.S. report on Page 89.

VOL. CXVII...No. 40,325 NEW YORK, THURSDAY, JUNE 20, 1968 10 CENTS

PRESIDENT SIGNS BROAD CRIME BILL, WITH OBJECTIONS

Asserts It Contains 'More Good Than Bad' and Will Lift 'Shadow of Fear'

ASSAILS WIDE WIRETAPS

But He Praises Massive Federal Help to Improve Local Law Enforcement

Text of Johnson's statement is printed on Page 23.

By MAX FRANKEL

Special to The New York Times

WASHINGTON, June 19—President Johnson signed the controversial omnibus crime bill tonight because he said it contained "more good than bad."

Expressing strong reservations, especially about the broad license it gives to state and local law enforcement agencies to tap telephones and engage in other forms of eavesdropping, the President said that despite its shortcomings the new law "will help to lift the stain of crime and the shadow of fear from the streets of our communities."

The heart of the measure, he noted, is the authorization for massive Federal grants to improve local law enforcement and methods, and this, the President indicated, is a great opportunity that should not be lost.

Repeal Is Urged

Mr. Johnson called for the repeal of the wiretapping provisions and indicated some reservation about elements of the law dealing with certain rules of evidence in Federal criminal trials.

But these provisions, which purport to overturn Supreme Court decisions on the rights of defendants, will not seriously affect the Federal practice, the President indicated, and can be so interpreted as to be constitutional.

The new law also contains controls on the sale of handguns, which the President previously called "a halfway measure" because it omitted rifles and shotguns.

Nonetheless, Mr. Johnson noted that the gun controls ended three decades of inaction by the Federal Government. He urged Congress to follow this up quickly by passing the controls over rifles and shotguns that he urged following the assassination June 5 of Senator

Continued on Page 23, Column 1

Over 50,000 March in Capital in Support of the Poor

The New York Times

Participants in the Poor People's Campaign "Solidarity Day" march massed around the Reflecting Pool in front of Washington Monument yesterday

Protesters Call for Sharing Of Nation's Affluence by All

By BEN A. FRANKLIN

Special to The New York Times

WASHINGTON, June 19—More than 50,000 orderly Americans marched here today to emphasize their demand for a just share of affluence and dignity for Negroes, Spanish-speaking minorities, American Indians and poor whites.

"The Solidarity Day" march of the Poor People's Campaign—a leisurely one-mile stroll on a hot, humid afternoon from the Washington Monument to a prolonged formal program of harshly worded speeches at the Lincoln Memorial—was a numerical success.

Forecasts by the march organizers had never asserted the attendance would be greater than 40,000. The official crowd estimate of 50,000 was provided by the police.

Impact Is Weighed

The demonstration's impact on Washington, Congress and the nation, however, remained in doubt. Most of the speakers this afternoon appeared to sense a national mood of irresolution, and they warned that the country's impoverished people were giving the affluent and the powerful a "last chance."

March leaders said that they were pleased by the turnout—particularly by the fact that about half the marchers were white—and that the day's success might serve to revitalize the Poor People's Campaign.

Some campaign leaders asserted that the throng, which began disembarking from 700 chartered buses and countless private cars before dawn this morning, had equaled or surpassed the 200,000 or more persons who attended the last great protest demonstration in the capital, the civil rights

Continued on Page 30, Column 1

SOME GAIN HINTED IN VIETNAM TALKS

Indication of Move Toward Private Sessions Is Seen at Paris Negotiations

By HEDRICK SMITH

Special to The New York Times

PARIS, June 19 — American and North Vietnamese negotiators stepped up their mutual public recriminations today, but at the same time prospects improved for moving to secret bargaining.

Spokesmen for both delegations said that the ninth negotiating session since May 13 on the Vietnam war had produced no break in the deadlock over American bombing of North Vietnam and other substantive issues.

But for the first time, the two sides withheld virtually all details of informal conversations they had during a 40-minute recess in the talks.

American officials, who have been pressing for secret discussions as a way of getting into meaningful bargaining, were clearly encouraged by this development.

Statements Are Guarded

Until now, conversations during breaks for tea have been devoted to small talk. Today, for the first time, neither side would say flatly that only small talk and no substantive issues had been raised as the delegations mingled informally in several small groups.

The tea breaks began at the sixth session, on May 31. They have steadily grown longer, another sign of encouragement to some American officials of the possibility that informal, private bargaining sessions may develop.

William J. Jorden, the American spokesman, said today that there had been "no arrangement" between the delegations to keep the subject matter of the teatime talk secret. But he refused to discuss it further

Continued on Page 2, Column 4

MOSCOW REBUFFS PRESIDENT AGAIN

Pravda Says Issues Besides War Bar Cooperation

By RAYMOND H. ANDERSON

Special to The New York Times

MOSCOW, June 19—An authoritative Soviet political commentator, Viktor Mayevsky, declared today that there were many reasons, besides the war in Vietnam, why the Soviet Union was wary of responding favorably to President Johnson's appeals for an improvement of relations.

Moscow has no intention, Mr. Mayevsky wrote in the Communist party newspaper Pravda, of developing friendly relations with the United States "to the detriment of the interests of socialism, the national liberation movement and the security of peoples."

President Johnson has made three public appeals in the last two weeks for greater Soviet-United States cooperation in world peace-making and economic and scientific development.

Another authoritative commentator, Vikenty Matveyev of Izvestia, the Soviet Government newspaper, turned a cold shoulder to the gestures last week, declaring that the war in Vietnam must be ended be-

Continued on Page 9, Column 4

NEWS INDEX

Audience at Hunter Jeers Moscow Rabbi

By IRVING SPIEGEL

Chief Rabbi Yehuda Leib Levin of Moscow was jeered and finally hooted off the stage of the Hunter College Auditorium last night after he declared that there was no anti-Semitism in the Soviet Union and that Soviet Jews held places of honor in the arts and sciences.

The rabbi succeeded in finishing his 50-minute speech—which was given in Yiddish—but the final 20 minutes of English translation could not be made because of the jeering. Rabbi Levin had paused about every 10 minutes for the translation.

The 74-year-old, white-bearded chief rabbi was frequently interrupted by catcalls from a small, vociferous minority

Continued on Page 21, Column 1

$600-MILLION CUT IN AID BILL VOTED

House Unit Pares Johnson's Request 20%—G.O.P. to Seek $1-Billion Slash

By FELIX BELAIR Jr.

Special to The New York Times

WASHINGTON, June 19—A foreign aid authorization of $2.36-billion—about $600-million below President Johnson's budget request—was approved today by the House Foreign Affairs Committee.

The vote of 24 to 9 sustained the 20 per cent cut proposed by the committee's chairman, Representative Thomas E. Morgan of Pennsylvania, in an effort to forestall an even heavier reduction when the measure comes up for debate on the House floor next week.

But before the measure could be brought to a vote in committee, some Republican members led by Representative E. Ross Adair of Indiana said that they would carry their fight for at least a $1-billion cut to the floor.

In announcing the committee action, Mr. Morgan conceded

Continued on Page 18, Column 3

Corallo, Fried and Motto Convicted in Marcus Case

By BARNARD L. COLLIER

A Federal jury convicted four out of five defendants in the Marcus bribery conspiracy case yesterday.

Former Water Commissioner James L. Marcus had already pleaded guilty to the charge of sharing a $40,000 kickback on a reservoir-cleaning city contract. Although the case took his name he was not on trial and not in the courtroom when the verdict came at 7 P.M.

Those found guilty as co-conspirators with Marcus were Henry Fried, 68-year-old millionaire contractor; his company, S. T. Grand, Inc.; Antonio (Tony Ducks) Corallo, 54, a man Marcus had testified was "a top guy in the Mafia," and Daniel J. Motto, 57, the president of Local 350 of the Bakers and Confectionary Workers Union in Queens.

Acquitted by the all-male jury, which deliberated three hours and ten minutes, was Charles J. Rappaport, 30, a former law partner of Herbert Itkin, who appeared during the trial as one of the Government's star witnesses and revealed that for six years he was an undercover agent for the Federal Bureau of Investigation.

Mr. Rappaport, who was sitting with his lawyer at the defense counsel's table, put his head in his arms and cried when his acquittal was read by the jury foreman, James C. Hunnewell. His blond wife, Rochelle, who had been in court during ten full trial days, sighed loudly and also broke into tears.

The other defendants took the decision without visible emotion. Fried sat hunched in a chair between two of his lawyers, the frown he had worn throughout the trial unchanged.

Judge Edward Weinfeld placed all of the convicted men under bail: $50,000 for Fried, $25,000 for Corallo and $10,000 for Motto. All of the defendants can receive up to five years in jail and be fined $10,000 when sentencing takes place on July 26.

The jury heard a two-hour five-minute charge by Judge Weinfeld shortly before it was sent for an hour lunch break. The jurymen began their first

Continued on Page 35, Column 1

Grand Central Tower Will Top Pan Am Building

By GLENN FOWLER

Detailed plans were announced yesterday for a 55-story-tall slab of concrete and granite that will be "floated" above the waiting room of Grand Central Terminal just north of 42d Street to create a companion skyscraper to the Pan Am Building astride Park Avenue.

The plans for the new $100-million office tower were made public by the architect, Marcel Breuer, and the builder, Morris Saady. The disclosure promised to revive the controversy that greeted the first announcement last September that the New York Central Railroad — now the Penn Central—intended to sell air rights over the landmark terminal to the highest bidder.

"It's the wrong building, in the wrong place, at the wrong time," Donald K. Elliott, chairman of the City Planning Commission, said yesterday after having seen the preliminary plans.

The planning commission, however, is not empowered to hold up construction of a building so long as it conforms to the city's zoning resolution. Mr. Breuer's plans require no variance from the zoning rules, commission members concede.

One possible effect of the new tower would be the permanent closing of the heliport

Continued on Page 36, Column 1

The New York Times (by Patrick A. Burns)

Marcel Breuer, architect, looking over a rendering of the building as it would appear over the 42d Street facade of Grand Central Terminal. The Pan Am Building is behind it.

Brownsville to Get 50-Block Renewal

By KATHLEEN TELTSCH

A 50-block renewal program is to be undertaken in the predominantly Negro Brownsville section of central Brooklyn to provide improved housing and jobs for residents.

The development of Marcus Garvey Park Village, named for the black nationalist leader of the nineteen-twenties, was announced jointly yesterday by city officials and community leaders as New York's first venture under the Federal Model Cities Program.

A key element in the plan calls for the city to acquire buildings and to collect rentals and then to transfer ownership within three years to local corporations of Brownsville residents. The corporations will be set up to

Continued on Page 75, Column 2

O'DWYER ASKS END OF HUMPHREY BID

Says Primary Vote Shows Vice President Should Let McCarthy Run Alone

By MAURICE CARROLL

Paul O'Dwyer, savoring his surprise victory as Democratic nominee for the Senate, said yesterday that Vice President Humphrey should withdraw as a candidate for President.

"If that isn't clear to him," Mr. O'Dwyer said, "it should be made clear to more realistic leaders in my party."

Mr. O'Dwyer said that he could not possibly support Mr. Humphrey for either the nomination or the Presidency.

An independent-minded former City Councilman, Mr. O'Dwyer helped form the Coalition for a Democratic Alternative, which opposes the Vietnam war, and his campaign was intertwined with the efforts of Senator Eugene J. McCarthy of Minnesota to win convention delegates from New York.

The O'Dwyer-McCarthy victories in New York, along with Mr. Humphrey's "vociferous" support of the Vietnam war, persuaded him, Mr. O'Dwyer said, that the Vice President should pull out as a candidate "and leave the race to Gene McCarthy."

With a smile, Mr. O'Dwyer turned aside all questions about his plans to run against Senator Jacob K. Javits, the two-term Republican incumbent who also won the Liberal line on Tuesday. There would be time for that after rounding up

Continued on Page 39, Column 1

M'CARTHY FORCES SEEK TO CONTROL STATE DELEGATION

Call on Democratic Party to Give Them at Least Half of the At-Large Seats

MAJOR VICTORY CLAIMED

Minnesota Senator Urges Also That Platform Reflect Peace and Poor Issues

By RICHARD WITKIN

Senator Eugene J. McCarthy's campaign chiefs here, elated by his solid primary victory, called on the Democratic State Committee yesterday to reflect this popular will in picking the more than 65 delegates-at-large to the August nominating convention.

One campaigner, Harold Ickes Jr., specified that Mr. McCarthy should get half or more of the delegates. He based this figure on his confidence that final tallies in Tuesday's voting would show the Senator winning "over a majority" of the 123 district delegates picked by the Democratic voters.

Later, John J. Burns, the party's state chairman and a strong backer of the late Senator Robert F. Kennedy, said the state committee would pick the at-large delegates at a meeting a week from Friday.

"We will try to be absolutely fair," he added.

Tabulation Continues

Though the McCarthy forces said their tabulations showed they could be "sure of at least 60" district delegates, an incomplete Associated Press tabulation in late afternoon showed the McCarthy count at 52.

The Associated Press said the figure for former pro-Kennedy candidates, who ran pledged to Kennedy principles, was 26. Victories also were posted by 19 "uncommitted" delegates and by five or six pledged to Vice President Humphrey.

The figures totaled 103, leaving 20 contests where the results were not yet final. Most of these races were upstate, where wide use of paper ballots slowed the count.

In a companion Republican primary, overshadowed by the Democratic battle, latest United Press International returns showed that candidates backing Richard M. Nixon, but pointedly not encouraged by him, had won at least four of 11 contests with pro-Rockefeller delegates.

Rockefeller Unopposed

Governor Rockefeller had been assured from the start of at least 70 of the 82 district delegate slots being filled, since candidates supporting him were unopposed. Former Vice President Nixon was assured a fifth supporter—another unopposed organization choice who announced for Mr. Nixon before the primary.

Senator McCarthy flew here from Washington late in the afternoon and warmly greeted Paul O'Dwyer, who had won the Democratic Senate nomination in a campaign closely linked to his own.

Interviewed in a cavernous

Continued on Page 38, Column 1

2 Medical Units Call Marijuana Harmful

By RICHARD D. LYONS

Special to The New York Times

SAN FRANCISCO, June 19—Marijuana smoking was condemned as "dangerous" today by two medical and scientific groups in one of the strongest statements yet made by such agencies on use of the drug.

Their report said that strict penalties should be imposed for the sale of the drug but users should not be treated as criminals solely on the basis of drug abuse.

A number of medical men, including Dr. James L. Goddard, outgoing head of the Food and Drug Administration, have expressed uncertainty about the harmfulness of marijuana.

Committees of the American Medical Association and the National Research Council, the research arm of the federally

Continued on Page 26, Column 1

"All the News That's Fit to Print"

The New York Times

LATE CITY EDITION

Weather: Mostly sunny, hot today; fair and warm tonight, tomorrow. Temp. range: today 89-72; Thurs. 91-73. Temp.-Hum. Index yesterday 80. Complete U.S. report Page 69.

VOL. CXVII..No. 40,375 · NEW YORK, FRIDAY, AUGUST 9, 1968 · 10 CENTS

NIXON SELECTS AGNEW AS HIS RUNNING MATE AND WINS APPROVAL AFTER FIGHT ON FLOOR; PLEDGES END OF WAR, TOUGHNESS ON CRIME

BIG BOARD URGES COMMISSION CUT ON LARGE TRADES

Exchange Concedes Federal Pressure Prompted Move for Its First Reduction

By EILEEN SHANAHAN

The New York Stock Exchange, conceding that it was acting under "Government prodding," proposed yesterday the first reduction in brokerage commissions in its 176-year history.

The reduction in commissions would apply only to stock transactions involving 1,000 or more shares, on which current commissions are considered excessive by both the Exchange and the Securities and Exchange Commission. Thus, many ordinary investors, who never buy or sell as many as 1,000 shares at once, would reap no direct benefit.

Among those, however, who would profit directly would be almost all persons with money invested in mutual funds or in private or corporate pension funds that invest in common stocks.

Fund Shareholder Would Gain

The reduction in brokerage commissions paid by mutual-fund managers on large stock transactions would put an additional $15 to $20 each year into the pocket of a typical mutual-fund shareholder with $5,000 invested in a fund with average securities trading.

Brokerage commissions are considered part of the fund's cost of doing business, and are part of the management fee, which is, in effect, subtracted from the value of the investor's holdings. If the commission comes down, there would be less to be subtracted, so the value of the investor's holdings would go up accordingly.

Traders of substantial blocks of stock would benefit not only from reduced charges on their trades on the New York Stock Exchange, but also on almost all of their other stock transactions. New York Stock Exchange brokerage commissions set the pattern for the rest of the industry.

Governors Approve Reduction

For the brokerage community as a whole, the reduction in commissions would amount to an estimated $150-million a year, or about 7 per cent of total stock-exchange commissions based on the volume of trading on the New York Stock Exchange last year. Assuming continuation of this year's pace of trading, the reduction would be even greater for 1968.

The commission-cutting proposal was announced at a news conference by Robert W.

Continued on Page 56, Column 3

U.S. Finds Wolfson And 3 Aides Guilty Of S.E.C. Violations

By H. J. MAIDENBERG

Louis E. Wolfson, who dazzled the world of high finance with his activities in the early nineteen-fifties, and three co-defendants were found guilty of violating the Securities and Exchange Commission Act by a Federal jury here yesterday.

The 55-year-old former scrap metal merchant and present chairman of the Merritt-Chapman & Scott Corporation was found guilty of perjury, subornation of perjury, obstruction of justice, concealing documents and filing false statements with the S.E.C. The company, a shipbuilding, construction, chemicals and money-lending concern, is now in liquidation.

He faces a maximum prison sentence of 14 years and a fine of $32,000. Fraud and stock manipulation charges against the multimillionaire financier were dropped by Federal Judge Edmund L. Palmieri early in the eight-

Continued on Page 56, Column 1

JULY PLAN TO OUST DUBCEK REPORTED

Sources in East Berlin Say Soviet and East Germany Considered an Invasion

By DAVID BINDER

Special to The New York Times

BERLIN, Aug. 8 — Highly placed sources in East Berlin disclosed today that the Soviet Union and East Germany seriously considered invading Czechoslovakia in mid-July.

One informant said, "I was really worried not so much by what was happening in Prague as what was happening here."

He went on to speak of a partial mobilization of the 650,000-man reserves of East Germany's People's Army, which has not yet been publicized; of the recall of hundreds of East German tourists, and of the virtual closing of the border with Czechoslovakia.

[In Warsaw, informed sources said that Soviet troops were still arriving in Poland despite the accords on Czechoslovakia. Page 4.]

An East Berlin source said

Continued on Page 5, Column 1

'NEW LEADERSHIP'

'Long Dark Night' Over, Nominee Says, Pledging Action

Texts of Nixon and Agnew speeches, Page 20.

Special to The New York Times

MIAMI BEACH, Aug. 8 — Richard M. Nixon called tonight for "new leadership" to restore the nation's prestige abroad and heal its wounds at home.

"The long dark night for America is about to end," the Republican Presidential nominee declared in his acceptance speech.

"The time has come for us to leave the valley of despair and climb the mountain so that we may see the glory of the dawn of a new day for America, a new dawn for peace and freedom to the world."

Mr. Nixon told the partisan audience of thousands and a nationwide television audience of millions that he would make the end of the war in Vietnam his first order of business.

Without offering specific solutions, Mr. Nixon suggested that only a new Administration "not tied to the mistakes and policies of the past" could bring a successful conclusion to the hostilities.

'Era of Negotiation'

Offering the hand of friendship to the nation's cold-war adversaries, he said that "after an era of confrontation, the time has come for an era of negotiation" with the leaders of Communist China and the Soviet Union.

On domestic issues, Mr. Nixon offered to solve the nation's internal difficulties by combining a firm approach to law and order with new remedies for the problems of poverty that would depend less on Government "billions" and more on activities of an enlarged private sector.

The speech was punctuated frequently by applause. The response was greatest after his appeals for law and order and his frequent references to what he portrayed as a decline in national prestige over the last eight years.

Early in his speech Mr. Nixon said that he had talked with Mrs. Dwight D. Eisenhower earlier in the day and that she had said that the best thing for the ailing former President

Continued on Page 21, Column 5

United Press International

G.O.P. CANDIDATES: Richard M. Nixon and Gov. Spiro T. Agnew of Maryland respond to cheers at Convention Hall

REBELS PUT DOWN

Fail in Effort to Have Convention Choose Romney Instead

By TOM WICKER

Special to The New York Times

MIAMI BEACH, Aug. 8—Richard M. Nixon accepted tonight the nomination of a Republican party that was surprised and to a large extent unhappy over his choice of Gov. Spiro T. Agnew of Maryland as his running mate.

Mr. Agnew was approved by the delegates on a roll-call vote in which Gov. George Romney of Michigan received 186 votes and 26 other delegates withheld their votes from the Marylander. Mr. Agnew got 1,128 votes.

Mr. Nixon, addressing a packed and cheering convention hall, pledged that his "first priority foreign policy objective" would be "to bring an honorable end to the war in Vietnam."

His Domestic Policy

Turning to domestic policy, Mr. Nixon promised a tough approach to crime and lawlessness, criticized the courts for going too far "to weaken the peace forces against the criminal forces" and pledged to maintain law and order.

Mr. Nixon's oration ended in a tremendous ovation and an enormous outpouring of orange balloons from the ceiling of the convention hall. Before and after his speech, he took Mrs. Nixon and his daughters, Patricia and Julie, to the podium.

Taking note of the battle over Mr. Agnew's nomination, Mr. Nixon said it had been a healthy thing for the party and that even after spirited contests for President and Vice President Republicans "stand united before the nation tonight."

Hoped for Unity

Mr. Nixon's aides said he had selected Mr. Agnew as his running mate in the belief that the Maryland Governor would help unite the party. The result was the opposite.

All day long, after the choice was announced, the delegates seethed and grumbled, particularly those in the moderate wing of the party and from the big urban states, who believed a Southern-oriented ticket could not win this fall.

When the convention was called to order at 7:30 P.M., a major revolt against Mr. Nixon's choice might have been set off had not Mayor Lindsay of New York seconded Mr. Agnew's nomination and firmly refused to have anything to do with the dissidents.

Preference for Lindsay

Mr. Lindsay was the alternative they preferred, and the latent support for him in the convention could be measured by the long and enthusiastic ovation he received when he went to the podium for his seconding speech. It dwarfed the tiny demonstration staged for Mr. Agnew when he was nominated by Representative Rogers C. B. Morton of Maryland.

Mr. Romney was nominated by the Nevada state chairman, George Abbott, and allowed his name to remain before the convention. He apparently made no effort either to head off or to assist the movement in his behalf.

His 186 votes included majorities of the delegations from Delaware, Michigan, Minnesota

Continued on Page 18, Column 1

3 NEGROES KILLED IN NEW MIAMI RIOT

Policemen Battle Snipers—Troops Hold 100 Blocks Amid Looting and Fires

Special to The New York Times

MIAMI, Friday, Aug. 9 — Two Negroes were killed yesterday and one early this morning as Miami policemen and Negroes exchanged gunfire in the northwest section of the city.

The police said that two of the victims were killed in a gun battle at an apartment house on 62d Street yesterday.

The third man was identified by the police as a sniper who was killed early today on a roof at 301 Northwest 22d Street, in the city's Central District, a Negro area.

In Liberty City, also a predominantly Negro section, where the original violence broke out two days ago, the police reported that conditions had become quiet. Today's violence erupted in adjoining Central District.

Police Lieut. Jay Golden said that the violence in the Central District was producing "fire-fights like in Vietnam."

Armed National Guard troops

Continued on Page 16, Column 1

Humphrey and McCarthy Welcome G.O.P.'s Ticket

Vice President Elated

By ROY REED

Special to The New York Times

WAVERLY, Minn., Aug. 8—Vice President Humphrey said today that the country would have a "clear choice" in this year's Presidential election if he was chosen by the Democrats to oppose Richard M. Nixon.

He also gave his first hint of a possible line of attack on the Republican ticket chosen this week in Miami Beach. Speaking of Mr. Nixon's selection of Gov. Spiro T. Agnew of Maryland as a running mate, he said:

"I have a feeling the choice represented a rather significant compromise. Mr. Nixon had a great deal of support from the South. Maryland is a border state, and I imagine the choice of Mr. Agnew was related to some of the problems in the Republican party."

Meets With Newsmen

The Vice President was barely able to conceal his pleasure at the prospect of running against Mr. Nixon and Mr. Agnew.

"We now have a Republican ticket we can go to the mat with," he said.

He refused to discuss his own possible running mate.

Mr. Humphrey met newsmen on the lawn of his lakeside home here a few minutes after the announcement that Mr. Nixon had picked Mr. Agnew.

The Vice President, dressed in a sports coat and turtle neck shirt and chatting informally, acknowledged that the Agnew

Continued on Page 22, Column 3

Senator Is Confident

By E. W. KENWORTHY

Special to The New York Times

WASHINGTON, Aug. 8 — Senator Eugene J. McCarthy had praise today for the selection of Richard M. Nixon as the Republican nominee for President.

"I think the choice of Nixon is a proper choice," he said at a brief news conference. "He is truly a Republican candidate."

Earlier, when two reporters called on Mr. McCarthy in his dark-walled Senate office, they found him in a relaxed mood after a day of strenuous Ohio campaigning yesterday in Columbus and Cleveland.

Books on His Desk

On his desk were copies of "Poems" by George Seferis, the Greek poet; Robert Lowell's "Near the Ocean," T. S. Eliot's "The Wasteland," and Robert Bly's "The Light Around the Body."

The Senator arrived home last night in time to watch on television some of the nominating speeches and demonstrations in Miami Beach, and he said he was giving some thought to an innovation when his turn came in Chicago.

"What," he asked, "would you think of something along the line of a Greek chorus for the nominating speech?"

"You mean," one of his visitors asked, "strophe and antistrophe—with the strophe saying 'a man who' and the antistrophe saying . . .?"

"That's right," Mr. McCarthy

Continued on Page 22, Column 5

LINDSAY RESISTS PLEA BY LIBERALS

Rejects a Move to Nominate Him and Accepts Invitation to Speak for Agnew

By RICHARD REEVES

Special to The New York Times

MIAMI BEACH, Aug. 8—Mayor Lindsay resisted today the pleas of a group of Northern liberals who urged him for nine hours to become a candidate for the Republican Vice-Presidential nomination against Gov. Spiro T. Agnew.

The liberals, who included Gov. John Chafee of Rhode Island and several Congressmen, began telephoning the Mayor within minutes after Richard M. Nixon announced that he had selected the Maryland Governor as his running mate.

The pleas continued as Mr. Lindsay prepared to step onto the convention platform to second the nomination of Mr. Agnew and began again as soon as the Mayor left the podium.

Mr. Chafee, who later switched his insurgent support to Gov. George Romney of Michigan, said that at no time did Mr. Lindsay waver in his determination to support Mr. Nixon's choice.

Mr. Lindsay's action in supporting the established party leadership contrasted sharply with his decision in 1964 not to support the party's Presidential candidate, Barry Goldwater.

Thus, the young Mayor stepped deeper into the main-

Continued on Page 21, Column 8

Jersey Bans New River Pollution

Court Tells 9 Towns in Morris to Stop Construction

By RONALD SULLIVAN

Special to The New York Times

TRENTON, Aug. 8 — Nine Morris County communities, several of which have rapidly developing residential and industrial complexes, were ordered today in State Superior Court to suspend any further building until they stopped polluting the Rockaway River.

The order was praised by Richard J. Sullivan, the director of the State Division of Clean Air and Water. He said it was the first time in memory that a group of New Jersey communities had been ordered to halt major construction in the interest of keeping the state's rivers clean.

"If you're looking for a trend in water pollution control," he said today, "this is the kind of thing that's going on now."

The order, which had been sought by Mr. Sullivan, was issued this morning by Superior Court Judge James Rosen in the Hudson County Courthouse in Jersey City.

It applies to Boonton Township and Borough, Denville, Randolph, Dover, Rockaway Borough and Township, Wharton and Victory Gardens, which lie in the Rockaway Valley watershed.

Sewers in the nine municipalities lead to the Jersey City waste treatment plant, which the city built in the early

Continued on Page 56, Column 3

The New York Times · Aug. 9, 1968

Court ordered all building halted in shaded communities

President Discloses An Ailment of Colon

By NEIL SHEEHAN

Special to The New York Times

AUSTIN, Tex., Aug. 8—President Johnson has had since 1960 a common intestinal condition known as diverticulosis, White House officials said today.

The officials disclosed the presence of diverticula — pouches cropping out from the President's large intestine, or colon—while giving a report on the results of the President's annual physical examination at the Brooke Army Medical Center in San Antonio.

The President's condition is not considered an illness, officials explained, because none of the diverticula have ever become inflamed from trapped intestinal matter, a disorder known as diverticulitis. Nor have they caused Mr. Johnson any discomfort, it was said.

Continued on Page 8, Column 1

Svetlana Alliluyeva Burned Her Soviet Passport

Will Seek U.S. Citizenship, She Writes to a Friend

By HENRY RAYMONT

Svetlana Alliluyeva has written a friend that she burned her Soviet passport last summer so that no one could ever think that she might return to Moscow. She also indicated that she intended to seek United States citizenship.

In an intense, personal and sometimes caustically witty letter, Miss Alliluyeva, Stalin's daughter, vowed she would never return to the Soviet Union, "a land of uninterrupted pain and trauma" for which, she said, she felt none of the nostalgia that Russians living abroad often develop.

Svetlana Alliluyeva's letter is printed on Page 14.

Writing with affection about friendships she has formed with American families in Princeton, N. J., where she has lived for almost a year, she said, "My life is now really free, full of interest and significance for me."

The 1,500-word letter, dated May 11, was sent to an unidentified elderly Russian woman living in Paris with a request that it be published as a reply to an article in the French newspaper L'Aurore.

The article, written by André Vigo, depicted Miss Alliluyeva, who is in her early 40's, as lonely, longing to return to her two children in Moscow, unable to adapt to American life and heavily guarded by the police. The article was based on a visit to Princeton, the author said.

"I should be resigned by now to being lied about," Miss Alliluyeva wrote, "but somehow I cannot get reconciled to the idea that from now on and forever there will be no escape for me from lies. As a result I continue to react strongly to articles of this kind."

Her letter was first published in Russian in a small exile journal in Paris called La Pensée Russe, and more recently in La Croix, a French Roman Catholic daily. It also appeared in Russian in the July 14 issue of Novoye Russkoye Slovo, a Russian-language daily in New York.

Reached at her home in Princeton, Miss Alliluyeva made available an approved English translation of the letter. The translation was by Paul Chavchavadze, a descendant of Georgian princes who emigrated to the United States and has written several books about Czarist Russia.

In the letter, Miss Alliluyeva acknowledged that she missed her children—Iosif, 21, born during her first marriage, to

Continued on Page 14, Column 1

NEWS INDEX

Keir Dullea starred in Stanley Kubrick's personal triumph, *2001: A Space Odyssey.* Kubrick spent $10.5 million on this project at a time when the picture industry was in grave economic trouble.

Barbra Streisand as Fanny Brice in *Funny Girl.*

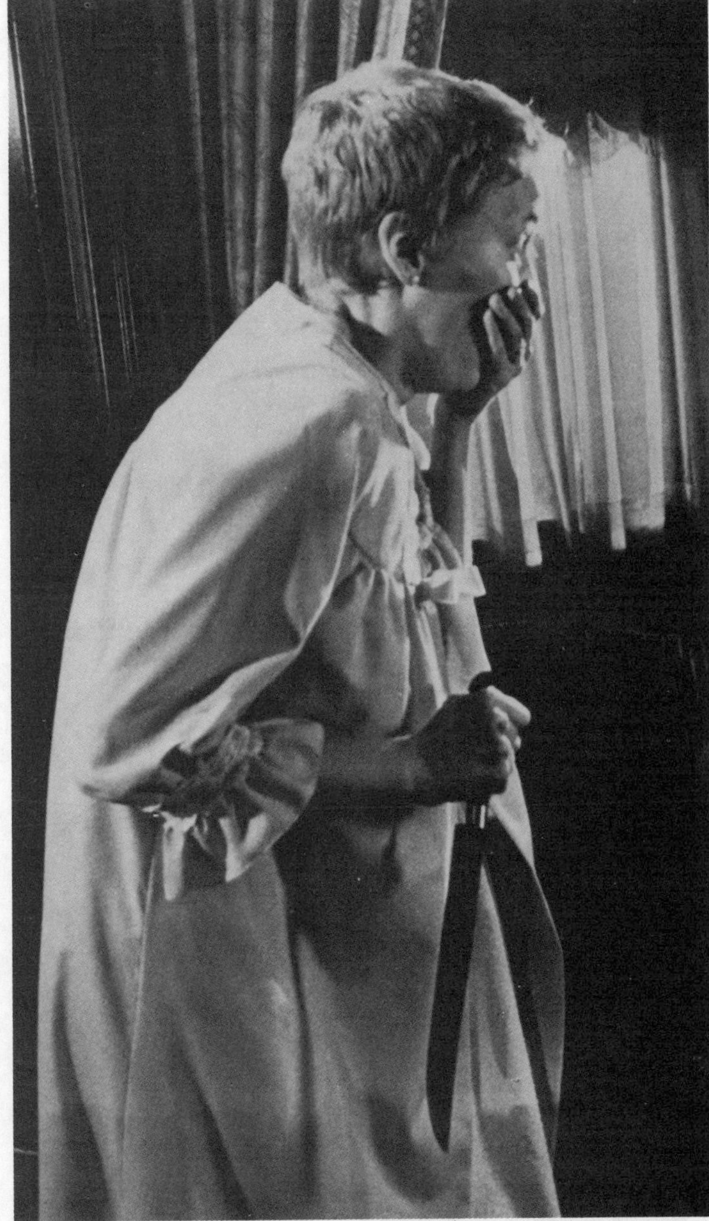

Mia Farrow shown in a chilling scene from Roman Polanski's *Rosemary's Baby.*

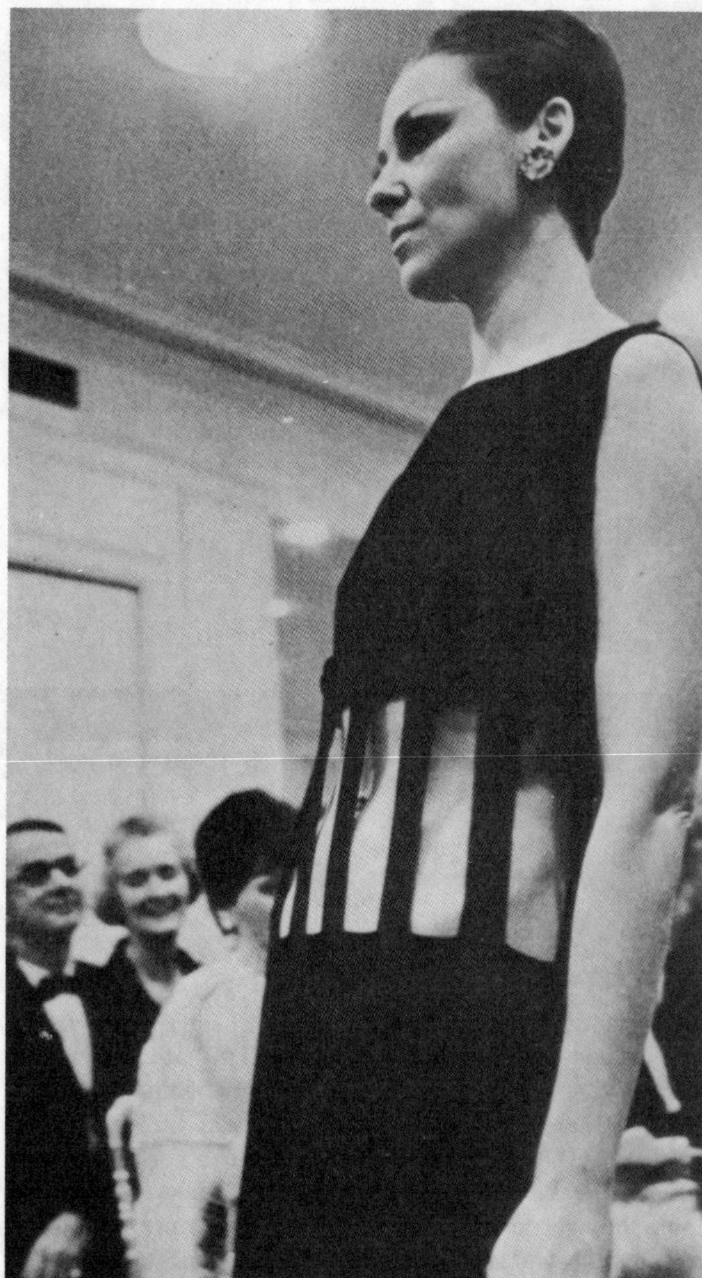

Norman Norell applied the "cage" treatment to his new line of fashion.

Frank Zappa (right) with the Mothers of Invention.

Aristotle Onassis with his new bride after the ceremony. Caroline is in back of Jackie, and John-John with a bowed head is in front.

Janis Joplin floored her audiences with her startling delivery when she hit the pop scene in 1968, but the high-powered fuse went short just two years later in a sudden, drug-induced death.

"All the News That's Fit to Print"

The New York Times

LATE CITY EDITION

Weather: Sunny, warm today; fair, seasonable tonight and tomorrow. Temp. range: today 89-73; Tuesday 91-72. Temp.-Hum. Index yesterday 81. Complete U.S. report on Page 90.

VOL. CXVII . No. 40,387 NEW YORK, WEDNESDAY, AUGUST 21, 1968 10 CENTS

CZECHOSLOVAKIA INVADED BY RUSSIANS AND FOUR OTHER WARSAW PACT FORCES; THEY OPEN FIRE ON CROWDS IN PRAGUE

13 INDICTED HERE IN RIGGING OF BIDS ON UTILITY WORK

Contracts Worth 49-Million Involved—14 Construction Companies Also Named

By MARTIN TOLCHIN

Fourteen major construction companies, 12 top corporate executives and one employe were indicted here yesterday on charges of rigging bids on utilities contracts totaling $49.8-million.

The defendants were accused of deciding among themselves who would be low bidder in the contracts with Consolidated Edison, the Brooklyn Union Gas Company, and the Empire City Subway Company—the latter a subsidiary of the New York Telephone Company.

The indictments charge that the defendants then accommodated the selected low bidder by submitting higher bids.

The companies included such important contractors as Lipsett, Inc., a leading demolition company that razed Pennsylvania Station, the Savoy Plaza Hotel and the Third Avenue El; the Slattery Contracting Company, which held the general contract for excavating the site of United Nations Headquarters and built subway spurs and the Lincoln Center reflecting pool, and the Thomas Crimmins Contracting Company, which did the excavation for numerous skyscrapers.

1959 Activities Covered

The companies received contracts to dig trenches for electrical conduits and gas mains and for paving work. The contracts totaled $49,788,165.

The four indictments, with a total of 28 counts, were an outgrowth of the investigation of James L. Marcus, former City Water Commissioner, who pleaded guilty in Federal court to receiving a $40,000 kickback on a city reservoir cleaning contract.

"Our interest in Marcus and [Herbert] Itkin led us to the inquiry that led to these indictments," Frank S. Hogan, New York County District Attorney, said.

He noted that the indictments alleged activities that began in 1959, "before the community at large was aware of Marcus and Itkin," and

Continued on Page 35, Column 3

Democrats Debate Position on the War in Vietnam

The New York Times

Secretary of State Rusk defended the Administration's policies at the hearing.

Associated Press

Senator George S. McGovern of South Dakota was critical of the Administration.

The New York Times (by George Tames)

Kenneth P. O'Donnell, left, who was an aide to President Kennedy, talks with Senator J. W. Fulbright, standing right, at the platform hearing. The Senator spoke against the war.

SOVIET EXPLAINS

Says Its Troops Moved at the Request of Czechoslovaks

By RAYMOND H. ANDERSON
Special to The New York Times

MOSCOW, Wednesday, Aug. 21 — Moscow announced this morning that troops from the Soviet Union and four other Communist countries had invaded Czechoslovakia at the request of the "party and Government leaders of the Czechoslovak Socialist Republic."

The announcement followed unofficial information here that Alexander Dubcek, the reform leader of the Czechoslovak party Presidium, had been overthrown.

In a statement authorized by the Soviet Government, the official press agency, Tass, declared at 7:30 A.M. Moscow time (12:30 A.M., New York time) that Czechoslovakia had come under a threat from "counterrevolutionary forces" involved in a collusion with foreign forces hostile to socialism.

Friendship Stressed

Tass said that troops from Bulgaria. East Germany, Hungary, Poland and the Soviet Union, acting from motivations of "inseverable friendship and cooperation," entered Czechoslovakia early this morning.

The troops will be withdrawn as soon as the threat to Czechoslovakia and neighboring Communist countries has been eliminated, according to Tass.

"The actions that are being taken are not directed against any state and in no measure infringe state interests of anybody," the statement said. "They serve the purpose of peace and have been prompted by concern for its consolidation."

"The fraternal countries firmly and resolutely counterpose their unbreakable solidarity to any threat from outside," the Soviet explanation continued. "Nobody will ever be allowed to wrest a single link from the community of Socialist states."

Polemics Resumed

The handwriting was on the wall for the Czechoslovak reform regime last Friday when the Soviet press abruptly resumed its bitter polemics against the country.

Czechoslovakia's seven-month-old experiment with democracy under Communist rule was explicitly doomed yesterday when the Soviet Communist party warned in an editorial that imperial intrigues must be "nipped in the bud."

Rumors swept Moscow yesterday that the Soviet party's Central Committee had met in secret session, presumably to endorse intervention. Official sources insisted, however, that

Continued on Page 14, Column 6

The New York Times Aug. 21, 1968

FIVE-POWER INVASION: Soviet planes carried troops into Prague (cross). Ground forces of bloc crossed Czechoslovak borders that are indicated by heavy line.

Versions of the Two Sides

Following are the texts of the Prague radio announcement of the Soviet-bloc invasion of Czechoslovakia, as monitored in Washington, and of a Soviet statement distributed in New York by Tass, the Soviet press agency.

Czechoslovak Radio Broadcast

To the entire people of the Czechoslovak Socialist Republic:

Yesterday, on 20 August, around 2300 [11 P.M.], troops of the Soviet Union, Polish People's Republic, the G.D.R. [East Germany], the Hungarian People's Republic and the Bulgarian People's Republic crossed the frontiers of the Czechoslovak Socialist Republic.

This happened without the knowledge of the President of the Republic, the Chairman of the National Assembly, the Premier, or the First Secretary of the Czechoslovak Communist party Central Committee.

In the evening hours the Presidium of the Czechoslovak Communist party Central Committee [had] held a session and discussed preparations for the 14th Czechoslovak Communist party congress.

The Czechoslovak Communist party Central Committee Presidium appeals to all citizens of our republic to maintain calm and not to offer resistance to the troops on the march. Our army, security corps and people's militia have not received the command to defend the country.

The Czechoslovak Communist party Central Committee Presidium regard this act as contrary not only to the fundamental principles of relations between Socialist states but also as contrary to the principles of international law.

All leading functionaries of the state, the Communist party and the National Front: Remain in your functions as representatives of the state, elected to the laws of the Czechoslovak Socialist Republic.

Constitutional functionaries are immediately convening a session of the National Assembly of our republic, and the Presidium is at the same time convening a plenum of the Central Committee to discuss the situation that has arisen.

PRESIDIUM OF THE CZECHOSLOVAK COMMUNIST PARTY CENTRAL COMMITTEE.

Announcement by Moscow

Tass is authorized to state that party and Government leaders of the Czechoslovak Socialist Republic have asked the Soviet Union and other allied states to render the fraternal Czechoslovak people urgent assistance, including assistance with armed forces. This request was brought about by the threat which has arisen to the Socialist system existing in Czechoslovakia and to the statehood established by the Con-

Continued on Page 14, Column 2

TANKS ENTER CITY

Deaths Are Reported—Troops Surround Offices of Party

By TAD SZULC
Special to The New York Times

PRAGUE, Wednesday, Aug. 21—Czechoslovakia was occupied early today by troops of the Soviet Union and four of its Warsaw Pact allies in a series of swift land and air movements.

Airborne Soviet troops and paratroopers surrounded the building of the Communist party Central Committee, along with five tanks. At least 25 tanks were seen in the city.

Several persons were reported killed early this morning. Unconfirmed reports said that two Czechoslovak soldiers and a woman were killed by Bulgarian tank fire in front of the Prague radio building shortly before the station was captured and went off the air.

[Soviet troops began shooting at Czechoslovak demonstrators outside the Prague radio building at 7:25 A.M., Reuters reported. C.T.K., the Czechoslovak press agency, was quoted by United Press International as having said that citizens were throwing themselves in front of the tanks in an attempt to block the seizure of the city.]

Move a Surprise

The Soviet move caught Czechoslovaks by surprise, although all day yesterday there were indications of new tensions.

Confusion was caused in the capital by leaflets dropped from unidentified aircraft asserting that Antonin Novotny, the President of Czechoslovakia who was deposed in March by the Communist liberals, had been pushed out by a "clique." The leaflets said that Mr. Novotny remained the country's legal President.

At 5 A.M. the Prague radio, still in the hands of adherents of the Communist liberals, broadcast a dramatic appeal to the population in the name of Alexander Dubcek, the party

Continued on Page 14, Column 1

NIXON INCREASES GALLUP POLL LEAD

Tops Humphrey, 45% to 29, and Maintains His Margin Over McCarthy, 42 to 37

Special to The New York Times

PRINCETON, N. J. Aug. 20—Richard M. Nixon stretched a slim mid-July edge over Vice President Humphrey to a 45-to-29 per cent lead in voter preference immediately following the Republican National Convention, according to the latest Gallup Poll.

Against Senator Eugene J. McCarthy—Mr. Humphrey's chief rival for the Democratic Presidential nomination—Mr. Nixon held a 42-to-37 per cent lead, almost the same margin he had in the previous test in mid-July.

Mr. Nixon's improved advantage over the Vice President was caused more by Mr. Humphrey's losses than by gains by Mr. Nixon. The Republican nominee was 5 percentage points higher than the preconvention survey, while Mr. Humphrey was 9 points lower.

Support for the independent candidacy of George A. Wallace of Alabama held up. He polled 18 per cent in the Nixon-Humphrey-Wallace test and 16 per cent in the Nixon-McCarthy-Wallace post-convention survey.

In interviewing between Aug. 8 and 11, the following question was asked of a representative sample of 1,526 adults in over 320 localities:

"Suppose the Presidential election were being held today. If Hubert Humphrey were the Democratic candidate, running against Richard Nixon, the Republican candidate, and George Wallace of Alabama were the candidate of a third party, which would you like to see

Continued on Page 34, Column 2

Guard Is Called Up To Protect Chicago During Convention

By DONALD JANSON
Special to The New York Times

CHICAGO, Aug. 20—Gov. Samuel H. Shapiro called up the National Guard today to keep order in the city during the Democratic National Convention.

At the request of Mayor Richard J. Daley, the Governor ordered 5,649 Illinois National Guardsmen to round-the-clock duty in Chicago beginning Friday to head off threats of "tumult, riot or mob disorder."

Meanwhile, an Army spokesman in Washington confirmed in a telephone interview that about 6,000 regular Army troops received rigorous riot-control training at Fort Hood, Tex., last week as a precautionary measure.

That exercise, he said, was called Operation Jackson Park, after the park in Chicago

Continued on Page 32, Column 2

Democrats to Seat Mississippi Rebels

By MAX FRANKEL
Special to The New York Times

CHICAGO, Aug. 20—Mississippi's regular delegation to the Democratic National Convention was barred from its seats tonight by an overwhelming vote of the Credentials Committee on the ground that it had failed to meet national standards to assure the full participation of Negroes in the political process.

A biracial delegation including many members who have fought many years for this moment will be seated in place of the regulars.

At the same time, the Credentials Committee rejected by various votes the delegate

Continued on Page 32, Column 6

KENNEDY BACKERS OFFER WAR PLANK

But McCarthy Group Balks at Compromise—Rusk Is for General Statement

Text of plank and excerpts from statement, Page 33.

By JOHN W. FINNEY
Special to The New York Times

WASHINGTON, Aug. 20—Supporters of the late Senator Robert F. Kennedy circulated in the Democratic platform committee today a compromise dovish plan on Vietnam calling for a halt in the bombing of North Vietnam, a cease-fire and negotiations between the Saigon Government and the National Liberation Front, the political arm of the Vietcong.

In the bitter fight developing within the platform committee, the proposed plank is designed to provide a common front for supporters of Senator Eugene J. McCarthy, Senator George S. McGovern and Senator Kennedy.

For the moment, however, some difficulty was being encountered in winning the approval of some McCarthy partisans, who were holding out for a plank that would be more critical of the Administration.

As the doves began to mount a concerted attack on the Administration's Vietnam policy, Secretary of State Dean Rusk was called in to defend the Administration position. Mr. Rusk,

Continued on Page 33, Column 2

NEWS INDEX

13 Points in Delta Are Shelled by Foe

By JOSEPH B. TREASTER
Special to The New York Times

SAIGON, South Vietnam, Wednesday, Aug. 21 — The Vietcong shelled 13 cities and military installations in the Mekong Delta this morning, extending their latest wave of attacks into South Vietnam's southern-most region.

Seven of the shellings were followed by ground attacks.

Initial reports were sketchy, but a United States military spokesman said that allied casualties and damage in all of the attacks appeared to be light.

To the north, allied troops are making an increasing number of forays into the southern

Continued on Page 4, Column 3

OUTLOOK GUARDED FOR EISENHOWER

His Condition Still Critical Despite 'Favorable Trend'

By FELIX BELAIR Jr.
Special to The New York Times

WASHINGTON, Aug. 20 — Former President Dwight D. Eisenhower clung resolutely to life today, but with a fragile grip that his doctors acknowledged could loosen at any time.

The condition of the 77-year-old General of the Army still was listed as "critical" and the outlook for his survival as "guarded." His doctors have used this term to mean uncertain or unpredictable.

A bulletin issued at Walter Reed Army Medical Center about 11 A.M. mentioned the development of a "favorable trend" in the pattern of abnormal heart rhythm.

The episodes of rapid irregularity in the heartbeat persisted, the doctors reported, but they were isolated and did not involve the sustained fibrillating, or fluttering, reported prior to last night.

At the time of the morning

Continued on Page 13, Column 1

Soviet Turns Back Clock

By JAMES RESTON

The Soviet invasion of Czechoslovakia has transformed world and American politics.

It occurred in the middle of the American Presidential election of 1968, as the Soviet invasion of Hungary took place during the Eisenhower-Stevenson Presidential election of 1956. The Soviet Union moved on Prague while the United States was preoccupied in Vietnam, as they moved on Budapest in 1956 while the British and French were preoccupied with the invasion of Suez. The latest move by Moscow startled Washington just as officials there were convening on new moves to reach an understanding with the Soviet Union on Vietnam.

News Analysis

Washington was prepared for a dramatic move by the Soviet Union against the new liberal regime in Prague, but not for anything quite so bold as an invasion by the Red Army.

It had been observing closely the increasingly violent attacks on the Czechoslovak Government in the Soviet press, and Under Secretary of State Charles E. Bohlen, former United States Ambassador to the Soviet Union and France, had warned of the possibility of a coup d'état, followed by Soviet military intervention in Czechoslovakia. But a direct invasion at this time was discounted.

In fact, the Johnson Administration, under attack on its Vietnam policy just before the Democratic Presidential nominating convention next week in Chicago, was discussing new moves to enlist the help of the Soviet Union for a compromise in Vietnam when the Red Army moved.

The first impression of the crisis was that this Soviet intervention in Czechoslovakia, like the first one at the end of World War II, would increase

Continued on Page 15, Column 1

JOHNSON SUMMONS SECURITY COUNCIL

Calls Emergency Session After Seeing Soviet Envoy

By B. DRUMMOND AYRES JR.
Special to The New York Times

WASHINGTON, Aug. 20—President Johnson met with the National Security Council in an emergency session tonight to discuss developments in Czechoslovakia after he received a visit from the Soviet Ambassador.

The Council meeting, which was held in the Cabinet Room in the West Wing of the White House, began at 10:15 P.M. and lasted for 55 minutes.

It was followed by a 15-minute meeting at the State Department between the Soviet Ambassador, Anatoly F. Dobrynen, and Secretary of State Dean Rusk.

There was no indication after either of the meetings of what course the United States would take in the crisis, which clearly came as a stunning surprise here.

During the recent weeks of tension around Czechoslovakia, the Administration has insistently maintained a hand-off attitude, arguing that any gestures of support from Washington would only complicate the Prague regime's status in the Communist camp. Any move to exploit the Soviet di-

Continued on Page 15, Column 1

"All the News That's Fit to Print"

The New York Times

LATE CITY EDITION

Weather: Sunny, mild today; fair and milder tonight and tomorrow. Temp. range: today 77-56; Wed. 75-57. Temp.-Hum. Index yesterday 69. Complete U.S. report on Page 70.

VOL. CXVII .No. 40,395 — NEW YORK, THURSDAY, AUGUST 29, 1968 — 10 CENTS

HUMPHREY NOMINATED ON THE FIRST BALLOT AFTER HIS PLANK ON VIETNAM IS APPROVED; POLICE BATTLE DEMONSTRATORS IN STREETS

SOVIET TO LEAVE 2 BLOC DIVISIONS ON CZECHS' SOIL

Svoboda Tells the Cabinet Other Forces Will Depart in 'Several Months'

By TAD SZULC
Special to The New York Times

PRAGUE, Aug. 28—President Ludvik Svoboda told his Cabinet today that the withdrawal of the Soviet-led occupation troops from Czechoslovakia would take "several months and stages" and that at least two divisions would remain permanently stationed on the West German border.

Authoritative sources that provided the account of the Cabinet meeting at Hradcany Castle quoted the President as having informed the ministers that no exact date had been set to begin the withdrawal of the forces of the Soviet Union and the four other Warsaw Pact countries that invaded Czechoslovakia a week ago.

The National Assembly adopted an eight-point resolution asking that a firm date be set forthwith for removal of the occupying forces and declaring that the Czechoslovak Army of 200,000 men was capable of guarding its own frontiers.

Prague Back at Work

Meanwhile, Prague was back at work, but a curfew was maintained and Soviet armored scout cars and motorized infantry trucks with machine guns mounted on their cabs continued to cruise through the city's crowded streets.

In a speech to the nation tonight, Premier Oldrich Cernik announced that today's Cabinet session had drafted a proposal to the Soviet Union, Poland, Hungary, Bulgaria and East Germany to begin "soon" the actual negotiations for the departure of their armies.

He said that within two weeks economic talks with the Soviet Union were to begin "during which compensation for damages" caused by the invasion would be discussed among other topics.

Czechoslovakia has long been

Continued on Page 3, Column 1

Associated Press
John Gordon Mein

U.S. ENVOY SLAIN IN GUATEMALA

Terrorists Shoot Mein After Ambushing Car—Johnson and Rusk Ask Inquiry

By Reuters

GUATEMALA, Aug. 28—The United States Ambassador, John Gordon Mein, was slain here this afternoon by unidentified youths who had ambushed his limousine.

The 54-year-old career Foreign Service officer tried to put up a fight, but fell under a hail of pistol and machine-gun fire, dying instantly. At least nine bullets struck his body.

As the Ambassador was driving along Avenida Reforma to the embassy, several youths leaped out of two small Japanese-made cars and opened the limousine's rear door to force him out. He resisted and they opened fire.

[In Washington, President Johnson and Secretary of State Dean Rusk expressed shock and grief and called on Guatemala to investigate the assassination.]

Campaign of Terror

Mr. Mein is believed to be the first United States Ambassador assassinated at his post.

The kidnapping of prominent people has been an element of the terror campaign that has been waged by extremist political elements in this uneasy Central American country, which has a population of more than 4.6 million.

The shooting occurred three blocks from the Biltmore Hotel, where Mr. Mein had attended a luncheon given by the Foreign Minister, Emilo Arenales Catalán. The scene was about 10 blocks from the embassy.

The Ambassador's chauffeur,

Continued on Page 16, Column 3

HUNDRED INJURED

178 Are Arrested as Guardsmen Join in Using Tear Gas

By J. ANTHONY LUKAS
Special to The New York Times

CHICAGO, Thursday, Aug. 29—The police and National Guardsmen battled young protesters in downtown Chicago last night as the week-long demonstrations against the Democratic National Convention reached a violent and tumultuous climax.

About 100 persons, including 25 policemen, were injured and at least 178 were arrested as the security forces chased down the demonstrators. The protesting young people had broken out of Grant Park on the shore of Lake Michigan in an attempt to reach the International Amphitheatre where the Democrats were meeting, four miles away.

The police and Guardsmen used clubs, rifle butts, tear gas and Chemical Mace on virtually anything moving along Michigan Avenue and the narrow streets of the Loop area.

Uneasy Calm

Shortly after midnight, an uneasy calm ruled the city. However, 1,000 National Guardsmen were moved back in front of the Conrad Hilton Hotel to guard it against more than 5,000 demonstrators who had drifted back into Grant Park.

The crowd in front of the hotel was growing, booing vociferously every time new votes for Vice President Humphrey were broadcast from the convention hall.

The events in the streets stirred anger among some delegates at the convention. In a nominating speech Senator Abraham A. Ribicoff of Connecticut told the delegates that if Senator George S. McGovern were President, "we would not have these Gestapo tactics in the streets of Chicago."

When Mayor Richard J. Daley of Chicago and other Illinois delegates rose shouting angrily, Mr. Ribicoff said, "How hard it is to accept the truth."

Crushed Against Windows

Even elderly bystanders were caught in the police onslaught. At one point, the police turned on several dozen persons standing quietly behind police barriers in front of the Conrad Hilton Hotel watching the demonstrators across the street.

For no reason that could be immediately determined, the blue-helmeted policemen charged the barriers, crushing the spectators against the windows of the Haymarket Inn, a restaurant in the hotel. Finally the window gave way, sending screaming middle-aged women and children backward through the broken shards of glass.

The police then ran into the restaurant and beat some of the

Continued on Page 23, Column 1

The New York Times (by Neal Boenzi)

AT CONVENTION: Cheering in the amphitheatre after Vice President Humphrey's name was placed in nomination

United Press International

IN STREETS: Police attempting to clear demonstrators on Michigan Avenue outside Conrad Hilton Hotel last night

VICTOR GETS 1,761

Vote Taken Amid Boos For Chicago Police Tactics in Street

Excerpts from the nominating speeches are on Page 22.

By TOM WICKER
Special to The New York Times

CHICAGO, Thursday Aug. 29 — While a pitched battle between the police and thousands of young antiwar demonstrators raged in the streets of Chicago, the Democratic National Convention nominated Hubert H. Humphrey for President last night, on a platform reflecting his and President Johnson's views on the war in Vietnam.

Mr. Humphrey, after a day of bandwagon shifts to his candidacy, and a night of turmoil in the convention hall, won nomination on the first ballot over challenges by Senator Eugene J. McCarthy of Minnesota and George S. McGovern of South Dakota.

The count at the end of the first ballot was:

Humphrey	1,761¾
McCarthy	601
McGovern	146½
Phillips	67½
Others	32¾

Violence Draws Attention

There was never a moment's suspense in the balloting, and throughout a turbulent evening, the delegates and spectators paid less attention to the proceedings than to television and radio reports of widespread violence in the streets of Chicago, and to stringent security measures within the International Amphitheatre.

Repeated denunciations of Mayor Richard J. Daley from convention speakers and repeated efforts to get an adjournment or recess were ignored by convention officials and Mr. Daley.

He sat through it all, usually grinning and always guarded by plainclothes security men, until just before the roll call. Then he left the hall. A few miles away, the young demonstrators were being clubbed, kicked and gassed by the Chicago police, who turned back a march on the convention hall.

Watched From Hotels

Most of the violence took place across Michigan Avenue from the convention headquarters hotel, the Conrad Hilton, in full view of delegates' wives and other watching from its windows.

From the convention rostrum, Senator Abraham A. Ribicoff of Connecticut, denounced "Gestapo tactics in the streets of Chicago."

Julian Bond, the Negro insurgent leader from Georgia, in announcing his delegation's

Continued on Page 20, Column 1

PRAGUE'S LEADERS WARNED BY SOVIET

It Says It Will Be Vigilant—Hints Doubt on Outcome

By RAYMOND H. ANDERSON
Special to The New York Times

MOSCOW, Aug. 28—The Soviet Union warned today that the reform leaders of Czechoslovakia, although allowed to return to Prague and to retain their positions after the negotiations here, were on a short leash and under the vigilant eyes of the Kremlin.

Soviet commentators asserted that a counterrevolutionary threat continued to exist in Czechoslovakia, and they indicated that Moscow had doubts that the Prague leadership could or would cope with the dangers adequately.

[In Bonn, the West German Government called for a complete restoration of Czechoslovakia's sovereignty and a pullback of all Soviet invasion forces. Page 6.]

Pravda, the Communist party organ, expressed indignation that underground radio stations in Czechoslovakia had broadcast criticism of the agreement worked out in Moscow between the Soviet leadership and a Czechoslovak delegation headed by President Ludvik Svoboda.

Yuri Zhukov, the political

Continued on Page 4, Column 3

Dubcek Was Put in Handcuffs: An Account of Confrontation

The following chronological account of the confrontation of Soviet and Czechoslovak leaders after the invasion of Czechoslovakia was written by Vincent Buist of Reuters.

PRAGUE, Aug. 28—Alexander Dubcek, the Czechoslovak Communist leader, was hustled out of his party headquarters last Wednesday, handcuffed and flown to a secret destination in Slovakia in a Soviet military aircraft.

All the way he sat on the plane's metal deck.

This was disclosed in an account of Mr. Dubcek's arrest and of the Moscow negotiations given to me today by an official of the Czechoslovak Communist party's Central Committee.

The official said Mr. Dubcek was in his private room speaking on the telephone when the Central Committee building was surrounded by Soviet paratroopers with light tracked vehicles last Wednesday morning.

The party leader was trying to find out details of the extent of the invasion as a Soviet security officer and two soldiers armed with light machine guns burst into the room.

They tore the telephone out of Mr. Dubcek's hands and ripped the wire out of the wall, the official said.

The party leader was taken away and locked in a room in

Continued on Page 2, Column 5

FIGHTING INTENSE IN SAIGON REGION

G.I.'s Battle Through Night With Foe on Infiltration Routes Near Capital

Special to The New York Times

SAIGON, South Vietnam, Thursday, Aug. 29—Sharp fighting flared around Saigon last night and this morning as United States infantrymen battled a sizable enemy force on flatland infiltration routes northwest of the capital.

The United States command said this morning that fighting had continued through the night with a company-size enemy unit 32 miles northwest of Saigon and 4 miles north of Trangbang.

So far, a total of 80 enemy soldiers have been killed in the fighting, American spokesmen said. Reports from the scene were sketchy, but United States spokesmen termed American casualties light.

101st Division Involved

According to the spokesman, the fighting began Tuesday after soldiers of the 101st Air Cavalry Division set up a cordon around an area and began moving in.

Fighting tapered in the evening, but by noon yesterday units of the division, trudging through muddy fields, came under sharp fire. Fighting continued into the morning.

Farther north, near another key infiltration route into Saigon, soldiers of the United States 25th Infantry Division fought two enemy companies seven miles southeast of Tayninh. During the four-hour bat-

Continued on Page 10, Column 1

Defeat for Doves Reflects Deep Division in the Party

By JOHN W. FINNEY
Special to The New York Times

CHICAGO, Aug. 28 — A deeply divided Democratic National Convention, after a climactic floor clash between the Administration's supporters and its critics, adopted today a White House-dictated plank supporting President Johnson's policy in Vietnam. The whole platform was then approved.

By a vote of 1,567¾ to 1,041¼, the convention rejected a plank advanced by Democratic doves calling for an unconditional halt in the bombing of North Vietnam. Instead, it adopted a plank that called for a bombing halt but only on conditional terms.

Excerpts from the debate on platform, Page 22.

The vote reflected the deep, emotional division within the party over the Vietnam issue. The division manifested itself in nearly three hours of increasingly acrimonious debate, conducted against a backdrop of sporadic chants of "Stop the war!" from the galleries and the New York and California delegations.

It was a division that Vice President Humphrey, in his bid for the Presidential nomination, had hoped to avoid. But he could not avoid it when Mr. Johnson intervened behind the scenes to toughen the language of the plank so that it would correspond to Administration policy.

In the wake of the policy confrontation, the major question was whether Mr. Hum-

Continued on Page 25, Column 1

The Party and the Police

By JAMES RESTON
Special to The New York Times

News Analysis

CHICAGO, Aug. 28 — The Democratic party was deeply hurt politically here tonight by the vicious clashes between demonstrators and the police in the streets of Chicago. Though the party itself had no direct responsibility for the incidents, it held its convention here knowing of the dangers of violence and counted on Mayor Daley and his police to handle the situation without embarrassment to the party. This gamble failed, despite all the barbed wire barricades, the police, secret agents and National Guardsmen. It was not only that Mayor Daley was condemned from the rostrum and stood in the aisles mocking Senator Abraham Ribicoff who had condemned the police action, but tens of millions watched the incidents on television to the obvious detriment of the Democratic party.

By the end of the night, Daley had become a symbol in the convention of the opposition within the party to the turbulent conditions of American life. So strong was the feeling against Mayor Daley and his police that even the name of Illinois was loudly booed when the roll of the states was called for nominations for the Presidency.

Thus the convention pre-

Continued on Page 20, Column 3

HUMPHREY AIDES LIST 4 FOR TICKET

Say Muskie, Harris, Alioto and Shriver Are Leading for the No. 2 Spot

By STEVEN V. ROBERTS
Special to The New York Times

CHICAGO, Aug. 28—Aides of Vice President Humphrey advanced four names today as leading candidates for the Vice-Presidential nomination: Senators Edmund S. Muskie of Maine and Fred R. Harris of Oklahoma, Mayor Joseph L. Alioto of San Francisco and Sargent Shriver, the Ambassador to France.

The list contained no surprises. All four men have figured in recent speculation.

However, Mr. Humphrey met in his hotel suite today with key political figures, including Mayor Richard J. Daley of Chicago, and aides said the Vice-Presidency was one topic of discussion. It was generally believed that the final decision would not be made until tomorrow.

It was considered a remote possibility that Mr. Humphrey would try to heal the deep breach in the party over the Vietnam war by choosing a prominent war critic. Senators Eugene J. McCarthy of Minnesota, George S. McGovern of South Dakota and Edward M.

Continued on Page 22, Column 2

NEWS INDEX

Gruening Defeated In Alaska Primary

By LAWRENCE E. DAVIES
Special to The New York Times

ANCHORAGE, Alaska, Aug. 28 — A dramatic, unexpected victory by a dark, good-looking, 38-year-old challenger has terminated the long political career of Senator Ernest Gruening, an 81-year-old warhorse known to his admirers as "Mr. Alaska."

Mike Gravel, a real estate developer from Anchorage and former Speaker of the state's House of Representatives, won the Democratic nomination for the Senate over Mr. Gruening in yesterday's primary election in Alaska.

Unofficial returns to Secretary of State Keith Miller in

Continued on Page 26, Column 5

James Lovell, Jr., William A. Anders and Frank Borman (left to right) of the Apollo 8 mission, starred in a rather unique Christmas special. Their televised orbit around the moon provided majestic photos of the lunar terrain as well as of earth.

Eve Arden (left) and Kay Ballard (right) starred in the *Mothers-in-Law*.

Hope Lange starred as the lady of the (haunted) house in *The Ghost and Mrs. Muir.* Edward Mulhare played the ghost of the man in the portrait lurking behind her.

When The Monkees were pulled off the air in 1968, the greatest short-term blitz of protest letters in history were sent to NBC.

"All the News That's Fit to Print"

The New York Times

LATE CITY EDITION

Weather: Sunny, mild today; fair, cool tonight. Fair, mild tomorrow. Temp. range: today 60-39; Thurs. 55-36. Full U.S. report on Page 93.

VOL. CXVIII . No. 40,459 | NEW YORK, FRIDAY, NOVEMBER 1, 1968 | 10 CENTS

ATTACKS ON NORTH VIETNAM HALT TODAY; JOHNSON SAYS WIDER TALKS BEGIN NOV. 6

LINDSAY, SHANKER COOL TO HOLDING A SPECIAL SESSION

But Teachers' Union Leader Agrees to Public Hearing as Proposed by McCoy

By LEONARD BUDER

Mayor Lindsay and the president of the teachers' union both reacted coolly yesterday to a suggestion that Governor Rockefeller convene a special session of the State Legislature to deal with the city school crisis.

Informed of their reactions, Governor Rockefeller said:

"Wonderful. All they have to do is settle it. I certainly don't want to call a special session but I am deeply concerned about the children and the parents."

Mr. Rockefeller has been under increasing public pressure to summon a special session because of the school crisis, which has led to three citywide teachers' strikes this fall. City pupils have had only 12 days of regular schooling since the term began on Sept. 9.

Albert Shanker, the president of the teachers' union said last night he would be willing to take part in a public hearing as proposed by Rhody A. McCoy, the administrator of the Ocean Hill-Brownsville school district.

McCoy for Public Hearing

Mr. McCoy had suggested earlier in the day that a public hearing be held before "some responsible and high-ranking public official" that would go into union charges that its members have been harassed and threatened in the district.

At issue in the dispute is the reinstatement of a group of union teachers in the predominantly Negro and Puerto Rican Ocean Hill-Brownsville district in Brooklyn.

The district's governing board originally defied the city Board of Education and refused to reinstate the teachers, asserting that they were a detriment to the district. It has now agreed to permit the teachers to return, but the union has questioned the local board's sincerity.

Dr. James E. Allen Jr., the State Education Commissioner, said last night that he was con-

Continued on Page 32, Column 2

Nixon Hopes Johnson Step Will Aid the Talks in Paris

By ROBERT B. SEMPLE Jr.

Richard M. Nixon expressed last night his hope that the halt in the bombing of North Vietnam would "bring some progress" in the Paris talks on the war.

But Mr. Nixon, who addressed a colorful and enthusiastic crowd of some 19,000 partisans gathered in lusty communion in Madison Square Garden, did not offer any further opinion on President Johnson's announcement of the bombing halt.

Pointing to Gov. Spiro T. Agnew of Maryland, his Vice-Presidential running mate, sitting on the stage behind him, the Republican Presidential nominee suggested that it would be unwise for either of them to say anything more because it might upset the delicate talks in Paris.

"Neither he nor I will destroy the chance of peace. We want peace," he said.

According to Nixon aides, the President telephoned Mr. Nixon at his New York apartment about 6 P.M., roughly four hours before the candidate spoke, to inform him of the substance of his address.

Mr. Nixon made his comments at what some observers called "the rally of all Nixon rallies." A man who has often been exposed to well-orchestrated gatherings, Mr. Nixon has not in this campaign seen a noisier and more demonstrative crowd.

One hour of the proceedings, including the candidate's speech, was televised over 247 stations of the American Broadcasting Company at a cost of roughly $200,000.

The show included appear-

Continued on Page 51, Column 1

CAUTION IS VOICED

U.S. Officials Expect the Sessions to Be Long and Difficult

By BERNARD GWERTZMAN
Special to The New York Times

WASHINGTON, Oct. 31—Administration officials cautioned tonight against expecting an early end of the war in Vietnam as a result of the agreement to stop the bombing of North Vietnam announced by President Johnson.

There was no mood of exultation in Washington as Administration officials met with newsmen at the White House, State Department and the Pentagon. Instead, officials were warning that the road ahead looked extremely difficult.

One high official, in fact, said that the next round of talks in Paris might turn out to be one of the most complicated diplomatic exercises in history, with the opposing sides spending much time attacking each other publicly and haggling over protocol details of seating, recognition, and prestige.

Details Are Secondary

The American view, however, is that these details are secondary to the major question, which was posed colloquially by one official: "Can the powers with guns in their hands sit around a table and make peace?"

No agenda has been arranged with North Vietnam on the forthcoming talks, to which the Government in Saigon and the National Liberation Front have been invited to participate.

There is some question whether South Vietnam will be able to assemble a delegation in time for the first session next Wednesday. But American officials said that if Saigon was not present, then the Front would not be allowed to take part.

Officials said that they expected the two sides to spend the first weeks, and perhaps months, on the issues of how the talks should proceed and what kind of agenda to follow.

Neither Saigon nor the Front recognizes the other as a competent spokesman for the South Vietnamese people. And the United States and North Vietnam have publicly shared the view of their allies.

Thus President Johnson said

Continued on Page 10, Column 6

ANNOUNCING HALT: President Johnson as he was seen on television yesterday

John Soto for The New York Times

PEACE CALLED AIM

Saigon and N.L.F. Can Join in the Enlarged Paris Discussions

Text of the Johnson speech is printed on Page 10.

By NEIL SHEEHAN
Special to The New York Times

WASHINGTON, Oct. 31—President Johnson announced tonight that he was ordering a complete halt to all American air, naval and artillery bombardment of North Vietnam as of 8 A.M. Friday, Eastern standard time (9 P.M., Vietnam time).

"I have reached this decision on the basis of the developments in the Paris talks," the President said, "and I have reached it in the belief that this action can lead to progress toward a peaceful settlement of the Vietnamese war."

"What we now expect—what we have a right to expect," the President said in a television broadcast, "are prompt, productive, serious and intensive negotiations in an atmosphere that is conducive to progress."

Face Shows Fatigue

His face showed fatigue as he made the announcement culminating weeks of secret negotiations.

Mr. Johnson did not announce any reciprocal military commitments from North Vietnam, which he has often said he must have in order to halt the air and naval bombardment that began on Feb. 7, 1965.

[Word of the President's action reached Paris about 2 A.M. Friday, and North Vietnamese negotiators said they might have a statement later in the day. Page 11.]

Washington officials said the bombing of infiltration trails in Laos would continue and that there was no prohibition against reconnaissance flights over North Vietnam.

'Reason to Believe' Foe

Senior Administration sources said the United States had "reason to believe" North Vietnam would not escalate the war in South Vietnam as a result of the bombing cessation.

They said Hanoi "clearly understood" that Mr. Johnson would resume the bombing if it attacked South Vietnamese population centers or took military advantage of the demilitarized zone.

On its side, North Vietnam had apparently not obtained the unconditional bombing halt it has consistently demanded.

Mr. Johnson said that in exchange for the bombing halt Hanoi had agreed to accept participation of the South Vietnamese Government at the Paris talks and the United States had in turn accepted the

Continued on Page 11, Column 1

Israeli Commando Units Attack Two Nile Bridges

By JAMES FERON
Special to The New York Times

JERUSALEM, Friday, Nov. 1—Israeli commandos struck deep into the United Arab Republic early today in retaliation for Egyptian incursions Saturday on the eastern bank of the Suez Canal.

A Government announcement said that Israeli commandos had attacked a transformer station and two bridges on the Nile between Aswan and Cairo and had returned safely.

Accompanying the announcement was a statement by Premier Levi Eshkol characterizing the Israeli incursion as a warning intended to underline the dangers of violating the cease-fire agreement between Israel and the United Arab Republic.

Egyptian commandos, he said, have been crossing the Suez Canal cease-fire line with the full knowledge and cooperation of the Egyptian Army.

By striking well within Egyptian territory, Mr. Eshkol said, Israel intended to demonstrate the capability of the Israeli Army in this type of warfare.

Result Not Described

The announcement of the Israeli foray did not describe the result of the raid. Read to correspondents at 2:30 A.M., it said:

"Israeli commando units attacked three objectives in southern Egypt tonight on the road between Cairo and Aswan about 230 kilometers [140 miles] north of Aswan.

"The objectives were a transformer station and two bridges on the Nile. Our forces returned safely."

This meant that the Israeli troops would have had to travel more than 200 miles from the southern region of the Sinai Peninsula, their closest base.

It also indicated that the

Continued on Page 17, Column 1

STATE WILL BUILD 4 HOSPITALS HERE

City to Run Them—8 Health Centers and 2 Housing Projects Also Planned

A state corporation created by the 1968 Legislature will build and outfit four new hospitals, eight neighborhood health-care centers and two housing projects for hospital staffs in this city at a cost of $276.4-million dollars, Mayor Lindsay announced yesterday.

The city will eventually pay off the construction costs, either in rents or by long-term purchase of the buildings, but the new plan can have them ready for use within five years, as against 10 to 15 years if the city were to build them, the Mayor said.

Mr. Lindsay said state and city health officials had resolved some legal and other problems and reached agreement that the new corporation, called the State Health and Mental Facilities Improvement Corporation, would finance the construction out of the $700-million bond issue authorized by the Legislature.

State and city officials will meet here Monday to work out remaining details, including de-

Continued on Page 32, Column 6

HUMPHREY HAILS DECISION AS WISE

Asserts 'Vast Majority' Will Support It—Aides Look for Campaign Upturn

By R. W. APPLE Jr.
Special to The New York Times

BATTLE CREEK, Mich., Oct. 31—Vice President Humphrey reacted cautiously but with scarcely concealed exuberance tonight to the news that President Johnson had ordered a halt in the bombing of North Vietnam.

"I've been hoping for months that it would happen," he said, "for months."

Standing on the ramp of his campaign plane at Newark Airport, Mr. Humphrey said that he fully supported Mr. Johnson's "very wise and prudent" decision and was sure "the vast majority of the American people will also support it."

Displays Good Spirits

Asked whether he thought the breakthrough would help his Presidential campaign, the Vice President replied:

"This is going to help people. I don't think it has much to do with the candidates as such. I suggest that you just look at the President's message and then study it."

But Mr. Humphrey then walked back to the press plane, past the spotlights that had been set up on the runway, and demonstrated that he was in the best spirits imaginable.

He hectored his press secretary, Norman Sherman, for not producing quickly enough a transcript of his remarks, joked with reporters, and made a "my-lips-are-sealed" gesture when asked about the possible political implications of Mr. Johnson's statement.

Will Refer to Vietnam

The plane's cabin was festooned with orange and black crepe paper, and the stewardesses were wearing black sweaters and miniskirts in anticipation of a Halloween party.

"Happy Halloween," the Vice President exclaimed when he spotted the stewardesses. "We've had tricks—and look at the treats."

Chatting informally with the newsmen, he said that he planned to refer "in guarded phrases" to the Vietnam developments during the rest of his campaign.

He also insisted that he had received no word earlier this

Continued on Page 51, Column 7

22 Days of Tension Led To Turning Point in Talks

By PETER GROSE
Special to The New York Times

WASHINGTON, Oct. 31—On Oct. 9, 1968, North Vietnam began asking the United States some serious questions. These questions and the American replies dominated 22 days of tense and tangled diplomacy, involving a dozen capitals, and led today to an order to cease all bombing of North Vietnam.

As the President announced his long-awaited decision, high Administration officials lifted the tight cover on the dossier of secret diplomatic exchanges, revealing a large part of the substance behind the public speculation around the world for weeks past.

A basic proposition of fewer than 100 words was the core of the diplomatic maneuvering. The formula was drafted by the Johnson Administration early in September, accepted by Hanoi last weekend and approved by the Government of South Vietnam this afternoon.

A Meeting at 2:30 A.M.

It was the basis of a White House meeting at 2:30 A.M. on Tuesday, when President Johnson called in his top Cabinet advisers to talk with the American military commander in Vietnam, Gen. Creighton W. Abrams, within minutes of the general's unannounced arrival.

The essence of the formula was to cut through the deadlock set up by Hanoi's insistance on a bombing halt without conditions and Washington's equal insistence that there could be no further cessation of bombing without reciprocity.

Here is how Administration officials say the diplomatic efforts unfolded:

For many months after the

Continued on Page 11, Column 5

ROCKET ATTACKS ON SAIGON KILL 21

Most Victims at Early Mass —Hue Is Also Shelled, With 9 Feared Dead

By GENE ROBERTS
Special to The New York Times

SAIGON, South Vietnam, Friday, Nov. 1—A series of the war's most damaging rocket attacks in terms of human life rocked Saigon last night and this morning as President Johnson was instructing the military to halt the bombing of North Vietnam.

South Vietnamese police officials said that more than 20 rockets had been fired, killing at least 21 Vietnamese civilians and wounding more than 70 others.

About 15 rockets also fell on Hue, the former imperial capital, killing 9 civilians and wounded 13, according to United States military spokesmen.

They also said that Mytho, the largest city in the Mekong Delta, had been shelled heavily with mortar rounds, but that there had been few casualties there.

U.S. Official Surprised

A high American official, who apparently knew that the bombing halt was being ordered, seemed incredulous when he received his first word of the Saigon attack from a newsman.

"You can't be serious," he said. Seconds later, he recovered his composure and said, "I'm sure there won't be any comment on this—at least for a while."

Ton That Thien, the South Vietnamese Minister of Information, denied that these had been rocket attacks when he was awakened after midnight by newsmen calling for comment.

Then, after becoming convinced that the reports were true, he said, "Hanoi has ruined Vice President Humphrey's chances now."

Most of the casualties in Saigon occurred at 6:30 A.M. today when a rocket struck the Xom Moi Roman Catholic Church just before mass.

"Beaucoup deaths—women, children, men," said the Rev. Nguyen Van Tri in a mixture of French and English as he twisted a key ring over and over in his palm and paced back and forth near the debris.

The church and its yard

COST FOR WELFARE NOW TOP CITY BILL

Exceeds Outlay for Schools by Using 26% of Budget

By RICHARD PHALON

Welfare has supplanted education as the city's biggest expense item.

Controller Mario A. Procaccino's annual report, released yesterday, shows that welfare costs in the fiscal year ended last June 30 rose to 26.6 per cent of the city's $5.29-billion expense budget, while education declined to 21.4 per cent of the total.

A year earlier, when the total budget was $800-million less, education was the big expense item. It amounted to 22.7 per cent of all funds, compared with 20.7 per cent for welfare.

In all, the city last year spent $1.4-billion on such welfare programs as aid to dependent children and stipends to the aged and handicapped. This compared with $931.8-million the year before.

The outlay for education was $1.1-billion, an increase of $200-million over fiscal 1967.

The cost curves on welfare have continued to rise in this fiscal year. The Human Resources Administration, which administers the city's welfare and antipoverty programs, is budgeted at about $348-million over last year. That outlay rep-

Continued on Page 32, Column [illegible]

Ramon Novarro Slain on Coast; Starred in Silent Film 'Ben-Hur'

Special to The New York Times

LOS ANGELES, Oct. 31—Ramon Novarro, the Mexican-born star of scores of Hollywood movies made in the nineteen-twenties and thirties, was found bludgeoned to death in his $125,000 Hollywood Hills home early this morning. He was 69 years old.

The actor's nude body was discovered on the king-sized bed in the master bedroom at 8:30 A.M. by Edward Weber, 42, Mr. Novarro's private secretary and long-time friend.

According to detectives of the North Hollywood division of the Los Angeles police department, there was evidence that Mr. Novarro, a slightly built man, had put up a strong fight for his life. Furniture was overturned and vases and other small articles were broken in the den, living room and bedroom.

Several hours after the body was discovered, and while two reporters were milling around outside the house, a young sightseer, Ted Grezlok, found a pile of bloody clothing in an ivy bed on the far side of the

Bob Martin

Ramon Novarro in 1964

LOST A-SUBMARINE FOUND OFF AZORES

Parts of the Scorpion's Hull Sighted at 10,000 Feet

By MARJORIE HUNTER
Special to The New York Times

WASHINGTON, Oct. 31—The Navy announced today that part of the hull of the nuclear submarine Scorpion had been located more than 10,000 feet below the surface of the Atlantic, 400 miles southwest of the Azores.

The discovery ended a five-month search for the atomic-powered submarine and her crew of 99 officers and men.

The Scorpion was last heard from May 21. When she failed to arrive on schedule May 27 in Norfolk, Va., a vast air and sea search was begun.

In announcing the photographic sightings today, Adm. Thomas H. Moorer, Chief of Naval Operations, said that a seven-man Navy court of inquiry would be reconvened in Norfolk. He set no date.

Findings by an inquiry last June have not yet been released.

Admiral Moorer said that reports of the photographic sightings came last night from a United States Navy oceanographic research ship, the Mizar.

"Mizar reports that the submarine's location has been con-

President Is Offered Million for Memoirs

Special to The New York Times

WASHINGTON, Oct. 31—President Johnson has received at least one, and possibly more, conditional offers of an advance in excess of $1-million for his memoirs.

One condition is understood to be that the first volume deal with the major events of his Administration, such as his decisions to begin the bombing of North Vietnam, to send American combat troops into the war, to announce that he would not seek another term and, now, to halt the bombing of North Vietnam.

Although the President has not firmly decided what he will do, he is said to have tentatively agreed to write such a volume in advance of a multi-volume series of memoirs. He also plans to write some magazine articles.

The President is understood to have indicated to prospec-

Channel 13 Ahead 20 Minutes on Talk

By MICHAEL T. KAUFMAN

Channel 13 broke an embargo and televised the President's speech 20 minutes before it was officially released last night.

The violation — which the educational station ascribed to honest error—resulted in angry and indignant protests by the White House and the commercial networks.

"No one told us that the film was embargoed," said Lee Hays, producer of Channel 13's nightly news show. He acknowledged that the unauthorized early showing of the film of Mr. Johnson's speech was put on the air at 7:40 P.M.

Neither he nor station officials were able to say whether the premature broadcast was picked up by any of the 16 other outlets of the Eastern Educational Network, which serves an area from Maine to Washington.

Within minutes after the em-

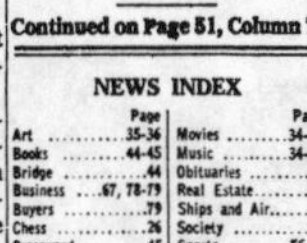

NEWS INDEX

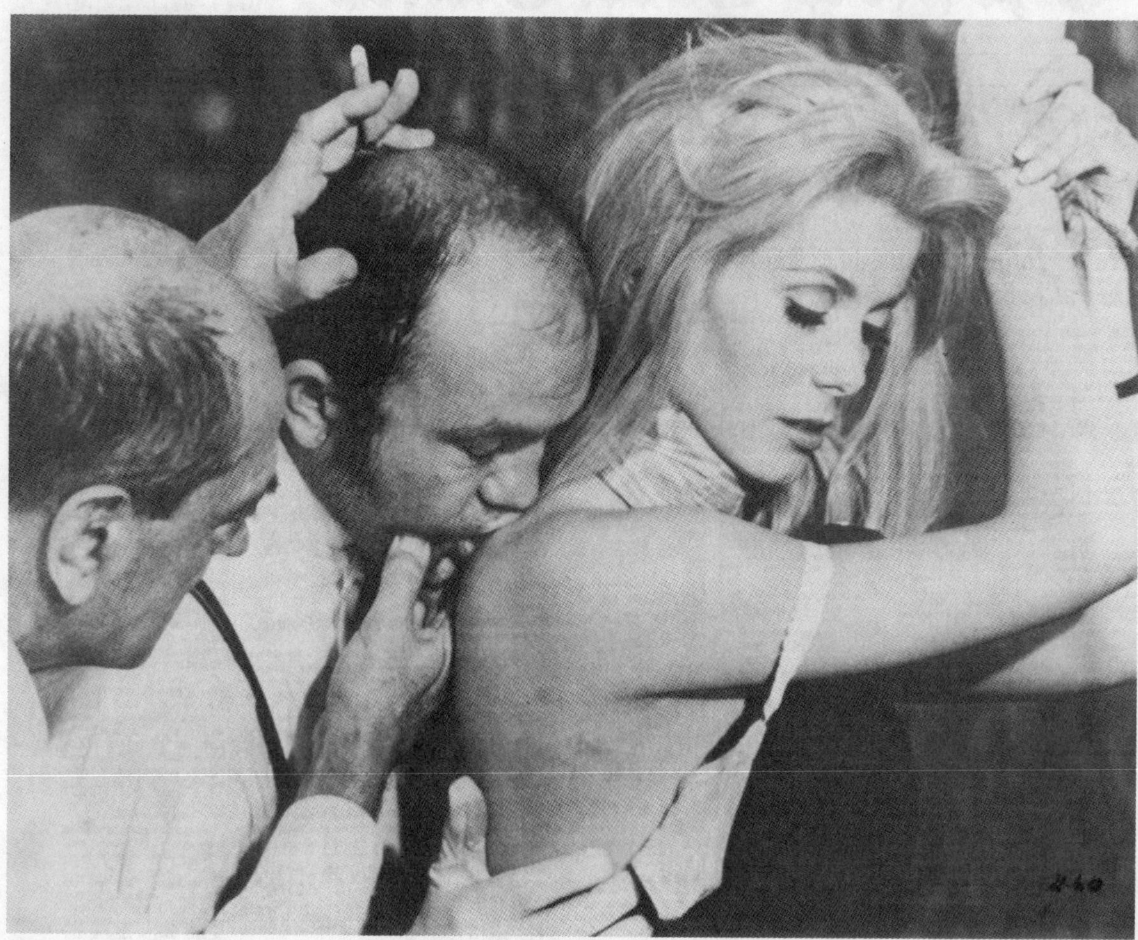

Luis Buñuel directed Catherine Deneuve in *Belle de Jour*, an elegant and elaborate essay in sexual fantasy.

Charlton Heston encountered an uncomfortable twist to evolution in *Planet of the Apes*. The two apes in the foreground are Kim Hunter and Roddy McDowell.

"All the News That's Fit to Print"

The New York Times

LATE CITY EDITION

Weather: Rain today and tonight. Cloudy, showers likely tomorrow. Temp. range: today 52-48; Wed. 54-45. Full U.S. report on Page 93.

VOL. CXVIII . . No. 40,465 NEW YORK, THURSDAY, NOVEMBER 7, 1968 10 CENTS

NIXON WINS BY A THIN MARGIN, PLEADS FOR REUNITED NATION

The New York Times (by Neal Boenzi)

SHE KNEW IT ALL ALONG: President-elect Richard M. Nixon holding crewelwork, a facsimile of Presidential seal embroidered by his daughter Julie, who stands beside her fiancé, David Eisenhower. Mrs. Nixon and daughter Patricia completed the family group at the Waldorf-Astoria yesterday.

NIXON'S ELECTION EXPECTED TO SLOW PARIS NEGOTIATION

Allied Diplomats Suggest All Sides May Adopt a Wait-and-See Stance

By HEDRICK SMITH
Special to The New York Times

PARIS, Nov. 6 — Allied diplomats suggested tonight that Richard M. Nixon's election victory would add, at least temporarily, to the delays and complications of getting meaningful Vietnam peace negotiations under way.

The American, the North Vietnamese and the National Liberation Front delegations here had no comment on the election results.

But allied diplomats close to the talks suggested that the Republican victory would probably bring eventual changes in the American negotiating team, encourage delays by the South Vietnamese Government, and induce a wait-and-see attitude by all sides until Mr. Nixon's own approach to the talks became clearer.

The uncertainty about the future relationship between the outgoing Johnson Administration and Mr. Nixon is considered the primary complicating factor.

Eyes on Saigon

"Everybody has to see how Nixon and Johnson are going to handle this period," said one Western diplomat.

The Saigon Government is reported to feel that the Johnson Administration pressed it too rapidly toward expanded talks embracing the Vietcong. It now is expected to use the change-over period in the United States to play for time.

South Vietnamese officials here made no secret that they consider Mr. Nixon more sympathetic than Mr. Johnson to their position.

They have recently dropped hints that they expect no active negotiating on issues of substance until early next year.

Western diplomats now speculate that President Nguyen Van Thieu may delay sending a delegation to the talks here until he has learned Mr. Nixon's views.

But a more common opinion is that Saigon will send a delegation soon and then try to stall until the Republicans take office in January.

The Republican victory,

Continued on Page 13, Column 1

POLICE SEIZE 125 ON C.C.N.Y. CAMPUS

AWOL Soldier Taken From Student Center 'Sanctuary'

About 250 members of the Tactical Patrol Force moved onto the City College campus early today at the request of the administration and arrested more than 100 students and the AWOL soldier they had been guarding in a student center.

Under the direction of Police Commissioner Howard R. Leary, Chief Inspector Sanford Garelik and a number of other high police officials, the arrests were carried out without violence following a warning from the administration to vacate the building.

In all, about 125 persons were arrested, including supporters of the peace movement and Pvt. William Brakefield, who had been in the Finley Student Center, at 133d Street and Convent Avenue, since last

Continued on Page 4, Column 4

Soviet Bids U.S. Confer; Calls for 'Normalization'

By HENRY KAMM
Special to The New York Times

MOSCOW, Nov. 6—The Soviet Union greeted the election of a new President of the United States today with a call for the "normalization" of relations between Moscow and Washington for the sake of world peace.

The demand was put forward in a speech on behalf of the ruling Politburo of the Communist party by First Deputy Premier Kirill T. Mazurov as election returns in the United States showed that Richard M. Nixon had won the Presidency. The occasion was the traditional speech in the Kremlin on the eve of the anniversary of the Bolshevik Revolution.

To underline the importance Moscow attaches to relations with the United States, Mr. Mazurov raised the issue twice. Noting Soviet proposals for mutual limitations on nuclear weapons and delivery systems, the official said:

"It is relevant to recall in this connection that we have expressed readiness to conduct negotiations with the United States on the entire range of these problems. But their positive solution does not depend on the Soviet Union alone."

Review of Soviet Actions

After a review of Soviet actions on the international scene, Mr. Mazurov returned to Soviet-American relations. He said:

"We have always attached great importance to the normalization of relations between the Soviet Union and the United States, which would be important not only to both of our countries but also to world peace."

A public offer to enter into negotiations with the United States for an accommodation on vital issues was regarded as a Soviet reaction to the

Continued on Page 14, Column 1

POSITION ON SINAI DEFINED BY ISRAEL

Note to Jarring Links Issue of Boundaries to Security Needs and Tiran Rights

By DREW MIDDLETON
Special to The New York Times

UNITED NATIONS, N.Y., Nov. 6—Israel has told the United Arab Republic that her attitude toward the boundary problem will be governed by her security needs and the maintenance of full protection of Israeli navigation in the Strait of Tiran.

This is the first time that Israel has defined with any precision her interest in the Sinai Peninsula.

Western diplomats inferred that if Israel's security requirements were fulfilled, including protection of shipping in the Strait of Tiran, the Government would not reject an arrangement that returned a demilitarized Sinai to Egypt. The peninsula has been occupied by Israel since the Israeli-Arab war of June, 1967.

This information was in a memorandum that Foreign Minister Abba Eban gave yesterday to Dr. Gunnar V. Jarring, the United Nations intermediary. Mr. Eban went over the text of the memorandum with Dr. Jarring at meetings yesterday afternoon and last night.

Ambassador Jarring was asked to transmit the memorandum to Mahmoud Riad, the Egyptian Foreign Minister. The clarification of Israel's approach to the boundary problem apparently was intended to rebut Mr.

Continued on Page 2, Column 3

NEWS INDEX

REPUBLICANS GAIN SAFE ALBANY EDGE

Lead in Assembly Put at 77-73 and in Senate at 33-24 Unofficially

By JAMES F. CLARITY

Republican officials said yesterday that they expected to have clear majorities in both houses of the 1969 Legislature.

The Republicans, on the basis of unofficial but reliable vote-counts in the elections for the 150 Assembly and 57 Senate seats, will probably control the Assembly by 77 to 73, and the Senate by 33 to 24.

The official counts of several close Assembly races were not expected to affect lower house control, which the Republicans appeared almost certain to have wrested from the Democrats in Tuesday's election.

Official Count Delayed

The official count of the close races was expected to be completed early next week. The G.O.P. Senate majority was assured, regardless of the final count in a few close races.

But the Republicans' control of the Assembly, which they had lost in 1964, did not appear to give G.O.P. leaders assurance that their programs and legislation or those proposed by Governor Rockefeller would necessarily sail through the Legislature because of the majorities in both houses.

Among the Republicans who captured Democratic seats in the Assembly were several conservatives who, by combining with conservative Democrats, could obstruct, if not defeat, legislation they considered liberally oriented, or objectionable for other reasons.

Three of the newly elected Republican Assembly members

Continued on Page 40, Column 5

The Election at a Glance

President

Needed for Election—270 Electoral Votes

	Number of States*	Electoral Votes
Humphrey	14	191
Nixon	30	287
Wallace	5	45
In Doubt: Alaska, Missouri.	2	15

*Includes District of Columbia.

The Senate

Newly Elected Senators		Make-up of New Senate	
Democrats	18	Democrats	58
Republicans	15	Republicans	41
In Doubt	1	In Doubt	1

The House

Democrats Elected	243
Republicans Elected	192

Senate's Liberal Coalition Survives Gains by G.O.P.

By DAVID E. ROSENBAUM

Republicans made a net gain of at least four Senate seats in Tuesday's election, but the balance between liberals and conservatives did not appear to have changed substantially from the present Senate.

One Senate race remained in doubt last night. In Oregon, Wayne Morse, a Democrat, who served four terms, was running a close race with State Representative Robert W. Packwood, a Republican. Observers said it might be days before the outcome was certain.

Depending on the Oregon race, the Democrats will hold 58 or 59 seats in the new Senate to 41 or 42 for the Republicans. In the present Senate there are 63 Democrats and 37 Republicans.

Four conservative Republicans and one conservative Democrat were elected to seats that had been held by liberals or moderates. On the other hand, there was a shift in favor of liberals in at least two states.

Thus it appeared that a majority could still be formed from liberal Northern Democrats and moderate Republicans to pass legislation on such issues as civil rights and aid to education.

The Republicans' net gain of only four seats in the House of Representatives dashed the party's hopes of capturing control of that body.

In the Senate the Republicans picked up seats that had been held by Democrats in Arizona, Florida, Maryland, Ohio, Oklahoma and Pennsylvania. Democrats took Republican-held seats in California and Iowa.

Among the new conservatives was Barry Goldwater, the Republican Presidential nominee in 1964. He defeated Roy L. Elson for the Arizona

Continued on Page 29, Column 2

Election Tables

Tables reporting the vote in national, state and local contests in Tuesday's election are now scheduled for publication in The New York Times tomorrow.

The Times had expected to print them today, but breakdowns in the News Election Service's national and regional computers made a total recheck of the election results necessary. This recheck is expected to be concluded today.

A Loser Concedes and Tries to Smile

By R. W. APPLE Jr.
Special to The New York Times

MINNEAPOLIS, Nov. 6—It was probably Hubert Horatio Humphrey's last hurrah in Presidential politics.

He had tried once before, in 1960, and had been crushed by the superb organization of John F. Kennedy in the West Virginia primary. Now he had lost again, this time to the man whom John Kennedy had defeated, in an agonizingly close finish.

Transcript of the Humphrey statement is on Page 22.

The Vice President—a hearty, sentimental man, given to laughter and to tears—tried to smile as he stood on the stage in the Leamington Hotel's ballroom this morning and listened to his faithful followers shout, "We Want Humphrey!" But what he brought forth was more a grimace than a grin. "Thank you very much," he said in a quavering voice. "It's nice to know."

Mr. Humphrey went through

Continued on Page 22, Column 1

Associated Press

Vice President Humphrey with his wife after conceding

GOAL IS HARMONY

President-Elect Vows His Administration Will Be 'Open'

By ROBERT B. SEMPLE Jr.

President-elect Richard M. Nixon turned yesterday from the business of winning elections to the business of assembling an Administration.

Weary but thankful, he appeared before an elated band of supporters gathered in the ballroom of the Waldorf-Astoria at 11:35 A.M. He expressed his gratitude for their efforts and his admiration for the "gallant and courageous fight" of his opponent.

Transcript of Nixon's remarks will be found on Page 21.

He also extended the hand of friendship to the disappointed partisans of Mr. Humphrey's cause—particularly the young.

Near the end of his eight-minute talk, Mr. Nixon took note of the division in the nation and pledged, in these words, to bend every effort to restore racial peace and social harmony:

"I saw many signs in this campaign. Some of them were not friendly and some were very friendly. But the one that touched me the most was one that I saw in Deshler, Ohio, at the end of a long day of whistle-stopping, a little town, I suppose five times the population was there in the dusk, almost impossible to see — but a teen-ager held up a sign, 'Bring Us Together.'

"And that will be the great objective of this Administration at the outset, to bring the American people together. This will be an open Administration, open to new ideas, open to men and women of both parties, open to the critics as well as those who support us.

"We want to bridge the generation gap. We want to bridge the gap between the races. We want to bring America together. And I am confident that this task is one that we can undertake and one in which we will be successful."

Several hours later the campaign entourage began to disassemble, its members heading home for a brief but long-overdue rest. The candidate himself flew southward for a three-day vacation in Key Biscayne, a peninsula just south of Miami where he rested occasionally during the campaign.

Although he has been urged

Continued on Page 21, Column 1

ELECTOR VOTE 287

Lead in Popular Tally May Be Smaller Than Kennedy's in '60

By MAX FRANKEL

Richard Milhous Nixon emerged the victor yesterday in one of the closest and most tumultuous Presidential campaigns in history and set himself the task of reuniting the nation.

Elected over Hubert H. Humphrey by the barest of margins—only four one-hundredths of a percentage point in the popular vote—and confronted by a Congress in control of the Democrats, the President-elect said it "will be the great objective of this Administration at the outset to bring the American people together."

He pledged, as the 37th President, to form "an open Administration, open to new ideas, open to men and women of both parties, open to critics as well as those who support us" so as to bridge the gap between the generations and the races.

Details Left for Later

But after an exhausting and tense night of awaiting the verdict at the Waldorf-Astoria Hotel here, Mr. Nixon and his closest aides were not yet prepared to suggest how they intended to organize themselves and to approach these objectives. The Republican victor expressed admiration for his opponent's challenge and reiterated his desire to help President Johnson achieve peace in Vietnam between now and Inauguration Day on Jan. 20.

The verdict of an electorate that appeared to number 73 million could not be discerned until mid-morning because Mr. Nixon and Mr. Humphrey finished in a virtual tie in the popular vote, just as Mr. Nixon and John F. Kennedy did in 1960.

With 94 per cent of the nation's election precincts reporting, Mr. Nixon's total stood last evening at 29,726,409 votes to Mr. Humphrey's 29,677,152. The margin of 49,257 was even smaller than Mr. Kennedy's margin of 112,803.

Meaning Hard to Find

When translated into the determining electoral votes of the states, these returns proved even more difficult to read, and the result in two states—Alaska and Missouri—was still not final last night. But the unofficial returns from elsewhere gave Mr. Nixon a minimum of 287 electoral votes, 17 more than the 270 required for election. Mr. Humphrey won 191.

Because of the tightness of the race, the third-party challenger, George C. Wallace, came close to realizing his minimum objective of denying victory to the major-party candidates and then somehow forcing a bargain for his sup-

Continued on Page 20, Column 1

Johnson Vows Aid In Power Transfer

By NEIL SHEEHAN
Special to The New York Times

SAN ANTONIO, Tex., Nov. 6—In a telegram of congratulations this morning, President Johnson informed President-elect Richard M. Nixon that he would do "everything in my power to make your burdens lighter on that day when you assume the responsibilities of the President."

Even as Mr. Johnson's telegram was being transmitted to Mr. Nixon from the President's ranch 65 miles north of here, the machinery had been set in motion for an orderly transition from the old Administration to the new.

Lawson Knott, the administrator of the General Services

Continued on Page 20, Column 3

"All the News That's Fit to Print"

The New York Times

LATE CITY EDITION

Weather: Mostly sunny, cold today; fair, warmer tonight and tomorrow. Temp. range: today 30-20; Tuesday 34-24. Full U.S. report on Page 62.

VOL. CXVIII—No. 40,513 NEW YORK, WEDNESDAY, DECEMBER 25, 1968 — 10 CENTS

3 MEN FLY AROUND THE MOON ONLY 70 MILES FROM SURFACE; FIRE ROCKET, HEAD FOR EARTH

PUEBLO CREWMEN GREETED ON COAST; CAPTORS ASSAILED

Relatives Weep and Scream—Captain Asserts North Koreans Are Inhuman

By BERNARD GWERTZMAN
Special to The New York Times

SAN DIEGO, Dec. 24 — The crew of the intelligence ship Pueblo returned to the United States today in time for Christmas with many of their families.

Led by Comdr. Lloyd M. Bucher, the 82 survivors arrived at the Miramar Naval Air Station outside this city and were met immediately by emotional, sometimes hysterical, greetings and embraces of wives, mothers, fathers and children.

The one man who did not return alive, Duane D. Hodges, was carried from one of the C-141 transports in a flag-draped coffin while the air station band played the Navy hymn.

Commander Bucher, apparently overwrought with emotion, spoke in a low voice as he told the more than 250 relatives, the 300 newsmen and the national television audience about the 11 months his crew spent in North Korean captivity.

Calls Captors Inhuman

He described North Korea as a land "completely devoid of humanity, completely devoted to enslavement of men's minds."

[In Washington, the Navy named Vice Adm. Harold S. Bowen to head a court of inquiry into the Pueblo incident.]

Commander Bucher said that, during the months in North Korea, "the thought that preyed on my mind was the embarrassment to my country because of the loss of one of its fine ships."

At a news conference held in the base theater at Navy Hospital here, Rear Adm. Edwin Rosenberg, the representative of the Commander in Chief, Pacific Fleet, in charge of the Pueblo's repatriation, repeated his past praise

Continued on Page 2, Column 1

At Least 22 Survive Pennsylvania Crash Of Plane With 45

Special to The New York Times

BRADFORD, Pa., Wednesday, Dec. 25—An Allegheny Airlines jetprop plane with 45 persons aboard crashed last night in rugged terrain during a heavy snowstorm while attempting to land at Bradford Regional Airport 15 miles south of here.

There were at least 22 survivors.

The twin-engine plane was Allegheny Flight 736, bound from Detroit to Washington. It had stopped in Erie, Pa., and had been scheduled to stop in Bradford and Harrisburg, Pa.

The wreck, about three miles southeast of the airport, was reported shortly before 9 P.M. by Allegheny Flight 734 out of Cleveland, which said it saw a fire.

It took rescue teams an hour to reach the scene on snowmobiles in freezing temperatures. Several inches of snow had fallen during the day in the heavily wooded area and

Continued on Page 62, Column 1

Pope Paul Says Mass In a Huge Steel Mill

By ROBERT C. DOTY
Special to The New York Times

TARANTO, Italy, Wednesday, Dec. 25—Pope Paul VI celebrated Christmas midnight mass here for 15,000 workers and members of their families in a huge, echoing rolling mill.

The Pontiff chose the vast Italsider steel plant at this developing industrial center in the heel of the Italian boot as the place to express "the fraternal and radiant presence of Christ among workers throughout the world."

Even while the Pope said mass at an altar consisting of a four-ton slab of steel supported on two broad sections of steel pipe, work continued elsewhere throughout the 2,000-acre plant, the largest in Europe.

Blast furnaces poured plumes of flame into a rainy

Continued on Page 34, Column 1

VIOLATIONS MAR TRUCE IN VIETNAM

80 Incidents Are Reported—22 Enemy Soldiers and an American Killed

By B. DRUMMOND AYRES Jr.
Special to The New York Times

SAIGON, South Vietnam, Wednesday, Dec. 25—The allies and the Vietcong put separate cease-fires into effect yesterday to mark Christmas, but not all the guns fell silent.

At 9 o'clock this morning, the American military command said there had been at least 80 "incidents" involving military contact since the allied cease-fire, scheduled to run 24 hours, went into effect at 6 P.M. yesterday.

The enemy cease-fire began at 1 A.M. yesterday and was scheduled to run for 72 hours. Allied military spokesmen said there were at least eight incidents involving military contact during the first hours of that stand-down.

In about 30 of the incidents, casualties were suffered by one or both sides. The allied spokesmen said that over-all South Vietnamese losses had been light. United States losses were broken down as one soldier killed and 38 wounded.

At least 22 enemy soldiers died.

It was not known whether North Vietnamese troops in South Vietnam were complying with the Vietcong cease-fire order. During previous holiday

Continued on Page 5, Column 3

Christmas Day

Today is Christmas Day. Following is a list of services that are affected:

Public and Parochial Schools—Closed.

Post Office—Closed except for special delivery.

Stores—Most retail and department stores closed.

Banks—Closed.

Stock Exchanges—Closed.

Sanitation—No regular refuse collection.

Parking — Sunday parking regulations in force, permitting parking in alternate-side parking zones and at most parking meters.

Libraries—Closed except for the Main Reading Room of the Library at Fifth Avenue and 42d Street, which will be open from 1 to 10 P.M.

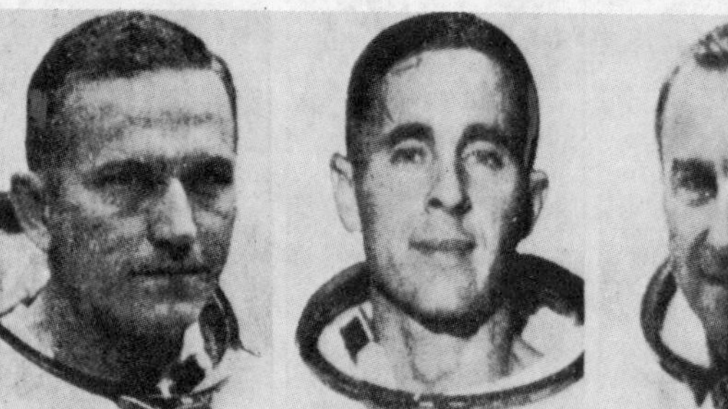

Col. Frank Borman — Maj. William A. Anders — Capt. James A. Lovell Jr.

Associated Press

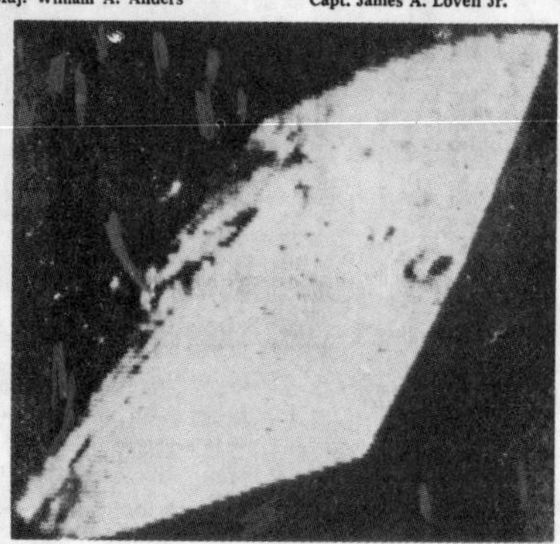

Associated Press

Moon pictures taken through the window of the Apollo 8 spacecraft that were telecast to earth last night. In picture at left of Sea of Crises area, the larger crater is 30 to 40 miles wide. The picture at right was last transmitted.

Astronauts Examine 'Vast, Lonely' Place; Read From Genesis

By JOHN NOBLE WILFORD
Special to The New York Times

HOUSTON, Wednesday, Dec. 25—The three astronauts of Apollo 8 yesterday became the first men to orbit the moon. Early today, after flying 10 times around that desolate realm of dream and scientific mystery, they started their return to earth.

They fired the spacecraft's main rocket engine at 1:10 A.M. to kick them out of lunar orbit

Excerpts from messages to and from Apollo, Page 36.

and to carry them toward a splashdown in the Pacific Ocean on Friday.

Through the static of 231,000 miles, as Apollo 8 swung around from behind the moon and started for earth, one of the astronauts dispelled any doubts, saying, "Please be informed there is a Santa Claus."

57-Hour Return Trip

It would be a 57-hour return trip from the most far-reaching voyage of the space age thus far—or of any other previous age. The astronauts had seen, as no other men had, the ancient lunar craters, plains and rugged mountains from as close as 70 miles.

At 4:59 A.M. yesterday, about 20 hours before the return trip, Col. Frank Borman of the Air Force, Capt. James A. Lovell Jr. of the Navy and Maj. William A. Anders of the Air Force, swept into an orbit of the moon by firing the spacecraft's main rocket. This occurred after they flew around the leading edge of the moon and were directly behind the earth's only natural satellite.

"We got it! We've got it!" exclaimed a mission commentator of the National Aeronautics and Space Administration as the spacecraft emerged from behind the moon 24 minutes later, and was clearly flying a safe and smooth orbit.

Businesslike Report

The calm and laconic Apollo explorers, however, were all business. Captain Lovell's first message to earth was simply:

"Go ahead, Houston. Apollo 8. Burn complete. Our orbit is 169.1 by 60.5—169.1 by 60.5."

The astronauts flew twice around the moon in the egg-shaped orbit, then dropped to a circular orbit nearly 70 miles above the ancient craters, plains and rugged mountains of the lunar surface.

As they beamed their first live television from orbit on Christmas Eve morning, they described the surface of the moon as a colorless gray, "like dirty beach sand with lots of footprints on it" and said it "looks like plaster of Paris."

At about 9:30 P.M. the astronauts began their second and last television show from lunar orbit. It ran some 30 minutes and showed the bright moon, in a pitch black sky, outside the spacecraft window.

Earth Like an 'Oasis'

Colonel Borman described the moon as a "vast, lonely and forbidding sight," adding that it was "not a very inviting place to live or work."

Captain Lovell saw the earth as a "grand oasis in the big vastness of space."

Major Anders was most impressed by "the lunar sunrise and sunsets."

As the telecast neared its end, Colonel Borman said "Apollo 8 has a message for you." With that, Major Anders began reading the opening verses from the Book of Genesis about creation of the earth.

"In the beginning," Major Anders read, "God created the heaven and the earth.

"And the earth was without form and void; and darkness was upon the face of the deep . . ."

Captain Lovell then took up with the verse beginning, "And God called the light day, and the darkness He called night."

Colonel Borman closed the reading with the verse that read:

"And God called the dry land Earth; and the gathering together of the water called He Seas: and God saw that it was good."

Sends Holiday Greetings

After that Colonel Borman signed off, saying:

"Good-by, good night. Merry Christmas. God bless all of you, all of you on the good earth."

Glynn S. Lunney, one of the flight directors here, told reporters earlier, "we have a completely 'go' spacecraft."

George M. Low, the spacecraft manager at the Manned Spacecraft Center, said he was "altogether happy" with the mission — the most ambitious and daring thus far in the nation's $24-billion Apollo project to land men on the moon next year.

Although the mission's object was not primarily scientific, Dr. John Dietrich of the space center's geology and geochemistry branch, said that the television pictures and astro-

Continued on Page 36, Column 1

FUEL DELIVERIES FALL SHORT HERE

City's Health Chief Warns of Danger to Sick—Flu Vaccine and Blood Low

By ARNOLD H. LUBASCH

A shortage of heat, vaccine and blood plagued the city yesterday as the Hong Kong flu epidemic continued, and the Health Commissioner warned that many sick people might die unless emergency fuel deliveries were made.

Mayor Lindsay, who said most drivers had stopped fuel deliveries for the holiday, joined Health Commissioner Edward O'Rourke in appealing for fuel deliveries today even though it was Christmas.

With the temperature dropping into the low twenties last night, hundreds of homes, apartment houses and commercial buildings remained without fuel, although oil companies sought to catch up on deliveries delayed by last week's strike.

The city's supply of flu vaccine ran out yesterday as efforts were made to arrange for further shipments before Jan. 2, when 40,000 more doses are scheduled to arrive.

A critical shortage of blood was reported by the Greater

Continued on Page 21, Column 1

NEWS INDEX

Orbit Shows Lunar Interior Is 'Lumpy'

Slight Wobbles Observed in Spacecraft's Course

By WALTER SULLIVAN
Special to The New York Times

HOUSTON, Dec. 24—For the first time human beings took a close look today at the earth's nearest celestial neighbor, viewing it from many angles to seek out clues to the events that formed its awesomely rugged terrain.

Until now man has always been forced to look at the moon from a single direction at a great distance, although in the last few years spacecraft have provided glimpses of the far side and close-up views of the earth-facing side.

Today the three Apollo astronauts sailed serenely over the giant craters, looking down their throats, marveling at their crumbling walls and countless strange features that have long puzzled astronomers.

They reported seeing many freshly formed craters, indicating that the cataclysmic events that have pocked the moon and sprinkled it with rubble are continuing. Some of the craters, the astronauts said, looked as though a giant pick had been hacking at a concrete surface, producing fine dust as well as other debris.

They became the first men to witness a lunar sunrise and found it a strange and unexpected experience. According to Capt. James A. Lovell Jr., about two minutes before sunrise a fine white haze appeared over the horizon where the sun was about to appear.

"It takes the fan shape," he said, "unlike the sunrise on earth, where the atmosphere affects it."

Meanwhile, analysis of the orbital flight by radio antennas on earth showed that, from time to time, the spacecraft wobbled slightly in its path. This confirmed earlier indications that the interior of the moon is "lumpy."

Some scientists, notably Dr. Harold C. Urey of the University of California, San Diego, a Nobel laureate, have suggested that the moon is like a giant raisin cake with lumps of dense iron embedded in material that is far less dense. Such a body could have been formed from a cloud of dust and smaller objects, including chunks of iron, during the formation of the solar system.

If the moon were uniformly dense and perfectly spherical, the gravitational field surrounding it would be perfectly symmetrical. It was this field that held the Apollo spacecraft in orbit. The fact that the spacecraft's road was slightly bumpy, so to speak, revealed an uneven distribution of mass within the moon. In particular, this was noted as the astronauts sailed over Copernicus, one of the largest and most spectacular craters on the moon. It was in darkness but was dimly illuminated by ghostly earthshine—sunlight reflected by the earth.

The lumpiness of the moon

Continued on Page 38, Column 1

A Reflection: Riders on Earth Together, Brothers in Eternal Cold

By ARCHIBALD MacLEISH

MEN'S conception of themselves and of each other has always depended on their notion of the earth. When the earth was the World—all the world there was—and the stars were lights in Dante's heaven, and the ground beneath men's feet roofed Hell, they saw themselves as creatures at the center of the universe, the sole, particular concern of God—and from that high place they ruled and killed and conquered as they pleased.

And when, centuries later, the earth was no longer the World but a small, wet, spinning planet in the solar system of a minor star off at the edge of an inconsiderable galaxy in the immeasurable distances of space — when Dante's heaven had disappeared and there was no Hell (at least no Hell beneath the feet) — men began to see themselves, not as God-directed actors at the center of a noble drama, but as helpless victims of a senseless farce where all the rest were helpless victims also, and millions could be killed in world-wide wars or in blasted cities or in concentration camps without a thought or reason but the reason—if we call it one—of force.

Now, in the last few hours, the notion may have changed again. For the first time in all of time men have *seen* the earth: seen it not as continents or oceans from the little distance of a hundred miles or two or three, but seen it from the depths of space; seen it whole and round and beautiful and small as even Dante—that "first imagination of Christendom"—had never dreamed of seeing it; as the Twentieth Century philosophers of absurdity and despair were incapable of guessing that it might be seen. And seeing it so, one question came to the minds of those who looked at it.

"Is it inhabited?" they said to each other and laughed—and then they did not laugh. What came to their minds a hundred thousand miles and more into space—"half way to the moon" they put it—what came to their minds was the life on that little, lonely, floating planet; that tiny raft in the enormous, empty night. "Is it inhabited?"

THE medieval notion of the earth put man at the center of everything. The nuclear notion of the earth put him nowhere — beyond the range of reason even—lost in absurdity and war. This latest notion may have other consequences. Formed as it was in the minds of heroic voyagers who were also men, it may remake our image of mankind. No longer that preposterous figure at the center, no longer that degraded and degrading victim off at the margins of reality and blind with blood, man may at last become himself.

To see the earth as it truly is, small and blue and beautiful in that eternal silence where it floats, is to see ourselves as riders on the earth together, brothers on that bright loveliness in the eternal cold—brothers who know now they are truly brothers.

1969

"All the News That's Fit to Print"

The New York Times

LATE CITY EDITION

Weather: Chance of showers today; clearing tonight. Fair tomorrow. Temp. range: today 87-62; Sunday 84-55. Full U.S. report on Page 80.

VOL. CXVIII...No. 40,637 NEW YORK, MONDAY, APRIL 28, 1969 — 10 CENTS

DE GAULLE QUITS AFTER LOSING REFERENDUM; SENATE LEADER TO SERVE PENDING ELECTION

COMPROMISE BILL FOR CITY SCHOOLS HITS ALBANY SNAG

G.O.P. Conservatives Balk Decentralization Proposal on Local Board Issue

By SYDNEY H. SCHANBERG

Special to The New York Times

ALBANY, April 27 — The topsy-turvy, on-again, off-again compromise on New York City school decentralization was off again today. The Republican legislative leaders were brought up short by new demands from a conservative Republican bloc just as they thought they had a bill ready for passage.

Frantic attempts to plug the leak in the latest compromise on the racially sensitive issue continued through the day, and when the leaders adjourned both houses tonight they expressed the hope that a school plan could be passed tomorrow. But most of the legislators were cynical after a week of false starts.

Governor Rockefeller and his staff were deeply involved with the negotiations.

Changes Demanded

It could not be learned what concessions, if any, the conservative Republicans had won. Negro and Puerto Rican legislators, supported by some white liberal colleagues, were also said to be demanding changes in the new compromise bill, but their requests were reported to be less difficult to solve.

Resolution of the volatile question of who will control the city's 1.1-million-pupil school system has been doubly frustrating to the leadership because it is the only major issue blocking adjournment of the 1969 legislative session.

After weeks of confusion, suspense and wildly fluctuating reports of agreement and collapse, the leaders last night called the weary members into an unusual Sunday session, presumably to pass a new compromise bill.

Protests Registered

But no sooner had the 72-page mimeographed bill been distributed to key legislators early this morning than conservative Republican Assemblymen from the city began to register their protests with Assembly Speaker Perry B. Duryea Jr. Mr. Duryea was reported to have made a commitment to consult with these conservatives before he would pass a bill.

Their basic objection was that the five-member elected Board of Education to be created under the bill would not have enough power and that too much power would be surrendered to a new chancellor of the city school system and to the 30 community school districts and their local boards, which would be established by the legislation.

"The inclusion of an elected board is a complete farce," said one of the conservatives,

Continued on Page 53, Column 2

Cooke in Rome for Elevation to College of Cardinals

United Press International

Cardinal-designate Terence J. Cooke, right, with James Francis Cardinal McIntyre in Rome

By ROBERT C. DOTY

Special to The New York Times

ROME, April 27—The Most Rev. Terence J. Cooke, Archbishop of New York, arrived in Rome today to be raised, with 32 other prelates, to the College of Cardinals, highest body in the Roman Catholic Church. Pope Paul VI will elevate the prelates in a four-day consistory stripped of some of its former pomp, and with an unprecedented oath of secrecy demanded of Cardinals for the first time. The Vatican provided no explanation of the decision to ask each new "Prince of the Church" to pledge that he "will not divulge to their damage or discredit the councils entrusted to me, either directly or indirectly, without the consent of the Holy See."

It was speculated that the Pontiff, who has expressed concern over the "practically

Continued on Page 4, Column 4

CHINESE AFFIRM HARD-LINE STAND IN PARTY REPORT

Lin Asks War Preparation —United Front to Oppose U.S. and Soviet Urged

By TILLMAN DURDIN

Special to The New York Times

HONG KONG, April 27 — The Chinese Communist party has adopted as its basic program a plan for continued hard-line revolutionary action, at home and abroad.

The program was set out in a 24,000-word report by Lin Piao, the party's deputy chairman, and adopted at the ninth party congress, which met in Peking the first 24 days of this month. It was made public tonight by Hsinhua, the official Chinese Communist press agency.

Mr. Lin, who is also Defense Minister, denounced the United States and the Soviet Union, and said that China must prepare for the eventuality of nuclear war with either country. He pledged continued support for revolutionary movements everywhere and called on nations to form a united front to resist Soviet and United States efforts to divide up the world.

Kosygin Offer Disclosed

The report said that the Chinese had rejected an offer by the Soviet Premier, Aleksei N. Kosygin, to discuss the Chinese-Soviet border dispute over the telephone. [Page 14.]

It asserted that the Cultural Revolution, initiated by the party chairman, Mao Tse-tung, in 1966 to purge Communist China of revisionist leaders and influences, had achieved a smashing victory. However, it declared that the revolution was not yet over and that further struggle lay ahead before complete political transformation in China and world revolution were attained.

The report underlined the new primacy of the military in the affairs of Communist China by quoting Chairman Mao as having said, "The main component of the state is the army." It proclaimed Mao Tse-tung's thoughts, in equal status with Marxism-Leninism, as the basis for all the actions of the people of China.

Mr. Lin gave his report, which sums up the genesis, development and future perspectives of the Maoist Cultural Revolution, on April 1. It was adopted by the congress after protracted discussion and some emendations on April 14.

The report is the basic

Continued on Page 14, Column 3

President de Gaulle voting in Colombey-les-Deux-Eglises

Associated Press

Alain Poher, right, President of Senate, being escorted by an official yesterday. He will be interim President.

VOTE WEEKS AWAY

President, in Office a Decade, Will Leave at Noon Today

By HENRY TANNER

Special to The New York Times

PARIS, Monday, April 28—Charles de Gaulle stepped down early today after more than 10 years as President of France. He acted after his regime suffered a numbing defeat in a referendum.

In a statement issued by his office at Elysée Palace, the 78-year-old President said: "I cease to exercise my functions as President of the Republic. This decision takes effect today at noon."

The announcement was made a few minutes past midnight (7 P.M., New York time). The general was at his country residence at Colombey-les-Deux-Eglises, where he traditionally votes.

Most Votes Counted

Interior Minister Raymond Marcellin announced at 1:20 A.M. that with all but 470,000 votes accounted for, the Government's bill for constitutional reform had been rejected by 52.87 per cent of the voters casting valid ballots. The bill was favored by 47.13 per cent.

Paris received the news of the voting and the resignation quietly, until students and the police clashed in the Latin Quarter and right-wingers staged brief demonstrations on the Champs-Elysées.

Premier Maurice Couve de Murville conceded defeat shortly before 11 P.M., less than three hours after the polls closed.

Looking drawn and tired, but keeping his cold voice under the iron control for which he was noted during 10 years as Foreign Minister, Mr. Couve de Murville said:

"A majority of the French people has pronounced itself against the reforms that were submitted to it, with all the political consequences that this rejection entails.

"Beginning tomorrow a new page will be turned in our history."

Alain Poher, President of the Senate, will become interim President of the republic at noon today.

Dictatorship Feared

This is the line of succession under the Constitution. A bitterly contested feature of the Government's defeated constitutional reform was that the interim Presidency would go to the Premier, who is appointed by the President. The opposition feared this could mean a giant step toward dictatorship.

Mr. Poher's task will be to organize presidential elections to be held no sooner than 20 days or later than 35 days from today.

The interim President's powers are limited. He cannot dissolve the Government or the National Assembly and he cannot ask for a vote of confidence in the Assembly.

Premier Couve de Murville and his Cabinet will remain the caretaker government for this period.

It was the President's personal decision to call the nation to the polls. Several of his Cabinet ministers and leading Gaullist politicians had advised strongly against it.

But the general has frequently felt the need to get new "proof of confidence" from the nation. A commentator in the

Continued on Page 12, Column 1

Albany Approves Change In City Hospital System

By RICHARD L. MADDEN

Special to The New York Times

ALBANY, April 27—The Assembly gave final legislative approval tonight to a bill setting up a public corporation to run New York City's 20 municipal hospitals. The measure, which passed 119 to 17, with one abstention, now goes to Governor Rockefeller for his expected approval.

The bill would create the New York City Health and Hospitals Corporation, which would be run by a 16-member board. Five of the members would be city officials, five others appointed by the Mayor, five by the City Council and the remaining member would be chosen by the others to be chief executive officer.

Although Mayor Lindsay and the Democratic-controlled City Council, which modified the Mayor's original proposal, had requested the measure, it still ran into some opposition on the Assembly floor.

Assemblyman Charles B. Rangel, Democrat of Manhattan, citing the recent threatened closing of Harlem Hospital, said that the proposed corporation would be a "buffer" between the Mayor and the people.

During the half-hour debate,

Continued on Page 53, Column 7

4TH POLICE SHIFT IS PUT OFF 3 DAYS

P.B.A. Given Chance to Try to Fill Duty Tour in South Bronx With Volunteers

The beginning of a new 6 P.M.-to-2 A.M. police patrol shift in the South Bronx will be postponed from today to Thursday to give the Patrolmen's Benevolent Association time to obtain volunteers for the duty tour.

The delay in implementing the new fourth platoon, which is designed to increase the number of policemen on patrol during the hours when the most crimes are reported, was announced yesterday by Police Commissioner Howard R. Leary after a meeting with John Cassese, president of the P.B.A.

There had been earlier reports that at least some of the affected policemen might call in sick to show their opposition to the new system. Then on Saturday, the department informed its 30,000 members that the union, its officers and its individual members would be subject to the new

Continued on Page 52, Column 6

U.S. IS REDUCING FLEET OFF KOREA

Pentagon Announces Move After Senator Says Ships Are Leaving the Area

By CHRISTOPHER LYDON

Special to The New York Times

WASHINGTON, April 27 — The naval task force mobilized to protect American reconnaissance flights off North Korea is being reduced in size, the Pentagon said tonight.

A high-level source said a significant number of ships were being withdrawn.

The Soviet Union made oral complaints last week, both in Moscow and in Washington, expressing concern over the presence of the United States fleet in the Sea of Japan near the Soviet port of Vladivostok.

The Pentagon announcement came a few hours after Senator Henry M. Jackson, Democrat of Washington, who is generally well informed about military affairs, said that the fleet, Task Force 71, had not been directed to the Yellow Sea, as the Pentagon announced yesterday, but had, in fact, been ordered to

Continued on Page 8, Column 1

Resignation Stirs Hopes For West European Unity

By ANTHONY LEWIS

Special to The New York Times

LONDON, Monday, April 28 —Initial Western European reaction to the resignation of President de Gaulle was an expression of hope for a new opening toward unity in Europe, mixed with fear of the unknown.

Despite all the public opinion polls of recent days, the resignation came as a shock. The politicians and officials who have had to deal with General de Gaulle over the years had come to feel that there was a kind of invincibility about him.

[Washington officials had no public reaction to General de Gaulle's resignation. Officials began preparing for allied consultations on European unity although no immediate shifts in French policy were foreseen. Page 13.]

There was no official comment from the British Government when the news of General de Gaulle's resignation came after midnight. Spokesmen for Prime Minister Wilson said that he would have nothing to say during the night.

Privately, those who have worked to bring Britain into the Common Market — and have been stymied by General de Gaulle's successive vetoes—felt an evident exhilaration. At last there was at least a possibility of change in the frozen French position on the issue of British entry into the Common Market.

No one here deceives himself that any successor will instantly open his arms to Britain. But the removal of General de

Continued on Page 12, Column 5

Nixon Hopes Youth Turns to Religion

United Press International

President Nixon, Mrs. David Eisenhower, his daughter, and the Rev. Edward G. Latch, chaplain of the House of Representatives, in the Rose Garden after White House service.

By FELIX BELAIR Jr.

Special to The New York Times

WASHINGTON, April 27—President Nixon spoke informally today about the value to the individual of religious faith and worship and about his hope that more young Americans would find in religion an answer to today's "crisis of the spirit" of which he spoke in his Inaugural Address.

The President talked to a few of the 200 guests who had just attended the fourth in a series of interdenominational religious services in the East Room of the White House. Over coffee in the State Dining Room, the President was asked if he had any particular purpose in holding services in the executive mansion.

Although he seemed surprised by the question at first, he did not hesitate. Religious faith, he said, is something he acquired from his mother, so it has always been a necessary part of his life.

But he has learned from experience that he could not, as President, attend a regular church service without becoming a source of distraction to the congregation and the cause of all manner of special preparations, including security, Mr. Nixon added.

Here at the White House,

Continued on Page 29, Column 1

President Barrientos of Bolivia Is Killed in Crash of Helicopter

By Reuters

LA PAZ, Bolivia, April 27—President René Barrientos Ortuño was killed today in a helicopter crash in the Bolivian interior. Vice President Luis Adolfo Siles Salines was sworn in as his successor.

The colorful 49-year-old Air Force general was returning from a village near the town of Arque in Oruru Province south of here after talking to peasants and inspecting government development projects.

According to reports, his helicopter took off from a baseball stadium, flew into telephone wires, plummeted into a stream and burst into flames. It took nearly 10 minutes for the flames to die down sufficiently for stunned villagers to approach the wreckage.

Three helicopter crewmen also were killed.

Mr. Siles, who had been serving as Senate President as well as Vice President, immediately went to the Presidential palace and was sworn in before military leaders and prominent government officials.

He pledged to serve the remainder of General Barrientos's term, until August, 1970, and ordered 30 days of national mourning.

He praised the late President for fighting for the rights of peasants and workers, and

Continued on Page 41, Column 2

New Pressures on the Franc Are Expected in Paris Crisis

By CLYDE H. FARNSWORTH

Special to The New York Times

PARIS, April 27—The resignation of President de Gaulle was expected to lead to renewed pressure on the French franc and perhaps a devaluation that would touch off general currency realignments throughout Western Europe.

International monetary authorities, through their highly developed support machinery, are prepared to offer maximum assistance for defense of the franc.

This, together with the Bank of France's $3.8-billion of reserves and $2-billion credit line with central banks, was expected to see the franc through the next few weeks.

But the question on most bankers' minds was whether a new French Government would remain committed to holding the franc at its current parity of 20 United States cents.

A new government generally likes to start with a clean slate when it inherits a weak currency, monetary specialists said.

President de Gaulle resisted devaluation during a currency crisis last November against the counsel of some of his advisers and, even with optimum conditions, he was never given more than a 50-50 chance of waging a successful defense.

Though still at relatively high levels, the French reserves

Continued on Page 12, Column 1

NEWS INDEX

The Mets' winning pitcher Jerry Koosman was crushed between catcher Jerry Grote and Tom Seaver, and an exhilerated cluster of victors.

New Yorkers went wild as the Mets were honored with a ticker tape parade after their surprising World Series victory.

Joe Namath inspired his team's victory over the Baltimore Colts in an upset at the Superbowl.

Bill Russell and Wilt Chamberlain (with the ball) spent most of the 60s in fierce competition. In 1969, Chamberlain, now with the Lakers, lost the NBA title to Russell and the Celtics.

Millions of Americans dropped what they were doing to attend mass demonstrations to let the Administration know they wanted the war stopped, on Vietnam Moratorium Day, October 15.

Casualties kept mounting, anti-war protests were increasing, but peace talks were going nowhere.

Lieutenant William Calley (right) was released from the stockade under President Nixon's order while his conviction for the murder of some 350 people was under review.

"All the News That's Fit to Print"

The New York Times

LATE CITY EDITION

Weather: Cloudy, chance of showers today. Fair tonight and tomorrow. Temp. range: today 72-62; Sunday 82-63. Temp.-Hum. Index yesterday 73. Complete U.S. report on Page 94.

VOL.CXVIII...No.40,679 NEW YORK, MONDAY, JUNE 9, 1969 10 CENTS

NIXON TO REDUCE VIETNAM FORCE, PULLING OUT 25,000 G.I.'S BY AUG. 31; HE AND THIEU STRESS THEIR UNITY

A MIDWAY ACCORD

Leaders Agree First Cutbacks Will Begin Within 30 Days

Text of the joint communiqué is printed on Page 16.

By HEDRICK SMITH
Special to The New York Times

MIDWAY ISLAND, June 8—President Nixon met with President Nguyen Van Thieu of South Vietnam today and announced that 25,000 American soldiers would be withdrawn from Vietnam before the end of August.

After the first two hours of five hours of talks on this Pacific island, Mr. Nixon emerged to declare that the Presidents had agreed that troop withdrawals would begin within 30 days.

And with Mr. Thieu standing at his side, Mr. Nixon held out the hope of further reductions in the 540,000-man American force when this first phase was completed.

Replacements Available

He said that the equivalent of a combat division could leave Vietnam because of progress in the training and equipping of South Vietnam's Army.

Both President Nixon and President Thieu underscored the point that the American forces being withdrawn would be replaced in the field by South Vietnamese forces.

Mr. Nixon termed the withdrawal a "significant step forward" toward a lasting peace in Vietnam. At the end of the five-hour conference, Mr. Thieu said that the step was "good news for the American people that Vietnamese forces replace United States combat forces."

Both in announcing the troop withdrawal and in presenting a joint statement to the press at the end of their meeting, the two leaders sought to emphasize their solidarity.

Differences Not Mentioned

Their joint communiqué made no allusion to differences in approach to the Paris negotiations, and President Thieu remarked afterward that it was "not true" that he had come to Midway to thresh out differences with the new American Administration. But little was noted in the public statements of either man that might quiet Saigon's fears about the ultimate intentions of the United States leadership.

Although the announcement of the troop withdrawal was aimed at placating domestic critics of the war and putting pressure on North Vietnam and the Vietcong to negotiate more seriously in Paris by seeking to demonstrate South Vietnam's growing strength, Mr. Nixon mentioned neither American war critics nor the enemy.

As if pleading for more patience from the American pub-

Continued on Page 16, Column 3

VAGUE ON ISSUES

Statement Is Believed Unlikely to Dispel Saigon's Unease

By TERENCE SMITH
Special to The New York Times

MIDWAY ISLAND, June 8—President Nguyen Van Thieu departed for Saigon today armed with a joint communiqué that appeared to do little to relieve the widespread uneasiness that prevails in South Vietnam over United States intentions concerning the war.

The 1,200-word joint statement issued by the two Presidents at the conclusion of their five-hour conference appeared too general to be of much use in dispelling the concern that has grown up in political and military circles in South Vietnam about the American plan to negotiate a settlement to the war.

In a brief speech delivered in conjunction with the release of the communiqué, the South Vietnamese leader sought to quell speculation that there were significant differences between his country's position on the peace talks and that of the United States.

Denial of Differences

"It is not true," he said, "that I had to come here to dissipate or discuss those differences." Later, he added: "We have had close consultation before and we have a very close understanding."

Speaking from the stage of the theater at the naval station here, Mr. Thieu also spoke of the "constant duty of the Vietnamese people to take over more responsibility and to alleviate the burden of the United States people to support us and defend freedom in Vietnam."

Expressing his country's gratitude for American sacrifices, Mr. Thieu said, "We never forget that the blood and human life are precious to anyone, to any people, at any time."

The communiqué was most notable for its omissions, particularly of items that Mr. Thieu had come to this Pacific island to obtain, such as a pledge that the United States would stand behind the present Government in Saigon and support the current South Vietnamese Constitution.

As it turned out, the statement included no references to the Constitution, to special elections, or to any of the other questions that have caused concern in Saigon since President Nixon unveiled his eight-point

Continued on Page 17, Column 1

MEET AT MIDWAY: President Nixon and President Nguyen Van Thieu of South Vietnam after their arrival.

Associated Press

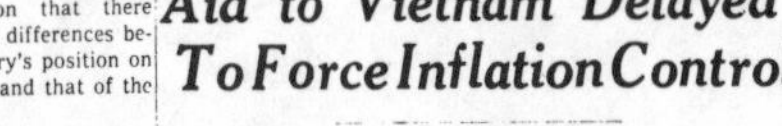

Aid to Vietnam Delayed To Force Inflation Control

By B. DRUMMOND AYRES Jr.
Special to The New York Times

SAIGON, South Vietnam, June 8—The United States has been applying economic pressure on the South Vietnamese Government to convince it of the need to control inflation.

According to American officials, $40-million in United States aid was withheld from Saigon during much of April and May while intense discussions were under way over means to halt price increases and to decrease deficits.

At the end of May, the South Vietnamese agreed to take steps against inflation, and the money was released.

In the last three months prices in South Vietnamese stores and market places have risen about 10 per cent. Prices have risen about 30 per cent every 12 months for several years.

Within a few days recently, the price of a glass of sugar-cane juice doubled, from 5 piasters to 10. A bag of rice that cost 270 piasters one month ago now costs 300 piasters. The official exchange rate is 118 piasters to the dollar. The black market rate is about 180 piasters to the dollar.

The South Vietnamese have agreed to reduce imports of such luxuries as television sets and dried fruits, and to increase imports of such essentials as machinery and fertiliz-

Continued on Page 14, Column 1

SOVIET GAIN SEEN IN MIRV PROGRAM

Pentagon Analysis of Tests Bolsters U.S. Advocates of Continued Testing

By WILLIAM BEECHER
Special to The New York Times

WASHINGTON, June 8 — A new analysis of Soviet missile tests in the Pacific is reinforcing arguments of those within the Administration who favor continuation of United States tests of multiple warheads.

The analysis, by intelligence experts in the Pentagon primarily, suggests that multiple warheads now being tested by the Russians may be capable of being guided to three scattered targets and powerful enough to destroy hardened missile silos.

Until now, United States specialists had believed the Russians were testing a three-part multiple warhead all three elements of which landed in a fairly tight, predictable pattern near one another, attacking only a single target.

Thus the new intelligence information, reliable sources say, suggests the Russians are further along than previously thought toward development of

Continued on Page 35, Column 1

PLAN WOULD HELP BIG STOCKHOLDERS TAKE HIGH OFFICE

Sales of Shares to Treasury Aimed at Removing Link to Conflict of Interest

SENATORS PREPARE BILL

McIntyre's Proposal Gives Appointee Chance to Serve Without Financial Loss

By WARREN WEAVER Jr.
Special to The New York Times

WASHINGTON, June 8—A novel plan that would permit millionaire stockholders to serve in high Federal office without risking conflict of interest or financial loss is being drafted in the Senate.

The plan is designed to meet the situation that arose when President Nixon named David Packard Deputy Secretary of Defense. He held $300-million worth of stock in an electronics concern that does about a third of its business with the Pentagon.

Mr. Packard, answering Senate criticism, set up a charitable trust for 3,550,150 shares of Hewlett-Packard Corporation stock with the Bank of America as trustee.

Under the new plan, an appointee would sell his stock to the Treasury, which, in turn, would gradually resell it in small pieces.

Bipartisan Backing

The legislative proposal, developed by Senator Thomas J. McIntyre, Democrat of New Hampshire, has bipartisan backing among leaders of the Senate Banking and Currency Committee. Senators William Proxmire, Democrat of Wisconsin, and Edward W. Brooke, Republican of Massachusetts, have endorsed the measure.

Senator McIntyre's idea has been submitted to President Nixon's top domestic advisers in the White House, and they were sufficiently interested in it to schedule a personal presentation to the President shortly.

If the plan wins the approval of Congress and the President, its first beneficiary may be Ray Watt, a California builder who was in line for appointment as the Federal Housing Administrator. He has been plagued by serious conflict-of-interest problems.

Mr. Watt and Mr. Packard both owned huge blocks of stock in corporations doing sub-

Continued on Page 27, Column 1

PREPARING FOR DEBATE: A studio technician adjusts Mayor Lindsay's chest microphone before the start of the program. In foreground is State Senator John J. Marchi.

The New York Times (by William E. Sauro)

New School Board Warns Of 'Disaster' in Budget Cut

By LEONARD BUDER

The new interim Board of Education, in its first public statement, warned yesterday that the city school system faced "major disaster" next fall because of insufficient operating funds.

The five-member board, which took office two weeks ago, said the indicated city expense budget for the fiscal year starting July 1 would force the system to reduce current services by $96-million.

"We are shocked at the dire prospects facing our schools in the next school year because of the most drastic budget cut ever received by the city school system," the board said.

Plea for Aid Made

The budget reduction, which has already stirred an outcry from school, parent and community groups, would have the following impact, according to school officials:

¶The elimination of 4,427 needed teaching and supervisory positions.

¶An expected increase in class sizes in many schools by an average of two pupils for each class.

¶A one-third reduction in the free lunch program for poor children.

¶A cutback in pupil transportation services.

"Even at this late date," the board said, "we hope earnestly that the city, state and Federal Government can help restore the budget at least to the point that will enable our schools to

Continued on Page 67, Column 4

LINDSAY, MARCHI CLASH IN DEBATE

Senator Charges Ineptness by Mayor, Who Says Rival Helped Deny City Funds

Mayor Lindsay was accused in debate yesterday with State Senator John J. Marchi of being unwilling to deal properly with crime and charged in turn that Mr. Marchi had helped to deny the city the money it needed to solve its problems.

The charges and countercharges occurred as the two Republican mayoral candidates, standing in three-sided television booths that looked a bit like witness stands, debated some of the issues for the first time. Each found the other inadequate to the task of governing the city.

The half-hour special live telecast on WCBS-TV began with Mr. Lindsay, who had won a coin toss.

In the two minutes allotted him for opening remarks, the Mayor said his administration, while not without its setbacks, had "started to do what has to be done." His years in office, he said, proved that the city "can be governed."

Mr. Lindsay, who is the mayoral candidate of the Liberal party, pointed to the addition of men to the police force, new subway construction, a balanced budget for four years running and an improve-

Continued on Page 50, Column 7

POLICE IN U.S. SEEK TO EASE HOSTILITY

Survey Finds That a Rise in Efforts to Reduce Racial Tension Sometimes Fails

By JOHN HERBERS
Special to The New York Times

WASHINGTON, June 8 —In cities across the nation, white policemen and black militant leaders have been holding "confrontation sessions" in which they probe each other's motivations and prejudices in an effort to lower the level of hostility between the two groups.

Many police departments have opened storefront centers in the slums, at which residents can voice complaints against the police or other public employes to policemen who have a reasonably sympathetic ear.

Virtually every department has stepped up efforts to hire more Negro policemen, and there have been a number of new community relations efforts, such as Operation Handshake, in which a new patrolman must spend several days in the community making friends before he begins enforcing the law.

An Explosive Issue

Despite these efforts, however, the hostility between the police and the Negro communities has worsened in some cities and in others remains the most explosive issue in race relations.

This information is based on a New York Times survey of 13 cities and on interviews with national leaders familiar with the situation. The cities surveyed were Boston, New York, Philadelphia, Chicago, Detroit, Pittsburgh, St. Louis, Houston, Miami, Kansas City, Mo.; Los Angeles, San Francisco and Oakland, Calif.

In the last year, the police departments have made efforts to institute new community relations programs, many of them following the recommen-

Continued on Page 37, Column 1

ROBERT TAYLOR, 57, IS DEAD OF CANCER

Associated Press

Robert Taylor

Special to The New York Times

SANTA MONICA, Calif., June 8—Robert Taylor, a Hollywood star for more than 30 years, died this morning of lung cancer at St. John's Hospital. He was 57 years old. With him was his wife, the German actress Ursula Thiess.

Hollywood's studio-sponsored star system created one of its most durable luminaries in Robert Taylor, who in 70 feature films, personalized the glamorous leading man adored by movie fans between the two World Wars.

Despite a shock of black, wavy hair, complete with an eye-catching widow's peak, a

Continued on Page 47, Column 2

NEWS INDEX

FLEE BATTLE IN TAYNINH: Refugees jamming road near the provincial capital 60 miles northwest of Saigon as allied troops sought to oust several hundred North Vietnamese who had taken a nearby hamlet. Article is on Page 17.

United Press International

Men of Dartmouth Are Troubled By Lingering Echoes of Protest

By MICHAEL STERN
Special to The New York Times

HANOVER, N.H., June 8—In any other year, the deep green and gold New England summer that is settling in here would be casting a sweet somnolent spell over the hearts and minds of Dartmouth men.

But this year, many of those hearts and minds are deeply troubled by still-fresh memories of chaotic springtime protests over R.O.T.C. on campus and the calling in of 90 state troopers last month to arrest students who had occupied Parkhurst Hall, the college administration building.

Vivid reminders of those events showed up here last week when 36 students—several with jailhouse haircuts—returned to the campus after having served 26 days of 30-day sentences for having defied a court order to leave the administration building. They got time off for good behavior.

Four others, whose trials had been delayed, left the campus this last week to begin their 30-day sentences and will not be released until July.

Still to come, beginning tomorrow, are hearings before the College Committee on Standing and Conduct, hearings that some condemn as a double jeopardy for the arrested students. The hearings are to determine what penalties will be imposed on those who overstepped Dartmouth's ground rules on free expression and dissent.

"Now is when the agony begins," said Prof W. W. Ballard, chairman of the committee, as

Continued on Page 67, Column 2

Paul Newman and Robert Redford starred as the likeable outlaws in *Butch Cassidy and the Sundance Kid.*

John Wayne won an Oscar for best actor for his role as Rooster Cogburn in *True Grit.*

Brenda Vaccaro and Jon Voight in a party scene from *Midnight Cowboy.*

"All the News That's Fit to Print"

The New York Times

LATE CITY EDITION

Weather: Rain, warm today; clear tonight. Sunny, pleasant tomorrow. Temp. range: today 80-66; Sunday 71-66. Temp.-Hum. Index yesterday 69. Complete U.S. report on P. 50.

VOL. CXVIII . No. 40,721 NEW YORK, MONDAY, JULY 21, 1969 X 10 CENTS

MEN WALK ON MOON

ASTRONAUTS LAND ON PLAIN; COLLECT ROCKS, PLANT FLAG

Voice From Moon: 'Eagle Has Landed'

EAGLE (the lunar module): Houston, Tranquility Base here. The Eagle has landed.

HOUSTON: Roger, Tranquility, we copy you on the ground. You've got a bunch of guys about to turn blue. We're breathing again. Thanks a lot.

TRANQUILITY BASE: Thank you.

HOUSTON: You're looking good here.

TRANQUILITY BASE: A very smooth touchdown.

HOUSTON: Eagle, you are stay for T1. [The first step in the lunar operation.] Over.

TRANQUILITY BASE: Roger. Stay for T1.

HOUSTON: Roger and we see you venting the ox.

TRANQUILITY BASE: Roger.

COLUMBIA (the command and service module): How do you read me?

HOUSTON: Columbia, he has landed Tranquility Base. Eagle is at Tranquility. I read you five by. Over.

COLUMBIA: Yes, I heard the whole thing.

HOUSTON: Well, it's a good show.

COLUMBIA: Fantastic.

TRANQUILITY BASE: I'll second that.

APOLLO CONTROL: The next major stay-no stay will be for the T2 event. That is at 21 minutes 26 seconds after initiation of power descent.

COLUMBIA: Up telemetry command reset to reacquire on high gain.

HOUSTON: Copy. Out.

APOLLO CONTROL: We have an unofficial time for that touchdown of 102 hours, 45 minutes, 42 seconds and we will update that.

HOUSTON: Eagle, you loaded R2 wrong. We want 10254.

TRANQUILITY BASE: Roger. Do you want the horizontal 55 15.2?

HOUSTON: That's affirmative.

APOLLO CONTROL: We're now less than four minutes from our next stay-no stay. It will be for one complete revolution of the command module.

One of the first things that Armstrong and Aldrin will do after getting their next stay-no stay will be to remove their helmets and gloves.

HOUSTON: Eagle, you are stay for T2. Over.

Continued on Page 4, Col. 1

VOYAGE TO THE MOON

By ARCHIBALD MACLEISH

PRESENCE among us,

wanderer in our skies,

dazzle of silver in our leaves and on our
waters silver,

silver evasion in our farthest thought—
"the visiting moon" . . . "the glimpses of the moon" . . .

and we have touched you!

From the first of time,
before the first of time, before the
first men tasted time, we thought of you.
You were a wonder to us, unattainable,
a longing past the reach of longing,
a light beyond our light, our lives—perhaps
a meaning to us . . .

Now
our hands have touched you in your depth of night.

Three days and three nights we journeyed,
steered by farthest stars, climbed outward,
crossed the invisible tide-rip where the floating dust
falls one way or the other in the void between,
followed that other down, encountered
cold, faced death—unfathomable emptiness . . .

Then, the fourth day evening, we descended,
made fast, set foot at dawn upon your beaches,
sifted between our fingers your cold sand.

We stand here in the dusk, the cold, the silence . . .

and here, as at the first of time, we lift our heads.
Over us, more beautiful than the moon, a
moon, a wonder to us, unattainable,
a longing past the reach of longing,
a light beyond our light, our lives—perhaps
a meaning to us . . .

O, a meaning!

over us on these silent beaches the bright
earth,
presence among us

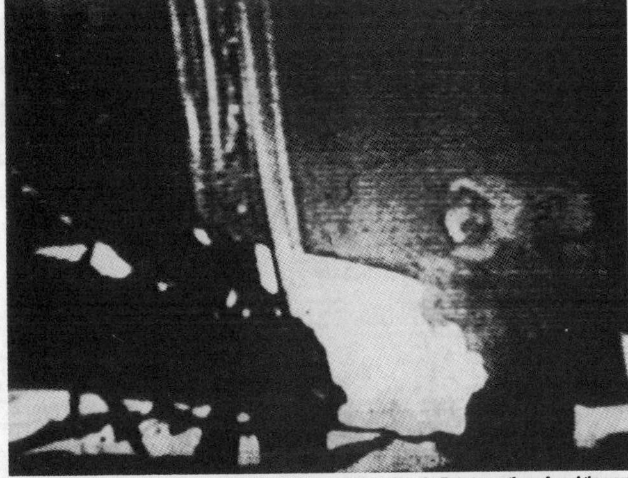

Neil A. Armstrong moves away from the leg of the landing craft after taking the first step on the surface of the moon

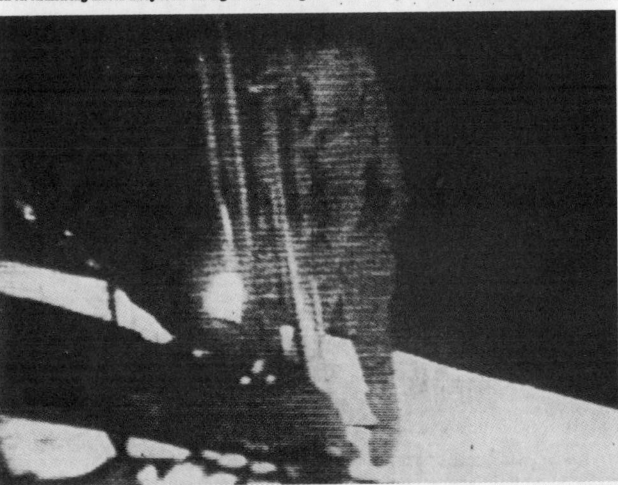

The New York Times from C.B.S. News

Col. Edwin E. Aldrin Jr. climbing down the ladder. The television camera was attached to a side of the lunar module.

Associated Press

Mr. Armstrong, right, and Colonel Aldrin raise the U.S. flag. A metal rod at right angles to the mast keeps flag unfurled.

A Powdery Surface Is Closely Explored

By JOHN NOBLE WILFORD

Special to The New York Times

HOUSTON, Monday, July 21—Men have landed and walked on the moon.

Two Americans, astronauts of Apollo 11, steered their fragile four-legged lunar module safely and smoothly to the historic landing yesterday at 4:17:40 P.M., Eastern daylight time.

Neil A. Armstrong, the 38-year-old civilian commander, radioed to earth and the mission control room here:

"Houston, Tranquility Base here. The Eagle has landed."

The first men to reach the moon—Mr. Armstrong and his co-pilot, Col. Edwin E. Aldrin Jr. of the Air Force—brought their ship to rest on a level, rock-strewn plain near the southwestern shore of the arid Sea of Tranquility.

About six and a half hours later, Mr. Armstrong opened the landing craft's hatch, stepped slowly down the ladder and declared as he planted the first human footprint on the lunar crust:

"That's one small step for man, one giant leap for mankind."

His first step on the moon came at 10:56:20 P.M., as a television camera outside the craft transmitted his every moved to an awed and excited audience of hundreds of millions of people on earth.

Tentative Steps Test Soil

Mr. Armstrong's initial steps were tentative tests of the lunar soil's firmness and of his ability to move about easily in his bulky white spacesuit and backpacks and under the influence of lunar gravity, which is one-sixth that of the earth.

"The surface is fine and powdery," the astronaut reported. "I can pick it up loosely with my toe. It does adhere in fine layers like powdered charcoal to the sole and sides of my boots. I only go in a small fraction of an inch, maybe an eighth of an inch. But I can see the footprints of my boots in the treads in the fine sandy particles.

After 19 minutes of Mr. Armstrong's testing, Colonel Aldrin joined him outside the craft.

The two men got busy setting up another television camera out from the lunar module, planting an American flag into the ground, scooping up soil and rock samples, deploying scientific experiments and hopping and loping about in a demonstration of their lunar agility.

They found walking and working on the moon less taxing than had been forecast. Mr. Armstrong once reported he was "very comfortable."

And people back on earth found the black-and-white television pictures of the bug-shaped lunar module and the men tramping about it so sharp and clear as to seem unreal, more like a toy and toy-like figures than human beings on the most daring and far-reaching expedition thus far undertaken.

Nixon Telephones Congratulations

During one break in the astronauts' work, President Nixon congratulated them from the White House in what, he said, "certainly has to be the most historic telephone call ever made."

"Because of what you have done," the President told the astronauts, "the heavens have become a part of man's world. And as you talk to us from the Sea of Tranquility it requires us to redouble our efforts to bring peace and tranquility to earth.

"For one priceless moment in the whole history of man all the people on this earth are truly one—one in their pride in what you have done and one in our prayers that you will return safely to earth."

Mr. Armstrong replied:

"Thank you Mr. President. It's a great honor and privilege for us to be here representing not only the United States but men of peace of all nations, men with interests and a curiosity and men with a vision for the future."

Mr. Armstrong and Colonel Aldrin returned to their landing craft and closed the hatch at 1:12 A.M., 2 hours 21 minutes after opening the hatch on the moon. While the third member of the crew, Lieut. Col. Michael Collins of the Air Force, kept his orbital vigil overhead in the command ship, the two moon explorers settled down to sleep.

Outside their vehicle the astronauts had found a bleak

Continued on Pages 2, Col. 1

Today's 4-Part Issue of The Times

This morning's issue of The New York Times is divided into four parts. The first part is devoted to news of Apollo 11, and includes Editorials and letters to the Editor (Page 16). Poems on the landing on the moon appear on Page 17.

General news begins on the first page of the second part. The News Summary and Index is on the first page of the third part, which includes sports news, obituaries (Page 51) and transportation news and weather reports (Pages 50 and 52).

Financial and business news begins on the first page of the fourth part.

Following is the News Index for today's issue:

"All the News That's Fit to Print"

The New York Times

LATE CITY EDITION

Weather: Clearing and warm today; fair tonight. Fair, warm tomorrow. Temp. range: today 85-64; Friday 76-61. Temp.-Hum. Index yesterday 69. Complete U.S. report on Page 50.

VOL. CXVIII.. No. 40,726 — NEW YORK, SATURDAY, JULY 26, 1969 — 10 CENTS

KENNEDY WEIGHS QUITTING, SEEKS ADVICE OF VOTERS; PLEADS GUILTY TO CHARGE

The New York Times

EXPLAINS ACTIONS: Senator Edward M. Kennedy on TV

MISHAP DESCRIBED

He Calls 'Indefensible' His Delay in Reporting to Police on Fatality

Text of Kennedy broadcast, transcript of hearing, Page 10.

By JOSEPH LELYVELD
Special to The New York Times

HYANNIS PORT, Mass., July 25—Edward M. Kennedy described tonight as "indefensible" his failure to report immediately a fatal automobile accident last week and said he was considering whether to resign his Senate seat.

He invited his constituents from Massachusetts "to think this through with me" and help him arrive at the right decision.

Senator Kennedy went on national television to present his account of the accident, in which a young Washington secretary, Mary Jo Kopechne, drowned when his car went off a bridge and overturned in a pond. The Senator spoke 10 hours after he pleaded guilty in a court on Martha's Vineyard to a charge of leaving the scene of the accident.

Sentence Is Suspended

His plea resulted in a suspended sentence of two months in jail, the minimum sentence provided in the law. The presiding judge said of Mr. Kennedy:

"He has already been and will continue to be punished far beyond anything this court can impose."

Mr. Kennedy, who until last week was considered one of the Democratic party's likeliest candidates for the Presidency in 1972, addressed himself early in his television statement to what he called "ugly speculation" linking him romantically with the 28-year-old Miss Kopechne.

"There has never been a private relationship between us of any kind," he declared.

He also denied that he was driving "under the influence of liquor" at the time of the accident.

When his car plunged off the wood bridge on Chappaquiddick Island, the Senator said, water entered his lungs and he "actually felt the sensation of drowning."

Returned to Scene

Later, he went on, he returned to the bridge with two companions, Joseph F. Gargan, a cousin, and Paul Markham, a former United States attorney, and attempted for a second time to dive for Miss Kopechne's body.

His account of a return to the scene after midnight could help resolve a discrepancy over the time of the accident between Mr. Kennedy's original statement and the testimony of a witness.

The witness, Christopher Look Jr., a Dukes County deputy sheriff, thought he saw a car carrying three persons turn down the dirt road to the bridge about 12:40 A.M. Saturday. Mr. Kennedy's original statement, made to the police when he first reported the fatality about 9 A.M. Saturday, placed the time of the accident at about 11:15 P.M. Friday.

Conduct Makes 'No Sense'

In his televised statement tonight, Mr. Kennedy said, "My conduct and conversations during the next several hours make no sense to me at all."

He added, "I regard as indefensible the fact that I did not report the accident to the police immediately."

Speaking slowly, the Senator recounted some of the irrational thoughts that he said raced through his mind after the accident. He said he wondered whether "some awful curse" really did hang over the Kennedys, or whether Miss Kopechne might still be alive.

He was, he said, "overcome by a jumble of emotions."

Mr. Kennedy said he had re-

Continued on Page 10, Column 1

People of Massachusetts Rush to Support Kennedy

Special to The New York Times

BOSTON, July 25—Tens of thousands of Massachusetts residents rushed to their telephones tonight to express what appeared to be heavy support for Senator Edward M. Kennedy in reply to his appeal for their advice.

The deluge of calls began after the Senator announced he was contemplating resigning and invited his constituents to assist him in making the decision.

Checks with the state's major newspapers and radio and television stations, which were flooded with calls and telegrams, showed that most—and in some cases an overwhelming majority—were in favor of Mr. Kennedy's remaining in office.

Many callers, however, said they were unconvinced by the Senator's nationally televised account of the car accident on Chappaquiddick Island a week ago in which a 28-year-old Washington secretary, Mary Jo Kopechne, was drowned.

[In Washington, Senate colleagues of Mr. Kennedy who could be reached for comment expressed the hope that the Senator would not resign. Page 11.]

A Heavy Response

The televised statement, made just 10 hours after the Senator had pleaded guilty to a charge of leaving the scene of the fatal accident, drew immediate and heavy response across the state.

Thousands of calls jammed the switchboard of the Boston newspapers—The Globe, The Record American, and The Herald Traveler—and the state's major radio and television stations.

The newspapers, which generally tend to be friendly toward the Kennedy family, reported that the sentiment of callers was running about 2 to 1 in support of the Senator.

"All hell's breaking loose

Continued on Page 10, Column 3

NIXON PLANS CUT IN MILITARY ROLE FOR U.S. IN ASIA

Starting Tour, He Promises Respect for Commitments, but Under New Forms

ARRIVES IN PHILIPPINES

President, at Guam, Asserts Nation Won't Be Drawn Into More Vietnams

Excerpts of summary of Nixon news conference, Page 8.

By ROBERT B. SEMPLE Jr.
Special to The New York Times

MANILA, Saturday, July 26—President Nixon declared yesterday that the United States would not be enticed into future wars like the one in Vietnam and would redesign and reduce its military commitments throughout non-Communist Asia.

Mr. Nixon promised, however, that the United States would continue to play a sizable role in the Pacific and would not forsake its treaty commitments.

This was the essence of views put forth by the President in an informal news conference before he set forth from Guam on the diplomatic leg of his global journey.

President Exhilarated

The President, who seemed exhilarated by the successful moon venture of Apollo 11, arrived here today for the first foreign stop of a tour taking him to Indonesia, Thailand, India, Pakistan, Rumania and, briefly, Britain.

During his short stop in Guam, Mr. Nixon set forth in considerable detail the purposes of his week-and-a-half trip and disclosed major points he would be making to the Asian leaders. He spoke for publication but asked that his words not be directly quoted.

The President defined his Asian policy in more specific and forceful terms than at any time since taking office. Some of his views had been expressed earlier in articles and in the political campaign last fall, but he went further today in emphasizing his intention of limiting United States commitments.

New Aid Is Hinted

Specifically, he said he might order a reduction of military operations in South Vietnam if that would help the negotiations to end the war.

The President also hinted that new forms of economic aid to the Asian nations might soon be forthcoming, but—perhaps mindful of growing ill will toward foreign aid at home and the constraints that inflation has placed on new Government spending—he carefully avoided promising an increase in aid.

The President spent the major part of his news conference, held at the naval officers' club in Guam, on questions relating to Vietnam and Asia, demonstrating that despite all the early publicity devoted to visit he will pay to Rumania Aug. 2, he himself was placing highest priority on the Asian

Continued on Page 9, Column 1

Souvanna Denies U.S. Invaded Laos

By DREW MIDDLETON
Special to The New York Times

PARIS, July 25 — Prince Souvanna Phouma, the Premier of Laos, today rejected as "completely false" North Vietnam's charge that his country had been invaded by 12,000 United States troops.

The charge was made yesterday by Xuan Thuy, head of the North Vietnamese delegation, at the 27th plenary session of the Paris peace talks.

The Laotian Premier also denied Mr. Thuy's charge that troops from Thailand were fighting on the Government side. Any interested power, he said, can send observers. "We live in a glass house," he said.

There are no American combat forces in Laos, the Premier said at a news conference, but there are at least 60,000 North

Continued on Page 3, Column 2

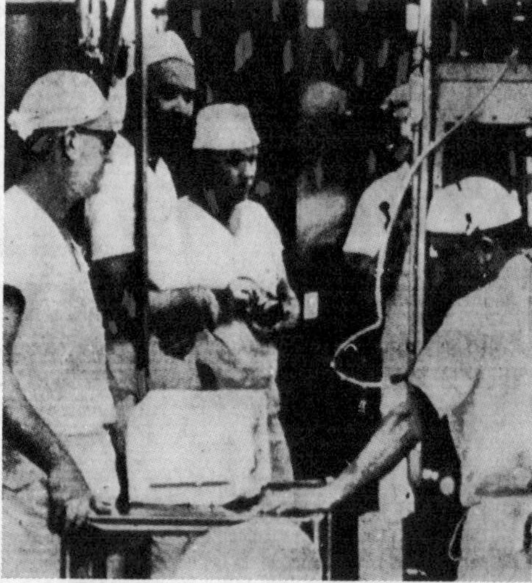

United Press International

TO STUDY SAMPLES FROM TRANQUILITY BASE: Technicians at the Lunar Receiving Laboratory in Houston with one of the two boxes of soil and rocks from the moon.

NIXON CONSIDERS A WAR SLOWDOWN

Says He May Order Cut in Operations if That Would Help the Peace Talks

By MAX FRANKEL
Special to The New York Times

MANILA, Saturday, July 26—President Nixon said yesterday that he might order a reduction of military operations in South Vietnam if that would help the negotiations to end the war.

Mr. Nixon implied that his military commanders preferred to continue applying the program of "maximum military pressure" on the enemy to search out and destroy concentrations of men and supplies. But he said he had to consider the situation in a wider, diplomatic context.

In a news conference on the island of Guam on the eve of his trip to four countries of South and Southeast Asia, the President guardedly acknowledged that he was reviewing battlefield tactics in Vietnam.

Change Is Weighed

He left the impression that he was weighing a change of tactics either to draw North Vietnam into more active negotiations or to reciprocate for the enemy's withdrawal from major engagements over the last month.

His military commanders are more expert tacticians than he is, Mr. Nixon said, and he naturally defers to their judgment on the conduct of a war.

But now that his Administration is engaged in negotiations, the President added, military tactics have become a part of the bargaining process. He and his aides are therefore re-evaluating military objectives and tactics, he said, mindful that diplomatic positions are developing on a parallel track.

He will announce the changes if any are made, Mr. Nixon said.

No Direct Quotation

Mr. Nixon stood in the same auditorium on Nimitz Hill in Guam where President Nguyen Van Thieu and Vice President Nguyen Cao Ky of South Vietnam drew new promises of support from President Lyndon B. Johnson two years ago. But the new President's emphasis was on turning a new leaf in Southeast Asia, learning from past mistakes and ending the war before too long, though no one could say how long.

The President was at first reluctant to discuss battlefield tactics. He said he had no plans to visit South Vietnam on the current trip but hoped to meet in Bangkok next week with the United States Ambassador to Saigon, Ellsworth Bunker, and perhaps also with the American military commander in South Vietnam, Gen. Creighton W. Abrams.

Just before leaving Washington Tuesday, he said, he

Continued on Page 9, Column 5

Apollo 11 Crewmen 'Fine'; Moon Rocks Go to Houston

Flight Surgeon Reports

By JAMES T. WOOTEN
Special to The New York Times

ABOARD U.S.S. HORNET, in the Pacific, July 25 — The Apollo 11 astronauts have passed their preliminary medical examinations and are relaxing in a quarantine trailer aboard this carrier. The three-man crew of the lunar mission will arrive in Pearl Harbor tomorrow for a plane ride to Houston.

"They're fine, as far as I can tell," said Dr. William R. Carpentier, the flight surgeon who is traveling in the small trailer with Neil A. Armstrong, Col. Edwin E. Aldrin Jr. and Col. Michael Collins.

"Actually, it looks as though I'm out of a job," the physician said.

His report to newsmen through a small window at the rear of the trailer, called the Mobile Quarantine Facility, included mention of the astronauts' activities after they awakened this morning from nine hours' sleep.

"They just sat around for a while, eating breakfast and reading The New York Times," Dr. Carpentier said. "Then I ran them through some physical exercises and — well, that was it."

As Dr. Carpentier spoke, Colonel Aldrin appeared behind him, dressed in a white T-

Continued on Page 12, Column 2

Studies to Begin Today

By JOHN NOBLE WILFORD
Special to The New York Times

HOUSTON, July 25 — The treasure of Apollo 11, two boxes of rocks and soil from the moon, arrived here today for the beginning of months of painstaking scientific analysis.

The aluminum boxes, each about the size of a small suitcase, were handled with the care usually accorded priceless jewels and a curiosity not unlike that aroused in the courts of Europe by explorers returning with tobacco, maize and Indians from the New World.

Scientists plan to open the boxes and get their first look at the lunar material tomorrow.

The Apollo 11 astronauts — Neil A. Armstrong, the civilian commander, and Col. Edwin E. Aldrin Jr. and Col. Michael Collins of the Air Force — are scheduled to arrive at nearby Ellington Air Force Base at 2 A.M., Eastern daylight time, Sunday.

The three men, still confined to their Mobile Quarantine Facility, will be taken to quarters in the same sealed building here at the Manned Spacecraft Center in which the rocks and soil are housed. The astronauts' quarantine is to last at least until Aug. 11.

The first box of the lunar

Continued on Page 12, Column 3

ISRAELIS SAY JETS HIT EGYPTIAN GUNS

Canal Raid Is 4th This Week —Cairo Claims 3 Planes

By JAMES FERON
Special to The New York Times

JERUSALEM, July 25—Israeli jets attacked Egyptian artillery positions along the Suez Canal today for the fourth time this week.

An Israeli army communiqué said that the planes were sent in at about 1 o'clock this afternoon to silence Egyptian guns. They bombed and strafed the positions for one hour and a half, the communiqué said.

[In Cairo, a military spokesman said that three of the attacking Israeli planes had been shot down by antiaircraft fire.]

The Israelis said that the operation was conducted without interference from the Egyptian Air Force. Twice this week Egyptian jets have responded with similar assaults on Israeli positions.

According to the communiqué, the Israeli attacks were aimed specifically at the sources of Egyptian artillery fire. This would make it a considerably smaller operation than the earlier raids when ground-to-air missile bases, a radar station and antiaircraft positions were attacked.

Limiting the operation to the

Continued on Page 6, Column 4

MOSCOW REPORTS GROWTH-RATE LAG

But Says Economy Showed a Pickup in 2d Quarter

By BERNARD GWERTZMAN
Special to The New York Times

MOSCOW, July 25—The Soviet Union disclosed figures tonight indicating that its economy had picked up momentum in recent months but was still lagging behind its planned annual growth rate.

According to official statistics on the first six months of the year, published in Izvestia, the Government newspaper, the industrial sector overcame severe difficulties caused in part by a bad winter, and recorded an annual growth rate of 7.8 per cent in the second quarter.

In the first quarter, industry expanded at a 6 per cent rate. This meant that the overall rate for the first half of the year was 6.9 per cent—the figure by which this year's output exceeds last year's. The planned rate for the year was 7.3 per cent. Last year at this time Soviet industry was growing by 9 per cent and in 1967 by 10.6 per cent.

In general, the statistics could bring little encouragement to officials and economists who have been complaining about bottlenecks and waste of resources in the economy. Another key index of the

Continued on Page 2, Column 3

PRIVATE COLLEGES TO GET STATE AID STARTING IN FALL

52 Nonsectarian Institutions to Share $24.1-Million—Church Schools at Issue

By M. S. HANDLER

Fifty-two private, nonsectarian colleges were declared eligible yesterday for state aid without conditions. A state official said it was the first time in the nation that such grants had been made.

The State Department of Education named the 52 institutions eligible under the so-called Bundy Law enacted by the Legislature last year and funded this year.

Under the law, the State will distribute $24,112,000 for the 1969-70 academic year. Of this amount, the 52 institutions will receive $17-million during the current fiscal year and the remainder in fiscal 1970-71.

Although the program goes into effect in September, the allocations were based on $400 for each bachelor's and master's degree and $2,400 for each doctoral degree awarded in the academic year ended in June, 1969.

Financial Relief Sought

The great majority of the eligible institutions are small or medium-sized colleges, many of them suffering severe or acute financial crises, caused by rising salaries and maintenance costs.

The state funding, although modest in most cases, will provide some relief and raised the hope among college administrators that, the principle of state aid having been established, the program would be expanded.

Thirty-three church-affiliated sectarian colleges and universities also applied for funds under the Bundy Law, but the Department of Education said a final decision on their eligibility was still pending.

The 1969 Legislature passed a bill to facilitate state aid to church-affiliated colleges and universities, but Governor Rockefeller vetoed the measure. He said he was obliged to do so because the bill would violate the State Constitution.

Rockefeller Committee

The Bundy Law was named for McGeorge Bundy, the president of the Ford Foundation, who headed a select committee appointed by Governor Rockefeller and the Board of Regents to study aid to private institutions. Other committee members were James B. Conant, president emeritus of Harvard University; John A. Hanna, the president of Michigan State University; the Rev. Theodore M. Hesburgh, the president of the University of Notre Dame, and Abram L. Sacher, the chancellor of Brandeis University.

The major private universities received the biggest allocations, of course, because they awarded the most degrees. The biggest allocations were to New York University, $4,400,000; Columbia, $3,234,000; Syracuse, $2,462,000; Cornell, $1,260,400, and Teachers College, Columbia University, $1,192,000.

Program a U. S. First

In announcing the grants, Ewald B. Nyquist, Acting State Commisssioner of Education, said the state was the first to provide unrestricted financial assistance to its private nonsectarian four-year colleges.

"I believe this new program will help maintain an appropriate balance between public and private institutions and sustain private initiative in providing educational opportunity for students of New York State," he said.

Mr. Nyquist termed the Bundy law "precedent-setting legislation."

It is the smaller institutions throughout the country that are said to be suffering severe

Continued on Page 15, Column 5

SENATE ABM FOES RELY ON M'INTYRE

They Hope That His Speech on Monday Will Retrieve the Initiative in Debate

By JOHN W. FINNEY
Special to The New York Times

WASHINGTON, July 25—The opposition to the proposed Safeguard antiballistic missile system, on the defensive for the last week, believes it is about to recapture the initiative by picking up the vote of Thomas J. McIntyre, one of the uncommitted Senators.

Senator McIntyre, a New Hampshire Democrat, is scheduled to announce in a Senate speech Monday that he will vote for the opposition amendment prohibiting any deployment of the Safeguard system in the coming year.

With Senator McIntyre included, the opposition believes it can count on at least 49 votes—or just two short of a bare majority—against the Administration's deployment plan.

Administration spokesmen in the Senate say they have a minimum of 51 votes for Safeguard deployment. But included in this claim appear to be some uncommitted or wavering Senators who may go with the opposition.

In the narrowly divided Senate, therefore, the outcome of the issue continues to turn on a few wavering or uncommitted Senators, such as Clinton P. Anderson, Democrat of New Mexico; John J. Williams, Re-

Continued on Page 4, Column 3

Rival Ice Cream Vender Held In Mister Softee Holdup Case

By MICHAEL STERN

A competitor of a Mister Softee ice cream distributor was named by the Bronx District Attorney yesterday as the "kingpin" of the six-man armed gang that held up a Mister Softee garage July 2 and incapacitated 39 trucks.

The competitor, a distributor of Freezer Fresh soft ice cream, was arrested on a five-count indictment handed up Thursday by a Bronx County grand jury.

"This was an effort to cripple a business rival," said Burton B. Roberts, the prosecutor. Mr. Roberts said Freezer Fresh had been losing drivers who sold its products on the streets of Brooklyn to the Mister Softee concern and had resorted to old-style gangland muscle tactics to recoup its position.

The accused man is Salvatore Fariello, 40 years old, of 2335 Legion Street, Bellmore, L. I., the father of three children. Also named in the indictment were Lawrence Siniscalchi, a Brooklyn carpenter, who was arrested Wednesday, and a third man who is now a fugitive.

Mr. Roberts identified the fugitive as Robert England, a 35-year-old laborer of 35 Vermont Street, Brooklyn, who also has three children. He was described as blond, blue-eyed, 5 feet 10 inches tall and weighing 195 pounds. He is being sought by the police along with three other suspects who have not yet been named.

The motive given by Mr. Roberts was the first official expla-

Continued on Page 15, Column 2

NEWS INDEX

1969

Judy Garland, star of both screen and stage, died of an overdose of sleeping pills at 47. But she left us a legacy—her daughter Liza Minnelli.

The bridge at Chappaquiddick where the enigmatic death of Mary Jo Kopechne occurred. The accused Ted Kennedy told a televised audience his version of the tragedy.

Former President Dwight Eisenhower waved from his hospital room on his 78th birthday. He died five months later.

Supreme Court Justice Abe Fortas was forced off the bench by open demands from the Senate and pressure from the press—a first.

"All the News That's Fit to Print"

The New York Times

LATE CITY EDITION

Weather: Cloudy, warm and humid, showers likely through tomorrow. Temp. range: today 88-75; Saturday 89-74. Temp.-Hum. Index yesterday 81. Complete U.S. report on Page 83.

SECTION ONE

VOL. CXVIII . . No. 40,748 — NEW YORK, SUNDAY, AUGUST 17, 1969 — 50 CENTS

60c beyond 50-mile zone from New York City, except Long Island. 75c beyond 200-mile radius. Higher in air delivery cities.

The New York Times (by Jack Manning)

MUSIC WAS THE MAGNET for throngs at Woodstock Music and Art Fair. Towers near the stage hold loudspeakers.

300,000 at Folk-Rock Fair Camp Out in a Sea of Mud

By BARNARD L. COLLIER

Special to The New York Times

BETHEL, N.Y., Aug. 16—Despite massive traffic jams, drenching rainstorms and shortages of food, water and medical facilities, about 300,000 young people swarmed over this rural area today for the Woodstock Music and Art Fair.

Drawn by such performers as Joan Baez, Ravi Shankar, Jimi Hendrix and the Jefferson Airplane, the prospect of drugs and the excitement of "making the scene," the young people came in droves, camping in the woods, romping in the mud, talking, smoking and listening to the wailing music.

Looking out over 20 acres of youths squeezed body to body, the festival's organizers, the state police and officials of the Sullivan County Sheriff's office agreed that the crowd was over 300,000.

Participants Well-Behaved

The crowd, which camped on the 600-acre farm of Max Yasgur near here for the three-day festival, was well-behaved, according to both the sponsors and the police, even though about 75 persons in the area were arrested, mostly on charges of possessing narcotics.

Most of the hip, swinging youngsters heard the music on stage only as a distant rumble. It was almost impossible for them to tell who was performing and probably only about half the crowd could hear a note. Yet they stayed by the thousands, often standing ankle-deep in mud, sometimes paying enterprising peddlers 25 cents for a glass of water.

Roadways leading from the site were lined tonight with thousands of weary-looking youths who had had enough, and were trying to reach places where they could get food or transportation.

During the first 24 hours of the fair, festival medical officers said that a thousand people had been treated at first-aid stations for various ailments, including exposure and a few accident cases. About 300 were ill because of adverse drug reactions.

Doctors Fly to Scene

A dozen doctors, responding to a plea from the fair's sponsors, flew from New York to the scene, about 70 miles northwest of the city, near the Catskill Mountain resorts of Liberty and Monticello.

Michael Lang, the 24-year-old producer of the event, said that the medical help was summoned not because of any widespread illnesses, but because of the potential threat of a virus cold or pneumonia epidemic among such a large gathering.

Parked cars jammed roadways in all directions for up to 20 miles, and thousands of festival-goers, weary after long walks to get here, had to spend the night sleeping on the rain-soaked ground. They awoke to find food and water shortages.

But Mr. Lang said this afternoon: "It's about the quietest, most well-behaved 300,000 people in one place that can be imagined. There have been no fights or incidents of violence of any kind."

A state police official agreed. "I was dumfounded by the size of the crowd," he

Continued on Page 80, Column 1

VARIED DRUG LAWS RAISING U.S. FEARS

Justice Agency Dismayed as Some States Crack Down While Others Ease View

By MARTIN ARNOLD

Many State Legislatures across the country, trying to come to grips with the nation's growing narcotic problems, this year are passing diverse and sometimes contradictory laws that are causing considerable dismay within the Justice Department.

"We are delighted with the concern over drug abuse but I'm afraid that the contradictory laws will hinder rather than help Federal narcotic enforcement," said Anthony J. Roccograndi, assistant chief counsel of the Justice Department's Bureau of Narcotics and Dangerous Drugs.

Actions by the States

Because of this concern, the Justice Department is trying to sell the various states on the idea of a model state drug control act, which would standardize narcotic and drug laws throughout the land and bring them into closer conformity with Federal laws.

But the department declines to specify precisely what it wants in the model act and is delaying intensive efforts to obtain support for one until Congress acts on the narcotic abuse proposals that President Nixon sent to Congress on July 14.

At least 20 states this year have either passed new laws on narcotic abuse or amended old laws while about 20 other states have seriously debated legislation.

Meanwhile, at least 10 states

Continued on Page 60, Column 1

Majority on Relief Are White on L.I. And in Westchester

By AGIS SALPUKAS

More than half the people receiving welfare money in Nassau, Suffolk and Westchester Counties are white, many of them ironic victims of a search for a better life in the suburbs.

"It's a myth that welfare recipients in the suburbs are mostly black, living in ghettos," said Joseph Barbaro, the Commissioner of Social Services of Nassau County, in a recent interview.

The myth has been sustained, he added, because white welfare recipients generally try to hide their circumstances. They avoid protest demonstrations, surplus food centers and, in many cases, continue to live in the middle-class houses that started their financial difficulties.

Their mortgage payments are often taken care of by welfare grants—because, according to welfare officials, most of the time it is cheaper than trying to relocate a family.

Instead of trying to "keep up with the Joneses" many now struggle to keep up minimal appearances out of fear that their immediate neighbors will dis-

Continued on Page 68, Column 3

MAYORS WELCOME NIXON'S AID PLANS BUT DOUBT IMPACT

Call Urban Proposals Steps in Right Direction, but Say Funds Are Inadequate

By ROBERT M. SMITH

Special to The New York Times

WASHINGTON, Aug. 16—The mayors of 11 major cities across the nation think the legislative approach that President Nixon has proposed might solve some of their problems, but they wonder what it will do for the major troubles that afflict their cities.

To a man, however, the mayors applaud the fact that the President has made new and concrete proposals to deal with the problems of the nation's urban areas.

As Atlanta's Mayor Ivan Allen Jr., a Democrat, put it: "The significance of President Nixon's welfare reforms is that they are the first real attempt to view the needs of the poor in light of current problems, not circumstances which existed in the Depression."

"They represent a change from an outmoded public assistance program to a flexible system for a rapidly changing society."

A Minimum Standard

The Mayor of Dallas, Erik Jonsson, said there were certain to be objections to the President's proposals, but they are "an intelligent, sincere approach to a beginning—the Administration has taken the position that they have to try."

As for the money that the proposals would bring in to the cities, Mr. Jonsson said, "The total may move a small mountain, but not a big one."

Mayors in several cities across the nation were asked by correspondents for The New York Times to give their views on President Nixon's urban package — the proposals on welfare reform and manpower training, revenue sharing and mass transit.

The mayors who commented were those of New York, Albany, Atlanta, Dallas, Baltimore, Houston, Jackson, Miss., New Orleans, Philadelphia, San Francisco, and St. Louis.

Some of the mayors said it was too early to gauge precisely how the new programs would affect their cities. However, most of them said the amount of money involved was inadequate to meet their problems.

For example, Baltimore's Mayor Thomas J. D'Alesandro 3d, a Democrat, noted that his

Continued on Page 69, Column 4

Associated Press

AT CHECKPOINT IN BELFAST: British soldiers check parcel before letting residents pass in a Catholic area.

Most Materiel in Vietnam To Go With U.S. Forces

By JAMES P. STERBA

Special to The New York Times

SAIGON, South Vietnam, Aug. 16 — Plans for the Vietnamization of the war effort call for the turnover of only a small fraction of the equipment now being used by United States forces here.

High-level military planners in charge of reductions in American troops and supplies said recently that the largest part of the fighting equipment—such as helicopters, tanks, trucks and artillery—was expected to be distributed among other American military installations in Southeast Asia or sent to other military assistance programs in the Pacific.

These planners stressed that the "legitimate needs" of the Vietnamese armed forces would be filled. In other words, the South Vietnamese would not be left to carry on the war without sufficient equipment.

Much Would Be Useless

However, the planners said that since the training of the South Vietnamese forces was not expected to be upgraded to anywhere near the level that of the United States forces, much of the advanced equipment used by Americans would be of no value to Saigon's forces.

According to one military official, 80 to 90 per cent of the "legitimate needs" of the South Vietnamese forces have already been filled. These needs include M-16 rifles, mortars and some light-artillery equipment carried by individual soldiers, jeeps, trucks and some aircraft.

Limited amounts of heavy, more advanced equipment can be expected to be turned over to the South Vietnamese in the next two years as operation and maintenance training programs are completed.

Only Part of Equipment

The key factor in the turnover program is the amount of time left for the Americans to train the South Vietnamese, the planners said. The longer the hostilities drag on, the more time there will be to train the South Vietnamese.

Both a peace settlement and a hastened American pullout would cause a curtailment in programs to upgrade the quality and increase the number of South Vietnamese specialists in the operation and maintenance of aircraft, radar networks, electronic-sensing gear, communications equipment and complicated vehicles such as diesel trucks and earth-movers and ships, these planners said.

But even if these programs are completed on schedule, they involve only a tiny fraction of the American equipment in South Vietnam.

The planners emphasized that United States military needs had first priority. Although priorities next on the list were not made known, officials said that teams from American military-assistance programs in

Continued on Page 8, Column 1

SHOTS AND FIRES PLAGUE BELFAST FOR THIRD NIGHT

Two More Catholics Die—Blazes Engulf Textile Mill and Plastics Factory

BUT CAPITAL IS QUIETER

British Troops on Patrol—Wilson to Cut Vacation for Talks in London

By JOHN M. LEE

Special to The New York Times

BELFAST, Northern Ireland, Aug. 16—Several shooting incidents plagued riot-torn Belfast today as armed British soldiers patrolled barbed-wire barricades around militant Roman Catholic areas. Armored cars with mounted machine guns were stationed in narrow side streets.

Fire engulfed a textile mill and plastics factory in a Catholic district. Militant Protestant youths erected barricades of burned cars and oil drums in their streets, and small boys joined in the looting of a burned-out candy store.

But late tonight Belfast was quieter than it had been in two days. Just before midnight the police said there had been no casualties today.

Pub Crowds Missing

Dark streets in the downtown area and in the segregated riot areas were empty of the usual Saturday night pub crowds. Hardly any traffic was moving and nothing was open. Even the militant Protestant areas, patrolled by the part-time special policemen, often criticized as Protestant partisans, were deserted.

John McGrath, a Catholic asphalt contractor, had trouble getting through the troops and police to his home, and he stopped for a moment and said: "It looks like the troops are finally calming it down, but the divisions are greater than ever."

Earlier, additional units of British troops were requested and sent into Belfast to reinforce those sent yesterday. An army spokesman refused to disclose their numbers.

Death Toll Put at 8

Two more men died from gunshot wounds received earlier, bringing the total riot deaths since Thursday to eight. All have been Catholics. A 15-year-old boy died last night.

The latest police figures for injuries in the 24 hours ending at 8 A.M. were 236 persons, including 4 policemen. Of these, 66 had been shot, mostly by shotguns.

The continuing violence and the mounting intervention of British troops have precipitated a three-way political crisis touching the British Government, the locally autonomous Government of Northern Ireland, which is united with Britain, and the Republic of Ireland to the south.

The Prime Minister of Northern Ireland, which is commonly known as Ulster, Maj. James

Continued on Page 3, Column 1

Today's Sections

Index to Subjects

Survey Finds Public Concerned That Discipline in Schools Is Lax

By M. A. FARBER

A major Gallup survey has concluded that the chief complaint against public schools is that students do not receive enough discipline, that the nation is about evenly divided in its willingness to pay more for the schools and that Americans are "ill-informed about education itself."

Spokesmen for the Gallup organization in Princeton, N. J., said that the survey, "based upon a representative sampling of all adults in the country," was the "most extensive" it had conducted on the subject. Officials of the National Education Association in Washington said it was also the most comprehensive survey they knew of.

Another Gallup poll, made public today, reported that 44 per cent of those interviewed believed that racial integration in the public schools was going "too fast," while 22 per cent said it was "not fast enough" and 25 per cent said it was "about right." That poll also showed that the percentage of white parents who would object to sending their children to schools with Negro pupils was generally declining.

The survey of adult public opinion and knowledge of public schools was conducted last February for C.F.K., Ltd., of Denver, a nonprofit educational group headed by Charles F. Kettering 2d.

The Gallup organization said it had found that the teaching profession "has probably never been held in higher esteem" and that the public had accepted the right of teachers to join

Continued on Page 66, Column 3

Student and Puerto Rican, 25, Appointed Trustees of City U.

Jean-Louis d'Heilly — Maria Josefa Canino

The New York Times

By MAURICE CARROLL

A 28-year-old student at the City University and a 25-year-old graduate were appointed by Mayor Lindsay yesterday to the Board of Higher Education.

The appointments gave the board, whose members average about 60 years in age, its first student and its two youngest members.

The student, Jean-Louis d'Heilly, first met Mayor Lindsay when he was organizing a demonstration against Mayor Lindsay.

The graduate, 25-year-old Maria Josefa Canino, has been active in Puerto Rican community organizations since she was a teen-ager.

Miss Canino succeeds Dr. John E. Conboy, who, according to the Mayor's announcement, asked not to be reappointed. The recent retirement of Henry E. Schultz, whose term ran until 1971, leaves board membership at 20, including the two new appointees.

Early on Friday morning, each of the new appointees got a personal telephone call from Mayor Lindsay to tell them of their appointments to the 21-

Continued on Page 36, Column 1

Refugees Gather at 2 Camps in Ireland

By ALVIN SHUSTER

Special to The New York Times

GORMANSTON, Ireland, Aug. 16—A 75-year-old man, his hands shaking and eyes staring, sat on the wooden bench in front of the army barracks numbered 47-A.

The voice over the loudspeaker blared the announcement that "dinner for civilians will be served at half past one in the dining room."

Children, as if on vacation, climbed over fences and played in the dirt before the white brick building marked with a hastily prepared sign, "Civilian Rest Center," and furnished with lounge chairs and a television set.

Soldiers carried the metal frames of army cots past mothers pushing baby carriages.

This army camp, built by the Canadians in World War I, is now the home of the latest members of the world refugee population. And, like other refugees elsewhere in the world, they tell stories of fear, violence, bitterness and bewilderment.

The camp, which was occupied until last week by reservists in summer training, is the larger of the two refugee centers set up this week by Ireland for Roman Catholics fleeing the sectarian violence in Northern Ireland.

Yesterday 22 refugees had arrived. By this morning, 150—about half of them children—were living in the austere and damp quarters as temporary refugees. They did not bring their worldly possessions, just enough for a few days. Their intention is to return to Northern Ireland when calm returns.

Moreover, they do not represent the total number of Catholics who have left their homes to come south during the crisis. Many others, perhaps hundreds, have traveled to Ireland to stay temporarily with relatives and friends.

For the moment there is little to do here. Dublin is 23 miles away, and the Irish Sea just a few minutes walk past the volleyball court and the officers' mess. But the weather was cloudy and cool today, and no one felt like swimming.

"The women here want to help," said an army officer. "They want to cook. But we are not used to that kind of help. We'll prepare their meals and help them all we can."

They came by car, train and bus, sometimes helped by Catholic civil rights workers. There are no restrictions at the border except for a routine check by Irish customs officials. British customs officials meet travelers from the south. There are similar checks at rail and air

Continued on Page 3, Column 1

The music festival at Woodstock brought together all elements of the Youth Movement of the Sixties.

Mick Jagger of the Rolling Stones on stage at Altamont where a Hells Angel guard mauled an overzealous fan. Another victim was a reputed Black Panther, murdered by an Angel at the scene.

It was the electric Jimi Hendrix's last year. He died in 1970 from an overdose of drugs.

Students at Berkeley headed for class alongside National Guardsmen who inhabited the campus after bloody rioting.

"All the News That's Fit to Print"

The New York Times

LATE CITY EDITION

Weather: Fair, cool today. Partly cloudy and cool through tomorrow. Temp. range: today 65-47; Wed. 64-46. Full U.S. report on Page 96.

VOL. CXIX..No. 40,908 · NEW YORK, THURSDAY, OCTOBER 16, 1969 · 10 CENTS

VIETNAM MORATORIUM OBSERVED NATIONWIDE BY FOES OF THE WAR; RALLIES HERE CROWDED, ORDERLY

The New York Times (by William E. Sauro)

OBSERVING MORATORIUM: Senator Eugene J. McCarthy, Minnesota Democrat, addressing crowds in Bryant Park

METS TRIUMPH, 2-1, ON ERROR IN 10TH; LEAD SERIES BY 3-1

Wild Throw Following Bunt by Martin Lets In Run—Orioles Gain Tie in 9th

SEAVER IS THE WINNER

Brilliant Catch by Swoboda Helps—Clendenon Hits Homer in 2d Inning

By JOSEPH DURSO

The New York Mets moved to within one victory of the pot of gold yesterday when they defeated the Baltimore Orioles, 2-1, in 10 innings and took a lead of three games to one in the World Series.

The victory was the third straight for the underdog Mets over the champions of the American League and it was laced with potent doses of the "magic" that has marked their fantastic surge to the top in 1969.

They led, 1-0, going into the ninth inning behind the three-hit pitching of Tom Seaver. Then they were caught when the Orioles tied the game, but were saved from losing it by a tumbling backhand catch by Ron Swoboda.

One Step Closer

Finally, an inning later, they scored the winning run with the help of the sun's glare, a 10-foot bunt and a wild throw to first base on an illegal play detected by neither the Orioles nor the umpires (Details on Page 59).

The Mets' latest adventure was witnessed by 57,367 persons, a record paying crowd for Shea Stadium, and it left them in a commanding position to win the championship of baseball one year after they had "advanced" to ninth place.

They will try to nail down the title this afternoon at 1 o'clock, with Jerry Koosman pitching against Dave McNally of the Orioles. If they don't, the Series will return to Baltimore for the final game or games this weekend.

The Mets' astounding success was matched by a series of unlikely upsets for the Orioles, who won their divisional championship by 19 games and were ranked as one of the most powerful teams of modern times:

¶Until the Orioles scored in the ninth inning, they had been shut out for 19 straight innings—and this was a team that had been held scoreless only eight times in 162 games this season.

¶Even after they teased home a run in the ninth, they still had crossed home plate only twice in their last 32 innings.

Continued on Page 58, Column 2

Bishop Sheen, 74, Resigns Post in Rochester Diocese

Will Return to New York for TV and Other Work —Successor Is Named

The New York Times

Bishop Fulton J. Sheen at news conference yesterday.

By JOSEPH LELYVELD

Special to The New York Times

ROCHESTER, Oct. 15 — The Most Rev. Fulton J. Sheen resigned today as Bishop of Rochester after a three-year tenure and was immediately succeeded by Msgr. Joseph L. Hogan, whose appointment was announced by Pope Paul VI in Rome.

"I am resigning the diocese," said Bishop Sheen who is 74 years old. "I am not resigning work. I am not retiring, I am regenerating." The Vatican announced his appointment as titular archbishop of Newport, England, which now exists as a diocese only on paper.

Bishop Sheen, who presented his successor at a news conference here this morning, ended his tenure on a general note of frustration and disappointment for himself and his flock.

Bishop Sheen said he could recite a "long litany" of his failures here. He said it was up to others to cite any successes he may have had, but he mentioned specifically the certified auditing of the diocese's finances, consultation with his priests on new appointments and the purchase of homes for 14 indigent slum families.

"I move too fast," he said, alluding to his concern with the conditions of slum blacks. "I'm a little too progressive."

A proselytizer used to reaching a mass audience of millions by means of television, Bishop Sheen was widely criticized in his upstate diocese for failing to communicate with ordinary parishioners.

"He stirred the whole dio-

Continued on Page 50, Column 5

A MIDDLE COURSE IS URGED BY COOKE AT BISHOPS' SYNOD

He Stresses Need for Both Papal Supremacy and the Principle of Collegiality

By ROBERT C. DOTY

Special to The New York Times

ROME, Oct. 15 — Cardinal Cooke, Archbishop of New York, urged the Roman Catholic Synod of Bishops today to consider the present period of "stress and strain" in the church "frankly and positively, with great charity."

The 48-year-old New York prelate, first from the United States to speak at the meeting here, made what most observers construed as a middle-of-the-road approach to the issue of balance between papal power and the collegial power of the bishops as a whole.

He spoke on the third day of the synod, which seems to be moving toward consensus on the idea that the Roman Pontiff, whatever his right to rule alone, should, as a practical matter, seek and follow the advice of the bishops on major problems affecting the entire church.

Birth Control Dissent Cited

At least three prelates have cited the storm of dissent that followed issuance of the renewed ban on birth control by Pope Paul VI in July, 1968, as the consequence of failure to associate the bishops with the decision-making process.

Cardinal Cooke limited himself today to describing the nature of the questions to be resolved without suggesting answers beyond a general proposal for "closer cooperative activity and improved communications" between the Vatican and the bishops.

Cardinal Cooke said that both the principle of supreme power of the Pope, declared by a church council a century ago, and that of "collegiality," rule of the church by the Pope with the bishops, were essential to a church in a time of transition.

Sharing of Power Stressed

Sharing of power by the bishops was important, he said, to a world increasingly conscious of the worth of the individual and increasingly suspicious of decisions made unilaterally, of adherence to tradition and of unity for its own sake.

On the other hand, he said, in an age of "socialization" and interdependence, papal authority provides the essential coordination of effort. An age of pluralism would threaten to become chaotic unless there were someone "to discern the truth and indicate what is essential to the faith," he said.

Cardinal Cooke went on to list the problems: the role of the bishops in guiding the church with the Pope, the role of the local bishop, and the proper interaction between the Pope and the bishops in delineating doctrine more clearly.

He suggested that the new international commission of theologians might help find the answers to these questions.

This was the solution proposed forcefully by Julius Cardinal Döpfner, Archbishop of

Continued on Page 4, Column 1

POLICEMAN SLAYS SOMALI PRESIDENT

Assassin Seized After Shot Kills Shermarke Instantly —Curfew in Mogadiscio

By Reuters.

MOGADISCIO, Somalia, Oct. 15—President Abdirashid Ali Shermarke of Somalia was assassinated today by a member of the police force, an official announcement said here.

The announcement said that a man had been arrested and accused of the murder at Las Anod in northern Somalia, where the President was touring an area stricken by drought. No reason for the assassination was suggested.

Authorities imposed a dusk-to-dawn curfew in Mogadiscio, the capital of the East African country, which became a republic in 1960.

The President, who would have been 50 years old tomorrow, was said to have died instantly. His body was being flown to Mogadiscio as the Somali Council of Ministers was called into emergency session.

Acting Premier Yassin Nur Hassan, speaking for the Council of Ministers in the absence of Premier Mohammed Ibrahim

Continued on Page 6, Column 1

Senate Unit Drops Two Oil Reforms From the Tax Bill

By EILEEN SHANAHAN

Special to The New York Times

WASHINGTON, Oct. 15—The Senate Finance Committee dropped from the tax reform bill today two sections that would have increased the Treasury's annual collections from oil companies by about $65-million.

The provisions that were dropped from the bill, which has been passed by the House of Representatives, involved the credit that American companies may take on their United States tax returns for taxes paid to a foreign government.

The decision to eliminate the two sections was made, according to committee officials, by a "rather decisive" margin.

Corporations other than oil companies are affected by the provisions, but to a much lesser degree.

The decision on the foreign tax credit is the first that the committee has reached in its work on the reform bill that involves the oil industry. It has not yet considered the question of lowering the 27½ per cent depletion allowance — or other reforms in the House bill that would raise the oil industry's taxes.

In other actions today, the

Continued on Page 40, Column 3

DISSENSION IN CITY

Lindsay Leads Protest and Is Met by Jeers as Well as Cheers

By HOMER BIGART

Peace rallies drew throngs to the city's streets, parks, campuses and churches yesterday in an outpouring of protest against the Vietnam war.

The Times Square area was hit by a colossal traffic jam during the evening rush hour as tens of thousands of demonstrators marched to the culminating event of the day—a rally in Bryant Park, west of the New York Public Library.

The park was saturated with people, many of them unable to see the speaker's stand or hear the denunciations of war by Mayor Lindsay and Senators Charles E. Goodell, Jacob K. Javits and Eugene J. McCarthy.

Mayor Lindsay had decreed a day of mourning. His involvement was bitterly assailed by his political opponents and by many who felt that the nationwide demonstrations were not only embarrassing President Nixon's efforts to negotiate an honorable peace but were giving aid and comfort to the enemy as well.

Flag Dispute at Shea

The Mayor encountered cheers and jeers as he led the protest in the city. State Senator John J. Marchi, his Republican-Conservative rival in the mayoral race, saw the demonstrations as "a strike against America" and "a New York version of Dunkirk."

The dissension even reached World Series level. At Shea Stadium, just before the start of the fourth series game between the Mets and the Orioles, an impasse threatened the pregame flag-raising ceremony.

The Mayor had directed that flags on all city properties be flown at half-staff. Shea Stadium is owned by the city.

But just before the ceremony, the military color guard and 225 wounded Vietnam war veterans announced they would not participate unless the flag was flown full-staff.

Baseball Commissioner Bowie

Continued on Page 20, Column 2

Protests Staged in Capital As Nixon and Aides Meet

Thousands Mark Day

By E. W. KENWORTHY

Special to The New York Times

WASHINGTON, Oct. 15 — President Nixon discussed Latin America, inflation and domestic hunger with his advisers today while thousands of Government workers, students businessmen, lawyers, and housewives in the nation's capital petitioned him to pursue peace in Vietnam.

Tonight the capital's Vietnam Moratorium was brought to the gates of the White House itself, when tens of thousands of persons marched to the President's mansion.

The day's culminating demonstration began with a rally on the grounds of the Washington Monument, where Mrs. Martin Luther King Jr. addressed a throng estimated by the park police at 22,000. From there a solemn procession began, led by Mrs. King, and it soon stretched from the monument grounds to the White House, where Mrs. King paused and lit a candle on a glass-globed stand and then moved on.

It was a quite, almost funereal march, but here and there could be heard soft singing and chants. It was predominantly young, predominantly white, but here and there could be seen the middle-aged and, throughout, a scattering of blacks, their candles flickering against a light, chill wind.

For more than two hours, the throng filed by threes out of the monument grounds and

Continued on Page 18, Column 2

A Pledge by Humphrey

By SETH S. KING

Special to The New York Times

MINNEAPOLIS, Oct. 15 — Former Vice President Hubert H. Humphrey said today he had promised President Nixon that, as the leader of the Democratic party, he would never say, "You are the man who lost the war."

"As head of the Democratic party—and, by God, I am the leader of the party—I didn't want him to worry about me stabbing him in the back later," Mr. Humphrey declared.

The former Vice President met with Mr. Nixon on Friday at the White House. After the meeting, Mr. Humphrey said that he believed Mr. Nixon was on the right path toward ending the Vietnam war and that he would support the President as long as he stayed on this path.

"I told him that if he takes the steps that are needed to end the war, he can depend on Hubert H. Humphrey to support him, and I said I would put that in a letter if he wanted it and sign it," Mr. Humphrey said.

The former Vice President said he was astounded that the President had not offered the North Vietnamese a cease-fire. He said it could be assumed that this had been discussed in Mr. Nixon's presence.

"I encouraged the President to speak to the nation about the war, and I hope that he will have something to say to us in the speech he had scheduled for

Continued on Page 18, Column 3

OPPONENTS REACT

Many Show Support for Nixon by Flying Flags Full-Staff

By JOHN HERBERS

Protests ranging from noisy street rallies to silent prayer vigils and involving a broad spectrum of the population were held across the nation yesterday in an effort to demonstrate the growing public opposition to the war in Vietnam.

Only scattered incidents of violence marred the outpourings of small and vast crowds in which the black armband was the standard symbol.

The Vietnam Moratorium—which began as a national protest by college students and spilled over to include such groups as the United Automobile Workers union and the Pittsburgh City Council—was termed an overwhelming success by its planners, the youthful members of the Vietnam Moratorium Committee.

But it also demonstrated the great divisions in American society created by the prolonged American involvement in Southeast Asia. The demonstrations generated counter protests in some areas, and some supporters of the war who had been quiet for months spoke out in anger.

Largest Protest So Far

It was the largest public protest of the many that have been held against the Vietnam war. Historians in the Library of Congress said that as a nationally coordinated antiwar demonstration it was unique.

There was no way to estimate immediately the total numbers involved, but counting the demonstrators, the children who stayed out of school, the workers who did not report for their jobs, those who did and wore armbands and those who prayed in homes and churches, possibly millions were involved.

The demonstrations drew largely on students and other youths, the middle class and professional groups. Blue-collar workers and Negroes did not participate in great numbers, even though unions such as the United Auto Workers and the United Shoeworkers of American endorsed the moratorium. In a number of communities blue-collar workers made up the active opposition to the moratorium.

The Pentagon's civil disturbance command post termed the

Continued on Page 18, Column 5

The New York Times (by Patrick A. Burns)

THE WINNING PLAY: J. C. Martin of Mets (9) racing to first base after laying down a bunt in the tenth inning. The throw from Pete Richert (34), Orioles' pitcher, hit Martin and bounced away, allowing Rod Gaspar to score from second. The umpire is Lou DiMuro.

Eisenhower Dollar Voted by Congress

By PETER GROSE

Special to The New York Times

WASHINGTON, Oct. 15 — Congress voted today to coin a new dollar that would honor former President Dwight D. Eisenhower, but the Senate and House of Representatives differed on whether it should be a silver dollar.

Flourishing a letter from Mrs. Eisenhower, a group of Western legislators got the Senate to override the Administration's proposal to produce a copper and nickel coin. A similar effort, backed by the same letter, failed in the House, which opted for the Administration's non-silver dollar.

Mrs. Eisenhower's letter disclosed that the former President had loved to collect and distribute silver dollars as

Continued on Page 24, Column 4

Pacification in Rural Vietnam Making Big but Fragile Gains

By TERENCE SMITH

Special to The New York Times

SAIGON, South Vietnam, Oct. 15—The road that runs south from Saigon to Cantho is clogged these days with trucks and cars that rattle along with careless abandon.

Sixteen months ago, in the wake of the Lunar New Year offensive, a drive along the stretch between Mytho and Cantho was a perilous adventure. Vietcong guerrillas regularly planted mines under the pavement and floated explosives under the bridges. In the evening and early morning snipers fired at passing cars from the trees lining the road.

Today, as an extensive auto trip has confirmed, the only danger along Route 4 is the traffic, which is dreadful, and the potholes, which can shatter an axle.

The improved security along the road is one of the more visible examples of the progress achieved over the last year by the allied pacification program. While the enemy has concentrated his attacks on military targets, the $600-million-a-year effort to secure and develop the South Vietnamese countryside has proceeded almost without opposition.

The gains during the period have been striking. Rural security has been greatly increased—although American officials concede that it is still fragile—and the Saigon Government's control now reaches deeper into the countryside than it has for at least two years.

The expanded security in the

Continued on Page 12, Column 1

NEWS INDEX

"All the News That's Fit to Print"

The New York Times

LATE CITY EDITION

Weather: Sunny and mild today. Fair, mild through tomorrow. Temp. range: today 59-38; Wed. 53-36. Full U.S. report on Page 94.

VOL. CXIX . . No. 40,822 © 1969 The New York Times Company. NEW YORK, THURSDAY, OCTOBER 30, 1969 10 CENTS

SCHOOL INTEGRATION 'AT ONCE' IS ORDERED BY SUPREME COURT; NIXON BID FOR DELAY REJECTED

FIRST BURGER CASE

'All Deliberate Speed' Decision Voided in Mississippi Action

Text of the Supreme Court's opinion is on Page 34.

By WARREN WEAVER Jr.
Special to The New York Times

WASHINGTON, Oct. 29—The Supreme Court ruled unanimously today that school districts must end segregation "at once" and operate integrated systems "now and hereafter."

The decision will unquestionably apply to Southern states where dual educational systems exist. The initial reaction of most legal authorities in the civil rights area was that it would not affect de facto segregation in Northern cities.

The Court replaced its 14-year-old decision that school desegregation should proceed with "all deliberate speed" with a new and much more rigorous standard: immediate compliance.

The effect of today's decision is to write a legal end to the period during which courts have entertained various excuses for failure to integrate Southern schools. Its basic message was integrate now, litigate later.

The decision was a stinging setback for the Nixon Administration. The Justice Department had argued less than a week ago that delays were permissible in requiring integration in some districts and that providing a continuing education should take precedence over enforcing social justice.

View Rejected

The Court rejected this view unanimously in a two-page unsigned opinion.

The Court, which had heard the case on an expedited basis, released its decree in printed form as soon as it could be prepared rather than wait until Monday, its customary decision day.

It was the first major decision handed down by the Court with Warren E. Burger sitting as Chief Justice. He is President Nixon's first appointee to the Court, a man chosen to help restore a measure of conservative balance to the tribunal.

The ruling specifically affected 33 school districts in Mississippi, but its broad language will be a precedent for all pending Court cases involving school segregation and in all future suits that may be filed.

In the Mississippi cases, the Supreme Court held, all requests for additional time to present desegregation plans should have been denied "because continued operation of segregated schools under a standard of allowing 'all deliberate speed' for desegrega-

Continued on Page 34, Column 1

PRESIDENTIAL SUPPORT: President Nixon with Representative William T. Cahill, Republican candidate for Governor of New Jersey, in Hackensack High School last night. Jason Laure

U.A.R. TO MEDIATE LEBANESE DISPUTE WITH GUERRILLAS

Beirut Negotiators in Cairo Are Reported Amenable to Loosening Controls

A CEASE-FIRE ARRANGED

Arafat Is Invited to Egypt to Represent Palestinians in the Discussions

By RAYMOND H. ANDERSON
Special to The New York Times

CAIRO, Oct. 29—The United Arab Republic announced tonight that it had agreed to undertake full-scale mediation in the conflict between the Lebanese Government and Palestinian guerrillas.

Lebanese negotiators, led by Gen. Emil Bustani, the head of the armed forces, who arrived here last night for urgent talks, were said to have offered specific measures for ending the dispute and "creating a good basis for a solution of the crisis."

No details of the Lebanese proposals were made public, but there were reports that the Beirut authorities were amenable to loosening controls over the guerrillas. However, Beirut was said to have wanted assurances of complete coordination, committing the Palestinians to inform the army of plans for operations across the frontier into Israel.

Government's Aim Reported

It was also said that the Government hoped to achieve an agreement restricting the guerrillas to certain sparsely settled regions.

[In Beirut, officials confirmed a report broadcast by the Fatah radio that the Lebanese Army and the guerrillas had agreed to a 24-hour cease-fire, which began at noon Wednesday. The object appeared to be to give the Cairo talks a chance to begin under favorable conditions.]

The Lebanese mission in Cairo was said to have assured the Egyptians of "complete understanding and goodwill to cooperate with the commandos."

Fighting broke out in Lebanon last week between the army and guerrillas, who left mountain retreats to take winter quarters in villages.

The clashes touched off an uproar of protest in the Arab world, followed by demands for full freedom of movement

Continued on Page 14, Column 1

PUGWASH EXPERTS OFFER ARMS PLAN

Scientists of East and West Seek to Avert Atomic War

By WALTER SULLIVAN
Special to The New York Times

SOCHI, U.S.S.R., Oct. 27—In a broad range of agreements, scientists from East and West, including some high in the Soviet hierarchy and former leaders of American defense research, have recommended measures to avert nuclear war.

Although the recommendations of the week-long talks here were unofficial, and speakers may not be identified, the issues touched on the negotiations on strategic arms limitations opening Nov. 17 in Helsinki, Finland.

The meeting here was the 19th Pugwash Conference on Science and World Affairs, so known because the first was held 12 years ago at Pugwash, Nova Scotia.

The sessions have shown the extent to which those in the Soviet and American establishments sympathetic to curtailment of the arms race are in agreement. However, as one participant put it, the Helsinki talks may boil down to two "domestic negotiations" between hawks and doves on each

Continued on Page 11, Column 1

Thieu Frees Monk; 300 Political Foes Will Get Clemency

By The Associated Press

SAIGON, South Vietnam, Oct. 29 — President Nguyen Van Thieu ordered the release from prison of a militant Buddhist monk today. A Government spokesman said the monk was the first of more than 300 political prisoners who would be released or whose sentences would be reduced as part of South Vietnam's National Day observance Saturday.

President Thieu ordered the release of Thich Thien Minh, a monk imprisoned last March on a charge of harboring draft dodgers and deserters. Earlier in the day, the Government freed 88 Vietcong prisoners, also apparently as a National Day gesture.

Mr. Thieu Minh was freed Thursday, United Press International reported.

A spokesman said that a total of 310 political prisoners would be released or their sentences commuted. Mr.

Continued on Page 19, Column 1

ROGERS DISPUTES FULBRIGHT ON LAOS

Asserts Congress Receives Full Information on U.S. Role in Secret Warfare

Special to The New York Times

WASHINGTON, Oct. 29 — Secretary of State William P. Rogers disputed Senator J. W. Fulbright today on his allegation that the State Department had not kept the Senate Foreign Relations Committee fully informed on American military operations in Laos.

Mr. Rogers told reporters after a closed committee hearing that he was surprised by the Senator's charge. "I thought Congress was familiar with what we are doing there," he said. "We thought Congress understood it."

Discussing the policy toward Laos, Mr. Rogers said he did not think that there was going to be a change now. Nixon Administration sources have said that a Foreign Relations subcommittee's inquiry into the Laotian issue had stimulated the Administration to begin rethinking policy on Laos.

Fundamental Issue Raised

Senator Fulbright, Democrat of Arkansas and chairman of the Foreign Relations Committee, insisted during the hearing that the Administration had not briefed him or the committee on the United States' involvement in the clandestine war in Laos. He made similar remarks yesterday in public.

The dispute underscored a fundamental issue on the making of American foreign policy: Just what does the Constitution demand of the Executive branch in seeking the advice and consent of the Senate in the conduct of foreign affairs?

More and more has been heard on the matter as doubts about the United States' participation in the war in Vietnam has grown. First the process by

Continued on Page 18, Column 3

Seale Put in Chains At Chicago 8 Trial

By J. ANTHONY LUKAS
Special to The New York Times

CHICAGO, Oct. 29—Bobby G. Seale, chairman of the Black Panther party, was gagged and chained to his chair today during the trial of the Chicago Eight.

Judge Julius J. Hoffman ordered the unusual restraints after Mr. Seale, one of the defendants charged with conspiracy to incite a riot during last year's Democratic National Convention, repeatedly shouted accusations and insults at the Federal district judge and the prosecution.

Earlier in the day, Federal marshals twice wrestled Mr. Seale into his seat. The second time, a marshal twisted the defendant's arm behind his back to hold him there. David T.

Continued on Page 39, Column 1

HOUSE COMMITTEE APPROVES AID BILL OF $2.19-BILLION

$390-Million Trimmed From Nixon's Original Request on Foreign Assistance

By FELIX BELAIR Jr.
Special to The New York Times

WASHINGTON, Oct. 29—The House Foreign Affairs Committee approved a $2.19-billion foreign aid authorization bill today after trimming about $390-million from President Nixon's original request.

The money ceiling included $1.79-billion for loans and grants for economic development and $400-million for military aid grants. President Nixon had originally asked for $2.58-billion, but additions to the measure in committee brought the total to $2.73-billion.

The committee's action was the culmination of four months of hearings and closed-door deliberations. The cuts of $467-million in economic aid and $75-million in military assistance were approved before the panel voted, 27 to 8, to report the bill to the House. Two members were recorded as voting present.

In addition to pruning the President's request, the committee made it difficult for the Administration to propose higher ceilings in next year's budget estimates. Economic aid categories that were cut most heavily were put on a two-year authorization basis.

Economic Loans Cut

Thus, the committee cut $200-million from the $675-million sought for economic development loans. It also cut $100-million from the $437-million asked for the Alliance for Progress and $100-million from the $515-million asked for supporting assistance to countries spending more for defense than they can finance without outside help.

The only economic aid category for which the Administration had asked a two-year authorization was the $463-million in the technical assistance program. This amount was cut by only 40.5-million.

But by writing in the two-year authorization for development loans and the Alliance for Progress as well as technical assistance, the committee served notice that the Administration would have to present an airtight case if it seeks an enlargement of these authorizations next year.

Apart from economic aid, a multiyear authorization was also requested for the

Continued on Page 10, Column 3

SENATE UNIT VOTES TO REDUCE TAXES OF SINGLE PERSONS

None Would Pay Over 20% Above Levy on Married With the Same Income

By EILEEN SHANAHAN
Special to The New York Times

WASHINGTON, Oct. 29—The Senate Finance Committee voted today to reduce the taxes of single persons, regardless of age, so that none would have to pay more than 20 per cent more in Federal income taxes than a married couple with the same income. Single persons now can pay as much as 40 per cent more.

The tax cut for single persons was the first relief measure agreed to by the Senate committee, which concluded today its work on the reform provisions of the tax bill and turned its attention to tax reduction.

Tomorrow, the committee is expected to vote about $9-billion to $10-billion in tax cuts for individuals at all income levels. That is approximately the same amount of tax relief contained in the reform and relief bill passed by the House of Representatives in August.

Discussing Tax Relief

The Senate committee's tax relief for single persons would save six million single taxpayers $445-million annually. The House bill would have saved them $650-million a year.

The committee spent much of today discussing different forms of tax relief, including an increase in the $600 personal exemption; a tax credit as a substitute for the personal exemption, and reductions in tax rates.

The Finance Committee's chairman, Senator Russell B. Long of Louisiana, said afterward that he thought the committee would vote "cut the minimum, to reduce taxes on individuals by as much as the House did." That will be $9.3-billion a year, after all the relief provisions were fully in effect—in 1972.

Senator Long added that "I really don't think the corporate

Continued on Page 65, Column 1

NIXON CAMPAIGNS ON CAHILL BEHALF

President Asserts G.O.P. Gubernatorial Candidate Can Deal With Crime

By RONALD SULLIVAN
Special to The New York Times

HACKENSACK, N. J., Oct. 29—Lending some of the luster of his office to the gubernatorial campaign of Representative William T. Cahill, President Nixon called tonight for a Republican victory before a cheering audience of nearly 4,000 jammed into the Hackensack High School gymnaisum.

Mr. Nixon said that crime was one of the major issues in the New Jersey campaign and that "there is not a better man to deal with crime than Bill Cahill."

The President told the crowd that he had telephoned Mr. Cahill's 16-year-old daughter, Patricia, who is in the University of Pennsylvania Hospital recuperating from head injuries suffered in an auto accident several months ago. He said he had told the girl:

"Your daddy's going to win."

His remarks brought loud cheers from the audience.

About 2,000 supporters stood outside the school, as did some 300 antiwar demonstrators holding lighted candles.

Mr. Nixon had flown to New Jersey in his Air Force jetliner, arriving at Newark Airport and then going by helicopter to

Continued on Page 41, Column 2

Mine Health and Safety Bill Is Passed by House, 389-4

By BEN A. FRANKLIN
Special to The New York Times

WASHINGTON, Oct. 29—The House of Representatives approved overwhelmingly today a tough measure to protect coal miners by requiring mine owners to adopt safety practices many of which have been recommended for 100 years.

House passage of the Federal Coal Mine Health and Safety Act of 1969, a bill hailed by its sponsors as the most comprehensive and far-reaching occupational safety measure since the Federal railway safety legislation of 75 years ago, came on a 389-to-4 roll-call vote.

It followed by four weeks the Senate's passage of a similarly strong mine safety bill, and the prospect is that the legislation will be strengthened further in a Senate-House conference despite bitter opposition by segments of the coal industry.

House action came almost a year after 78 miners were killed in explosions at the No. 9 mine of the Consolidation Coal Company at Farmington, W. Va., The accident stirred demands for reforms in the industry.

The House bill contains the first all-inclusive Federal prohibition of underground smoking or the use of open-flame lights in the 100 years in which Congress has infrequently considered the high rate of death and injury in the mines.

The measure includes requirements for fully illuminating underground work areas and for cabs with supporting

Continued on Page 38, Column 4

BOARD VOTES PLAN FOR WELFARE ISLE

Critics Charge Undue Haste on Plan to Construct 5,000 Housing Units There

By EDWARD C. BURKS

A $200-million plan to develop two new towns on Welfare Island was approved by the Board of Estimate yesterday, despite angry charges of steam-roller tactics.

The plan for 5,000 housing units, town squares and waterfront promenades on the long-neglected island in the East River was made public just 20 days ago.

A 99-year lease, putting the development of most of the two-mile-long, 147-acre island in the hands of the New York State Urban Development Corporation won the unanimous approval of the Estimate Board after a three-hour hearing.

Delay Is Denied

Community planning board members and others who spoke at the City Hall hearing pleaded vainly for more time to study the complicated lease terms or to offer possible alternate proposals.

A main concern of the community planners was that the city would be abdicating its right of review of the detailed designs still to come.

As a result, the board then voted to amend the lease, increasing the influence of elected city officials on the 18-member subsidiary corporation that will be in charge of design, construction and management of the new community.

The main aspects of the general plan are:

¶The 5,000 housing units will be in four-to-12-story buildings

Continued on Page 50, Column 5

Brandt's Foes Say His Stand On East Germany Perils Bonn

By LAWRENCE FELLOWS
Special to The New York Times

BONN, Oct. 29—In a spirited, occasionally turbulent session of the Bundestag today, the opposition accused Chancellor Willy Brandt of threatening the very foundations of the state by proposing that West Germany accept East Germany as a separate and sovereign nation.

"We will see the landslide that we have tried together to hold back for 20 years," said Kurt Georg Kiesinger, whom Mr. Brandt, a Social Democrat, succeeded last week.

"Where is this trip taking us?" asked Rainer Barzel, the opposition whip.

Before the day was out the atmosphere was extremely heated as the lower house of Parliament debated the policy statement made yesterday by Mr. Brandt.

In it he listed his priorities in domestic and foreign policy, including efforts to improve relations with Eastern Europe, which he said would involve acknowledgement of the territorial integrity of the countries concerned, among them East Germany.

As members rushed forward to hurl accusations and questions, Mr. Barzel, a member of the Christian Democratic party, moved an adjournment to allow "heads to cool." An unexpected motion, it was an outside chance to embarrass the Government with a minor defeat on its first day of real action in Parliament.

Associated Press
Rainer Barzel, opposition whip, speaking in Bonn.

The deputy whips raced through the building, hurrying members back to the floor. In the confusion the doors were locked too early and the voting

Continued on Page 6, Column 1

Right of Peaceful Student Dissent Is Affirmed by City School Board

By LEONARD BUDER

A policy statement defining the personal and political freedom of high-school students, including recognition of the right to peaceful dissent, was informally approved yesterday by the Board of Education.

Board officials said that the statement, which is still subject to revisions, was the first of its kind ever formulated for the city school system.

It came amid continuing student agitation here, as well as elsewhere in the country, for a greater role in school affairs. At the same time many principals and teachers have voiced concern that yielding to student pressures would erode their authority and jeopardize the effectiveness of the schools.

Text of the board's resolution is printed on Page 37.

The new code would have a varied impact on the city's 90 academic and vocational high schools and their 275,000 students. A headquarters official said that some schools had already developed "fairly liberal" student policies on their own, while others followed a more conservative line.

The statement recognizes the right of senior high-school students to have a voice in school matters that concern them, generally frees school newspapers from official censorship and upholds the right of students to wear buttons, armbands and

Continued on Page 37, Column 1

Democrats Languid In Procaccino Race

By MARTIN TOLCHIN

Large segments of the city's Democratic organization are making only a half-hearted effort on behalf of Mario A. Procaccino, the party's candidate for Mayor.

For the first mayoral campaign within the memory of veteran Democratic politicians, precinct captains in Brooklyn and Queens have not received their customary $25 to $30 to ring doorbells on behalf of the party's candidates and to stand outside polling places to corral passers-by into the voting booths.

Large outdoor signs and banners—paid for by local Democratic organizations—that have been hallmarks of every general election campaign are missing. Locally sponsored rallies are

Continued on Page 40, Column 1

NEWS INDEX

1969

Lawyer William Kunstler with three defendants of the Chicago Conspiracy trial, Abbie Hoffman, David Dellinger and Jerry Rubin.

Charles Manson was a fanatical leader of an obedient cult, which aided him in the bloody murder of seven persons.

Bobby Seale (left) was detached from the Chicago conspiracy trial because he used "bad words." Many believed that the gagging of Seale was an example of the breakdown of justice in the country. He is shown here with Huey Newton.

Actress Sharon Tate and her unborn child were victims of the Manson family.

Dennis Hopper, Peter Fonda and Jack Nicholson starred in *Easy Rider.*

Jane Fonda starred as a tragic victim of society in *They Shoot Horses, Don't They?*

Robert Ryan (top, center) and his cut-throat bounty hunters posed for a publicity shot for *The Wild Bunch.*

"All the News That's Fit to Print"

The New York Times

LATE CITY EDITION

Weather: Fair and continued cold today, tonight. Fair tomorrow. Temp. range: today 41-26; Saturday 47-34. Full U.S. report on Page 95.

SECTION ONE

VOL. CXIX . No. 40,839 — © 1969 The New York Times Company. — NEW YORK, SUNDAY, NOVEMBER 16, 1969 — 60c beyond 50-mile zone from New York City, except Long Island. 75c beyond 200-mile radius. Higher in air delivery cities. — 50 CENTS

250,000 WAR PROTESTERS STAGE PEACEFUL RALLY IN WASHINGTON; MILITANTS STIR CLASHES LATER

The New York Times (by Barton Silverman)

Demonstrators at foot of the Washington Monument. Some wave flag of National Liberation Front of South Vietnam.

A RECORD THRONG

Young Marchers Ask Rapid Withdrawal From Vietnam

By JOHN HERBERS

Special to The New York Times

WASHINGTON, Nov. 15—A vast throng of Americans, predominantly youthful and constituting the largest mass march in the nation's capital, demonstrated peacefully in the heart of the city today, demanding a rapid withdrawal of United States troops from Vietnam.

The District of Columbia Police Chief, Jerry Wilson, said a "moderate" estimate was that 250,000 had paraded on Pennsylvania Avenue and had attended an antiwar rally at the Washington Monument. Other city officials said aerial photographs would later show that the crowd had exceeded 300,000.

Until today, the largest outpouring of demonstrators was the gentle civil rights march of 1963, which attracted 200,000. Observers of both marches said the throng that appeared today was clearly greater than the outpouring of 1963.

At dusk, after the mass demonstration had ended, a small segment of the crowd, members of radical splinter groups, moved across Constitution Avenue to the Labor and Justice Department buildings, where they burned United States flags, threw paint bombs and other missiles and were repelled by tear gas released by the police. There were a number of arrests and minor injuries, mostly the result of the tear gas.

Exodus Begins

At 8 P.M., most of the demonstrators, who had come from all parts of the country, were on buses, trains and cars leaving the city. By 11 P.M., the police said all was quiet in the city.

About 3,000 youths were unable to get to their buses, which were parked by the Tidal Basin, because of the tear gas and heavy traffic, so the city operated an emergency shuttle service of sightseeing buses.

The predominant event of the day was that of a great and peaceful army of dissent moving through the city.

At midday, under clear skies and in the face of a cold north wind, a solid moving carpet of humanity extended from the foot of the Capitol, 10 long blocks up Pennsylvania Avenue to the Treasury Building, four blocks down 15th Street and out across the grassy hill on which the Washington Monument stands.

The crowds brought to Washington a sense of urgency about a Vietnam peace and impatience with President Nixon's policy of gradual withdrawal. This theme, which was repeated throughout the day in various forms, was expressed

Continued on Page 60, Column 1

Parade Marshals Keep It Cool

By MAX FRANKEL

Special to The New York Times

WASHINGTON, Nov. 15—It was a campus crowd. It was chilled. It was huge. It was obviously proud of its size, tolerant about its diversity and almost smug about its self-control. It was parading a sense of right, and the most important thing for most of the marchers was simply to have been there.

Arms were thrust especially high, the fingers forming a V, outside the sealed portals of the Justice Department. You see, they were saying to nervous officialdom, peacefulness, it's easy. Was it worth arguing for a week whether to march along Constitution instead of Pennsylvania?

The radical minority that has been spoiling for a fight came back to Justice at dusk to bash in some windows and force this capital's efficient police to hurl out the tear gas again. Thousands milled around to watch the efforts to raise the Vietcong flag and hundreds here and dozens there sniffed the gas that pursued the looters and bottle throwers around town tonight.

But the mean or just plain rowdy here this weekend have been flotsam on a sea of serene people who frown upon all violence, in Vietnam or Washington. During the daylight activities, the marchers and their monitors in the police were all smiles.

Smiles were especially broad for the thousands of marshals along the route, young men and women indistinguishable from the marchers except for the armbands that made them the symbols of self-discipline.

"Keep warm by keeping cool, friends," the marshal in blond curls kept saying. He snapped pictures of his friends as they passed and swapped reassurances with the police sergeant whenever he came along.

The marshals evoked cheers. "What do we want?" "Peace." "When do we want it?" "Now."

The marshals gave out advice. "Keep moving please." "Hold hands if you're chilly." "Just six more blocks, three of them in the sun."

The marshals locked arms to contain the militants, prancing in ranks of 15, thrusting Vietcong banners high above the much more common Stars and Stripes (and one hearts and stripes). When the Yippies chanted obscenities a chorus of marshals would sing out in counterpoint with the Beatle song "Give Peace a Chance."

The marshals modestly accepted the crowd's offerings—peanut butter and jelly on white and Fig Newtons.

The pace was that of a football crowd filing into the stadium. The age, too. The adults, alumni perhaps of other marches, in two's and three's, feeling very young and gay,

Continued on Page 62, Column 1

Nixon Sees 4 Aides During the Protest

By JAMES M. NAUGHTON

Special to The New York Times

WASHINGTON, Nov. 15—President Nixon talked about the Vietnam war with four key advisers today as the police and bumper-to-bumper buses isolated the White House from massed antiwar marchers.

As the talks took place, thousands of peace demonstrators filed up Pennsylvania Avenue to within one block of the White House. At 15th Street the marchers

Continued on Page 61, Column 5

TEAR GAS REPELS RADICALS' ATTACK

Capital Police Retaliate as Youths Hurl Bottles and Rocks at U.S. Buildings

By JOHN KIFNER

Special to The New York Times

WASHINGTON, Sunday, Nov. 16—Young radical demonstrators hurling rocks and bottles at Government buildings in the heart of the Capital were turned back last night by barrages of tear gas.

The District of Columbia police fired volley after volley of gas after a militant splinter group from the main antiwar march pelted the Justice Department and twice ran a Vietcong flag up the building's main flagpole.

Police officials reported that there had been at least 93 arrests, including three on felony charges. Hospitals reported that 97 demonstrators were treated for various causes, primarily the effects of the gas.

In nearly all of the encounters, the police did not use their clubs or make physical contact with the demonstrators, relying instead on gas.

After the demonstration at the Justice Department was broken up in a dense cloud of CS, a chemical gas used in Vietnam that causes burning sensations in the eyes and skin, choking and nausea, clumps of young people wandered through the main streets of Washington.

Some were shaken and distraught, but others ranged

Continued on Page 60, Column 6

APOLLO 12 SWINGS ONTO A WIDER PATH TOWARD THE MOON

Course Correction Is Made to Fulfill Requirements for Landing Wednesday

CRAFT PASSES MIDPOINT

Color TV Beamed to Earth —Clock Only Casualty of Power Lapse in Lift-Off

By JOHN NOBLE WILFORD

Special to The New York Times

HOUSTON, Nov. 15—With a short blast of its rocket, the Apollo 12 spacecraft swung out tonight on a wider, slower and somewhat riskier course toward the moon.

The three moonbound astronauts moved smoothly beyond the midpoint in their outward journey, transmitting a color telecast to the earth, checking out spacecraft systems and generally relaxing after their tense, rain-soaked launching yesterday at Cape Kennedy, Fla.

Flight controllers here reported that the 96,000-pound spacecraft was functioning almost flawlessly. An on-board clock was apparently the only casualty of the electrical failure that hit Apollo 12 shortly after lift-off.

Apollo 12, man's second mission to land on the moon, is aiming for lunar orbit Monday night. Then two of the astronauts are to ride the squat, four legged landing craft, dubbed the Intrepid, to a touchdown on the moon's Ocean of Storms early Wednesday morning for a 32-hour visit for scientific exploration.

Equipment Is Checked

At 5:43 P.M., Eastern standard time, today, Comdrs. Charles Conrad Jr., Richard F. Gordon Jr. and Alan L. Bean, all Navy pilots, began transmitting television from inside the cockpit as they checked out equipment and squared away for the rocket firing.

The three astronauts were wearing caps with long bills decorated in Navy braid. Commander Conrad's cap was topped with a small propeller, which he flipped into motion for the television audience 133,000 miles away on the earth.

A snowstorm of ice particles swirled outside the spacecraft window, the frozen debris from an earlier venting of waste water.

Inside the cabin, lights blinked rapidly on the DSKY—the display keyboard for the computerized guidance and navigation system.

Commander Conrad, the Apollo 12 command pilot, and his crew were setting the switches, closing circuit breakers and checking computer data

Continued on Page 66, Column 3

City's New Master Plan Calls Middle Class Vital

Asserts 'Crucial Challenge' Is to Keep Whites While Improving the Lot of Poor Blacks and Puerto Ricans

The "crucial challenge" facing the city is its ability to retain its largely white middle class while elevating low-income blacks and Puerto Ricans, according to the first volume of the long-awaited Master Plan for New York.

The 90,000-word installment of the "Plan for New York City," made public yesterday by the City Planning Commission, proposes the strengthening of the city's role as a national center with a goal of "several hundred thousand more office workers in the business districts in the next 10 years."

Donald H. Elliott, the chairman of the City Planning Commission, described the nonbinding Master Plan as a "realistic and pragmatic" guide to urban policy for "the next five or ten years."

The comprehensive document discusses a broad range of city problems and attempts to outline a development strategy for dealing with them.

It envisions a city in which electrically powered taxicabs operate, private cars are restricted from some business streets, more recreational facilities are built to join housing and piers on the waterfront, and a new rail tunnel runs under the Hudson.

It urges more training and jobs for the underemployed, classes for 3-year-olds, a network of neighborhood medical services and mixed residential and industrial buildings.

The plan, much revised from portions of a first draft obtained by The New York Times last February, voices hope on some problems, pessimism on others.

For example, the plan states: "The plain fact is that no one yet knows how to make a ghetto school work." It also warns that the city's parochial schools are in "serious financial difficulties," and maintains that the city must choose between subsidizing them or ex-

Continued on Page 84, Column 3

Arms Parley in Helsinki Is Set to Open Tomorrow

By BERNARD GWERTZMAN

Special to The New York Times

HELSINKI, Finland, Nov. 15—The chief disarmament negotiators of the United States and the Soviet Union arrived here today and expressed guarded hope for success in the preliminary talks on limiting strategic arms, which begin Monday.

Both Gerard C. Smith, director of the Arms Control and Disarmament Agency, and Vladimir S. Semyonov, a Deputy Foreign Minister, stressed the preliminary nature of the Helsinki talks, which most diplomats expect to last about three weeks.

In these talks, the expected topic is the framework, time and place for further negotiations on halting the arms race in offensive and defensive systems of strategic weapons.

Both delegations arrived under dark gray skies in a cold drizzle, the usual weather in this northern capital at this time of year. It was already dark at 3:30 in the afternoon when Mr. Semyonov's train arrived.

Earlier, upon arriving aboard a United States Air Force jet, Mr. Smith repeated Secretary of State William P. Rogers's words that the purpose of the talks "is to have a free discussion about how the substantive negotiations will be conducted."

At the same time, Mr. Smith left open the possibility that the preliminary talks might move directly into specific issues. Lacking advance indication on what the Soviet Union might propose, Mr. Smith seemed careful to avoid foreclosing any options.

"We do not rule out the pos-

Continued on Page 14, Column 1

Nixon Aide Says Agnew Stand Reflects White House TV View

By E. W. KENWORTHY

Special to The New York Times

WASHINGTON, Nov. 15—Vice President Agnew's speech charging the television networks with biased news reporting "reflected the views of the Administration," Clark R. Mollenhoff, special counsel to President Nixon, said today.

Controversy meanwhile, continued to swirl over the Vice President's remarks, both in the United States and abroad. Six former Government officials and 11 law school deans signed a statement expressing alarm over the "inflammatory" remarks attributed to Mr. Agnew and other high officials. [Details on pages 78 and 79.]

Mr. Mollenhoff said there had been discussion within the White House staff "for a long time" about the way network reporters and news commentators had dealt with various issues.

Mr. Mollenhoff was responding to questions about a Washington dispatch in today's issues of The Des Moines Register, for which Mr. Mollenhoff worked before he joined the

Continued on Page 78, Column 3

Irate Black Athletes Stir Campus Tension

By ANTHONY RIPLEY

Special to The New York Times

DENVER, Nov. 15—Rising militancy among black athletes is reaching out to touch most college campuses where blacks take part in intercollegiate sports.

Though much less explosive in their actions than their fellow black students, roused black athletes in increasing numbers are gambling their principles against their educations.

There is an element of self-destruction in this. It has led to dismissals and a cutback in recruiting, and for many blacks from poor families a college education means a football

Continued on Page 85, Column 1

Associated Press

A row of buses blocked access to the White House. Coffins held cards with names of Americans killed in South Vietnam.

More Than 100,000 on Coast Demonstrate in Moderate Vein

By WALLACE TURNER

Special to The New York Times

SAN FRANCISCO, Nov. 15—Upwards of 100,000 people from many walks of life and widely varying political persuasions staged today the biggest peace demonstration ever seen in the West.

They began to gather in the darkness last night, and some of them marched as far as seven miles through this cool, gray city to the rally in Golden Gate Park. Others drove, hitchhiked or rode buses hundreds of miles to reach here today.

In their talk, the speeches they heard and the signs they carried, they repudiated President Nixon's plea that they quietly follow his leadership toward ending the war in Vietnam. Many of them also specifically repudiated Vice President Agnew's criticisms of peace demonstrations.

Again and again throughout the day it was plain that the moderates in the diverse group that planned this demonstration had kept control. The marchers were chaperoned by upward of 1,000 monitors who kept them in line and made them wait at stop lights.

But the strongest indication that the moderates were in control came at the rally when David Hilliard, chief of staff of the militant Black Panther party, was booed. Mr. Hilliard at-

Continued on Page 61, Column 1

Today's Sections

Index to Subjects

*Included in all copies distributed in New York City and suburban area.

Bob McGrath (center) and Loretta Long (right) were among the stars of *Sesame Street,* an educational program that finally appealed to kids.

Mary Tyler Moore in a skit about women's rights on a CBS Special, *Dick Van Dyke and the Other Woman.*

Flip Wilson embarrassed his host on the popular talk show, *The Dick Cavett Show.*

"All the News That's Fit to Print"

The New York Times

LATE CITY EDITION

Weather: Variably cloudy and windy today, tonight and tomorrow. Temp. range: today 35-40; Wed. 63-52. Full U.S. report on Page 93.

VOL. CXIX..No. 40,843 · © 1969 The New York Times Company. · NEW YORK, THURSDAY, NOVEMBER 20, 1969 · 10 CENTS

ASTRONAUTS IN 2 MOON WALKS; ESTABLISH SCIENTIFIC STATION

CONGRESS CLEARS BILL PERMITTING A DRAFT LOTTERY

Move to Let Nixon Set Up New System by Decree Is Hailed by White House

Special to The New York Times

WASHINGTON, Nov. 19 — The Nixon Administration's draft lottery bill was approved by the the Senate today and sent to the White House for the President's signature.

It was the first major piece of new legislation that the Administration has obtained from Congress during 10 months in power. The White House Press Secretary, Ronald L. Ziegler, described Mr. Nixon as "highly gratified" that he might now move ahead with draft reform.

The measure was passed on a voice vote, with only one Senator, Mike Mansfield of Montana, the Democratic floor leader, heard in the negative.

He said earlier that he regarded the proposed new draft system as "inequitable" and "just a restructuring of pressure" on draftees.

Containing only one sentence, the bill repeals a 1967 law that prohibited the President from using a random selection system to decide which young men should be chosen first for the armed services.

Will End Present System

Its enactment will permit Mr. Nixon to abolish the present draft system, under which men are eligible continuously from their 19th to their 26th birthdays and the oldest are chosen first to fill the national quotas.

The President has promised to put into effect instead a system under which an order of draft eligibility will be established by lot each year for those reaching 19. Those at the top of the list will serve a year either at once or at the end of their college deferment.

After the lottery is held, those

Continued on Page 15, Column 1

Rockefeller Bars A Special Session For Redistricting

By WILLIAM E. FARRELL
Special to The New York Times

BINGHAMTON, N. Y., Nov. 19 — Governor Rockefeller ruled out today the possibility of a special session of the Legislature this year to reapportion the state's 41 Congressional districts.

Mr. Rockefeller also said he personally did not favor a move by the Republican leaders of the Legislature to try to redistrict the State Senate and the Assembly in time for the 1970 elections.

In an interview after a dedication ceremony here for a $40-million governmental civic center, Mr. Rockefeller was asked whether he would call a special session to comply with a ruling by the United States Supreme Court earlier this year. The Court said the state's Congressional districts must be redrawn to better comply with the one-man, one-vote doctrine in time for next year's elect-

Continued on Page 56, Column 5

TWO STATES AGREE TO TAKE CONTROL OF THE NEW HAVEN

Pact With the Penn Central, Subject to Other Approval, Opens Way for Repairs

By PETER KIHSS

A "memorandum of intent" has been agreed upon for bi-state take-over of the New Haven Railroad's West End lines, on which 24,000 Westchester County and Connecticut residents travel to the city daily.

The agreement, concluded by the Metropolitan Transportation Authority, the Connecticut Transportation Authority and the Penn Central Company, includes a new plan for the two authorities to lease the New Haven tracks from Grand Central Terminal to Woodlawn.

This would enable the state agencies to make eventual improvements on that segment, thereby providing some benefit for the 24,000 commuters of the Harlem Division who use the trackage and 12,000 on the Hudson Division who use part of the same segment.

Money Is Ready

The agreement, still subject to various state and Federal approvals after an announcement that is expected to be made next week, opens the way to use of $56.8-million already committed by the Federal and State Governments for major capital improvements on the long-ailing New Haven.

The two transportation authorities would collect the revenues on the New Haven commuter line, which is informally estimated to be grossing about $25-million a year, and would shoulder the expenses, currently estimated to be causing a deficit of about $3-million a year. The Penn Central would run the line for a management fee, indicated as about $100,000 a year.

The outlines of the agreement became known here as the Senate in Washington yesterday approved a compact between New York State and Connecticut to make such an agreement possible.

House Vote Is Next

The compact was approved by the New York State Legislature last year and by Connecticut's Legislature this year. It must still be approved by the House of Representatives by Dec. 31.

House members from Connecticut and New York failed Monday to get unanimous consent to approve the amendment then. Representative Albert W. Johnson, Republican of Pennsylvania, asked a delay "until we can get some information as to what the potential Federal cost is going to be" in the New Haven rehabilitation.

In the Senate, where ap-

Continued on Page 95, Column 3

Associated Press

ANOTHER MAN ON THE MOON: Comdr. Alan L. Bean climbing down ladder attached to leg of lunar landing module

INSPECT SURVEYOR

They Take Its Camera and Collect Rocks—Re-enter Module

By JOHN NOBLE WILFORD
Special to The New York Times

HOUSTON, Thursday, Nov. 20 —The two astronauts of Apollo 12 tramped about the moon's surface yesterday and early today with the exuberance of boys, collecting rocks and setting up on that ancient world the first scientific observatory designed for long life.

Comdr. Charles Conrad Jr. and Comdr. Alan L. Bean of the Navy took two long walks outside their spacecraft, the Intrepid, which was standing near the rocky rim of a crater on the Ocean of Storms.

In the second, man's first far-ranging moon hike, the two astronauts walked over to the inner slope of a crater to snip souvenirs from an unmanned spacecraft, Surveyor 3, which has been resting there for two and a half years. The Surveyor stood about 600 feet from their landing craft.

After reaching the Surveyor, the astronauts took pictures of it and wiped part of it with a cloth.

Find Color Changed

"Surveyor looks in very good shape," they reported back to Mission Control at the Manned Spacecraft Center here. But they said that the craft's color appeared to be more tan than it had been on earth.

From the Surveyor they removed its camera, the first to take, and send back to earth, color pictures of the moon's surface.

They also cut off from the three-legged craft the mechanical claw-like scoop with which it had dug shallow trenches in the first remote-controlled test of the consistency of the lunar soil. The scoop still held some dirt. Also removed were some aluminum tubing and cables.

Then they returned to the Intrepid at 2:43 A.M. They had spent nearly eight hours on the surface in their two walks.

Prize for Accuracy

The Surveyor remnants will be the astronauts' prize for landing so close to their target. When they are returned to earth, they should give scientists clues as to how materials fare under the harsh heat and cold of the lunar environment.

Commander Conrad, the 39-year-old command pilot, began the second excursion by stepping down the landing craft's ladder onto the surface at 11:01 P.M. yesterday. He was followed 10 minutes later by Commander Bean, the 37-year-old co-pilot.

They bubbled with conversation, laughed and enjoyed themselves as they set about doing the exploration tasks they had traveled 250,000 miles to do. A camera failure, however, blacked out part of the first moon walk and all the second for television viewers on earth.

Rolls Rocks on Slope

The two astronauts wore white pressure suits, bubble-top helmets, gloves, boots and oxygen-supplying back packs. They ranged far from their landing craft, stopping often to pick up rocks, take core samples from beneath the lunar topsoil, and snap pictures.

At one point, Commander Conrad found some rocks of grapefruit size and rolled them

Continued on Page 30, Column 2

Walking—and Talking—on the Moon

Following are conversations between controllers in Houston and Comdrs. Charles (Pete) Conrad Jr. and Alan L. Bean, who made their two moon walks yesterday and early today after landing the lunar module, Intrepid, in the Ocean of Storms. All times given are Eastern Standard.

CONRAD (6:39 A.M.)—I'm headed down the ladder.

BEAN—O.K., wait. Let me get the old camera on you, Pete.

CONRAD—Man, is that a pretty-looking sight, that LM [landing module].

BEAN—O.K., O.K., got the old camera running.

CONRAD (6:45 A.M.)—Down to the pad. . . . Whoopie, man, that may have been a small step for Neil, but that's a long one for me. I'm going to step off the pad. Right. Up. Oh, is that soft. Hey, that's neat. I don't sink in too far. I'll try a little—boy, that sun's bright. That's just like somebody shining a spotlight in your eyes. I can walk pretty well, Al, but I've got to take it easy and watch what I'm doing. Boy, you'll never believe it! Guess what I see sitting on the side of the crater. The old Surveyor!

BEAN—The old Surveyor, yes, sir.

CONRAD (laughter)—Does that look neat. It can't be any further than 600 feet from here. How about that.

HOUSTON—Well planned, Pete.

CONRAD—I have the decided impression I don't want to move too rapidly. But I can walk quite well. The Surveyor really is sitting on the side of a steep slope. I'll tell you that.

BEAN—Boy you sure are leaning forward, Pete.

CONRAD—Hey, lean forward, I feel like I'm going to fall over in any direction.

BEAN—You're leaning—

CONRAD—Hey, Houston, one of the first things that I can see, by golly, is little glass beads. I got a piece about a quarter of an inch in sight and I am going to put it in a contingency sample bag.

CONRAD—O. K., I got the table out, testing the MESA [Modularized Equipment Storage Assembly] . . . Very nice. Very nice. Hey, Al.

BEAN—Yep.

CONRAD—I could work

Continued on Page 31, Column 6

2 SENATORS SPLIT ON HAYNSWORTH

Williams of Delaware Says He Is Against Nominee—Aiken to Vote for Him

By WARREN WEAVER Jr.
Special to The New York Times

WASHINGTON, Nov. 19—The middle ground in the dispute over Clement F. Haynsworth Jr. narrowed still further today as two of the Senate's most influential Republicans split over supporting President Nixon's controversial nominee to the Supreme Court.

Senator John J. Williams of Delaware, who has made a career out of investigating impropriety by public officials, announced that he would vote against Judge Haynsworth because "the restoration of the confidence of the American people in the integrity and fairness of our courts is of paramount importance."

A few hours after Mr. Williams had spoken on the floor, Senator George D. Aiken of Vermont, dean of the Senate Republican delegation, issued a seven-sentence statement announcing his support of the nominee. He said that it was his personal policy, violated only once, to vote for all Presidential nominees.

Both Republicans had been members of the steadily dwindling group of undecided Senators. So had Senator J. Caleb Boggs of Delaware, who also announced today in favor of confirmation. His decision had been reported yesterday.

The day's decisions brought

Continued on Page 23, Column 1

CYCLAMATE PANEL WOULD EASE CURB

Bids Finch Seek Warning Label on Food and Drink Instead of Withdrawal

By RICHARD D. LYONS
Special to The New York Times

WASHINGTON, Nov. 19 — A panel of experts has recommended that the Department of Health, Education and Welfare soften its curb on the artificial sweetener cyclamate.

The panel, a group of doctors named by Robert H. Finch, the Secretary of Health, Education and Welfare, has recommended that foods and soft drinks containing the chemical be labeled with a warning, rather than withdrawn.

The recommended label would tell the user that he should consume the product only on the advice of a physician.

It was not known if Mr. Finch, who announced the withdrawal order a month ago, would agree to the advice of the panel, which has been in touch with the department's chief medical administrator, Dr. Roger O. Egeberg.

Indications emerged last week that the restriction, which was prompted by the discovery that large doses caused bladder cancer in rats, might be softened.

On Friday, Mr. Finch extended the grace period within which foods packed with cyclamate had to be removed from the market, from Feb. 1 to Sept. 1, 1970.

When cyclamate was banned last month, Dr. Egeberg, Assistant Secretary for Health and Scientific Affairs, announced at

Continued on Page 22, Column 3

A 'Silent Majority' Backs Nixon In U.S.I.A. Film Sent Abroad

By TAD SZULC
Special to The New York Times

WASHINGTON, Nov. 19 — The Nixon Administration has carried to potential television audiences in 104 foreign countries a message suggesting that the President's Vietnam policies are backed by a "silent majority" of Americans.

Since last Monday, the United States Information

Excerpts from shooting script of the film, Page 27.

Agency has shipped abroad 200 prints of a 15-minute television film, "The Silent Majority," showing scenes from last week's antiwar demonstrations in Washington interspersed with comments appearing to support Mr. Nixon's stand and emphasizing the importance of the "silent" citizens.

It ends with the statement that "the loudest sound is not the only one that should be listened to."

The film, which cost $20,000 to produce, has a basic English soundtrack, but copies sent overseas also include versions dubbed in nine languages: Spanish, French, Portuguese, Vietnamese, Arabic, Korean, Tagalog, Indonesian and the Mandarin dialect of Chinese.

U.S.I.A. officials said that additional versions were being dubbed in 13 other languages and that more prints were being sent out daily. The film is being dispatched to 104 countries—35 in Africa, 17 in Europe, 14 in the Far East, 14 in the Middle East and 24 in Latin America.

The agency, which presents United States policies and the American way of life to overseas audiences, is now preparing through its Motion Picture and Television Department a short film biography of Vice President Agnew and a 90-minute documentary on the United States presence in Vietnam.

Agency spokesmen said that no film portrait of a United States Vice President had been produced by the U.S.I.A.

The Vietnam film, also costing $20,000 was directed by John Ford. It was begun during the Johnson Administration.

The "Silent Majority" film

Continued on Page 27, Column 1

PAYOFF OF $12,500 LAID TO DE SAPIO

Itkin Says He Was Told Part of It Came From Fried

By EDITH EVANS ASBURY

A Federal jury and judge heard testimony yesterday that Carmine G. De Sapio, former Tammany chief, made three cash payments totaling $12,500 in 1967 to Herbert Itkin, to be shared with James L. Marcus, then Commissioner of Water Supply, Gas and Electricity in the Lindsay administration.

The testimony was given by Itkin, a labor lawyer and self-described Federal informant, in the trial of Mr. De Sapio and Anthony (Tony Ducks) Corallo on charges of conspiring to bribe Marcus and extort contracts from Consolidated Edison.

Henry Fried, a Mount Kisco contractor who was described as the source of part of the money by Mr. De Sapio, according to Itkin's testimony, was also named in the indictment but obtained delay of his trial because of illness. Marcus and Itkin were named as co-conspirators but not defendants, and both have been called as witnesses on behalf of the Government.

The first payment, $5,000, was given to him at Mr. De Sapio's apartment, at 11 Fifth Avenue, on Nov. 24, 1967, Itkin testified. He said the second payment, $2,500, and the third, $5,000, were handed to him by Mr. De Sapio in the latter's office at 151 East 55th Street.

The money was paid in return for the signing and dis-

Continued on Page 50, Column 1

TOP 11TH-GRADERS URGED FOR C.C.N.Y.

Copeland Says Move Would Offset Influx of Unprepared

Dr. Joseph J. Copeland, the acting president of City College, proposed last night that next year, exceptionally qualified high-school juniors be admitted to the college as part of efforts to "counterbalance the influx of unprepared students" expected under the City University's new open-admissions policy.

In a speech at the annual dinner of the college's alumni association in the Roosevelt Hotel, Dr. Copeland said fears of lowered academic excellence as a result of open enrollment "must be faced honestly and not dismissed with glib or simplistic answers."

He said the formula, which was adopted last week by the Board of Higher Education, would "not be as good as the optimists think."

"We can only hope that it will not be as bad as the pessimists find it," he said.

Under the plan, all high-school seniors who apply with academic averages of 80 or above or who rank in the top half of their graduating classes will be assured entry to one of the university's senior colleges. All other high-school graduates will be eligible to attend a two-year community college.

The plan was approved by the board two days after it was proposed by Dr. Albert H. Bowker, chancellor of the City University. Earlier formulas for implementing open admissions had

Continued on Page 36, Column 1

G.I. Says He Saw Vietnam Massacre

By ROBERT M. SMITH
Special to The New York Times

WASHINGTON, Nov. 19—An Army sergeant said tonight that he saw American soldiers gun down "women and children and old men" in a South Vietnam village last year.

Sgt. Michael A. Bernhardt said in a telephone interview that the slaying were carried out by "most of the men" in his company—C Company of the First Battalion, 20th Infantry, 11th Infantry Brigade.

"They were women and children and old men mostly," Sergeant Bernhardt said of residents of Songmy village who were killed in March of 1968. "I didn't notice any military-age males there," he said.

The incident described by the sergeant, who is now stationed with a basic training company at Fort Dix, N. J., is under investigation by the Army. The Army has charged First Lieut. William L. Calley—a platoon leader in Company C—with the murder of "a multiple number" of civilians.

It has also charged a sergeant in the platoon, David Mitchell, with assault with intent to murder.

Sergeant Bernhardt said he refused to take part in the shooting of the villagers.

According to the sergeant's account, the commander of C Company—whom he refused to name—gathered the men together for a briefing before they were to advance on the village, which Sergeant Bernhardt called Mylai 4.

"The company commander had us in a group," he said, "and gave us a briefing before we went on the mission. The briefing was to the effect that the village and the occupants were to be destroyed.

"He said they were all V.C. [Vietcong] and there were no innocent civilians in the area."

The sergeant, who at the time of this mission was a private and an automatic rifleman, said that no one had protested.

Asked whether he thought at the time that all the villagers were Vietcong, he said, "It was ridiculous, but apparently some of them believed."

There appears to be some confusion concerning the name of the village involved in the

Continued on Page 14, Column 4

Metropolitan Elects Dillon as President

By GRACE GLUECK

C. Douglas Dillon, the investment banker who was a high official in the Eisenhower, Kennedy and Johnson Administrations, has been elected president of the Metropolitan Museum of Art. He succeeds Arthur A. Houghton Jr., president of Steuben Glass and the museum's president since 1964, who has been elected chairman of the board of trustees. Both men will assume their new posts Jan. 1.

The 60-year-old Mr. Dillon takes office during one of the greatest expansion periods in the Metropolitan's history. The museum, now

Continued on Page 58, Column 4

NEWS INDEX

Neil Armstrong's "one small step" led the world to a new frontier—and even beyond—to the Seventies.